Governor Edwin W. Edwards
1972-1980, 1984-1988, 1992-1996

I0891842

# The Louisiana Purchase Bicentennial Series in Louisiana History

Glenn R. Conrad, General Editor

VOLUME I
THE FRENCH EXPERIENCE IN LOUISIANA

VOLUME II
THE SPANISH PRESENCE IN LOUISIANA, 1763 - 1803

VOLUME III
THE LOUISIANA PURCHASE
AND ITS AFTERMATH, 1800 - 1830

VOLUME IX
LOUISIANA SINCE THE LONGS
1960 TO CENTURY'S END

VOLUME X
A REFUGE FOR ALL AGES:
IMMIGRATION IN LOUISIANA HISTORY

VOLUME XIII
AN UNCOMMON EXPERIENCE:
LAW AND JUDICIAL INSTITUTIONS
IN LOUISIANA, 1803 - 2003

VOLUME XVI
AGRICULTURE AND
ECONOMIC DEVELOPMENT
IN LOUISIANA

# The Louisiana Purchase Bicentennial Series in Louisiana History

VOLUME IX

# LOUISIANA SINCE THE LONGS 1960 TO CENTURY'S END

EDITED BY

MICHAEL L. KURTZ

CENTER FOR LOUISIANA STUDIES
UNIVERSITY OF SOUTHWESTERN LOUISIANA
LAFAYETTE, LOUISIANA
1998

**Front Endsheets:**

Governor Foster: Courtesy Governor's Office, State Capitol, Baton Rouge, Louisiana
Governor Edwards: Courtesy Louisiana Department of State, Division of Archives, Records Management and History

**Back Endsheets:**

Governors Roemer, Treen, McKeithen, and Davis: Courtesy Louisiana Department of State, Division of Archives, Records Management and History

Library of Congress Catalog Number: 96-84494
ISBN Number: 1-887366-26-1



Published by The Center for Louisiana Studies
P.O. Box 40831
University of Southwestern Louisiana
Lafayette, LA 70504-0831

# CONTENTS

## ABOUT THE EDITOR

**Michael L. Kurtz** received his doctorate in history from Tulane University and since 1967 has taught at Southeastern Louisiana University, where he currently serves as Dean of the Graduate School. He is co-author of *Louisiana: A History* and of *Earl K. Long: The Saga of Uncle Earl and Louisiana Politics* and author of numerous articles on recent Louisiana history. He is a past president of the Louisiana Historical Association.

# ABOUT THE SERIES

It was in the spring of 1992 that first thought was given to the matter of how best the Center for Louisiana Studies might commemorate the bicentennial of the Louisiana Purchase in 2003. For the next few months the Center's staff and members of its Advisory Council intermittently discussed the possible project, but no consensus was forthcoming. Perhaps the reason being that the Purchase looms so monumentally in United States history there are seemingly few memorials of proper proportion to commemorate the event's bicentennial.

Nevertheless, as time passed the outlines of a project began to take shape. To properly mark the occasion the Center for Louisiana Studies should produce a lasting tribute not only to the people who crafted the Louisiana Purchase but also to the people who, during the last two hundred years, have had a role in transforming that vast wilderness into the heartland of America. But the Center's focus is not mid-America for all practical purposes, it is Louisiana, the state that took its name from the Purchase territory. Therefore, the Center's project would concentrate on a Purchase bicentennial memorial that embraced the full range of Louisiana history.

There was another reason for this decision. In March of 1999 the Gulf Coast and the Mississippi Valley will mark the tercentennial of the founding of the French colony of Louisiana and the beginning of the region's historical era. Thus, if the Center's endeavor for the Purchase bicentennial was to be a history of Louisiana, then it should tell not only about the American experience in the area but also the Native American, French, Spanish, African, British and other influences that helped to lay the foundations for the present-day state.

Questions arose: Will the Center's Purchase bicentennial memorial be yet another history of Louisiana? If so, should it be another survey or should it be a more detailed account? Who would write this account of our times and those of our forebears? What interpretation would emerge from such a monograph? Who was expert enough to incorporate a harmonious blend of the political, economic, and social ingredients of our society?

Another year slipped by while we pondered these and other questions concerning the Center's memorial to the Purchase bicentennial and the tercentennial of the founding of the colony. After more discussion, there began to emerge a collective concept that was at once imaginative, exciting, and, above all, challenging. As a fitting memorial for the Louisiana Purchase bicentennial, the Center would organize and direct the publication of a major historical series. Marking the anniversaries, however, should not be the only reason for such an endeavor.

As discussion of the nature of the series evolved, it became obvious that there was an overriding reason for it. The series, to be known as the LOUISIANA PURCHASE BICENTENNIAL SERIES IN LOUISIANA HISTORY, would be a fine sampling of twentieth-century scholarship, particularly the scholarship of the last half of the century which embraced new methodologies leading to broader interpretations of the state's history. Here, in a multi-volume series the student of Louisiana history would be exposed to a wide range of scholarship reflecting multiple interpretations of historical events.

Thus, the decision was made; the Series would bring together in one place the very best articles, essays, and book parts that have been published about Louisiana in the twentieth century, particularly the latter half of the century. Its focus would be to inform scholars, teachers, students, and laypersons on far-ranging topics of Louisiana history drawn from a great reservoir of scholarship found in media ranging from scholarly to popular to obscure.

Most important to the development of such a series, however, was the person or persons who would select the "very best" to incorporate into the Series. The answer came quickly, only widely recognized experts, acting as volume editors, would determine from the broad spectrum of sources those essays which reflect the best in research, writing, and interpretation on topics in Louisiana history.

Initially, twenty broad topics of Louisiana history were identified, and the Center plans to publish these twenty volumes between 1995 and 2003. There may be additional volumes, if they are warranted. It should be noted, however, proper presentation of some topics in Louisiana history cannot be confined to a single book; hence, some volumes may incorporate several parts in order to present the full spectrum of scholarship on the subject. Finally, the volumes will not be published in sequential order, although Volume I, *The French Experience in Louisiana* was the first to appear. Each volume will be announced upon publication.

THE LOUISIANA PURCHASE BICENTENNIAL SERIES IN LOUISIANA HISTORY presents a great source of information for anyone interested in the history of the colony and the state. It stands as an appropriate memorial to the men and women who shaped the colony and state down to the dawn of the twenty-first century.

Glenn R. Conrad, General Editor

# INTRODUCTION

The year 1960 may be viewed as a watershed year in the history of twentieth century Louisiana. The death of Earl K. Long in September brought to an end the tumultuous and controversial political regimes that he and his brother, Huey, had established. The federal court-mandated racial desegregation of two public elementary schools in New Orleans in November ushered in the era of civil rights. The inauguration of Jimmie Davis as governor in May produced the last efforts of hard-line segregationists to maintain a dying system of discrimination and repression.

In the nearly four decades since 1960, Louisiana has experienced revolutionary change in virtually every aspect of its existence. For the first time in their history, African Americans enjoyed equal treatment before the law and developed a strong influence in the state's political system. Such outstanding blacks as Dutch Morial and his son, Marc, both mayors of New Orleans, William Jefferson and Cleo Fields, both members of the U.S. House of Representatives, and state legislators Diane Bajoie, Johnny Jackson, Alphonse Jackson, and Dorothy Mae Taylor became powerful elements in the political process. The new state constitution of 1974 contained a strong provision mandating sexual equality. Together with legislative acts and constitutional amendments abolishing such vestiges of the male-controlled past as the "Head and Master" law giving the husband the domineering influence in marriage, and the radical revision of the Forced Heirship principle that had dealt harshly with widows, the status of women in modern Louisiana improved dramatically. Politically, Edwin Edwards became the dominant force in the state, serving a record four terms as governor and leaving his indelible mark on the system. The Republican party took advantage of the growing conservatism of much of the populace to become a true rival to the Democrats, with such men as Congressmen Bob Livingston and Billy Tauzin achieving positions of importance in the national government, and such state leaders as House Speaker John Hainkel and Governor Mike Foster dominating state politics in the last years of the twentieth century. The influence of women in Louisiana politics increased dramatically with such prominent leaders as Congresswoman Lindy Boggs, U. S. Senator Mary Landrieu, and Lieutenant Governor Kathleen Babineaux Blanco attaining state and national distinction.

Throughout the nearly four-decade long period, Louisiana experienced a series of economic upheavals. In the 1960s and 1970s, a booming oil industry, its profits swelled by the enormous inflation in energy costs of the 1970s, poured billions of dollars into the state's coffers, enabling Governors Jimmie Davis, John McKeithen, and Edwin Edwards to fund hefty increases in state spending on health, education, and welfare without imposing prohibitive taxes on the citizenry. The early 1980s, however, witnessed a collapse of the oil boom, as prices plunged, and tens of thousands lost their jobs. Correspondingly, state spending on social programs declined, and Louisiana dropped to the bottom of the South in such categories as teachers' salaries, educational expenditures, employment, and health care. This, in turn, led to Buddy Roemer's dramatic defeat of Edwin Edwards in the 1987 governor's election.

The revival of the economy came in the mid-1990s, as the energy industry recovered its former status, and gambling fever swept the state. The formal approval in 1990 by state voters of a constitutional amendment authorizing a state lottery generated the development of such other forms of legal gambling as video poker, riverboat casinos, and a permanent land-based casino. Despite many problems associated with gambling, the industry poured billions of dollars into the economy and contributed to the revival of such places as Lake Charles, Shreveport, and Bossier City. Despite strong competition from riverboat casinos in neighboring Mississippi, legalized gambling had a profound impact on Louisiana. The combined annual amounts of money bet on riverboat casinos and video poker machines totaled more than $1 billion. The industry employed thousands of people and pumped tens of millions into local and state coffers. Opponents of legalized gambling claimed that these amounts would have been spent on more productive areas of the economy had gambling not existed. Furthermore, they asserted that the plague of compulsive gambling afflicted tens of thousands of people and ruined innumerable lives.

From kindergarten through graduate school, education in Louisiana remained near the bottom of the nation in the quality of instruction and in the amount of state resources spent on it. The number of days in the school year declined. School teachers found themselves receiving inadequate training, and by 1996, more than 40 percent of all public school teachers in the state were not certified to teach in the area they were assigned. With teachers' salaries ranking forty-third in the nation and the country's highest high school dropout rate, Louisiana clearly had fundamental problems to resolve. Colleges and universities found themselves increasingly forced to endure substantial cuts in state appropriations which resulted in high tuition, low salaries, neglect of physical plant maintenance, and crowded classrooms.

The environment became an increasingly significant topic of discussion. The decline in population of such endangered species as the Louisiana black bear, the annual erosion of the state's coastline, the ravaging of its wetlands, and the toxic pollution from the petrochemical industry made environmental concerns the subject of great attention. Along both sides of the Mississippi River between Baton Rouge and New Orleans, experts attributed an alarmingly high incidence of lung cancer to industrial pollution.

Environmental groups did contribute to preservation movements that resulted in considerable popular interest in the Atchafalaya Basin, the Kitsachie Forest, and the Gulf Coast.

Culturally, Louisiana remained one of the nation's leaders. In the arts, Anne Rice became one of the best-selling authors in the country with her series of vampire novels. Walker Percy won respect as one of America's greatest writers, and T. Harry Williams and Stephen Ambrose wrote highly acclaimed historical works. Musicians Harry Connick, Jr. and Aaron Neville gathered numerous fans from across the country for their unique musical styles. Almost every weekend, Louisiana communities attracted tens of thousands to their festivals featuring jazz and musical heritages, African American, Cajun, and other ethnic cultures, and a bewildering variety of foods, ranging from strawberries to andouille to crawfish to pralines.

This, the final volume chronologically, in the *Louisiana Purchase Bicentennial Series*, provides a selection of readings covering some of the main historical trends and events since 1960. It is not intended to be comprehensive, and many significant reading selections have been omitted. Rather, the selection of readings from both scholarly and popular authors is meant to offer the reader a sampling of writings about some of the most significant people, places, and events that have contributed to the development of Louisiana in the last four decades of the twentieth century. It is divided into sections: politics; the economy; the environment; race; education; and some reflections on late twentieth-century Louisiana.

The first section covers politics because in Louisiana, politics has always dominated the agenda. In the initial selection, Edward F. Haas relates one of the unique features of state politics, the heavy dosage of humor underlying campaign appeals and press conferences by elected officials. Indeed, the term colorful has been applied to a host of state politicians, and in this reading, Haas's presidential address before the Louisiana Historical Association, he provides an amusing and insightful look at the innate wit of many state politicians. In the second reading, Thomas A. Becnel describes the changes in political philosophy undergone by one of Louisiana's longtime political powers, U. S. Senator Allen Ellender. The third selection encompasses brief biographical sketches of three of Louisiana's governors during the period covered by this volume: John McKeithen by Arthur W. Bergeron, and Edwin Edwards and David Treen by Joseph B. Parker.

A native of Marksville, Edwin W. Edwards dominated state politics for nearly a quarter of a century and won election to the governorship a record four times. Colorful, controversial, charismatic, Edwards aroused intense passions in the electorate and left a legacy of both genuine accomplishment and questionable methods. In the fourth selection under politics, Melody D. Bonnette describes the difficulties that Edwards encountered during his third administration, both his doomed efforts to deal with Louisiana's severe fiscal crisis of the mid-1980s and his federal grand jury indictment and subsequent trials on various charges of political corruption. The fifth selection presents lively commentary by political writer John Maginnis about state politics and about Edwards's successful campaign to unseat incumbent David Treen in the 1983 gubernatorial election.

The last two selections in the politics section cover the most controversial figure in recent Louisiana politics, former Ku Klux Klan supporter David Duke. The sixth reading by Elizabeth A. Rickey provides an insider's account of the failure of the leadership of the Louisiana Republican party to reject Duke's attempt to run as the party's candidate for governor in 1991. The seventh reading by journalist Tyler Bridges covers what he termed "the race from hell," the highly inflammatory 1991 gubernatorial primaries, with Edwin Edwards and David Duke emerging as the leaders after the first primary and facing each other in the runoff. Both Rickey and Bridges vividly describe the atmosphere of hatred, bigotry, and ugliness that Duke's candidacy engendered in Louisiana, and the attendant national publicity, much of it highly negative and critical, brought down on the state during the campaign. Duke's surprising victory over former governor Buddy Roemer in the first primary left the voters with a choice between him and Edwards. In the runoff, Edwards easily won, but only because his opponent was David Duke.

In the next section, the Economy, three readings offer insights into various aspects of Louisiana's economic development during the period since 1960. In the first selection, Lee J. Melton, Jr. provides a probing insight into the factors affecting Louisiana's economy in the 1960s. In the second reading, Loren C. Scott relates the dynamics of the state's dramatic economic growth during the 1970s. The third article, also by Loren C. Scott, describes various factors, including demographic changes, that have affected the state's economic structure for the past quarter century.

The next section, the Environment, contains five readings covering different features of Louisiana's complex ecological system. In the first reading, Anthony J. Mumphrey, Jr., and Frederick W. Wagner describe some of the environmental problems, as well as some of the economic impacts, of the development of the outer continental shelf in Lafourche Parish. In the second selection, Robert Fritchey relates some of the threats to the lifestyle of the brown pelican, the state bird. Third, the Louisiana Advisory Committee details some of the problems that industrial development engenders, particularly its damaging impact on black citizens. Fourth, John Randolph Kemp narrates the story of some of the unique denizens of the Manchac Swamp area, including the daily problems they confront, as well as the environmental features of that great Louisiana ecological system. Finally, Martin Reuss details some of the issues associated with flood control in the great Atchafalaya Basin.

The next section, Race, treats one of Louisiana's and the nation's most serious issues. In the first reading, Arnold R. Hirsch provides an insightful account of the changing nature of race and its impact on politics in the state's largest city. The next reading, by Christopher B. Strain, relates the story of the Deacons for Defense and Justice, an organization of blacks in Bogalusa who acted as a deterrent to the Ku Klux Klan and other segregationist groups during that city's racial problems of the 1960s. In the third reading, Adam Fairclough relates the development of black political power in

Louisiana after the passage of the Voting Rights Act of 1965. The fourth reading, by Roman J. Heleniak, recounts the highly significant speech by President Lyndon B. Johnson, given in New Orleans during the 1964 presidential campaign, in which Johnson urged fellow southerners to stop their habitual use of the race issue to inflame political passions. Fifth, Kent Germany describes the legal and social problems associated with public school desegregation in Lincoln Parish. Sixth, Elliott Leyton provides a chilling account of the murderous rampage of Mark Essex, a man driven to acts of extreme violence by his experiencing of repeated instances of racial bigotry. Finally, Adam Fairclough discusses some of the challenges that continue to face Louisiana in the area of race.

Five articles treat the subject of the next section, Education. Morgan D. Peoples provides a lively, entertaining account of the career of the legendary president of Grambling State University, Ralph Waldo Emerson "Prez" Jones. Donald E. DeVore and Joseph Logsdon discuss the changing nature of public education in New Orleans after public school desegregation. In his presidential address before the Louisiana Historical Association, Michael L. Kurtz provides a summary of some of the problems affecting education in Louisiana. Brady M. Banta relates the story of the decades-long struggle of Shreveport to obtain a medical school. Finally, Judith F. Gentry, James H. Dormon, and Thomas D. Watson analyze the lack of sufficient attention to History among the state's colleges and universities, and they offer a suggestion for improvement.

In the final section, labeled Some Reflections on Late Twentieth-century Louisiana, a potpourri of articles covering various features of Louisiana history since 1960 is presented. In the first reading, Henry Hurt details some of the mysterious activities of Lee Harvey Oswald during his five-month sojourn in New Orleans during the spring and summer of 1963, activities that raise serious questions about the Warren Commission's contention that Oswald acted alone in assassinating President John F. Kennedy, and he discusses the controversial investigation into the assassination by Orleans Parish District Attorney Jim Garrison. The second and third readings, by Burk Foster, consider certain aspects of crime. The fourth reading, by Dr. John Salvaggio, describes some of the political and financial problems faced by New Orleans's Charity Hospital. In the fifth reading Vivien W. Chen provides interesting epidemiological data on the high cancer rate in the southern half of the state. Sixth, Glenn R. Conrad provides a nostalgic look at the passing of old institutions, such as the "mom and pop" stores that used to line Main Street. Prescott N. Dunbar tells the story of the rise of the New Orleans Museum of Art from its modest beginning to its current status as one of the nation's leading galleries. Ann J. Pond describes one of innumerable festivals, the annual New Orleans Art for Arts' Sake gala. Barbara C. Ewell offers a reinterpretation of the influence of women writers in Louisiana. Jared W. Bradley gives a sympathetic account of one of modern Louisiana's most renowned writers, Walker Percy. Journalist Wiley W. Hilburn, Jr., writes a series of interesting accounts of some of the wonderful variety of life in North Louisiana. The final three readings, by Barry Jean Ancelet, Rhodes J. Spedale, Jr., and Laurence Bergreen, treat certain aspects of Louisiana's rich musical tradition.

In the past four decades, like the rest of the nation, Louisiana experienced many changes, yet she retained many of the essential features of her unique past. This combination of strong adherence to tradition with a ready acceptance for change, has made the state one of America's most interesting. It is hoped that these readings will provide the reader with an appreciation of the difficulties, the challenges, and the opportunities that have confronted Louisiana since 1960.

# PART I

## POLITICS

# BLACK CAT, UNCLE EARL, EDWIN AND THE KINGFISH: THE WIT OF MODERN LOUISIANA POLITICS*

Edward F. Haas

Louisianians may have serious misgivings about their government, but few will deny that they enjoy politics. A. J. Liebling, a perceptive observer from New York, noted: "in Louisiana, anyone from a society woman to a bellhop will talk politics."[1] Iris Kelso, veteran political reporter for the *New Orleans Times-Picayune,* recently agreed that politics was her "state's favorite spectator sport."[2] Huey Pierce Long, too, contended that politics was a magnificent game. The Kingfish once told Richard W. Leche, a disciple who lacked his leader's savvy and verve for the contest, that politics was "the sport of kings."[3] Eugene Schlossberger, a professor of Philosophy at Louisiana State University in Baton Rouge and former resident of Pennsylvania, though acknowledging the validity of Kelso's claim, viewed Louisiana politics with a decidedly less regal perspective. In an interview with *USA Today,* Schlossberger argued: "Politics plays the role in Louisiana that TV wrestling does in the rest of the nation. It is fixed. It is flamboyant. It is surreal. It is our spectator sport."[4]

The philosopher's remarks, however, neglected a vital aspect of Louisiana politics that Senator Tom Connally understood well. In 1934, after a clash with the Kingfish, the Texan made this recommendation to his Washington colleagues: "I advise anyone who thinks he knows something about politics to go down in Louisiana and take a postgraduate course."[5] Connally recognized that the Pelican State was one of the nation's toughest political arenas; those who mastered the game there were among the best. A. J. Liebling also recognized the underlying sophistication of the state's favorite sport. The New York journalist contended that "Louisiana politics is of an intensity and complexity that are matched . . . only in the republic of Lebanon."[6]

*First published in *Louisiana History*, 29 (1988): 213-27. Reprinted with the kind permission of the author and the Louisiana Historical Association.

Schlossberger, nonetheless, correctly assessed an entrenched and significant segment of modern Louisiana political culture. Residents of the Pelican State have come to view politics as an "entertainment outlet." For them, politics has been a traditional and reliable source of fun.[7] In 1968, for instance, New Orleans journalist Hermann B. Deutsch deemed politics in the state's largest city "The Greatest Free Show on Earth."[8] He, like Frank Skeffington, the sage protagonist in Edwin O'Connor's classic novel, *The Last Hurrah,* believed that "a big political campaign, if it's run right, is one of the greatest shows on earth."[9] In Louisiana, many people have customarily added to their political pleasure with bets on electoral contests and thus tapped into the state's third largest industry, illegal gambling. In such cases, the show was not always free.

At the core of the Louisiana political spectacle has been humor. In 1982, political scientists David M. Landry and Joseph B. Parker noted: "Political pranks are common in Louisiana, and storytelling is a way of life."[10] Citizens of the Pelican State have learned to expect jocularity from their political leaders and have had little cause for disappointment. The ranks of state politicos have routinely included individuals of the keenest wit, the unintentionally funny, sagacious spinners of downhome wisdom and the simply bizarre. Among the most notable have been the Long brothers, Huey and Earl, "Coozan" Dudley LeBlanc, and, of course, Edwin Washington Edwards, but other lesser figures such as B. B. "Sixty" Rayburn, Victor H. Schiro and Allen "Black Cat" LaCombe have made their contributions to the legacy of political humor in Louisiana.

This fascination with political humor was first evident during the antebellum period when political rallies were exciting events that commonly included, according to Robert Patrick, "barbecues, glee clubs and all that sort of thing."[11] Candidates for public office frequently traveled together from village to village and developed a sense of camaraderie that manifested itself in practical jokes and barbed exchanges. On the campaign trail, humorous quips and satirical poetry—often quite bad satirical poetry—were typically the order of the day. Louisiana audiences grew accustomed to political candidates who sang songs, related entertaining stories and told jokes. Rural folk with few amusing diversions to break the monotony of toil undoubtedly looked forward to these political gatherings with great relish.[12]

During the last decade of the antebellum era, emotionalism and flamboyance persisted in Louisiana politics, but the issues of slavery, states rights, and secession were serious matters that invoked what scholars have called "a rhetoric of desperation."[13] After the Civil War, the Old South legend, the myth of the Lost Cause, white supremacy, and the New South creed did not lend themselves to humor.[14] Late nineteenth-century journals such as the *Mascot* in New Orleans commonly included excellent political cartoons and rich satire, but the disfranchisement of black men and poor whites, convict-leasing, and the state lottery did not amuse Louisianians.[15] The frivolity that frequently prevailed among Louisiana Democrats behind the closed doors of the Choctaw Club in the Crescent City was not evident in their public presentations.[16]

During the twentieth century, wit returned to Southern politics. In 1917 New Orleans Mayor Martin Behrman, a conservative Democrat, reputedly remarked upon the closing of Storyville, a protected red-light district, "You can make prostitution illegal in Louisiana, but you can't make it unpopular;" however, the true sires of Southern political humor were the demagogues who often turned the stump into comic opera.[17] Born of the Populist struggle against Bourbon rule, the demagogues' style featured the "tricks of the ham actor," the use of "jokes, anecdotes, and personalized invective," "profuse emotionalism" and a "carnival-like atmosphere of the oratorical occasions."[18] In Louisiana the foremost practitioner of these techniques was Huey Pierce Long of Winn Parish.[19]

Long, like the Populists, spoke in the vernacular of the common man and used his wit to polarize his backers and his foes. The Kingfish was a master of personal ridicule. Long once contended that if you put former governors J. Y. Sanders, Ruffin G. Pleasant and John M. Parker in "a room with a polecat, the polecat will break out in about two minutes."[20] A similar remark about Shreveport Mayor Lee E. Thomas led to a slander suit.[21] The Kingfish, maintaining that Martin Behrman and John Sullivan were henchmen in the service of Wall Street, stated: "If Behrman took a dose of laudanum [a narcotic], Sullivan would get sleepy in ten minutes."[22]

Long commonly used derogatory nicknames to characterize his opponents. Sullivan, a horseracing devotee, became "Bang Tail"; Robert Ewing of the *New Orleans States*, an aggressive, outspoken critic, earned the label "Colonel Bow Wow." Long called Marshall Ballard of the *New Orleans Item* the "Imperial Wizard of Pen-Pushers" and T. Semmes Walmsley, the tall, balding, bony-faced New Orleans mayor, "Turkey Head." He deemed Edward Rightor, a socially prominent Crescent City attorney, "Whistle Britches," supposedly because the anti-Longite rubbed his pants legs together when he walked, making a distinctive sound, but insiders always cited Rightor's proneness to flatulence.[23]

The Kingfish, when necessary, resorted to allegory. He once contended that Herbert Hoover was a hoot owl and President Franklin D. Roosevelt, whose name Long always purposely mispronounced, a scrootch owl. The hoot owl, said Huey, "bangs into the nest and knocks the hen clean off and catches her while she's falling." A scrootch owl "slips into the roost and scrootches up to the hen and talks softly to her. And the hen just falls in love with him, and next thing you know there ain't no hen."[24]

Earl Long rivaled his older brother's talent for political castigation. Uncle Earl once said of his opponent Jimmie H. Davis, author of "You Are My Sunshine": "How you going to debate a clown like that? All he gives them is music." Earl contended that the singer "won't say nothing, he won't do nothing and if he gets in, he [still] won't do nothing."[25] Long denounced Attorney General Jack Gremillion with the observation, "If you want to lose anything real good, just put it in Jack Gremillion's law book."[26] In his final campaign against Harold McSween, Uncle Earl contended that McSween is "the only man I know who can talk out of both sides of his mouth and whistle at the same time."[27]

Earl, too, combined subtlety with wit. In Protestant North Louisiana, Long addressed charges that New Orleans Congressman T. Hale Boggs was a Communist.

Uncle Earl mockingly defended his adversary with the comment that Boggs "ain't no Communist. He's too good a *Catholic* to be a Communist." For those who missed the point, Long added, "He's got a brother that's [*sic*] a *Catholic priest*" and "he's Knights of Columbus."[28] When Sam Houston Jones suffered an injury in an automobile accident during a political contest with Earl, Long quipped, "I quit campaigning to see he got the best medical attention. I knew if old Sam died they might put a good man in the race who'd beat us both."[29]

During another campaign, Long sent his workers to mix with the crowds at Jones rallies and whisper to each other that the candidate was a good man, but nobody liked him. The tactic was so effective that Jones deviated from one prepared address to assert angrily that people did indeed like him.[30] In 1956, Long's false praise for gubernatorial rival Fred Preaus, an automobile dealer, was equally ruinous. Earl assured his audience that Preaus was "a fine fellow. If I wanted an automobile I'd go to him to buy one," then Long abruptly changed pace, "but now if I wanted *three* automobiles, that would be too big a deal for him to handle."[31]

At other times, the Long brothers dismissed guile and employed blatant profanity. When Dr. Hiram W. Evans of the Ku Klux Klan promised a visit to Louisiana, Huey declared bluntly, "Quote me as saying that that Imperial bastard will never set foot in Louisiana, and that when I call him a sonofabitch I am not using profanity, but am referring to the circumstances of his birth."[32] Evans wisely did not show. During one heated legislative debate, a livid Uncle Earl unthinkingly blurted, "Willie Rainach ain't nothing but a little __________ [expletive deleted]." Quickly realizing the magnitude of his slip, Long apologized, "Ladies and gentlemen, excuse me, I meant 'sapsucker.'"[33] When friends advised him to watch his mouth, Earl replied that without profanity he would be like his cousin who joined the Baptist Church and lost ninety percent of his vocabulary.[34]

Huey and Earl often used humorous denunciation of their foes to cement their ties with the common folk of Louisiana. When Representative Riley Joe Wilson claimed that he had gone barefoot as a child, the Kingfish responded, "I can go Mr. Wilson one better; I was born barefoot."[35] In 1940, Brother Earl explained his failure to receive the endorsement of the *New Orleans Times-Picayune* with the admonition, "It's because I can't eat a sixteen[-]course dinner with a fork about as big as your little finger without spilling some of it on your vest. Sam Jones can do that."[36] Long advised his constituents: "Vote for a man that [*sic*] looks like ye, and works like ye—and smells like ye on Saturday night."[37] "Old high hat[,] sweet smelling[,] silk stocking Jones" obviously did not qualify.[38] Nor did Robert Kennon whose blood, said Uncle Earl, was "65 percent champagne and 35 percent talcum powder."[39] Neither did Harold McSween, whom Earl called "Catfish Mouth." According to Long, "The heaviest thing he ever picked up was a golf ball."[40]

Uncle Earl's favorite target, however, was Mayor deLesseps Story Morrison of New Orleans, whom Long alternately deemed "Dellasoups," "Little Boy Blue, the debutante's delight" and "Storytelling" Morrison.[41] The Winn Parish native denounced the youthful mayor as "a boy in a man's job" and claimed that Morrison wore a toupee—"tuppy," as Uncle Earl called it—bought expensive suits and used cologne.[42] The New Orleanian tried to retaliate, but his strategy usually fizzled. The Crescent City mayor, for instance, once attacked Long's television appearances, saying that to get Uncle Earl to speak his lines correctly, aides had to "put him in a corset, powder his face," and shoot "the film in short takes."[43] Long responded deftly, "How can I compete with Della Soups on television? I ain't even got one of them make-up kits. . . . "[44]

The success of the Kingfish and Uncle Earl prompted others to follow their lead. In 1963, John J. McKeithen, one of Earl Long's pupils, revived the toupee ploy in his gubernatorial contest with Morrison—although McKeithen pronounced the word "too-pay." The New Orleanian became so incensed that once during a rally he pulled hard on his thinning hair to prove that it was real.[45]

Twenty years later, David Treen and Edwin Edwards traded numerous barbs in their run for the governorship. Edwards focused on Governor Treen's supposed indifference to the poor people, "They can't find a job and can't find anyone to talk to. Have any of you ever called Dave Treen? Go ahead and try it and see if he calls you back. By the time you hear from him again, I'll be in the [Governor's] Mansion answering the phone."[46] On another occasion, Edwards blasted Treen's direct mailings by holding up a letter and asking what was the color of the governor's signature. When the audience shouted, "Blue," Edwards responded quickly, "Same color as his blood."[47] Treen denounced Edwards's falsehoods with the contention, "When his mouth's not moving, he's not lying."[48] During a debate, the governor asked, "Why do you continue to talk out of both sides of your mouth?" Edwards retorted, "So that people like you with nothing between their ears can understand what I say."[49] Edwards pressed the issue of Treen's intellect with his most devastating remark: He "takes an hour and a half to watch *60 Minutes*."[50] Political tout Joe Robino later suggested that the two verbal combatants rent the Louisiana Superdome to mud wrestle.[51]

Much of Louisiana political humor has been inadvertent. When in 1929 Longites contended that Chief Justice Charles O'Neil was biased against Huey Long and should recuse himself from any impeachment proceedings, O'Neil countered, "Don't they think that I'll give the thieving sonofabitch a fair trial?"[52] Responding to charges of corruption, Richard Leche once exclaimed, "I deny the allegations and I defy the alligator."[53]

Allen LaCombe, a hapless candidate who acquired the nickname "The Black Cat" for his ineptitude at handicapping horses and politics, also displayed a talent for unintentional humor. In the 1959 governor's race, "Black Cat" enjoyed his greatest political success due to his placement on the ballot. LaCombe "got Number Seven, right between Davis and Morrison [the frontrunners]." He calculated, "I have to get at least three thousand votes by mistake. I figure to run a good sixth."[54] Even in triumph, he was wrong; he finished fifth.

In 1962, LaCombe, though "drawing unemployment compensation," ran for mayor of New Orleans. During a television debate, "Black Cat" advised viewers forthrightly, "Don't vote for me 'cause they've got a lot of good men in this race." They listened. He ran last.[55]

The undisputed king of political malapropism, however, was Victor H. Schiro. Schiro once lectured a group of local businessman, "We people in New Orleans are sitting on some of the biggest assets in the world." During a political dinner, the mayor introduced Governor McKeithen and his wife, became flustered and declared that the first lady's love for "Big John" was beaming from "every wrinkle in her face." Amid the chaos of Hurricane Betsy in 1965, the Crescent City chief executive reputedly counselled confused residents, "Don't believe any false rumors unless they come from me."[56]

Huey Long, too, produced unintentional humor, often when he discussed the Bible. When an associate suggested the use of a biblical quotation, the Kingfish, warming to the idea, sent an aide to buy him "the best damned Bible they've got." He once told reporters, "You never see anybody getting into trouble that [*sic*] lives up to the Bible." Not spying his sacred volume immediately, he complained, "By the way, where the hell is that Bible I had anyway."[57] Long's belief in ministers, however, did not match his devotion to the Holy Scriptures. "Bible's the greatest book ever written," Long insisted, "but I sure don't need anybody I can buy for six bits and a chew of tobacco to explain it to me. When I need preachers, I buy 'em cheap."[58]

Edwin Edwards, a Nazarene preacher as a young man, often used religious wisecracks to advance his notable reputation for high living. While exiting Notre Dame Cathedral in Paris, Edwards encountered a nun from Louisiana who jokingly said, "Governor, I'm going to give you a French kiss," indicating, of course, location, not technique. Edwards answered, "Okay, Sister, just don't let me get in the habit."[59] On Pope John Paul's visit to New Orleans in September 1987, the governor announced, "The Pope has not agreed to extend his stay three days to hear my confession." It "would not be long enough."[60] In August 1987, he told the congregation of the Union Bethel African Methodist Episcopal Church in New Orleans, "I didn't come here as a saint trying to be a governor, but as a governor trying to be a saint. It's hard."[61] When a reporter asked the Reverend Clarence D. Bates about his support for Edwards, a man who gambled, chased woman, laughed about lying and was constantly under investigation for corruption, the minister responded, "Well, he doesn't drink or smoke."[62]

Edwards's raucous lifestyle gave rise to numerous amusing comments. When a reporter asked if Korean businessman Tongsun Park supplied congressmen with women, Edwards replied that he was unaware of that, "but it's certainly better than cash." After the governor informed the press that a respected politician had a mistress, a newsman asked, "You're telling us that he cheats on his wife." Edwards answered, "He's not as good at it as I am, but he does."[63] In 1983, he boasted, "The only way I could lose this next election is if I was caught in bed with a dead woman or a live boy."[64] When Edwards stood trial on federal charges of corruption, investigators revealed that he had frequently used the fictitious name of T. Wong on his gambling trips to Las Vegas and Reno, prompting reporters to joke that it was "just a case of a good man gone Wong."[65] In his concession speech to Charles E. "Buddy" Roemer on October 24, 1987, the governor quoted the Chinese proverb: "If you wait by the river long enough, the body of your enemy will float by." Political analyst John Maginnis noted tongue in cheek, "Spoken like a Wong."[66]

Novelist Nancy Lemann observed that "in Louisiana we elect our governors to be kings. The nuttier the better, that they should then turn into megalomaniacs, provide public entertainment, and have public breakdowns."[67] No one matched Earl Long in the latter category. Despite his incarceration in Texas and Louisiana mental institutions, Uncle Earl maintained his sense of humor. On route to a mental hospital in Galveston, he commented that he felt "like a muley bull coming out of a dipping vat."[68] He subsequently recalled that there were "not enough clothes on me to cover a red bug, and a week later I was enjoying the same wardrobe."[69] When Long managed to transfer to a state asylum in Mandeville, Dr. Charles Belcher, the superintendent, greeted him, "I'm Dr. Belcher, Governor." Uncle Earl shot back quickly, "The hell you *are*—you *were* Dr. Belcher."[70] A. J. Liebling once said that Long "was beset by arteriosclerosis, several small strokes, oscillatory blood pressure and an irreverent gleam in his left eye."[71]

An anti-Longite predicted during Long's 1960 campaign for Congress, "He [is] . . . likely to die before the primaries, sure to get licked if he survived, certain to be thrown out by the State Supreme Court if nominated, and bound to be in jail before he could be inaugurated."[72] Harold McSween, noting Long's escapades in mental hospitals and his close and intimate association with stripper Blaze Starr, argued derisively that his adversary belonged in public office only "if the knowledge of whiskey-drinking, chasing women, and the bug house are qualifications."[73] Long responded to the charge of chasing women, "I'm not a married man, I can go out with a pretty woman if I want to. I'm 64 years old and just had the worst operation a man could have. What would I do with a woman if I caught one?"[74] This disclaimer, nonetheless, did not mean that Uncle Earl was quitting the chase. After Long became involved in a French Quarter auto accident, a policeman asked for the governor's driver's license. Earl looked through his pockets and handed a license to the officer. The policeman, checking the card, said, "Governor, this . . . is a hunting license." Long answered, "What do you think I'm doing in the French Quarter?"[75]

Louisiana politicos have also been homespun philosophers. Uncle Earl once stated that Governor Orval E. Faubus of Arkansas, a segregationist, was a fine man, "but nobody had told him about the Civil War."[76] His thoughts on money and death were simple, "If I'm going where I hope to go, I won't need it. And if I go anyplace else, it'll burn up anyway."[77] He contended that there were "two types of people you can't satisfy, teachers and prostitutes."[78] He additionally stated that there were "two things a man ought never do. Write a letter to a woman and put money in a bank." His political strategy was also basic: "Don't write anything you can phone, don't phone anything you can talk face to face, don't talk anything you can smile, don't smile anything you can wink, and don't wink anything you can nod."[79] When a reporter claimed that Long had said one thing on Monday in Baton Rouge and exactly the opposite two days later in Lake Charles, the governor replied, "That's easy to explain. On Monday, I lied."[80]

Others were equally wise. Huey Long indeed was utilitarian. He advised the printer of his political circulars, "Don't use any of that damn smooth stuff, use some that they can use on their backside[s] after they get through reading it."[81] When a state legislator asked "Coozan" Dudley LeBlanc if Hadacol, his patented elixir, had ever made anyone well, LeBlanc, patting his hip pocket, replied, "I don't know about that, ma' fren,' but it sure has helped old Dud's pocket book." The Cajun politico, nonetheless, asserted that Hadacol was good for a variety of ailments, but it could not be used as antifreeze in automobile radiators.[82] When associates recommended that Robert Maestri respond to press criticism, the New Orleans mayor retorted that the suggested strategy was futile because "I buy ink by the bottle, they buy it by the tank car."[83] During a discussion of the state's woeful fiscal situation, Senator B. B. "Sixty" Rayburn maintained, "If you ain't got no cash, you ain't got a cash-flow problem."[84] Applauding the judge's establishment of a gag rule during the first Edwards trial, James Neal, a defense counsel, remarked, "You don't have to explain anything you ain't never said."[85]

The most humorous stories, however, have commonly involved the seeming essence of Louisiana politics: payoffs, patronage, and election fraud. Richard Leche spoke for many Louisiana politicos: "When I took the oath of office, I didn't take a vow of poverty."[86] When a reporter asked Representative Peter Hand what was in a particular legislative bill, the lawmaker answered, "About one thousand dollars for me."[87] A Crescent City political hack who held the patronage job of sidewalk inspector complained to his supervisor that someone was tailing him everyday at work. The superior screamed, "You dumb S. O. B., that's your assistant. He's following you to make sure you don't lose the sidewalk."[88]

Earl Long and Edwin Edwards certainly understood patronage and power. Uncle Earl professed that those who supported him in the first primary got jobs, those who backed him in the second primary got good government.[89] When a powerful sheriff died in office, a newsman sarcastically asked the governor which of his "good friends" would receive the interim appointment. Earl growled his response, "The first one of my good friends who gets here with $10,000."[90] After his election in 1983, Governor Edwards explained that there were three types of people whom he could appoint to public office or help get state business: "qualified friends, unqualified friends and enemies," adding emphatically, "I'm still working on the first group."[91]

Both men spoke lightly of corrupt practices. Uncle Earl declared, "It's a terrible thing when a man shows up crooked, but when Christ was on earth he picked 12 men and got a son-of-a-gun among them."[92] Edwards once told newsmen, "There is a big difference between what's illegal and what causes you people to raise your eyebrows."[93] He reminded voters, "Edwin Edwards may be rancid butter, but I'm on your side of the bread."[94] Earl's brother Huey shared their world view. Admitting the recent conviction of Representative Joe Fisher, a loyal associate, on federal charges, the Kingfish remarked, "He's a good friend of mine, but I've got too many relatives in the pen to make any comments about it."[95]

Long thought similarly about election fraud. A. O. Rappelet, for example, got his political initiation at age eighteen when he voted for the Kingfish twenty times in one day.[96] When in 1932 John Overton, another Long cohort, ran for the United States Senate, Huey, late at night, telephoned Sheriff L. A. Meraux of St. Bernard, a parish notorious for its peculiar returns, to inquire how many votes Overton had received. Meraux replied that, though the hour was late and the polls closed, they were still voting. A shocked Kingfish shouted, "We already won. For God's sake, stop counting." Long fully understood the implications of the sheriff's answer. Two years earlier, St. Bernard had delivered 3,979 votes for Huey and nine ballots for his opponent although there were only 2,510 registered voters in the parish.[97]

Meraux and his colleagues bore close kinship to the Louisiana judge and his political crony in a story that Huey's son Russell often related. One night the two politicians were strolling through a cemetery, copying down names to add to the voting rolls, when the compatriot could bear no more and "pleaded with the judge to leave, even though 10 tombstones remained to be inspected." The judge, however, refused, pointed to the remaining grave markers and declared, "Wait a minute. These people have just as much right to vote as the others."[98]

Nancy Lemann has reiterated the popular theory behind these shenanigans: "The people of Louisiana would rather be entertained than served with ethics."[99] Gus Weill, a veteran of many political wars, however, advanced his own perspective on the state's favorite spectator sport. He ruminated that "Circus tents are like political campaigns. You ever think of that? It's the same feeling of carnival, of magic, and the next day it's pulled down and gone. All illusion."[100] During his campaign for governor, "Buddy" Roemer, in a similar, though more critical vein, called Louisiana politics "Flashdance."[101] On October 24, 1987, the people of Louisiana, through the election of Roemer, broke with their obstreperous past, ended the festivities and introduced themselves to the stark reality of the morning after. In the ensuing days and weeks, the most optimistic began to hope that Russell Long was correct when he compared democracy in the Pelican State and elsewhere to a raft: "Your feet are always wet, but you never sink."[102] The Kingfish's son, however, undoubtedly never anticipated that his father's legacy would be a political whirlpool of cosmic proportions.

## Notes for "Black Cat, Uncle Earl, Edwin and the Kingfish"

[1]A. J. Liebling, *The Earl of Louisiana* (New York, 1961), 18.

[2]*New Orleans Times-Picayune*, January 19, 1988.

[3]Richard W. Leche, January 30, 1960, Interview Collection, Box 3, Folder 34, T. Harry Williams Papers, Department of Archives and Manuscripts, Louisiana State University, Baton Rouge.

[4]*USA Today*, April 17, 1987.

[5]T. Harry Williams, *Huey Long* (New York, 1969), 686.

[6]Liebling, *The Earl of Louisiana*, 18.

[7]David M. Landry and Joseph B. Parker, "The Louisiana Political Culture," in James Bolner, ed., *Louisiana Politics: Festival in a Labyrinth* (Baton Rouge, 1982), 10-11.

[8]Hermann B. Deutsch, "New Orleans Politics—The Greatest Free Show on Earth," in Hodding Carter, ed., *The Past as Prelude: New Orleans, 1718-1968* (New Orleans, 1968), 305.

[9]Edwin O'Connor, *The Last Hurrah* (Boston, 1956), 72.

[10]Landry and Parker, "Louisiana Political Culture," 2, 11; *Times-Picayune*, February 29, 1988.

[11]Edwin A. Davis, *Louisiana: A Narrative History* (Baton Rouge, 1961), 191.

[12]Ibid., 191-93.

[13]Waldo W. Braden, "Introduction," in Waldo W. Braden, ed., *Oratory in the Old South, 1828-1860* (Baton Rouge, 1970), 5.

[14]Waldo W. Braden, "Repining Over an Irrevocable Past: The Ceremonial Orator in a Defeated Society, 1865-1900," in Waldo B. Braden, ed., *Oratory in the New South* (Baton Rouge, 1979), 12; T. Harry Williams, *Romance and Realism in Southern Politics* (Athens, Ga., 1961), 6. See also Paul M. Gaston, *The New South Creed: A Study in Southern Mythmaking* (New York, 1970).

[15]See William Ivy Hair, *Bourbonism and Agrarian Protest: Louisiana Politics, 1877-1900* (Baton Rouge, 1969), chs. 10-11. See also New Orleans *Mascot, an Independent Journal of the Day*.

[16]Edward F. Haas, "John Fitzpatrick and Political Continuity in New Orleans, 1896-1899," *Louisiana History*, 22 (1981): 16, 21.

[17]Williams, *Huey Long*, 131.

[18]Cal M. Logue and Howard Dorgan, "The Demagogue," in Cal M. Logue and Howard Dorgan, eds., *The Oratory of Southern Demagogues* (Baton Rouge, 1981), 1-2, 5-6.

[19]V. O. Key, Jr., *Southern Politics in State and Nation* (New York, 1949), 3.

[20]*Times-Picayune*, June 19, 1930.

[21]Williams, *Huey Long*, 269, 451.

[22]Ibid., 204.

[23]Ibid., 204, 341, 427, 605-606; *New Orleans Item*, December 19, 1923.

[24]Williams, *Huey Long*, 812.

[25]Ed Cocke, "It Sounds Like Sunshine Time Again," *New Orleans*, 4 (1970): 56.

[26]Liebling, *The Earl of Louisiana*, 162.

[27]G. Dupré Litton, *The Wizard of Winnfield* (New York, 1982), 122.

[28]Ibid., 26.

[29]Ibid., 17.

[30]Thomas M. Brahney interview, January 30, 1971, deLesseps S. Morrison Collection, Department of Manuscripts and Archives, Tulane University, New Orleans, Louisiana.

[31]Richard B. McCaughan, *Socks on a Rooster: Louisiana's Earl K. Long* (Baton Rouge, 1967), 151. See also Litton, *The Wizard of Winnfield*, 30.

[32]Williams, *Huey Long*, 703; Hermann B. Deutsch, "The Kingdom of the Kingfish," in *Item*, September 19, 1939.

[33]John Maginnis, *The Last Hayride* (Baton Rouge, 1984), 177.

[34]Morgan D. Peoples, "Earl Kemp Long: The Man from Pea Patch Farm," *Louisiana History*, 17 (1976): 384.

[35]Williams, *Huey Long*, 205.

[36]F. Edward Hébert and John McMillan, *Last of the Titans: The Life and Times of Congressman F. Edward Hébert of Louisiana* (Lafayette, La., 1976), 143.

[37]Peoples, "Earl Kemp Long," 369; *Baton Rouge Sunday Advocate*, October 18, 1987.

[38]Litton, *The Wizard of Winnfield*, 17.

[39]*Sunday Advocate*, October 18, 1987.

[40]Litton, *The Wizard of Winnfield*, 122; Peoples, "Earl Kemp Long," 389.

[41]McCaughan, *Socks on a Rooster*, 151; Liebling, *The Earl of Louisiana*, 26, 92; Edward F. Haas, *DeLesseps S. Morrison and the Image of Reform: New Orleans Politics, 1946-1961* (Baton Rouge, 1974), 120-21; *Sunday Advocate*, October 18, 1987.

[42]Haas, *Morrison*, 225.

[43]Peoples, "Earl Kemp Long," 388.

[44]Litton, *The Wizard of Winnfield*, 30.

[45]Susan Everett Fenwick, "That Ol' Mr. *Times-Picayune:* A Political Analysis," *New Orleans*, 4 (1970): 55-56.

[46]Maginnis, *The Last Hayride*, 12.

[47]Ibid., 268.

[48]*Sunday Advocate*, October 18, 1987.

[49]Maginnis, *The Last Hayride*, 225.

[50]Ibid., 202.

[51]Ibid., 179.

[52]Williams, *Huey Long*, 383.

[53]Hébert and McMillan, *Last of the Titans*, 109.

[54]Liebling, *The Earl of Louisiana*, 165.

[55]Ed Cocke, "Things Just Might Be a Little Screwed Up or The Black Cat's Predictions for 1970," *New Orleans*, 4 (1969): 55-57.

[56]Louis de la Foret, Bob Krieger, and Ross Yockey, "The Sayings of Chairman Vic," *New Orleans*, 4 (1969): 35-37. Schiro later maintained that he had told the people: "Don't listen to anybody or any rumors. Mine is the only voice you should listen to. I'll give you the exact facts. When it's dangerous, I'll tell you to move. But don't listen to anybody or any rumors." George Gurtner, "The Hurricane Mayor Still Answers His Phone," *New Orleans*, 12 (1977): 23. For the McKeithen story, see Jack McGuire interview, September 1, 1987, Victor H. Schiro Interview Collection, Louisiana Historical Center, Louisiana State Museum, New Orleans, Louisiana.

[57]Williams, *Huey Long*, 135, 592, 648.

[58]Hermann B. Deutsch, *The Huey Long Murder Case* (Garden City, N.Y., 1963), 25.

[59]Maginnis, *The Last Hayride*, 15, 338.

[60]*Times-Picayune*, June 25, 1987.

[61]Ibid., August 31, 1987.

[62]Maginnis, *The Last Hayride*, 113.

[63]Ibid., 27, 28.

[64]*USA Today*, April 17, 1987.

[65]Nancy Lemann, *Ritz on the Bayou* (New York, 1987), 99.

[66]John Maginnis, "All in a Transition: Roemeristas, Resumés," *New Orleans City Business*, 8 (November 9, 1987): 33.

[67]Lemann, *Ritz on the Bayou*, 12.

[68]Peoples, "Earl Kemp Long," 374.

[69]Liebling, *The Earl of Louisiana*, 24.

[70]Litton, *The Wizard of Winnfield*, 48.

[71]Liebling, *The Earl of Louisiana*, 81.

[72]Ibid., 22.

[73]Peoples, "Earl Kemp Long," 389.

[74]Ibid., 374-75.

[75]Litton, *The Wizard of Winnfield*, 111.

[76]Liebling, *The Earl of Louisiana*, 138.

[77]McCaughan, *Socks on a Rooster*, 26.

[78]Litton, *The Wizard of Winnfield*, 40.

[79]McCaughan, *Socks on a Rooster*, 156.

[80]Peoples, "Earl Kemp Long," 374.

[81]Joseph B. David, June 25, 1957, Interview Collection, Box 3, Folder 30, T. Harry Williams Papers.

[82]Floyd Martin Clay, *Coozan Dudley LeBlanc: From Huey Long to Hadacol* (Gretna, La., 1973), 164, 174.

[83]Author's conversation with Eugene Fogarty, July 1, 1987.

[84]*Times-Picayune,* March 12, 1987.

[85]Author's recollections.

[86]Maginnis, *The Last Hayride,* 26.

[87]Iris Kelso and Rosemary James, "When the Caucus Ruled the World," *New Orleans,* 5 (1971): 48.

[88]Ibid., 22.

[89]*Times-Picayune,* July 26, 1987.

[90]John Maginnis, "The Downside of Freedom," *Gris Gris,* 3 (1987): 12, 14.

[91]Maginnis, *The Last Hayride,* 160.

[92]McCaughan, *Socks on a Rooster,* 68.

[93]Maginnis, *The Last Hayride,* 24.

[94]*Times-Picayune,* August 7, 1987.

[95]Ibid., April 28, 1935; Williams, *Huey Long,* 819.

[96]A. O. Rappelet, March 5, 1963, Interview Collection, Box 3, Folder 38, T. Harry Williams Papers.

[97]Williams, *Huey Long,* 539, 599.

[98]*Times-Picayune,* January 11, 1987.

[99]Lemann, *Ritz on the Bayou,* 12.

[100]Maginnis, *The Last Hayride,* 216.

[101]*Times-Picayune,* September 24, 1987.

[102]Ibid., January 11, 1987.

# THE GREAT SOCIETY UNDER SIEGE (1966-68)*

Thomas A. Becnel

In the midst of political battles over civil rights and agriculture, [Senator Allen] Ellender prepared for his sixth election campaign. He had completed nearly five full terms in Washington and felt confident about his reelection chances. The new civil rights legislation affected registration and voting patterns in Louisiana, but no apparent champion of black or liberal causes had emerged to challenge him. His position on sugar, rice, and cotton legislation had strengthened his hand with his constituents. He was seventy-five years old, but his active schedule and energetic ways led people to assume that he was much younger.

Ellender's team of veteran campaigners was in place for his reelection bid. Edward Wright managed the Louisiana front from his law office in Houma. Wright had extensive lists of past contributors, campaign workers, and "friends" and contacts throughout the state. Next to the names on one list were such comments as "has written a number of times and seems anxious to help," "may want to be paid," "the Sen. is a little skeptical about him, because he runs down so many people," or "old friend of the Senator's."[1]

Not until April did Ellender finally learn who his opponents would be in the Democratic primary scheduled for August 13. Camille Gravel, a liberal attorney from Alexandria, announced rather late. A Roman Catholic and the father of ten children, the fifty-year-old Gravel, a former assistant district attorney and a member of the Knights of Columbus, had been a strong backer of John Kennedy in 1960. He and Ellender had clashed then over civil rights programs of the Democratic party. The winner would face the Republican opponent, if there was one, in the November general election.

Labeling Ellender a tool of special interests, Gravel called him a senator *from* Louisiana, not a senator *for* Louisiana. A servant of big farmers and an opponent of Medicare, Ellender served big business and opposed benefits for workers, Gravel said,

*First published as Chapter 17 in Thomas A. Becnel, *Senator Allen Ellender of Louisiana* (Baton Rouge: Louisiana State University Press, © 1995), 244-57. Reprinted with the kind permission of the author and the publisher.

more candidly than the Ellender camp would have admitted. Calling himself a "progressive" moderate Democrat, Gravel said Ellender's "sorry voting record" showed he had voted against every minimum wage increase and against every Social Security extension.[2]

In some ways Ellender had become a political hybrid. Although he had a typical white Southerner's attitude toward race and labor, he did not always support the Southern line on presidential appointments or on foreign policy and the Cold War. Conservative congressional-rating organizations, which gave liberal Jacob Javits of New York a zero and conservative Richard Russell of Georgia an eighty-three, rated Ellender in the high forties or low fifties. Liberal rating groups, which usually gave Javits high scores, gave Ellender ratings in the low to midtwenties, whereas conservatives like Milton Young of North Dakota and James Eastland of Mississippi scored five or less. In other words, Ellender did not fall into a neat category for classification. On most issues he was conservative; on others surprisingly liberal. The liberal *New Republic* on twelve roll call votes in the Eighty-ninth Congress gave Javits and Walter Mondale of Minnesota scores of eleven, Young a two, and Eastland a zero. Ellender scored a four. In 1965 he had voted to support Lyndon Johnson's position 44 percent of the time. He supported the Democratic party position only 35 percent of the time. But 77 percent of the time he supported positions endorsed by a conservative coalition of Republicans and Southern Democrats.[3]

In an urban industrial area Gravel's charges might have swayed voters, but in conservative Louisiana, Ellender's voting record enhanced his popular appeal. He had voted against repeal of the Tonkin Gulf Resolution, for delaying implementation of the $1.60 minimum wage law until 1969, and for Everett Dirksen's constitutional amendment to circumvent one-man, one-vote guidelines by allowing one house of the state legislature to be apportioned on a geographical basis. Demonstrating a knack for turning negative criticism into positive campaign strategy, Ellender claimed that a 1966 political coup in Ghana proved his widely criticized statement about the inability of African nations to govern themselves without outside help to be true. To think, Ellender said, he had been declared unwelcome in some parts of Africa three years earlier for voicing an obviously sensible view.[4]

Two other opponents entered the Senate race against Ellender, state senator W. J. DeBlieux of Baton Rouge and Troyce Guice, thirty-three, an automobile dealer from Ferriday. Staffers in Ellender's office said Crowley congressman Edwin Edwards would back his opponents. As the filing deadline approached in late June, Wright hoped Ellender would face token opposition and would require only a token campaign. This seemed likely after his most serious opponent, Gravel, withdrew from the race, apparently because he failed to generate much support. Ellender would not be popular with black registered voters, his campaign team realized, but white Democrats still comprised the largest bloc of potential supporters. When campaigning for black support, Ellender and Wright used friendly sheriffs in the various parishes to court the black vote in subtle ways. Through the sheriffs they found small political jobs for part-time black preachers in exchange for a few favorable comments about Ellender. They also bought advertisements in black newspapers and contributed money to black churches.[5]

As usual Ellender had little difficulty financing his election campaign. In August he thanked New Orleans businessman Louis Roussell and former Huey Long financier Seymour Weiss for contributions made to his campaign fund.[6] Once television became an important part of American life, and media exposure vital in shaping political thinking, Ellender hired professionals to conduct polls and prepare television, radio, and newspaper advertisements. These innovations added considerably to the cost of campaigning.

The company Ellender and Wright chose to manage the 1966 campaign, Bauerlein, of New Orleans, proposed a budget exceeding $100,000 most of which would go to media time and lineage in major urban areas. A slightly reduced alternative budget called for spending only $92,000; another budget called for spending nearly $260,000. Between June 17 and August 15, Wright wrote seven checks to Ken Gormin of Bauerlein for a total of about $86,000. Ellender planned a radio and television blitz during the last two weeks of the campaign.[7]

Flo LeCompte regularly forwarded funds received in Ellender's Washington office to Wright in Houma. After receiving a cash contribution, LeCompte said, "At the Senator's suggestion, I deposited the cash to my personal account and then wrote a check to Allen J. Ellender Campaign Fund." Medical doctors contributed to the fund "for a friend of organized medicine." The Democratic Senatorial Campaign Committee sent Ellender a check for seven thousand dollars. Campaign headquarters received more than thirteen thousand dollars in contributions and loans from New Orleans and funneled most of it back to the Crescent City Democratic Association through its agent, Pete Gagliano.[8]

Ellender's lopsided victory on August 13 represented more than 74 percent of the total votes cast in the statewide primary. In some parishes he received 85 percent of the vote. In a handwritten note to Ellender marked "personal & confidential," Wright told his old friend, "You got plenty of votes and cash, too." Total receipts came to $126,524, Wright said; expenditures totaled $114,955—newspapers $50,287, television $31,626, radio $23,565, the Houma office $1,382, and other $8,095. The balance came to $11,569, which could be carried over for future campaigns or used as personal funds. In September, Ellender told a New Orleans fund-raiser to send any surplus funds to Wright in Houma. "As you may know, any surplus there will be transferred to my 'Reports from Congress' account, which I use for public service purposes."[9]

Because Ellender faced no Republican opposition, his successful campaign was behind him long before November elections. In the meantime, he could plan a few fishing trips in Louisiana with [his brother] Willard and his old friends. Ellender spent the weekend after his victory in Houma with his family. On Monday Allen Jr. and two of the grandchildren drove him to the airport in New Orleans. Before the day was over, he was on Capitol Hill considering minimum wage increases and legislation for rent supplements.[10]

The United States by then had become more deeply involved in Vietnam. "Personally, I went on record as far back as 1954 against the involvement of U. S. forces in Viet Nam, and advised President Eisenhower against it," he wrote in 1965. "We have almost no commercial ties there, and no historical ties," he said in 1963. "On the other hand, we stand to lose a great deal, including men, material, money, and a large amount of national prestige."[11]

When the Tonkin Gulf Resolution first came up for discussion in 1964, Ellender posed pointed questions to J. William Fulbright, chairman of the Senate Foreign Relations Committee, who was pushing the resolution. Demanding specific details of the PT boat attacks on the *Maddox* in the Gulf of Tonkin, Ellender tried to determine whether the U. S. Navy had provoked an attack. At one point in the discussion he introduced a resolution to limit the president's war-making powers, but he withdrew it later on the advice of Fulbright, who assured him the Tonkin Gulf Resolution applied to defensive operations at sea, not to land operations. In the end, Ellender joined all but two senators in voting for the resolution.[12]

By May, 1965, Ellender realized, the United States was engaged in a major war. Whenever Johnson sought additional funding and manpower, he invited Ellender and about thirty other members of Congress to the White House for briefings on Vietnam. By July, Ellender was saying he had no choice but to support the president, who had taken a gamble in Vietnam. Ellender disliked antiwar demonstrations and believed they were encouraged by a small minority of Americans. He supported the bombing north along the seventeenth parallel, sending more men into combat, and increasing the draft.[13]

Ellender had no plan for ending the war. When Senator Wayne Morse of Oregon called for a U. S. withdrawal from Vietnam, Ellender seemed to concur, as though he had favored such a move for some time. Nevertheless, Ellender voted against all end-the-war amendments. Although Vietnam was not the logical place to fight communism, Ellender and Richard Russell thought, once U. S. land forces had been committed to the area, they should have a chance to finish the job. Ellender felt the United States should fight to win or get out completely.[14]

Ellender favored using air strikes against North Vietnam to improve American chances for success. "We can't possibly win in North Vietnam without air power," he said. Late in the year, he labeled the struggle a war the United States "cannot afford to fight and cannot afford to quit." American aid money, he complained, "is being used to fill the coffers of the Vietnamese government." Ellender favored continuing the bombing until the North Vietnamese agreed to talks. Meanwhile, Ellender received his share of favors, according to the president's "Congressional Favors File."[15]

On the home front, the war in Vietnam erupted into a major confrontation involving civil rights and law and order. Attracting world attention and dominating domestic concerns, the war overshadowed other areas of foreign policy. Ellender gradually acquiesced to escalation, criticizing instead riots, demonstrations, and unrest at home.

During his reelection campaign, Ellender had prepared a forceful speech supporting LBJ's hard line against Ho Chi Minh, possibly for later use in the campaign. But he never delivered it. Immediate decisive action was the way to prevent major disaster in the future, he asserted. Claiming the time for debate was over, he said the United States should "go all out or get out." Ellender criticized European allies who did not support American efforts in Southeast Asia. By the summer of 1967 Ellender had become more vocal, more specific regarding Vietnam. "We've paid until it hurts," he said, lamenting the cost of sending two Korean divisions to Vietnam. "We must not only pay for their logistices, but also the support of their widows and children," he said. Predicting a cease-fire by the end of 1967, Ellender said, "We should get our men home through an honorable solution in Vietnam."[16]

Senate Armed Services Committee chairman Richard Russell influenced Ellender's thinking on Vietnam more than did Foreign Relations Committee chairman J. William Fulbright. Russell favored bombing North Vietnam and blockading Haiphong harbor and the Vietnam coast. Ellender's mail included emotional observations about war casualties. A New Orleans correspondent wrote dramatically: "Die, lads, 337 of you die now, this week, it's for us." The president and military leaders were doing everything possible to win the war, Ellender told him.[17]

Despite growing skepticism about foreign affairs in general, Ellender usually defended President Johnson. Explaining in March why he did not support a move to rescind the Tonkin Gulf Resolution, he said, "It may well be that those in opposition to our course in Vietnam are attempting to use the confusion which existed at the time, to reinforce their attacks on current policy."[18]

At the opening of the Ninetieth Congress on January 7, 1967, Ellender was exceeded in seniority only by Carl Hayden of Arizona and Richard Russell of Georgia. Hayden was ninety and planning to retire at the end of the session; Russell's emphysema was becoming more incapacitating. When Hayden and Russell were indisposed, Ellender directed Appropriations Committee hearings. Starting in 1967, Ellender spent most of his time working with the Appropriations Committee. Because the 1965 Agricultural Act was working well, he and Freeman agreed there was no need for a new farm bill. Ellender focused on the president's greatest burden—Vietnam. In exchange for support from Ellender, Johnson granted many favors. Convinced the budget was getting out of control when LBJ asked for $9.4 billion in January, Ellender nonetheless acquiesced, figuring the admirals and generals would get what they wanted. In June, Congress voted for an additional $70.3 billion for defense, mostly for Vietnam.[19]

Ellender's statements of opposition to the war in Vietnam were inconsistent with his votes to finance and expand the war. Undoubtedly, Johnson flattered him; he also agreed to his farm proposals and granted many favors asked for his constituents. Perhaps

Ellender, thinking Johnson's antiwar opponents responsible for political chaos at home, believed the president's only hope for domestic tranquillity was victory in Southeast Asia.

White House files from 1966 to 1968 indicate extensive political and social meetings between the president and Ellender. For instance, on October 16, 1967, a White House aide told another aide of Ellender's eagerness to cook shrimp curry for the president. The next day he handed the president Ellender's luncheon list with two open spots he could fill with whomever he wanted. Unlike Richard Russell, who distanced himself from Johnson during the civil rights struggles, Ellender maintained close ties to his old Senate sidekick, who happened to be the most powerful political leader in the world.[20]

In January, 1968, Ellender approved LBJ's plan to halt the bombing of North Vietnam if prospects for meaningful talks improved. In February, Johnson promised to increase rice production allotments, which would benefit Louisiana farmers. In March, Johnson announced his support for Ellender's rural economic development bill, which had failed in two previous attempts. In September, Johnson invited Ellender to accompany him on Air Force One to New Orleans for a presidential address to an American Legion convention. Ellender approved LBJ's hard-hitting speech and, later in the month, got the president to reduce sugarcane acreage cuts for Louisiana.[21]

Meanwhile, the country, torn by rioting and political dissension, prepared for the presidential election. Johnson, under increasing pressure from opponents of the war in Vietnam, announced in March, 1968, he would not seek reelection in November. Calling him a "patriot" for stepping aside in order to achieve peace, Ellender said Johnson was not to blame for the war in Vietnam. In April the assassination of Martin Luther King, Jr., touched off racial riots in a number of U. S. cities. Hubert Humphrey, once considered the favorite of liberals and Johnson's likely successor, faced challengers who disliked the administration's war policy. Robert Kennedy and George Wallace vied for leadership among Democrats. In June, Kennedy was assassinated just as his challenge to Humphrey for the nomination had been enhanced by primary victories, notably in California.

In July, Humphrey won the nomination at the Democratic convention while police and demonstrators engaged in violent confrontation. George Wallace and Curtis LeMay promptly formed a splinter independent party. Meanwhile, Republicans nominated Richard Nixon and Spiro Agnew to lead their party in the election.[22]

All the while Ellender criticized antiwar demonstrations, marches, and protests, equating them with civil rights activities. He fumed when boxer Cassius Clay refused to be drafted and black militant Stokely Carmichael encouraged rebellion from exile in Havana. He supported a bill to ban flag burning. Calling black activist Rap Brown "that racial troublemaker," Ellender said, "I would not put him in the jailhouse, I would put him under it." Ellender refused to vote for funds for the War on Poverty because of demonstrations in Washington, D.C., demonstrations that, he thought, should not receive extensive television coverage. Giving money to cities, Ellender said in March, 1969, would not stop violence, which he attributed to an atmosphere of lawlessness associated with racial sit-ins and marches.[23]

Ellender viewed the 1968 presidential race with little or no enthusiasm. Hubert Humphrey, like Adlai Stevenson in the 1950s, was too closely associated with civil rights for his liking. In addition, Humphrey had endorsed Johnson's Vietnam policy, which was becoming increasingly untenable. Third-party candidates George Wallace and Curtis LeMay were not a viable alternative in the view of Ellender, who scheduled an extensive fall and winter tour of the Far East. Weary of the chaos, rioting, and political turmoil, Ellender turned his back on the counterculture tearing the country apart.

As he grew in seniority, Ellender took more seriously his inspection tours of foreign lands. After five visits to the Soviet Union, his surprisingly liberal view of détente with the USSR had become more pronounced. At first Ellender considered Nikita Khrushchev a clown, but later changed his mind and viewed him instead as a diamond in the rough. "It seems to me that we have as much to fear from ignorance, prejudice, selfishness and bias in our own nation," Ellender observed, "as we have from a similar condition on the part of the Russian leadership." On another occasion he stated in his Acadian style: "I often wondered why in hell we don't get together with the Russians?"[24]

American taxpayers were financing Ellender's home movies of his travels abroad, Drew Pearson and Jack Anderson claimed in 1967. Ellender used his own camera, but the Senate Recording Studio handled film processing for him: it sent film for processing and splicing to the USDA; then it added Ellender's voice narration to film for Louisiana television stations. The USDA sent a bill to the recording studio for processing the film.

After "Washington Merry-Go-Round" criticized the policy, Ellender paid the recording studio with a check for $6,165, explaining that it was "only because I desire to have all the charges at hand so that full payment could be rendered at one time." Extant records do not indicate clearly when Ellender began to pay for processing film. As early as 1956, he had paid for film from his "Reports from Congress" account. While answering charges by Pearson and Anderson in the summer of 1967, Ellender voted to censure Senator Thomas Dodd of Connecticut for spending political contributions on personal items.[25]

Ellender had voiced opposition to the war but voted to sustain it. Rather than take the lead in resistance to the war, he acquiesced to the charms of LBJ and convinced himself that antiwar demonstrators were really civil rights protesters committed to a new cause. Many of his constituents resisted civil rights legislation, supported the war, and opposed gun control. Thus, he took a safe political stance, maintained the friendship of Johnson, and garnered many government programs for his home state, although he stressed cutting waste and reducing government spending. He had not varied much from his position of support for Huey Long, Franklin Roosevelt, or Harry Truman.

Ellender continued to oppose gun control legislation, even when the measure received renewed support after the assassinations of Martin Luther King, Jr., on April 4 and Robert Kennedy on June 6. Russell Long and Wayne Morse in the Senate agreed with Ellender; Lyndon Johnson, Eugene McCarthy, and Attorney General Ramsey Clark all favored gun control. Ellender told constituents he considered gun control a local issue, but he favored curbs on mail-order purchases of weapons.

Ellender explained to critics how he decided issues. "I try to think problems through an then act accordingly," he wrote, explaining his opposition to Medicare, the antipoverty program, and gun control. In opposing the antipoverty program Ellender was refusing aid to some of the rural poor who had received few farm benefits and had been driven from the land. Many now resided in urban slums. He seemed no more sympathetic or inclined to help them now. He would vote to confirm the nomination of Abe Fortas to the Supreme Court as he had voted to confirm every other nominee except Thurgood Marshall.[26]

From time to time Ellender received hate mail and death threats, which the FBI investigated. In July and again in August, 1966, a former mental patient wrote intimidating letters. One letter threatened to "decimate by torture your entire family."[27] If Ellender worried about the threats from the deranged antagonist, whose name was deleted in the FBI files released to the author, he kept his concerns to himself.

Ellender's only sister, Walterine, died at Terrebonne General Hospital on February 21, 1967. She was seventy and had lived in Houston until 1959, when her husband, Charles Caillouette, retired. Walterine and Charles had moved into the family home [Allen's father] Wallace had built on Hope Farm Plantation. Ellender flew in from Washington to attend the funeral at St. Ann's Church in Bourg, a short distance above the Ellender lands along the banks of Bayou Terrebonne. Lyndon Johnson sent Ellender a sympathy note.[28]

Several months later, on May 20, while Ellender was in Ruston to deliver the graduation address at Louisiana Tech University, his brother Willard died suddenly of a heart attack at home. Willard, sixty-one, had recovered from a mild attack in 1961. He and his cousin Dr. Ernest Ellender, Jr., had established the Ellender Memorial Hospital. Allen and Willard had remained close through the years. The brothers had often hunted and fished together, enjoying long conversations while cleaning and cooking their fish and game. "His sudden death was a great shock to the family and is a loss that will be deeply felt for a very long time to come," he wrote. "He was more like a son to me than a brother, and his sudden death comes as quite a shock," he told another. "I cannot yet realize he is gone."[29]

Although Ellender was nearly seventy-seven when Walterine and Willard died, he contemplated his own mortality only briefly. He had already made provisions for disposing of his property; his life-style continued unchanged. Occasionally he seemed tired and complained of not feeling well, Flo LeCompte noticed. He blamed periodic bouts of indigestion on unwise eating habits or on straying from his simple diet to indulge in Mexican food or other exotic culinary delights. Ellender visited Bethesda Naval Hospital on May 11, 1967, at 8:30 p.m., according to a memo President Johnson received and which provided no other information. Perhaps he experienced indigestion.[30]

After serving twenty-five years in the nation's capital in Ellender's office, Flo LeCompte returned to Louisiana in 1967 to help care for her ailing sisters and her ninety-three-year-old father. LeCompte did not terminate her employment with "the Senator" (as she always called him); instead she ran his Houma office. Home at night to help care for her family, LeCompte spoke to Ellender on the telephone every day when he was in Washington. When he was in Louisiana, she drove him around and performed secretarial chores in the office. She returned to Washington occasionally for visits.[31]

Ellender had lost [his brothers] Claude, Willard, and Walterine. Wallace Jr. was his only remaining sibling. After [his wife] Helen died in 1949, Ellender had turned to Claude and Thelma; after Claude died in 1956, he had visited with and engaged in outdoor activities with Willard. He conferred often with Wallace Jr. about farm operations, but he had a much closer personal relationship with Willard. After Willard's death, Ellender sometimes asked Irving Legendre, Jr., who had married Willard's daughter Byrne, to take him fishing. The relationship was good for Ellender; Irving deferred to the senator and took him to new fishing spots in neighboring Lafourche Parish where the Legendres lived. Ellender liked to spend time at the Legendre summer home on Grand Isle where the atmosphere was informal and the fishing was good.

The Legendre "camp" was large and usually filled with visitors, family, and young people. Ellender enjoyed cooking for them and lecturing them on world affairs. His nieces and nephews sat around attentively, but they disliked having their uncle quiz them on geography or world politics. Ellender amazed the young people who gathered about him with his energy. He often stayed up late at night talking or reading, but rose early the next morning to begin the day's fishing. He never asked to come in early as long as the fish were biting. His typical fishing attire was a long-sleeved white shirt buttoned at the neck, cotton gloves, and an old hat purchased in Europe in the 1930s and worn because it was "too good to throw away." His expertise in fishing had not improved over the years, but he made up for the shortcoming with enthusiasm.[32]

From time to time Ellender wrote friendly letters to former president Harry Truman. After returning from the Far East, he told Truman that the North Koreans and Chinese were "arrogant." Had Douglas MacArthur followed Truman's advice in Korea in 1950, the situation would be better today, he suggested. As usual, the FBI received reports of Ellender's jaunts, especially his fifty-three days touring and filming in the Soviet Union. An agent in Hong Kong described Ellender's knowledge of the Soviet Union as "superficial at best." Furthermore, Ellender was "naïve in matters of relationships between countries," had become "very senile," and showed a "strong hostility toward the Bureau and the Director." Hoover may have been gathering information to counter Ellender's report of FBI operations abroad.[33] Ellender may have been naïve or wrong, but he was not senile.

The Ellender clan gathered for the Christmas of 1968 at Wallace Jr.'s.[34] As usual, Ellender's hectic schedule allowed insufficient time for visiting with family. Before long he had to depart for Washington for the opening of the Ninety-first Congress in January, 1969. He would have to contend with a new president, Richard Nixon, who had inherited a multitude of problems.

## Notes for "The Great Society Under Siege (1966-68)"

[1]Box 1838, Allen J. Ellender Papers, Nicholls State University Library, Thibodaux, La., hereinafter cited as AEP.

[2]Random newspaper clippings gathered by Ellender's clipping service, Box 1838, AEP.

[3]*Congressional Quarterly Weekly Report*, July 22, 1955, November 4, 1966; *New Republic*, October 22, 1966.

[4]*New Republic*, October 22, 1966; *Alexandria* (La.) *Town Talk*, March 8, 1966, Box 1838, AEP.

[5]Random 1966 newspaper clippings, and office note to Allen Ellender, April 22, 1966, all in Box 1838, Elward Wright to C. R. Morrison, June 6, 1966, Box 1836, and figures from Board of Registration, East Baton Rouge Parish, Box 1834, all in AEP; Elward Wright, interview, November 8, 1979.

[6]Allen Ellender to Seymour Weiss, August 1, 1966, and Ellender to Louis Roussell, August 4, 1966, both in Box 1834, AEP.

[7]Boxes 1837 and 1838, AEP, contain detailed correspondence and financial records pertaining to the 1966 election.

[8]Florence LeCompte to Elward Wright, July 19, 23, August 19, 1966, Ellender to Wright, July 26, 1966, all in Box 1838, AEP, Box 1834, passim, AEP.

[9]Elward Wright to Allen Ellender, August 27, 1966, Ellender to Albert V. LaBiche, September 13, 1966, both in Box 1834, AEP; random newspaper clippings in Elward Wright Papers, in the possession of Thomas Wright, Houma, La., hereinafter cited as EWP.

[10]Patricia Gorman, *New Orleans States-Item*, August 15, 1966, in "1966" Scrapbook, AEP.

[11]Mimeographed text of radio reports, September 7, 1963, May 8, 1965, both in Box 1486, AEP.

[12]Allen Ellender, interview by T. Harrison Baker, July 30, 1969, in Oral History Collection, Lyndon Baines Johnson Library, Austin, Tex., 16-17.

[13]Ibid., 16; mimeographed text of radio report, May 8, May 15, May 29, July 31, 1965, January 15, February 15, 1966, all in Box 1488, AEP.

[14]*Congressional Quarterly Weekly Report*, July 29, 1972; Tristan Coffin, *Senator Fulbright: Portrait of a Public Philosopher* (New York, 1966), 217-18; miscellaneous newspaper clippings, February, 1964, in "1964" Scrapbook, AEP; Gilbert C. Fite, *Richard B. Russell, Jr., Senator from Georgia* (Chapel Hill, 1991), 437, 440, 448; "Allen J. Ellender Oral History Interview," by Larry Hackman, August 29, 1967 (John F. Kennedy Library, Washington, D.C.; facsimile copy in Nicholls State University Library, Thibodaux, La.), 29.

[15]Miscellaneous newspaper clippings, January, 1965, in "1965" Scrapbook, AEP; mimeographed text of radio report, January 15, 1966, Box 1488, AEP; Diary Cards, December 9, 1964, February 20, July 28, 1965, in Appointment Files, Box 24, and "Ellender, Allen J.," Congressional Favors File, various dates, Box 9, all in Lyndon Baines Johnson Library, Austin, Tex., hereinafter cited as LBJ.

[16]Speech, February 24, 1966, Box 1841, AEP; *New Orleans States-Item*, February 10, 28, 1966, both in "1966" Scrapbook, AEP; *New Orleans Times-Picayune*, June 7, 1967, *New Orleans Item*, June 7, 1967, both in "1967" Scrapbook, AEP.

[17]Fite, *Richard Russell*, 454; Path Miller to Allen Ellender, May 26, 1967, and Ellender to many constituents, March 1967, all in "Foreign Relations (Vietnam) Legislation" Folder, Box 901, AEP.

[18]Allen Ellender to Claribel H. Weaver, February 8, 1968, and Ellender to Henry O. Williams, Sr., March 4, 1968, both in "Foreign Relations, Vietnam" Folder, and Ellender to Ernest Meredith, April 24, 1968, in "1968 France Legislation" Folder, all in Box 919, AEP; "Weekly Report from Congress," February 3, 1968, Box 1494, AEP.

[19]*New Orleans States-Item*, April 29, 1968, Edgar Poe, *New Orleans Times-Picayune*, May 5, 1968, both in "1968" Scrapbook, AEP; "Weekly Report from Congress," April 27, May 4, 1968, Box 1494; "Weekly Report from Congress," January 21, 28, February 11, March 4, June 3, 17, 1967, all in Box 1493, AEP; Mike Manatos to Lyndon Johnson (memo), June 21, 1967, in Allen Ellender Name File, Box 60, White House Central Files, LBJ.

[20]Diary Cards, February 3, 24, March 11, May 18, July 19, 1966, January 9, March 1, July 25, October 9, 11, 18, 1967, January 31, March 13, September 9, 10, 1968, in Appointments File, Box 24, LBJ; Mike Manatos to Lyndon Johnson (memo), April 22, 1966, Marvin Watson to Johnson (memo), February 16, 1967, Johnson to Allen Ellender, February 22, 1967, Manatos to Johnson, October 16, 17, 1967, all in Allen Ellender Name File, Box 60, White House Central Files, LBJ.

[21]"Weekly Report from Congress," January 27, February 3, March 2, 16, September 14, 21, 1968, all in Box 1494, AEP.

[22]"Weekly Report from Congress," April 6, 1968, ibid.

[23]"Weekly Report from Congress," June 11, 1966, Box 1838, May 13, 19, June 24, August 26, September 2, 16, 1967, Box 1493, March 2, 9, June 29, 1968, Box 1494, all in AEP; *New Republic*, October 22, 1966.

[24]"Allen J. Ellender Oral History Interview," by Larry Hackman, August 29, 1967 (John F. Kennedy Library, Washington, D.C.; facsimile copy in Nicholls State University Library, Thibodaux, La.), 26-28; quotations are from *Congressional Quarterly Weekly Report*, July 29, 1972.

[25]*Congressional Record*, 90th Cong., 2d Sess., Vol. 114, Pt. 22, September 26, 1968, 28285-88; *New Orleans Times-Picayune*, June 24, 1967, *Charleston* (W.Va.) *Gazette*, July 23, 1967, both in "1967" Scrapbook, AEP; George Arceneaux, Jr., to Florence LeCompte, October 10, 1956, in "Personal—1956 World Tour" Folder, Box 1843, AEP.

[26]*Congressional Quarterly Weekly Report*, June 21, 1968; Allen Ellender to Lloyd Gaubert, August 13, 1968, and Ellender to many constituents, September 20, 1968, both in "1968 Firearm Legislation" Folder, Box 919, AEP; "Weekly Report from Congress," June 15, 1968, Box 1494, AEP.

[27]FBI File 9-45583.

[28]*Houma* (La.) *Courier*, February 24, 1967; Charles Caillouette, interview, November 23, 1979; Lyndon Johnson to Allen Ellender, February 22, 1967, in Allen Ellender Name File, Box 60, White House Central Files, LBJ.

[29]Ellender to R. E. Thompson, June 26, 1967, in "Fire Ants, Dept. Agriculture, 1967" Folder, Box 418, AEP; Ellender to Julian C. Miller, June 26, 1967, in "Sweet Potatoes, Dept. Agriculture, 1967" Folder, Box 419, AEP; *Shreveport Times*, May 30, 1967, *Houma* (La.) *Courier*, June 2, 1967, both in "1967" Scrapbook, AEP.

[30]James Cross to Juanita Roberts (memo), May 12, 1967, in Allen Ellender Name File, Box 60, White House Central Files, LBJ.

[31]Florence LeCompte to Mona Jennings, January 11, 1967, in "Ellender Personal" Folder, Box 1197, AEP; Florence LeCompte, interview, June 20, 1991.

[32]Irving Legendre, Jr., interviews, June 18, July 10, 1980.

[33]Allen Ellender to Harry Truman, December 29, 1968, "General—Ell—Ellery" Folder, Box 87, Truman Library, Independence, Mo.; [?] to Director, December 5, 1968, FBI File 62-81810; Allen Ellender "Press Releases" Folder, Box 1498, AEP. See Kenneth O'Reilly, "The FBI and the Politics of the Riots, 1964-1968," *Journal of American History*, 75 (1988): 91-114, and Athan G. Theoharis and John Stuart Cox, *The Boss: J. Edgar Hoover and the Great American Inquisition* (Philadelphia, 1988), for examples of how the crafty Hoover survived the wrath of several U. S. presidents.

[34]Charles Caillouette, interview, November 23, 1979.

# THE LOUISIANA GOVERNORS: FROM IBERVILLE TO EDWARDS*

Joseph G. Dawson III, ed.

## *John J. McKeithen*
Governor, 1964-1972

McKEITHEN, John Julian (b. Grayson, Louisiana, May 28, 1918), state representative, member of the Public Service Commission, and governor. The son of a contractor and farmer, McKeithen attended public schools in Caldwell Parish. After brief studies at High Point College, a Methodist-supported institution in North Carolina, he returned to his native state and received the B. S. and LL. B. degrees from Louisiana State University in 1942. Shortly after graduation, he enlisted in the United States Army, and he served honorably during World War II, until his discharge as a first lieutenant in 1954. McKeithen married Marjorie Howell Funderburk on June 14, 1942, and they have six children.

In 1945, McKeithen opened a law practice in Columbia, Louisiana. Three years later, he was elected to the Louisiana House of Representatives, where he served until 1952. During his service in the house, he acted as a floor leader for Governor Earl K. Long. In 1952, he was an unsuccessful candidate for the Democratic nomination for lieutenant governor on the ticket of Judge Carlos Spaht. McKeithen was elected to the Public Service Commission from Huey P. Long's old north Louisiana district in 1954 and was reelected in 1960. While on the commission, he followed Long's example by attacking a large corporation—in his case, Southern Bell Telephone Company. During his term, he successfully fought to keep the five-cent rate for local pay calls.

McKeithen defeated the former New Orleans mayor DeLesseps S. Morrison for the Democratic nomination for governor in 1964. He then turned back a strong challenge by

*Excerpts first published in Joseph G. Dawson III, ed., *The Louisiana Governors: From Iberville to Edwards* (Baton Rouge: Louisiana State University Press, © 1990), 267-80. Reprinted with the kind permission of the editor and the publisher.

the Republican candidate, Charlton Lyons, in the general election. McKeithen's inauguration occurred on May 13, 1964.

During the 1963-1964 gubernatorial race, McKeithen had run as a reformer, promising to "clean up the mess in Baton Rouge." His first term did have a strong reform flavor to it. He got a state code of ethics established and a board to enforce it. He compiled a central list of state employees, as well as an inventory of state property. He appointed a commission headed by the former governor Sam Jones to examine the appointive powers of the governor. In 1964, the governor of Louisiana appointed more people to office than any other governor in the United States except New York's. The Jones commission consolidated some offices and made others elective. More jobs were put under state civil service. McKeithen worked hard to get new industry for the state and was truly a supersalesman for Louisiana. Tax concessions were expanded to induce new industry to come to the Pelican State. In 1966-1967, McKeithen conducted a "right to profit" campaign.

McKeithen confronted a racial crisis in Bogalusa in 1965. A showdown between the Ku Klux Klan and the Congress of Racial Equality, backed by the militant Deacons for Defense, seemed certain. Local citizens asked McKeithen to intervene, and he called for a cooling-off period. To preserve law and order, he set up the biracial Louisiana Commission on Human Relations, Rights, and Responsibilities. His moderate position helped to quiet the situation. He realized that if tension and violence were allowed to build and spread, they would hurt the state's image and might discourage new businesses from locating in the state. Racial violence threatened to erupt again in the summer of 1967. McKeithen announced that he would not tolerate any disturbances and threatened to have authorities shoot people caught rioting, looting, and fire-bombing.

McKeithen persuaded the legislature to pass two constitutional amendments of significance in 1965, and the people of Louisiana approved them both in the following year. One called for the state to construct a domed stadium, the Superdome, in New Orleans. In exchange for this, McKeithen got support in the Crescent City for the second amendment, which allowed governors, including him to serve consecutive terms.

Toward the close of McKeithen's first four years, there were charges of widespread labor-union racketeering in the Baton Rouge area. National publications, such as *Fortune*, publicized what it called the "big shakedown in Baton Rouge." McKeithen appointed members to the Labor-Management Board of Inquiry to investigate the charges. The whole affair hurt his efforts to attract new industry, and it became the chief issue of the gubernatorial primary in late 1967.

Congressman John R. Rarick, from the Sixth District, an archconservative and McKeithen's chief opponent in the Democratic primary, accused the governor of allowing racketeers and organized crime to influence state government. Nevertheless, McKeithen won a crushing victory over Rarick, carrying every parish in the state. With no Republican opposition, McKeithen easily gained a second term and became the first Louisiana governor in the twentieth century to succeed himself.

The McKeithen administration received additional criticism in the national press in 1969 and 1970. Several prominent magazines, most notably *Life*, reported Mafia influence in state government. McKeithen appointed a Mafia probe commission to study the alleged link. By 1972, thirty-nine state, parish, and local officials were under indictment for various crimes.

McKeithen's accomplishments during his second term included reform of the Department of Corrections and improvements in the state prison at Angola. To aid the development of the state's colleges and universities, he set up the Coordinating Council for Higher Education. State employees received a uniform insurance program. Highway construction expanded greatly, as did other capital improvements. Despite legislative opposition, the governor finally succeeded in obtaining tax increases to pay for the expanded programs.

After McKeithen left office in 1972, he ran as an independent candidate for the United States Senate but was defeated by J. Bennett Johnston. McKeithen returned to the practice of law and farming in Columbia.

McKeithen's election marked an end, for better or for worse depending upon one's perspective, to the bifactional politics that characterized Louisiana elections from the time of Huey Long. The division between supporters and opponents of the policies and programs of Longism had given the state's voters a clear-cut choice while it existed. McKeithen, in his 1963-1964 campaign, reached across bifactional lines with various public images and attracted voters from both camps.

McKeithen succeeded in enacting a number of reforms while he was governor, particularly during his first term but also into his second. In addition, he attracted a large number of industries to Louisiana. Those industries did bring jobs and money into the state, but they employed relatively few semiskilled and unskilled laborers, who made up the bulk of the state's work force. The people who held most of the skilled jobs came from out of state. For the times, McKeithen adopted a moderate stand on racial problems, and though some racial confrontations occurred, the state did not have the major racial violence that affected other parts of the South.

Although charges of racketeering and organized crime clouded McKeithen's two terms, he was never personally accused of any wrongdoing. He was a popular governor, as evidenced by the passage of the gubernatorial succession amendment and his crushing defeat of Rarick in 1968.

## *Edwin Edwards*
Governor, 1972-1980, 1984-1988

EDWARDS, Edwin Washington (b. Marksville, Louisiana, August 7, 1927), city councilman, state senator, congressman, and governor. Edwards' life became for a time a twentieth-century political success story.[1] This son of a sharecropper, after elementary and secondary education in public schools, attended Louisiana State University, where he received his law degree at age twenty-one. According to one of his close associates, Edwards was so poor that he had to hitchhike to New Orleans to take the bar examination.

In 1949, after admission to the bar, Edwards established his law practice in Crowley. He married the former Elaine Schwartzenburg, by whom he has four children, and quickly became active in local political affairs. He was elected to the Crowley city council in 1954. He held that position until 1964, when he was elected to the Louisiana Senate. Then, in 1965, he won an election to fill an unexpired term in the United States House of Representatives. He was reelected in 1966, 1968, and 1970.

In 1971, Edwards entered the race for governor in a field of seventeen candidates in the Democratic primary. He led in the first primary with 23.8 percent of the vote, largely as a consequence of very strong support in his native south Louisiana. He defeated J. Bennett Johnston in the runoff by less than eight thousand votes and then defeated the Republican, David C. Treen, in the general election, in February 1972, with over 57 percent of the vote. Once in office, Edwards pushed through the legislature a bill that put Democrats and Republicans on the same ballot, in an open primary. In 1975, he benefited from the new procedure, defeating five opponents with 63 percent of the vote.

In 1979, Edwards was blocked by the state constitution from seeking a third consecutive term, but he made it clear that he would go for another term in 1983. In fact, he opened a campaign office in Baton Rouge upon leaving the governorship and immediately launched his run for a third term. He made himself available as a speaker to virtually every organization in the state and started raising money for the sizable war chest required in Louisiana's gubernatorial campaigns. The 1983 governor's race was a historic first in Louisiana. It pitted an incumbent governor, David Treen, against a former governor, Edwards. It contrasted personalities and styles: Treen, the low-keyed governmental technician, versus the flamboyant Edwards. It was a bitter race in which Treen sought to depict Edwards as corrupt and dishonest. Edwards largely ignored the charges, focusing his campaign on Treen's inaccessibility and alleged ineptitude. Edwards reported expenditures of approximately twelve million dollars and Treen approximately six million—figures that likely translate into the highest spending per voter for any governor's race ever conducted in the United States. When the results were in, Edwards buried Treen with 62 percent of the vote, and a majority in sixty-two of sixty-four parishes.

Within a few months of his third inauguration, Edwards faced a stiff political challenge. In late February, 1985, he was named, along with his brother Marion and other business associates, in a fifty-one-count federal indictment, which listed charges of mail fraud, obstruction of justice, and public bribery. The indictment focused on Edwards' alleged involvement in a complicated scheme that granted preferential state certifications to companies involved in business dealings with Louisiana's state hospitals. The allegation was that Edwards had illegally received $1.95 million, which, if he had been found guilty, could have been reclaimed by federal authorities under provisions of the Racketeering Influenced and Corrupt Organizations (RICO) Act. Edwards immediately proclaimed his innocence, sure that he would not be convicted on any charges.

On March 8, 1985, he entered a plea of not guilty in federal court in New Orleans. United States Attorney John Volz, a Republican, conducted the case against the governor, and Edwards often said to reporters that his indictment and trial were politically motivated by Volz and the Republican party. During the course of the trial, Volz attempted to show that Edwards' gambling losses, sustained at a number of Nevada casinos, put the governor in need of money to pay back his growing debts. Meanwhile, after a lengthy trial, Marion Edwards was acquitted of the charges against him. In December, 1985, when the jury failed to reach a unanimous verdict, Judge Marcel Livaudais declared a mistrial in the case against Governor Edwards. The ruling of a mistrial was interpreted by Edwards as confirmation of his innocence, but Volz soon moved for a new trial. The second trial resulted in an acquittal.

Edwards has no doubt earned special treatment in political histories of Louisiana. He was the first governor elected to three terms. He was only the second twentieth-century governor to succeed himself—thanks to a constitutional amendment passed in 1966. He was the first French-speaking, Cajun governor in over a century. Although Edwards has an Anglo-Saxon name, his mother was a Brouillette, and he retains from his childhood in Cajun country a distinct Cajun accent and the zest for life characteristic of Louisiana's French descendants.

Louisiana voters have established clearly over many decades their preference for colorful—even flamboyant—politicians. In large measure, they found in Edwards the quality they admire. Always impeccably dressed and manicured, Edwards has few peers among politicians when it comes to one-liners, and in public he is never without a stage presence. Many call him charismatic. While his detractors might deny his charisma, few would deny that he is a master showman-politician. For example, he once called a press conference to reveal that he had failed to report a campaign contribution from a South Korean lobbyist. When a reporter asked why he did not return the money, Edwards replied without hesitation or a trace of a smile that he did not know whom to return it to since "all Koreans look alike" to him.

Running for an unprecedented fourth term in the open primary of October, 1987, Edwards met an unexpectedly strong set of challengers. The field included Billy Tauzin, a former Edwards floor leader in the state legislature; Jim Brown, the secretary of state; Bob Livingston, the Republican congressman from New Orleans; and Charles ("Buddy") Roemer III, the Democratic congressman from Shreveport. Perhaps all of the state's economic problems and Edwards' own political difficulties of the third term began to catch up with the governor.

In the primary balloting on October 24, Edwards finished second, with 28 percent of the vote, to Roemer, who gathered 33 percent. Roemer had rushed into contention in the final three weeks of the campaign, gaining major newspaper endorsements and showing well in a widely televised multicandidate debate. A result of the first primary would have forced a runoff between Edwards and Roemer, but Edwards shocked the state and disappointed many of his supporters by announcing his withdrawal from the race on October 25, thus throwing the election to Roemer. The possibility—maybe the likelihood—of failing to muster the required backing in a hard-fought second primary was evidently not appealing to Edwards. If Roemer had gained most of the support from the other major candidates, he would have won the runoff. The various political polls and the division of the votes among the other candidates on October 24 (Livingston with 18 percent, Tauzin with about 10 percent, and Brown with about 9 percent) seemed to indicate that reform, or at lease the call of newspaper editorials to elect "anybody but Edwards," would carry the day against the incumbent.

The transition period between administrations (then stretching from the primary in October, 1987, to March, 1988) was controversial and filled with contention. Roemer made many proposals to reorganize state agencies and revise the state budget. Edwards went along with some proposals but neglected or rejected others. Roemer was inaugurated on March 14, 1988.[2]

Edwards' governorship could boast of numerous accomplishments. He pushed a plan for a constitutional convention through the legislature in the first session after his election. That convention (dubbed CC-73) drafted a new constitution, which was approved by the voters and became effective in January, 1975. The Constitution of 1921, which it replaced, was among the longest in the nation, cluttered with detail and burdened with the hundreds of amendments approved in the half century of its existence. In accordance with the provisions of the new constitution, Edwards initiated a major reorganization of the executive branch. Over eighty agencies were abolished, and those remaining were rearranged on the model of the federal government. In addition, Edwards was the first governor since Reconstruction to include blacks in high positions in his administration. In this area, his administration marked a clear break with the past, when blacks held state jobs only at the menial level.

Edwards used tax revenues on oil and gas to increase state spending. He succeeded in getting enacted a legislative proposal that restructured the severence tax on crude oil to a percentage of the price of each barrel, from a flat fee per barrel. When energy prices soared during the 1970s, the Louisiana treasury was a direct beneficiary of the price-setting power of the Organization of Petroleum Exporting Countries (OPEC). In Edwards' third term, however, this policy came back to haunt him, for oil prices went into a free fall that resulted in massive revenue shortages for the state treasury. Edwards was the moving force behind the Louisiana Superport, an offshore facility designed to handle oil supertankers. During his first two terms, the state's expenditures increased dramatically (163 percent), and still the budget was balanced consistently and with relative ease. But this third term was plagued with budgetary problems from the beginning.

Edwards also worked for a change in election procedures, which he pushed through the legislature during his first term. When he won office in 1972, he had to get through two Democratic primaries and then defeat a Republican candidate in the general election. Edwards quickly set himself to changing that procedure in order to make his reelection easier. He got the legislature to pass a new "open elections" arrangement that put Democrats, Republicans, and independents on the same ballot, with two heats if no candidate received a majority in the first balloting. This procedure was for all elected offices in the state. It worked well for Edwards in 1975, when he won with ease in the first heat. But in 1979, it turned out to help the Republican party, which it was originally designed to thwart. The Republican, Treen, defeated a divided field of five Democrats. The electoral arrangement did serve, however, to stymie the development of Republican representation in the state legislature.

Few observers took a neutral attitude toward Edwards. His critics are as intense in their feelings as his admirers are. The critics find much to criticize. Edwards' terms as governor have found him in several near-entanglements with scandal. His campaign contribution from a Korean lobbyist appeared to some to be of questionable legality. His commissioner of administration, Charles Roemer, was convicted and sentenced to prison in a bribery kickback scheme to place a state insurance contract with a company owned by Carlos Marcello, alleged to be an underworld boss. Edwards was never implicated in that scandal. Camille Gravel, Edwards' close friend and political confidant, once said, "Edwin's greatest strength—and his greatest weakness—is his ability to come within a millimeter of the law without breaking it."[3] By evading conviction in two federal trials, he has proved Gravel's assessment.

Edwards remained one of Louisiana's most popular and colorful figures throughout his years as governor. His first two terms showed excellent political management in the flush times of high oil prices and, consequently, high income from state severance taxes. The state needed a new constitution, and Edwards used his executive authority and power to press for a convention that produced an excellent state charter, certainly an outstanding improvement over the outmoded Constitution of 1921. Furthermore, Edwards accomplished a major reorganization of the executive branch and appointed a significant number of blacks to various offices in state government.

In his third term, however, he faced fiscal and personal crises. Although he claimed that he could manage state resources better than Governor Treen, oil revenues plummeted because of the drastic decline in international oil prices, leaving the state with a staggering revenue shortfall, with inadequate funds to continue some state programs, and with the need to trim the state budget instead of expanding programs and funding departments at higher levels, as had been possible during his first two terms. Moreover, the federal racketeering charges made Edwards a figure of national notoriety. The colorfulness of his character throughout his years in office, the problems of his third term, and his withdrawal from the campaign of 1987 indicate that Edwards will remain controversial in Louisiana history.

## *David Treen*
### Governor, 1980-1984

TREEN, David Connor (b. Baton Rouge, Louisiana, July 16, 1928), congressman and governor. Treen is an anomaly among Louisiana governors.[4] Louisiana's first Republican governor in the twentieth century may turn out to be the state's least colorful governor of the century too. In a state that prefers its governors to entertain as well as govern, Treen is a serious-minded man with a passion for detail and little inclination toward showmanship.

Treen attended public schools in East Baton Rouge, Jefferson and Orleans parishes and graduated from Fortier High School, in New Orleans, in 1945. He received both his undergraduate and law degrees from Tulane University and served as a defense and prosecuting counsel in the United States Air Force for two years. He is married to the former Delores Briski, and they have three children.

Treen became involved in politics in the late 1950s. He was initially involved in the States Rights party—running one time under its banner for the United States House of Representatives. He switched to the Republican party, and became chairman of the Jefferson Parish executive committee for several years as well as a member of the state central committee for most of the 1960s and 1970s. Later that year he was elected to Congress from the Third District (largely suburban New Orleans), to become the first Republican elected to Congress from Louisiana in the twentieth century. He was reelected in 1974, 1976, and 1978.

In 1979, Republican leaders responded to Louisiana's "open election" system—in which all the candidates of all the parties ran on the same ballot, with two heats if no candidate won by a majority in the first canvass—by deciding to field just one Republican in the governor's race, against a number of Democrats. That approach worked well. Five major Democrats were in the race, and Treen, by virtue of being the senior elected Republican in the state, was the Republican candidate. The Democratic candidates generally conceded Treen a place in the second round and fought tenaciously to be there with him. In the first heat, Treen ran first. He faced Louis Lambert, of the Public Service Commission, in the new round, since Lambert had narrowly edged out Lieutenant Governor James Fitzmorris for second place. But the tone of the campaign for the second position was so bitter and intense that the four unsuccessful Democrats gave their endorsement to Treen. All four had substantial campaign debts that Treen helped pay off, and all were appointed to positions in Treen's administration. Some of Treen's critics who thought that he did not know how to play Louisiana's tough game of politics may need to reexamine their opinion. Treen defeated Lambert by fewer than ten thousand votes.

As governor, Treen got a legislative program passed that aimed at improving education. The program included pay incentives for teachers who added to their training, and it imposed higher standards for qualifying to teach in the state. Treen negotiated a settlement with the United State Department of Justice in a long-standing dispute over Louisiana's dual system of predominantly white and predominantly black colleges and universities.

Governor Treen also worked out a plan for flood control and environmental preservation in the Atchafalaya Basin. He obtained the initial legislation for purchasing privately owned land there, but the plan's ultimate success will depend upon action by the national government. Appropriations of more than one billion dollars are necessary to implement the flood-control design. Treen sponsored legislation intended to protect Louisiana's coastal wetlands, but that bill failed.

Treen's governorship had a significant, though perhaps ironic, result for blacks, who may have perceived Treen as a segregationist antipathetic to their interests. He received less than 1 percent of their vote in his unsuccessful race for governor in 1972 and only about 3 percent in 1979. Nevertheless, he appointed more blacks to positions under gubernatorial control than any previous governor has done. Thus he can be credited with a large role in the attempt to change the perception of the Louisiana Republican party from that of a WASPish club to that of a broad-based, competitive party.

Treen had more than a few problems as governor. He came to the office with no experience in state or local government and none as an administrator. His government seemed confused and indecisive as it slowly made its way through the shakedown period of its early weeks. Perhaps Treen's greatest problem was the financial difficulty that the oil glut of the early 1980s created. Because of the dependence of Louisiana's revenue system on severance taxes levied upon oil, the decline in both the production of oil and its prices created a financial nightmare of shrinking revenues during much of Treen's tenure. In addition, there were cutbacks in available federal revenues as a consequence of budget reforms pushed by Treen's fellow Republican, President Ronald Reagan.

Undoubtedly, one of Treen's major problems as governor was his personality and political style. A political observer contends that Louisianians like their politicians like their food: hot and spicy. Treen was neither. And he followed a succession of governors who had provided voters with plenty of entertainment. Instead, Treen exhibited a passion for detail and methodical decision making. Those traits led journalists and politicians to conclude that he was plodding and indecisive. Most of his recent predecessors were gregarious types who enjoyed traveling, speaking, and shaking the hands of voters across the state. Treen seemed uncomfortable in those roles. Instead he preferred to be behind a desk, enmeshed in the details of running the governor's office. As a consequence, he may have turned down more speaking and ribbon-cutting invitations than any other governor in recent times.

In 1983, Treen sought a second term and was opposed by his predecessor, Edwin Edwards. Treen's campaign struggled uphill from the beginning. A Republican in a predominantly Democratic state running against one of the greatest campaigners in Louisiana history, he had the burden of presiding as governor during a severe budget crisis and at a time when unemployment in the state was well above the national average. The problems were a result of the state's heavy dependence upon oil and gas for both employment and tax revenues at a time when an overabundance of oil plagued the industry. Treen began the campaign trailing badly in the polls, and though he fought tenaciously to hold on to the governorship, he was able to gain only 36.8 percent of the vote, and a majority in only two parishes.

Treen's defense of his stewardship as governor was that "leadership is not demonstrated by flamboyance or by glibness. It is demonstrated by accomplishments."[5] Time will tell whether his accomplishments put him among Louisiana's significant chief executives. How the Republican party does in the state in the next few decades will show whether Treen has brought his party to the level of a viable competitor with the Democrats or whether his governorship was only a once-in-a-century aberration akin to an eclipse of the sun or a close encounter of planets.

Notes for "The Louisiana Governors: From Iberville to Edwards"

[1]The author is indebted to several journalists who have written for the *New Orleans Times-Picayune/States Item*, for their factual and interpretive accounts of Edwards' performance in office and on the campaign trail. The writers include James Gillis, Charles Hargroder, Alan Katz, Iris Kelso, Newton Renfro, and Jack Wardlaw.

[2]Some representative reports on the 1987 election and its aftermath: *Baton Rouge Morning Advocate*, October 31, 1987, March 14, 1988; *Houston Chronicle*, October 26, 1987; *Washington Post National Weekly Edition*, November 9, 1987; *Wall Street Journal*, March 14, 1988.

[3]Alan Katz, "The Upcoming Trial of the Century," *New Orleans Times-Picayune*, March 3, 1985.

[4]The author is indebted to several journalists who have written for the *New Orleans Times-Picayune/States Item*, for their factual and interpretive accounts of Treen's performance as governor. The writers include James Gillis, Charles Hargroder, Alan Katz, Iris Kelso, Newton Renfro, and Jack Wardlaw.

[5]Jack Wardlaw, "Treen's Legacy," *New Orleans Times-Picayune*, October 26, 1983.

# POLITICAL CRUCIBLE*

Melody D. Bonnette

Edwin Edwards, Louisiana's most favored son and consummate politician, would certainly need to prove his mettle in his third term. Indeed, when he took over the reins of state government in 1984, it was a different situation than the one he left in 1980. Not only was the state treasury empty, but he had to contend with a $180 million budget deficit. To be sure, the era of big budget surpluses had ended and new ways of financing would need to be devised. Also, the legislature enjoyed a heady independence not known during Edwards's administrations—one that it may not want to relinquish. Thus, Edwards's fiscal problems, heightened because he had promised a10 percent pay raise to school teachers and public employees, loomed precariously on the legislative horizon. As serious as these problems appeared, they paled, though, in comparison with Edwards's forthcoming legal battles with the federal courts and the tenacious district attorney, John Volz.

Yet, in spite of these serious fiscal problems, or perhaps because of them, Edwards left in January for his notorious seven-day trip to Paris, to begin a celebration that would culminate with an inaugural ball two months later at the New Orleans Superdome. With an entourage of 617 that included thirty-five news reporters, a majority of the legislature, and an NBC television crew, the group boarded two jumbo jets, the "Gabrielle Special" and "Evangeline Special," and headed for Paris.

Along with an itinerary that promised a whirlwind tour of Paris and the surrounding area, Edwards planned brief business meetings. He signed a cultural exchange agreement in Brussels that provided for exchanges "to further the French cultures of Louisiana and Belgium."[1] Edwards had a private audience with French President François Mitterrand during which he jokingly told Mitterand that the $15 million campaign for governor last year cost about as much as the United States paid to France for Louisiana in the first place.[2] In addition, he met with Renault executives about the possibility of building a

*Chapter 4 from Melody D. Bonnette, "The Louisiana Phoenix: A Study of the First Three Gubernatorial Administrations of Edwin W. Edwards" (M. A. thesis, Southeastern Louisiana University, Hammond, La., 1994), 147-202. Published with the kind permission of the author.

bus assembly plant in Louisiana, pledging to buy at least one hundred buses per year as part of an agreement to entice the prospective owners to locate the plant in New Orleans.

Part of the itinerary included optional side trips as well. Some of the group, including Edwards, chose to travel to Monte Carlo for an evening of gambling. Although the casinos in Monte Carlo, with its nineteenth-century dome of stained glass and gold leaf, were more elegant, smaller, and sedate than those in Las Vegas, Edwards broke precedent and entertained the crowds with his loud cries of "Roll' em, Mister!" Louisiana's most famous gambler did well and won $15,000 at the dice table.[3] When asked by one reporter if he could balance the state budget with his winnings he replied, "There isn't enough money for that in this whole damn casino."[4] Violating other gambling etiquette and causing the pit bosses some initial consternation, Edwards's four children borrowed chips from each other to bet on their father, something not done in a proper European dice game. Other events included a cocktail party at the Eiffel Tower, an evening at the famed Le Crazy Horse nightclub which featured nude dancers, though nothing new to French Quarter natives, a cruise down the River Seine, and sightseeing in Monaco and Reims. The Hotel Crillon, a favorite of Ernest Hemingway's in the 1920s and where he wrote most of his great novels, became a favorite spot for many of the travelers.

There were inspirational moments also, such as Edwards laying a wreath at the tomb of France's unknown soldier at the Arc de Triomphe and his induction into the Society of Beaujolais. One of the more touching moments for Edwards was a special mass at the famed Notre Dame Cathedral. Awed by the beauty of the ancient church, Louisiana visitors offered solemn prayers and received Holy Communion while the historic cathedral rang with "amens" and spirituals led by a Louisiana gospel singer living in Paris. Edwards later complained that the press wrote more about his gambling winnings than about the Notre Dame visit: "I spent more time at Notre Dame chapel than at the Monte Carlo tables, but Monte Carlo got more press."[5]

The high point of the trip, a glittering black-tie $71,000 dinner held at the Palace of Versailles, "a glittering edifice of more than 400 rooms surrounded by gardens and filled with priceless works of art," the home of King Louis XIV, the Sun King, left the group in awe as they walked through the Hall of Mirrors and through the king and queen's chambers to the vast dining hall.[6] Although the crowd agreed that French cuisine was no match for famed Louisiana Creole cuisine, they gave a standing ovation for the lavish dinner that began with smoked salmon and champagne and culminated with a parade of waiters, in seventeenth-century attire complete with powdered wigs, carrying plates of baked Alaska topped with sparklers.

The festive dinner, setting a record as the largest formal dinner at the palace in more than a century, honored Governor-elect Edwards.[7] The crowd, all wearing their lapel pins that showed a profile of Edwards and the inscription "Sun King" beneath it, christened Edwards king for the night, a role that Edwards called his destiny. He toasted his supporters: "It was destined, I thought, when I was born, to be king, and tonight I can be." Mocking the pomp and pageantry, Edwards donned a white periwig purchased from a waiter for $50 and paraded around the room upon which the crowd responded, "Hail, Edwin the First!"[8]

Political columnist Iris Kelso described the historic trip to Paris as "the experience of a lifetime." Indeed, it was not everyday that one could stand next to the governor and gamble at the dice table. She claimed that there would never be another experience quite like the famed trip to Paris, which she viewed as "a unique moment in Louisiana's history." Kelso saw this trip as an ideal way to get the Edwards administration off to a good start. To be sure, intangible benefits could be gained from such a successful venture, most notably, image. "Edwards's unique ability to create an event of this nature and make it work [added] to his aura of political invincibility."[9] This illusion of being a political superman would aid him greatly when the legislative session opened in April, especially considering the fact that Edwards planned to ask for a massive tax program. In addition, with almost one-half of the legislature on the trip, Edwards developed good personal relationships with many of the newer lawmakers and rekindled old friendships, once again an attempt to garner support for his forthcoming tax package. Along with legislative support, Edwards's reputation as being an accessible governor, the antithesis of Governor Treen, appeared most believable. One well-known story put it in perspective:

When a north Louisiana man was asked why he paid $20,000 for himself and his wife to travel to Paris with the governor-elect he responded with a story about Governor Treen. He said he and some other leading citizens from his parish arranged a meeting with the governor to discuss a problem important to his area. He said Treen greeted the delegation with, "You have exactly five minutes." Although the requests were eventually granted, it left the leaders with a bad taste in their mouths. This man who paid $20,000 to go to Paris does not think he will have that much trouble getting Edwards to listen to his problems.[10]

The trip to Paris generated a large amount of publicity. As one newsman asked after Edwards returned from his trip in late January, "Does anyone remember who holds the office of governor right now?"[11] Edwards returned from Paris and its fond memories with the perfect one-liner about his trip. When asked about the biggest benefit of the trip to Paris, he glibly responded, "Five million dollars."[12] Thus, he returned from a successful fundraising trip that retired the last of his campaign loans of the past election and claimed his place in Louisiana history.[13]

Edwards's inauguration ceremonies, in March, began with a private mass at St. Joseph Cathedral in memory of Nolan, his late brother, and Gene Jones, Edwards's body-guard, who died the previous summer of a heart attack.[14] An inaugural parade, led by Edwards, wound through the streets of Baton Rouge amidst a light drizzle. When heavy rain and blustery winds tore the bunting draping the inaugural stand on the Capitol steps, the ceremony moved inside. Thus, the swearing-in ceremony took place in the crowded chamber of the House of Representatives, with spectators spilling outside into the halls and onto the steps. Although many appeared dismayed at the thunderstorms, Iris Kelso saw it otherwise. She interpreted the inclement weather as a reminder to Edwards, to the legislators, and to the public that Edwards was indeed just a man. And in spite of his political magic that caused legislators to view him as a phenomenon, he was just a governor, if there was such a phrase in Louisiana political jargon. To be sure, Kelso saw the rain as a reminder that "not all of his occasions are stellar, nor all of his performances award-winning."[15] This view seemed in stark contrast to the legislator who joked to Edwards during a meeting concerning the tax proposal, "Governor, you got 75 percent of the vote in my parish. If you want to tax breathing, I'm with you."[16]

Edwards took the oath of office first in English, administered by his son, Steven, then in French, by his brother, Marion. His inaugural speech was an inspirational appeal to lawmakers to "look to the state's needs no matter what the short term political consequences." He promised that if the legislature followed his advice and passed his proposed tax program, then "before the next election there will be happiness and the people will be glad we did it."[17] The inaugural ball that followed broke tradition by being held at the New Orleans Superdome instead of Baton Rouge. As in the past, invitations, automatically sent to campaign workers, were also given to anyone that asked.[18] Edwards showed up a few hours after the ball began and, amid blue and gold streamers and oversized color pictures of Edwards that hung from the oversized television screens, he told the crowd of over 80,000, "Eat, drink, and be merry, because tomorrow we go to work."[19]

To that end, Edwards, as his first official act as governor, called for a special legislative session to begin in mid-March. After months of debate and speculation over the need for a special tax session, Edwards, minutes after he finished his inaugural address, called for a seven-day legislative session to rework the state's tax program.[20] He defended his call for the special session in order to deal with the $200 million deficit for the current year and the estimated shortfall of $450 million in revenue to finance the state's operating budget for the upcoming fiscal year. He stated that there were important programs that needed to be funded and that he did not want them to lapse before the regular session. He planned to propose a "megabucks" tax proposal, designed to raise between $500 million and $1 billion a year, and in "one fell swoop end the fiscal crisis that has gripped state government since 1982."[21]

Handling the tax agenda at a special session, a keen political move by Edwards, afforded numerous advantages. Most importantly, he had the power to limit the agenda to taxes, thereby heading off the "horse trading and confusion" that results from mixing taxes with myriad issues that accompany a regular session.[22] In addition, if the major part of his tax package passed during the special session, Edwards's fiscal problems would be lessened and he could concentrate on other areas of his legislative agenda during the regular legislative session. Finally, with a limit of seven days for this special session, this short time period would be advantageous in keeping the momentum going for his tax package. To be sure, there would not be much time for objections from the legislators or their constituents.

Still, it promised to be an uphill fight to get two-thirds majority in each house, but one that Edwards felt he could win. Riding the momentum of his overwhelming victory and taking advantage of the fact that his influence with the legislature was at its peak, he knew that many of the lawmakers wanted to be part of the Edwards landslide. To be sure, some legislators regarded him as a "political genius" and wanted to be "close to the glamour, the action, the success."[23] The legislators realized that they might possibly have to deal with Governor Edwards for the next eight years, a formidable thought to anyone who planned to oppose him so early in his administration. Likewise, he did not overtly threaten the legislators who did not support him with political reprisals. Instead, he simply stated, "You can't get run over if you're on the train." Thus, from his vantage point, it was the best possible time to push his new agenda, a tax increase of 36.3 percent.[24]

When the special session began, Governor Edwards, whose speeches were usually laced with humorous anecdotes, asked the legislators in a somber, detailed address to approve the biggest tax increase in the history of Louisiana. Funding would then be available to give the teachers and state employees a pay raise, implement a statewide drainage plan, strengthen the state retirement systems, and build state and local prisons. It would also provide monies to begin a biotechnology program at Louisiana State University, upgrade education, clean up the environment, and repair highways. To finance his agenda, Edwards proposed eleven taxes that would produce revenues of more than $1.1 billion a year.[25] Taxes included a one-cent increase in the state sales tax; an increase on the taxes on soft drinks, beer, liquor, cigarettes, and gasoline; an increase in the severance taxes on timber, pulpwood, sand and gravel; and a tax on the storage of hazardous wastes. He also included in his tax program a plan, contingent upon statewide voter approval, to reduce the amount of federal taxes that corporations could deduct from their state income taxes.

Edwards, though, encountered problems with a special feature of his tax package, the new $250 million "single business tax," intended to replace four taxes, the corporate income tax, the corporate franchise tax, the sales tax businesses pay on their purchases, and the property taxes paid on inventory. His plan to replace these taxes with a flat 3 percent tax on transactions after expenses did not garner much support. Opponents of the new business tax stated that the elimination of these four taxes would actually cost the state more revenue than the new tax would bring in. Thus, Edwards chose to forgo a fight on this tax, strongly opposed by the business community, and eliminated this new tax from his tax package.

Edwards, considered to be a "master political manipulator," centered his argument on the theme that the pain of new taxes would be less than that of reduced services and that it all would be worth it in the end.[26] He warned the legislators that if they chose to resist him completely he would cut state agency budgets and curtail vital state programs even more than former governor Treen had done. He stated, "No tax you could vote for could hurt you that much." If the legislature chose to only finance the shortfall, he reminded them that it would not address the issue of statewide drainage, educational improvements, or employee pay raises. Instead, he urged them to approve every proposal: "The worse you could do is give me half. Then all we could do is balance the budget and nobody would believe me when I told them there was no money for anything else."[27]

Edwards also promised at least $100 million in spending cuts by removing, through attrition, approximately 6,000 state employees hired within the previous year.[28] To be sure, Louisiana ranked eighth among the fifty states and first among the nine Southern states in state employees per 10,000 population. Therefore, Louisiana had 188 employees for every 10,000 people, compared to an average of 133 in other Southern states and all but ten others nationwide. Also, while the trend in other states was to cut back on the number of state and local employees, Louisiana continued to add to its figures. But Edwards backed off from this plan when a search of the 6,000 jobs revealed that many of the employees were ineligible for firing, others performed essential duties, and the rest had their salaries paid by the federal government. In addition, Edwards came across a law that restricted wholesale firings. Thus, Edwards suggested that the final number of employees laid off would be "significantly less" than his original figure of 6,000.[29]

Edwards promised the lawmakers that if they approved his entire package he would not ask for any more taxes on consumers until he left office, possibly in 1992, and that no new taxes would be needed until after the year 2000. He told the legislature that with this new tax package approved, they could all have an "easy instead of a miserable time for the next eight years."[30] Plus, if the state reaped a windfall in a longstanding suit against the federal government involving offshore oil revenues, he offered the possibility that some taxes could be repealed, perhaps just before the 1987 elections.

Although this was the first year of the new term for the wary lawmakers, the possibility of eliminating taxes before the next election appeared as hopeful news indeed. To be sure, many of them knew about the 56.8 percent increase in state taxes passed in 1948 because of Governor Earl Long's mighty rule over the legislature, and the subsequent fallout the following election year when many of those who supported this monumental tax increase were not reelected. Edwards attempted to counter this fear with a powerful, altruistic call during a dramatic forty-minute speech at the House podium, where governors seldom venture except during a joint session. He asked them to examine their motives: "Maybe some of you will put political careers on the line. The question is, are we so driven by the restless inner demons of ambition that we are unwilling to take any risk to save our people?"[31]

Overall, Edwards's tax plan, the biggest one ever proposed to the Louisiana Legislature, met with mixed reviews. Some legislators predicted that the tax package would emerge from the special session triumphant. House Speaker John Alario called the tax package "a broad-based tax program [where] everyone pays a little bit, but no one pays a great deal."[32] Iris Kelso viewed his tax agenda as much more than a test of Edwards's popularity. Rather, she saw it as an indication that perhaps Louisianians had realized that they must pay taxes for public services, a new way of thinking in Louisiana.[33] Senator

Fritz Windhorst of Algiers agreed, stating, "We've had indications for the last several years that we would have to find some new sources of revenue. That time has come."[34]

The majority of the legislature, though, did not agree. In spite of an impressive array of business, labor, and governmental groups supporting Edwards's tax plan, the lawmakers approved only a portion of Edwards's tax package. Edwards proposed $1.138 billion in new or increased taxes, but received an estimated $753.9 million instead. Regardless, it was the largest tax increase in Louisiana history in terms of actual dollars. Based on the Fiscal Office estimate, every resident of Louisiana would experience an increase in taxes of approximately $170 a year.[35] The state sales tax, the biggest tax passed at the session, was expected to generate an additional $315.3 million, an increase from three cents on the dollar to four cents.[36] Edwards, well aware that an increase in the sales tax placed restrictions on local governments to use the tax for their own purposes, predicted that, with the invigorated oil and gas industry revenues projected within a few years, his first order of business would be to repeal the one-cent sales tax increase, thereby freeing local governments to use it if necessary. The legislature approved the increase proposed by Edwards on the tax on gasoline to sixteen cents per gallon, and also passed a tax increase on alcohol and cigarettes, in spite of Edwards's earlier campaign promises.[37] Only one of his tax proposals actually failed, the one-cent per can soft drink tax, expected to generate $11 million. Also, Edwards withdrew his tax proposal on real estate transactions and occupational licenses, under intense pressure from lobbyists and legislators. Another bill that doubled the severance tax on timber and pulpwood passed, but Edwards vetoed it, planning to refile it in another form for consideration at the regular session.[38] The rest of Edwards's proposals passed with some fiscal changes.

Political columnist Iris Kelso praised Edwards for his "bold, visionary approach" to Louisiana's future. She argued that with a new, strong fiscal base Louisiana could begin to prepare for the time when oil and gas revenues would no longer be able to give state government its basic support.[39] Yet, the reworked tax package passed by the legislature did not cover the programs that Edwards had promised his constituents. Although Edwards exerted enough influence to get more taxes passed than any other chief executive in Louisiana history, it was yet another reminder, like the rain on inauguration day, that Edwards was not invincible.[40]

Thus, for Edwards the legislative session was a pyrrhic victory, one achieved at a high cost. The legislature gave Edwards approximately three-fourths of his $1.1 billion tax agenda, a remarkable feat for a governor of any state, but not the ultimate success he hoped for. So when the regular legislative session opened two weeks later, he told the legislators to "bite the bullet some more," because without the approval of his entire tax package, he needed an additional $13 million in taxes and more than $200 million in spending cuts. In a one hour and fourteen minute opening address, devoted mostly to an attack on the lawmakers who opposed his tax program, he reminded the legislature that just giving the teachers and the state employees the pay raises he promised them during his election campaign would cost $240 million.[41]

Edwards felt the harsh reaction from the taxpayers concerning the special session, especially towards the one-cent sales tax increase and the eight-cent increase in the gasoline tax, the third highest rate in the country.[42] Consequently, Edwards looked for ways to cut spending so that all or part of these two highly unpopular taxes could be rescinded in the regular session. To that end, he suggested repealing a portion of the exemptions to the state sales tax, including food and drugs. These exemptions, which totaled more than $600 million a year, could be used to finance the teacher pay raise and curtail some of the tax increases passed by lawmakers in the special session. He defended his position concerning these possible changes, arguing that the sales and gasoline taxes "were not my original proposals." Edwards said he would be willing to abolish the two tax increases and instead remove the exemptions on the sales tax simply because "it's fairer."[43]

Meanwhile, teacher organizations threatened to participate in classroom walkouts and mass marches to the state capitol. They demanded the 10 percent pay raise that Edwards promised in his $1.1 billion tax plan, in spite of the fact that the legislature failed to include it in the $734 million adjusted budget. Thus, after postponing one walkout because of Edwards plea for more time to come up with a workable proposal, teachers converged on the Capitol, the first such gathering since 1977, to press for a raise.

Amid a chilly reception at the Capitol steps, Edwards told the more than 12,000 teachers gathered there that he had begun his "last, best effort" to find money for pay raises. He proposed a plan that would raise the corporate franchise tax, cut a portion of the exemptions from the state sales tax in half, and repeal half of the eight cent per gallon gasoline tax increase. The net effect of these three proposals would increase revenue by $293 million, enough to fund a state employee and teacher pay raise.[44] He reminded the teachers that it was the legislature and not himself that had eliminated his promised teacher pay raise. When asked if he would consider a special session if necessary, he stated, "We will do whatever it takes. We cannot turn our backs on the teachers of this state."[45]

Calling it a "shift in priorities," Edwards revised his original strategy and proposed a new plan that benefited only teachers and other educational personnel, not state workers. At last the legislature approved the amended teacher pay plan, the first across-the-board pay raise since 1981. This change, along with only a 7 percent pay increase and a $1,200-a-year limit on the amount any teacher could receive, lowered the cost to $130 million. The new plan involved the original corporate franchise tax increase, expected to produce $86 million, with the balance coming from budget cuts in educational improvement programs and increased fees for state services.[46] Overall, enough revenue would be raised to fund the much-needed pay raise for educators. Likewise, Edwards postponed his plan to seek pay raises for state employees, ostensibly because state civil service personnel had not yet devised a pay plan for its workers.

Although the teacher pay raise dominated the first half of the regular session, other legislation passed as well. Former Governor Treen's $92 million Professional Improvement Program (PIPS) for teachers would be phased out by 1990. In its place, a study to develop a career ladder plan to replace PIPS began, in which teachers judged to be outstanding would receive higher salaries, along with added responsibilities.[47] Also, the approval of multi-parish banking allowed bank holding companies to purchase banks anywhere in the state, beginning in 1985. The Office of Minority Business Enterprise, created to help minority-owned businesses participate in state government purchases of goods and services, would be given preference if the minority-owned businesses fell within 5 percent of the lowest bid.[48] Also, the legislature created a Governor's Scholar Program, to honor and reward with in-state scholarships, academic achievement of the state's most meritorious students.[49] In addition, the legislature agreed to a standardized aptitude test for teacher certification.[50] Edwards, though, cited as the biggest accomplishment of the difficult session the proposed constitutional amendment that drew little attention from the media. The proposed amendment, a key part of Edwards's economic development package, set a cap on spending and limited the growth of government "so we will never again find ourselves in the position we were in 120 days ago, with $500 million worth of "unmet needs."[51]

When the session ended, Governor Edwards and lawmakers alike found the session "challenging, trying, and grueling." Former House Speaker John Hainkel, Jr., called it "the worse session I've ever seen, period." Senator B.B. "Sixty" Rayburn said he found the 1984 session more difficult than Governor Earl Long's memorable 1948 tax session.[52] Other lawmakers complained that this session concentrated more power in the hands of the administration, thus relinquishing the independent spirit they had experienced during the Treen administration. For instance, a bill easily passed through the legislature that gave the governor greater control over various boards and commissions. As a result, not only did members of these agencies have terms concurrent with the governor, but they could be replaced at any time, "at the pleasure of the governor."[53]

In spite of these complaints and the failure to have his entire budget package approved, Governor Edwards praised the legislature at a post-session news conference: "The public will never be aware of what we have saved them from if we had not taken the actions we have. We have literally kept the institutions of Louisiana from falling apart . . . The state was on the verge of financial collapse." Edwards, somewhat satisfied with the outcome, stated that "the real winners were the people of Louisiana."[54]

It had been a trying first few months of Edwards's third term. He survived two difficult legislative sessions, threatened walkouts by teachers, and the largest tax increase in Louisiana's history. To be sure, the broad-based coalition that had elected him, business and labor, liberals and conservatives, and blacks and whites, all had their own agendas. It was up to Edwards to balance their individual needs with the needs of the state, quite a formidable task, even for the experienced Edwards. As he ruefully observed at the end of his first ninety days of his third term, "The last easy thing I did was take the oath of office."[55] Yet, despite the difficulties, this ultimate legislative success, albeit, not the one he had hoped for, placed Edwards in a position to carry out an agenda that could establish him in the history books as a truly great governor—if he could stay clear of the grand jury.

At the beginning of his third term as governor, Edwin Edwards told his constituents that "this one's for history."[56] Acknowledging the past scandals that plagued his previous administrations, he pledged that this term would be different and that this term would be his best. Likewise, his brother, Marion, spoke of a "scandal-free administration."[57] To that end, Edwards proclaimed September 2, 1984, as "Integrity Day" shortly after he took office. It was, however, shortlived. Two days later controversy arose over a story that ultimately engaged Edwards in what would eventually be known as "the trial of the century."[58]

U. S. Attorney John Volz began an inquiry into new hospital and nursing home proposals shortly after Edwards issued a ninety-day moratorium on state approvals, formerly called certificates of need, in order to revise the state health plan.[59] This plan contained the guidelines that the state followed to determine whether a new health care project was needed in a proposed area. If approved, the project became eligible for substantial federal funds, such as Medicare and Medicaid, to cover capital costs. Edwards wanted changes in the plan so that it would provide for more facilities and increased competition in the health care industry. However, when Edwards imposed the moratorium, he also ordered eight applications approved. In addition, five of these new hospital proposals had been submitted by one firm, Health Services Development Corporation (HSDC), owned by Metairie lawyer James Wyllie, Jr., and Ronald Falgout, an official in the state health department during Edwards's previous administration. The governor's action sparked protest from those whose applications had been denied, especially when the administrator of the U. S. Health Resources and Services Administration claimed that the eight applications approved did not meet the guidelines established in the state health plan.

After intense public criticism over the involvement of his personal friends and supporters in the approval of state health care facilities, Edwards, at a news conference, announced that HSDC offered to return the certificates of need approved by Edwards. He stated, "I did not realize it would take on the proportions that it has."[60] Protests, though, continued when it became public that Edwards's nephew, Charles David Isbell, handled the real estate transactions on some the HSDC projects, and that Edwards was a silent partner in Isbell's real estate firm. Edwards then admitted receiving one million dollars from HSDC, while he was out of office, for his assistance in getting state approval of three health care projects in Baton Rouge, Houma, and Gonzales between 1981 and the summer of 1983. This latest revelation resulted in a full-blown investigation, launched by the Justice Department and led by John Volz. Edwards, once again the target of a grand jury investigation, his twelfth to be exact, maintained his innocence, stating, " . . . I feel very comfortable with what I've done; after all, I was a private practitioner at the time and a businessman and I had every right to do what I did."[61] After testifying before the grand jury for four hours though, a different picture emerged. Edwards admitted personal interest in not three, but four health care facilities in the state which netted him approximately two million dollars for his work with HSDC, not the original one million dollars he earlier had claimed. Also, he previously stated that he was only a lawyer-consultant for HSDC, he amended that description after his grand jury testimony to include real estate agent and potential investor. He explained, "I was serving in a number of roles and capacities."[62] After hearing testimony from Edwards's relatives, friends, current and former staff members, HSDC officials and employees, and disgruntled hospital developers, the grand jury indicted Edwards and six others on fifty-one counts of racketeering, mail fraud, wire fraud, and obstruction of justice. The indictment purported that a conspiracy to violate the provisions of the Racketeer Influenced and Corrupt Organizations law (RICO) took place and that the defendants schemed to use the office of governor to enable them to profit personally by state action on health projects that totaled approximately ten million dollars.[63] Thus began the historic trial, "Criminal 85-078, United States of America versus Edwin Edwards, et al."[64]

An amazing cast of characters emerged from the complex web of business dealings and onto the fifty-two pages of the federal grand jury indictment. The indictment charged that Edwards concealed his involvement in the hospital projects so that he could later help the enterprises when he returned to office; that he received approximately two million dollars in legal fees for his assistance; and that, when he returned to office for his third term, he used his position to have other hospital projects approved. The indictment charged that James J. Wyllie, Jr., who received more than $2.6 million as part-owner of the four hospital ventures, concealed the true ownership of the hospital companies to allow the enterprise to benefit from Edwards's position when back in office; that he compiled applications for state approval of hospital projects and then steered them through the approval process; and that he contacted major hospital companies around the country to buy the corporations that had received state approval. Ronald Falgout was indicted for executing secret counter-letters that indicated that he held part of the stock in the hospital companies for the benefit of Edwards and his brother, Marion. The indictment alleged that Falgout told state health employees that Edwards had an interest in approval of certain projects submitted by the enterprise and implied that their careers might be jeopardized by their actions on these particular projects.

The grand jury indictment also included the governor's brother, Marion Edwards, who received approximately one million dollars for his involvement in the hospital projects. It charged that after the governor's election Marion received his brother's share of the projects. The indictment stated that Marion assured potential buyers of Wyllie's and Falgout's credibility and favor with the governor. In addition, Marion allegedly tried to persuade buyers that property bought through Charles David Isbell could receive state approval for hospital projects. The indictment also charged that Gus Mijalis, Edwards's long-time friend, had, along with Edwards, introduced the developers of certain nursing homes to Falgout, who obtained state approval for them. Mijalis, who earned $100,000 for his role in the approvals, also was alleged to have asked the developers to hide his role from the grand jury. The indictment charged that Charles David Isbell, the son of the governor's sister, Audrey Isbell, acted as the real estate agent on behalf of at least seven hospital corporations. The last figure in the grand jury indictment was Perry Segura, an architect and close friend of Edwards. The indictment alleged that Segura held stock in his own name for Edwards. He also provided architectural drawings required for state approval of the hospital projects, with the promise of a kickback of a portion of the architectural fees to Falgout and Wyllie.[65]

The indictment of Governor Edwards, the second Louisiana governor to be formally accused of violating federal law, the first Louisiana governor to be charged while in office, and the sixth governor nationwide to be indicted since 1920 sent shock waves throughout Louisiana.[66] It marked a dramatic reversal of fortune for Edwards, coming only one year into his unprecedented landslide victory of his historic third term. To be sure, a poll taken by the *New Orleans Times-Picayune* revealed that 72 percent of those surveyed believed that Edwards's indictment hurt the state's image, with only 35 percent saying that they would vote for Edwards if the election were held that day.[67]

Edwards outwardly appeared unaffected about the indictment. After a visit to his doctor for a check-up, he joked with reporters, "I'm healthier now than I was a year ago. I'll be able to live out any sentence I might receive that might result from this." He consistently maintained that the investigation was simply an attempt by Republicans to discredit him and that he had done nothing illegal.[68] Many observers suggested that unless Edwards resigned or could be quickly cleared of any misconduct, impeachment proceedings were a distinct possibility. U. S. Republican Representative Bob Livingston, concerned about Louisiana's image nationwide called for Edwards to step down, citing that he "is the highest elected official of our state . . . Every day that he remains in office after this indictment is a day that further tarnishes our national image."[69] Although the legislature had the power to impeach, no state law automatically required a high official to resign if facing criminal charges. One veteran House member predicted that the House would take no action until a verdict had been reached by the federal district court.[70] However, should Edwards be forced to leave office, the constitution provided that he would be succeeded by the elected lieutenant governor, Bobby Freeman.[71]

Edwards, in an attempt to calm the fears of those concerned about who would run the state during the trial, announced that the day-to-day operations would be in the hands of Stephanie Alexander, his commissioner of administration and newly appointed executive secretary to the governor, C. W. Roberts, Edwards's executive counsel, and Sid Moreland, his executive assistant. Roberts stated that "everything will operate just as it does now. The only difference is that the governor won't be there."[72] Edwards made it clear that he intended to remain in charge throughout the trial and continue to serve the people of Louisiana. He stated, "The chain of command is well forged. Government will go on." Edwards then announced that although he could not "conceive of the possibility of a conviction," if convicted he planned to resign, without waiting for an appeal.[73] In a news conference, Edwards, in a failed attempt at levity, began, "I don't cry and I don't sigh, and this will be over, by and by." Aware of the silence in the room, he assured the public that he would be found innocent of all charges and that there was no evidence to support the indictments.[74]

Legislators anticipated tumultuous months ahead for Louisiana's government. With an eighty-five day legislative session beginning shortly, some foresaw an indicted Edwards possibly having a difficult time dealing with the legislature, still disturbed over the previous year's tax increase. Representative Kevin Reilly, Edwards's floor leader, stated that the grand jury probe had already "paralyzed" Edwards and left the legislature a "headless body." He continued, "It's awfully difficult when there is no leadership."[75] Other politicians called the indictment serious but not enough to call for Edwards's resignation or impeachment. House Speaker John Alario shared the view with other legislators that the legislature would have to work harder, but that they were prepared to do it. U. S. Senator J. Bennett Johnston agreed, stating that Louisiana would undergo adverse publicity, but that the state needed to "pull together as it has never done before." A worker at the state Capitol summed up the sentiment of many Louisianians: "Other people expect this of Louisiana. I expect this of Louisiana. Citizens of Louisiana expect this of Louisiana. I'm embarrassed—but I'm going to enjoy the hell out of the trial."[76]

The regular legislative session began in April, with Governor Edwards, in his opening address, assuring the legislators that he would survive his legal troubles. He took a business-as-usual approach and, as usual, dominated the legislature, pushing through a tough agenda, thus proving that he could function successfully while under the dark cloud of a federal indictment. One of the biggest hurdles the legislature overcame was the approval of a bill to keep the New Orleans Saints football team in Louisiana. Both the state and the city of New Orleans agreed to repeal their sales taxes on Superdome events, while the state also granted the new team owner Tom Benson concessions worth approximtely $2.47 million a year, in exchange for a lease binding the team to play in the Superdome until the year 2001, wherein new negotiations would then take place.[77] Edwards also sought passage of a measure to have the state superintendent of education appointed by the State Board of Elementary and Secondary Education (BESE), rather than an elected office, starting in 1988. Louisiana would thus end its arrangement established in 1922 wherein the state had two elected education heads, the board and the superintendent.[78]

In addition, the Louisiana Educational Quality Trust Fund (LEQTF), a permanent trust fund, established from the bulk of anticipated windfall money, became one of Edwards's most important victories during the session. The state expected to receive a windfall of $605 million, following the settlement of a dispute with the federal government over money from oil and gas activities on federal tracts, called the 8(g) region, in the submerged outer continental shelf which borders Louisiana tracts. The interest from the hundreds of millions of dollars expected in mineral revenues was thus dedicated to fund educational improvements.[79]

Some of the most difficult days for the legislators and the governor alike involved, not surprisingly, the state budget. In spite of an earlier $900 million tax increase, deficits were projected to reach roughly thirty million dollars. Edwards reminded the legislators that he predicted one year ago that the state's fiscal problems were not over when they failed to approve his $1.1 billion tax increase package. Consequently, the legislature agreed to across-the-board cuts totaling $134.8 million to keep the state from operating in the red during the fiscal year.[80] Spending cuts became the only option to balance the budget since tax increases were prohibited in odd-year regular sessions. Most legislators supported the proposed budget initiated by Edwards, who called it "a budget that tries our souls."[81] State Representative Raymond LaBorde of Marksville, an Edwards floor leader, stated, "He had the courage to do something the legislature didn't have the courage to do."[82]

Indeed, courage was the quality that Edwards would need as his day of reckoning finally arrived. Assembled for the trial of Edwards and his co-defendants was "the most dazzling coterie of legal hotshots ever to grace a Louisiana courtroom."[83] The defense team included some of the best trial lawyers in New Orleans as well as some with national reputations. It included, among others, James Neal, who, as a prosecutor, won convictions of Teamster boss Jimmy Hoffa and some of the Watergate conspirators. In private practice he gained notoriety as the successful defense lawyer in the trial of the doctor of Elvis Presley and also in the celebrated Ford Pinto case.[84] Also, Neal's assistant, Camille Gravel, a "controversial, behind-the-scenes figure in Louisiana politics," was seen by many observers as "the best trial attorney there."[85]

The prosecution, on the other hand, had the status, reputation, and the resources of the federal government at its disposal. Led by the aggressive and intense prosecutor John Volz, who started out as assistant district attorney in Orleans Parish under Jim Garrison and later became a U. S. Attorney where he boasted a perfect record of victories, many observers saw him as a "conspicuous presence in the courtroom."[86] He received national attention when he won convictions of some of the most powerful and prominent figures in Louisiana, including Brilab participants Carlos Marcello and Charles Roemer.

The trial, presided over by Judge Marcel Livaudais, Jr., his first major criminal case, finally began. Indeed, both sides had a difficult task before them. The twelve-member jury, described as a "working-class" jury, consisted of seven whites and five blacks, which included nine blue-collar workers, two housewives, and a student.[87] They had to be led through a tangled thicket of federal, state, and local regulations governing hospital approvals. Also, the federal racketeering and fraud laws, statutes which were vague and difficult to understand, had to be grasped as well. In order to prove that the defendants engaged in racketeering, an organized pattern of crime, the prosecutors had to prove that each defendant broke at least two federal laws, in this case, mail fraud and wire fraud.

With security tight inside the closed, packed federal courtroom, with no cameras or recording devices permitted, John Volz began his opening remarks. He painted a picture of a group of men who, he claimed, used their political connections to control state approvals of new hospital construction. "They bribed the governor of this state . . . they bribed Mr. John Landry, a health department employee. That ladies and gentleman, in a nutshell, is what this case is about."[88]

Jim Neal painted a different picture of Edwards and his co-defendants in his opening statement. He accused the prosecution of applying corrupt motives and illicit intents to "shrewd and legal business deals." Neal, in his booming southern drawl, warned the jury not to let the two people he represented, the private citizen Edwards, who made money, and Governor Edwards, who had not taken any money from his co-defendants, become confused as one.[89]

Volz began his prosecution by attempting to "weave an intricate tapestry of secret letters, midnight telephone calls, clandestine meetings, phony land deals, state employee promotions, payoffs, safe deposit boxes, extortion, and bribery." He told the jury, "A shrewd business deal? You don't go to those extremes to cover up a shrewd business deal. You go to those extremes to carry out a crime."[90] Prosecutors first showed that Edwards earned two million dollars from the sale of four hospital corporations while out of office. Volz then put his key witness on the stand, John Landry, a health department employee who claimed that he received a bribe for approving a hospital project in which Edwards held one-third interest. Following the approval, Landry said he received a promotion after Edwards returned to office in 1984. During the cross-examination, defense attorney's focused on Landry's conflicting statements to the grand jury during two appearances. Under questioning, Landry acknowledged that he had lied during his first grand jury appearance and also while giving a deposition during a health department hearing. Later, under more questioning by the defense, Landry acknowledged that his promotion only increased his salary by $42.50 a week.[91] After his testimony, the defense was jubilant. Volz's star witness, whose singlehanded testimony was supposed to decide the case, was perceived as a flawed witness. Moreover, when the defense called the secretary of the Department of Health and Human Resources to the stand she testified that she, not Edwards, promoted John Landry. When asked what role Governor Edwards took in the promotion, or bribe according to the prosecution, she replied, "Nothing that I know about."[92]

Volz also tried to prove that Edwards purposely hid his ownership in certain hospitals by listing other defendants as the owners, and by not including his ownership in campaign financial disclosure forms filed in 1983 and 1984, thereby defrauding the public. The defense attorneys argued that the use of counter-letters was not illegal under Louisiana law and were used, in this case, to keep people in the Treen administration from finding out about Edwards's ownership and jeopardizing the project's success.[93] Also, both Edwards's tax attorney and bookkeeper testified that the omission of Edwards's ownership of the hospitals, a violation of a state law, was unintentional.

The prosecution also tried to prove that Marion Edwards, who earned one million dollars from the sale of a fifth hospital, was actually the "bagman" for his brother when Edwin Edwards became governor for a third term. Volz presented the fact that when the governor's son, Stephen, wanted to buy a $200,000 fishing boat, he went to Marion for the money, who Volz alleged held the money for Edwin. Stephen, defending his behavior, testified that he asked his uncle for the money because "he didn't have the guts" to ask his father for it.[94]

The prosecution's most convincing evidence centered around Edwards's approval of three nursing home projects after he became governor. Shreveport nursing home operator Kevin Gamble testified that Edwards offered to help him obtain approvals for the three projects. Edwards reportedly told a co-defendant to check the need for the three nursing homes and "bicycle" them through the state system. The same day that they were approved, Edwards ordered a moratorium on further approvals. Prosecutors maintained that the moratorium effectively stopped competitors from building their own nursing homes and hospitals. But defense attorneys rejected the accusation and instead portrayed Edwards as "doing what he does every day as governor, simply helping constituents make their way through a maze of state regulations."[95]

Volz then presented, in a two-hour electrifying testimony, the alleged motive for establishing the purported hospital approval scheme, the gambling debts of Governor Edwards.[96] Using a chart that showed the dates of Edwards's gambling trips, how much he owed, when he paid the debts, and how they were paid, the prosecution attempted to prove that Edwards's gambling activities were an obvious motive for his involvement. According to testimony by an FBI agent, Edwards took fifteen gambling trips to Las Vegas, Reno, and Lake Tahoe and lost more than two million dollars, as much as $500,000 during one trip, between 1981 and 1984. A retired Caesar's Palace casino employee testified that Edwards gave him a suitcase, on two different occasions, filled with a total of $780,000 in cash to pay off two gambling debts. In addition, a former Las Vegas Desert Inn casino employee testified that he picked up a manila envelope stuffed with $100,000 from an Edwards aide to pay off another gambling debt. Furthermore, an FBI agent testified that Edwards used a number of aliases when gambling at the casinos, including T. Lee, Ed Neff, T. Wong, and B. True.[97]

The testimony by the defense painted an entirely different picture of Edwards's gambling activities. Led by Neal, Vern Welch, the assistant general manager for operations at Harrah's Lake Tahoe casino, amended the chart, prepared by the prosecution, to include Edwards's gambling winnings, not just his losses, which actually showed that Edwards won more than he lost. Welch also testified that gambling chips from one casino are honored at other casinos, thus supporting the argument made by the defense that Edwards's debts did not accurately represent his losses at a given casino. Likewise, Volz's desire to impugn Edwards's character by introducing the gaming evidence did not succeed. During jury selection, the majority of the prospective jurors, when questioned about their views of high-stakes gambling, stated that they were not offended by gambling and that "what he [Edwards] does with his money is his business."[98]

After ten weeks, forty witnesses, and twenty-two days of often-times tedious, complex testimony, Governor Edwards finally took the witness stand. After weeks of boring, intricate details concerning the state's health planning system, spectators and jurors alike appeared eager to witness the "high drama" promised when Edwards and Volz squared off. As one reporter observed, "His appearance on the witness stand was like the coming of a messiah who would lead the people out of the deadly Valley of Bore."[99] To be sure, Edwards entered this stage of the trial on a high note. Previously, the prosecution had been hurt by the testimony that Edwards had nothing to do with the promotion of Landry in the state Department of Health and Human Resources. Also, the prosecution's contention that Edwards participated in the hospital scheme to pay off gambling debts was damaged when an employee of Harrah's casino testified that Edwards did not owe $686,000 to the casino, but actually had won $562,500, weakening further Volz's accusation that Edwards had gambling debts to pay off.[100]

Spectators had been waiting for this showdown—the governor's quick wit against Volz's volatile line of questioning. The testimony was often interrupted by objections from Edwards's attorneys, laughter from the jurors, and occasional boos from the spectators. Once there was even a burst of applause. Edwards showed off his adroitness as a witness, quoting page numbers from his own grand jury report from memory. Edwards often appeared better prepared for the cross examination than Volz did. At one point, Volz had to stop a line of questioning because he did not have the correct page number. Without missing a beat, Edwards said, "It's page ninety-three." Volz checked, and found that Edwards was correct.[101]

It was an intense, yet welcome moment when the jury, then sequestered, finally began their deliberations. Many viewed the anticipated decision as the "biggest political decision in Louisiana's recent history."[102] The stakes could hardly be higher. For Governor Edwards, who gave eight to one odds that he would be found innocent, knew a guilty verdict could mean an end to a brilliant political career.[103] To be sure, he had stated earlier that if convicted, he would resign. If Edwards were to be exonerated, though, he would still be damaged politically, perhaps enough to not seek re-election. In addition, a mistrial, which would allow the possibility of a retrial, would also have a detrimental effect. Either way, the decision by the jury could have the effect of starting the 1987 gubernatorial campaign earlier than usual.

In a bizarre turn of events, Judge Livaudais convened a Saturday court session to discuss an incident involving one of the jurors. Clifford West, while being escorted from the Hotel Intercontinental, searched for the television cameras and twice made a thumbs-down gesture through the window of the van he was riding in. Defense attorneys, after being shown a recording of the incident, made a formal request that West be dropped from the jury, stating that during the trial West had often been spotted making bizarre gestures. For instance, during Edwards's testimony, West pretended to be rolling dice. After a defense witness testified that Edwards won instead of lost at Nevada casinos, West rubbed his index fingers together in a "naughty, naughty" gesture toward the prosecutors. Although this behavior was indeed bizarre, other jurors succumbed to the boredom and pressure of the long, tedious trial as well. One juror rolled up a prosecution's exhibit like a telescope and peered through it at the defense and the prosecution's attorneys. Another juror pulled a rubber band off a transcript of Edwards's grand jury testimony and stretched it over his forehead, leaving it there for several minutes.[104] Judge Livaudais succumbed to the tedium also. One observer noted, "During the course of some of the testimony, he sinks so far down in his chair that only his head is visible from the back of the courtroom."[105] Judge Livaudais, though, refused the motion, and West continued as one of the jurors deciding the fate of Governor Edwards.

The jury, not surprisingly, had a difficult time during their deliberations. Indeed, the thirteen-week trial had mounds of documented, complex evidence—eight volumes of prosecution exhibits and six volumes of defense exhibits—along with forty pages of jury deliberation rules. The jury repeatedly sent out questions to Judge Livaudais, ranging from procedural questions to requests for grand jury testimony. Also, the jury knew that in order to find the defendants guilty, they needed a unanimous vote "beyond a reasonable doubt." Six days later, the jury sent out a note stating that "after days of deliberation, we are at a point of deadlock with no foreseeable progress." Judge Livaudais then issued an "Allen charge" or a "dynamite charge" urging the jury to reach a decision.[106] Two days later, the jury finally agreed on one thing, they were indeed deadlocked.

Judge Livaudais thus declared a mistrial and an exultant Governor Edwin Edwards, one of the most resilient politicians in Louisiana history, bounded down the courtroom steps, flanked by his family, with tears of joy in his eyes. He stated, "I have just won the sixteenth most important election in my life by the greatest margin ever. After all this, I simply want to say how sweet it is."[107] He moved quickly to re-establish his damaged credibility and regain control of the state. It would not be a simple task. A statewide poll taken shortly thereafter revealed that 52 percent of the people polled would not vote to re-elect Governor Edwards, while 30 percent believed that Edwards was guilty of the racketeering and fraud charges against him.[108] He called a press conference and made it clear that he intended to complete his term as governor, as well as run for re-election in 1987. In addition, he promised to unveil a new plan to revitalize the economic base of the state of Louisiana."[109]

Edwards, coming off a trial in which revelations about his high stakes gambling practices received nationwide attention, boldly announced his new plan to a packed ballroom in the New Orleans Hilton Hotel: casino gambling in the New Orleans area, a statewide lottery, and gambling on cruise ships in the Mississippi River. According to Edwards, it would solve the state's fiscal dilemma by creating 100,000 new jobs, bringing in revenues totaling more than $500 million yearly, and by creating "a Superbowl every weekend" because of the thousands of tourists the gaming industry would attract.[110] He announced plans to call a special legislative session once he had the support to push his gambling agenda through the legislature.[111]

Even with his renowned ability to sway the legislature, Edwards faced an uphill battle. The legislature would have to drop the legal barriers in order to approve casino gambling and a state lottery. The 1974 constitution contained a specific ban on lotteries.[112] It would therefore take a two-thirds vote of each house and a statewide referendum to initiate a lottery, while casino gambling could be legalized by a simple majority of the House and Senate. Also, Edwards ran into solid opposition from a coalition of religious leaders, fearful of further damage to the state's image, as well as on moral grounds. Law enforcement officers and private citizens shuddered at the claims that crime would increase a whopping 300 percent.[113]

Although the governor painted a bleak picture of the state's future if the legislature refused to act and promised budget cuts that would cripple state services and lay off 10,000 employees, Edwards could not garner the support necessary to ensure a victory.[114] Therefore, Edwards canceled his plan for a special legislative session. He stressed that although he had postponed his special session, he had not given up his plan to legalize gambling.[115] Rather, he simply changed his strategy.

Edwards challenged the legislature to put his proposals before the voters in a public referendum—and promised to resign if the proposals were rejected. He stated, ". . . If we don't do something about our problems, none of us are going to be reelected in 1987 anyway."[116] This time, though, the legislature refused to fall into line, especially when he angered them by claiming that the legislature was incapable of balancing the budget without casino and lottery money. Moreover, he promised to veto their budget, which he expected to contain tax increases and budget cuts to erase a predicted $500 million deficit. One legislator responded, "No governor has ever vetoed a budget before, and nobody has passed a budget over his veto—but there's a first time for everything."[117]

The announcement of a retrial came at a particularly bad time for the governor.[118] The opening of the legislative session, less than a month away, posed massive problems for Edwards, even without a retrial. He left the legislature with no plan for dealing with a growing fiscal crisis, except for a highly unpopular revenue package that involved legalized casino gambling, a statewide lottery, and a 20-mill state property tax.[119] Nevertheless, John Volz refused to give up. Saying justice was not served, he announced that he planned to retry Governor Edwards and his co-defendants on fraud and racketeering charges. Edwards, visibly angered at the news, stated once again that Volz, who planned on leading the prosecution through the retrial, was conducting a political vendetta.[120]

After two weeks of intense questioning, a jury of nine men and three women, consisting of eight blacks and four whites, were selected for the retrial. Although the majority of the jurors chosen were, as before, blue-collar workers, they were older and better educated than the jury in the first trial.[121] In an unusual move, Judge Livaudais ordered the sequestration of the twelve jurors and four alternates for the duration of the trial, at an approximate cost of $250,000.[122] Despite the cost and the inconvenience, Livaudais stated that "the closeting is necessary so jurors can avoid the temptation of looking at news reports and the risk of someone approaching them [about the trial]."[123]

The retrial, as expected, appeared as a virtual rerun of the first trial. Both sides agreed that the theory remained unchanged: The prosecution contended that Edwards and his co-defendant manipulated the state's hospital approval program for their own gain. The differences consisted of subsidiary issues, such as a sequestered jury, a trimmed-down indictment that eliminated four charges from the original fifty-count joint indictment, and the exclusion of Edwards's gambling testimony. There were also fewer defendants because of the acquittal of Brooks, Segura, and Isbell at the end of the first trial. A change in the governor's defense team occurred as well. Edwards chose Michael Fawer, who represented co-defendant Brooks in the first trial, as his defense attorney after James Neal failed in an attempt to delay a forthcoming trial in order to represent Edwards.[124]

The prosecution offered no new evidence, no markedly different testimony, and no new key witnesses. As in the first trial, no traceable pattern of payments proved, beyond a doubt, that Edwards, or others, took bribes for hospital approvals. Thus, the case was once again open for interpretation: Was it a conspiracy or just aggressive business deals? Volz, attempting to avoid the pitfalls he fell into during the first trial, changed his strategy. This time, he stated in his opening statement there was no smoking gun. Rather, the pieces would eventually fit together like a puzzle. Also, Volz chose not to call John Landry to testify, a decision that brought outrage from the defense. Volz defended his action, stating that Landry had not told the "whole truth" during the first trial. The defense countered that Landry was not called because his testimony did not implicate Edwards.[125]

The defense, in a bold tactic, rested its case, without calling any defense witnesses. They simply claimed that they had nothing to contradict, thus sending a message that the defense did not feel the government presented a case strong enough to even refute.[126]

Assistant U. S. Attorney Barnes, presented a three-hour closing argument. She summed up the prosecution's position by stating that Edwards sold out the citizens of Louisiana and "he didn't come cheaply. He lied, showed undue favoritism to his friends, peddled influence, and was bribed by his co-defendants to manipulate the state's hospital approval program for his gain and theirs." Volz challenged the jury to "send a message that no man is above the law . . . they are not untouchable . . ."[127] He then presented the jury with a picture of a puzzle, shaped like Louisiana, that alluded to his earlier opening statements. As he spoke, an FBI agent added pieces to the puzzle, each bearing a different theme of the prosecution's case, such as bribes, pay-offs, cover-ups, and co-conspirators. One letter in each title was enlarged, thereby spelling out the word FRAUD when Volz ended his closing argument.

The defense stated in their closing arguments that the case was simply built on "guilt by gossip, guilt by suspicion . . . and that the defendants need not disprove what the government has not proved." Camille Gravel told the jurors that the purpose of this ordeal had been to brand Edwards as a racketeer and that although Edwards may not be a saint, he was certainly not Satan either. Rather, "he's not a man without faults, but he's also got enormous virtues."[128]

The jury in the seven-week retrial deliberated approximately twelve hours over two days before reaching a verdict. An air of anticipation filled the courtroom as the jurors filed in, showing no signs of emotion. The courtroom deputy read the verdict: "The jury unanimously finds the defendant, Edwin Edwards, as to all counts, not guilty."[129]

Spectators and defendants alike jumped to their feet. Edwards embraced his attorneys, then his wife, children, and his brother, Marion. The other verdicts were then read one by one. The four other co-defendants, Marion Edwards, James Wyllie, Ronald Falgout, and Gus Mijalis were also acquitted.

On the courthouse steps, Edwards, greeted with applause and cheers from the spectators, launched into a familiar theme of Edwards's for the last nineteen months: that he was a victim of a Republican prosecutor. He reacted to Volz's closing argument that the jury send a message to the people of the state that corruption will not be tolerated. He stated, "The message is very plain . . . This is a courtroom, and not a political headquarters." He continued, "We were found innocent without having to utter one word in our defense, without having to produce one witness or one document." Edwards, with the legislature ever-present on his mind, then stated, "The first order of business is to get back to Baton Rouge."[130]

It was a unique legislative session that Edwards returned to—there had been no governor standing in the wings to give advice or lobby for his programs. In Edwards's own words, he had been "shackled to a chair" in a New Orleans courtroom for the first half of the legislative session. Edwards, rather naively, reasoned that his absence would give the legislature "a unique opportunity to show its independence."[131] The legislature, still angered over the governor's accusations that it was incapable of solving the state's fiscal woes, capitalized on the opportunity. Earlier, leaders in both houses let it be known that they planned to end the session as quickly as possible—in other words, to balance the budget by cutting expenditures—just in case Edwards's retrial might end early, thereby increasing the likelihood of the governor returning and raising revenues through gambling and not making the budget cuts. Thus, when Edwards returned from his retrial, the legislature, which had voted earlier to table a legalized gambling bill without bringing it up for debate, presented him with a balanced budget that included $437 million in budget cuts, with no legalized gambling revenues.

Edwards, who remained convinced that legalized gambling was the answer to the fiscal crisis, responded by stating that he planned to call a special session when legislators realized that they needed to rescind their budget cuts and raise revenues through legalized gambling. Insulted by the rejection of his budget plan, Edwards spurned the legislature, keeping a low profile after the session ended. He then called for a special session, the first one since the tumultuous tax session in 1984, to tackle the state's fiscal problems. Desperately trying to get his gambling agenda passed, he dropped his initial proposal for casino and riverboat gambling, recommending only the approval of a statewide lottery that could produce revenues of $150 million a year, along with an additional 3 percent across-the-board-cut for all state agencies.[132] The legislature, though, refused to quiet their new-found voice. To that end, the legislators called an unprecedented meeting in order to present a unified front on the following day, when legislative leaders would meet with Governor Edwards to discuss the fiscal options available. Despite a personal plea from Edwards, who guaranteed that 75 percent of the proceeds from the lottery would be earmarked for education, with the balance going to health care, the House rejected the governor's proposal for a state lottery.[133] It was a stunning blow for Edwards, mighty ruler of the legislature for almost two decades.

Had Edwards, Louisiana's Phoenix, who remained unscathed and victorious for over three decades, finally been consumed in the conflagration of Louisiana politics? In the past, Edwards had endured an inferno of allegations, indictments, and trials, always emerging politically intact. But could he survive an independent legislature—especially one with no money to spend? Or would his political life end at the conclusion of his historic third term?

Perhaps Edwards, who had been conspicuously absent from Baton Rouge because of his two trials on racketeering charges, had indeed lost some of his spark. And rightly so. Few politicians could survive the problems that Edwards endured during his first three terms as governor. The shadow of scandal, from Koreagate, Brilab, DCCL, to Edwards's trial and retrial, climaxing with a mutinous legislature, had taken its toll on this accomplished politician. Yet, little was ever been proven against the verbose, often defiant Edwards, in spite of a plethora of grand jury investigations. Indeed, his achievements, notoriety, and his efficacy are beyond question. To be sure, the seamier side of Edwards has often been looked upon as entertainment, if not unanimity, by many Louisianians.

Yet, Edwards's recent brush with the law was not the only explanation for his lack of control over the legislature. His announcement to push for legalized gambling, not only before he had the legislative support he needed, but before the legislators had actually grasped the enormity of the financial crisis ahead, was highly uncharacteristic of Edwards, ever mindful of the political climate. To be sure, having to cancel a special session only added to his lack of influence with the legislature. Then, his suggestion for a referendum to let the public decide whether or not they wanted legalized gambling also failed to survive the House and the Senate. When an amended form of the governor's gambling proposal could not be passed in a later special session, the legislature, heady from its encounter with independence from the governor, refused to return to their compliant ways.

Perhaps for another politician, possibly one not as gifted as Edwards, such problems would have signaled the end of a political career. Yet for the Louisiana Phoenix Edwin Edwards, this difficult third term served only as a crucible, not consuming him, but rather, shaping him, for his future flight into the incredible realm of Louisiana politics. Many legislators hailed the body's independence from Governor Edwards, calling the historic session the "Legislature's Magna Carta." Others agreed, stating that Louisiana had witnessed a revolution in politics.[134] A political revolution? Indeed, the revolution had just begun.

## Notes for "Political Crucible"

[1]*New Orleans Times-Picayune*, January 24, 1984.

[2]Ibid., January 25, 1984. In 1803 President Thomas Jefferson paid $15 million for the acquisition of the Louisiana Territory from France which doubled the size of the United States.

[3]Ms. Iris Kelso, Telephone interview by the author, New Orleans, Louisiana, March 7, 1994.

[4]*Times-Picayune*, January 23, 1984.

[5]Ibid., January 29, 1984.

[6]*Baton Rouge Morning Advocate*, January 24, 1984; January 29, 1984.

[7]*Times-Picayune*, January 22, 1984. The crowd added another superlative to their record—the only crowd to ever dine at Versaille and dance to the tune of "Dixie."

[8]Ms. Iris Kelso, interview by the author, Telephone, New Orleans, La., March 7, 1994.

[9]*Times-Picayune*, January 22, 1984, January 26, 1984.

[10]Ibid., January 29, 1984.

[11]Ibid.

[12]Ibid., January 26, 1984.

[13]The state chairman of the Republican party in Louisiana, George Despot, attempted to get the Internal Revenue Service to audit the income tax returns of all those who accompanied Governor-elect Edwards to Paris. The IRS refused, stating that "We do not, and will not, examine a taxpayers return because of political affiliation or charges made by a political opponent." Press release, Office of the Governor Edwin W. Edwards, February 24, 1984, Edwin W. Edwards Collection, Louisiana State Archives, Baton Rouge, Louisiana.

[14]"The Inaugural Ceremonies of State Officials of Louisiana," March 1984, Baton Rouge, Louisiana, Edwin W. Edwards Collection, Louisiana State Archives, Baton Rouge, Louisiana.

[15]Ms. Iris Kelso, Telephone interview by the author, New Orleans, Louisiana, 7 March 1994; *Times-Picayune*, March 15, 1984.

[16]*Times-Picayune*, March 15, 1984.

[17]Governor Edwin W. Edwards, *Inauguration Speech*, March 12, 1984, Tape recording, Edwin W. Edwards Collection, Louisiana State Archives, Baton Rouge, Louisiana.

[18]Press release, Office of the Governor Edwin W. Edwards, February 7, 1984, Edwin W. Edwards Collection, Louisiana State Archives, Baton Rouge, Louisiana.

[19]*Morning Advocate*, March 12, 1984.

[20]Press release, Office of the Governor Edwin W. Edwards, February 12, 1984, Edwin W. Edwards Collection, Louisiana State Archives, Baton Rouge, Louisiana. Critics questioned the need for a special session that would begin in March, when the regular legislative session, designated to begin only one month later, might possibly handle such matters.

[21]*New Orleans Gambit*, January 14, 1984, Edwin W. Edwards Collection, Louisiana State Archives, Baton Rouge, Louisiana; *Shreveport Journal*, March 12, 1984, Edwin W. Edwards Collection, Louisiana State Archives, Baton Rouge, Louisiana.

[22]*Times-Picayune*, February 12, 1984.

[23]Ibid., March 18, 1984.

[24]*Shreveport Journal*, March 21, 1984, Edwin Edwards Collection, Louisiana State Archives, Baton Rouge, Louisiana.

[25]*Times-Picayune*, March 20, 1984.

[26]Michael L. Kurtz and Morgan D. Peoples, *Earl K. Long: The Saga of Uncle Earl and Louisiana Politics* (Baton Rouge, 1990), 1; *Times-Picayune*, March 27, 1984.

[27]*Times-Picayune*, March 14, 1984; March 18, 1984. Treen had previously cut 4.4 percent from the state agencies' operating budget. *Morning Advocate*, February 17, 1984. Edwards warned of budget cuts as high as 25 percent.

[28]Press release, Office of Governor Edwin W. Edwards, February 24, 1984, Edwin W. Edwards Collection, Louisiana State Archives, Baton Rouge, Louisiana. Under Civil Service rules, new employees hired within one year were considered probationary and could be fired, depending on their job classification. *Morning Advocate*, March 20, 1984.

[29]*Public Affairs Research Council of Louisiana, Inc.* 272 (September 1984): 4; *Times-Picayune*, March 17, 1984; March 21, 1984.

[30]*Times-Picayune*, March 18, 1984.

[31]Ibid., March 20, 1984; March 4, 1984.

[32]Ibid., March 20, 1984.

[33]Ms. Iris Kelso, Telephone interview by the author, New Orleans, Louisiana, March 7, 1994; *Times-Picayune*, March 18, 1984.

[34]*Times-Picayune*, March 18, 1984.

[35]Ibid., March 27, 1984. Governor Earl Long's tax increase in 1948 was larger as a percentage of the state budget.

[36]*Acts State of Louisiana*, Extraordinary Session, Vol. 2 (1984): 2424-2431.

[37]Ibid., 2418, 2383, 2389, 2428-2431. Edwards proposed the tax increase on alcohol and cigarettes in spite of his campaign rhetoric during the 1983 motorcade wherein he accused Treen of taxing beer and cigarettes stating, "Although I don't smoke or drink, I'm not going to punish those that do." *Baker Observer*, October 13, 1983.

[38]*Acts State of Louisiana*, Extraordinary Session, Vol. 2 (1984): 2405.

[39]Ms. Iris Kelso, Telephone interview by the author, New Orleans, Louisiana, March 7, 1994; *Times-Picayune*, March 25, 1984.

[40]*Times-Picayune*, April 14, 1984.

[41]Ibid., June 3, 1984.

[42]*PAR Analysis* 272, September 1984:3.

[43]*Times-Picayune*, April 6, 1984.

[44]Ibid., May 18, 1984. The balance of the revenue would be used for drainage and flood control.

[45]Ibid., May 25, 1984.

[46]Ibid., June 8, 1984. The corporate franchise tax, contingent upon voter acceptance of the tax increase, would be levied on a corporation's capital stock. The proposed constitutional amendment would double the tax from $1.50 to $3.00 per $1,000 of capital stock. *Times-Picayune*, June 21, 1984.

[47]*Acts State of Louisiana*, Regular Session, Vol. 2 (1984): 1880-1885.

[48]Ibid., Regular Session, Vol. 1, (1984): 1472; *PAR Analysis* 272 (September 1984): 1-12.

[49]*Acts State of Louisiana*, Regular Session, Vol. 1 (1984): 590-91.

[50]Ibid., Regular Session, Vol. 2 (1984): 2054.

[51]*Times-Picayune*, July 8, 1984.

[52]Ibid., July 8, 1984.

[53]*PAR Analysis* 272 (September 1984): 12.

[54]*Times-Picayune*, July 8, 1984.

[55]Ibid., May 27, 1984.

[56]*Lake Charles American Press*, November 2, 1983, Edwin W. Edwards Collection, Louisiana State Archives, Baton Rouge, Louisiana.

[57]*Morning Advocate*, October 23, 1983; *Times-Picayune*, October 28, 1984.

[58]*Times-Picayune*, March 3, 1985.

[59]Under this federal program, a certificate of need, or an 1122 certificate, is needed to receive Medicare and Medicaid subsidies. The certificate, granted by the state, says that a health care facility is needed and will not be underused. Ostensibly, the 1122 Program was established to ensure that federal money does not build unnecessary health care facilities. Since Medicare and Medicaid comprise as much as 40 percent of a hospital's patients, the reimbursements can total tens of millions of dollars. *Times-Picayune*, September 15, 1985.

[60]*Morning Advocate*, March 1, 1985.

[61]From 1973 through 1985, twelve grand jury probes investigated Edwards: 1973-75 income tax; 1974 campaign finances; 1974-75 campaign finances; 1974-75 campaign finances; 1975 Family Health Foundation; 1975 campaign finances; 1977-78 Tongsun Park; 1980 Brilab; 1983-84 DCCL; 1983-84 Norvell Rhodes case; 1984-85 Texaco; 1985 state hospital approvals. *Times-Picayune*, March 1, 1985.

[62]*Times-Picayune*, March 1, 1985.

[63]The RICO statute is used in the prosecution of group crime committed through the formation of an enterprise. Enacted in 1970, the RICO statute had been used in the prosecution of white-collar crime, including cases of political corruption. In order to be a violation of RICO there must be a "pattern of racketeering." Howard Abadinsky, *Organized Crime*, 2nd ed., Nelson-Hall Series in Justice Administration (Chicago, Nelson-Hall, 1985), 269-272.

[64]*United States of America v. Edwin W. Edwards et al*, Criminal Docket No. 85-078, Sect. E Mag. 4, United States District Court, Eastern District of Louisiana, 1985.

[65]*United States of America v. Edwin W. Edwards et al*, Criminal Docket No. 85-078, Sect. E Mag. 4, United States District Court, Eastern District of Louisiana, 1985.

[66]*Times-Picayune*, March 1, 1985; *New York Times*, March 1, 1985. The state's only other governor prosecuted by federal officials was the late Richard W. Leche, convicted in 1940 of mail fraud charges growing out of allegations that he illegally received money for awarding a state road-building contract. Leche resigned as governor during the Louisiana scandals in 1939, three months before he was indicted. He was sentenced to a ten-year prison term but was released after serving a little over three years. In 1953 President Harry Truman pardoned Leche. It is also noteworthy that the prosecutions of Leche and Edwards were the work of federal prosecutors rather than state district attorneys.

[67]*Times-Picayune*, March 8, 1985.

[68]*Dallas Times*, March 1, 1985, Edwin W. Edwards Collection, Louisiana State Archives, Baton Rouge, Louisiana.

[69]*Times-Picayune*, March 1, 1985.

[70]*Morning Advocate*, March 2, 1985, Edwin W. Edwards Collection, Louisiana State Archives, Baton Rouge, Louisiana. If the House did vote to impeach, the Senate would then conduct a trial. It would require a two-thirds majority of the Senate's thirty-nine members to convict. Under the 1974 state constitution, though, a Louisiana governor does not have to resign even if convicted. In theory, a Louisiana governor can continue to serve even if he is serving time in prison.

[71]To complicate the issue further, earlier that year a federal grand jury began investigating allegations of bribery that involved Bobby Freeman's involvement in a 1984 World's Fair contract. It was announced later by U. S. Attorney John Volz that the investigation was over and that Freeman would not be prosecuted, thus clearing the way for a possible succession, if necessary.

[72]Governor Edwin Edwards, News conference, location unknown, March 1, 1985, Tape recording; *Morning Advocate*, March 8, 1985; *Times-Picayune*, September 16, 1985.

[73]*Morning Advocate*, March 2, 1985.

[74]Governor Edwin Edwards, News conference, location unknown, March 1, 1985, Tape recording. In an untimely slip of the tongue, Governor Edwards, during his first news conference after the indictment, stated, "I am equally confident that I would not undergo the trauma of a trial if I were not positive that we would end up victoriously and be found guilty at the conclusion of the proceed—listen to me . . . be found . . . be found guiltless at the conclusion of the proceedings."

[75]*USA Today*, March 1, 1985, Edwin W. Edwards Collection, Louisiana State Archives, Baton Rouge, Louisiana.

[76]*Times-Picayune*, March 1, 1985.

[77]Ibid., May 26, 1985.

[78]*PAR Analysis* 278, October 1985: 5.

[79]*Acts State of Louisiana*, Regular Session, Vol. 2 (1985): 2047-50; *PAR Analysis* 278, October 1985: 3.

[80]*PAR Analysis* 278, October 1985: 2.

[81]*Times-Picayune*, March 16, 1985.

[82]Ibid., February 14, 1985.

[83]Ibid., October 27, 1985.

[84]James Neal successfully defended Elvis Presley's doctor from charges of prescribing drugs that caused the singer's death. In addition, Neal successfully defended the Ford Motor Co. from charges it built Pinto cars knowing they had a gas tank problem that could lead to death. Nancy Lemann, *The Ritz of the Bayou* (New York, 1987), 23; *Times-Picayune*, September 15, 1985.

[85]*Times-Picayune*, October 27, 1985.

[86]*Morning Advocate*, September 19, 1985. Jim Garrison gained notoriety for his unsuccessful prosecution of New Orleans businessman Clay Shaw on charges of conspiring to assassinate President John F. Kennedy. It should also be noted that John Volz, originally a Democrat, switched to the Republican Party midway through his career.

[87]*Baton Rouge State Times*, September 28, 1985, Edwin W. Edwards Collection, Louisiana State Archives, Baton Rouge, Louisiana.

[88]*Morning Advocate*, October 1, 1985; *Baton Rouge State Times*, October 1, 1985, Edwin W. Edwards Collection, Louisiana State Archives, Baton Rouge, Louisiana.

[89]*Baton Rouge State Times*, October 1, 1985, Edwin W. Edwards Collection, Louisiana State Archives, Baton Rouge, Louisiana.

[90]*Times-Picayune*, October 1, 1985.

[91]*Monroe New-Star-World,* October 9, 1985, Edwin W. Edwards Collection, Louisiana State Archives, Baton Rouge, Louisiana.

[92]*Times-Picayune,* November 26, 1985.

[93]A counter-letter is a legal document that says property owned by one person actually is owned by another.

[94]*Morning Advocate*, November 6, 1985.

[95]*Monroe News-Star-World,* November 8, 1985, Edwin W. Edwards Collection, Louisiana State Archives, Baton Rouge, Louisiana.

[96]Judge Livaudais denied a defense motion to exclude the gambling evidence, stating that the questioned evidence would be deemed admissible in court if properly authenticated during the trial. Prosecutors were allowed to introduce the gambling evidence to show that Edwards had a history of high-stakes financial dealings. Before the gaming evidence was introduced, though, Judge Livaudais cautioned the jury that Edwards's gambling was completely legal, it was not mentioned in the indictment, and should be disregarded when deciding the guilt or innocence of the other defendants. *Times-Picayune*, August 28, 1985; November 8, 1985; November 10, 1985.

[97]*Times-Picayune,* November 8, 1985; November 27, 1985; *Baton Rouge State Times,* November 27, 1985. Both the prosecution and the defense agreed that the aliases were not used to hide the governor's identity and that he was well known at the casinos.

[99]*Times-Picayune*, December 3, 1985.

[100]Ibid., December 1, 1985.

[101]Ibid., December 4,1985.

[102]Ibid., November 24, 1985.

[103]*Wall Street Journal,* March 1, 1985.

[104]*Baton Rouge State Times*, December 5, 1985; *Times-Picayune*, December 15, 1985.

[105]*Times-Picayune*, November 3, 1985.

[106]Ibid., December 17, 1985. An "Allen charge" or "dynamite charge" is routinely read as a last resort to a jury that seems on the verge of hopeless deadlock.

[107]*Morning Advocate,* December 19, 1985. The jury voted ten-to-two to acquit Edwards on some charges and eleven-to-one on others. Earlier, Judge Livaudais ordered the acquittal of defendants Brooks, Isbell, and Segura on all of the fifty charges against them, and on one charge against Mijalis. *Morning Advocate,* December 10, 1985. Since 1954, Edwards had a perfect record of fifteen election victories. He considered this mistrial his sixteenth victory.

[108]Ibid., December 23, 1985.

[109]Press release, Office of the Governor Edwin W. Edwards, January 17, 1987, Edwin W. Edwards Collection, Louisiana State Archives, Baton Rouge, Louisiana.

[110]*Alexandria Daily Town Talk,* January 7, 1986, Edwin W. Edwards Collection, Louisiana State Archives, Baton Rouge, Louisiana; *Morning Advocate*, January 29, 1986.

[111]Prior to this proposal, individuals or groups of legislators attempted a variety of bills designed to open up Louisiana to more legalized gaming activity. None met with any success. This time the issue met with unparalleled intensity simply because it was initiated by the governor.

[112]*Louisiana Constitution*, art. XII, sec 6.

[113]*Morning Advocate*, April 2, 1986.

[114]*Wall Street Journal*, January 13, 1986.

[115]*Monroe News-Star-World*, January 28, 1986, Edwin W. Edwards Collection, Louisiana State Archives, Baton Rouge, Louisiana.

[116]*Alexandria Daily Town Talk*, January 30, 1986, Edwin W. Edwards Collection, Louisiana State Archives, Baton Rouge, Louisiana.

[117]*Morning Advocate*, February 26, 1986; *Times-Picayune*, February 27, 1986.

[118]*Christian Science Monitor*, January 13, 1986.

[119]*Monroe News-Star-World*, February 27, 1986, Edwin W. Edwards Collection, Louisiana State Archives, Baton Rouge, Louisiana.

[120]*Times-Picayune*, January 12, 1986.

[121]*Morning Advocate*, April 8, 1985.

[122]*Baton Rouge State Times*, March 20, 1986. During the first trial, the jury was sequestered only during the ten days they deliberated, at a cost of $17,000. *Times-Picayune*, March 24, 1986.

[123]*Times-Picayune*, March 20, 1986.

[124]Neal was defending movie director John Landis on involuntary manslaughter charges related to the death of three actors during the filming of "Twilight Zone—The Movie." *Times-Picayune*, March 5, 1986.

[125]*Baton Rouge State Times*, April 21, 1986, Edwin W. Edwards Collection, Louisiana State Archives, Baton Rouge, Louisiana.

[126]*The Daily Advertiser*, April 24, 1986, Edwin E. Edwards Collection, Louisiana State Archives, Baton Rouge, Louisiana.

[127]*Times-Picayune*, May 7, 1986; May 9, 1986.

[128]Ibid., May 10, 1986.

[129]*The Baton Rouge Sunday Advocate*, May 11, 1986.

[130]*Times-Picayune*, May 11, 1986.

[131]Ibid., May 23, 1986.

[132]*Alexandria Daily Town Talk*, September 24, 1986, Edwin W. Edwards Collection, Louisiana State Archives, Baton Rouge, Louisiana.

[133]Governor Edwin W. Edwards, Legislative address, Tape recording, date unknown, Edwin W. Edwards Collection, Louisiana State Archives, Baton Rouge, Louisiana.

[134]*Times-Picayune*, June 26, 1986.

# THE LAST HAYRIDE*

John Maginnis

Like the nozzle of a giant garden hose on the loose, the Mississippi River for centuries fanned left, fanned right and spewed its silty waters over its lower delta, creating at its mouth a swampy, boggy netherworld, half land, half sea: a teeming estuary for the trappers and fishermen who would live off its inlets, coves and bayous, but also a sinister, dangerous labyrinth for sinister, dangerous men who would need a safe place to hide near the open sea. Today, the wild swampland of Barataria, below New Orleans, provides drug smugglers the same port of entry first used nearly 200 years ago by Jean Lafitte, the Pirate King.

Don't call the old boy a pirate without expecting an argument. One of the few shadowy facts most natives know of the state's history was that Lafitte was no pirate, but a privateer, operating with letters of marque from the South American port of Cartagena to prey on the merchant vessels of Spain. The semantics, however, were lost on his victims. Jean Lafitte and his brother Pierre, with their fleet of fast ships and trained seamen, were smugglers on a grand scale, pioneers in the annals of American organized crime and an affront to the newly installed U. S. government in New Orleans.

Governor William Claiborne was having a hard enough time winning the hearts and minds of the hostile, suspicious, French-speaking subjects who had just been sold down the river for $15 million cash by their protector Bonaparte. The last thing the American governor needed was an independent, well-armed rival fleet exercising its own foreign policy for profit just offshore. There wasn't much, however, Claiborne could do about the pirate force. Locating the banditti's base in Barataria wasn't easy; engaging the expert marksmen in swamp guerrilla warfare just meant more dead Americans. But what galled Claiborne even more than the elusiveness of Lafitte was his broad-based popular support in the city of New Orleans. He couldn't catch him in the swamp and he couldn't touch him in the city. There the strikingly handsome, impeccably dressed, glib and flirtatious Lafitte was a favorite among the French leaders and ladies. So confident was Lafitte in

*Excerpts first published in John Maginnis, *The Last Hayride* (Baton Rouge: Gris Gris Press, ©1984), 1-9; 10-32; 325-42. Reprinted with the kind permission of the author.

his popular support that he could openly make fools of the American authorities. When Claiborne just could not tolerate the presence of the privateer any longer and put a $500 price on Lafitte's head, there appeared in the Place d'Armes that night another poster offering a $1,500 reward for the capture and delivery of the American governor to Lafitte at Grand Terre.

The proper, humorless American governor was amazed that the French and Creole citizens of the new territory would readily accept a man so clearly outside the bounds of law and good government. But it wasn't his glamor or charm or even the French tolerance for rascality that made Lafitte a local hero and stymied any American moves against him. French New Orleans revered Jean Lafitte because he gave these struggling pioneers something the brave new democracy of the United States could not: a European-style standard of living made possible through his smuggling trade.

New Orleanians would make regular trips into Barataria along one narrow finger of dry land to advertised auctions at The Temple, Louisiana's first discount shopping center, built on an island of shells where two bayous emptied into Little Lake near the present town of Lafitte. There they could buy the finest European merchandise that the victimized Spanish fleet could offer, from lace to furniture to slaves, at prices far below the exorbitant rates charged by merchants in the city. Lafitte's low, low overhead—he didn't get it wholesale, he got it free—helped create for the new settlers a standard of living far above what they could otherwise expect to scratch out in this lonely, hostile, far-flung outpost of European civilization.

Lafitte was Louisiana's first Robin Hood. He stole treasure from the Spanish, snuck it past the Americans and sold it cheap to the French. So important was Lafitte to the economic lives of the first settlers that if the Congress were to have allowed free elections in the newly acquired territory, the American Claiborne would have had a hard time holding onto his job against the wealthy French privateer.

Despite his playfully condescending attitude toward the American governor, it was Jean Lafitte's patriotism rather than his merchandising that has secured his place in Louisiana mythology. When British forces threatened New Orleans in 1815, the city's newly arrived defender, General Andrew Jackson, needed only two weeks to realize the Battle of New Orleans could not be won without Lafitte's fleet, cannon and artillerymen. The general and the pirate linked forces in one of the great upsets in American history, even if it did take place after the war was settled by treaty. In the afterglow of the shocking victory, President Madison pardoned Lafitte, who resumed business as usual. But the mores of the new country were taking hold in the old city, where the founding French families who had endured so much were steadily being overrun by the Americans. Soon not even New Orleanians distinguished between pirates and privateers, especially since Spain was now an ally against the hated British. Lafitte transferred his operations to Galveston. But soon, after one of Lafitte's captains sank an American vessel, the game was up even there. When an American warship appeared off the Texas coast, Lafitte outfitted his best ship, picked a crew of his most loyal men and set sail into the mists of history.

Though he never returned, his legend endured. Lafitte is revered and remembered as a patriot, a romantic rogue and the purveyor of the good life, which he so grandly expropriated from the foreign colonialists. To the French settlers, far from their homeland and betrayed by Napoleon, Lafitte was a bridge between cultures, as he could deliver the everyday comforts that made life in the New World more bearable. He fulfilled the people's wishes and when he was no longer needed, he disappeared as mysteriously as he first came.

It would be a long time before anyone would again share the wealth on such a grand scale. The reason is that without a cooperatively hapless Spanish navy to pick on, there wasn't much wealth to share. For the balance of the nineteenth century, Louisiana fell into the long poor line of Southern states dominated by rich planters and city merchants who engineered a low tax, low service state government that allowed them to keep their stranglehold on the state's economy. Louisiana, like other states, had a flash of populist fervor at century's end, but it was stamped out in Louisiana even more viciously than elsewhere, mainly because of the ruthless style of politics that had taken hold. Meeting the challenge of a grassroots populist rebellion of white and black farmers in the 1896 gubernatorial election, the Democratic oligarchy was forced to great lengths to preserve the way of life it held dear. Historian William Ivy Hair quotes a North Louisiana Democratic daily newspaper sounding the call to arms: "It is the religious duty of Democrats to rob Populists and Republicans of their votes whenever and wherever the opportunity presents itself and any failure to do so will be a violation of true Louisiana Democratic teaching. The Populists and the Republicans are our legitimate political prey. Rob them? You bet! What are we here for?" Observing those tenets of "true Louisiana Democratic teaching," the planters and merchants, known as the Bourbons, reversed a troublesome liberal trend toward Negro suffrage, brought populist farmers to heel and managed to keep a lock on power and wealth in Louisiana for another generation.

It took another accident of geography and exploitation by a new colonial power to bring the poor state a new economic savior. Huey Long's populist demagoguery could not have gone as far as it did unless he had other people's money to spend. Like Lafitte, Long preyed on a new colonial power, John D. Rockefeller's Standard Oil, which was tapping and refining the newly discovered oceans of fossil fuels beneath the swampy soil. Huey came out of the piney hills the avenging demagogue and, having seized hold of state government and slapped a one cent a barrel severance tax on "the Standard," he unleashed a torrent of public works and created a powerful central government that smashed forever the tax-nothing, do-nothing Bourbon mindset.

More than wealth was pouring out of the ground. With it came enormous power for Huey Long. With oil money he remade state government in his image, forging a benevolent and ruthless dictatorship that provided a full range of state services for the people—from modern roads to free hospitals and old age pensions—and an overflowing trough for his legions of good friends and soldiers. The more oil money that came in, the grander Huey's schemes to spend it, the larger and more beneficent state government grew, the louder the cries Long was creating a socialist welfare state in this former backwater bastion of Bourbonism. Huey was indeed the modern-day Robin Hood: the greater his power, the wider his ambition, the more outrageous his public behavior. He was playing to his audience, the teeming masses of poor folk, in this state and across the country, who took special delight not only in his taxing the rich but in his thumbing his nose at the genteel sensibilities of the privileged class.

Huey Long revolutionized Louisiana politics by taking from the rich, keeping some for himself and his friends and giving more to the poor than government ever had before. Whatever national threat Huey posed to the Established Order passed with his assassination. But in Louisiana, Huey the Martyr set in motion a tradition of populism, power and public works—for as long as there would be other people's money to pay for it.

Huey set the standard for his successors to govern by: a massive, centralized government powered by oil, a wealth-sharing plan for politicians and cronies, and high political theater for the people. Sometimes Louisianians would get too much of a good thing. After the Kingfish died, no strong central figure could keep the rascality within acceptable bounds, the U. S. Justice Department could no longer look the other way, and the Louisiana scandals of 1939 forced Governor Dick Leche to resign in disgrace, sent the president of LSU to jail and caused the oil-fueled binge, so amply documented in Harnett B. Kane's *Louisiana Hayride*, to crash and burn. From those ashes rose a few fitful attempts at reform, but with the rise to power of Earl Long in 1948 a new hayride was hitched up.

The basic form remained the same: high state services led by charity hospitals and free school lunches; low governmental efficiency marked by favoritism, waste and a manageable degree of corruption; and ribald political theater. Uncle Earl was no Kingfish but he was twice the showman his older brother had been. Earl could say and do the darnedest things, and when Miz Blanche finally had the state police cart him off to a mental hospital, only to have the old buzzard fire the director of hospitals and set himself free to go on a recuperative gambling fling through the Western states and Mexico, the rest of the country was predictably shocked and repulsed. *There goes Louisiana politics again: how can those poor people stand it?*

The one who took the trouble to find out, the great A. J. Liebling in *The Earl of Louisiana*, had one hell of a good time and left with the firm conviction that Earl Long was the most effective liberal in the South and one of the leading American statesmen of his time. He saw Louisiana as a misplaced Mediterranean state, as American Lebanon with its diverse and conflicting religious and ethnic factions. He saw this diversity giving the gumbo of Louisiana politics its flavor, but the body, said Liebling, was oil. Liebling's book, as close as anyone's come to explaining the phenomenon, became the primer for any outside journalist visiting the state, as they do each election year to get a taste of *joie de vivre* and to gawk at high-priced, theatrical political campaigns. The general story line they come away with is *Louisianians love their politics like they do their gumbo, hot and spicy, and they applaud chicanery and corruption as good political theater*. It's an easy story to write. About two dozen of them, basically the same, were written and broadcast during this last election. But it misses an important point, the why part.

Not even the best political sideshow could play in this state if there wasn't a good economic reason for it. Louisiana keeps electing colorful, populist rogues because it can afford them, or perhaps, can't afford to do without them. Louisiana government is based on high services, low efficiency, and colorful theater for two basic reasons: 1) a built-in constituency for populism, that is, lots of poor folks, and 2) a middle class that doesn't have to pay the bill. The oil companies do.

Louisiana's individual citizens are among the least taxed in the country. The state income tax is negligible, the residential property tax is laughable. A family who owns a $75,000 home outside the city limits of Baton Rouge pays zero in local and state property taxes. Families with $125,000 homes pay less in one year than a similar family in Houston pays in one month. Severance taxes in Louisiana historically pay for one-third to two-fifths of the total state bill, depending on what kind of year they had in the oil patch. And there's no state sales tax on food and drugs.

The middle class, in effect, has been bought off. Since the average taxpayer pays hardly any taxes except on sales, what does he or she care what the politicians do with the money? So the state is first provider of many services that don't even exist in other states. So the public schools are underfunded, the roads inadequate and there are more people on the state payroll doing nothing than are employed by other states three and four times the size of Louisiana. So waste is rampant and sweetheart contracts and consulting fees are dished out to friends and contributors. The Louisiana middle class, the same people who in other states stage periodic tax rebellions and crucify any politician brushed with scandal, feel no reason to complain. And so they don't.

The great myth, nurtured by Liebling, is that Louisiana people, as a group, love their politics and gossip about it incessantly in political cafes on every street corner. The truth is, the vast majority of people in this state don't give a damn about politics. They neither pay for it nor care much for it—it's rampant apathy, not interest, that gives politicians the free rein they have to perform as outrageously as they do. Even the underclass, the recipients of the more liberal state services, take them for granted. The people who do care about politics are the politicians and their symbiotic allies, the businessmen-contributors. The political contributor in Louisiana approaches politics as he would any investment. With the accepted rule of politics being to do business with one's friends in any way legally or otherwise possible, it pays to make friends with the right people. That's the accepted rule anywhere, except that in Louisiana, with most folks not even paying attention, there's more latitude in what's possible. And there is no more important friend (read: investment opportunity) to cultivate than someone who may one day be governor.

Since the oil money flows directly into the state treasury instead of to local taxing bodies, power is centralized in the state capital to a greater degree than in any other state. Within the state capital, the power of the governor dwarfs all others'. In terms of the powers vested in chief executives in other states, the governor of Louisiana has no peer. He directly controls 1,340 appointments, including cabinet secretaries and undersecretaries and the members of 135 boards and commissions regulating everything from mineral production on public lands to cosmetologists and embalmers. Through these boards and his own fiats, the governor can influence private industry and directly steer massive construction jobs and lucrative professional contracts to his friends. Earning the friendship of the governor can pay big dividends, perfectly legal and legitimate, in the form of highly profitable supply contracts (sure, there is a bid law, but bid specifications can be massaged), state leases, emergency requisitions, architect and engineer selections, issuance of tax-free bonds for private investment, nonbid professional services and friendly decisions and inside information from regulator boards—to name just a few favors a governor can bestow on his friends.

There is no real balance of power with the legislature, a body for many years regarded as nothing more than a debating society set in place to conform to the mandates of the U. S. Constitution. On paper, the legislature has power, but the real power of the purse is held by the governor. In order to get in the local projects they need for reelection, legislators tend to cooperate with the governor on the total package. Whom he can't control with the carrot he can always beat with the stick—the ultimate power of the veto. The governor can line item veto, that is, excise any single appropriation important to an individual legislator or delegation. The mere threat of a governor's veto on the right project can bring almost any legislator to heel on another issue. Practically, there is no overriding a governor's veto. Sure, if you can get two-thirds majorities in both houses you can override a governor's veto. Not to say it couldn't happen, it's just that it hasn't in this century. That's one hell of a stick.

Louisiana elects more statewide officials than does any other state. But there is little sharing the power because of the governor's control of the budget—everyone's budget. Say some brave attorney general wants to launch an investigation of the Mineral Board. He may find, at the start of the new fiscal year, that funds for investigators, nay, even attorneys, have been cut from his budget.

The state bureaucracy is massive. In 1900, a group photo of the employees at the Old State Capitol contained 30 faces. In 1983, 125,000 people, including schoolteachers, worked for the state. Another 12,000 employees of local governments, from firemen to deputy sheriffs, received state supplemental pay. And though most of them are civil service employees, immune to the spoils system, they nevertheless know who's boss, for the legislature only grants pay increases when the governor says so.

That's the primary reason why so much is spent in state elections, because so much is at stake. State government is big business in Louisiana. Doing business means having friends, and in this business, friends don't come cheap.

Louisiana government is built around the banana republic principle of one strong man, accountable only to the vote of the people and unfettered by the checks and balances found in established democracies. The system appears to invite more corruption but in another way controls it. Louisianians learned a hard lesson from the horrendous scandals of 1939. In the four years after the death of the Kingfish, the pigs at the trough got out of control, and the U. S. Justice Department had to finally step in. There were too many small-time operators tapping into the unguarded state treasury. Huey was wise enough and strong enough to see that no one stole too much. Knowing full well if there's government there will be graft, a prudent citizenry demands a strong governor to broker the deals, contain corruption to acceptable levels and in general keep everything running smoothly.

There's another reason—as much psychological as economic—why Louisianians don't mind vesting that kind of power in one strong politician-king. The lessons of the Civil War weren't lost on Louisiana. Keeping the Union whole meant keeping the South down. Today, as then, the South, with its abundant natural resources, continues to be an economic vassal of the industrialized East. More jobs may be coming to the Sunbelt but the profits from the giant refineries and petrochemical plants continue to go back north, if not overseas. Louisiana is as much an economic colony of New York today as it was when owned outright by Spain and by France. The severance tax on the state's extracted natural resources is all the tribute that can be exacted from the new colonialists. Louisiana embraced Huey Long and tolerated his excesses for the same reason it did Jean Lafitte: not just because they enhanced the quality of life but because they took a piece from the colonialists' purse to do it. Since then, Louisiana continues to look to one strong man who can keep straight the business of politics at home and exact some tribute from the outside interests that ultimately control the state's destiny.

The rest of the country may sneer at Louisiana politics, but Louisianians can at least be comforted knowing that those critics of this political system are footing a large part of the bill for all its wonderful excesses. It's as close as they can come to revenge.

Eighty miles north of Baton Rouge, you don't expect to hear French spoken in the bar at the edge of the courthouse square. This far north of Baton Rouge, you wouldn't expect to find a bar on the edge of the courthouse square. Though the area is actually in Central Louisiana, to South Louisianians, impatient with geographic subtleties, Central Louisiana is to North Louisiana as Central America is to South America: foreign soil. In a state divided in culture, custom and cuisine between north and south, anything beyond a 30-minute drive above U. S. 190 is North Louisiana, land of Baptists, hills and cotton.

But that doesn't explain the old men, joking and cursing in French, drinking at a bar that is closer to the courthouse steps than is the First Baptist Church. But this is Marksville, in Avoyelles Parish, an exception to the Louisiana line of demarcation. Geographically it is the buttonhole of the state, the center point where the Red River and the hills of the north meet the Atchafalaya and the plains of the south. Agriculturally, its soybean and cotton fields belong to the north, while culturally and historically it is French Louisiana, the northernmost tip of the Cajun Triangle, which abruptly ends at the banks of the Red River. That's the line. Within Avoyelles Parish, one is defined by being from either the "Cajun side" or the "Redneck side" of that river.

Safely on the Cajun side, in the bar on the courthouse square, the visitor, lulled by the first beer of the hot, humid afternoon and the soft Cajun patois filling the room, is jarred by a foreign sound—spoken English. The young bearded fellow at the bar is breaking the house language, but the substance of his remarks seems to fit the atmosphere. "Yeah, I ran six or seven shady deals with a clean face, so I had to grow this beard to run a few more."

The old boys laugh in appreciation at the ingenuity, and a few more patrons sidle up to the bar. A bigger crowd than usual for a weekday. But it's not your every day in Marksville—tonight its favorite son is coming home.

The daylight is fading just enough so you don't have to squint, once outside the bar. A city cop directs traffic at the corner, rerouting cars away from the closed street behind the courthouse. A country western band (from the redneck side of the Red) on the courthouse steps wails out "I Can't Stop Loving You" as farmers and townsfolk, parking their cars and pickup trucks, begin to fill up the paved yard of the courthouse. Some older citizens are settling down on the courthouse lawn as volunteers dish out hotdogs and Cokes to all takers. "The square couldn't hold the crowd for Earl," an old-timer reflects, "but this ain't bad." No, it isn't, for a hot summer evening, with the sun just about to set, and nothing to bring out the crowd of well over 1,000 from their air conditioning and prime time TV but some free hotdogs, a redneck band and Edwin Edwards.

At just past seven o'clock, there is a stir on the edge of the crowd. Edwin Edwards has materialized across the street and is shaking hands with about a dozen blacks, who, conditioned by their age and the way things used to be, feel more comfortable on the far side of the street.

The band plays on as Edwards, followed by his usual entourage of driver, aides, a few reporters, local supporters and, in a rare campaign appearance, his son Steven, crosses the street and presses into the crowd, which quickly engulfs him. Edwards doesn't glide through this crowd as smoothly as he does elsewhere on the campaign trail. He's less the snappy, urbane, self-assured man of power he is before most strangers on the trail—today he's the Edwards boy come home to the people who watched him grow up. He looks into each face to jog his memory of a name of someone he grew up with, or worked with, 30 years ago.

"Remember me?" quizzes the old fellow.

Edwards reaches back. "Sure, you used to run the cleaners next to the Western Auto."

"Still do."

Some he's never seen before but knows exactly who they are. "You're Shirley Gremillion's daughter." He points to the pretty teenager. "I'd know those eyes anywhere."

Some Marksvillians have set up their folding chairs on the lawn nearest the building, waiting for their old playmate to pass their way. "The last thing we thought he would be was governor," says one. "Sure, he said it, we just didn't believe him." Even his reputation as a ladies' man is lost on these who knew him first. According to Ellen Moulard, "We used to chase him and try to kiss him. But he'd get under the house and stick his tongue out at us. Oh, if we'd have caught him, we'd have eaten him up."

The entourage seems to be snaking aimlessly through the crowd, but by the time he mounts the steps, he has covered the entire square and shaken every outstretched hand. Now he stands before the crowd with his arm around a man in a shortsleeve shirt, who, with thinning dark hair and deeply tanned, weatherbeaten face appears to be older than Edwards. Yet the two are close in age and lined by a searing childhood experience that forms the subject of this evening's opening parable.

> Many of you already know this man, Glen Dunlap. I met him many years ago when his father paddled across the river in the night and came to our family's store and knocked on the door. There with him was this seven-year-old whose fingers had just been crushed by a falling pile of logs. I remember staying up all night with my mother, soaking Glen's hands in warm water to ease his pain. We didn't send for the doctor because it was the middle of the night, we were sharecroppers and you just didn't do that. I remember thinking how important it was to help people, that my mother was always there to help when they needed it.

A fitting parable, the perfect jumping-off point of attack the incumbent governor, and uncaring man, the crowd is told, who reduced the state allowance to senior citizens in nursing homes from $50 a month to $40. With his hand on Glen Dunlap's shoulder he swears, "I would rather my arm wither and fall off before I cut the little spending money that poor widows have who just want to live out their twilight years in peace and dignity." He sees so many Louisianians who need help and can't get it. "They can't find a job and can't find anyone to talk to. Have any of you ever called Dave Treen? Go ahead and try to and see if he calls you back. By the time you hear from him again, I'll be in the Mansion answering the phone."

His words aren't new but the context is fresh, as though the memory of the boy with the crushed fingers has inspired his impromptu riff on the importance of a governor who cares. The crowd in the darkness of the courthouse lawn is with him, enthusiastic and involved. His words cut back through the years and the money and the power and all that separates him from his backwater beginnings, striking that chord with his old neighbors, reminding them what it was like growing up—together—at the bottom of the social order. They remember. No matter that Edwin Edwards now belongs to a different world of power and money—he came from theirs. One of the senior bar patrons who has worked his way up to the front of the crowd raises his Falstaff in salute: "Un de nous autres." *He's one of us*. It wasn't the first time I had heard that phrase, in French or in English, while following Edwin Edwards across the state. Every candidate strives for that kinship, whether pitching rednecks or Eskimos. Edwin Edwards' special gift is that it comes not only because of his nature but because of his background. For in Marksville, where north meets south, where divergent cultures, languages and values converge and coexist, to be one of us is to cover a lot of ground. The paradoxes of Louisiana are commonplace in Avoyelles Parish, nowhere more so than in the house Boboy Edwards built on the banks of the Red River.

Edwin Edwards calls Marksville his hometown, but that was merely the location of the nearest post office. Edwards was born in the little community of Johnson, in an area which, fitting the vague and shifting geography of the upland delta region, in earlier days, at different times took the names of the nearby communities of Catville and a place called Riddle.

His mother, Agnes Brouillette, was pure Cajun French. She married Clarence Edwards, whose mother was Cajun but whose father came from Welsh stock by way of the Kentucky and Tennessee migration into North Louisiana's hill country three generations before. The five Edwards children—Audrey, Allen, Edwin, Marion and Nolan—are three parts Cajun and one important part Redneck.

There were three class distinctions in the country: sharecropper, farmer and merchant. Clarence Edwards, "Boboy" to his friends, at one time or another was all three. When his second son Edwin was born in 1927, he was strictly sharecropping cotton. But he inherited a few acres, bought a few more and finally built a small one-room general store that traded with other sharecroppers.

Boboy only had a third grade education because, as the second child of eight, he had to quit school at 13 when his father died and his mother delivered twins two months later. Yet as an avid reader of dictionaries and encyclopedias, he could firmly articulate his rock-hard beliefs. Edwin Edwards credits his father's eloquence and outspokenness for his own talent for public speaking, though Boboy did hold a particularly dim view of politicians.

From his isolated farm he watched his sons grow up to be worldly men—late in life he satisfied his own urge to see what lay beyond the Red River. "In the mid-'50s sometime," recalls his son Edwin,

> he got up one morning and told our mother that he was going to take a trip. Mother asked him where he was going and he said he didn't know. When was he coming back? Couldn't say. He just left one day. He bought a bus ticket and went out to California and up to Oregon and Washington and down through the west. Sometimes he rode the bus, other times he hitchhiked. We didn't hear from him until two or three months later when he came home.

Agnes Edwards was a woman country people came to for help, whether for first aid emergencies for children or midwifing babies. By her count, she helped deliver 1,800 infants, often holding a lantern as she reassured a nervous expectant father as he rowed her across the Red River to meet the doctor. Farm life was a grind for Agnes. Through most of her child-rearing years she worked over a wood stove in a house with no electricity or running water.

There wasn't much for a kid in Johnson to do but farm chores. Edwin, the middle child, developed an odd quirk for a farm boy, an obsession with cleanliness, one that he keeps to this day. His sister Audrey remembers Edwin would not let anyone else clean his own plate and utensils. Once when the family visited neighbors and the hostess began to dish out ice cream, Edwin pulled out his own cup and spoon and ordered, "Just put it in here." His abhorrence for getting his hands dirty pushed him to get out of the cotton fields at the first chance and into the city for a job at the Western Auto store after school. As he would later tell approving farm audiences during campaigns: "I wasn't very smart, but I knew as a six-year-old I didn't want to farm. You have to work too hard. I wanted to be a politician and a lawyer so I wouldn't have to work."

Education was revered in the Edwards home. "Anything less than a B on a report card meant a whipping from my father," says Marion. Edwin and Marion rarely fell below the mark and graduated as valedictorians of their classes at Marksville High. They were as adept at getting along with their schoolmates. Neither Edwin nor Marion remembers ever getting in a fight with other children.

Though half Cajun himself and in many ways a freethinker who encouraged the children to make their own decisions, Boboy's redneck side commanded an absolute intolerance of alcohol or tobacco. Once he caught the three younger boys smoking a pipe one Sunday behind the barn. They were severely whipped and sent into the fields to pick 100 pounds of cotton—and no throwing a watermelon in the sack to make the weight. Edwin got the point. Though he would later embrace the live-for-the-moment *joie de vivre* of the Cajuns, his abstinence from intoxicating substances remains as hard-shell as any Baptist's.

On that Cajun side of the Red River, Catholicism was practically the state religion. Not in the Edwards household. Agnes, of course, was devoutly Catholic. Boboy was officially Presbyterian, but, more to the point, anti-Catholic. And though he allowed the priest to baptize the children, he wasn't silent about his hatred for the Church of Rome. As brother Marion remembers, "The only bitter arguments in our household were over religion." That split within the family, along with the natural curiosity of farm children with nothing better to do, drew Audrey, Edwin and Marion to the makeshift church that Nazarene missionaries set up across the road. "We went because it was there, because it was something to do," says Marion. "I remember thinking it was the greatest thing in the world when they gave me a little 15-cent Bible." The children were regulars at the Nazarene services and as teens even preached at brush arbor revivals, which provided young Edwin his first audiences. Miss Agnes was very upset and cried to the priest, who said the children were committing mortal sins. But she got no support from her husband, who delighted in and encouraged his offspring's desertion of the One True Faith.

He remembers as a child gravitating toward the courthouse, where he saw all elements of parish life pass through the doors, but mostly the lawyers and the politicians, people who make their living talking, dealing, negotiating—not picking cotton or even stacking car filters in the Western Auto. He decided what he wanted to be, and his girlfriend Elaine Schwartzenburg was the first person he told: "I'll be governor one day."

Since ambition that large was hard to nurture in a little town like Marksville, a teenaged Edwin got his first crack at politics at Pelican Boys State in the summer of 1943. The annual summer training camp at LSU gave young leaders of tomorrow their first intoxicating whiff of power. "You can't believe the power trip," one former child politico confided, "of blowing a whistle and seeing 500 16-year-olds cross the street." Edwin cut his political teeth not as a candidate but as campaign manager for a skinny kid from Baker named Ossie Brown, who, with the help of his energetic, fast-taking bilingual manager, was elected governor. (Edwards likes to point out that Ossie would not win another election until 1972, when as governor he helped his old friend get elected district attorney of East Baton Rouge Parish.)

After LSU and law school and marriage to Elaine, he moved from Marksville—no new fortunes to be made there—south to Crowley, where his married sister Audrey lived. He hung up his shingle and he prospered. He quickly made friends around the courthouse, especially with an equally smooth-talking young attorney named Edmund Reggie, whose taste for politics and the good life matched Edwin's. Edwards started his unbroken string of winning elections with a city council post in Crowley. In 1964, he entered the state Senate, where he impressed Governor John McKeithen, who tapped the 36-year-old Cajun as an administration floorleader. When Seventh District Congressman T. A. Thompson died in a car accident, young Senator Edwards, with McKeithen's help, won the special election and was on his way to Washington in 1965.

Edwin Edwards didn't pretend to be interested in the painfully slow workings of the Congress: he introduced few bills, skipped most debates and racked up one of the worst attendance records on the Hill. But he learned fast how the power game was played in Washington and how very much clout rested with the seniority-heavy Louisiana delegation. Clout that could help him achieve his own goals. The only real way an ambitious congressman could get any political mileage back home was to deliver some plum project that would boost his district's economy. Edwards had no seniority, and no pull in the bureaucracy or in the White House. All Edwards had going for him was the friendship of the rest of the delegation. But what friends to have. Senator Allen Ellender of Houma, who delighted in conversing exclusively in French with the freshman congressman, chaired the Agriculture Committee and was the second ranking Democrat on the all-important Appropriations Committee. Senator Russell Long, chairing the Senate Finance Committee, had the last word on all foreign trade legislation. In the House, Otto Passman chaired the foreign aid subcommittee of Appropriations while Hale Boggs on the

Ways and Means Committee had the ear and total confidence of its chairman Wilbur Mills. They had been just drinking buddies to T. A. Thompson, but to Edwin Edwards, whose special gift was in knowing how to use the power of others to help himself, they were giants who, with some cultivation and imagination, could give the young congressman the necessary political boost.

What the Seventh District needed most was a new market for its rice, which was stacking up in the mills as its price steadily dropped. South Korea bought a lot of rice, primarily from the closer California ports. It also bought a lot of airplanes, bombs and guns for its military arsenal. President Park Chung Hee had sent a young businessman named Tongsun Park to Washington to persuade American congressmen, by whatever means necessary, to better appreciate South Korea's needs. Park became good friends with Edwin Edwards, as well as with Otto Passman, whose subcommittee was so vitally important to Park's mission. Park was more than happy to broker the rice deal to please his friends. With the help of the other powerful Louisiana congressmen, all the right skids were greased with foreign aid, foreign trade, and appropriations. All that was needed was for the Agriculture Department to approve a $31 million long-term, low interest loan for the purchase. Dealing with the bureaucrats was tricky, but Passman knew just where to push. He went to the White House to ask his friend Richard Nixon a favor. As Nixon picked up the phone to call the Agriculture Department, the president thought he was accommodating his good friend Otto Passman, not realizing how much he was in on the making of the next Louisiana governor.

In 1971, all over Acadiana, rice mills emptied and ships filled up at the Port of Lake Charles bound for Seoul. As the price of rice shot up, Louisiana rice farmers, on the brink of a disastrous year, made record profits. Their congressman had come through for them when they needed help and they felt strongly they owed him a debt of gratitude. So did their bankers, investors and suppliers. The young congressman had just ingratiated himself with most people with money in Southwest Louisiana. And he already knew how they could return the favor.

History will judge John McKeithen one of the state's greatest governors. Too bad he didn't end that way with the voters. He was the pivotal governor who broke state politics with the hidebound first half of the 20th century and lit a new industrial fire under a lagging economy. In the view of business leader Ed Steimel, McKeithen was the "all-time greatest industry hunter" whose overwhelmingly persuasive salesmanship and promise of cheap natural gas attracted scores of the great petrochemical plants that transformed the stretch of river between Baton Rouge and New Orleans into the Little Ruhr Valley of America.

McKeithen contributed even more to the state as a racial peacemaker. He started out mouthing "separate but equal" but ended up presiding over the peaceful integration of Louisiana public schools and colleges. As a politician, he earned his place in the state hall of fame by lulling voters into approving a two-term constitutional amendment to allow governors to succeed themselves.

Big John was, still is, a big man, with an overpowering personality and an ego that wouldn't quit. He thought big. And he didn't shrink from a fight. Finally, those two qualities and the nature of Louisiana politics did him in. By the end of John's second term, the state was tiring of his bigness. His Superdome was causing super financial and political headaches. The legislature was balking at the spate of taxes he shoved through it. And the people were just a little embarrassed by John's vice presidential ambitions and the way he skulked off from the 1968 Democratic convention when those dreams were summarily dashed in Chicago. McKeithen's diminished popularity was finished off by a devastating *Life Magazine* article tracing links between McKeithen's staff and Mafia boss Carlos Marcello.

McKeithen, in many ways a reform governor when he entered office in 1964, was leaving with the people calling out for more reform. McKeithen blazed many trails but he wasn't able to break the jinx of governors who left office less popular than when they came in.

Louisiana never saw a field of candidates like the menagerie lined up for the 1971 race. The 17 qualifiers included:

> —former governor and country western star Jimmie Davis, the favorite of the sheriffs and the former race-baiting sweetheart of the rednecks, whose greatest contributions to the state in his two prior terms were the infamous Sunshine Bridge that spanned the Mississippi and dead-ended in a canefield and a graceless, antebellum style Governor's Mansion built on the Interstate;
> —two cousins of Huey Long, Congressman Speedy Long and Gillis Long, who had run a heartbreakingly close third in 1963 and was about to do it again;
> —grocery store magnate John Schwegmann, who used his grocery bags for political advertising;
> —highly popular Lieutenant Governor Taddy Aycock, who should have never dared to test the Peter Principle;
> —gadfly raconteur Puggy Moity, widely assumed to be paid by Gillis Long to pull black and Cajun votes away from Edwin Edwards by saying terrible things about him (Puggy's weekly half hour live TV spots were hilarious bad taste—his tagging Edwards "Tweety Bird" got Edwards' goat more than anything else said about him);
> —*Life Magazine* writer David Chandler of Mafia exposé fame, running for governor to write a book about it;
> —and two self-labeled reform candidates, the moderate, good government state senator from Shreveport, J. Bennett Johnston; and the French-speaking congressman from Acadiana [Edwin Edwards] who was supposed to be good at raising money.

It would be the most free-spending election in Louisiana history, especially with the new feeder at the election trough, TV advertising. Edwards would claim to have spent $1.5 million on the whole election—an astronomical sum at the time. But as there were no campaign finance reporting laws, who knows how much was spent? Certainly not

Edwards or his brother Marion, who conducted fund raising from his suite in the Monteleone in New Orleans. As Edwards would recall in the midst of a future investigation, "We sat in that hotel room and raised thousands of dollars in the morning and gave it away that afternoon and the next day I couldn't tell you where half of it came from or went."

Yet plenty of contributors counted on his remembering. According to his campaign sidekick Clyde Vidrine in his salacious memoirs, *Just Taking Orders*, Edwards was outright promising specific state positions to contributors. Edwards would later dispute the amounts, but the promises, he said, were not illegal. As far as a political campaign went, very little was illegal in 1971.

Bennett Johnston, with his established business and oil support, had good financial backing, but more than that, he had the appeal of the dynamic new urban conservative, an articulate and progressive North Louisiana not strapped with a hick accent and a neanderthal view of race relations. The emerging middle class saw in Bennett a break with the old way of politics in this state, a decent guy who wasn't in with the courthouse gangs and their backroom deals, and folks liked that. Bennett was pure. He represented the fiscal conservative and good government ideals espoused by Republicans without having to carry that Republican baggage with him.

When the smoke cleared, and there was a lot of that, the two reform candidates led the field, Edwards with 23 percent of the vote, Johnston with 19. Bennett—otherwise known as "Bennett Who?" on election night—had the momentum going for him. Not only did he carry North Louisiana but did surprisingly well with white voters in New Orleans and Baton Rouge. But his strength was also his problem. Not only did he present the image of being unsullied by bargaining with courthouse gains, it was a true image. Bennett couldn't or wouldn't cross over and get in the back door and deal with Jimmie Davis' sheriffs or offer to help pay Gills Long's campaign debts or make any of the traditional second primary moves by which winning coalitions are formed.

Edwin Edwards was not so handicapped. No sooner had Johnston turned off some sheriff or potential contributor than Edwards was camped out at the door. Not only did he offer to help pay Gillis' campaign debts but promised to gerrymander a congressional district to fit Long's black voting strength. Edwards was the labor candidate, the country candidate, the Cajun candidate, the Catholic candidate (he kept the Nazarene connection very quiet in South Louisiana) and the favorite of the blacks. But it took more than that to beat back the emerging white middle class conservative vote. Edwards' secret was that he could use his assets without being trapped by them.

Though a French-speaking candidate, with an English surname he could plug for votes in many North Louisiana towns where an Edwin Brouillette best not even stop.

Though the Catholic candidate, he could preach in piney woods revival tents.

Though the sharecropper's son espousing populism in rural parishes he could champion the oil and gas industry and reassure any Chamber of Commerce group that he was here "to comfort the afflicted but not to afflict the comfortable."

Though he could cut his deals with the sheriffs and black bosses, he could go on TV promising reform and an "era of excellence."

When it came right down to it, he got his vote out and Bennett didn't. Edwards did well where he was supposed to, plus he cut into North Louisiana just enough to eke out a 4,500 vote win, a margin of less than one-half of one percent or about one vote per precinct.

No sooner had he put away the Republicans' draft candidate named David Treen in the general election that Edwin Edwards moved to take hold of the levers of power like they had never been gripped in 40 years. He had called for reform in government, so had Johnston, but Edwards' idea of reform was to remold the whole structure and form of state government to meet the modern needs of government as well as his own.

The people wanted a new constitution—a convention was at work within a year. Publicly, he gave that body plenty of leeway but behind the scenes he tightly controlled it through the substantial number of appointments he made to the convention. His talent was in achieving the semblance of good government reform that at the same time enhanced his already considerable power. In rearranging the mire of 258 state agencies into a cabinet form of government, he didn't eliminate any jobs but concentrated his own power by creating a new top level of bureaucracy under the governor's exclusive control. He won a critical showdown in clipping the prosecutorial wings of the state attorney general on local criminal matters. The move enormously increased the power of the district attorneys, who could keep the state attorney general out of local criminal investigations unless he could get a judge to sign an order. In the past, local corrupt politicians had nothing to worry about as long as the attorney general was your Jack P. F. Gremillion-type (of whom Uncle Earl once said, "If you want to hide something from Jack Gremillion, put it in a law book"). But this key clause, personally lobbied by Edwards, effectively limited the damage an aggressive and ambitious attorney general—like this new guy Billy Guste, who had just been elected—could do if seized by some frenzied Watergate reform spirit. Nowhere was local jurisdiction more important than in the seat of state government, now the turf of Edwards' old friend from Pelican Boys State, newly elected Baton Rouge DA Ossie Brown.

Structure was great, but what Edwards needed was money for pay raises, roads and bridges. Concrete is the currency of power, the carrot of legislative leadership. To be the kind of powerful and benevolent governor of his self-image, he'd need lots of money. The obvious place to go was the oil companies. Every populist governor thinks of that, but the oil lobby makes every penny per barrel of severance tax squeezed from them a bloody battle. Instead of nickel and diming around with the severance tax, Edwards moved to change the flat tax of 18 to 26 cents per barrel to 12.5 percent of value. Initially, the oil companies put up a vicious fight, but when Edwards turned the full weight of his office against them, they scattered before him. And as the post-Arab embargo price of oil shot through the roof, so did severance tax receipts. Even with the production of oil beginning its long-term decline in the '70s, the value tax became a revenue gusher that fueled an exponential, unprecedented leap in the size of state government. In Edwards' first year in office, the state spent less than $1.9 billion. At the end of his second term, the budget topped $4.5 billion.

The volume to value switch was a master political stroke and the most important economic legacy of Edwards' tenure, the most effective revenue raiser in the history of the state—as well as the most politically acceptable. It enabled Edwards to eliminate the state property tax and the state sales tax on food and drugs. In his first year in office, he was responsible for both the largest tax increase and the largest tax decrease in state history. The oil companies passed the tax along to customers, the consumers in the 49 other states, forcing the rest of the United States to involuntarily bankroll a massive program of public spending by Edwin Edwards. Huey Long would have approved. And Jean Lafitte, wherever he was, would have been proud.

Edwards took to power easily, almost casually. No early riser, the longer into his term, the less time he spent at the Fourth Floor office at the Capitol, increasingly conducting the state's business from his den in the Mansion. He delegated huge chunks of authority primarily to Commissioner of Administration Charlie Roemer, the sly and ambitious North Louisiana plantation master and computer king, a man who knew how to run things. Impatient with details, the governor wanted his options spelled out on one sheet of paper, "a half page if you can do it." He made up his mind fast or he would do nothing. He knew what he was doing.

The den in the Mansion wasn't as impressive and imposing as the high-ceilinged, dark-paneled office at the Capitol, but it was far more efficient. Instead of having to deal with one appointment at a time, at the Mansion he could scatter the petitioners in several rooms around the first floor, make rounds like a doctor and then have everyone to lunch in the dining room.

Rather than adopt John McKeithen's dynamic LBJ-approach to power—the governor who would sniff out controversy, dive into the middle of it, bust heads, twist arms and force a consensus—Edwards, the boy who had never been in a fight, would go a long way to avoid an argument. When a problem had to be resolved, Edwards put the disagreeing parties in one room, told them how he felt about it but stressed it was their decision to make and then left them to slug it out.

The governor's most enviable power is to say yes. Edwards used that power a lot. His style was to agree to just about any reasonable request and then to send it through the bureaucracy where, if the plan was found to be unfeasible, there would be someone else to say no. Edwards got the credit or some flunky got the blame.

He was criticized for delegating so much authority to people he could not always control, mainly Charlie Roemer, whose ambition and ego rivaled the governor's. The commissioner of administration had his own personal agenda and with his broad powers over awarding professional contracts, writing friendly bid specifications and hiring, Roemer began clutching for power that Edwards did not even know about. An Edwards aide remembers the governor in a rage over the newest Roemer scam to hit the press. "I can't believe that sonofabitch did that," Edwards would say, but when the reporters called, Edwards backed his man up. Instead of reining in Roemer, Edwards gave him more rope and finally Charlie hung himself in the federal government sting operation called Brilab. When the news broke that Roemer was on tape accepting a bribe from an undercover FBI agent posing as an insurance executive, Governor Edwards claimed to be as surprised as anyone and was just as much in the clear. In delegating such broad powers he was also distancing himself from those appointees who eventually self-destructed.

He made decisions fast. Sometimes, it seemed, too fast. He once told an aide, "Half my decisions are right, a quarter could go either way and a quarter are wrong. But you can adjust them later. The important thing is to keep things moving." Sometimes the decision was not to decide. Even when he knew what had to be done, he delayed until his own sense of "the tides," the timing of current events and public opinion, told him it was okay to proceed.

Throughout his first two terms, Edwards was fond of telling reporters, "There is a big difference between what's illegal and what causes you people to raise your eyebrows." The eyebrows started rising in his first year when he proudly announced he had an interest in something called TEL Enterprises, owned by his aide Clyde Vidrine and his Highway Board chairman Lewis Johnson, who were proposing to build a 62-story New Orleans office tower to be called One Edwards Square. Edwards saw nothing unusual about a governor playing a role in a speculative real estate venture but as the press scrutiny continued and the TEL deal looked shakier, Edwards treated the press to some of his finest broken field explaining. He denied he owned part of TEL or ever did, clarifying his "interest" in TEL as merely the interest of a friend in another's success.

Edwards brushed off the TEL fiasco but he began distancing himself from his old friend, who had signed on very early in Edwards' rise to power. With TEL crumbling, Vidrine resigned as the governor's aide. As his financial problems mounted, Clyde found he could not even get his old friend Edwin on the phone. He was being cut off. In his anger, Clyde committed a political sin worse than incompetence, worse than dishonesty, worse than even getting caught. He talked.

He started with New Orleans investigative reporter Bill Lynch, and then went on to the FBI. Clyde Vidrine was piercing the vital veil, secrecy, and the public was scandalized and titillated by what they read: that Edwards had sold top state positions to old cronies and high bidders, that cash prices had been fixed on state positions and that you could get anything done in government for a price. Anything. The dirtier the more expensive, claimed Clyde, who said permits for hazardous waste dumping were especially lucrative rake-offs.

A federal grand jury in Baton Rouge began investigating Vidrine's allegations amid a flurry of rumors of Edwards' pending indictment. (Ossie Brown even empaneled a parish grand jury, for what that was worth.) A dinner guest at the mansion in October 1974 witnessed an uneasy Edwards waiting for word from the federal courthouse while delaying his departure to cut the ribbon to open the Baton Rouge State Fair. Picking at his food,

Edwards wondered aloud to aides and family how he could publicly discredit Vidrine. Edwards knew that Vidrine, an admitted reformed alcoholic, had been hitting the bottle again under the pressure of his failed business deals and the investigation. If Edwards could just find a competent, respected source to say that. An aide reminded the governor he had recently appointed Clyde's brother Ramson coroner of Evangeline Parish. "That's it." Edwards snapped at the old Mafia technique of turning your opponent's brother against him. "Anyone would believe the guy's brother, right?" he said, passing the suggestion around the table. At about that time, an aide reported that the grand jury had dismissed Vidrine and adjourned for the day without taking any action. Edwards smiled, getting up from the table. "Well, let's go dedicate that fair."

During the next week, state policemen delivered to TV stations copies of a letter from Dr. Ramson Vidrine calling for his brother's commitment and claiming Clyde's "alcohol-soaked brain" was the cause of his delusions. Obstruction of justice questions were raised but not pursued over how the governor was involved in the coroner's attack on his brother.

The federal investigation wound on but eventually stalled on Vidrine's credibility problems. It would be a pattern that would pull Edwards through other scrapes. In a showdown of one person's word against Edwards', the governor's practice of only dealing with people shadier than himself paid off.

Edwards had the last word on Clyde's reputation, but Clyde would get back with a last word of his own. His book, *Just Takin' Orders*, caused a great sensation when published in 1977. Not only did it describe Edwards' fund-raising techniques, it also richly detailed Edwards' gambling escapades and extramarital flings. Clyde said it was all true, Edwin said it was all lies, and Louisianians flocked to the bookstores. More than anything for Edwards, the book was an embarrassment, a lingering one at that. When *60 Minutes* made their first phone calls here in 1983 for leads in researching the planned segment on Edwards, a daily newspaper reporter suggested they begin with *Just Takin' Orders*.

Edwards' other first term eyebrow raiser followed press reports the IRS was investigating his gambling trips to Las Vegas. This was the kind of scandal Edwards could handle, for gambling was his vice removed. He could cavort in Las Vegas or Reno casinos or those near his Lake Tahoe condominium without any snooping reporters. "I don't think the people where I come from care if I get into a dice game or a poker game once in a while." They didn't even seem to mind press reports that he used a plane leased to a state agency for one trip, that a plane from Harrah's picked him up from another or that the IRS investigated both his winnings and reports someone else had paid off $200,000 of his losses. He denied ever losing more than $8,000 at one time or winning more than $6,000. "I don't make a living off gambling and no one makes a living off me gambling." When a reporter met him at the airport on a trip home from Nevada, he answered the reporter's queries on his trip succinctly. "That's none of your goddam business. Print it just like that: none of your goddam business." When the *Shreveport*

*Journal* asked its readers if they approved of Edwards accepting free plane trips and hotel rooms from casino owners, a resounding 51 percent of respondants in this queen city of the Bible Belt said yes with such comments as "It is much better than congressmen spending the taxpayers' money to take trips all over Europe" and "No public official should be required to become a father image."

Controversies that would flatten other politicians seemed to roll off his back as easily as his nonapologetic quips about them rolled off his tongue. Governor Dick Leche of *Louisiana Hayride* fame was fond of saying, "When I took the oath of office, I didn't take a vow of poverty." The same would go for Edwards and vows of chastity. Once again he was the beneficiary of good timing. Just as Edwin Edwards was popping up on the state scene in 1971, the '60s were just hitting Baton Rouge. The drug culture and the sexual revolution were stripping away some of society's pretenses and relaxing the pressure on public officials to lead exemplary private lives. Which was fine for Edwin Edwards, because the stories had been circulating since the campaign—not just stories but eyewitness, firsthand accounts—of women who had been propositioned by Edwards, straight on and out of the blue. As candidate and then governor, he had the perfect vantage point for meeting women all over the state, and just as many contributors were promised appointments, so were potential girlfriends offered state jobs. Those who weren't looking for work might receive a color TV or jewelry the next day instead of roses. His former aide and constant companion Clyde Vidrine would later write of Edwards' insatiable sexual appetite and his use of the state payroll to build a harem within close reach.

When not able to make the advance himself, the governor would use aides, friends and state troopers to approach different women. *Say, Governor Edwards would like to meet you. He can pick you up at your apartment at eight tonight.* The trysts were brief—aides and troopers did not have to wait long in motel parking lots for him to come and go, refreshed and rejuvenated and ready to go speak to some Rotary Club or the League of Women Voters. Aides and friends came to accept his appetite. "He enjoys the game, of setting it up, of sort of sneaking around to arrange a rendezvous. I think that part has as much to do with it as the sex." His busy schedule normally prevented any longer interludes, but when he could get away for a weekend with a girlfriend, he could, observed one traveling companion, "spend 18 hours a day in the sack."

His was such a public game that he had fun implicating others, turning to a legislator upon meeting his wife to say, "I didn't know you were married." Or poking at other politicians' carefully preserved images of righteousness, once casually telling a group of reporters that he knew for a fact that a respected state politician had a mistress.

"You're telling us," a reporter asked, "that he cheats on his wife?"

"He's not as good at it as I am," answered Edwards, "but he does."

When he tired of the secretarial pool, there was always the campus. Sorority Row was a favorite cruising ground. A young woman remembers standing on the front porch of her sorority house when a white Oldsmobile rolled to a stop, the back widow rolled down and Edwards asked her if she wanted to go out. She went back in.

Rejection didn't faze him. After all, he once told a legislator, two out of ten women are dying to go to bed with you, but you have to ask the other eight in order to find the two. His material was not very original—how could it be after a while? On more than one occasion he gave a woman he was pursuing a pair of expensive sunglasses and told her, "Your eyes are too beautiful to look into if I can't have you. . . ."

He was fortunate not to suffer any embarrassing public scenes or paternity suits from his affairs. Perhaps because "affair" is too permanent a term. "Encounter" may be a better description, brief ones at that. No one held the center spot as the other woman for more than a few days. Some encounters became running encounters that went on for months or longer. Some turned into friendships. He's watched over the careers of past lovers with the loyalty he's extended to good contributors. Roughly in his mind they equated, as when he commented on stories that Tongsun Park often supplied congressmen with women, "I'm unaware of that, but it's certainly better than cash."

Philandering is a habit normally associated with politicians, but so is hypocritical puritanism. Edwards never fell into that trap. You could say or write what you wanted of his personal life but you didn't call him a hypocrite—how could you? His passes became so well known that women, from waitresses to society matrons, all but came to expect them, were even at times disappointed not to have the chance to say no, or yes. Far from trying to dampen the rumors, Edwards fanned them with his own double entendres and self-incriminating asides. Asked by reporters outside a federal courthouse if he thought his phone was tapped, he said no but added, "Except by jealous husbands." His image and his resulting immunity were so firmly established by the end of his first term that he could tell a reporter the only personal scandal that could hurt him would have him "caught in bed with either a dead girl or a live boy.

The larger question was not why the voters accepted it but why his wife took it. That's a private question for Elaine Edwards in her very public life. Surely when he told her when they were teenagers that he would be governor she had no idea it would come to this. The politician's family's life in the fishbowl is strain enough. Elaine Edwards, a private person, has had to endure so much more.

It's another of the paradoxes of Edwin Edwards: his open promiscuity and his tight family bonds. From brothers to mother to children, the Edwards family has presented a highly visible united front and a strong campaign force. Elaine has been the key—through everything, above everything, public scandal or behind the back whispers, she stuck by his side. Still, there have been the uneasy moments, even in public. Women who have greeted the governor, even if being introduced to Edwards for the first time, have reported feeling a burning hole in the head coming from the direction of Elaine's stares. It's not, friends would say, that Mrs. Edwards felt any competition. "Elaine is not at all threatened by those women. She regards them with contempt, but it's more like disgust, knowing they will be out in tomorrow's trash."

A report noted as Edwin Edwards was sworn in for his second term that the governor appeared bored and listless. Having passed a new constitution, reformed the state tax structure and survived Clyde Vidrine, what more excitement could he expect? But looming on the horizon was the spectre of Koreans bearing gifts, which would be his closest brush yet with the U. S. Justice Department.

Tongsun Park had been very, very good to Edwin Edwards. The rice deal he helped broker propelled Edwards into the Mansion. Tongsun made friends all over Capitol Hill, so many in fact that the U. S. Justice Department would later indict Park on 36 counts of federal corruption charges. When the *Washington Post* reported in 1975 that Justice was investigating a $20,000 campaign contribution from the Korean, Edwards bitterly denied the allegations as more witch-hunting and said he received nothing from Tongsun Park. But the *Post* reports persisted into the next year, as did the federal investigation, until Edwards, following an acrimonious, drawn-out cat and mouse exchange with reporters, finally said, "Look, do you want to know what really happened?"

"Why do you think we've been asking you questions for 45 minutes?"

Then Edwards offered perhaps his most bizarre explanation ever. Park had given him nothing, as he had always maintained, although the Korean did give his wife Elaine $10,000 cash to buy gifts for herself and her daughters. Elaine didn't even tell him about it, he said, until a couple of years later, but he never thought much of it. After all, he told the press conference, to a person of his means $10,000 was not that great a sum and it would only be important "to a reporter." Asked what his wife did with the money he replied, "My daughters are trying to find that out now." A year later, another admission, this time that an employee of Park's gave $10,000 to Edwards' 1971 campaign. When reporters asked why it took so long to tell the whole story, he said, "Nobody in this press corps has ever asked me, 'Did any other Korean make a contribution to you?'" The federal grand jury indicted Congressman Otto Passman, who was later acquitted, but it did not indict Edwards since it could find no actions on his part to return Park's favors.

The Park affair, however, marked a low point in Edwards' relationship with the press. Press conferences turned into increasingly bitter battles of attrition with the truth. In the heat of persistent questioning, Edwards' pique showed and sometimes his mouth got out of control. After one Mansion press conference, while showing reporters the $1,000 Korean table inlaid with mother-of-pearl given the family by Park, the governor said he saw nothing wrong with current press reports of American businessmen bribing foreign officials. "The present supermoralistic attitude that you shouldn't be making these payments has cheated American businessmen of the right to compete in foreign countries." The headline writers had a field day with such screamers as:

GOVERNOR EDWARDS IN FAVOR OF BUSINESS BRIBES

Edwards later recanted the statement but the damage was done. The combination of his Korean semantics and the bribe quotes did not set well with a public that thought it had heard just about everything from Edwin Edwards. At a 1976 campaign stop with Jimmy Carter in New Orleans, Edwards was roundly booed and met with shouts of "Give back the table."

For all he had been through in two terms, Edwards' popularity was only dented. A 1977 poll showed Edwards' approval rating slipping to an all-time low: 55 percent. Out-of-state reporters were astounded at his resilience. He went hard against the grain of post-Watergate morality, the new political purity in vogue everywhere else, but his attitude of *laissez les bons temps rouler* perfectly expressed the spirit of the times at home. These were the go-go years of unprecedented industrial expansion and personal income growth in Louisiana. Everyone was making money and no one seemed to mind that Edwards and his friends were doing very well too, or that the state budget had more than doubled during his eight years. Why should they mind? Personal taxes had gone down. And so what if the governor gambled and chased women? Suffocating Southern puritanism had never taken strong hold in South Louisiana anyway. And now a new anything-goes spirit was sweeping away the confining strictures in business and personal life. Edwin Edwards was not only in step with the times in Louisiana, he symbolized them. Here was a man who talked fast, lived fast and made things happen, for himself and for others. The '70s were great years for Louisianians straight across the economic scale. Whatever Edwin Edwards was doing to help things along, folks didn't want him to stop.

Toward the end of his second term, it was apparent Edwin Edwards would achieve what no other governor, save Huey Long, had: to leave office more popular than when he came in. All that was left was to ensure in 1983 he could come back.

He kicked off massive construction projects with every dollar he could raise or borrow. They included the long-awaited North-South highway, a Mississippi River bridge at Luling, a second downtown bridge for New Orleans and overflowing pork barrels of lesser projects. He took credit for announcing the projects while leaving the next governor to pay for and build them, which should take just enough time so that Edwards could be back in office to cut the ribbon. He took care of some long-waiting constituencies, finally endorsing the flagging Equal Rights Amendment in his last year, after having refused to push it in his first seven. He shocked good government advocates by enacting several good government reforms, most of which would not go into effect until he left office. These included disbanding the gubernatorially appointed Budget Committee in favor of more legislative control on appropriations, tightening the state procurement code and decreasing the size of the Mineral Board. It took Edwards eight years to implement these reforms that would limit the power of the governor, especially the next governor. In the name of reform, he transferred some appointive positions to civil service, but in effect he was cementing his own people in sensitive posts all over government and the next governor would not be able to root them out. These new civil servants also formed the nucleus of Edwards' superb intelligence network for the next four years. In his final days in office, he even started the clock ticking on several time bombs he knew would detonate sooner or later. Asked why he named Pam Harris chairman of the

Parole Board, Edwards said that she was "the kind of Republican who will give Dave Treen trouble."

He was even getting along better with the press, bouncing back from an all-time nadir during Koreagate. That thaw was put to the test in the 1978 Capitol Correspondents' Gridiron Show, which had unusually good material to work with after the publication of Vidrine's *Just Takin' Orders*. There was no lack of bad taste that night on the part of the reporters as they reenacted spicier tales from the book. The governor sat through the show poker-faced as usual, but his wife appeared far less amused. They were surprised she didn't walk out in the middle of some skits. But she was saving her response for the end. At the close of the show, when Edwards took the mike for the governor's traditional rebuttal, he pulled out a copy of Clyde's book and said there was someone with even more to say, inviting Elaine onstage.

Audience and cast held their breath as a stern Elaine Edwards faced the audience, took Clyde's book from her husband and said that since so much of the show was lifted from this book, she would like to point out some obvious factual errors. Then she read the passage about a party in a motel where Edwin made a point of stopping at Clyde's door five times to show off each one of the girls he was taking to his room.

"Well, of course, that's untrue," said Elaine to a stunned audience. "Anyone who knows my husband knows he would have been asleep after the first one."

Audible gasp. Then cast and audience spontaneously broke into applause and rose in standing ovation as Edwin stood by beaming proudly. *That's my girl. . . .*

They begin their days together, when Edmund Reggie picks up Marion in Crowley and then stops at Billy Broadhurst's and sets off to Baton Rouge. Crossing the Atchafalaya Swamp, they talk about people and jobs, making or breaking the hopes and plans of the hundreds who want to be a part if not own of piece of the new administration of Edwin Edwards. Officially, Edwards' brother and his two longtime friends are members of the executive committee of the transition team. In reality, they are the shadow cabinet, trusted draftsmen connecting the broad strokes of the grand design by the Great Architect. The three have been with Edwards since the first race for the Crowley City Council 30 years before. They are still his chief operatives, meeting with him first thing at the transition office (formerly state headquarters) on Silverside Lane and reviewing the order of the day. Marion is primarily concerned with retiring the $4.3 million in $25,000 and $50,000 notes given by members of the Committee of 200. Broadhurst and Reggie are screening the major appointments to executive positions, the boards and commissions, as well as planning the first legislative package with another veteran confidant Camille Gravel. Another executive committee member, Ann Davenport, though not returning to her old job as executive secretary, is overseeing the hiring and training of a new Fourth Floor staff to work as smoothly as the one Davenport oversaw four years ago.

The governor-elect has promised a new kind of state administration, different from the previous one or, for that matter, the one before that: open, fresh, clean, responsive, responsible, attracting only the best and the brightest and even the equal opportunity employer. For all the freshness and newness, Edwards still likes things to work. Hence, the job of the old hands, to set the new faces in place and have them ready for a running start March 12.

The change in atmosphere from the old campaign office to the new transition office is apparent from the first step inside the door where the visitor is now met by a couple of state policemen and Kermit Richard, the official greeter who knows who needs to be specially cared for. Everyone else is sent down the hall for a visitor's badge. Upstairs, the once supercharged but relaxed atmosphere has settled to a dignified rush. Even Gus Mijalis, whose casual swagger and easygoing good humor epitomized the former tone of the campaign of friends, appears positively buttoned-down and elegant peering over his glasses with a bundle of important papers in hand. Aides who two months ago were setting up drivers and country western bands and campaign contributors are now immersed in weightier task, setting a new government in motion, and not just any government, but a new political order, "a hallmark against which all future administrations will be judged," as the office inspirational has it.

The generator of all this dare-to-be-greatness looks around for a spare room to chat with his visitor. Interviewing Edmund Reggie is like throwing paper airplanes into a fan—he greets each question with a windstorm of enthusiasm followed by gusts of tangential thoughts and spontaneous observations. As good as Reggie's b.s. is, he is merely the animator for the Great Architect.

> Edwin gives us a real sense of direction. He has the composite in his mind, he sees the complete picture. And the amazing thing is that after eight years in office and four years running for it, he's coming up with the freshest, most far-reaching most innovative ideas I've ever heard to move the state forward. He keeps telling us to not be afraid to reach higher, to do something progressive, to go farther than the accepted limits of what state government can do.

The recurring theme is that Louisiana will see a different kind of administration. How different? "Well, last time we had Clyde Vidrine, so we have to guard against that." The difference this time, says Reggie, will be in the people.

> We are putting together a cabinet and subcabinet with people who would be attractive to private industry. Edwin sold them on coming in on state pay and at salaries that won't be increased. And not because someone is the son of a contributor. Edwin's coming in without a single commitment. That's one blessing of raising and spending $13 million. He had all the money to run with. Now he doesn't have to use the state treasury to pay off any promises.

Reggie disappears down the hall and returns with his "precepts of understanding" all major appointees must commit to: no salary increases for the foreseeable future, decreasing the number of employees in each department, giving Edwards in January a comprehensive plan to realistically reduce departmental expenses without reducing legislatively mandated programs. "If they can't say they'll do a better job for less, they're not the people we're looking for. That's the test."

Also, he reads in, no spouse, relative or children will be hired by or have any business with an official's department. And all will observe an open door policy, meeting the public and returning all phones calls on the day they are received. "The governor does that himself. If he does that for the whole state, then every secretary in every office will do the same. There will be no more kingdoms. . . . We'll all respond in the same way to the public. Edwin is so against bureaucratic arrogance."

Reggie whips up his rhetoric in a grand crescendo. "I am staggered and amazed by the enthusiasm of the man and by the fresh, imaginative ideas he wants implemented. He's more full of ideas than he was in 1972." Time will tell what Edwin and Edmund are full of, but the transition staff at least, getting the full Reggie treatment, can't help but be believers.

The aide looks around one time and confides, "I tell you what pisses me off is the way he's been so damned nice to some people who did nothing for us." Within the heady atmosphere of the victors' camp, some loyalists, though conceding Edwards does a fine job of taking care of his friends, still can't understand his reluctance to punish his enemies. It was much more fun during the campaign when Edwards gave no quarter, finding, even funding, candidates to run against and pin down Treen supporters. But his massive landslide has allowed him the luxury of granting political pardons. "There is not a vindictive bone in his body," says Judge Reggie. Not many stupid ones either. Edwards knows when and with whom to make peace—as long as the vanquished come bearing the olive branch. Yet sometimes absolution is not his to give. When asked at a press conference if any of Treen's black appointees will be kept on, Edwards refers the question to the back of the room where Dorothy Mae Taylor and Sherman Copelin are sternly shaking their heads in unison.

Rapprochement takes many forms. Following tradition, *Advocate* publisher Doug Manship hosts a dinner party at the City Club for Edwards and the newspaper's editors, at which the two old enemies toast and joke with each other. Manship will tell friends, "I don't know why he wants the job," but he extends his editorial good will and will ultimately endorse Edwards' $1 billion tax package.

Stranger than that, while Anna Edwards is planning the inauguration she receives a call from John Spain, archfiend news director of Channel 2, the very man who sent John Camp after Edwin Edwards. Spain just wants to offer Anna any assistance in media coordination, credentials, pool coverage, anything he can do to help. The press corps gawks as Spain assumes all press coordination chores for the politician who had publicly reviled him a few short weeks before. Either Spain or Spain's boss Manship had decided that eight years is a long time for a cold war and that a fresh start is in order.

Edwards is breaking important new ground for women and blacks in government by making good on his promise of a balanced administration top to bottom. Stephanie Alexander is a far cry from the wily, ambitious and imprisoned Charlie Roemer as commissioner of administration, and pediatrician and hospital administrator Dr. Sandra Robinson offers a style and an approach to the state's largest department, Health and Human Resources, that are light-years distant from those of Edwards' last DHHR head, whip-cracking George Fischer. But Edwards' most surprising top appointment is neither female nor black, rather a white guy named Ron Faucheux as secretary of commerce.

In New Orleans that news shakes City Hall where Dutch Morial, having vanquished or tamed all rivals for his sovereignty in the city, and who has also always received appropriate reverence and a wide berth from candidate Edwin Edwards, is now humiliated by Edwards' awarding a plum cabinet post to Faucheux, Morial's bitter opponent in the racially spiked mayoral race of 1982 and a prominent figure in Dutch's hall of black candles. Slain by Dutch, Faucheux's career was in a heap, alongside any citywide ambitions of other white candidates in black-dominated, Dutch-ruled New Orleans. Faucheux had stalked the lieutenant governor's race but decided not to run. And therein lay his reward. As a favor to his staunch labor ally Victor Bussie, Edwards had talked Faucheux out of the lieutenant governor's race with the lure of the future cabinet job, thus taking a lot of pressure off embattled incumbent Bobby Freeman, who was both labor's candidate and their insurance policy should something untoward happen to Edwards. Some Edwards staffers were at first surprised and disgruntled because of Faucheux's minor contribution to the campaign, but later nodded with respect and approval when they got the full picture. "It was a clever case," says one, "of Edwin letting labor borrow on his assets." It was also the opportunity for Edwards to send a clear message to Dutch Morial. Candidate Edwards had bowed and scraped to humor Dutch, to keep him out of the governor's race, to keep the black vote united, even catching a lot of flak for endorsing Morial's unlimited terms. Throughout the campaign, Edwin Edwards showed Mayor Morial the utmost respect and honor. But now Edwin Edwards, coming to power, is letting Boss Dutch know who's really boss.

Through his appointment process, Edwards is keeping another promise, to invite public comment or criticism before announced appointments are finalized. Every release of proposed appointments bears the curious disclaimer, "Any person knowing just reasons why any such persons should not be so appointed is asked to speak now or forever hold his peace." Edwards completes nearly all of his cabinet appointments—that is, all the blacks and women he's going to name—in time for *60 Minutes* to film them for the upcoming show. So complete is Edwards' demographic mix, it's getting to be a joke. He introduces his new secretary of the Department of Culture, Recreation and Tourism as a Cherokee Indian, even though Noelle LeBlanc's Indian ancestor preceded generations of New Orleans uptown society. No matter, an Indian's an Indian on the vita. At one point Edwards even introduces his new director of the office of veterans' affairs, a handicapped black Republican, who turns out to be everything Edwards could ask for, except a veteran.

His name is quietly withdrawn. During that same show and tell for the cameras, at which black and female faces far outnumber one lonely white guy, an irreverent aide pokes a reporter and asks, "Where's the Jew?"

Edwards achieves peace on his own terms with the state press corps but doesn't presume the good will carries beyond the border. That's the way it's always been. Even at the height of his popularity in his first two terms, Edwards and his Cajun rogue image played to bad reviews in the Eastern press. Even on his best behavior, he's been snubbed, as when he approached the podium at the 1976 Democratic National Convention to second the nomination of Jerry Brown and the networks switched to commercials. Visiting journalists in the 1983 campaign couldn't resist the easy cliche of the cocky politician-king who dazzles his subjects with corruption and excess. But Edwards' remarkable landslide could not be denied. On election night, *USA Today* was planning a story for the Monday edition, and NBC's Ken Bode had been in to prepare a report for the Sunday news show. Then late election night, half a world away, a terrorist drove a loaded truck bomb into the marine barracks in Beirut, sending shock waves through the nation's press for the next weeks, wiping out all else from news budgets, burying the Edwards victory in the rubble of that disaster.

When the *60 Minutes* piece aired in early December, it fell in neatly with the pack. The 13-minute segment ignored the immensity of the Edwards victory and the appointment of his balanced cabinet to home in on the 12-year-old allegations of Clyde Vidrine. There's Clyde and an embittered Lewis Johnson interviewed on camera by Ed Bradley, who feigns civics textbook incredulity at the idea that a governor would actually appoint a large contributor to an important state job. The report focused on the 1971 money angle, especially Edwards' disputing the claimed amount of Jerome Glazer's contributions—"My version is it was $45,000. I think Clyde skimmed $30,000 from the money." That kind of talk was just too sexy for producer Joe Bernstein to pass up—so it forms the meat of the show. It may have been more interesting to try to explain how Edwards was twice overwhelmingly reelected after those allegations first surfaced. That, the story leaves you to assume, is because Louisianians are ignorant and hopelessly duped by Edwards' cult of personality. The truncated, unbalanced report raises more questions than it answers and though it does no new damage to Edwards' already tarnished reputation, the show does manage to insult the state as a whole and to deepen the national misunderstandings of Louisianians' approach to government.

Edwards' final campaign finance report weighs in at 20 pounds for 1,867 pages, listing over 10,000 contributors and over 19,000 individuals who received a check from the Edwards campaign. That includes the thousands of part-time workers receiving $20 to $50 for canvassing, taking people to the polls, telephoning. Edwards wheels the documents across the parking lot to the Ethics Commission office to make a point that the law's requirements are a "particularly silly exercise in good government" and call for his "taking a long look at the campaign finance law." In practical terms, he questions how "one person who receives a $20 check for working election day can alter the course of the election or history and we don't need to keep track of every check."

A gaggle of candidates who had just filed their reports wait outside in the parking lot for Edwards to finish his media event. Among them is Butch Baum, who ran a respectable but not respectable enough second to Agriculture Commissioner Bob Odom's landslide. Well, it was all a good experience for Butch, who made a lot of new friends and contacts. But only one thing bothers him about the election.

> Well, what really disappoints me is how poorly I did here in Baton Rouge. Odom beat me 80,000-27,000 right here in my home. You know, I just couldn't figure it and it got me a little mad. So I went back through my records and did you know that in the past 15 years I have donated $1,653,000 to charities here. And the son of bitches wouldn't even vote for me . . .

says Butch looking off in hurt disgust. "But I guess it worked out all right. I've saved $25,000 since the election. When the charities call me now, I just tell 'em, *Call Bob Odom!*"

"Your Worship," the governor-elect greets Archbishop Philip Hannan in the Little Capitol's dining room. Edwards is back already to his old Mansion tradition of breaking bread at noon with everyone from legislators to out-of-state journalists to the reigning Arkansas Pork Queen. The afternoon appointments follow. It's the same idea in a scaled-down version during the transition. Today's lineup includes the good archbishop who has driven up from New Orleans, press secretary-designate Meg Curtis, Wayne Ray, Marion and Thibodaux contributor C. O. Calogne, about to be appointed to the Mineral Board.

After the archbishop says grace, he expresses his own gratitude that the governor-elect is on board to help him talk some sense into the Italians dealing with the World's Fair. Seems the archbishop, having been guaranteed one of Michelangelo's sculptures for the Vatican Pavilion of the World's Fair, is now running into thorny problems with the Italian government, which apparently is using the sculpture as a pawn in its ongoing domestic political crisis. Seems the Italian government, which has final say on the movement of the Vatican's precious artwork, has reneged on its earlier agreement with the archbishop and now says it can't possibly send the priceless sculpture for fear of breakage. The Italians have offered to send another sculpture, but you don't rise to archbishop in the Catholic church without knowing how to play politics. "I told them what I am going to do," says the archbishop, unfolding his napkin. "The entire pavilion is designed with the spot for the Michelangelo as the focal point. I told them we will simply leave the pedestal empty with a card explaining the absence of the Michelangelo. Then we'll let them explain."

Edwards compliments the prelate on his grasp of the jugular. The archbishop's confession seems to relax the governor-elect into treating his excellency to a spate of his latest ethnic jokes. And since the subject is Italians, "Did you know the Italian Army recently held maneuvers for the Third World War? They spent three week practicing this"—Edwards puts his hands up over his head. The archbishop smiles politely into his salad. But just in case he didn't catch that one, "Do you know why the new Italian Navy has glass-bottomed boats? So they can see the old Italian Navy."

Edwards especially loves telling Italian jokes to Italians. "This is all in your honor, C. O.," he nods to his contractor friend.

"Governor," protests Calogne, "as long as you've known me, you continue to think I'm Italian. I'm a descendant of a French prince."

"C. O., the only thing worse than an Italian is one who won't admit it."

At this point the archbishop might consider putting Edwards on that empty pedestal in the Vatican Pavilion to do his Italian routine. Instead, the prelate diplomatically shifts the conversation to Project Harvest, the ambitious humanitarian effort to get surplus food at the market and from restaurants into the hands of the urban needy. Edwards follows the discussion with interest, then interjects a question. "Did you hear about the Italian girl that says, 'Mama, Mama, I'ma preg-a-nant.' 'Don't worry,' says her mother, 'maybe it's not yours.' "

A good comic knows how far he can ride a gag, but of course Edwards can't let the routine end without "What's black and blue and floats in the river? A Cajun who tells Italian jokes."

The luncheon guests sigh in relief, but the host is on a roll. After the Italian jokes, can the pope jokes be far behind? Did his worship hear the one about the Pope sending 300 septic tanks to his native Poland? "He got a telegram back that said, 'Have the tanks. As soon as we learn how to drive them, we'll attack the Russians.' "

Okay, the archbishop chuckles at that one. What else is he going to do? Edwards and Hannan have been friends for years—the archbishop has presided at all the Edwards kids' weddings. He understands Edwards' distaste for boring formalities. And a big part of it may well be that Edwards, having spent three years being uncharacteristically nice to everyone ("I'll even be nice to reporters," he said during the campaign in Morgan City, "and when I get back in, I'm gonna be a real son of a bitch."), is getting back to his old self again. Edwards, who escaped the lower class with a straight shot to the upper class, doesn't truck with middle class morality and convention. And the son of Boboy Edwards doesn't kiss rings of Catholic archbishops. Nor does Philip Hannan, who understands the prerogatives and uses of power, expect him to, as the two skilled politicians disappear into Edwards' office to plot the next move against the unsuspecting bureaucrats in Rome.

Marion would like to sell about 20 more seats on the plane. "We don't have to, but it will be nice." Nice indeed. So far the Paris fund-raiser will gross $5 to $5.5 million and will net $4 to $4.2 million to pay off the notes secured by the letters of credit from the Committee of 200. The campaign treasurer is rightly proud of himself for having conceived, implemented and sold this spectacular fund-raiser, the capstone of the most expensive campaign in the history of American state politics. He considered a rerun of the 1972 trip to Mexico City and South America, but Marion knew the monstrous debt would require an even more magnificent promotion. And what could be more logical than a return to the homeland, the source of Louisiana politics' grand excesses?

With two jumbo jets almost filled, Marion's main task now is fighting a rearguard action against everyone trying to scramble aboard for the $2,100 special deal that the press and legislators are getting. Marion is on the phone to a friend of Bob Odom, explaining that the press reports were wrong, that not all state officials get the reduced price, only legislators. He is only selling $10,000 tickets, but, well, look, "I can raise $5,000 if he can raise $5,000. . . . Yet, someone gave me $5,000 to help someone who needs it to be able to go, so if you can get that $5,000. . ."

"Sherman Bernard wants to go too," says Mike Baer, cupping his hand over his phone.

"Same deal," says Marion, cupping his hand over his.

Sam Thomas, a coordinator of the trip, says every effort has been made to accommodate travelers, including their E-Z credit terms: "$2,100 down and five payments of $2,000. We all know it's not how much that counts but what are the terms," he laughs going out the door.

Marion says it's been tough holding the line, but it's been held. "By the time this trip is over, I will have raised more than what Jefferson paid for Louisiana in 1803. That was $15 million. By the time this trip is over, I will have raised $17 million [$13 million for the campaign and $4 million to repay the amounts raised by letters of credit]." And you don't beat Napoleon's take by selling at-cost tickets. "Look, no one's getting a free ride. Everyone's got to pay. The governor, his ticket is paid for. Same for my family, my wife. Everyone is paid for," although some very thoughtful wealthy contributors and industries paid for tickets for Edwards to use or give away.

Baer puts down the phone in triumph. "Got him! He and his wife are going. $20,000."

Marion has cast his net wide, asking many who did not contribute to the campaign but who now are looking for some way to get on the bandwagon after the parade has passed. "Some Treen supporters have even called us and asked if Republicans can come along," laughs Judge Reggie. No problem at all, this is an equal opportunity scam.

Many were asked. Like the lobbyists who opened their mail to find two artfully designed tickets to the Paris fund-raiser and the letter instructing that a $20,000 check be returned because Governor Edwards knows you will want to go along. And it did no good to ditch the invite, for it was followed up by a phone call a week later from a campaign aide inquiring if the check was in the mail yet. "I've never seen the squeeze on lobbyists like this before," says the veteran. "You have to admire the way they have organized this." Lobbyists are the perfect target for a postelection fund-raiser. The private organizations that work for private companies do their business with the legislature and with the regulatory boards, representing their clients as would a lawyer. Their unofficial, privately funded role in state government leaves them open for an appeal of this sort, with the ever so slight suggestion of an offer you can't refuse. It's not merely a question of one's clients getting roughed up in the legislature or the bureaucracy, it's a matter of being left out of the action. Many of the state's boards and commissions have by tradition or law included representatives from several of the different industries and interest groups that are overseen by the boards. In many cases, complains the lobbyist trying to be objective, "It's lousy government, fox in the henhouse stuff," but it's ingrained in the system and no lobbyist can afford to have his people left off a board. The Edwards team knows the system as well as anyone, says the lobbyist. "They know what you want. They have systematically put together all the boards and commissions and who they know wants input to what selections. There are people in government for 40 years who don't know that, but the Edwards people do." And they hope to capitalize on the lobbyists' self-interest by encouraging them to buy tickets or to get their clients to pony up. "it's the smartest thing I've ever seen," says the lobbyist, "I'm still shocked at how sophisticated it is."

Yet, despite a good effort by Marion's sales team, few lobbyists sign up for the trip. Their entertainment expense accounts just go so far. The greater concern among lobbyists is the fear that Edwards and company are moving in on their turf. You just have to look at the new lobbying organizations being formed. George Fischer, having played no role in the transition, has formed a lobbying company along with his old aide (and Edwards' old press secretary) Jim Harris. Marion Edwards has gone into public affairs/lobbying, taking a vice president's post at Freeport-McMoRan, a giant company with sulfur plants and oil and gas interests in Louisiana. Ann Davenport and Vicki's husband Larry Cormier have formed a lobbying group and are already handling some legislators' fund-raisers.

Davenport, Cormier, Fischer, and Harris all held posts in prior administrations. This time they're back in the action but not on the state payroll, so they don't have to worry about all the disclosure requirements and nagging ethics rules that have come to make state service a real drag for the governor's connected friends. This time around, Edwards can take care of his friends at arm's length, without the state having to pay for it, at least not directly. The parallel world of lobbyists, of private firms paid by private companies to inform and influence legislators, boards and bureaucrats, operates free of the strictures of state service. The combination of the lobbyists' freedom and access and the governor's friendship can work in ways smoothly subtle but devastatingly effective. Say your company or industry association has some important legislation coming up this season—now, who's your lobbyist again?

Before Dave Treen can gracefully leave office, there is the final untidy business of calling a special session to cure the impending deficit whose existence Treen downplayed when not denying it during the campaign. His cool, reasoned remarks to the opening joint session are hailed by many as his most impressive address as governor. "Yeah, just like MacArthur," breezes one legislator, "he saves his best speech for last."

But it won't be enough. House members are impressed by the lame duck governor's speech but stop dead in their tracks at Treen's request to reimpose the state income tax rates he cut three years before. Faced with legislative intransigence, Treen swallows hard and calls in the old master to whip the boys into shape. Showing up in blue jeans and windbreaker, Edwards casually moves to take charge of the special session, encouraging and cajoling the legislators, some of whom are lame ducks themselves, to start wiping out the major initiatives of the Treen administration. Not only is the full income tax reimposed, retroactive to cover 1983, but the congressional lines are redrawn in the Orleans area to create a majority black congressional district and to cut away 80 percent of Republican Bob Livingston's neighboring district. Also, the legislature suspends creation of Treen's Department of Environmental Quality, a measure Treen will ignore anyway.

"It's the lemming Legislature," the sardonic reporter labels it. "It's so funny, I mean these guys won't go to the bathroom without calling Edwards. In the House, they're so-o-o upset at the idea of electing Joe Delpit Speaker pro tem," she says of Edwards' choice of the black Baton Rouge representative for the No. 2 leadership post, "but they won't dare vote against him." She's right, they don't.

On the Senate side, the solons have adjourned for the day after waving through the entire Edwards-Treen corrective package with barely a dissenting vote. Relaxing on the side of the chamber are two former Young Turks of the Senate, Tommy Hudson and Tony Guarisco. Entering their third terms, neither is that young anymore and Hudson, for one, has changed nationality. Turks don't get elected to Senate leadership positions and Hudson is campaigning hard for Senate president pro tem. But Guarisco's flame still burns brightly for lost causes and new conspiracies to alert the world against. "Did you see they're installing missiles at the White House and any plane that comes close gets destroyed, no questions asked?" Hudson, the frequent visitor to Washington, is looking at Guarisco like he just fell off the onion truck. "Oh sure, Hudson," Guarisco continues, "you probably think it's great. Look at you, I bet you're a part of it."

"Tony, have you ever seen an aviation map of D.C.? They've got this black rectangle from the Capitol to the White House with the warning that any plane that strays into that air space gets blown away. That's nothing new."

"Yeah, well, now they're gonna do it with missiles," huffs Guarisco. "That's Reagan for you."

"Guarisco's our Spartacus." Hudson pats his old roommate on the back. "On the very first vote, the Edwards people are looking to see who will come out against them and here's Tony in the back lighting a match to his foot."

Guarisco holds both arms behind his back. "They're gonna lash me to that pillar. I'll have to eat heavier before the regular session starts so that I'll last a few days longer."

John Hill passes by and asks Hudson, "Has Edwin told you who you'll be voting for for pro tem?"

"I just sent my ballot to him," smiles the candidate, doing his lemming imitation. "Now, John, you're so cynical. Don't take that to mean I'm going to let Edwards tell me what to do. No, he's just going to go ahead and do it."

At Tour D'Argent, after a day of touring Paris, playfully posing with fur-draped models from the House of Revillon, signing a cultural and trade agreement with government officials at the Chamber of Deputies and having a private audience with President François Mitterrand, Edwin Edwards sidles over to Bob Courtney near the TV cameras and asks, "Heard anything on Ossie Brown?"

That Edwin Resplendent, triumphant in Paris, the touring statesman with his bulging entourage of 600, could even bother to worry over the Baton Rouge DA's impending indictment suggests the governor-elect's mind is not all on his trip. So how is the royal tour going?

"Oh, I've done just what Marion told me to do. I've been good, I've gone to all the functions and smiled at people and shook hands, but tell you the truth, I want to get the . . out of here and go home."

Anyone who would raise a toast in Paris and say, "I was destined, I thought, when I was born, to be a king, and tonight I can be," can't be expected to tolerate long separations from his people. The royalty theme is carried to the limits of good taste and beyond, especially the little lapel pins with the profile of Edwards and the inscription "Sun King." Whenever the awe-inspiring events crammed into each day—from laying a wreath at the tomb of France's unknown soldier to Edwards' induction into the society of Beaujolais—got to be just too overwhelming, Edwin could be counted on to puncture the pomp and pageantry. After waiters in 17th-century garb bearing candelabras led the gawking 600 through the Palace of Versailles and served them *Saumon Marine a l'Aneth Sauce Moutarde Brune*, Edwards tablehops and poses for pictures wearing a waiter's periwig. And when it came to wisecracks, the king of repartee could not have had better set-ups. Exiting Notre Dame Cathedral, Edwards is greeted by a Louisiana nun, now living in France, who jokes, "Governor, I'm going to give you a French kiss."

"Okay, Sister, just don't let me get in the habit."

He even provides CBS with the perfect closing line for its story. Asked the most important thing he got out of the trip, he can't resist. "Five million dollars."

Finally the governor-elect is able to relax and have some back-home kind of fun: shooting craps at Monte Carlo. With its dome of stained glass and its gold-leaf, the 19th-century gaming room at the Monte Carlo Casino is not exactly Harrah's, so Edwards tries to impart some continental manners to his rowdy buddy Gus Mijalis. "Don't holler if you don't have the number, dummy," Edwards yells at his exuberant friend.

"That's me, a nine! A nine!" Mijalis shouts back.

"You can holler, you can holler," yells Edwards.

The biggest news of the trip—a banner headline in the *Morning Advocate*—comes an hour later when Louisiana's most famous gambler finishes a $15,000 run. To hell with decorum, the governor-elect slaps the table and instructs the dealer, "Give me my money. Give me my money. Give me a wheelbarrow for my money."

Organizers Marion Edwards and Sam Thomas are dubbed the generals of the trip. They keep the tour moving—campaign style. When 100 more of the Louisianians than expected show up for a night at the Lido, Marion slips the *maitre d'* $1,000 and seats appear from nowhere.

Daughter Vicki commands her share of attention on the trip. She even makes the network news, displaying her barefoot-in-the-bayou charm in responding to the reporter's question "Did you pay $10,000 to come on the trip?"

"Hell, no, I'm the governor's daughter."

She makes some head-turning entrances as well. When she walks into the gaming room in Monte Carlo in a stunning black and gold gown with a gold-glittered, black ostrich plume swooping back over her ear, reporter Jack Wardlaw observes, "Looks like tonight's entertainment is going to be Vicki singing *Carmen*."

*Time* and *People* are along for the ride to capture *The Beverly Hillbillies Go to Paris* spirit of the occasion. Most of the travelers, though, are not new to Paris or insensitive to her charms. Nita Thomas, walking through Versailles' Hall of Mirrors, where the chandeliers are dimmed to candlelight level, is enthralled. "I feel like Cinderella going to the ball. It is like a fairy tale." On the whole, the supporting cast of 600 acquit themselves quite well. "On their best behavior" is the term most often used to describe their comportment. Still they can't resist a little silliness. At dinner at Le Train Bleu, all are minding their manners until legislators Jesse Deen and LaLa Lalonde climb atop the center table to have their picture taken next to the brass rooster atop the decoration. A reporter gasps to Representative Clyde Kimball, who laughs it off. "Hell, I'll probably take it home with me," says Clyde, as he slips an ashtray into his pocket. On the ride back to the hotel, the merrymaking legislators sing "Jolie Blonde" and then, of course "You Are My Sunshine" as the bus rolls down the moonlit Champs Elysees.

"How about a Dave Treen letter opener, still left over from the inauguration?" Lanny Keller is handing out mementos to reporters on the governor's last day at the office. But there's a catch. "You have to take one of his boring books, too." They've been left over since Treen was in Congress. Boxes of files are still being hauled downstairs but the pace for some staff members has in fact quickened this last day. Ray Lamonica breaks his hurried stride to explain, "There's so much left to do. You can't have something signed by one secretary and by another governor. Everything started by this administration has to be finished here." And today. For Treen will spend Friday in New Orleans doing TV interviews and will go home that night to his condo on the golf course at Beau Chene, the picturesque St. Tammany development where he and Dodie will eventually build.

Treen welcomes reporters into the high-ceilinged, dark wood office, the old Court of Appeals library, designed with intimidation in mind. Treen is in good spirits if not particularly good form—his voice is going fast as he croaks out answers to the final formula questions for the wire service and the TV reporters.

*If you had it all to do over again . . .*

"I would not make any different decisions, but I would probably try to find someone who was an expert on TV projection to get across the idea to the public what a warm, sensitive, hilarious, witty person I really am."

*That's odd since at a party you're so relaxed and make everyone feel so comfortable.*

"Yes, I know, but it just seems that in press conferences, I don't know, I look too serious, too stiff, but it is sort of an adversarial relationship."

*What will you be thinking about when you walk out of this office the last time tonight?*

"I really can't answer what I'll feel like. This office really hasn't done what I thought it could do in terms of ego inflation. It's a nice office, nice-looking, but I associate it with all the burdens of the job. I've never had a chance to sit on the sofa over there and look around the office and enjoy it."

*And leaving the Mansion?*

"We left with mixed feelings. Dodie and I were both surprised that we didn't feel sadder about leaving it. But we had a very nice weekend alone, just the two of us, in the condo. It was very nice."

The governor looks forward to another nice weekend playing golf, then returning to Baton Rouge for the inauguration. If all that goes as quickly as he hopes, "I can still tee off in the afternoon and get in 18 holes."

He interrupts so Robyn Eckings can do some cutaways for her public TV interview. While Robyn re-asks her questions for the tape, Treen throws in joke answers that sound more appropriate than his on-the-record comments.

*Do you blame anyone for your defeat?*

"Four hundred thousand voters."

Then there are the little readjustments to normal, mortal existence outside the power and glory of office. "I'll have to get used to carrying my car keys and wallet again," he says, thumbing through his modest Member of Congress billfold. For transportation there's the 1971 Cutlass convertible—indeed it is the real Treen family car, not a prop kept around to look good on financial disclosure reports. At the end of the day, however, Billy Nungesser presents his friend with the keys to a new Cadillac, a going-away present from some of his friends and supporters.

Leaving the governor to toil and grind through his final hours in power (let the record show that Dave Treen finally left his office at 2:30 a.m., March 9), the reporters take the gold-door governor's elevator to the basement. "I couldn't help but feel sad seeing him there," says one. "He is such a nice guy and I don't think people ever understood him." No, they didn't, but neither did Treen show us much of himself to understand. Dave Treen remained to the end his own man, refusing to allow the demands of power and politics to push him onto the public stage to display his charm and project the correct image of the sincere public servant getting the job done. The people didn't need to see an actor, a stand-up comic or a self-assured power broker: Dave Treen, the man, was impressive and likable enough to form a better personal bond with the people. But he was too imprisoned by that office which he never had enjoyed to project the real Dave Treen to the people of this state who want more than a public servant as governor, who want a personality who shows he is a leader and knows how to use the awesome powers granted him by the voters. To have projected that image, even the correct image, would have required Treen to give over a part of his life for public consumption. And that, Dave Treen, an intensely private man thrust into an intensely public life, was not ready to do. The really successful politicians readily and completely give over their private lives to their public. They live onstage, never shrinking from the camera's eye, revealing a carefully concocted and constrained persona or, like Edwin Edwards, letting it all—or most of it—hang out for the amazement and entertainment of the public.

In a way, you have to admire the public man who refuses to go public with his life. Just as many appreciate the fact that Dave Treen was not adept at politics and would rather be right than governor. We admire and respect those people, but history shows we don't elect them. And if by some chance we do, we get rid of them at the first opportunity. It's no putdown of the gifted politicians or the people—it's a matter of electing the right person for the right job. Treen had something to contribute to public service. His talent was to study an issue, pick it apart, hear the conflicting arguments, ignore the outside pressures and decide what was right. He was not meant to be the one with the vision, the dream, the one to gather his resources and set his course and to move a constituency toward his goal. By his style and character, he was judge and not a leader. Dave Treen could not have been a better person, but because of who he was he could not have been in a worse job.

The Reverend Clarence D. Bates died in early February and was honored in a raucous, free-wheeling and joyous memorial service at the Greater First Pentecostal Church in Alexandria. Sister Vesta Mangun led the congregation in singing "I'll Fly Away" as mourners were swept away in homage to the colorful ward-heeling preacher, Uncle Earl's old state trooper, Edwin Edwards' staunchest defender and Central Louisiana's most creative political moralist. His work on this earth done, he'll be sorely missed, but in a way old Clarence, though never one to shrink from any seemingly irreconcilable contradiction between faith and politics, nevertheless is probably relieved and happy to receive his final reward before having to rise to his greatest challenge: explaining the newest outrage to emanate from Edwin Edwards' lips. . . .

# THE NAZI AND THE REPUBLICANS: AN INSIDER VIEW OF THE RESPONSE OF THE LOUISIANA REPUBLICAN PARTY TO DAVID DUKE*

Elizabeth A. Rickey

David Duke is a man of many faces. He has been a state legislator from the Eighty-first District in Metairie, a recent candidate for the high offices of president, U. S. Senate, and governor, and a professional racist. His emergence on the political scene as a Republican has thrown the Louisiana Republican party into confused immobility. The hesitant response of Republican party leaders to Duke has helped to gain him precisely what he wants: mainstream respectability. In so doing, David Duke does damage to the conservative agenda by redefining it in his own image, an image that defines issues in a racial context.

I have gained a certain notoriety by trying to put the pieces of Duke's life—or lives—together. I did so hoping that my Republican colleagues in Louisiana would blanch when they learned what this man is all about. Instead, their response to the candidacy of this Nazi sympathizer has been curious at best and morally irresponsible at worst. They turned their heads or said "So what?" The moral crisis facing the Louisiana Republican party and its national parent is indeed a struggle for the soul of our party. This crisis began when the state leadership chose to ignore Duke's neo-Nazi philosophy. This chapter is the story of my unsuccessful attempt to have the leadership repudiate it.

In December 1988, I was pursuing a doctoral degree in political science at Tulane University in New Orleans and had been recently elected to the Louisiana Republican State Central Committee. One of my colleagues on the State Central Committee, John Treen, was running for a legislative seat in Metairie. A special election had been called for January 1989 to fill the vacancy, and John was one of many persons seeking the position. His major opponent was Jefferson Parish School Board member Delton

*From Douglas R. Rose, ed., *The Emergence of David Duke and the Politics of Race*. Copyright © 1992 by the University of North Carolina Press. Used by permission of the publisher and author.

Charles. David Duke's last-minute entrance into the race as a Republican was viewed more as a curiosity than a threat. However, Treen asked me to look into Duke's background so that he could be prepared in case the former Klansman became a serious contender.

Tulane University has one of the few collections in the nation of left- and right-wing political information, with an extensive collection on David Duke and his writings. I immersed myself in Klan and Nazi literature, and the more I read, the more appalled I was. Duke had left a paper trail that was twenty years long; there was no doubt that he was a professional racist and Nazi sympathizer. His claim that this was all in his "past" was blatantly untrue.

As a native Louisianian, I had heard of David Duke for years and dismissed him as a kook. No one took him seriously, at least in my circle of friends, and his frequent publicity stunts were just another sideshow attraction in the circus of Louisiana politics. Without knowing of his Nazi leanings, I was repelled by his leadership in the Knights of the Ku Klux Klan. In my family, the Klan was regarded as a terrorist organization, not as an upholder of Southern tradition. My great-grandfather, John Henry Womack, for twelve years around the turn of the century was sheriff of St. Helena Parish, a Klan stronghold in the late 1800s. A story that deeply impressed me was that he once held off a Klan lynch mob gathered at the parish jail in Greensburg, Louisiana. My grandfather, only twelve years old at the time, recalled that his father, John Henry, directed him to bring a wagon to the back of the jail, to hide the black man under a bale of hay, and to take him to Clinton in the next parish. It was the dead of night, and roads were treacherous back then, especially at night, but my grandfather transported the man to safety. The black man had been wrongly accused of raping a white woman, and my great-grandfather was keeping him in the jail for his own protection. The bravery on the part of my great-grandfather and grandfather stuck with me, and I viewed Klansmen with contempt, as cowards who liked to terrorize and denigrate people.

As I read *The Crusader*, Duke's Klan newspaper, I saw racist cartoons, racist jokes, and articles on the superiority of the white race. My overwhelming impression of Duke from his writings was of a mean-spirited, unkind man, contemptuous of his fellow human beings, and deceitful. He was not a person to be considered a serious candidate for anything except a mental institution.

However, what really stopped me cold was Duke's obvious fascination with Adolf Hitler and Nazism. My father had served as a lieutenant colonel in the Third Army under General George S. Patton. He landed at Normandy and was a part of the Battle of the Bulge. Papa was very proud of his service to his country and used to tell me stories about the war. More than once, he told me of the camps where innocent civilians had been starved to death or left to die of typhus and other diseases by the Nazis. He spoke of how people were killed in the extermination camps just because they were of a particular religion. My father died when I was ten, but I never forgot how important it was to him that he had helped to liberate Europe. The lessons he had taught me of those evils and horrors left an indelible imprint.

So when it dawned on me that Duke was not only a white supremacist but also a devotee of Hitler and National Socialism, I was affronted. What particularly incensed me was Duke's continual denial, over a twenty-year period, that the Holocaust ever happened. I resolved to expose this man for the hatemonger that he is. I was sure that once my colleagues on the Republican State Central Committee heard that a Nazi was in their midst, they would all rise in collective indignation and denounce him.

David Duke won the state legislative seat in February 1989, if only by some two hundred votes. He prevailed in spite of endorsements for his opponent, John Treen, by President George Bush and former president Ronald Reagan. Billy Nungesser, as chairman of the Louisiana Republican party, had issued a lukewarm denunciation of "opportunists" and reaffirmed the party's support of Treen as the endorsed candidate. Chairman Lee Atwater had sent resources from the Republican National Committee (RNC) to assist the Treen campaign. All of these efforts helped to slow Duke down but did not prevent his narrow win over John Treen.

Within a week of Duke's victory, at the end of February, Lee Atwater polled the members of the RNC's executive committee, and they voted unanimously to censure Duke. Although widely approved outside of Louisiana, this action was roundly denounced by many Republicans in the state. Mail started flooding the party's state headquarters on North Sixth Street in Baton Rouge. Among the letters received are these two examples:

> Because of the despicable attack upon Mr. Duke by Lee Atwater and other national Republican leaders, I have decided to withhold my support of the Republican Party until such time as this position is reconsidered and reversed. [Bogalusa]
>
> I would like to see J. Bennett Johnston defeated at any cost, but Lee Atwater must apologize to David Duke for his past action on national television. After the apology I will forward a check for $100.00. [Pineville]

## March 1989

On March 4, 1989, I was sitting in a jammed meeting room at the Bismarck Hotel in Chicago. I was a registered guest of the Populist Party National Convention, an amalgam of former Klansmen, neo-Nazis, and other right-wing extremists who had organized in 1984. The leader of the Populist party was Willis Carto, the shadowy head of the Liberty Lobby, a virulently anti-Semitic organization in Washington, D.C., and the Institute for Historical Review, whose sole purpose is to argue that the Holocaust never happened. Carto was a longtime associate of David Duke's, beginning in 1968 with the National Youth Alliance, a neo-Nazi organization. The Populist party had, for all intents and purposes, funded Duke's successful bid for the Louisiana legislature just two weeks before. Only 18 percent of Duke's contributions came from within Louisiana, and he received contributions from all fifty states. Carto's personal assistant, Patricia Katson, was now employed in Louisiana as Duke's legislative assistant.

Duke had run as the Populist party candidate for president the year before. He was on the ballot in twelve states, finishing fifth. He switched to the Republican party just weeks after his defeat in the presidential race and had tried to cover up his associations with right-wing extremists during his campaign for the state legislature. Yet here he was, the newly elected Republican representative from Louisiana, "coming home" to thank the Populists for their support.

What am I doing here? I thought to myself. To my right was a group of skinheads—neo-Nazi youths with shaved heads and wearing heavy jackboots. On my left was a man who appeared to be in a brownshirt uniform. At the podium the speaker was ranting about the Japanese. Suddenly, he announced that he just received information that infiltrators from the B'nai B'rith were in the room. He suspiciously looked my way as if to warn me and said that there were people in the room to take care of people like them—and pointed at the skinheads sitting next to me. This was not your typical political convention.

Of course, I had had an inkling that things were amiss when I discovered that the Chicago chapter of the American Nazi party had provided security for the convention. In fact, my friend Linda and I had had to get through a security phalanx to be admitted into the closed meeting where Duke was going to speak. The press was forced to stay one floor below, so I felt rather vulnerable as I ascended the staircase to the meeting room. We were stopped on the stairway and I flashed my convention badge. The Nazi guard asked me if I was from the press, and I responded indignantly, "Of course not, I'm a Populist!" The next guard was eyeing us suspiciously so I went up to him and pretended that I knew him: "How are you—haven't seen you in awhile! How's your family?" The man looked confused; he was too embarrassed to tell me he did not know who I was and ushered us in.

I had a tape recorder under my coat, stuck in my skirt. The device kept working its way down. I had a vision of it falling to the floor so I grabbed the nearest chair and sat down. Breathing a sigh of relief, I turned my attention to the speaker. All of a sudden I heard a loud "CLICK." Linda started coughing to cover up the sound as people turned to see what the noise was. I had forgotten to turn the tape over. I got up, walking sort of bent over so the tape recorder would not drop out of my shirt, and scuttled into the nearest bathroom. I managed to fix the tape recorder and secure it better, then returned to the meeting.

The mood in the room was tense. The speakers were all angry—angry about minorities, angry about the media, just plain angry. As much as Linda and I tried to keep our sense of humor, we later admitted how frightened we were. We also knew we were there without benefit of the media as protection, so we tried to look as inconspicuous as possible. However, Linda is Asian-American and we did not blend in. It seemed funny later, but at the time we might as well have been blacks at a Klan meeting.

As David Duke was being introduced, I got up and went to the back of the room in case he recognized me. He stood before the group and said, "We did it!" The room erupted in applause and shouting. "My victory in Louisiana was a victory for the white majority movement in this country." I stood transfixed. Duke's bodyguards, members of the American Nazi party, surveyed the crowd like members of the Secret Service—they wore dark glasses and three-piece polyester suits. One of them stared at me during the Duke speech and I felt obliged to clap and yell, "Duke! Duke! Duke!" At the end of his speech, Duke said "Listen, the Republican Party of Louisiana is in our camp, ladies and gentlemen. I had to run within that process, because, well, that's where our people are." I looked at the crowd, mostly male—skinheads, Klansmen, T-shirted. It seemed incredible that I was listening to a man who had run as a Republican just two weeks ago and was now telling these bigots that his victory was a victory for them. It was like I was in on a dirty little secret.

When Duke had finished, Linda jumped up and said rather loudly, "I've had enough of this!" I tried to hustle her out, muttering under my breath, "Be quiet, they're watching us," while I smiled and spoke to people as we left. It was a nerve-wracking experience. We were both so rattled that we skipped the press conference afterward. This is when Duke was photographed shaking hands with Art Jones, chairman of the American Nazi party. Jones got into a scuffle with a reporter, pushing him and calling him a "low-life scumbag."

Duke returned to Louisiana and apologized to the legislature for the incident in Chicago. In a letter addressed to all the representatives he explained that Jones was some "Nazi kook" whom he had never seen before and that the Populist party meeting was a "conservative anti tax" rally. Moreover, he continued:

> Because of my controversial Klan background and my dabbling in far-right politics as a teenager, the media saw this as a great opportunity to suggest that I have connections with the politics of extremism. I reject categorically racial or religious intolerance. Furthermore, I am diametrically opposed to the totalitarian policies of both Communism and Nazism. Both those ideologies I find personally abhorrent.
>
> . . . I also repudiate any efforts of extremist groups to capitalize on my election victory. My victory was a victory for true equal rights and greater understanding and not intolerance and discrimination.

One of my friends in the legislature sent me a copy of Duke's letter. It was unbelievable audacity for the darling of the Populist party to tell the Louisiana legislature that he repudiated "any efforts of extremist groups to capitalize on my election victory." That was the whole purpose of his talk in Chicago—to present his victory in Louisiana as a blueprint for other extremists to use in their campaigns.

I immediately went to see the state Republican party chairman, Billy Nungesser. He was troubled by Duke's visit to Chicago. I believe that he was genuinely turned off by the Nazi incident but wanted to keep a lid on things. Nungesser's approach to leadership is to control and contain, and he feared that publicizing this event might give Duke the attention he craved. I must say, though, that while his arguments seemed tactically sound, I was disturbed that he did not seem to share my visceral distaste for David Duke.

## April 1989

I gave one interview to WWL-TV on the Chicago convention and this aired at 10:30 P.M. on Sunday, April 1. In that time slot it was not widely seen and only contained a brief statement of mine on the subject. This program, however, was sent to the Republican National Committee, and I was contacted by Dan Beck, a former Southern field coordinator who had been in Louisiana for the Treen race. He told me that Lee Atwater was deeply concerned about David Duke, and that the RNC wanted to send a field person to meet with me and look at the research I had on Duke. I agreed to help them out, and the staff person called me and arranged a day and time to fly to New Orleans. Meanwhile, I thought that it would be appropriate to notify the state chairman that an RNC representative was coming to meet me, so I called Billy Nungesser to inform him of this. He became agitated and told me he did not want any of "those national people" down here messing around. He thought that it would backfire if Duke found out that the national party was involved again. Nungesser's ears were still ringing from the calls he received from irate Republicans who were angry over the national party's censure of Duke.

Nungesser told me that he was going to call Atwater and tell him to call off the dogs, that he intended to handle the situation. I agreed that it was reasonable to try and work things out ourselves. Billy talked about raising money to research the issue, and I was assured that he wanted to address this problem. The visit by the RNC staffer was canceled.

Meanwhile, my friend and Tulane University colleague, Lance Hill suggested that we try and see if Duke was still selling Nazi books now that he was a state legislator. Many people argued with us that Duke had changed, that his Nazi "stuff" was in the past. Hill, a student of the far right for ten years, was curious to find out whether Duke was using his legislative office as a vehicle to promote his book business.

Lance phoned the number listed under National Association for the Advancement of White People (NAAWP) in the directory. The phone was answered, "David Duke, District 81." Lance then asked the receptionist if they had a copy of *The Turner Diaries* for sale. *The Turner Diaries*, written by William Pierce, a longtime Nazi activist and one of Duke's mentors, is a novel about guerrilla warfare and violence against Jews and blacks. According to the Anti-Defamation League of B'nai B'rith, *The Turner Diaries* was the blueprint for the Order, an underground terrorist group founded by members of Pierce's

National Alliance. The Order was responsible for a series of criminal and terrorist activities in 1983-84; it is most notorious for its assassination of Alan Berg, a Denver talk-show host in 1984.

The NAAWP receptionist asked Lance to hold for a minute and returned to say that, yes, they did have a copy of the book. He asked for the price and thanked her.

Lance and I decided that I would go over to Duke's office and buy *The Turner Diaries*. A colleague of mine at Tulane, David Hagy, went along with me because I was not comfortable going by myself. We entered the basement office at 500 North Arnoult. The reception area was empty except for a desk and a broken chair. There were wires hanging down from the ceiling, and people kept walking through the reception area without acknowledging our presence. Finally, David stopped one of the people and said we were interested in purchasing a book. The receptionist looked a little suspicious, so I said that we wanted to buy *The Turner Diaries*. She got the book and gave me a receipt from American Books. Then we left.

## May 1989

On May 24 and 26 we purchased more books and some tapes from Duke's legislative/NAAWP offices. I sent another researcher so that suspicion would not be aroused. I instructed the buyers to ask for *Imperium* by Francis Parker Yockey, *Hitler Was My Friend, The Myth of the Six Million, The New Mythology of Equality, Hate Nanny* by Odis Cochran, and two cassette tapes: the *Three Bigots* and *George Lincoln Rockwell v. NAACP*.

The researcher who went on May 24 said that she was greeted in the reception area by a woman in her late twenties. The researcher said that she wanted to buy some books and the receptionist told her to wait. She disappeared into a storage area. The researcher observed that the office was "shabby." There was a small, well-worn desk and a single telephone on the desk. On one side of the desk were stacks of newspapers and on the other side were cardboard boxes. At the rear of the office was a washing machine and clothes dryer. In a back room one wall was lined with shelves containing stacks of David Duke and NAAWP T-shirts. The floor was littered with debris.

After about five minutes, a man entered from the storage room. He introduced himself saying, "My name is Chris Winter, like the season." The researcher asked for *Hitler Was My Friend* under the pretext that the book was for boyfriend. Winter went back into the storage room.

A few minutes later he returned with Hitler's *Mein Kampf* (published by Angriff Press in Los Angeles, California, and distributed by American Books, P. O. Box 10453, New Orleans, Louisiana 70181), stating that he was out of *Hitler Was My Friend*. Winter was animated as he explained that *Mein Kampf* was the "one book" about Hitler everyone should read. The researcher bought the book for seven dollars. When Winter returned with her change, he gave her several NAAWP pamphlets and copies of *NAAWP News*, urging her to pass the literature around to her friends.

When she asked to browse through the books in stock, Winter declined. He then accompanied her out to her car. As she was leaving she noticed in her rear-view mirror that he was copying down her license plate number.

Two days later the researcher returned for another buy. Chris Winter greeted her warmly. He asked her to wait because he had something for her. He returned with a copy of *Imperium* and a cassette tape entitled *Rockwell v. NAACP*. The researcher bought both at fifteen dollars each. She and Winter then struck up a conversation. She commented on books lying on the desk and began to browse through them. Winter gave all of them to her for free. The titles included *Zoological Subspecies of Man, Racial Difference in Mental Growth and School Achievement, Ethnic Group Differences, The Control of Evolution in Man, Race Differences—20 Years Later, Did Six Million Really Die? The Truth at Last, The Racial History of Scandinavia, Heredity and Environment: Major Findings from Twin Studies of Ability, Personality and Interests*, and *The American Melting Pot: Its Meaning to Us*.

Now we had the evidence that Duke was (1) still selling Nazi books and (2) doing so under the auspices of his legislative office. Lance and I pondered what to do at this point. We consulted with the Reverend James Stovall, of Baton Rouge, the executive director of the Louisiana Interchurch Conference. I had first spoken with Stovall by telephone after Duke's election, and he was very supportive of our efforts. Stovall set up a meeting in Baton Rouge with state representatives Kip Holden, Randy Roach, and Mitch Landrieu to discuss the situation. Also present was Leonard Zeskind, research director of the Center for Democratic Renewal in Atlanta (formerly known as the Anti-Klan Network). We discussed how best to release the materials—whether it should be done by political leaders, religious leaders, or a combination of both. We did not reach any definitive conclusions, except an agreement that Duke's involvement with them should be publicized.

It was my opinion that I should bring this up at the upcoming Republican State Central Committee meeting on June 3. I also wanted to propose a motion of either censure or investigation into the charges that Duke was using his legislative office to distribute Nazi books. I had submitted a motion of investigation to Billy Nungesser on May 22, 1989. He phoned me right away, very concerned. He told me that I was going to stir up a hornet's nest and help Duke by giving him publicity. He did not want to raise the matter at the meeting and inferred that my motion would never make it out of committee. I agreed to find another way to bring it up.

## June 1989

On June 3, the Louisiana Republican State Central Committee met in the chamber of the House of Representatives at the state capitol in Baton Rouge. Although word was not officially out about the books, a few people did know of them. I had the books with me in my bag and showed them to interested persons. David Duke was at the meeting, wandering around the floor of the House chamber, shaking hands. I had yet to meet him. I was sitting with John Treen when Duke approached John with his hand outstretched. John refused to shake his hand and proceeded to lambast Duke for spreading rumors that he (Treen) had been arrested. Treen also let him have it for spreading the false rumor that he was a child molester and let Duke know that he was facing a lawsuit on that one. Duke denied ever making those comments. John said, "You are a lying, character-assassinating son of a bitch." I decided that Treen did not need any help; he was handling Duke quite nicely. I left them in heated discussion.

A few minutes later, however, Duke followed me across the chamber. He held out his hand and said, "Hi, I'm David Duke." Then he said, "You know, I never had seen Art Jones before in my life." Obviously, he was aware that I had attended the Chicago convention where Nazi party chairman Art Jones was photographed shaking his hand. I replied, "Oh, come on. He was one of your bodyguards."

"I swear, Beth, I had never seen the guy before in my life."

"Then what were you doing at a convention where Nazis were hanging out?"

At this point, the meeting was called to order and I had to take my seat.

Duke was behind the railing of the chamber holding hands with a Nordic-looking blonde. He stared at me throughout much of the session. Finally, toward the end of the meeting, I got up to get coffee. The sergeant at arms informed me that I could not bring coffee on the floor of the House, so I sat on a couch behind the railing. The next thing I knew this voice says "Beth." I turned to my right and there was Duke, seated next to me on the couch. He had his arm around the back of the couch and was leaning toward me.

He wanted to talk about the books I had bought from his legislative office. I said I thought it was awful that he sold propaganda claiming the Holocaust never happened. He told me that I just misunderstood him, that he meant no harm to Jewish people. He also told me that it was his belief that race was the defining element for civilizations, and that race mixing had caused the downfall of many civilizations. As he talked about race, his face took on an eerie glow and he became more animated. I sat there sort of fascinated, and I finally said, "You really believe all this, don't you?" And he replied, "Oh, yes, it's a religion for me." Then I asked him about his mentor, Jim Lindsay, who was murdered in 1975. Lindsay was a Nazi and Klan activist in the New Orleans area and a surrogate father to Duke. Lindsay's estranged wife was charged with the murder but was acquitted. I said, "David, I find it a strange coincidence that Lindsay was murdered and you became grand wizard of the Klan."

"Yes, some people think I killed him," Duke said. I told him that I did not think so, but that I did not believe Lindsay's wife was guilty either. Duke responded, rather bitterly, that of course she was. (Later, I thought that it was an odd conversation to have with a legislator in the state capitol.)

At this point we had been talking for about twenty minutes. I looked up and, much to my amusement, noticed that about half of the members of the State Central Committee had swiveled in their chairs to watch Duke and me instead of the speaker at the podium. The sergeant at arms, Tommy Gaudet, was signaling to me asking me if I was okay. I nodded affirmatively. Gaudet would have been glad to muscle Duke away if necessary, I gathered.

The meeting closed and Duke said that he wanted to introduce me to his girlfriend. He brought me up to her and said, "This is Ginger Swenson. She has a degree from Loyola." I was a little startled by this strange introduction.

Afterward, Jason Berry, a local writer who is an expert on hate groups, suggested that we take advantage of the Simon Wiesenthal exhibit that was being set up in the rotunda of the state capitol. The Wiesenthal Center of Los Angeles, California, was taking an exhibit of photographs of the Holocaust around the country. Jason said it would provide an excellent backdrop for a press conference. On June 6, when the exhibit opened to the public, the media reported that a Holocaust survivor confronted Duke, who was lingering in the rotunda looking at the photographs.

That night in New Orleans, people who were concerned about the election of David Duke met at Loyola University. The group later evolved into the Louisiana Coalition against Racism and Nazism. After the meeting, where we discussed the Nazi books, I decided to strike quickly. Lance prepared a press release, and the next morning David Hagy and I drove to Baton Rouge to present our case to the media.

Hagy and I met the press in the hallway outside of the House committee rooms where, coincidentally, Duke himself was in a meeting that day. As we distributed our packets Duke appeared and began signing autographs for admirers. He was oblivious to us until Robyn Eckings of WVUE-8 in New Orleans grabbed my copy of *Did Six Million Really Die? The Truth at Last* and waved the book in his face on camera. When Eckings asked, "Are you selling this out of your legislative office?" Duke's face reddened, and he asked her excitedly who had brought her that book. Eckings pointed at me. Duke, with obvious agitation, turned and asked me why I was doing this.

"You're treating me like Salman Rushdie!" he said to me, then turned on his heel and hurried away from us, pursued up the stairs by camera crews and reporters until he reached the sanctity of the floor of the legislature, where the press is not allowed. This bizarre reference to the author of *The Satanic Verses*, hiding from Muslim assassins, was vintage Duke, always the martyr. Reporters told me later that Duke called his office in Metairie from the House floor and warned his staff not to sell any more books.

The "Nazi books" incident was considered a successful hit at Duke's claims that he had changed. Chairman Nungesser called to congratulate me after he saw the media coverage. However, he said that the State Central Committee should not say anything about Duke. Nungesser still clung to the idea that Duke was not a racist but just an opportunist.

I began to suspect that there was more agreement with Duke on the race issue than I had heretofore believed. (An example of Nungesser's position on Duke later surfaced in the *New Republic* of September 18-29, 1989, when he was quoted as saying that Duke was "an opportunist, rotten to the core" but argued that censuring him would only give him publicity and only stoke the antiestablishment fire. Nungesser further claimed that only a small core of Duke's supporters was racist, and that the rest of the people were drawn to Duke because of his position on taxes, affirmative action, and so forth.)

On June 22, the still-unnamed Louisiana Coalition against Racism and Nazism held a meeting at my apartment. Present were Lance Hill, the Reverend James Stovall, Professor Lawrence Powell of Tulane, Professor Paul Sanzenbach of Louisiana State University, and myself. We were discussing strategies for dealing with David Duke.

About ten o'clock the phone rang and a voice said, "Beth, this is David Duke." At first I thought it was a joke, but the voice was unmistakable. It was a strange coincidence. I told him that I had company and asked if he could call later. He called back in thirty minutes and we talked for three hours. In the background he kept playing a song by Mike and the Mechanics entitled "Can You Hear Me Running?"; he said it was one of his favorites. Ever the media creature, he was providing his own incidental music.

We talked about Franklin D. Roosevelt's "treason" at Pearl Harbor, a man named Dr. Schweiler who claims that there is no equality between the races, India and its caste system, Greek culture, blondes in India, how Iceland is a superior culture, sperm banks, Duke's love of nature, hiking in Vientiane (Laos) during the Vietnam conflict, and on and on. When I got off the phone, I was very tired and a bit disoriented. Duke was now no longer an abstract entity but a real person.

## July-August 1989

Over the next few weeks I spent a good bit of time in Baton Rouge observing Duke and his working relationship with members of the legislature. He and I got together several times to talk, and now and then he would sit with me in the back of the chamber. It was difficult at times to maintain a psychological distance from him, because he is a master of political courtship. He would call me occasionally at home and talk about Jews and blacks.

I asked him one day what he wanted from me and he said, "I want you to hold a press conference and say you were wrong about me." I replied that that was an unlikely prospect considering the fact that I totally disagreed with his racial theories. Suddenly, his demeanor changed from affable to a bit menacing. "Well, Beth, remember, I haven't attacked you—yet."

On August 4, Duke invited me to a lunch meeting at the Ming Palace restaurant in Metairie. He brought with him two books, *The Six Million Reconsidered* and *The Grand Dragon*—the former is about how the Holocaust did not happen, and the latter is a novel about a Jewish reporter who has an overnight fling with a grand dragon of the Ku Klux Klan. *The Grand Dragon* is supposed to be based on a real-life incident. Its author—a woman—was a writer for *The Times* of London. Duke claimed that it is based on him but denied ever sleeping with the writer. In any case, he was very proud of the book and seemed oblivious to the unflattering portrait it paints of him. Any kind of publicity makes him happy, apparently.

On the way to the restaurant our conversation turned to the "Nazi books" episode. Duke told me that whenever I "pull a stunt like that," I would "stir up the Jews." He complained about receiving death threats and said that incidents such as publicizing the fact that he sold Nazi books were "going to get me killed." I told him I would not feel responsible if he were assassinated, and he said, "I hope you'll feel a little guilty if I get killed." I told him that I would feel a little guilty if that would make him happy. That is the patented Duke charm for you—guilt.

As we ate, he propped up the *Six Million* book on the table in front of his plate and pointed out passages from the Talmud that he claimed proved the Satanic qualities of the Jewish people. Talking about Nazi Germany, he said: "Rudolf Hess was a great man, because of his loyalty to Hitler and because of his attempts at peacemaking. He should have received the Nobel Peace Prize for his flight to England." He especially admired Hess's skill as a pilot and observed what a fear it was to make that flight successfully. He concluded somberly, "One of the greatest travesties of justice was his imprisonment in Spandau Prison." I remembered that the *NAAWP News* and other right-wing publications often featured the campaign to have Hess released. Hess, who stunned the world in 1940 by flying to England solo to offer terms personally to Winston Churchill, had been Hitler's closest deputy since the 1920s, but by 1940 he was losing favor in Hitler's inner circle.

Then came the bone chiller. "And Dr. Mengele," Duke said.

"Oh, you like him, too?" I asked. Josef Mengele was the monsters' monster among the Nazi death camp sadists, the surgeon who treated prisoners, even children, like laboratory rats.

Duke leaned over on his elbow with a confiding look and said, "Beth, he had a Ph.D.! Do you think he would have jeopardized his career by performing experiments on people with so many witnesses around? Come on!"

"It would seem illogical," I replied, feeling a little queasy. Duke's seeming naiveté can be stomach turning. His calm sincerity gives one the sense of dining with an ax murderer.

He talked some about Mengele's research on twins and how interesting it was. Then he began to rail about the injustices done to Adolf Eichmann, the death camp superintendent captured in South America in the 1960s and executed after his trial in Israel in 1961. Now my head was spinning. Here I was, seated at a normal restaurant in the heart of suburban New Orleans, and this normal-looking man was arguing like a personal injury lawyer for Nazis. It was surreal.

Duke was on a roll now. Auschwitz, he said, was never an extermination camp, merely a labor camp. The stench in the air, he said, was from the manufacture of rubber, not from bodies. On a napkin he drew a map of the Mauthausen "labor" camp, explained that he had visited the place, and assured me that there was no such thing as "gas showers." Zyklon-B, the killer gas, he said was only a pesticide used to kill lice and was used only for delousing. If Zyklon-B had been used to kill people, it would have required massive doses of the stuff, which would leave a residue known as "Prussian Blue." He said he had personally examined the walls of the camp and there was no evidence of Prussian Blue.

"What about all of the bodies?" I asked. His answer was that most of the people had died of typhus, some of starvation—as if cruelty were natural. Besides, he claimed, a lot of the photographs of bodies were "doctored" and fakes. As he got deeper into the story, his eyes lit up and he became more and more animated.

"You see, Beth, the extermination camps were a myth concocted by Hollywood to help create the state of Israel." When I asked him why Hollywood would invent such a story, he replied, "Because [it is] controlled by the Jews!"

Duke also talked about how there was no "Final Solution" as history tells us. There is no record of Hitler ordering the extermination of the Jews, he said. The Final Solution was merely a plan to segregate the Jews from the rest of society, much like we segregated the Japanese during World War II. He used Hitler's own reasoning that Jews were enemies of the state who supported communism.

"Oh, come on, David. You don't believe all of this?" I said.

"Beth, don't you think that transporting the Jews to Poland and other far away locales would be stupid if Hitler wanted to kill them? Why would he transport these people all over the place, make a big deal out of it if they were going to be killed? They were just going to labor camps." He said this as if human slavery were a reasonable alternative and as if the bones of millions and the testimony of both victims and ex-Nazis had not convinced a generation of Hitler's guilt.

At this point I had had enough. He invited me to continue the discussion at his office but I declined, wanting to get away from him. During our meeting Duke had informed me that he would be making his annual pilgrimage to Bavaria that month (August). I laughed and told him I thought that was pretty funny—he did not see the humor in this. Duke does not have a sense of irony.

## September 1989

He disappeared for the next four weeks and we were out of touch. When he returned, he looked somewhat different. His face seemed redder and tighter. I knew that Duke was a fan of cosmetic surgery (he lauds it in his sex manual, *Finders Keepers*), and he told me that he had had a nose job a long time ago. He said it was because he had fallen asleep at the wheel while delivering newspapers in New Orleans as a teenager—his car ran into a tree and he broke his nose. He insisted that it wasn't cosmetic surgery but a necessary medical procedure to fix his nose.

Anyway, Duke had a new face. (I later heard that he had had a chemical peel and needed to be out of sight for a while. When ABC's "Prime Time Live" came to town in October, he said that he had gone to Brazil to look at rain forests and write articles on ecology.)

The next Republican State Central Committee meeting was scheduled for September 23, 1989. There was a lot speculation as to whether a motion to censure Duke would be introduced. At first, I had no plans to do so, but my colleague Neil Curran, a member of the evangelical wing of the party, said that he intended to introduce a censure motion. Neil had worked in John Treen's legislative race against Duke and shared my distress over Duke's anti-Semitism and bigotry. He felt strongly that Duke's agenda was opposed to the Judeo-Christian ethic, and he had openly denounced Duke since the election.

Curran was unfairly characterized as a man with a vendetta because of Treen's loss to Duke. Actually, his revulsion was based on an entirely different reason. After sifting through research on Duke for hours on end, he came to a realization that this man was trying to build a white power movement under the nose of the Republican party.

The week preceding the State Central Committee meeting, Curran was featured in several articles about the pending censure. One in particular, written by Jason Berry for *Gambit*, a New Orleans weekly, received a lot of attention. Curran was taking a lot of heat for his decision, and I felt that it was important that I publicly sign on and support him. On Wednesday, September 20, Curran and I met and drafted a resolution condemning Duke's politics of racism and bigotry, spelling out detailed examples of his recent ties to neo-Nazi groups. The resolution called for censure by the state Republican leadership. We realized that censure carried little weight but felt that it was important that a moral statement be made. It was, after all, a decision our national leadership had reached without flinching.

The chairman of the Resolutions Committee was state representative Charles Lancaster of Metairie, an apparent Duke sympathizer. Since Lancaster was not very likely to be pleased at the prospect of moving a Duke censure vote through this committee, particularly with national TV cameras focused on him, Curran assumed that Lancaster would try to derail the resolution on a procedural move. He checked with the parliamentarian for the committee, Robert Edgeworth, to make sure the resolution was being submitted in a timely and correct manner.

Edgeworth assured Curran that as long as the resolution was delivered into the hands of Chairman Lancaster in advance, then it was properly submitted. Assuming the worst, Curran also got a ruling from the parliamentarian that if Lancaster tabled the resolution in committee, Curran—as a member of the Resolutions Committee—could still bring it up for discussion in the form of a minority report.

The night before the vote, I arrived at the Ramada Inn in Baton Rouge, where out-of-town members were staying. Stopping by Secretary of State Fox McKeithen's hospitality suite, I encountered Bill Nungesser. He was very displeased with the censure move and said that he wanted to speak privately with Curran and me. Later that evening, we met with him and the Reverend Billy McCormack in the hospitality suite of state Senator Ben Bagert. The meeting was tense and lengthy.

The presence of McCormack was particularly significant, since he represented the powerful evangelical bloc of the GOP central committee, the so-called born-agains. The born-agains had been elected, district by district, across the state during the March 1988 Super Tuesday presidential primary in Louisiana to support televangelist Pat Robertson's bid for the Republican presidential nomination.

The nickname of the evangelical members denoted a certain naiveté about politics, since most of them were freshmen members of the committee as well as newly registered Republicans who switched parties so they could run for the central committee. Though it was new to politics, there was nothing amateurish about the numbers the Robertson flock had rolled up across the state the year before. At least 60 of the 140 members of the GOP State Central Committee were now born-agains who voted as a bloc, and they were becoming sophisticated in finding the dozen or so votes necessary to achieve a majority.

McCormack, their leader, a Baptist minister who insisted on being called "Dr.," planted himself in the only available chair in the room. Nungesser sat on one of two beds, while Curran and I sat together on the other facing him. Chain-smoking and talking in a voice like Marlon Brando in *The Godfather*, Nungesser browbeat Curran and me for two hours. He always calls me "Baby" when he is not mad at me and "Beth" when he is. Tonight, I was Beth.

"You have no right to do this!" he said repeatedly. How dare people like Curran and myself assume the role of declaring David Duke a moral disgrace to the state party? That was the gist of the interrogation, which Curran and I had expected. McCormack just watched this performance, for the most part, from his "throne" as Nungesser did his damnedest to overpower us. We could have left, of course, but felt it was important to hear them out.

It was important, too, not to be argumentative, so we kept the response simple: "We just want to follow in the footsteps of the national Republican Party and censure David Duke."

After a while, Nungesser lost his patience and declared that, in fact, the national party had never censured Duke at all. He was quite insistent about this. I was reminded of

Duke himself, pressing me to apologize for exposing his racist activities. Only Nungesser was anything but charming in his demeanor to Curran and me.

As you go down the Duke food chain, things get less and less charming. I discovered this at the Chicago Populist party convention, where the delegates resembled nothing so much as a casting call for extras in another Mad Max sequel.

"Billy," I told the party chairman, under the eye of the born-agains' leader, "he was censured by the national party a week after the election. It was all over the newspapers."

He maintained that I was imagining things.

This was ridiculous. I was getting angrier and angrier. Curran, thank God, kept his composure, even when Nungesser implied that the censure vote was just a publicity stunt for those of us proposing it.

Finally, I blew up.

"Listen, Billy, yesterday I received a phone call that said if I get up in front of the committee tomorrow and move to censure Duke, the caller will put a bullet in my head."

Suddenly, McCormack, who had been listening impassively to all this, sat up and relieved the nonplussed Nungesser. It was your classic bad cop/good cop routine—first the rubber hose and then the prayers.

The reverend doctor said something to the effect that I had gone through a lot. Duke, he said, convincingly, was evil. That much we should all agree with. Nungesser was silent for the first time since we had entered the room.

I felt that McCormack was genuinely distressed over the situation and wanted to address it, so we discussed a compromise. What we worked out was that Nungesser would recognize Curran, have him read the motion of censure, and then offer a motion to form a committee to investigate the charges for purposes of censure at the next meeting. This way, we would go around the Resolutions Committee and its reluctant chairman, Charles Lancaster. We shook hands all around, and then McCormack asked us to join hands and pray over our decision. It was a strange moment—Nungesser, Curran, McCormack, and I huddled together holding hands, praying for God's blessing.

I went to bed that night believing that we had reached an agreement and that at least McCormack, if not Nungesser, was aware of the problems Duke posed for the party. But unbeknownst to me, the next morning Nungesser and Lancaster had figured out their own compromise, pulling McCormack in on the deal. "Tag" Livingston, a New Orleans central committee member and retired rear admiral, was selected to derail our resolution by moving to have it tabled. McCormack's people a near-majority of the State Central Committee, were instructed to vote to table it. I was sitting in my seat thinking that everything was still in order. I noticed Lancaster huddled in the back of the House chamber with Duke, which disturbed me, but I shook it off. Then, someone came up to me and said that Nungesser and McCormack were double-crossing me. I was told that Curran and I would be allowed to read the resolution but that it would be tabled.

I was furious. McCormack was sitting two seats in front of me, and, resisting the urge to grab him by his hairpiece, I grasped his chair and spun it around. "You deceived me," I said in a low voice. "Then you prayed with me, and I believed that you wanted to help."

"Beth, I swear, I have nothing to do with the motion to table," McCormack replied, looking a little shaken.

"Don't hand me that, reverend, you control the votes in that caucus," I replied. "What bothers me more than anything is that you are a minister, and you lied to me. I will never forget this," I said and went back to my seat. I then sent a message up to Chairman Nungesser by courier. It read:

> Dear Billy,
>
> You double-crossed me. I will never ever let you forget this.
>
> Sincerely yours,
> Beth Rickey

At this point messages started flying between the podium and the area where Neil and I were seated. The thing that really floored me was that in the very act of the double-cross, Nungesser and McCormack were denying any responsibility. Sometimes I thought they were as nervy as Duke, denying in the face of hard evidence.

Neil and I were recognized by the chairman. Knowing that we had been shanghaied, I just stood next to Neil. The moment Neil finished reading our resolution, Tag Livingston jumped up and moved that it be tabled. It was seconded. Nungesser called for a voice vote and declared that the ayes had it. A division of the House was called and I asked that the committee be polled so that the members could go on record. Nungesser ruled me out of order. We proceeded to a secret ballot and the results were never published. I later learned that only about 25 out of the 140 members voted with Neil and me.

After the meeting, Livingston was asked why he moved to table the motion. He said that although Duke was a "charlatan," further investigation of his record would keep him in the eye of the media, thereby enhancing his celebrity. I told the press that I was very disappointed in the party's inability to confront a racist in their midst.

As I left the chamber I was nearly assaulted by angry people. I have gone head-to-head with Duke supporters on radio talk shows, and I have interviewed Klansmen and neo-Nazis, but nothing compares to the insulting behavior I encountered from fellow Republicans on the State Central Committee. You would have thought that I had just made a motion to censure Ronald Reagan. I thought one little old lady was going to hit me, she was so mad.

An irate member of the evangelical caucus followed me down the steps of the capitol. I tried to ignore his shouts but he pursued me all the way to my car. The man accused me of staging all of this to make money to get publicity for myself. At this point I stopped in my tracks, turned around, and said, "I don't like Nazis. I especially don't like them running around in the Republican party. If you have a problem with that, then I suggest that there is something seriously wrong with you and the other 114 members of the State Central Committee who voted to ignore this matter." The last thing I remember hearing as I got into my car was, "Now wait a minute, I never said I liked Nazis!"

What a twilight zone, I thought. I had been standing in front of the state capitol in 1989 arguing with someone over condemning an open racist and Nazi sympathizer. I just did not understand how anyone could look at David Duke, listen to him for any length of time, know of his background, and not want to put garlic around their neck.

# THE RACE FROM HELL*

Tyler Bridges

As soon as David Duke lost the Senate election to Bennett Johnston in October 1990, his legions of ardent supporters and opponents both asked: Will he run for governor the following year? With his strong showing in defeat, Duke had established himself as a formidable potential challenger to the incumbent governor, Charles (Buddy) Roemer III.

Roemer, however, was unconcerned. He thought Duke had run strongly against Johnston because voters didn't care much who they put in the Senate—they seemed to view it as a job in far-off Washington held by someone they had little contact with—and had used the election to vent their anger by sending a message to Washington. Louisianians, in contrast, cared deeply about who served as their governor, Roemer felt, because the governor directly affected their taxes, their children's schools, their highways, the safety of their streets, and many other things big and small. In Louisiana, the governor is "the Kingfish," a legacy from Huey Long, wielding enormous power to reward friends and punish enemies by offering or withholding government contracts and patronage appointments to powerful state boards.

Early polls comforted Roemer. They showed him with about 35 percent of the vote, Edwin Edwards with 25 percent and Duke 15 percent. Roemer also dismissed Duke's Senate showing—and the fact that Duke in 1991 raised as much money as Johnston—because he thought Johnston was a lackluster candidate. Roemer had no doubts that he would tear Duke apart if Duke entered the governor's race. Roemer was the dragon-slayer, a title bestowed on him after he won election in 1987 by defeating Edwin Edwards—who had served longer as governor than any of his predecessors and had been the state's most powerful governor since Huey Long. Roemer ran first in the October 1987 primary in a five-man field with 33 percent of the vote. Edwards finished second with 28 percent and, at 1:30 a.m. on election night, shocked his supporters by announcing he would not contest the runoff. Suddenly, Buddy Roemer was governor.

*First published as chapter 9 in Tyler Bridges, *The Rise of David Duke* (Jackson, Mississippi: University Press of Mississippi, © 1994), 194-237. Reprinted with the kind permission of the author and the publisher.

A four-term congressman from Northwest Louisiana, Roemer had won by promising to take on the sacred cows and shake up the system. "The Roemer Revolution," he called it. He had started the race the longest of long shots, at 1 percent in the polls. But he catapulted ahead of the other four candidates in the final month of the campaign when the state's major newspapers endorsed him, and he aired tough-talking, plainspoken television ads in which he pledged to clean up Louisiana's corrupt politics, improve education, fight crime, cut taxes, eliminate wasteful government spending, and crack down on polluters that had made the state the most befouled in the Union.

"We must free Louisiana from the grip of political corruption," he exhorted. "And that's going to take more than just new faces, new rhetoric or new style. It's going to take a revolution in Louisiana's politics, government, education and economy—and that's what my campaign is all about."

By making his appeal directly to voters through television ads and news stories, Roemer, an evangelical, mesmerizing speaker, eschewed the traditional approach of seeking endorsements from elected officials, local power brokers and the courthouse crowd. He also broke with tradition by refusing to accept cash donations, contributions over $5,000 per donor—at the time there was no dollar limit—and contributions from political action committees.

Roemer was raised on the 2,000-acre Scopean Plantation, ten miles south of Bossier City, by parents who were unusually passionate about educating their five children. "They would pore over books and learn world history before school in the morning, debate issues of the day at the breakfast and supper tables and sweat in the North Louisiana cotton and soybean fields in the afternoon," *Times-Picayune* reporter John McQuaid wrote in a penetrating 1987 profile of Roemer.

> There was no television in the house. A green blackboard mounted on a wall in the dining room became the battlefield for regular mealtime debates on anything from foreign policy to physics. . . . The parents raised their children with a mission: They would take their citizenship seriously, and would lend their intelligence to public service. Buddy Roemer, the eldest, undertook the mission with singular zeal.

Valedictorian of Bossier High School's class of 1960, Roemer headed off to Harvard at age sixteen, where he earned an undergraduate degree and a master's degree at the business school. He returned to work for the family business and also formed two banks. He became active in politics in 1971 when his father, Charles Roemer II, managed the campaign of a reform candidate from Acadiana named Edwin Edwards. After winning, Edwards named Charles Roemer the commissioner of administration, the state's most powerful position after the governor.

Buddy Roemer, who managed North Louisiana during the 1971 Edwards campaign, founded a political consulting firm and managed several successful campaigns before winning a seat in the United States House of Representatives in 1980. During his seven years in the House, he earned a reputation as a maverick who repeatedly angered the

Democratic leadership by refusing to go along with their programs. "Often wrong, never in doubt," House Speaker Thomas (Tip) O'Neill said of Roemer. Bucking the Democratic leadership played well at home, however, as he was reelected three times without opposition.

As a political consultant, Roemer received government contracts and additional favors from Edwards and other public officials he had helped elect. But as an antiestablishment member of Congress, Roemer grew uncomfortable with Louisiana's political tradition. He also blamed that tradition for ruining his father. Charles Roemer in 1981 was sent to federal prison along with New Orleans Mafia boss Carlos Marcello for conspiring to sell influence in the awarding of state insurance contracts. During the fifteen months Charles Roemer served in a federal prison in Fort Worth, his son often visited him on trips back to his congressional district.

Buddy Roemer, a bantamweight at five feet seven inches and 145 pounds, attacked Louisiana's political system with a vengeance during the 1987 gubernatorial campaign, aiming much of his fire at Edwin Edwards, whom he blamed for his father's troubles. "I want a governor who puts our pocketbook ahead of his," Roemer said repeatedly. He and his group of young, idealistic aides—dubbed the Roemeristas—took office, and for more than a year they won a string of legislative victories that reshaped the state: teacher pay increases, a teacher evaluation program, tougher environmental enforcement, strict limits on campaign financing. To balance the state budget, Roemer sold off government airplanes, cut many popular programs and borrowed $1 billion. He had staved off Louisiana's bankruptcy, and now he moved to his biggest gambit yet—a restructuring of the state system that he said would put Louisiana on solid fiscal standing for years. It was put before the voters in April 1989. And with newly elected state representative David Duke leading the charge against it, the measure was defeated.

It was a crushing blow for Roemer and his so-called revolution. His enemies in the legislature counterattacked, calling him arrogant, snide, and sanctimonious. Allies of Edwards, they plotted against Roemer and began derailing his reform measures. The revolution was becoming untracked. But the worst was yet to come for Roemer. One day in September, his wife, Patti, a former state fair queen who had grown to hate the demands of political life, walked out of the governor's mansion with their ten-year-old son, Dakota. Roemer was heartbroken. "It was probably the first time in the governor's life that he felt a little bit out of control," said Danny Walker, a Baptist minister and close family friend who became his spiritual adviser.

Roemer was an unusual elected official. He was a diabetic who needed two shots of insulin a day. He was a loner who didn't like other politicians. He brought books to football games and often failed to return phone calls, which infuriated many people, especially supporters. When he went to his favorite restaurant in Baton Rouge, a Mexican food place called the Superior Bar & Grill, he would barely talk with any of the other patrons and would sit at a table with his back to the crowd. Roemer's media consultant, Raymond Strother marveled at his behavior. The many politicians Strother had advised would have worked the room, shaking hands with everyone, and would then have sat facing the crowd so that people would come by to visit.

Patti Roemer's leaving reinforced her husband's antisocial manner. Roemer went into a shell. He canceled appointments and sat by the mansion's swimming pool during the day with strict instructions that he not be disturbed. At night he had trouble sleeping. He desperately missed his wife, and all he cared about was winning her back.

In January, Walker organized a three-day inspirational seminar called "Adventures in Attitudes" and invited the governor's top aides and Patti. Early on during the retreat, Walker urged everybody to put a rubber band around their wrist. "From now on and the rest of the seminar, when somebody says a negative thought about himself or puts you down, you go, 'Cancel. Cancel.'" Roemer's aides rolled their eyes in disbelief—and Patti on the second day fled.

Roemer didn't give up. He took ballroom dance lessons, went to therapy, and read self-help books provided by Walker. The most important was a New Age bestseller, *All I Really Need to Know I Learned in Kindergarten*, by Robert Fulghum. Following Fulghum's prescription, Roemer sought to "honor" everybody by listening attentively, showing them respect, and trying to fulfill their requests. "Honor," read the sign he hung over his office door.

By now legislators, already unhappy with Roemer's disdain for them, were in open revolt. But with Walker's advice, Roemer decided he could win them over with a positive approach borrowed from Fulghum. He unveiled it in April as he gave the opening address for the 1990 legislative session.

Roemer apologized for his "inflexibility and insensitivity." "Please forgive me, if you can," he asked the legislators. He talked about "listening" and "honor" and "sharing." He said: "Let's say goodby to 'me' and hello to 'we'. . . . Let's say goodbye to the negative and welcome the positive." Then he invited the legislature to "light the campfire . . . I think it's time to gather 'round, hold hands, laugh, share dreams, find common ground, discover our fellowship, refocus our vision, feel the power of the tribal family and start afresh." Twice he referred to Patti as if they were still a couple. Legislators snickered when reporters asked for their reaction afterward. "I think Danny Walkerism had come into play," said state Senator Hank Lauricella. It was, several others legislators said derisively, Roemer's "campfire" speech.

Roemer's problems with the legislature worsened, and by the time the governor's race got under way at the beginning of 1991, legislators throughout the state were bad-mouthing him to their constituents. Still, Roemer and his advisers thought he would easily win reelection. He was a terrific campaigner—few people could give a better speech—and, his aides figured, the field looked weak. The challengers were Louis Lambert, the Democratic chairman of the Public Service Commission, who had faded from view after narrowly losing the 1979 governor's race to Dave Treen; Aaron Broussard, the can-do Democratic mayor of the New Orleans suburb of Kenner, who was unknown statewide; David Duke, whom the Roemer campaign dismissed because of his Nazi and

Klan past; and Edwin Edwards, whom voters had overwhelmingly rejected four years before.

Edwards was the latest in a long line of flamboyant governors from a state that, with its conservative Protestants in the north and its freewheeling, Roman Catholic Cajuns in the South creating a Byzantine political gumbo, seemed to have more in common with a Latin American country than with the rest of the United States. "Every man a king" and "Share the Wealth," Huey Long had shouted during his near-dictatorial reign, when he handed out free textbooks, paved roads, built charity hospitals, and enriched himself and his biggest supporters. Long ruled from 1928 when he was elected governor until he was gunned down in 1935 in the towering state capitol he had just built. Huey's brother, Earl, later served as governor three times and continued the populist tradition, handing out food to the poor that he had just bought at country stores and increasing spending for education and the indigent. In his final term, Earl Long had a mental breakdown, took up with a stripper, and attacked segregationists.

The next great heir of Louisiana's populist tradition was Edwin Edwards, who had been born in a rural part of central Louisiana, the son of a tenant farmer and a midwife. When Edwards was a boy during the Great Depression, his family lived on butter, beans, flour, and other staples from the government. His early hero was President Franklin D. Roosevelt. "I remember when government made it possible for electricity to be brought to my house," he said in a 1991 interview. "I remember when government made it possible for a bus to pick me up and drive me eight miles into town. I remember when government made it possible for me to eat a free, hot lunch at school. I remember when government made books available to me that I otherwise would not have been able to have."

After getting a law degree from LSU, Edwards moved to Crowley, a small town in southwestern Louisiana. With his bayou charm, razor-sharp intelligence, and intuitive understanding of human nature, he built a successful law practice and won a string of elections that took him from the Crowley City Council to the Louisiana Senate to Congress. In 1971, he put together a coalition of blacks, blue-collar workers, and Cajuns to edge Bennett Johnston in the Democratic runoff. Edwards then trounced David Treen, the Republican candidate, in the general election. He was the state's first Cajun governor and the first to have openly courted blacks.

It was a good time to be governor of Louisiana, particularly if you like to manipulate the levers of the power and government, as Edwin Edwards did so artfully. The state's oil-based economy was strong, and he had plenty of money to do what he liked best—spend on new roads, bridges, ports, hospitals, and schools.

Like Huey Long, he was populist who championed the poor and underprivileged. And like Long, he cut deals to steer work to favored businessmen, who provided the money he needed to run his campaigns. When news articles raised questions about these deals, some of which seemed to benefit Edwards personally, he dismissed the complaints with a wink and a few one-liners. When asked about accepting illegal campaign contributions, he said, "It was illegal for them to give, but not for me to receive." When questioned about his frequent trips to Las Vegas, he admitted that he loved to gamble, and he cracked more jokes. When questioned about tales of his womanizing, as when a book claimed he once made love with six women in a night, Edwards smiled and said, "No it wasn't that way. He [the author] was gone when the last one came in."

With the state's economy humming, practically everyone laughed along with Edwards, and in 1975, he was overwhelmingly reelected. "I think people realize that public officials are human and that we have our faults, our inadequacies," he explained once, "and if we don't try to be hypocritical or santimonious about it, I think they'll forgive us for it."

State law required Edwards to step down after two terms, and he was succeeded by David Treen, the state's first Republican governor since Reconstruction. When Edwards was eligible to run again in 1983, he challenged Treen, who was running for reelection. Treen was an honest and fair governor but indecisive and an unwilling deal maker. Edwards sliced him apart. Treen, Edwards said, was "so slow it takes him an hour and a half to watch '60 Minutes.'" Edwards was so confident of his election that he said he couldn't lose unless he was caught "in bed with a dead girl or a live boy." He was right. Voters returned him to the governor's mansion with 63 percent of the vote. Although the challenger, he outspent Treen $16 million to $6 million. After the election, Edwards paid off a $4 million campaign debt by filling two 747s with supporters, at $10,000 a head, for a week-long trip to France. On a side trip to Monaco, Edwards won $15,000 shooting craps.

But when he took office in 1984 as Louisiana's first three-term governor, oil prices were dropping, and the state's finances were soon a shambles. Edwards rammed a $730 million tax increase through the state legislature, but it wasn't enough to stem the red ink. He had to cut cherished government programs. The good times were over.

Edwards over the years had been investigated by more than a dozen grand juries but had always escaped indictment—until 1985. A federal court indicted him on charges that he was paid $1.9 million by hospitals while Treen was governor in return for favors when, as expected, he became governor again in 1983. Prosecutors charged that Edwards needed the money to pay off $2 million in gambling debts from Nevada casinos. Casino executives testified that Edwards paid off his debts with suitcases stuffed with cash at the governor's mansion. Edwards attempted to hide his losses, prosecutors added, by gambling under the aliases of T. Wong, T. Lee, B. Tune and Ed Neff. The high point of the trial came when Edwards took the stand. He denied the allegations, and almost all of the jury believed him. The judge declared a mistrial. Federal authorities decided to prosecute him a second time. This time he was acquitted.

While Edwards had won a legal victory, he was badly damaged politically. With the Oil Bust pushing Louisiana's unemployment rate into double digits and the state nearly bankrupt, voters no longer laughed at Edwards's escapades. When he ran for reelection in

1987, the magic touch was gone, and he conceded to Roemer without even contesting the runoff. Most everybody thought his political career was over.

Edwin Edwards, however, nursed the idea that he could be elected governor again. Even as he dropped out on the night of the 1987 primary, he began plotting to win back the governor's mansion four years later. He would run again for several reasons. One was his belief that Roemer's preachy style would wear thin with voters and that Roemer would be unable to keep his 1987 campaign promises. Edwards knew that every so often Louisiana, like a boozer swearing off alcohol, elected a reform governor but four years later always replaced him with a populist. "Let the good times roll," after all, is the state's motto.

Another reason Edwards would run again was that he loved being the Kingfish. He reveled in the crowds of people who flocked to him wherever he went, asking for help or just wanting to say hello. As governor, Edwards could help his core constituency: the poor, the elderly, minorities. He could also help his friends and, many said, himself financially. There was another basic reason he wanted to defeat Roemer in 1991: beginning with his election to the Crowley City Council in 1954, he had won twenty-two elections in a row before the 1987 loss. He wanted to avenge that defeat and end his forty-year political career as a winner.

Edwards declared his candidacy on February 8. Silver haired, tan, and sixty-three years old—looking like an aging card shark—he defended his own record and promised "to learn from my mistakes." He would be, he said, "a different Edwin Edwards." He added: "I like to believe I've evolved mentally and emotionally. . . . I think I'm a little more serious, and these are serious times. . . . I am going to be very careful about not falling into some of the traps I fell into when I was less experienced."

Edwards also bitterly attacked Roemer. Playing on Roemer's 1987 campaign slogan, he spoke under a banner that read, "I'm the Solution to the Revolution." Roemer, Edwards said, "promised us an ethical, scandal-free government and gave us Danny Walker voodooism."

While he concentrated his fire on Roemer, Edwards got in a few jibes at Duke. "I cannot believe that anybody who had worn a Nazi uniform or a Klan sheet is respectable," he said. "That is too unlike the philosophy of Americans and Louisianians." Privately, he joked that he and Duke were similar in that "we're both wizards under the sheets." Edwards and his wife Elaine had gotten divorced in 1989 after forty years of marriage. He now had a new lady, a twenty-six-year-old LSU nursing student named Candy Picou. She was blonde and slender and looked like a model. "A man is as old as the woman he feels," Edwards joked to a crowd of supporters one night during the campaign.

David Duke had decided during the Senate campaign that his next step politically would be to run for governor if he lost to Johnson. Several of his advisers told him that he was much better suited to be a legislator than an executive, since it was far easier to demand changes than actually try to implement them. His closest adviser, Jim McPherson, told him he should run for reelection in 1991 and for Congress the following year. But as he sat in the legislature, Duke had been impressed with how much power the governor wielded. And throughout the Senate campaign, he constantly ran into people who implored him not to go off to Washington, telling him that they needed him in Baton Rouge, cleaning up the state's problems. There was another reason Duke wanted to run for governor: with his belief in destiny, he thought that his strong showing in the Senate election showed he was on his way to saving the white race and that winning the governorship was the next step.

Duke in January told reporters that he would run for governor, although he didn't make his formal announcement until March. As in the Senate campaign, he would run as a repackaged right-wing, antiestablishment populist, and he would continue to try to distance himself from what he called "youthful intolerance" and "youthful mistakes." As in the Senate election, he would focus on racially based issues, speaking in code. He would oppose affirmative action and minority set-asides, call for the end of forced busing, advocate reducing the welfare benefits of women who bear illegitimate children, and demand that welfare recipients work for their checks. He would not discuss issues involving Jews.

As a gubernatorial candidate, Duke, who turned forty-one on July 1 that year, would stress additional issues to broaden his appeal and to speak more directly about pocketbook issues: opposition to new taxes, opposition to reducing the state's $75,000 homestead exemption, support for a clean environment, the need to cut government spending, opposition to abortion, the need to get tough on crime. He would still hold old-style campaign rallies throughout the state, but he wouldn't need to hold as many—or speak as long—because voters now knew him. Most of his top campaign aides would be the same as in 1990: Jim McPherson, David Touchstone, Babs Wilson, Howie Farrell, and Kenny Knight.

Buddy Roemer at the beginning of 1991, meanwhile, was preoccupied not only with running state government but also with deciding whether to switch political parties. Roemer in Congress had never been comfortable with the Democratic party. Known as one of the Boll Weevils—the group of conservative Democrats who provided crucial backing for President Reagan—he voted with the Reagan administration more often than almost any other Democrat. He had not even attended the 1988 Democratic Convention.

Republican members of the Louisiana delegation for several years had tried to persuade Roemer to switch parties. But it wasn't until a conversation with President George Bush in early 1990 that Roemer began to consider the idea seriously. Roemer and Bush had become friends when Bush was vice president, and they frequently played paddle ball in the House gymnasium. The paddle ball games continued when Bush was president and Roemer was visiting Washington as governor.

One day Bush told Roemer that he would love to have him join the Republican party. When the idea came from his friend the president, Roemer listened. There were follow-up phone calls from Bush and John Sununu, Bush's chief of staff. "You're a road warrior," Sununu told him. It was heady stuff for Roemer, especially in the last part of

1990, as Bush's popularity soared because of his tough response to Saddam Hussein's invasion of Kuwait.

For months, Roemer kept it hidden that he was considering changing parties, something no sitting governor in American history had ever done. He informed his aides at the beginning of 1991. On January 25, he invited them to the governor's mansion for dinner along with his family, and he asked everyone for their advice. As he went around the table, person after person—his mother, father, and aides alike—advised that switching would hurt him with voters, particularly among blacks. Roemer's polling corroborated their words. He would lose four percentage points running as a Republican. But still dismissing Duke's candidacy, Roemer thought he could withstand the four-point loss. By switching, he figured, he could also keep out one of the major Republicans—most notably, David Treen—who were considering running and who would take away more than four points.

Another consideration in Roemer's mind far outweighed the impact of his switch on the governor's race, but it was something he kept secret. He wanted to run for president in 1996, but he thought he had little chance to win the Democratic nomination. The party's rank-and-file voters, who dominate the primary process, would dismiss him as too independent, he feared. Roemer, however, did like his odds for winning the Republican nomination. He could run as a fiscal conservative and social moderate, a break-the-mold Republican who would reduce spending, hold down taxes, protect the environment and strongly support civil rights. Roemer announced the party switch on March 11 on the front steps of the governor's mansion.

While President Bush very much wanted Roemer to become a Republican, the state GOP chairman, Billy Nungesser, did not. Nungesser thought Roemer was too liberal. But what bothered Nungesser even more was that Roemer had kept him in the dark about the party switch and now seemed to expect to take control of the state party. Nungesser retaliated by speaking bitingly about Roemer to reporters. Shortly afterward, Nungesser met with Roemer at the governor's mansion. A heated argument ensued. "Goddammit, Nungesser," Roemer shouted, "if you don't get into line and cut this shit out, I'm going to kick your [expletive deleted] ass out of the mansion." Roemer's outburst shocked Billy Rimes, his legislative lobbyist. Rimes had never before heard Roemer curse in front of his mother, who also attended the meeting.

As Nungesser hurried away from the mansion, he resolved to undercut Roemer. And as state party chairman, he had ample opportunity. After Roemer switched, all the potential heavyweight Republican candidates deferred to him except one: Clyde Holloway, a three-term congressman who represented a rural area of central Louisiana. While national Republican leaders urged Holloway to stay out, the party's small but vocal antiabortion wing implored him to run. Comprised mostly of fundamentalist Christians, antiabortionists badly wanted to defeat Roemer because he had vetoed two bills in 1990 that would have prohibited virtually all abortions in Louisiana—three years after he firmly placed himself in the antiabortion camp. Nungesser joined the right-to-lifers in urging

Holloway to challenge Roemer. On April 17, Holloway announced his entry into the race.

Nungesser was to create more problems for Roemer. He went ahead and scheduled a state Republican convention in June to endorse a gubernatorial candidate. Roemer wanted the convention canceled, believing that as the incumbent Republican candidate, he should automatically win the party's endorsement. Besides, with a legislative session coming up, he didn't want to spend the time and money needed to woo Republicans and capture the endorsement. The Republican State Central Committee on May 11 backed Nungesser, however, and agreed to hold the convention on June 15 in Lafayette. Duke and Holloway applauded the decision and said they would contest the endorsement; Roemer said he would not. Two months after becoming a Republican, Roemer seemed like a man without a party.

These developments thrilled David Duke. At the beginning of the race, he thought he would make the runoff against Buddy Roemer. Now he thought Roemer had been so badly damaged that he would face Edwin Edwards. He preferred this prospect because he thought so many voters hated Edwards that given a choice between the two, they would vote for Duke.

On May 18 Holloway and Duke competed in the GOP's statewide caucuses, where 55 percent of the delegates would be chosen for the convention four weeks later at the Lafayette Cajun Dome. Holloway came out on top at the caucuses, winning about 330 of the delegates selected to Duke's 220. Duke could claim victory, however, because he had won nearly ten times as many delegates as at the Senate caucuses eighteen months before. He was becoming more socially acceptable.

And while Holloway won the party endorsement at the state convention on June 15, Duke flexed his muscle when GOP leaders tried to prevent him from addressing the delegates. He sidled up to the back of the stage, sidestepped a guard trying to block him, and dashed up to the microphone, arms aloft in victory. Dozens of his supporters rushed up to the stage, waving placards and chanting his name, "Duke! Duke! Duke!" Nungesser shouted for order, but Duke's supporters continued their noisemaking for ten minutes. They quieted down only when Duke was allowed to speak later in the afternoon. The boisterous Duke demonstration unnerved Neil Curran, a Republican stalwart who had worked for John Treen in the District 81 race. "It's like we're attending a party convention in Germany in the 1930s," he thought, "and Hitler is coming to power."

With the Republican party badly divided between Roemer, Holloway, and Duke, Edwin Edwards's electoral prospects were starting to improve a bit. But they still didn't look good. The first half of 1991 had not been an easy time for the proud man who had dominated the state's politics for a generation. Some friends he called asking for campaign donations told him to stay out, believing that he couldn't beat Roemer in the runoff. Others didn't call him back. Even two of his top campaign aides, Al Donovan and Bob d'Hemecourt, thought he couldn't defeat Roemer.

But Edwards soldiered on, confident that he would prove the skeptics wrong. By late July he had shored up his base in the Democratic party with the withdrawal of Louis Lambert and Aaron Broussard from the race. Both had run out of money. They were soon followed by Kathleen Blanco, a Public Service Commission member and Democrat who had become a candidate in May. With Lambert, Broussard, and Blanco gone, Edwards could corral their supporters.

Holloway, meanwhile, was going nowhere. As with Ben Bagert the year before, the state Republican party endorsement meant little. Holloway could not raise the $2 million needed to wage an effective campaign, and he could only count on his base of support, the state's fundamentalist Christians, who accounted for but 10 percent of the state's voters.

Like Lambert, Broussard, and Blanco, Holloway was discovering that it was a three-man race. Roemer, Duke, and Edwards each enjoyed such a large block of support in a highly polarized electorate that no one else could mount a successful challenge. In general, blacks, Cajuns and union workers backed Edwards; businessmen, environmentalists, pro-choice groups, and good-government reformers supported Roemer; and blue-collar whites and disaffected Republicans backed Duke. When the votes were counted on October 19, primary election night, one of the three would be the odd man out. Most political experts thought the man would be Duke. They expected Roemer to run first and Edwards second in the primary, and then Roemer would triumph in the runoff.

Roemer, however, was having more problems. In June, the legislature approved another strict antiabortion bill. Roemer vetoed it. But this time the legislature overrode him—the first time that had ever happened to a Louisiana governor. Roemer ran into more problems when he vetoed a reapportionment bill he had promised the night before to sign, lawmakers called him a liar. Edwards and Duke jumped on these developments, saying Roemer had alienated so many legislators that he could no longer get his measures approved.

Duke, however, was hardly one to argue this point. He was still far more effective at winning publicity than at getting his racially oriented bills passed. He did have better success with the legislature in 1991 than in his two previous years, as fewer legislators wanted to oppose him. The house adopted five of his seven bills, but most were severely watered down by amendments. His most publicized bill, which would have given each woman on welfare $100 a year to have the Norplant birth control device implanted in her arm, was amended to provide instead for distribution of birth control information to welfare recipients. Duke in 1991 did get his first bill through the legislature. It was an innocuous measure prohibiting jurors from accepting payment from movie producers or book publishers seeking an account of the jury's proceedings.

During July and most of August, the campaign rolled on with little drama. With the state's economy still in the doldrums and with Roemer's $5,000-per-contributor limit now state law, none of the candidates yet had the money needed to wage a high-octane television campaign. Where Edwin Edwards raised $16 million in 1983, Edwards, Duke, and Roemer were hoping in 1991 to raise $2 million to $3 million each. There was another reason for the lack of drama during July and most of August: Roemer, the focal point of the race, was not campaigning. While Edwards, Duke, and the minor candidates were appearing at campaign forums across the state, Roemer was spending most of his time in Baton Rouge governing the state. This was a deliberate strategy by Roemer's campaign advisers, who believed that forums simply let his opponents trash him in front of the media. Besides, they knew that the media would stop covering them if he didn't show up.

Roemer finally announced his candidacy on August 27. Cast in the unfamiliar role of the incumbent who presided over state government, Roemer, forty-seven, tried to update the themes of four years before. He portrayed himself as a reformer who had taken on the state's entrenched interests but needed another term to complete the job. "Louisiana is not going back to the days when our children's futures were held hostage to a bankrupt and inadequate state education system," Roemer said.

> Louisiana is not going back to the days when the quality of the air we breathed and the water we drank was taken for granted. And Louisiana is not going back to the days when money ruled our politics, when backroom deals determined our policy, and when the interests of our people and our state's future took a back seat to the interests of the politicians and special interest groups.

Roemer simultaneously launched a massive television ad campaign, echoing the themes of his announcement. The campaign began to heat up. There were now fewer than sixty days before the October 19 primary. The betting was still on a Roemer-Edwards runoff. They were now tied with 25-30 percent apiece in the polls, followed by Duke with 15 percent and the rest of the voters undecided or divided among the minor candidates.

With Roemer formally getting in the race on August 27, Duke stepped up his campaigning, making stops over the next two weeks in Vivian, Oak Grove, Chatham, Bossier City, New Orleans, DeQuincy, Maryville, Sugartown, Ragley, Washington, Morgan City, Kenner, and New Orleans again. On September 11, he returned to LSU to speak at Free Speech Alley—where he had gotten his start in politics in 1969 as a skinny sophomore who called himself a Nazi and called for the eradication of Jewish influence in America. In those days, students dismissed Duke as a kook and jeered him off the soapbox. Now, twenty-two years later, with resculpted features and carrying the promise that he was a changed man, Duke would get a far different response.

Hundreds of students packed the alley in front of the LSU Student Union, despite the sweltering September humidity. Dozens more leaned against the union's second-floor balcony. "I'm here because I believe in freedom of speech, ladies and gentlemen," Duke began, fearful perhaps that the students would shout him down as they had during his days at LSU. The crowd buzzed, but no one tried to challenge him. Duke plunged ahead. "I'm likely to be governor of this state next year." The students cheered and whooped with delight—something Duke had not heard at Free Speech Alley before. He paused in surprise and smiled. "The most precious thing you have is your right to freedom," he cried out, picking up steam. "I believe in less government, not only in the Soviet Union but for us right here in Louisiana. I think it's about time people stand up and say things honestly." The students cheered and whooped some more. And so it went.

Black students scattered throughout the crowd of 700 muttered angrily throughout Duke's thirty-minute appearance, forcing him to shout to be heard. One student held a sign behind him that read, "Nose Job Nazi." Another sign read: "No thanks Mr. Duke—we have enough racists in government already!" But the blue-and-white "Duke Governor" signs outnumbered them, and roars of approval repeatedly interrupted Duke. "Amen, I'm tired of spending my tax dollars on them!" a young woman in a fraternity shirt shouted when Duke attacked the "massive welfare underclass that is growing every day." Shannah Smith, a twenty-two-year-old hospital technician standing nearby, shook her head in agreement. "We work so they can have baby after baby," she called out.

"Duke! Duke! Duke!" the students chanted when he attacked affirmative action and race-based college admission policies and promised to "preserve the distinct quality of LSU," a predominantly white university. Duke received a royal homecoming, and it wasn't over when he finished his speech. Students crowded around him as he made his way to the shade of a nearby oak tree. For the next half hour, he signed autographs and answered more questions.

Billy Hankins stood apart from the crowd, shaking his head in dismay. Hankins had been one of Duke's top aides during the Senate campaign, but no longer wanting to be around Duke's extremist friends, he was now working for Clyde Holloway's campaign. He had stopped by LSU because he wondered how students would react to his former boss's performance. "This is ridiculous," Hankins said, as he surveyed the adoring students surrounding Duke. "Look, at all these people out here for Duke when Clyde is the better conservative."

Duke pressed on with his offensive. Eight days after his Free Speech Alley appearance, he broadcast his first TV ad of the campaign, a thirty-minute spot. As in the Senate ad the year before, he mixed his traditional race-based pitch with an appeal to fed-up voters wanting safer streets, a healthier economy and a better educational system. In a new approach to disarm his opponents, Duke in the gubernatorial ad suggested that they were the ones guilty of intolerance. After Duke's two teenage daughters briefly appeared at his side, he said,

> It's only been the love of my wonderful family and the strength that Christ gives me that enables me to stand tall in spite of the unfair attacks I've weathered. I sometimes wonder about those self-righteous people who speak about loving everyone and then hate me. Those of you who hate me for my past, I ask you honestly: Have you ever hurt a friend or loved one? Have you ever spoken words you'd take back if you could? Have you ever changed your opinion? If you haven't, I guess you can throw the first stone. I ask only that you treat me as you'd have others treat you.

Throughout the ad, Duke portrayed himself as the candidate of change, and he returned to that theme for his close. "I'm the only viable alternative to those tax and spend policies of the past," he said. "I'm the only one with a chance to break through for the principles we share. Please help me make that breakthrough possible for all of us."

As in the Senate ad, Duke flashed an 800 number for viewers to call to make a contribution, and in yet another novel approach, he told them they could call a 900 number to subscribe to the *David Duke Report*. He said the call would cost fifteen dollars. He did not disclose that he owned the *David Duke Report*; he admitted this several days later in an interview. South Central Bell still prohibited candidates from using 900 numbers for contributions, but did not stop calls for the *David Duke Report*, since Duke pocketed the money as a private business owner. Politics, after all, was how he made a living. Duke's message was hitting home. White Louisianians who had voted for Buddy Roemer four years earlier because they were angry and wanted a change were still angry and were now turning to Duke as the shake-things-up candidate. The polls did not reflect this, as Duke's support remained at 15 percent. But Roemer's twenty-four-year-old daughter, Caroline, saw the awful truth of Duke's strength on September 29 when she rode in the Louisiana Sugar Cane Festival parade in New Iberia. She had been traveling the state for several months as part of a Women for Roemer group that was founded after her father vetoed the abortion bill.

Duke rode directly in front of Caroline Roemer in the parade, perched on the back seat of a convertible. During the first half of the parade, most everybody in the five-deep crowd was white, and they all seemed to be holding Duke signs and chanting his name. When Caroline Roemer passed, they shouted, "Where's Buddy?" "Where's the governor?" Some people shouted, "Go home!"

Caroline Roemer began to get a sinking feeling in her stomach. Duke was so popular, she thought, it was almost cultlike. And with her dad not attending a parade that featured not only Duke but also Edwards, she realized that voters felt ignored by him. "We're in big trouble," she thought to herself. "Dad's advisers need to get out of Baton Rouge, they need to stop reading polls and see how much support Duke has." Caroline Roemer was further unnerved when, near the end of the parade, Duke drove by a large section of black parade-goers. They yelled obscenities and threw bottles, none of which hit Duke. The police moved in and Duke's car sped ahead to avert a possible riot. "What's happening to Louisiana?" she wondered.

When Caroline Roemer got back to the governor's mansion, she ran upstairs to find her father. He was playing poker with Danny Walker and several others. "Hey, how'd it go?" he asked nonchalantly.

"I'm scared, I'm frightened," she said, choking back tears. She described what had happened. "There was not one Buddy Roemer sign. All I saw were David Duke signs. I think you're underestimating him." She turned and hurried from the room.

Buddy Roemer left the card game several minutes later to comfort her. "Was it really that bad?" he asked.

"Yes, it was overwhelming," she said. "I realize now that we have to do something. On the two-hour drive there, I didn't see one Roemer sign."

"But, Caroline, the polls are showing us way ahead."

"I think they're wrong," she responded. "I think people are lying. They won't admit they're voting for Duke. I've been traveling to small towns for three months. I pass a general store and see Duke signs where four years before there were Buddy Roemer signs."

Buddy Roemer shook his head and asked quietly, "How can we stop him? I don't know what to do."

Caroline Roemer was not the first person to implore her father to take on David Duke. Raymond Strother, Roemer's media consultant, had been warning him for weeks that Edwards's vote was solid and that Duke was threatening to take away Roemer's white voters and keep him out of the runoff. Strother, who was staying at the mansion, beat this drum so incessantly that Roemer began ducking him.

When Roemer switched parties in March, he not only joined the GOP but also recruited officials from the Republican National Committee to run his campaign. The campaign manager was Sam Dawson, who had been a disciple of RNC Chairman Lee Atwater in their native South Carolina, and the press secretary was Gordon Hensley, an accomplished spinmeister. Fred Steeper handled the polling.

Strother, fifty-one, had spent the first half of his career in Louisiana before moving to Washington and had produced the tough-talking ads that had helped propel Roemer to the governorship in 1987. He had always worked for Democrats and had agreed to sign on with Roemer in 1991 only because they had been together four years before. But because he was a Democrat, the Republicans were slow to listen to his warnings about Duke. It wasn't until October that Strother convinced Dawson and Steeper that Duke posed a major threat. He got them to agree to hold two focus groups one evening on the so-called West Bank—a section of Jefferson Parish across the Mississippi River from New Orleans—among white, blue-collar swing voters in an attempt to plumb their real attitudes toward Duke.

Strother, Dawson, and Steve Lombardo, Steeper's research director, watched the session from behind a two-way mirror. To get at voters' real feelings about Duke, the Roemer aides had the moderator ask a series of questions about a hypothetical candidate. "What would you think of a candidate who had evaded the draft during the Vietnam War and lied about it later?" he began.

"I can't imagine a man who wouldn't serve his country," one man said.

"What would you think of a candidate who had plastic surgery?" the moderator asked.

"I'd wonder about his sexuality," another man said.

"What would you think of a candidate who hadn't paid his taxes?" the moderator asked.

"I pay my taxes," a woman said, "and I expect a politician to."

"What about a candidate who has never held a job?"

"How can anybody understand our problems if they've never held a job or sweated for a living?" a man asked.

Clearly, this hypothetical candidate would have a snowball's chance in hell of getting elected.

As the first group filed out, Strother told Dawson and Lombardo that he wanted to try something different with the second group to ferret out and gauge more accurately the pro-Duke sentiment. This time the moderator would discuss the hypothetical candidate and then identify him as David Duke. When the second group was asked how they felt about Duke's having evaded the draft, a man leaped to his defense. "Everybody of that generation was trying to evade the draft," he said. "I went to Vietnam, but I would have evaded going there if I could have."

When asked about the plastic surgery, a woman said, "What's wrong with a politician having plastic surgery? Movie stars do it. And politicians, after all, are movie stars."

What about Duke's not paying taxes?

"Only dumb people pay taxes," a woman said. "Politicians and millionaires don't because they're smart. Duke must be smart."

What about his never having held a job?

"He's a politician," one man said. "Politicians don't work."

What about his having been in the Klan?

"It was when he was a kid," a man said. "Kids do crazy things."

What had been unacceptable character flaws in an unidentified candidate were now acceptable when it was revealed to be Duke. In his nearly thirty years in politics, Strother had never seen anything like it. He was shaken and turned to Dawson, "It's over for Buddy," he said.

But perhaps it wasn't. Responses to questions about the impact of a Duke election on the economy provided a glimmer of hope for Strother and Dawson. When the moderator asked the focus group about the fears of many that a Duke election would hurt the state economically, that it would drive away conventions, tourists, and potential business investors, several people agreed. "People will lose jobs," one man said.

Strother met with Roemer the next day. "If you don't do something immediately about David Duke," he said, "you're going to lose. I've just seen the handwriting on the wall in two West Bank focus groups."

"Well, what would you do?" Roemer asked.

If it had been 1987, Strother would have put Roemer in front of a television camera and let him in his plainspoken, evangelical way tell viewers that he didn't want his ten-year-old-son—and their children either—to be educated in a state governed by a racist and anti-Semite. But in 1991, test runs of Roemer ads before focus groups had shown that people didn't want to listen to him. Using so-called People Meters, in which focus group viewers used hand-held dials to rate how favorable they felt second by second throughout the commercial, Strother had found that whenever Roemer himself appeared in the ads, the rating declined. Looking at those results, Strother had come to the startling conclusion that viewers thought Roemer was so smart and mesmerizing that they tuned him out to avoid buying into his message. They didn't want to be convinced.

Unable to use Roemer, Strother decided to put together ads with ordinary people warning of how a Duke election would cost the state jobs and business investment. Strother decided to use slightly upscale people in the ads—the kinds of people who would decide whether Duke or Roemer made the runoff. He produced six ads and wanted to flood the airwaves with them. Strother thought Roemer could be saved if every time that viewers turned on the television set, they saw fellow citizens warning that Duke's election would mean economic catastrophe.

Strother screened the ads for Roemer and Danny Walker at the mansion. When he was through, Walker shook his head. "There's nothing to be gained by being negative," he said. "There's nothing to be gained by winning the wrong way. You can't put these on."

Roemer didn't comment but asked Strother to screen them once more. "I know you're upset about David Duke," he told Strother after watching them again. "But having a bunch of yuppies on TV talking about losing their jobs won't hurt David Duke. The numbers don't show it."

"You have to put them on," Strother pleaded. "I can't point to numbers because we can't poll Duke accurately. We need to go after upwardly mobile voters because they're going for Duke."

Roemer cut him short. "We're not going to run them," he said. He wheeled around and left the room.

Strother looked down and frowned. "It's really over now," he thought to himself.

Buddy Roemer's political future hung in the balance, but he couldn't bring himself to do what was necessary to win: launch a full-scale attack against David Duke. One reason was that, still emerging from the throes of a midlife crisis, Roemer seemed tired of being governor. His aides chafed at how little he campaigned. On the final Sunday before the election, he spent the day watching two football games at the mansion. Another reason was that Roemer didn't feel comfortable attacking a candidate personally. He had always prided himself on that.

But most important, Roemer didn't understand racism and couldn't bring himself to believe that the people of Louisiana preferred Duke to him. When Roemer was growing up at the Scopena Plantation, the black farmhands ate at the dinner table and swam in the swimming pool. Such a thing was unheard of in conservative Bossier Parish. Roemer's parents instilled in him unswerving support for racial tolerance, a belief he embraced. Roemer left the room when somebody told a racist joke, and his best friend was a black man. To an intellectual like Roemer, racism just didn't make sense.

He knew that a core group of racists in the state—perhaps 15 percent of the electorate—backed Duke. But he did not think that reasoned, intelligent people could walk into the voting booth and pull the lever of a bigot and anti-Semite. Couldn't they tell that Roemer was working day and night to turn Louisiana around? Couldn't they tell that Duke was nothing but a hater? Couldn't they tell that Duke had nothing to offer but a few slogans and a bunch of vague promises? And didn't the polls reflect this? They showed Duke running a weak third.

Although he was blind to it, Buddy Roemer was on the ropes, and a businessman named Jack Kent was secretly preparing to deliver the knockout blow. Kent owned Marine Shale Processors, a controversial Morgan City company that incinerated hazardous wastes. It was a benign process, Kent held. Roemer's Department of Environmental Quality had a different view and way trying to shut down Marine Shale. The company, DEQ said, emitted dangerous pollutants into the air. Kent decided that he could no longer survive with Buddy Roemer as governor. But he could with Edwin Edwards—or even David Duke. Edwards had been a friend for many years and would never have tried to put him out of business, while Duke was promising to relax DEQ's enforcement of small businesses. Kent decided to attack Roemer in a massive television campaign in the final two weeks before the election.

Deno Seder, one of the country's best negative ad political consultants, was sitting in his Washington office on September 27 when the phone rang. "Stay where you are," an anonymous caller said. "The man with the cheese is on his way to Washington."

"Who's that?" Seder asked.

"Jack Kent," the caller replied and hung up.

Seder was perplexed. "Who's Jack Kent?" he wondered.

Several hours later his phone rang again. This time it was Kent. He had just arrived in Washington on his private jet. "I'm on my way over," Kent said.

They met for several hours and Kent explained what he wanted. "What would $500,000 get me?" he asked.

"Three to five points off of Roemer," Seder replied. That would probably be enough to spell Roemer's political doom. Kent hired him.

Seder was a smart choice. Having spent twenty years in Louisiana before moving to Washington, Seder knew both the state and Buddy Roemer intimately. They had worked as partners on political campaigns in the 1970s, and Seder had served as Roemer's media consultant during his 1980 election to Congress. But eleven years later when Kent offered him the chance to end his old friend's political career, Seder jumped at the opportunity. Seder worked only for Democrats and thought Roemer was fair game as a party-switcher. Besides, Kent was offering him a ton of money.

Seder quickly hired a team of producers and editors and, working nonstop over the next five days, they produced five attack ads. Each had a similar them: the "Revolution" had failed, and Roemer was just another politician who made promises and couldn't keep them. Seder flew to Louisiana and showed Kent the ads. Kent like theme. "Let's skin him up a little bit," he said. Before he permitted the ads to air, however, Kent decided to try to cut a deal with Roemer. He sent an emissary to meet with P. J. Mills, Roemer's chief of staff, and tell him about the ads. Kent will pull the ads, the emissary told Mills, if Roemer calls DEQ off Marine Shale.

Roemer got angry when Mills outlined Kent's deal. "I didn't become governor to make deals like this with people like Jack Kent," he said. "If he's violating the law, we should do everything we can to make him stop." When Kent got word of Roemer's response, he immediately swung into action, buying nearly all the advertising time on television still available in the two weeks before the primary. And on October 7 he began flooding the airwaves with Seder's missiles.

Sam Dawson got hold of the five ads that day and watched them at Roemer's Baton Rouge campaign headquarters. "Shit!" he exclaimed after screening them. "These are good." A frustrated Dawson could feel Roemer voters sliding into Duke's column. Not many but enough to make the difference. Strother quickly rushed a counterattack on the air that charged Kent's ad was a political payoff for his friend Edwards. But the Roemer campaign couldn't match Kent's firepower.

Duke was rising, Roemer's nightly tracking polls during the final week showed. The final poll, taken on Tuesday night, October 15, showed he now trailed Roemer by ten points with 12 percent of the voters undecided. Edwards led with 31 percent of the vote, Roemer had 30 percent, Duke 20 percent, and Holloway 6 percent. Duke's campaign staffers could feel that he was surging by the intensity of the crowds that turned out to see him in the final week. People stood on the side of the road just to watch him drive by on his way to the next campaign stop.

Without accurate polls to go by, not privy to the realization of Dawson and Strother and skeptical of Duke's oft-repeated claim that he would win, nearly all political pundits were still predicting a Roemer-Edwards runoff. But a few—like *Times-Picayune* columnist James Gill—were raising the possibility of the unthinkable. If Roemer loses, Gill wrote shortly before the primary, "we will have to decide whether to turn the clock back four years with Edwards, or 100 years with the other guy." Edwards-Duke, he concluded, would be "the gubernatorial runoff from Hell."

The day before the October 19 primary was a Friday, and Roemer spent it campaigning in Jefferson Parish and New Orleans. He was beginning to comprehend Duke's strength. "My greatest nightmare, as a person who loves the state, would be having to choose between Edwin Edwards and David Duke," he told a lunchtime crowd in New Orleans. "I want to ask each of you to call 10 people tonight. If you do that, we cannot lose." Edwards spent the day in his suite at the Monteleone Hotel in New Orleans, calling his political allies to ensure that his supporters turned out to the polls the next day. Duke held a huge rally that Friday night in the New Orleans suburb of Kenner. He was confident that he would fulfill his destiny the following day. "We [in Louisiana] have been last in so many things," he told a cheering throng. "Maybe that's why you're committed to making Louisiana first in something else. You're committed to letting Louisiana lead the way for millions across this country who think like you do and think like I do. And who are waiting for us to lead the way."

When the initial returns came in Saturday night, Roemer took the lead. Then Duke jumped out front. With one-third of the precincts reporting, Edwards now ran first, Duke second and Roemer third. And that's how it ended. The final returns were:

| | | |
|---|---|---|
| Edwin Edwards | 523,195 | 33.8 percent |
| David Duke | 491,342 | 31.7 percent |
| Buddy Roemer | 410,690 | 26.5 percent |
| Clyde Holloway | 82,683 | 5.3 percent |
| Sam Jones | 11,847 | 0.76 percent |
| Ed Karst | 9,663 | 0.62 percent |
| Fred Kent | 7,385 | 0.48 percent |
| Anne Thompson | 4,118 | 0.27 percent |
| Jim Crowley | 4,000 | 0.26 percent |
| Albert Powell | 2,053 | 0.13 percent |
| Ronnie Johnson | 1,372 | 0.09 percent |
| "Cousin" Ken Lewis | 1,006 | 0.06 percent |

Edwards had held onto his base of blacks, blue-collar whites, and Cajuns. Duke, building on his core group of racist adherents, had convinced enough Roemer supporters in rural and suburban areas that he—not Buddy Roemer—would provide the changes they wanted. Once again, he had flown under the pollsters' radar. In four weeks, Louisiana voters would have to choose between Edwards and David Duke—the runoff from hell.

At the Sheraton hotel in Shreveport, shortly after the final outcome was known, Caroline Roemer walked into her father's suite. She burst into tears. "It's OK, it's OK," Roemer said as he gave her a hug.

"It's not OK," she replied. "We were beaten by David Duke and Edwin Edwards. I feel so humiliated."

"My strategy was wrong," Roemer said ruefully. "I thought we were winning."

You could almost feel a shudder pass through Louisiana on the morning after the October 19 primary. Only Edwin Edwards stood between David Duke and the governor's mansion. And the white people who had accounted for nearly all of the votes for Buddy Roemer and Clyde Holloway in the primary—and who would decide the governor's race in four weeks—reviled Edwards as a corrupt has-been. These whites, who made up about 30 percent of the electorate—were left to ponder: who was less worse, a bigot or a crook? On the day after the primary, a Sunday, it seemed anybody's guess which way they would go. "It's almost too hard a decision," Roemer supporter Marie Sarrat, a Metairie school administrator, said, in a comment echoed by many others.

While a Duke-Edwards runoff paralyzed many people, it immediately energized thousands more. On Monday, October 21, registrars of voters throughout Louisiana reported long lines of people waiting to register. On Tuesday, the final day to register for the November 16 runoff, the lines stretched even longer. People began queuing up on Tuesday throughout the state hours before the registrars of voters offices opened, and the lines remained long throughout the day and into the evening. At New Orleans City Hall, the line snaked through a block-long hallway and spilled out onto a sidewalk. In Jefferson Parish, the line around the Gretna Court House lapped itself by midafternoon, and when the office was supposed to close at 8:00 p.m., more than 2,000 people were still waiting. It took until after midnight for everybody to register. "It was amazing," marveled registrar Sam Altobello. "People waited four and five hours in line to register."

Many people were registering to elect Duke. "Everybody I know is voting for Duke," said James Heckathorn, as he waited in line to register in St. John the Baptist Parish, thirty miles west of New Orleans. "I like what he says. . . . I think people on welfare ought to have to work for it, too." But even more people registered that Monday and Tuesday to vote against Duke. For blacks, in particular, the primary results served as a wake-up call. In neither the 1990 Senate election nor the gubernatorial primary did Duke's candidacy prompt an outpouring of concern among blacks. They viewed him with alarm but didn't get excited, since they didn't think he could win. Besides, many disillusioned blacks said, Duke wasn't much worse than Ronald Reagan or George Bush. In both the Senate and gubernatorial primary elections, the black turn-out was about ten percentage points below the white turnout.

The runoff would be another story as blacks flocked to registrars of voters offices on Tuesday. In Baton Rouge, student leaders at predominantly black Southern University knocked on dormitory doors to remind classmates to register and rented buses to transport them to the registrar of voters office. The Southern University band serenaded the students as they waited in line throughout the afternoon. The Red Cross handed out water. Restaurants donated food and drinks. One person standing in line, twenty-five-year-old Darryl Robertson, said he had never voted before. "But I don't want to see David Duke become the governor. I don't want to see David Duke become anything because I think David Duke represents racism to the fullest."

Students from Grambling State University, another predominantly black institution, inundated the Lincoln Parish Registrar of Voters office in Ruston. In Alexandria, one of the last people to register was an eighty-seven-year-old man named George Heggin. When Heggin had last tried to register fifty years before, he had been turned away. His skin was the wrong color. What prompted Heggin to register in 1991? Duke, his wife said.

The flood of people registering to vote stunned state officials. "We've never seen anything like it," said Jerry Fowler, the Louisiana Commissioner of Elections. "Everyone wants to be able to vote in this election." In all, 68,335 Louisianians—nearly half of them black—registered to vote on that Monday and Tuesday, a two-day record. The large numbers of blacks registering alarmed Duke and his top advisers, but they still felt confident they would triumph. They had met at his Metairie home on Sunday morning to discuss the four-week runoff campaign. Duke told his advisers that he thought the election would be close but that he would win. Since the Roemer and Holloway voters had backed Republican candidates, Duke figured, they would likely vote for him in the runoff. He was a Republican and Edwards was a Democrat. Besides, he reasoned, the up-for-grabs voters were white, and he had a higher white vote in the primary (40 percent) than Roemer (33 percent) or Edwards (18 percent). Duke also thought that the runoff campaign would be fought over issues, his strength. How could Edwards attack him for his past when Edwards's own past was so tarnished?

Duke did not like strategy sessions—he cared about ideas, not tactics—so he ended the morning meeting without mapping out a plan. He figured that his approach thus far had succeeded; why not continue it? He called a press conference in New Orleans and unveiled what passed for his runoff strategy—praise of Roemer and more promises to shake up the status quo. "I like what Buddy Roemer said. We had to put education first in our state and reform the political process. We had to end the special-interest control of politics." He added: "One person described me as the Boris Yeltsen of American politics. I like that. I'm certainly opposed to the way the establishment has conducted and run our government both in Louisiana and the nation."

Across town that Sunday morning, Edwin Edwards and his top advisers were meeting in suite 1545 of the Monteleone Hotel in the French Quarter. Edwards, too, felt confident. He had gotten 88 percent of the black vote in the primary and expected nearly 100 percent of the black vote against Duke. If blacks, who comprised 27 percent of the electorate, turned out in large numbers, he could win without a majority of the white vote.

Unlike Duke, Edwards at his meeting formulated a plan to bring the Roemer voters into his fold. It called for getting the backing of Roemer, his top aides, his business supporters, and Republican party leaders. Edwards hit the phones to ask for their support and began promising to continue some of Roemer's reform programs. He proclaimed himself a "new" Edwin Edwards, one who would not cut deals, direct government benefits to friends, or embarrass the state with ribald behavior. "I'm anxious to make things better than they were the last time I was in office," he said. "I don't want to live the rest of my life with a legacy of bad marks I had eight years ago, six years ago."

Edwards got a lucky break later that day that helped formulate his anti-Duke strategy. At the New Orleans Saints-Tampa Bay Buccaneers game at the Louisiana Superdome that afternoon, Raymond Strother, Roemer's media adviser, by chance ran into two of Edwards's top campaign aides, Bill Morgan and Billy Broadhurst. Morgan, a longtime friend of Strother's, produced Edwards's TV ads. Broadhurst, who had become infamous in 1987 for chartering the yacht *Monkey Business* with former Colorado Senator Gary Hart and model Donna Rice in an incident that helped torpedo Hart's presidential aspirations, acted as the campaign's all-purpose troubleshooter. As they watched the game from a luxury suite, Strother told them what the Roemer campaign's extensive research had found: Duke was invulnerable on his Nazi and Klan past, as voters had already decided whether or not this mattered. Duke couldn't be attacked for his failure to pay property taxes or for his opposition to affirmative action or minority set-asides. "But we found that you can hit him on the economic issue," Strother related. "We think you can hit him hard on it, but Roemer just wouldn't do it."

Both Morgan and Broadhurst relayed Strother's advice to Edwards the next day. Edwards passed along this information to key Roemer backers during the next several days as he moved to line up their support. One of the first people he called was David Treen. His campaign polling showed that Treen's endorsement mattered as much to Roemer's supporters as did Roemer's. The longtime titular head of the Louisiana Republican party, Treen had no doubt about whom he would support. There was only one option, he thought. Edwin Edwards had defeated him twice for governor, in 1972 and 1983, and stood for everything Treen opposed. But David Duke was worse, Treen felt. Duke was a moral blot on the Republican party that had to be removed as soon as possible, or the party would forever be branded racist.

Treen and Edwards met on October 27, eight days after the primary. On October 29, Treen called a press conference. "The implications of this election for the future of Louisianians are profound—more so than I can ever recall," he said.

> Some have counseled me to stay out of this run-off election, to make no public statement of my views, to remain neutral. . . . While some of what he says touches on issues with which Republicans are concerned, his true agenda is far from ours. His true agenda is repugnant in the extreme. . . . To my Republican friends, therefore, I say: Do not be persuaded in favor of Duke simply because he has adopted the Republican label. David Duke must be defeated. He cannot be defeated by voters staying at home out of disaffection with both of the candidates for governor.

Edwards met with Buddy Roemer the same day that Treen made his announcement. Roemer strongly disliked Duke but feared that Edwards would undo the reforms he had carried out during his term. Several days after the primary, he expressed reservations to his chief of staff, P. J. Mills, about backing Edwards publicly. "If you don't say something about how bad David Duke is," Mills admonished him, "it will hurt your career in the future." On October 31, two days after meeting with Edwards, Roemer called a press conference and announced he would vote for Edwards. "Duke has no chance to help this state," Roemer told reporters. "Edwards has one chance. I pray to God that he takes it."

Meanwhile, independent of the Edwards campaign, businessmen who had backed Roemer were beginning their anti-Duke efforts. Most of them had done little to defeat Duke in the Senate race except perhaps make a $1,000 campaign contribution to Bennett Johnston. Nobody thought Duke had a chance for Senate. But now that Duke appeared to have even odds of becoming the state's chief executive, the business establishment was rising up against him. It was a decision based on dollars and cents, not morals.

One of the business leaders leading the charge against Duke was Pres Kabacoff, a New Orleans developer who had signed up for the Roemer Revolution in early 1987 when Buddy Roemer stood at 1 percent in the polls. On the night of the 1991 primary, when he saw that Duke had knocked Roemer out of the runoff, "It took me about two seconds to decide: 'I'm going with Edwin Edwards,'" Kabacoff remembered later. "I thought that if Duke won, Louisiana would be set adrift from the Union. The federal government would shut down Louisiana to show it would not work with a Nazi." Kabacoff contributed $5,000 to the Edwards campaign and urged friends and contractors who worked on his development projects to do likewise. Later in the runoff, he appeared in a television ad warning that Duke's election would cost the state thousands of jobs.

It took a day for the election results to sink in with New Orleans businessman David Dixon, another strong Roemer backer. Dixon, an antiques dealer who in the 1960s had spearheaded the drive to get New Orleans a professional football team and get the Louisiana Superdome built, had flown to New York City the day after the primary. As his friends there expressed horror at the thought of a Duke victory, Dixon realized, "This guy ruins our state if he wins. It's almost like Adolf Hitler is running."

When he returned to New Orleans two days later, Dixon began raising money to defeat Duke. He took in $25,000 and planned to give it to an anti-Duke group led by New Orleans attorney Moise Steeg. But when Steeg told him that his group was still getting organized, Dixon decided to act on his own. With an additional $40,000 of his own money, he cut a television ad the next day standing in front of the Superdome. "David Duke's supporters are already claiming that his election would not hurt tourism and convention business in this state," Dixon said. "They're absolutely right. He won't hurt it, he'll eliminate it."

A group of business leaders joined the fray with a press conference on October 25. Noting that the election was big news not only across the country but overseas as well, Jim Bob Moffett, chairman of Freeport-McMoRan, Incorporated, said, "If Duke is governor, national conventions scheduled for Louisiana would be canceled. Sports events would be turned away, businesses would move, top university researchers and professors would leave, and jobs would be lost." Tourist leaders chimed in a week later to say that many groups scheduled to hold conventions in New Orleans had promised since the primary to go elsewhere if Duke were elected.

Duke came under fire on another front—from the *New Orleans Times-Picayune*, the state's biggest newspaper and the only daily in New Orleans. Some people had criticized the paper for not going all out earlier to defeat Duke, but the editors of the *Times-Picayune* felt that journalistic rules of fairness prevented them from doing that. The primary election result changed their thinking. On the Monday after the primary, the paper's editors met and decided that they would not treat this as a conventional gubernatorial election. Duke was an extraordinary candidate in American history—no other neo-Nazi had come so close to being elected governor of a state—and the situation demanded an extraordinary journalistic response. The paper's editors decided they would launch a no-holds-barred assault against Duke, with hard-hitting news stories and slashing editorial columns. The paper would not omit negative information about Edwin Edwards, with whom the paper had warred for years, nor would the paper puff him up. The *Times-*

*Picayune* in fact reprinted embarrassing testimony from Edwards's 1985 trial. But the paper would devote its resources to exposing Duke's past, not Edwards's.

The paper fired its first shot with an editorial that appeared the day after the primary:

> The limelight of the world is on our state, and we are not a pretty sight to behold—by many measures last or near bottom in education, literacy and living standards. And now we have a first: elevating an extremist of the caliber of Mr. Duke to direct contention for the governorship. But the story is not yet played out. The clear-headed people of this state—and we happen to think there are still many—must now muster their resolve to see that on Nóv. 16, Mr. Duke is not elected governor. It's time to sober up.

In the days that followed, the paper launched daily bombing raids on Duke, revealing new details of his extremist activities. The paper also published a five-part series of editorials entitled "The Choice of Our Lives" that detailed graphically why Louisiana could not elect Duke. The *Times-Picayune* became such an adversary for Duke that late in the campaign Duke broadcast a television commercial attacking the newspaper. The newspaper's coverage was important not only because it reached about one-third of the state's voters but also because it emboldened newspapers and television stations throughout the state to follow its lead. The *Baton Rouge Morning Advocate* and the *Shreveport Times*, in particular, stepped up their critical coverage of Duke.

Duke was under attack on many fronts, but at the midway point of the runoff, many people still feared he could win. There were too many signs of massive Duke support throughout the state to count him out.

When Duke visited the luxury suites at the Saints game on the day after the October 19 primary—the game at which Strother outlined the Roemer campaign's findings about Duke—men fell over themselves trying to shake his hand. Duke then went in search of more voters. He walked through a tunnel that led to the terrace stands. In between plays, he popped his head out of a portal and waved to the group of fans sitting in that section. Few politicians would have dared to do this, because fans at sporting events typically boo them. But when Duke waved a greeting, the Saints fans roared back their approval. He went to another section and got the same rousing response. For the next half hour, he worked his way around the Superdome's stands, eliciting some boos but mostly cheers at each stop. This response did not bode well for Edwards.

There were more signs that Duke might pull off the unthinkable. A stream of Roemer supporters, including elected officials, called David Touchstone, Duke's northwest organizer, to climb aboard the Duke campaign. "The people who have to vote for Edwards for him to win are voting for Duke," reported business lobbyist C. B. Forgotston. "They're educated people, they're not hicks. But they're mad as hell, they're saying, 'Fuck the establishment. Throw the bums out.' That's what Duke stands for."

Duke also seemed to have found an effective way to distance himself from his extremist activities. He had become, he said, a born-again Christian. Yes, he may have been intolerant in the past, he said, but now he was a new man, thanks to Christ. Many people correctly saw this claim as a cynical ploy to win votes. But in a conservative state yearning for a savior, many others bought it. Duke had begun calling himself a Christian during the 1990 United States Senate election. But he played the religion card far more heavily in the gubernatorial runoff, crediting Christ in every speech with helping him overcome his past ways. "I want to thank the force in my life that's really enabled me to stand up through all the smears and the personal attacks and all the dirty politics that Louisiana is famous for," he told one cheering crowd. "I want to thank the influence of my Lord and Saviour Jesus Christ. I could not have gone on and continued to stand tall without the prayers He's answered."

Duke may pull it off and win, thought Lance Hill, executive director of the Louisiana Coalition Against Racism and Nazism, which had continued to dog Duke during the gubernatorial campaign. Hill's sources were reporting that good-government conservatives—the kinds of Roemer supporters that Edwards needed—were backing Duke. As he brooded over this on the bus to work one morning, a woman talking harshly about the election interrupted his thoughts. "They talk about Duke's past," she told a friend, spitting out the words. "Look at Edwin Edwards. Nobody wants to come to a state with a crook in charge."

Hill had a enduring faith in the basic wisdom and decency of the American people. But the anger and hate in the woman's voice scared him. "What if I'm wrong?" Hill thought. "What if this isn't some heroic effort to defeat David Duke? What happens if it's a tragedy?" A poll released on October 29 by Mason-Dixon Opinion Research reinforced Hill's apprehension. Edwards was leading Duke but by only a 46 to 42 percent margin. Mason-Dixon had adjusted the numbers to try to account for the hidden Duke vote, but who could be sure? And the 12 percent of voters who were undecided seemed likely to go with Duke: 59 percent of them viewed Duke as more honest and trustworthy than Edwards, and 70 percent thought Edwards's past was worse than Duke's.

A joint appearance by Duke and Edwards the next day at the annual state convention of the American Association of Retired Persons provided more evidence that Duke might triumph. The welfare system encourages women without husbands to have babies instead of encouraging birth control, Duke told the senior citizens, making a familiar charge. Politicians had learned not to challenge Duke's antiwelfare pitch because it resonated so strongly with voters. But Edwards knew Duke's charge was silly and couldn't resist saying so. A welfare mother with two children receives only $190 a month, and two-thirds of that comes from the federal government, Edwards said. For a third child, she receives an extra eleven dollars a week, he added.

"Can you really in good conscience think that this woman is going to sit around the table and wonder how she can get pregnant again to collect another $11 a week?" Edwards asked.

"YES!" the seniors yelled back.

"He's appealing to your base emotions," Edwards said of Duke, but boos cascading from the crowd drowned him out. Edwards paused and said, with emotion rising in his voice, "Who is going to be next? The disabled? The old? You better think about it."

It was Duke's turn to speak. "The elderly who have contributed all their lives have been forgotten by a welfare system that encourages laziness," he said. "And there is no more important freedom than the freedom to live without fear." The seniors erupted in cheers.

"You have worked, sacrificed and produced all your lives while the welfare system expands because people won't work," Duke added. "Many of the children turn to crime because the system doesn't encourage them to work." The crowd cheered again.

When the sixty-minute forum ended, seniors surrounded Duke to clap him on the back and shake his hand. "Man, we've got Edwards," exulted Duke aide Jim McPherson. "We're going to win."

Edwards, normally unflappable, was rattled. "In my entire career," he told aide Al Donovan as he hurried out a back door, "I've helped people like these seniors by making sure their needs are met. They have no earthly idea what Duke's ulterior motives are. If Duke gets elected, he'll do an about-face and these will be the people he'll hurt the most."

Three days later, Edwards and Duke met in the first of two statewide televised debates. The date was November 2, the runoff's midway point. Duke was nervous beforehand. He knew that Edwards, with his razor-sharp mind and quick wit, had made a career out of cutting up his political opponents. But with his years of experience appearing on television and radio, Duke would prove a formidable debating opponent. Throughout the hour-long event, Edwards seemed tentative and flat, while Duke hammered away at him confidently. "If you like what's been going on over the past 20 years, go ahead and vote for Edwin Edwards," Duke asserted. "You'll get more of the same: more environmental destruction, you'll get lower salaries for teachers, more crime in our streets, our schools will continue to decline. We need change. Please let's make a change in this election—a change to turn Louisiana around."

By the luck of the draw, Edwards gave his closing statement first. Expecting to face Roemer, Edwards was like a fastball hitter who unexpectedly had to face a curveballer. Duke was catching him off stride. Duke was unlike Bennett Johnston, Dave Treen, or Buddy Roemer, the gubernatorial candidates Edwards had faced before. Edwards in a perfunctory close could come up with nothing better than a promise to bring together the state's divergent factions to solve Louisiana's problems, including a slack economy and a projected $1 billion budget deficit. In his close, Duke went on the attack again. He pulled a sheaf of papers from his coat pocket and said they were a sampling of the hundreds of pardons Edwards had granted to dangerous criminals during his three terms as governor. "Edwin Edwards freed more violent criminals in this state over the last 20 years than all the other governors in this century combined in Louisiana," Duke said. The statement was an exaggeration, but it was dramatic, and because Duke went last, Edwards could not respond.

Arnold Hirsch, chairman of the University of New Orleans history department, scored Duke the debate victor. "Any time Duke is able to stand up in that setting wearing a coat and tie and looking like a major candidate, being treated respectfully and deferentially, it helps his legitimacy and buttresses his argument that he's a mainstream candidate," Hirsch said. "He doesn't look dangerous, he doesn't sound dangerous—what's all the fuss about?" Duke and his aides celebrated after the debate. In two weeks, they told themselves, Duke would be elected governor. They looked ahead expectantly to the second statewide debate, which would be held in four days. Duke would finish Edwards off that night, they thought. The debate, which was held on November 6, would prove to be the pivotal event of the runoff, but it would not turn out as Duke and his aides expected. Edwin Edwards, Louisiana's master politician for the past generation, would see to that.

By now Edwards had tired of Duke's challenge. He thought he should not just win but win big over a former Nazi and Ku Klux Klan grand wizard. Yet his latest tracking poll showed him with 52.7 percent of the vote, enough to win but perhaps only barely if voters were still lying about supporting Duke. Edwards cleared his schedule the afternoon of the debate to prepare. He met at his Baton Rouge home with Billy Broadhurst, his longtime friend and former law partner. They spent a couple of hours discussing key issues and how Duke would likely respond to them and how Edwards ought to respond. They agreed that Edwards had to be more aggressive and forceful than in the first debate. Edwards should focus on Duke's extremist activities, they decided, and portray the election as a moral choice between a longtime public servant and an unqualified candidate who had sown discord all his life. Edwards wouldn't make the same mistake as Bennett Johnston. He would assault Duke's character.

When he and Broadhurst had completed the debate preparation, Edwards excused himself and sat alone for twenty minutes writing on a yellow legal pad. He was working on his closing statement, and he wanted to be sure it packed a wallop. He thought of Duke and said to himself, "This is the time I'm going to show the difference in our lives. I spent my life helping and building, and you spent your life tearing down and burning."

Duke at that moment was driving to an American Legion hall in Uptown New Orleans. His top adviser, Jim McPherson, wanted Duke to take it easy that day and spend the time before the debate preparing and collecting his thoughts. But after winning the first debate, Duke felt overconfident going into the second one. He was spending the day as he had every other since the primary election, campaigning nonstop. It was to be a fateful error.

A dozen anti-Duke protesters were waiting for him outside the American Legion hall. When Duke, McPherson, and his two bodyguards pulled up to the curb, the protesters surrounded the car, screamed insults, and cursed him.

"Nazi, Nazi!"

"Klan bastard!"

"Shithead!"

"Fuck you, Duke!"

Duke and his three associates paused for a minute and then pushed their way into the hall. Inside was a small group of elderly men and women. Over the protesters' shouts, which were audible within the building, Duke gave a short speech and asked for their support. He then apologized, saying he had to leave. It was 4:00 p.m.—two hours before the debate was to begin in Baton Rouge, eighty miles away.

They pushed their way through the protesters again and sped off. They had to get to Baton Rouge quickly, or Duke might arrive late for the debate. But the driver, it turned out, didn't know New Orleans well, and they got lost on their way to Interstate 10, which would take them to Baton Rouge. They lost precious minutes. When they found I-10, they got stuck in rush hour traffic. As they crawled toward Baton Rouge, Duke was talking excitedly in the back seat about the hostile reception he had received outside the American Legion hall. He should have been calmly preparing for the debate.

They finally cleared rush hour traffic and sped ninety miles an hour to Baton Rouge. Duke every few minutes anxiously checked his watch to see whether they would arrive before the 6:00 p.m. starting time. The debate was to be held at Louisiana Public Broadcasting. At 5:50, Edwards had already been through makeup and was standing on the set reviewing his notes. The four journalists on the panel were reviewing their questions. And Duke was on the outskirts of Baton Rouge hurtling at ninety miles an hour toward the television station. He—and everybody at LPB—was wondering whether he would get there on time. The car screeched to a halt at the station. Duke jumped out and rushed through a throng of waiting reporters. It was 5:59—one minute to airtime. He dashed onto the set. As he was miked up, he ran his hand through his unkempt hair. And then the debate began.

Duke's lack of preparation showed immediately. In his opening statement, he was unfocused and rambling. It was downhill from there, as he came up against an aggressive set of reporters and a well-prepared Edwards. Several minutes later, Norman Robinson, a news anchor at WDSU-TV in New Orleans, asked Duke to name his main legislative goals as governor. When Duke instead went into his standard antitax spiel, Robinson interrupted Duke to say he wasn't answering Robinson's question. A short time afterward, another panelist, Richard Baudouin of the *Times of Acadiana*, asked Duke how many jobs he would cut from the government rolls to balance the budget. When Duke went into his government-is-too-big pat answer, Baudouin interrupted him to ask for specifics. Yet another panelist, Jeff Duhe, an LPB correspondent, interrupted Duke after Duke gave a vague answer to the question of what jobs he had held. "This is a job," Duke responded. "This is work."

"Are you saying," Duhe asked, interrupting him again, "you're a politician and you run for office for a living?"

Duke sputtered an answer.

Edwards then jumped in. "The fella never had a job," he said. "Look, this is an important business. There is $9 billion involved and 75,000 employees. These professional politicians who make a living by running for public office and living off of contributions aren't qualified to be governor."

The emotion and intensity of the debate were at a fever pitch. And now Norman Robinson was about to elevate them even higher. Since being asked several days earlier to serve on the panel, Robinson had debated with himself how aggressively he should question Duke. As a news anchor who had to be liked by both blacks and whites, he felt that he should ask blank questions to avoid offending viewers. But as he ruminated, he decided that first and foremost he was a journalist and had been one for nearly nineteen years. He had to ask tough questions. And as a black man, he had to ask Duke a question that would cut to the heart of his racial appeal.

As Robinson, forty, had watched Duke throughout the campaign, he had been reminded of his boyhood in Toomsuba, Mississippi, a town of 500 residents. As a boy, he had watched whites run his uncle out of town and his grandfather off his land. His uncle's offense was hitting a store owner who called him "nigger." Robinson was once beaten with a chain by two white boys because he drank water from their pump.

Duke gave him that same dry taste in his mouth and uneasiness in his gut he had had as a boy who always feared that he might offend white people by what he said, how he looked at them, and how long he stayed in one place. Duke, to Robinson, represented the reemergence of the unbridled, unapologetic, raw hatred of whites, he had known as a boy. "We've gone though the Civil War," Robinson thought at one point during the campaign, "the Civil Rights movement, the country has been turned upside down. We've supposed to be in an age of enlightenment, and here we are fighting the same old hurtful politics of the past."

As the hour-long Duke-Edwards debate progressed, Robinson thought again of all these things. He would have one last chance to ask Duke a question. The moment arrived. "Mr. Duke, I have to tell you I am a very concerned citizen," Robinson began. "I am a journalist, but first and foremost I am a concerned citizen. And as a minority who has heard you say some very excoriating and diabolical things about minorities, about blacks, about Jews, about Hispanics, I am scared, sir."

Robinson paused. "I have heard you say Jews deserve to be in the ashbin of history. I've heard you say that horses have contributed more to the building of America than blacks did. Given that kind of past, sir, given that kind of diabolical, evil, vile mentality, convince me, sir, and other minorities like me to entrust their lives and the lives of their children to you."

Duke frowned. He then reached for a pat answer. "Mr. Robinson, I don't think there is a human being on this earth or in this state who hasn't at some time been intolerant in their life." Jesse Jackson, he added, had spit in white people's food while working at a restaurant as a young man.

Robinson broke in. "Sir, we are talking about political, economic genocide. We're not talking about intolerance. We are not talking about spitting on people, sir. As a new-found Christian, a born-again, are you here willing now to apologize to the people, the minorities of this state, whom you have so dastardly insulted sir?"

"Of course I apologize for things I have said that have been intolerant and improper," Duke replied.

Robinson was unsatisfied. "Do you repudiate the Klan? And the neo-Nazis?"

"I do repudiate the Klan and any other racist organization or intolerant organization that exists in this state or this country," Duke said blandly. He then segued into his anti-affirmative action spiel. "There is violence in our streets every day directed at white people as well as the other way around," Duke added.

"As well as against black people?"

"Look, Mr. Robinson, I don't think your are really being fair with me," Duke said testily.

"I don't think you are really being honest, sir," Robinson replied.

Duke campaign aide David Touchstone, watching the debate in Shreveport, exulted at the harsh exchange, convinced that it would prompt undecided whites to vote for Duke. Henry Dillon III, who was organizing a get-out-the-vote effort among blacks in New Orleans, also cheered the Duke-Robinson exchange but for different reasons. "Robinson's stuck a hole in the aura of Duke's invulnerability," he thought. "This is going to motivate a lot of blacks to vote."

The televised debate was now nearly over. Duke made his closing statement. He was defensive and unfocused. It was Edwards's turn. He pulled out the statement he had written that afternoon. "This man has attacked us for 20 years," Edwards said.

> Now, all of a sudden, he wants to stop the attacks. While David Duke was burning crosses and scaring people, I was building hospitals to heal them. When he was parading around in a Nazi uniform to intimidate our citizens, I was in a National Guard uniform bringing relief to flood and hurricane victims. When he was selling Nazi hate literature as late at 1989 in his legislative office, I was providing free textbooks for the children of this state. When he was writing porno books, I was signing anti-pornographic legislation.

He paused.

> I have been in this business for a long time. I have a record, and he has a record. I suggest to you he has given us 20 years of hate and hurt, and I don't think he has earned the right to ask you to be governor. Let him go back to our communities if he in fact has a new-found religion. And let him spend some time providing some healing and help to overcome what he has done to us for all these years, giving us this reputation in the nation and the rest of the world. Then after he has done community service and served mankind with some help, then let him come back to us 20 years from now when he has matured and truly shown us that he is a different, new man. Maybe at that time we'll think about letting him be governor of our state. But until then, don't let him divide us. Don't let him separate us from the rest of the nation. Don't let him make a mockery of Louisiana. We're too important, and we're

> too good for that. The people of this state need a governor as good as the people of this state, not someone whose reputation, deserved or not, around the nation is one of hate and division. I don't want my Louisiana to fall into that morass. We went down that road one time a long time ago, and we suffered for it for many decades. We'll not let David Duke take us down that same road again. Not ever.

The debate was over and with it David Duke's chances of being elected governor. His weak showing and Edwards's brilliant closing statement had destroyed his momentum. Louisianians watching on TV throughout the state breathed a sigh of relief. They felt that the barbarians had been repulsed at the gate—but that they could not rest easy because the barbarians might attack again at any moment.

Duke tried to regroup, but he was to come under a withering attack during the final ten days before the November 16 runoff. The anti-Duke movement had raised millions of dollars in the previous two and one-half weeks—the amount of money normally only a popular presidential candidate could raise during such a short period of time—and would ensure that no one could watch television in Louisiana during the election's final ten days without seeing ads warning that the state faced economic catastrophe if Duke was elected. Defeating Duke had become a crusade.

Much of the anti-Duke money had been pouring into the coffers of the Edwards campaign and the Louisiana Democratic party—not just from Louisiana but from throughout the United States. In a year when only three states held elections, the Duke-Edwards race had become front-page news throughout the country and dominated radio talk shows nationwide. The *New York Times* was publishing at least one article a day, as if it were a local race. When Louisianians traveled out of the state, they found that all anybody wanted to talk about was the governor's race.

Duke, meanwhile, was appearing repeatedly on the evening news and national television shows: "Good Morning America," "Nightwatch," "Larry King Live," "Donahue," "Crossfire," "Today." His appearances prompted thousands of people from around the country to contribute to his campaign. But it scared many others, particularly Jews, into thinking that he could win. While Duke's supporters made $5 and 10 contributions, his opponents gave $1,000 or more.

Donald Spector, a professional fund raiser hired by the Louisiana Democratic party to tap into big donors during the runoff, had never seen people make contributions so eagerly. They were frantic at the thought that Duke might win. "There was a feeling of life and death," Spector remembered later. "It wasn't just about winning or losing a race." When Spector called business executives of major companies seeking contributions during normal campaigns, they usually returned the call a couple of days later, and then it was only their secretaries who made the call. When Spector called seeking money for the anti-Duke campaign in 1991, the business executive themselves called him back immediately.

Steven Ross, chairman of Time-Warner, worked feverishly to defeat Duke. Ross, who was dying of cancer, gave the Louisiana Democratic party $25,000, and he wrote letters and called friends, beseeching them to make contributions. Dustin Hoffman sent $25,000; Michelle Pfeiffer gave $1,000. So did Dan Akroyd, Kirstie Alley, James Garner, Norman Lear, and Herb Alpert. Five Democratic senators joined the effort, sending out an appeal for the Louisiana Democratic party. They got back eight boxes worth of letters, in a response rate that was fifteen times higher than normal.

When Edwards visited New York City on November 5, he raised $200,000. "I'll do whatever I can to help," contributors told him throughout the day. Many people felt they had to stop David Duke in Louisiana, or his success would be repeated in New York, Connecticut, and other states. Edwards in the primary had raised $1 million, barely enough to mount a successful campaign. But in the runoff, checks flowed into his campaign at a dizzying rate. Eating lunch at Tujague's restaurant in the French Quarter one day during the runoff, Edwards's friend and adviser Bob d'Hemecourt recalled how at the beginning of the campaign they had been strapped for funds. He asked Edwards: "Do you remember when you personally got on the phone and wanted to know where the $5,000 check enroute from Lafayette was? You needed the money to pay an expense."

"Yeah, I remember," Edwards said with a laugh.

"Well, I have $700,000 in my briefcase that we picked up in the last two days," d'Hemecourt chortled.

During the final ten days of the campaign, Duke was under attack by not only Edwards, businessmen, the Louisiana Coalition Against Racism and Nazism, and the state's newspapers but also the Louisiana Democratic party, which kicked off a massive anti-Duke television campaign on November 8, two days after the second debate. The ads were produced by Deno Seder, who wanted to ensure that he had not helped knock out Buddy Roemer in the primary only to see Louisiana end up with David Duke.

The state Democratic party ads concentrated on the economic angle, but several attacked Duke for his Nazi activities. In the most effective spot, Major General Ansel Stroud, commander of the Louisiana National Guard, stood in full dress uniform in front of an American flag and said, "I joined the army in 1944 to fight against the Nazis. And I'm going to fight the Nazis in this election." Another ad broadcast excerpts from Duke's 1986 taped interview with doctoral candidate Evelyn Rich in which Duke told neo-Nazi Joe Fields it could take decades to bring down the United States government. A third ad, as it showed a photograph of Hitler in stiff-arm salute, told viewers: "Vote for Duke. Create a Fuehrer." Separately, New Orleans businessman David Dixon was running his anti-Duke ad, and Bobby Hebert, the Cajun working-class hero who quarterbacked the New Orleans Saints, cut a thirty-second spot in which, without mentioning Duke by name, he told voters to reject racism.

Altogether, the anti-Duke ads were running virtually around the clock. "It has to be the largest single advertising buy ever in American politics against one person," Raymond Strother said. "There's so much of it. I don't see how he can withstand it." Meanwhile, business owners wrote their employees, warning that a Duke election would spell economic doom. "Vote for Governor Edwin Edwards," the general manager of the

New Orleans Hilton wrote his employees. "It may be the most important vote you cast in your lifetime." Anti-Duke bumper stickers sprouted on cars throughout the state. "No Dukes" was the favorite, but other popular ones were "Vote for the Lizard, not the Wizard" and "Vote for the Crook. It's important." President Bush denounced Duke as a racist and anti-Semite, and national Republican party leaders chimed in.

David Duke was thick-skinned after a lifetime of enduring slings and arrows. But the massive onslaught in the runoff was taking its toll. Usually surefooted on television, Duke stumbled on Sunday, November 10, when he appeared with Edwards for the final time during the campaign, on NBC's "Meet the Press." It was six days before the runoff, and all the world was watching. Timothy Russert, NBC's Washington bureau chief and a panelist on the show, was determined not to let Duke manipulate "Meet the Press" panelists as he had unprepared interviewers on so many other television shows. He researched Duke thoroughly to come up with tough questions that would keep Duke from giving his canned answers.

The show was a verbal slugfest. Duke and Edwards, sitting side by side in a New Orleans television studio, frequently interrupted each other to charge the other with improprieties and to launch spirited defenses. But neither candidate had scored an advantage until Russert late in the show asked Duke to identify the three manufacturing companies with the most employees in Louisiana.

"I couldn't give you their name right off, sir," Duke said, stumbling for words.

"You don't know who the biggest employers in the state of Louisiana are?" Russert asked incredulously.

"Well, I don't have the statistics in front of me," Duke said.

Jim McPherson, sitting a few feet away off camera, was silently imploring Duke to turn the question around and make his points, as he had done time and time again throughout the campaign. "Tell him there aren't enough jobs," McPherson said under his breath. "Tell him that when you're governor, there'll be new industry. Tell him how many jobs Louisiana lost while Edwards was governor." But Duke, worn down by the attacks, came up empty.

Russert followed up with another question. "How many people in your state live below the poverty line?" he asked.

"I don't have the exact numbers in front of me, sir," Duke said, faltering again. "I don't carry around an almanac with me."

"It's 24 percent," a playful Edwards, sitting next to him off camera, whispered, giving the correct answer. Duke looked at him blankly and turned back to the camera but said nothing.

A few minutes later, the show ended. As Edwards and Duke were taking off their microphones, Duke said to Edwards, "Well a week from now it will be a very close election. Whichever way it goes, I want to stay in touch with you."

"Well, number one," Edwards responded, "it's not going to be a close election. And you can visit me at the mansion anytime you want." A few minutes later, he told reporters, "Heavens to Betsy, if he doesn't know where the jobs in Louisiana are now, how is he going to be more effective in getting the jobs tomorrow or the next day?"

Duke had taken a pounding during the past week, and there would be no letup in the final five days of the campaign. On Monday, November 11, Bob Hawks, a former Tennessee state legislator who had worked for Duke for several months, quit his campaign and charged that Duke's claim of a recent conversion to Christianity was a hoax.

Hawks, a devout Christian, said that while Duke praised Christ in public, in private he never displayed any religious fervor or read the Bible. "I would hear it in his words where he was stage-center, which included talking to the media and from platforms," Hawks said, "but failed to hear it from his daily life." The incident damaged Duke's credibility with a key constituency, Protestant evangelicals. It also reminded them that nine days earlier, he had claimed to belong to the Evangelical Bible Church—only to have to admit the next day that it did not exist. Actually, he explained, he participated in a nondenominational Bible study with a small group of individuals who met in different homes.

Duke had further stumbled when, pressed to identify the moment when he had become a born-again Christian, he said it had happened at age thirteen. If so, he had been an admirer of Hitler and had been a Klan grand wizard after finding Christ, a claim that did not square with many Christians. "It is not possible that someone who found Christ 28 years ago could have burned the cross, could have twisted the cross into a Swastika," Neil Curran, an Evangelical Christian and Republican party activist, told reporters.

On Wednesday, two days after Hawks blasted Duke, Duke suffered a final body blow. Ros Davidson, a Scottish journalist, told the *Times-Picayune* that Duke had said Jews were a plague on the white race during a 1990 interview with her—at a time when he was claiming to no longer hold extremist views. While Duke was normally careful not to display his true anti-Semitic views to reporters, Davidson said she thought he opened up with her because she was Scottish. Because his forebears were from Scotland, he told her, he felt a special affinity for the country. "You know the [Ku Klux Klan] fiery cross is a symbol adopted from Scotland," he told Davidson.

Despite the battering, Duke wasn't giving up. That Wednesday night, his largest crowd yet of the campaign, more than 2,500 people, turned out for a rally in Lafayette, a traditional Edwards stronghold. "On Saturday," Duke shouted, "the silent majority is not going to be silent any longer." Edwards at a New Orleans rally on Thursday night scoffed at that notion. "David Duke says the polls can't tell about his strength because he flies below radar," Edwards said. "Forty-eight hours from now, he's going to crash." His own tracking poll showed him with 59 percent of the vote, up from 51 percent two days before.

Three polls released that week, after attempting to adjust for Duke's hidden vote, showed Edwards leading by seven to ten points. Who was right, Duke with his silent majority or Edwards and the pollsters? "We're all holding our breath for tomorrow's election," a woman told the *Dallas Morning News* on Friday. Duke held the final rally of his long campaign that night at an American Legion hall in the New Orleans suburb of Jefferson. He predicted victory the next day and denounced Edwards and the *Times-Picayune.* Afterward, hundreds of people spilled into the parking lot, not wanting to go home. Neither did Duke. Lit up by the floodlights of half a dozen TV cameras, he stood on the back of a truck, waving to his supporters, who were chanting, "Go to hell, *T-P*, go to hell!" Duke finally left to be interviewed by Ted Koppel on "Nightline." It would be another night when he didn't get much sleep.

Henry Dillon III didn't get any sleep that night. Executive director of the Louisiana Voter Registration/Education Crusade, a nonprofit group based in New Orleans that registered black people to vote, Dillon was exhausted but too excited to rest. For four weeks, since Duke had made the runoff, he had helped organize a get-out-the-vote effort on a scale he had never dreamed possible. And he was not alone in ensuring that blacks turned out in record numbers. Black political organizations in New Orleans and other major cities throughout Louisiana had organized similar drives. The Edwards campaign financed many of these groups, spending hundreds of thousands of dollars to hire workers to knock on doors in the days before the election and turn out voters on election day. Many blacks traditionally worked in get-out-the-vote efforts because of the money they were paid. But money didn't matter in this election. Defeating Duke had become a moral imperative for blacks. Everywhere Henry Dillon went in New Orleans during the four-week runoff, blacks wanted to talk only about the governor's race. "What do I have to do to stop Duke?" they asked him. National black groups, meanwhile, sent thousands of dollars to aid the get-out-the-vote effort.

On election day, November 16, Dillon began deploying his forces before the sun came up. Hundreds of people put up Edwards signs throughout the city. By 6:00 a.m., when the polls open, they were manning a fleet of vans that would take people without transportation to the polls. Blacks in New Orleans traditionally voted later in the day. But Dillon's workers found this morning that blacks throughout the city were waiting to vote at polling stations when they opened.

"If Duke wins, it'd be just like the '60s," said Jay Jackson, a thirty-three-year-old maintenance man, as he waited to vote at 7:30 a.m. in New Orleans. "Different water fountains, all that stuff. We'd be slaves again."

A little later, Dillon was at his headquarters when a group of students walked in. They wanted to help out. "We don't have any more money to pay you," Dillon said.

"We're not here for money," one woman said. "We just want to know how we can beat Duke."

At 11:00 a.m., a group of drivers sent by Lance Hill to black precincts to take voters to the polls found to their astonishment that there was no one to drive. Everyone had voted. In Baton Rouge, Duke campaign aide David Touchstone saw hundreds of black people displaying red "Stop Duke" signs in their car windows and long lines of black voters at the polls. He shook his head in resignation. "We can't possibly win now," he thought.

This day, blacks would turn out in record numbers: 78.3 percent of registered blacks voted, a rate nearly as high as whites' 79 percent turnout. Overall the turnout was 78.7 percent, an extraordinarily high rate in an era when only 50 percent of registered Americans voted to elect their presidents. It was the highest rate in a Louisiana election since a 79.3 percent turnout for the 1964 second Democratic primary.

Polls on election day were scheduled to close at 8:00 p.m. People across the state nervously turned on their TV sets to get the results. The election that had weighed on their minds for days and days was now over. At two minutes before 8:00 p.m., a dozen Duke supporters at Mama's Place, a neighborhood bar in Duke's legislative district in Metairie, thought their man was about to make history. "I think it's beautiful that the white people stuck together on this one like the niggers did," said Lois Brondum, "Mama" in the bar's name. "I can't wait for Duke to win. I just can't wait." At seconds past 8:00, Bob Schieffer came on the air for CBS. "Edwin Edwards has won the Louisiana governor's race by a substantial margin," Schieffer said, citing exit polls.

Duke's supporters at Mama's Place fell silent. The crowd of people in Edwards's suite at the Monteleone whooped and hollered. Bob d'Hemecourt shook Edwards's hand. "Congratulations," he said, "you did it again."

Word spread immediately throughout the French Quarter. A brass band materialized from somewhere and led a group of revelers to the Monteleone, playing "When the Saints Go Marching In." The final result was:

| | | |
|---|---|---|
| Edwin Edwards | 1,057,031 | 61 percent |
| David Duke | 671,009 | 39 percent |

Duke could run from his past, but he could not hide from it. In the end, truth had won out. Duke was unfit to be governor.

Along with the huge black turnout, the economic issue had proven decisive for Edwards. Exit polls showed that 94 percent of the people who listed losing business as a top concern voted for Edwards. When asked to pick their top two concerns in the election from a list of nine possibilities, 37 percent named business. The economic issue swung Roemer's supporters into Edwards's camp. Three out of every four Roemer supporters voted for Edwards. Edwards won not because voters liked him but because he convinced them that Duke posed a grave threat to their well-being. Nearly half of the people who pulled Edwards's lever did so because they did not want Duke to be governor, exit polls showed. Six in ten voters said they thought Edwards was a crook.

The *Times-Picayune* and the television advertising bombardment overwhelmed Duke in the New Orleans metro area, where one-third of the state's voters lived. Edwards crushed Duke in New Orleans with 87 percent of the vote, and he won a whopping 59 percent vote in conservative Jefferson Parish. Edwards even defeated Duke in his Metairie legislative district with 56 percent of the vote. Duke won only nineteen of Louisiana's sixty-four parishes, with most of them in the rural northeast corner of the state. Duke had not just lost but lost big. Analysts pointed out that he had received a lower percentage of votes than in the Senate race. He was going backwards politically, they said. There were some bright spots for Duke. He had won 55 percent of the white vote, despite the massive negative assault, exit polls showed. He carried 56 percent of the Republican vote and 56 percent of the Cajun vote.

At 9:30 p.m., Edwards went down to the Monteleone grand ballroom to make his victory speech. "Tonight, Louisiana became first," he told a cheering throng, "first to turn back the merchant of hate, the master of deceit. I ask the nation, the national press, I ask all those whose opinions we respect, to write and to say of us that Louisiana rejected the demagogue and renounced irrational fear, dark suspicion, evil bigotry and division and chose a future of hope and trust and love for all of God's children."

An hour later, a subdued Duke conceded before his supporters at the Baton Rouge Hilton. "Right doesn't win every battle, but right always triumphs in the end," he said. "This is just the beginning, not the end." Surrounded by a phalanx of bodyguards, he moved onto the floor to thank his supporters and give interviews to the dozens of reporters covering his election-night party. In one brief interview, he blamed his defeat on "power, money, endorsements, the media and economic blackmail. . . . All the factors working together were too much to overcome."

Two hours later, Duke was still circling the littered ballroom, looking for hands to shake and reporters to talk to. He wasn't ready yet to yield the spotlight.

# PART II

## THE ECONOMY

# SOME FACTORS AFFECTING THE ECONOMIC DEVELOPMENT OF LOUISIANA*

Lee J. Melton, Jr.

The interest in economic development since World War II has been phenomenal. It can only be compared to that displayed in the period of "mercantilism" when the national states of Western Europe were emerging, and for sheer magnitude and intensity it surpasses anything the world has ever seen. Why is that so? In part, it is a matter of contact. Poverty is both absolute and relative. It is possible to be poor in the relative sense and still be content—for what one has never seen, one does not miss. However, in this day of rapid transportation and even more rapid communication, the populace of underdeveloped areas have observed what can be done and are no longer content with their lot.

For that matter, even the advanced areas wish to experience further growth, for human wants are insatiable and higher levels of living create the desire for even higher levels. Every society is beset with demands for goods and services that cannot be fully met, with the result that all demands have to be curtailed in part, or some completely, or both. Economic growth leads to greater area income—a bigger pie, so to speak—and to a degree lessens the problems associated with the recipients of the smaller shares.

This fervor for economic growth is not an unmixed blessing. History indicates that a high order of economic development is the exception, not the rule, and further that it is painful, expensive, and usually slow. To the extent that efforts are expended for increased development and fail, the dissatisfaction and disappointment of the people involved may constitute a barrier to further efforts. This danger notwithstanding, it can for purposes of policy be ignored, for there is no choice but to try.

Developed or advanced areas fall into three classifications: those that are continuing to advance; those barely maintaining their position; and those losing ground. The underdeveloped areas may be grouped under four categories: those not developing and

*First published as chapter 1 in Thomas R. Beard, ed., *The Louisiana Economy* (Baton Rouge: Louisiana State University Press, © 1969), 21-40. Reprinted with the kind permission of the editor, author, and publisher.

with little or no potential for development; those not developing but apparently possessing great potential for development; those that are developing but with a limited potential; and those developing and possessing great potential for continued growth.

Although we tend to classify a nation, region, or state as a whole, even the best contain all the categories of advancement and underdevelopment. So do the worst. Only the proportions differ.

As a state, Louisiana must be classified as one of the least developed parts of the most developed nation in the world. Yet, in certain of its geographic areas Louisiana has achieved levels of growth that are among the highest, just as in others the level is among the most miserable. There is a tendency on the part of those writing or speaking for public consumption to become extremely optimistic over the possibility of Louisiana quickly closing the gap that now exists between it and national levels of economic achievement. For this reason the folklore persists that the state is something of a Sleeping Beauty, requiring only the kiss of a searching prince to initiate the upward spiral. The princes of the industrial world—these days called locational experts—have been carrying on constant investigation of the economic potential of various areas in the state. Louisiana has not been overlooked; she has been looked over and found wanting.

## THEORIES OF ECONOMIC DEVELOPMENT

The interest of the economist in the growth and development of the economy of a nation, state, or region is as old as the discipline itself. Formerly called political economy—still the most descriptive term—the study of economics recognized that the welfare of the group and its continued advancement to a higher order of economic achievement was a public goal. So, from the beginning, there have been attempts to explain the process of economic growth and to formulate a theory of such growth that would possess universality in its applicability. All such attempts have, so far, been unsuccessful, and it is suspected that efforts to develop a general theory of economic development will continue to disappoint the social scientist. Nevertheless, from the centuries of thought and investigation that have gone into these matters, partial theories of economic development have been formulated, and from such theories may be extrapolated certain key elements that have significant bearing on the rate of economic growth, even though the degree of importance may vary from one situation to another.

### *A natural process?*

The fathers of the school of classical economics were deeply interested in the matter of economic growth, but—as a group—they considered it something of a natural process. There were dissenters, of course, and Malthus, for one, pointed out that there was nothing at all natural about it.[1] Certainly, history has not indicated that economic development is simply a process of natural evolution. Further, the gap between the developed countries and the underdeveloped ones is not narrowing, it is widening. It is not inevitable, then, that Louisiana will undergo economic growth at a rate sufficient to overcome the differential in per capita income in this state compared to the national average, much less surpass it. It is conceivable that the differential might even worsen. Unless the climate for economic development is improved and the seeds of its existence sown in greater quantity, Louisiana might well remain at the lower end of the spectrum of per capita income in the United States.

### *Geographic determinism*

Geographic determinism is the limitation placed on economic development by the natural environment. Indeed, it goes beyond this and makes the economy a somewhat hopeless victim of natural physical forces. No competent economist has ever denied that physical environment is a strong conditioning force—exceedingly so—but enough examples abound of nations with few resources and relatively high levels of development achievement to justify the hypothesis that the geographic conditioners of an area may impede development but cannot, of themselves, prevent it if other factors are favorable.

Natural resources and geographic factors have posed no great barriers to economic growth in Louisiana. On the contrary, much—if not most—of the growth to date has been directly related to the exploitation of mineral resources, with the result that the economic complex is perhaps oriented disproportionately toward the processing of raw materials and producers' goods.

### *Capital formation*

The test of essentiality is a rather poor one, and to state that one factor of economic development is more important than another is fraught with peril. Nevertheless, the one factor that is mentioned more than any other—and this has been true throughout the history of economic thought—is that of capital formation. Certainly it is a critical factor. For the underdeveloped country the lack of capital may present an almost insurmountable obstacle. For Louisiana, this is not so. As a part of a well-developed nation possessing the greatest store of capital goods in the world, there are no political barriers to the flow of capital into Louisiana. Only the opportunity for use more profitable than other alternatives outside the state is required. For those with a fetish about locally raised capital, the low per capita income in the state probably precludes significant increases in the rate of local accumulation.

*Entrepreneurship*

Many have considered the role of the entrepreneur as the critical element in economic growth.[2] This assumes, of course, some sort of free enterprise system which permits this type of individual to function, for the profit motive and the possibility of sufficient returns are the voices calling these unique individuals to the market place. To a considerable degree, entrepreneurship is a function of the social climate; it does not thrive where the attitudes of the populace and the governmental units are hostile. In the past Louisiana has been frequently accused of anti-business bias. Much of this clamor has been simply the effective use of an offensive weapon by the variety of business interests operating in the state. But it is true that much anti-business bias has been prevalent, a not unusual occurrence in an agrarian state with a traditionally rural population.

As in the case of any area whose economic development has failed to keep pace, Louisiana has the advantage of imitating the innovational procedures of its more successful sister states to close the lag in the time gap, and it is possible to import innovators after the gap has been closed. Still the encouragement and development of greater amounts of indigenous entrepreneurship is to be encouraged. A note of caution at this point. A government policy or attitude that is not in keeping with what business would prefer is nearly always considered "anti-business" by the representatives of business interests. The proper role of government is to be neither pro-business nor anti-business, nor pro or con any other segment of the economy for that matter. Its proper role is concern for the interests of the group as a whole, without bias for any segment. However, insofar as the encouragement of any group can be undertaken which promotes the welfare of the larger state family, it should be done.

The causes which enable or compel an individual to act as an entrepreneur are not fully understood, but among them appears to be an intense need for achievement, and there is ample evidence that this motivational factor has been much less plentiful in underdeveloped areas than in the advanced. The inference is that for economic development to proceed at a more rapid pace, the number of individuals with the entrepreneurial complex will have to be greatly increased. What appears to be the origin of such individuals? Probably neither the most depressed economic group nor the highest echelon of the well-to-do will furnish it. It appears to come mostly from the lower-middle-class members wishing to advance. As Louisiana broadens this group, the base for potential entrepreneurs increases proportionately. Certainly, the sociological barriers to growth have constituted a major force in the past, and the impact of these barriers will last well into the future.

*Dualism*

Frequently in underdeveloped areas there appear to be two distinct sectors of the economy. This is usually the aftermath of the backward area coming into contact with more advanced regions. In the resulting clash of systems the techniques of the advanced group will be grafted on a segment of the less developed economy, but other sectors will remain unaffected, insulated by economic, sociological, psychological, and cultural factors that appear either impervious or highly resistant to change. The consequence is that one policy of a uniform nature can be adopted to promote growth in such a situation.[3]

Any casual examination of Louisiana economy reveals a pattern of striking contrasts. Pockets of industrial complexes representative of economic advancement of the highest order are not far removed from areas of abject poverty and the absence of economic growth, or its probability under present conditions. It is not particularly startling that this should be so. The nature of much of the industrialization that has taken place makes it almost axiomatic. While not without some carry-over impact, the influence of the raw materials processing industries appears to have had negligible impact on the indigenous activities. This is the typical response of underdeveloped areas to the extraction and processing of raw materials, even when done by the most advanced techniques. The spill-over effect is sometimes disappointing. The phenomenon is often observed in agriculture, with the most advanced techniques existing side by side with what constitutes subsistence agriculture.

The cleavage between the advanced and less developed sectors of the Louisiana economy has diminished to a considerable degree. Nevertheless, degrees of difference in the levels of, and the rates of, economic development do exist between various parts of the Louisiana economic complex. One does not have to accept the theory of sociological dualism to appreciate the role of cultural, sociological, and psychological factors in economic development. Indeed, the provincial attitude of the Louisiana populace may prove a more formidable barrier to economic advancement then purely economic obstacles.

### *The big push*

Professor Harvey Leibenstein has placed major emphasis on what he termed "the critical minimum effort."[4] Put succinctly, this thesis holds that an underdeveloped area is characterized by a certain degree of apparent stability. In order to achieve sustained growth, it is necessary that stimulants to development be of a certain minimum size. At any one time there are forces at work in the economy tending to increase per capita income and there are forces at work tending to decrease per capita income. In the former group are increased savings and investment, higher levels of work skills, resource discovery and utilization, increases in entrepreneurial numbers and energy, and economies of scale. The latter includes increases in surplus population, failure of firms and entrepreneurs to realize expectations, institutional rigidities, and resistance to new ideas and change. The critical minimum effort must be of such magnitude as to set off income generating forces that are sufficient to overcome the deterrents and reinforce themselves in succeeding periods.

It behooves planners for economic development not to undertake too much too soon, and to concentrate efforts in carefully selected areas and activities rather than to utilize a shotgun approach to all areas and activities.

### *Take-off into sustained growth*

Walt W. Rostow has traced rather carefully the stages through which a nation passes on its journey to economic development.[5] The Rostow treatment indicates the necessity of separating the stages of economic development and ascertains certain common characteristics of particular stages as they have occurred in different countries. The stages are: (1) the traditional society; (2) preconditions for take-off; (3) take-off; (4) drive to maturity; and (5) age of high mass consumption.

Because the lack of economic development in Louisiana is a relative proposition and we feel impoverished as a state only in relation to states with an even higher degree of economic achievement, Louisiana is already in the fifth stage. After all, a part of a complex cannot long remain isolated from the other parts. Still, it might be conceived that Louisiana is in the take-off period insofar as an era of rapid industrialization is concerned. While it is probable that the preconditions have been met in at least minimal fashion, it is regrettable that an even better educational and institutional base has not been provided. Even so, an adequate base probably exists. It is possible, however, to accelerate economic growth and to extend the ultimate potential for development if increased attention is given to the educational and institutional base.

### *Backwash effects*

Elaborate theses have been developed to indicate that the commercial intercourse between developed and underdeveloped areas (especially as it concerns manufacturing areas and producers of raw materials and primary products) might have certain backwash effects on the underdeveloped member.[6] By backwash is meant that there may be a small multiplier effect from the export industries of the underdeveloped area, that the terms of trade from the raw materials may steadily worsen, and that specialization in the raw materials curtails the promotion of industry that might otherwise occur and the spill-over effects that would accompany such industrialization. This argument is usually presented as a case for protectionism by underdeveloped nations to help force economic growth. The state of Louisiana is virtually powerless to impose effective restrictions on imports from and exports to other states in the union, but—insofar as it is within the power of planners to affect the course of private business—emphasis should be put on increasing the value added by Louisiana processors.

### *Continued development*

One problem that is of constant concern to the advanced areas of the world, and of this country, is the matter of maintaining growth. This is perhaps not so acute a problem for Louisiana in the direct sense. In the indirect sense it is very real, however, for it is a problem for the nation as a whole, and the effects must overflow into the state economy. The essence of the problem is that the voluminous amounts of investment needed to keep the advanced economy at a level of full and growing employment will in turn, bring about tremendous increases in the level of productive capacity, which will call for still more investment.[7] In other words, this ability of the advanced economy to produce a market surplus of many goods and services sometimes makes further economic growth difficult in a given period of time. For an underdeveloped area within a national economy of advanced development—and this is Louisiana's position vis-à-vis the United States—this means that surpluses outside its borders diminish the demands for its exports and increase the available supply of goods for import, thus impeding the growth of both its raw materials sector and its finished goods sector. Recessions in the United States' economy can have particularly severe repercussions for Louisiana, as the demands of the nation for the raw materials and semifinished goods produced in this state are reduced, at least in relative terms, and the competitive surplus of such manufactured goods as Louisiana does produce becomes more abundantly available.

## SPECIFIC FACTORS IN LOUISIANA'S ECONOMIC DEVELOPMENT

### *Introduction*

If the discussion is moved from general concepts of economic development to a critical examination of more specific factors, what are the forces currently exerting the greatest influence on the economic development of Louisiana, and how may these forces be marshalled in such a way as to maximize the growth potential of the state and its component parts?

What one might call the ingredients of economic development can be divided into two broad categories: the natural and the human or man-controlled. The natural includes such things as land area and its quality, climate, and resources. The better the natural base, the more favorable the growth potential. It should be stressed that the potential for growth and the rate of growth may be two entirely different things. Examples abound of areas that are "have-nots" and yet have still achieved significant economic development. Nevertheless, the natural base—if inadequate—does serve to severely limit the ultimate level of economic development. At least this has been true in the past. Improved transportation, and therefore, the increased ease and decreased cost with which resources can be moved from one geographic location to another, is lessening the pull of natural resources. The importance of natural ingredients notwithstanding, if such a lack exists, there is little that can be done about it. If the framework of natural resources is inadequate, the role of the man-controlled factors, which is always critical, simply becomes more so.

The man-controlled ingredients, because they are amenable to change, are perhaps of more long-run significance to the area seeking economic development. Unlike the natural ingredients they can continually be increased and augmented. The man-controlled ingredients include population, both quantity and quality; technology; the rate of capital accumulation; and the institutional structure. All of these are basically functions of the quality of population. If there is any secret to economic development, it surely lies in the qualitative aspects of the population. Low quality of population is a common ingredient binding all underdeveloped areas—whatever else their differences—in a common union.

When comparing one underdeveloped region with another, one subject for examination would be the institutional framework established for the solution of the various economic and social problems. Although the structure of Louisiana is not basically different from that of any other state, the utilization, quality, and attitudes of institutions sometimes differ a great deal.

### *Natural ingredients*

Geographically, Louisiana is located roughly between latitudes 29.5 degrees N and 33 degrees N and from the 94th meridian eastward to the Mississippi River as the northern part of that boundary and to the Pearl River as the southern part. Elevation ranges from sea level in the coastal areas to over 500 feet above sea level in the hills of the northwest.[8] The total area of the state encompasses 48,523 square miles, ranking it thirty-first among the states. This area consists of 45,106 square miles of land and 3,417 of water.[9] Only four other states have a greater area of water within their borders.

Mean annual precipitation ranges from 46 inches in Caddo Parish in the north to 66 inches in parts of the south, with a median of approximately 56 inches. Snow and sleet are of little importance in Louisiana, rarely reaching damaging proportions although snow does occur more frequently than is generally realized. The average annual temperature varies from 66$^{\circ}$ F in the northern portions of the state to 69$^{\circ}$ F in the southern parts. In January the lowest average is 49$^{\circ}$ F in the northwest and north-central and 57$^{\circ}$ F in the southeast. The highest July averages extend from 83$^{\circ}$ F in the north and north-central to 81$^{\circ}$ F in the east-central. The average number of days with freezing temperature, or lower, ranges from twenty-four at Shreveport to four at New Orleans.[10]

Rains of flood-producing proportions may occur at any time of the year but are most likely to come during late winter and early spring and least likely in the fall. Tropical storms and tornadoes are a threat to life and property in some areas.[11] Water conservation measures, flood control, and accurate weather forecasting, however, have greatly diminished the loss from such forces.

The climate of Louisiana, then, suits the state to a wide variety of agricultural and industrial pursuits.

The commercial requirements of present-day industry and agriculture, added to the private needs of individual citizens, severely tax the water resources of the nation. These demands will obviously become more acute as population grows. Louisiana has been fortunately endowed with ground and surface water resources. However, the popular idea that Louisiana has water to waste is simply not true. Although Louisiana is considered to be a "water-rich" state, there are several areas where little or no fresh ground water is available.[12] Further, the requirements for surface water have increased to the point where improper utilization could severely limit industrial expansion.

The large inland water area of Louisiana and its coastal position are conducive to an extensive harvest of fish and seafood, which in 1962 amounted to 766,540,000 pounds valued at $28,923,000, second highest in the South and Southwest.[13]

The forest land of Louisiana covers 15,999,000 acres. Of the Southern states, only North Carolina contains more live saw timber.[14] The production of lumber, pulp, and forest products ranks as one of the state's major economic activities.

In total mineral production, Louisiana stands second in the nation. Further, Louisiana contains the second largest amount of proven crude oil and natural gas reserves and is the second largest producer of both of these minerals. Louisiana's output of carbon black is exceeded by only one other state. The state is also a major producer of salt and a principal source of sulphur.[15]

Louisiana has sources of clays, stone, lime, shell, and sand and gravel.[16] Deposits of other major minerals such as coal and iron ore are of no commercial significance.

In summary, it may be said that Louisiana is indeed rich in some mineral resources, particularly oil and natural gas, but that it is only adequately endowed with others, and woefully lacking in still others. The fact remains, however, that Louisiana has a natural endowment equal to, and in some cases superior to, many other states that have shown a more rapid rate of growth. A fact to keep constantly in mind about those resources which Louisiana does have in abundance is that while compelling resources will attract, other factors must be given superior weight if alternative sources are available. It should further be recalled that resources are becoming more transportable, so that transformation does not have to occur at source. Nevertheless, we may work under the hypothesis that the natural base of Louisiana is adequate to sustain far more rapid rates of growth than have occurred in the past.

### *Man-controlled ingredients*

While technological progress and capital accumulation are critical factors in economic development, their lack does not have the same implication for a state which is a member of a well-developed national economy than it does for underdeveloped areas that are entities in their own right. Louisiana has available to her the technical and capital resources of the nation in that there are no legal obstacles to their importation. The barriers to capital and technical flows into Louisiana are barriers of opportunity. To the extent which opportunity is not blocked by lack of a specific natural resource, the impediments must be sought in the population and in the institutional framework.

### a) *Population*

The projected population of Louisiana for 1965 was 3,544,000, consisting of 2,420,000 white and 1,124,000 nonwhite.[17] From an educational standpoint the level is quite low. The Census of 1960 indicated that in excess of 20 percent of those twenty-five years of age or older were classed as functional illiterates (fifth grade education or below), and it is this age group which constitutes the bulk of the labor force.[18] This means that many of those in the unemployed category must actually be considered unemployable, and—unless the skill level of this group is raised—the proportion of those unemployable will increase as the demands of industry for workers with high capacities continue to grow.

Because areas experiencing rapid economic development normally undergo increases in population, population increments frequently come to be regarded as desirable in and of themselves. Each new family is thought of as representing a certain amount of additional purchasing power in the community and as a source of increased demand for goods and services. Overlooked is the fact such population also represents a demand for additional social services. So long as the ability of the increment to produce is equal to or in excess of its consumption, well and good. However, a part of the increased population frequently represents nothing more than an additional drain on the resources of the community. As the shift from rural to urban residence continues, many Louisiana communities will no doubt find their population increasing, but much of it may consist of displaced agricultural labor which will constitute a burden rather than an asset.

It is predicted that by 1970 Louisiana's population will have increased to 3,830,000.[19] As indicated in the previous paragraph, this may prove to be a mixed blessing. The ability of many of these people to consume may not be matched by their ability to produce. Louisiana cannot afford the burden of increased population unless the proportions of high quality-low quality population undergo marked change.

### b) *The community*

Some communities have industrialization thrust upon them because of factors beyond their control. Still, the frequency with which industry has some choice of communities—at least within a region—is increasing. It therefore behooves any community to make itself more attractive to those enterprises which might conceivably locate there.

For that matter, community improvement is a desirable objective for its own sake. High quality schools, streets, utilities, fire and police protection, drainage and sanitation, medical facilities, public transportation, and recreational areas enhance the productivity of those already living in a community as well as providing the inducement for industry.

Zoning for effective land use can transcend city boundaries and become a parish, as well as a state, matter. Nevertheless, the principles applicable to one governmental subdivision are equally applicable to all. Maximum land-use efficiency requires overall planning and sensible restrictions on use. Failure to act in this respect means a hodge-podge of residential, commercial, and industrial use that detracts from both productivity and beauty. Historically, Louisiana communities have been notoriously lacking in the planning and enforcement of such policies.

Economic development means change, and change is never altogether painless. Older firms in a community become of less significance and import. Because political influence so often flows from economic concentration, the power complex of the community may be altered, or at least such alteration may be threatened. As a consequence, the attitudes toward economic growth will not be uniform. Some will prefer that conditions remain static, for their relative position is strongest when conditions remain just as they are. The significance of these attitudes must never be underestimated, for the controlling complex—through land ownership, political influence, and control of local financial institutions—may possess ample power to thwart the events upon which economic development is predicated. These impediments are perhaps more critical for small industry than for large. There is no definitive solution to deal with them.

### c) *Social-overhead capital*

The provision of social-overhead capital—that is, facilities that must be provided by public authority such as education, highways, and various public works—is a vital ingredient in the process of economic development. Louisiana has poured relatively more of its resources into education and highways than the bulk of the other Southern states. In per capita terms, however, state-local expenditures on education rank below the national average, and highways expenditures rank only slightly above average.[20] Instead of holding its own, or advancing, the state has been losing ground.

Although state contributions to education, in relation to ability to support, have been admirable, contributions at the local level have been extremely small. Additional needs will—and now—require that larger contributions come from local sources than has been the case in the past. Since it has been estimated that education expenditures can yield as much as a 30 percent return on investment, any concerted effort to promote economic growth will call for heavy expenditures in this area.[21]

Effective transportation is indispensable to economic development, as all economic, social, and political activities require interaction over distance. While all forms of transportation are important in the economic complex—though the degree of importance of particular types of transportation varies from industry to industry and in the aggregate—private ownership provides the ways utilized by only one mode, the railroad. Highways, waterways, and airways are maintained by government. In the case of the highways, user charges in the form of taxes are utilized to recoup the bulk of the expenditures, although highway studies have consistently indicated that certain categories of highways users do not pay charges consistent with their responsibility for highway costs.[22]

The upkeep of airways is primarily the responsibility of the federal government, and there has been no reluctance on the part of the central government to appropriate money for such purposes whenever there is the slightest demonstrable need. The primary demand on the state for social-overhead capital in the field of transportation will be highways.

Lack of transportation is not now, nor is it likely to be in the future, a problem of insurmountable magnitude standing in the way of Louisiana's economic development. Although transport facilities may not be as extensive in Louisiana as in some other sections of the country, they are as adequate to meet current needs as one usually finds. The provision of highways, particularly, nearly always runs behind, or at best only slightly ahead, of public desire. When highways are properly priced to include all the social and economic costs involved—which is seldom if ever the case—the effective demand for additional highway improvements may not be so great as ordinarily thought.[23] Even so, when transport demand increases, facilities to provide the wanted services will keep pace.

Although utility services are more often than not provided by privately owned companies operating under public regulation, these services are frequently lumped into the category of social capital because their availability is critical to the well-being of the populace and the functioning of the economy. Many of Louisiana's citizens are as yet without adequate utility service. Some are without a telephone, electricity, convenient fuel, or safe water; others simply lack desired quantities of such services. This inadequacy flows from Louisiana's level of economic development and low-income status, and will be overcome only as the level of development and income rises. Lack of utility service in Louisiana is a function of economic under-development and not a basic causal factor.

### d) *Government*

Much has been made of the unfavorable impression created by Louisiana's political climate. Granted, it has not been the best in the eyes of most unbiased observers, and pleas for, and promises of, good government have permeated political campaigns for generations. A stable political situation is always desirable for economic growth, other things being equal. Without belittling the importance of good government, the factor of stability is perhaps equally important. Industry can, and will, tolerate government that is less than optimum if that government has consistency so that one can adjust to the rules of the game. Even so, good government, like community improvement, is desirable in its own right. The fact that it plays a part in the promotion of economic development is an added benefit.

The aspect of Louisiana government which is most closely related to the attraction of industry is tax structure and policy. One constantly hears tales of the industry that is kept out of Louisiana solely because of high state taxes. In many respects the thesis that Louisiana is a high tax state is a myth. Louisiana, true, did rank ninth among states in per capita tax revenues in 1965.[24] However, in terms of both state and local taxes per capita, Louisiana ranked thirty-sixth, a position more in keeping with its economic status.[25] The difference in the two rankings is to be explained by the role of the state as a centralized collection agency for taxes, a considerable portion of which is remitted to parishes and local governments. Reform of the property tax assessment procedure and equalization of such assessments between parishes is badly needed to end the capriciousness of this levy, but the overall tax picture is not nearly so unfavorable to the attraction and development of industry as is often indicated by those whose primary purpose is to remove or reduce all indirect business taxes. Certainly, the state of Louisiana and its various subdivisions have the obligation to operate those services desired by the citizenry as economically as possible. Obviously, any industry would benefit from a reduction in its tax burden, but the readily discernible needs of the state for social-overhead capital indicate that tax rates will rise rather than fall.

In their eagerness to attract industry from other areas and under the stress of competition—real or imagined—with other potential sites, states and localities are often tempted to offer inducements in the form of tax relief or exemption or through the subscription of funds to construct plants, purchase equipment, and the like. Studies have shown that such concessions are of doubtful significance in the attraction of desirable industry.[26] Certainly, a state should be wary of offering undue tax concessions. A worthwhile enterprise should have a stake in the state and community and be willing to pay its own way. Louisiana currently has enough home-grown poverty. There is no necessity to import more.

### e) *Regionalism*

The poor are nearly always sensitive, singly and in the aggregate, and the underdeveloped area is no exception to the rule. This sensitivity often works itself out in the form of isolationism and a strong nationalistic feeling. The South has frequently exhibited this regional antagonism and the more underdeveloped the Southern state, the stronger its force. This resentment of outsiders which leads to a "go-it-alone" delusion is one that must be mitigated or eradicated if Louisiana is to realize its full potential in the attraction of the capital and technology necessary to overcome the gap between it and the more developed states.

### *Market size and quality*

One aspect of the Louisiana economy long lamented is that the state's raw materials are processed into producers' or semi-finished consumers' goods and then transported to destinations outside the state for finishing. Louisiana has had considerable success in attracting these extractive and producer goods industries, but the supply of raw materials and semi-finished goods flowing out of the state from these industries is enormous. It would be desirable if more processing took place and, consequently, more value were added within the borders of the state. This unfavorable situation is principally a market phenomenon. Lack of population concentrations and low per capita incomes mean inadequate consumer demand to support such market-oriented production. This type of enterprise will not be attracted in desired quantities until economic development has advanced far enough to raise per capita incomes to more adequate levels.

## CONCLUSIONS

The principal factor holding back the rate of economic growth in the state of Louisiana is the skill level of its people. Poverty begets poverty. The forces of low income, illiteracy, inadequate nutrition, low standards of sanitation and health care, and the second-rate social institutions by which they are accompanied tend to reinforce themselves through succeeding generations unless a concerted effort is made to end the cycle. Louisiana has made significant efforts, relative to its financial resources, to initiate programs designed to this end. Yet, its position relative to that of the national average has deteriorated in several crucial respects. The malady requires dosages of greater intensity and frequency to maintain even the status quo. To gain, and gain quickly, may require greater amounts of private capital importation and greater expenditures of state and federal funds for social-overhead than has been the case in the past.

The image that Louisiana government has projected to the nation has not been favorable. The criticisms have not been without foundation. Efficient government is the reflection of a demanding electorate. The voters of Louisiana have been subjected to government of about the quality they deserve. It might not be unkind to say that they have received the kind of government they have insisted upon. It is to be hoped that rising standards of education will produce an electorate that will demand more effective administration on the part of elected officials. There is some indication that this may be happening.

One noteworthy feature of government deficiency has been the frequent absence of fiscal responsibility. Apart from the makeup of the legislature and the various state administrations, a contributing factor has undoubtedly been the bonuses from state-owned mineral lands which have periodically bailed the state out of a final reckoning with financial reality. The immense growth in the needs of state and local institutions has created financial requirements which, it would appear, will not much longer permit the capriciousness of past fiscal policy. In any event, the rate of economic growth will be related to the adoption of prudent tax and expenditure measures.

The provincialism of much of the populace of the state, coupled with the vested interests that control the economic complex in so many of the rural areas and smaller communities, has made the reallocation of resources required by rapid economic development difficult. Changes will be inexorably forced in the long run, but a willingness to accept change, even to welcome it, could accelerate economic gains.

The resource base of Louisiana is sufficient to maintain a far more rapid rate of economic development than has occurred in the past. Further, the state has an advantage of location that gives it access to the growing markets of the southern United States and to those of Latin America.

It should be reemphasized that the principal barriers to Louisiana's development are human and institutional, and these change slowly, even under the pressures of modern society. It is to be expected, however, that the changes that are now taking place will continue and that they will be accelerated. The rest of the nation is undergoing the same pressures for more rapid economic growth. The rate at which Louisiana closes the relative gap between its level and that of the nation will probably be, barring unexpected and unpredictable events, a slow and tedious one. In terms of absolute growth, there is no insurmountable barrier to a significant and rapid rise in the level of Louisiana's economic accomplishments.

Notes for "Some Factors Affecting the Economic Development of Louisiana"

[1]T. R. Malthus, *Principles of Political Economy* (New York, 1964), 311-14.

[2]J. A. Schumpeter, *The Theory of Economic Development* (Cambridge, Mass., 1934), 61-90.

[3]J. H. Boeke, *Economics and Economic Policy of Dual Societies* (New York, 1953), 289.

[4]Harvey Leibenstein, *Economic Backwardness and Economic Growth* (New York, 1963), 94-106.

[5]W. W. Rostow, *The Stages of Economic Growth* (Cambridge, Mass., 1961).

[6]B. Higgins, *Economic Development* (New York, 1959), 345-53.

[7]E. D. Domar, "Expansion and Employment," *American Economic Review*, 37 (1947): 34-55.

[8]U. S. Weather Bureau, *Climates of the States—Louisiana* (Washington, D.C., 1959), 1.

[9]U. S. Bureau of the Census, *Statistical Abstract of the United States* (Washington, D.C., 1964), 169.

[10]U. S. Weather Bureau, *Climates of the States*, 2-3.

[11]Ibid.

[12]Department of Conservation, *Ground Water of Louisiana* (Baton Rouge, 1960), 47.

[13]U. S. Bureau of the Census, *Statistical Abstract of the United States*, 696.

[14]Ibid., 681.

[15]U. S. Bureau of Mines, *Mineral Yearbook* (Washington, D.C., 1962).

[16]Ibid.

[17]A. L. Bertrand and J. Wright, Jr., *Louisiana's Human Resources* (Baton Rouge, 1964), Pt. 3, page 7.

[18]U. S. Bureau of the Census, *1960 Census of Population* (Washington, D.C., 1961), I, Pt. 20, Table 47.

[19]Bertrand and Wright, *Louisiana's Human Resources*, 7.

[20]U. S. Bureau of the Census, *Governmental Finances in 1964-65* (Washington, D.C., 1966), 46.

[21]Howard G. Schaller, *Decade of Decision* (New Orleans, 1965).

[22]One example, particularly pertinent, is William D. Ross, *Financing Highway Improvements in Louisiana* (Baton Rouge, 1955).

[23]James M. Buchanan, "The Pricing of Highway Services," *National Tax Journal*, 5 (1952): 97-106.

[24]U. S. Bureau of the Census, *Compendium of State Government Finances in 1965* (Washington, D.C., 1966), 11.

[25]U. S. Bureau of the Census, *Governmental Finances in 1964-65*, page 45.

[26]William D. Ross, *Louisiana Industrial Tax Exemption Program* (Baton Rouge, 1953).

# THE LOUISIANA ECONOMY IN THE 1970s: A DECADE OF GROWTH AND INTERNAL SHIFTS*

Loren C. Scott

**Data for the past decade show Louisiana as a state that is profoundly influenced by oil and gas industry. Parishes that host the offshore oil industry have lept into prominent positions in terms of per capita income in the state. Those parishes between Baton Rouge and New Orleans have attracted industries which rely heavily on natural gas and vast supplies of water, and consequently their income and population have risen rapidly. Parishes located in rural areas with a heavy agricultural base have lost economic ground relatively to other parishes, and Orleans Parish, the most populous in the state, has been experiencing some special economic difficulties of its own. The state, as a whole, appears to be on a strong growth track.**

It has not been that uncommon, in the past few years, to hear someone refer to Louisiana as a "banana republic." Such a phrase congers up visions of a stagnant, backward, one-product economy.

However, as one examines the economic history of Louisiana during the 1970s, he is struck by the picture drawn of a vibrant, shifting, multi-dimensional economy. The influence of the energy crisis and the resultant growth in the importance of the oil and gas industry are strikingly revealed. Increased farm size and mechanization can be clearly seen in some of the population data. The strength lent to our state economy by the dual combination of natural gas and the Mississippi River are manifested in the development in the 1970s of an area of the state that some have nicknamed the "Little Ruhr." Other interesting changes are also apparent.[1]

*First published in the *Louisiana Business Review*, 45 (1981): 7-12. Reprinted with the kind permission of the author.

The data used to paint this decade-long picture of the state's economy come from two sources: (1) estimates of per capita income for each parish in 1978 made by the Bureau of Economic Analysis (BEA) of the U. S. Department of Commerce, and (2) the preliminary

**TABLE 1**

**Per Capita Income and Population Data for the United States, Louisiana and Its Parishes**

| Area | Per Capita Income | | | | | Population | | | |
|---|---|---|---|---|---|---|---|---|---|
| | 1978 (Dollars) | Percent Change, 1969-1978 | Percent of U.S. Average 1978 | Parish Rank 1969 | Parish Rank 1978 | 1980 (Thousands) | Percent Change, 1970-1980 | Parish Rank 1970 | Parish Rank 1980 |
| UNITED STATES | $ 7840 | 114% | — | — | — | 226,504.8 | 11.1 | — | — |
| LOUISIANA | 6738 | 137 | 86% | — | — | 4,194.3 | 15.1 | — | — |
| Acadia | 5483 | 163 | 70 | 40 | 32 | 56.6 | 8.6 | 18 | 19 |
| Allen | 4508 | 116 | 58 | 39 | 53 | 21.4 | 2.8 | 42 | 45 |
| Ascension | 6235 | 168 | 80 | 28 | 19 | 51.5 | 38.9 | 24 | 21 |
| Assumption | 5819 | 185 | 74 | 41 | 29 | 22.1 | 12.3 | 43 | 43 |
| Avoyelles | 4082 | 123 | 52 | 52 | 62 | 41.7 | 10.4 | 23 | 25 |
| Beauregard | 5430 | 144 | 69 | 31 | 34 | 29.6 | 29.5 | 37 | 35 |
| Bienville | 4573 | 131 | 58 | 44 | 52 | 16.4 | 2.2 | 52 | 54 |
| Bossier | 6390 | 143 | 82 | 16 | 16 | 80.9 | 22.8 | 13 | 13 |
| Caddo | 7379 | 130 | 94 | 6 | 7 | 252.0 | 9.5 | 4 | 4 |
| Calcasieu | 7271 | 145 | 93 | 8 | 8 | 168.7 | 16.0 | 5 | 5 |
| Caldwell | 4163 | 154 | 53 | 61 | 57 | 10.7 | 14.7 | 62 | 60 |
| Cameron | 6384 | 143 | 81 | 17 | 17 | 9.3 | 12.9 | 64 | 63 |
| Catahoula | 4202 | 158 | 54 | 62 | 56 | 12.2 | 3.9 | 58 | 58 |
| Claiborne | 5353 | 134 | 68 | 29 | 35 | 17.1 | 0.6 | 48 | 51 |
| Concordia | 5772 | 145 | 74 | 26 | 30 | 22.9 | 1.3 | 39 | 41 |
| DeSoto | 5133 | 139 | 65 | 35 | 42 | 24.6 | 8.0 | 38 | 38 |
| East Baton Rouge | 8020 | 132 | 102 | 3 | 2 | 368.5 | 29.2 | 3 | 3 |
| East Carroll | 4136 | 129 | 53 | 56 | 59 | 11.8 | –8.4 | 57 | 59 |
| East Feliciana | 5033 | 175 | 64 | 54 | 44 | 18.8 | 6.6 | 47 | 48 |
| Evangeline | 4304 | 139 | 55 | 57 | 54 | 33.4 | 4.5 | 30 | 31 |
| Franklin | 3830 | 128 | 49 | 60 | 64 | 24.1 | 0.7 | 35 | 39 |
| Grant | 4290 | 133 | 55 | 53 | 55 | 16.7 | 22.5 | 54 | 53 |
| Iberia | 6889 | 184 | 88 | 22 | 12 | 63.8 | 11.1 | 16 | 16 |
| Iberville | 6108 | 158 | 78 | 24 | 22 | 32.0 | 4.0 | 31 | 33 |
| Jackson | 5457 | 131 | 70 | 25 | 33 | 17.4 | 9.1 | 51 | 49 |
| Jefferson | 7850 | 116 | 100 | 1 | 3 | 450.6 | 33.2 | 2 | 2 |
| Jefferson Davis | 5219 | 135 | 67 | 32 | 40 | 32.1 | 8.6 | 33 | 32 |
| Lafayette | 8492 | 205 | 108 | 9 | 1 | 148.3 | 32.9 | 8 | 6 |
| Lafourche | 6680 | 166 | 85 | 20 | 14 | 82.4 | 19.6 | 11 | 12 |
| LaSalle | 4979 | 167 | 64 | 49 | 45 | 16.8 | 26.0 | 55 | 52 |
| Lincoln | 5836 | 148 | 74 | 27 | 27 | 39.7 | 17.5 | 27 | 27 |
| Livingston | 5954 | 148 | 76 | 23 | 26 | 58.1 | 59.5 | 25 | 18 |
| Madison | 3870 | 110 | 49 | 50 | 63 | 14.7 | –2.5 | 53 | 55 |
| Morehouse | 5261 | 146 | 67 | 37 | 39 | 33.8 | 4.0 | 29 | 30 |
| Natchitoches | 4714 | 135 | 60 | 43 | 49 | 39.2 | 11.4 | 26 | 28 |
| Orleans | 7744 | 120 | 99 | 2 | 4 | 556.9 | –6.2 | 1 | 1 |
| Ouachita | 6313 | 130 | 81 | 11 | 18 | 137.5 | 19.2 | 7 | 7 |
| Plaquemines | 6788 | 160 | 87 | 18 | 13 | 26.0 | 3.2 | 34 | 36 |
| Pointe Coupee | 5189 | 170 | 66 | 47 | 41 | 24.1 | 9.5 | 40 | 45 |
| Rapides | 5988 | 125 | 76 | 14 | 24 | 134.3 | 13.8 | 6 | 8 |
| Red River | 5325 | 148 | 68 | 36 | 37 | 10.3 | 12.1 | 62 | 61 |
| Richland | 5329 | 171 | 68 | 45 | 36 | 22.1 | 1.5 | 41 | 42 |
| Sabine | 4656 | 156 | 59 | 55 | 51 | 25.2 | 35.4 | 45 | 37 |
| St. Bernard | 7217 | 111 | 92 | 4 | 9 | 63.7 | 24.5 | 19 | 17 |
| St. Charles | 7167 | 163 | 91 | 12 | 10 | 37.4 | 26.7 | 33 | 29 |
| St. Helena | 4104 | 172 | 52 | 64 | 60 | 9.9 | –0.4 | 60 | 62 |
| St. James | 6955 | 171 | 89 | 19 | 11 | 21.5 | 8.8 | 44 | 44 |
| St. John the Baptist | 6126 | 180 | 78 | 33 | 20 | 31.9 | 34.1 | 36 | 34 |
| St. Landry | 4702 | 148 | 60 | 48 | 50 | 84.2 | 4.7 | 9 | 11 |
| St. Martin | 4936 | 191 | 63 | 59 | 46 | 40.1 | 23.5 | 28 | 26 |
| St. Mary | 7466 | 181 | 95 | 13 | 6 | 64.5 | 6.2 | 15 | 15 |
| St. Tammany | 6440 | 135 | 82 | 10 | 15 | 109.9 | 72.8 | 14 | 9 |
| Tangipahoa | 5079 | 141 | 65 | 38 | 43 | 79.0 | 19.9 | 12 | 14 |
| Tensas | 4856 | 165 | 62 | 51 | 47 | 8.5 | –12.8 | 61 | 64 |
| Terrebonne | 7504 | 183 | 96 | 15 | 5 | 94.7 | 24.6 | 10 | 10 |
| Union | 5286 | 160 | 67 | 42 | 38 | 20.9 | 13.2 | 46 | 46 |
| Vermilion | 6118 | 172 | 78 | 30 | 21 | 48.4 | 12.4 | 20 | 22 |
| Vernon | 5831 | 78 | 74 | 5 | 28 | 53.1 | 1.4 | 17 | 20 |
| Washington | 5508 | 126 | 70 | 21 | 31 | 44.4 | 5.8 | 21 | 23 |
| Webster | 6028 | 101 | 77 | 7 | 23 | 43.4 | 8.7 | 22 | 24 |
| West Baton Rouge | 5965 | 174 | 76 | 34 | 25 | 18.9 | 12.2 | 48 | 47 |
| West Carroll | 4096 | 141 | 52 | 58 | 61 | 12.8 | –1.9 | 56 | 57 |
| West Feliciana | 4153 | 165 | 53 | 63 | 58 | 13.6 | 26.0 | 59 | 56 |
| Winn | 4728 | 141 | 60 | 46 | 48 | 17.2 | 5.3 | 50 | 50 |

Source: Computer Printouts, U.S. Department of Commerce, Bureau of Economic Analysis, Regional Economics Information System, April 1980. (Per Capita Income information)

State Data Center Newsletter, Department of Experimental Statistics, Louisiana State University, January 1981. (Population information)

census count on population in each parish in 1980. Since Bureau of Economic analysis income estimates are only available through 1978, all income comparisons made in this article are for the period 1969-78.[2]

Section two of this article concentrates on an examination of state and parish level per capital incomes between 1969 and 1978. The third section deals with population shifts that have occurred between 1970 and 1980. The final section contains a summary and conclusions.

## Per Capita Income Shifts

Table 1 contains data on per capita income levels for the U. S., Louisiana, and each of our sixty-four parishes. Column two contains per capita income growth rates between 1969 and 1978, and column three expresses each parish's per capita income as a percentage of the average U. S. per capita income. Finally, in columns four and five, the parishes are ranked according to their per capita income levels in each of these two years.

**Louisiana Vis-à-Vis the Nation:** In 1978, the average (undeflated) per capital income for the U. S. was $7,840 while the comparable figure for Louisiana was more than a thousand dollars lower at $6,738. However, the 1969-78 period was a relatively good one for Louisiana as the data in column two reveal. Louisiana's per capita income grew noticeably faster than did that of the U. S. (137 percent versus 114 percent). Consequently, while the state ranked forty-fourth in per capita income among the fifty states in 1969, Louisiana had taken a healthy jump to the thirty-seventh position by 1978.[3]

**Per Capita Income Parish Level:** The position of thirty-seventh in the country is, of course, still below the national median, and a careful glance down column three of Table 1 demonstrates the impact of that rather low ranking. Only three parishes in the state, Lafayette, East Baton Rouge and Jefferson, have per capita incomes that match or exceed the national average. *Over one-half of the parishes in Louisiana have per capita incomes that are less than 75 percent of the national average.* Furthermore, the per capita incomes of two parishes, Franklin and Madison, are less than one-half of the national average.

Table 2 ranks the top ten parishes in the state by per capita income in both 1969 and 1978. The shifts that have taken place in the top ten parishes indicate the increasingly paramount role taken by the oil industry during the 1970s. Lafayette Parish, considered the headquarters city of the offshore oil industry, is now the richest parish in the state by the per capita income standard. Terrebonne and St. Mary parishes, which are also closely tied to offshore petroleum exploration, have also jumped into the top ten list.

Two parishes which have remained in the top ten and have pretty much held their relative positions over the decade are East Baton Rouge and Calcasieu (Lake Charles)

TABLE 2

Highest Ten Parishes, Ranked by Per Capita Income, 1969 and 1978

| Rank | 1969 | 1978 |
|---|---|---|
| 1 | Jefferson | Lafayette |
| 2 | Orleans | E. Baton Rouge |
| 3 | E. Baton Rouge | Jefferson |
| 4 | St. Bernard | Orleans |
| 5 | Vernon | Terrebonne |
| 6 | Caddo | St. Mary |
| 7 | Webster | Caddo |
| 8 | Calcasieu | Calcasieu |
| 9 | Lafayette | St. Bernard |
| 10 | St. Tammany | St. Charles |

*Source: Table 1 and Bureau of Economic Analysis printouts, April 1980.

Parishes. (East Baton Rouge ranked first in the state in 1976). Both of these parishes have economic bases with strong connections to the petroleum refining industry. As a matter of fact, the Exxon refinery in Baton Rouge is the second largest in the country.[4]

The improvement in ranking of these petroleum-oriented parishes has come at the expense of the parishes in the New Orleans and Shreveport areas. Jefferson, Orleans and St. Bernard parishes—which are in the New Orleans Standard Metropolitan Statistical Area (SMSA)—ranked one, two and four in 1969. Per capita income levels in these three parishes continued to grow at rates near the national average between 1969 and 1978. However, the per capita income levels of Louisiana's other parishes grew so much faster than the national average that the per capita income positions of Jefferson, Orleans and St. Bernard parishes fell to third, fourth and ninth, respectively.

As Map 1 illustrates, nine of the top ten parishes ranked by per capita income are located in South Louisiana. For sometime now the parishes in the northern area of the state have been losing ground to those in South Louisiana. A good example of this north-to-south shift is the Shreveport parish of Caddo. Caddo enjoyed the highest per capita income in the state in 1940.[5] Since that time its ranking has consistently fallen to its present position of seventh. Webster Parish, which is also in the Shreveport area, ranked seventh in the state in 1969 and is now no longer in the top ten. This deterioration in the Shreveport area ranking may soon be arrested, however, since General Motors is due to open a major truck assembly facility in Caddo Parish in the near future. This event will create a large number of new high-wage jobs in the area. For example, the average weekly earnings in the Motor Vehicles and Car Bodies Industry in the U. S. in 1978 was $388.40. In contrast, the average weekly earnings for all private, nonagricultural workers was a much lower $203.70.[6]

MAP I

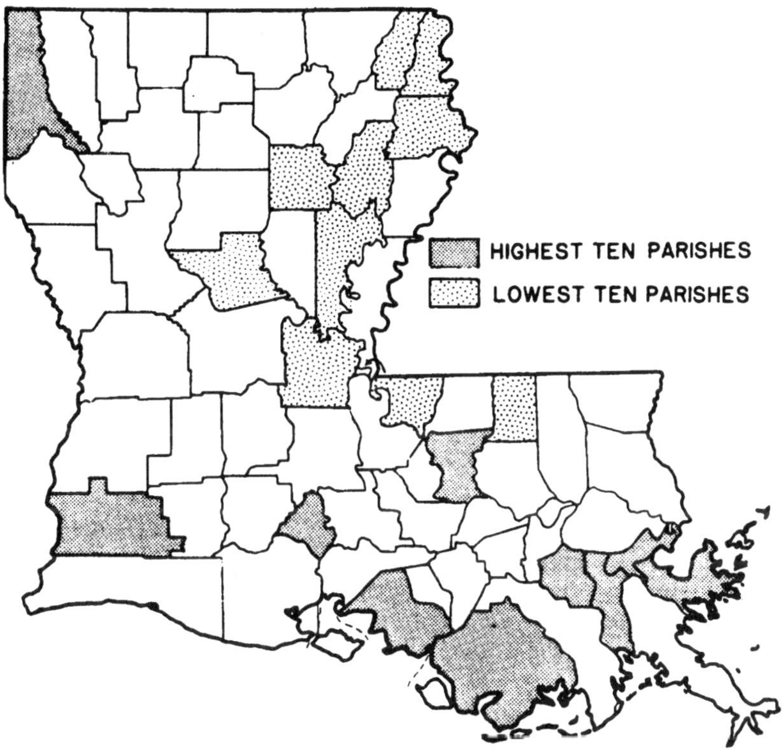


HIGHEST AND LOWEST TEN PARISHES RANKED BY PER CAPITA INCOME: 1978

Occasionally there are external events which tend to move an economy off its normal growth path. Federal military spending has tended to have such an influence on the Louisiana economy. For example, in 1969 while the Vietnam War was in progress, Vernon Parish, the location of Folk Polk, did exceedingly well with a per capita income ranking of fifth in the state. Furthermore, this small west-central parish had the highest per capita income in Louisiana in 1968, when the war was near its peak.[7]

However, after the conclusion of the Vietnam involvement, Vernon Parish had experienced the largest drop in per capita income of any parish in the state, falling to a rank of twenty-eighth in 1978. Similarly, Webster Parish, the location of a major munitions plant, fell from its seventh place ranking in 1969 to twenty-third in 1978.

Rapides Parish, the location of England Air Force Base, dropped from the fourteenth position to twenty-fourth during the same time period.

Finally, Table 3 lists the ten lowest parishes in terms of per capita income in 1969 and 1978. As it turns out, membership in this group has changed very little over time. Seven parishes appear in both the 1969 and 1978 rankings. From their position in Map 1 one can conclude that all of these parishes are in rural areas and most are located in the Mississippi River delta region of the state. According to these data, Franklin Parish with a per capita income of only $3,830, 49 percent of the national average, is the poorest in the state.

TABLE 3

Lowest Ten Parishes in Per Capita Income, 1969 and 1978

| Rank | 1969 | 1978 |
|---|---|---|
| 64 | St. Helena | Franklin |
| 63 | W. Feliciana | Madison |
| 62 | Catahoula | Avoyelles |
| 61 | Caldwell | W. Carroll |
| 60 | Franklin | St. Helena |
| 59 | St. Martin | E. Carroll |
| 58 | W. Carroll | W. Feliciana |
| 57 | Evangeline | Caldwell |
| 56 | E. Carroll | Catahoula |
| 55 | Sabine | Grant |

Source: Computer printouts, Bureau of Economic Analysis, U. S. Department of Commerce, April 1980.

TABLE 4

Percent of Employment in Various Sectors, 1978

| Rank 1978 | Per Capita Income Parish | Percent of Employment in Farming | Percent of Employment in State and Local Gov. |
|---|---|---|---|
| 64 | Franklin | 8.3 | 22.6 |
| 63 | Madison | 13.5 | 19.1 |
| 62 | Avoyelles | 5.5 | 21.0 |
| 61 | W. Carroll | 9.5 | 24.5 |
| 60 | St. Helena | 8.3 | 27.8 |
| 59 | E. Carroll | 17.7 | 13.9 |
| 58 | W. Feliciana | 5.0 | 28.8 |

Table 4 (cont.)

| Rank 1978 | Per Capita Income Parish | Percent of Employment in Farming | Percent of Employment in State and Local Gov. |
|---|---|---|---|
| 57 | Caldwell | 3.8 | 24.1 |
| 56 | Catahoula | 8.9 | 32.5 |
| 55 | Grant | 3.1 | 22.0 |
| n.a. | State average | 1.3 | 14.6 |

Source: Computer printouts, Bureau of Economic Analysis, U.S. Department of Commerce, April 1980.

n.a.—not applicable

A cursory examination of the economic bases of these parishes gives some clue as to the reason for their poor ranking. The data in Table 4 indicate the percentage of each parish's employment that exists in the farm and the state and local government sectors. Only about 1.3 percent of all wage and salary employment in Louisiana is in the farm sector. All of the parishes in question have noticeably higher proportions of their employment in that area. Not only are wages and salaries in the farm sector typically lower than average, but also between 1969 and 1978 farm income in the state grew only 20 percent while total income grew at a much faster 153 percent rate. Similarly all of these parishes, except East Carroll, have a much higher concentration of employment in state and local government than is the average for the state. Over the 1969-78 period, income in this sector grew by 140 percent, 13 percentage points lower than total state income.

## Population Changes[8]

**Louisiana Vis-à-Vis the Nation:** As one moves from a consideration of per capita income activity to population changes it would be expected that the order of magnitude of the shifts would be considerably smaller, especially when examining only a ten year period. This is because changes in the population of a state depend primarily upon birth rates, death rates and migration trends. Generally, these factors change slowly over time.

As the data in the second half of Table 1 demonstrate, this has basically been true for Louisiana. Preliminary data from the 1980 census count reveal that over the 1970-80 period the Louisiana population grew by 15.1 percent to a level of almost 4.2 million persons. This growth rate was significantly larger than the 11.1 percent growth rate for the nation as a whole. No doubt Louisiana benefited from the Snowbelt to Sunbelt population shift which occurred in the nation during the past decade. This led to the state's relatively larger population growth rate.

**Population Changes at the Parish Level:** An examination of the last two columns in Table 1 lends credence to the notion that relative population shifts occur rather slowly. Notice that there was very little change in the population ranking of each parish between 1970 and 1980. Only five parishes underwent ranking changes of four positions or more. Most involved rank changes of only two or three levels. (In contrast, the average shift in per capita income ranking among the parishes was six positions, and the rankings of thirteen parishes changed by ten or more positions.) Since the 1940s, Orleans Parish, with over one-half million residents, has been the most populous parish in Louisiana. Tensas Parish, with only 8,500 citizens, is the smallest parish in the state in terms of population size.

Despite the absence of marked changes in rankings, most of Louisiana's parishes experienced a noticeable change in *absolute* population size between 1970-80. Six parishes actually lost population over the decade and thirteen parishes experienced very slow population growth, that is, their growth rates were under five percent. As can be seen in Map 2, most of these "slow growth" parishes tend to be located in rural areas where there is a greater than average economic dependence on agriculture. Note, for example, that nine of these parishes are located in the Mississippi River delta region. A major movement has been taking place in farming in these parishes to consolidate smaller farms to take advantage of economies of scale in population. Throughout the state there has been a very significant movement towards larger size farms and, as a result, toward a smaller number of farms. This had led to a rural-to-urban population shift and the resulting pattern of population movements shown in Map 2.

The population movements in two of the slow growth parishes cannot be explained by the rural-to-urban shift hypothesis. The very weak 1.4 percent population growth in Vernon Parish is traceable directly to the wind-down of activities at Fort Polk with the end of the Vietnam War.

Orleans Parish, on the other hand, is suffering from a serious case of urban flight. Its population, which has been declining since the mid-1960s fell by 6.2 percent in the past decade. To a large extent, this outward population movement can be explained by a desire on the part of those who work in the parish to reside in outlying areas and avoid all the problems inherent in living in a very large inner city such as New Orleans. Clearly, the large growth in St. Tammany, St. Bernard, and Jefferson Parishes can be traced to this suburban shift. In particular, St. Tammany's population grew an astonishing 72.8 percent, the largest growth rate of any parish in the state in 1970s. One indication that most of this growth came from commuters to Orleans Parish is the fact that *fifty-eight percent of the labor and proprietor's income earned by residents of St. Tammany Parish was earned outside of the parish!* Comparable figures of thirty-one and forty-three percent, respectively, for Jefferson and St. Bernard Parishes lend credence to the "suburban shift" hypothesis.[9]

MAP 2

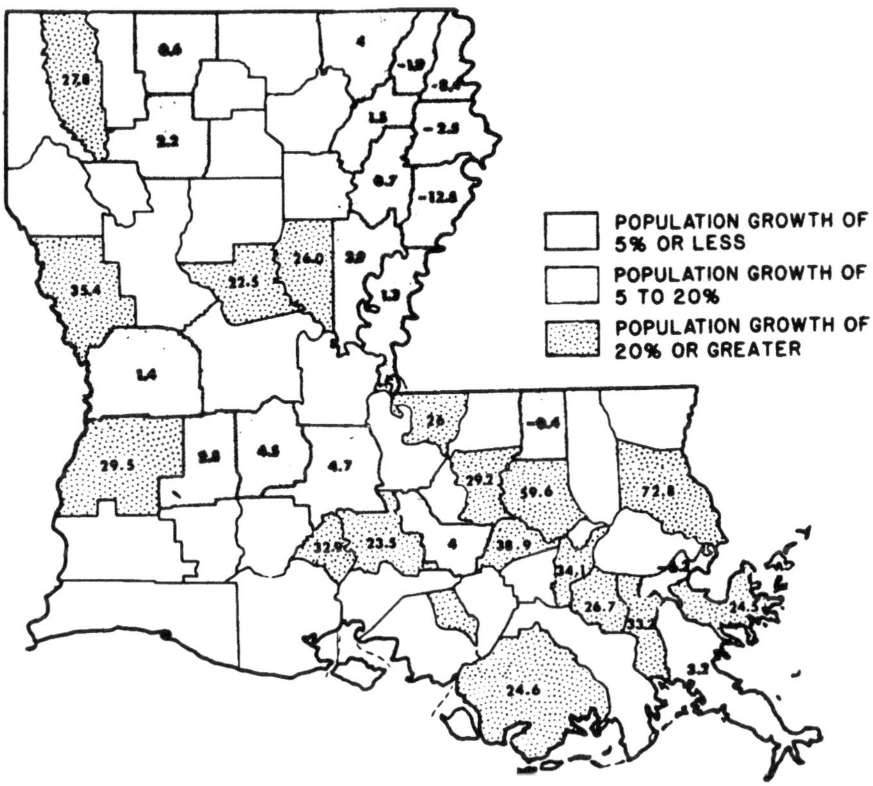


POPULATION GROWTH IN LOUISIANA PARISHES : 1970 – 1980

It should be noted, however, that not all of the population loss of Orleans Parish can be attributed to a simple suburban shift. Jobs in the basic industries have also been declining in that parish at an alarming rate. *The Preliminary Report of the 1977 Census of Manufacturers* reports that Orleans Parish lost 6,800 jobs in the manufacturing sector between 1972-1977.[10] Hopefully, the implementation of the ten-year capital improvements program by the New Orleans Port Commission and the 1984 World Exposition will give that parish a much needed economic shot in the arm in the 1980s and reverse its present trend.

Four other high population growth parishes shown in Map 2 experienced growth primarily because of suburban shifts from large cities nearby: Livingston (near Baton

Rouge), Beauregard (near Lake Charles), Bossier (near Shreveport) and Grant (near Alexandria). The percent of labor and proprietor's income earned outside of each of these parishes was 73, 28, 23 and 43 percent, respectively.

Three parishes, Lafayette, Terrebonne and St. Martin, have encountered rapid population growth recently because of the boom that has occurred in the offshore oil and gas industry since 1970. Closely related to this factor has been the very rapid growth in those parishes that lie along the Mississippi River between Baton Rouge and New Orleans. The rapid population growth parishes of Ascension, St. John the Baptist and St. Charles, enjoy the benefit of two important natural resources, natural gas and a large volume of water. The combination of these two resources has attracted a number of major plants along the River between these two cities. As a matter of fact, 35 percent of the total value of ten-year tax exemptions awarded in the state between 1970-79 was awarded solely in the six parishes that lie along the River between Baton Rouge and New Orleans.[11] Petrochemical, petroleum refining, and food processing plants are so numerous that the area has been nicknamed the "Little Ruhr."[12]

## Summary and Conclusion

The Bureau of Economic Analysis income data, and the 1980 Census data reveal a picture of a state which has been on a strong growth track since 1969. The prodigious growth in the oil and gas industry has continued the shift in the pattern of growth rates from the northern to the southern half of the state. The discovery of the Tuscaloosa Trend gas field extending through the south-central area of Louisiana and the mammouth investments in offshore oil exploration will probably cause this shift to continue throughout the 1980s. As the state's economy continues to reap the spill-over benefits of oil and gas deregulation, it would not be surprising to see Louisiana rise from its present per capita income rank of thirty-seventh in the U. S. to perhaps a position in the low thirties by 1990.

Finally, this paper has highlighted at least two major problem areas in the state's economy which need to be addressed. One is the lapse in economic activity taking place in Orleans Parish. Adoption of the Port Commission's ten-year capital improvements program and the hosting of the 1984 World Exposition should go a long ways toward remedying conditions in that area. Secondly, the entire central area of the state has suffered from a lack-luster economic performance in recent years. The construction of the north-south highway is absolutely essential to the economic development of this region, as anyone who has travelled the area by car can attest. With the natural financial and human resources that Louisiana will have in the 1980s, these problems seem hardly insurmountable.

## Notes for "The Louisiana Economy in the 1970s: A Decade of Growth and Internal Shifts"

[1]In an earlier paper the author used Bureau of Economic Analysis data to analyze shifts in the Louisiana economy over the longer 1940-1976 period. See: Loren C. Scott, "The Changing Structure of the Louisiana Economy: 1940-1976," *Louisiana Business Review*, 42 (1978): 2-6.

[2]These data are available for public use and inspection in the Division of Research, Room 3139, Center for Engineering and Business Administration of the LSU campus.

[3]Preliminary figures have recently been released by the Bureau of Economic Analysis showing that in 1979 Louisiana's per capita income had increased to $7,477—an improvement which has led to a new ranking of thirty-fifth in the nation. See: Louisiana Department of Commerce, Office of Commerce and Industry, *Louisiana Business* (1980): 1.

[4]For a review of the impact of this important industry on the state's economy, see: Loren C. Scott, "The Petroleum Industry in Louisiana," *Louisiana Business Review*, 41 (1977): 2-4.

[5]Scott, "The Changing Structure of the Louisiana Economy."

[6]U. S. Department of Labor, Bureau of Labor Statistics, *Employment and Earnings, United States, 1907-78*, Bulletin 1313-11 (Washington, 1979), 3, 355.

[7]Loren C. Scott, Thomas R. Beard, and Jan W. Duggar, "Economic Profiles, Personal Income, and Earnings Data for Louisiana State Planning Districts, SMSA's and Non-SMSA Parishes in Louisiana," Occasional paper #2 (Baton Rouge, 1971), 77.

[8]Data in this section are based on the preliminary 1980 population count data published in the *State Data Center Newsletter*, Department of Experimental Statistics (Baton Rouge, 1981).

[9]Bureau of Economic analysis, Personal Income computer printout, April 1980.

[10]U. S. Department of Commerce, Bureau of the Census, *1977 Census of Manufacturers, Preliminary Report* (Washington, 1979), 3.

[11]Louisiana Department of Commerce, Office of Commerce and Industry, computer printouts provided to the author.

[12]This refers to the enormous industrial complex that lies in the Ruhr Valley in Germany.

# A QUARTER OF A CENTURY OF CHANGE*

Loren C. Scott

Look in the rear view mirror of the Louisiana economy and what do you see? For the past 25 years . . . something akin to a roller coaster ride. Are we better off than where we started a quarter of a century ago? A good check is to examine our **real per capita income (RPCI)** . . . dollars received per person after adjusting for inflation.

## A Look At The State

Louisiana's RPCI is tracked over the 1970-95 period in Figure 1, and lo and behold . . . there is the roller coaster. Things were so good from 1970-81 that even terrible business decisions could be covered up by a booming economy. Spurred by a ten-fold increase in energy prices and a rapidly expanding, high paying chemical industry, Louisiana grew twice as fast as the national economy. Not only did our RPCI rise, but also our ranking among the 50 states jumped from 44th to 31st . . . an almost unheard of improvement.

### Down the Hill

Then, over 1982-87, the state went through the worst recession in its recorded history, losing 147,000 jobs or 9 percent of its employment. By way of reference, during the Great Depression U.S. non-agricultural employment fell only 7.5 percent. Plummeting energy prices and a loss of one-third of the jobs in our chemical plants sent our RPCI into a 6-year downward spiral, dropping our ranking among the states to 47th . . . just above Mississippi, New Mexico, and Utah.

*First published in *Louisiana Business Magazine*, 2 (1996): 6-9. Reprinted with the kind permission of the author.

## Back Up Again

Fortunately, there has been another hill for the roller coaster, and unlike the ones at the amusement park, this second hill has sent us even higher. Spurred by an expansion in our manufacturing sector and good growth in our feeder sectors, we began to set new records in our RPCI in 1990. The picture in Figure I is telling. **Despite the conventional wisdom that we are all worse off today than in the 70s, Louisiana citizens are clearly not only much better off, but also our relative rank among the states has improved to 41st.**

## Parish Trends

"But what about where I live?" you say. Recently, the Bureau of Economic Analysis (BEA) in the U.S. Department of Commerce released new income and population data at the parish level. There is quite a lag in these numbers . . . 1994 are the latest available.

These data are handily summarized in Table 1. The interested reader can scan down this table, find his/her parish, and determine (1) its per capita income in 1994, (2) the parish's rank compared to the U.S. average, (3) how that per capita income ranked in 1970 and in 1994, (4) the parish's 1994 population, (5) the change in its population since 1970, and (6) its population rank among the 64 parishes in both 1970 and 1994. These data tell us a lot about the areas of strength and weakness in our economy and about changes that have occurred **internally** in Louisiana over the past quarter of a century.

## Per Capita Income: We Still Have a Long Ways to Go

Scanning the per capita income portion of Table I leads to several conclusions. First, despite our recent solid recovery, and despite achieving a rank of 41st among the 50 states, we still have a long ways to go. **Every single parish in Louisiana has a per capita income below the national average.** Number one ranked Orleans Parish has a per capita income of $20,767 ($83,068 for a family of four) but is still over four percentage points below the national average.

## The Big Winners

Secondly, economic wealth in Louisiana is unevenly distributed **by parish.** For example, there are 64 parishes, yet only 11 have per capita incomes that equal or exceed the state average. Fifty-three parishes have per capita incomes below the *state* average!

How is this possible? Partly it is a matter of sheer numbers. As seen in Map 1, all of the richest 11 parishes are in metropolitan statistical areas (MSAs). They are either central city parishes (Calcasieu, Orleans, East Baton Rouge, Rapides, Lafayette, Caddo) or bedroom communities of central city areas (St. Tammany, Ascension, St. Charles, Jefferson, Bossier, St. Martin). Though there are only 11 of them, these parishes contain 56 percent of the state's population.

## Table 1

### Per Capita Income & Population Data for the U.S., Louisiana, and Louisiana Parishes: 1994

| | Per Capita Income | | | | Population | | | |
|---|---|---|---|---|---|---|---|---|
| Area | 1994 | % of U.S. Avg. | Rank 1970 | Rank 1994 | 1994 (000s) | % Change 1970 to '94 | Rank 1970 | Rank 1994 |
| U.S. | $21,696. | | | | 260,341 | 28.1% | | |
| Louisiana | $17,622. | 81.22% | | | 4,315 | 18.2% | | |
| | | | | | | | | |
| Acadia | $14,039. | 64.71% | 39 | 49 | 56.9 | 9.00% | 18 | 21 |
| Allen | 11,256 | 51.88% | 38 | 64 | 23.3 | 12.02% | 42 | 39 |
| Ascension | 17,785 | 81.97% | 28 | 10 | 63.9 | 71.77% | 24 | 18 |
| Assumption | 13,578 | 62.58% | 42 | 54 | 22.7 | 15.23% | 44 | 41 |
| Avoylles | 13,103 | 60.39% | 54 | 58 | 39.8 | 5.29% | 23 | 29 |
| Beauregard | 15,690 | 72.32% | 22 | 23 | 31.4 | 37.12% | 37 | 33 |
| Bienville | 14,371 | 66.24% | 46 | 44 | 16.1 | 0.63% | 51 | 52 |
| Bossier | 17,777 | 81.94% | 12 | 11 | 89.4 | 36.70% | 13 | 12 |
| Caddo | 19,831 | 91.40% | 5 | 5 | 246.8 | 7.07% | 4 | 4 |
| Calcasieu | 17,929 | 82.64% | 7 | 8 | 173.3 | 19.27% | 5 | 6 |
| Caldwell | 14,165 | 65.29% | 57 | 46 | 10.3 | 10.75% | 62 | 59 |
| Cameron | 14,491 | 66.79% | 10 | 41 | 8.9 | 7.23% | 64 | 63 |
| Catahoula | 14,657 | 67.56% | 59 | 38 | 11.3 | -4.24% | 58 | 58 |
| Claiborne | 13,675 | 63.03% | 35 | 52 | 17.4 | 2.35% | 48 | 50 |
| Concordia | 14,372 | 66.24% | 36 | 43 | 20.8 | -7.56% | 39 | 45 |
| DeSoto | 15,645 | 72.11% | 34 | 24 | 25 | 9.65% | 38 | 37 |
| E. Baton Rouge | 20,484 | 94.41% | 3 | 2 | 396.3 | 38.91% | 3 | 3 |
| E. Carroll | 13,066 | 60.22% | 61 | 59 | 9.5 | -26.36% | 57 | 61 |

| Per Capita Income | | | | | Population | | | |
|---|---|---|---|---|---|---|---|---|
| | | % of | Rank | Rank | 1994 | % Change | Rank | Rank |
| Area | 1994 | U.S. Avg. | 1970 | 1994 | (000s) | 1970 to '94 | 1970 | 1994 |
| E. Feliciana | 14,747 | 67.97% | 52 | 35 | 20.4 | 15.25% | 47 | 47 |
| Evangeline | 13,469 | 62.08% | 56 | 55 | 34 | 6.25% | 30 | 31 |
| Franklin | 13,949 | 64.29% | 55 | 51 | 22.4 | -6.28% | 35 | 42 |
| Grant | 13,376 | 61.65% | 58 | 56 | 17.8 | 28.99% | 54 | 49 |
| Iberia | 16,053 | 73.99% | 24 | 18 | 70.8 | 22.70% | 16 | 16 |
| Iberville | 16,059 | 74.02% | 26 | 17 | 31 | 0.65% | 31 | 35 |
| Jackson | 14,790 | 68.17% | 25 | 32 | 15.7 | -2.48% | 52 | 53 |
| Jefferson | 20,170 | 92.97% | 2 | 3 | 456.6 | 33.98% | 2 | 2 |
| Jefferson Davis | 13,157 | 60.64% | 31 | 57 | 31.4 | 6.08% | 32 | 33 |
| Lafayette | 19,376 | 89.31% | 9 | 6 | 176.6 | 57.82% | 8 | 5 |
| LaFourche | 14,912 | 68.73% | 20 | 31 | 86.9 | 25.58% | 11 | 13 |
| LaSalle | 14,421 | 66.47% | 43 | 42 | 13.8 | 2.99% | 55 | 54 |
| Lincoln | 16,255 | 74.92% | 29 | 15 | 43.2 | 27.06% | 27 | 25 |
| Livingston | 15,631 | 72.05% | 23 | 25 | 77.9 | 113.42% | 25 | 15 |
| Madison | 14,732 | 67.90% | 49 | 36 | 12.5 | -16.67% | 53 | 56 |
| Morehouse | 15,055 | 69.39% | 32 | 30 | 32.1 | -0.93% | 29 | 32 |
| Natchitoches | 14,123 | 65.09% | 48 | 48 | 37.3 | 5.67% | 26 | 30 |
| Orleans | 20,767 | 95.72% | 1 | 1 | 484.1 | -18.32% | 1 | 1 |
| Ouachita | 16,515 | 76.12% | 16 | 14 | 146.4 | 26.75% | 7 | 8 |
| Plaquemines | 16,831 | 77.58% | 11 | 13 | 25.5 | 0.79% | 34 | 36 |
| Pointe Coupée | 15,158 | 69.87% | 44 | 29 | 23 | 4.55% | 40 | 40 |
| Rapides | 17,804 | 82.06% | 17 | 9 | 126.5 | 6.75% | 6 | 9 |
| Red River | 14,780 | 68.12% | 27 | 33 | 9.3 | 1.09% | 63 | 62 |
| Richland | 15,500 | 71.44% | 37 | 26 | 20.6 | -5.50% | 41 | 46 |
| Sabine | 14,344 | 66.11% | 62 | 45 | 23.5 | 25.67% | 45 | 38 |
| St. Bernard | 16,137 | 74.38% | 4 | 16 | 67 | 30.60% | 19 | 17 |
| St. Charles | 18,669 | 86.05% | 18 | 7 | 45.7 | 54.39% | 33 | 23 |
| St. Helena | 12,244 | 56.43% | 64 | 62 | 9.9 | 1.02% | 60 | 60 |
| St. James | 15,941 | 73.47% | 19 | 19 | 21 | 7.14% | 43 | 44 |

| Per Capita Income | | | | | Population | | | |
|---|---|---|---|---|---|---|---|---|
| | | % of | Rank | Rank | 1994 | % Change | Rank | Rank |
| Area | 1994 | U.S. Avg. | 1970 | 1994 | (000s) | 1970 to '94 | 1970 | 1994 |
| St. John the Baptist | 15,794 | 72.80% | 30 | 21 | 41.7 | 75.21% | 36 | 28 |
| St. Landry | 14,561 | 67.11% | 53 | 40 | 82.2 | 2.49% | 9 | 14 |
| St. Martin | 12,367 | 57.00% | 60 | 61 | 45.7 | 40.18% | 28 | 23 |
| St. Mary | 14,705 | 67.78% | 15 | 37 | 57.2 | -6.23% | 15 | 19 |
| St. Tammany | 19,965 | 92.02% | 13 | 4 | 167.2 | 162.48% | 14 | 7 |
| Tangipahoa | 14,566 | 67.14% | 41 | 39 | 91.3 | 37.92% | 12 | 11 |
| Tensas | 15,731 | 72.51% | 51 | 22 | 6.9 | -28.87% | 61 | 64 |
| Terrebonne | 15,327 | 70.64% | 14 | 27 | 100.4 | 31.76% | 10 | 10 |
| Union | 15,843 | 73.02% | 50 | 20 | 21.5 | 16.22% | 46 | 43 |
| Vermillion | 14,010 | 64.57% | 33 | 50 | 50.8 | 17.87% | 20 | 22 |
| Vernon | 13,622 | 62.79% | 6 | 53 | 57 | 5.56% | 17 | 20 |
| Washington | 14,780 | 68.12% | 21 | 34 | 42.9 | 2.14% | 21 | 26 |
| Webster | 15,205 | 70.08% | 8 | 28 | 42.2 | 5.50% | 22 | 27 |
| W. Baton Rouge | 17,337 | 79.91% | 40 | 12 | 20.1 | 18.24% | 49 | 48 |
| W. Carroll | 12,646 | 58.29% | 47 | 60 | 12 | -7.69% | 56 | 57 |
| W. Feliciana | 11,558 | 53.27% | 63 | 63 | 13.1 | 21.30% | 59 | 55 |
| Winn | 14,135 | 65.15% | 45 | 47 | 17 | 3.66% | 50 | 51 |

Source: Bureau of Economic Analysis, U.S. Department of Commerce, CD-ROM, July 1996.

Major city areas contain many high wage occupations which less populated, rural areas may be too small to support. Examples would be high-end medical services, CPAS, engineering firms, consultants, attorneys, etc., and high-wage occupations mean higher per capita incomes.

There is another factor crucial to the superior performance of some of these 11 parishes. Some have attracted **high wage manufacturers** to their area. In the past 10 years, $8.8 billion in 10-year industrial tax exemptions have been awarded in just four of these 11 parishes . . . Ascension, East Baton Rouge, Calcasieu, and St. Charles. That represents almost 40 percent of the total value of exemptions awarded in the entire state.

The great majority of these exemptions has been awarded for new or expanded chemical plants or petroleum refineries. The average weekly wage in Louisiana's manufacturing sector in June was $600. Comparable wages for chemicals and refining were $1,022 and $816, respectively. Having these industries within its boundaries gives a significant boost to a parish's per capita income.

## The Bottom End

Map I also shows the five poorest parishes in Louisiana . . . West Carroll, St. Martin, St. Helena, West Feliciana, and Allen. Per capita incomes in these five are almost one-half the national average and are less than $12,700.

No one story explains this unfortunate ranking. Partial clues are found in Table 2 which provides data on the percent of income originating in government, manufacturing, and farming in these bottom ranked parishes.

## The Farm Factor

Three of the parishes have a significantly higher portion of their earnings coming from the farm sector. While there are no doubt very wealthy farm **owners** in these parishes, farm **laborers** are at the lower end of the wage scale. The U.S. average weekly wage of a farm worker in 1993 was $200, well under the poorest paying manufacturing subsector in Louisiana. Too, farm earnings have under-performed relative to other sectors of the economy. While total earnings in Louisiana have grown by 588 percent since 1970, farm earnings increased a much smaller 201 percent.

## The Government Factor

Secondly, four of the five are characterized by a much heavier dependence on government for earnings as compared to the state average. This is not always harmful to a parish's per capita income. For example, both East Baton Rouge and Lincoln Parishes have a relatively heavy dependence on government earnings, yet they are highly ranked (number 2 and 15, respectively). However, major universities are located in both of these parishes, with payrolls at the upper end of the government pay scale.

In the bottom 5 parishes, on the other hand, government employment is more likely to be in the lower-wage **local** government. In October, 1992 (the latest data available), local government workers earned on the average $1,800 a month as compared to $2,116 in manufacturing. The obvious exception to the local government concentration is West Feliciana Parish where state government employment dominates. However, that employment is heavily concentrated in Angola State Prison where, again, wage rates are relatively low.

**TABLE 2**

**PERCENT OF EARNINGS ORIGINATING IN GOVERNMENT, MANUFACTURING, AND FARMING IN THE BOTTOM 5 PARISHES IN PER CAPITA INCOME: 1994**

| 1994 RANK | PARISH | PERCENTAGE OF INCOME EARNED IN | | |
|---|---|---|---|---|
| | | GOVERNMENT | MANUFACTURING | FARMING |
| 60 | West Carroll | 23.8 | 8.7 | 26.4 |
| 61 | St. Martin | 16.7 | 35.8 | 2.6 |
| 62 | St. Helena | 36.7 | 15.1 | 3.7 |
| 63 | West Feliciana | 27.5 | 21.6 | 0.5 |
| 64 | Allen | 40.8 | 12.0 | 0.6 |
| NA | State Wide | 17.8% | 14.7% | 1.1% |

Source: See Table 1.

## Low Wage Manufacturing

Normally, one would expect a high concentration of manufacturing employment to be the key to upward movement in the rankings. Yet there is St. Martin, ranked 61st, with over a third of its jobs in manufacturing. But equally important is the **kind** of manufacturing. St. Martin's manufacturing sector is dominated by a large textile manufacturer and several small food processors. These are the two **lowest** paying sectors in manufacturing. In June of this year, the average weekly wage in manufacturing was $600. In textiles/apparels and food processing, the comparable wage figures were a much lower $287 and $375, respectively.

## Quarter Century Shifts: The Wartime Parishes

An analysis of the per capita income rankings in 1970 and 1994 reveals a number of interesting shifts. First, many readers will be surprised to find that in 1970, the 6th most prosperous parish in the state was Vernon. Where the heck is Vernon, you say? Located on the Texas border about half way between Lake Charles and Shreveport, Vernon Parish is the home of Fort Polk. Remember 1970? It was the height of the Viet Nam war. Similarly, note that Webster Parish was the 8th wealthiest parish in 1970. Webster is the home of a large ammunitions plant. Certain parishes in Louisiana greatly benefit from war times.

Just as they wildly benefit from wartime, these same parishes have been pummeled by the outbreak of peace! Vernon has dropped from 6th all the way to 58th in the per capita income rankings . . . the largest decline experienced by any of the 64 parishes. Webster similarly fell 20 places down to the 28th spot.

### Quarter Century Shifts: The Gulf Exploration Parishes

A second significant shift occurred in those parishes very directly tied to off shore exploration activities. Four parishes . . . LaFourche, Terrebonne, St. Mary, and Cameron . . . were ranked in the top 20 parishes in 1970. All have fallen noticeably in the rankings as of 1994.

For these parishes the story is very different from the wartime parishes. These four rose to even higher positions during the booming days of the early eighties before falling to their present levels. Too, because of the resurgence in exploration activity in the Gulf, these parishes wig probably enjoy another ranking boost when newer data come out.

### Why Has My Parish's Ranking Changed?

Another interesting discovery from reviewing the rankings data is that there is quite a bit of shifting over time, especially among those parishes in the 20th to 50th range. What is going on here?

The answer has to do with the distribution of the per capita income numbers. Note that just to rise 11 spots, from 11th to first in the rankings requires quite an improvement in a parish's economy. Per capita income must rise almost \$3,000 (from Bossier's \$17,777 to Orleans's \$20,767).

But notice that the distance between the 50th ranked parish (Vermilion at \$14,010) and the 20th ranked parish (Union at \$15,843) is only about \$1,800. Thus, a very small change in a parish's economy can have a major impact on its ranking within this very wide 30-spot range. For example if Vermilion Parish had been able to improve its per capita income by just \$ 1,000, its ranking would have leapt 20 places from 50th to 30th. This small change phenomenon helps to explain the performance of the two parishes which enjoyed the largest jumps in the rankings since 1970 . . . Union (50th to 20th) and Tensas (51st to 22nd).

## The Population Shifts

The final set of data in Table 1 are those involving population. The livelihoods of many businesses depend on a growing base of customers, and the easiest source of new customers is an expanding population. Carving out a larger market share from a stable or declining population is a much tougher way to go.

Map 2 aids us in analyzing population growth patterns in Louisiana over the last quarter of a century. There is a set of 11 parishes where owners of retail and service firms should have a large grin on their face. These are parishes whose populations have grown twice as fast as the state average, that is in excess of 36 percent. Three factors are involved in these extraordinary population growth patterns.

### The Urban-To-Suburban Shift

For seven of the 11 the real key to their growth has been a urban-to-suburban shift. These parishes adjoin a major central city parish and have become bedroom communities for persons who want to have in a less urban setting and commute to work in the city. St. Tammany Parish is a spectacular example of this phenomenon. This parish's population has increased by a whopping 162 percent since 1970, the record performance by far among the 64 parishes. St. Tammany is the bedroom community for New Orleans, and Tangipahoa and, to some extent, St. Charles serve a similar role for the most populous city in Louisiana.

The urban-to-suburban shift is a central element behind the second fastest growth parish in Louisiana . . . Livingston . . . whose citizens heavily commute into Baton Rouge. At least part of Ascension's 72 percent increase can be attributed to being a commuting haven for Baton Rouge workers. Bossier (for Shreveport), Beauregard (for Lake Charles), and St. Martin (for Lafayette) can also trace their unusually strong growth to this urban-to-suburban shift.

### The Industrial Corridor

A second source of unusually strong population growth has been the previously mentioned industrial corridor between Baton Rouge and New Orleans. This region has been the recipient of huge injections of physical capital going back to the late 1960s. Flying over the Mississippi River between these two cities, one is almost awed by the proliferation of plants that have located in the area. Many workers have eschewed that long commute into the major cities and have chosen to Eve closer to work. This certainly pumped up the population numbers for Ascension, St. John the Baptist, and St. Charles Parishes.

### Central City Growth

Finally, it is interesting to note that of the eight major cities in Louisiana, only two experienced really rapid growth over the past quarter of a century . . . Baton Rouge and Lafayette. Baton Rouge has enjoyed one of the best employment growth patterns in Louisiana, especially in recent years. As the state capital and the home to two major state universities, it has benefitted from the expansion of the state government sector. Too, East Baton Rouge Parish contains the largest concentration of chemical industry workers in the state, and this has added both growth and a measure of stability to the parish. Lafayette received nearly three-quarters of its population boost during the 1970-81 years when the energy sector was in its heyday.

### The Decliners: The Delta Parishes

Map 2 also delineates those parishes that had the unusual experience of **losing population** over the past quarter of a century. These 12 parishes fall into three distinct groups.

Nine are in the Mississippi Delta area of Louisiana. These nine, along with Jackson Parish, have economies that are generally dominated by farming. Back in 1950, farming in these parishes was characterized by a large number of small farms with little mechanization. Over time, these farms have been consolidated into a much smaller number of large farms that are highly mechanized and require much fewer workers. The result? Workers have been out-migrating from these parishes to more urban areas where job prospects are better.

### The Decliners: Orleans

It may surprise some readers to learn that Orleans Parish, though it is still the most populous in the state, has lost over 18 percent of its population since 1970. Actually, this is nothing new for Orleans. It has been losing population for at least four decades.

What has been happening should be clear from Map 2. This parish, more than any other has suffered from the urban-to-suburban shift. St. Tammany Parish has been the biggest recipient of this outflow, but large population gains have also been enjoyed by nearby St. Charles, Jefferson, St. Bernard, and another parish across the lake . . . Tangipahoa. Concerns about public schools, taxes, and, frankly, white-flight have fueled this shift.

**The Decliners: St. Mary**

Like Orleans, St. Mary Parish has a unique story of its own. Located on the Gulf of Mexico, this parish was whip lashed by the energy boom-bust cycle. Its population rose from 60,000 in 1970 to 66,800 at the height of the boom in 1982. It then went into a steady slide to its present level of 57,200. The recent recovery in the offshore exploration industry may yet reverse this trend.

Looking into the rear view mirror at the past quarter of a century has revealed a tumultuous period in the history of the Louisiana economy. We have seen big winners and big losers. We have seen that despite experiencing the deepest and longest recession in our state's history, the overwhelming trend is ever upward. Louisiana citizens are much better off today than in 1970.

Finally, ask yourself this question: Who, looking into a crystal ball in 1970, would have ever predicted the radical swings we went through from 1970-95? It makes those of us involved in forecasting ask for an extra large slice from the "humble" pie.

Figure 1: Real Per Capita Income - Louisiana
(Rank Among 50 States)

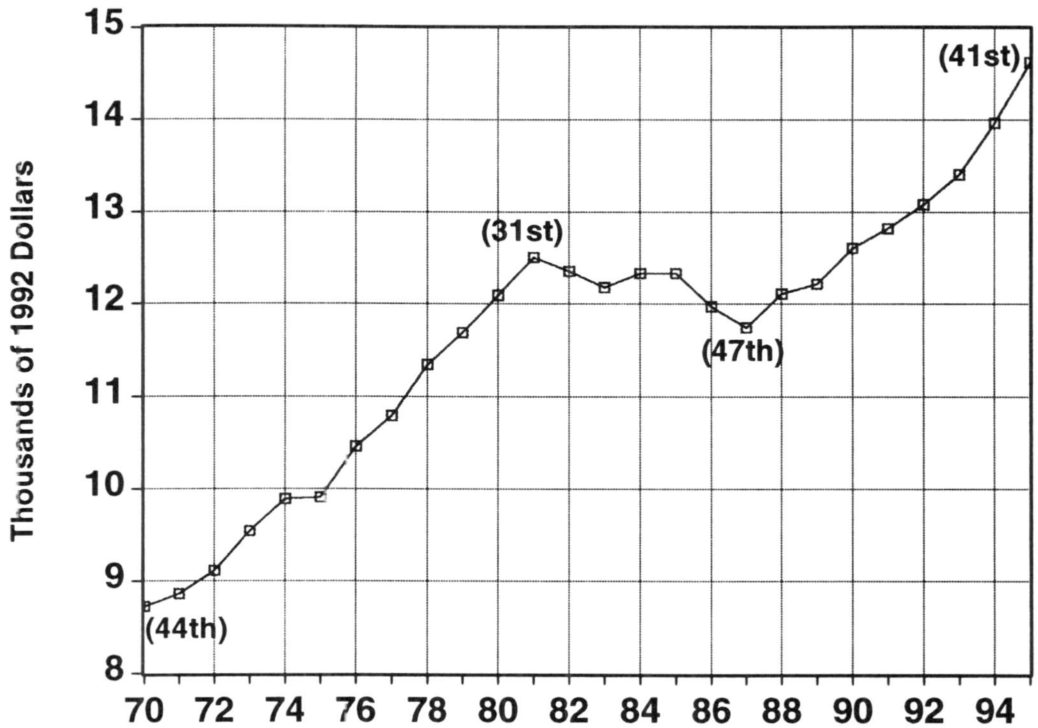


Source: Bureau of Economic Analysis, U.S. Department of Commerce

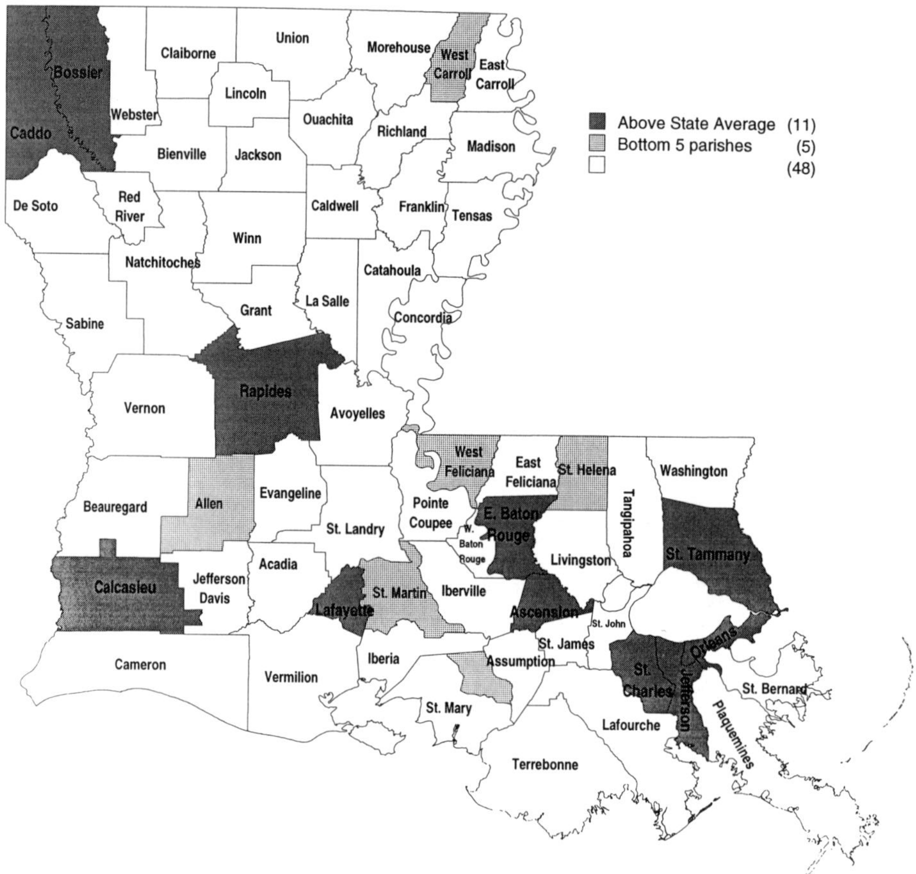


**Map1: Parishes with Per Capita Income Above the State Average and Bottom 5 Parishes: 1994.**

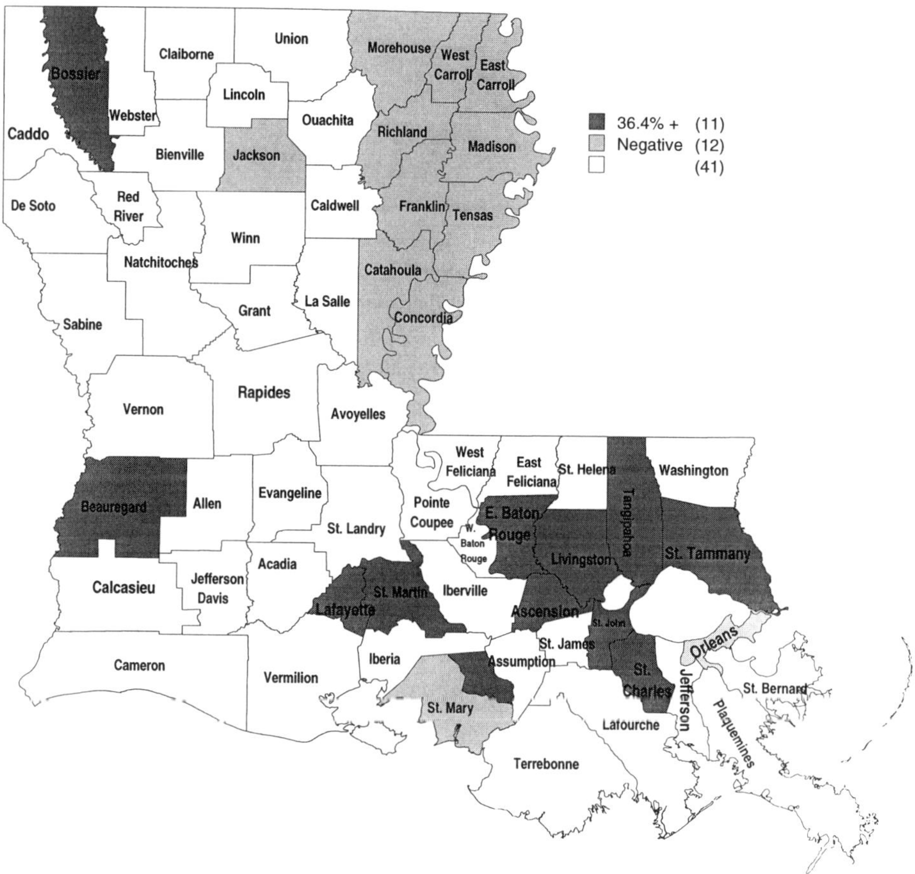


**Map 2: Fastest and Declining Population Growth Parishes in Louisiana: 1970 - 1994.**

# PART III

## The Environment

# THE IMPACT OF OUTER CONTINENTAL SHELF DEVELOPMENT IN LAFOURCHE PARISH*

Anthony J. Mumphrey, Jr., and Frederick W. Wagner

### THE IMPACT OF OCS DEVELOPMENT ON SEAFOOD, FUR, AND RECREATION IN LAFOURCHE PARISH

In this chapter, a brief description of the shrimp, oyster, menhaden, fur, and recreation industries in Lafourche Parish is presented, along with a discussion of OCS related impacts on these industries.

### LIVING WETLAND RESOURCES

Wetlands serve as a nursery, habitat, and source of nutrients for many seafood and fur animals. Destruction of wetlands leads to diminished production from these organisms. Natural and man-made phenomena cause stresses and destruction of the wetland environment. Natural stresses result from wave erosion, hurricanes, natural sedimentation from rivers and streams, natural pollution (such as oil seeps and natural phosphorus), certain marine organisms, geologic subsidence and other factors. Man-made changes in the wetlands which have caused environmental stress include pollution from urban runoff, industry, and pesticides; channelization and drainage and filling of wetlands for urbanization, agriculture and mining, which cause loss of habitat and productive capabilities. Channeling and dredging in the marsh and estuary areas are necessary for access to offshore and onshore oil facilities, laying pipelines, and constructing oil wells. As a consequence, various ecological changes occur along with oil industry development.[1]

Mumphrey et al.,[2] list the following ecological changes in coastal zones caused by channelization and dredging by the petroleum industry:

*Excerpts first published in Anthony J. Mumphrey, Jr., and Frederick W. Wagner, *The Impact of Outer Continental Shelf Development in Lafourche Parish* (New Orleans: University of New Orleans Urban Studies Institute, 1976), 162-96.

1. interfering with sheet water flow through the marsh;

2. allowing rapid salinity changes with the resultant death of vegetation and erosion of the marsh;

3. allowing destruction of marsh by wave action;

4. decreasing productivity by the presence of straight vs. sinuous channels that accelerate removal of freshwater and also confine water movement;

5. destruction of barrier islands with resultant increased destruction of marsh.

The flushing rate (movement of fresh water from wetlands into bayous and to the gulf) increases when north-south bayous are straightened and deepened. This results because the water does not have time to unload sediment and nutrients in the wetland area. The faster movement of water in the bayous and canals also causes erosion along the unstable banks of the streams. Other channels that are dug east-west across the marsh create spoil banks that interrupt the normal north-south sheet-like flow of water. This flow of water is important because it disperses nutrients and detritus over the wetlands. Additionally, man-made channels disrupt nursery areas of many commercially important marine animals (e.g., shrimp and menhaden). Dredging and channeling for the building of oil wells and pipelines can often destroy vegetation and habitats of marsh animals. (See Mumphrey et al., *Louisiana Metropolitan Wetlands*, 86-89, for a more complete discussion.) Burying pipelines and the revegetation of their paths through the marshes mitigates, but does not eliminate the effects of the associated channels.[3] Also, creative dispersal of spoil banks can mitigate some of the effects of channelization.

Where deep, straight canals are cut, salt wedges can result and extend far inland, causing the death of vegetation which results in the loss of nutrients, habitat, and erosion in the wetlands. These large, straight canals carry high velocity seawater (waves) during hurricanes and destroy vegetation. After a hurricane, the spoil banks tend to trap the saline seawater in the wetlands and prohibit it from draining. The result is the destruction of more vegetation and erosion. Also, the dredging of canals near barrier islands helps speed their destruction. Normally, these islands protect the plant and animal life of the wetlands from destruction by storm-generated tidal surges and diminish wetland erosion.[4]

The seafood and fur industries in Lafourche Parish are rather large. Therefore, preservation of wetlands productivity is important to the parish economy. The average employment in fishing for 1975-1976 is 250 (from Table 1). Commercial seafood landings in Lafourche Parish are shown in Table 2. Table 8 presents employment data on the fur industry.

## The Shrimp Industry

Louisiana's most important fishery in dollar terms is shrimp. The catch for the years 1940 to 1974 are shown in Table 3. Since trawling is performed over extensive acres of water, oil platforms do not affect the size of the shrimp catch. Of the several species caught in state waters, brown shrimp (*Penaeus aztecus*) and white shrimp (*Penaeus setiferus*) are the most important. During the 1958 to 1971 seasons, brown shrimp totaled 41% of the total Louisiana shrimp production. White shrimp, at one time, contributed 95% of the total offshore Louisiana catch. However, because of increased amounts of fresh water into estuary nursery grounds, where shrimp spend considerable time, there has been a decline in the catch since 1952.[5] Figure 1 shows that white shrimp spawn in the open gulf during May through July. After that, the larvae return to bays and estuaries and mature to adults in the safety of nursery grounds. The adults then return to the gulf in the early spring and live in waters less than 100 feet deep.[6]

TABLE 1
EMPLOYMENT IN SEAFOOD INDUSTRIES IN LAFOURCHE PARISH
FOR 1975-1976 BY QUARTER

| SIC Number | Description | 1975-1 | 1975-2 | 1975-3 | 1975-4 | 1976-1 |
|---|---|---|---|---|---|---|
| 0910 | Commercial fisheries | 86 | 109 | 120 | 118 | 79 |
| 0912 | Finfish | 5 | 5 | 10 | 7 | 10 |
| 0913 | Shellfish | 90 | 129 | 154 | 139 | 126 |
| 0989 | Fish hatcheries, farms, and preserves | 8 | 13 | 15 | 18 | 10 |
| | TOTAL | 189 | 256 | 299 | 282 | 225 |

Source: Louisiana Department of Employment Security, n.d.

TABLE 2
COMMERCIAL SEAFOOD LANDINGS
FOR GOLDEN MEADOW-LEEVILLE PORT

| Year | Size (1000 lbs.) | Value ($) |
|---|---|---|
| 1972 | 37,900 | 9,100,000 |
| 1973 | 32,565 | 8,626,000 |
| 1974 | 26,819 | 8,000,000 |
| 1975 | 23,395 | 11,260,000 |

Source: National Marine Fisheries Service, 1973-1976.

TABLE 3
LOUISIANA SHRIMP CATCH, 1940-1974

| Year | Quantity (1000 lbs.) | Value (1000 $) |
|---|---|---|
| 1940 | 90,820 | 3,645 |
| 1941 | NA | NA |
| 1942 | NA | NA |
| 1943 | NA | NA |
| 1944 | NA | NA |
| 1945 | 103,352 | 12,402 |
| 1946 | NA | NA |
| 1947 | NA | NA |
| 1948 | 79,966 | 16,827 |
| 1949 | 77,046 | 17,662 |
| 1950 | 70,630 | 14,696 |
| 1951 | 78,164 | 17,587 |
| 1952 | 75,854 | 15,722 |
| 1953 | 81,589 | 16,427 |
| 1954 | 77,709 | 15,451 |
| 1955 | 68,986 | 13,745 |
| 1956 | 56,886 | 15,316 |
| 1957 | 31,917 | 9,660 |
| 1958 | 39,760 | 13,080 |
| 1959 | 57,036 | 12,803 |
| 1960 | 61,758 | 15,881 |
| 1961 | 31,027 | 8,913 |
| 1962 | 43,585 | 14,985 |
| 1963 | 80,809 | 19,789 |
| 1964 | 59,382 | 18,794 |
| 1965 | 62,593 | 19,584 |
| 1966 | 62,276 | 24,390 |
| 1967 | 75,325 | 24,575 |
| 1968 | 67,768 | 25,623 |
| 1969 | 82,888 | 33,358 |
| 1970 | 90,948 | 34,614 |
| 1971 | 92,481 | 43,285 |
| 1972 | 83,035 | 47,066 |
| 1973 | 58,653 | 44,513 |
| 1974 | 59,591 | 32,206 |

Source: U.S. Fish and Wildlife Service, 1955-1969 and National Marine Fisheries Service, 1970-1974, 1975.

Since fishermen have extended their trawling grounds into deeper gulf waters, the brown shrimp has become more important than the white. Brown shrimp are associated with muddy substrates of peat and sandy mud. They bury themselves during the day and at night they feed in the gulf's surface waters. Trawlers bring in their greatest catches during summer nights. Brown shrimp spawn in the open gulf waters during fall and early winter. Larvae reaching the estuary nursery grounds remain until maturity when adults return to the open water in June (Figure 1). Brown shrimp are more tolerant of high salinities than white, 19 ppt (parts per thousand) being an optimum salinity.[7] Growth of the brown shrimp is dependent on moderate temperatures, 20$^0$C or greater, and salinity near 19 ppt.[8]

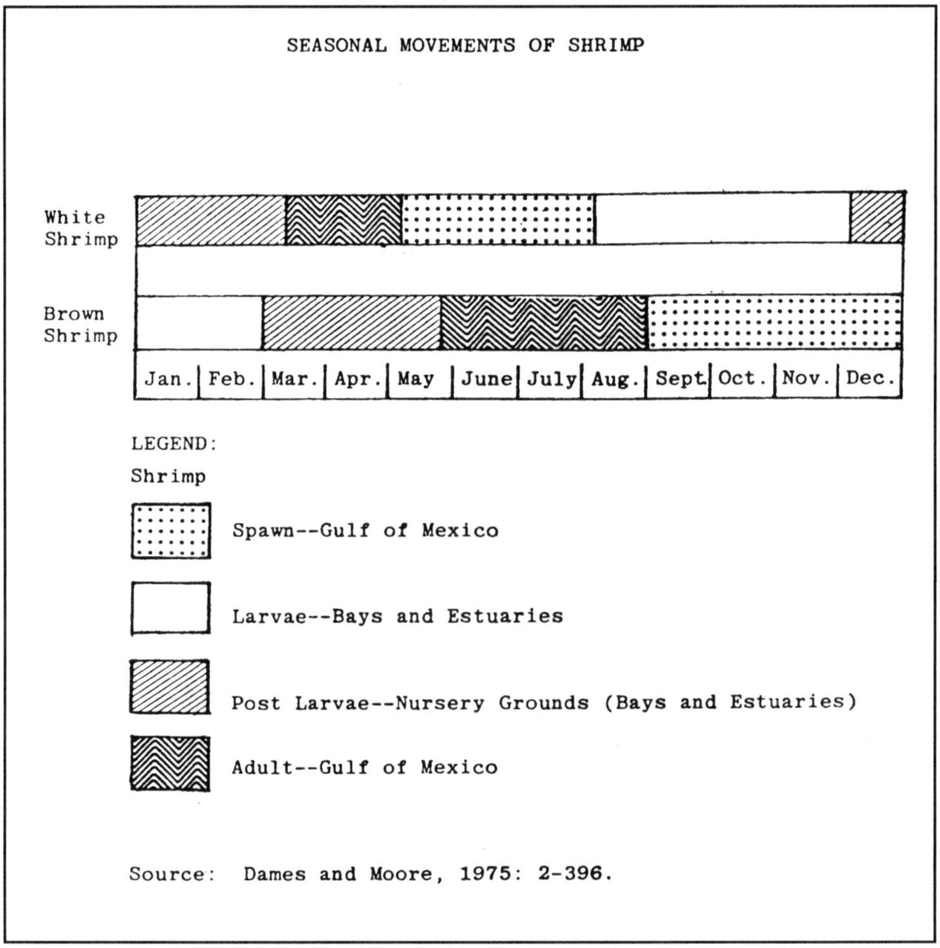


Figure 1

Estuarine nursery grounds provide shrimp with safety until they reach maturity. Plants, animals, and inorganic and organic detritus in the nurseries provide food for the shrimp. The estuarine nursery grounds are affected in two major ways by man's activities. First, changes in salinity and chemical composition of water are the results of channeling. Secondly, loss of vegetated marsh areas by channeling and dredging reduces the shrimp supporting capacity of the estuaries.[9]

Another problem which may affect the shrimp catch is the laying of pipelines. Pipelines laid in bays and offshore waters are either buried in the seabed or are eventually covered by the substrate (ocean floor material that supports plant or animal life). Occasionally, before pipelines are covered, or when they become uncovered by water current action, trawlers face navigational hazards. Nets become caught and snagged on exposed lines. For the same navigational reasons, trawling is not performed near oil platforms. However, many people believe the pipelines do not interfere with overall yields. Willingham et al., concluded "offshore pipelines . . . didn't appear to diminish yields of aquatic organisms."[10] Many shrimpers say the best trawling, areas are along underwater pipelines. Shrimp and other smaller fish hide from predators and feed in the abundant growths of seaweed found on both sides of a pipeline.[11]

The largest shrimp production areas are in Terrebonne and Lafourche Parishes with Barataria and Caminada Bays being the traditional center of brown shrimp production in Louisiana.[12] Only slightly less important are Timbalier and Terrebonne Bays. The average inshore production of brown and white shrimp for 1959 to 1972 in the Barataria and Caminada Bay areas was approximately 28% of the annual inshore brown shrimp catch in Louisiana.[13] Table 4 shows the brown shrimp catch in Barataria and Caminada Bays for 1959 to 1972.[14] 1970 yielded the largest catch with 4.95 million pounds. At the 1974 per pound value of $0.54 computed from Table 3, a catch of about 4 million pounds is valued at about $2 million.

While shrimp catches are important, processing is a necessity to distribute the various shrimp products. Shrimp producers sell shrimp in several forms including fresh headless, fresh peeled, fresh heads-on, frozen peeled, frozen heads-on, frozen heads-off, canned and dried. Four seafood companies in Lafourche Parish provide fresh and frozen shrimp.[15] The Louisiana Advisory Commission recommends that the dockside value of commercial catches be multiplied by a factor of between 2.5 and 3.5 to obtain the total worth of production after value added in processing. Using a factor of 3, a catch of 4 million pounds is valued, after processing, at $6 million.[16]

## The Oyster Industry

The Eastern or Atlantic oyster, *Crassostrea virginica Gmelin*, is the only commercially valuable oyster taken in Louisiana waters.[17] Although *Crassostrea virginica* may live in a salinity range of 10 to 30 ppt, it is usually found in salinities of 10 to 15 ppt. The reason for greater populations in a lower salinity range is the low salinity intolerance of oyster predators, such as the fungus *Dermocystidium* marinum and the conch (commonly called oyster drill), *Thais haemastoma*.

*Dermocystidium marinum* infects oysters usually during high temperature periods and in salinities above 10 ppt. Infection is usually lethal to the host oyster, but also may cause loss of weight, castration, and failure to grow normally. A change to a lower salinity achieved by fresh water flushing of the estuary is believed to be the best way to rid the oyster bed of the fungus.[18]

The conch *Thais haemastoma hayse* is common in the northern gulf waters. *T. haemastoma* feeds on oysters and other mollusks by drilling holes in the shell or penetrating the shell from the edge by secreting enzymes that soften the mollusks' shells. The conch has a high reproductive rate and high survival rate of larvae. A salinity of 10 ppt or lower will prevent the conch from entering waters and exposure to a salinity of 7 ppt or lower for one or two weeks is known to kill it. *T. haemastoma* breeds in Louisiana during a period beginning no later than the end of March and ending in July. The conch's tendency to climb on rocks or structures above ground to attach its eggcases has led many oystergrowers to erect stakes in the oyster grounds to trap the animal.[19]

TABLE 4
BARATARIA AND CAMINADA BAYS,
BROWN SHRIMP CATCH, 1959-1972

| Year | Catch (millions of pounds) |
|---|---|
| 1959 | 2.75 |
| 1960 | 2.99 |
| 1961 | 1.03 |
| 1962 | 1.50 |
| 1964 | 1.05 |
| 1965 | 2.59 |
| 1966 | 2.88 |
| 1967 | 3.55 |
| 1968 | 3.69 |
| 1969 | 4.37 |
| 1970 | 4.95 |
| 1971 | 4.68 |
| 1972 | 4.21 |

Source: Barrett and Gillespie, *Commercial Shrimp Production*, 26.

Louisiana's oyster production depends on "seed" oysters taken from state-managed seed grounds east of the Mississippi River and transported to private grounds for cultivation. Cultivating oysters has become more important in Louisiana with the depletion of natural oyster reefs. Some believe that the decline in productivity in the natural oyster reefs is due to overfishing more than the effects of salinity changes. Mackin and Hopkins define an oyster reef as "an area of not less than 500 square yards of the bottom of any body of water upon which oysters are found or have been found within a term of five years . . . in quantities which would warrant taking them for profit by means of tongs."[20] The largest natural oyster reef is the Point au Fer reef in the Atchafalaya Bay.[21]

The first seed plantings were tried in 1886 near the end of the Mississippi River delta with the Garden Island Bay oyster culture. Plantings were later begun below Quarantine Bay in an area known as the "Salt Works".[22] Natural reefs were used to provide seed oysters.

Oysters are dredged from the seed areas and transported to public and private leases for cultivation. Since 1904, an individual may obtain in his name up to one thousand acres in total of oyster lease cultivation grounds from the state.[23] Corporations may hold in total more than one thousand acres by having each of its various stockholders hold one thousand acres. Individuals or corporations who own factories are allowed to hold five hundred oyster lease acres for the first factory, two hundred and fifty acres for the second factory, and none for other factories. This is in addition to acres held as oyster cultivators. Leases are valid for fifteen years.[24] Figure 2 shows the principal lease and seed grounds in southeast Louisiana.

Louisiana oysters tend to grow faster, spawn more abundantly, and have a larger population in salinities up to 30 ppt. The abundance of natural predators in higher salinities forces the oyster to keep to lower salinity waters. Mackin and Hopkins believe the best oyster producing areas are high salinity waters where freshets (fresh water intrusions) drive out or kill predators. Oysters can withstand freshets by shutting their shells for long periods.[25]

The oil industry has had two main effects on the oyster populations of Louisiana, one direct and another indirect. Oil pollution directly affects the commercial value of the oyster. Oysters are sessile (attached to the substrate) filter feeders. Oysters ingest crude oil in feeding and concentrate it in their systems. The ingestion of oil does not affect their feeding process; however, an oily taste is imparted, making them undesirable in markets. Over time, however, if the oil is dispersed, the oysters will eventually lose the oily taste. In a study done on the effects of an oil spill from a Mecom Oil Company well, Mackin and Sparks found that after two months, the oil taste had "probably disappeared" from a great number of the population in the most contaminated area (located in Grand Isle Block, Freeport Sulphur vicinity), because of the breakdown of the oil.[26]

Salinity changes have been caused indirectly by the oil industry through channeling and dredging for access to offshore oil facilities. The increases in salt water allows the oyster predators to enter oyster grounds and often cause serious damage. Also, dredging that covers oyster beds or dislocates oysters from the substrate can cause destruction of the oyster reef.

Table 5 shows the catch and value of oysters in Louisiana for the years 1940 through 1974. In 1940, 12,412.2 thousand pounds of oysters were taken at a value of $694,875. In 1963, 11,563.2 thousand pounds of oysters were valued at $3,720,113 and in 1974, 9,971 thousand pounds were valued at $6,347,912. The 1968 catch was the largest catch at 13,122 pounds and was valued at $5,305,000.

In Lafourche Parish, 15,157 acres were leased for oyster cultivation in 1976.[27] Barataria Bay produces 357 pounds of oyster per acre leased. This is second only to Lake

Borgne (539 pounds per leased acre). In terms of production alone, Barataria Bay is valued first. An approximate 49% of the oyster meat produced in Louisiana during the 1963-67 period was from Barataria Bay.[28] If this proportion still holds, then Barataria Bay in 1974 produced 4.9 million pounds of oysters with a value of $9.3 million after processing.

## The Menhaden Industry

Since its beginning in Louisiana in 1948, the menhaden fishery has been an important commercial fishery in the state and recently is second only to shrimp. The two major species caught are *Brevoortia patronus* and *Brevoortia gunteri*. In 1974, 524,363,440 pounds of menhaden were caught in the four-parish area, including St. Mary, Assumption, Terrebonne, and Lafourche. Value of the catch was $19,027,142.[29] After processing, the value was approximately $57 million. Table 6 shows that the entire state's menhaden catch has greatly increased since 1948, based on the market for the fish and unrelated to the oil industry. Because extensive areas of the gulf are trawled for menhaden, the size of their catch is unrelated to the oil and gas platforms.

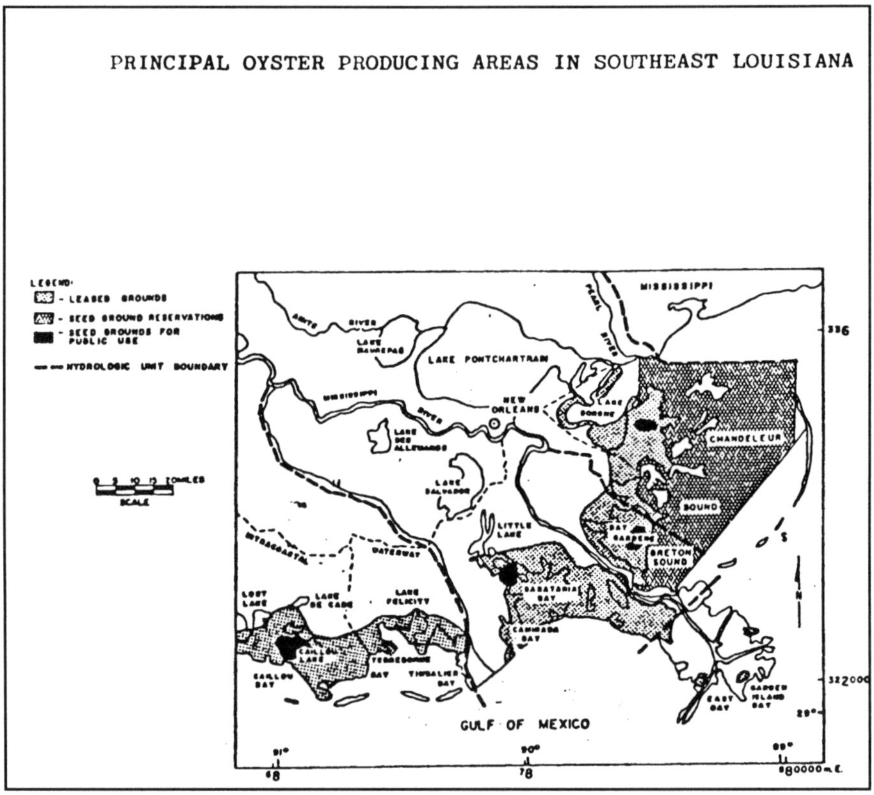


Figure 2. Source: Dames and Moore, 1975: 2-407.

TABLE 5
LOUISIANA OYSTER CATCH, 1940-1974

| Year | Pounds (in thousands) | Unprocessed Value |
|---|---|---|
| 1940 | 12,412.2 | $ 694,875 |
| 1941 | NA | NA |
| 1942 | NA | NA |
| 1943 | NA | NA |
| 1944 | NA | NA |
| 1945 | 9,884.1 | 2,829,007 |
| 1946 | NA | NA |
| 1947 | NA | NA |
| 1948 | 9,016.3 | 3,157,393 |
| 1949 | 9,687.5 | 3,459,341 |
| 1950 | 8,715.4 | 2,842,603 |
| 1951 | 8,163.7 | 1,902,647 |
| 1952 | 11,401.6 | 3,075,141 |
| 1953 | 9,435.3 | 2,672,664 |
| 1954 | 8,361.1 | 2,350,270 |
| 1955 | 9,394.9 | 2,753,177 |
| 1956 | 10,056.1 | 2,238,034 |
| 1957 | 10,489.3 | 2,756,098 |
| 1958 | 8,264.8 | 2,425,917 |
| 1959 | 9,667.5 | 2,645,124 |
| 1960 | 8,310.8 | 2,303,997 |
| 1961 | 10,139.2 | 2,849,090 |
| 1962 | 10,160.3 | 3,316,554 |
| 1963 | 11,563.2 | 3,720,113 |
| 1964 | 11,401.1 | 2,976,152 |
| 1965 | 8,342.7 | 2,401,607 |
| 1966 | 4,764.0 | 2,156,000 |
| 1967 | 7,743.0 | 3,414,000 |
| 1968 | 13,122.0 | 5,305,000 |
| 1969 | 9,178.0 | 3,969,000 |
| 1970 | 8,639.0 | 3,631,000 |
| 1971 | 10,528.0 | 4,638,000 |
| 1972 | 8,805.0 | 4,457,000 |
| 1973 | 8,953.8 | 5,545,022 |
| 1974 | 9,971.2 | 6,347,912 |

Source: U.S. Fish and Wildlife Service, 1955-1969 and National Marine Fisheries Service, 1970-1974, 1975.

The industrial fish industry is relatively new in the Gulf of Mexico. Bottom fish or "trash-fish" are used for feeding a variety of agricultural and domestic animals. In 1952, a pet food plant opened in Pascagoula, Mississippi, starting the bottom fish industry in the gulf. At least 65 bottom fish species are caught for processing, most of which are of the

Sciaenid family.[30] Industries use menhaden oil for manufacturing margarine and in a wide variety of industrial products and processes. Fish meal and solubles from menhaden are used for agricultural purposes.

TABLE 6
MENHADEN CATCH FOR LOUISIANA

| Year | Catch (1000 pounds) | Value (in thousands $) |
|---|---|---|
| 1948 | 88,110 | NA |
| 1949 | 165,914 | NA |
| 1950 | 207,755 | NA |
| 1951 | 209,574 | NA |
| 1952 | 283,373 | 2,765 |
| 1953 | 307,492 | 3,690 |
| 1954 | 270,094 | 3,727 |
| 1955 | 298,309 | 4,594 |
| 1956 | 320,521 | 4,840 |
| 1957 | 162,817 | 2,459 |
| 1958 | 241,813 | 3,627 |
| 1959 | 442,740 | NA |
| 1960 | 470,108 | NA |
| 1961 | 581,682 | 6,748 |
| 1962 | 689,157 | 7,994 |
| 1963 | 633,484 | 7,862 |
| 1964 | 599,538 | 9,046 |
| 1965 | 682,435 | 11,790 |
| 1966 | 555,852 | 9,558 |
| 1967 | 510,414 | 6,134 |
| 1968 | 622,291 | 7,740 |
| 1969 | 856,251 | 12,764 |
| 1970 | 959,810 | 18,931 |
| 1971 | 1,237,093 | 20,015 |
| 1972 | 928,252 | 15,279 |
| 1973 | 894,931 | 37,221 |
| 1974 | 1,079,304 | 39,539 |

Source: U.S. Fish and Wildlife Service, 1955-1969 and National Marine Fisheries Service, 1970-1974, 1975.

Most of the commercial fish important to Louisiana industry rely on estuaries for food or live part of their lives in the estuaries. Table 7 shows the migratory behavior of selected coastal organisms. Fish are subjected to two stresses from the oil industry: pollution from oil spills and destruction of estuary nursery and feeding grounds. Channeling and dredging have increased salinity in most of the estuary and marsh areas of Louisiana. Changes in salinity cause changes in flora, plankton, and overall habitat. Levee building for drainage and flood protection decreases the amount of freshwater runoff from land. This, in turn, leads to a depletion in nutrients necessary for plankton life (menhaden food). Straightening channels and bayous increases the flushing rate and turbidity of the stream or stops sheetwater flow, resulting in diminished wetland nutrients. Increased turbidity affects ability of many plankton species to float.[31]

Fish populations can be damaged in five major ways by oil spills:

1. coating and exposure to hydrocarbon concentrations in excess of 0.1 ppm cause eggs and larvae to die;
2. adult fish, especially anadromous fish, die or fail to reach spawning grounds if spill occurs in a critical, narrow, or shallow waterway;
3. contaminated spawning of nursery grounds causes loss of a local breeding population;
4. productivity and spawning patterns are changed;
5. local food species of adults, juveniles, fry, or larvae are affected.[32]

TABLE 7

MIGRATORY BEHAVIOR OF COASTAL ORGANISMS

| Month | Movement into Estuaries (or nearshore zone) | Movement from Estuaries |
|---|---|---|
| Jan. | Southern Hake, Red Drum (peak) | Menhaden, Spadefish |
| Feb. | Stingray, Brown Shrimp Post-larvae, Menhaden, Spadefish | |
| Mar. | Gulf Killifish, Spot, Cutlass-fish, Hogchoker, Butterfish, Rough Silverside, Flounder, Tonguefish | Bluc Catfish, Sheepshead Minnow, Long-nose Killifish |
| Apr. | Gafftopsail Catfish, Sea Catfish, Bluefish, Bumper, Sand Seatrout, Southern King-fish, Shipjack Herring (in and out same month), Adult Croaker, Black Drum (peak), Pinfish, Atlantic Threadfin, Toadfish, Midshipman | Bighead Searo-bin |
| May | Striped Anchovy, Lizardfish Sardine, Spanish Mackerel, White Shrimp Postlarvae | Menhaden, Southern Hake |
| June | Needlefish, Pompano, Crevalle Jack, Leatherjacket, Atlantic Moonfish | Butterfish |

Table 7 (cont.)

| | | |
|---|---|---|
| July | Ladyfish, Lookdown | |
| Aug. | | Ladyfish, Atlantic Threadfin |
| Sept. | | Adult Croaker, Rough Silverside |
| Oct. | Menhaden, Sheepshead Minnow, Bighead Searobin | Sardine, Bluefish, Leatherjacket, Atlantic Moonfish, Sand Seatrout, Cutlassfish, Spanish Mackerel |
| Nov. | Blue Catfish, Juvenile Croaker | Striped Anchovy, Gafftopsail, Sea Catfish, Needlefish, Pompano, Crevalle Jack, Bumper, Lookdown, Pinfish, Tonguefish, Toadfish, Midshipman, White Shrimp Juveniles |
| Dec. | Longnose Killifish | Stingray, Lizardfish, Gulf Killifish, Spot, Southern Kingfish, Flounder, Hogchoker |

Source: Dames and Moore, Inc., *Louisiana Offshore Oil Port*, 2-373.

Moore and Dwyer[33] describe five ways individual organisms respond to the effects of oil pollution. The first is direct lethal toxicity, resulting in death. Cellular and subcellular processes, especially membrane activity, are interfered with by the hydrocarbons released by crude oil. The most toxic of the hydrocarbons (the chemical components of petroleum) are the lower boiling point aromatics. These stay in the environment the longest. The larvae and juveniles of species are more sensitive to toxic matter than the adults. Adult marine organisms respond to lethal toxic levels from concentrations of soluble hydrocarbons in the 1-100 parts per million (ppm) range. Larvae stages may be affected by levels as low as 0.1 ppm.

The second response is sub-lethal disruption of physiological or behavioral activities. Disruption of cellular and physiological processes does not include immediate death, though it may occur in the long-run. Feeding and reproduction of species are possibly affected.

Direct coating of oil is the third response. This can cause smothering of the species and/or interference with feeding and movement. Oil can also destroy the water proofing and insulating properties of animals with feathers and fur. Oil can be ingested as animals try to clean themselves. Bird mortality, as a result of direct oil coating, has been well documented along the California coast.

The fourth response is the incorporation of hydrocarbons in food chains. This includes tainting of edible organisms such as oysters and clams. Accumulation and concentration of polycyclic aromatic hydrocarbons is a major concern, especially since this includes carcinogens.

The final response listed is changes in biological habitats, especially alteration of substrate characteristics. The substrate is the ocean floor material that supports plant or animal life. Species living passively on the substrate (not depending heavily on the substrate for support) may have little or no interference with their habitat. Flora and fauna living in the substrate or actively dependent on it may have adverse effects.[34] Although the quantity and types of oil that may prevent a species from utilizing a substrate are unknown, data indicate concentrations of 10 to 100 parts per billion (ppb) of low to medium boiling point aromatic hydrocarbons may interfere with the species' relationship to the substrate. Chemical sensing and communications upon which anadromous fish depend will be interfered with by the presence of aromatic hydrocarbon derivatives in such concentrations.[35]

## The Fur Industry

O'Neil and Linscombe[36] studied the fur industry of Louisiana and found that the state leads the United States in fur productions, amounting to 40 to 65 percent of the total catch per year. Fur trapping began in Louisiana in the 18th century with the founding of New Orleans. Furs were transported to the city and shipped to all parts of the world. Mink, raccoon, otter and alligator were hunted in Louisiana coastal marshes during the 1800s. Burning of the marsh to make alligator habitats more accessible to hunters and other factors such as salinity changes caused changes in the marsh vegetation. These man-induced changes to the marsh produced a favorable environment for the muskrat. During the early 1900s, efforts were begun to trap muskrat in large numbers.

Nutria were first brought to Avery Island, Louisiana, in 1938 from Argentina by Mr. E. A. McIlhenny. During captivity, some nutria escaped and others were intentionally released. This resulted in the establishment of a sizeable population in South Louisiana by 1943. The presence of nutria has offset changes in marsh vegetation and has consequently caused the muskrat population to decline.[37] The nutria is now Louisiana's most valuable fur animal. Table 3.8 gives an indication of the importance of fur trapping to employment in Lafourche Parish. Table 3.9 shows the Louisiana fur catch for the 1974-1975 season. After processing, its value is greater than $30 million.[38] Assuming that the proportion of fur taken in Lafourche Parish is equal to its proportion of the area of the coastal parishes—6%[39]—the processed value of fur animals to Lafourche Parish is over $1.8 million.

TABLE 8
FUR LICENSES SOLD IN LAFOURCHE PARISH
DURING THE 1973-1974, 1974-1975, AND 1975-1976 SEASONS

| Year | Fur Dealers ($150/year) | Fur Buyer ($25/year) | Fur Trapper ($2/season) |
|---|---|---|---|
| 1973-1974 | 2 | 12 | 432 |
| 1974-1975 | 2 | 12 | 517 |
| 1975-1976 | 2 | 13 | 496 |

(Fur dealers must also deposit $500 to insure payment of severance tax—O'Neil and Linscombe, *The Fur Animals*. Fur trappers may be employed part-time in trapping in addition to other work.) Sources: H. Cauvin, Lafourche Parish Sheriff's Office, Thibodaux, Louisiana, telephone interview, July, 1976; Louisiana Wildlife and Fisheries Commission, Fur Division, New Orleans, unpublished data on fur license.

TABLE 9
LOUISIANA FUR CATCH, 1974-1975 SEASON

| Category | Number of Pelts | Approximate Price to Trapper | Unprocessed Value |
|---|---|---|---|
| Muskrat (Eastern) | 240, 214 | $ 3.25 | $ 780,695.50 |
| Muskrat (Western) | 60,000 | 4.50 | 270,000.00 |
| Mink | 32,319 | 4.50 | 145,435.50 |
| Nutria (Eastern) | 1,000,000 | 4.50 | 4,500,000.00 |
| Nutria (Western) | 502,617 | 5.50 | 2,764,393.50 |
| Raccoon (Coastal) | 70,000 | 4.00 | 280,000.00 |
| Raccoon (Upland) | 90,863 | 7.00 | 636,041.00 |
| Opossum | 30,447 | 1.50 | 45,670.50 |
| Otter | 6,118 | 25.00 | 152,950.00 |
| Skunk | 298 | 1.00 | 298.00 |
| Fox | 3,471 | 16.00 | 55,536.00 |
| Bobcat | 775 | 25.00 | 19,375.00 |
| Beaver | 276 | 5.00 | 1,380.00 |
| Coyote | 342 | 10.00 | 3,420.00 |
| TOTAL PELTS | 2,038,379 | | $9,655,195.00 |
| Nutria Meat | 9,000,000 lbs. | .09 | $ 810,000.00 |
| Muskrat Meat | 250,000 lbs. | .09 | 22,500.00 |

Table 9 (cont.)

| Category | Number of Pelts | | Approximate Price to Trapper | Unprocessed Value |
|---|---|---|---|---|
| Raccoon Meat | 930,000 | lbs. | .30 | 279,000.00 |
| Opossum Meat | 250,000 | lbs. | .25 | 62,500.00 |
| TOTAL MEAT | 10,430,000 | lbs. | | $1,174,000.00 |
| TOTAL PELTS AND MEAT | | | | $10,829,195.00 |

Source: Louisiana Wildlife and Fisheries Commission, Fur Division, *Comparative Takes of Fur.*

Muskrat and nutria live in coastal marsh areas and have a diet consisting of three-cornered grass, salt meadow cordgrass, cattail bullwhip, alligator weed and other grasses. (Muskrat may also eat small amounts of fish, mussels, insects, and snails). Three-cornered grass (*Scirpus oeneyi*) is found in brackish marshes in dense, uniform stands often covering large areas. Marshes of three-cornered grass produce more than 80 percent of the muskrat catch and many of the nutria.[40]

Fur bearing animals are affected in several ways by man's activities in the coastal zone. Habitat land loss for fur animals consists of land disturbed by dredging and channeling operations and the resulting spoil banks. An indirect effect on habitat is the increased salinity in the marsh resulting from channeling. Salinity changes affect vegetation important to the animals, such as three-cornered grass.[41] Channeling may also create migrational and home range barriers for animals. Crossing spoilbanks will subject many animals to increased predatory vulnerability.[42] Temporary displacement and interruption of animal activities may accompany pipeline construction and surveillance in backfilled canals. Multipurpose canals may result in animals being periodically subjected to noise and sight of moving objects which may effect the behavior of local populations. Animals avoid areas where aircraft and vehicular traffic occur. The presence and noise from vehicular traffic in canals may affect the survival of some animal populations.[43]

Two positive side-effects of dredging and channeling can be found in the marsh lands. First, trappers and hunters make use of open canals to reach unaccessable trapping and hunting grounds. Secondly, stable spoil banks will become revegetated with shrubbery, creating new habitats for a diversified population.[44]

## RECREATIONAL RESOURCES

The developed recreation resources in Lafourche Parish are outlined in a study entitled the *State Comprehensive Outdoor Recreation Plan* (SCORP) by the Louisiana State Parks and Recreation Commission.[45] The study includes an inventory of facilities and their locations. Table 3.10 shows the SCORP listing of these recreational facilities. The SCORP list shows two wildlife management areas, with no facilities offering boating, hunting and fishing in Lafourche Parish (Figure 3.3). The Pointe-au-Chien Wildlife Management Area was acquired by the Louisiana Wildlife and Fisheries Commission in 1968, and consists of 22,595 acres, located in both Lafourche and Terrebonne Parishes. Wisner Game Management Area (26,310 acres) was leased to the State of Louisiana in 1968 by the Edward Wisner Donation Advisory Committee.[46] A third wildlife management area, Salvador, is located within St. Charles Parish and forms the parish boundary line with Lafourche. The area was purchased in 1968 by the Louisiana Wildlife and Fisheries Commission and consists of 27,499 acres.[47] One National Wildlife Refuge, East Timbalier, is a barrier island located off the Lafourche Parish coastline. The refuge contains 337 acres.[48]

Notes for "The Impact of Outer Continental Shelf Development in Lafourche Parish"

[1]A. J. Mumphrey et al., *Louisiana Metropolitan Wetlands: A Planning Perspective* (New Oreans, 1975), 41-95.

[2]Ibid., 86.

[3]C. A. Willingham et al., *Interim Report—1973—on a Study of Selected Coastal Zone Ecosystems in the Gulf of Mexico in Relation to Gas Pipelining Activities to Offshore Pipeline Committee, January, 1974* (Columbus, Ohio, 1974).

[4]Mumphrey et al., *Louisiana Metropolitan Wetlands*, 89-93.

[5]B. B. Barrett and M. C. Gillespie, *Primary Factors Which Influence Commercial Shrimp Production in Coastal Louisiana* (New Orleans, 1973).

[6]P. Viosca, Jr., *The Louisiana Shrimp Story* (Baton Rouge, 1957), 8-9.

[7]Barrett and Gillespie, *Commercial Shrimp Production*.

[8]C.J. White, *Effects of 1973 River Flood Waters on Brown Shrimp in Louisiana Estuaries* (New Orleans, 1975).

[9]J.T. McGinnis et al., *Final Report on Environmental Aspects of Gas Pipeline Operations in the Louisiana Coastal Marshes to Offshore Pipeline Committee, December, 1972* (Columbus, Ohio, 1972), 3-24.

[10]Willingham et al., *Interim Report*, 135.

[11]John LaPlace, "Will the Drip, Drip, Drip Get Us?", *New Orleans Times-Picayune*, June 16, 1976.

[12]Dames and Moore, Inc., *Environmental Analysis: Louisiana Offshore Oil Port* (New Orleans, 1975); White, *Effects of 1973 River Flood*.

[13]White, *Effects of 1973 River Flood*.

[14]Barrett and Gillespie, *Commercial Shrimp Production*.

[15]Department of Commerce and Industry, *Louisiana Directory of Manufacturers* (Baton Rouge, 1975).

[16]Louisiana Advisory Commission on Coastal and Marine Resources, *Louisiana Wetlands Prospectus* (Baton Rouge, 1973), 187-88.

[17]J. F. Pollard, *Experiments to Re-establish Historical Oyster Seed Grounds and to Control the Southern Oyster Drill* (New Orleans, 1973).

[18]G. Mackin, "Oyster Disease Caused by *Dermocystidium Marinum* and Other Microorganisms in Louisiana," *Publications of the Institute of Marine Sciences*, 7 (1962): 132-229.

[19]Paul S. Galtsoff, "The American Oyster, *Crassostrea virginica Gmelin*," *Fishery Bulletin of the Fish and Wildlife Service*, 64 (1964): 433.

[20]G. Mackin and S. H. Hopkins, "Studies on Oyster Mortality in Relation to Natural Environments and to Oil fields in Louisiana," *Publications of the Institute of Marine Sciences*, 7 (1962): 1-131.

[21]Ibid.

[22]Ibid.

[23]Ibid.

[24]John Lay, Louisiana Wildlife and Fisheries Commission, Oyster, Waterbottom and Seafood Division, New Orleans, Louisiana, personal interview, July, 1976.

[25]Mackin and Hopkins, "Studies on Oyster Mortality."

[26]G. Mackin and A. K. Sparks, "A Study of the Effect on Oysters of Crude Oil Loss from a Wild Well," *Publications of the Institute of Marine Sciences*, 7 (1962): 230-61.

[27]Louisiana Wildlife and Fisheries Commission, "Leased Water Bottoms Acreage," unpublished data, Division of Oysters, Waterbottoms, and Seafoods, Survey Section, New Orleans, Louisiana, 1976.

[28]U.S. Coast Guard, Department of Transportation, *LOOP Deepwater Port License Application*, vol. 1 (Washington, D.C., 1976), 2.4-2.9.

[29]National Marine Fisheries Service, U.S. Department of Commerce, NOAA, *Louisiana Landings, Annual Summary, 1974* (Washington, D.C., 1975).

[30]F. Dunham, *Study of Commercially Important Estuarine-Dependent Industrial Fisheries* (New Orleans, 1972).

[31]R. Patrick, "Diatom Communities in Estuaries," *Conference on Estuaries* (1967).

[32]Council on Environmental Quality, *OCS Oil and Gas: An Environmental Assessment*, A Report to the President, vol. 1 (Washington, D.C., 1974), 107, 109.

[33]S. F. Moore and R. L. Dwyer, "Effects of Oil on Marine Organisms: A Critical Assessment of Published Data," *Water Research*, 8 (1974): 819-27.

[34]Council on Environmental Quality, *OCS Oil and Gas*, 106.

[35]Ibid., 106-7.

[36]T. O'Neil and G. Linscombe, *The Fur Animals, the Alligator, and the Fur Industry in Louisiana* (New Orleans, n.d.).

[37]Ibid., 23.

[38]Louisiana Wildlife and Fisheries Commission, Fur Division, *Comparative Takes of Fur Animals in Louisiana, 1940-1975* (New Orleans, n.d.).

[39]Mumphrey et al., *Louisiana Metropolitan Wetlands*, 100.

[40]McGinnis et al., *Final Report on Environmental Aspects*, 2.20.

[41]Ibid., 3.17-3.18.

[42]Ibid., 3.18.

[43]Ibid., 3.19.

[44]Ibid., 3.18.

[45]Louisiana State Parks and Recreation Commission, *State of Louisiana Comprehensive Outdoor Recreation Plan 1975-1980* (Baton Rouge, 1974); Louisiana State Parks and Recreation Comission, unpublished data, 1974.

[46]Louisiana State Parks and Recreation Comission, unpublished data, 1974.

[47]Louisiana Advisory Commission on Coastal and Marine Resources, *Louisiana Wetlands Prospectus*.

[48]Louisiana State Parks and Recreation Comission, unpublished data, 1974.

# PLIGHT OF THE PELICAN*

Robert Fritchey

Louisiana lawmakers passed legislation in 1958 that named the "Pelican," the bird that had already graced the state seal, the official state bird. Of course, this honor had been intended for the brown pelican, the conspicuous and permanent resident of the state's coastal waters. But the precise wording of any bill is extremely important, and the legislators' omission of the modifier "brown" allowed the department of motor vehicles to put an American white pelican on Louisiana license plates one year. The white pelican is a migratory bird that, like a tourist, only visits the state in the fall and winter.

By 1966, when lawmakers finally corrected their omission, Louisiana's state bird was nearly extinct.

What happened to the brown pelican? The bird's demise was so sudden that no one is absolutely sure, though circumstantial evidence points strongly to its poisoning by agricultural pesticides.

A subsequent restocking program led to the re-establishment of this species of pelican in Louisiana. And to the irony that all of the Pelican State's official birds descend from those trucked here from Florida.

The brown pelican ranges as far north as the Carolinas on the Atlantic Coast, well into California on the Pacific Coast, throughout the Caribbean and down both coasts through Central America as far south as Brazil and Ecuador. Still, Louisiana quite fittingly came to be known as the Pelican State.

In the old days, a visitor to any part of the Louisiana coast at any time of the year couldn't fail to notice great flocks of the birds as they dove after fish, lumbered by in long, undulating lines or posed philosophically on sandbars and pilings. The state produced most of the brown pelicans along the entire northern gulf, with major breeding colonies at the mud lumps at the mouth of the Mississippi River; Grand Gosier Island in the Chandeleur chain; North Island, just west of the chain; Isle au Pitre, farther to the

*First published in *Louisiana Life* (Autumn 1994): 45-50. Reprinted with the kind permission of the author and publisher.

northwest; Raccoon Point, at the western extremity of the Isles Dernieres; and East Timbalier Island.

Because of the remoteness of these rookeries, early ornithologists made few actual counts of the birds, although Herbert K. Job in 1915 counted ten or twelve thousand breeding pelicans on East Timbalier alone, and in 1920 A. M. Bailey reported 50,000 on the mud lumps.

Some biologists reported that the birds were becoming less abundant as early as the 1940s, but brown pelicans didn't elicit any real concern until the mid-1950s when people started to find their macabre corpses. Visitors to Dauphin and Petit Bois Islands in Alabama and Mississippi found about 25 dead adults in 1956. Fifty more corpses were reported from Isle au Pitre and several more on the Candeleur Islands the same year. In 1959, a biologist with the Louisiana Department of Wildlife and Fisheries found many dead pelicans, along with dozens of dead gulls and terns, on a mud lump near Pass a Loutre. A return visit to the mud lumps in 1960 turned up still more dead pelicans.

Thousands of birds nested on the Chandeleur rookeries during the breeding season of 1958, when ornithologists counted about a thousand nests on North Island alone. But the number of nests on North Island dwindled rapidly, to about 100 in 1961, the last year Louisiana's native birds were known to have nested. In 1962, only six adult pelicans and no nests were seen on North Island, and the following year no brown pelicans were to be seen there or anywhere else in the state. The brown pelican had simply vanished.

During the years when Louisiana's pelicans were disappearing, no chemical analyses of their eggs or tissues were ever conducted, so the exact cause of their death is not known. However, 1943 to 1963 had been a time of ever-increasing use of agricultural pesticides in the Mississippi Valley. Farmers applied several million pounds of DDT to crops—primarily cotton—each year in the Mississippi Delta alone. In addition to this deadly chlorinated hydrocarbon, its close chemical relatives such as aldrin, dieldrin, endrin, and chlordane were also being spread by the millions of pounds, usually by airplane.

Rainfall flushed the poisons from the soil and carried them into the streams and bayous, then the rivers, and finally into the gulf.

At the same time the pelicans were dying during the 1950s and 'bos, dramatic die-offs of fish began to appear along the Mississippi and Atchafalaya Rivers and in many of the oxbow lakes paralleling the Mississippi. In 1960, at least 30 large fish kills were reported. Authorities often seemed reluctant to attribute the cause of these kills to agricultural pesticides but, when a chemical plant in Memphis spilled a huge volume of endrin into a tributary of the Mississippi, more than five million fish died as the chemical made its way down the river to the Gulf of Mexico. This was in 1963, the same year the pelican disappeared from Louisiana.

The brown pelican's sudden disappearance awakened everyone to the polluted environment we were living in. In doing so, the bird made the ultimate sacrifice for Louisianians, the sort of mythical self-sacrifice for which the pelican had been known since the Middle Ages. After all, as the persistent pesticides worked their way up the aquatic food chain to the mullet and menhaden that the pelicans were ingesting, they also worked their way into the seafood that Louisiana residents loved to eat.

Conciding with the 1962 release of "Silent Spring," Rachel Carson's indictment of DDT and other chlorinated hydrocarbons, the pelican's disappearance helped bring about the eventual banning of such pesticides. More pelicans would have to die in the meantime, however.

Faced with the embarrassing loss of its state bird, the Louisiana Department of Wildlife and Fisheries took action in 1968. The department organized a January meeting at Rockefeller Wildlife Refuge with representatives from the U. S. Fish and Wildlife Service, the Audubon Society, and other state and national conservation organizations to plot their strategy. The "Pelican Committee" decided to activate immediately a research and restocking program, and appointed biologist Ted Joanen of the Fur and Refuge Division to lead the effort. Joanen was a likely candidate to lead such an effort—he was already conducting research on the Louisiana alligator and would nurture this species from a 1967 entry on the federal endangered species list to an abundance that today supports a valuable and sustainable industry.

In the summer of 1968, Joanen, Larry McNease and other department biologists traveled to Cocoa Beach, a small town on Florida's Atlantic Coast, not far from the Kennedy Space Center. Their destination was the thriving brown pelican colony on nearby Merritt Island. There they captured 50 fledglings—juveniles just about to fly—and brought them back to Louisiana.

The team took half the birds to Grand Terre, an island just to the east of Grand Isle where Wildlife and Fisheries conveniently had a research station. The other half went to Rockefeller Refuge in Cameron Parish. Hand fed until their release, 15 were turned loose from Grand Terre in September, and another 15 from Grand Chenier Island at Rockefeller in October.

Joanen's group clipped the wings of the remaining 20 birds, hoping that the presence of 10 grounded birds at each site would encourage the free-flying pelicans to remain in the area.

The plan worked on Grand Terre. The birds quickly learned to fish the rich waters of Barataria Bay; after a day's foraging, they invariably returned to join the flightless flock that was enjoying menhaden, mullet and croaker provided for them by their keepers.

By the time the Rockefeller birds were released, however, they'd become so used to receiving handouts that they made little attempt to get out and fish on their own. To force them to support themselves, the Rockefeller biologists eventually cut off their free meals. By this time, winter had come. The Rockefeller flock fared well until the following March when several winter storms hit the refuge. Shortly thereafter, the birds started dying and, within a month, all were dead.

In 1969, another 50 Florida pelicans were split between Rockefeller Refuge and Grand Terre. This time the Rockefeller birds were allowed to fly free as soon as they were able. They responded by quickly disappearing, never to be seen again, dead or alive. At this point efforts to restore the species to western Louisiana—which had never been a major nesting area—came to an end.

Meanwhile, at Grand Terre, 160 miles east of Rockefeller, the newly released birds happily winged off to join those that had thrived through the winter and began diving into the bay for fish. Why the Barataria Bay colony flourished and the Rockefeller birds did not was a question that needed to be answered.

Joanen took the birds that had died in 1968 to LSU for postmortem examinations. The brains, livers, and other vital organs of the dead birds held high concentrations of DDE, a break-down product of DDT, which was still being heavily applied to coastal and river-bordered agricultural lands

Louisiana was not the only state losing its brown pelicans in the 1960s. The other small colonies in Texas, Mississippi and Alabama were also in grave trouble. In the fall of 1968, a rapid decline in Florida's birds occurred suspiciously close to those areas that had been sprayed with DDT-related heptachlor and dieldrin to control the proliferating fire ant. Brown pelican populations were also crashing in California, where DDT use was clearly implicated.

The brown pelican was finally placed on the federal endangered species list in 1970, just two years after our federal symbol, the bald eagle, was listed. Like the brown pelican, the bald eagle was a top-of-the-food-chain species that was feeding on fish laced with concentrated doses of pesticide. In 1963, the year Louisiana's brown pelican vanished, American's bald eagle population had fallen to a low of about 400 pairs.

## FIRST NESTS

Biologists continued to import additional pelicans from Florida to Grand Terre Island, which had been found to be relatively clean of insecticide residue. The birds were thriving, but hadn't yet begun to reproduce on their own.

In the spring of 1971, it happened. Biologists learned that brown pelicans mate after their third year, when some of the "Class of '68" nested on Camp Island, a small shell reef a short distance from Grand Terre. Eleven of the 20 eggs in their first nesting hatched, but high tides wiped out this first nesting effort. A second nesting was also washed away.

Although Camp Island barely rose above water level—today it is completely gone—one end of it was a few feet higher than the end the birds were using. Had the pelicans been nesting there generations before, they would no doubt have been utilizing this higher section. But with no older birds to follow, these young pioneers had to learn the hard way.

By luck, they did relocate to the higher ridge that fall. In their third effort of the year they laid 20 eggs which produced eight precious fledglings, the first in Louisiana in 10 years.

The following year, the pelicans returned to nest on Camp Island again. High tides again wiped out their first effort, drownng several dozen hatchlings. The birds' second and third efforts did yield 14 more fledglings.

In 1973, when the pelicans again tried to nest on the vulnerable Camp Island, Joanen and his biologists did everything possible to discourage them. They periodically visited the island to scare the birds away, and they strung up wires, hung with aluminum pie plates to further annoy the pelicans.

Some of the birds got the message and mvoed over to Queen Bess Island, a slightly higher oyster bar with a thick growth of black mangroves. There they fledged 26 birds.

The year 1974 was a good one for the brown pelicans in Barataria Bay. Although they hadn't yet learned to nest on the higher ground or in the mangroves at Queen Bess, the elements were kind to them and they fledged 104 young.

By 1975, with a population of nearly 400 birds, things were looking up for Louisiana's brown pelicans. DDT had been banned in the early 1970s and the water was getting cleaner. But in the spring, disaster struck again.

The bodies of about 100 white pelicans were found on the coast in early March. Two of the dead birds picked up near the mouth of the Mississippi were sent to LSU for analysis. The findings? High concentrations of the chlorinated hydrocarbons PCB (polychlorinated biphenyl), DDE, dieldrin and endrin.

The brown pelicans, however, didn't appear to be affected. Biologists felt that it was the combination of the pesticides and the stress of the white pelicans' long migration that had killed them and they remained optimistic about the local population of brown pelicans. That optimism soon faded.

A mid-1975 check of the brown pelican's total population revealed that almost a quarter were gone, dropping their numbers from about 450 to only 350. Analyses of the tissues of some of the dead birds that were found disclosed the presence of at least eight different pesticides: endrin, dieldrin, toxaphene, DDE, BHC (benzene hexachloride), HCB (chlorobenzene), PCB and heptachloride epoxide.

"All of the birds tested contained what we regard as lethal doses of endrin," stated then Louisiana Department of Wildlife and Fisheries Secretary Burton Angelle in a national press release. "We have ample evidence that much of the endrin is coming down the Mississippi River from states north of Louisiana." Until that die-off, he explained, the annual reproductive rate of brown pelicans had equaled natural mortality, maintaining a fairly stable population level.

"We are discouraged," said Angelle at that time, "but we haven't given up. Project Pelican will continue."

The annual importation of Florida pelicans did continue, but nesting by resident birds met with one disaster after another. The reason was always the same—the pelicans were building their nests on the lowest areas of Queen Bess, where high tides regularly swept over them. Only one fledling was produced in the seasons from 1975 through 1977.

Finally, in 1978, the birds moved to the highest end of the island, where many built nests in the mangroves, several feet above the highest tides.

The newly elevated colony of pelicans boosted its number by 128 in 1978 and each successive year was even more productive, with a total of 430 fledged in 1982.

With the brown pelican colony in Barataria Bay flourishing, biologists in the late 1970s reintroduced more than 500 birds to Isle au Pitre and North Island, the site of Louisiana's final nesting by native birds in 1961. They later introduced 150 pelicans to Isles Dernieres—"Last Islands"—the traditional nesting site south of Houma—and re-established the bird's other traditional nesting colonies as well. The restocking program was discontinued in 1980.

According to Fur and Refuge biologist Larry McNease, overflight surveys are now conducted a few times a year to track the brown pelican's population. He conservatively estimates the state's current population at about 25,000. "In 1993, we counted a total of 5,186 nests and 8,695 fledglings," said McNease. "And this year it looks like the numbers may be even better."

## MORE PROBLEMS

For the moment, the specter of death by poisoning no longer haunts Louisiana's state bird. This threat has been replaced by another equally as ominous.

The brown plican lays its eggs—about three at a time—in makeshift nests on the ground or in low shrubs. Like several other sea birds, the pelican builds its nests only on islands, a strategy that protects them from predators like raccoons.

Most of Louisiana's islands are rapidly washing away. Against a steady backdrop of rising sea level, natural subsidence and the dearth of rebuilding sediments, destructive storms continually assault these islands. In addition, each decade this century has been marked by at least one freeze severe enough to kill the mangroves which, like the brown pelican, cling to a precarious existence near the northernmost limits of their range. When stripped of the tenacious mat of mangroves that hold them together, the islands erode at an even faster pace.

The survival of Louisiana's brown pelican now hinges on our ability to reverse the destruction of such fragile islands.

The state Department of Wildlife and Fisheries and the U. S. Army Corps of Engineers offered a preview of our potential success when they reclaimed a 15-acre area of Queen Bess from the waters of Barataria Bay a few years ago. Queen Bess had shrunk by half in the 10 years from 1978 to 1989. Scoured down to little more than a crescent-shaped ridgelet of oyster shell, the island offered its nesting colony of birds less than first-class accommodations.

After connecting the two tips of the crescent-shaped island with a long rock dike, the Corps pumped the enclosed area full of mud dredged from the Barataria Waterway, the navigation canal that offers Lafitte shrimpers a straight shot to the gulf.

The success of the Queen Bess project paved the way for even larger land-building efforts on sandy barrier islands like Isle Dernieres. Another project, in which the Corps surrounded the area where an island used to exist with rocks and filled it high with sand, opened the possibilities to creating artificial islands for the birds.

If the Pelican State's namesake is to continue to survive, it needs the help of man. But preserving the brown pelican is more than an expensive exercise to benefit a single species. By providing an early warning that man was poisoning his environment, the brown pelican helped save many other species of wildlife and illustrated the link between his fate and that of man himself. Now, by fighting to preserve our state bird's island habitat, we're also fighting to save our own.

# THE BATTLE FOR ENVIRONMENTAL JUSTICE IN LOUISIANA . . . GOVERNMENT, INDUSTRY, AND THE PEOPLE*

Louisiana Advisory Committee

*Today in Louisiana more plants and largely black communities do share the same neighborhood. . . . but in no case have minority communities been targeted for the siting of chemical manufacturing plants in Louisiana. . . . so the relevant question is what are we doing to be better neighbors now? Partnerships are working in many areas, so it is important that we look at the work being done and the job that lies ahead.*[1]

## National Perspectives

In both separate and joint efforts, black, Hispanic, Asian, and American Indian groups are battling pollution hazards by arguing that their neighborhoods have become America's industrial dumping grounds. These groups and sympathetic whites have joined together under the banner of environmental justice.[2] Minority groups have developed into a new movement that is applying the language and strategies of the civil rights movement to counter environmental and health hazards in their communities as varied as toxic dumping and lead poisoning. A body of information that shows that minorities suffer the most from pollution and benefit the least from cleanup programs is transforming environmental politics. Many civil rights and traditional environmental organizations have reexamined their agendas and constituencies, and some are giving grassroots groups advice and support.[3]

The movement was triggered in 1982 by a national protest by the predominantly black community in Warren County, North Carolina. The decision to locate a highly toxic PCB landfill there sparked a heated debate regarding the site selection process for

*Excerpts taken from the Louisiana Advisory Committee to the U.S. Commission on Civil Rights, "The Battle for Environmental Justice in Louisiana . . . Government, Industry, and the People" (September, 1993).

hazardous waste facilities. The location of such a health-threatening facility in a predominantly black community, despite its scientific unsuitability, raised the question of how such decisions are made and "how many other racial and ethnic communities were similarly affected by hazardous wastes."[4]

Subsequent studies were conducted to assess the nature and extent of this problem. According to Benjamin Goldman, disproportionate shares of environmental contamination exist racially and economically. His study suggests that the racial and socioeconomic disparities in siting of commercial hazardous waste facilities uncovered by the United Church of Christ Commission for Racial Justice study, *Toxic Wastes and Race in the United States; A National Report on the Racial and Socioeconomic Characteristics of Communities with Hazardous Waste Sites*, also hold true for most other pollution and mortality factors as well. Mr. Goldman concludes that poor, black, Hispanic, and Native American communities are consistently hit more severely by pollution and death. In areas of the country that ranked the worst across all of the industrial toxic measures, minorities were more than twice the percentage of the population than the average for the rest of the country.[5]

Dr. Paul Mohai and Dr. Bunyon Bryant reviewed other studies to see if they showed a consistent pattern of environmental injustice based on race and socioeconomic factors. Their review also examined the distribution of commercial hazardous waste facilities in the Detroit metropolitan area. The authors concluded that both income and race are factors in the distribution of environmental hazards, but of the two factors, race appeared to have a more important relationship to environmental inequities.[6]

Although numerous studies have been done, several landmark national studies document this phenomenon. They include:

> In 1983 the U. S. General Accounting Office (GAO) surveyed commercial hazardous waste landfills located in eight southeastern States. Four offsite hazardous waste landfills are located [in] the region. The report, *Siting of Hazardous Waste Landfills and Their Correlation with Racial and Economic Status of Surrounding Communities*, found that blacks constituted the majority of the population in three of the four communities where the commercial landfills are located. At least 26 percent of the population in all four communities have income below the poverty level and most of their population is black. The release of this report marked the first official recognition by the Federal Government of the relationship between race and the sitting of hazardous waste disposal.[7]
>
> In 1987 the Commission for Racial Justice of the United Church of Christ (CRJ) released its study entitled *Toxic Waste and Race in the United States*. This study focused on the demographic patterns associated with commercial hazardous waste sites. Among the many findings that emerged from this study the following are most salient: (1) communities with commercial hazardous waste facilities were found to have twice the percentage of racial minorities as communities without such facilities; (2) communities with more than one facility or with the largest toxic waste dumps have three times as many people of color; (3) three of the five largest landfills with

toxic waste in the country are in black and Hispanic communities; and (4) race was the single most predictor of where commercial toxic waste treatment, storage, and disposal occur nationwide. This study was the first national report to document comprehensively the presence of hazardous waste sites in racial and ethnic communities throughout the United States.[8]

In 1990, in the book *Dumping in Dixie, Race, Class, and Environmental Quality*, Dr. Robert Bullard explored the thesis that southern black communities, because of economic and political vulnerability, have been routinely targeted for the siting of noxious facilities and environmental hazards. He documents the efforts of blacks fighting such sitings in Houston and Dallas, Texas; Emelle, Alabama; Institute, West Virginia; and Alsen, Louisiana.[9]

In 1990 the EPA responded to environmental inequities raised by a body of social scientists and civil rights leaders called the Michigan coalition. Through the ensuing dialogue, the EPA Environmental Equity Workshop was established within the agency to assess evidence that racial minority and low-income communities bear a higher environmental risk than the general population. The work of EPA through the Equity Workshop resulted in the 1992 report *Environmental Equity, Reducing Risk for All Communities*. Some of the pertinent findings cited are: (1) there are differences between racial groups in terms of disease and death rates, but there are limited data to link environmental exposures to these differences and there are limited data on environmental health effects by race and income; (2) racial minority and low-income populations experience higher than average exposures to selected air pollutants, hazardous waste facilities, contaminated fish, and agricultural pesticides in the workplace; (3) environmental and health data are not routinely collected and analyzed by income and race; (4) although risk assessment and management procedures are not in themselves biased against certain income or racial groups, these procedures can be improved to better take into account equity considerations. Overall, the findings suggest that minority communities experience greater than average exposure to some environmental pollution, such as lead, air pollutants, toxic waste, and tainted fish, but race is not as significant as poverty in determining which communities face the highest risk.[10]

The *National Law Journal* conducted a study in 1992 on EPA's enforcement efforts, indicating glaring inequities between white and racial minority communities. The report concluded that there is a racial divide in the way EPA cleans up toxic waste sites and punishes polluters. White communities see faster action, better results, and stiffer penalties than communities where blacks, Hispanics, and other minorities live. According to the report, unequal protection often occurs whether the minority community is wealthy or poor, therefore, concluding that race is the main predictor of how well environmental laws are enforced.[11]

In part due to the *National Law Journal* findings, the Enforcement Management Council of EPA is reviewing the *National Law Journal's* findings to determine their validity and recommend changes, if necessary, to the agency's enforcement policies and procedures. The Council's report will be completed in the summer of 1993.[12]

On the other side of the debate are views that discount the concept of environmental racism. Mr. Kent Jeffreys of the Competitive Enterprise Institute testified before the Committee on the Judiciary, Subcommittee on Civil and Constitutional Rights, U. S. House of Representatives, that socioeconomic factors and cheap land values where racial minorities largely live contribute most to the environmental problems suffered by racial minorities. He stated:

> Racism exists. Environmental problems exist. These facts, however, do not reveal whether or not environmental racism is occurring. Regardless of whether any particular case fits the definition of environmental racism, the fact remains that environmental problems—from a minority perspective—are rather trivial in comparison to the larger economic and civil liberty issues: solve these and you have solved most, if not all, of the environmental inequities. . . . Much has been said of potentially harmful levels of lead in the bloodstream of inner-city minorities. Yet, the primary risk of "lead poisoning" in urban areas comes from the mouth of a gun rather than a water faucet or a paint can. Murder is the leading cause of death among young male African Americans. While over 400 people were murdered in D. C. last year, not a single person died because of groundwater contamination from a hazardous waste site. Environmental issues must be placed in perspective. . . .[13]

Mr. Jeffreys concludes that respect for contracts and private property and less Federal legislation will solve much of the dilemma over racially disparate environmental results.[14]

Kyle McSlarrow, and environmental lawyer and a witness at the same hearing, stated that the poverty and political powerlessness of these communities should not be excluded as causes. He said:

> Some argue that race alone determines these outcomes, not income. This oversimplifies a much more complex issue, nor is it clear that race as opposed to income levels or political power is the most relevant factor. It must be obvious to us all that in this country race and income are too often closely related. It is difficult to disaggregate these factors when determining causes. . . . I do not believe that the case has been made that environmental protection laws have been enforced inequitably. I disagree moreover, with the largely self-defeating attempt to pin the causes on race to the exclusion of other factors.[15]

As a solution Mr. McSlarrow supports stronger property rights laws and state laws that subject siting decisions to an environmental risk analysis.[16]

Although most in industry concur that racial minorities reside disproportionately in and around industrial and hazardous waste facilities, a concerted national dialogue by industry about this issue is absent. However, there are exceptions. Corporations such as Waste Management Incorporated (WMI) have taken a public stand. Charles McDermott of WMI stated that racial minorities and the poor do bear a disproportionate share of the burden associated with pollution.[17] He said even some WMI sites have been held up as examples of discriminatory siting practices. In response to these charges, WMI examined this situation using the same methodology as in the Commission for Racial Justice study, and determined that 76 percent of WMI's disposal facilities are located in communities with a white population equal to or greater than the host state average.[18] Moreover, he stated, there is little evidence that emissions from waste facilities pose the greatest risk to the average minority community. Mr. McDermott suggested that companies must do a better job of communicating to communities about perceived risks versus actual risks, explaining the many advancements in pollution prevention.[19]

At the national level, the U. S. Chemical Manufacturers Association has taken the lead in launching an environmental initiative called Responsible Care. This program is a mandatory pledge from all industry members to improve and ensure the responsible management of chemicals. It is an effort to tie environmental responsibility into business practices. The U. S. Chemical Manufacturers Association describes the 10 principles outlined in the program as an environmental bill of rights for all people. The Louisiana Chemical Association (LCA) supports this initiative and has made it a part of its program to improve performance.[20]

Although many other environmental efforts by industry and business have occurred and are occurring throughout the country, there is still concern that industry has not participated in a full and open discussion on environmental equity issues.[21] As stated by Mr. McDermott: "There must be an honest and fair discussion of risk, a reexamination of how decisions are made, and special attention paid to the interests of the least powerful if the important questions about environmental fairness that have been raised are to be translated into meaningful action. . . ."[22]

A new presidential council appointed by President Clinton aimed at enhancing economic growth while protecting the environment, may provide an opportunity for industry to take part in a meaningful discussion on environmental equity. This council, which includes a number of chemical companies, was brought together in an effort to bring together interested parties who had not come together to exchange ideas before. It is hoped that among the many issues to be addressed by the council, that the allegations of environmental racism along the Mississippi River industrial corridor will be looked at.[23]

## The Setting in Louisiana

On June 1, 1990, the Louisiana Advisory Committee voted to conduct a fact-finding study on environmental issues in black communities. This study was undertaken based on reports of the disproportionate impact of hazardous and/or industrial pollution and the siting of hazardous and industrial facilities in poor black communities, particularly in the area in and around the lower Mississippi River between Baton Rouge and New Orleans referred to by some as the industrial corridor and by others as "Cancer Alley."[24]

Since the initiation of the Advisory Committee's study, EPA's Office of Pollution Prevention and Toxics has also prepared a report on toxic air emissions in the lower Mississippi River industrial corridor. The report concludes that many of the facilities emitting large amounts of chemicals are in areas with predominately minority populations. Moreover, populations within 2 miles of facilities releasing 90 percent of total industrial corridor releases feature a higher proportion of minorities than the state average.[25]

Louisiana is one of the largest U. S. producers of oil and natural gas and home of an enormous petrochemical industry. It has a national first place ranking for total toxic discharges into the air, water, and land, immediately raising concerns about environmental protection. With the exception of Texas and New Jersey, Louisiana is home to more chemical companies than any other state in the United States.[26] According to the 1991 EPA nationwide Toxic Release Inventory, Louisiana reported the largest toxic releases and transfers of chemicals into the environment (air, water, land) of any state, 459 million pounds of chemical releases or 13.5 percent of the national total.[27] The chemical industry contributes 89 percent of the total releases and transfers in Louisiana and 80.4 percent of the state's total air releases. Although Louisiana's emissions have dropped almost 50 percent over 5 years, further reductions are needed. For example, Louisiana decreased its discharge of toxic air pollutants by 30 percent over a 4-year period, but still has to reduce it another 20 percent by 1996 to comply with the state's air toxics law.[28] Louisiana ranked first in the Nation in total chemical releases, first in water releases, second in underground injection releases, and sixth for total air releases.[29]

Almost two-thirds, or 64.8 percent, of the state's voters are dissatisfied with the quality of Louisiana's environment.[30] Although the emissions affect everyone, the impact of industrial development appears to fall disproportionately on predominately black areas of Louisiana. This development is visible between Baton Rouge and New Orleans where smokestacks and pipelines of oil refineries and petrochemical plants are situated close by predominately black and often poor communities such as Alsen, St. Gabriel/Carville, Geismar, Mount Airy, Morrisonville, and Willow Springs. Many black residents in towns such as Revilletown have been bought out by Georgia Gulf; Good Hope was uprooted by a refinery in St. Charles; Morrisonville was relocated by Dow; and Sunrise was bought out by Placid Refining Company. Recently, residents of the St. Gabriel/Carville area have voiced strong opposition to the proposed location of the Supplemental Fuel Inc. (SPI) hazardous waste processing plant in a predominately black area. Allegations of environmental racism have been made, and the NAACP has been asked to help oppose the proposed site. The Louisiana House of Representatives, the Police Jury of Ascension and Iberville Parish have all passed resolutions opposing the SPI facility.[31]

Another factor affecting the quality of life for these communities is the unknown health risks. Residents of these communities now believe many of their health problems, such as cancer, respiratory ailments, central nervous disorders, birth defects, and spontaneous abortions, are directly related to their exposure to industrial contamination.[32] However, studies conducted on causes of suspected health effects do not show that industrial pollution exposures are the cause of these ailments.[33]

Industries adamantly reject the notion that race is or has been a factor in facility siting. Plant selection, they say, is based on availability of natural resources, land, and transportation needs.[34] Louisiana Chemical Association officials report that companies are reducing chemical waste and are taking proactive steps to work with communities to solve problems and be good neighbors. LCA President Dan Borne stated:

> In the past, the chemical industry has not adequately addressed its neighbors' anxieties, fears, and complaints. At times, we have not always reached far enough beyond our fence lines to provide information and extend a hand of help and opportunity. . . . Industry thought it was enough to provide jobs, pay taxes, and obey environmental laws and regulations. . . . Today a cultural change is taking place in the chemical industry, and it is a change for better. . . .[35]

Industry officials stated that emission reductions have come about through new waste reduction and minimization techniques. The chemical industries noted that they are committed to further reduction. LCA companies hope to achieve an overall 50 percent reduction in air toxics by 1996.[36]

According to the 1991 toxic release inventory, 10 parishes with the largest amount of releases and transfers are: Jefferson, St. James, Ascension, Calcasieu, East Baton Rouge, St. Charles, St. Mary, Iberville, Caddo, and Ouachita. Sixty percent of these parishes are located along the Mississippi River industrial corridor.[37] The top 10 emitters for total releases/transfers in 1991 were: American Cyanamid, Jefferson Parish; Agrico Chemical Faustina, St. James Parish; Agrico Chemical, St. James Parish; Arcadian Corp., Ascension Parish; BASF Corp., Ascension Parish; Citgo Petroleum Corp., Calcasieu Parish; CF Industries, Ascension Parish; Uniroyal Chemical Co., Ascension Parish; Rubicon, Inc., Ascension Parish; Dow Chemical Company, Iberville Parish.[38] At least 38 major chemical companies and 112 industrial sites are located in the industrial corridor. Discharges are calculated upwards to 400 million pounds of waste into the environment each year. At last count, there are approximately 800 suspected and confirmed hazardous waste sites in Louisiana and 12 Superfund sites.[39]

Coupled with this industrial pollution and toxic waste, a 1991-92 study by the Institute of Southern Studies on the environmental health of individual states showed that Louisiana ranked 48 in effectiveness of its environmental policies and 45th for general health quality of its citizenry.[40] Dr. Paul Templet, former director of the Louisiana Department of Environmental Quality (DEQ), admitted, "The State is at the bottom in regulations and at the top in toxic discharges."[41]

Despite its responsibility for attacking some of the worst environmental problems in the Nation, DEQ has been underfunded and criticized for ineffective enforcement efforts. Under the leadership of former Governor Roemer and DEQ head Paul Templet, from 1988 to 1991, the department was revitalized through increased funding, staff, and enforcement activities. As described by Dan Borne, "DEQ grew from a sleepy observer to an active participant."[42]

The current DEQ administration is viewed with a skepticism by environmental groups because of alleged close ties with industry. DEQ is accused of holding closed meetings and failing to provide pertinent information to citizens about health concerns and the status of the state's environment. Although DEQ was able to develop into an effective and credible department under the former administration, some are concerned that these gains will be lost under the current administration.[43]

Most recently, a DEQ official criticized EPA for releasing the "Toxic Releases in the Lower Mississippi Industrial Corridor" report, which concluded that chemical facilities are located most often near black populations along the Mississippi River between Baton Rouge and New Orleans. The DEQ official feared that the report would place a negative connotation on the state and emotionalize the issue in the local and national press. The official suggested to EPA to be "extremely cautious in publishing information regarding environmental equity and specific geographic regions," specifically, the lower Mississippi corridor.[44]

## The Economy

To get a better sense of environmental problems in Louisiana, one must understand the economic base on which the state depends and from which it benefits. Louisiana is the nation's third largest producer of chemical products.

The chemical industry is among the biggest sources of earnings in the state's manufacturing sector and produces more products for export than any other manufacturing industry. The chemical industry is also the largest single employer in the Louisiana manufacturing sector. Eighty-seven percent of chemical industry jobs are located in the corridor between Baton Rouge and New Orleans, and in Lake Charles.[45] The chemical industry employed 29,200 persons in 1990. For each job in the chemical industry, economists estimate eight more jobs are created in the economy.[46] On the other hand, the industry benefits from industrial property tax exemptions worth millions of dollars each year. According to the Louisiana Department of Economic Development, as of June 10, 1993, eligible industries throughout the state were exempted from approximately $12,315,110,207 in taxes. Of this total, the chemical industry's share was $5,240,590,084.[47] The oil and gas industry is directly responsible for 26 percent of the revenue received by the state and employs 6.1 percent of the state's total work force. More than 13 percent of the wages earned in Louisiana come from the oil and gas industry.[48]

## South Louisiana and the Mississippi River Industrial Corridor

The most heavily industrialized area of Louisiana is along the southern lower reaches of the Mississippi River stretching from Baton Rouge to New Orleans. South Louisiana includes 35 of the state's 64 parishes and approximately 72 percent of the population of

3.2 million. Racial and ethnic minorities comprise 1,067,327 or 35 percent of the population, of whom 86 percent are black. (See Table 1)[49] In 1988 the lower Mississippi River industrial corridor area contained 81 toxic releasing facilities, almost a third of all facilities in the state.[50]

Another area of extensive industrialization is along the Calcasieu River in Lake Charles. The Calcasieu area has at least 27 facilities that release toxic waste into the environment. Sprinkled among the chemical plants are some of the nation's largest oil refineries such as Exxon in Baton Rouge, Citgo Petroleum in Calcasieu Parish, American Cyanamid in Jefferson Parish, and BASF Corporation in Ascension Parish, to name a few.[51] An investigation by the *Baton Rouge Morning Advocate* showed that black communities in South Louisiana are more likely located next to heavy industries that pollute. However, the study concluded that economic status was more of a common denominator than race.[52]

Dan Borne, president of the Louisiana Chemical Association, stated:

> Plants and largely black communities do share the same neighborhoods, but it is not because industries have made a decision to discriminate against blacks. . . . Many LCA companies built on old plantation sites where the surrounding community probably was, and may still be, predominately black. Some facilities were built in rural areas that had no communities around them until years later. In some cases, the surrounding community had been mostly white, then changed over time.[53]

Dr. Beverly Wright, sociologist, Xavier University, noted:

> For a very long time minority and poor communities have been the prime targets for nondesirable but necessary byproducts of an industrial society. These neighborhoods are seen as the paths of least resistance, making them more likely candidates for bridge or highway buyouts, toxic and solid waste landfills, and incinerators for chemical plant locations.[54]

Dr. Paul Templet, an environmental professor at Louisiana State University and former secretary of DEQ, stated: "While pollution may be colorblind in that it affects everyone negatively, there are indications that minorities may bear a larger burden of the total risk."[55]

Darryl Malek-Wiley of the Gulf Coast Tenants Association said: "What it generally boils down to is the politically powerless communities are the ones most dumped on. Often the targeted communities are minorities."[56]

Theresa Roberts, an environmentalist from Ascension Parish, observed: "Race plays a large part, but politics and the economic situation of the community also are factors."[57]

As these viewpoints indicate, positions differ on why black communities are more directly exposed to industrial pollution. Some say race, some say politics, or economics, or both. LCA and officials of DEQ argue that decisions on where sites are located are not based on racial considerations but are determined by various factors related to geography and sound business criteria that match the manufacturing and service needs of the industry.[58]

## Table 1

*Racial/Ethnic Composition of South Louisiana by Parish*

| Region | Parishes Covered | Population |
|---|---|---|
| New Orleans | Jefferson, Orleans and St. Bernard | 1,011,875 |
| Baton Rouge | Ascension, Assumption, E. Baton Rouge, E. Feliciana, Iberville, Livingston, Pointe Coupée, St. Helena, Tangipahoa, W. Baton Rouge and W. Feliciana | 732,315 |
| Southeast LA | LaFourche, Plaquemines, St. Charles St. James, St. John, St. Tammany, Terrebonne and Washington | 499,422 |
| Lafayette | Acadia, Evangeline, Iberia, Lafayette, St. Landry, St. Martin, St. Mary and Vermillion | 554,665 |
| Lake Charles | Allen, Beauregard, Calcasieu, Cameron and Jefferson Davis | 259,425 |

| Parish | Total | White | Black | Hispanic | Other Race |
|---|---|---|---|---|---|
| Ascension | 58,214 | 44,480 | 13,268 | 923 | 466 |
| Acadia | 55,882 | 45,532 | 10,179 | 372 | 171 |
| Allen | 21,226 | 16,308 | 4,496 | 671 | 422 |
| Assumption | 22,753 | 15,273 | 7,349 | 292 | 131 |
| Beauregard | 30,083 | 25,242 | 4,489 | 417 | 352 |
| Calcasieu | 168,134 | 128,181 | 38,445 | 1,847 | 1,508 |
| E. Baton Rouge | 380,105 | 240,614 | 132,328 | 5,761 | 7,163 |
| E. Feliciana | 19,211 | 10,022 | 9,083 | 186 | 106 |
| Evangeline | 33,274 | 24,405 | 8,701 | 270 | 168 |
| Iberia | 68,297 | 46,940 | 20,154 | 1,320 | 1,203 |
| Iberville | 31,049 | 16,519 | 14,385 | 598 | 145 |
| Jefferson | 448,306 | 351,170 | 79,042 | 26,611 | 18,094 |
| Jefferson Davis | 30,722 | 24,721 | 5,836 | 201 | 165 |
| Lafayette | 164,762 | 125,340 | 36,846 | 2,613 | 2,576 |
| Lafourche | 85,860 | 72,371 | 10,703 | 1,249 | 2,786 |
| Livingston | 70,526 | 66,269 | 3,920 | 642 | 337 |
| Orleans | 496,938 | 173,554 | 307,728 | 17,238 | 15,656 |
| Plaquemines | 25,575 | 18,522 | 5,944 | 590 | 1,109 |
| St. Bernard | 66,631 | 62,199 | 3,111 | 4,183 | 1,321 |
| St. Helena | 9,874 | 4,725 | 5,127 | 46 | 22 |
| St. James | 20,879 | 10,484 | 10,357 | 107 | 38 |
| St. John Baptist | 39,996 | 25,039 | 14,419 | 954 | 538 |
| St. Martin | 43,978 | 28,806 | 14,532 | 502 | 640 |
| St. Mary | 58,086 | 37,688 | 18,337 | 1,128 | 2,061 |
| St. Tammany | 144,508 | 126,806 | 15,917 | 3,170 | 1,785 |
| Tangipahoa | 85,709 | 60,601 | 24,527 | 951 | 581 |
| Terrebonne | 96,982 | 75,082 | 16,032 | 1,376 | 5,868 |
| Washington | 43,185 | 29,669 | 13,376 | 239 | 140 |

(Table 1 cont.)

| Parish | Total | White | Black | Hispanic | Other Race |
|---|---|---|---|---|---|
| W. Baton Rouge | 19,419 | 12,329 | 6,993 | 206 | 97 |
| W. Feliciana | 12,915 | 5,672 | 7,149 | 203 | 94 |
| Cameron | 9,260 | 8,685 | 503 | 143 | 72 |
| Pointe Coupée | 22,540 | 13,196 | 9,275 | 166 | 69 |
| St. Charles | 42,437 | 31,638 | 10,253 | 1,070 | 546 |
| St. Landry | 80,331 | 47,532 | 32,392 | 639 | 407 |
| Vermillion | 50,055 | 42,237 | 6,956 | 592 | 862 |

Source: Louisiana Department of Economic Development, 1990 Census and Population Characteristics

A survey conducted in 1989 by the Environmental Social Science Research Institute at the University of New Orleans showed that 75 percent of black respondents in Louisiana are very concerned about the environment compared to 59 percent of the white respondents.[59] This is evident by formation of environmental groups with large black memberships such as the Gulf Coast Tenants Association, Ascension Parish Residents Against Toxic Pollution, Victims of a Toxic Environment, North Baton Rouge Environmental Association, Citizens Against Nuclear Trash, and the River Area Planning Group.

Efforts are underway to study and document suspected environmental problems in black communities impacted by industrial development. Dr. William Arp of Louisiana State University received funding from DEQ to conduct a study on environmental equity that included a review of the industrial corridor between Baton Rouge and New Orleans. The study will focus on attitudes and perspectives of black residents and industry located in this area.[60] Dr. Beverly Wright, a sociologist at Xavier University, is conducting a study on community voluntary involvement purchases (buyout and relocation).[61] Additional environmental equity initiatives are being pursued by DEQ in the form of a health study to examine adverse health effects in selected areas of South Louisiana.[62]

## Notes for "The Battle for Environmental Justice in Louisiana . . . Government, Industry, and the People"

[1]Dan Borne, president, Louisiana Chemical Association, remarks, fact-finding meeting before the Louisiana Advisory Committee to the U. S. Commission on Civil Rights, (Baton Rouge, February 19-20, 1992), 2:526 (hereafter cited as *Transcript*).

[2]Roberto Suro, "Pollution-Weary Minorities Try Civil Rights Track," *New York Times*, January 11, 1993.

[3]Ibid.

[4]Kelly Colquette and Elizabeth Henry Robertson, "Environmental Racism: The Causes, Consequences, and Commendations," *Tulane Environmental Law Journal*, 5 (1991): 157-58.

[5]Benjamin A. Goldman, *The Truth About Where You Live: An Atlas for Action on Toxins and Mortality* (New York, 1991), 282-83 (hereafter cited as *The Truth About Where You Live*).

[6]Paul Mohai and Bunyon Bryant, "Environmental Racism: Reviewing the Evidence," paper delivered at the University of Michigan Law School Symposium on Race, Poverty, and the Environment, January 23, 1992.

[7]U. S. General Accounting Office, "Siting of Hazardous Waste Landfills and Their Correlation With Racial and Economic Status of Surrounding Communities," 1983 (hereafter cited as *GAO Report*).

[8]United Church of Christ, Commission for Racial Justice, *Toxic Wastes and Race in the United States: A National Report on the Racial and Socioeconomic Characteristics with Hazardous Waste Sites* (1987), xiii, xiv (hereafter cited as *Toxic Wastes and Race*).

[9]Robert Bullard, *Dumping in Dixie, Race, Class, and Environmental Quality* (Colorado, 1990), 45-78.

[10]U. S. Environmental Protection Agency, *Environmental Equity, Reducing Risks for All Communities*, 1: 2-3, 6, 11; Michael Weisskopf, "Minorities' Pollution Risk is Debated," *Washington Post*, January 16, 1992.

[11]*National Law Journal Report*, p. S-2.

[12]See Clarice Gaylord, director, Office of Environmental Equity, letter to Bobby Doctor, Acting Staff Director, USCCR, re: Responses by the Environmental Protection Agency to Questions by the U. S. Commission on Civil Rights on Environmental Equity and Civil Rights Enforcement, April 13, 1993 (hereafter cited as Responses by EPA to USCCR Questions).

[13]Kent Jeffreys, testimony before the Subcommittee on Civil and Constitutional Rights, U. S. House of Representatives, March 3, 1993.

[14]Ibid.

[15]Kyle McSlarrow, environmental attorney, testimony before the Subcommittee on Civil and Constitutional Rights, U. S. House of Representatives, March 4, 1993.

[16]Ibid.

[17]Charles McDermott, *Transcript*, 2:667-76.

[18]Charles McDermott, testimony before the Subcommittee on Civil and Constitutional Rights, U. S. House of Representatives, March 3, 1983.

[19]Ibid.

[20]Robert D. Kennedy, "Corporate Priorities Driven by Environmental Concerns," *Birmingham News*, August 24, 1991; Dan Borne, *Transcript*, 2:527, see app. G.

[21]Charles McDermott, *Transcript*, 1:42.

[22]Charles McDermott, testimony before the Subcommittee on Civil and Constitutional Rights, U. S. House of Representatives, March 3, 1993.

[23]Mark Schleifstein, "Council may Study Louisiana Environmental Issues," *The Times-Picayune*, June 15, 1993.

[24]Louisiana Advisory Committee Project Proposal, "Environmental Equity," June 1991.

[25]"Toxic Releases Inventory and Emissions Reductions 1987-1990 in the Lower Mississippi Industrial Corridor," U. S. Environmental Protection Agency, Office of Pollution Prevention and Toxics, May 14, 1993 (hereafter cited, "Toxic Releases in the Lower Mississippi River Industrial Corridor").

[26]James O'Byrne and Mark Schleifstein, "The Chemical Industry's Toxic Toll," *The Times-Picayune*, February 17, 1991.

[27]U. S. Environmental Protection Agency, *The 1991 Toxic Release Inventory National Report* (May 1993), 3.

[28]Bob Anderson, "LA Leads U. S. in Toxic Discharges," *The Advocate*, May 26, 1993.

[29]"Toxic Releases in the Lower Mississippi River Industrial Corridor."

[30]Jack Wardlow, "Louisiana Environment Not So Hot, Most Voters Say In Poll," *The Times-Picayune*, April 3, 1993.

[31]Bob Warren and Stephen Casmier, "The Poor Begins to Draw Battle Lines," *The Times-Picayune*, February 20, 1991; Carol Moormon, "Residents Protest Waste Processing Plant," *The Advocate*, July 9, 1993.

[32]Joel Nitzkin, *Transcript*, 1:248, 251, 253, 256; James O'Byrne and Mark Scheifstein, "Invisible Poisons: No One is Sure About Effects on Our Health," *The Times-Picayune*, February 18, 1991.

[33]Ibid.

[34]Dan Borne, *Transcript*, 2:518-709.

[35]Ibid., 520-21.

[36]Ibid., 527.

[37]"Louisiana Toxic Release Inventory, 1991," December 1992, 21-22.

[38]Ibid., 50.

[39]William Arp and Valerie Jones, "Survey and Analysis of Environmental Concerns Within African-American Communities," Center for Energy and Environmental Studies, Southern University, November 16, 1992, page 3; Tammy Guillotte, "Hazardous Waste Sites Targeted by DEQ, EPA," *Louisiana Environmentalist* (March-April 1993),11.

[40]Bob Hall and Mary Lee Kerr, Institute for Southern Studies, *The 1991-92 Green Index: A State-by-State Guide to the Nation's Environmental Health* (Durham, N.C., 1991).

[41]James O'Byrne and Mark Schleifstein, "Regulators Struggle to Keep Up," *New Orleans Times-Picayune*, February 17, 1991.

[42]Ibid.

[43]Mary Lee Orr, executive director, Louisiana Environmental Network, Transcript, vol. 1:360; "Secrecy Clouds DEQ Reputation," *Baton Rouge Morning Advocate*, February 22, 1992.

[44]See Gary Johnson, memorandum to Jenny Henderson-LaBar, Louisiana Department of Environmental Quality, "Review of Toxic Release Inventory, Lower Mississippi Industrial Corridor," November 18, 1992.

[45]Loren C. Scott, "The Chemical Industry in Louisiana," presented to the Louisiana Chemical Association (January, 1991), i.

[46]Ibid.

[47]Steven Windham, Louisiana Department of Economic Development, memorandum to Farella Robinson, USCCR, June 10, 1993.

[48]Louisiana Mid-Continent Oil and Gas Association, "Louisiana Oil and Gas Facts" (September 1991), 3.

[49]Vivien W. Chen et al., "Cancer in South Louisiana," *Journal of the Louisiana State Medical Society*, 144 (April 1992), 149-56.

[50]*The 1988 Toxic Release Inventory National Report* (September 1990), 3.

[51]Louisiana Toxic Release Inventory, 1990.

[52]Bob Anderson, "Plant Sites: Is Racism An Issue?" *Baton Rouge Morning Advocate*, May 13, 1992.

[53]Ibid.

[54]Beverly Wright, *Transcript*, 18.

[55]Paul Templet, *Transcript*, 111.

[56]Anderson, "Plant Sites: Is Racism An Issue?"

[57]Ibid.

[58]William Kucharski, deputy secretary of DEQ, *Transcript*, 226-46; Dan Borne, president, LCA, *Transcript*, 522.

[59]Shirley Laska, "Louisiana Environment Attitudes," The Environmental Institute, University of New Orleans, 1989.

[60]Arp and Jones, "Survey and Analysis of Environmental Concerns With African-American Communities."

[61]Beverly Wright, telephone interview, November 10, 1992.

[62]See William Kucharski, deputy secretary of DEQ, letter to Farella Robinson, civil rights analyst, USCCR, October 28, 1992.

# MANCHAC SWAMP: THE PLACE AND ITS PEOPLE*

John Randolph Kemp

"Wilderness, or wildness, is a mystique," once wrote famed landscape photographer Ansel Adams. "As the fisherman depends upon the rivers, lakes and seas, and the farmer upon the land for his existence, so does mankind in general depend upon the beauty of the world for spiritual and emotional existence."

For centuries, poets and artists have explored their souls through nature. During the nineteenth century, artists such as New Jersey-born Joseph Rusling Meeker were enchanted by the dramatic sunsets and the warm, ethereal haze of foggy morning light in Louisiana's swamplands. The intense golden blush of a sunrise cutting through the low-hanging mist and thick cypress stands gave life to paintings and rhyme to sonnets. To borrow from Pat Conroy's best-selling novel *The Prince of Tides*, it is "a place where butterflies and angels are born."

Today, artists and photographers continue to search for personal expression in Louisiana's swamps, the state's only remaining wilderness areas. C. C. Lockwood has gained national attention for his striking wildlife photographs taken in the vast Atchafalaya Swamp of south central Louisiana. Over the last decade, another photographer has quietly compiled a rich portrait of a less-known Louisiana wilderness, Manchac Swamp. Julia Sims, one of only a few women professional wildlife photographers in the United States, has found expression and peace among the trappers, snakes, alligators, and hundreds of species of birds and flowers that inhabit this mysterious-sounding place with deep roots in Louisiana's past.

It is all the more mysterious because, at least to some extent, it lies hidden in plain sight. The elevated, twin-span Interstate 55 between the Louisiana towns of Ponchatoula and LaPlace crosses over a large section of the swamp, which surrounds Lake Maurepas and forms an hourglass-shaped barrier between Maurepas and its larger companion, Lake

***Manchac Swamp: Louisiana's Undiscovered Wilderness*, photography by Julia Sims and text by John Randolph Kemp. Photographs copyright © 1996 by Julia Sims and text copyright © by John R. Kemp.

Pontchartrain. Here southbound motorists weary of Mississippi's endless loblolly pine forests and rolling clay hills get their first dramatic glimpse of South Louisiana's vast, grassy coastal prairie, which stretches from the Pearl River and Mississippi Gulf Coast to the Sabine River and Texas.

At the heart of Manchac Swamp, the interstate arches over Pass Manchac, a history-steeped waterway that links Lake Maurepas with Lake Pontchartrain. Europeans first encountered the pass in 1699 when Pierre Le Moyne, sieur d'Iberville, and his brother Jean Baptiste Le Moyne, sieur de Bienville (who later founded New Orleans), explored and colonized Louisiana for France. Iberville, ever the diplomat, named Lake Pontchartrain in honor of Louis XIV's minister of marine, Louis Phélypeaux, comte de Pontchartrain, and Lake Maurepas in honor of the comte's son and successor, Jérôme Phélypeaux de Maurepas. The word *manchac* first appeared in French reports in 1699 and on colonial maps in 1732. Most accounts suggest that it derives from the French *manche*, meaning "pass" or "strait," and the Mobilian or Choctaw *imashaka*, for "back way" or "rear entrance." From the many shell middens found throughout the swamp and from accounts by colonial explorers, archaeologists know that Native Americans such as the Tangipahoans hunted and fished in Manchac for centuries prior to the arrival of Europeans and well into the eighteenth century. As late as the 1860s, Choctaws, who had migrated into Southeast Louisiana a hundred years earlier, had a settlement where Pass Manchac enters Lake Pontchartrain.

Pass Manchac was once an international border. During the eighteenth and early nineteenth centuries, when colonial Louisiana and the Gulf Coast bounced back and forth among France, Spain, Great Britain, and finally the United States, the pass formed part of the boundary between Louisiana and colonial West Florida, which stretched from Baton Rouge to Pensacola. During the Civil War, Manchac was an outpost for Union troops from Michigan, who feasted on roasted alligator tail while enduring the "fetid bayous. . . . musquitos, moccasin snakes," and "death-laden air of these horrible places."

Today, Pass Manchac has the less glamorous role of separating Tangipahoa and St. John the Baptist Parishes. Places such as Galva, Ruddock, and Frenier, once bustling whistle-stops along the Illinois Central Gulf Rail Road, are now little more than names on a map or exits along the interstate. Only the small Manchac community at the juncture of Pass Manchac and Lake Maurepas continues to thrive, home to a handful of trappers and commercial fishermen and the site of numerous weekend camps as well as several fish markets and a popular restaurant.

Some travelers hurry along Interstate 55, eager to put the swamp behind them. Others let their imaginations wander through the cypresses, willows, tupelo gums, and grass prairies, or slow down to take in a sunset of almost Wagnerian visual drama and colors to humble even the greatest painter. To the east, a full moon rising from the swamp throws a broad yellow path across the shadowy water. To the west, Lake Maurepas' electric blue-green surface shimmers as the sun drops below the horizon. The afterglow radiates in a cobalt-blue sky while wisps of gray clouds witness the spectacle.

In minutes the sky darkens as approaching night hammers the last light into a thin, burning crimson line across the horizon.

The lyrical and transcendent beauty of nature is everywhere—in the sunset silhouetting the abandoned Manchac lighthouse, in the delicate irises and lilies struggling for survival on the tangled swamp floor, and in the chevron-winged egret preening her long, wispy white plumes with the grace of a ballerina's pirouette. Even in a spring thunderstorm, the swamp is iridescent against the heavy flannel-gray sky, towering black thunderheads, and veils of rain that sweep across the watery prairie. "The South is all for nature," wrote the French poet Charles Baudelaire. "For there nature is so beautiful and bright that nothing is left for man to desire, and he can find nothing more beautiful to invent than what he sees. There art belongs to the open air." He was describing southern Europe but could just as easily have been writing about the swamps of South Louisiana.

Unlike the pine forests a few miles to the north, the swamp has pronounced seasons. The dark greens of the oppressively hot summers are transformed by autumn. Cypresses turn russet, swamp maples and gums blaze bright red. Winter brings starkness; leaves fall away and the swamp stands desolate in brown and gray. Then comes spring with all its splendor and life. The swamp in springtime is a grand aviary with bald eagles and great blue herons nesting, stick-legged egrets stalking prey in slow motion, red-tailed hawks gliding on warm breezes, and treetops filled with the discordant songs of a thousand birds. Tender leaves cover the trees, and the swamp floor is filled with a thick field of purple irises and swamp lilies. Each season has its personality and singular beauty.

"I don't know what it is, I just love it," says Sims. "I get lost, but I mean that emotionally. I feel absolutely right. I especially love early mornings when there is a light fog. It is so still and silent. Every sound is individual and so clear. They are comforting. It's like being above the tree line in another world. You don't get that feeling on a bayou, on a river. You just get it back there. It's healing."

But danger also lurks in the dark waters beneath the soft green carpets of floating duckweed and the fallen trees whose rotting branches sway above the water's surface like large bony fingers. "I'm terrified of snakes," Sims admits, grimacing as if touched by a cold wind. "I'm afraid of alligators. If you're not afraid of a ten-foot alligator sitting on her eggs, something is wrong with you."

She remembers one afternoon when she sat in her camouflaged blind photographing a white heron rookery. She took off her hip boots to get comfortable. Her feet, clad in white socks, dangled just above the water. Then came the blood-curdling roar of two nearby alligators eyeing the rookery and a good meal. "If you've ever heard an alligator bellow, you'll never forget it. The ground literally shakes." As the gators closed in, Sims looked down to see the white socks, which could easily have been mistaken for tasty young herons. "I couldn't move fast enough. I sat there the rest of the time on my feet, Indian style."

She knows the swamp better now. "I try to use good judgment," she says simply, then adds: "But my biggest fear is people." To get a good photo of the great horned owl in its nest, she will spend the night deep in the swamp where no one ever goes except local trappers. But if the nest is on a waterway traveled by strangers, forget it. "No question! People are my greatest fear."

Like some of the swamp creatures she photographs, Sims herself is a member of a rare breed—female wildlife photographers. "It's a wild land out there, and I like that. But I'm not sure how many ladies would do this. I'm not trying to prove anything. You have to love it to do it, and it's hard. It's physically hard carrying all that stuff back in the swamp." The "stuff" includes the heavy steel scaffolding she uses to photograph nests as much as seventy feet up in the trees. This is where the men come in. The scaffolding is transported by airboat to the nesting sites by Sims's trapper friend Donald Clark and her husband, Joe Arthur Sims. Several trips are needed to get it all back there. The two men assemble the platform and then leave Sims behind with her Nikons.

When Sims is after those remarkable nighttime shots of owls entering their nests, Joe Arthur drops her off just before dark and picks her up at first light the next morning. She sits alone in the scaffolding all night, waiting for a quick glimpse of an approaching owl against a moonlit sky. When there is no moon, she shines a dim light on the nest to reveal any activity taking place. Often, the sounds made by the baby owls alert her to the arrival of the adult. As the owl descends, Sims trips the camera's shutter release and the electronic flash fires. The owls seem oblivious to the sudden bursts of light. "After all," Sims points out, "they see lightning all the time."

As an alternative to a night on the scaffolding, Sims sets up a device that shoots a pencil-thin beam of infrared light across the nest to a reflector. When the owl crosses the invisible beam, it triggers the shutter and flash. Sims picks up her camera the next morning.

Despite her airboat, cameras, lights, and scaffolding, Sims tries not to disturb the natural setting. "You are disturbing! There's no question. Your presence is always making a disturbance. But I will go to any degree to make that disturbance the least I can create. That's why we build our blinds in stages." Birds and other animals, she observes, "are like we are. Some are shy, and some will tolerate anything."

With degrees in secondary education and social work, Sims did not start out to become a professional photographer or to photo-document the Manchac Swamp. She and her husband simply enjoyed being out there. Photography came later. Sims's interest in the outdoors began while Joe Arthur was in the army and stationed in Germany. "We took up hiking in the mountains, and that opened up a whole new world to me. When we got back to Louisiana, we couldn't do that. So we took up canoeing. I enjoyed that, but it didn't give us the same feeling as being up in the mountains." Then a friend took them deep into the Manchac Swamp in his airboat. "I had lived in Louisiana all my life, and I had never been that far back in a swamp." The next day the Simses bought an airboat.

Sims's fascination with Louisiana's wetlands began when she was a child growing up in Baton Rouge, where she was born on February 17, 1942. Her family made frequent automobile trips along Airline Highway to New Orleans. "I remember hanging out the car window as we drove through Lutcher and seeing all that beautiful swamp. I can remember thinking, 'What's back there?' There was just that wall. To think, now I'm back there. Maybe even then there was something there that drew me."

At first, photography was an excuse to spend time in the swamp: "I couldn't go out there and not do anything." Then, gradually, the camera made Sims a participant in the natural drama. After taking a beginner's photography course at Newcomb College in New Orleans, she signed up for wildlife photography workshops around the country, learning from some of the best in the business. By the mid-1980s she had a contract with a top New York stock-photo house. Her work has also appeared in *National Geographic* and an impressive list of other publications and galleries.

Although most of Sims's wildlife photography is done in Manchac, she also has worked in the Honey Island, Atchafalaya, and Houma Swamps and along the barrier islands off the Louisiana coast. "But there's no need for me to go to those other swamps. The Manchac Swamp is my backyard. An alligator is an alligator. Plus, I have good contacts in Manchac." Those contacts are the nutria trappers and alligator hunters who live in the swamp or along its outer ridges. "I get along with some pretty rough people. Rough not in a bad way, but they've been trappers all their lives, their fathers and grandfathers were trappers."

When Sims first saw these shadowy figures skimming in their fast boats across the misty swamp, she knew they would be crucial to her work. They know the swamp better than anyone. Getting to know them, though, was not easy.

> They didn't want to have anything to do with me. They thought here's this lawyer's wife. But in time, they saw me out there before daybreak when it was twenty degrees. They saw me out there before daybreak when mosquitoes were everywhere. They saw me out there when it was ninety degrees. I was fighting the same elements they were fighting. We love the same thing.

The trappers now compete with one another in searching out interesting or rare wildlife for Sims to photograph. In return, she gives them photographs of the animals. "Their camps and trailers are wall-to-wall photographs. That's what they want. They're a neat breed. You have people who are streetwise. These people are swampwise." In the past, some trappers shot everything in sight. The egrets and herons that now fill photographs on hunting-camp walls were once little more than target practice on a lazy afternoon. "They don't do that any more. I've never asked them not to. They just don't." But Sims cautions would-be wildlife photographers not to head into the swamp without determining who holds leases to the land. "They'd shoot you. They will shoot you!"

Despite that cautionary note, Sims speaks of the people she has come to know in the swamp as genuine folk heroes.

> They have had an influence on me. I appreciate the hard work they do. I appreciate anybody who works at what they love to do. They love it with a passion. That's why they are not depressed people. Joe Arthur says whenever I come back from being with them, I'm always so upbeat. He's says I look like hell, but I'm upbeat. They're always looking forward to something.

They are also vanishing—as endangered in their way as any rare species in a changing environment. The swamp-dweller in his boat, earning his living by every wile of hunting, trapping, and fishing, is a classic figure of Louisiana folklore. But such people were never as numerous as legend paints them, and today they are a dwindling few. "This is really the last generation," says Sims. "Their children won't be doing it."

The best way to understand the richness of Manchac Swamp is to know its people. Here are some of them.

## JAMES "PONCHO" DUHE

"Poncho" Duhe was born in Reserve, Louisiana, in 1936 and speaks with a strong Cajun accent. Poncho—a nickname tagged to him in childhood—is tall with broad shoulders, a ruddy complexion, blue eyes, thinning red hair, and callused hands strong enough to crush oyster shells. He is friendly, at times gentle, but always dead serious about his work. People in the swamp speak with guarded respect about Poncho. They talk about the time the airplane-style propeller on his airboat jammed. When he tried to free the blade, it kicked over, striking him across the back three times and pinning him against a tree. The blade cut deep into his back, broke ribs, collapsed one lung, and severely damaged his spleen. He wrapped the deep gashes with his shirt and walked three miles through the swamp to get help. He drank two glasses of whiskey straight and went to the hospital. A week later, he was back trapping.

Like his father, Ambrose "Tatoon" Duhe, Poncho has spent most of his life in the swamp. "My old man used to do it, all his life, but he got too old. He stayed back here until he was eighty years old. He didn't want to keep up with it, so I took it over." Tatoon died at the age of eighty-six.

Poncho does his trapping and hunting on nine thousand acres of thick swampland leased from a lumber company. He works his lease, which stretches along the southeastern shore of Lake Maurepas, from a fishing camp his father built many years ago. Located on the Reserve Canal not far from where the canal empties into Lake Maurepas, the weathered wood-frame camp, named "Tatoon's Hunting Club," is filled with alligator skulls and mounted ducks, raccoons, and deer heads—trophies of two generations of hunting in the swamp. But Poncho's bedroom walls are now covered with Sims's photographs.

Like others who make their living in the swamp, Poncho follows the "seasons" the word refers less to the calendar than to the natural and ever-various cycles of life in the swamp.

> Everybody axed me if I get lonely or if it gets boring. It never gets boring. I do different t'ings at different times. I fish during the summertime and the springtime, crawfish. I do the alligator eggs in mid-July. I get a dollar each for them. I sell them to alligator farms as far away as Alexandria, Louisiana. Then after that I usually have a crop of young alligators that I turn loose. And after that I go into the alligator season in September. That lasts another month. October, I go to squirrel and rabbit huntin'. In winter comes the deer huntin'. Then I do my trappin' in December, January, and February. I don't do the same t'ing like I had a job to get up at the same time.

Poncho once had regular jobs—on oil rigs, in sugarcane fields, and doing automobile body work—but they took too much time away from trapping and hunting. "This is all I do right now."

One September morning, the second day of alligator season in South Louisiana, Poncho and his crew were in their airboats deep in the swamp checking Poncho's alligator lines. He had caught eleven alligators the day before; he had state permits for at least thirty-four more.

Poncho's boat glided through the wilderness along trails of water as black as Louisiana crude, crossing mud flats, sunken stumps, and cypress logs. A grove of palmettoes swayed lazily in a rare September breeze like cardboard handfans on a hot Sunday morning in church. The steamy air was only slightly thinner than swamp water and smelled of mud and rotting vegetation. The square-nosed boat pushed muddy waves over upcroppings of dark cypress knees as it cut through islands of floating water hyacinths, lime-green duckweed, and sawgrass. Raised-headed cottonmouth moccasins, sleek green frogs, and young alligators fled the deafening roar of the airboat's engine. Poncho, sitting high in the pilot's seat, maneuvered through tricky turns with the calm confidence of someone born to the wilderness. He pointed out signs of alligators. By the paths swimming gators cut through the duckweed and water grass, he can tell how large they were and how long ago they passed.

Poncho's alligator lines are nothing more than heavy cord tied to a branch at one end with a large baited hook at the other. The bait, usually chicken wings or thighs, hangs two or three feet above the water to keep smaller alligators from hooking themselves. As Poncho eased his boat among the trees, some lines hung as he had left them, the bait untouched. He nodded; this was not unusual. Some hooks dangled empty: owls had taken the bait. Still others were pulled taut into the black water. This usually meant a snared gator. Small ones hooked in the mouth were thrown back for another time. Large ones were fair game.

Toward the end of the run, Poncho came upon a line stretched tight. He pulled, and the weight was like a submerged stump. The gator would not budge. Poncho's friend and cousin Donald Cambre lent a hand. The huge, reluctant creature rose slowly. As its head broke the water's surface, the gator began to thrash wildly, rolling over and over, its whiplike tail slashing mud in all directions. Wide, powerful jaws opened and hissed a threatening defiance at the two men until three shots from Poncho's rifle ended the five-minute drama. The dead gator measured ten feet nine inches in length.

## CHARLES "DAGO" KRAFT

One late Sunday afternoon in early February, Charles Kraft was in the small wooden skinning shed at the end of a cluttered path behind his house, off a narrow road west of Ponchatoula and fifteen minutes from Pass Manchac. A lifelong trapper and fisherman in Manchac Swamp, "Dago"—his nickname to everyone—worked in the skinning shed almost every afternoon during nutria season.

A single fluorescent light illuminated the dark, dank one-room structure. Steel-jawed traps hung from one wall. A dried beaver pelt was nailed next to the door. A flirtatious calendar girl stared out from another wall above drying nutria skins. On two sides of the shed, row after row of drying nutria, mink, and otter pelts hung to dry. Below one rack of hides, hundreds of dried pelts lay stacked like firewood.

At a small, brown-stained table in the center of the room, Dago cleaned his day's trappings. His razor-sharp knife gliding over the pelts' pink inner surface, he cut away meat and unwanted tissue with the deftness of a surgeon. At the back of the shed an ancient, rusty clothes dryer clanked along in metallic rhythm, drying fresh skins. When each pelt was clean, Dago stretched it over a cypress drying board, nailed it in place, hung it to dry, and reached into the machine for the next one.

Dago, with tangled black hair and skin tanned as dark as a dried pelt, looked exactly the part of one of the last remaining trappers in Manchac Swamp. He was talkative but shy, rarely making eye contact with those around him. As he nailed skins to the drying board, streams of sweat ran down his brown, whisker-stubbled chin like a heavy rain across burned swamp grass. "About forty years ago," he said, "I stayed out there in that swamp about fifteen years. I run away from school and I stayed in the swamp. I got as far as the sixth grade. Dey kept me after school one day and I jumped out the window, went down to the swamp, and never come back out of there."

Trapping has changed considerably over the years, Dago said.

> I started trappin' when I was twelve or fourteen, and dey didn't have no nutria in those days. Didn't have nothin' but mink and muskrat. Dey ain't got a muskrat in that swamp now. Dey just disappeared. Lots of coons, nutria—and minks are just startin' to come back. Da prettiest fur dey got is a beaver, and dey won't buy it. Dey never would buy beaver down here.

Mink pelts that once sold for $22 to $25 now fetch $4 to $8. Mink farms have knocked the bottom from under mink trappers. The price for nutria hides is much lower—so low that in 1993 Kraft did not bother to set his traps. "It was the first time in forty years I didn't trap. It wasn't worth nothin'. Dey wouldn't buy 'em."

As if conscious of belonging to a disappearing way of life, Kraft noted that he preferred to run the traplines on his lease in an old-fashioned pirogue, rather than use one of the now-popular motorized Go-Devils or airboats: "I don't like dem airboats." He added that his son, Charles, is not a trapper, but a crabber in Pointe a la Hache, near the mouth of the Mississippi River.

As Dago talked, Luther Morehouse walked into the shed. Morehouse, who lives in Slidell, has been a fur buyer for over thirty years. He was there to buy Dago's pelts, but like all good storytelling Cajuns, he was prepared to reminisce:

> I remember back in the days when buyers came from all over the country to buy pelts. Dey ain't no more nutria like dey used to have. You used to come over here and you'd see thirty-seven thousand of 'em. It'd take 'em four days to count and grade 'em. One man shot dice out there and lost all his money, thousands of dollars. One roll, double or nothin'. That was about twenty-five years ago. All the big dealers who use to be in the business are all dead. Yeah, we had some nutria there one time. Dey might come back.

After Luther's departure, Dago, too, spoke of the long view.

> I'd rather trap than anything. That's the best thing I did ever like to do in my life. I just love it back there. Been in it all my life. But it done changed ten times since I've been in it. It's wide open now. I've seen deer, you couldn't shoot from here to that door right here without hitting one, it was so thick. You'd have to cut your way through. Deer, hogs, everything. It's wide open now, everyt'ing died. I don't know what killed it. Dey say salt water killed it, salt water ain't killed it. I don't know. I feel sick back there now, da way it looks. It looks bad.

Perhaps his mood reflected thoughts of what he might learn the following day at the doctor's office. The next day came and his fears were reality: he had cancer and faced a long series of operations. A few months later Dago was back on the lake crabbing. But a year after that Sunday afternoon in the skinning shed, the cancer finally triumphed, and the old-time Manchac trappers were fewer by one.

## ERICK AND JUSTILLIA MARIE PONVILLE LIGHTELL

Erick and Justillia Marie Lightell live at the end of a long shell road in the little settlement of Frenier Beach. Their house is a camp raised high off the ground on creosote pilings in the traditional style of the south Louisiana marsh. Less than a hundred feet from their front door, waves from Lake Pontchartrain slap against a breakwater of broken concrete slabs. Jet airliners interrupt the silence as they work their flight patterns around nearby New Orleans International Airport.

Erick and Marie have lived in Manchac Swamp for as long as they can remember. Erick was born in St. Bernard Parish, just south of New Orleans, but at the age of four went to live with his grandfather, Oscar Lightell, at Frenier Beach on property owned by the Guste family of New Orleans. Oscar worked for the Gustes and made extra money selling catfish, shrimp, and trout and trapping mink, coon, and otter.

Marie was born in LaPlace. Her family moved to Manchac when she was a very young child. "My brother and daddy use to trap along Highway 51." Her strong rhythmic Cajun accent snapped out the words in short bursts like slapping mosquitoes on a warm summer night.

> We had a palmetto house, and it had cardboard for floorin'. When my mama went into labor, dey called Doctor Gross. He crossed the canal. My daddy went and get him. He said, 'Oh! It's goin' to be cold in here for dat baby and your wife, she gunna catch pneumonia.' So after the baby was born, he took her and put her in a box, my sister in a box, near the stove. The box was catchin' on fire. My mama said, 'Where's my baby?' Doctor Gross said, 'I wrapped her up and trow her in a box.' And daddy said, 'Yeah, but that box is on fire.' My mama used to tell us that story all the time.

Marie's ninety-year-old mother speaks only French. When she goes to the hospital or doctor's office, Marie accompanies her as a translator.

Marie's father built the palmetto house when she was about five or six. It had three bedrooms and a kitchen. Palmetto fronds overlapping on a pole frame formed the roof and sides—a style of construction adapted by French colonists from the Indians. "It didn't rain in it, and it was nice and warm." The family lived there until the early 1950s when the highway department moved them out to make room for a new Highway 51. With free lumber given by a friend, Marie's father built another house nearby. Twenty years later, they were in the way once more. The interstate was coming through and highway officials "told us to move again, so we moved back by my sister's house in LaPlace." After the Lightells' son was born, the Guste family gave them permission to build a camp on the Frenier Beach property. What began as a weekend camp eventually became a home.

The Lightells are as much a part of the swamp's rhythm as the changing tides. Erick sells catfish, lizards, snakes, and frogs and runs crab traps in Lake Pontchartrain. Marie makes and sells stuffed crabs and flounders. Like many others in Manchac, the Lightells tend to look away shyly when talking with strangers, rarely making eye contact.

The couple's large living room, with windows overlooking the lake and nearby fishing camps, is filled with photographs of their son Erick, known by friends and family as "Poule d'eau" (pronounced 'pool-doo" in Louisiana, and a common nickname for children in French-speaking parts of the state, the term names a small waterfowl, the American coot). The bright, cheerful photographs were a melancholy contrast to the framed obituaries that hung across the room. "I don't know how it happened," Marie said, her voice painfully balanced between despair and attempted good spirits. "He was by himself. I don't know if he fell overboard or what. He was crabbing. It was on a Good Friday." In one corner stood a vase filled with brown, wilted flowers—the bouquet of red roses Poule d'eau gave his mother a few weeks before he drowned. "You see, I still got them. They all dried up, but I told him I was never goin' to trow them away."

Despite their loss, the Lightells still love the swamp: its beauty, and the freedom it brings to their lives. "It's quiet," says Erick. "I think about a lot of stuff. I worked before on different jobs and I just didn't like it. Here, you are your own boss. Nobody's on your back all the time. You wanna go, you go. You don't wanna go, you don't." To Erick the swamp is at its best in the early morning. "Everything is quiet, everything is starting to wake up. You see more animals moving around early in them morning." Winter mornings, "especially when there's a frost on the ground," are the most peaceful times to him. Marie prefers summertime, when the trees are in full green.

Like everyone who knows Manchac Swamp, the Lightells have noticed great changes taking place. "Every year things change more and more," Erick says. He describes those changes one by one. Erosion is the biggest problem: "The lake taking up everything, eating up the land. After a while the washout will be all the way out here. No protection, just getting bigger and bigger. We also catch more she-crabs coming from the Gulf. I've never seen that before. The lake is getting more salty than before."

## VIRGINIA MAY SALTZMAN RAKOCY

The middle-aged Chicago couple could not resist the sign hanging in front of Virginia Rakocy's little white cinder-block seafood market at Manchac. Driving along Interstate 55, they could see her sign below, advertising everything from alligator to coon meat. When the couple walked in, they quickly were aware that this was no ordinary fish market. Tags in the display cooler identified wild pig, coon, nutria, muskrat, alligator, and turtle, along with catfish and soft-shell crabs. Five alligator skulls rested atop the cooler, their dark bony eye sockets and fearsome teeth confronting anyone entering the screen door. The couple bought five pounds of alligator meat and in a few minutes were back in their white Cadillac heading home to Chicago.

Virginia, who runs the market with her fisherman son Andrew "Rocky" Rakocy, is an elegant woman with penetrating eyes and a lilting laugh. Half the people in the Manchac area call her "the bait lady," but somehow only the last word seems to fit. Born the year World War I broke out in Europe, she has lived in Manchac her entire life except for a brief time during World War II when she worked in Monterey, California. Over the years, she has fished, worked as a waitress in a Manchac restaurant, and during the late 1940s and early 1950s, served as postmistress at Manchac's tiny Akers Post Office (named for Will Akers, a longtime railroad telegrapher at the Manchac bridge). Three times a day, she met the trains to pick up or send out the mail. The trains also took on fresh fish for New Orleans and other towns and cities along the track.

"You are just so free here," says Virginia of her long life in Manchac. "I guess I just love the changin' seasons. It keeps me so occupied. You just look forward to the alligator season, the deer huntin' time, the trappin' time, the crabbin' and fishin' time. There's just always somethin' to keep you lookin' forward to."

Virginia's late husband, Andy, drove a school bus up to Ponchatoula for over thirty years. "He had fifty-five children at times. After the second road came through, they took people's land and many of them moved to town. A few young people stayed." Shortly after Andy started driving the bus, Virginia opened a small seafood market under a shed alongside the highway and in front of the house she and her family lived in for over forty years. "I started selling crabs, a little bait, and all that right under that shed." She pointed outside to the small shed, where local fishermen and trappers still congregate to socialize and talk about their catch, prices, or any other topic of the day. "I get three or four bushels of crabs a day now, when I use to get forty bushels a day."

Virginia's family, the Saltzmans, came to Manchac from Blind River, in Livingston Parish, on April 10, 1896. She has spent many years compiling notes on the history of Manchac and its families. She reads from her notebook: "They crossed Lake Maurepas to Manchac and bought 365 acres at 25 cents an acre. The Saltzmans learned how to fish here. At Blind River they were farmers and mink trappers; they also cut cypress to make roof shakes for houses." She has notes on Manchac's early families, the Barbiers, Succows, Renos, DeGruyses, Windeckers, Straders, Cortezes, and Guichets—the latter being one of the few African-American families to settle in Manchac. She also had stories about the German families at Frenier—Groetes, Windeckers, Slussers—who grew cabbage on their small farms and from it made sauerkraut that they shipped to New Orleans, Chicago, and St. Louis. The farms are all gone now. Most were destroyed by the devastating 1915 hurricane.

Virginia was too young to remember that storm, which took many lives and wrecked almost every building in Manchac. But she does remember Hurricane Betsy in 1965. 'The only thing I don't like and really don't like is hurricanes." She put one hand to the side of her head to emphasize the story about to come. When Hurricane Betsy hit in 1965, Virginia, Rocky, Andy, and Andy's grandfather huddled in the house, listening to a battery-operated radio.

> We heard the announcer say, 'The eye of the hurricane is here!' I didn't realize what the eye of a hurricane was. It was about midnight or later, I seen this big bright light coming across the lake on the railroad bridge. I said, now that's the eye of a hurricane. So we got our raincoats and hats, and I made grandpa put on his rain coat. I said, 'This *must* be the eye of the hurricane.' Then I heard a roar and sure enough I knew it was the eye. It turned out to be a freight train.

Her head rocked back as she laughed at her own innocence.

Virginia talked about Manchac and its beauty before the interstate blocked her view of Lake Maurepas and its shoreline. "This interstate wasn't here." She pointed an accusatory finger out the front door to the raised concrete roadway. "Out on that point there was some beautiful cypress trees and the moss was hanging. They would be green—just beautiful. You could feel the cool in the evening. I would go out there and just watch. That old canal wasn't there. . . . There's nothin' beautiful on that lakeshore any more. Not like it was. It just don't look the same."

## DONALD CLARK

"There's a word that describes Donald," Sims says, but after struggling to find that one word, she settles for several: "He literally becomes part of the environment, and his eyesight is unbelievable." Clark catches birds and snakes with his bare hands. The creatures seem oblivious to his presence.

> One day I was with him and his wife out in the Prairie in a marshy area. All of a sudden Donald ran his boat up on the ground, jumped over Ruth, and just took off running. Next thing you know, he has a mallard duck under his arm. He ran around a little more and then he had two mallard ducks under his arm. He can just approach these animals and they don't leave.

Clark, a retiring and shy man with a mop of dark brown hair, makes his living following the seasons in the swamp. He started working in Manchac at the age of eight with his stepfather, Robert Kliebert, who owned a turtle farm in Hammond. After finishing high school, Donald "graduated from school to the swamp." He hunts nutria and catches catfish, crickets (for bait), lizards, and snakes by day and frogs at night. When he is not hunting, fishing, or frogging, he often can be found building scaffolding to provide Sims a closer look at the nest of a horned owl or red-shouldered hawk. Over the years, he has given her another set of eyes in the swamp.

Clark is one of the few trappers who work the Manchac Swamp on foot. He owns boats, but when he nutria hunts, he takes off and walks five or six miles. He shoots nutria rather than trapping them, skins them on the spot, and leaves the flesh for other animals. He also walks the railroad track through the swamp, catching lizards and snakes. He has been bitten twice by venomous cottonmouth moccasins. His remedy is one every scout learns—cut the bite and bleed it. But he does his best to avoid cottonmouths. "You can smell them, they stink. You can smell them when you are around them."

Like others who spend their lives in Manchac Swamp, Clark is fiercely independent. "It's somethin' I like. You don't have to listen to nobody." He once worked as a scaffold builder for Shell Oil. In 1985 the company sent him to Arizona, but he quickly returned to Louisiana and Manchac. He uses only enough words to make his point: "No swamp. Nothin' to do but work. When they ain't workin', they drink."

Although Clark does not talk much to strangers, he breaks through his reticence when the subject is the swamp and the beauty he sees out there especially in the morning light with the "sun coming up and a misty fog on the ground." He often picks wildflowers by the root and transplants them in his yard. Clark refuses to take money for helping Sims build scaffolding or spot wildlife. Instead, he wants photographs of the creatures he long took for granted. "The real thing is always prettier. But with a picture, you can always remember it when you can't go back." Sims believes her photography has changed Clark's attitudes toward the swamp and its wildlife. He once told her that before he met her, he was not too concerned about what he shot out there. Now he has books about birds and often phones Sims to talk about the different species in his bird feeder.

## MICHAEL HENRY FANNALY

"I love it. You can get back there and it's real quiet. You're by yourself and you're part of nature. I see things in my life that Julia would love to have on film. You just see things other people will never see. I can leave my truck and in five minutes see more things than any person can, paying twenty dollars to go on one of those swamp tours."

Michael Henry Fannaly, born in 1953 of Irish and German descent, is tall with a thick athletic build and wavy ginger hair. His blue eyes and every inch of his clean-shaven, ruddy face enjoy a smile. A lifetime of pulling shrimp nets and crab traps and paddling pirogues has given him thick fingers and strong hands. His life as a commercial fisherman in Manchac and Lake Pontchartrain began when he was eleven years old. "I use to put the crab traps right up in front of the pass [Manchac] and get a few crabs and sell them to Middendorf's Restaurant. I got thirty-five cents a dozen. They'd bring them up and sell them for fifty cents a dozen. Back then, thirty-five cents was a lot of money." After high school, Fannaly had ideas of becoming a marine biologist. He spent two years studying botany at Southeastern Louisiana University in nearby Hammond, but then got married and headed back to the swamp.

When Fannaly is not crabbing, he is shrimping, fishing, trapping alligators and nutria, or catching frogs and crawfish on his nine-thousand-acre lease, which stretches along Lake Maurepas from Pass Manchac south almost to the Reserve Canal. He has held the lease for more than a dozen years. Before that, leases were rare among the trappers and fishermen. "It was open land. Fishermen and trappers had unwritten agreements as to individual territory. You just honored where he went. If he had a run, you just stayed off it."

Fannaly has seen many changes in Manchac since he was an eleven-year-old with a few crab traps. Not only is the swamp's very nature changing, but trappers and fishermen are having a more difficult time making a living. Fannaly outlines the problem with the ease of a broker discussing the stock market:

> The product I catch is worth more, but there's not as much of it. Ten years ago, you could go and just about walk across the lake on crab traps. You couldn't find a place to put them because there were so many. Last fall, when I crossed from the pass to the south end of the causeway [Lake Pontchartrain Causeway], I ran across one line. People have thinned out that much in the last few years.

Fannaly also believes that crabbing in Lake Pontchartrain has been seriously hurt by overharvesting and by seafood brokers from northern states buying up everything that is caught.

> When we first started crabbing, you couldn't sell a gumbo crab [small crab]. The only thing you could sell was a number one crab. Anything else, we would throw them back. When these dealers came down, they put a price on what they call factory crabs. You can't afford to throw them back. You're talking thirty-two dollars a bushel. That's a lot of money. These crabs are going to Bayou La Batre, Alabama, and the picking plants, and that's the crabmeat that you buy.

The fur business also is not what it was. Manchac Swamp was once filled with muskrat, otter, and mink. A few remain, but most are gone. The three-cornered grass that muskrats once dined on was destroyed by salt water and nutria. Even the formerly high-rolling nutria business has declined dramatically since its peak in the 1970s. "Fur sales used to be a big deal down here. Buyers came from New York, all over. They bought whatever I had. It's been five years since we had one of those. Use to be a good deal for everybody involved. Now, there's just very few people trappin'. The hardest thing is finding somebody to buy them."

Fannaly believes the day may come when he can no longer make a living crabbing or trapping in Manchac. But whatever happens, he will not give up the swamp where he has spent most of his life. "This is all I've ever done. If I couldn't do it full time, I guess I would spend most of what I made going down there duck huntin', deer huntin'. I'd be down there one way or another."

## DENNIS GUY AND HAYDEN RENO

Dennis Guy and his wife, Denise, live near French Settlement at the end of a long, dusty dirt road bordered on both sides by swamp. Their house is on the Chinquapin Canal, which leads to Bayou Chene Blanc and eventually Lake Maurepas. Guy's yard is filled with machine parts, a large metal-roofed shed covering a sawmill, and cypress "sinker" logs scoured from nearby bayou and lake bottoms. The massive tree trunks scattered about the yard resemble felled columns from some toppled Athenian temple transported to a Louisiana swamp.

The dark, crusty logs, which have lain on the water bottoms for almost a century, generally run three to four feet in diameter. Many are more than a thousand years old. Against the side of the Guys' two-story, alpine-style home, which Dennis built himself totally from sinker cypress, leans a cross section of a cypress log almost five feet in diameter. The tree was a sapling in the time of Christ. Guy built his house entirely with planks from this and other ancient logs found nearby. Walls and floors throughout the house are made from this exquisite wood with the warm color of buttered honey. Individual floorboards measure as much as twenty-six inches wide.

Guy is in his early fifties and has the build of a man who wrestles water-soaked logs out of the mud. His face is leathery brown and his graying hair is an unruly mass. When he smiles, the crinkles around his green eyes break into a worn sunburst.

Guy, who works by himself, has been milling sinker cypress logs for over a decade. Finding them and wrestling them up from water bottoms is hard work. First he scouts likely spots—along the edge of Lake Maurepas, the nearby bayous where logging was heaviest, and train crossings where logs were hoisted from the water to waiting flatcars. Standing in his boat, Guy eases along "feeling" the bottom with a pole. When he strikes something that feels like a log, he jumps overboard and dives to the bottom to test the object with his hands. "I stick my hands in the mud like a turtle." Guy burrows his wiggling hands in the mudless air to show how it is done.

To raise the sinker, Guy uses his homemade pontoon boat, a cleverly designed little craft made entirely from found parts. The pontoons are joined together by a superstructure of steel pipes. Pulleys and cables hang from the metal frame. At one end of the main cable sits a large winch seasoned by rust and motor oil. Steel logging tongs hang at the other end. Guy lowers the tongs to grip the log, then hoists it until it rests directly between the pontoons, where he secures it with heavy steel cables. "I spent as much as ten days getting a log up once," he says matter-of-factly. "I fought it until I finally got it."

Once the sinker is in place, Guy tows the pontoon rig back to his mill. He uses his backhoe to drag the log from the water. When the wood is dry enough for milling, he muscles the log into position for the saw with the help of cables, winches, and pry bars. He uses a bandsaw rather than a circular saw because the bandsaw creates less waste. The blade moves lengthwise down the log, slicing off wide boards like a sharp knife cutting through a slab of cured bacon. Guy mills only cypress, which he sells by word of mouth to builders, cabinetmakers, and anyone else who enjoys working in the material. "There's no prettier wood than this," he says firmly.

Hayden Reno would agree. One balmy June morning Hayden, his wife Debbie, and their son, Hayden, Jr., were aboard their homemade pontoon rig in Manchac Swamp pulling a large sinker log from the muddy bottom of Black Bayou. The rig creaked and rocked in the shade of an eight-foot-thick hollow cypress on the nearby bank. The tree's hollow core saved it from the lumberman's axe a century ago. Yet the tree still lives.

The Reno name has been known in the Manchac area since those early logging days, and Hayden Sr. has lived in Manchac Swamp all his life. For more than eighteen of his thirty-seven years he made his living following the "seasons" in the swamp fishing, frogging, trapping alligators, and pulling sinker cypress logs from the bottom. Although he is now the full-time caretaker at Southeastern Louisiana University's Turtle Cove Environmental Research Station at Pass Manchac, he still hauls his rusting pontoon rig out into the swamp and bayous to pull logs.

"I used to pull ten thousand feet a week out of these canals," Hayden said while adjusting a cable around the water-soaked log dangling between the pontoons. "I got log sinkers around here I got hid. I got logs bigger than that." He nodded at the three-foot-thick log in his cable rigging. "That log went all the way across the canal. I wouldn't leave it in shallow water, so I hid it. I just got it in my head where I leave logs. I used to get in the canal and just walk. I used to do it every day. I used to come pull logs all day by myself and spend all day from sunup to dark."

Falling cypress prices, aging equipment, and "cold winters" finally persuaded Reno to look for more dependable work, but he still gets out in the swamp as often as possible. "It's in my blood," he says, glancing at his son playing on the huge, waterblackened cypress log. "Somethin' about this swamp and water. I just love it. I like in the spring when it's still cool. I love it in the winter. It's all dead and you can see things. You can find all kinds of stuff from loggin' days. I should have been back here a hundred years ago."

## LOUIS HENRY BARBIER

From an airplane overflying Manchac Swamp, the effects of a century of cypress logging are painfully visible. Within sight of the New Orleans skyline to the southeast, vast grassy prairies soak in coffee-black water where a thick cypress forest once stood. What remains today are thousands of dark stumps rotting in the mire, third-growth cypresses struggling for survival, thousands of felled trees graying in the hot sun, and narrow logging canals cutting across the watery landscape like long-festering wounds.

To satisfy south Louisiana's and the nation's appetite for cypress, logging companies almost leveled the entire Manchac area between the late 1890s and 1956, when the last log was cut for the mills. They crisscrossed the landscape digging canals such as Main Canal, Ruddock Canal, and Galva Canal to move their steam-powered pullboats deeper and deeper into the swamp. From each canal, small feeder ditches radiate off in every direction like spokes in a wagon wheel. From the air, these watery radiants glisten like silver starbursts in the late afternoon sun.

Cypress logging was a major industry in Louisiana, especially in Tangipahoa and St. John the Baptist Parishes. Manchac prospered, and boom towns such as Frenier, Ruddock, and Strader popped up along the railroad line that had opened the swamp and its vast forests to the world (the first highway, a dirt road, did not come along until 1926). By 1910, Frenier had almost two hundred residents, a small Catholic church, and by 1914, a school. Ruddock's population in 1915 was over seven hundred. Workers filled the towns and lumber mills. When they were not cutting trees or milling lumber, they fished, trapped, and gathered Spanish moss, which in those days was widely used in stuffing mattresses and padding upholstery. But in September of 1915, life in Manchac changed forever. The great hurricane of 1915 roared through. After it passed, Ruddock and Frenier no longer existed and more than 275 people were dead, mostly in south Louisiana (in Frenier alone, 25 people were killed when the railroad depot, in which they had sought refuge, collapsed). The once-thriving communities were never rebuilt, and the swamp long ago reclaimed the few surviving house pilings.

Louis Henry Barbier of Ponchatoula was in New Orleans when the 1915 storm hit, but he remembers the hurricane that hit Manchac and southeastern Louisiana on September 21, 1909, as if it were only yesterday.

> My mother, my uncle George, and my sister and my brother were there when the storm hit. The water was washin' in the front door. We thought we were gone. All the camps down there gone. On the big lake [Pontchartrain], that had big timber, big cypress timber, it was just like a break boat went along there. I'll bet that storm blowed every bit a hundred and twenty miles or thirty miles an hour. You could hear it come across the South Pass when it hit our place—just like a freight train.

The storm, which packed winds up to 125 miles per hour, claimed more than 350 lives, again mostly in south Louisiana.

Born in Madisonville, Louisiana, on May 17, 1896, Barbier remembers the thick cypress swamp well. The son of a French-speaking Swiss immigrant, he grew up on Jones Island in Manchac Swamp. Just before the turn of the century, his father purchased seventeen acres on the island. There he built a house and raised a family. The little homestead had a smokehouse, vegetable gardens, and fruit and pecan trees. Barbier's father made his living trapping, fishing, and hunting alligators. "I remember he killed some sixty-odd alligators in one night. He took the hides and left the carcasses in the swamp." Hides then sold for twenty-five cents a linear foot (today a large gator fetches more than forty dollars per foot). "They had all kinds of stuff down there. I came out one day with sixteen minks, twenty-two coon hides. We had to skin 'em back there in the swamps. They were too heavy to carry out. Them days I was a big man. I could pick up half a deer and walk out the swamps with them." Barbier's grandmother operated a small stall in the New Orleans French Market selling game and fish her husband caught in Manchac. "We use to paddle along Pass Manchac right at the edge of the swamp and kill us a couple of squirrels while goin' home. Now you can't see a squirrel or a rabbit or nothin' else. They all killed out. The young generation ruined the world. That's what they done." His voice grew angry as his hands dug deep into the armrest of the overstuffed chair while pulling his frail body up closer to the edge of the seat. "They kill everything they see. When the poules d'eau and the ducks would come down there, the pass would be black with them."

Barbier, whose small frame house in Ponchatoula is filled with faded family photographs, remembered when the logging companies practically clear-cut Manchac. In fact, he worked for the companies. "I was about seventeen or eighteen when they done all that. They just pulled boats in there. I worked on a pullboat, cuttin' timber. I would cut the tree around." Ringing the trees cut off their sap flow and killed them. They were then left standing for as long as a year before being logged and floated to the mills. During that time the wood dried, losing weight and thus becoming easier to handle. The technique of ringing cypresses was learned by the early French settlers, probably from the Indians. "We got fifteen cents a tree, that's all we got," Barbier recalls. "Them big trees, sometimes took you an hour to go around them."

Life in Manchac was hard and medical care scarce. Barbier's mother died of pneumonia when he was fifteen. "We had to wait a day before we could get a doctor." His father sent him to live with an aunt in New Orleans. After returning from service in World War I, Barbier and his bride, Allie, from Osyka, Mississippi, moved to Manchac, where he took a job at Edward Schlieder's elaborate Turtle Cove fishing camp on Pass Manchac. Schlieder was an executive with Salmen Brick and Lumber, one of several companies that held vast timber leases in the swamp. Barbier later worked as a lightkeeper's assistant at the Manchac lighthouse, an important navigational landmark then located on dry land where the pass entered Lake Pontchartrain. Today the lighthouse, which Barbier swears is haunted, stands abandoned and in ruins several hundred yards out in the lake.

Barbier began as the assistant keeper and later became head keeper, a job he held until the Coast Guard abandoned the lighthouse in 1958. He recalls stormy nights and rowing a small boat through treacherous seas to service seven beacon lights in Lake Pontchartrain and four in Lake Maurepas. He remembers the steamboat *Alexander Stuart* and the schooner *Malvena Anderson* and other steamers and schooners that hauled freight to and from New Orleans through Pass Manchac. He remembers twin-engine towboats "pulling a mile of timber at a time through the pass." Cypress logs were chained together in huge "rafts" that were pulled through the Pass and then across Lake Pontchartrain to the mills. "Sometime those logs would get heavy, so they would cut them loose. They would sink to the bottom. The bottom of the pass down there is filled with big timber." He described the cemetery that still can be seen "near North Pass and the big oak tree," where sixteen members of the Barbier, Saltzman, Reno, and Jones families are buried. "I got an uncle, two brothers, and a grandmother buried down there." Virginia Rakocy's four-month-old son, who died of pneumonia in 1934, also is buried there. An elaborately carved wooden plaque once marked his grave, but it was destroyed during Hurricane Betsy. A simple wooden cross now throws a gray shadow across the burial site.

Sadness rises in Barbier's voice when he talks about the changes he has seen in the swamp over nearly a century. "When I drive across the Manchac bridge, I shake my head sometimes . . . nothing but a lake. Ain't no more timber in there . . . cleaned it all out. I don't even try to go down there anymore."

## A DYING SWAMP

Louis Henry Barbier, Poncho Duhe, Virginia May Rakocy, Michael Fannaly, Hayden Reno, Erick and Marie Lightell, and others who have lived their lives in and around the Manchac Swamp know that the swamp is slowly dying. Fannaly describes the Manchac of the late 1950s and early 1960s:

> When I was a kid, you could go off the side of South Pass and you could get lost there. It was actually that thick-myrtle bushes, palmettoes, the trees and cypress were alive. They weren't big, but everything was alive. They used to have plenty of deer and ducks. They used to have so many ducks, you'd go in some places, you couldn't hear yourself talk. It's all more or less open now. The salt water, I think, more or less killed it. Just after Hurricane Betsy in 1965, that's when things really started dying off.

Scientists and state agencies are working on several fronts to save Manchac Swamp, which, according to Louisiana Department of Wildlife and Fisheries plant ecologist Latimore Smith, contains some of the oldest tidewater red cypresses in the country. Between 1975 and 1977 the state created the Manchac Wildlife Management Area with the purchase of more than 8,000 acres of swamp and marsh, including the once-broad, grassy plains called the "Prairie." In 1982 the Joyce Foundation of Chicago donated 13,569 acres of swampland to the Louisiana Department of Wildlife and Fisheries. The department then leased another 2,040 acres from landowners to form the Joyce Wildlife Management Area. In addition, biologists at the Turtle Cove Environmental Research Station have initiated a program to plant cypress seedlings, hoping to rebuild the forests. They have planted thousands. Many have survived, but most have been eaten by nutria.

The station's director, Robert Hastings, is not optimistic that Manchac can be saved. Hastings, a wiry man with close-cropped graying hair and beard, claims that natural and human-engendered forces are slowly killing the swamp. Clear-cut logging, which continued as late as the 1950s, is not the only culprit. Hastings enumerates other factors: natural land subsidence; rising sea levels caused by long-term global warming; the digging of logging and highway canals; the Mississippi River levee system, which prevents natural sediment deposits in the swamp; and the depredations of nutria, a South American rodent that spread explosively in the Louisiana wild after being released by accident from a breeding farm in the 1930s.

Lake Pontchartrain's salinity is a complicating—and complicated—factor. It increased somewhat after the completion in 1963 of the Mississippi River-Gulf Outlet shipping canal, which connects New Orleans and the Gulf of Mexico, but Hastings suspects that salt water entering the lakes from the Gulf during hurricanes causes far more damage than long-term trends. In 1985 Hurricane Juan brought a six-foot tidal surge into the lake. Everything in Manchac flooded. When the water receded, salt was left behind in the soil. High salinity in the lake may be good for shrimp and the seafood industry, Hastings says, but it is deadly for cypress.

Scientists generally agree that land subsidence, the lack of new sediment, deposits from the Mississippi River, and the intrusion of Lake Pontchartrain's naturally brackish waters are harming the swamp's cypress shoreline. Not all scientists, however, accept Hastings' salinity theories. In a 1985 article, estuarine ecologist Walter Sikora, then at Louisiana State University, and oceanographer Bjorn Kjerfve of the University of South Carolina pointed toward natural land subsidence as the main culprit. As the land slowly subsides, they wrote, more and more water from the lake enters deeper into the swamp, killing fresh-water vegetation. Their study also found that salinity increased only slightly in eastern Lake Pontchartrain after the Gulf Outlet opened, and hardly at all near Manchac to the west. As for hurricanes, Sikora and Kjerfve suggest that any temporary increase in salinity caused by seawater incursion is more than offset by the heavy rainfall that accompanies hurricanes, flushing the lakes with fresh water from area rivers.

Whatever the cause or causes, the cypress swamps around the rim of Lake Pontchartrain have eroded at the rate of 15 to 23 feet a year since 1970. By comparison, the Manchac area lost only about 300 feet of shoreline between 1897 and 1952. As late as 1953, the Prairie was just that, a broad grassland. In the 1970s, it was 70 percent water. By 1990, it was 90 percent water.

Professor Hastings believes Manchac's slow death is inevitable.

> It cannot be stopped. It can, however, be slowed down. We have to remember that the earth is a very changing environment. It is not stable. . . . Manchac is disappearing along with much of the rest of the Louisiana coast. The estimated rate for all Louisiana is about thirty-five square miles per year. The distance from Lake Pontchartrain to Lake Maurepas by Pass Manchac is seven miles. The loss of the Prairie is definitely imminent. Only twenty-five or thirty yards of land separate it from the lake. If we lose the Prairie, that means two of those seven miles are lost.

If Hastings' dire prediction comes true, Pontchartrain and Maurepas eventually will become one large body of water and Manchac will be little more than a memory on old maps and in Julia Sims's photographs.

Photography, Ansel Adams once wrote, has an obligation "to help us see more clearly and more deeply, and to reveal to others the grandeurs and potentials of the one and only world which we inhabit." Manchac is Julia Sims's world—an undiscovered one for most of us—and through her photographs we can see its fragile yet timeless grandeur.

# ENVIRONMENTAL ISSUES, OLD AND NEW*

Martin Reuss

While the controversy over the Atchafalaya Basin's future ownership remained the key question facing government bureaucrats, experts of all stripes, and the general public, other related issues also galvanized opinion and proved nearly as contentious.

One ever-vexing challenge was managing the huge amounts of sediment that settled in the Atchafalaya Basin. The problem joined environmental, navigation, and flood control concerns. Corps plans called for 1.5 million cfs to pour through the Atchafalaya Basin during a project flood. Yet the 869,000 cfs of water which flowed through the basin at the height of the 1973 flood threatened the guide walls along the lower floodway and the floodwall at Morgan City. The basin "bathtub" had nowhere near the capacity thought necessary.[1] The agreement with the National Wildlife Federation prevented the Corps from completing its 100,000-square-foot center channel, and levees were still below grade along stretches of the lower floodway because of sinking foundations. Somehow, room had to be found for more than 600,000 cfs of floodwater, but time was not on the Corps' side. The sediment deposited in the basin raised the elevations of flow lines from year to year. An intrepid swamper blazing a direct path leading from Charenton on the western edge of the basin to Bayou Pigeon on the eastern edge would have trekked over as much as 15 feet of silt accumulated since just 1917. The Corps was understandably anxious.[2]

In every solution, the operation of the Old River Control Structure played a major role. Any operational changes (including those for the planned auxiliary control structure) would affect the discharge downstream on the Atchafalaya River and, consequently, the characteristics of the future channel and the deltaic growth occurring at the river's mouth in Atchafalaya Bay. For those reasons, the engineers were wary of tinkering with the system. Yet, both environmental and economic arguments favored changing the operation of the control structure. Farmers in the Red River backwater area wanted the flow

*First published in Martin Reuss, *Designing the Bayous: The Control of Water in the Atchafalaya Basin, 1800-1995* (Alexandria, Va.: U. S. Army Corps of Engineers, 1998), 312-22. Reprinted with the kind permission of the author.

into the Atchafalaya River reduced during May, June, and July in some years. That would lessen the amount of water on the land during crop planting. On the other hand, the FWS wished to increase flows during the same months in drier years to benefit downstream fishery interests. The EPA also desired to increase the diversion, but for purely environmental reasons—to maintain the aquatic nature of the Atchafalaya ecosystem.[3]

By early 1979, the Corps was considering ten different plans to operate the control structure. One plan considered a 40 percent diversion down the Atchafalaya River. The other plans maintained the 70-30 percent split but provided for the control structure to be operated in different ways to reduce flooding in the Red River backwater area. Some options would have resulted in environmental degradation, and several would have required the construction of additional flood control structures.[4] In the end, the Corps of Engineers resisted all suggestions for significant modifications but kept open the possibility that some short-term changes might be made periodically. Allowing more water through the structure risked exactly what the Corps rested its reputation on preventing—letting the Mississippi establish a new channel through the Atchafalaya Basin—while diminishing the water would exacerbate the sedimentation problem. Their investigations convinced the engineers that they had hit on the best overall plan. The 70-30 split at Old River let the Atchafalaya increase its own carrying capacity, and by mid-1979 Colonel Sands had decided that dredging a large new channel for the Atchafalaya was no longer necessary; the Atchafalaya's main channel was "dredging itself out."[5] Moreover, new Corps engineering and environmental studies indicated that dredging a 100,000-square-foot center channel would adversely affect more than 20,000 acres of woodlands and wetlands, thus confirming some of the fears first expressed by the environmentalists.[6]

Sands' decision eliminated the issue which had been a flashpoint ever since it was first formally advanced in 1963, and that had led to the involvement of the National Wildlife Federation and other private and public agencies in the EIS process. However, the new approach hardly diminished the involvement of various organizations in the Corps' EIS efforts. By 1979, the Atchafalaya planning process had a life of its own. New issues had arisen and the basin had become a rallying point for environmentalists around the country. The public–private involvement continued.

In its final feasibility study[7] and EIS of 1982, the Corps modestly recommended dredging 29 million cubic yards of material from only 17.6 miles of the Atchafalaya's main channel between river miles 116 and 90 (mainly in the Grand and Six Mile Lake area) to help the river enlarge itself—the Corps called it "channel training"—and continuing to divert 30 percent of the combined flow of the Mississippi and Red rivers at the latitude of Old River into the Atchafalaya River.[8] The Fish and Wildlife Service acquiesced to this decision, although the agency expressed the hope that flows could be increased at selected times to prevent degradation of the fish habitat.[9] The Environmental Protection Agency also eventually supported the Corps' Old River decision but pushed even more energetically for the creation of its pet project—the management units—to control the spread of sediment within the basin. Not only would water quality improve,

EPA insisted, but the approach also promised to improve crawfish production and bring more fur-bearing animals to the lower basin.[10]

Despite EPA's enthusiasm, the effectiveness of management units was another intensely debated environmental issue. The Corps of Engineers believed that EPA claimed too much. Even the environmental planners in the Corps were dubious. They did not believe that the management units could work in the southern (lower) part of the basin at all and were unconvinced about several other units. "We sat around a room at various times and argued and yelled and screamed at each other, but it was all biologists," recalled Suzanne Hawes, who was chief of the environmental branch in the New Orleans District.[11]

Discussions of management units, heated or not, continued into 1981, with the Corps almost invariably taking a more conservative approach. Issues included the effectiveness of sediment traps, the realignment of distributary channels, and, as always, the design of the hydrographs.[12] Gas and oil interests also expressed concern that the units would interfere with their operations.[13] Whenever the Corps suggested eliminating some management units from further consideration, EPA authorities objected. One EPA letter protested the "unilateral" nature of the Corps' decisions and observed, "We look forward to discussing the restoration of the full complement of management units with you."[14] Finally, reflecting much debate and compromise, the management units themselves were modified before they were listed in the Corps of Engineers' 1982 feasibility study and EIS. Bayou Fordoche had been renamed Henderson Lake, and two small units, Lost Lake and Cow Island Lake, were identified in the zone separating Henderson Lake from Warner Lake. Both the West Atchafalaya and Morganza units were dropped and The Crevasse and Upper Belle River were consolidated. The result was the following list:[15]

| West of the Atchafalaya River | East of the Atchafalaya River |
|---|---|
| Henderson Lake | Alabama Bayou |
| Warner Lake | Bayou des Glaises |
| Lost Lake | Pigeon Bay |
| Cow Island Lake | Flat Lake |
| Cocodrie Swamp | Upper Belle River |
| Beau Bayou | |
| Buffalo Cove | |
| Six Mile Lake | |

Of the 13 management units, the Corps determined that five— Buffalo Cove, Henderson, Beau Bayou, Flat Lake, and Cocodrie Swamp—had the best chances of success. In the feasibility study, the Corps recommended that Buffalo Cove and Henderson Lake be used as pilot units, to be developed and closely monitored by the Corps in conjunction with the FWS, EPA, and appropriate state agencies.[16]

The debate over the management units epitomizes one of the poignant ironies of the Atchafalaya Basin. The basin had long ago lost its claim to be an entirely natural ecosystem; for two centuries humans had exploited its resources and channeled its waters. Flood control activities had transformed the topography, altered flora and fauna, and had left little in the basin untouched. Yet, the Environmental Protection Agency, in its desire to restore the basin's natural rhythms, advanced a plan that would subject the region to a degree of human management previously unknown.

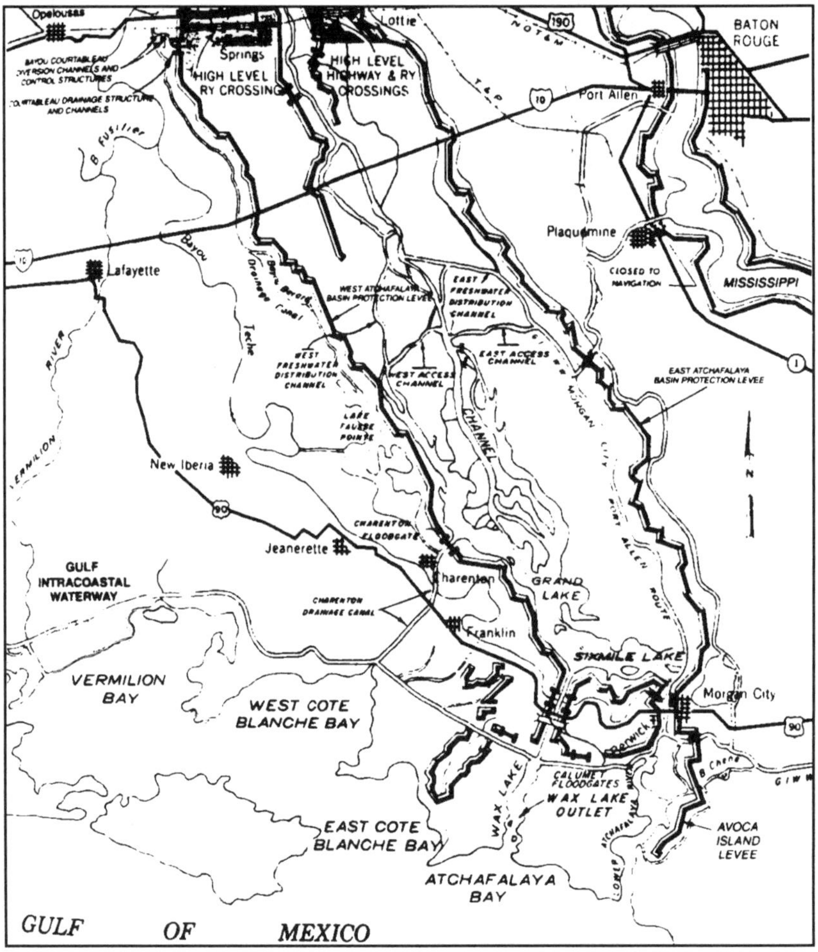


The Lower Atchafalaya Basin and the intracoastal waterway

Another controversy raged over the extension of the Avoca Island Levee (see map). The Corps had completed the original levee in 1953 to control backwater flooding south and east of Morgan City in the marshlands of Terrebonne Parish. The levee extended from Bayou Boeuf just below Morgan City southward to a point just above Cutoff Bayou. While the structure initially lowered backwater flooding, its effect was partially offset by the delta building at the mouth of the Atchafalaya and the general deterioration of the lower part of the river. To overcome the problem, the Corps proposed incrementally extending the levee 16 miles or more to the south depending on the exact route chosen—designated as bay shore, channel, or marsh. All three routes were divided into six reaches to be built at approximate ten-year intervals. The channel and marsh routes extended directly into Atchafalaya Bay, while the bay shore route adhered more closely to the shoreline.[17]

However, opponents blasted the project. They pointed to numerous adverse environmental and economic impacts, and they challenged the project's overall cost-effectiveness. Environmental agencies demanded new and often expensive scientific studies to detail the project's probable impact, while engineers insisted that more studies were unnecessary. At both the state and federal levels, the debate opened a chasm between engineering and environmental agencies.

The Fish and Wildlife Service listed numerous adverse consequences of the Avoca Island Levee extension. The extension would cut off freshwater flows from the Atchafalaya River into the western Terrebonne Parish marshes, destroying productive marsh habitat. As a consequence, the nursery grounds for shrimp, crab, and fish would deteriorate or be eliminated. Nutria and muskrat populations would harm the commercial trapping industry. Further negative effects included a degradation in delta development, the acceleration of saltwater intrusion, the deterioration or destruction of a natural hurricane buffer zone, more conversion of marshland into farmland, and more development in flood prone areas.[18]

The FWS's state counterpart, the Louisiana Department of Wildlife and Fisheries, generally supported the findings of the federal agency (except for differences over federal land acquisition in the basin). A similar alliance occurred on the developmental side. The state Office of Public Works supported the Corps' position that if the extension were not constructed, Morgan City and the surrounding area would suffer economic consequences. While many Atchafalaya-related issues divided the environmental and developmental agencies, probably none brought the differences into higher relief than the controversy over the Avoca Island Levee.

Differences over the levee extension festered for some time, but the dispute intensified in the summer of 1979 when the Louisiana Department of Transportation and Development (DOTD), which embraced the Office of Public Works, ran into strong opposition from both the state and federal wildlife agencies. At a meeting of the Atchafalaya Basin Agency Management Group at the end of May, a DOTD representative expressed his agency's support for the extension, but his rationale, in the words of a Fish and Wildlife official, "was not apparent" and in fact conflicted with several revised guidelines in the state's coastal resources program.[19] The Office of Public Works responded that the FWS did not appreciate economic, cultural, social, or safety concerns. However, J. Burton Angelle, secretary of the Louisiana Department of Wildlife and Fisheries, jumped into the dispute with a letter suggesting that the Office of Public Works did not understand the more limited role of the FWS—to protect, preserve, and enhance fish and wildlife resources. Angelle also noted, "It has not been demonstrated that significant adverse economic impacts will result if the Avoca Island Levee extension is not constructed."[20]

Environmental organizations opted for a system of 28 ring levees around populated areas instead of the Avoca Island Levee extension. The Environmental Protection Agency, Fish and Wildlife Service, National Oceanic and Atmospheric Administration, National Marine Fisheries Service, Louisiana Department of Wildlife and Fisheries, and various fishery organizations supported this approach. [21] While the Corps admitted that this plan would completely protect areas within the ring levees, the agency expressed concern that the approach left unprotected most of the land subject to backwater flooding. The Corps concluded that the proposal would require the relocation of 1,900 residential, commercial, and public structures.[22]

The debate over the cost-effectiveness and necessity of the levee extension continued, as did numerous scientific studies to gather more information about the project's impact on the ecosystem. In particular, the FWS complained about a lack of hydrologic data. That agency was frustrated because Colonel Sands had by 1980 indicated that he supported construction of the first reach (about 14,000 feet) of the extension along the bay shore route, which was the least environmentally damaging of the three routes. Although the FWS had by its own account inadequate information, the agency observed that this construction would result in two major adverse impacts. First, it would result in approximately 84,000 acres of wooded wetlands north of the Intracoastal Waterway becoming sufficiently dry to be converted to other land uses. Second, it would mean greater saltwater intrusion.[23] As the FWS admitted, these problems could be mitigated through the erection of various control structures or through land easements or acquisitions. When the Corps appeared intent on recommending the levee extension despite environmental objections, the FWS modified its strategy to emphasize mitigation features rather than the complete elimination of the project. Sands was responsive; indeed, the Corps was working on some of the same solutions. He noted in early 1981 that the Corps would ensure that the project would not affect "existing salinity and sediment distribution patterns in the western Terrebonne Parish marshes."[24] Yet, the Corps, too, had insufficient data to assess the project's precise impacts.

In June 1981, the Corps published a new five-volume draft feasibility report and environmental impact statement on the Atchafalaya Basin floodway system (a preliminary draft had been circulated for agency review in March 1981). This report responded to Secretary Veysey's decision five years earlier to combine the engineering and environmental features into one plan, and it replaced the earlier DEIS of 1976. As Colonel Sands had earlier hinted, in the report's "tentatively selected plan" (TSP), the Corps recommended the construction of the first reach of the Avoca Island Levee extension.[25] Once more, the Corps held five public review meetings around the state, and again the agency received ridicule and scorn but also strong support. In Morgan City, residents of Terrebonne Parish applauded every criticism of the Corps. "The Corps of Engineers is apparently the executor of the curse on Terrebonne Parish," parish resident and state legislator Murray Hebert said. "You've been attempting for years to do away with us, and this seems like the final blow." Warming up, Hebert continued, "Thanks to the Corps' work Terrebonne Parish is an endangered species. . . . I know they're [*sic*] brighter minds with brighter plans."[26] At the meeting, oystermen also complained that the extension would alter salinity, destroying oyster grounds.

The Corps admitted in the TSP that it had inadequate information about the effect of the Avoca Island Levee extension on natural resources and that more studies were necessary. While the Corps' figures did not come close to the 84,000 acres that the FWS tentatively estimated, the TSP conceded that thousands of acres of marshland would be lost because of the impact of construction, the reduction of river overflow, and the isolation of newly developed delta—some 3,200 acres—which would eventually return to the bay.[27] The FWS vehemently denied a Corps suggestion in the TSP that the controversy surrounding the construction of the levee extension had been resolved. "This could not be farther from the truth," responded David Soileau, acting field supervisor in the Lafayette office, who once more advanced the ring levee option.[28] He observed that the levee extension would "protect residents and property in the area immediately north and east of Morgan City from only *backwater flooding problems* caused by the Atchafalaya River." However, he went on, such flooding accounted for only half of the flooding problems in the area. The rest came from tidal and headwater flooding, neither of which would be lessened by the Avoca Island Levee extension.

On the other hand, the ring levees would give 100 percent flood protection.[29] In its formal report dealing with the Avoca Island Levee extension, the FWS also correctly noted that the "Limited Structural Measures"—the ring levees—would comply with President Jimmy Carter's 1978 executive orders dealing with floodplain management and the protection of wetlands.[30] The state Department of Wildlife and Fisheries sided with the FWS completely: "In our view the extension of the Avoca Island Levee would cause an unacceptable amount of environmental damage while failing to provide adequate protection from flooding to the residents of the backwater area. . . . Ring levees remain a much superior flood control and environmental alternative and are more cost-effective."[31]

The intensity of the opposition to the Avoca Island Levee extension surprised the Corps, and Colonel Sands attempted to be sensitive to both environmental and engineering concerns. While the final feasibility study and environmental impact statement of January 1982 argued that only an extension of the Avoca Island Levee would "provide protection over the entire area of backwater influence east of the floodway," it did not specify the length the extension should be. Instead, the Corps admitted that more biological and engineering studies—to be completed by 1985—were necessary before the exact length could be determined.[32] What Sands had not anticipated was that the seven-man Mississippi River Commission, pressured by an enormous letter-writing campaign by Morgan City interests, would overrule him on the subject and in April 1982 would recommend the immediate extension of the Avoca Island Levee.[33] This story and its aftermath is part of the final chapter of this history.

The controversies surrounding the Atchafalaya Basin in the 1970s partially resulted from new planning procedures more congenial to the environmental era, procedures which emphasized constraints rather than development. They limited use in order to preserve the ecosystem, but they could not always reconcile all the conflicting purposes and problems involved in the project. An even more daunting task was to agree on priorities. As the story of the Atchafalaya Basin shows, if planners cannot agree about the relative importance of *all* project purposes, the appropriate application of technical and nontechnical data, and acceptable environmental impacts, confusion and acrimony are almost guaranteed. Even if all parties do initially agree, they need to be prepared for subsequent modifications; new objectives—and objections—continuously emerge. By the end of the 1970s, awareness that science and engineering could not solve essentially social and economic questions was growing. These were political matters that required political negotiation.

## Notes for "Environmental Issues, Old and New"

[1]Johannes L. van Beek, Ava L. Harmon, Charles L. Wax, Karen M. Wicker, *Operation of the Old River Control Structure, Atchafalaya Basin: An Evaluation from a Multiuse Management Standpoint*, EPA-600/4-79-073 (Las Vegas, 1979), 25.

[2]Kermit L. Hebert, *The Flood Control Capabilities of the Atchafalaya Basin Floodway*, rev. ed. (Baton Rouge, 1973), 55. Hebert originally submitted this paper in partial fulfillment of the requirements for a master of science degree, and it was first published in 1967. Subsequently updated, the study remains a standard source on the subject.

[3]Van Beek et al., *Operation of the Old River Control Project, Atchafalaya Basin*, 28; U.S. Army Corps of Engineers, New Orleans District, *Feasibility Study, Main Report and Final Environmental Impact Statement*, in *Atchafalaya Basin Floodway System, Louisiana: Feasibility Study*, 4 vols. (New Orleans, 1982), 1:33, hereinafter cited as *Feasibility Study*.

[4]"Atchafalaya Under Scrutiny: Alternatives for Operating Old River Project," *New Orleans Times-Picayune*, January 19, 1979.

[5]*Feasibility Study*, 1:33–34; Sands' quotation is from the *Franklin Post*, August 24, 1979, as cited in Lee Pendergrass, "Stewards of the Waters: The Corps of Engineers New Orleans District, 1977–1988" (unpublished manuscript, New Orleans District, U.S. Army Corps of Engineers, May 1989), 173.

[6]*Feasibility Study*, 2:B-33.

[7]The feasibility study addressed both authorized and "preauthorized" elements—those which still required congressional approval, including environmental, real estate, and recreational elements. The general design memorandum dealt only with authorized features, principally flood control. However, pursuant to Assistant Secretary Veysey's guidance in 1976, it included studies of alternate plans to accomplish the project purposes. House and Senate committee resolutions had directed the study of preauthorized features. See ibid., 2:A–3 to A–4. For additional explanation, see Chapter 11, pages 281–82.

[8]*Feasibility Study*, 2:60–64.

[9]Cary W. Kerlin, Lafayette Field Supervisor, FWS, to Colonel Sands, September 21, 1979; Gary Hickman, Lafayette Area Manager, FWS, to General Thomas A. Sands, Reporting Officer, Atchafalaya Basin Project, January 13, 1982, both in U.S. Fish and Wildlife Service Files, Lafayette, Louisiana. [Hereinafter cited as FWS.]

[10]Pendergrass, "Stewards of the Waters," 172.

[11]Suzanne Hawes, interview by author, March 5, 1986.

[12]Cary W. Kerlin, Lafayette Field Supervisor, FWS, to Colonel Sands, September 21, 1979; Adlene Harrison, Regional Administrator, EPA, to Colonel Sands, March 4, 1981; Gary Hickman, Lafayette Area Manager, FWS, to General Thomas A. Sands, Reporting Officer, Atchafalaya Basin Project, January 13, 1982, all in FWS.

[13]*Feasibility Study*, 1:EIS-221.

[14]Frances E. Phillips, Acting Regional Administrator, EPA, to Colonel Sands, May 4, 1981, Hawes Files, Office of History, Headquarters, U.S. Army Corps of Engineers, Alexandria, Virginia).

[15]*Feasibility Study*, 1:46, 67–68.

[16]Ibid., 1:67.

[17]Information on the early history of the Avoca Island Levee comes from U.S. Army Corps of Engineers, New Orleans District, "Draft Environmental Statement: Atchafalaya Basin Floodway, Louisiana," 5 vols, February 1976, 3:39; *Feasibility Study*, 2: C–44.

[18]"Probable Adverse Impact of Construction of the Avoca Island Levee Extension," FWS fact sheet, no date, FWS.

[19]David W. Fruge, Acting Field Supervisor, Lafayette, to Jerry Dyson, Program Administrator, Office of Public Works, June 27, 1979, FWS.

[20]J. Burton Angelle, Secretary, Louisiana Department of Wildlife and Fisheries, to Roy Aguillard, Assistant Secretary, Office of Public Works, July 26, 1979, FWS.

[21]Bobby G. O'Barr, Chairman, Gulf of Mexico Fishery Management Council, to Colonel Sands, August 20, 1981, FWS; D. K. Ekberg, Chief, Environmental and Technical Services Division, National Oceanic and Atmospheric Administration, to Colonel Sands, August 20, 1981, FWS.

[22]*Feasibility Study*, 1:80–81.

[23]Cary W. Kerlin, Field Supervisor, Lafayette, to Colonel Sands, District Engineer, December 17, 1980, FWS.

[24]According to Cary Kerlin in a letter to Colonel Sands, March 5, 1981, FWS.

[25]U.S. Army Corps of Engineers, New Orleans District, "A Feasibility Report/Environmental Impact Statement on the Atchafalaya Basin Floodway System, Louisiana: An Interim Report of the Atchafalaya Basin (Water and Land Resources), Louisiana Study combined with a Phase I General Design Memorandum. Draft Main Report and Environmental Impact Statement," 5 vols. (New Orleans, June 1981). Volume I describes the tentatively selected plan on 189–202.

[26]Bob Marshall, "Landowners had Loudest Voice at Basin Meeting," *New Orleans Times-Picayune*, July 19, 1981.

[27]D. K. Ekberg, National Oceanic and Atmospheric Administration, to Colonel Sands, April 29, 1981, FWS.

[28]Soileau, Acting Field Supervisor, Lafayette, to Colonel Sands, May 3, 1981, FWS.

[29]Ibid.

[30]U.S. Department of the Interior, Fish and Wildlife Service, Division of Ecological Services, "Atchafalaya Basin Reports: Avoca Island Levee Extension and Water Management & Land Use Controls" (Lafayette: Field Office, May 1981), 40. The executive orders were issued in June 1978. EO 11988 dealt with floodplain management, and EO 11990 pertained to wetlands protection.

[31]Jesse J. Guidry, Secretary, Department of Wildlife and Fisheries, to Kai Midboe, Office of Intergovernmental Affairs, Office of the Governor, May 5, 1981, FWS. Guidry was the recent appointee of the new Republican governor, David Treen.

[32]*Feasibility Study*, 1:67; and 2:B-74.

[33]"Commission Overrules Experts; Supports Levee Project at Morgan City," *Alexandria Daily Town Talk*, April 21, 1982.

PART IV

# RACE

# SIMPLY A MATTER OF BLACK AND WHITE: THE TRANSFORMATION OF RACE AND POLITICS IN TWENTIETH CENTURY NEW ORLEANS*

Arnold R. Hirsch

## The Voting Rights Acts and the Evolution of Black Politics

The Voting Rights Act of 1965 gravely altered the political landscape and was felt far beyond the political arena. In 1964, 63 percent of the city's eligible white population was registered to vote, but only 28 percent of the blacks could make that claim; the latter represented but 17.5 percent of the registered electorate. By the summer of 1966, 42 percent of the black eligibles had signed up (the comparable white figure remained at 63 percent) and blacks constituted 25.2 percent of the city's registered voters. With New Orleans only belatedly feeling the tug of white flight, the potential for future demographic—and political—shifts seemed enormous.[1]

Equally striking, however, were the ways in which the Voting Rights Act served as a social force. Blacks could exert political influence only through discipline, organization, and a high degree of racial solidarity. Those who mobilized voters made increasingly explicit racial appeals, reinforced the prevailing racial dualism, obfuscated all other sources of identification, and accelerated an ongoing process now generations old. The heat of repeated political battles, fought out increasingly along racial lines as color came to replace party as an organizing principle on the local level, served as a forge, purging elements that failed to line up on one side or the other of the great racial divide. If racial interests were not always clear—or perhaps subject to manipulation—there was no doubt that they moved more frequently to center stage.

The 1965 mayoralty showed the transforming power of the Voting Rights Act as well as the dogged persistence of powerful local traditions. Jimmy Fitzmorris, a Chep Morrison protégé and Vic Schiro's major opponent, found every chink in the mayor's

*First published as Chapter 6 in Arnold R. Hirsch and Joseph Logsdon, eds., *Creole New Orleans: Race and Americanization* (Baton Rouge: Louisiana State University Press, © 1992), 288-319.

racial armor, promising to hire without regard to race, end discrimination in city hall, reopen the city's swimming pools, and appoint a biracial human relations committee. Schiro, who had picked up the race issue as a matter of convenience, now took out ads in the *Louisiana Weekly* and cut deals with the old black auxiliaries in the Morrison manner.[2]

Despite his recent record, the incumbent had enough success to ensure victory. A. L. Davis had been fired and arrested by Schiro but supported him along with the rest of the Orleans Parish Progressive Voters League (OPPVL); so did A. P. Tureaud and Avery Alexander. Fitzmorris's ties to labor won him the endorsement of Chink Henry and the Crescent City Independent Voters League (CCIVL), and he added to that the backing of the *Louisiana Weekly* and those who were not impressed by the mayor's "grandstanding." It was not enough. The important point, however, was that his first post—Voting Rights Act campaign was carried out, according to the *Louisiana Weekly*, in the "absence of the hobgoblins of race hate." It was also notable that the black vote remained fragmented. It was neither sufficient nor independent enough to strike out on its own.[3]

The Voting Rights Act also stimulated the opportunistic creation of a new range of black organizations. The two most important groups were the Community Organization for Urban Politics (COUP) and the Southern Organization for Unified Leadership (SOUL). If, as the *Louisiana Weekly* claimed, blacks found themselves "plunged into a sea of political maneuver," COUP and SOUL were two quickly fashioned vessels carved from different, long-standing tendencies within the larger black community. Designed to capitalize instantaneously on New Orleans's radically altered political opportunities, both groups were narrowly and conventionally political. Literally born out of the need to corral black voters in particular legislative races, they eschewed systemic change in favor of the more immediate rewards the system now had to offer. They thus differed not only from the National Association for the Advancement of Colored People (NAACP) but even from the older political groups, which, although they had sought tangible advantage, also maintained some sense of pushing a communal agenda. Setting themselves up as intermediaries to broker the black vote, the new groups became convenient channels for white politicians who were still isolated from a black community they could no longer ignore.

SOUL, as its acronym clearly implied, embodied the heightened racial consciousness and militance of the civil rights era. Its links to that movement were explicit because the organization itself was the political offshoot of New Orleans' Congress of Racial Equality (CORE). CORE attorney Nils Douglas originally ran for the state legislature from the downtown Ninth Ward in 1963, but it was his next stab at that seat, initiated a year after the passage of the Voting Rights Act, that served as the impetus for SOUL's creation. Though unsuccessful, Douglas became the first black candidate to lead the pack in a first primary since Reconstruction; and SOUL, which survived the election, became an important downtown black political organization.[4] Fully accepting, indeed championing,

America's duochromatic social framework, SOUL stressed racial identity and mobilization as the best way to squeeze concessions out of the "system."

Similarly, COUP coalesced around Charles Elloie's unsuccessful Seventh Ward race for state representative. Led initially by CORE-affiliated attorney Robert Collins, COUP brought together young black professionals who represented the "assimilationist" and conservative tendencies found in that downtown creole stronghold. Its key leaders such as Henry Braden IV and Sidney Barthelemy had not been conspicuous in the civil rights movement, and indeed, as their Urban League orientation demonstrated, they were more adept at cultivating white contacts. If SOUL tried to capture the new racial assertiveness, COUP traveled the more well-worn path of accommodation and relied heavily on white familiarity and support.[5]

Most notably, however, the first real breakthrough made possible by the Voting Rights Act resulted not from these institutional initiatives but rather from the intersection of the new opportunity structure and the most deeply rooted independent black force in New Orleans—the "unassimilated" creole leadership of the NAACP. Victory came with Dutch Morial's election to the Louisiana legislature in 1967. Always a man in a hurry, Morial became the first black elected to the Louisiana House of Representatives in the modern era as well as the first black graduate of Louisiana State University Law School (in 1954) and the first black assistant United States attorney in New Orleans. He would later append to these accomplishments a veritable string of other firsts: first black to serve as Juvenile Court judge, first on the Fourth Circuit Court of Appeals, and, ultimately, the first black mayor of New Orleans. Dutch Morial was himself a civil rights revolution.

Morial's initial forays into electoral politics came well before the Voting Rights Act. He campaigned in 1959 for a seat on the Democratic State Central Committee and did so again in 1963 from the downtown Ninth Ward. Intended both to stimulate and benefit from augmented black voter registration (the NAACP conducted a registration drive in the lower Ninth Ward in late 1962), Morial's second race coincided with the failure of another black candidate to make the runoff for the Louisiana legislature by a single vote in the uptown Twentieth District (Wards 1 and 2). By the end of 1964, Morial had established a legal residence in that district at 1242 Magazine Street, and by mid-1967 the NAACP Youth Council was conducting a voter registration campaign headquartered at 1242 Magazine that included Wards 1 and 2. Morial won his election in the first primary by a majority of 107 votes and then won the suit brought by a disgruntled white opponent who challenged his residential qualifications. A Seventh Ward creole, an unsuccessful Ninth Ward candidate, Morial found his first safe electoral haven in uptown New Orleans. The *Louisiana Weekly* concluded that he provided "new direction and a new political freedom to Negro voters . . . throughout the entire city."[6]

In his background, his vision, and his willingness to challenge racial barriers—his determination to confront the "fanaticism of caste"—Morial remained the most prominent legatee of the creole protest tradition. Born in 1929, he represented a new generation, one yet another step removed from the pitched battles of Reconstruction and the embittered resistance to the imposition of Jim Crow, but nonetheless with a clear connection to that legacy. His link, mentor, and law partner was none other than A. P. Tureaud, and if, like Tureaud, he was fair-complexioned enough to have "passed," there is no doubt that he "identified black." If anything, the passage of time blurred the distinctions that might have tempered that identification. The last of six children, Morial was the only one in his family who spoke no French. And he had no memory of his family's antebellum status. But as John Higham has noted of European ethnic groups, "it has been possible to shed the outward marks of foreign origin without undergoing total assimilation. Some differences of attitude or world view linger after the group itself has ceased to figure largely in a person's consciousness." So it was with Morial.[7]

Morial's identification with and service to New Orleans' black community was reciprocated with deeply felt pride and admiration. Morial moved freely through black New Orleans during the civil rights era, recruiting plaintiffs with the assistance of the Interdenominational Ministerial Alliance, raising funds in churches of all faiths, and mobilizing marchers for the demonstrations of the early 1960s. The civil rights movement was thus an ethnic crucible melding black New Orleans into a single whole to a greater extent than it had been since the colonial era. As the local attorney, along with Tureaud, most closely identified with the dismantling of Jim Crow in New Orleans, and the president of the NAACP (1963-1965), he remained in the forefront of black protest, and his entry into the political arena was, as he put it, merely the "logical extension" of his earlier career. He consequently enjoyed "a degree of acceptance" in the community even as that community took greater pride in its "blackness." For Morial, however, the goal of the struggle against invidious racial distinctions remained the obliteration of caste or color privilege, not the mere manipulation of the existing racial order. His fight became, in his own words, "more of a moral and human rights thing that affects all people." It was a vision that owed more to his cultural antecedents than it did to the emerging racial consciousness of the 1960s.[8]

The full implications of the Voting Rights Act rose into sharp relief with the city elections of 1969-1970. Because of the chief executive's two-term charter limitation, the race for city hall was wide open. Ultimately, a councilman-at-large Moon Landrieu won that campaign by garnering over 90 percent of the black vote and only a minority of the white vote in a rare general election in which a surprisingly strong Republican showing resulted from explicit white concerns over rising black political strength. Landrieu's success in solidifying the black vote while endorsed by the new black political organizations also seemingly overturned a tradition of endemic fractiousness and permitted the perception that the new groups were, indeed, major players. Finally, that same election witnessed Dutch Morial's citywide race for councilman-at-large, a seemingly premature effort inasmuch as blacks constituted no more than 30 percent of the electorate, yet one that came surprisingly close, failing by only about 5,000 votes out of 160,000.

These developments were important not for their individual significance but for their interrelationship and consequences for black empowerment and independence.

In running for mayor, Moon Landrieu seemed to be a natural choice for the black community. As a freshmen legislator in Baton Rouge during the school crisis of 1960-1961, Landrieu opposed the segregationists, denying them the unanimity they ardently sought. As a leader in the city council (1965-1969) he responded sensitively to black needs, facilitating the removal of the Confederate flag from council chambers and pushing through the ordinance establishing a biracial human relations committee near the end of Vic Schiro's second term. And as a candidate for mayor he promised passage of a public accommodations ordinance that would enhance the protection offered by existing federal law and the appointments of blacks to key positions in government. Landrieu, moreover, actively sought to run on a citywide ticket with an at-large black candidate for the city council; and when Dutch Morial's candidacy preempted the field, Landrieu offered Morial his endorsement. Supported by SOUL, COUP, and much of the newer black political leadership, Landrieu positioned himself well in the black community.[9]

But in a crowded first primary field of twelve, Landrieu drew no more than 39 percent of the black vote, sharing it with Judge David Gertler, Bill Guste, councilman John Petre, and runoff opponent Jimmy Fitzmorris. Gertler and Guste had connections among New Orleans' blacks, and the traditional political fragmentation of that community clearly persisted in the 1969 mayoralty. It was only in the runoff—after Fitzmorris calculatedly rejected Landrieu's guarantees on public accommodations and appointments and failed to endorse Dutch Morial—that the black community rose as a unit to defeat a contender who was clearing running as the "white candidate." That solidarity only increased when Republican Ben Toledano pursued Landrieu in the general election, his candidacy fueled by white anxiety over the decisive leverage black voters demonstrated in the Democratic primary.[10]

The belated consolidation of the black vote, however, belied its earlier diffusion and Landrieu's apparent efforts to wrap it up early in the campaign. Despite later denials, Landrieu had close ties to a new uptown group, the Black Organization for Leadership Development (BOLD), that sponsored a "Black Primary" in the hopes of eliminating intrablack competition while mobilizing for the upcoming mayoralty. On the surface, the September 27, 1969, Black Primary seemed little different from earlier efforts to stimulate racial and political solidarity. It targeted the overlapping uptown councilmanic District B and Fourth District assessor's races where, given New Orleans's relatively mixed neighborhoods, intrablack divisions meant continued white victories. In calling for a privately held Black Primary, BOLD wished to encourage black interest and unity and also certainly hoped to improve the chances of one of its own leaders, Jim Singleton, in the District B race.

But there were other motives as well. Black candidate and one-time NAACP president Bennett Ross attacked the Black Primary and tied it to Moon Landrieu. "What the Black Primary sponsors are really interested in is having two candidates, one in the assessor's race and one in the councilmanic race, who will carry the banner of a particular mayoralty candidate. . . . The sponsors of the Black Primary, BOLD, the vehicle of SOUL, T[otal] C[ommunity] A[ction], and the Urban League [desire only] . . . to . . . garner a few votes for their man for mayor." In linking BOLD to SOUL, he noted the irony that many of the primary's organizers were not registered to vote in the district and came from the Eighth and Ninth wards, where they "all enjoy[ed] healthy helpings at the white man's feeding trough."[11]

SOUL, TCA, and the Urban League all had strong ties to Landrieu. The Urban League, particularly, provided much of his moderate-to-liberal business support and connected him to a particular segment of the emerging black leadership; he would turn to that link time and again in selecting young black professionals to serve in his administration. And though SOUL's support of Landrieu was never in doubt, its deep involvement in the Black Primary became evident when organizer Don Hubbard left his downtown bailiwick to assist in SOUL's unsuccessful effort, as the *Louisiana Weekly* put it, "to extend its political influence uptown via the Black Primary."[12]

Ironically, the Black Primary turned out fewer than 15 percent of the area's sixteen thousand black voters, stirring less interest and unity than did the subsequent galvanizing negative candidacies of Jimmy Fitzmorris and Republican Ben Toledano. Landrieu's solid black support materialized only in the second primary and the general election. It was also stark testimony to the overwhelming significance of the Voting Rights Act. Capturing roughly 90 percent of a 75 percent black turnout against Fitzmorris and nearly 99 percent of a 77 percent black turnout against Toledano, Landrieu received more black votes than white in each instance.[13]

There is no question that Morial's nearly successful citywide race for the city council greatly aided Landrieu by bolstering black registration and turnout. Morial did not endorse Landrieu in the first primary, but he did in the second, and the two campaigned from then on as a "ticket." Landrieu contended that he "did everything [he] could" to get Morial elected. But Morial—obviously feeling the sting of a narrow defeat—remembered that they appeared together only in black neighborhoods and believed that he lent considerably more to Landrieu's campaign than vice versa. Reflecting on the event years later, Landrieu admitted that Morial "may be right." In his postelection statement, though, Dutch Morial captured the significance of the 1969 campaign. "Our people have exerted an influence in the recent election," he declared, "that will not soon be forgotten."[14]

## The Landrieu Years

Moon Landrieu, like so many other postwar New Orleans political figures, was a Chep Morrison protégé. He nonetheless differed from Morrison in significant ways. First, there was the simple question of timing. Morrison governed at the beginning of the civil rights era whereas Landrieu did not assume office until the 1960s were a receding—if still vivid—memory. There is no question that Landrieu's vision was sharpened by the struggles he witnessed in the turbulent decades preceding his election as mayor, and as a consequence he did not suffer the political paralysis that doomed Morrison when he found himself whipsawed by the winds of change and gales of reaction. Despite continuing bitter resistance, Landrieu saw and brought the future to New Orleans. Second, if Landrieu's political calculus proved unerring, his actions on racial matters could not be dismissed as merely self-serving. He displayed political courage and a moral vision that was alien to Morrison, for example, in confronting the rabidly segregationist Louisiana legislature during the school crisis.

There is no question that Landrieu saw the necessity of breaking with tradition on race. Indeed, where Morrison extolled the "customs and mores" of the South, Landrieu believed that his "single greatest accomplishment" was the "significant progress" made in opening up opportunities for blacks "through the political process." There was much to substantiate the claim. At the beginning of 1970, blacks occupied only 19.4 percent (1,833 out of 8,219) of the positions in the city's classified civil service; eight years later they claimed 43 percent (4,304 out of 10,009). Landrieu also kept his promise to name black department heads—director of property management Andrew Sanchez and twenty-nine-year-old welfare director Sidney Barthelemy were the first—and he went even further by naming Robert Tucker an executive assistant and ultimately appointing Terrence Duvernay as chief administrative officer.[15] And if the new black presence in government was unprecedented, Landrieu also did not hesitate to use his political leverage to create opportunities in the private sector as well.

Such unprecedented actions contributed greatly to Landrieu's standing and popularity in New Orleans and enabled him to run for reelection in 1973 without serious opposition. He won the first Democratic primary with about 75 percent of the vote and discouraged Republicans from contesting the general election. When he left office in 1978, he received a nearly unanimous chorus of accolades from the local press.[16]

The real key to Landrieu's popularity, though, was not simply his perceptive shattering of obsolete customs but his skillful maintenance of those that were still useful. If, in the post-civil rights age, racial relationships had to be restructured, it was Landrieu's ability to work within existing political traditions and within the fully Americanized racial dichotomy that fostered change without pain. Landrieu was able to offer new opportunities to blacks without grievously antagonizing whites because he was cutting large new slices off an expanding economic pie. Landrieu's exceptional skill in obtaining significant federal revenues provided a new source of funding that he directed into black channels with great political dexterity. And on the state level, especially after black votes helped elect Governor Edwin W. Edwards in 1971, additional largesse came from Baton Rouge. One of the largest plums of the Landrieu years—the Louisiana Superdome—was a state project that conveniently fell into his lap. The result was that Landrieu did not have to take anything away from existing interests to reward new friends. And in specifically providing new opportunities for blacks, Landrieu did not have to face the more daunting and politically dangerous task of providing opportunity generically across the board. White interests could be protected in their traditional bailiwicks, and even those initially hostile to Landrieu's precedent-shattering initiatives could ultimately be recruited as allies.

Landrieu's adroit political maneuvering led at least one journalistic critic to swim against the tide of praise bestowed on the outgoing mayor in 1978 by referring to him as the "major domo of New Orleans sleaze." Bill Rushton's unflattering portrayal focused not on Landrieu's racial breakthroughs but on a "series of urban policies whose sole beneficiaries were his major campaign contributors."[17] In dealing with black New Orleans, the practice of traditional politics meant the creation of a patronage network in which rewards were doled out in the established manner—the servings were larger and more regular, but the ladle remained in white hands.

Landrieu felt that he was merely engaging in individualistic, tangible, and pragmatic politics—the essence of American urban governance. He provided opportunity on a nondiscriminatory basis—he "opened up" the system. But that was precisely the point. By providing access, he muted the call for systemic change. Black Louisiana politicians could behave as white Louisiana politicians did; indeed, those who adapted most quickly to the existing political ethos would most assuredly reap the largest prizes. New Orleans' reified system of ethnic patronage politics remained—as elsewhere—essentially conservative and incapable of fundamentally altering conditions for the city's poor masses.

The initial conduit for federal poverty program money in New Orleans was Total Community Action, Inc. It was created in 1965 as an agency outside city hall because Vic Schiro wanted no part of the controversial program and did not see its possibilities. The vacuum at the top enabled councilman-at-large Landrieu, according to *Times-Picayune* reporter James Gillis, to "exercise considerable influence . . . in connection with the Great Society programs." Ostensibly nonpolitical, TCA created a multi-million-dollar string of neighborhood centers, child development centers, and job and recreational programs; but as columnist Iris Kelso noted, its payroll quickly became "the backbone of many black political organizations." Key black Landrieu allies such as Edwin Lombard, Sidney Barthelemy, and Jim Singleton were, at one time or another, TCA board members; others, such as Sherman Copelin, Don Hubbard, Dorothy Mae Taylor, Robert Tucker, and Terrence Duvernay, were employees; and board member Barthelemy held four different positions with TCA between 1967 and 1969. TCA was, as reporter Gillis asserted and Black Primary critic Ross contended, a "political haven for a large number of Landrieu's black supporters." Similarly, Singleton, Copelin, Duvernay, and Lombard found occasional sustenance through the Model Cities program. And during the Landrieu years, Henry Braden IV directed the federally funded "New Orleans Plan" through the local Urban League. Barthelemy, Braden, and Tucker were all founders of COUP and central Urban League figures; Singleton and Taylor represented BOLD; and Copelin, Hubbard, Lombard, and department head Sanchez carried SOUL's banner. Only the tip of the proverbial iceberg, these agencies, programs, and jobs altered the character of black politics in New Orleans.[18]

Consciously cultivating a newer, young generation of black leaders, Landrieu made them the most direct beneficiaries of the civil rights struggles even as their success diverted their energies into narrower, shallower political channels. SOUL, the political progeny of CORE, showed the nature of the transformation. After his first election, Landrieu recalled that veteran civil rights leader Lolis Elie, Robert Collins, and Nils Douglas "didn't want anything and didn't know what to ask for" from the new mayor; they were concerned about appearing "co-opted." Elie never did take anything, and Landrieu steered the others away from symbolic prizes toward less visible but potential more remunerative positions.[19] The older SOUL leadership, however, was soon supplanted by former CORE activist Don Hubbard and Dillard University graduate Sherman Copelin, who completed the transformation of a civil rights initiative into a conventional political organization. SOUL's new guiding spirits would never be at a loss in suggesting just reward for services rendered. The frequent and calculated use of the rhetoric of racial militance proved insurance enough against charges of co-optation.

COUP had an ever shorter road to travel. Its leaders, for the most part, had not been active participants in the pitched battles for civil rights, had already established close ties to the white community, and, indeed, entered Landrieu's office with a bill of particulars. Landrieu recalled exchanging words with Sidney Barthelemy over some specific demands before reaching an accommodation. COUP's directorate, in short, echoed the sentiments of the *Louisiana Weekly* when it extolled, rather than condemned, the "spoils system." "We must 'play the game' just as others have played it," the *Weekly* declared. "We know that in order to rise within the system you must use the system to your advantage."[20]

The *Louisiana Weekly's* euphoria over the strategic placement of a new generation of black leaders at the beginning of Landrieu's administration gave way to questions at its close. By 1978, it noted COUP's success in getting Sidney Barthelemy elected state senator and then councilman-at-large, in Henry Braden's elevation to Barthelemy's vacated senate seat, and in Robert Collins' appointment as the first black federal judge in "the Deep South Eastern District." "The important question now," the *Weekly* asserted, "is . . . will COUP measure up and be able . . . to create long standing economic opportunities not only for its immediate supporters, but for the black community at large?" The obvious answer, of course, was that COUP's agenda was already on the table. Indeed, Rodolphe Desdunes' castigation of early twentieth century black political operatives seemed prophetic and applicable to the current crop of "political leaders who worked on the principle that personal recognition is race elevation, and that the race is never so well represented as when he holds a sinecure as a 'representative Negro.'" COUP's domination of the city's CETA program (funded under the federal Comprehensive Employment and Training Act) epitomized their approach. Injecting heavy doses of nepotism and favoritism into the hiring process, they provided more immediate support for their college educated, middle-class associates than for the hard-core unemployed.[21]

SOUL's leadership proved even more adept at blending race and politics for profit. In a curious mix of newfangled militance and old-style politics, its directorate allegedly stimulated charges of "genocide" to threaten the publicly funded Family Health Foundation's (FHF) family planning mission while issuing "demands" for patronage. Nils Douglas and Don Hubbard, among others, eventually found slots on the FHF payroll, and Model Cities director Sherman Copelin reportedly received over $50,000 in payoffs designed to overcome community suspicions and facilitate the construction of FHF clinics in Model Cities neighborhoods. Such financial arrangements coincided with the cessation of intimidating demonstrations and ultimately resulted in the indictment and conviction of FHF executives who engaged in creative bookkeeping to cover their costs. "Unindicted co-conspirators" Copelin and Hubbard earned immunity for their testimony and rallied the black community on their behalf by attacking the "antagonistic reporting" of the white media.[22]

In many ways, however, it was the creation of Superdome Services, Inc. (SSI), that was the literal and symbolic capstone to the transformation of black politics in the Landrieu era. A freshly minted corporation whose initial ownership was more than three-quarters black, SSI received the contract to provide security, janitorial, and ticket services for the Superdome. James Gillis subsequently reported that "the formation of SSI was initiated from the office of Mayor Landrieu and the task of putting it together was assigned to Dan McClung, one of Landrieu's executive assistants." He created a corporate umbrella under which virtually all the mayor's black allies gathered and through which they used their political leverage to economic advantage. Within its first year of operation, SSI had nearly 250 permanent employees and tapped a pool of hundreds more. Directed by Sherman Copelin and Dan Hubbard, it constituted a small patronage army.[23]

Almost from the beginning, there were complaints about the inflated costs of SSI's negotiated "cost-plus" contract and its after-the-fact ratification by a state legislature dominated by Edwin Edwards. Charges of inefficiency and incompetence also dogged SSI during its early months. As the calls for investigation began to mount, Copelin's and Hubbard's involvement in the FHF scandals came to light.

Edwards' and Landrieu's political adversaries, as well as the local press—particularly the *Times-Picayune*—made the most of the charges. But both Landrieu and Copelin ably defended SSI from accusers they believed to be politically and racially motivated. The mayor pointedly noted that "it was perfectly acceptable" to enter negotiated contracts with established white interests that had the proper "social connections" and that the furor over such routine procedures erupted only when blacks became the beneficiaries. Responding to charges of SSI's inefficiencies, Copelin similarly raised questions about "sweetheart deals" with favored Dome users that did not provide enough revenue to service events. In sum, neither side entered the dispute with clean hands and each provided the other with ample ammunition.[24]

The political legacy of the Landrieu years, then, was—echoing Chep Morrison's experience—a mixed one. In granting access to government and dispensing the traditional, tangible rewards of politics, Landrieu had no parallel. But the black political community remained fragmented, held together only by the centripetal pull of its major white benefactor. Large numbers of black interests came together only in their support of Landrieu and in SSI—a profit-seeking venture that "was an in-house City Hall operation involving Mayor Landrieu's political subordinates.[25]

Moreover, it was ironic that black identification with scandals in TCA, FHF, CETA, and SSI did so much to undermine Landrieu's truly constructive efforts at overturning traditional white racial attitudes. The indictments and convictions that marked the various scams uncovered at TCA and FHF and the political exploitation of the CETA program and SSI burdened black politics with the image of corruption, reinforcing old prejudices.[26]

Even more significant, though, was the price paid by the black community in its loss of independence. To the degree that black political advances were tied to Landrieu's efforts and success, that administration's interests took precedence over all others. And there is no question that at least in the conventional political organizations, Landrieu's presence dominated.

The electoral breakthroughs of the Landrieu years were virtually all tied to the mayor's exertions. Israel Augustine's successful citywide judicial race in 1970 was notable for the biracial support it received because of Landrieu's strong backing and the campaign orchestrated by Landrieu's law partner Pascal Calogero. Similarly, in 1973, SOUL's Edwin Lombard (a "relatively unknown 27-year old attorney," according to the *Louisiana Weekly*) became the second black parochial (parishwide) official since Reconstruction when Landrieu appeared on television to boost his campaign for clerk of the Criminal District court—a move welcomed by Landrieu's executive assistant Dan McClung, who was guiding Lombard's effort. And lest anyone confuse such success with the black organizations' independent ability to churn out the vote, eleven other black candidates running for parochial offices suffered stunning first primary defeats. The 1973 campaign, as the *Louisiana Weekly* regretfully acknowledged, demonstrated black political weakness rather than strength. Finally, Sidney Barthelemy became the first black Louisiana state senator in nearly a century when Governor Edwards appointed the incumbent to the judiciary. In a district evenly split between white and black voters, Barthelemy ran successfully against three white opponents with Landrieu's backing in a 1974 special election and was unopposed in the following year's regular contest.[27]

None of this, of course, inspired black independence. Indeed, even the "militant" SOUL's ties to Landrieu were so close (as when it backed Pascal Calogero in his 1972 race for the state supreme court against black attorney Revius Ortique) that in some quarters its members were called "Moon's Coons." It was not surprising, then, that when black community groups marched to protest police brutality and the Landrieu administration's inattention to that problem in 1977, civil rights forces such as NAACP and Southern Christian Leadership Conference strode in front, while the conventional political organizations such as BOLD, SOUL, COUP, and OPPVL—and the Urban

League (derisively called the "Bourbon League" by some of the NAACP's creole leaders)—were conspicuously absent.[28]

Even the appearance of A. L. Davis on the New Orleans city council in 1975 resulted from white discretion rather than the mobilization of black political strength. A vacancy on the council resulted when a member assumed a seat on the Municipal Court. With the reapportionment of the council in litigation—its 1973 elections were canceled and the case was not resolved for another three years—the six remaining white councilmen selected Davis to represent the majority black district. And when special council elections were finally held in 1976, Mayor Landrieu supported the status quo even to the point, it was rumored, of short-circuiting challenges by SOUL-backed candidates not only uptown but also in SOUL's own backyard, where a white incumbent had to face a new constituency that was nearly 50 percent black.[29]

Nothing else rendered the patron-client relationship so clear, and nothing threatened it until the two-term limitation forced the black political organizations to look to the future. Both COUP and SOUL acted entirely in character. COUP was clearly grooming Sidney Barthelemy to be the city's first black mayor and opted for the traditional route that had served both Vic Schiro and Landrieu. First he would make a race for councilman-at-large and later pursue the big prize. Never having strolled through a political door that had not been safely held open for him, Barthelemy chose a cautious path—he would wait.

SOUL, despite its militant posturing, took a different route. It set out to anoint and make itself indispensable to the next white mayor. It found a ready ally in state senator Nat Kiefer, a fellow downtowner, who was a floor leader for Edwin Edwards and chairman of the investigative committee probing improprieties at the Superdome. Eagerly pursuing the mayoralty, Kiefer was obviously in a position to help—or hurt—SSI and SOUL and had, in the process, made a bitter enemy of Moon Landrieu. As Sherman Copelin and Don Hubbard read the future and moved into Kiefer's orbit, Landrieu used his still considerable influence to cultivate his own loyal faction within SOUL and precipitated a struggle for dominance. The bitter infighting led to litigation that eventually confirmed Copelin's and Hubbard's control of the organization. The fratricidal warfare for SOUL's soul on the eve of the 1977 mayoralty indicated the depths to which white leaders were implicated even in the group's internal politics.[30]

## Dutch Morial and the Survival of Creole Protest

Unlike the leaders of COUP and SOUL, Dutch Morial was neither disposed to wait until the white electorate seemed ready for a black mayor nor willing merely to accept largesse from white sponsors in need of black support. Throughout the Landrieu administration, Morial had maintained a low political profile. He returned to his legislative seat following his defeat in the 1969 city council race and remained there until the end of the 1970 legislative session, when Gov. John McKeithen elevated him to the Orleans Parish

Juvenile Court. Following a successful race for the Fourth Circuit Court of Appeals in 1972, Morial spent the Landrieu years literally and figuratively on the bench, insulated from the day-to-day political maelstrom that swirled about city hall. He seemed, for example, to be the only major black political figure not involved with SSI or some other Landrieu-affiliated project. When he announced his candidacy for mayor in 1977, he literally seemed to have come from nowhere and quickly became a wild card that disrupted the professionals' carefully laid plans. For those unfamiliar with the history of New Orleans' black community—a community that now constituted about 43 percent of the total electorate—his candidacy seemed quixotic at best.[31]

Certainly COUP and SOUL knew about Morial. Moon Landrieu recalled a 1969 campaign meeting when it became clear to him that Morial "never played with these guys" and that there was no "personal affection" between them. Trying to solidify support for his at-large council race, Morial had launched into what Landrieu considered an "astounding talk." Morial told them that he would not give them a penny and that they should be raising money for him rather than vice versa. As far as Landrieu could see, Morial "threw down the gauntlet" before those groups for "no reason"; and as far as he could tell, Morial did not get the effort out of the black organizations a "different approach" might have achieved. How valuable a more devoted effort would have proven is arguable. What was clear was that Morial still refused to "play with these guys." Landrieu did. Each had his reasons.[32]

The difference between Morial, on one hand, and Copelin, Hubbard, Braden, and Barthelemy, on the other, was best described by Rodolphe Desdunes seventy years earlier when he elaborated on the "two distinct schools of politics" that characterized the "Latin Negro" and the "Anglo Saxon." Differing in "aspiration and . . . method," the former made "every effort to acquire merits" while the latter tried "to gain advantages." Raising the ghosts of an earlier generation of Latin-creole leaders, Desdunes also spoke of the "moral Negro" who fought to "have the Negro *respected* rather than *protected*." Such leaders, in his mind, contrasted most favorably with the more "practical," self-serving political leadership he saw emerging at the end of Reconstruction.[33] Similarly, in his perceptions, values, and, ultimately, goals, Morial *was* different from the professional black politicians. Consequently, despite the apparent unity of race, the leaders of COUP and SOUL found it easier to work with Moon Landrieu than Dutch Morial; they understood one another and shared the same assumptions. Morial, as Landrieu recalled that 1969 meeting, seemed to have his "own agenda." Indeed, he did. And it is no wonder, then, that Morial's performance should seem so incomprehensible to Landrieu, who was primarily concerned about winning an election. Morial was, too—but in his own way, on his own terms, and for his own reasons. When he offered his black counterparts nothing more than a chance to fulfill their "sense of duty" in supporting his candidacy, Landrieu considered it a needless provocation.

There was also a particular racial vision that survived in the creole radicalism embodied by Morial that remained at odds with the prevailing American social order.

Although Morial and others like him displayed fierce pride in their racial heritage, they wanted to create a society free of what Desdunes called the "dissensions of caste." Indeed, it was an article of faith for Desdunes that "Negroes, in treating of essential principles, should cease to be Negroes, in order to live, think, feel and act as true Americans, just as Brown, Garrison, Lovejoy, Phillips, Lincoln and Long[fellow], ceased to be whites, that they might become the instruments of loving humanity. The white man's history is the black man's study."[34] Morial's struggle was to transcend racial barriers and to make such distinctions meaningless. Displaying a finely tuned racial consciousness and more genuine militance than most in confronting a society that adhered to invidious racial distinctions, Morial pursued neither black separatism nor chauvinism but a single society, open to all on the basis of merit, free of the chains of race prejudice.

In contrast, the very existence and success of COUP and SOUL depended on the persistence of a racially divided and highly race-conscious environment. COUP set itself up to mediate between black and white, occupying a middle ground as "black" leaders who enjoyed—and were enamored with—"white" support. The bridge between two societies, these brokers seemingly had no purpose beyond securing their own favored position and that of their sponsors. Any serious effort to redistribute society's resources would effectively end their role as mediators, as would the emergence of a unified society in which race was irrelevant. Their stake was in the status quo. Race for SOUL's leaders was a lever to be used to pry concessions from whites in the post-civil rights era. For them, too, it was therefore absolutely essential that society remain racially segmented and highly race conscious. A society that operated on the basis of racial difference and distinction was not, for them, abhorrent—it provided their living. They were amply rewarded for accepting the American racial dualism and for working within its framework. If, to whites, COUP and SOUL represented cooperation and confrontation, respectively, neither challenged the fundamental structure of the prevailing political order.

With Morial out of the political limelight for much of the 1970s, the articulation of that vision—as well as evidence of its tenacious persistence—came from the institutional incarnation of creole radicalism in New Orleans, the local branch of the NAACP. Although Morial was not visibly active in its deliberations, the NAACP took stands on desegregation in higher education and on reapportionment with which its former president had "no quarrel" and that set Morial and the NAACP apart from those more comfortably ensconced in a fully Americanized racial order.

In the early 1970s, the NAACP reopened the issue of maintaining a dual system of higher education nearly a century after P. B. S. Pinchback offered his support for the Redeemers' state constitution in exchange for the creation of Southern University. In proposing the creation of a unitary system, the NAACP was well aware that in the years following Pinchback's accommodation strong black interests had arisen that "were adamant in their opposition to any action that would eliminate separate black schools or alter their identity." But though it urged the maintenance and expansion of private black institutions, the NAACP did not believe that black colleges "should . . . [get] significant support from public funds" because such support placed these schools under white control. Its conclusion that blacks would receive equity only when "state authorities cannot single out black people in separate facilities" led to an inescapable recommendation for merging the black and white schools despite the acknowledged "difficulties and sacrifices." In making that choice, the NAACP approvingly quoted W. E. B. DuBois' comment that the *Brown* decision presented blacks with a "cruel dilemma." "They must eventually surrender race solidarity and the idea of American Negro culture," DuBois asserted, "to the concept of world humanity, above race and nation."[35]

Similarly, the reapportionment controversy that wrecked the city council in the 1970s led the NAACP to articulate a vision that was rejected by the more Americanized segments of the community, both black and white. When following the 1970 census, the all-white New Orleans city council proposed a reapportionment plan that was an obvious racial gerrymander, it triggered four years of litigation. Suggested compromises included the expansion of the seven-member council to nine, or even eleven, in efforts to satisfy sitting councilmen and guarantee a certain number of new "black" seats. Both the *Louisiana Weekly* and the black political organizations championed expansion as the best "method of getting two or three blacks on the City Council," but the NAACP rejected that course. Allison Chapital voiced the association's determination not to "support any plan merely to have one or two hand-picked machine politician blacks placed on the Council." The NAACP proposed instead the retention of the existing system that elective five councilmen from districts and two at large and outlined what it perceived to be an equitable redrawing of the district boundaries. Under the NAACP proposal there would be one district with a black voting majority, the possibility of two others (if blacks worked at registration—here was an opportunity, not a guarantee), and the need, in any case, to build multiracial coalitions in a small number of large districts. It never had a chance. Councilman Jimmy Moreau adopted the format of the NAACP plan, altered its substance to minimize black influence, and successfully urged its acceptance on his colleagues. The Moreau Plan was eventually upheld by the U. S. Supreme Court in 1976.[36]

Given their differences, it was not surprising that the black political organizations greeted Morial's announced 1977 candidacy with less than overwhelming enthusiasm. And they certainly must have been taken aback by his willingness to risk a citywide race so soon after two other blacks—Robert Tucker and Sidney Cates—suffered crushing defeats in their races for the at-large seats in the special city council elections of 1976. For the political professionals and conventional thinkers, the time was not right and Morial was not their man. Still, he persisted, and in charting that course he presented the black organizations with a "cruel dilemma" of their own.

For SOUL, the decision was easy because it had already been made. In backing Nat Kiefer in his 1975 race for the state senate, SOUL had made one of its rare breaks with Moon Landrieu, evidently deciding that the waning influence of a lame-duck mayor presented fewer possibilities than did support for the heir apparent. SOUL also saw the advantage in having a white mayor. Landrieu, despite his record, still felt dependent on the black organizations to mobilize their communities on his behalf. He could not appeal over them or work around them the way Dutch Morial could. The result was that even though Landrieu was determined "not to replace white incompetents with black incompetents," his power to discipline his black allies—as was evident in the SSI case—was sharply circumscribed by their political leverage. He needed them—as, presumably, any white mayor would. SOUL's leaders, moreover, had learned valuable (and lucrative) lessons in provoking white anxiety and intimidating the leaders of the Family Health Foundation. Facing a black mayor—particularly one who refused to guarantee patronage as a matter of principle—was another matter. Although some sense of ethnic difference still persisted (Sherman Copelin joked about needing a visa to get into the Seventh Ward), Morial represented, more than anything else, a threat to SOUL's interests. Indeed, in one of the rare instances of agreement between Morial and media critic Iris Kelso, both perceived that a Morial victory would mean that "there won't be any more black political leaders who can mau-mau the Mayor, claim to represent blacks, and walk off with all the rewards."[37]

COUP had additional considerations. There were long-standing personal rivalries, particularly between Morial and the Bradens, that grew out of their shared communal base, the old creole Seventh Ward. But their common base also made it difficult for COUP to oppose a "favorite son" who promised to become the city's first black mayor. Still, Sidney Barthelemy's ambitions and the fear that COUP's support for two blacks at the top of the ticket (Morial for mayor, Barthelemy for councilman-at-large) might appear to be an attempted black takeover (they were still worried about alienating whites) made Morial's endorsement anything but automatic. Finally, after debating three hours and taking five ballots, COUP issued a lukewarm endorsement for Morial. Patron-client ties were still very much in evidence at Nat Kiefer's allies, as well as those tied to the candidacy of Chep Morrison's son Toni, tried unsuccessfully to win approval for their sponsors. COUP president Monk Dupre sounded almost apologetic when it was all over: "We didn't want to be considered racist . . . and we wouldn't have endorsed Dutch just because he is black. But he is qualified."[38]

The jockeying for the black vote was completed when Moon Landrieu furnished campaign assistance and an endorsement for Toni Morrison. Once a member of the Young CCDA, Landrieu was now in a position to give Chep's son a boost. As the fourth major mayoral candidate, Joe DiRosa, made little pretense about pursuing black voters, Morial, Kiefer, and Morrison were left dueling over that turf.

Interestingly, Kiefer had not only pocketed SOUL's support but had that of the CCIVL, BOLD's Dorothy Mae Taylor and Jim Singleton, and, remarkably, the *Louisiana Weekly*. He had done his homework. Toni Morrison, moreover, had Landrieu's help in picking up A. L. Davis and the OPPVL. And though Morial had COUP's less-than-ringing endorsement, it was clear to columnist Iris Kelso that "COUP doesn't really want Dutch Morial to be elected mayor." Despite running without the substantive or (with one exception even the nominal support of the major black political interests, Morial led the field and picked up 58 percent of the black vote. The primary tally was all the more remarkable given the real fear that Morial might be unelectable in the runoff. Blacks still represented only a minority of registered voters, and many of those given to shrewd calculation undoubtedly tried to pick a white winner in preference to going down with a black loser. Morial surprised them all. His long years of service, his identification with the cause of civil rights, and his independence stood him in good stead. His unshakable black base emasculated the Kiefer and Morrison campaigns and pushed him into the runoff with Joe DiRosa.[39]

Even after his strong showing, Morial's candidacy hardly became a racial crusade for the professionals. COUP's reticence remained evident, and SOUL's Hubbard displayed his "pragmatism" by asserting that "politics is the art of the possible. I'm interested in backing somebody who can win." That political leaders who made a career out of promoting racial causes and the city's only black newspaper (the *Louisiana Weekly* issued no endorsement in the runoff) could still distance themselves from Morial's campaign against an opponent who railed at "junglebunnies" when given black voter registration figures was grave testimony to their differences and the tortured calculation of self-interest. But the elimination of Kiefer and Morrison also left those whites who were appalled at DiRosa's antiestablishment rhetoric (one columnist labeled him the "bête blanc") and less than comfortable with his own ethnic heritage nowhere to go but to Morial—the candidate whose manners, polish, erudition, and intellectual attainments made him appear the "aristocrat" in this race. When it was over, Morial had piled up 97 percent of a 78 percent black turnout and nearly 20 percent of a 75 percent white turnout. It was enough to produce a 6,000-vote victory (out of 175,000 cast)—a tally similar to DiRosa's margin of victory over Morial in 1969.[40]

Morial's electoral strength had immediate ramifications for the major black political organizations. SOUL's close identification with Kiefer left it particularly exposed. As the campaign heated up, SSI had finally proven enough of an embarrassment to Governor Edwards that he called a meeting of interested black leaders to declare "all political accounts at the Dome paid in full." He brought in the Hyatt Management Corporation to handle Dome affairs in the summer before the mayoral balloting and SSI maintained its presence only by reducing operating costs by $1 million and cutting its staff of two hundred in half. The Hyatt canceled the SSI contract within days of Kiefer's defeat. The timing suggests that it was the loss of SSI's patron that freed Hyatt from any remaining political constraints and rendered SSI vulnerable. The housecleaning began even before the runoff election.[41]

COUP was hit in an even more spectacular fashion. Less than six months after Morial took office, police conducted a raid on the New Orleans Regional Service Center, eventually rounding up some forty-three CETA employees, almost all of whom were COUP members or supporters. COUP officials Henry Braden, Sidney Barthelemy, and George ("Nick") Connor (who had some relatives picked up in the sweep) denounced the raid as politically motivated and part of a personal vendetta that revealed the new mayor's taste for revenge. Whatever private pleasure Morial derived from COUP's discomfiture, the attempt to write off the raid as evidence simply of personal pique was more self-serving than the raid itself.[42]

Morial and his new police chief, Jim Parsons, claimed that the raid was triggered by a series in the *States-Item* that illustrated how the CETA program had been "marked by nepotism" and abused by "bureaucratic and political mercenaries . . . [who] rip[ped]-off much of the funds for their own personal gain, and [left] the poor and unemployed worse off than before." For Morial (who was characterized as "rigidly honest" in an FBI report before his 1965 appointment as an assistant U. S. attorney) such freebooting was anathema, and he had already told his own staff that they had "better keep their hands clean." While his new director of manpower, Sandra Gunner, "laid down the law to the agencies that got jobs under the CETA . . . program," Parsons set up a special Integrity Unit to investigate white-collar crime and corruption in government. COUP was less the victim of a personal vendetta than of the loss of its former political protection and its own practices. Within a year, the U. S. Conference of Mayors selected Morial's Office of Manpower and Economic Development as a national model because of its oversight of CETA operations. It was named the "most improved" and "best in the state" by the Department of Labor's regional Dallas office.[43]

This opening round of sparring led to eight years of virtual political war between Morial and COUP. More than occasionally manifested in bickering between the mayor and councilman Sidney Barthelemy, it was most spectacularly evident in COUP's outright opposition to Morial's reelection in 1982 and the mayor's subsequent successful effort to defeat Henry Braden and Nick Connor in their state legislative races the following year. Both sets of contests demonstrated Morial's appeal to the black electorate and the bankruptcy of a political organization whose influence, seemingly, did not reach beyond its shrinking patronage rolls. In the first instance, COUP backed a black challenger, state senator William Jefferson, who garnered 7 percent of the vote and actually received more support from whites than blacks. In the runoff, COUP endorsed Morial's white opponent, Ron Faucheux, and stood helplessly by as Morial swept black precincts. The success of Morial's retaliatory purge simply emphasized the point. Black voters indicated decisively where they stood in the Morial-COUP dispute.[44]

If SOUL's relations with the mayor lacked the personal rancor that fueled the Braden-Morial feud, there were still enough serious differences to lead SOUL to support William Jefferson's 1982 challenge. Jefferson's anemic standing in the polls, however, led the pragmatists in SOUL to bail out before election day and slink back to the Morial fold. Other than that abortive effort, SOUL devoted most of its energies during the Morial years to finding a safe electoral haven for Sherman Copelin. Indeed, SOUL's move back to Morial was a desperate effort to salvage Copelin's candidacy as a councilman. Still tainted by his connection to the FHF scandal, Copelin could not overcome an opponent who carried—and quoted—his damaging grand jury testimony. In the end, the outraged voters of District E elected a white who later would be driven from office under his own legal cloud in preference to a black who received immunity for his indiscretions.[45]

It was Copelin's appointment as interim assessor for the Third Municipal District (Wards 7, 8 and 9) in 1984, however, and his race for election to that seat in his own right in early 1985 that highlighted his differences with Morial and demonstrated the cynicism with which the race issue could be raised. Copelin was appointed to the vacancy by the sitting Board of Assessors after a vigorous lobbying effort by Governor Edwards. He received Edwards' backing after "knifing" black challenger Israel Augustine in his race against Congresswoman Lindy Boggs, and that of assessor Connie Comiskey after promising SOUL's support in her own race against BOLD's Ken Carter. It was enough to overcome Morial's efforts on behalf of his chief administrative officer, Errol Williams, a "squeaky clean" candidate, who, according to political columnist Clancy DuBos, had professional credentials that were unmatched. When a Morial-endorsed Williams proceeded to challenge Copelin in the March, 1985, election, Copelin—conveniently forgetting how he had won that seat in the first place—attacked the mayor and his opponent for threatening "black unity." Haunted by his own past, and, perhaps, damaged by Edwards' indictment during the campaign, Copelin failed to make the runoff against the ultimately victorious Williams.[46]

Theoretically, a mayor who waged daily battle with the traditional black political organizations, cleaned up scandalous and wasteful public programs, and promoted professional excellence as opposed to sustaining politically connected incompetence should have received a warm welcome in the white community—particularly in the historically reform-oriented uptown neighborhoods. There was much else to recommend Morial to whites as well. He was a fiscal conservative who preached the gospel of self-reliance both to the city as he tried to cut its dependence on federal revenues and to young blacks out on the street looking for work. Indeed, after he had broken a police strike in his first year in office and joined with the more progressive elements of the business community to promote economic growth in the private sector, the *Wall Street Journal* referred to him as a "black Calvin Coolidge."[47]

But it was particularly his views on race and his philosophical predisposition to emphasize merit and competence over color that should have put the white community's fears of a black mayor to rest. In a speech before the Metropolitan Area Committee shortly after his election, Morial clearly articulated a twentieth-century variant of the old radical creole abhorrence of caste. "I have no intention of politicalizing the incoming administration," he assured his listeners, "on the narrow grounds of reverse prejudice. It does not serve this city, or the cause of black people, to tolerate prejudice or discrimination in any form. It is the daily struggle of minorities. We will never be its exponent. We will always be its enemy." Once in office, he acted on that premise. It was, in fact, his firing of the black organizations' political appointees and their replacement by blacks and whites from management, the professions, and academia that caught the eye of the *Wall Street Journal*.[48]

Morial's racial views, however, had a corollary that the white community found more difficult to accept. If blacks could not expect a free ride in his administration, the new mayor had even less tolerance for entrenched bastions of white privilege and power. An equitable, "color-blind" society had to be truly "opened up," and whites would have to grant access, not to the back of the patronage bus, where blacks could be collectively gathered in a handful of designated "black" enterprises, but to everything, across the board. Morial was not turning down the racial "heat" by stressing merit; he was turning it up by asking whites to deliver on their professed convictions. Could they "cease to be white" as Garrison, Phillips, and Lincoln did in Desdunes' forgotten memory? The answer came in the deadly drone of election data. Morial received a respectable 20 percent of the white vote in 1977 but slipped to perhaps 13 or 14 percent in his successful 1982 reelection campaign, and that total was cut in half again when he failed to change the city charter to permit more than two terms. By the end of his administration the mayor was almost totally estranged from all but a relative handful of white New Orleanians.

The mayor's unparalleled popularity among blacks, his declining standing among whites, and the subsequent racial polarization of New Orleans' electorate stemmed not simply from Morial's demands for an open city. First, whereas Moon Landrieu was able to carve new "black" opportunities out of greatly expanded federal and state assistance, Morial sought to open *every* door to potential black access in a time of budgetary stringency. Virtually coinciding with the "Reagan revolution," Morial's administration tried to do more with less. Considering the political heat turned on a popular Landrieu when he tried to toss some new "plums" (such as the SSI contract) to black supporters, it was inevitable that Morial's attempts to cut into existing white business even as local budgets were being slashed would produce cries of outrage.

Second, there was the matter of style. It was not just what Morial did but the way he did it that infuriated many whites and captivated blacks. Morial's own distinctive history, achievements, and competence provided him with a confidence and assertiveness that, in the context of race relations in New Orleans, whites often read as arrogance. It was a label hung on the mayor during the campaign, and it dogged him throughout his administration. His constitutionally short fuse and absolute refusal to be either awed or intimidated by the pillars of the white community when he became engaged in unseemly controversies made him vulnerable to the charges of political adversaries who found it more convenient to point to personality than self-interest as the fundamental cause of confrontation.

An incident that occurred in the 1977 campaign is illustrative. At a joint appearance with Toni Morrison in Corpus Christi Church, the spiritual center of the Seventh Ward, Morial savaged his opponent after the memory of Chep Morrison was invoked to appeal to black voters. According to one reporter, Morial "completely [blew] his cool and [took] off after Toni Morrison with a vengeance," excoriating "his Daddy's record" and turning on a black Morrison supporter with the epithet "Uncle Tom." Morrison responded calmly by talking about how his father taught proper "manners." The reporter, obviously stunned by Morial's outburst, left the meeting concluding that "this is one audience . . . Morrison wooed and won." Yet the returns from the Seventh Ward told another story. Morial obviously knew his audience far better than did either Morrison or the press. He gave voice to a community that was heartened, not appalled, by his actions.[49]

Finally, Morial's concept of an "open" New Orleans included a redefinition of the mayor's role that was sharply at odds with practices that had been traditional for at least a century. In asserting a primary role in urban governance for the city's democratically elected chief executive, Morial's race—or at least the public's fascination with it—obscured the real dynamics of a fundamental political challenge to the social and economic oligarchy that dominated public affairs not from any elected posts but from perches of social privilege and seats on the "independent" agencies and commissions, such as the Sewerage and Water Board, Dock Board, and Board of Liquidation, City Debt, that controlled key city functions. Indeed, in his speech before the Metropolitan Area Committee, Morial told what was coming. He made pointed reference to Tulane University political scientist Charles Chai's 1971 study "Who Rules New Orleans?" and informed the committee that he was "astounded" that the mayor was not included among the list of "influentials" compiled after discussions with community leaders. It was inconceivable to him that "a majority of the people [consulted] failed to even mention the mayor as a man essential to the communal equation." He added diplomatically that he "would like to think that this perception has changed." What he meant, of course, was that it would be changed. No longer of that class, nor willing to serve its narrow ends, a democratically responsive, independent chief executive represented a real threat to the traditional elite's interests; it was a challenge that would have provoked a political firestorm for any mayor—black or white—who dared to stake out such a position.[50]

Ultimately, those blacks and whites who were alienated by the mayor tried to pigeonhole him by invoking America's racial dualism in ways that revealed little besides their own race-bound predilections. Black critic Tom Dent, for example, denounced Morial's "isolation" from black political organizations, attacked "Creoles" generically as those who "suffered from confusions and indecision about racial identity" (this was undoubtedly a reference to the fully acculturated creoles who, enamored with standards of color, extolled their "whiteness" in the age of Jim Crow and often rushed to "blackness" in the civil rights era—in either case, it was Dent who was confused in trying to attach that tendency, however indirectly, to Morial), and asserted that Morial's "prime distinction" was that he was a black mayor who did "not act like a black man." Others echoed the charge, claiming that he adhered to a "Superblack" theory that rewarded only overqualified blacks and that he retained too many white advisers and appointees.[51]

Such criticism highlighted the historical "trick bag" that enveloped Morial. If his battle was to transcend racial barriers, his political success rode the crest of an unprecedented wave of racial consciousness and solidarity. As a pragmatic politician, Morial exploited racial issues with considerable skill, wringing every ounce of electoral advantage that could be had from them and producing a certain incongruity between ends and means.

Morial's very success was dependent on a historical phenomenon that denied and undercut his vision; having ridden a racial surge into office, he could not move the city beyond such confining conceptualizations—he was its prisoner as well as its beneficiary. Not all in the black community shared his vision, and their differences became more apparent once the candidate became the mayor. Some who accepted and inverted the American racial order displayed a sense of betrayal when they applied their own color-based standards of achievement to the Morial administration. If the mayor personally retained the overwhelming loyalty of the vast majority of black voters, that dissonance may still explain why no larger movement appeared to sustain the ideals he brought to city hall. The notion of a caste-free society succumbed to the overpowering presence of a segmented, highly race-conscious social order. Creole radicalism had no place in the American city.

White columnist Iris Kelso similarly displayed her own acceptance of the prevailing racial dualism when she asserted that "Dutch Morial's problem is that he's too white for the blacks, and too black for the whites." Her analysis was couched in stark racial terms, and she clearly had no idea how Morial fit such a scheme. Unable to shake her color-bound mind-set, she had no way to take the measure of a man who could not be held simply to racially based standards of appearance or political conduct. Nor could she conceive of any other paradigm.[52]

The mayor's good friend and president of Xavier University, Norman Francis, also noted Morial's racial marginality, but did understand him. "He's been white in a black man's world and black in a white man's world," according to Francis. To be recognized for his abilities, he has had to "constantly . . . break through the color barrier." Indeed, it was the desire to obliterate, not merely manipulate, that barrier that drove Morial. And it was his longing for acceptance on the basis of his abilities alone that led him to express anguish at his declining white support despite his best efforts to be mayor for "all the people."[53]

The struggle to succeed Dutch Morial was an intrablack affair that saw COUP's Sidney Barthelemy defeat William Jefferson, a Protestant north Louisianian. Campaigning as the candidate who could unite the city and overcome the "divisiveness" of the Morial years, Barthelemy offered peace and a smile. He became New Orleans' second black mayor, but he was catapulted to office on the back of a nearly monolithic white voting bloc. Carrying barely more than a quarter of the black vote, Barthelemy swept 85 percent of the whites. He had turned the biracial coalition of Moon Landrieu and Dutch Morial inside out. Where the previous mayors combined a liberal white fragment with overwhelming black backing, joining the most progressive elements of both races, Barthelemy blended the most conservative segments of each, grafting a slender layer of black support onto a massive white base. White New Orleans had found itself a black mayor.

A final irony occurred after Sherman Copelin, stymied in his efforts to become a councilman and an assessor, found the lower Ninth Ward's 90 percent black Ninety-ninth

Legislative District congenial enough to send him to the state House of Representatives in 1986. Within a year, *New Orleans Times-Picayune* columnist Allan Katz praised Copelin as "one of the most effective members of the legislature" and noted that "key elements of the white establishment that once scorned him now value Copelin and speak of how useful he is in Baton Rouge." It was a remarkable turnaround. In an earlier, trouble time, SOUL colleague Don Hubbard had reveled in the fevered opposition he and Copelin aroused in the *Times-Picayune*. "The black community knows who the *Times-Picayune* is; they know what that paper represents," Hubbard boasted. "When they start to pat us on the back, then our people will know we've sold out to the establishment." Indeed. It was no accident that the white community found itself propping up the weakest and most venal black leaders. They offered no threat to the status quo.[54]

What white New Orleanians could not tolerate was the "divisive," "abrasive," and independent Dutch Morial. Seemingly before it began, black politics in New Orleans had met its Thermidor; but by 1986 any allusion to the French Revolution would have seemed out of place. In the end, Morial's significance was not simply that he was New Orleans' first black mayor but that he was probably the last of the radical creoles.

The Americanization of New Orleans, including the imposition of an unwavering racial dualism, was now virtually complete. If the white creoles, overwhelmed by demography and history, fiercely seized their "whiteness" at the dawn of the Jim Crow era, the struggle to lift that veil nearly one hundred years later did much to submerge what remained of a stubbornly persistent sense of ethnic difference in the black community and compelled abandonment of even unconscious patterns of thought and behavior that had been nourished under different circumstances. The ultimate irony was that the defeat of segregation was accomplished only by an explicitly racial counterattack, an onslaught that killed Jim Crow but, when the dust had settled, left only "blacks" and "whites" facing each other across a daunting racial divide. The peculiar history of the creoles may have made them key agents in that struggle, but it also rendered them anachronistic. By the late 1980s, there were few willing to question—much less challenge—the "fanaticism of caste."

## Notes for "Simply a Matter of Black and White: The Transformation of Race and Politics in Twentieth Century New Orleans"

[1]Allen Rosenzweig, "The Influence of Class and Race on Political Behavior in New Orleans, 1960-1967" (M. A. thesis, University of Oklahoma, 1967), 16-17.

[2]*Louisiana Weekly*, October 9, 30, 1965.

[3]Ibid.

[4]Furnell Chatman, "Black Politics: A Concept in Search of a Definition," *New Orleans*, 5 (1971): 29ff.; Tom Dent, "New Orleans Versus Atlanta," *Southern Exposure*, 7 (1979): 64-68.

[5]Daniel C. Thompson, *The Negro Leadership Class* (Englewood Cliffs, N.J., 1963), 36-37.

[6]Untitled handwritten report, November, 1962, in NAACP Papers; *Louisiana Weekly*, June 10, November 11, 1967; *New Orleans Times-Picayune*, November 6, 1967.

[7]John Higham, *Send These to Me: Jews and Other Immigrants in Urban America* (New York, 1975), 12; interview with Dutch Morial by Arnold R. Hirsch, April 24, 1987.

[8]Interview with Morial, April 24, 1987.

[9]Interviews with Moon Landrieu by Arnold R. Hirsch, May 8, 13, 1987; *Louisiana Weekly*, November 8, December 6, 13, 20, 1969.

[10]*New Orleans Times-Picayune*, October 16, November 9, 1969, April 8, 1970; *New Orleans States-Item*, December 15, 1969.

[11]*Louisiana Weekly*, August 19, November 18, 1967, September 13, 27, 1969; Chatman, "Black Politics," 29ff.

[12]*Louisiana Weekly*, September 13, October 4, 11, 1969.

[13]*New Orleans Times-Picayune*, December 14, 1969; *Louisiana Weekly*, April 18, 1970.

[14]Interview with Landrieu, May 13, 1987; interviewing with Dutch Morial by Arnold R. Hirsch, June 20, 1987; *Louisiana Weekly*, January 10, 1970.

[15]*New Orleans Times-Picayune*, October 2, 1977, March 12, April 19, 1978, July 31, 1979; *Louisiana Weekly*, May 9, 16, July 11, 1970, October 16, 1971, February 26, 1972, March 3, 1973, August 28, 1976; James Gillis, "No Race Wall at City Hall," *Dixie Magazine*, *Times-Picayune*, June 4, 1972, 44ff.

[16]*Figaro*, March 15, 1978.

[17]Bill Rushton, "New Orleans Elects a Black Mayor," *Southern Exposure*, 6 (1978): 5-7.

[18]Gillis, "No Race Wall at City Hall"; *Figaro*, May 17, August 9, 30, 1978, December 10, 1979; *New Orleans Times-Picayune*, November 4, 1975, August 21, 1979.

[19]Interview with Landrieu, May 13, 1987.

[20]Ibid., *Louisiana Weekly*, March 4, 1972.

[21]R. L. Desdunes, *A Few Words to Dr. DuBois: With Malice Toward None* (New Orleans, 1907), 8, 13; *Louisiana Weekly*, June 10, 1978; *New Orleans States-Item*, August 17, 1978.

[22]Martha Ward, *Poor Women, Powerful Men: America's Great Experiment in Family Planning* (Boulder, Colo., 1986), 93-96, 122-25; *Louisiana Weekly*, March 29, 1975.

[23]*New Orleans Times-Picayune*, October 31, November 14, 1975, January 11, 1976; *Louisiana Weekly*, March 2, 1974.

[24]*Louisiana Weekly*, April 6, 1974, April 5, October 10, 1975; *New Orleans Times-Picayune*, September 26, 30, October 23, November 6, 12, 14, 1975; *New Orleans States-Item*, November 20, 21, 1975.

[25]Garry Boulard, "Power Brokers: Black Political Organizations," *New Orleans*, 20 (1985): 46ff.; *New Orleans Times-Picayune*, April 25, 1976.

[26]*Louisiana Weekly*, October 18, 1975; *New Orleans States-Item*, December 27, 1975.

[27]*Louisiana Weekly*, August 22, 1970; November 3, 17, December 22, 1973; March 9, 16, 1974; *New Orleans Times-Picayune*, April 21, May 1, 1974.

[28]*Louisiana Weekly*, September 27, 1975, March 26, 1977.

[29]Ibid., September 4, 1976.

[30]Ibid., November 13, 20, 27, 1976, January 8, March 5, 12, September 10, 17, 197.

[31]*Figaro*, March 9, 1977.

[32]Interview with Landrieu, May 13, 1987.

[33]Desdunes, *A Few Words to Dr. DuBois*, 7, 8, 13.

[34]Ibid., 5.

[35]"Report of the Louisiana NAACP Special Committee on Desegregation of Public-Supported Higher Education in Louisiana" (Mimeo, November 12, 1972, in author's possession).

[36]*Louisiana Weekly*, February 19, 26, March 18, September 16, October 21, 1972, March 17, April 28, 1973.

[37]*Figaro*, March 9, October 12, December 7, 1977.

[38]Interview with Henry Braden III by Arnold Hirsch, June 29, 1987; *Figaro*, September 7, 1977.

[39]*Figaro*, October 5, 1977.

[40]Ibid., March 9, August 3, October 5, 19, November 9, 1977; *Louisiana Weekly*, November 19, 1977.

[41]*Louisiana Weekly*, June 25, October 15, 22, 1977.

[42]*New Orleans Times-Picayune*, October 20, 1978; *New Orleans States-Item*, October 20, 1978; *Louisiana Weekly*, October 28, 1978.

[43]*New Orleans States-Item*, August 17, 18, 1978; *Figaro*, May 31, August 30, 1978; *Louisiana Weekly*, August 18, 1979.

[44]*Gambit*, February 20, 1982; *Louisiana Weekly*, February 20, 27, March 6, 1982, October 29, November 19, 26, 1983.

[45]*Gambit*, January 30, March 6, 1982.

[46]Ibid., October 6, 1984, January 12, March 16, 23, April 6, May 11, 1985.

[47]*Wall Street Journal*, May 1, 1979.

[48]Ibid.; *Figaro*, January 25, 1978.

[49]*Figaro*, October 5, 1977.

[50]Charles Y. W. Chai, "Who Rules New Orleans?" *Louisiana Business Survey*, 2 (1972): 2-7; *Figaro*, January 25, 1978.

[51]Dent, "New Orleans Versus Atlanta;" *Figaro*, November 16, 1977.

[52]*Figaro*, March 9, 1977.

[53]*New York Times*, November 14, 1977.

[54]*New Orleans Times-Picayune*, August 23, 1987; Boulard, "Power Brokers," 51.

# "WE WALKED LIKE MEN": THE DEACONS FOR DEFENSE AND JUSTICE*

Christopher B. Strain

On a sultry July evening in 1965, a cavalcade of cars driven by members of the Ku Klux Klan barreled into a predominately black neighborhood of Bogalusa, Louisiana, as they had done on countless nights before. The twenty-five car motorcade sometimes sped, sometimes cruised ominously through the streets. Leaning out of car windows, Klansmen taunted black residents, hurled racial epithets, insulted black women, and brandished pistols and rifles. When the Klansmen fired randomly into the homes of black Bogalusa residents, a fusillade of bullets met them in return. The unwelcome visitors quickly fled the neighborhood. It was the Klan's first encounter with the Deacons for Defense and Justice.[1]

Shrouded in mystery, the Deacons have defied definition, although several observers have tried. In 1965, Roy Reed described the Deacons as "the newest of the Negro civil rights organizations . . . an armed, semi-secret, loosely organized federation . . . a tough-minded league of Negroes, formed to defend members of their race from white terrorism." Howell Raines mistakenly labelled them as "the South's first organized black vigilantes." Cleveland Sellers described the Deacons as "a group whose responsibility was to defend their communities or themselves against attack." Charles Sims, president of the Bogalusa chapter of the Deacons, called his organization "a defense guard unit." While all of these definitions touch upon the Deacons' activities, self-protection was the group's *raison d'être*. The Deacons should thus properly be characterized as an advocacy group for self-defense.[2]

The group first organized in March, 1965, as a nonprofit corporation in Jonesboro, Louisiana, after Klansmen had driven through Jonesboro with a police escort to distribute leaflets. A handful of local black men, all United States Army veterans, decided that if the white power structure would condone and abet such activity, they must do something

*First published in *Louisiana History*, 38 (1997): 43-62. Reprinted with the kind permission of the author and the Louisiana Historical Association.

to help themselves. The next day, the men met to discuss how to protect their community. They subsequently purchased citizens band radios and ammunition and established nocturnal patrols of the black community.

Having addressed their most pressing concerns, the group's members turned their attention to organizational matters, electing Percy Lee Bradford as president and naming the association. The men, many of whom were devout Christians, agreed on the name "Deacons" as a reflection of their religious backgrounds and their self-ascribed roles as servants of the community and defenders of the faith.

A chapter of the organization was soon established at Bogalusa, Louisiana. Both branches quickly grew and expanded. Though Jonesboro remained the Deacons' official headquarters, the organization's locus of power quickly shifted from Jonesboro to Bogalusa, where the Deacons gained national media attention.[3]

To understand the Deacons, one must examine the environment and circumstances that fostered the group's creation. Organization of the Deacons constituted an empowering reaction to an antagonistic power structure. The movement incorporated both official and unofficial elements of resistance. The popular, media-generated image of the Deacons as gun-slinging vigilantes is inaccurate. A closer look at the movement in Bogalusa, Louisiana, in the mid-1960s shows the Deacons in different light.

Bogalusa, a small town approximately two hours by car from Biloxi, Mississippi, boasted 22,000 residents in 1965. It was originally a sawmill town, which accounted for its location on the edge of the Pearl River swamps. In 1965, however, a paper mill operated by the Crown-Zellerbach Corporation dominated the town's economy and landscape, giving it an unmistakable appearance and odor. The town otherwise was unremarkable and indistinguishable from other Louisiana towns of its size. Howell Raines unflatteringly characterized Bogalusa as "a rarity among the small towns of the South in that it has no redeeming touch of grace, beauty, or elegance to surprise the eye or rest the spirit."

In Bogalusa, Charles Sims and the Deacons for Defense and Justice made their indelible mark on the black struggle for equality in America; according to historian George Lipsitz, the Deacons "made Bogalusa one of the places in the South where armed self-defense supplemented tactical nonviolent direct action in the civil rights movement. . . . Their discipline and dedication inspired the community, their very existence made black people in Bogalusa think more of themselves as people who could not be pushed around."[4]

The civil rights movement came to Bogalusa, as it came to other small towns around the South: it arrived rather quietly in the form of local, grassroots activism, without the fanfare and bluster of national leadership and media attention. Local blacks protested segregation and sought to integrate local facilities. Additionally, they criticized the lack of economic opportunities, police brutality, "separate-but-equal" public services and accommodations, and poor educational opportunities. White Bogalusans resisted stubbornly, and the black activists met little success, though their persistent efforts attracted the attention of outside parties.

The mettle of local activists attracted the Congress of Racial Equality (CORE) to Bogalusa in January 1965, though other factors beckoned CORE as well. Bogalusa held a reputation as a bastion of white supremacy. The Ku Klux Klan tyrannized the area, and CORE, like other national civil rights organizations, relied on massive white resistance to advance its cause. White opposition galvanized protest, focused media attention, generated national sympathy, and inadvertently propelled the movement toward success—but at a cost: the struggle for black equality in Bogalusa destroyed what little racial harmony existed there.

Tension mounted as CORE stepped up its demonstration marches in early 1965. Several hundred protestors, mostly local high school students, marched on April 9 to advocate equal educational opportunities in local integrated schools and other issues. When marchers reached the downtown area, police ordered them to return to the local union hall after white spectators manhandled a white journalist and several marchers. Blacks sporadically picketed downtown businesses while negotiators representing the United States Community Relations Service and local businessmen attempted to mediate the conflict. The United Conservatives of Louisiana, a group akin to the White Citizens' Council, staged a rally in early May which attracted thousands and featured Sheriff Jim Clark of Selma, Alabama; Clark, however, withdrew at the governor's request. City officials augmented the city's police force of thirty-four men with twelve deputized firemen and an equal number of county sheriff's deputies. In addition, the governor dispatched 300 highway patrolmen to the area, and the Federal Bureau of Investigation also sent approximately thirty agents to the scene. Bogalusa braced itself for a large-scale, violent confrontation.[5]

On May 23 Mayor Jesse H. Cutrer, Jr., announced the repeal of all city segregation ordinances. He also promised that blacks would be hired for the police force, and possibly other government agencies. "Everyone must recognize the fact that federal laws supercede city and state laws in the field of civil rights," he stated. "We must obey the law, no matter how bitter the taste." Reaction to Cutrer's proclamation ranged from lukewarm to openly hostile. While pressuring the municipal government to follow through on Cutrer's statments, James Farmer of CORE cautiously praised the action. "The fight is not ended," Farmer warned prophetically. "The most difficult part is ahead." Local white citizens sought to remove Cutrer from office and moved for a recall election. White youths attacked a newspaper photographer sent to cover a pro-integration rally and destroyed his equipment. State and city police quelled street fights which broke out between blacks and whites in downtown Bogalusa. Police also arrested two white men for attempted arson outside the local Baptist church where James Farmer was to speak. The policemen expropriated a two-gallon can of gasoline from the suspects—as well as an unrepentant confession.[6]

The desegregation of Bogalusa turned out to be a pyrrhic victory. On June 2, newly hired Deputy Sheriff O'Neal Moore was shot to death in his car while on patrol in Varnado (outside of Bogalusa) by a gunman in a passing pick-up truck. He and his partner, Creed Rogers, who was wounded in the shooting, were two of Washington Parish's first African American peacekeepers. Authorities arrested a white Bogalusa resident, Ernest Ray McElveen, and charged him with murder.[7]

This electrically charged atmosphere of animosity and hair-trigger violence, fueled by white hatred and black frustration gave birth to the Deacons. Up to this point, the Deacons had been quietly making their presence known: watching events from a safe distance, formulating their policies, bolstering membership, and supplementing their growing arsenal of firearms. After announcing the repeal of city segregation ordinances, Mayor Cutrer warned in a veiled threat to the Deacons: "Anyone, white or Negro, who attempts to violate the rights of another or cause bodily harm will be promptly arrested, charged and prosecuted." After Moore's murder, several Deacons, in their first public display of arms, guarded the homes of local black leaders.[8]

Moore's death presaged the Deacons' rapid acceleration to the forefront of the movement in Bogalusa. Friends and family scheduled Moore's funeral for June 9, the following week, and James Farmer planned to speak at the service. He flew into the New Orleans International Airport, where four state police detectives and four Deacons met him. The detectives warned Farmer of a Klan plot to assassinate him in Louisiana, and offered to provide protection for him, though Charles Sims, who did not fully trust the detectives, insisted that Farmer ride with him. Sims, along with three other Deacons, chauffeured Farmer from New Orleans to Bogalusa—approximately 65 miles—with a pistol on the car seat beside him. Upon his safe arrival in the troubled city, Farmer praised the Deacons. "CORE is nonviolent," said Farmer, "but we have no right to tell Negroes in Bogalusa or anywhere else that they do not have the right to defend their homes. It is a constitutional right." An estimated fifty Deacons attended Moore's funeral.[9]

The Deacons subsequently expanded their organization through the establishment of branches in Homer and Tallulah, Louisiana, as well as chapters in Mississippi and Alabama. Expansion spawned one of the most perplexing and enduring mysteries about the organization. No one outside the group then knew—and no one knows today—how many men joined the Deacons. Ernest Thomas, Jonesboro chapter vice-president and full-time organizer for the Deacons, claimed in June 1965 that the group had more than fifty chapters in various stages of organization in Louisiana, Mississippi, and Alabama. He also said that "with hard work" the organization could spread to every Southern state in "six or seven months." Thomas, however, declined to disclose the number of members, in keeping with the Deacons' strategy of variously concealing and distorting membership figures. "It would not make sense to tell you we got four hundred men here," Thomas said in June of the following year, "and let 'the man' bring eight hundred." The Deacons limited public knowledge of membership for tactical purposes: surprise, intimidation, and self-preservation. They cultivated the image of an underground fraternal, organization which permeated the entire South. Only a handful of Deacons officially disclosed their membership, including Charles Sims, Ernest Thomas, Percy Lee Bradford, Bogalusa vice-president Royan Burris, and director of public relations Robert Hicks.[10] Observers speculated that membership ranged from five thousand to fifteen thousand, but these numbers were probably inflated.

In their charter and by-laws, the Deacons reaffirmed the principles of American democracy, thus resembling other civic-minded agencies. Their charter, recognized under Louisiana state law, commissioned the group "to instruct, train, and teach citizens, and especially minority groups, in the principles of democracy." The group required each prospective member to study and understand its by-laws before he could join. Each member took an oath, and pledged his life "to the defense of justice" and the defense of Negroes and civil rights workers wherever they required protection. Members paid $10 to join and $2 per month afterwards.[11]

The organization furnished members with ammunition, which it purchased in bulk quantities by means of an NRA-sponsored discount, but members provided their own guns. "Everybody owns his own piece," explained Thomas. Owning a gun, or two or three, was not uncommon among blacks in rural and small-town Louisiana during the 1960s; indeed, it was an old Southern custom among whites and blacks alike. Louisiana was known as the "Sportsman's Paradise," and, as Charles Sims pointed out, "they do a lotta huntin' around there." Sims further explained that "having a weapon's nothing new. What bugged the people was something else—when they found out what was the program of the Deacons." Of course, what made the Deacons unusual was their use of guns to counteract white aggression. The national media later zeroed in on the Black Panther Party in Oakland, California, as the first blacks in America to arm themselves; clearly, blacks were always armed—even before the Panthers—though perhaps not openly.[12]

When the Deacons first organized, members utilized the firearms they already owned—primarily shotguns, and a few handguns. Ernest Thomas sought to standardize weaponry to realize further savings, and favored the .30 M-1 Carbine and .38 Special revolver. How well the Deacons were armed, however, is a matter of conjecture. Thomas surreptitiously hinted that the Deacons stashed grenades in Jonesboro, and that they had used contacts in Houston and Chicago to acquire machine guns. Local police fretted that the Deacons possessed automatic weapons.

Although Gov. John J. McKeithen ordered the seizure of guns found in cars belonging to both Deacons and Klansmen, Louisiana state police recognized that confiscation of guns was illegal. Protected by the constitutional right to bear arms, the Deacons operated within the law. Of course, machine guns and hand grenades were a different matter: these items were illegal and subject to seizure. It thus seems unlikely that the Deacons would have owned such contraband; Deacons were attuned to the law, and would have done nothing to jeapordize unnecessarily their organization or its mission.[13]

It is noteworthy that the Deacons did not advocate using their guns for anything other than self-defense. Sims assured anyone who would listen that the Deacons would not start a fight, but would fight back "in concert" if attacked by whites. "They [whites] bring the fight to us," Sims maintained. "We don't take it to them." Deacons used their guns solely for self-defense, and for the defense of Civil Rights advocates, many of whom were pacifists. Given their menacing public image, it is surprising to learn that the Deacons reaffirmed the principle of nonviolent direct action. Many participated in nonviolent protest *without* weapons. Charles Sims felt that political and economic progress for blacks in America would be achieved through negotiations, not violence. When asked in an interview in August, 1965, how activists could best advance the movement, or achieve its aims most quickly, without the use of nonviolence, Sims said, "I believe nonviolence is the only way."[14]

Sims ignited the Deacons' meteoric rise to prominence. His charisma and leadership anchored the organization, and his persona symbolized the Deacons' no-nonsense approach to the struggle for black equality. Unlike many other civil rights leaders, Sims did not hail from a middle-class background. He was a part-time insurance salesman and a tough, hard-nosed man with a pre-movement police record which included assault and carrying a concealed weapon. If his pistol jabbed him in the ribs when he sat down, Sims would nonchalantly toss it—along with his car keys and cigarettes—onto the nearest table with a clatter, alarming anyone near. With disarming forwardness, and mock intimacy, Sims called prominent civil rights leaders (as well as white reporters) by their first names, calling well-known black author Louis Lomax "Louis," and CORE national president James Farmer "Jim." Showing that he was not within the circle of accepted civil rights leadership, Sims mistakenly referred to SNCC's Julian Bond as "Julius," though he respectfully called King "Dr. King." Stiff-necked and brooding, with a dark sense of humor, Sims did not take the civil rights movement or his role in it lightly.[15]

Under Sims' watchful eye, the civil rights movement in Bogalusa and the tension which accompanied it came to a head in July 1965. During a civil rights march on a downtown street, a flying bottle struck seventeen-year-old Hattie Mae Hill in the head, causing a gash. Leneva Tiebeman, a white nurse, rushed Hattie to a car driven by two Deacons, Henry Austin and Milton Johnson, who monitored the march from their automobile. White toughs hassled the girl and the nurse, who sought to take Hattie to a first-aid station in the black community. Miss Tiebeman hustled Hattie into the backseat of the car. When Austin and Johnson leaned from the car window, twenty-five-year-old Alton D. Crowe, Jr., of nearby Pearl River struck them both repeatedly in the face. Austin shot Crowe in the chest and neck. Police yanked both Austin and Johnson from the car, cuffed them on the car's hood, and took the two men to an unidentified locale for protection from angry whites, who shouted at policemen and attacked news photographers.[16]

That same night, again, two rallies occurred: one held by the Bogalusa Civic and Voters League, which coordinated black protest in Bogalusa, and the National States

Rights Party, featuring Atlanta attorney J.B. Stoner, who declared the "nigger" the "enemy" of his organization. Stoner urged whites to fire their black domestic help to speed black emigration from the South. Over the next few days, pressure built, tension increased. Bigots and extremists prevailed as moderate voices faded into the background. Gunplay and sporadic street violence occurred between blacks and whites. Then, on July 10, Federal Judge Herbert W. Christenberry enjoined Bogalusa police from using threats or violence to prevent blacks from exercising their civil rights, ordered police to protect civil rights activists from harassment by whites, and refused to grant city officials a restraining order temporarily stopping demonstrations. City attorney John C. Martzell reaffirmed the right of the Bogalusa Civic and Voters League (BCVL) to march, "but if it does," he warned, "as conditions now exist in Bogalusa, it may result in gang warfare." Agreeing with Martzell, A. Z. Young, president of the BCVL, voluntarily called off a march scheduled for that day, but rescheduled it for the following one.[17]

On July 13, Governor McKeithen, concerned with the damaging effect of demonstrations on the state's effort to attract Northern industry to Louisiana, flew to Bogalusa to make a personal appeal for the cessation of protest activities for a thirty-day "cooling-off period." Promising that demonstrations would be "stepped up," Bogalusa's black leaders rejected the plea, saying that the governor offered "nothing in return." With self-absolving sorrow, McKeithen washed his hands of the matter and lamented, "I think they have made a tragic mistake." Vice President Hubert Humphrey and John Doar, head of the Civil Rights Division of the Justice Department, participated in the negotiations—to little avail—via telephone. Protest efforts in Bogalusa ironically succeeded in breaking the apparent stalemate by finally attracting the attention of state and national officials.[18]

As the Deacons extended their reach, reaction to them grew proportionally. On August 2, both the Southern Christian Leadership Conference and the Deacons prepared to move into the Greensboro, Alabama, area. Two weeks prior, a small delegation of Deacons from Bogalusa visited Eutaw, twenty miles northwest of Greensboro to talk with local blacks about establishing a Deacons chapter there. Like SNCC and CORE, the Deacons sought to organize where the Ku Klux Klan was strong. Their move into Greensboro foreshadowed not only future conflict with the Klan, but also with Martin Luther King, Jr.

By August 1965, the Deacons had moved into Arkansas, Texas, and Illinois, with plans to organize in Georgia, North Carolina, and Florida. The organization sponsored activities later that month in the following Mississippi locales: Natchez, Greenville, Columbia, and Jackson, where Charles Sims led a ten-man delegation invited to discuss the possibility of establishing a chapter there. Sims told a crowd of three hundred black men at the Negro Masonic Hall on Lynch Street: "It is time for you men in Jackson to wake up and be men." Sims claimed he had been "shot five times and shot at about ten," and he was not afraid to come to Jackson.

Gender stereotypes and macho language often shaped the burgeoning debate over the place of guns in the movement, as well as the ongoing argument concerning self-defense.

Sims' rhetoric reflected this trend. The Deacons excluded women from their organization, which was, in many ways, an expression of manhood. "Everything we done," Sims said, "we walked like men." Royan Burris, after repelling Klan invaders in Bogalusa, explained: "They finally found out that we really are men, and that we would do what we said, and that we meant what we said." Dr. Stephen E. Salenger of Los Angeles, a psychiatry resident who spent time in Jonesboro as a member of the Medical Committee for Human Rights, said in an interview that he believed a white segregationist called a black man "boy" to disrespect and "de-sex" him, or at least to deny that the black man was a physical or sexual threat to his own supremacy. To combat this attitude, Salenger claimed, the Deacon flaunted the gun—a phallic symbol—to assert his own sexual competence and his contempt for the white man's power. Regardless of the psychological implications, the Deacons undeniably asserted themselves in terms of masculinity.[19]

Events picked up across the border in Mississippi in June 1966. Civil rights leaders flocked to the Meredith March Against Fear after James Meredith was shot from ambush on the highway. The march from Memphis to Jackson—an individual crusade begun by Meredith on June 5 as a display of defiance against white oppression—gained momentum as Dr. Martin Luther King, Jr., of the Southern Christian Leadership Conference, Floyd McKissick and James Farmer of CORE, Stokely Carmichael of the Student Nonviolent Coordinating Committee and others marched from the location where Meredith was gunned down (near Como) and spearheaded the demonstration as it pressed deeper into Mississippi. The Deacons also participated, but only after much debate, and much turmoil. It was there in Mississippi, during the Meredith March Against Fear, that the Deacons controversially exploded onto the national scene.[20]

Charles Sims and his Deacons played a pivotal role in the Meredith March Against Fear (also known as the Greenwood March), which stands as a watershed of the national civil rights movement, and the flashpoint for the ongoing question concerning the place of violence within the movement. Because of the Deacons' controversial image and use of guns, civil rights leaders disagreed as to whether or not the Deacons should participate in the Greenwood March. Cleveland Sellers has described SNCC's decision to continue Meredith's march across Mississippi in his book *The River of No Return*. According to Sellers, Stokely Carmichael argued that the march should "deemphasize white participation, that it should be used to highlight the need for independent black political units, and that the Deacons . . . be permitted to join the march." Roy Wilkins and Whitney Young were "adamantly opposed" to Carmichael. "They wanted to send out a nationwide call to whites; they insisted that the Deacons be excluded and they demanded that [SNCC] issue a statement proclaiming . . . allegiance to nonviolence." Martin Luther King, Jr., held the deciding vote. While he favored mass white participation and nonviolence, he was committed to the maintenance of a united front. King sided with Carmichael. Wilkins and Young withdrew their support and did not participate in the march.[21]

Sellers' account of the debate seems reliable, though other historians disagree over what transpired, particularly over King's involvement in the discussion. According to biographer Stephen Oates, King "pleaded with his Deacon brothers to remain true to nonviolence," but "the Deacons didn't 'believe in that naked shit no way,'" and would not be swayed by King. SNCC and CORE concurred with the Deacons, but King "pressed on":

> He was not saying that Negroes shouldn't protect themselves and their houses when attacked. Yet self-defense was not the point here. The point was whether they should carry guns in an organized demonstration. To do so would only confuse and obscure the moral issues, and it would not expose Mississippi injustice. If Negroes came marching through the state brandishing .38s and rifles, they were bound to precipitate a calamitous confrontation. Whites from the governor down would use it as an excuse to start shooting Negroes at random.

Carmichael and Floyd McKissick disagreed with King. McKissick asserted that "nonviolence had outlived its usefulness in this racist country" and that "Negroes ought to break the legs off the Statue of Liberty and 'throw her into the Mississippi.'" King confirmed this account of the contested debate in his book *Where Do We Go from Here?*[22]

Biographer David J. Garrow's account directly contradicts those of Sellers and Oates. Garrow contends that King remained "largely silent throughout the long and contentious discussion." Carmichael antagonized Roy Wilkins and Whitney Young, yet King kept quiet:

> King's silence gave assistance to Carmichael's goal of dissuading the NAACP and the National Urban League from taking part . . . [B]y remaining silent King allowed SNCC's divisive desires to run their course. Carmichael interpreted King's silence as either intentional or unintentional support for SNCC. 'When we were acting really impolite . . . King made no move at all. He kept quiet.'

If King indeed did remain silent during the discussion, and did not "plead" for nonviolence and the exclusion of the Deacons, how do we interpret his close-mouthed reaction? King's silence could be seen as tacit approval of the Deacons and what they represented. Sellers said that "everyone realized that without [the Deacons], our lives would have been much less secure." Perhaps "everyone," including King, appreciated the Deacons' protection, and recognized their participation as complementary, rather than antithetical, to the larger movement.[23]

Sims' own testimony holds the key to unlocking the mystery surrounding the Deacon debates and King's enigmatic behavior. Sims claimed that "a lot of things happened on the Meredith March that was never told." Sims described the funeral of Armstead Phipps, an elderly participant who collapsed and died of a heart attack during the protest march. King was asked to preach at his funeral "way up in the Delta." King agreed to go to the service, but he would not go unless Sims "carried him."

> And he knowed the only way for me to carry him in the Delta, I had to carry him with my gun and my mens, not his. He can let his men trail along at the tail end, but in front and behind, it was gon' be me. And that was the only way he'd go. So, when the chips were down, I won't say the man woulda picked up a gun, but I'll say this, he didn't run one away, 'cause I was with the man.

Sims had spurned King just a year before. When asking civil rights leaders to come to Bogalusa in 1965, Sims said, "I want everybody here except Martin Luther King. If he came and they gun him, I couldn't protect him, because he don't believe in me." Sims apparently changed his opinion of King after the two men discussed self-defense and the goals of the movement. A year later, during the Meredith March, Sims told King, "Now you do yo' thing and I'm gonna back you up in doin' you thing, 'cause this is my job." Sims admitted that he respected and admired King as a "brilliant" man. According to Sims, King recognized a place for the Deacons within the movement. Both men saw the complementary nature of civil rights activism and armed self-defense by blacks.[24]

During the march, the Deacons provided protection for the marchers, stopping suspicious whites loitering near the march route and demanding that they state their business. They walked the ridges of hills adjacent to the road. Ernest Thomas observed the march from his car—featuring a windshield sticker that read "Friends of the Deacons." Thomas and the Deacons guarded the campsites at night with rifles, pistols, and shotguns, and provided armed escorts for marchers who travelled at night to the airport in Memphis. Reverend Theodore Seamans, pastor of Woodbridge Methodist Church in Woodbridge, New Jersey, saw weapons in the Deacons' cars. He spoke for many when he said, "I was astounded and made my views known. The movement is no place for guns."[25]

On June 21, armed whites and blacks skirmished in Philadelphia, Mississippi, where three young civil rights activists—James Chaney, Michael Schwerner, and Andrew Goodman—had been slain two years earlier. There is no evidence, however, to suggest that the black gunmen involved in this exchange of gunfire were Deacons.

The Deacons, however, were subjected to a verbal barrage later that day when King lashed out at the Deacons in a speech in Yazoo City. In a thinly veiled reproof directed toward the Deacons, King admonished those who used the same methods of violence as "our oppressor"; he did so to reassure the public of the movement's commitment to non-violence. Also that same day, James Meredith announced that he would rejoin the march in Canton, but evaded a direct reply to the question of whether he would carry a gun. Yet Meredith disavowed the Deacons, saying, "I don't know them. I don't know that they have any capabilities. I don't favor any group. I don't favor the Deacons."[26]

During the Meredith March, Stokely Carmichael introduced the phrase "Black Power" in a speech in Indianola, birthplace of the White Citizens' Council. The day after the Greenwood rally, SNCC printed up leaflets and placards with the Black Power slogan at the SNCC print shop in Atlanta. Historians generally consider the Greenwood March as a watershed event in the Civil Rights movement, an event in which the concept of Black Power split the radical and moderate factions within the movement. While the introduction of Black Power did drive a wedge between some younger and older activists, it united others. Sellers noted that while King was forced by "political circumstances" to distance himself and SCLC from Black Power, the Meredith March confirmed King as a "staunch ally" of the SNCC and a "true brother." It is notable that Sims did not condone Black Power and the multivalent ideas for which it stood. "The slogan Black Power didn't do a damn thing but hurt the movement," argued Sims. "I don't wanna live under Black Power. I don't wanna live under white power. I want equal power, and that's what I push."[27]

As quickly as they soared to notoriety, the Deacons faded into obscurity. After the Meredith March, they all but disappeared from the national media. The Deacons made one last major news splash in September 1967 before they slipped into oblivion. The local NAACP chapter led a march in Woodville, Mississippi, to protest Negro teachers who did not favor blacks running in Democratic primaries. At the march, police disarmed Deacons who were present.[28]

As the Deacons faded from the scene, the Federal Bureau of Investigation targeted the organization to be "disrupted" and "neutralized," along with SNCC, SCLC, CORE, the Revolutionary Action Movement (RAM), and the Nation of Islam. Director J. Edgar Hoover addressed a memo headed "Personal Attention to All Offices" on August 25, 1967, concerning what he termed "Black Nationalist Hate Groups." The Deacons were later downgraded as a primary target, displaced by the other groups because of the national scope of these organizations and their "most violent and radical" orientations."[29]

Contrary to FBI sources, the Deacons tried to avoid provoking a clash of arms, though their opponents argued that by simply arming themselves, the Deacons exacerbated an already explosive situation. Did possession of weapons create violence? Perhaps, but it also effectively deterred it. Discussions of armed self-defense and demonstrations of a willingness to fight back sometimes fueled progress in the struggle for black equality. Sims found that he could often avert violence by merely exhibiting a weapon. "The showing of a weapon stops many things," he said. "Everybody want to live and nobody want to die."[30]

A fine line exists between self-defense and aggression. Yet, Roy Reed termed the Deacons' means of dealing with oppression "noble belligerence,"[31] noting that the Deacons toed the line of aggressive violence.

The Deacons' rapid disappearance begs an explanation. Perhaps, after the group quickly organized, they dissipated as the character of the movement became more "violent" and more militant. Perhaps the movement outgrew the Deacons. Perhaps as the goals of the larger movement incorporated the ideals of the Deacons, the group no longer had a place within the movement. No longer needed for protection, the Deacons became obsolete. In the mid-to-late 1960s, fewer and fewer activists had qualms about self-defense, which became a common assumption for blacks, or about picking up a gun to further the aims of the movement. It is also possible that the Deacons faded from public view because of ideological differences with other activists, exemplified by King's repudiation of the group and their own disillusionment with Black Power advocates.

Or maybe Sims masterminded an invisible empire not unlike the Ku Klux Klan. Sims claimed that the group had chapters all across the country, though COINTELPRO FBI files do not confirm organization on a national level. The FBI carefully monitored black militant groups in major United States cities after 1967, and the Bureau did not record Deacon activities in their files. Of course, this does not mean that the Deacons necessarily ceased to exist; the FBI of the 1960s was a thorough, but imperfect investigative agency. Some observers have surmised that the Deacon organization was simply driven underground. Secrecy regarding Deacon membership has fueled this speculation.[32]

The organization left an enduring legacy in American race relations. "Anytime a Negro and a white man have any kind of round up and the Negro decide he going to fight him back," Sims once said, "he's a Deacon." Sims further complicated defining the organization by extending its membership to all those who stood up to "the man." The Deacons became—in a theoretical sense—a mindset, a broad concept of empowerment and self-protection.

The Deacons punctured the double standard of self-defense in America. They homed in on the lesser amounts of protection offered blacks by Southern polity and made a conscious effort to change the discrepancy. "I think the Louisiana state law says a man can carry a weapon in his car as long as it is not concealed," said Sims. "We found out in Bogalusa that that law meant for the white man, it didn't mean for the colored. Any time a colored man was caught with a weapon in his car, they jailed him for carrying a concealed weapon. So we carried them to court." Sims noted that police only interfered when the empowered black man asserted his civil rights. For example, the police in Philadelphia, Mississippi, made no move to interfere in black-white clashes "until half a dozen Negroes began to fight back." Sims also observed that "in the southern states, the police have never done their job when the white and the Negro are involved—unless the Negro's getting the best of the white man." James Farmer summed it up best when he explained: "Understand, the Deacons don't replace legal law enforcement—there is no such thing as legal law enforcement in much of the South that will protect a Negro citizen." The law eventually helped the Deacons, who helped themselves in a situation where inclusive law and order had broken down.[33]

Strikingly self-aware, Charles Sims and the Deacons were acutely conscious of their role in history. Sims felt that standing up to white supremacists by defending their homes and by participating in rallies signalled the birth of "a brand new Negro." Sims explained, "We told [the Southern white man] that a brand new Negro was born. The one he'd been pushin' around, he didn't exist anymore . . . We definitely couldn't swim, and we was as close to the river as we could get so there was but one way to go." Monitoring the mounting frustration and increasing militance of blacks in America in the mid-1960s, the Deacons took the political pulse of the country.[34]

## Notes for "'We Walked Like Men': The Deacons for Defense and Justice"

[1]Joanne Grant, *Black Protest: History, Documents, and Analyses: 1619 to the Present* (New York, 1968), 359.

[2]Roy Reed, Atlanta correspondent for the *New York Times*, was the only writer to take an interest in the Deacons during their heyday. I have relied heavily on his insight into the Deacons' activities. Reading his material, characterized by dramatic flair and foreboding dread, I gather that he respected and understood the Deacons, but paradoxically viewed them as misguided and "foolhardy." Roy Reed, "The Deacons, Too, Ride by Night," *New York Times Magazine*, August 15, 1965; Roy Reed, "Armed Negro Unit Spreads in South," *New York Times*, June 6, 1965; Raines, *My Soul Is Rested*, 416; Henry Hampton and Steve Fayer with Sarah Flynn, *Voices of Freedom: An Oral History of the Civil Rights Movement from the 1950s Through the 1980s* (New York, 1990), 286; Grant, *Black Protest*, 357.

[3]Reed, "Armed Negro Unit Spreads in South," 25; Reed, "The Deacons, Too, Ride by Night," 10-11.

[4]*Southern School News*, May 1965, vol. 11, no. 11, 5; Raines, *My Soul Is Rested*, 416; George Lipsitz, *A Life in the Struggle: Ivory Perry and the Culture of Opposition* (Philadelphia, 1988), 96.

[5]*Southern School News*, May 1965, vol. 11, no. 11, 5, June 1965, vol. 11, no. 12, 14.

[6]*Facts on File*, May 1965, 197; *Southern School News*, June 1965, 14; *New York Times*, May 24, 1965.

[7]*New York Times*, July 1-7, 1965.

[8]*New York Times*, May 24, 1965; *Facts on File*, July 1-7, 1965, 246-47.

[9]*New York Times*, June 6, 1965; James Farmer, *Lay Bare the Heart: An Autobiography of the Civil Rights Movement* (New York, 1985), 287-91.

[10]*New York Times*, June 6, 1965; "Marchers Upset by Apathy," *New York Times*, June 14, 1966; Grant, *Black Protest*, 63.

[11]Reed, "The Deacons, Too, Ride by Night," 11; Grant, *Black Protest*, 359; *New York Times*, June 6, 1965.

[12]Sonia Sanchez, formerly associated with the Black Panther Party, noted:

> The whole image that went around the world of Panthers going into the [California state] assembly with guns was something that said, simply, 'Don't mess with me.' And I remember talking to some old folks at the time. They said, 'Well, girl, that ain't nothing new. We always owned guns. We just kept them in our top drawer, you see.' The whole point of the newspaper articles was simply that this was a new phenomenon, that we never thought black men had guns. But if you went south or out west, black folks always had guns someplace in the house.

Sanchez quoted in Hampton, *Voices of Freedom*, 370; *New York Times*, June 6, 1965; Raines, *My Soul Is Rested*, 418; Grant, *Black Protest*, 361.

[13]*New York Times*, June 6, 1965; Reed, "The Deacons, Too, Ride by Night," 10-11.

[14]The Deacons never picked up their guns in the name of the civil rights movement; i.e., they never used their weaponry as official representatives of the movement. They did not target whites for retaliatory violence, or advocate disruption of the white community through violent means. The Deacons' guns were, in a sense, secondary to their promotion of personal self-defense. "I want to say when I confront a white man," warned Sims, "I would be just as dangerous to the white man without a weapon as I would be with a weapon, if he didn't treat me right." Grant, *Black Protest*, 358, "Rights Activities Spread in the South," *New York Times*, August 1, 1965; "Deacons Organize Chicago Chapter," *New York Times*, April 6, 1966.

[15]Farmer, *Lay Bare the Heart*, 257; Reed, "The Deacons, Too, Ride by Night," 22; Raines, *My Soul Is Rested*, 420.

[16]Roy Reed, "White Man is Shot by Negro in Clash in Bogalusa, La.," *New York Times*, July 9, 1965.

[17]A. Z. Young and the BCVL welcomed protection from the Deacons. "I know the Klan would have already come in here and killed or whipped the leaders of the movement if it weren't for the Deacons," Young noted.

"The Deacons give them something to think about." Young quoted in Lipsitz, *A Life in the Struggle*, 95; *New York Times*, July 9, 1965; Reed, "U.S. Court Enjoins Bogalusa Police," *New York Times*, July 11, 1965; Reed, "Moderates Fail to Aid Bogalusa," *New York Times*, July 11, 1965.

[18]Reed, "Negroes Reject Bogalusa Truce," *New York Times*, July 14, 1965.

[19]Gender stereotype marked discussion of self-defense within the movement like a red flag. Self-defense became a function of manhood. Bishop Charles Eubank Tucker blessed marchers and re-assured, "Any Negro or white has the right to defend himself with arms. Any man who didn't ought to take off his pants and wear skirts." See "Marchers Upset by Apathy," *New York Times*, June 14, 1966. The Deacons, too, used similar language. "It's time for black men," Ernest Thomas implored, "to start taking care of their black women and children." See "Marchers' Ranks Expand to 1,200," *New York Times*, June 20, 1966. Sims expressed himself in much cruder terms:

> See, the southern white man is almost like Hitler in the South. He been dictating to the Negro people, 'Boy, this,' and 'Uncle, that,' and 'Granma, go here,' and people's been jumpin'. So he gets up one morning and discovers that 'boy' was a man, and that he can walk up and say something to 'boy' and 'boy' don't like what he say, he tell him to eat himself—you know?

Grant, *Black Protest*, 362, 364; *New York Times*, April 6, 1966; Reed, "Deacons, in Mississippi Visits, Implore Negroes 'to Wake Up'," *New York Times*, August 30, 1965; Raines, *My Soul Is Rested*, 421; Reed, "The Deacons, Too, Ride by Night," 11, 22.

[20]"Mississippi March Gains Momentum," *New York Times*, June 10, 1966.

[21]Cleveland Sellers, *The River of No Return: The Autobiography of a Black Militant and the Life and Death of SNCC* (New York, 1973), 162.

[22]Stephen B. Oates, *Let the Trumpet Sound: The Life of Martin Luther King, Jr.* (New York, 1982), 397-98.

[23]David J. Garrow, *Bearing the Cross: Martin Luther King, Jr. and the Southern Christian Leadership Conference* (New York, 1986), 477; Sellers, 166. Adam Fairclough has suggested that Carmichael encouraged animosity between King and Wilkins "to ensure that SNCC did not become absorbed in a broad coalition that watered down its more radical aims." He also has suggested that King allowed his long-standing dislike of Wilkins to influence his judgement regarding the Deacons. Adam Fairclough, *To Redeem the Soul of America: The Southern Christian Leadership Conference and Martin Luther King, Jr.* (Athens, 1987), 313-15.

[24]Sims quoted in Raines, *My Soul Is Rested*, 421-22; Reed, "The Deacons, Too, Ride by Night," 24.

[25]Sellers, *The River of No Return*, 165-6; *New York Times*, June 10, 14, 1966.

[26]"Philadelphia, Miss. Whites and Negroes Trade Shots," *New York Times*, June 22, 1966.

[27]For a full treatment of Black Power ideology, see Stokely Carmichael and Charles V. Hamilton, *Black Power: The Politics of Liberation in America* (New York, 1967); see also chapter 3. The concept of Black Power as expressed by Stokely Carmichael and Willie Ricks truly angered Charles Sims. For Sims, Black Power had a different meaning. "[T]he cats that was hollerin' Black Power, I was protectin' and guardin' they damn ass. I don't see nothin' they was doin' to even be talkin' 'bout no Black Power. The Black Power, we had it. In them thirty rounds of ammunition on a man's shoulder, we had the Black Power." Raines, *My Soul Is Rested*, 422, 423; *New York Times*, June 22, 1966; Sellers, *River of No Return*, 169.

[28]"Mississippi March by Negroes Halted," *New York Times*, September 5, 1967.

[29]The Declassified Documents, FBI Counterintelligence Program (COINTELPRO) File, August 27, 1964—April 28, 1971, Deacons for Defense and Justice File, serial 5; see also Kenneth O'Reilly, *Racial Matters: The FBI's Secret File on Black America, 1960-1972* (New York, 1989).

[30]Grant, *Black Protest*, 361.

[31]The Deacons could have slipped across the brink of self-defense at any time, crossing into the morally questionable realm of aggressive violence. Where the two planes intersected was not always clear, as Charles Sims illustrated:

> See, we had made up our mind on one thing. I know where just about every honkie here live. If he'd attacked any my mens, he couldn't go to his house and sleep no more, 'cause if he do, I don't know what would have happened to him. I won't say we'da killed him. I got more sense than to use *those* words, but I'm not sure what *would* have happened.

Sims came perilously close to promising retributive violence, but did not. Undoubtedly, the threat existed, regardless of whether Sims verbally expressed it or not. Reed, "The Deacons, Too, Ride by Night," 22; Raines, *My Soul Is Rested,* 419.

[32]Raines, *My Soul Is Rested,* 421; Grant, *Black Protest*, 363.

[33]Grant, *Black Protest*, 358, 364; *New York Times,* June 22, 1965; July 9, 1965.

[34]Grant, *Black Protest*, 359, 362.

# RACE AND DEMOCRACY: THE CIVIL RIGHTS STRUGGLE IN LOUISIANA, 1915-1972*

Adam Fairclough

## MAKING RIGHTS REAL

Less than a year after the Voting Rights Act, arguably its greatest triumph, the civil rights movement split apart when two of the most dynamic organizations raised the banner of "Black Power." Sparking furious debate as to its precise meaning, Black Power fundamentally altered the character of SNCC and CORE, its principal proponents: they abandoned integration, repudiated nonviolence, and rid their ranks of white people. By the end of 1966, however, both organizations were in headlong decline, and the days of the "freedom summers," when hundreds of idealistic whites had gone South to work in "the movement," were fading into the romantic mists of a bygone era. In Louisiana, as elsewhere in the South, CORE was soon reduced to a shadow of its former self; by the summer of 1966 it had only five staff members left in the state. With black leaders at each other's throats, with Vietnam fast becoming the dominant political issue, and with white perceptions of race now colored by burning ghettos and the incendiary rhetoric of black nationalism, many commentators pronounced the civil rights movement dead.

Some CORE veterans felt profoundly alienated by their organization's embrace of black nationalism, and they resented CORE's takeover by people who had little or no experience in the Southern movement. Ronnie Moore decided that CORE's idealistic spirit had died. That spirit had been grievously wounded when committed staff members like Jim Peck, Jerome Smith, Rudy Lombard, Dave Dennis, and Richard Haley were fired by the national office or else quit out of disillusionment. It expired altogether when, in the name of a shallow slogan, CORE disowned its most fundamental principle, nonviolence.

*Excerpt first published in Chapter 13 of Adam Fairclough, *Race and Democracy: The Civil Rights Struggle in Louisiana, 1915-1972* (Athens, Ga.: The University of Georgia Press, © 1995), 381-417. Reprinted with the kind permission of the author and publisher.

> I am and always have been in favor of self-defense of one's home, but I have always held that direct action which includes picketing, mass demonstrations, etc., must be non-violent. Not only for philosophical reasons must this exist, but it must exist for practical reasons. I know the reality of nonviolence because I have worked in the South and I have inhaled tear gas. I have witnessed police brutality; I have ducked bullets, therefore, I know when it was wise to pick up guns and when it was wise to be non-violent. And a man who says shoot at all times is either an idiot or a damn fool.

Moore, along with several other seasoned staff members, went to work for CORE's Scholarship, Education, and Defense Fund for Racial Equality (SEDFRE) which remained wedded to interracialism.[1]

Still, the cry of "Black Power" touched an emotional and intellectual chord among black Americans. It intensified racial pride, discarded the word "Negro" to the dustbin of linguistic history, and ushered in radically different styles of militancy. Black Power made the ideals of nonviolence seem anachronistic and mawkish. Dreams of a "beloved community" gave way to calls for black unity; the vision of a "salt-and-pepper" society faded before an insistence on "blackness." And a cult of the gun displaced the pacifist orientation of the civil rights movement. Nonviolence, it is true, had always hinted at the possibility of violence, but Black Power positively relished that possibility. The language of violence—ominous threats of retaliation, blood-curdling calls for revolution, grim predictions that this or that city was "about to blow" soon became common argot in the black community.

Throughout Louisiana blacks appeared more assertive, at times even aggressive. Boycotts were often accompanied by intimidation, demonstrations sometimes degenerated into battles against the police, and by the end of the decade riots were breaking out in the most unlikely places—even in Lake Providence, a repressive north Louisiana town where black violence would have been unthinkable a few years earlier. When a new generation of black college students initiated a wave of protests between 1969 and 1972, the symbols of black nationalism and the language of insurrection permeated their rhetoric. High school students invoked Malcolm X and called for the teaching of black history even as they entered newly integrated schools. Not even the NAACP could insulate itself from Black Power insurgency: by 1968 the association was in turmoil at the national level, and sometimes at the local level too, over demands that it abandon interracialism and change the words in its title from "Colored People" to "Black People."

Some aspects of Black Power ran against the grain of Louisiana's Creole heritage. In Acadiana, for example, where white priests ministered to black Catholics and where white and black families sometimes openly acknowledged their blood relationships, notions of black separatism usually fell on stony ground. In St. Mary Parish, for example, black candidates garnered white support and even ran on integrated tickets. In the area around Opelousas, CORE worker John Zippert succeeded in organizing a farmers' marketing cooperative that counted thirty-five whites among its two hundred members. Some

NAACP branches in southern Louisiana began to attract a significant number of white members.[2]

Yet the term "black" also had particular resonance in Louisiana, where Negroes had traditionally been highly sensitive to variations in skin color, and where the Creoles of New Orleans, generally lighter in complexion than the rest of the Negro population, still remained a distinctive and self-conscious group. Stokely Carmichael's celebration of black skin, thick lips, and "nappy hair"—African rather than European physiognomy—praised precisely those features that were disdained by many Creoles. Indeed, "Black Power" challenged the very concept of "Creoleness." It even sometimes implied that the old "lighter is better" standard should be replaced by a "blacker is better" ideal. However, the issue was less skin color than racial identity. The dilemma of the "tragic mulatto" caught between the black and white worlds had long been a literary cliché; Black Power now challenged light-skinned Creoles to abandon their alleged social exclusivism once and for all and to identify with the black struggle unambiguously.[3]

The extent to which Black Power traumatized Creoles and transmuted the Creole self-image can easily be exaggerated. Most Creoles had long ago identified themselves as "Negroes"; indeed, Creoles like A. P. Tureaud, Arthur J. Chapital, and Ernest N. Morial had led the civil rights struggle. Moreover, the civil rights movement of the early 1960s had already heightened racial solidarity, acting, in the words of historian Arnold Hirsch, as "an ethnic crucible melding black New Orleanians into a single whole." Resentment of Creoles persisted, but it had more to do with class than with color: many viewed Creoles as a pushy and clannish elite that tended to dominate black leadership. "The friction was there," recalled NAACP field secretary Harvey Britton, "but it was a subtle friction within the black community that made things difficult in terms of cohesiveness on issues, because it was always deciding which group called out the particular troops at a given point in time."[4]

It would also be an error to draw too sharp a distinction between the activism of the "civil rights era" and that of the "Black Power era." If the civil rights movement disintegrated as a coherent national force, it survived, albeit in an attenuated form, in the states, cities, and rural areas, where blacks continued to struggle for jobs, integrated schools, and political representation. Indeed, the evidence of Louisiana contradicts the notion that the civil rights movement suddenly collapsed after Black Power supposedly split it asunder.

Local activism did not grind to a halt when the SNCC and CORE workers departed. For one thing, many independent local movements survived and prospered because they continued to receive support from various sources. The Southern Regional Council launched a third Voter Education Project in 1967, channeling more registration grants to local voters leagues. The Lawyers Constitutional Defense Committee continued to represent local movements in court, with Richard Sobol and Alvin Bronstein covering Louisiana from offices in, respectively, New Orleans and Jackson, Mississippi. The Scholarship, Education, and Defense Fund, which in 1967 split from CORE to become an independent organization, directed a leadership training program that instructed thousands of local activists in politics and government. Finally, the federal government itself gave sustenance to local movements. The machinery set up to enforce the 1964 Civil Rights Act encouraged complaints against employment discrimination, and it helped blacks to desegregate schools, hospitals, and public accommodations. The Voting Rights Act led to the appointment of federal registrars, invited complaints against unfair electoral practices, and generated a flood of reapportionment suits. Finally, the government's "War on Poverty" funded community organizations and, by creating jobs that were thinly disguised patronage, facilitated political mobilization. Thus outside help did not dry up.[5]

The impact of CORE's demise, moreover, was mitigated by the NAACP's revival. Indeed, the association consciously took advantage of its rival's organizational collapse, sharpening its appeal to black youth who, fired by the rhetoric of Black Power, often had nowhere else to go but the NAACP's Youth Councils. The NAACP's growth was particularly marked in those towns and cities where blacks, either through apathy or fear or a combination of the two, had been previously quiescent. In New Iberia, Lake Charles, Opelousas, New Roads, Baton Rouge, and Shreveport vigorous NAACP branches attacked police brutality, employment discrimination, and school segregation. To a great extent, of course, the NAACP had recourse to litigation, exploiting new avenues of legal redress opened up by civil rights law. Yet the NAACP of the late 1960s also displayed a hard-hitting edge that had been largely absent in the early 1960s: it was more militant, more confrontational, and more oriented towards direct action. Somewhat paradoxically, the NAACP also benefited from the tendency of white leaders to treat the association as their preferred channel of communication with the black community. Governor McKeithen's creation of a biracial commission in 1965 typified this new, conciliatory attitude, for the commission was heavily loaded with NAACP stalwarts.

If reports of the civil rights movement's death proved greatly exaggerated, the influence of black nationalism was similarly overstated. An inspirational slogan rather than a coherent ideology, Black Power operated on the level of culture and rhetoric rather than as a programmatic commitment to violence or racial separatism. Black Power meant all things to all people: therein lay both its popularity and its weakness. As a rallying cry for black unity it exercised great appeal, but it provided no clear strategy and failed to provide strong alternative, let alone revolutionary, leadership.

Black Power verbalized threats and articulated anger, but activists tended to utilize such oratory as a means of enhancing their bargaining power rather than encouraging violence. In fact, Black Power rhetoric frequently implied violence rather than explicitly threatening it. When, for example, A. Z. Young led a march from Bogalusa to Franklinton in 1966, FBI agents carefully monitored the fiery speeches at the concluding rally, but reported that "no mention was made of violence as an answer to problems." A year later, listening to a mass meeting in Bogalusa, Miriam Feingold noted how

> the movement combines country-style Negro religion with black power rhetoric. Meetings here start with several long prayers and . . . a hymn or two, and even "We Shall Overcome" sounds like a Negro hymn! Then the president of the [Bogalusa Voters] League gives a rousing speech, sprinkled with anti-white sentiments. . . . There's even violent, riot-like talk, but just as quickly people condemn looting and burning, realizing, they say, that the wrong people get killed.

By and large, advocacy of violence remained at the level of symbol rather than serious intention. Threats of armed insurrection were accorded spurious credibility by "long, hot summers" of riots and the white press's fawning, credulous coverage of self-styled black revolutionaries. It is a striking fact that the Deacons for Defense faded away at precisely the time that the rhetoric of armed struggle was intensifying. More to the point, the avowedly revolutionary Black Panther Party, which established a presence in New Orleans in 1970, failed to attract much support. Only when it became the object of police repression did blacks spring to its defense.[6]

Moreover, just as SNCC, CORE, and SCLC had often used demonstrations as a form of political drama, gearing their tactics towards the news media, there was a conscious element of "street theater" in how local activists deployed the symbols of Black Power. National figures like Stokely Carmichael and H. Rap Brown were useful "bogeymen" to dangle in front of appalled whites: blacks could revel in their firebrand declamations without subscribing to their revolutionary messages. John Martzell recalled entering a barbershop in Tallulah, Madison Parish, and unexpectedly encountering Ron Karenga, inventor of the Kwaanza celebration and one of the foremost black nationalists of the day. "He had a dashiki, and a big leather belt, and a .357 Magnum, sitting there in the barber chair, with his hands across his chest and his eyes closed." By then, however, Martzell understood "the subtle theater" of such situations. "I wasn't overly impressed, and I couldn't really picture Ron Karenga spending a whole lot of time in Tallulah." Such cynicism could be dangerous, but it contained some insight: at the state and local level the civil rights struggle continued as before; the style changed, but the substance remained much the same.[7]

The late 1960s, to be sure, saw much less emphasis upon integration and much more upon the development of community institutions. This shift, however, was a natural transition rather than an abrupt change. Certainly, much of the idealism surrounding integration faded, and interracialism as an end in itself became far less prominent. Yet blacks continued to press for integration in the broad sense of access to public accommodations, public services, employment, and government. The struggle for school integration, far from being abandoned, actually intensified in the late 1960s and came to a head in 1970, a year often seen as the high-water mark of black separatism. Likewise, Black Power's emphasis on institution building was a development of a long historical tradition, one that went back to the Reconstruction era, and in some communities still further, rather than a novel concept. To some extent, of course, institution building represented a departure from the integrationism of the period 1954-65. The NAACP's goal of integrating higher education evoked widespread opposition from people who did not wish to see Louisiana's black colleges lose their identity by being absorbed into a unitary system. Similarly, black teachers were deeply divided over whether the LEA should merge with the LTA, the white teachers' association.

Yet in many cases blacks were not so much opposing integration as the manner in which integration was implemented, particularly if it meant the destruction of community institutions. Thus blacks often supported school integration while at the same time opposing the closure of black schools and the sacking of black principals. In fact, the NAACP's dogmatic integrationism had always aroused misgivings, and most Southern blacks, it is fair to say, regarded integration as a means to an end rather than an end in itself. Hence Black Power, as many observers noted at the time, provided ideological cover for some fairly conservative and traditional attitudes. It is doubtful that the popularity of the Black Power slogan indicated a fundamental change in how blacks in the South viewed their goals. As Clayborne Carson has argued, "Rather than claiming that a black power movement displaced the civil rights movement," historians should stress the underlying continuities between the two periods.[8]

The most obvious continuity was political action. In a much discussed article published in 1965, Bayard Rustin argued that the civil rights movement should abandon direct action and redirect its energies "from protest to politics." Such a shift, facilitated by the Voting Rights Act, did indeed take place, but it was neither abrupt nor complete. Political action had been a central thread of black protest for more than twenty years, and universal suffrage had been a major goal of the civil rights movement. Black political participation massively increased in the wake of the Voting Rights Act, but it built upon a solid foundation of methods, leaders, and organizations. The other side of the coin was a continuing readiness to employ direct action when the occasion demanded it. If, in the late 1960s, politics and litigation became the major vehicles of black activism, that was because they overtook, rather than displaced, the direct action methods of earlier years. Blacks never discarded direct action entirely, and the years 1966 to 1970 saw a resurgence of boycotts and demonstrations around such issues as employment, school integration, police brutality, and student autonomy.[9]

The persistence of "protest" alongside the growth of "politics" had a great deal to do with the simple fact that whites continued to resist black demands for equality. White racism did not suddenly disappear with the passage of civil rights laws. Such laws declared blacks to be legally and politically equal, but they were not self-implementing. Blacks still had to struggle against white recalcitrance, utilizing whatever method or combination of methods—political action, direct action, litigation—seemed most appropriate. Indeed, the struggle to translate the Civil Rights Act and the Voting Rights Act into tangible equality continues to this day and shows no sign of coming to an end.

The Voting Rights Act dealt a severe blow to Louisiana's racial order, but it did not usher in the political millennium. White resistance to black voting did not evaporate overnight. In New Orleans, the number of black voters increased by thirteen thousand between August and October 1965, but the registrars showed no hurry to process the applicants, keeping thousands "waiting patiently under a blazing sun or in drizzling rain." The Reverend A. L. Davis filed suit against the Orleans Parish registrar, accusing him of deliberate delaying tactics, but Judge Frank Ellis rejected the complaint. In Shreveport, registrars continued to be infuriatingly inconsistent over identification: during the weeks following the Voting Rights Act they rejected 337 black applicants for inadequate identification, but only 15 white applicants. In the five parishes that received federal examiners, black registration shot up. However, all five local registrars refused at first to accept the federally registered voters, and state judges actually enjoined the registrars from enrolling them.

In parishes without federal examiners, rises in black registration showed extreme variations. For example, Madison saw a dramatic increase, while Morehouse and West Carroll saw the number of black voters, already small, actually decline. Most parishes witnessed steady but not spectacular growth. Even when they registered, blacks could still face obstacles casting a ballot. In Washington Parish, some complained of being barred from the Democratic primaries because the registrar had listed their party affiliation as "none." Throughout the state, but especially in North Louisiana, illiterate voters were refused assistance at the polls.[10]

Local registrars fell into line, however, when they saw the futility of continuing to reject black applicants. Although the Justice Department appointed federal examiners sparingly—much to the disappointment of civil rights organizations—the threat of being circumvented did have the desired effect on most parish registrars. The federal courts, moreover, swiftly disposed of challenges to the Voting Rights Act and, in *U.S.* v. *Louisiana*, ordered local election commissioners to aid illiterate voters. In 1967, under pressure from the Justice Department, the state told registrars not to apply the "good character" tests enacted in 1960. Finally, Governor John McKeithen had no desire to see federal examiners sent to Louisiana, and he prodded recalcitrant parish authorities to mend their ways.[11]

Across Louisiana, James McCain reported in 1967, "registration is not a serious obstacle anymore." Even Leander Perez, who in 1967 stormed into the office of the federal examiners and spewed a stream of vitriolic abuse, proved powerless to prevent blacks from voting in Plaquemines Parish. Five years after the passage of the Voting Rights Act the number of black voters had almost doubled, and the proportion of blacks who were registered grew from 30 to 60 percent. That represented a net increase of about 154,000.[12]

Faced with the sudden enlargement of the black electorate, white politicians faced a dilemma. Should they exploit racial polarization in order to solidify the white vote? Or should they reach out to black voters and abandon the politics of segregation?

The alternatives, of course, were rarely that simple. For one thing, the black vote was not an undifferentiated "bloc"; most black communities boasted at least two rival political factions, and new ones were appearing all the time. Then again, white politicians could tone down, but few were willing to entirely abandon, appeals to white racism: Southern whites still enjoyed a privileged position vis-à-vis blacks and many, feeling no sense of guilt over past discrimination, wished to retain as much of the status quo as possible. Moreover, as blacks pushed against the barriers of segregation and discrimination, social and economic conflict intensified. Competition for jobs, for example, was becoming more direct and more intense, with whites fearful that black advances would come at their expense. In the cities, residential segregation was becoming increasingly pronounced, as whites moved out of older, mixed neighborhoods to the newer, racially exclusive suburbs. Above all, the great majority of whites never reconciled themselves to school integration, an issue that by 1970 affected virtually every family in the state. Underlying such specific issues was a general feeling among most whites, ranging from mild uneasiness to pronounced fear, that a secure racial order had given way to a world in which blacks did not know their place, were threatening, dangerous, out of control.

How a politician balanced the often competing demands of black and white voters depended on many factors. Politicians had to consider the local electoral arithmetic. That candidates could win election with only a minority of the white votes was not an entirely new circumstance in Louisiana. Now, however, many could win with an even smaller minority if they won the greatly expanded black vote. As Walters and Cleghorn noted in 1967, "When a politician knows he can afford to lose 62 per cent of the old electorate, a figure which usually had been regarded as a landslide, his political bearings are suddenly shifted." Indeed, seeing the writing on the wall, almost a third of the South's congressmen supported the Voting Rights Bill. All those from the Deep South already had large black constituencies and, seeing that passage was inevitable, recognized that their future survival depended on black votes. It was no coincidence that the two Louisiana congressmen in favor of the bill, Hale Boggs and Jimmie Morrison, represented the congressional districts with the highest proportion of black voters. Without minimizing their political courage in casting "yes" votes—Jimmie Morrison's may well have cost him his seat in Congress—calculated self interest clearly influenced their decision.[13]

The extent of a politician's ambition also influenced how he responded to black and white constituents: the desire for higher office tomorrow, for example, might well affect how he acted today. In the case of Chep Morrison, the desire to be governor had led to a more robust defense of segregation than he might otherwise have espoused. In John McKeithen's case, national aspirations had the reverse effect: the governor's racial moderation after 1964 owed at least something to his ambition to become the Democratic vice presidential candidate in 1968. When McKeithen failed to achieve this goal, he had to focus his sights on state politics once again and his subsequent opposition to school integration could be explained, in part, by the need to shore up his support among segregation-minded whites.[14]

Some politicians stubbornly rejected the idea of courting the black electorate. "I won't stoop to entice these niggers," vowed representative Vail M. Deloney of East

Carroll Parish. "They either vote for me or they don't." Some went still further and contemptuously spurned "the illiterate bloc vote." John R. Rarick, challenging Congressman Jimmie Morrison in 1966, made a virtue of the fact that he received practically no black support: "Morrison gets nearly 200 Negro votes to one for his opponent." Enjoying the enthusiastic backing of the Klan (some believed that he was a Klan member himself) Rarick terminated Morrison's twenty-four-year congressional career in the most overtly racist campaign since Willie Rainach's bid for governor. Morrison's fate showed the danger of a "white backlash." Candidates had to be careful not to court black voters so ardently as to alienate too many whites, who in 1970 still made up nearly four-fifths of Louisiana's electorate. Indeed, white registration increased by a quarter of a million between 1965 and 1970, rising to 80 percent of its potential. Hence while blacks made up over a third of the voting-age population in 1970, they still accounted for only 21 percent of the voters.[15]

Most white politicians, however, quickly softened their segregationist rhetoric and wooed blacks with shameless abandon. McKeithen led the way. Having alienated black voters almost to a person in his campaign against Chep Morrison, McKeithen had a keen appreciation of the Voting Rights Act's import. "Every time I'd go and ask him to do something," Jesse Stone remembered, "he'd say, 'How many people are registered to vote up there?' So I had to carry . . . the numbers and information in my pocket all the time." In 1965 McKeithen wanted black support for a constitutional amendment that would allow him to succeed himself in office. In creating the state biracial commission and urging compliance with the Civil Rights Act, McKeithen shed his segregationist clothes and donned the garb of racial moderate. Blacks not only voted for the constitutional amendment but also overwhelmingly backed McKeithen in 1967, when he crushed John Rarick to win a second term as governor, enjoying "the greatest margin of victory in modern Louisiana history."[16]

Even some vehement opponents of the civil rights movement managed to cling to office by forging alliances with newly influential black leaders. In Shreveport, for example, George D'Artois, the hard-nosed commissioner of public safety, gained the backing of both Alphonse Jackson, president of the LEA and Shreveport's first black legislator, and Jesse Stone, Shreveport's most prominent black lawyer. In his last campaign in 1972 D'Artois received a good percentage of the black vote. Similarly the right-wing, ultrasegregationist district attorney for Baton Rouge, Sargent Pitcher, attracted not a few black votes with the help of allies like Acie Belton, longtime leader of the Second Ward Voters League.[17]

That blacks voted for the likes of George D'Artois seems incongruous, to say the least, but such choices had less to do with venality or gullibility than with hard-headed political calculation. Unless they could muster the voting strength to elect black candidates, blacks had to vote, as they had done in the past, on a "lesser of two evils" basis. And often the devil you knew, especially the one already in power, was better than the devil you did not. The personal factor also came into the equation. It was almost a cliché among blacks in the South that the racist you could trust was preferable to the liberal you could not. Although D'Artois was a hard man, Jesse Stone explained, when he made a promise he always kept it. Similar logic influenced the choice of some blacks to support Victor Schiro when he ran for reelection in 1965. A segregationist, albeit a genial one, Schiro's record as mayor of New Orleans was hardly such as to endear him to black hearts. Moreover, his opponent, councilman Jimmy Fitzmorris, clearly outbid Schiro when it came to making specific promises to blacks. Yet Schiro received the endorsement of A. P. Tureaud, Rev. A. L. Davis, and Rev. Avery Alexander, who helped to deliver between a third and a quarter of the black vote. Politics in Louisiana, of course, had always been notable for opportunism and a readiness to switch sides: political alliances were governed as much by political horse-trading as by declarations of principle. Even newer and ostensibly more militant organizations like SOUL tended to play by the old rules. As SOUL founder Nils R. Douglas put it, explaining his dealings with a segregationist politician, "I am willing to make a compact with the devil if we had the remotest chance of securing our goal."[18]

Faced with a choice of lackluster white candidates—in the 1965 mayoral race, for example, between two former segregationists of doubtful sincerity—it is perhaps not surprising that black voters in New Orleans failed to speak with a united voice. In the absence of exciting elections and attractive candidates, moreover, a large pool of potential voters showed little interest in politics: by 1966 fewer than half of those eligible had registered. These nonvoters were disproportionately poor; many lived in the city's public housing projects. Reporting on an NAACP registration drive in the Ninth Ward, which contained two of the largest and most rundown projects, Wilfred Aubert explained the difficulty of motivating such people.

> These are people who have suffered many years of deprivation, neglect and misery because the city administration has failed to keep its democratic promise to all its citizens. Therefore, they look upon everyone with suspicion and mistrust. . . . Poverty and fear have caused them to become indifferent and they live a life of despair. Progress in this area is very slow. . . . We must reach their natural leaders, such as the ministers, the barbers . . . the barkeepers and other persons whom they trust.

Given something positive to vote for, however, the ghetto poor would indeed register, and black voters would prove capable of remarkable solidarity. A large and solid black vote elected Maurice "Moon" Landrieu, a white racial liberal who succeeded Victor Schiro in 1970, and Ernest "Dutch" Morial, who became the city's first black mayor eight years later. Until black registration reached a critical mass of about 30 percent of the total electorate, however, the black vote in New Orleans remained, to quote Arnold Hirsch, "neither sufficient nor independent enough to strike out on its own."[19]

In some of the rural parishes, the electoral arithmetic began to favor blacks very soon after the Voting Rights Act, making the election of black candidates a real possibility.

Old patterns of deference, however, did not die overnight, and blacks often went down to defeat because black voters failed to back them. In some cases, white candidates simply bought votes for $5 or $10 apiece—a timeworn practice that continues to this day—and paid blacks $25 to $50 to act as campaign workers. But not a few blacks continued to support whites simply out of habit and ultracaution. "Many said that the time was not right [for black candidates]," Ernest Middleton recalled of his 1966 campaign in St. Mary Parish. "Still others argued that the candidates were not the right people or were not qualified. . . . Still others felt that Negroes couldn't help Negroes." Black ministers, Middleton thought, were especially negative. Moreover, religious sectarianism sometimes lurked beneath the surface in South Louisiana, further hampering black unity. In St. Mary Parish, for example, a white Catholic priest, Father Frank Ecimovich, played a key role in encouraging black candidates. However, Baptist and Methodist ministers felt threatened by Ecimovich's popularity and viewed his efforts "as an attempt of the Catholic Church to take over the town."[20]

Perhaps the most remarkable example of black voters failing to support black candidates occurred in the town of Lake Providence, in East Carroll Parish, in the election of 1970. Although blacks composed about two-thirds of the voters, whites were elected to the posts of mayor and town marshal—a result that caused some disappointed blacks to smash the windows of downtown stores in anger and frustration. Yet NAACP field secretary Harvey Britton disbelieved charges that whites had rigged the vote, arguing that "the Negroes lost because the black community did not support them."[21]

The fractured black vote sometimes reflected divisions within the local black leadership, which, as James McCain lamented in 1967, "is partially split in a few parishes." Factionalism was especially prevalent where CORE-backed groups clashed with NAACP branches and other established organizations, or else challenged the right of certain individuals, usually teachers and ministers, to represent the black community.[22]

The War on Poverty sometimes exacerbated these quarrels, although its divisive effects should not be overstated. While conflicts over control of community action programs (CAPs) could be extremely bitter, the overall effect of the antipoverty program was to stimulate black political action. Many civil rights activists found secure niches in CAPs, employment that enabled them to bridge the transition from the civil rights movement to electoral politics. The War on Poverty also provided patronage jobs that nourished and sustained black political organizations. The classic example was Total Community Action (TCA), the poverty program in New Orleans, which gave employment to any number of political activists, especially those connected with the newer groups like SOUL, COUP, and BOLD. These organizations supported Moon Landrieu in his successful bid for mayor and garnered a further rich crop of patronage in return. Not coincidentally, Landrieu had exercised considerable influence in the selection of TCA's board members.[23]

Yet the War on Poverty also occasioned acrimonious disputes within some black communities, especially when rival groups vied for representation on the CAP boards and competed to win sponsorship of the preschool educational program, Head Start. CORE workers viewed the War on Poverty, with its provision for "maximum feasible participation" by the poor themselves, as a vehicle for radicalizing the poor in an overtly political way. The Southern Consumers' Education Fund, on the other hand, wished to downplay the connection between the War on Poverty and the civil rights movement, stressing the need to create efficiently run programs that would be immune from political attack. Founded and headed by Father Albert McKnight, a black Catholic priest born in Brooklyn and now living in Lafayette, this organization became the funding agent for the Head Start program in half a dozen parishes, and it soon found itself opposing CORE's demands in Shreveport and elsewhere. In Bogalusa the antipoverty program became a bone of contention between three organizations, with the Bogalusa Voters League, the Louisiana Education Association, and the NAACP all vying for representation on the board of the CAP. When the BVL failed to gain control, its representative resigned from the board, denouncing the remaining blacks as "Uncle Toms."[24]

CORE liked to depict such rows as conflicts between the black poor and the black middle class, but the issue was rarely that simple. In reality, CORE's claim to represent the black proletariat rested on shallow ground: as CORE workers sometimes conceded in private, the local groups that it backed often had little solid support and, far from being "independent," were heavily dependent on CORE for political guidance. Moreover, the terms "middle class" and "Uncle Tom" were not accurate descriptions but infinitely elastic terms of abuse. Thus interorganizational rivalries over the poverty program in many cases bore little relationship to class stratification within the black community.

It is nonetheless clear that white politicians exploited such rivalries by including some blacks and excluding others, with the obvious intention of controlling the poverty program as tightly as possible. In some cases this meant favoring the NAACP over CORE-backed groups; in others it meant selecting teachers and shutting out the NAACP. But black teachers were not always docile mouthpieces of the "white power structure." In St. Mary Parish, for example, teachers associated with the LEA successfully challenged a CAP board that had been handpicked by the local sheriff.[25]

Even a coherent black vote, however, could not guarantee the election of black candidates, for strenuous political mobilization by blacks often led to equally vigorous countermobilization on the part of whites. The 1967 results in Iberville Parish were especially disappointing, for the Iberville Industrial Voters League had confidently expected to be "the first group to make a major political breakthrough" in Louisiana. Over the years the voters league had received more support from CORE, SEDFRE, and the VEP than any other group in the state; by 1967 black registration exceeded 80 percent and composed 40 percent of the total electorate. In the first big test of black voting strength, however, all twenty-four black candidates lost. Here, as elsewhere, the requirement to gain an outright majority of the votes proved the bane of black candidates, who invariably led in the first primary only to lose in the runoff.[26]

Blacks also faced efforts by white officials to dilute the black vote by manipulating the electoral system. The most common device, employed throughout the South, was to substitute unitary electoral districts for ward-based ones. In 1968 the state legislature permitted such "at-large" elections for police juries and school boards, a system that militated against the election of blacks in all but a handful of majority-black parishes. The result was that five years after the Voting Rights Act blacks composed only a minuscule proportion of the state's elected officials, fewer than 1 percent. Only after 1970, when litigation by blacks and intervention by the Justice Department produced a more equitable electoral system, did the situation change markedly for the better.[27]

Nevertheless, if blacks failed to gain anything like a fair share of the political offices in Louisiana, the fact that they began to win even a few had great symbolic significance. In many parishes and cities people of color held office for the first time since Reconstruction. The astonishing transformation wrought by federal reform of the South's voting system was especially striking in the majority-black cotton parishes along the Mississippi River. In Madison Parish, for example, no blacks had voted before December 1962; less than seven years later Zelma Wyche, jailed half a dozen times for his civil rights activities, was elected police chief of Tallulah.[28]

Madison Parish was a textbook example of how the civil rights struggle persisted at the local level. The same men who had petitioned for the vote in the 1940s and sued for the vote in the 1950s and early 1960s now organized the black vote to win a share of political power. They also wielded direct action to integrate public accommodations and break the color line in employment. The decline of the civil rights movement as a national force did not slow them down. The advent of Black Power did not alter their goals, deter them from accepting white help, or persuade them that the federal government was an enemy. And rather than abruptly shifting "from protest to politics," they utilized demonstrations alongside litigation and political action.

CORE worker Cathy Cortez was not overly impressed by the leaders of the Madison Parish Voters League. These men were too timid, she thought, too trusting in the "good white folks." It had taken them fifteen months to finally accept CORE's help, and even then they were reluctant to embark upon direct action.[29]

But the nucleus of the Voters League, eight or ten men in their fifties and sixties, were a determined group of people. They went back a long way: some were veterans of the East Carroll Parish resettlement fight of 1938-39; some were veterans of the Second World War. Since 1947, when they founded the Voters League, they had stuck together through thick and thin. "There were lean years when we didn't do anything," one recalled. "But we were constantly trying to do something." Doggedly pursuing right-to-vote suits, their patience finally paid off in 1961: they won a federal injunction against Katherine Ward, the registrar of voters. By then they had become a tightly knit group that had firmly established its leadership credentials. Moreover, being the only civil rights organization in the parish (there was no NAACP branch) the league did not have to contend with the factionalism and disunity that sometimes prevailed in other communities.

As in Bogalusa, the arrival of white CORE workers to organize the testing of public accommodations—still off-limits to blacks nearly a year after the Civil Rights Act—provided blacks with the inspiration to confront the white authorities. The beating of white CORE worker Gary Craven on the streets of Tallulah galvanized the black community and, in the words of Zelma C. Wyche, led blacks to follow through with "every kind of 'in' you could mention." Sixty-one people were arrested testing the Post Inn Café, and it took only ten hours for the black community to raise sufficient cash to have them bailed out. In 1966 the league supported a student boycott of a new but unfinished and allegedly dangerous high school; in September two hundred blacks marched to the offices of the school board to protest against the maintenance of segregated school buses.

The league also instituted a boycott of Tallulah businesses that refused to hire black sales clerks. It was "probably the most successful boycott ever held in the state of Louisiana," thought John Martzell. "When the boycott was going on you could have shot a shotgun down Main Street and not hit anyone—empty, bare." Seventeen businesses closed their doors rather than succumb to the pressure. The A & P supermarket endured 111 days of boycotting and picketing before acceding to the league's demands. By the end of 1965 the league had the support of sixteen black ministers; the weekly mass meetings rotated among the various churches. In the meantime the league intensified its voter registration efforts; assisted by the federal examiners, black registration soon overtook white.[30]

Faced with black political control of both Tallulah and Madison Parish, whites stared into the future with horror. "All the white officials are implacable segregationists," an LCDC lawyer discovered. "Judge [Cliff] Adams explained that the whites are in a minority and have to fight back." Fight back they did. In October 1965 the leaders of the Voters League suffered a rash of fires: Moses Williams saw his tire shop go up in flames; Rev. Willie Haynes saw his church razed; the arsonists also struck at several homes. Few doubted that the Klan was setting the fires. But blacks were not intimidated. "Seems like every time they did something mean to one of us," Rev. Haynes told a reporter, "all the rest of us just pushed harder."[31]

As the number of black voters steadily mounted, white officials resorted to some devious stratagems. Harrison Brown beat an incumbent school board member in the Democratic primary, but the clerk of elections, Jerome K. Post, gathered 510 absentee ballots for a hastily entered "write-in" candidate. These absentee ballots accounted for a quarter of the total white vote and caused Brown's defeat in the general election. It transpired that Post and his deputies had traveled to plantations and nursing homes, not only soliciting votes from the old and the infirm, but also allowing able-bodied people who had no intention of being out of the parish on election day to vote in their own homes. Post did not, needless to say, display similar diligence in securing absentee ballots from blacks. Judge Ben C. Dawkins ordered a new election, but the registrar of voters then disqualified 479 people, the majority of them blacks drawn from a list of "felons" obligingly supplied by the sheriff.

When Zelma Wyche ran for the office of town marshal in 1967 after Jimmy Rogan died in a car crash, he narrowly lost because his name had been disconnected from the Democratic lever on the voting machines. Throughout his campaign Wyche had urged blacks to vote the straight Democratic ticket, and over 500 people did just that, failing to record a vote for Wyche because they did not realize they were required to pull a separate lever for the marshal's race. A white candidate coasted to victory. Wyche only learned of the change on the morning of the election and he challenged the result. When Dawkins ordered a new election, he won. Even then, however, he had to file another lawsuit before receiving his commission. In 1970 blacks again went to court after the registrar purged a large number of blacks, but only a handful of whites, for failing to report changes of address. Once more Dawkins insisted on new elections.[32]

A veteran of World War Two who made his living as a barber, Wyche had long nurtured an ambition to become Tallulah's police chief. A tall, bespectacled, heavyset man in his late forties, Wyche inspired local blacks through force of personality and sheer guts. A natural leader who could only find his true potential once CORE had defied the white authorities and raised the sights of the black community, Wyche soon became the dominant figure in the Voters League. He displayed amazing coolness in the face of white threats. On several occasions whites leveled shotguns at him; he did not flinch.

Wyche's courage and audacity were conspicuously displayed on July 28, 1966, when he entered a truck stop on Highway 80, a notorious Klan haunt, to demand service. A white employee had closed the restaurant "to keep down trouble," locking the door and wedging a chair against the handle. Wyche forced his way in and demanded to see the manager. After he left, a white logger appeared in the doorway, aimed a gun, and threatened to "blow his brains out." Everyone else took cover (about fifty blacks had gathered outside the restaurant) but Wyche stood his ground, calmly facing the man until the police arrived. The incident cost Wyche a conviction for battery and a four-month jail sentence. "Get out of my face, man," Wyche had told his alleged victim, a white doctor. "We're not working on this nonviolence deal no more."[33]

Such statements seemed to resonate with the militancy of "Black Power." After the Klan arson attacks of October 1965 the Voters League made it abundantly clear that it would not take white violence lying down. Shouting through a bullhorn after the burning of Moses Williams's tire shop, Wyche warned, "You burn us one more time and we're gonna burn you right back. You hurt one of us and we're going to hurt the first white person we run across." The Voters League did not form an armed self-defense group along the lines of the Deacons, but neither did it discourage certain members from carrying guns. The influence of "Black Power" could also be seen in the league's decision to field all-black tickets, a departure from its earlier insistence on supporting white candidates as well as black ones. CORE worker Bruce Baines had returned to Tallulah from the Meredith March convinced that dogmatic adherence to CORE's interracial idealism would only slow black political advance. After initial resistance, the league accepted Baines's logic. Since 1966, Wyche explained, "It's been our objective to take every seat that we could take—and when it all boils down, we're gonna take *every seat* in the village *and* the parish."

If Wyche found the rhetoric and symbolism of Black Power useful, he had little sympathy for its separatist tendencies or clarion call for violent revolution. Like A. Z. Young and Robert Hicks, the leaders of the Bogalusa Voters League, Zelma Wyche personified a new assertiveness, even aggressiveness, that characterized the Southern civil rights movement during the second half of the 1960s. But like Hicks and Young, he articulated goals that remained basically assimilationist or integrationist. Blacks in Madison Parish wanted equity within the American system: decent schools and public services, effective political representation, an end to segregation and police brutality, a fair share of the economic pie. Living in a majority-black parish where whites fought them every inch of the way, the Voters League was an all-black movement. But its decision to field all-black tickets did not entail a rejection of white allies or a repudiation of interracialism: it merely reflected political reality. "We found . . . that the whites in this community did *not* want black people in office," said Wyche, "even though we were trying to be fair."[34]

Far from adopting the "go-it-alone" policy advocated by SNCC, Wyche and the Voters League welcomed outside help, black and white. It regarded the federal government as an ally, and with good reason: the Justice Department appointed federal examiners in 1966 and two years later intervened on behalf of Wyche in his suit against the clerk of elections. In 1970 the government again sued the registrar of voters when 159 blacks were stricken from the rolls. Although white civil rights workers were no longer needed once local blacks had gained sufficient self-confidence, the Voters League continued to rely on white lawyers from the LCDC. The league also called upon SEDFRE to provide political education and training. Upon his election as police chief in 1969, SEDFRE staff members helped Wyche develop a police community relations program. Five years later it sent a team of experts to advise Adell Williams, Tallulah's first black mayor.[35]

A long-established nucleus of activists and a towering individual leader gave blacks in Tallulah cohesion and strength. In Ferriday, Concordia Parish, by contrast, organizational rivalries and the absence of effective leadership fostered weakness and disunity. The result was a fragmented movement that failed to achieve the dynamism of either the Madison Parish Voters League or the Bogalusa Voters League. The Ferriday movement failed, too, to attract the kind of vigorous federal intervention that had so helped blacks in Tallulah and Bogalusa. The absence of a history of black organization and leadership helps to explain this contrast: Ferriday had no NAACP branch, no strong union local, no active voters league, no leaders of the caliber of A. Z. Young, Robert Hicks, Gayle Jenkins, or Zelma Wyche. Yet Ferriday presents a not atypical example of a relatively weak local insurgency that, thanks to the impetus attained by the wider civil rights movement, still managed to change the status quo.

The slowness of indigenous black leadership to emerge owed something to the character of Ferriday itself, a sawmill town close to important oil fields. Loggers and roustabouts were tough men, and Ferriday, the boyhood home of Jerry Lee Lewis and Jimmy Swaggart, offered them the kind of entertainment that gave it the reputation of a "wide open" town. According to John Martzell, "In a state filled with mean towns . . . Ferriday is the meanest." Ferriday also lay within the economic hinterland of Natchez, Mississippi, and the Natchez area boasted one of the most murderous Klan units in the South. In December 1964 members of this group killed Frank Morris by torching his shoe repair shop; in August 1965 an explosion destroyed Hope Well Baptist Church; in November a bomb blew out the windows of Robert Lewis's home. (Lewis, leader of the new NAACP branch, was then arrested for "aggravated assault" when he stood outside with a shotgun). At the end of the year a black-owned Esso service station was burnt to the ground. In Natchez itself the president of the NAACP was seriously injured in a bomb attack. In 1967 the branch treasurer, Wharlest Jackson, died in a car explosion.[36]

So if blacks in Ferriday seemed more fear-stricken than those in Bogalusa, despite the fact that they composed a majority of the town's population, they had reason to be. "Bogalusa was a picnic compared to Ferriday," according to one FBI agent. When CORE workers arrived in the town in July 1965, they found a community "paralyzed, unable to act for fear of reprisals or terrorism." No minister would let them hold meetings in his church. Not a soul would house them: they had to commute from Alexandria through seventy miles of dangerous countryside. When the board of the NAACP state conference met in Ferriday, it began its deliberations well before noon "so that we can be out of Ferriday before dark for safety's sake." The CORE workers eventually found accommodation in the town, but they felt it prudent to change their address every few days. Molotov cocktails hurled from passing cars were an everyday occurrence.

When it became clear that the CORE team would not be intimidated, however, a local movement began to crystallize. At first the Ferriday Freedom Movement comprised students from the Negro high school, but in time a few adults lent support. As happened in Bogalusa and Tallulah, the beating of white CORE workers in broad daylight electrified the black community, prompting the first civil rights march in the town's history. "The Negro community feels guilty about letting 2 beatings occur in their neighborhood," wrote Meldon Acheson, a white summer volunteer, "so I walk around with my black eye and people can't get involved fast enough!"

Members of the Ferriday Freedom Movement integrated the lunch counter at Walgreen's drugstore and obtained cards from the public library. Several applied for admission to the local trade school, and in February 1966 three young children integrated a white elementary school. The movement called upon blacks to boycott the Arcade Theater, a movie house that still made blacks enter through a separate door and sit in the balcony. "I think they've started to move," Acheson reported, "and it's only a matter of time before they get their 'first-class' citizenship. . . . The determination of the youth, and their example of overcoming fear, has begun to catch hold of their parents." In the spring of 1966 black youths responded to a Klan circular by distributing a leaflet of their own in white neighborhoods. It consisted of a poem and contained the following lines:

> As I lay asleep in my bed
> The KU KLUX KLAN put a letter at my head.
> As I began to read it my anger grew bigger,
> Because the first line read, "Dear Nigger." . . .
> They've scared the people and have them upset.
> But I'll get one of those peckerwoods yet.
> They still think that I'm scared of ghosts,
> But I'll send them to hell with the DEVIL as their host.
> When things are good and going on alright
> PECKERWOOD stay from around my house at night.
> Because after reading the FIREY CROSS,
> I'M still the boss.
> To find out who's best you need a good distinguisher,
> So I hope you understand - THE FIREY CROSS EXTINGUISHER.

These sentiments were a far cry from the nonviolent gospel that CORE had tried to spread in the early 1960s.[37]

Meldon Acheson, a native of Iowa then attending the University of Arizona, had been an idealistic member of the Tucson CORE group. The ubiquity of guns in the black community and the matter-of-fact way in which the other CORE workers accepted their presence shocked him at first, but he soon learned to live with guns. "Most projects here in the dangerous areas have arms in the house to 'protect' against night attacks," he explained to his parents. But the Klansmen "are as afraid of us as we are of them," he reassured them; the guns were never likely to be fired in anger. To David Whatley, the twenty-year-old leader of the Ferriday Freedom Movement, the threat of the Klan was all too real and guns an absolute necessity. "Only by the Grace of God and the tiresome and lonely Gardshifts [*sic*] that we are undergoing every night from six o'clock until six thirty A.M. and later" had he survived a winter of Klan attacks. Whatley became the first and only African-American in Ferriday's previously all-white high school. "He goes through a lot each day," a CORE worker reported. "Books spit on, clothes wet when in gym, and the usual heckling."

As CORE's presence faded in 1966, a newly formed NAACP branch took up some of the slack. At first it had to meet in a vacant lot but eventually, by subjecting ministers to pressure and persuasion, it obtained the use of a church. In August 1966, after the bombing of a member's home, the branch announced a boycott of virtually all the town's white-owned businesses. The protest was inspired, in part, by the highly effective boycotts across the Mississippi River in Natchez and Port Gibson, both of them also organized by the NAACP. Rudy Shields, who directed the Natchez boycott, advised the

Ferriday NAACP on how to conduct the campaign. The instigation of the boycott heightened tension considerably: the Natchez boycott had diverted much trade to the town, and Ferriday's white merchants now faced the prospect of ruin. During one of his visits Shields was arrested for "molesting a customer"; when NAACP president Robert Lewis led a protest march to the city hall he was met by twenty policemen and Mayor L. W. Davis, submachine gun in hand.[38]

By the end of 1966, however, the boycott was increasingly ineffective, and the movement no nearer its goal of forcing the city into face-to-face negotiations. Part of the problem lay in weak and fragmented leadership. The Ferriday Freedom Movement coexisted uneasily with the NAACP; the NAACP youth council was at odds with the elderly branch president; a Civic League organized by Father August Thompson was trying to promote biracial talks; and a shadowy Deacons for Defense group lurked in the background. In addition, a group of young blacks calling themselves "the Spirits" took it upon themselves to enforce the boycott through intimidation; their activities threatened to discredit the movement. Gloster Current sent Harvey Britton to resolve the impasse, and Britton recalled his shock upon first encountering the Spirits.

> [The NAACP] had a church meeting and a young man got up and talked about a couple of teachers who had broken the boycott, and the fact that the Spirits had visited them, and that they now understood. And my first thought was, 'Here I am in a religious setting. I have a highly motivated group of young people in the church. . . . And faith is the thing that is moving them.' And then the young man said, 'And when all the windows in the cars were broken out, they understood.'

Britton denounced such activities in no uncertain terms. Years later, he laughed at the naive stereotype that he, as someone born and bred in the North, had held of black Southerners.[39]

Britton's decision to lift the boycott, and the waning of Klan influence under FBI pressure and public disapproval, paved the way for a rapprochement between the "white power structure" and representatives of the black community. Various outside parties had tried their hand as mediators, including the federal Community Relations Service and the Louisiana Biracial Commission, but Father Thompson was the key individual in bringing the two sides together. A black Catholic priest who had lived in Ferriday since 1962, he made valiant and ultimately successful efforts to unite the black community behind a list of negotiable demands. In April 1967 the city finally set up a biracial committee, black voters electing seven people and the mayor selecting five of them. It was hardly the millennium, but it did constitute a victory for the black people of Ferriday.

Political power, however, proved elusive. When Father Thompson appealed to Governor McKeithen to use his influence on the whites, the governor, always the practical politician, told the priest that blacks should concentrate on voter registration. "You can have all the civil rights marches you want, but put your energies into getting people to vote. And I'll make sure that no-one screws around with you." But in 1966 the city council prescribed runoff elections, which ended the "first past the post" system. It also prohibited "single-shot" voting, which prevented blacks from concentrating their ballots on favored candidates. Together with the system of at-large elections, these rules enabled whites to translate their bare majority in voter registration into complete control of municipal government.[40]

When black organizations competed for leadership, as in Ferriday, the establishment of a united front was always difficult. It was made yet more difficult by the position of the national NAACP, whose officers had always been extremely wary of cooperation with other groups. Now, more than ever, they wished to discourage local coalitions, fearing that NAACP branches might become tainted by association with the likes of SNCC and CORE, whose move toward black separatism created an ideological breach that they regarded as unbridgeable. At the NAACP's national convention in July 1966, Roy Wilkins denounced Black Power in the most forceful terms he could muster, characterizing it as "a reverse Mississippi, a reverse Hitler, a reverse Ku Klux Klan." But organizational self-interest, as much as doctrinal purity, dictated New York's distrust of other groups. As always, competition for publicity and money militated against coalitions in which the NAACP might become submerged. Now, moreover, New York calculated that the growth of black nationalism in SNCC and CORE would give the NAACP an opportunity, in the words of director of branches Gloster Current, to pick up "mature and balanced young people" from the "defections in their ranks."[41]

Local NAACP members did not necessarily share New York's hostility to other groups and sometimes expressed impatience with the sectarianism of Wilkins and Current. "I don't care who does the job in northeast Louisiana," wrote the head of the Ferriday branch, "just as long as the black man becomes a free man in this society." Mary Jamieson, appointed to the post of Louisiana field director at the start of 1966, shared these sentiments. A young white woman from Long Island, Jamieson had become active in the NAACP while a teacher at Holy Rosary, a black Catholic high school in Lafayette. She subsequently became the first white student at Grambling College. Jamieson recognized CORE's dominance in certain areas and tried to work closely with the local organizations that CORE had sponsored. In Ferriday, for example, she facilitated the election of David Whatley, head of the Ferriday Freedom Movement, to the vice presidency of the NAACP youth council. In Bogalusa, she wanted to revitalize the weak branch by harnessing the strength of the Bogalusa Voters League; NAACP lawyer Marion Overton White collected over one hundred memberships when he addressed a BVL meeting in August 1966.[42]

Jamieson's ecumenical approach, however, soon earned her reprimands from Gloster Current. Refusing to accept the memberships sent in by White, he warned her to avoid associating with the Deacons for Defense. That meant steering clear of the BVL. He also reproached her for issuing a joint press statement with CORE worker John Zippert. "It is best for the NAACP to proceed independently," insisted Current, even if that meant organizing some communities later rather than sooner. "We should organize slowly," he explained, "and as our movement is strengthened, some of the people who used to work with us are undoubtedly going to return." In October 1966 Current fired Jamieson.[43]

Harvey R. H. Britton, Jamieson's successor, was much more sensitive to the concerns of the national office, and he developed a close rapport with Current. A native of New York City, Britton had trained as a radio and television repairman before serving three years in the Army. He then attended a college in West Virginia, first as a preministerial student, then as a sociology major. Graduating in 1966, he joined the association as a temporary field director assigned to New Haven, Connecticut. After organizing a successful membership drive, Current sent him to Louisiana on a six-month posting. When Britton arrived to take up the post in January 1967, his knowledge of Louisiana was virtually nil. Twenty-six at the time, with a shock of wavy hair that accentuated his youthful appearance, Britton ended up serving as the state field director for nine years.[44]

He found the NAACP in a parlous condition. Of the fifty or so branches, half had fewer than one hundred members; a dozen had failed to meet for at least five years. Much of Britton's incessant traveling was wasted, for many branch officers had no idea how to respond to his requests for information. The association had still not fully recovered from the "chilling effect" of the 1956 injunction: in 1967 there were barely eight thousand members in Louisiana, fewer than in 1955. Schoolteachers were still very reluctant to take out memberships. Ministers, too, rarely supported the NAACP, and the preachers who headed branches tended to be old and incapable. Perhaps the most startling evidence of the organization's weakness was its lack of success in reestablishing strong branches in some of the biggest cities. Branches in Shreveport and Baton Rouge barely limped along; the Monroe and Lafayette branches were all but defunct; the Alexandria branch was in "constant decay."

With the exception of Lake Charles and the small branch in Lake Providence (which the Reverend John Henry Scott had led for almost thirty years) only the New Orleans branch had a record of stability. With a membership of more than three thousand, and with experienced officers whose service to the organization went back, in some cases, twenty, thirty, and forty years, the New Orleans branch provided a core of leadership in the state. But the prominence of the Crescent City branch, Britton thought, had a disadvantage: its leaders tended to dominate the state organization, deterring less experienced, less educated, and less articulate branch presidents from attending and participating. Hence the rural branches, which composed the bulk of the membership, had little contact with or influence within the Louisiana State Conference of Branches (LSC). The large membership of the New Orleans branch, moreover, belied its factionalism and general torpidity. In Britton's view only five branches in the entire state, all of them rural, functioned effectively.[45]

Yet Louisiana, Britton discovered, was the quintessential NAACP state, regardless of whatever other groups were popular at a particular moment. The NAACP's comparatively small membership was misleading, he later explained; "our members were more members-at-large, members in faith, members in that vein, as opposed to financial contributors or people who came to meetings." With deep roots in local communities, the NAACP had the prestige and the connections to mobilize support around gut issues.

Gut issues were never in short supply, but it took leaders to articulate them. One or two dedicated and able activists could transform a moribund branch into a vigorous campaigning organization. And that could happen virtually anywhere, irrespective of the community or its history of race relations. Conversely, with the retirement or departure of key individuals a branch could just as swiftly lapse into inertia. The four strongest branches of the mid and late 1960s, Opelousas, New Roads, New Iberia, and Shreveport, illustrate this life cycle of birth, spectacular growth, and then decline.

Charles E. Bryant and Marion O. White organized the St. Landry Parish branch in August 1963, and it soon became the second largest in the state. Bryant, a schoolteacher, and White, a lawyer, challenged the cozy modus vivendi that had existed since the early 1950s, when whites permitted black voter registration only to co-opt the black vote through a combination of vote buying, petty patronage, and alliances with Negro ministers. Sheriff D. J. "Cat" Doucet, regularly reelected by a strong black vote, personified this paternalistic style of politics. Attacking segregation head-on, in short order the NAACP integrated buses, lunch counters, restaurants, and the courthouse. White filed over thirty lawsuits in the field of public accommodations, and the branch orchestrated dozens of sit-ins. Bryant himself was repeatedly arrested—according to one tally, over forty times. When restaurants evaded integration by becoming "private clubs," white NAACP supporters and lightskinned mulattos obtained membership cards. The city fathers "pretended to be nice," White recalled, creating a biracial committee and asking him and Bryant to serve. They assented, but made it clear that they would not be deflected from their NAACP-work. In 1965 Bryant came within a whisker of being elected to the city council; two years later he ran for sheriff and, by chipping away at Doucet's black support, helped a white candidate to end the remarkable career of "The Cat."[46]

In the small town of New Roads, in Pointe Coupee Parish, the NAACP underwent a transformation under the leadership of Emmitt J. Douglas, a barber and businessman. In 1966 the branch instigated a boycott of selected white merchants, maintaining daily picketing for several months. One of the targets, a pharmacist, sued Douglas for $450,000 in damages and had thirteen pickets arrested on a complaint of intimidation. The dispute climaxed in a march of two thousand people, and it ultimately wrested some jobs from the grudging merchants. In 1967 the branch organized a boycott of local schools to protest the survival of segregation under a so-called freedom of choice plan. An impetuous man and a rousing public speaker, Douglas went on to serve as president of the State Conference of Branches, bringing to that position the kind of assertive leadership that it had not seen since Dr. E. A. Johnson held the post in the early 1950s. Working with younger activists like Llewellyn Soniat and Raphael Cassimere, both of whom had risen through the New Orleans Youth Council, Douglas gave the NAACP high visibility across the state and bucked up underperforming branches. His flamboyant personality and tendency to shoot from the hip landed him in trouble with both friends and foes. He managed to offend both Gloster Current and Charles Bryant, and in 1969 the Baton Rouge district attorney indicted him for inciting a riot. But he gave the state organization a much-needed shot in the arm.[47]

New Iberia provided the most striking example of a branch that came out of nowhere. Defunct since the state's injunction in 1956, it was rechartered in 1964 on the initiative of Dr. James H. Henderson, Lester Scurlock, and T. A. Bolden. "We were determined that we were going to do something." recalled Henderson, a native of North Carolina who had practiced dentistry in the town since the mid-1950s. "And we got out and we talked. We went to all of the churches, we went to the P.T.A. meetings. . . . And I guess we showed sincerity in what we were after, and I remember people just fell into line, and when someone came up and tried to block us, we rode right over him." Franzella Volter, secretary of the branch twenty years earlier when J. Leo Hardy had been beaten and run out of town, became secretary once more. The fastest-growing branch in the state, it soon boasted about a thousand members, an impressive number for a town of thirty thousand where blacks made up only a quarter of the population. Few teachers joined, and fewer ministers; the bulk of the members, according to Henderson, were working class. Numbers, however, told only part of the story. Under Henderson's leadership, the branch picketed downtown stores and outlying shopping centers, forcing the hiring of black clerks. It also utilized the 1964 Civil Rights Act by filing over sixty complaints with the Equal Employment Opportunity Commission; targets included the famous McIlhenny Company, purveyor of Tabasco sauce to the world. Henderson and Volter served on the board of the LSC and helped to organize branches in Lafayette and St. Martinville.[48]

The rapid rise, and equally rapid decline, of the Shreveport branch provided a good illustration of how the fortunes of the NAACP often depended upon one or two individuals. At the time of Martin Luther King's death Shreveport was still a monument to segregation and still maintained one of the most repressive racial orders in the South. George D'Artois, the commissioner of public safety, had squelched attempted demonstrations in September 1963, and he had kept up a blanket ban on all forms of direct action, including picketing, ever since then. The most influential politician in the city, he had the entire community, white and black, cowed. By the end of 1968, however, a young writer and actor, B. J. Mason, had revived the branch, defied D'Artois, and dispelled some of the fear that had immobilized blacks.

B. J. Mason was a twenty-four-year-old graduate of Grambling College and a gifted writer who worked part-time on the *Shreveport Sun*, Louisiana's oldest black newspaper. With Harvey Britton's encouragement, he took over the branch in May 1968 and made plans to challenge the ban on picketing. Mason presided over his first mass meeting in a church that stood opposite the police station; on May 17 he personally handed D'Artois a ten-point plan for improving police-community relations. Instead of rejecting the proposals out of hand, the commissioner, no doubt with an eye on the growing black vote, listened politely and agreed to institute some changes. On June 9, Mason and three others picketed Stan's Record Shop, a store that catered to blacks but stocked racist titles ("Kajun Ku Klux Klan") and employed no Negroes. The police did not arrest them—the first time blacks in Shreveport had been allowed to picket. Soon, as Mason described the scene, "students, ministers, mothers, and common laborers were to be seen marching quietly and slowly in eighty-plus degree temperatures. . . . One old shabbily-dressed black woman laugh[ed] hysterically amid cries of 'Thank God! Thank God! Thank God!'" After a nineteen-day boycott the proprietor agreed to hire five blacks. Other stores were singled out for "selective buying" campaigns, and pickets sauntering up and down the sidewalks became a common sight.

Mason then organized a Youth Council and installed one of the most enthusiastic pickets, Larry N. Cooper, as its president. Cooper called for the teaching of black history and was arrested for "disturbing the peace" while picketing a white high school. On September 18 he led a three-mile march, attended by several thousand youths, from Booker T. Washington High to the offices of the school board. Known to all as "Boogaloo," Cooper was a born orator, and he employed the rhetoric of "Black Power" to great effect. His brand of militancy also appealed to the not-so-young. "The Youth Council . . . had men in there 45 and 50 years of age," Harvey Britton recalled.

Faced with the fastest-growing NAACP branch in the state, which in December 1968 announced a "Black Christmas," a boycott of the downtown shopping area, D'Artois made a determined effort to break up the Youth Council. Police stopped and questioned everyone entering Cooper's apartment; they trailed cars and bugged meetings; they booked drivers for nonexistent traffic offenses; they arrested Cooper himself eighteen times. Determined to go through with the boycott, the NAACP scheduled a march through the downtown business district for December 14. D'Artois denied them a permit and deployed two hundred police—virtually the entire force—to stop it. About 250 people, led by Mason, Britton, and four ministers, covered a block before being halted by the police phalanx. After a tense confrontation, they turned around and regrouped at the church. The branch officers decided to try again the following week.

In any other Southern city, the protest would be judged a failure, but in the context of Shreveport it represented at least a partial victory. The marchers had not been intimidated, nor had they been arrested. The boycott was holding. The NAACP had not exactly clipped D'Artois' wings, but it had stood up to him. "For the first time," Britton told Gloster Current, "meaningful restraints have been placed upon the Safety Commissioner; and the fear of many Negroes . . . has been removed. In Shreveport, one of the strongholds of racism in northern Louisiana, long supported and enforced by city officials, the stage has been set for meaningful change." It seemed an overoptimistic assessment: on December 21 the police arrested Mason and thirty-five others when they attempted to hold another march. Soon afterward, internal wrangling paralyzed the NAACP: Larry Cooper was expelled; Mason suddenly quit as branch president. Shreveport remained a tough city and D'Artois was still firmly ensconced in power. Yet blacks had breached a psychological barrier and now massed the votes to attack a political one.[49]

By the second half of the 1960s the NAACP had acquired a certain legitimacy in the eyes of many influential whites; they viewed it as a useful point of contact and communication. "The black and white antagonists always maintained a relationship with one another, always spoke to each other," Harvey Britton recalled. "So the NAACP was seen as a legitimate vehicle by the white community to transmit information to the black community, even though it may not have been as receptive to the information coming *back* through the NAACP." Only rarely was there no communication at all: usually, Britton stressed, "You see them on the street, and you say, 'How're you doing?' 'What y'all gonna do next?' That kind of stuff." Sometimes, too, whites accepted the NAACP as the bargaining agent for the black community. It was a striking contrast to the late 1950s, when the state had attempted to destroy the organization. By 1965, however, key people of influence in the state finally admitted that black insurgency would not go away, and they preferred to deal with the NAACP rather than CORE. Governor John McKeithen's decision to create a statewide biracial commission typified this realization, and the recognition he accorded the NAACP through the commission was a rather blatant attempt to isolate CORE. The personal rapport between McKeithen and Emmitt Douglas helped to cement the state-NAACP relationship: both men were born politicians of the joke-telling, back-slapping variety.

Significantly, McKeithen tapped Jesse N. Stone, Jr., to help organize the commission's black representation. Like McKeithen, Stone came from North Louisiana and had been raised in a hard school of race relations; although firmly identified with the NAACP, he was used to dealing with white segregationists in a friendly and diplomatic way. Yet McKeithen almost torpedoed his own initiative by insisting on personally selecting some of the commission's black members, something that even the NAACP moderates balked at. They were dissuaded from boycotting the commission when Stone told them that however many members McKeithen named, the governor had agreed that he, Stone, would be able to name twice as many. To nobody's surprise, the black members of the commission included some fairly conservative people by the standards of 1965 black militancy, but they also included a fair cross section of the NAACP's leadership.[50]

Through the biracial commission McKeithen established personal contacts with many of Louisiana's NAACP-oriented black leaders, and he made himself accessible to them. Tall, funny, and personable, the governor resembled Lyndon Johnson in both his skill in dealing with people in a "one-to-one" situation and his appreciation of the growing black vote. Men like Emmitt Douglas and Harvey Britton got to know him well. They even grew to like him. His metamorphosis from segregationist to racial moderate had a calming influence on race relations during the second half of the 1960s.

McKeithen relished the considerable power of Louisiana's governorship and, in contrast to Jimmie Davis, did not hesitate to exercise it. Harvey Britton remembered calling on the governor and asking him to appoint the first black person to a draft board, pointing out that a vacancy existed in Shreveport. McKeithen picked up the phone and ordered the appointment made. A few minutes later the phone rang and, apparently, someone in Shreveport questioned the order. "Yes, yes! Me! The governor!" McKeithen barked. "That's who said put him on the board! Me! The governor! I said put him on the board!" Slamming the phone down he turned to Britton and said, "They don't understand sometimes. I'm the governor!"[51]

The commission's staff members, John Martzell and Jesse Stone, could draw upon McKeithen's authority to defuse racial conflicts. In May 1969, for example, police in Leesville arrested eighteen members of the NAACP State Conference who, having heard that black servicemen from Fort Polk were experiencing off-base discrimination, had set up an improvised "Military complaints center" in a tent. The mayor of Leesville, "Fatty" Fertita, had vowed to keep the NAACP out of his city, and he did not appreciate McKeithen's friendly suggestion that he release the prisoners. Told to mind his own business and stay out of Leesville's affairs, McKeithen exploded. "As long as I'm governor of the state," he told Fertita, "you do what I say or you move that damn city to Texas." He then vowed to send in the state police and the National Guard, placing the city under martial law, unless the prisoners were set free. "At which point," Harvey Britton remembered, "the town of Leesville turned around and said to us, 'Out. Look, y'all gotta go.'" After being incarcerated in a filthy jail for two days, the prisoners were released on bond. Many years later, asked about this incident, McKeithen denied having threatened Fertita. Yet two weeks after their "very friendly" telephone conversation, the governor sent a large contingent of state police to Leesville to ensure that the city did not interfere with an NAACP mass rally.[52]

The biracial commission could only formally mediate a dispute if local white officials asked for its assistance, but when it did intervene, it often got results. In one North Louisiana town, for example, Jesse Stone persuaded a white family business, the target of a boycott, to talk with the Reverend Elijah Brass, their hated antagonist. When he first entered the family store to encounter "a group of white men seated round a pot-bellied stove," the outlook for brokering the dispute seemed unpropitious: the head of the family started the conversation by saying that Brass ought to be shot. In this case, however, as in many others, all it took was an outside mediator, backed by the authority of the governor, to bring the two sides together. Here, too, such mediation was a godsend to the black protagonists, who were desperate to settle before their protests collapsed. "I'm so glad to see you; I don't know what to do," Brass told Stone. "I've been to the cemetery today and I was praying to my dead father because I've got these people out here and we can't stay out and I just don't know what to do." To Stone, getting blacks out of the streets was often the best thing that could happen: "They were tired and ready to come home."[53]

Sometimes it only took one phone call from the governor to defuse an apparently trivial dispute that, in the increasingly hysterical atmosphere of the late 1960s, might have had tragic consequences if left to fester or approached in a ham-fisted way.

The student strike at Grambling College was one such instance. Founded in 1901 as a private high school, converted into a junior college in 1928, and by 1967 a four-year college with about four thousand black students and six white ones, Grambling was the personal fiefdom of Ralph Waldo Emerson Jones. Like many presidents of state-funded black colleges, Jones wielded autocratic power and, as long as he obeyed the dictates of the state board of education, could count on staying in his post until he chose to retire. "A simple, quiet Negro village in the scrub-pine obscurity of the Deep South," Grambling had scarcely been touched by the civil rights movement, or by any of the other cultural and political currents of the 1960s. The college made a fetish of athletics: it boasted more graduates who played professional football than any other college except for Notre Dame; Grambling's baseball team was coached by President Jones himself. The college's rules were not merely paternalistic but oppressive: students had to eat breakfast at 6:00 A.M. underneath signs telling them to "Take bite-size mouthfuls." Women were not allowed to wear slacks, drive cars, or smoke in the student union. Off-campus dating was forbidden; dormitories were locked at 10 P.M.[54]

In the spring of 1967 Jones agreed to liberalize the rules after a student protest. By October, however, the changes had not been implemented, and students instituted a boycott of classes. Contending that Grambling's ethos elevated the sports field over the classroom, the protesters attacked the preferential treatment received by athletes and argued that Jones should resign as college president if he continued to coach the baseball team. Over half the student body boycotted classes; about a quarter threatened to withdraw from college. Students blocked the entrances to the administration building and demanded action on their grievances.[55]

McKeithen dispatched Martzell and Stone to sort out the mess. They arrived at Grambling on October 27, the day of the Grambling-Texas Southern football game, to find that the students had effectively taken over the university. "Dr. Jones lived not unlike a Balkan prince," Martzell discovered. "We sat down to dinner, and they brought in . . . an incredible layout of food—you wouldn't believe it." Perusing the students' list of demands, Martzell could hardly believe that any college still maintained such trivial and onerous rules. Apprised of the situation by phone, McKeithen agreed: "If that's what's going on, I'd [expletive] revolt myself!" As gently as they could, Stone and Martzell told Jones that the governor thought he should concede the demands. Jones meekly agreed. The National Guard arrived on the campus, a few students were expelled, and the boycott collapsed.[56]

Much of the commission's work remained invisible. It organized area committees, for example, that could be quickly contacted by the commission's staff. When the unlikely figure of Rev. Avery Alexander appeared in North Louisiana to lead a march from Haynesville to Jonesboro, a route that led through the racist bastion of Homer, John Martzell quietly alerted influential whites and asked them to ensure the marchers' safety. He also persuaded the sheriff of Claiborne Parish to release Alexander after his arrest for parading without a permit. "They were protected and marched to their heart's content,"

Martzell recalled. According to Troy Middleton, the press followed a deliberate policy of not reporting the commission's interventions, "to prevent offering opportunities to rabble-rousers to come in and preach their hate doctrines."

During the five years of its existence, the statewide commission inspired and facilitated biracial negotiations in many Louisiana communities. Indeed, biracial committees—the bêtes noires of segregationists in the early 1960s became all the rage during the second half of the decade. Alexandria created one in 1967; Mayor Victor Schiro of New Orleans appointed one in the same year. They already existed in Baton Rouge, Lake Charles, Lafayette, Hammond, Jonesboro, Opelousas, and New Iberia. Of all the major cities in the state, only Shreveport bucked the trend.[57]

Yet Jesse Stone expressed skepticism about the value of biracial committees. Too often, he believed, blacks made the establishment of a BRC the centerpiece of their demands. They then entered negotiations only to be fobbed off with vague promises, token concessions, or inaction.

> The biracial committee, I thought, occupied too prominent a place in what they were trying to do. But there was this real desire on the part of black people to sit at the table and talk things out on a "man-to-man" basis when we really had no experience in bargaining and dealing with the white man. . . . And every time blacks and whites sat down at the bargaining table, blacks lost. We would proceed by telling the white people off, feeling good, but with them shaking their head and saying "this is a good meeting," you know, with nothing accomplished.

The setting up of a biracial committee tended to become an end in itself, rather than simply one means to an end. And this was in some measure true, he feared, of the state commission. Assessing the commission's accomplishments many years later, Stone confessed to some disappointment.[58]

For the whites on the state commission, getting to know Louisiana's black leadership, or at least an important segment of it, was an important learning experience. John Martzell was convinced that the frank discussions helped erode the ignorance that resulted in racial stereotypes. "One of the best ways to break down the myths about two groups is to put the groups together, and they laugh, and say, 'You mean you believe that!'" Yet most of the black members were worldly wise in dealing with whites and had little need of such education. And they became increasingly suspicious that the commission was being used to damp down racial fires rather than produce tangible improvements in the lives of Louisiana's black citizens.[59]

McKeithen's response to the Bogalusa-to-Baton Rouge march of August 1967 provided a typical example of the commission's basically reactive role. This march was also an excellent example of how local activists combined the traditional tactics of the civil rights movement with the new rhetoric of Black Power to successfully induce near-panic in the federal and state authorities.

The Bogalusa-to-Baton Rouge march had many bizarre and even comic aspects, not the least of which were its origins. In July 1967 A. Z. Young wrote to McKeithen requesting a meeting with the biracial commission to discuss the "steadily worsening" situation in Bogalusa. Due to what John Martzell described as a "bureaucratic foul-up," the letter was filed away without ever coming to McKeithen's attention. When he failed to receive a reply, Young thought he had been deliberately snubbed, and he announced that the Bogalusa Voters League would march on the state capitol. A hastily improvised list of demands focused on the lack of Negroes in state employment, drawing particular attention to the absence of a single black state policeman.

The scenario had all the ingredients of a political Molotov cocktail. The route of the march ran through the predominantly white portion of the Florida Parishes, an area populated by "tough, Mississippi-type rednecks," a good many of whom belonged to the Klan. During the Selma-to-Montgomery march of 1965 the presence of thousands of troops had not prevented the Klan from murdering Viola Liuzzo, a white woman. The possibility of Klansmen attacking and even killing marchers during the 106-mile trek twice the length of the Selma-to-Montgomery march—was all too real. The worst potential flashpoint was Denham Springs, in Livingston Parish, which Martzell characterized as "the Klan country of all Klan country."

Equally worrying, the march took place during the worst "long, hot summer" of the 1960s, in the immediate aftermath of devastating and bloody riots in Newark and Detroit. Every city in the country was trembling with tension. Baton Rouge, the march's destination, was widely regarded as the Louisiana city most likely to blow up, with a poorly organized black community almost at the boiling point over police brutality. The 271-man Baton Rouge police force had only twelve black officers, and these men were still in effect segregated on the job, traveling in separate patrol cars. When Mayor W. W. Dumas ordered the force to pair the black officers with whites, he had to rescind the directive when the whites threatened to strike. To cap it all, H. Rap Brown, the chairman of SNCC, was due to speak to the marchers from the capitol steps. Brown had recently been arrested for inciting a riot in Cambridge, Maryland, and had described the riots as "just dress rehearsals for revolution." The fact that Brown had grown up in Baton Rouge would give his visit further incendiary potential.[60]

The nine-day march passed without serious violence, but it produced some nasty moments. After dozens of whites tried to break through police lines to get at the marchers as they entered Livingston Parish, the head of the state police, Colonel Thomas Burbank, persuaded the Klan to leave the marchers alone as long as they went clear through the parish the next day. But when A. Z. Young insisted that they rest a day before resuming the march, the Klan repudiated the agreement, and Burbank, incensed that Young had broken his word, threatened to withdraw the state police. "The federal government went absolutely bonkers," recalled Martzell, threatening to send in paratroopers if the state failed to provide adequate protection. McKeithen ordered Burbank to continue guarding the marchers and, in addition, called up more than eight hundred

National Guardsmen. Deploying the part-time soldiers was a shrewd move. "Those crazy rednecks out there," McKeithen explained, "they'll jump on a policeman but they'll never jump on an American soldier. They're so patriotic they'll just never do it." When he learned that the adjutant general proposed leading the march atop a tank and wanted his men to carry loaded rifles, the governor could barely contain himself with laughter. "These guys are the National Guard," he told Martzell. "I'm not going to give those guys any bullets!"

As the marchers passed through Denham Springs, soldiers flanking them on both sides, white onlookers jeered but kept their distance. Moreover, by the time the marchers arrived in Baton Rouge, "Rap" Brown had been arrested for carrying a gun onto a plane (the FBI had had him under close surveillance and nabbed him in New York). Police with shotguns patrolled Baton Rouge's black neighborhoods and fifteen hundred National Guardsmen stood at the ready. The feared riot did not take place.[61]

If the march proved a law enforcement triumph, it left the black members of the biracial commission seething with frustration. Only when A. Z. Young vowed to repeat the protest, threatening simultaneous marches that would converge on Baton Rouge from "the four corners of the state," did McKeithen convene the commission to discuss the question of state employment. The governor was especially embarrassed by the fact that Colonel Burbank had recently hired 150 state policemen, all of them whites. His explanation for this state of affairs, that sacrosanct civil service rules were to blame, did not impress the black members, who also questioned his claim to have improved the lot of blacks in state employment generally. Only the threat of demonstrations, complained Rev. T. J. Jemison, had moved the governor to address the problem. "The Commission will not receive one ounce of credit. The Bogalusa march will be the cause of a [black] state trooper, not the Human Relations Commission. . . . I regret that we have pussyfooted so long." Henry Carroll of Monroe put the matter more bluntly: "We are serving as Uncle Toms." A few months later, civil service rules having been bent, the state police hired two black troopers. As Jemison commented acerbically, "If white men want to do it, it is done."[62]

Some blacks had opposed the commission from the outset. To CORE lawyer Nils Douglas, it was a "do-nothing committee" that merely testified to the governor's fancy political footwork, his attempt to be all things to all men while remaining, at heart, a white segregationist. McKeithen certainly had the ability, as Camille Gravel noted, to mix political oil and water. Gravel once visited the governor's mansion to find him holding simultaneous meetings with blacks and Klansmen, each group oblivious of the other's presence in the building. The biracial commission enabled McKeithen to institutionalize this policy of playing both ends against the middle. According to a 1966 survey of racial attitudes in Louisiana, whites expected the commission "to act as a kind of safety valve which will keep the lid on the situation and maintain as much of the status quo as possible." Blacks, on the other hand, wanted the commission to be a vehicle "for solid accomplishment." Judged solely in political terms, McKeithen walked this tightrope with great success: in 1967 he romped home to a second term, garnering 82 percent of the total vote and an even greater percentage of the black vote. This lopsided vote, however, overstated black enthusiasm for McKeithen: the governor was running against Congressman John Rarick, the Klan-backed candidate of the far right. Perhaps the most common opinion was that of James Henderson, the commission member from New Iberia. "I think he was as sincere as any white man in this state could have been at that time—but that doesn't mean that politically he didn't try to use us."[63]

By 1967 Stone and Martzell had become frustrated by McKeithen's use of them and the commission for crisis management. "Louisiana is doomed to future discord," they warned, "if the Commission's principal function in the public eye is 'keeping the lid on.'" Poverty and unemployment were now the biggest problems facing blacks, and they demanded urgent action. "Viewed in the coldest light the fact is that, by and large, Negro Louisianians are the State's poorest producers; and, by and large, white Louisianians are to blame. The question is what can be done about it." They believed that the biracial commission, in its present form, could do little. Even its chairman, Troy Middleton, agreed that the commission had exhausted its usefulness as an advisory body.[64]

The commission's inability to substantially improve the position of blacks in state and municipal employment underscored their point. Between 1964 and 1971 the number of black people employed by the state increased by about 4 percent. According to one careful study, however, this increase "did not improve the occupational position of the Negro state employee." To be sure, visitors to state government offices in Baton Rouge could now see a few black typists and secretaries where before there had been none. But black clerical workers numbered only fourteen out of nearly twenty-five hundred. The majority of black state employees remained in the lowest occupational category, that of unskilled laborer. Very few indeed were hired in supervisory, technical, and professional positions. For example, the one thousand or so examiners, inspectors, and investigators employed by state agencies included only seven blacks. The situation in city government was little better. A 1967 survey of Baton Rouge showed that blacks held 16 percent of the municipal jobs but made up 65 percent of the laborers. The fire department was over 97 percent white, a handful of black firemen serving in one "Negro" station. In Shreveport the disparities were even more pronounced: 82 percent of black city employees were classified as "service maintenance" compared with 13 percent of white employees.[65]

The stagnating economic position of the black population testified to the magnitude of the so-called crisis of victory confronting the civil rights movement. The goals of civil and political equality under the law had largely been accomplished: public accommodations had been desegregated, the battle for the vote had been won, discriminatory statutes based on race had been erased. But if the civil rights movement had toppled the legal scaffolding of white supremacy, the edifice itself remained largely intact. Civil rights legislation so far had singularly little effect on the distribution of wealth and the structure of the employment market; indeed, the individualistic ethic implicit in the Fourteenth Amendment and the 1964 Civil Rights Act reflected a deeply rooted ideological commitment to free market capitalism, to the belief that the removal of artificial racial barriers would enable blacks to enter the economic mainstream under their own efforts.

Some blacks subscribed to this optimistic faith. Revius Ortique, chairman of the New Orleans Community Relations Council, saw "an unparalleled era of opportunity in employment" for blacks; J. Harvey Kerns, secretary of the New Orleans Urban League, agreed that "never before have the opportunities for competent Negroes been so great." Others offered a more pessimistic assessment. The NAACPs Arthur Chapital warned that the language of equal opportunity would ring hollow if decent jobs were not available, and employers would not create jobs for blacks by displacing whites. Even in a theoretically "color blind" job market, he added, blacks, worse educated and worse trained than whites, would find it difficult to compete. Harvey Britton's experience in trying to secure secretarial help for the NAACP office in New Orleans exemplified this problem: most applicants lacked basic skills, he complained; those hired proved to be poor workers.

The explosion of riots in the urban ghettos of the North and West underlined the failure of the civil rights movement to bring tangible economic improvements to the lives of most black people. Politicized by the rhetoric of freedom and equality, the black poor felt massively disappointed when so little changed after the great legislative victories of the movement. The failure of the War on Poverty to alleviate their economic plight—especially when hopes had been raised so high by President Johnson's grandiose promises of a "Great Society"—added to that sense of disillusionment. In the wake of Watts, Chicago, Newark, and Detroit, black leaders gradually woke up to the fact that the urban poor constituted social dynamite and that the mainstream civil rights organizations had made virtually no effort to organize them. As Nils R. Douglas pointed out, the movement had owed its success to strategy and leadership rather than weight of number; "The crucial masses remain substantially untouched."[66]

The NAACP's failure to relate to those masses derived partly from the association's predominantly middle-class leadership, which found it difficult to identify and communicate with the ghetto poor. It also derived from the NAACP's basic orientation, the product of a long history of focusing on discriminatory laws and practices. "They lacked imagination outside of the civil rights movement," he recalled of the New Orleans branch leaders. "Anything that did not speak literally to 'I see civil rights,' they couldn't deal with." The legacy of Cold War anticommunism, when the NAACP had deliberately divorced itself from the labor-left agenda, nurtured a lingering suspicion of anything that hinted at socialism or economic radicalism. The war in Vietnam, moreover, reinforced fear of communism among the older leaders. In New Orleans, the Youth Council's wish to endorse Martin Luther King's criticisms of the war evoked strong opposition from the branch.

The NAACP's shortcomings should not be judged too severely. In truth, the social and economic problems of the black ghettos were of overwhelming magnitude and complexity. If they defeated the best efforts of the federal government, with all its poverty experts and billions of dollars, it is scarcely to be wondered that the NAACP—for all its prestige, a shoestring operation, with a small staff and modest funds—did not know where to begin. Besides, the NAACP always found that more immediate and more emotional issues needed addressing. Much of the time it found itself reacting to specific incidents and situations; long-range planning remained an unaffordable luxury. "There just wasn't time for that," Britton recalled. "It was still a time for access—'you've got to get in here, you've got to get in there, you've got to stop police brutality.'"[67]

## Notes for "Race and Democracy: The Civil Rights Struggle in Louisiana, 1915-1972"

[1]Ronnie Moore to Marvin Rich, "The State of CORE," August 8, 1966, Congress of Racial Equality Papers, Scholarship, Education and Defense Fund for Racial Equality files, microfilm at Alderman Library, University of Virginia, Charlottesville, hereinafter referred to as SEDFRE; August Meier and Elliot Rudwick, *CORE: A Study in the Civil Rights Movement, 1942-1968* (New York, 1973), 411.

[2]Raymond J. Lockett, "A History of Black Leadership and Participation in Local Politics in St. Mary Parish, 1950-1970" (M.A. thesis, Southern University, 1971), 41, 57; John Zippert, "Chronology of Events in the Formation and Development of the Grand Marie Vegetable Producers Cooperative," July 20, 1966, SEDFRE.

[3]Judith R. Berzon, *Neither Black nor White: The Mulatto Character in American Fiction* (New York, 1978). For expressions of the cliché by black writers, see, for example, Frank Smalls, "The Octaroon"; Pauli Murray, "Mulatto's Dilemma"; Octave Emy, Jr., "Song of the Mulatto," all in *Opportunity*, March, June, November, 1938. *Opportunity* was published by the National Urban League.

[4]Arnold R. Hirsch, "Simply a Matter of Black and White: The Transformation of Race and Politics in Twentieth-Century New Orleans," in Hirsch and Joseph Logsdon, eds., *Creole New Orleans: Race and Americanization* (Baton Rouge, 1992), 292-316; Virginia R. Dominguez, *White by Definition: Social Classification in Creole Louisiana* (New Brunswick, N.J., 1986), 172-74; Harvey R. H. Britton, interviewed by Adam Fairclough, November 4, 1987, 13.

[5]For a brief history of the LCDC, see Jack Bass, *Unlikely Heroes* (Tuscaloosa, 1990), 293.

[6]Report, "Proposed March of Bogalusa Voters League in Bogalusa, Louisiana, to Franklinton, Louisiana," August 11, 1966, FBI file 157-5844; Feingold to Russell, August 12, 1967, reel 1, Feingold Papers. In 1968 the FBI concluded that the Deacons for Defense were now "of little or no significance" and discontinued its surveillance; see R. W. Smith to William C. Sullivan, March 26, 1968; SAC, New Orleans, to Hoover, December 13, 1968, FBI file 157-2466.

[7]John Martzell, interviewed by Adam Fairclough, October 1, 1987.

[8]Clayborne Carson, "Civil Rights Reform and the Black Freedom Struggle," in Charles W. Eagles, ed., *The Civil Rights Movement in America* (Jackson, Miss., 1986), 26-27.

[9]Bayard Rustin, "From Protest to Politics: The Future of the Civil Rights Movement," *Commentary*, 39 (1965): 25-31.

[10]*New Orleans Times-Picayune*, November 7, 1965; A. L. Davis to Marvin Rich, November 3, 1965, SEDFRE; *Louisiana Weekly*, August 21, 28, September 4, October 2, 1965; *Blacks United for Lasting Leadership* v. *City of Shreveport*, 71 F.R.D. 623 (1976); Commission on Civil Rights, *The Voting Rights Act: The First Months* (Washington, D.C., 1965), 38; *U.S.* v. *Louisiana*, 265 F. Supp. 603 (1966); John Doar to James H. Morrison, August 13, 1966, box 74, folder 15, James H. Morrison Papers, University of Southeastern Louisiana, Hammond; Jack P. F. Gremillion to Louis Lyons, August 3, 1966, box 986, Louisiana Attorney General's Papers, Louisiana State Archives, Baton Rouge.

[11]*U.S.* v. *Louisiana*; John Kenneth Price, "The Impact of Black Voter Participation on the Politics of Louisiana and Virginia" (Ph.D. dissertation, University of Texas at Austin, 1978), 93.

[12]James T. McCain to Marvin Rich, "Louisiana and South Carolina Reports," December 18, 1967, SEDFRE; "Leander H. Perez, Sr.," FBI file 44-37688; David J. Garrow, *Protest at Selma: Martin Luther King, Jr., and*

*the Voting Rights Act of 1965* (New Haven, 1978), 19, 200; Voter Education Project, "Voter Registration in the South: Autumn, 1970," December 1970, Southern Regional Council Papers, microfilm at Alderman Library, University of Virginia, Charlottesville, hereinafter cited as SRC; James R. Bobo and Jesse M. Charlton, Jr., eds., *Statistical Abstract of Louisiana* (New Orleans, 1974), 246.

[13]Pat Watters and Reese Cleghorn, *Climbing Jacob's Ladder: The Arrival of Negroes in Southern Politics* (New York, 1967), 33-34; Mark Doherty, "Hale Boggs and Civil Rights: A Case Study of a Southern Moderate" (B.A. honors thesis, Tulane University, 1983), 66-67.

[14]Jack Bass and Walter DeVries, *The Transformation of Southern Politics: Social Change and Political Consequences Since 1945* (New York, 1977), 167-70.

[15]Jules Witcover, "Who's Afraid of Those Negro Voters?" *New Republic*, October 30, 1965, 10; "'Black Power' v. Americanism," Rarick campaign flyer; speech of James H. Morrison, July 25, 1966, reprinted from *Congressional Quarterly*, both in James H. Morrison Papers; *New South* (Fall 1966): 101-3.

[16]Jesse N. Stone, interviewed by Adam Fairclough, April 3, 1992, 5; Watters and Cleghorn, *Climbing Jacob's Ladder*, 35-36; Bennett H. Wall, ed., *Louisiana: A History* (Arlington Heights, Ill., 1990), 349.

[17]Stone interview, 4-7; Ronnie Moore to Acie Belton, August 23, 1966, SEDFRE.

[18]Stone interview, 6; Hirsch, "Simply a Matter of Black and White," 291; Nils R. Douglas to Marvin Rich, December 27, 1966, SEDFRE.

[19]Hirsch, "Simply a Matter of Black and White," 289; Addison C. Carey, "Black Political Participation in New Orleans" (Ph.D. dissertation, Tulane University, 1971), 55-56; Wilfred Aubert, "Narrative Report," July 26, 1967, folder 289, National Association for the Advancement of Colored People, New Orleans Branch Records, Earl K. Long Library, University of New Orleans, hereinafter cited as NAACP (NO).

[20]Lockett, "History of Black Leadership," 33-54. In 1979 a federal grand jury indicted over thirty people in Leesville for conspiracy to buy votes in the election that put Claude "Buddy" Leach into Congress. They included the town's mayor and top officials, as well as a former president of the NAACP branch. Most pleaded guilty or were convicted.

[21]*Lake Providence Banner-Democrat*, May 22, 1970; Harvey Britton to Nathaniel Jones, May 25, 1970, box 8, folder 6, Papers of the NAACP Field Director for Louisiana, Amistad Research Center, Tulane University, New Orleans, hereinafter cited as NAACP (LA).

[22]James T. McCain to Marvin Rich, "Louisiana and South Carolina Report," December 18, 1967, SEDFRE.

[23]Hirsch, "A Simple Matter of Black and White," 298.

[24]"Field Report on Project Head Start," July 1965, SEDFRE; David Dyer Massey, "The Federation of Southern Cooperatives," *Southern Exposure* (Fall 1974): 39-47; Harris David to Sargent Shriver, July 8, 1966; notes on Bogalusa poverty program, June 8, August 19, 1966, reel 9, Lawyers Constitutional Defense Fund Committee files, microfilm at Amistad Research Center, hereinafter cited as LCDC.

[25]Mike Lesser, "Let's Have a People's Conference," May 1965, box 9, folder 12, CORE Papers, Southern Regional Office files, State Historical Society of Wisconsin, Madison, hereinafter cited as CORE (SRO); Lawrence Stewart to Harvey Britton, August 7, 1965, box 1, folder 1, NAACP (LA); Lockett, "History of Black Leadership," 12.

[26]William H. Samuel to Ronnie Moore, October 11, 1967; "Roster of Negro Candidates," 1967, both in SEDFRE.

[27]Stanislaus Anthony Halpin, Jr., "The Anti-Gerrymander: The Impact of Section 5 of the Voting Rights Act upon Louisiana Parish Redistricting" (Ph.D. dissertation, George Washington University, 1978), 174; Commission on Civil Rights, *The Voting Rights Act: Ten Years After* (Washington, D.C., 1975), 205-6.

[28]Marvin Rich, "Civil Rights Progress out of the Spotlight," *Reporter*, March 7, 1968; Charles L. Sanders, "Black Lawman in KKK Territory," *Ebony* (January 1970), 57.

[29]Catherine Cortez to Oretha Castle, Field Report, November 8-10, 1964, box 3, folder 2, Monroe Project files, CORE papers, State Historical Society of Wisconsin, Madison.

[30]*Louisiana Weekly*, November 13, 1965; Zelma Wyche, Moses Williams, Harrison H. Brown, Jr., Rev. F. W. Wilson, Rev. T. I. Israel, interviewed by Miriam Feingold, [1966], recording, Feingold Collection, State Historical Society of Wisconsin, Madison; L. H. Whittemore, *Together: A Reporter's Journey into the New Black Politics* (New York, 1971), 206-7; "Madison Parish School Boycott Injunction," January 14, 1966, *Madison Parish School Board* v. *Madison Parish Voters League* file, reel 98, LCDC; New Orleans to Director, September 1, 1966, teletype, FBI file 157-6-33-4410; Martzell interview, 20.

[31]Armin Rosecranz to Harris David, April 17, 1966, Madison Parish file, reel 48, LCDC; Sanders, "Black Lawman," 64.

[32]Files on *Brown* v. *Post*, *U.S.A* v. *Post*, *Wyche* v. *Post*, reel 74, LCDC; Research Project, University of Chicago Law Review, *Voting Rights: A Case Study of Madison Parish, Louisiana* (Chicago, 1971), 764-74; Frank T. Read and Lucy S. McGough, *Let Them Be Judged: The Judicial Integration of the Deep South* (Metuchen, N.J., 1978), 314-15.

[33]Donald A. Juneau, Memo, December 20, 1965, in Zelma Wyche: Aggravated Assault file; Note of Evidence, September 28, 1966, and other materials in *Louisiana* v. *Wyche* file, all in reel 73, LCDC.

[34]Whittemore, *Together*, 206-8; Bruce Baines, unidentified interviewer, [1984?], recording, Amistad Research Center.

[35]University of Chicago Law Review, *Voting Rights*, 767-76; *A SEDFRE Report: Tallulah, Louisiana*, n.d., SEDFRE.

[36]Elaine Dundy, *Ferriday, Louisiana* (New York, 1991); Martzell interview, 19; *Louisiana Weekly*, December 4, 1965; CORE news release, December 19, 1965, box 1, folder 2, CORE Papers, State Historical Society of Wisconsin, Madison, hereinafter cited as CORE (FFM); SAC, New Orleans, to Director, "Ferriday Freedom Movement," August 4, 1965, FBI file 517-5133; Keesing's Research Reports, no. 4, *Race Relations in the USA* (New York, 1970), 214.

[37]John Hamilton to Richard Haley, [May 1966], box 1, folder 5, CORE (FFM); Meldon Acheson to parents, July 10, 1965; "The Firey Cross Extinguisher," Meldon Acheson Papers, CORE (FFM); Louisiana State Conference of Branches, minutes, February 27, 1966, folder 134, NAACP (NO).

[38]Meldon Acheson to parents, July 10, 14, 30, August 10, 1965; Acheson to Garry Greenberg, July 27, August 17, 1965, all in Acheson Papers; David Whatley, Field Report, n.d.; John Hamilton to Richard Haley, May 18, 1966, both in box 1, folder 5, CORE (FFM); Robert Lewis to Mary Jamieson, June 28, 1966, box 1, folder 7; NAACP news releases, August 8, 31, 1966, box 34, folder 24, all in NAACP (LA).

[39]John Hamilton to Richard Haley, Field Report, April 2-7, 1966, box 1, folder 5, CORE (FFM); David Whatley to Mary Jamieson, June 21, 1966; Harvey Britton to Gloster Current, January 15, 1967, box 1, folders 7, 13; Britton to Rhennie Whittle, October 24, 1969, box 7, folder 4, all in NAACP (LA); Britton interview, 1.

[40]Calvin Kytle to Wiley Branton, July 22, 1965, box 3, Lee White Papers, Lyndon B. Johnson Library, Austin, Texas; Frank J. Price, *Troy H. Middleton: A Biography* (Baton Rouge, 1974), 378; Harvey Britton to Mayor L. W. Davis, March 23, 1967; Britton, Monthly Report, April 13, 1967, box 2, folders 3, 4, NAACP (LA); Martzell interview, 19; *Wallace* v. *House*, 337 F. Supp. 1192 (1974).

[41]Roy Wilkins quoted in Adam Fairclough, *To Redeem the Soul of America: The Southern Leadership Conference and Martin Luther King, Jr.* (Athens, Ga., 1987), 320; Current to Branch Department Staff, May 31, 1966, box 1, folder 5, NAACP (LA).

[42]A. P. Tureaud, interviewed by Joseph Logsdon, tape 20; Mary Jamieson to Current, June 20, 1966; Jamieson to Richard L. Dockery, n.d., box 1, folders 7,10, NAACP (LA).

[43]Marion Overton White, interviewed by Patricia Rickels, 1979, recording, University of Southwestern Louisiana, Lafayette; Current to Jamieson, June 16, 22, September 26, October 13, 1966, in box 1, folders 9-11, NAACP (LA).

[44]Britton's biographical details in Britton to Donald Avery, March 7, 1967, box 2, folder 2, NAACP (LA); Britton interview, 13-14.

[45]Britton Monthly Report, October 17, 1967, Annual Report, November 29, 1967, box 3, folders 3, 4; Monthly Report, April 15, 1968, box 4, folder 1, all in NAACP (LA). On the reluctance of teachers to join the NAACP, see Anthony G. Pierre (Lafayette) to Jamieson, April 27, 1966, box 1, folder 3; Linton J. Carmouche (Marksville) to Britton, October 22, 1968, box 5, folder 2; Robert Clark and Dessie Lee Patterson (De Soto Parish) to Britton, April 5, 1969, box 6, folder 2, all in NAACP (LA).

[46]Brendan Sexton and Bill Brown, Parish Scouting Report, Opelousas, St. Landry Parish, November 22, 1963, box 7, folder 1, CORE (SRO); White interview; "A Brief History of the St. Landry NAACP," [1967], box 38, folder 7, NAACP (LA); Mary Alice Fontenot and Vincent Riehl, *The Cat and St. Landry: A Biography of Sheriff D. J. "Cat" Doucet of St. Landry Parish, Louisiana* (Baton Rouge, 1972), 145-46.

[47]James H. Henderson, interviewed by Adam Fairclough, September 28, 1987; Louisiana State Conference of Branches, minutes, February 27, 1966, folder 134, NAACP (NO); Emmitt J. Douglas, "Newsletter," April 21, 1967; Britton to Current, April 26, 1967, both in box 2, folder 5; Britton to Charles E. Bryant, August 1, 1968; Current to Britton, August 8, 1968, both in box 4, folder 8, all in NAACP (LA); *Baton Rouge Morning-Advocate*, August 13, 1969.

[48]Henderson interview; Britton, Monthly Report, February 14, 1968, box 3, folder 7, NAACP (LA).

[49]Stanley J. Lewis to B. J. Mason, June 27, 1968; Mason to Lewis, July 27, 1968, box 4, folder 7; Britton to Current, June 25, 1969, box 6, folder 7; Shreveport NAACP, news releases, May 2, July 30, 1968, box 38, folder 9; Britton, Monthly Report, November 19, 1968; Britton to Current, December 16, 1968, box 5, folders 3, 4; B. J. Mason to Alfred Mitchell, March 4, 1969, box 5, folder 8; Britton, Monthly Report, May 15, 1969, box 6, folder 9, all in NAACP (LA); *Shreveport Sun*, June 13, 1968; Notes on picketing of Sliman's liquor store, December 12-29, 1968; Petition for Writ of Habeas Corpus and Bail, May 1969, *Cooper* v. *Goslin* file, reel 16, LCDC; Britton interview, 7; Willie Burton, *On the Black Side of Shreveport: A History* (Shreveport, 1983), 109-12.

[50]Britton interview, 5; Meier and Rudwick, *CORE*, 349; Stone interview, tape 2, 2.

[51]Britton interview, 1, 11.

[52]Harvey Britton, "Chronicle of Events Leading to the Establishment of an NAACP Military Complaints Center In Leesville, Louisiana, May 17, 1969," May 22, 1969; Britton to Gloster Current, "NAACP Mass Rally, Leesville, June 1, 1969," June 3, 1969, box 6, folders 5, 6, NAACP (LA); Britton interview, 4; John J. McKeithen, interviewed by Adam Fairclough, recording, October 7, 1987.

[53]Stone interview, 2, 7.

[54]George Frazier IV, "100 Yards and 60 Minutes of Black Power," *Esquire* (October 1967): 95-99; list of demands, April 7, 1967; R. W. E. Jones and William M. Zanders, Agreement, April 10, 1967, all in Grambling College file, reel 75, LCDC.

[55]"The Grambling Protest Movement," n.d.; The Informers, "Awaken Black Brothers and Sisters," leaflet, n.d.; notes of Interdepartmental Council meeting, October 26, 1967; *Monroe Morning World*, November 1, 1967; *Wall Street Journal*, November 3, 1967, all in reel 75, LCDC.

[56]Martzell interview, 22-23; *Shreveport Times*, November 1, 1967.

[57]Price, *Troy H. Middleton*, 377-78; Martzell interview, 21; *Homer* v. *Alexander* file, reel 1, LCDC. Creation of the Alexandria BRC is mentioned in Louis Berry, Annual Report of the State Attorney, January 8, 1968, box 3, folder 6, NAACP (LA). The New Orleans BRC was appointed in August 1967; eight white members were nominated by labor, religious, and civil organizations; an equal number of black members by colleges, civil rights organizations, labor, and the ministerial alliance. In early 1968 another six member of each race were chosen in public elections, with voters casting ballots by race (New Orleans Human Relations Council Files, New Orleans Public Library; hereinafter cited as HRC).

[58]Stone interview, tape 1, 7-8.

[59]Martzell interview, 18-19. Interestingly, while the commission's white director, Martzell, recalled that the commission met frequently and that the meetings were useful, according to Stone, the black associate director, the commission met infrequently and the meetings did not achieve all that much.

[60]Ibid., 16; *New Orleans Times-Picayune*, August 15, 1967; Brown quoted in Keesing's Research Reports, *Race Relations in the USA*, 252.

[61]Martzell interview, 12, 16-17; *New Orleans Times-Picayune*, August 15-21, 1967.

[62]Louisiana Commission on Human Relations, minutes, August 28, 1967; meeting of subcommittee with Civil Service Commission, minutes, November 7, 1967, both in box 21, folder 24, Alexander Pierre Tureaud Papers, Amistad Research Center, Tulane University, New Orleans, hereinafter cited as APT.

[63]Nils R. Douglas, "An Impartial Look at the Biracial Commission and the Present Status of the Negro Under Governor McKeithen," n.d.; Speech to Lyceum Committee, Tulane University Center, December 9, 1966, both in Douglas Papers; Camille Gravel, interviewed by Jim Brown, "Louisiana Politics" series, NOETC Higher Education Channel, broadcast February 17, 1992; Louis, Bowles, and Grace, "Study of Racial Attitudes in Louisiana, Fall of 1966: Principal Findings," 11, box 5, Gene Geisert Papers, Orleans Parish School Board files, Earl K. Long Library, University of New Orleans; Henderson interview.

[64]Martzell and Stone, "Position Paper on the Louisiana Commission on Human Relations, Rights, and Responsibilities," February 9, 1967, box 21, folder 27, APT; Price, *Troy H. Middleton*, 380.

[65]John Hampton Carson, "A Quantitative and Qualitative Analysis of Racial Employment Discrimination in Louisiana, 1950-1971" (Ph.D. dissertation, Louisiana State University, 1973), 99-127; *Baton Rouge Morning Advocate*, August 13, 1969; *Blacks United for Lasting Leadership* v. *Shreveport*, 71 F.R.D. 623 (1976).

[66]*Louisiana Weekly*, January 2, 1965.

[67]Britton, Monthly Report, October 17, 1967, box 3, folder 3, NAACP (LA); Britton interview, 2-3.

# LYNDON JOHNSON IN NEW ORLEANS*

Roman J. Heleniak

It was 9:30 in the evening of a day that included stops in Louisville, Kentucky, and Nashville, Tennessee, before the guest of honor arrived in New Orleans. His travels did not end there; he would be at his ranch by midnight.[1] But before he could find rest at the Texas White House, Lyndon Baines Johnson had important matters to attend to in the Crescent City. His energy still flowing after a day of motorcades, countless handshakes, political discussions and public appearances, the president seemed eager to make his last major speech of the day. Surrounded by Secret Service men and Louisiana state police, LBJ and his party moved from a hotel suite to the Grand Ballroom of the Jung Hotel, where 1,500 of Louisiana's Democratic faithful waited for him. Despite his height, Johnson could not see past the small army that flanked him on all sides and did not know where he was headed. "Where're we goin'?" he bellowed. Before he got an answer, he roared, "I want to know where're we goin'." Not satisfied with the mumbled answers of those around him, he, in his best Johnsonian earthiness shouted, "I don't care if we go to a whorehouse, I just wanta know where we are goin'."[2]

Ten minutes later, after numerous introductions of local and state dignitaries, the president began his address, according to many, his finest speech of the campaign.[3] Loyal assistant, Jack Valenti, of sound sleeping fame, would remember the occasion more than ten years later as the "most dramatic moment" of Johnson's reelection bid.[4]

Speaking with an accent that advertised his Texas and Southern origins, the former power of the Dixie-dominated 'club' of the United States Senate delivered his only major speech of the campaign on the incendiary issue of civil rights.[5] What he had to say was especially important to blacks and Southern whites. The rush of national and international events unfortunately prevented Johnson's speech from getting the public attention it merited. To begin with, both Lyndon Johnson and his opponent Senator Barry M. Goldwater delivered several major speeches a day in separate sections of the

*First published in *Louisiana History*, 21 (1980): 263-75. Reprinted with the kind permission of the author and the Louisiana Historical Association.

nation as the presidential campaign entered its final weeks. The pell-mell spate of datelines and stories made sober reportage difficult, if not impossible.

Even more important, however, were the events which preceded and followed the campaign stop in New Orleans. On September 27, the Warren Commission published the results of its investigation of John Kennedy's assassination. Grassy Knoll enthusiasts, 'single bullet' doubters, and assorted critics and defenders of the report avidly plunged in, and the commentary has not ceased to this day. Then, beginning on October 14, the next several days saw the bringing to the surface of the October 7 arrest of LBJ's closest and oldest associate, Walter Jenkins, on charges stemming from a sordid episode in a men's room; the fall of Nikita Khrushchev in the Soviet Union; the collapse of the Conservative government in Great Britain; and the detonation, by the Red Chinese, of their first atomic bomb.[6] In the shock-laden decade of the 1960s, that October stands out as one of the vintage months.

Yet, for all the significance of those events, they do not diminish the importance of Lyndon Johnson's rousing speech, which can be seen not only as a reaffirmation, on LBJ's part, of his quest for racial harmony but also his personal effort to lead the South into the mainstream of modern American life.[7]

Politically, LBJ had little to gain from the Louisiana phase of his Southern tour. Jack Valenti may have exaggerated only slightly when he labeled Johnson's civil rights address before a Southern audience, albeit an integrated one, an "act of sublime courage."[8] But Johnson knew that he had little or no chance to carry the Pelican State. The same polls which indicated LBJ's national lead over Goldwater at more than twenty percentage points *also* gave the Arizona Senator a solid base in the South from South Carolina to Louisiana.[9] Moreover, Governor John McKeithen, even before Johnson came to Louisiana, informed the president that the "Negro thing" would cost him the state. McKeithen was not dissuaded by the large crowds that greeted Johnson in New Orleans. "Mr. President these people love you because you're President and respect you," but, he cautioned, many of these same onlookers would vote for Goldwater.[10]

Johnson, of course, realized this, and he would not tailor his remarks to appeal to segregationist sympathies. In part, this Southern campaign visit dovetailed with the president's tactic of presenting himself to the voters as the national leader of *all* the people. Journalists Rowland Evans and Robert Novak described it as pure Johnsonian consensus: "America is one family, not North or South, not Republican or Democratic, not white or black. . . ."[11]

Johnson echoed this theme before a crowd at the Union Passenger Terminal, where he met Lady Bird Johnson at the completion of her long whistlestop tour of the South, by invoking the words of one of the great native sons of the South: "In the words of Robert E. Lee, I am going to say tonight, let's try to get our people to forget their old animosities and let us all be Americans."[12]

A reasonable enough statement, but during the summer and fall of 1964 "old animosities" were hardly waning. The United States appeared to teeter on the brink of racial anarchy.

Johnson's signing, on July 2, of the most important civil rights law since Reconstruction did not usher in the millennium. It only marked the beginning of one of those "long hot summers" that frayed American nerve ends and contributed to the fear that our society was becoming hopelessly polarized. It was a time when the cry "burn, baby, burn" could be heard between the reports of gunfire in the streets of many Northern cities. A time when the sounds of explosions destroyed black churches shattered the silence of rural nights in Mississippi.[13]

*Newsweek*, on the cover of the same issue that reported LBJ's signing of the 1964 Civil Rights Act, featured a photography of two tough-looking Mississippi lawmen grimly waiting for the "invasion" of that state by an army of civil rights workers. The same issue also carried the sinister, but not surprising, news that the burned-out automobile which belonged to three missing civil rights workers had been found near Philadelphia, Mississippi.[14] Several pages later, political pollster Louis Harris analyzed the potentially explosive "backlash" issue Would white voters blame the liberals and advocates of civil rights for the riots in urban ghettos?[15]

The tragic events of the summer of 1964 placed Americans who advised caution and calm on a very narrow perch. For example, those who counseled patience with the South and that given enough time the people of Dixie would accept the new law of the land, were jolted by a series of nightrider outrages. The slayings of James Chaney, Andrew Goodman, and Michael Schwerner in Neshoba County, the shotgun slaying of black educator Lemuel Penn on a lonely Georgia road, and the church bombings near McComb, Mississippi, all received extended coverage in the media. The South seemed a long way from compliance.

But those fond of pointing at the South and saying "I told you so" had a difficult time explaining the string of racial conflagrations in the cities of the North, including the *other* Philadelphia.[16] Being a sportsminded people, Americans digested the news as they did the morning box scores. So many killed there, scores injured here, property damage in the millions in another place. The figures were frightening.

Equally disturbing were the new voices of black America and their message. Whether it came from street-wise militants of the inner city or from established Negro writers such as LeRoi Jones and James Baldwin, the message was both perplexing and disturbing—a hatred of white America. So intense was this animosity that many blacks called for the creation of separate society for Negroes.[17] Meanwhile, proponents of civil rights and the Johnson administration assaulted the citadels of the American South's "separate but equal" society. If it sounds somewhat confusing, it was. Theodore White had written that in the election year of 1964 "probably no other question agitated Americans more than the question, What Do They Want?—'they' being the Negroes."[18]

Johnson's campaign visit in New Orleans would, therefore, serve several purposes. One, it would clarify his administration's commitment to a society of equal opportunity and full legal rights for all Americans. Two, as William O'Neill has written, and others have noted, Lyndon Johnson hated racism and regarded the Southern obsession with the Negro issue as a folly, a folly which had acted as a curse upon the South and had prevented the best impulses of its people from being manifested. The civil rights issue had also virtually excluded Dixie politicians from attaining the presidency, as Johnson discovered in 1960. The president would appeal to the people of the South to let their finest instincts govern their actions.[19] Three, Lyndon Johnson was running for reelection. Not only did he want to win, he wanted to rack up one of the great landslides in the history of presidential politics. He especially desired to avoid being humiliated in his own backyard, the South.

To win even a portion of the Southern states in 1964, with the Civil Rights Act containing his signature, would not be dismissed as impossible by Johnson. He would appeal to the South's traditional reverence for the Constitution. Once the South realized that the guarantee of civil rights for blacks was constitutional, much of the opposition would diminish. He would talk straight on the civil rights issue and would not, to use a Southern expression, "pussy-foot around." He would also remind Southerners that there were other issues in the campaign. Lastly, Johnson hoped that he could win the vote of those Southerners who *always* voted Democratic and those who would feel loyalty to Johnson because he was from the South.[20]

The task of convincing a large majority of the white voters of the South to forget their strong views of civil rights and vote the Democratic ticket was probably impossible in the supercharged atmosphere of 1964, but Lyndon Johnson had going for him one asset, one trump card, that few other presidents have had—a first lady who was a remarkable politician, a seasoned and gifted campaigner and a thoroughly Southern woman.

Claudia Taylor Johnson, universally known as "Lady Bird," was the person most responsible for Lyndon Johnson's appearance in New Orleans. Lady Bird dreamed up the ambitious whistlestop tour that would begin in Washington, take her and her party across eight states and 1,600 miles of the South and conclude in New Orleans on the fourth day. It stands out as one of the most remarkable political achievements of any president's wife.[21]

Not only did Lady Bird propose the trip, but along with Lindy Boggs, Liz Carpenter, and Virginia Russell, the wife of the governor of South Carolina, she did most of the planning.[22]

The ladies only had three weeks to prepare before the "Lady Bird Special" left Washington headed South. Mrs. Johnson immediately contacted the governors of those states her train would ramble through. Hopefully her courtesy would result in their cooperation.[23]

Lyndon Johnson, who insisted that Lady Bird use the talents of the women who worked for the White House to plan the tour, became involved himself. He gave his approval to every decision and, of course, made suggestions. It was LBJ who insisted that the Lady Bird Special visit the tiny town of Ahoskie, North Carolina. The White House received a wire from the hamlet begging Lady Bird to stop there when her train moved through North Carolina:

> Dear Mrs. Johnson,
>
> Please stop in Ahoskie. No important person has visited here since Buffalo Bill, and no passenger train has stopped in 12 years.

LBJ ordered "Stop there!" He added that "if they want you that bad, you'll get everyone from three counties." To which Linda Bird chimed in, "Well, we will have some kind of wild west show."[24] Johnson's instincts were correct, this small town was one of the highlights of the tour. When the First Lady visited Ahoskie, the local weekly greeted her with a full front-page photograph of herself and the homey headline, "How Do Lady Bird!"[25]

LBJ had to make one other major decision in conjunction with Lady Bird's tour—where he would make his appearance. He did not have to think twice, it would be in New Orleans. He told Liz Carpenter that by meeting Mrs. Johnson at the end of the swing the public and press would not lose interest in the tour. The New Orleans speech would also serve as the final touch on his own Southern campaign.[26] In keeping with Johnson's propensity to spring surprises, the news that he would be in New Orleans was released immediately. As late as September 22, the *Times-Picayune* could only speculate that the Crescent City might be accorded a presidential visit, but the paper could not get any information from Lindy Boggs or Press Secretary George Reedy.[27] However, confirmation was received by J. Marshall Brown, Louisiana National Democratic Committeeman, just two days later.[28]

LBJ's visit promised to be historic in more ways than one. According to Charles "Pie" Dufour, New Orleans journalist and historian, LBJ would be only the eighth president to visit New Orleans.[29]

New Orleans was not selected because Louisiana stacked up as one of Johnson's strongholds. On the contrary, the state seemed engulfed by a wave of pro-segregationist and anti-Johnson feelings that fall. With public opinion so strong, understandably, some of the political leaders of the state either opted for Goldwater or tried to establish a discreet distance between themselves and the president. Even Senator Allen Ellender, who was not afraid to be known as a friend of Johnson, had some problems.[30] Before the Democratic convention, Senator Hubert Humphrey wrote to Jack Valenti warning that Ellender was unhappy because the Louisianian was not getting much attention from the White House. Humphrey advised that "in view of this political situation in Louisiana, it appears to me that the President's seeing Allen Ellender and it being well publicized in Louisiana could be useful. . . ."[31]

If Ellender pouted from a lack of White House attention, John McKeithen, at least publicly, appeared eager to avoid contact. When Lady Bird called to inform him of her Louisiana visit and to invite him to ride on the train with her, the governor, to use a Louisiana word, "crawfished." He declined the train ride but said he was "working for the Democrats, you understand" but could do more by doing other things. The perceptive Lady Bird *did* understand.[32]

On the surface, McKeithen's "working for the Democrats" appeared counter-productive. Before the Democratic convention, McKeithen, along with George Wallace of Alabama, Paul Johnson of Mississippi and Orval Faubus of Arkansas, boycotted a meeting of Southern governors in Washington called by Lyndon Johnson. The Dixie governors, according to an "unofficial source," used this absence to protest any pro-black settlement of the dispute involving the seating of the Mississippi and Alabama delegates at the Atlantic City convention.[33]

A few days later, McKeithen publicly urged the Louisiana delegation to leave the convention over the seating compromise. The next day, however, J. Marshall Brown, a close ally of the governor, said that the state delegation would vote against the compromise but gave no indication that the Louisianians would walk out.[34] McKeithen balanced himself on a fence between the state's segregationists on one side and the national Democratic party on the other. He refused to openly support Johnson and chose, instead, a position of neutrality.[35]

Behind the scenes, Louisiana's "hep me" man played a different game. He had several telephone conversations with Johnson during the campaign. The talk was candid, and McKeithen bluntly informed Johnson he would lose Louisiana because of the civil rights issue. But, at the same time, he assured the president that he would vote for the Democratic ticket.[36]

McKeithen was also able through J. Marshall Brown to short-circuit an attempt by Leander Perez to manipulate the selection of loyalist Democratic electors. Brown informed the White House that "the Governor had the situation in hand at all times."[37]

Johnson's decision to appear in New Orleans forced the governor to expose himself politically. He had to make a choice. He could decide to be on hand when the president arrived and lose political points with white voters opposed to LBJ's civil rights stand, or he could avoid the president by leaving the state as he did when Goldwater campaigned in Louisiana and possibly strain his relationship with Johnson.[38]

Because of his hegira when Goldwater visited Louisiana, many felt the governor would do the same thing to Johnson. McKeithen played out the charade until October 1 when he announced that, of course, he would be on hand to greet the president as a "matter of courtesy."[39] He has since remarked that he never had any intention of *not* being in New Orleans to meet LBJ.[40]

With the governor's agreement to be present, Johnson had managed to attract most of the state and New Orleans political leadership to his campaign visit. Only F. Edward Hebert and Joe Waggonner were missing from Louisiana's congressional delegation.

The strong support of the Democratic political leadership of Jefferson and Orleans parishes, the endorsements of both city newspapers, and the novelty of a presidential visit combined to produce large crowds to greet the president. Furthermore, political polls showed Johnson winning New Orleans while he was losing elsewhere in the state. The president could hardly have chosen a better site in the Deep South to deliver a major address on civil rights.

This should not be construed to mean that New Orleans Democratic leaders requested such a speech. On the day LBJ arrived in New Orleans, Bill Moyers sent a telegram to Jack Valenti, traveling with the president, which stated that "several people in New Orleans, including our advance men, feel the President should not refer to 'civil rights.'" Moyers suggested that if Johnson had to deal with the touchy subject he should talk about "constitutional rights."[41]

Moyers, who was coordinating speech writing activities and forwarding proposed texts and ideas to the president, obviously did not know what Johnson would say in New Orleans. Even Jack Valenti was surprised. Perhaps, the only person to have advance information about LBJ's plans was Richard Russell, who, understandably, did not like the idea.[42]

While the local leaders did not show any enthusiasm for presidential words on civil rights, there was more than casual concern that Johnson would make some comment on the long-standing tidelands issue. Charles Ferguson of the *States-Item* speculated that McKeithen was certain to mention the tidelands to LBJ when they met in New Orleans.[43] The White House was certainly aware of the issue. Several times aides to the president discussed the question in memos. As late as October 8, White House aide Douglas Cater suggested to Bill Moyers that the president ought to make some mention of the tidelands when he spoke in New Orleans.[44] But LBJ's visit did not bring the tantalizing Goloconda any closer to the grasp of Louisiana. McKeithen never got the chance to discuss it with LBJ, because the president was too busy working the friendly crowds.[45] Johnson did not mention the subject either, and it was no oversight. In a proposed draft of the New Orleans address forwarded to Valenti for revision, the following statement appeared: "The differences inherited from other years on Tidelands can be, ought to be—and will be resolved." Valenti revised this out of the text.[46]

In fact, much of what LBJ said in New Orleans would not be recognized by presidential speech writers. For example, Walter Heller of the Council of Economic Advisors had suggested that Johnson use the New Orleans trip to praise the economic achievements of the last thirty-six years and to pledge even more of the same.[47] Few of Heller's ideas were used.

Another proposed text would have had Johnson build his speech around Thomas Jefferson and Andrew Jackson, two illustrious men important to Louisiana history.[48] Although this proposal was dated October 7, only two days before the New Orleans address, the format was not used by LBJ.

Actually, Johnson delivered two speeches at the Jung. The first one was the address expected by those close to the president and a copy was released to the press before Johnson spoke. It was the standard campaign address that, with some deletions, could have been delivered in any city, in any state. Parts of it were no doubt familiar to more than one presidential ghost writer. Nevertheless, it generated a warm response. After completing his prepared remarks, Johnson, encouraged by the friendly and enthusiastic audience, tossed his papers aside and began to speak without notes and from the heart.

LBJ talked about the South, it problems, its potential, its future. Some of the ideas were first expressed by LBJ in 1938 in a radio address entitled "The South Will Rise," when he sadly noted that the South was the scene of grinding poverty, a region that saw its rich natural and human resources plundered by outsiders.[49] The 1938 speech reads as if it could have been given by Huey Long. It was no accident. When LBJ addressed the crowd at the Jung he selected the fabled Kingfish as the Louisianian to talk about, not Jefferson or Jackson. Johnson said he owed a personal debt to Long, adding, "I never heard him make a speech that I didn't think was calculated to do some good for some people who needed some speeches made for them and could not make them for themselves."[50]

Warming to the receptiveness of his listeners, Johnson got to his main point, the 1964 Civil Rights Act. "I signed it and I'm going to enforce it," he bluntly warned. He added, "I think any man worthy of being president is going to do the same thing." He had more to say. The South had never taken advantage of its potential, because the South was divided and distracted by the race issue. To illustrate this point LBJ told a favorite story of his about a former U. S. senator from Texas who was raised in another Southern state.[51] This man confided to Sam Rayburn that he was tired of racial politics, and that, before he died, he wanted to go back to his old state and speak. "Poor old state, they haven't heard a Democratic speech in 30 years. All they ever hear at election time is Negro, Negro, Negro."[52] Was there a Southerner in that room who had never heard such a speech? Would they ever hear it again? Not if LBJ had his way. He pressed on. Race should not be an issue, only "equal opportunity for all, special privileges for none." The only problem facing Americans is whether they are "going to live or die."[53]

Although Johnson continued to speak for several minutes, he had made his most important remarks. A Southern president in a Southern city had laid it out in plain language. The South had to end its obsession with race and get on with the job of living. Lyndon and Lady Bird Johnson believed the South could do it.

Shortly before Mrs. Johnson began her tour, she spoke from her heart to her campaign workers and explained why this whistlestop trip was so important to her and her husband:

> I know the Civil Rights Act was right, and I don't mind saying so. But I'm tired of people making the South the whipping boy of the Democratic Party. There are plenty of people who make snide jokes about the corn-pone and red-necks. I'm no hard-sell person. But what I want to say to those people is that I love the South, I'm

> proud of the South, I know there have been great achievements there. And I want them to know as far as *this* President and his wife are concerned, the South belongs to the United States. For me this is going to be a journey of the heart.[54]

Lyndon Johnson died in 1973 and did not live to see the full realization of his dream of a New South. But in 1976, a Georgia peanut farmer was elected to the highest office in the land in a closely contested election. The margin of victory was provided by the same Southern states that voted for Goldwater in 1964. A combination of Southern blacks and Southern whites had returned the New South to the voting pattern of the old. Lyndon Johnson would have been pleased.

## Notes for "Lyndon Johnson in New Orleans"

[1]Daily Diary, October 9, 1964, Lyndon B. Johnson Library.

[2]John McKeithen to Roman Heleniak, January 25, 1978, Columbia, Louisiana.

[3]William Manchester, *The Glory and the Dream: A Narrative History of America, 1932-1972* (New York, 1975), 1030.

[4]Jack Valenti, *A Very Human President* (New York, 1975), 161.

[5]Theodore H. White, *The Making of the President, 1964* (New York, 1965), 364.

[6]Manchester, *Glory and the Dream*, 1029-30.

[7]Eric F. Goldman, *The Tragedy of Lyndon Johnson* (New York, 1969), 293-94.

[8]Valenti, *A Very Human President*, 162.

[9]Goldwater carried Louisiana with 57% of the vote, Mississippi with 87%, Alabama with 70%, Georgia with 54% and South Carolina with 59%. Johnson's campaign aides only had hopes of winning Georgia. Rowland Evans and Robert Novak, *Lyndon B. Johnson: The Exercise of Power* (New York, 1968), 506.

[10]JMcK to RH, Memo, Cliff Carter to LBJ, September 21, 1964, White House Central File, Lyndon B. Johnson Library.

[11]Evans and Novak, *Lyndon Johnson*, 500.

[12]Speech given at Union Passenger Terminal in New Orleans, October 9, 1964, Statements of the President, Lyndon B. Johnson Library.

[13]From June through September, thirty-three Negro churches were destroyed in Mississippi. *Newsweek*, October 12, 1964.

[14]Ibid., July 13, 1964.

[15]Ibid.

[16]Ibid., July-August, 1964, scattered references.

[17]William O'Neill, *Coming Apart: An Informal History of the 1960's* (New York, 1976), 167-69.

[18]White, *Making of the President*, 305.

[19]O'Neill, *Coming Apart*, 118.

[20]Goldman, *Tragedy of Lyndon Johnson*, 288-89.

[21]Ibid., 425.

[22]Elizabeth Carpenter, *Ruffles and Flourishes* (Garden City, N.Y., 1970), 195.

[23]Claudia T. Johnson, *Lady Bird Johnson: A White House Diary* (New York, 1970), 195.

[24]Carpenter, *Ruffles and Flourishes*, 146.

[25]Nan Robertson in the *New York Times*, October 7, 1964.

[26]Liz Carpenter to Roman Heleniak, February 7, 1978, Austin, Texas.

[27]*New Orleans Times-Picayune*, September 22, 1964.

[28]Ibid., September 24, 1964.

[29]Charles Dufour in the *New Orleans States-Item*, October 9, 1964.

[30]Allen J. Ellender to T. Harrison Baker, Oral History Collection, Lyndon B. Johnson Library.

[31]Memo, Hubert H. Humphrey to Jack Valenti, August 4, 1964, White House Central File, Lyndon B. Johnson Library.

[32]Claudia Johnson, *White House Diary*, 197.

[33]*New York Times*, August 23, 1964.

[34]Ibid., August 24, 1964; ibid., August 25, 1964.

[35]*New Orleans Times-Picayune*, September 16, 1964.

[36]JMcK to RH.

[37]Memo, Harold Leventhal to Cliff Carter, September 1964, White House Central File, Lyndon B. Johnson Library.

[38]McKeithen was advised by some of his aides to avoid meeting with Johnson because the President was not popular. JMcK to RH.

[39]*New Orleans States-Item*, October 2, 1964.

[40]JMcK to RH.

[41]Telegram, Bill Moyers to Jack Valenti, October 9, 1964. Statements of Lyndon B. Johnson, Lyndon B. Johnson Library.

[42]Goldman, *Tragedy of Lyndon Johnson*, 290.

[43]*New Orleans States-Item*, October 9, 1964.

[44]Memo, Douglas Carter to Bill Moyers, October 8, 1964. Files of Douglas Carter, Lyndon B. Johnson Library.

[45]JMcK to RH.

[46]Proposed speech, Statements of Lyndon B. Johnson, Lyndon B. Johnson Library.

[47]Memo, Walter Heller to Willard Wirtz, October 1, 1964.

[48]Proposed speech, October 7, 1964. Statements of Lyndon B. Johnson, Lyndon B. Johnson Library.

[49]Radio broadcast, "The South Will Rise," Station KNOW, Austin, Texas, August 24, 1938.

[50]*New Orleans States-Item*, October 10, 1964.

[51]Jack Valenti has written that the man was Senator Joseph Bailey, a native of Mississippi who moved to Texas. Valenti, *A Very Human President*, 161; Liz Carpenter, however, is not sure that Bailey was the only man LBJ told this story about. LC to RH.

[52]Interestingly, at least five authors have misquoted LBJ on this important line. Carpenter in *Ruffles and Flourishes*, 169, and Valenti in *A Very Human President*, 161, have Johnson saying "nigger, nigger, nigger." O'Neill in *Coming Apart*, 118, Goldman in *Tragedy of Lyndon Johnson*, 294, and Manchester in *The Glory and the Dream*, 1030, all have Johnson saying the more polite southernism, "nigra, nigra, nigra." An audio tape available at the LBJ Library clearly shows that LBJ used the word Negro.

[53]*States-Item*, October 10, 1964.

[54]Carpenter, *Ruffles and Flourishes*, 149-50.

# RACE AND RELUCTANCE: FEDERAL-LOCAL RELATIONS IN THE PUBLIC SCHOOL DESEGREGATION OF LINCOLN PARISH, LOUISIANA, 1965-1971*

Kent Germany

In September, 1957, the words "lynch her," "nigger," "not . . . in our school" echoed across the yard at Little Rock's Central High School.[1] Living rooms and breakfast tables would soon host images of white Southerners in skirts and ties hurling epithets and saliva on innocent black students attending school by permission of the 101st Airborne. Central High was the first serious test in the South of the *Brown v. Board of Education* decisions. A high point of massive resistance, the battle in Little Rock defined President Dwight D. Eisenhower's civil rights record and exposed to the world the obstinacy of Southern bigotry. Violent obstructions to desegregation would follow in other Southern cities.

In a region recoiling from what it saw as an ominous assault on its way of life, these first desegregation attempts often met vindictive white protest. However, legal decisions bolstered by the Civil Rights Act of 1964 pushed the fight for integration into a new phase. Extensive court orders, public forums, and judicial conferences replaced the episodes of violence, harassment, and political grandstanding. Coffee, sweat, and ink replaced blood and spit.

During this second phase, along with hundreds of other local bodies throughout the South, the Lincoln Parish, Louisiana, school system came under the attention of the Fifth Circuit Court of Appeals, the Supreme Court, the Department of Justice, and the Department of Health, Education, and Welfare (H.E.W). Unlike the previous stage of desegregation, these later federal efforts abolished acceptance of tokenism, opting for full compliance. In the summer of 1966, taking advantage of the Civil Rights Act of 1964, the Justice Department used a complaint from local black citizens to sue the Lincoln

*First published in the *Journal* of the North Louisiana Historical Association, 25 (1994): 134-59. Reprinted with the kind permission of the author and publisher.

Parish School Board.[2] Justice Department maneuvers and federal judicial decisions over the next five years prompted Federal District Judge Ben C. Dawkins, a segregationist who admitted he "outgrew" the practice during these and related cases, to force full desegregation from the school boards under his jurisdiction. In Lincoln Parish he consistently found "faithful" adherence.[3] The initial lawsuit produced only cosmetic desegregation of students and faculty in 1966, but subsequent arm-twisting of local officials would lead to total eradication of a dual system.

Because school systems were locally controlled, the responsibility for integration fell upon each parish's (or county's) school board. Initially, the Lincoln Parish School Board preferred a slower, voluntary method, but, as the federal mandates became more specific, the board complied with adequate speed, the only realistic choice. Overwhelmed by the momentum of the overall desegregation movement, the parish of Lincoln offered no extraordinary resistance. Although the board and many of the parish's citizens favored keeping segregation as intact as possible, the inevitability of the outcome diminished tensions and helped shape a successful unitary system. In August, 1971, seventeen years after the first *Brown* decision and five after the initial local suit, more than seven decades of segregated schooling yielded to full integration.

Almost one hundred years earlier, during Reconstruction, Louisiana law provided for desegregated public education, but beyond New Orleans almost all schools were segregated. Conservative Democratic resurgence in 1877 and the prevalence of Jim Crow laws in the 1890s solidified the dual system. Accepted socially and politically, the segregation of schools received constitutional legitimacy in 1896 when the U. S. Supreme Court, in *Plessy v. Ferguson*, erected the "separate but equal" doctrine.[4] Compounding a poor racial situation, there was little support for public education in post-Reconstruction Louisiana, especially for African Americans, and the twentieth century held little hope for change.[5]

In Lincoln Parish, during the early twentieth century, inadequate funding plagued all schools. Some advances were made in the system, but black schools continued to be crude and deficient, separate and unequal. Significant changes came in 1948 when Louisiana elected Earl K. Long as governor, and the Lincoln Parish School Board chose Morelle Emmons as its new superintendent. Lincoln Parish operated about fifteen one to two-room black schools scattered throughout the countryside, compared with only one all-white school of this type.[6] Passage of a local bond issue and Governor Long's massive spending program for education upgraded the level of black teachers' salaries and allowed for the consolidation of the two-room schools into one modern black high school and several neighborhood elementary schools.[7] Superintendent Emmons described this as "immeasurable progress," and he claimed it inspired pride and contentment among whites and blacks.[8]

The first successful court challenge to segregated secondary and elementary schools came almost five years later, in 1954, when the U.S. Supreme Court made its first *Brown* decision, which annulled the "separate but equal" doctrine and asserted the inherent inequality of segregated schools. This verdict pronounced segregation unconstitutional, but it gave no orders for compliance.[9] One year later, the Court's second *Brown* ruling required schools to "make a prompt and reasonable start toward full compliance." Public schools should be put "on a racially non-discriminatory basis with all deliberate speed."[10] "Deliberate speed," as it applied to the actions of white local authorities in the Deep South, could accurately be described as deliberately slow. By 1957, no African-American had been admitted to a white school in any of the so-called "recalcitrant states."[11]

Recalcitrance would linger in the rural parish of Lincoln until 1966. The *Brown* decisions effected almost no change in the local school system, which continued to operate as a completely segregated district. All schools functioned under one board and one superintendent, but black schools and white schools had different supervisors, buses, and curricula. "Each went on . . . like the other one didn't exist," a Lincoln Parish educator recalled.[12]

Without "noticeable criticism" from either community, for the twelve years following the initial *Brown* ruling, the Lincoln Parish board operated its dual system.[13] During this period decisions reached in the Fifth Circuit Court of Appeals led the way to token integration. Early in 1964, in *Evers v. Jackson Municipal School District*, the Fifth Circuit ruled that the Fourteenth Amendment did not order integration, but only prohibited "enforced racial segregation." This opened the way for the so-called Freedom of Choice plan, which allowed any student to choose to attend a school of the opposite race. By 1965, Fifth Circuit Judge and Louisiana Republican leader John Minor Wisdom wrote that "footdragging public school boards" needed "to move with celerity toward desegregation."[14] In January, 1966, the circuit court approved the Freedom of Choice plan only if the school boards gave students adequate notice and also abolished same-race schools within the same geographic zones.[15]

At a hearing on July 28, 1966, Judge Dawkins instructed the Lincoln Parish School Board to submit a desegregation plan for the upcoming year. Citing a lack of choice in the matter, the board unanimously endorsed the Freedom of Choice plan, announcing to the public that any child in the first, second, third, tenth , eleventh, or twelfth grades who wanted to transfer should apply at the school board office.[16] All requests would be granted unless space was not available in the desired school. No application could be "unreasonably denied," and refusal could not "be based on race or color [or] . . . technical errors." The resolution sought to comply further with judicial requirements by abolishing school districts drawn according to race and by emphatically prohibiting any influencing of a student's or parent's selection. Beginning the following year, choice would extend to all grades.[17]

In constructing this first desegregation plan, the school board conceded there were differences between black and white students, but it wanted to consider more than numbers and formulas. Hoping to eliminate the word "race" from the schools, the administration worked to remove the potential for conflict. Officials believed that, because whites and blacks were so far in levels of academic achievement, integration would be best accomplished gradually, that "50 students" would "successfully compete and participate" more readily "than . . . 500." With time, as black students would become aware of their ability, integration would accelerate, and the dual system would disappear.[18] Although this plan would have prolonged the desegregation process, parish administrators believed that it would be more effective in the long-term.[19]

During the 1966-1967 school year, the Freedom of Choice plan underwent its first test. At his own or her own discretion, any student in the appropriate grade was free to enroll at a school of the opposite race, but few did. Only three black students, two girls and one boy, ventured to the all-white Ruston High School in the fall of 1966. They became the first enrolled African American students in history to walk the halls of an all-white school in Lincoln Parish, and their entry passed without much incident.[20]

African American students did not stampede the parish's all-white schools. Of more than three thousand eligible black students, only 96 in 1967 and 116 in 1968 chose to go to trade schools.[21] The low transfer ratio may be due to a number of factors. Pointing to their self-described success in upgrading the dual system, administration officials contended that black students were simply content "to stay in a school of their own race." To enter a predominantly white school would require an African American student to give up established traditions, pride in athletic teams, and generally comfortable circumstances. In fact, one student at all-black Lincoln High could not "remember anything but joy for being [there]."[22] Some civil rights groups asserted that "fear of retaliation" kept black students from changing schools, but there is no evidence that supports such a claim in the case of Lincoln Parish.[23] Apparently, African American students preferred the familiarity of their established schools to the uncertainties of converting to previously all-white ones.

Whatever the reason for it, the lack of crossover prompted more action, as did the board's token of compliance with Judge Dawkins' April 6, 1967, directive, in which he ordered faculty desegregation.[24] At a conference on February 21, 1968, Dawkins informed the board that he expected "specific action" by a "specific date," and that each school should have two teachers of the opposite race. Twelve days later, the Lincoln Parish School Board unanimously resolved to support this plan.[25] The Lincoln board was moderately successful in integrating its school faculties. By 1969 only three schools out of nineteen contained a single-race faculty, and the number of teachers in opposite-race schools increased to thirty-four.[26]

Forthcoming cases led also to the total integration of the parish's student population.[27] Perhaps, the most important judicial decision of the second phase of desegregation came in Judge Wisdom's *Jefferson County* decisions, which affected all subsequent determinations because Wisdom directed specific actions, leaving no legal rock under which a wily school board could hide.[28] Another pivotal decision was the Warren Court's *Green v. New Kent County*, which ruled that Freedom of Choice could be used by boards only if the result was a "unitary System."[29] The Fifth Circuit followed *Green* with *Adams v. Mathews*, in which it found that Freedom of Choice was working too slowly and, therefore, ordered school boards to construct alternative plans.[30] In January, 1969, Judge Wisdom decreed in *Cleveland v. Union Parish School Board* that the school boards in the Western District of Louisiana must accomplish "lock, stock, and barrel desegregation" by the 1970-1971 school year.[31] Four months later, on May 28, 1969, the Fifth Circuit court delivered the death blow to segregation in Lincoln Parish. The decision in *Hall v. St. Helena Parish School Board* effectively abrogated Freedom of Choice, instructing the district judges to ensure the implementation of desegregation plans, and admonishing local school boards to "act affirmatively to abolish all vestiges . . . of segregation" and shoulder "responsibility for . . . administering" the dissolution of the dual system.[32]

This decision sent many of the white citizens of Lincoln Parish scrambling to push for retention of the Freedom of Choice plan, but, except for an occasional anonymous telephone call or a lone picketer at the school board office, most of the community acted "without viciousness."[33] Instead of public harassment, residents responded with political pressure. In early June, two citizens groups emerged to lobby for extension of Freedom of Choice. Neither group publicly discussed race as an issue. Instead, they claimed to resist a reduction of standards and a loss of local control.[34] "HEP" or "Had Enough, Parents?," a group led by Jim Davis, came forward first, but it was soon replaced by a larger, better organized group known as the Lincoln Parish Citizen's Committee for Quality Education (CCQE).[35] Headed by Louisiana Polytechnic Institute chemistry professor, Donald Roberts, the CCQE emerged as a grassroots political organization with several hundred members, and it ultimately spread to thirty-seven other parishes.[36] The movement's strength demonstrated a widespread desire to continue the Freedom of Choice plan, as well as a still-strong rumbling in support of segregation and state rights. Nevertheless, the CCQE, not powerful enough to stem the drive behind desegregation, soon turned to the advocacy of private schools.[37]

Despite the moves to block federal action, not all groups opposed desegregation. In July, 1969, black and white citizens from Ruston and Grambling formed the Lincoln Parish Community Relations Council (CRC) to demand that the board "bend its efforts toward total integration" and to plead for the community to escape from its "vacuum of prejudice."[38] Although the CRC did not emerge as a powerful political group, it served as a voice of reason for accepting the inevitability of integration and a protest against prolonging the status quo.

Following the *Hall* decision, Superintendent Emmons and Lincoln Parish District Attorney Ragan Madden realized that it would not be possible to salvage Freedom of Choice.[39] For Superintendent Emmons, the decision was a "hit in the face." By ignoring the board's previous efforts, the court, which Emmons charged was interested "only in housing children," had alienated the education community.[40] An indication of the local leaders' perception of federal attitude came from one parish educator who remarked that the typical federal representative was not "interested in whether they [the students] learn[ed] anything or not. . . [but] interested in who they are sitting by."[41] Parish officials had no time to sulk, however, because, on June 6, 1969, a new era for education commenced when Judge Dawkins ordered thirty-five Louisiana school districts to work with the United States Department of Health, Education, and Welfare (H.E.W.) to submit an acceptable plan by July 5.[42]

On June 23, at 8:15 a.m., two representatives from the Office of Education, Hal Jacob Kennamer and Leon Crowley, having arrived quietly in Lincoln Parish, walked into the school board office and seized information needed to create the H.E.W. plan. Both Kennamer and Crowley were former educators, but they inspired little confidence in Superintendent Emmons, who thought they lacked administrative competence. It was not until late that afternoon that Kennamer and Crowley consented to meet with Emmons, and at that time they told him that they could not accept input from him, nor could they give any comment, or consult the board in any manner regarding their plan. Having interpreted Dawkins's order to mean that H.E.W. and the board would work together, school officials resented the two men's attitude.[43] Hoping to avoid federal dictation of the terms of desegregation, the board began to formulate its own plan. Although board members would have preferred to retain the Freedom of Choice plan, they now recognized the need to present an alternative one to the H.E.W design.[44] Ten days later, Kennamer and Crowley presented their own plan to Dawkins and the Lincoln Parish School Board, stating that its date of implementation could not be negotiated, although Lincoln Parish School Board was free to present a different plan, as long as it achieved full integration.[45] As to the atmosphere of this meeting, Assistant Superintendent Thomas Judd later recalled, "I'm the only person in the world, I guess, who has been called a white racist and a nigger-lover on the same day in the same court trial."[46]

In order to eradicate the dual system, the representatives from the Office of Education proposed to restructure the entire school district. In Lincoln Parish outside the population center of Ruston, there was three smaller communities with schools, Dubach, Simsboro, and Choudrant. Kennamer and Crowley's plan, shown in the following table, would place schools in those areas in jeopardy:

Table 1.
H. E. W. Proposed Plan, July, 1969

| Lincoln Parish Schools | Grades Set for Desegregation |
|---|---|
| Ruston High School | All parish students, grades 10-12 (except Dubach) |
| Dubach School | Grades 9-12 and 1-2 |
| Ruston Elementary | All Ruston first graders |
| Lincoln Elementary | Closed |
| St. Rest School | Closed |
| Hico School | Closed |

Students in the other outlying areas of the parish would attend elementary and junior high schools in the closest town. In Ruston, the rest of the elementary students would be grouped into schools containing two grades each, based upon geographic zones. Addressing faculty composition, H.E.W. ordered each school to have an "approximately equal" ratio of white and black teachers.[47]

The Kennamer-Crowley plan would end the dual system, but to do so it ignored realities that were important to the local officials, who reacted strongly against it. Complaining that Kennamer and Crowley had produced an administratively unworkable plan, Tom Judd exclaimed, "I'm in shock!" To him the proposal was "dead wrong" and would be so regardless of who was involved. Board member T.W. Green expressed the fear students would drop out of school, rather than be bussed all over the parish, while Morelle Emmons remarked that the plan "wrecked the schools . . . [and] the communities . . . you [H.E.W.] couldn't have done a worse job even if [former Soviet Premier Nikita] Khrushchev had been in on it."[48] Emmons feared that the plan would cause social turmoil in Ruston and destroy the sense of community that the outlying towns derived from their high schools.[49]

The day after the unveiling of the federal plan, Superintendent Emmons called a special session of the school board to outline an alternative plan to preserve the quality of education, advance the "welfare of our children," and consider more than "cold statistics." The board voted unanimously to ask Judge Dawkins to accept its desegregation plan or, at least, to arbitrate.[50] Some mediation would be necessary because the board's proposal (see table 2) was entirely different, a recast version of Freedom of Choice, combined with a gradual, forced integration. Any student not mentioned were to be placed according to choice.[51]

Table 2.
Lincoln Parish School Board Proposal, July 1969

| Lincoln Schools | Grades Set for Desegregation |
|---|---|
| Choudrant High School | Grades 1 and 7 |
| Dubach High School | Grades 1 and 9 |
| Simsboro High School | Grades 1 and 9 |
| Ruston Schools | All Student, Grades 1 and 9 and All Girls, Grade 7 |

The relaxation of civil rights policy by the new administration of President Richard M. Nixon convinced Dawkins, on July 7, 1969, to extend by sixteen days the deadline for filing acceptable plans.[52] Within this period Dawkins asked the board's representatives and the federal government's representatives to meet with him in closed conference on Wednesday, July 16. Here, the judge explained Nixon's plan to both groups, and then ordered the H.E.W. to work with the school board to formulate a plan in keeping with the new approach.[53] Thomas Judd recalled that, after the meeting, Dawkins told him and a Justice Department official to resolve the impasse. Over coffee at the Busy Bee Cafe, the two men developed a plan "a little different than everybody else's," which became a blueprint for a proposal submitted by Judd and Emmons to the board, which adopted it unanimously.[54] Thirteen days later the board and H.E.W. representatives met in Judge Dawkins' private chambers. Without further argument, Dawkins approved the school board's plan, professing that it met Constitutional requirements and that it would dismantle the parish's dual system.[55] The modified plan called for implementation in two phases, the first during 1969-1970 school year, and the second during the 1970-1971 year.[56] The 1969-1970 plan closely resembled the school board's first plan (see Table 3).

Table 3.
The First Phase of the July, 1969 Desegregation Plan for Lincoln Parish Schools, 1969-1970[57]

| Lincoln Schools | Grades Set for Desegregation |
|---|---|
| Choudrant, Dubach, and Simsboro Schools | Same as July, 1969 Plan (see Table 2) |
| Ruston High School | Grades 10 and 11 with Choice Given to 9 and 12 |
| Greenwood Elementary | Closed, students dispersed to other schools |
| Lincoln Elementary, I.A. Lewis and Glenview schools | Remain Unchanged |

The second phase beginning in the fall of 1970 would increase integration (see Table 4).

Table 4. The Second Phase of the July, 1969 Desegregation Plan for Lincoln Parish Schools, To Be Implemented August, 1970[58]

| Lincoln Schools | Grades Set for Desegregation |
|---|---|
| Choudrant Students | |
| St. Rest (Choudrant) | Grades 1-3 |
| Choudrant High School | Grades 4-12 |
| Dubach Students | |
| Dubach High School | Grades 1, 8-12 |
| Hico School | Grades 2-4 |
| Hopewell School | Grades 5-7 |
| Simsboro Students | |
| Simsboro High School | All Students |
| Hopewell School | Closed |
| Ruston Students | |
| Lincoln Elementary | Closed |
| Cypress Springs, Hillcrest, and Ruston Elementary | Grades 1-5 at each school |
| Glenview Junior High | All Girls, Grades 6-8 |
| I.A. Lewis | All Boys, Grades 6-7 |
| Lincoln High School | All Boys, Grades 8-9 |
| Ruston High School | All Girls, Grade 9 and All Students, Grades 10-12 |

Before the fall, 1970, assignments could be implemented according to phase two of the plan accepted in June, 1969, new political and judicial developments led to changes in it. In mid-March, further policy relaxation on the part of the Nixon administration, as well as new court decisions allowing the "neighborhood concept," caused the school board to ask for the chance to alter its plan for the 1970-1971 school year.[59] In search of approval for their modifications, which emphasized grouping students according to geographic zones, Emmons, Judd, and Board President Robert Holladay traveled to Washington, D.C., for a meeting with Jerris Leonard, head of the Civil Rights Division of the Justice Department, who promised not to contest the change.[60] Soon afterwards, on June 12, 1970, Judge Dawkins gave verbal agreement to the modified plan (see Table 5).[61]

Table 5. Final Modifications in the Desegregation Plan for Lincoln Parish Schools[62]

| Lincoln Schools | Action Taken |
|---|---|
| Hopewell and Hico Schools | To Be Consolidated and to House Grades 1-6 |
| I.A. Lewis School | To House All Sixth Grade Students |
| Greenwood School | To Become a School for Reading Help |
| Ruston High School | To Receive All Students, Grades 9-12 |

On August 5, Dawkins issued his formal acceptance, stating that the plans fell "within permissible constitutional limitations" and adequately established a "unitary system."[63] Dawkins commended the board for fully implementing the 1969-1970 plan and for having "demonstrated the utmost faith" in promoting the education of the children while adhering to the court's orders.[64] In making stipulations, the judge outlawed any discrimination or "racially identifiable" policies, demanded a progress report every year, and ordered the creation of a biracial committee.[65] Except for one small alteration in the summer of 1971, this decision stood as law, and the educators in Lincoln Parish returned to the daily tasks of running a school system.

In 1971, the same bells rang for both whites and African Americans.[66] Integration was completed. Just as the spitting, yelling, and grandstanding had eventually stopped in Little Rock, so had the judicial decrees, government directives, and hurried local responses ceased in Lincoln Parish. Once an acceptable plan had been implemented in local schools, H.E.W., the Justice Department, and the federal courts turned their attention away from rural north central Louisiana, rarely intervening after 1971.[67] The relative acceptance of desegregation by Lincoln Parish revealed a foundational change in Southern race relations. Race-baiting, state-rightism, and massive resistance no longer ruled the day.

Lincoln Parish's bout with desegregation was a story of grudging recognition of the unavoidable. Most of the parish leaders wanted to employ slower methods, but a new political, legislative, and judicial environment offered them no alternative. The lack of serious incidents also showed at least a latent acceptance of the transformation. Similar to much of the South, the parish originally delayed efforts to mix its schools racially, but the parish leaders eventually provided a sufficient solution. Overall, response mollified federal authorities, and at the same time avoided massive protest. Almost twenty years after it began, the paper chase of desegregation had come to an end.

## Notes for "Race and Reluctance: Federal-Local Relations in the Public School Desegregation of Lincoln Parish, LA, 1965-1971"

[1]Juan Williams, *Eyes on the Prize: America's Civil Rights Years, 1954-1965* (New York, 1987), 101-2.

[2]Attorney General Nicholas Katzenbach had received a complaint that black schools were inferior, that black students "were being deprived of equal protection." See *Ruston Daily Leader*, July 29, 1966.

[3]J.W. Peltason, *Fifty-Eight Lonely Men: Southern Federal Judges and School Desegregation* (New York, 1961), 133; *U.S.A. v. Lincoln Parish School Board*, Civil Action No. 12,071, August 5, 1970, found in Superintendent's file, Lincoln Parish School Board Office, Ruston, La.; and Judge Ben C. Dawkins, Jr., interview by Norman Provizer, June 5, 1979, interview OH 42, transcript, Louisiana State University-Shreveport Oral History Collection, Noel Memorial Library, Department of Archives and Special Collections, 4-5.

[4]C. Vann Woodward, *The Strange Career of Jim Crow* (New York, 1966), 24; William Ivy Hair, *Bourbonism and Agrarian Protest: Louisiana Politics, 1877-1900* (Baton Rouge, 1969), 121; and *Plessy v. Ferguson*, 163 U.S. 537 (*United States Reports* [New York, 1896]). For a study of African-American education in New Orleans, see Donald E. DeVore, "Race Relations and Community Development: The Education of Blacks in New Orleans, 1862-1960" (Ph.D. dissertation, Louisiana State University), 1989.

[5]Hair, *Bourbonism and Agrarian Protest*, 60-62, 123-27. For a summary of the overall history of desegregation, see Walter G. Stephan, "A Brief Historical Overview of School Desegregation," in Walter G. Stephan and Joe R. Feagin, eds., *School Desegregation: Past, Present, and Future* (New York, 1980), 3-23. Some dated, but useful studies are Betty Porter, "The History of Negro Education in Louisiana," *Louisiana Historical Quarterly*, 25 (1942): 728-821; and Thomas A. Green, "The History of Education in Lincoln Parish, Louisiana" (M.A. thesis, Louisiana State University), 1929.

[6]Loyace Braggs, at present a Lincoln Parish School Board member, attended Lincoln High School, the all-black parish high school, from 1940-1945. In an interview in February, 1993, she said that the physical conditions of the school were "poor" and "unreliable," but the educational atmosphere was good. See Thomas Knapp, "Not So Far Back-Black History," *Ruston Morning Paper*, December 18, 1993.

[7]Morelle Emmons, interview by the author, October 29, 1992, Ruston, La., tape recording, in possession of the author, Ruston; and Michael Kurtz and Morgan D. Peoples, *Earl K. Long: The Saga of Uncle Earl and Louisiana Politics* (Baton Rouge, 1990), 131, 268. Emmons stated that seven black elementary schools were built. Also at this time, Col. George T. Madison, Superintendent of Louisiana Schools, helped to establish a first through twelfth grade lab school at Grambling College.

[8]Emmons interview; Morelle Emmons, deposition taken October 30, 1968, for *United States of America v. Lincoln Parish School Board et al.,* Civil Action No. 12,071, in Superintendent's File, Ruston, La., 178, hereinafter referred to as LPSB Minutes. Emmons related that he had received no complaints from the parish about the condition of schools.

[9]*Brown v. Board of Education of Topeka*, 347 U.S. 483, *United States Reports* (Washington, D.C., 1954).

[10]*Brown v. Board of Education of Topeka,* 349 U.S. 294 and 300, *United States Reports* (Washington, D.C., 1955).

[11]W.D. Workman, Jr., "The Deep South," in Don Shoemaker, ed., *With All Deliberate Speed: Segregation-Desegregation in Southern Schools* (New York, 1957), 88.

[12]Tom Judd, Lincoln Parish School Board Employee and Assistant Superintendent, 1955-1972, interview by the author, October 21, 1992, Ruston, La., tape recording, in possession of the author, Ruston. Ray Bratton, a coach and teacher at all black Lincoln High School during desegregation, recalled a lack of a "sense of frustration." He also attributed any discrepancy in funding to differences in the numbers of students. See Thomas Knapp, "Looking Back Locally into Black History," *Ruston Morning Paper*, February 4, 1993.

[13]Judd interview.

[14]*Evers v. Jackson Municipal Separate School District,* 328 F.2d 408 *Federal Reporter* (St. Paul, Minn., 1964); *Singleton v. Jackson Municipal Separate School District,* 348 F.2d 729 (1965), *Federal Reporter* (St. Paul, Minn., 1965).

[15]*Singleton v. Jackson*, 355 F.2d 871 (1966), *Federal Reporter* (St. Paul, Minn., 1966). The boards should assign a student who makes no choice to the "school nearest [his or her] home." See also *United States v. Jefferson County Board of Education*, 372 F.2d 836 (1966).

[16]Judd interview; Emmons interview; LPSB Minutes, August 2, 1966, 25-27.

[17]LPSB Minutes, August 3, 1966, 25-27; "Notice to the Public," *Ruston Daily Leader*, April 26, 1967.

[18]Morelle Emmons, deposition in *U.S.A. v. Lincoln*, LPSB Minutes, 179.

[19]Judd interview; Emmons interview.

[20]"At Rotary Club: Morelle Emmons Outlines Plans of Board Under New Regulations," *Ruston Daily Leader*, August 7, 1969.

[21]*Hall v. St. Helena Parish School Board*, 417 F.2d 801 (1969), appendix, *Federal Reporter* (St. Paul, Minn., 1970), reports that in 1967-1968, 3,126 black and 3,630 white students went to parish schools. The percent of blacks in formerly all-white schools was 3.07. In 1968-1969, the number of blacks increased to 3,139, with whites climbing to 3,682, and the percentage of crossover to 3.7. No white students transferred to all-black schools.

[22]J. Harvie Wilkinson III, *From Brown to Bakke: The Supreme Court and School Integration, 1954-1978* (New York, 1979), 109, suggests that African Americans did not change because most could not shed ingrained social mores. Emmons interview; Judd interview; and Thomas Knapp, "Looking Back," *Ruston Morning Paper*, February 4, 1993.

[23]Student Non-Violent Coordinating Committee (SNCC), *Special Report*, September 30, 1965, 24, as quoted in Gary Orfield, *The Reconstruction of Southern Education: The Schools and the 1964 Civil Rights Act* (New York, 1969), 128.

[24]Black teachers accounted for 3.76 percent of the faculty in formerly all-white schools. White teachers constituted 4 percent of the faculty in formerly all-black schools. See *Hall v. St. Helena Parish School Board*, 417 F.2d 801 (1969), appendix.

[25]Lincoln Parish School Board, minutes of meeting, 1966-1973, 142; "More Integration Due for Teaching Faculty," *Ruston Daily Leader*, March 6, 1968, 1. Mr. Emmons remarked that he placed David Wright, a "personable and attractive" African American, at an elementary school, that Wright soon became a favorite among his students, and that his success "opened the door" for more promising race relations. Emmons interview.

[26]*Cleveland v. Union Parish School Board*, 406 F.2d 1340 and *Hall v. St. Helena*, 417 F.2d 801 (1969).

[27]For well-researched interpretations of the Supreme Court's and Fifth Circuit Court's decisions regarding desegregation, see Lino A. Graglia, *Disaster by Decree: The Supreme Court Decisions On Race and the Schools* (Ithaca, N.Y., 1976), 18-90; Jack Bass, *Unlikely Heroes* (New York, 1981); and Wilkinson, *From Brown to Bakke*, 11-78.

[28]Bass, *Unlikely Heroes*, 297-310.

[29]*Green v. County School Board of New Kent County*, 391 U.S. 430, 431. Decided May 27, 1968.

[30]*Adams v. Mathews*, 403 F.2d 182 (1968). The court also attached a deadline. Plans must be ready before the 1968-1969 year or shortly thereafter.

[31]*Cleveland v. Union Parish School Board*, 406 F.2d 1332. Decided October 25, 1968.

[32]*Hall v. St. Helena Parish School Board*, 417 F.2d 801 (1969). This decision involved twenty-nine school districts from Louisiana, of which Lincoln Parish was one.

[33]Judd interview; Emmons interview.

[34]The sentiment of this group was expressed by Mrs. R.W. Winters, in "Letter to the Editor: Readers Debate Issues of Public Education," *Ruston Daily Leader*, August 1, 1969, who wrote, "The federal government may take my money . . . my land, my home, my car, but I refuse to surrender my children."

[35]The ten parents in "HEP?" were apparently playing upon Governor John McKeithen's campaign pronunciation of "help." See "Board Views Court Rule, Special Session Expected Within 10 Days," *Ruston Daily Leader*, June 4, 1969.

[36]"Local Citizens Committee Formed to Support Freedom of Choice," *Ruston Daily Leader*, June 5, 1969; "Citizen's Meet at Ruston High School," *Ruston Daily Leader*, June 6, 1969; "Committee Initiates Program to Organize Regional Meeting," *Ruston Daily Leader*, August 9, 1969.

[37]"Education, Tech Professor Leads Fight for Choice Plan," *Ruston Daily Leader*, July 15, 1969.

[38]"Community Relations Council, Parish Group Urges Total Integration," *Ruston Daily Leader*, July 2, 1969.

[39]"Board Views Court Rule: Special Session Expected Within Ten Days," *Ruston Daily Leader*, June 4, 1969. Also instrumental in the parish's defense was special counsel Harry Kron, former assistant Attorney General for Louisiana, who was hired September 3, 1968. See LPSB Minutes, September 3, 1968, 169.

[40]Emmons interview; Morelle Emmons, speech given to the faculty of Lincoln Parish, Fall, 1969, Private Papers of Morelle Emmons, Ruston, La.

[41]Judd interview.

[42]"Court Orders Boards to Submit New Plans," *Ruston Daily Leader*, July 6, 1969.

[43]LPSB Minutes, July 3, 1969, 224.

[44]"School Mixing Plan Due Thursday," *Ruston Daily Leader*, July 2, 1969; Judd interview; and LPSB Minutes, July 3, 1969, 224.

[45]LPSB, July 3, 1969, 221-24; and Tom Kelly, "HEW Plans Shock Board Members," *Ruston Daily Leader*, July 3, 1969.

[46]Judd interview.

[47]Tom Kelly, "HEW Plans Shock Board Members," *Ruston Daily Leader*, July 3, 1969.

[48]Ibid.

[49]Emmons interview.

[50]LPSB Minutes, July 3, 1969, 221.

[51]The students could choose from the following schools: in Choudrant, St. Rest School or Choudrant High; in Dubach, Hico School, Hopewell School, or Dubach High; in Simsboro, Fellowship School or Simsboro High; in Ruston, Hillcrest, Cypress Springs, Lincoln, Greenwood, or Ruston Elementary; I.A. Lewis or Glen View Junior High; or Lincoln or Ruston High. LPSB Minutes, July 3, 1969, 221-28; and *Ruston Daily Leader*, "Board Submits Own Desegregation Plan," July 7, 1969.

[52]This extension applied to all affected school districts in the Western District of Louisiana. See "Boards Get 16-Day Extension," *Ruston Daily Leader*, July 8, 1969; and Marian Wright Edelman, "Southern School Desegregation, 1954-1973: A Judicial-Political Overview," *Annals of the American Academy* (1973): 39-40.

[53]"Officials 'Explore' School Plans," *Ruston Daily Leader*, July 17, 1969; "Board, HEW Officials Discuss Modified Plan," *Ruston Daily Leader*, July 18, 1969.

[54]Judd interview.

[55]*United States v. Jefferson County Board of Education*, 372 F.2d 836; *Adams v. Mathews*, 403 F.2d 181 (1968); *Hall v. St. Helena*, 417 F.2d 801 (1969)—all asserted that a plan met constitutional standards if it "worked." By working, a plan had to abolish all vestiges of the dual system.

[56]"Court Order Implements Integration Plan," *Ruston Daily Leader*, August 5, 1969; "Lincoln Schools Plan Approved," *Ruston Daily Leader*, July 30, 1969.

[57]"Integration Plan for Fall Is Told," *Ruston Daily Leader*, August 5, 1969; and "Desegregation Plan," found in the Superintendent's file, Lincoln Parish School Board, Ruston, La.

[58]"Total Integration Required in Lincoln for 1970-71 Year," *Ruston Daily Leader*, August 5, 1969; and "Desegregation Plan," Superintendent's file, Lincoln Parish School Board, Ruston, La.

[59]"School Board to Ask Dawkins for Change In Integration Plan," *Ruston Daily Leader*, March 4, 1970. Edelman, "Southern School Desegregation," 39-40, asserted that Nixon caused the Southern desegregation movement to wane because of his public disapproval of a Supreme Court decision ordering the integration of thirty-nine Mississippi school districts.

[60]"Revised School Plan, Board to Meet Officials in D.C.," *Ruston Daily Leader*, March 20, 1970; "Board Assures Black Citizens of No Purge Against Teachers," *Ruston Daily Leader*, June 3, 1970.

[61]LPSB Minutes, May 25, 1970, 254, and June 24, 1970, 257.

[62]See *U.S.A. v. Lincoln*, July 23, 1971, *consent decree*; LPSB Minutes, March 17, 1970, 247; and Judd interview.

[63]*U.S.A. v. Lincoln* "Conclusions of Law," August 5, 1970, court decree made by Judge Ben C. Dawkins, Jr., found in Lincoln Parish School Board Office, Superintendent's file, Ruston, La.

[64]*U.S.A. v. Lincoln*, "Findings of Fact," August 5, 1970, Superintendent's file, Ruston, La.

[65]*U.S.A. v. Lincoln*, August 5, 1970, Superintendent's file, Ruston, La. The bi-racial committee consisted of six black and six white members of the community. Its job was to advise the board on matters involving race, and it could not compel action. Emmons claims that it was not too effective. See also Tom Kelly, "Bi-Racial Committee Named, Parish Advisory Group On Schools, *Ruston Daily Leader*, October 7, 1970.

[66]As a result of the court-ordered desegregation plan, a reactionary private school movement created two new schools. An almost reflexive action to integration movements in the South was the establishment of private schools, and in Lincoln Parish the knee jerked readily. Realizing that Freedom of Choice would not be reinstated, white citizens created Southland and Cedar Creek private schools. The Southland School, which opened in Dubach on an "emergency basis" and attracted students from neighboring parishes as well as Lincoln, lasted only a few years. Cedar Creek School, on the other hand, has survived until the present. Organized by prominent businessmen from the Ruston area, Cedar Creek's declared purpose was to "supplement the present local system" and give parents more control of their children's education. The founders insisted that all students would be welcome, but no blacks enrolled. Because of much of the private school enrollment came from outside the parish, Lincoln's public schools suffered little loss of students. See "Open House Scheduled By Southland Academy," *Ruston Daily Leader*, March 17, 1970; "Cedar Creek School Will Open in the Fall," *Ruston Daily Leader*, January 22, 1970; "Confrontation: Public, Private Officials Meet," *Ruston Daily Leader*, March 4, 1970; LPSB Minutes, March 3, 1970, 245; and Emmons Interview.

[67]Judd recalled that the Justice Department sent some representatives to Lincoln once during the mid-1970s. Investigating some racial turmoil surrounding the election of the homecoming court, they found the situation being handled adequately and left after a short stay.

# HATE WHITE PEOPLE-BEAST OF THE EARTH: MARK JAMES ROBERT ESSEX*

Elliott Leyton[1]

"The quest for freedom is death—then by death I shall escape to freedom."

Mark Essex[2]

The mental life of mass murderers is not so difficult to decipher once we have uncovered the social messages which constitute the ciphering key. Many such killers do contrive to leave a kind of enigmatic wake behind them, because the date at which they are stopped is when they are riddled with police bullets (as was the case, for example, with Charles Whitman's shootings from the University of Texas tower in 1966). Yet it is a grievous error to believe that dead men tell no tales, and Essex is perhaps the finest illustration of this point. It is an equally monumental error to dismiss Essex, as so many have done, as a kind of deranged "sniper," and hope to leave it at that. He was much more.

During his killing spree, Essex seemed to address himself to some fundamental issues in American life. His "sniping" was an integral part of a coherent campaign. Moreover, he tried to "explain" it in his earlier comments to friends and family, in his writings on his apartment walls and ceilings, and in his shouted remarks as well as his homicidal actions during the actual assault. His central rebellion, despite the wretched and racist form it actually took, was an interesting one, aimed directly at what he perceived to be the racist white establishment in America. Appropriately then, he tried to kill its most visible and powerful representatives, those uniformed, generally white, agents of social control—the police (although he did not shrink from murdering civilians, so long as they were white). He conducted his explosion of radical creativity with considerable style and *finesse*: he challenged the entire police and military forces of the great city of New Orleans. The ensuing gunfight came close to destroying an entire city block, and he

*First published as Chapter 7 in Elliott Leyton, *Hunting Humans: Inside the Minds of Mass Murderers* (New York: Pocket Books, 1988), 241-75. Reprinted with the kind permission of the author and Beverley Slopen Literary Agency.

escaped to freedom in death, leaving behind him ten dead, twenty-two wounded, and millions of dollars worth of property in ruins. More important to his purpose, he created many admirers for himself in the radical community—and left in his wake an air of imminent insurrection felt so intensely by both the public and the authorities that something might almost have come of it. In his own terms, it was both an exit with *panache* and an achievement of which few young persons dared dream.

## KILL PIG DEVIL

His first kill was on New Year's Eve of 1974. He hid across the street from the New Orleans' police department's Central Lockup and opened fire with his Ruger .44 magnum semi-automatic carbine. His first four shots were fired in rapid succession and narrowly missed the head of police cadet Weatherford, blasting cement chips off the wall around him. After the briefest pause during which cadet Weatherford took cover, cadet Al Harrell, one of the few young blacks in the New Orleans police, came into view. Essex unleashed a volley of shots at the nineteen-year-old. The third shot struck Harrell in the chest, passing through "the anterior thorax causing severe lacerations to the heart," as the death certificate later read. The .44 magnum bullet was not yet spent, and after it passed through Harrell's body, it struck Lieutenant Horace Perez in the ankle. Perez blacked out. Observing the assault, a detective called both for an emergency ambulance and for all available police to rush to the Lockup. Within seconds, they were swarming over the area with shotguns and revolvers ready, fanning out into the area from which the shots had been fired. Their assailant had disappeared.[3]

A few moments later, police officers Edwin Hosli and Harold Blappert were investigating a ringing alarm in a company office a few blocks from the Lockup. Carrying flashlights, and unaware of the recent shooting, they prepared to check out the building. Essex was hiding inside the office. His first shot struck Hosli in the abdomen, ripped through one kidney, collapsed a lung and perforated the bowels, spilling fecal matter through the body cavity. It would take Hosli two months to die. A second shot shattered the squad car's windshield, and a third ricocheted off the hood and penetrated the windshield, while a fourth struck the building behind the officers.[4]

Within minutes, more than thirty police surrounded the office: six men fired shotguns with heavy loads at the door, disintegrating it, and then sent in a dog. A subsequent search of the premises revealed that the assailant had entered the hemp factory by shooting the lock off the door. Blood stains on the window glass through which Essex had left the office indicated that he had been wounded, and bloody handprints on the windowsill suggested that he had tried to dry the blood. Among the items he left behind was a brown leather purse with a black owl painted on its side containing fifty .38-caliber bullets.[5]

Apparently anxious to ensure that police knew where he was going, and to draw them into an ambush, Essex left a trail of bullets—two together always pointing in the same direction—at periodic intervals along his path of retreat from the hemp factory to the front of the First New St. Mark Baptist Church. There he waited. Incredibly, as police arrived in front of the church and found the cartridges, they were pulled out of the neighborhood by a police administrator who was concerned with the high level of tension in this black area. During the "cool-off" period that the administrator wanted, the assailant disappeared from the church.[6]

Although he would not kill for another week, he did not remain inactive. During the afternoon of January 1, 1975, he seems to have set two fires in nearby warehouses in the heart of the city: the fires smoldered for five days, and 200 firefighters were called in to douse the flames. He seems to have returned periodically to the church over several days: on the evening of January 3, police received a complaint that a man was hiding in the church. When they searched the church, one policeman recalled, "the evidence our man had been there was unbelievable. Hidden in the ladies' bathroom, we found a cloth sack filled with .38 caliber rounds. We also found bloodstains on several doors and window sills."[7]

On the morning of January 7, he walked into a grocery store managed by Joseph Perniciaro, who had reported seeing him to the police (it was not determined how Essex had received this information). He entered the store carrying a rifle and called to the manager, "You, you're the one I want," and shot him in the chest. Essex ran for several blocks, then stuck his rifle through the window of an idling car and told the driver, who was black, to get out. "I don't want to kill you," the driver remembered him saying, "but I'll kill you too." Essex drove off, heading toward the downtown Howard Johnson's Hotel, which would be the scene of his ultimate demonstration to the authorities.[8]

He parked his car, and climbed the hotel's outer staircase to the eighth floor—but was refused entry by the hotel staff. On the ninth floor, he rapped on the outer door and asked a maid: "Let me in, sis, I got something to do," she remembered him asking. She refused, and he climbed the outer staircase once more. He finally gained entrance on the eighteenth floor where, carrying his rifle, he brushed past three black employees with the remark, "Don't worry, I'm not going to hurt you black people, I want the whites." A twenty-seven-year-old white doctor of medicine, Robert Steagall, stepped into the corridor as Essex passed his room. They struggled with one another until Essex shot him in the arm and chest. When Steagall's wife, Betty Steagall, rushed at them screaming, and knelt next to her husband, Essex shot her through the head. He then entered the Steagall's room, set fire to the drapes, and ran down the hall back to the staircase. The fires began to spread, smoke billowing from the rooms.[9]

Frank Schneider, the front-office manager, and Donald Roberts, a bellman, were on their way up to investigate the sounds and smoke. As they stepped out of the elevator on the eleventh floor, they saw Essex standing a few yards away. Schneider and Roberts ran for the nearest exit. "We heard one shot and that was the one that went over my head as I was running low," Roberts said later. "Then the second shot apparently got Frank, who was running behind me; and I kept running." Schneider had been shot in the head and killed.[10]

Walter Collins, the hotel's general manager, and Luciano Llovett, a maintenance man, went up to investigate the reports of a man in the hotel with a rifle. On the tenth floor, Collins saw a youth with a gun and started to run. The bullet hit him in the back and he collapsed to the floor. When he heard Essex leave the corridor, he began crawling on his elbows and knees toward the landing.[11]

Patrolmen Michael Burl and Robert Childress were the first policemen to reach the hotel. As they ascended the hotel's elevator, the first fire engines began to arrive outside the building. Fire Department Lieutenant Tim Ursin was climbing a ladder up the side of the building when Essex appeared on one of the balconies and fired at him: the bullet struck Ursin in the left arm, scouring a wound so severe that his left forearm later required amputation. Essex continued firing when any policemen or firemen showed themselves.[12]

A chaotic scene soon developed (although it was nothing compared to what was to come): explosions from Essex's .44 carbine mingling with sporadic return fire from police, screams from the hotel guests trapped in their rooms, and billowing smoke from the burning floors. The chaos deepened as police began firing at random at the hotel's upper floors—in contravention of all notions of fire control. For his part, Essex continued to prefer uniformed targets; so much so that he even allowed a detective, who appeared to be a civilian, to pass unscathed through the killing ground. By eleven o'clock that morning, one hundred policemen had surrounded the hotel. That number would swell to over 600 policemen from Louisiana, Texas, and Mississippi, as well as FBI, Treasury, and other federal agents (totaling twenty-six state, local, and federal law enforcement agencies), before the affair was finished.

Patrolman Charles Arnold climbed to the tenth floor of an office building across the street from the hotel. When he pushed open a window, Essex fired a shot which shattered on Arnold's shotgun and tore into his jaw, knocking him to the floor. Arnold later told Essex's biographer, Peter Hernon, that as he spat out pieces of jawbone, teeth, and blood, someone had looked at him and said, "Good Christ! He blew your whole face off." As the firing continued, Robert Beamish, a forty-three-year-old broadcasting executive, tried to sneak past the swimming pool out of the hotel, but Essex spotted him and shot him in the stomach, blowing out his belly button. Beamish jumped or fell into the pool, where he remained for two hours. Inexplicably, Essex continued to pass up some targets, whimsically allowing some to pass unscathed.[13]

Now he raced through the upper floors of the hotel shooting and setting fires in as many rooms as he could manage. Firemen who were trying to fight the fires found themselves exposed to increasingly uncontrolled shooting from the police. The absence of police fire control severely exacerbated the danger to the growing number of tourists who had begun to gather around the hotel to witness the event—some of them, presumably radicalized blacks, shouted "Right on!" each time the sniper fired.[14]

Patrolman Kenneth Solis was using a loudspeaker to direct the tourists to take cover when Essex shot him in the right shoulder under the rib cage, shattering the shoulder and exposing splintered bone. Another bullet hit Sgt. Emmanuel Palmisano as he ran across the plaza to help Solis: the bullet fractured Palmisano's left arm, entered his body under the armpit, traveling down his back and grazing his spine. Patrolman Philip Coleman responded to the cries for help from the wounded by driving his squad car across the plaza, sunk low in the driver's seat. Patrolman Paul Persigo died instantly from a shot through the mouth as he stood gazing at the hotel's upper floors. An unidentified man in a civil defense helmet was shot in the right arm as he walked along the street; and when ambulance driver Chris Caton ran out to rescue him, another bullet hit Caton in the back, crushing his shoulder blade, collapsing one lung, and exiting under the armpit. Civilians armed with rifles, some clad in ill-fitting military uniforms, were beginning to show up near the hotel and began to join in the attack on Essex—adding to the air of farce enveloping the scene.[15]

A crowd of several hundred young blacks was now on the street. They acted as a kind of cheering section for Essex: each time he fired, the crowd moved forward a few paces, chanting, "Kill the pigs, kill the pigs," and, as Hernon wrote: "As the tempo of the gunfire increased, these chants became louder, fiercer. Several empty bottles were thrown. . . . Many of the blacks were drinking wine from bottles in brown sacks. 'Hang on, baby,' one of them shouted. 'When it gets dark, we gonna help you.'"[16]

Deputy Supt. Louis Sirgo of the New Orleans police led a small assault team up to the top floors of the hotel. On the stairs above the sixteenth floor landing, a shot from Essex's carbine fractured Sirgo's spinal cord, breaking the vertebral column and perforating his left lung, liver, and right kidney. He died within minutes. Essex continued firing as he ran from floor to floor, lighting more fires (most often by igniting each suite's telephone book and placing it under a curtain or mattress), while nervous and utterly uncoordinated police barely managed to avoid shooting at each other.[17]

When Officer Larry Arthur of the tactical squad smashed through the locked door opening on to the hotel roof, Essex shot him in the abdomen and shouted, "Free Africa! Come on up, pigs!" Essex would not leave the roof alive. For the rest of the siege, he would pop in and out of the concrete cubicles which protected the doorways to the roof, jumping out from them to fire at different angles and then taking shelter again as the torrent of inaccurate and uncoordinated fire from the police bracketed his position. During a lull in the firing, Essex was heard to scream, "Happy New Year's, pigs! I've killed four of you motherfuckers. Come on up and I'll kill four more." At midafternoon, police fired a dozen tear-gas canisters at the roof. The gas settled on the roof and then dispersed without effect. To taunt them, Essex shouted, "I'm still here pigs!" Meanwhile, elected officials were beginning to panic. They thought Essex's attack might not be just one individual's idiosyncratic action: "The thing that worried us the most," said one councilman, "was the question, what if this was the beginning of something much bigger? We wondered whether a revolution was coming, whether other blacks would come to the sniper's assistance." Essex would have been pleased.[18]

When a small and unarmored police helicopter circled near the hotel, a volley of shots from Essex drove it off. Soon after, however, a U.S. Marine Air Reserve CH-46 ex-Vietnam armored helicopter, carrying two Marine sharp-shooters armed with M-14 .308s and three policemen with AR-15 .223s, flew to the scene through rain and fog. For what remained of the day, the helicopter would make a total of forty-eight passes over the hotel, and do so in the midst of undisciplined fire from police and civilians. On one swoop, police in the helicopter mistakenly opened fire on a stairwell in which police officers were hiding. "The rounds just poured on us," one of the policemen later said. "They riddled the door, the hole, everything. Plaster and concrete went flying down those stairs. It was amazing no one was killed."[19]

As the gunners on the helicopter poured magazine after magazine into the cubicles, a radio-station announcer broadcasted a "request" from police for citizens with large-caliber rifles to come to their aid. This fabricated request produced a "large number of morons, marginal types, all of them armed to the teeth" at the hotel, all offering to "get the sniper." The police evicted the vigilantes, but the following morning, another group was discovered approaching the hotel by stealth. Incredibly, according to police, one woman telephoned them to offer blankets for the sniper, whom she thought was "probably freezing up on that roof." Their response to the offer has not been recorded. At no point during this operation did any police strategist apparently consider the obvious way to conclude the assault (which would have prevented all police and civilian casualties): to simply clear the area of all human targets, and wait out the sniper.[20]

Meanwhile, Essex continued to address his fire and his abuse at the police. "Come on up, you honky pigs!" he shouted. "You afraid to fight like a black man?" The police responded in kind, shouting, "Fuck you! Fuck you. Fuck you. Fuck you." Once again, the helicopter swooped down on the wrong stairwell and opened fire on the police crouching there. A black policeman briefly tried to talk Essex into surrendering, but Essex merely shouted, "Fuck you. Power to the people!"[21]

The last moments of Mark Essex came at just before nine that night. As the helicopter dove at him once more, he ran out of a cubicle and fired, then ran back inside: at that point he seems to have been hit. As the helicopter pilot remembered it: "I guess the guy figured it was over. They were pouring a lot of lead in there, and he ran out firing." He was met by the full-automatic fire from the helicopter, as well as the heavy rifles (including .375 and .458 "elephant guns") from the hundreds of police on adjoining roofs. One of the gunners in the helicopter, firing on full automatic, said Essex

> came out, running toward the helicopter, firing as he came. He was looking straight at us, holding the gun at the waist and firing. He took two or three steps before we opened up. I hit him a whole clip from the thighs to the neck. He was running at full tilt and his momentum carried him another five or ten feet. Then the bullets caught him and held him up, sort of like when you shoot at a pie plate and keep it rolling.

Firing his high-velocity Weatherby rifle from the roof of the Bank of New Orleans, another officer said: "The guy came out and turned around to shoot . . . that's when I fired. I hit him in the buttock, and he tumbled forward and dropped his rifle. Then some guys with the big stuff, the .375s and .458 elephant guns, opened up. One of those shells hit his leg. It looked to me like it blew it off." The officers with perhaps the best view of Essex's last stand said:

> I think what happened is that some tracers burned up after hitting the walls of the cubicle. Whatever it was, he came out running and screaming and his left arm was up, the fist clenched. It looked like he was running on a charcoal grill. With all that shooting, there was a ring of red fire around him. The bullets actually held him up, twisting him around. Then he went down on his back about twenty feet from the cubicle. Everyone kept shooting.[22]

The heavy fire from the helicopter and the adjoining roofs shattered a water pipe on the roof, unleashing a four-foot wall of water which roared down the stairwell in which the police were watching, and sweeping them off their feet in a wave of weapons, bandoliers, clothing, and police. Moreover, the officers believed there might be a second sniper on the roof, and they continued to "see," "hear," and shoot at the "second sniper." As Hernon described the scene: "Long into the night, police yelled insults from the Rault Center and other buildings as they tried to bait the gunmen into revealing their positions. 'Where does it hurt Leroy?' they shouted, their voices lost in the darkness. 'Hurts all over, don't it.' No one answered from the roof. 'Power to the people, nigger.'" Reports then came in that another sniper had definitely been spotted on the roof. The police opened fire once more, their spotters observing the flashes of the bullets hitting the building, but interpreting them as muzzle flashes from a second sniper. In the rising crescendo of police fire, nevertheless, there could still be heard the distinctive sound of a Thompson .45-caliber submachine gun firing on full automatic, and the steady boom of a .375 Holland and Holland big game rifle.[23]

To compound this farce, late that night, the police sent in the K-9 corps. The dogs climbed to the roof, but one of them was so sickened by the tear gas that it simply curled up on its side. A second dog's trainer refused to let it go out alone on the roof, frightened that "they'll kill my dog." A third dog's trainer agreed to send his dog, but the dog would not oblige. At 5 a.m., the helicopter made another strafing run in the gathering light pouring fire into the cubicles, but succeeded only in awakening the five policemen who had fallen asleep in the stairwell. Then began the inevitable process in which the police began to shoot at each other. When one officer gingerly stuck his helmet on a stick and climbed slowly out on the roof, police without radios opened fire on him, mistaking him for the sniper. When a police team stormed the roof a little before two in the afternoon, police from City Hall opened fire on them. Soon the assault team was joined by thirty other zealous officers, standing shoulder to shoulder in a semicircle around the boiler room: they opened fire together and the ricochets careened around the roof, wounding nine of them, three seriously. Essex would have loved it.[24]

His body lay twisted on the roof. One leg was virtually severed from his body; the torso was a crushed pulp; the face had been almost shot away; but the left hand was still clenched in a fist. Officers in the morgue later counted at least 200 bullet holes in Essex's body and noted that the gall bladder was the only organ not destroyed by the small arms fire. All that remained in his pockets were two bullets and one firecracker. An inquiry later determined that he had fired between 100 and 150 rounds to kill nine persons and seriously wound another ten during the hotel assault. Police found his stolen car parked within a block of the Central Lockup. In the glove compartment was printed material from the state's Department of Employment on discrimination in hiring practices. In the trunk, police found a duffel bag on which the word WARRIOR had been printed by hand in black ink.[25]

## A CURIOUSLY HAPPY CHILDHOOD

The conscious mental life of our civilization, conditioned as it is by notions that it is primarily childhood that produces the man, makes us assume that we will find something bizarre in Essex's family or community to explain his murderous behavior. It would be most satisfactory if we could demonstrate that he had come from a brutalizing family, or a community discolored by ugly racism—and that these experiences had established subconscious drives to manufacture a manhood crushed in childhood. Yet we search in vain for such evidence. Indeed, the evidence from both family and community points resolutely in another direction.

Essex was a young black raised in a thoughtful, progressive, and gentle home, in a community that was insulated from all the vilest excesses of urban or southern racism. We do not know the precise details of the ideological atmosphere in which he was raised, although we can state with little fear of contradiction that it was non-violent. What we can be certain of is that the gentility of his family and community failed to prepare him to accept numbly with suitable meekness the racism he would encounter later on in the navy, or prepare him for the limitations to his chances in life that he would confront in the outside world. What is the process whereby a gentle and non-racist youth is transformed into a violent racist—one who hates with such ferocity that he can kill not only the uniformed white authority figures, but also shoot in the head a young woman kneeling dazed beside her husband's body? To comprehend this transformation, we must follow Essex through his brief and tortured life. To do so, we must examine the artifacts of his life through the prism of the system of social class and race in American life. We will make no progress if we dwell merely on the superficial elements that have engaged some commentators (such as Essex's tiny stature) who have argued that his actions stemmed from his personal inadequacies. It takes more than diminished height, or the reputed sharp tongue of a mother, to finance an explosion of mass murder.

To reach below the surface of Essex's life is to marvel at the uncommon happiness of his childhood. He was a cub scout and well regarded by most, if not all. He spent many hours fishing for perch and catfish in the waters near town; and a teacher described him as a "crack shot on rabbits and squirrels." He attended a neighborhood primary school and a high school in the downtown business district. As only twenty-nine of the school's one thousand students were black, his minority status constituted no threat to the established white order of Emporia, Kansas. Certainly his relations with other white youngsters were good, for they were his playmates in childhood and his dates during adolescence. The family home was no ghetto slum: it was a detached single story house in a faded suburb, with a large playground across the street.[26]

His family's social-class affiliation is critical. Essex's father was no unemployed slum-dweller conditioned to accept his station in life. His father was a foreman, not a worker, in a small, family-owned firm in Emporia, and they could well afford their lower-middle-class style of living. Ironically and more destructively, he grew up with the deadly misapprehension that his race might not matter very much in the larger scheme of things—or even not at all. His family obviously discussed the racist evils of the society at large; but his own experience of it was once or twice removed. Even when his brothers and sisters left Emporia, they went to other places where the racism was subtle and subdued—a brother found a measure of peace in Cedar Rapids, as did sisters in Los Angeles and Waterloo, Iowa. Most critically, as the son of a foreman who owned his own respectable home, he must have felt it was possible for him to make a life as a man in his society—a belief that no slum-dwelling urban black could sustain beyond puberty—and even form dangerous ambitions (whether or not they were beyond his personal gifts). Thus the crisis that must hit many blacks in adolescence did not hit Essex until he was an adult and in the navy—a far more difficult time for an individual to absorb the social message that he or she is worthless, especially a young man reared on self-respect. If a class or race is to be systematically subordinated, its self-respect must be looted systematically in childhood: in this special sense, the system failed.

Neither was there any agency in the community adequate to decode that social message. Emporia's factories and slaughterhouses did not deny a place to blacks: only one black owned his own business, but many labored in the factories and slaughterhouses. The community's roots in the anti-slavery movement were deep. The town had sent a 144-man regiment to fight the Confederacy during the Civil War, and the ruins of John Brown's log cabin remain as a monument only a few miles to the east. The majority of the community were of Welsh and English stock, shaping a milieu that was deeply religious, prosperous, and puritanical (Emporia was the first "dry" community in the Midwest). Less than 2 percent of its 28,000 people were black; and if the black and Chicano families lived in the shabbier eastern end of town, the system that kept them there was subtle and without violence. A further safety-valve was that the community exported its most aggressive and ambitious blacks who searched elsewhere for their dreams, for they were not content with Emporia's mediocre horizons. This was not at all the stuff of the destruction of the spirit and the body that Elliot Liebow described in *Tally's Corner*, his classic study of the black slums in Washington, D.C.[27]

Essex was an average student in school—and it was this essential mediocrity, combined with his inappropriate ambition, which would (as much as his soul-destroying encounter with white racism) doom him to his fate. He had a special aptitude for technical subjects, and his teachers and schoolmates remembered him as a "smiling, friendly boy who was always laughing and joking," who dated both black and white girls, and whose ambition was to be a minister. A former girlfriend said: "He really didn't talk about wanting to be anything else. I know his mother was really happy about him wanting to become a minister." He spent one unsatisfactory semester at Kansas State College, after graduating from high school, and then enlisted in the navy in 1969, partly to avoid the draft and certain assignation to Vietnam. He scored in the top 25 per cent in the navy's entrance examination—which emphasized technical matters—and, impressed with the navy's programs, he signed up for four years. Hernon said Essex was "elated" when he discovered he was to be sent to San Diego. That elation would soon disappear, for he was about to be exposed to a hurricane.[28]

## THE MANUFACTURE OF DESPAIR

"There is no place in this white man's navy for a self-respecting black man."

Mark Essex[29]

The metamorphosis of Essex from a cheerful young Midwestern black into a deeply embittered and increasingly committed young pseudo-revolutionary was accomplished within a few months in the U.S. Navy. He enlisted on January 13, 1969, and arrived in San Diego in early February for three months at the Naval Training Center. By April, Hernon wrote, Essex "had finished boot camp with an outstanding performance rating and was encouraged to take advanced training in a specialty." His superiors encouraged his essentially middle-class aspirations and assumptions, and advised him to enroll in the Naval Dental Center. After completing their three-month course in x-ray procedures and oral surgery, he was rated outstanding and assigned to the Dental Clinic at the Naval Air Station at Imperial Beach in July. There he established a solid working relationship with the young dentist to whom he was assigned, and who would later describe Essex as

> a pretty good athlete. . . . He was a good team man, sort of an all-American boy. In those days he was just the nicest person in the world. He was concerned about everybody around him, concerned about learning his job. . . . He was the kind of person I liked to have around, a happy-go-lucky kid who was very hard to get rattled. I'm very demanding, especially when it comes to dentistry. I demanded a lot out of him and he delivered. His folks flew out to visit him early in his tour. They were just

> fine people. I really liked them. They were nice, down-home people who really enjoyed living and loved their son.

A co-worker described Essex in similar terms: "He was an easygoing guy. He would sing to himself and be real friendly with everyone. I remember when I first got to the clinic he took time out and helped me. He showed me how to work with the doctors."[30]

Despite his positive attitudes and sunny personality, an epidemic of racial harassment on the Imperial Beach base began to trouble him. He wrote to his parents to complain that the navy "is not like I thought it would be, not like in Emporia. Blacks have trouble getting along here." When Essex discussed the problem with his black friends on the base, they advised him to adjust to the reality, to work hard enough to receive promotion, and thus be removed from contact with the worst racists. Essex took the advice to heart and was promoted from recruit to seaman in less than a year; but the harassment continued, and as Hernon observed, "it was increasingly clear that blacks were second-class citizens in the Navy, and it was hard for him to understand why no one seemed willing to change things."[31]

Nurtured in the blandness of Emporia, his assumptions about himself as a full citizen and human being were being bombarded, and he had no ready defense for such an assault. When he took an extra job as bartender at the enlisted men's club, he found that while white bartenders could go anywhere without permission, he could not enter certain rooms without first asking a white sailor. The car he bought to celebrate his twenty-first birthday was halted by security guards each time he entered or left the base: invariably he had to produce his license, registration, and insurance as if they did not know him. Frequently, he was ordered out of the car as guards searched its every seam, elaborately unscrewing even the door panels to make their racist point. When he began to date a Mexican woman and took her to the enlisted men's club, "conversation stopped, heads turned, and its wasn't long before the half-whispered [racist slurs and] comments began to circulate."[32]

The rebellion first surfaced when Essex and his three black bunk mates were put on report for "excessive noise in the barracks." They were accused of playing a stereo late into the night, and forced to face a disciplinary hearing. They were convinced that they were being discriminated against, since whites played their stereos just as loudly and without punishment. Essex and his friends decided to fight the charge and demanded a summary court-martial, which would allow them to argue their case. Essex's patron and boss, the dentist, conducted his own private investigation into the affair and was convinced the matter was a clear case of racial discrimination. The sailor who filed the complaint, he said, "was a guy who was obviously just a prejudiced individual. He didn't like blacks in general. . . . He told me that he walked into Essex's room and here was 'all this nigger shit.'" The dentist told the commanding officer about his findings and the court-martial proceedings were halted. But Essex was not satisfied, for he and his friends were then separated and assigned to different barracks. It was vindication not compromise that he sought.[33]

Essex felt he and his friends had been "sold out," and thought that once they had been isolated in their new barracks, "it was really going to hit the fan." As Hernon wrote,

> His prediction proved accurate. The riding continued unabated. He was a pariah who lived in virtual silence. No one openly called him 'nigger.' They didn't have to, for he was subjected to every petty indignity imaginable—endless bed checks, extra guard-duty tours, and constant admonitions to turn down his stereo even when the volume was so low he could barely hear it. There were even laughs when he cut his low-riding bush haircut, which he kept well trimmed for fear of being put on report for violating grooming regulations.

At the enlisted men's club, the once-muted racial tension escalated into louder and more vicious racial slurs; and the same slurs hounded him into the mess hall or gymnasium until his work at the dental clinic began to suffer and he was forced to take sedatives.[34]

Two black friends of Essex during that period later told the *New York Times* that

> all the young blacks around the base were being hassled. Essex felt that he was getting a particularly rough deal and that he wasn't going to take it lying down. White sailors in the enlisted men's club came down hard on Essex, regarding him as a 'cocky nigger.' . . . But what really burned Essex up was the riding he got from petty officers and other officers. They would write him up for the smallest infraction and usually he would get a Captain's Mast while the white got off scot free. We all had that sort of experience.

Another friend commented that "Essex came into the Navy expecting to be treated in the same decent way he always had been treated back in Emporia, and he found it wasn't like that all."[35]

The first explosion of violence from Essex took a remarkably long time to emerge; but in August of 1970, a racial slur triggered a fistfight. As the incident was reconstructed, a white petty officer had remarked to Essex about black "smilin' and shufflin'," and prolonged the taunting until Essex jumped on the man's chest and began flailing at him with his fists. The fight was interrupted by a passing officer, but the chain of thought it had provoked was not. As Hernon noted of this release from the colonial mentality:

> For the first time in his life he had struck a white man, a fact so unbelievably startling that its significance was only now beginning to ring in his brain. The blow had seemed as natural as a thunderstorm in summer and as he thought about it, re-creating the fight in his imagination, savoring it, he realized that what he had done was more than justifiable; it was heroic.

But Essex paid a heavy price for that blow: everywhere on the base, he was now a marked man, a black who had struck a white NCO. A friend remembered him concluding that "if a black sailor can't get a fair shake when he's in the right, then to hell with the whole United States Navy."[36]

In increasing despair, Essex went absent without leave on the morning of October 19, 1970, one month after the base commander had halted his court-martial. Even with the sleeping pills, he had been unable to sleep, lying awake and dreading another day of racial harassment and denial of self. Sitting in the bus depot waiting for a bus to Emporia, he decided it was necessary for him, purely as a matter of self-preservation, to get out of the navy. He telephoned his parents and told them, "I'm coming home. I've just got to have some time to think." He spent his days in Emporia thinking "about what a black man has to do to survive." According to Hernon,

> the intensity of his bitterness at first surprised, then worried his parents, but when they gently tried to caution him about the dangers of hatred, his head would jerk up as if pulled by strings. 'What else is there?' he would say. 'They take everything from you, everything. Your dignity, your pride. What can you do but hate them?' He vowed that he was unwilling to wait any longer to be treated 'like a man.'[37]

Mrs. Essex later recalled for Hernon that her son "'told us he didn't see how he could go back to the Navy and start it all over again.' While she cautioned moderation, he replied that he was not being treated with 'moderation,' but 'like a nigger.'" The distraught parents asked their minister to intervene: "He told me," the minister recalled, "how badly the Navy had treated him and how fed up he was. We talked a lot about discrimination and I remember him telling me how he had seen 'the whole picture' in the Navy. He was very, very bitter. I'll tell you, I was worried about the boy after we talked. So were his parents." Eventually, however, their counsel prevailed, and Mark returned voluntarily to the navy after a month's absence without leave. "He had had his time to think," Hernon wrote. "He had had his chance, as he would say later at his court-martial, 'to talk to some black people.'" Essex reported to his base's military police and awaited his court-martial.[38]

## The Trial

"I have two years left and when I get out I want to become a dentist."

Mark Essex[39]

Before trial, Essex—not yet utterly alienated from white society—explained his dilemma to his patron, the dentist Hatcher. "I just couldn't hack it anymore, and I felt like everybody was out to get me," Hatcher remembered him saying. "I really had to go home and get my head straight, and my mom and dad told me that I had to do it this way. So here I am. You do whatever you have to do and then, that's it I'm getting out." When Hatcher tried to argue that Essex should not run away from the problem, Essex replied, perhaps with greater wisdom: "Nothing is going to change, doctor. The same old hassles will go on, and me and all the other blacks will keep on coming out on the bottom." Clearly, he had already made his dual decision to leave the navy and to conclude that nothing could be changed—at least not by conventional action.[40]

The trial was appropriately Kafka-esque. Essex's lawyer based his defense on the prejudice issue and used the dentist Hatcher as his primary witness. Hatcher, Essex's superior officer on the base, testified that Essex was

> by far . . . the best [assistant] that I have worked with. He is outstanding in his professional performance and duties [and] . . . in my relationship with him he has proven to be a very personable, very warm person. He is sincerely worried about other people, about their needs, about their problems [and] . . . he constantly volunteers his services because he wants to help people.

Hatcher further testified that the story behind Essex's absence without leave could be traced to his being put on charge for excessive noise in the barracks:

> The men felt that they were being unjustly accused because of their color, and . . . my investigation showed that the man who made the original complaint was a very biased individual, and very obviously racially prejudiced. He had very possibly, to my way of thinking, influenced the other witnesses . . . so that the picture given to the court-martial was a very biased one. The captain, after hearing this, talked to the man who made the original complaint . . . and decided the whole case was a matter of injustice.[41]

"He [the Captain] at this time ordered that the court-martial be stopped," Hatcher's testimony continued,

> and brought the four men before him and made what I think he felt was an honest attempt to get at the problem [but] . . . I think that the feeling from all four of them was that it was just another whitewash of the situation, that, in fact, the Captain was not going to be able to do anything . . . I think that Essex, in this case being the most sensitive and the most responsible of the four, felt that he had been sold out, and he was very despondent over it. Immediately after the initial complaint was lodged and was brought to the XO's mast, they [the four sailors] were separated. . . . They put Essex in a room with totally incompatible people and the harassment started almost immediately, and he was again forced into a situation, this was before the court-martial even came about, that was nothing but a constant hassle, and this in his living spaces, the only place . . . he could go to relax. The harassment occurred in the mess hall lines, recreation areas, and so forth. So all put together, he was a very upset person during this time. . . .

The remarkable Hatcher continued with a denunciation of the harassment that Essex had experienced, and of his own doomed attempts to abridge it.[42]

When it came time for Essex to testify, he essentially concurred with Hatcher. "I am the accused," he said chillingly.

> I believe that Dr. Hatcher explained most of everything as to the reason that I went UA. When we asked for a court-martial, the four black people felt that it was a case of discrimination. We had certain things happen to us before we went to trial . . . I went UA because I just needed time to think . . . I had to talk to some black people because I had begun to hate all white people. I was tired of going to white people and telling them my problems and not getting anything done about it. I am twenty-one years old. Almost every time I drove on the base they would search my car. I had a fight in front of chow hall. Some friends of mine were going back to the barracks, and I was going to chow and they asked me to bring back some chicken for them, and I asked them what color the chicken was to be, and they said that it should be black. Well, someone said to me, 'Why does it have to be black, what is wrong with white?' and I jumped on his chest . . . I have two years left and when I get out I want to become a dentist.[43]

For the crime of fleeing from racist abuse, Essex was sentenced to forfeit ninety dollars of his pay each month for two months, was "restricted to the limits of the Naval Air Station . . . for a period of 30 days," and was "reduced to the pay grade of E-2." The presiding judge could only say that "the prejudice issues that were raised by the defense, while not excusing your offense, do materially explain your actions." Essex left the room with an emotionless expression and the conviction that the system had failed and excluded him. Several weeks later, Essex was asked to sign a document acknowledging that he had been considered "for an administrative discharge for reason of unsuitability due to character behavior disorder." Shortly after this ultimate degradation, the station's commanding officer recommended that Essex be

> separated from the naval service . . . [as his] further retention in the service would not be in the best interests of the Navy. Essex continues to display flagrant disregard for Military authority, despite frequent counseling at the departmental and command level. Essex's impulsive behavior, and inability to accept the responsibilities of military service have rendered him a severe liability to this command.

Thus the system vindicated itself in this extraordinary document, and "explained" Essex's reaction to intolerable racist abuse as a "behavior disorder." Therein lay the intolerable affront that Essex would redress by carefully planned behavior in which he would accept the responsibilities of quite another form of military service.[44]

## THE CREATION OF AN IDEOLOGUE

"It's a revolution!"

Mark Essex[45]

The emotional preconditions for his task were created in the profound contradictions embedded in the social order. These were transmitted with the utmost rigor to young Essex. It now remained for him to explore whatever ideological alternatives were available to him in order to reconstruct his damaged sense of self. He appeared to find it in the burgeoning black radicalism of the time. However, like all our multiple murderers, as a true ideological conservative he would not join a revolutionary movement. He would only absorb its rhetoric and style in order to carry out a personal vendetta, an individualized protest against the exclusion of this marginal middle-class black from his own aspirations. It should come as no surprise that his rebellion took such a racist form, for the spirit of the times gave ideological—even divine—sanction to racist excess. All this must have been intoxicating for a maturing martyr and rebel.[46]

It is not clear exactly what Essex's movements and contacts were during his post-navy career. The journalist Tobias thought that "there was scattered evidence to suggest that Essex had connections with black militant groups," but admitted that "it was not clear." Still, Tobias concluded that since there was an abundance of black revolutionary literature in Essex's apartment, there "seemed little doubt that Essex was intimately connected with black extremist factions." There was insufficient evidence for such a conclusion. Tobias noted that Essex spent "most of the time" between his discharge from the navy in February 1970, and April of 1972, with his parents in Emporia, but added that "he took mysterious trips to New York and New Orleans supposedly to 'visit old Navy friends.'" Whatever the actual contacts with militant groups may have been, "Essex left Emporia somewhat abruptly and went to New Orleans where he joined a militant Black Muslim friend from the Navy." One police report commented that

> during this entire investigation into the background of Mark Essex, no firm physical evidence was found which would link him to any of the known subversive or militant groups, although his possible involvement with several such groups was hinted by more than one source interviewed. There can be no doubt that Essex was well trained both in firearms and urban guerrilla tactics . . . and while the investigation failed to develop the sources of and scope of any such training, there is some evidence to indicate that he did undergo a period of training shortly after his release from the Navy.

Despite the paucity of evidence, there was no doubt in the police investigators' minds that Essex's behavior had been a coordinated and well-considered campaign, part of a group's terrorist strategy. As one detective remarked, "this was expert, well planned, well executed, and demonstrated the techniques of urban modern guerrilla warfare."[47]

We will never know the precise details of whether he was involved in personal encounters with revolutionary groups; but it matters not, for the important thing is that in his post-navy maturation, he was exposed to the writings and thoughts of black revolutionary intellectuals, and that his state of mind was such that he was willing to kill and die for such notions. Since no action was followed after his death, it is unlikely that his terrorism was anything other than an individual *communiqué*. The origin of his ability to make such a social statement lay in the shock of his sudden exposure to white racism. An ugly or lame child may grow accustomed to such stigmatization: it is the beauty whose face is suddenly destroyed or the athlete whose body is crippled by accident who experience the sharpest pain—a shame requiring terrible expiation.

Essex cannot have been exposed to radical thought during his adolescence in Emporia—or if he was, it made no impact upon him. He would only have felt the intense and Christian sense of injustice which his mother articulated in her no-nonsense way. It was in the navy, Hernon wrote,

> that Essex began to read about the black movement, something he had rarely done in Emporia. With interest he followed in the newspapers the legal battles of Huey Newton and Bobby Seale, who had founded the Black Panther Party in 1967 . . . [and of a] five-hour gun battle in Los Angeles between police and eleven Panthers, including three women.[48]

At this time too, he formed new associations. What the sociologists call "the significant other," the influential friend, was to be Rodney Frank, a New Orleans black with an extensive arrest record who was in the navy at Imperial Beach with Essex. It was Frank who would interpret Essex's experience for him. According to the police report, "Fellow sailors and superior officers reported that Essex began to have a change of attitude as he became more closely associated with Rodney Frank. Frank, who was described as being militant and antagonistic, later became a Black Muslim, and his attitude towards the white population may have influenced Mark Essex's thinking." A later FBI report noted that Essex, while in the navy, also "associated with and received black militant literature from a member of the Black Panther Party," and Hernon said that Essex

> mingled off-base with other tough-talking blacks in the San Diego area. These individuals . . . undoubtedly felt their relationship with Essex was one of student-teacher: the naive black from backwoods America needed to be informed what it was like to be beaten down by the system. What influence they had on Essex is not known; whatever it was, it became increasingly clear to Dr. Hatcher and others that the young sailor had changed.

Hatcher even dated the change to Essex's twenty-first birthday on August 12, 1970. "The change was very sudden," he remembered.

> It seemed to come in a matter of weeks . . . I have a feeling that he got in with a group of blacks who really felt they were being put down. . . . Several times he talked about going downtown and meeting with some guys who were putting out an underground newspaper. . . . Once the harassment started, after the fight and after he started getting into trouble, the conversations we had were very terse. He was almost a defeatist at that point. He was really down on the system. And as I said, it really came overnight. It was very quick, and I couldn't understand it. . . . During that first year all our conversations had been happy ones. But then they became very short. He was kind of defensive, belligerent sometimes.

Essex's torment was profound: as his sister later put it, he was in the midst of the process in which "the Navy became his own private hell."[49]

Hernon correctly noted that Essex was "a casualty of history," and reminds us of the prevailing mood of protest within the armed forces at the time, in which black sailors also began to rebel.

> Fights swept U.S. military bases and naval stations. In Vietnam, black GIs drafted to fight in a war in which they didn't believe were accused of blowing up—fragging—white officers. Morale disintegrated. . . . Resistance organized, and groups with names like 'Black Liberation Front of the Armed Forces' were established. Sabotage increased. In May of 1970, for example, nuts, bolts, and chains were dumped down the main gear shaft of the U.S.S. *Anderson* while she was in San Diego. Other ships were similarly damaged. The revolt of Seaman Essex was the revolt of every black in uniform.[50]

According to the New York City police's Intelligence Division, Essex went to New York in February, shortly after his discharge from the navy, and established contact there with the most militant wing of the Black Panthers. "At that time," the black undercover detective recalled, "that was the headquarters for the Eldridge Cleaver faction of the Panther Party. He must have gotten the revolutionary rhetoric hot and heavy." He spent three months there, at a time when the Panther Party was in serious financial trouble, due to a severe drop in membership, that Stokely Carmichael, an early hero of the party, had remarked that "the Panthers are practically finished." Out of fashion, the Panthers were divided by the inevitable ideological disputes and had split into two rival factions. The dispute was so divisive that soon after Essex arrived in New York, a shooting war broke out between the two factions and several members were killed.[51]

Still, there was no need to be a member, or a part, of any revolutionary party when the monthly publication of the Cleaver wing, *Right on*, contained the ideology and instructions for the developing urban guerrilla. "There were, for instance, discussions of revolutionary tactics; 'how-to' techniques for killing 'pigs,' including where to shoot them (in the head) and what kinds of weapons to use . . . diversionary tactics, how to manufacture bombs and incendiary devices; first aid; and propaganda." The fashionable revolutionary texts were Chairman Mao's *Red Book*, Che Guevara's *Guerrilla Warfare*, and Carlos Marighella's *Mini-Manual of the Urban Guerrilla*. Marighella stresses that the "perfection of the art of shooting makes him a special type of urban guerrilla—that is, a sniper." Similarly, reference was often made to a "Vanguard Party, capable of leading the black masses into an open, violent revolt to overturn the 'racist capitalistic superstructure,'" and to a "'Black Messiah' who would carry a rifle, not a cross." In this maelstrom, Essex's adult identity was forged. He had little choice by then, for as one undercover officer remarked: "Essex probably peddled the paper, and I'd be surprised if he didn't pick up a lot just by reading it. It's all part of the indoctrination. You read about revolution and killing pigs; you talk about it constantly until it's almost a kind of narcotic."[52]

Hernon speculated quite reasonably that Essex must have become "disillusioned" by his time in New York. "The Panthers were weak, hopelessly divided—instead of shooting 'pigs' they were shooting one another—and for a young, increasingly angry black, polarized by violent rhetoric and conceivably interested in armed revolution, it must have been a serious disappointment to see his heroes in such disarray." He left New York just before militant blacks attacked four city policemen, killing two of them. At home he read and re-read *Black Rage*: "As a sapling bent low stores energy for a violent backswing, blacks bent double by oppression have stored energy which will be released in the form of rage—black rage, apocalyptic and final." Not long after one thousand state troopers opened fire on rioting Attica prisoners, killing twenty-eight prisoners (mostly black), Essex purchased the recommended Ruger .44 magnum carbine and began to practice using the weapon. Late that summer, he decided to move to New Orleans. He left quietly, without telling his parents, for he was certain they would not approve of such a move. With him went his Ruger carbine and his .38-caliber Colt revolver.[53]

In New Orleans, he joined his navy friend, Rodney Frank. While Frank joined the Black Muslim Mosque and sold its newspaper, *Muhammad Speaks*, Essex made one final attempt to grasp a tolerable social status and proscribe his coming suicide. He enrolled in a government training program for underprivileged persons, studying vending machine repair with pay. This was no easy way of simply obtaining funds, and Essex's instructors reported that he was an enthusiastic and dedicated student. Still, his anxiety reflected itself in his mindless watching of television hour after hour. As well, he was now studying his "heritage," reading books on Africa and learning words from Zulu and Swahili, even dropping them into conversations and adopting the Swahili word for "bow" as his nickname. In late October, he returned to Emporia for a brief visit, and appeared to be in good spirits.[54]

When he returned to New Orleans, his inner contradictions tortured him with headaches and nightsweats. "Thrust up to the edge of an abyss, he could see no way to cross. More and more he stayed to himself, withdrawing to his apartment to watch television or to read." Soon he would grasp fully the insufficiency of his attempt to embrace the identity of a repairer of vending machines. The incident which ultimately committed Essex to his radical course was the police shooting of two black university students at a campus demonstration in Baton Rouge on November 16. With that, Essex committed himself to becoming a god. Late in December, he sent his declaration to a television station: "Africa greets you . . . on Dec 31 1974 appt 11 the Downtown New Orleans Police Dept will be attack . . . Reason—many. But the deaths of two innocent brothers will be avenged. And many others . . . P.S. Tell Pig Gurusso [the police chief] the felony action squad ain't shit." The letter was signed with his Swahili nickname, "Mata" (bow). He attended his final vending-machine repair class, then wrote his parents a letter vowing total war against whites. "Africa, this is it mom," he wrote. "It's even bigger than you and I, even bigger than god. I have now decided that the white man is my enemy. I will fight to gain my manhood or die trying." Having committed the remainder of his destiny, like a Kamikaze warrior, he distributed his most prized possessions among friends—although he did not, apparently, inform them of his intent.[55]

During that period, it would seem, he daubed the walls and ceilings of his apartment with slogans of his hate and rebellion.

> The largest wall was practically covered with the word 'AFRICA,' which was painted in wavy letters three feet high and bordered with a black margin. Beneath it, in red, was written, 'My destiny lies in the bloody death of racist pigs.' The words 'destiny' and 'death' were underlined. In some places the paint had run in streaks. Next to the slogan 'Revolutionary justice is black justice' was the word 'blood,' and above that the letters 'KKK.' Also painted in red, 'Blond hair, blue eyes.' The words 'hate' and 'kill' were splashed everywhere, seemingly at random. Next to the word 'Africa' was scrawled, 'Hate white people—beast of the earth.' Inside the giant C of 'Africa' Essex had carefully penciled in, 'The quest for freedom is death—then by death I shall escape to freedom.' Near the ceiling was spelled out, 'The Third World—Kill Pig Nixon and all his running dogs.' No inch of wall space was spared.

There were also many words, many of them garbled and misspelled, from Swahili. Essex had left his last will and testament, and done so with an uncharacteristic trace of humor; for when the detectives entered the apartment and looked up at the ceiling, they read his painted insult to them: "Only a pig would read shit on the ceiling."[56]

## THE AUTHORITIES RESPOND

"Essex was caught between two worlds which retarded the maturation of his self-identity."

Ronald Tobias[57]

Hard upon his actions there followed an inevitable deluge of self-serving responses from the authorities, both judicial and intellectual. Leftist ideologues established the legitimacy of his grievance and linked it to the obvious form of society but, typically, ignored the sufferings of his victims. For their part, the rightist ideologues devoted their efforts in equally predictable fashion to exonerate society of all blame and lodge responsibility for the crime in some flaw (such as the retardation of the maturation of his self-identity) in Essex. "He was overwhelmed by the sudden insistence of black survival in a hostile environment where the whites controlling it were less permissive than they had been in Emporia," said Tobias. This unreasonable insistence that blacks should survive, this non-permissive navy attitude toward blacks, seemed to have been at the root of Essex's retarded maturity, thought the spokesmen of the right.

Yet it was not simply journalists who drew such flaccid conclusions. During Essex's first psychiatric examination, when he was in trouble in the navy in early February of 1971, the navy psychiatrist had admitted that there was "no clinical evidence of delusion, hallucinations, inappropriate affect, impaired reality testing, thought disorder, or organic brain disease," but found Essex's judgment to be "poor, impulsive, and immature." The doctor concluded that Essex had an "immature personality" and represented "a liability to himself and to the United States Navy." Then, in a prophetic observation, he wrote: "The patient gives a history of no previous suicidal gestures which were done to manipulate those about him of his environment. At this time, he denies that he wishes to kill himself. However, he alludes to the fact that he 'might do something' if he doesn't get what he wants."[58]

After the shooting, the state's Attorney-General told newsmen that he was "now convinced that there is an underground, national, suicidal group bent on creating terror in America. Their purpose is to cause the people to be dissatisfied, to bring race against race, black against white, young against old, to cause internal chaos." This sentiment was echoed by the U.S. Attorney-General, who promised that "the full force of the Department of Justice would be behind a national investigation" to uncover the conspiracy. Louisiana Governor Edwin Edwards told reporters that "he would consider state laws to reinstate capital punishment for certain 'heinous crimes.' He also said that he had 'no information whatsoever on a nationwide conspiracy to kill policemen.'"[59]

More analytically, a black assistant to the Mayor commented:

> This event will be what we make of it. There are lessons to be learned. The police will learn tactical lessons. Hopefully, by the same manner, I think people all around this country will learn . . . there are real hard problems to deal with. [Many young blacks] were drawing a link to that man on the roof and blacks pursuing their legitimate grievances.

In a similar vein, a black activist told Hernon that

> A lot of white people have written Mark Essex off as just a crazy nigger, an extremist. They forget what Malcolm had to say about extremists. He said, 'You show me a black man who isn't an extremist and I'll show you one who needs psychiatric attention.' . . . He was a man who was terribly frustrated and decided to fight. Most blacks deal with frustration in other ways, or if we are violent, we've been brainwashed to the point where we channel our violence against one another. It was different with Essex. And as I watched the shooting at the hotel that Sunday, I kept thinking, why doesn't that happen more often? I don't think Essex believed he was

> going to kick off a revolution as some have suggested. I think he just wanted to act. He didn't give a damn any more about what would happen; he wasn't looking at the result. . . . The system had fucked him over. The only thing he thought he could do to the system was to try to destroy it, and if he died trying, he died.[60]

More traditionally, Louisiana psychiatrist Dr. William Bloom de-politicized and diminished Essex's rebellion by analyzing him in terms of a short and impotent person. "He was very short," he told a journalist,

> and yet he had a very big gun. . . . There's not a great deal of difference between his drawing of a sword and the image of him striking death with his .44 magnum carbine. The gun probably helped him compensate for his feelings of powerlessness. If he saw himself as a crusader, striking back, he would not have to feel disenfranchised. His concept of self-esteem is very important. By acting in the spirit of a black revolutionary, he may well have been acting against injustices which he perceived to have been done against him. The slogans which he sprayed across the walls of his dingy apartment certainly indicated he hated the police as symbols of the white power structure. By killing them, he would assert his manhood and gain esteem from some elements of the black community. And by gaining esteem, he could defend his fragile identity, which probably was the biggest fight. . . . After looking at his apartment and seeing all of those racist slogans painted on the walls, I would say that Essex had no clarity of concept; the slogans from various revolutionaries were mixed together.

Bloom admitted that "we can't seem to build any case that Essex was neurologically defective or psychotic. As far as I know, there were no signs of mental illness in his family." Still, he concluded that "I do think, however, that there were indications he was suicidal."[61]

The most important document in the intervention of the state in this case was undoubtedly that prepared by police Superintendent Giarrusso, who moved to exonerate the state. "For his [Essex's] acts," Giarrusso wrote, "he paid with his life and, thus, inflicted pain and suffering on his own family." Drawing attention to the fact that one of Essex's victims had been black, another had been a woman, and that a third one was younger than Essex, he concluded: "They all shared the commonality of membership in a society, a society that Mark Essex had rejected because, in his opinion, it had failed to meet its expectations." Giarrusso cautioned that "an attempt may be made to explain Essex's violent acts against his fellow human beings by the presentation of evidence carefully selected to support the premise that society was the compelling contributor to those acts and, if not responsible therefore, at least to blame." For Giarrusso, this notion seemed easy to refute: "In not accepting that premise, I reject the selected evidence offered in its support. To do otherwise, in my opinion, would fix upon society, instead of individuals, the blame for all criminal acts." Yet where did he find the idea that both cannot be blamed; or that in blaming one, the other was therefore exonerated? It mattered not, for his task was not to understand a phenomenon, but merely to blame the actor. "Mark Essex's footnote in history should state clearly that he murdered and executed, without justifiable cause of purpose; that society did not fail him, but that he failed society; that if society inflicted any indignities upon him, such indignities were minuscule by comparison."[62]

In the final analysis, it was the two sociologists who asked the important questions. The social scientist, William Swanson, commented that Essex's apparently suicidal behavior could be linked to other phenomena:

> I do think that Essex was suicidal. I think that he was suicidal in the sense that he did think he could start something, that he might begin a revolution . . . start something that was big. I think that he thought that when he went up on the roof of that hotel that he wasn't coming down. He was suicidal in the sense that he was willing to sacrifice himself for the cause. That may not have been realistic but not delusional in that he thought he was a Black Messiah, the chosen one. There are many examples of this kind of suicide throughout history. It's called altruistic suicide, and one of the best examples is the Kamikaze pilot of the Second World War.

More fundamentally, sociologist Daniel Thompson pierced the heart of the issue when he observed: "The problem for society to ponder out of all this is a fundamental one. How is it to deal with such supreme alienation? It doesn't matter whether the individual be black or white, although in Essex's case it's obvious that his blackness precipitated his action. The question is, what do you do with the man who is alone, cut off, willing to die?"[63]

## INTERNMENT

"Man seems to take justice into his own hands when god or secular authorities fail. It is as if in his passion for vengeance he elevates himself to the role of god and of the angels of vengeance."

Erich Fromm[64]

If we rely on conventional explanations for such outrageous behavior, we are inevitably left perplexed. Essex was no troubled victim of an abusing family, displacing hatred of father on an innocent society. Neither was he a deranged individual suffering from some mental disease, for even his inquisitors cleared him of any serious charges of this nature. Yet this pleasant young man from a prosperous and loving home killed and wounded several dozens of his fellow human beings—including one of his own race—and came close to obliterating an entire city block. In passing, he exposed the incompetence of the city's security forces (as he had said he would do in his *communiqué* to the media).

Essex shares the self-absorption and simple-mindedness of all our multiple murderers, but he is the only one of their number whose protest *seems* to be more than entirely personal, the only one who appeared to act politically, which is to say on behalf of others besides himself. Indeed, this won him much sympathy in certain circles, for he seemed to represent the needs and aspirations of the disenfranchised black masses. Yet the only difference between Essex's rebellion and that of our other multiple murderers is that many people could identify with, even approve, his outrage at his particular exclusion (in a way they could not, for example, with the failed entrance to the lower-middle classes that haunted DeSalvo). In fact, however, his protest proceeded from precisely the same individual reasons as that of all the others in this book. He had no revolutionary social theory other than a racist hatred, no concept of organized response beyond the .44 magnum.

One is led inexorably to the conclusion that if he had remained in Emporia and achieved his high school ambition of becoming a minister, or even perhaps risen to be a junior executive in a meat-packing plant (instead of venturing into the racist trap of the U.S. Navy) he would have remained forever the gentle and delicate young man he was when he walked through the gates of the San Diego naval yard for the first time. One suspects that if he had been able to fulfill his earlier dream of becoming a dentist, or even if he had come to terms with his considered career in vending-machine repair, he and his victims would have survived. Thus the killing stemmed as much as (or more) from his mundane personal career crisis as from any revolutionary ideas: he could not tolerate the lowly rank that his society and his limited personal talents would make available to him.

His final hours were theatrical and entirely in keeping with the fashionably violent codes of his culture. John Wayne would have understood his explosion into purple ceremony. He had decided that only through monstrous acts could he feel that he addressed himself to what historians of crime Peter and Favret call "the rule of lies and the foul machine at whose whim his fellows, the disinherited of the earth, are and have always been crushed, each day, each life." But the act that was a discourse fell hard on perpetrator and victim alike, along with all their intimates. No repayment, despite the many millions of dollars in law suits against the city, could return what had been stolen. The victims were buried during *days* of funerals: among the first was Patrolman Paul Persigo, at thirty-three, the youngest accredited Rose Show Judge in the United States. He did not deserve to die; and neither did the others who followed him into their graves.[65]

Essex was too proud to face a life he perceived as "devoid of all future, deprived of all prospects," or to thereby endure "the unlivable, day in and day out." In Emporia, his parents gave a hint of the moral rectitude that provided the ideological basis for their son's decision, the means by which a young man described by a lifelong friend as "sort of a soft kid, a delicate sort of man," was transformed into a heartless killer. "Young blacks are not going to accept the white racist society," his mother told a reporter. "It's a clear signal, a clear signal for white America to get off the seat of its pants and do something. I don't want my son to have died in vain. If this terrible thing will awaken white America to the injustices that blacks suffer, then some good will come out of it." His sister added that after "Jimmy went into the Navy, he really saw what life, the world was all about. He saw that white people control the world, and blacks were being oppressed by the white man. He didn't like society the way it is. He wanted to change things. The Navy to Jimmy was his own private hell." Undoubtedly it was, alas, but he changed nothing: however, it mattered not, for his goal had been merely to release his own personal anger, to stage his private rebellion.[66]

The warrior with 200 bullet holes in his body was buried in an unmarked grave in Emporia. A few days after the funerals, one of the policemen who had been in the Marine helicopter which had attacked Essex, shot a slum black who had tried to kill him. As attendants placed the youth in the back of the ambulance, a woman's voice rose over the darkened New Orleans slum: "Sniper comin' back. Sniper comin' back to get you all." As if to confirm this—and to deny the reality that many died for nothing—young blacks sometimes search for Essex's unmarked grave and, finding it, stand beside it in silence.[67]

## Notes for "Hate White People-Beast of the Earth: Mark James Robert Essex"

[1]Essex did not leave us much, but what does remain is reprinted in Peter Hernon's splendid study, *A Terrible Thunder*, a spellbinding account of the case rich in quotations from Essex and recollections of Essex's behavior. Ronald Tobias' *They Shoot To Kill* is very much a secondary, and occasionally inaccurate, source. I am grateful to Harriet and Elliot Liebow who, in introducing me to the slums of Washington D.C., gave me some sense of the black experience in urban America.

[2]Peter Hernon, *A Terrible Thunder: The Story of the New Orleans Sniper* (New York, 1978), 255.

[3]Ibid., 47, 19-22. [4]Ibid., 49. [5]Ibid., 55-56. [6]Ibid., 68. [7]Ibid., 93, 95-96.

[8]Ibid., 110-11. [9]Ibid., 112-14. [10]Ibid., 116. [11]Ibid., 117-18. [12]Ibid., 123.

[13]Ibid., 126-29. [14]Ibid., 134-38. [15]Ibid., 140-54. [16]Ibid., 156.

[17]Ibid., 161-63, 172-74. [18]Ibid., 176-78, 180-82, 184.

[19]Ibid., 198. [20]Ibid., 200-203. [21]Ibid., 204, 210. [22]Ibid., 211-13.

[23]Ibid., 223, 226-31. [24]Ibid., 232-34, 243-44. [25]Ibid., 246-53.

[26]Ibid., 52. [27]Ibid., 50-52. [28]Ibid., 52-53, 22-23. [29]Ibid., 66.

[30]Ibid., 23, 24-25. [31]Ibid., 25. [32]Ibid. [33]Ibid., 38.

[34]Ibid. [35]Ibid., 39-40. [36]Ibid., 18-19. [37]Ibid., 46, 52, 53.

[38]Ibid., 53-54. [39]Ibid., 63. [40]Ibid., 58. [41]Ibid., 59-60.

[42]Ibid., 60. [43]Ibid., 62-63. [44]Ibid., 63-64. [45]Ibid., 146.

[46]For popular accounts of the extreme form these radical black offshoots took, see Clark Howard, *Zebra* (New York, 1980), and Robert Tannenbaum and Philip Rosenberg, *Badge of the Assassin* (New York, 1979).

[47]Ronald Tobias, *They Shoot to Kill: A Psycho-survey of Criminal Sniping* (Boulder, Colo., 1981), 81-82, 89, 107.

[48]Hernon, *A Terrible Thunder*, 25-27.

[49]Ibid., 36-37, 38. [50]Ibid., 53-54, 64-65. [51]Ibid., 71-72. [52]Ibid., 73, 74.

[53]Ibid., 74, 81. [54]Ibid., 87, 90-91. [55]Ibid., 98-99, 101-2. [56]Ibid., 256.

[57]Tobias, *They Shoot to Kill,* 112.

[58]Hernon, *A Terrible Thunder,* 281.

[59]Ibid., 239-40. [60]Ibid., 260-61, 277. [61]Ibid., 279-80.

[62]Ibid., 278-79. [63]Ibid., 280-81, 216. [64]Ibid., 101. [65]Ibid., 177.

[66]Jean-Pierre Peter and Jeanne Favret, "The Animal, The Madman, and Death," in Michel Foucault, ed., *I, Pierre Rivieré, having slaughtered my mother, my sister, and my brother . . . A Case of Parricide in the 19th Century* (New York, 1975); Hernon, *A Terrible Thunder*, 264, 266-67.

[67]Hernon, *A Terrible Thunder,* 283.

# STRUGGLE WITHOUT END*

Adam Fairclough

In 1991 a gubernatorial campaign in Louisiana riveted the nation's attention. David Duke, a Nazi sympathizer and a former leader of the Ku Klux Klan, had won the Republican nomination for governor. Finishing second in Louisiana's "open" primary election and beating Charles "Buddy" Roemer, the incumbent, into third place, he stood a real chance of becoming the state's chief executive. That bizarre and alarming prospect drew a question mark against the supposed achievements of the civil rights movement.

Duke's message could not have been simpler: blacks were backward, lazy, violent, and immoral; far from being treated unfairly, they were so pampered by "affirmative action" and welfare handouts that whites were the real victims of racial discrimination. Head of a "National Association for the Advancement of White People," which he founded in 1981, Duke made little effort to disavow his Klan and Nazi credentials beyond bland admissions of "dabbling in far-right politics as a teenager." However, despite vague assertions that he now "reject[ed] categorically racial or religious intolerance," Duke continued to espouse Nazi racial doctrines, argued that the Holocaust was an historical myth, and sold Nazi and racist literature from his NAAWP headquarters. In 1989 he won a seat in the state legislature. In 1990 he garnered over two-thirds of the white vote in his race for the U.S. Senate. And in November 1991, in a bid for the governor's office, he again received the endorsement of a clear majority of Louisiana's white voters.[1]

The reemergence of race as the dominant issue in two state elections was an astonishing development. With the collapse of legalized segregation and the ending of the white monopoly on political power, race had long ceased to be, outwardly at least, the primary organizing principle of state politics. Indeed, it had become conventional wisdom that although politicians might make subtle appeal to racial prejudice, to openly inject the race issue into a political campaign was the height of folly. By the early 1970s

*Excerpt first published in Chapter 15 of Adam Fairclough, *Race and Democracy: The Civil Rights Struggle in Louisiana, 1915-1972* (Athens, Ga.: The University of Georgia Press, © 1995), 463-78. Reprinted with the kind permission of the author and publisher.

the strength of the black vote had become so obvious that white candidates risked alienating it at their peril.

The 1971 election of Governor Edwin W. Edwards demonstrated, for the first time, the decisive influence of the black vote on the state level. To be sure, Edwards, a French-speaking Cajun, also benefited from the relative growth of South Louisiana and the consequent muting of the religious issue: by 1980 the southern parishes accounted for 68 percent of the state's population; Louisiana was ready for a Cajun and a Catholic. Equally important, Edwards had no segregationist past to live down. "Race means nothing to him," thought Camille Gravel. "Never has." Ever since his election to the city council of Crowley in the 1950s—the first council in the state to have black members—Edwards had been accustomed to treating blacks as significant political players. In 1971 he gathered black support with unselfconscious ease. With the backing of SOUL in New Orleans and the support of Jesse Stone and Alphonse Jackson in Shreveport, Edwards garnered more than two-thirds of the black vote in the 1971 Democratic primary, narrowly winning a tight contest against state senator J. Bennett Johnston. And in the general election against Republican Dave Treen, Edwards's black support surpassed 90 percent.[2]

Politicians of all stripes quickly adjusted to the realities of biracial politics. When J. Bennett Johnston ran for the U.S. Senate in 1971, mounting a campaign devoid of racist appeals, black voters rewarded him with solid and decisive support. In backing Johnston, blacks also punished John McKeithen, who stood as an independent, for his raucous defense of school segregation during his second term as governor. Even die-hard segregationists could understand the new electoral demography. Otto Passman, congressman from the Monroe area since 1946, had long boasted the most conservative and pro-segregation voting record in the state. In 1973, however, after surviving a serious challenge in a district where blacks constituted a third of the voters, he earned an approval rating of 39 percent from the Congressional Black Caucus, a higher score than any congressmen from Alabama or Mississippi. State representative Risley Triche underwent a similar metamorphosis. The Assumption Parish legislator had been a loyal henchman of Leander Perez; in 1960 he fought tooth-and-nail to stop the integration of schools in New Orleans. In 1972, however, he supported two bills designed to outlaw job discrimination. "We now find that we were wrong," he explained, referring to his stand on segregation in 1960. "I want my family and my citizens and my friends and my constituents . . . to grow out of racism and bigotry." The price of refusing to change was illustrated by the fate of Congressman John Rarick. First elected in 1966 as the favored candidate of the Ku Klux Klan, he lost the 1974 primary, and hence his seat, to a racial liberal.[3]

It seemed, for a time, that white politicians were prepared to make amends for Louisiana's racist past, and that something like a consensus on racial equality might soon emerge. In 1969 the New Orleans city council enacted a public accommodations ordinance that finally integrated the city's bars. In 1971 the state legislature abolished the state sovereignty commission, whose sole purpose had been the defense of segregation.

The legislature also repealed eleven segregation laws, a symbolic act of reconciliation (the statutes had already been nullified by the federal courts) all the more significant for being initiated by Dorothy Mae Taylor, the first black woman to be elected a state representative. A new state constitution fashioned in 1973 incorporated a "Right to Individual Dignity" that forbids discrimination because of race, religion, idea, belief, and political affiliation.[4]

The passing of the old racial order was most dramatically illustrated, perhaps, in the collapse of the Perez dynasty in Plaquemines Parish. This mineral rich area had been, for all practical purposes, the personal fiefdom of Leander Perez, whose fierce racism and unscrupulous methods ensured that political opponents were powerless and the black population so cowed that dissidents feared for their lives. After the death of the patriarch in 1969, power passed to two sons, Chalin and Lea, who continued to hold sway for another ten years. In 1979, however, fourteen years after the Justice Department sent federal registrars into the parish, a black man was elected to the parish council. In the same year three black oystermen, angered by the curtailment of their fishing rights by a new state law, organized the Fishermen and Concerned Citizens Association. The FCCA openly challenged the commission council, and for the first time in living memory blacks demonstrated outside the parish courthouse, demanding the removal of council president Chalin Perez. The following year the vice president of the council, Luke Petrovich, rebelled against the Perez brothers (who by now were engaged in a bitter feud) and initiated an investigation of parish finances.

As Lea and Chalin continued their fratricide, Petrovich waged a relentless campaign to uncover the way in which the Perez family had, over a period of fifty years, enriched themselves from mineral revenues that rightly belonged to the parish. When the sordid details of this massive fraud finally came to light, the name Perez had turned to mud. In 1983 the parish council canceled the annual public holiday that marked Leander Perez's birthday, and in 1987 it renamed Judge Perez Drive and Lake Judge Perez. Anxious to avoid a trial in the state courts, the Perez family eventually agreed to relinquish control of 60,000 acres of land and pay the parish $10 million in back royalties. The settlement involved a mere fraction of the estimated $78 million in illegal profits that the family had siphoned off since 1936, but it represented a damning admission of guilt and drove a final nail into the Perez political coffin. For decades, Plaquemines Parish had voted the way Leander Perez had wanted it to, turning in the most fraudulent results in the state. But in 1991 the parish recorded a majority for Edwin Edwards, a result that would have been unthinkable when Perez was alive. Perez's shadow shortened even more when River Oaks Academy, one of five private schools he had set up in 1966 to avoid integration, closed its doors because of falling rolls. The other four "segregation academies" had already gone out of existence.[5]

By the 1980s the segregationist redoubts of old had crumbled. West Feliciana Parish, which in 1963 did not have a single black voter, became the only parish in Louisiana to record a majority for George McGovern in the 1972 presidential election. In 1979

William Bailey, longtime head of the Washington Parish NAACP, became president of the Bogalusa city council. By 1993 black mayors were serving in twenty towns and cities, including Ferriday, Lake Providence, Tallulah, Opelousas, and, of course, New Orleans. All told, Louisiana boasted 636 black elected officials, a figure exceeded only in Mississippi. Overall, blacks held 12.8 percent of all elective offices. In 1993 thirty-one blacks served in the state legislature, accounting for 21.5 percent of all the seats. In 1990 William Jefferson, former student leader at Southern University, became Louisiana's first black congressman, taking the New Orleans seat vacated by Lindy Boggs. Louisiana now has two black congressmen.[6]

Black political gains reflected more than raw voting strength measured by the sheer number of black voters; they also testified to the importance of the federal government in ensuring that black votes were translated into something approaching fair representation. With each decennial census, blacks brought suit in federal court to redistrict electoral boundaries in order to increase the number of majority-black districts. At the same time, the Supreme Court's decision in *Allen* v. *State Board of Elections* (1969) enabled blacks to challenge official efforts to rig the electoral game against black candidates. In affirming that Congress intended the Voting Rights Act to prevent discrimination in the electoral process, as well as in the act of voting itself, the Court unleashed a flood of private suits against unfair electoral practices. Moreover, as Frank Parker notes, the *Allen* decision "greatly increased the voting rights enforcement role of the Justice Department," which now had clear authority to scrutinize proposed changes to the electoral laws of states and localities. The lawyers of the Civil Rights Division, writes Steven Lawson, soon became adept at spotting and challenging "sophisticated practices designed to diminish the influence of the black electorate." Despite its courting of Southern white voters, the Nixon administration did not make a vigorous effort to reverse the momentum of black advances; at the national level, too, the civil rights movement had apparently evoked broad consensus rather than spirited backlash.[7]

Just as its contemporaneous *Alexander* decision proved the turning point in making school integration a social reality, the Supreme Court's ruling in *Allen* ensured that black representation went far beyond tokenism. Its most obvious consequence was that blacks successfully opposed a large number of "at-large" electoral plans at the city and parish level under which, except in rare instances where blacks were a majority, whites would continue to monopolize elective offices. Throughout the state, judges imposed single-district plans (although sometimes retaining a couple of at-large seats) on police juries, school boards, and city councils. One such decision led to a black majority on the New Orleans city council, which, until 1975, had been all white.[8]

The results of *Allen* were especially striking in North Louisiana, where whites had been most resistant to black voting and were fighting a vigorous rearguard action to keep black representation to a minimum. After being reversed by the court of appeals in a pivotal case involving East Carroll Parish, Judge Ben Dawkins sedulously struck down schemes that discriminated against black voters. Disallowing an at-large system for the

Caddo Parish police jury, he insisted that "this substantial proportion of black citizenry should not have its vote diluted . . . and that it was entitled to black representation as nearly as possible to that proportion." In his most important voting rights decision, Dawkins ended a white monopoly of political power in Shreveport that had endured for a century. Declaring that Shreveport's at-large elections deprived blacks of political representation, Dawkins accused the city's white officials of systematically discriminating against blacks in every sphere of municipal life. They had virtually excluded blacks from the better-paying city jobs; their efforts to provide low-rent public housing had been minimal; their neglect of black neighborhoods was shamefully visible in ill-lit, badly drained, potholed streets. At-large elections, Dawkins argued, perpetuated "official unresponsiveness to the physical and economic needs and desires of Shreveport's black populace." Under a new city charter establishing single-member districts, three blacks won election to the city council in 1978.[9]

In a political world dominated by bloc voting, of course, whites could still place a ceiling on black representation no matter how equitable the electoral system. But if whites still routinely opposed black office seekers, the black vote could often make or break white candidates. "Maybe we could not get a person elected we wanted elected," explained Jesse Stone, "but we could defeat anybody we wanted to defeat. And that's what we did. We decided, for example, that no one who holds public office in Shreveport at this time . . . is ever going to go further along than where he is right now." The ability to mobilize black voters in this way made Shreveport representative Alphonse Jackson one of the most powerful politicians in the state. According to one study, the Jackson organization "has helped elect congressmen, sheriffs, district attorneys and mayors." It might have added governors and U.S. senators. But the showpiece of black political power was New Orleans, where a combination of bloc voting by blacks and crossover voting by whites enabled Ernest N. Morial to win the mayor's office in 1977 despite the fact that whites composed a clear majority of the electorate. Four years later Morial won reelection, again receiving near solid black support and substantial, albeit reduced, white minority support.[10]

Given the political clout wielded by black voters, it seems strange that a racial extremist like David Duke could become a serious candidate for statewide office. Biracial coalitions, however, have been difficult to construct and have always been vulnerable to the vicissitudes of white opinion. Despite appearances, race never disappeared as a political issue; it could be played down, but it could not be ignored or erased. The reappearance of overt racism also reflected, in addition to lingering rank prejudice, the failure of conventional politics to bring blacks and whites together in any real sense. Racial bloc voting does not simply reflect racial prejudice or racial chauvinism; it mirrors the inequalities and divisions that continue to inform the relationship between blacks and whites.

The persisting economic gap between the races is perhaps the most obvious source of inequality. Scholars have argued endlessly about the extent of black economic progress since the Civil Rights Act of 1964. Optimists point to the rapid growth of the black middle class, a loosely defined category that now embraces between a quarter and a third of the black population. Pessimists view black economic gains as illusory, pointing to the much larger group who suffer from unemployment and poverty and noting that the overall income gap between the races has not closed. As Steven Lawson argues, despite the gains chalked up by the middle class, "the majority of blacks had made little progress in catching up with whites." In 1992 the median income of black families stood at 58 percent of the white level, a wider gap than in 1968. According to a 1991 survey, the median white household has *ten times* the net assets of the median black household. In New Orleans, one of the poorest cities in the nation, 37 percent of black families were below the poverty level compared with 9 percent of white families. Only Mississippi has a greater percentage of poor people than Louisiana.[11]

The most ominous and controversial aspect of black poverty has been the growth of a so-called black underclass of people who have little or no hope of ever escaping from poverty. The "underclass" concept, popularized in the 1980s, revived the old association of black poverty with social pathology. It stresses that the poor are held back not only by unemployment and lack of skills, but also by crime, drug addiction, family instability, and other behavioral problems. The "underclass" is impossible to define precisely or quantify, and the term should be treated circumspectly. Still, the increasing social, physical, and economic isolation of the very poor is all too visible in urban America, and Louisiana's cities are no exception. In New Orleans, for example, the exodus of upwardly mobile blacks to formerly white neighborhoods and new suburbs has weakened both the social cohesion and the physical fabric of many older black areas. The desegregation of Canal Street and the opening of suburban shopping malls has led to the virtual extinction of black business districts.

The gap between the black middle class and the so-called underclass might, logically, militate against racial bloc voting by blacks and whites. Indeed, sociologist William Julius Wilson has argued that it is economic class, far more than race, that governs the position of blacks in contemporary America. Educated blacks, he contends, have little difficulty in finding well-paid jobs, and the major corporations are going out of their way to recruit them. Hence the unemployed, underemployed "underclass" is not so much the victim of white racism as of economic change. With the decline of traditional "smoke-stack" industries and the consequent shrinkage of blue-collar employment, the unskilled and uneducated are marginalized, languishing in low-wage service industries or dropping out of the labor market altogether to live on the criminal fringes of society in the decaying central cities.

If class, therefore, were to become the main determinant of political behavior, then political alliances would increasingly cut across the racial divide. After all, as the black population becomes increasingly stratified according to economic class, the basis for political unity becomes increasingly tenuous; once the novelty of electing a black candidate wears off, there is a natural tendency for the black vote to lose its cohesion. In

New Orleans, for example, blacks failed to unite around a black candidate to succeed Ernest Morial as mayor: in a race contested by two blacks, the man favored by most whites, Sidney Barthelemy, won the election with only a quarter of the black vote. According to Arnold Hirsch, the Barthelemy coalition "blended the most conservative segments of each [race]."[12]

Class, rather than color, might also explain the ambivalent white perceptions of black people. Whites might fear and abhor the "underclass," but also respond positively to "respectable" middle-class blacks. This was certainly the belief of the strategists who constructed Douglas Wilder's campaign for the lieutenant governorship of Virginia. Explained one of them: "People were convinced that prejudice was based solely on the element of color. Our feeling was that that kind of prejudice was on the wane and that the real prejudice that had to be overcome was one based more on class." Whites *would*, they calculated, vote for a smooth, educated, affluent black lawyer. Wilder won his campaign for the lieutenant governorship and went on to become the first black governor of a Southern state. In both races he could not have won without substantial white support.[13]

It is a fallacy, however, to argue that nonracial factors alone account for the reality that blacks still lag behind whites. Class and race do not constitute political opposites: they intersect in complex ways and in some respects reinforce each other. Even in an ideal world where racism did not exist, the overlapping of race and class would still tend to divide whites and blacks. And in practice, when the mental world of white people is already well stocked with negative images of black people, the high rate of black poverty and the association of blacks with crime make it difficult for many whites to view African Americans as individuals rather than as members of a racial group. Color-blind judgments are rendered still more difficult by the fact that residential segregation, now more marked than ever, physically separates blacks and whites into two social worlds.

White perceptions of crime illustrate how real fears combine with racial stereotypes to reinforce divisions. The explosion of violent crime that took place during the 1970s and 1980s is an undeniable fact. Before 1966, the annual homicide figure for New Orleans never exceeded one hundred; after 1970 it never fell below that number. During the second half of the 1980s, with the spread of "crack" cocaine, the black homicide rate soared, in some cities almost doubling. During the first nine months of 1990, 229 people were murdered in New Orleans; 203 of the victims were blacks. In 1993, with 389 homicides, New Orleans became the murder capital of the United States. Louisiana had become one of two Southern states, and one of seven states nationwide, where more people died by the gun than died on the roads.

Spiraling crime rates are a matter of legitimate public concern for blacks and whites alike. There is a strong tendency among whites, however, to make fear of crime their primary response to African Americans. This association of blacks with crime helps to perpetuate racial segregation. It also fuels repressive criminal justice policies that have a disproportionate impact upon black people. Hence while the overall crime rate actually *declined* somewhat during the 1980s, America's prison population more than doubled.

With over one million prisoners, the United States has the highest rate of incarceration in the world, and blacks make up almost 47 percent of those behind bars. America's renewed enthusiasm for capital punishment shows a similar effect: blacks make up 39 percent of all death-row inmates. Since the resumption of executions in 1976, the twelve leading death penalty states include all but one of the ex-Confederate states. Louisiana has executed more prisoners than any other state except Florida and Texas; in proportion to its population, it is America's leading executioner.[14]

In the white suburbs on the peripheries of predominantly black cities, fear of crime is almost an obsession, and politicians have not been slow to exploit it. Jefferson Parish, which borders New Orleans to the south and west, is typical of such areas. Almost as populous as the city itself, Jefferson is a bastion of the "white flight" mentality. In 1986 its sheriff, Harry Lee, ordered his deputies to stop and question any blacks who were seen driving through white neighborhoods in "rinky-dink cars." Two months later the commission council erected barriers across Willow and Hickory streets at the Jefferson Parish line, preventing vehicular access to and from New Orleans. The resulting furor caused both actions to be rescinded, but their authors suffered no political harm at all in a parish that is 90 percent white. In 1989 David Duke won a seat in the legislature representing Metairie, an area of Jefferson Parish in which blacks compose less than 1 percent of the population.[15]

The black vote has not, therefore, fragmented along class lines as much as one might expect. The growing black middle class has not lost its race consciousness; it remains aware of its economic vulnerability and recognizes that its advancement has resulted from racial unity as much as from individual initiative. "Although increased competition for public office sometimes proved divisive," notes Lawson, "blacks generally remained united in their unfinished goal of achieving racial equality." As long as they suffered from discrimination and prejudice, "race persisted as a crucial category for determining political choices." And middle-class blacks had ample reason to believe that whatever their economic status, they would still need to unite with other blacks to oppose racism. True, public expressions of crude racial prejudice had become unacceptable, even in the South. Granted, the only whites who openly advocated segregation were regarded as cranks. But blacks suspect a large dose of racism, albeit vicariously expressed, in the white obsession with crime, in white opposition to busing, in "white flight" from the cities, in white attacks on "affirmative action" policies, and in the general white indifference to the problems of cities and poor people.[16]

The growth of the Republican party in the South illustrates the difficulty of isolating class and race as distinct political categories. The Louisiana Republican party has not based its appeal on overt racism, but it recognizes that its strength resides almost exclusively in the white electorate, especially in suburban enclaves like Jefferson Parish (where David Duke ran as a Republican). Thus in 1979 the party elected its first governor, Dave Treen, a former Citizens Council stalwart, by splitting the interracial coalition put together by Edwin Edwards and solidifying the white vote. Nationally, too, the Republicans have become a virtually all-white party: Ronald Reagan received only 6 percent of the black vote in 1980 and barely 10 percent in 1984. The Republican party has therefore had little to lose by being unresponsive to black demands, and much to gain by opposing them. Usually, moreover, they have been able to frame their policies in such a way that, although having a disproportionately adverse impact on blacks, they are racially neutral. As Alphonse Pinkney laments in *The Myth of Black Progress*, "As long as conservatism dominates the country, there can be no progress in the area of race relations."[17]

It would be fatuous to equate conservatism and racism, yet considerations of race pervade Republican strategy and tactics at both the state and national level. During the 1986 U.S. Senate race, for example, the Republican National Committee tried to reduce the black electorate by as many as eighty thousand voters in an effort to defeat Democratic candidate John B. Breaux. The Republican "ballot integrity" program was reminiscent of the voter purge conducted by the white Citizens Councils in the late 1950s. Like that earlier effort, a federal court judged it illegal. Two years later the Republican party sensationalized the crime issue during George Bush's election campaign by framing a television commercial around a black rapist. The infamous "Willie Horton" spots typified the way in which an ostensibly nonracial issue was given a racial slant in a manner plainly calculated to arouse white fears.[18]

By catering to the white vote and writing off the black vote, the Republican party has helped to legitimate a new form of covert or coded racism. "White racial attitudes have definitely hardened during the Reagan-Bush era," writes Lawrence Powell. "Duke is the beneficiary of twenty years of Republican bottom fishing for Wallace votes." Duke sounded many of the themes that had been popularized by the Republican party; indeed, judged solely on policies, it would be difficult to distinguish Duke from Jesse Helms, archconservative senator from North Carolina, and other right-wing Southern Republicans. It could even be argued that whites voted for Duke in spite of, rather than because of, his Klan and Nazi background; hence Duke advised his supporters to "stay away from the 'N' word" on the grounds that voters were repelled by racial hatred.[19]

Yet to interpret Duke as another right-wing Republican would be to underestimate the breadth and character of his appeal. Duke's electoral support in Jefferson Parish differed from that of mainstream Louisiana Republicans: he drew most of his votes from working and middle-class whites, many of them registered Democrats, not from the affluent whites who formed the backbone of the traditional Republican vote. Duke exerted a class appeal that mobilized white voters from the bottom up, not the top down. And, unlike mainstream Republicans, he explicitly encouraged those voters to project their resentments onto the black population. Lawrence Powell argues, and common sense would indicate, that it was precisely *because* of his well-known Klan background that whites of this class responded to Duke so enthusiastically.[20]

If the Republican party helped to sow what David Duke reaped, the reemergence of overt racism at the end of the 1980s still requires a fuller explanation. Perhaps, as Powell speculates, the backdrop of sharp economic decline made whites in Louisiana especially susceptible to Duke's brand of right-wing populism. Between 1974 and 1981 Louisiana enjoyed an economic boom of unprecedented magnitude: per capita income grew from 79 percent of the national average to 90 percent; nonagricultural employment increased by almost a quarter. When oil prices plummeted in 1981, however, the bubble burst, and Louisiana entered a recession of exceptional severity. By 1981 unemployment had climbed to 13.1 percent, twice the national average, and by 1988 per capita income had declined to 75 percent of the national average. As the unemployment lines lengthened, moreover, the Reagan administration slashed federal aid to the cities. New Orleans, for example, saw its annual subventions decline from $123 million in 1980 to $65 million in 1982; by 1987 the city faced a crippling budget deficit of $30 million.

Instead of class conflict, hard times produced two highly charged, racially polarized state elections. Duke "successfully focused blue- and white-collar economic resentments on programs of racial preference and the black 'underclass,'" writes Powell. And the growth of the black middle class, instead of fostering a feeling of common interest that transcended race, merely accentuated white racial resentments. Middle-class blacks lived in different areas and had little contact with white suburbanites. Moreover, as blacks were demanding a larger slice of the pie, the pie was shrinking. In a straitened economy, with rising unemployment and a contracting public sector, the economic fortunes of the black middle class became closely linked to political patronage, state spending, affirmative action, and minority "set-asides." Race-specific programs to favor black job applicants and promote black employees became one of the most politically divisive issues of the 1980s. Whites believed—and the Republican party encouraged them to believe—that "racial quotas" directly and unfairly disadvantaged them. By the time David Duke appeared on the scene it had become almost an article of faith that black gains meant white losses.[21]

Yet economic hardship and white racial resentments were hardly peculiar to Louisiana. Perhaps one should also look to Louisiana's political culture as an explanation for the Duke phenomenon. The collapse of white supremacy and the rise of the Republican party has not led to a stable two-party system. Quite the reverse: the past quarter of a century has seen the bifactionalism of the Long era give way to an anarchic multifactionalism in which party labels mean little. An "open primary" law, under which all candidates run in the same primary, regardless of party, further discourages party cohesion. The 1979 gubernatorial election, writes Paul Grosser, exemplified Louisiana's "no-party politics run amok." After the first primary, the four losing Democratic candidates all endorsed the Republican, former Citizens Council stalwart Dave Treen, and campaigned against the Democratic front-runner. After Treen's election, his Democratic backers all received plum appointments in the governor's new administration.

Dishonest elections also continue to tarnish Louisiana politics. A 1974 congressional race produced so many fraudulent votes that a state court set aside the result and ordered a new election. In 1976 Congressman Rick Tonry resigned his seat after being indicted for election fraud; two years later he began a jail sentence. The gubernatorial primary of 1978 aroused widespread suspicion, later shown to be justified, that voting machines had been tampered with. The following year a federal grand jury indicted over twenty people in the Leesville area for conspiring to buy votes on behalf of Congressman Claude Leach.[22]

Louisiana's political culture is also, as ever, riddled with corruption. In 1973 a federal judge sentenced former state attorney general Jack P. F. Gremillion to a three-year jail sentence for perjury after he falsely denied his financial interest in a savings and loan company. In 1976 a grand jury charged Shreveport public safety commissioner George D'Artois with stealing $30,000 in city funds; he was also charged with the contract murder of a political enemy. Refusing to submit to arrest, he was physically removed from his office after a sensational armed siege. (He died before standing trial.) Allegations of corruption have swirled around Edwin Edwards throughout his gubernatorial career; he twice stood trial in federal court on charges of fraud and racketeering, but juries acquitted him on each occasion. A 1980 "sting" operation by the FBI revealed the extensive influence of Mafia boss Carlos Marcello with many leading politicians and public officials. Charles Roemer, a top Edwards aide and father of future governor Buddy Roemer, went to jail for corruption. In 1991 a jury convicted Insurance Commissioner Doug Green of taking $3 million in bribes.

Black politicians have no immunity against greed, and many have readily adapted to the "enrich yourself" mentality that pervades public life. The leaders of New Orleans political organization SOUL, writes Arnold Hirsch, proved "adept at blending race and politics for profit." They demanded money in return for financial support, misused antipoverty funds, and made dubious profits from public ventures like the Superdome. Members of the state parole board gave convicts preferential treatment in exchange for money. Perhaps the most egregious case of corruption involved former civil rights lawyer Robert F. Collins. Appointed to the federal bench by President Carter, the first black federal judge in the South, Collins went to jail for taking a $16,500 bribe.[23]

Dishonesty and unprincipled opportunism provide a poor foundation upon which to build a healthy democratic politics. It is common to hear that Louisianians love a rogue, and that corruption in public life is tolerated and even admired. In his memoirs of a long political career, William J. Dodd argued that "a big-time state-politician who failed to get rich and make his friends rich has been considered stupid." There is little evidence, however, that voters approve of flagrant greed and dishonesty in the state's highest officials. Corruption has not so much been tolerated by the state's voters as foisted upon them by a corrupt political system that seems incapable of reforming itself.[24]

Chaotic factionalism, stolen elections, and endemic corruption have nurtured the kind of cynicism that makes voters warm to a candidate, in this case David Duke, who seems to offer a principled stand and a clean break with the past. The corruption of Edwin Edwards's third administration alienated white voters, causing his political base to fracture along racial lines in 1987. After the failure of Buddy Roemer to ease Louisiana's wretched financial condition, many white voters needed only a little prompting to turn their economic woes into resentment against blacks. The coalition that gave Edwards, the notorious corruptionist, a precedent-breaking fourth term had little rationale other than that of denying the governorship to David Duke. The anti-Duke sticker that adorned car bumpers in 1990—"Vote For the Crook, It's Important"—provided a rueful but telling comment on the straitened moral climate of Louisiana politics.

David Duke and Edwin Edwards exemplify the Janus face of contemporary Louisiana. Yet Duke's astonishing popularity among whites in 1990-91 should not obscure the most salient fact about his two bids for statewide office: he lost. Blacks voted in unprecedented numbers to oppose Duke: in the 1991 governor's race, black turnout actually exceeded white. Black Louisianians stopped Duke's career in its tracks, burying his hopes of statewide office and thwarting his national political ambitions. And the black vote, truly functioning as a coherent "bloc," ensured the return to the governor's mansion of Edwin W. Edwards, for twenty years the leading exponent of biracial politics. If the meteoric rise of Duke underlined the continuing vitality of white racism, his equally swift fall demonstrated the extraordinary durability and popular appeal of Edwards. It is doubtful that historians will ever write about "the Duke era." The last quarter of a century of Louisiana politics, however, can already be called "the Edwards era."

To be sure, the rise of David Duke revealed disturbing continuities in Louisiana politics, but the 1991 gubernatorial election revealed, even more clearly, how the electoral game had changed since the heyday of segregation. In 1959, to cite the last example of a campaign based solely on the race issue, Willie Rainach had prompted all the other candidates to gang up against Chep Morrison, the racial moderate. In 1991 Duke's racist campaign persuaded all the other candidates to rally around Edwards. And while the division between North and South Louisiana could be discerned in the Duke-Edwards result, it was not nearly so clear as in previous elections where race had been the dominant issue. Duke carried a bloc of rural parishes in the northern half of the state, but he failed to carry Shreveport, the traditional bastion of Louisiana conservatism. He won Winn Parish, the seat of the Long dynasty, but failed to carry Claiborne, Rainach's home parish and the birthplace of the Citizens Councils. While Duke won two former Klan strongholds in the Florida Parishes, Washington and Livingston, he lost Plaquemines Parish, the old fiefdom of Leander Perez. Duke was soundly beaten, in fact, in every part of Louisiana.[25]

The extraordinary diversity of the coalition that mobilized against him suggests that David Duke was anything but an ordinary segregationist. Only the most profound fear of the consequences of a Duke win could have persuaded business leaders, conservative Republicans, and former Dixiecrats to resurrect Edwin Edwards from his political grave. Much of the white opposition to Duke was a vote against racial extremism and a vote against Louisiana becoming a pariah state, but it was also a vote for conservatism and for the continuation of white control wherever possible. In a racially polarized mayoral election in 1990, for example, voters in Shreveport chose Hazel Beard, a white woman and a Republican, over Dr. C. O. Simpkins, the black civil rights leader who had recently returned to the city after a twenty-five year residence in New York. But the city also returned majorities against David Duke, and an outbreak of cross-burnings led to the swift apprehension and punishment of the Klan perpetrators.

Paradoxically, Duke's statewide campaigns may well have had the beneficial effect of introducing much-needed order into Louisiana's politics and of clarifying the race issue after two decades of obfuscation. Writing in 1989, historian Glen Jeansonne argued that "given the opportunity to vote class interests, as opposed to religious or racial interests, Louisianians have consistently voted the latter two." The elections of 1990 and 1991 broke that pattern, and may well mark a turning point in the state's political development.[26]

In New Orleans, the white elite's commitment to racial egalitarianism was soon put to the test. No sooner had Duke been defeated than a controversy over Carnival erupted. An ordinance passed by the majority-black city council in December 1991 gave Carnival krewes a year to demonstrate that they did not restrict their membership on the basis of race, gender, or religion. If they failed to do so, the city would, in effect, make it impossible for them to parade. Two of the oldest and most prestigious krewes, Comus and Momus, canceled their 1992 parades in protest, others threatened to pull out, and for a time the future of Carnival was in doubt. The council responded to white anguish by appointing a committee, in which whites outnumbered blacks, to examine the controversial ordinance and try to finesse a compromise. Carnival went ahead, and blacks and whites mingled on the sidewalks, yelling "Throw me something, mister!" with no evident racial tension. New Orleans is probably the only city in America where race can be all but forgotten amid two weeks of madcap hedonism. Yet race endures as a fact of life in contemporary Louisiana, just as it does in the United States as a whole. Race and racism are not entities that can be weighed and measured; they are complicated amalgams of social relationships and social identities. They change and mutate over time; they are refracted through class and culture. Race is part of the warp and weft of American society. Like politics itself, in a democracy the struggle for racial equality is a struggle without end.[27]

# Notes for "Struggle Without End"

[1]Elizabeth A. Rickey, "The Nazi and the Republicans: An Insider View of the Response of the Louisiana Republican Party to David Duke," in Douglas D. Rose, ed., *The Emergence of David Duke and the Politics of Race* (Chapel Hill, 1992), 64-74. Duke took 58 percent of the white vote in 1990 and 55 percent in 1991.

[2]Bass and DeVries, *Transformation of Southern Politics*, 167-68; Price, "Impact of Black Voter Participation," 115-18; Alexander P. Lamis, *The Two-Party South* (New York, 1990), 110-11; Jewel L. Prestage and Carolyn Sue Williams, "Blacks in Louisiana Politics," in James Bolner, ed., *Louisiana Politics: Festival in a Labyrinth* (Baton Rouge, 1982), 307-8. Edwards rewarded his black allies with important appointments. Jackson, elected to the state legislature in 1971—the first black representative from north Louisiana—became Edwards's floor manager. Stone became president of Southern University. A. Z. Young, former leader of the Bogalusa Voters League, received a top administrative position in the Department of Health and Human Resources.

[3]Bass and DeVries, *Transformation of Southern Politics*, 177, 180. The victor in the runoff, W. Henson Moore, was a conservative Republican with the reputation of a racial moderate.

[4]Ibid., 176; Price, "The Impact of Black Voter Participation," 177; *New Orleans Times-Picayune*, June 9, July 6, 1972; Anne L. Simon, "Inequality Under the Law: The Louisiana Story," *Southern Studies*, 16 (1977): 293-96; Mark T. Carleton, "The Louisiana Constitution of 1974," in Bolner, ed., *Louisiana Politics*, 27. The New Orleans public accommodations ordinance was passed in December 1969 and came into effect the following month.

[5]Pat Bryant, "A Long Time Coming," *Southern Exposure*, 10 (1982): 83-89; *New York Times*, February 25, 1980, May 11, 1981; *New Orleans Times-Picayune*, February 24, March 20, August 3, December 11, 12, 1987.

[6]*Bogalusa Daily News*, December 5, 1979; Dundy, *Ferriday*, 194-96; Joint Center for Political Studies, *Black Elected Officials: A National Roster* (Washington, D.C., 1993). Reapportionment created another black-majority district stretching along the Mississippi and Red River.

[7]Frank R. Parker, *Black Votes Count: Political Empowerment in Mississippi after 1965* (Chapel Hill, 1990), 97-100; Steven F. Lawson, *In Pursuit of Power: Southern Blacks and Electoral Politics, 1965-1982* (New York, 1985), 135-40, 189-90.

[8]Halpin, "The Anti-Gerrymander," 206-8.

[9]*Blacks United for Lasting Leadership* v. *City of Shreveport*, 71 F.R.D. 623 (1976); Burton, *The Black Side of Shreveport*, 122-23.

[10]Stone interview; Louisiana Governmental Studies, *The Grass Roots Guide, Vol 2: Lobbying the Louisiana Legislature, 1988-1992* (Lafayette, 1988), 140-41, copy in Louisiana Collection, Tulane University, New Orleans; Alvin J. Schexnider, "Political Mobilization in the South: The Election of a Black Mayor in New Orleans," in Michael B. Preston, Lenneal J. Henderson, Jr., and Paul Puryear, eds., *The New Black Politics: The Search for Political Power* (New York, 1982), 227-31; Hirsch, "Simply a Matter if Black and White," 314. According to Stone, an exception was made for Pike Hall, who became a justice of the state supreme court.

[11]Steven F. Lawson, *Running for Freedom: Civil Rights and Black Politics in America since 1941* (Philadelphia, 1991), 262; Wright, "New Orleans: A City That Care Forgot," 60-61; *Washington Post*, January 11, 1991; *New York Times*, April 10, 1994.

[12]William Julius Wilson, *The Declining Significance of Race: Blacks and Changing American Institutions* (Chicago, 1978), 93-103; Hirsch, "Simply a Matter of Black and White," 317-18.

[13]*New York Times*, January 12, 1986; Lamis, *Two-Party South*, 288-89, 316-18. Wilder picked up 44 percent of the white vote in 1986 and 41 percent in 1989.

[14]Vincent Maruggi and Susanne D. Harti, eds., *Statistical Abstract of Louisiana* (New Orleans, 1981), 133; *Washington Post*, October 14, 1990, January 5, 1991; *New Orleans Times-Picayune*, November 17, 1993; *Guardian* (London), June 1, 1994; Coramae Richey Mann, *Unequal Justice: A Question of Color* (Bloomington, 1993), 46, 202-3, 222-23.

[15]*New Orleans Times-Picayune*, January 11, February 22, 24, 1987; Lawrence N. Powell, "Slouching toward Baton Rouge: The 1989 Legislative Election of David Duke," in Rose, ed., *The Emergence of David Duke*, 16-17,

[16]Lawson, *Running for Freedom*, 244.

[17]Alphonso Pinkney, *The Myth of Black Progress* (Cambridge, England, 1984), 179.

[18]*New Orleans Times-Picayune*, October 25, 1986; Lamis, *The Two-Party South*, 277-78.

[19]Powell, "Slouching toward Baton Rouge," 16-17; Douglas D. Rose with Gary Esolen, "DuKKKe for Governor: 'Vote for the Crook. It's Important,'" in Rose, ed., *The Emergence of David Duke*, 211.

[20]Powell, "Slouching toward Baton Rouge," 22-25.

[21]Ibid., 28-29; James R. Adams, "The Sunbelt," in John B. Boles, ed., *Dixie Dateline: A Journalistic Portrait of the Contemporary South* (Houston, 1983), 148-49; Wright, "New Orleans: A City That Care Forgot," 61; Monte Piliawsky, "The Limits of Power: New Orleans," *Southern Exposure*, 12 (1984): 72.

[22]Paul Grosser, "Political Parties," in Bolner, ed., *Louisiana Politics*, 258-77; Wall, *Louisiana*, 365; Lamis, *The Two-Party South*, 114-16, 355; *New York Times*, July 6, 18, 21, 1979, January 5, 1980. The "open primary" rule, moreover, provides that the top two candidates in the first primary, regardless of party affiliation, should face each other in the runoff election. The rule has made a nonsense of the two-party system.

[23]*New York Times*, May 20, September 26, 1971, January 5, 1973; Lamis, *The Two-Party South*, 280; Hirsch, "Simply a Matter of Black and White," 300-302; *Washington Post*, June 30, 1991; John H. Davis, *Mafia Kingfish: Carlos Marcello and the Assassination of John F. Kennedy* (New York, 1989), 486-92, 549; *Southern Exposure*, Summer 1991, 2. If they do not take bribes or steal public monies, politicians still commonly exploit public office to favor friends, relatives, and business associates. In 1992, for example, it emerged that state legislators, who each have the right to award a Tulane scholarship to a deserving student, have routinely chosen their own family members. Mayor Sidney Barthelemy awarded one to his son.

[24]William J. Dodd, *Peapatch Politics: The Earl Long Era in Louisiana Politics* (Baton Rouge, 1991), 5-6.

[25]*New Orleans Times-Picayune*, November 17, 18, 1991; Iris Kelso, "Black Solidarity Wins it for Edwards and Louisiana," *New Orleans Times-Picayune*, November 18, 1991; Rose and Esolen, "DuKKKe for Governor," 227-31. Black turnout reached nearly 80 percent, 3 or 4 percentage points above white turnout.

[26]*New Orleans Times-Picayune*, May 29, November 8, 1990, February 1, 1992.

[27]Ibid., January 12, 19, 20, 21, 22, 1992.

# PART V

## EDUCATION

# RALPH WALDO EMERSON "PREZ" JONES: "THE COUNTRY DOCTOR OF HIGHER EDUCATION IN LOUISIANA," 1926-1977*

Morgan D. Peoples

"We're gonna miss you, 'Prez'," the Grambling State University student newspaper flashed in banner headlines in its edition of February 4, 1977. The well-known and beloved president of Grambling State University had announced his retirement after fifty-one years of dedicated service to that institution, the past forty-one years as president. "A natural love affair" had ended as the president neared the end of his career, and the grateful college newspaper heaped praise upon the man:

> From the time Ralph Waldo Emerson Jones took over until now, he has carried on a natural love affair with 'his university.' He's seen it grow from just a few frame buildings to its present status. He's been through hard times with it and also good times. Of all his many accomplishments here, perhaps the most important of all was the loving care he has given everyone and everything at Grambling.[1]

It was difficult for the students and faculty of Grambling to say goodbye to someone they cherished so dearly. But, his retirement was assuaged because everyone new he would not be leaving the community of Grambling. The administrator disclosed his future plans when he declared: "This is my home and I couldn't imagine ever living any place else."[2]

So, snuggled at the foot of a typical upland North Louisiana hill, several hundred yards from the center of the hustle and bustle of Grambling State University, he spent the remainder of his life in an unpretentious home, comfortable and relaxed. He refused to accept, however, the inactive and lonesome existence experienced by many retirees. In 1981 he celebrated his seventy-sixth birthday, but he had the enthusiasm of a man twenty years younger. His schedule was still filled with speaking engagements all over the

*First published in *Louisiana History*, 25 (1984): 367-90. Reprinted with the kind permission of the author and the Louisiana Historical Association.

country as well as visits to or with friends and former students. His "joy for living" was expressed in these words in a personal interview in 1981:

> I intend to live as long as my old slave grandfather did. He died at the age of 102, and I think he could have lasted several more years if he had not been married for the second time to a 65 year old woman.[3]

And to be in his presence one concluded that he appeared to have many good years ahead of him.

Ralph was proud of his grandparents and spoke reverently of them:

> My grandfather and grandmother were slaves. Right there at Laurel Hill after you pass St. Francisville. Grandfather was named for the slave owner. He learned to read and write and used the Bible for a textbook, the only textbook slave-owners let the people have. His master said to him, 'Herman, you are a good man, if you want to, you can buy your freedom.'

Herman raised vegetables and sold them until he raised $300 to buy his freedom. Then, during the Civil War he joined the Union army and fought under General William Tecumseh Sherman in Georgia. Later, the former slave sent his three children to Leland College, Baker, Louisiana, where Ralph's mother and father met.

Ralph Waldo Emerson Jones was born in Lake Charles, August 6, 1905, the third child of John Sebastian and Maria Morrison Jones, both college graduates and teachers. Ralph's father was a well-known pioneer Louisiana Negro educator. He was, for many years, a teacher and principal in the Lake Charles black school before moving in 1914 to Southern University in Scotlandville as director of the Academic Department. John Sebastian Jones was affectionately known by two generations of students at Southern as "Dean Jones."[4] His son, in four decades of guidance at Grambling, was universally known as "Prez."

Young Ralph grew up amid a rich and varied cultural atmosphere where he read poetry, history, and mastered the intricate manipulation of several musical instruments. Nevertheless, he enjoyed playing baseball more than any other activity. As a young man in Baton Rouge he was often called upon to play in funeral jazz bands, so popular in South Louisiana cities until recent years. Unlike the New Orleans bands that played "When the Saints Go Marching In" on their return from the cemetery, the tune most often played during Baton Rouge funeral recessionals was "Free as a Bird."[5]

Young Jones worked his way through Southern University, receiving a certificate in auto mechanical drawing, and a degree in tailoring in 1925. After his graduation he still lacked the burning ambition within him to pursue a teaching career. Yet, a few months later he began such a teaching career at a small black school, Lampkin College, Alexandria, Louisiana. During that school year, 1925-1926, Jones received no pay at Lampkin because it was a doomed private school; however, because of this unhappy experience Ralph began to create his own image and formed a new view of the world about him.[6]

Ralph Jones began his tenure in the little whistle-stop town of Grambling in 1926 and continued his long, dedicated academic career there until his retirement in 1977, fifty-one years later. The campus newspaper in its special Bicentennial Edition, May 1976, paid homage to the "man called Prez" by declaring that he was "five men in one." According to the newspaper, he was knowledgeable, courageous, full of physical stamina, a warm humanitarian, and a wonderful human being.[7]

When the fledgling educator arrived upon the campus in 1926, it consisted of a few wooden buildings lighted with kerosene lamps. Students slept two to a bed and furnished their own bedding, even stuffing their own mattresses with straw. Study tables were made by the students. Slop jars and demijons were popular since only outdoor toilets were available, and "number three" tin wash tubs were used for bathing. Both men and women worked on the farm to produce their food that consisted mostly of grits, cornbread, flour, navy beans, and occasionally, some meat and gravy. Wood, cut and delivered by the boys, was used for heating and cooking; water was hauled from nearby wells. Board was ten dollars per month. Teachers' salaries, when they were paid, came from the proceeds of a touring minstrel show, or some other kind of fund raiser. It is no wonder that the Grambling school became known as "The college where everybody is somebody."[8]

Jones performed his herculean tasks in the North Louisiana backwoods with the Booker T. Washington approach: "You have to work hard if you have to pay someone to let you work hard." The school wanted a band but had no instruments so Ralph wrote Sears, Roebuck and Company requesting seventeen horns on credit. Much to his surprise, he received them. Nobody knew anything about the horns or the music except Professor Ralph Jones. He taught band members all the intricate procedures required to play the instruments, and when any member of the band was absent from a practice or concert, the band leader picked up and played that particular instrument. Often football players were members of the band, and during football halftime shows, they marched in their football uniforms. Growth of the band was so phenomenal that by 1977, the Grambling State University Marching Band had 150 members equipped with the finest instruments money could buy. In fact, the Grambling Band has strutted all over the world and has been acclaimed in every country where it has performed.[9]

A way to describe the kind of zest reflected in such a long successful career is to show that "Prez" was a man of many faces—a veritable Lon Chaney. In each face, Jones revealed his clever and original sense of humor, as well as his unwavering dedication to certain moral values he never omitted from his life.

His most important visage was his "Family Face," used while working with the thousands of underprivileged blacks from all over Louisiana and other parts of the country at Grambling State University. He wore this face from September, 1926, until his death, April 10, 1982.

Ralph Jones considered that good fortune overtook him in 1926 when President Charles P. Adams, president for 35 years of Louisiana Negro Normal and Industrial Institute, as Grambling was known in its early years, hired him as a new teacher. However, according to the sharp-witted Jones, it was "accidental." President Adams greeted him with: "You're not the man I thought you were, but I'm going to employ you anyway." The president then began to assign him his duties:

> You will teach mathematics, chemistry, and physics. There is a boy's dormitory where you as a single teacher can live and be Dean of men. We need someone to record grades and you can be our Registrar. I want you to start a band, organize a football team and baseball team.

After each assignment, Ralph replied, "Yes, sir." According to Jones, what else could a small man weighing 120 pounds say to a man who was six feet nine inches and weighed 300 pounds? Anyway, in those days everyone had to carry a heavy load. It was no time for the "inflexible specialist." The very existence of the school for the next decade "was problematic and in every sense hanging in the balance."[10]

In a special article written for the *Alexandria Town Talk* in 1976, Sue Eakin of LSU-Alexandria, wrote the following description of the man who guided progress and development at Grambling State University for over forty years:

> The president of Grambling State University is a dedicated educator, a poet with a wizard's command of the English language . . . a ham who could have won an Oscar, a royal ambassador for whomever he represented at the time—black people (especially students), Louisiana, the United States of America—this man has spoken before the United Nations, represented his country abroad. . . .
>
> . . . Now he is a legend in his own time, and a warm delightful human being, able to speak the language of whomever he turns his attention to at the moment—a child, janitor, the Queen of Iran, or the legislature.[11]

No one, including Ralph Waldo Emerson Jones, remembered when or how he was first called "Prez." However, for forty-one years everyone who knew, intimately, the jovial Grambling president, affectionately referred to him by the nickname. Once when he was in a Japanese hotel a young Japanese businessman rushed up to him and called him "Prez." He was a former graduate of Grambling who had received close guidance from President Jones when he was a student there. Several years later on a street in Monrovia, Liberia, the same thing happened.

His strong arm and keen eye were put to work at the helm of Louisiana Negro Normal and Industrial Institute in 1936, after President Charles P. Adams bowed out as gracefully as he could. It was more than a change of administrators. The school was being forced to move in a new direction. Indeed, it had to take a new direction or perish. "I became president of Grambling College in 1936," he wrote years later in a summary of his career, "at a point in time when we had three clear choices: become just another black college; come up with a unique program; or just simply slowly die out altogether."[12] The new president inherited an institution made up of three wooden buildings, 17 faculty members, and a budget of $55,000 per year from the Louisiana State Department of Education.

From its origin in 1901 to 1928 the institution offered only one year of college credit. In the latter year Governor Huey Long gave it a financial boost and elevated it to junior college status. Then, eight years later Prez started a period of tremendous growth. Almost miraculously, when he stepped down as president forty-one years later, Grambling State University contained forty-four modern brick buildings on a 382-acre campus with a net worth of over forty million dollars. A library, housing 123,000 volumes with a seating capacity of 800, served most effectively the intellectual needs of the university. Student enrollment had grown from twelve in 1901 to 4,200 and the faculty had grown to four hundred well-qualified instructors. From May, 1944, to May, 1976, Grambling awarded 12,093 four-year college degrees.[13]

Fortunately for Jones in the beginning, he inherited a group of dedicated teachers to labor with him in what seemed to be an impossible task. Most of them had been trained at Southern University or Tuskegee Institute in industrial education, home improvements, and agriculture; and from them evolved the famous "Grambling Spirit" that has not only endured to the present day but also has grown with the university. "Knowledge for use and knowledge in use" became the slogan. But the spirit said—and still does—"Take what you have and make what you want."[14]

The new program instituted by President Jones, which saved the college, consisted of a statewide field service that toured the backwoods, teaching such basics as hygiene, how to fix harness, how to build beds and partitions in the one room frame houses, how to improve gardens, and how to plant flowers. Unfortunately, the service met stiff opposition from some planters who thought the black teachers came to exert pressure on their sharecroppers to revolt against them or to leave them. As the first group left the campus, President R. W. E. Jones addressed them with these words: "Okay, you're a country teacher! If there are no sanitary toilets, nutritious foods, comfortable homes, good schools, don't sit down and cry about it, get moving and correct these situations."[15]

Reva Williams, a student under both President Charles P. Adams and President Ralph Jones, praised the latter's accomplishments:

> It wasn't until after R. W. E. Jones arrived that the state gave us some electric lights, some extra land, and the state also bought the farm from its owner and gave it to the school. We didn't have any hard surface streets and the sand was so deep that parked cars would stall in the sand. . . .[16]

Kerosene lamps were replaced by electric lights in 1937, and a water system was added at the same time. Outdoor toilets were used until 1939. But, in 1940 the institution was upgraded by the Louisiana legislature to senior college status. Four years later the college awarded its first four-year degrees.[17]

Prez continually harbored a deep desire to help every black student that showed up at Grambling. He thought an institution such as the North Louisiana Negro college was best qualified to deal with their special needs. As a consequence, and principally through Jones' efforts, the rural institution of higher learning became known as the "Biggest Little College in America."[18] In 1964 it was the fourth largest Negro college in the United States, and when integration was mandated during the 1950's-1960's Grambling College hired more white professors than any other black institution in the country.[19]

Even the president's home on the campus was opened to poor black students. Ralph and Mildred Shaw Jones housed and financed at least ninety students through Grambling College over a period of forty years, at the same time they were raising two boys of their own who became successful in their chosen professions and assets to their communities.[20]

Today, Grambling University is known nationally for its football, basketball, baseball teams, and its band; yet the institution stresses mind over muscle in its curricula. Business courses are the most popular classes on the campus. Furthermore, 40 percent of the faculty hold the doctor of philosophy degree. University status was granted to the college in 1974 by the State Board of Regents and approved by the Louisiana legislature. Still, in 1977 there were only 40 whites numbered among the 4,200 students—a condition that still confronts many state college and university administrators in 1983.[21]

Some critics insisted at intervals that the institution placed too much emphasis on athletics. Prez never avoided the issue, neither did he answer critics satisfactorily. In the early spring of 1969, when he was called before the Louisiana Legislature and was questioned about this accusation, he proclaimed seriously, but with a touch of his proverbial sense of humor: "I'm proud of our alumni who have become doctors and lawyers and educators. But I ain't seen anyone yet who would pay six dollars to watch a physics class."[22]

Indeed, a roster of the alumni of the university reads like a "Who's Who of Professional Football, Baseball, and Basketball." Prez, himself, organized the first football and baseball teams in 1926. Coach Eddie Robinson, in forty-one years as head football coach, has seen over 160 of his former Tiger footballers advance into the professional ranks. Every weekend during the National Football League season, Grambling graduates excel, and Robinson-coached teams have played all over the country and in Japan. President Jones developed a great respect and admiration for Coach Robinson and his players. He never missed a game they played either at home or on the road. "These football players today, they're big and fast," Prez once quipped, "I'm afraid to go in the dining room at meal time."[23] There were also some big men in Grambling's roundball program. Willis Reed and Bob Hopkins left their marks in professional basketball, both as players and coaches. Coach "Prez," himself, as baseball mentor, developed many outstanding professional baseball players such as Tommie Agee, Cleon Jones, and Ralph Garr.[24]

Ralph Jones was never a pompous college president who sat in his office shuffling papers, worrying over routine, everyday affairs. Every spring found him in his "flannel uniform," "golfing out fungoes" to the outfielders and infielders, and instructing pitchers and catchers. He chuckled as he admitted that he once umpired in the old Negro American League during the era when the incomparable "Satchel" Paige was a star pitcher in that league. Actually, he coached the first football team, the first baseball team, and trained and drilled the first band at the school in 1926 all at the same time. Sears, Roebuck and Company also shipped, on credit, the necessary football uniforms used by the inexperienced young blacks.[25]

Because of his long years of devoted service to sports, Prez was elected to the NAIA Hall of Fame and was named the National Association of Intercollegiate Athletics Coach of the Year in 1963. His main reason for staying in baseball coaching so long was, as he said, "to help others achieve." In fifty-one years of coaching he posted a record of 815 wins to 216 losses, a record unsurpassed in American college annals in any sport.[26]

Prez's love for his students was tested severely during the campus upheavals of the 1960s. During the time when many American college students were marching, taking over university buildings, and rioting, President Ralph Waldo Emerson Jones was quietly, but successfully maintaining control over these potentially destructive activities at Grambling State College. He used his great power of persuasion on most occasions, talking students out of making protest marches to Ruston or taking over college buildings. On one hot, summer day he summoned a large group of dissidents, planning a march into Ruston, into the air-conditioned auditorium, whose caretaker had been informed to turn the thermostat down as low as it would go. Prez then addressed them:

> I want you to soak up all this cool air you can while you are in here. If you decide to march to Ruston, I would be deeply grieved. That Lincoln Parish Jail does not have air-conditioning. Then, if the State Board of Education decides you ain't gonna be a student at Grambling anymore, you know you ain't got no air-conditioning at home, either.[27]

Many students had already started to review his sensible remarks. Then, as he began to leave the stage, he carried the day with these words: "Don't ever forget that your girl friends are here on this campus." Slowly and quietly the thoroughly subdued crowd filed from the auditorium, drained of most of the angry protest they had harbored a few minutes earlier.

Despite Prez's efforts a serious campus uprising occurred in October 1967. Participating students claimed they were ashamed of Grambling's low academic standards, and they were marching in protest. However, Public Relations Director Collie Nicholson blamed the uprising on "Black Power" advocates from Detroit, Houston, and New York City who came to Grambling for the sole purpose of stirring up trouble. Before it was finally settled, Louisiana National Guardsmen were called to the campus to seal off all entrances during the night of October 30, 1967. They were withdrawn the next day without a confrontation with the protesters. During the entire episode most of the students attended class, and Prez Jones kept a low profile. He even attended a football game on the campus without recognizing protest activity on the sidelines. Within a few days the uprising had run its course, and classes returned to normal.[28]

The second face used by "Prez Jones" was his "Felicitous Face." He donned this face anytime he sensed an opportunity to gain revenue or to enlist new supporters for the growing "whistle stop institution." At these times the varied talents he possessed were put into service: a keen sense of humor; his affability (unfortunately, some contemporary impatient blacks called it "Uncle Tomism"); his unequalled oratorical ability; and his ability to see and fulfill with strong desire the needs of his institution. Dr. Floyd L. Sandle, dean of the Division of Academic Studies for several years at Grambling, speaking at graduation ceremonies, May 15, 1977, aptly gave the dedicated president the title of "Country Doctor of Higher Education in Louisiana," a title he accepted with pride.[29]

Financial support of the black North Louisiana college was not always given equal consideration in relation to the other state colleges and universities; and, at times, public money was appropriated reluctantly to Grambling. Yet, Prez managed to wring out of the legislature about everything he requested. In one of his regular trips to the legislature at Baton Rouge, seeking money for his college, he reported after returning to his office: "I [have]been down to the legislature. . . . it is TOUGH down there. . . . The legislature doesn't have any money hid. If they had some hid, Ralph Jones would find it." He often laughed about how he "performed" for the legislature, the governor, or the legislative budget committee.[30]

A classic example of how completely Prez swayed the legislature with his showmanship and oratory occurred in 1946 when the Grambling administrator appeared before a regular session of the legislature to get the name changed from Louisiana Negro Normal and Industrial Institute to Grambling College. Prez began his request by seriously pointing out the changes, goals, curricula, and accomplishments of the school. At that point he sensed that he was not getting his message to the lackadaisical, day-dreaming legislators. It was then he decided to resort to his play-acting ability, and he did so in these words:

> Gentlemen, as you know, we have a very fine football team at Grambling, thanks to Coach Eddie Robinson. We are beating all the black colleges in the South, and, occasionally, we beat some of them in the North. However, we've got a serious problem you can solve for us. Let's suppose that we're playing Alcorn A&M and the score is 0 to 0. Alcorn has the ball, first and goal, on our ten yard line. Gentlemen, before our peppy little cheerleaders can get out there and yell: [Here he took the position of a cheerleader and cavorted through the movements as he talked.] 'Hold that line, Louisiana Negro Normal and Industrial Institute,' the other team's done scored!

The antics caused the legislators to erupt into gales of laughter. He had them ready for his main punch line, which he delivered very dramatically:

> What we want, gentlemen, is to change our name to 'Grambling'! And then them cheerleaders can quickly yell in any real emergency: 'Hold that line, Grambling!'

The request was quickly granted by a unanimous voice vote.[31]

Prez always made special efforts to get along well with Louisiana governors. His record reflects his success. But, he and three-term governor, Earl K. Long, developed an especially close relationship. Maybe it was because each man was blessed with a sharp sense of humor. As a result, Prez was always able to get about whatever he requested from Governor Long. "Ole Earl" always chuckled when he called Prez, "Ralph Waldo Emerson Jones, Himself!" He usually added, everytime they met, "and what in the hell do you want this time, Ralph?"[32]

Gov. Earl Long first met Prez when the new governor came to Grambling in 1948, shortly after his inauguration. Doctor Felton Green, Earl's nephew from Ruston, drove the tempestuous governor to the Grambling campus. When they arrived, "Ole Prez" was waiting for his guest, like a fox in his den. No host could have been more cordial. After an enjoyable visit in his office, he took his distinguished guest on an extended tour of the campus. Naturally, he showed the governor all the places needing improvement. After returning to his office in the administration building, Prez politely asked Earl's nephew if he could speak with the governor alone. The permission was granted. They spent about an hour behind the closed door before "Ole Earl" came out and indicated to his nephew that he was ready to depart. After leaving the building, the Louisiana chief executive exclaimed, in his usual gravelly voiced, abrupt, and profane manner: "You know what? That black son-of-a-bitch conned me out of a million dollars! *But, he needed every penny of it!*"[33]

President Ralph Jones was among the people selected to visit Earl Long at Pea Patch Farm near Winnfield. Prez laughed about his reaction when he first met the governor there: "There I sat at Pea Patch Farm, me and the governor of the state of Louisiana! Governor Long stretched far back in his rocking chair wiggling his toes, barefoot . . . the governor. . . ."[34] Sometimes, it was during these visits that he and Governor Long worked out Grambling's budget for the next fiscal year.[35]

When the governor decided to close the State Tuberculosis Hospital, located near Grambling, Long arrived to decide how to dispose of the furnishings, buildings, and a prize herd of Jersey cows. Prez got word of the governor's presence through his efficient "grapevine." It was, then, only a matter of minutes until he arrived at the scene. "Ole Earl" spied him as he approached. "Well, well, if it ain't Ralph Waldo Emerson, Himself? What in the hell do you want over here, Ralph?" he exclaimed with apparent mock irritation. Prez replied, "Governor, that's not fair? You know I came over here just to greet you on your visit to North Louisiana." Earl then retorted, "Hell, I know you better than that, Ralph! What do you want?" Prez answered, still expressing an affected air: "Governor, you know you have already taken good care of the faculty and students at Grambling College through your generous appropriations, and we are grateful to you for it and that's why I'm here! But, since you insist there is one more thing Grambling students need—*it's milk for their breakfast cereal.*" Earl, realizing he had met his match concluded: "Take the damned Jersey cows, Ralph. They're yours!"[36]

Ralph Jones was never without his third face—"His Friendly Face." His friends included people of all races and colors without distinction. During the days of segregation Grambling College choirs sang in Ruston churches, and Ruston civic clubs competed with each other to be invited to meet on the Grambling campus.[37] At the same time Prez was just as gracious to black groups in the all-black town of Grambling, the home of Grambling College. Even in 1981, in retirement, Ralph Jones avoided any talk of racial prejudice or "Uncle Tomism." He dismissed the subject saying "I always judged a man by what's in him, not by the color of his skin. As for Uncle Tomism, I've never been bothered by what some people say about me."[38]

During his long tenure as president, Prez could not say "no" to needy student applicants. He enrolled any student at the institution, although he might arrive "with a suitcase and not a single penny." In 1971, 80.3 percent of Grambling students received student aid—that was 2,685 out of 3,342 students who had scholarships, grant, loans, or jobs. Besides that, over 200 more were veterans who attended college under the G. I. Bill of Rights.[39] Because of these conditions a deficit accumulated at Grambling State University during the 1970s. It finally grew to the huge sum of 4.5 million dollars. However, it was a condition with which the state legislative budget committee was kept informed regularly. They knew the money creating the deficit was being used to help needy students at the all-black institution. Shortly before Prez retired in 1977, the Louisiana Legislature absorbed the deficit, but at least one sanctimonious Shreveport senator castigated the old educator unmercifully. In the end the legislature ordered the university to eliminate deficit spending immediately and begin to "live within its means."[40]

Allegorically, Prez's most impressive face was, "The Famous Face of Prez Jones." This man was known all over the world, and numbered among his acquaintances many of America's most famous people.

Always a spellbinder, Prez Jones had no peer as a speechmaker. As a result he addressed audiences in cities in all parts of the world and in every major city of the United States. Some of his most notable speeches were delivered when he addressed a teachers group at Tehran University, soldiers in West Berlin, the United Nations, and citizens of Tokyo, Honolulu, and Monrovia, Liberia.[41] He spoke at Brown University, Providence, Rhode Island, during its bicentennial celebration in 1964, appearing with such notables as Secretary of State Dean Rusk and Harvard University President Nathan M. Pusey. Wherever he appeared, at the smallest black school in Louisiana or the United Nations, his sense of humor made every speech a gem of oratory, and he always captivated his audience.[42]

Grambling's football team and band took Prez to more national and worldwide sites than any college president in American history. Large jets whisked them to New York, Houston, Japan and Honolulu. Well-known national networks filmed programs at

Grambling. CBS filmed a segment for the "Morning Show" in 1976. Heywood Broun was on the campus a few years earlier. NBC sent crews in 1977; while at ABC, Howard Cosell has never missed an opportunity to plug the little college on NFL Monday Night Football.[43]

During the forty-one years he was president, Ralph Jones hosted educators from all over America as well as others from many foreign lands. Writers, legislators, and representatives from state colleges and universities came to seek first-hand information about what had made programs at Grambling so effective. Throughout the decade of the 1950s Grambling stayed in the national limelight through articles in national publications featuring the teacher-training program.[44]

Prez became well acquainted with four American presidents. He knew President John F. Kennedy and supported him because he espoused minority causes. President Lyndon Baines Johnson cultivated his acquaintance, and called him on his special telephone more than once. President Richard Nixon called him to the White House along with fifteen other Negro college presidents to discuss the black colleges' needs. Earlier, Prez met Jimmy Carter at a meeting of the Southern Baptist Convention, long before Carter became a resident of the White House. Jones told Carter at the time: "You'll hold a high office one day." Jimmy was too surprised to express an intelligent answer.[45] Even Prez must have been taken by surprise when Jimmy won the presidency.

In 1976 he was the guest of the empress of Iran.[46] Later that year he made a ten-day study of the schools of Iraq. He assured the Louisiana Board of Regents before he departed on the trip to Iraq that he would stay out of the war in Lebanon. "I'm a peace maker. I'm non-violent," he said.[47] Ranking high among his many honorary services was his appointment by President Nixon as a member of the American official party sent to attend the inauguration ceremonies of the new president of Liberia in 1972. The Grambling College Band was also selected as one of the official bands for the inauguration parade. Sitting behind Mrs. Pat Nixon on the official platform during the ceremony, Prez was emotionally touched when "the band" marched by the reviewing stands. His description of the scene revealed his deep love for his institution as well as his country:

> . . . And that Grambling band strutted out there with the 'Stars and Stripes Forever' and something inside me churned. I'd been in this country [America] all my days, but never was as proud as when the band struck up the 'Stars and Stripes Forever.' And, I realized I was living the American Dream . . . I realized how much I loved the United States.[48]

A few hours later he laughed at himself about a boner he had just pulled. On a tour through a Monrovia department store, Prez and other members of his party, spent time "just browsing around. . . ." When the party started to leave, a member of the group reminded Prez that to be polite he should purchase some item. Complying with the request he grabbed, at random, a piece of merchandise, and took it to the well-dressed young male clerk at the check-out counter. The young man looked at the item and at

Prez, and then said, "Sir, are you certain you want to buy this product?" Such a remark caused Jones to bristle and brought a curt retort from him: "Of course I want to buy this article, I came 10,000 miles over here and who are you to tell me that I don't want to buy this item. I certainly do want it. How much is it?" He paid the clerk a dollar and picked up the package and stalked out of the store. On the street he decided to see what he had bought. Imagine his surprise when he withdrew a bottle of suntan lotion from his shopping bag.[49]

Even before retirement, June 30, 1977, many well-known people from all parts of the country began to bestow honors and accolades upon him. One admirer compared him to "Moses." An ABC program, June 26, 1977, reported that "Prez IS Grambling State University because he made it what it is." He was honored at a special dinner at the Shreveport Civic Center by the Black Trade Fair, February 16, 1977. A friend told him at one of the banquets honoring him that he had obtained "the humanitarian diploma."[50] Louisiana Governor Edwin Edwards exclaimed, "Ralph Waldo Emerson Jones will be missed. He is a part of the institution in the future." Former State Superintendent of Education William J. "Bill" Dodd proclaimed that he was one of Louisiana's greatest public educators.[51]

The list of honors tendered the retiring college president was too long to compile. However, the one that meant the most to him was the presentation of the keys to "the Old Black Chrysler" that he had driven so long and so far during the time when the college and its future were very much in doubt. It was almost as symbolic to him of the love of the students and faculty as the name: "*Prez.*"[52]

R. W. E. Jones summed up his personal gratitude to the people who supported him for over fifty years, when he told a misty-eyed audience: "Praise then be to Almighty God, for those great souls who have cajoled, and encouraged, and aided this very fortunate human to try and do just a little something that may be classed as worthy."[53]

Prez, in his fifty-one years at Grambling, achieved the pinnacle of success few men ever reach. When the time arrived for him to relinquish his position, he did so with the full realization that his life had been well spent in the service of education for deprived black youths of Louisiana. He expressed deep emotions that had formed during a half-century of his life in his "American Dream Speech," 1973, when he said, in part:

> I have seen deprived, depressed, poverty stricken, misguided, and frustrated youths by the thousands find themselves. And I have seen the great American dream of equality, opportunity, and justice come to wonderful and beautiful reality in a little out-of-the-way place that happened to be the homesite of Grambling College.[54]

For the first five years after his retirement in 1977 he maintained a full and active schedule. Rocky Mountain Baptist Church of Grambling, where he was a deacon for fifty years, claimed much of his retirement service. He accepted many speaking engagements; yet, Prez never missed a Grambling football game. During the filming of the movie, "The White Tiger," at Grambling State University in 1981, Prez made an appearance on the scene and laughingly commented. "I've got to meet that Belafonte fellow [actor Harry] and tell him how to play the part of Eddie Robinson. He doesn't know Eddie like I do." Also, during these years he received two more honorary degrees to put alongside the doctorate awarded to him by Louisiana Tech in 1971. Southeastern, Washington D. C., and the University of Baltimore made the new presentations.[55]

Then, during the week before Easter, 1982, Prez was stricken with an acute gall-bladder attack. A routine operation was performed at Lincoln General Hospital in Ruston. Prez came out of the operation in his usual good physical condition. He was recuperating normally until, suddenly he was stricken by an embolism of the lungs, an unexpected complication, that resulted in his quick death. The date was April 9, 1982, Good Friday night. Ralph Waldo Emerson Jones had completed his life at the age of 76.

Sunday's local newspaper proclaimed: "Lincoln Parish, Louisiana, and the nation has lost a friend. 'Prez' is dead."[56] Tributes for the famous educator poured in from all directions. E. E. Cole, former vice president of Grambling State University, said that Jones had accomplished so much for the institution that it was not easy to single out any one thing as the greatest; however, he thought that his greatest contribution might have been "the teacher education program initiated in 1936." Eddie Robinson, Grambling's football coach, loved Prez "like a father." According to Robinson he was still Grambling's number one football fan, attending practice every day since his retirement in 1977.[57]

A former student, Nevada Jenson Hill, compared the incomparable Prez to many bible characters in the following tribute:

> Solomon—the greatest king of Israel—Grambling State reached its zenith under him.
> 'You have stood as Abraham stood, as the father of faithful Gramblinites.
> A Daniel, when you expressed a desire to go to jail for Grambling State University.'
> He was like Christ because he fed the hungry . . . gave sight to the educationally blind . . . helped the poor.
> 'A David, you killed many financial giants with one stone.
> To Grambling you were Paul of Macedonia, asking other teaching apostles to come over and help out. Unlike Joshua, who fought until the walls came down, you always fought for walls to go up.'[58]

Area sportswriters added their tributes. One Shreveport editor asserted that:

> . . . Prez was one heck of a politician. He had to be. When he came to his school, public support of black colleges was an afterthought. The programs he built argued in favor of greater support, granted, but a lot of it depended directly on Prez's own force of personality. He could, no doubt about it, talk a state administration or legislative committee into providing money where a lesser man would have failed or gotten at best a token brushoff.[59]

O. K. "Buddy" Davis, Ruston sports editor and a close friend of Prez, penned the following words of praise:

> Prez was color blind.
> He was guided by love. He was guided by knowledge of the young lives he knew he had a hand in shaping, and he was guided by an uncanny sense of what was good for all people—black and white.
> Prez was a master of what he did best: talking to folks. . . .
> There will never be another Ralph Waldo Emerson Jones. The mannerisms, the wit that made him so homespun and yet among the wisest of men will be remembered now.
> He wrote the Grambling Alma Mater and stood straighter than anybody else when it was sung.
> He had the ears of governor, presidents, foreign heads of state.[60]

Davis so idolized Jones that he thought he should have been named this nation's ambassador to the United Nations.

One of the most elaborate funerals ever held in North Louisiana was observed at eleven o'clock on Monday, April 12, 1982, at the T. H. Harris Auditorium on the Grambling State University campus. Over four thousand people filed by the bier of the beloved Grambling president as it lay in state for three hours before the funeral.

Over two thousand people packed the auditorium for the impressive final services. Interment followed at Grambling Memorial Gardens, a quiet place close to Prez's greatest love, Grambling State University.[61]

A fitting and lasting monument to such a dedicated and unselfish man has not yet been planned. It will be impossible to include all the contributions of one who gave fifty-one years of his life to building good citizens at a once remote institution of higher learning. Indeed, it could be stated that the world beat a well-traveled path to his door at Grambling, Louisiana. That Prez Jones was "the Country Doctor of Louisiana Education" can be substantiated by driving through the campus of Grambling State University.

Several years before he retired he penned his philosophy of how one succeeds. As he put it:

> Success cannot be awarded from the outside. It is something that must emanate from the inside. The plaudits and the glory shall come from the outside after one has climbed the hill, but the climbing one must do himself, very often alone and unnoticed and often criticised along the way.[62]

Prez climbed that hill and achieved success from the inside. The glorious contributions he made to a university, an area, a state, a nation, and the world will not soon be forgotten.

## Notes for "Ralph Waldo Emerson "Prez" Jones: 'The Country Doctor of Higher Education in Louisiana,' 1926-1977"

[1]*The Gramblinite*, February 4, 1977.

[2]Ibid., and May 6, 1977.

[3]Personal interview, Ralph Waldo Emerson Jones, Grambling, Louisiana, February 5, 1981.

[4]Shirley Huffin Ayatey, "John Sebastian Jones and the *Louisiana Colored Teacher's Journal, 1925-1947*" (M. A. thesis, Louisiana Tech University, Ruston, Louisiana, August, 1969), 1-8; Francis Fletcher and Ralph L. Ropp, eds., *Lincoln Parish History* (Merceline, Mo., 1976), 282; *Time*, 109 (March 21, 1977): 96; Thelma Smith Williams, *Grambling, A Pictorial History* (Grambling, 1980), 116.

[5]Personal interview, R. W. E. Jones.

[6]Copy of a State of President R. W. E. Jones, Grambling, Louisiana to the Book Division, Johnson Publishing Company, 820 Michigan Avenue, Chicago, Illinois, 2-3 (author has a xeroxed copy in his possession); undated newspaper article, R. W. E. Jones Collection, A. C. Lewis Memorial Library, Grambling State University, Grambling, Louisiana. Prez and B. T. Woodard owned a pressing shop in Grambling in 1928. Later tailoring was added to the school's curriculum. See *The Gramblinite*, May, 1976.

[7]*The Gramblinite*, May, 1976.

[8]Ibid., *Time*, March 21, 1977, p. 96. As late as 1970 students were required to wear their best clothes to the college cafeteria every Sunday. See *The Gramblinite*, October 25, 1970.

[9]Ibid., personal interview, R. W. E. Jones.

[10]Copy of Statement of R. W. E. Jones to Book Division, p. 3; Earl Maxey, "The Development of Grambling College" (M. A. thesis, Tuskegee Institute, Tuskegee, Alabama, August, 1950), 72; personal interview, R. W. E. Jones.

[11]Cited in *The Gramblinite*, May, 1976.

[12]Copy of Statement by R. W. E. Jones, 3; Earl Maxey, "The Development of Grambling College," 72; personal interview, R. W. E. Jones.

[13]*Citizens' Guide*, Grambling and Lincoln Parish Ruston-Grambling League of Women Voters, Ruston, Louisiana, 1975, 11; personal interview, R. W. E. Jones; *The Gramblinite*, May, 1976; *Time*, May 21, 1977, p. 96. One source said Adams had only four students and three teachers. See *The Gramblinite*, May, 1976.

[14]Copy of Statement of R. W. E. Jones to Book Div., 4; Maxey, "Development of Grambling College," 57; *Ruston Daily Leader*, July 17, 1962; *The Gramblinite*, May 1976; *Time*, March 21, 1977, p. 96.

[15]Ibid.

[16]Cited in *The Gramblinite*, May, 1976.

[17]*The Gramblinite*, May, 1976; Maxey, "Development of Grambling College," Appendix B and 58; *A Report of the History and Philosophy of Grambling College* (compiled by a Special Committee, Grambling College, Fall, 1955), A. C. Lewis Memorial Library, Grambling State University, Grambling, Louisiana.

[18]Maxey, "Development of Grambling College," 1.

[19]*Ruston Daily Leader*, July 3, 1964; *The Gramblinite*, May, 1976.

[20]Personal interview, R. W. E. Jones.

[21]*The Gramblinite*, May 1976; *Time*, March 21, 1977, p. 96.

[22]*The Shreveport Times*, April 6, 1969; *Time*, March 21, 1977, p. 96.

[23]Clipping, Shreveport newspaper, undated, vertical file, A. C. Lewis Memorial Library, Grambling State University, Grambling, Louisiana.

[24]Ibid.; *The Gramblinite*, October 15, and November 19, 1976.

[25]Ibid.; *The Gramblinite*, March 4, 11, and June 24, 1977; *The Shreveport Times*, April 6, 1969. One supporter of the football team in the early 1930's noted that although Grambling's colors were black and gold, the players were supplied with so much of Louisiana Tech's castoff equipment Grambling players wore all kinds of combinations of red, blue, white, black, and gold.

[26]Clipping, Shreveport newspaper, undated, A. C. Lewis Memorial Library, Grambling State University, Grambling, Louisiana; *The Shreveport Times*, April 6, 1969; *The Gramblinite*, October 15, and November 19, 1976.

[27]Personal interview, R. W. E. Jones.

[28]See *Ruston Daily Leader*, October 26, 27, 30, 31, 1967; *Monroe Morning World*, October 29, 1967.

[29]*Ruston Daily Leader*, May 16, 1977.

[30]Cited in *The Gramblinite*, May, 1976; *Time*, March 21, 1976, p. 96; Personal interview, an anonymous member of the Louisiana Legislative Budget Committee, 1972-1976, Ruston, Louisiana, January 26, 1981.

[31]Personal interview, R. W. E. Jones; personal interview, R. L. Ropp, Ruston, Louisiana, October 10, 1956; *The Gramblinite*, February 4, 1977; Doris Dorcas Carter, "Charles P. Adams and Grambling College" (M. A. thesis, Louisiana Tech University, Ruston, Louisiana, May, 1971), 33 (footnote). Special tape on "Prez" Jones made by William J. "Bill" Dodd, Baton Rouge.

[32]*The Gramblinite*, May, 1976, personal interview, R. W. E. Jones.

[33]Personal interview, Dr. Felton Green, Ruston, Louisiana, December 16, 1980. Author's emphasis.

[34]Cited in *The Gramblinite*, May, 1976; personal interview R. W. E. Jones.

[35]Personal interview, R. W. E. Jones.

[36]Ibid.

[37]*Ruston Daily Leader*, May 16, 1977. Former Acting Governor James A. Noe, Monroe, gave freely to Grambling State University, and the college newspaper acknowledged the university's loss at his death in 1976. See *The Gramblinite*, March 5, 1971.

[38]Personal interview, R. W. E. Jones.

[39]*The Gramblinite*, March 5, 1971.

[40]*Ruston Daily Leader*, May 25, 1977; personal interview, anonymous member of the Louisiana Legislative Budget Committee, 1972-1976, Ruston, Louisiana, January 29, 1981.

[41]Personal interview, R. W. E. Jones. As president he enthralled Grambling students with his homespun oratory. "Prez" continued to accept speaking engagements after his retirement. For example, he spoke to the student body at S. M. U. on February 16, 1981.

[42]*The Gramblinite*, December 18, 1964. One of his greatest speeches was made at a commencement ceremony at a high school in LeCompte, Louisiana at seven o'clock in the morning. Prez literally "brought back to life" students and parents who were deadened by a night of celebrating. Most other orators would have given this situation up as a hopeless failure before its beginning, but Prez had the audience in gales of uncontrolled laughter within five minutes. From a personal interview, Professor James Henderson, Grambling State University, Grambling, Louisiana, January 28, 1981.

[43]*Time*, March 21, 1977, p. 96; *The Gramblinite*, September 24, 1976 and June 24, 1977.

[44]Copy of Statement of R. W. E. Jones, 5; J. Andrew Gaulden, *Negro Louisiana*, 1 (1953).

[45]*Ruston Daily Leader*, May 25, 1970; personal interview, R. W. E. Jones.

[46]Cited from an article by Sue Eakin, *Alexandria Town Talk*, reprinted in *The Gramblinite*, May, 1976.

[47]*The Gramblinite*, November 5, 1976.

[48]Cited in *The Gramblinite*, May, 1976.

[49]Personal interview, R. W. E. Jones.

[50]*The Gramblinite*, June 24, 1977 and February 28, 1977; *Ruston Daily Leader*, June 13, 1977.

[51]*The Gramblinite*, February 4, 1977; special tape made by "Bill" Dodd, Baton Rouge, Louisiana.

[52]Ibid., June 24, 1977.

[53]Ibid., March 13, 1970.

[54]Undated Clippings, vertical file, R. W. E. Jones, A. C. Lewis Memorial Library, Grambling State University, Grambling, Louisiana.

[55]*The Ruston Daily Leader*, April 12, 1982. In March, 1970, during the ceremony at Louisiana Tech that bestowed the honorary degree upon Prez, State Superintendent of Education William J. "Bill" Dodd, appropriately stated that: "This is the first official act in this state to reward the magnificent contribution of a native Louisianian without regard to anything except his greatness as a man and his success as an educator." See *The Ruston Daily Leader*, March 5, 1970.

[56]*The Ruston Daily Leader*, April 11, 1982.

[57]*The Times*, Shreveport and Bossier City, April 10, 1982.

[58]*The Ruston Daily Leader*, April 16, 1982.

[59]*The Times*, Shreveport and Bossier City, April 13, 1982.

[60]*The Ruston Daily Leader*, April 13, 1982.

[61]Ibid., April 12 and April 13, 1982.

[62]Copy of Statement of President Jones to Book Div., 4.

# A NEW AND UNCERTAIN ERA*

Donald E. DeVore and Joseph Logsdon

Desegregation failed to produce immediate widespread change within the New Orleans public school system, but the presence, during the 1960-61 school year, of four black students at two formerly all-white schools contained the seeds of change. By the close of the decade of the sixties—a decade as momentous in the nation's history as the twenties or the thirties—desegregation of the schools neared completion. And in the following decade, school officials completed the equally thorny task of faculty desegregation. To be sure, the men and women who guided school policy after 1960 addressed other issues as well—pressure from teacher groups for more pay, increased benefits, and improved working conditions, escalating costs and a declining tax base, and public criticism because of low student performance.

Uncertain of the future and buffeted by winds they could not control, school board members continued their policy of protecting the status quo and of resisting rapid change advocated by external forces. They did so without the services of Superintendent [James] Redmond, for he was one of several casualties of the desegregation crisis. It was somewhat ironic that the second person chosen as superintendent from outside the school system, or the New Orleans area, would find his administration almost totally absorbed in school desegregation. But his fate was inexorably tied to that issue even before he assumed his new position. Shortly before Redmond's arrival, NAACP leader Daniel Byrd had thought it "best to start out rough on him so that when he takes over he will have some respect for the [NAACP] Education Committee."[1]

The incessant debate and focus on desegregation stalled Redmond's hopes of producing educational improvement and reform. He did manage, however, to ensure the success of two reforms initiated the year before his arrival—the complete abandonment of the antiquated practice of sexual segregation in the high schools and the adoption of the 6-

*First published as chapter 7 in Donald E. DeVore and Joseph Logsdon, *Crescent City Schools: Public Education in New Orleans, 1841-1991* (Lafayette, La.: Center for Louisiana Studies, 1991), 251-91. Reprinted with the kind permission of the authors and the University of Southwestern Louisiana.

3-3 grade plan. In addition, his leadership proved instrumental in the opening of Benjamin Franklin in 1957, a high school for intellectually gifted students.

Unlike one of his predecessors, Lionel Bourgeois, Redmond refrained from direct involvement in school board elections. But he probably watched with dismay the replacing of avowed reform board members who secured his appointment with those concerned only with preventing desegregation. After the Brown decision an aggressive legislature and governor as well as segregationist board members usurped his leadership. Although Redmond remained at his post through the 1960-61 school year, he was a powerless lame-duck superintendent. In January 1961, just a few months after desegregation began in New Orleans schools, he submitted his resignation. Before the opening of schools for the next term, he accepted an offer to head the Chicago public schools and left New Orleans. In the midst of the desegregation crisis the task of leading the school system again fell to O. Perry Walker.

After the beginning of desegregation on November 14, 1960, Judge J. Skelly Wright, acutely cognizant of the effects his court orders had on race relations in the community, continued to pursue his policy of gradual desegregation. Thus, when the school year opened in 1961, Wright's grade-a-year desegregation plan remained in force. Eight black first-graders, along with the four black students admitted in November 1960, now attended desegregated schools. Four additional elementary schools—Benjamin, Lusher, Wilson and McDonogh 11—joined Frantz and McDonogh 19 as desegregated institutions. The twelve black students attending racially mixed schools in the fall of 1961 were spared the hostility and anger that had greeted Tessie, Leona, Gail, and Ruby in November 1960. And the almost total white boycott of classes at McDonogh 19 and Frantz that had remained in effect during the 1960-1961 school year was not replicated at Benjamin, Lusher, McDonogh 11, and Wilson. Nonetheless, enrollment at the four schools suffered a decline, for the school board allowed white students to transfer from any school affected by desegregation.[2]

Nearly ten years after the filing of the Bush suit and eight years after the Brown decision, only twelve black students were attending desegregated schools in New Orleans. That was not what Judge Wright had in mind when he had sanctioned a grade-a-year plan. Consequently, on April 3, 1962, he issued his most sweeping order to date:

> Beginning with the opening of school in September, 1962, all children entering, or presently enrolled in the public elementary schools of New Orleans, grades 1 through 6, may attend either the formerly all white public schools nearest their homes or the formerly all Negro public schools nearest their homes, at their option.[3]

Judge Wright took the additional step of forbidding the board to issue transfers based on race. He also prohibited the board from any longer using the pupil placement tests which effectively blocked most black admissions to formerly white schools.

The fire storm that Judge Wright anticipated broke immediately. Board president Theodore Shephard, away from the city on school business, returned to New Orleans intent on calling a special meeting of the board to consider appealing the court order. Three of the other four members—Matthew Sutherland, Lloyd Rittiner, and Louis Riecke—voiced support for the appeal. The lone other member, Emile Wagner, Jr., expressed disgust with the way his board colleagues, along with the board's attorney Samuel Rosenberg, had handled the desegregation crisis and refused to support the idea of an appeal. On the other hand, Wagner thought Wright's newest ruling would hasten the abandonment by whites of the public school system.[4]

Many white citizens in the community shared Wagner's view, and successful boycotts of classes at McDonogh 19 and Frantz appeared to justify their predictions. But surprisingly, the anticipated white exodus from the public schools did not occur. To be sure, schools in neighboring St. Bernard Parish absorbed some of the former Frantz and McDonogh 19 students, and a private school, with assistance from the state and the local school board, opened in the Frantz and McDonogh 19 school district. Even so, however, white school enrollment in the elementary schools declined by less than twelve hundred between 1960-61 and 1961-62. And overall white enrollment decreased by less than three hundred. But total white enrollment mattered very little to most white parents and leaders—what mattered was the effect of desegregation on specific schools. White parents in school districts not affected by desegregation generally sympathized with parents opposing desegregation, but they kept their own children in public schools. Enrollment figures for the first several years of desegregated schools show that whites adjusted to or at least tolerated limited racial mixing in the schools.[5]

After his 1956 ruling ordering the desegregation of the New Orleans public schools, Judge Wright suffered verbal abuse, threats of violence, and social ostracism. His April 1962 order to accelerate the desegregation process only added to his personal woes. Obviously such feelings did not extend to Washington D. C., for in 1962 he was offered appointment as judge in the Court of Appeals for the District of Columbia. He accepted the position, though the decision was not an easy one, for he knew successful school desegregation in New Orleans, even if attainable, remained several years in the future. In a section of his last local decision, in *Bush* v. *OPSB*, though referring to the responsibility and travails of the school board, Wright might as well have been talking about himself. "The school board here," he stated:

> occupies an unenviable position. It's members, elected to serve without pay, have sought conscientiously, albeit reluctantly, to comply with the law on order of this court. Their reward for this service has been economic reprisal and personal recrimination from many of their constituents who have allowed hate to overcome their better judgement. But the plight of the Board cannot affect the rights of school children whose skin color is no choice of their own.[6]

With the departure of Judge Wright, Frank B. Ellis became the presiding judge and would hear the board's appeal for a stay order and a new trial. Before the 1961-1962 school year came to a close, Judge Ellis had made two significant rulings. He first granted the board a stay order effectively suspending Judge Wright's decision until he considered the board's request for a new trial. Obviously pleased with the order, board members tempered their elation with caution. Louis Riecke, for example, expressed satisfaction with the order but did not "think it's something . . . we can form a circle and clap hands about." And Rittiner viewed Ellis's ruling as a vindication of the board's efforts to desegregate the schools "with all deliberate speed."

Counsel for the plaintiffs, in the long-running Bush suit, immediately filed a motion with the U. S. Fifth Circuit Court of Appeals to vacate Judge Ellis's order. Chief Judge Elbert P. Tuttle, acting for the court, denied the request on the grounds that the plaintiffs rights "are not in serious jeopardy." Judge Tuttle made it clear, however, that "in denying the motion at this time I do so without prejudice to the rights of the movants to present the matter to the next panel of the court of appeals. . . ." Tuttle thought it best for the appeals court not to intervene until Judge Ellis ruled on the motion for a new trial, scheduled for May 8, 1962.[7]

On Tuesday morning, May 8, attorneys for the plaintiffs and the defendants arrived in court to present their arguments. A move by the city, the state, and the local police department to join the case as defendants created additional drama in the trial that many citizens believed just as important as the judicial proceeding that had led to the May 1960 court order to desegregate. City attorney Alvin J. Liska maintained that widespread desegregation of the elementary schools would cause social unrest, worsen race relations, and place strain on a police department already undermanned and underfinanced. Ellis expressed sympathy with the city's plight and invited Liska to submit amicus curiae briefs, but he refused the city's request to join the case as a defendant.[8]

In support of the board's motion for a new trial, Rosenberg argued that Judge Wright had greatly exceeded the intent of the Supreme Court decision in the Brown case. According to Rosenberg, local school officials had made a good faith effort to desegregate the schools and they were in the best position to assess the impact of desegregation on the public school system. Rosenberg's statements reflected the posture taken by the board since it had agreed to accept the grade-a-year desegregation plan: impress upon the court its willingness to comply with the order to desegregate but stress that community hostility and the maintenance of a good public school system necessitated the gradual, go-slow approach in place since 1960. Aware that part of the push for desegregation had originally stemmed from inadequate and overcrowded school facilities for black students, Rosenberg attempted to argue that the overcrowding in black schools had occurred because of a rising birth rate and migration to the city, not because of discrimination. Studies since the Grace report, however, had repeatedly demonstrated that the allocation of educational dollars and classrooms on a discriminatory basis had, in fact, caused the overcrowding. Rosenberg also knew, as did his local legal counterparts, Alexander P. Tureaud and Ernest Morial, that the issue of overcrowding had long since ceased to be central. Integration itself was now the issue. Although new to the case, Ellis also recognized the new central issue. Two weeks later he issued his decision.[9]

In the meantime, the board held a regular meeting on May 14 at which it departed from past desegregation policy. Throughout the desegregation crisis the board had refused, even when directed by the court, to formulate a plan to eliminate the dual system of education. By 1962, it was obvious that the courts might tolerate a gradual approach but only within the context of active compliance. In other words, courts throughout the country wanted local school boards to initiate specific timetables to comply with Brown. On May 14 the Orleans Parish School Board took the first step in that direction. The board passed a resolution allowing students entering the first grade in the 1962-63 school year to attend the school of their choice, though the board still maintained dual school districts. And a motion by Matthew Sutherland directed Superintendent Walker to eliminate race-specific attendance districts for the first grade, beginning in September 1963. Board members hoped their resolutions would conform to the court's desire for active compliance.[10]

The resolutions emerged as sound strategy, for in his ruling on May 23, Judge Ellis made a reference to the resolutions as a apparent attempt by the board to comply with Brown. Without those resolutions, his statement that it is "an irresistible conclusion that the Board has never actually complied with any order of this court . . . , nor had it ever entered into compliance with the Brown mandate as originally conceived," probably would have resulted in an affirmation of Wright's order for immediate desegregation of grades one through six. In the end, however, although he denied the board's request for a new trial, Ellis modified the previous ruling and withdrew the order to desegregate all elementary grades. In addition to the tentative steps taken by the board to comply, Ellis's belief that accelerated desegregation would create administrative and community problems also influenced his decision to scale back desegregation to the grade-a-year plan. Judge Ellis, to a greater degree than his predecessor, would weigh community sentiment in making all his rulings. The pace of school desegregation envisioned by Ellis matched that of school officials and, by then, many members of the city's white leadership.[11]

The court ruling gave school officials the time they claimed was needed to implement desegregation while maintaining educational standards. The board's task, over the next few years, involved convincing Ellis that its desegregation policy complied with the all deliberate speed test. Nonetheless, Tureaud and the other lawyers for the plaintiffs continued their court fight, for they believed the board's all deliberate speed policy represented nothing but delay and evasion. And student desegregation figures between 1962 and 1964 justified their skepticism. For example, in the school year following Ellis's decision (1962-63), only 107 black students attended desegregated schools. And again the board continued the practice of dispersing them among several schools to keep low the number of blacks attending any one formerly all-white school: the 107 black students attended twenty different schools. During the next school year the number of black students reached only 392 and the following year only 873.[12]

Such figures kept the case in court. But it was a slow fight. Several months or a year often elapsed between court appearances. The routine fell into a pattern. Tureaud and his people sued to speed up desegregation; Rosenberg and his people attempted to demonstrate the insurmountable problems that would result.

In August 1964, still displeased with the slow pace of desegregation as well as with the board's redrawing of school district boundaries, NAACP attorneys again went to court. Tureaud, along with James Nabritt from the NAACP Legal Defense Fund, wanted the court to order the school board to accelerate desegregation, stop gerrymandering the school districts, and adopt a long-range desegregation plan. During the proceedings, attorneys for the NAACP once again started attacking the board's few and slow desegregation efforts. But Judge Ellis wanted more than the customary attacks. He suggested that Nabritt and Tureaud produce specific alternate plans of their own, ideally plans drawn with assistance from recognized educational experts.

The task of securing the services of experts progressed slowly, but eventually Dr. Roger Bardwell, superintendent of School District 59 in Illinois and Dr. David Salten, superintendent of schools in New Rochelle, New York, agreed to work with the plaintiffs.[13]

"Any new matters, any new materials that may give the court a clearer insight, a clearer vision into what ought to be done," Ellis stated at the opening of additional hearings in April 1965, "the court is willing to listen to and accept. . . ." He envisioned three or four days of testimony, at the most, and warned the attorneys not to introduce points already contained in the trial record. Dr. Bardwell took the stand first and answered a series of questions designed to determine if the court would accept him as an expert witness. His training and professional experience won his acceptance as an expert in school administration but not in matters related to school desegregation. Considering Bardwell's background, superintendent of a virtual all-white suburban school district, the court's rejection of him as an expert in school desegregation could not have come as much of a surprise to Nabritt and Tureaud. Nonetheless, he proved to be a good witness for the plaintiffs and frequently, in response to questions by Nabritt, challenged the board's desegregation plan.[14]

Nabritt wanted Bardwell's testimony to support the plaintiffs' contention that overcrowding in the black schools, a lower average per-pupil cost, and a higher pupil-to-teacher ratio resulted from the continuation of a racially dual system of education. In response to a question from Nabritt, Bardwell, referring to charts and graphs he had compiled, answered that a significant imbalance existed in pupil-to-teacher ratios at black and white schools. Judge Ellis asked: "But you cannot discount the fact that the problem is aggravated by the fact that there is a material difference in number, can you?" Bardwell answered: "I can't, but I would add that there is a material difference in the allocation of the resources that are available to education in this parish." Bardwell also contended, later challenged by Rosenberg, that since 1954 the board had enough money for construction to prevent overcrowding. He suggested that overcrowding existed in black schools and underutilization in white schools because the board continued to build race-specific schools.[15]

Bardwell next ventured into an area that would later loom large in school desegregation—busing. Bardwell maintained that busing students to achieve a balanced pupil-to-teacher ratio and reduced class size represented sound administrative strategy that the board should pursue. Ellis asked if busing was practical, and Bardwell answered affirmatively, pointing out that thirty percent of his students were bused. Bardwell noted that the board already used busing, but to promote segregation. Using official school board figures, he pointed out, for example, that every school day hundreds of blacks rode buses to Benjamin School while passing two underutilized white schools, Wilson and Lafayette. School facilities, he stated, responding to a question from Nabritt, "are not being used as efficiently as they could be if there were more integration between the schools."[16]

At that point, Judge Ellis felt compelled to intervene. He then went into an extended summary of the court's previous efforts at desegregation. In his estimation, he said, he thought the court had done a splendid job in advancing school desegregation and noted that "serious problems" would occur from plans to accelerate desegregation. Ellis completed his summary assessment and asked Bardwell, in Ellis's words "a man of integrity," what he would do to accelerate desegregation? Bardwell, a resident of Illinois and aware of his "alien" status, began his response cautiously by acknowledging the sensitive problem of race relations in New Orleans. But he thought it would be best, he forcefully stated, "to fully integrate all of the schools in one year." "All of them?" Ellis asked in apparent disbelief. "All, right through the high schools," Bardwell insisted. "Well," Ellis added, "the court would like to appoint you as a special master to come down here and do that, and I think that you would end up in an institution for the insane."[17]

Judge Ellis's comments were more than an angry flourish. They represented his belief that school desegregation, if successful, had to proceed slowly. He had a pessimistic view of the long-range effects of desegregation and noted that desegregation of schools in Washington, D. C. had resulted in whites abandoning the system. He feared plans to accelerate desegregation would produce the same results in New Orleans. The entire struggle, he went on to say, would have been futile if, after several years of school integration, the system became resegregated because of parental choice. Ellis knew the law, as expressed in Brown and subsequent decisions, but he also knew white New Orleanians, as dramatically demonstrated in the boycott and eventual white abandonment of McDonogh 19.[18]

After Bardwell concluded his testimony, the other expert witness, Dr. Salten, took the stand. Dr. Salten was even more emphatic about immediate and total desegregation of all grades. He thought such a step would help the board in planning for future construction. Pleased with that response, Nabritt hoped for more. He asked Salten to express his views on faculty desegregation. Even Nabritt was unprepared for Salten's response. "I would think," he stated, "that this is a step which could be taken tomorrow morning . . . the fact that white children are exposed only to white teachers, and Negro children are exposed only to Negro teachers, is to me educationally unsound, and actually damaging to the future of not only the Negro children, but of the white children as well."[19]

When court reconvened the next day, Salten sought to moderate his position on total desegregation beginning in the 1965-66 school year. Although he still preferred immediate desegregation, he suggested a two-year plan. He recommended abolishing the dual system in the first, fifth, seventh and tenth grades the first year and the remaining grades the second year. Ellis asked Salten to comment on how well desegregation had worked in his own city of New Rochelle. Salten conceded, as he had done earlier, that problems had occurred. "And don't you recognize that the problem here is ten times, or twenty times more serious than the problems you had in New Rochelle, as far as public acceptance or reaction is concerned," Ellis wanted to know. Salten answered yes, and Ellis continued, "well, why don't you bring this out when you are indulging in all of your philosophical concepts as to the planning, and everything of that sort? Do you completely ignore the practicalities of the situation?"[20]

Salten remained convinced that rapid desegregation would prove less traumatic than the gradual, grade-a-year plan in use. Neither Rosenberg's cross-examination nor Ellis's pointed queries caused him to deviate from that position, and he continued to insist that complete faculty and student desegregation should start immediately. Unable to sway Salten, Rosenberg attempted to attack his credibility by mentioning the lack of time Salten had to study the problem of school desegregation in New Orleans. Therefore, Rosenberg charged, Salten could not make informed recommendations concerning increased student and teacher desegregation. Judge Ellis agreed with that assessment, and Salten's testimony had little, if any, influence on his ruling.[21]

Nonetheless, at the conclusion of the two-day hearing, Ellis substantially altered the pace of school desegregation. He ordered the board to establish single school districts for the fourth and fifth grades in 1965, the sixth and seventh in 1966, eighth and ninth in 1967, tenth and eleventh in 1968, and twelfth in 1969. Thus, beginning in the 1969-70 school year, New Orleans would have a totally desegregated public school system. Under the previous grade-a-year plan such would not have occurred until four years later, in 1973. The decision left neither the board nor the plaintiffs totally satisfied—it was more than the board had wanted to give and less than the plaintiffs had hoped to receive. Both sides, however, realized it could have been worse. And student desegregation, with slight alterations, followed that time schedule.[22]

When Judge Ellis made his April 1965 decision, 873 blacks attended thirty formerly all-white schools, the overwhelming majority of them in grades kindergarten through third. Only forty-seven of the total attended grades four or above. In addition, only one secondary school, Benjamin Franklin, had black students. Moreover, desegregation had been one way—blacks to formerly all-white schools. Only one white child, a student at Moton Elementary, had elected to attend a formerly all-black school. Despite the fears of white flight, white enrollment actually increased, at least for a time, after the start of desegregation. In the 1960-61 school year, white enrollment stood at 38,112 and by the

1964-65 school year had climbed to 39,314, after a decline in 1961-62 following desegregation. But the 39,314 white students in the public schools in 1964-65 represented the high point before the anticipated decline set in. Even the decline, however, proved not as rapid as many of the doomsayers had predicted.[23]

At the start of the 1966-67 school year, the junior high schools came under the desegregation plan. All eleven of the formerly all-white schools admitted black seventh grade students that first year. McMain, located on South Claiborne Avenue in the uptown section of the city, had the largest black enrollment, 229. Gregory, located on Pratt Drive in the downtown part of the city, had the lowest black enrollment with thirty-nine. In the following year, eight former exclusively white high schools, joined Franklin in admitting black students.[24]

Table I[26]

*Total Public School Enrollment, 1960-1961 to 1980-1981*

| Year | Black Students | White Students | Total |
|---|---|---|---|
| 60-61 | 52,581 | 38,112 | 90,693 |
| 61-62 | 55,820 | 37,845 | 93,665 |
| 62-63 | 59,223 | 38,728 | 97,951 |
| 63-64 | 62,598 | 38,645 | 101,243 |
| 64-65 | 64,893 | 39,314 | 104,207 |
| 65-66 | 67,059 | 38,657 | 105,716 |
| 66-67 | 70,225 | 37,609 | 107,834 |
| 67-68 | 72,028 | 36,773 | 108,801 |
| 68-69 | 74,435 | 36,411 | 110,846 |
| 69-70 | 76,079 | 35,860 | 111,939 |
| 70-71 | 76,502 | 33,349 | 109,851 |
| 71-72 | 77,289 | 30,453 | 107,742 |
| 72-73 | 77,660 | 26,379 | 104,039 |
| 73-74 | 76,929 | 22,614 | 99,543 |
| 74-75 | 75,986 | 19,773 | 95,719 |
| 75-76 | 75,400 | 18,688 | 94,088 |
| 76-77 | 75,431 | 17,933 | 93,364 |
| 77-78 | 74,646 | 16,788 | 91,434 |
| 78-79 | 73,855 | 15,155 | 89,010 |
| 79-80 | 73,008 | 14,079 | 87,087 |
| 80-81 | 72,367 | 13,293 | 85,660 |

Source: Facts and Finances, 1960-1981.

In the 1969-70 school year, public school enrollment reached an all-time high of 111,939: 76,079 black students and 35,860 white students. Black enrollment had increased by slightly more than fifty percent during the past decade, while in the same period white enrollment had declined by approximately thirteen percent. Black enrollment continued to surge, peaking at 77,660 in 1972-73. But rising black enrollment after 1969 could not offset the rapid decrease in white enrollment. The long-feared white flight finally occurred during the second decade of desegregation, 1970-79. In the 1979-80 school year, only 14,079 whites attended the public schools. Within ten years the system had lost over twenty thousand white students. Looked at another way, in the 1960-61 school year blacks comprised 58 percent and whites 42 percent of total school enrollment. By the 1980-81 school session, black enrollment had reached 84.48 percent and white enrollment had declined to 15.52 percent. Thus twenty years after desegregation, the majority of black public school students were attending predominantly black schools.[25]

Overall public school enrollment figures for the ten years after the start of student desegregation show a steady but not drastic decline. So, it would appear that student desegregation alone did not account for eventual white abandonment of the public school system. True, the quickened pace of student desegregation after 1970 probably led to an increase in white flight, but the real answer probably lies in the start of faculty desegregation.

Faculty desegregation first started in the 1966-67 school year when the board assigned three black teachers to formerly all-white Kennedy High School and eleven whites to four formerly black schools, McDonogh 35, Bell, Clark, and Booker T. Washington. Meaningful faculty desegregation, however, occurred later, as the schedule for court-mandated school desegregation came to an end. By the 1969-70 school year the board still had not gone very far in desegregating the faculty. It appeared that faculty desegregation was destined to share the same go-slow, court-intervention fate of student desegregation. But in the early 1970s, the board began to display the good faith effort that Judge Wright had so courageously sought between 1956 and 1962. As a result, by the mid-1970s desegregated faculties existed at all schools.

But that progress was not without problems. The board attempted to desegregate the faculty by transferring experienced and newly hired teachers to other-race schools. A look at staffing of eighteen randomly selected schools for the years 1969 through 1972 illustrates the point. Eleven of the schools were elementary schools, five formerly white and six formerly black. The racial mix at the six formerly black schools in 1969 was 209 black teachers and no white teachers. In the five formerly white schools in 1969, the racial composition was 106 white teachers and nine black teachers. Through voluntary transfers, the numbers improved slightly during the next two school sessions. Twenty-eight blacks taught at the five formerly white schools in 1970-71 and thirty-one in 1971-72. In the formerly black schools the number of white teachers stood at eight in 1970-71 and twenty-seven in 1971-72.[27]

Similar faculty desegregation patterns prevailed at the secondary schools, as shown by analyzing seven of them: formerly all-white Abramson, Easton, Karr, and McMain; formerly all-black Bell, Clark, and Green. At the latter group of schools, the board employed 170 black and 13 white teachers in 1969-70, 152 black and 31 white in 1970-71, and 142 black and 30 white in 1971-72. The same racial imbalance existed at the formerly all-white group of schools for the same three years: 285 whites and 20 blacks,

250 whites and 55 blacks, and 235 whites and 67 blacks. Though the board had full discretion in the assignment of teachers, it had wisely chosen to give voluntary transfer a chance to succeed, for school officials realized that the teacher corps usually resented transfers. But the policy of voluntarism had failed to achieve faculty desegregation.[28]

Table II[29]

*Faculty Desegregation at Selected Schools, 1969-1972*

| | *1969-1970* | | | | *1970-1971* | | | | *1971-1972* | | | |
|---|---|---|---|---|---|---|---|---|---|---|---|---|
| School | T | B | W | % | T | B | W | % | T | B | W | % |
| Abrams | 24 | 1 | 23 | 4 | 23 | 5 | 18 | 22 | 21 | 5 | 16 | 24 |
| Bore | 24 | 22 | 22 | 9 | 25 | 7 | 18 | 28 | 22 | 8 | 14 | 35 |
| Crossman | 23 | 2 | 21 | 9 | 23 | 6 | 17 | 26 | 21 | 5 | 16 | 24 |
| Edwards | 46 | 46 | 0 | 0 | 37 | 34 | 4 | 8 | 32 | 31 | 1 | 2 |
| Guste | 39 | 39 | 0 | 0 | 36 | 36 | 0 | 0 | 31 | 27 | 4 | 3 |
| Lawless | 54 | 54 | 0 | 0 | 42 | 41 | 1 | 2 | 37 | 32 | 5 | 14 |
| McDon 7 | 16 | 4 | 12 | 25 | 15 | 4 | 11 | 28 | 14 | 6 | 8 | 41 |
| McDon 32 | 24 | 24 | 0 | 0 | 23 | 19 | 4 | 18 | 27 | 20 | 7 | 25 |
| Moton | 36 | 36 | 0 | 0 | 35 | 35 | 0 | 0 | 35 | 27 | 8 | 23 |
| Schaumburg | 28 | 0 | 28 | 0 | 29 | 6 | 23 | 21 | 26 | 7 | 19 | 30 |
| Wicker | 10 | 10 | 0 | 0 | 9 | 9 | 0 | 0 | 8 | 6 | 2 | 25 |
| Abramson | 96 | 4 | 92 | 4 | 107 | 16 | 91 | 5 | 102 | 22 | 80 | 22 |
| Bell | 80 | 75 | 5 | 6 | 83 | 69 | 14 | 17 | 76 | 62 | 14 | 18 |
| Clark | 50 | 44 | 6 | 12 | 57 | 45 | 12 | 21 | 55 | 43 | 12 | 22 |
| Easton | 58 | 6 | 52 | 10 | 62 | 14 | 48 | 23 | 59 | 14 | 45 | 24 |
| Karr | 92 | 2 | 90 | 2 | 80 | 11 | 69 | 14 | 88 | 16 | 72 | 18 |
| McMain | 59 | 8 | 51 | 14 | 56 | 14 | 42 | 25 | 53 | 15 | 38 | 28 |

Source: "Information Report on Staff Desegregation."

During the voluntary phase of faculty desegregation, the board had several opportunities to staff entire schools because five new schools opened in 1970 and in 1971. Three were elementary schools and their students would reflect the racial composition of their location. Crocker and Edison, located in predominantly black areas, had staffs of 73.7 percent black teachers and 26.3 percent white teachers and 66.7 percent black teachers and 33.3 percent white teachers when they opened in 1970. In that same year, Eisenhower Elementary School started operation in a white subdivision in Algiers with a faculty 80 percent white and 20 percent black. One of the two secondary schools, Livingston, located in the rapidly developing eastern section of the city, the area of choice for many young black and white professionals, had 39 white teachers and 20 black ones when it opened in 1971, a percentage of 66.1 to 33.9. The other secondary school, Walker, also located in Algiers, replaced Behrman, a previously all-white high school, and had a white to black faculty percentage of 77.7 to 22.3. Additionally, the board appointed a black educator, Dr. Alvin J. Aubry, as principal.[30]

The board's appointments at the five new schools revealed several things. The most important of which was some commitment to advance faculty desegregation, especially at previously all-black schools. For example, using the same six randomly selected black elementary schools, only eight (4.4 percent) of the 182 teachers in the 1970-71 school year were white. But the two newly opened schools in black neighborhoods—Crocker and Edison—had thirty percent white faculty. And at the other three new schools, the board selected blacks to staff 25.7 of the teaching positions.

Although the board's efforts pushed the number of integrated faculties above that achieved through voluntary transfers, black leaders and the federal court insisted on greater and quicker faculty desegregation. Accordingly, on July 10, 1972, the board voted to use administrative transfers to achieve a ratio of sixty to forty black to white teachers in elementary schools and fifty-five to forty-five in secondary schools. The board also appointed a committee—the Advisory Committee on Implementation of Further Staff Desegregation—to make recommendations on implementation of the new policy.[31]

In August, school officials transferred over eight hundred teachers, nearly nineteen percent of the entire teaching staff. Opposition to the new transfer policy materialized almost immediately. Some of the affected teachers brought a class action suit against the board on August 17, 1972. In the suit—*Harry G. Caire, et al.* v. *Orleans Parish School Board*—the plaintiffs charged that "the orderly planning and operation and more particularly the effective teaching capacity in the Orleans Parish School System for the coming year had been severely impaired" because of the board's transfer of hundreds of teachers. They sought judicial relief to prevent "permanent damage to the education of the children involved." The attorney for the plaintiffs, Lawrence Smith, failed to win a restraining order, and a trial was scheduled for August 25.[32]

Attorneys for the board, including Franklin V. Endom, thought the case lacked merit and that the board possessed the authority and, in this instance, the legal obligation, because of court mandated orders, to transfer teachers. Endom, in his motion to have the suit dismissed, placed the suit in its proper context by arguing that "it is clear from reading the complaint that petitioners are really asking the court to delay the implementation of the Board's program to further desegregate the faculties for one school year." District Court Judge Herbert W. Christenberry, who had taken over the Bush case, ruled that the federal court lacked jurisdiction and dismissed the suit on August 28, 1972, without commenting on the merits of the case. Before he remanded the case to state court, however, he made it known that "if the state court grants any relief, particularly of an injunctive nature, which the court finds frustrates or is in derogation of the orders entered by this court in the case of *Bush v OPSB*, No. 3630, this court shall . . . stay such court action."[33]

After Christenberry's ruling, disposition of the suit became the responsibility of the Civil District Court for the Parish of Orleans. Judge Gerald P. Fedoroff scheduled a special hearing for September 15. In his brief to the court, Lawrence Smith tried to convince the court that the point of the "suit was not and is not to substantially delay or block integration of the faculties." The plaintiffs, Smith contended, wanted the board to "reverse its arbitrary and capricious decision to act in such haste and to plan properly before integrating the faculties on a massive basis." When the trial started, however, attorneys for both sides requested an indefinite delay in the trial, for they had agreed to implement a plan by which school officials would consider specific transfer cases with power to grant relief. Judge Federoff granted the request.[34]

The decision to review transfer cases individually led to charges of administrative bias, and the board established a grievance committee to resolve such cases. Lawrence Smith continued to act as an intervenor in transfer disputes and worked with Rosenberg and Alfred Hebeisen, assistant superintendent for personnel, in setting the claims. Most of the teachers who formally objected to the transfers cited personal reasons or charged that the board had acted unfairly. Charges of unfairness usually centered around seniority status in the system or within a particular school. The board eventually made several changes in assignment, but such changes did not substantially alter the faculty desegregation plan.[35]

School officials took several steps to help ensure successful faculty desegregation. They accepted several of the recommendations of the advisory committee, which included specific guidelines for transferring teachers, the formation of a bi-racial advisory committee, and enactment of a training program for teachers, principals, and administrators. Moreover, school officials elicited comments from teachers who had already served on desegregated faculties.[36]

How successful was the board's effort? In terms of producing a greater racial balance of faculty in the schools, the plan was a success. But progress towards improved race relations and an increase in meaningful contact between the races was more limited. Perhaps it was best summarized by Henry M. Williams, associate superintendent for human relations. Reflecting on the fact that black and white students tended to sit apart in classrooms and segregate themselves in the cafeteria and on the playground, Williams commented: "Polarization seldom disappears of its own accord. Unattended, it is more likely to increase than abate. There must be a genuine desire to overcome this divisive phenomenon and a willingness on the part of schools to work consistently with methods and procedures that unite students and faculty on bases other than race."[37]

By 1973 the membership of the school board had changed several times since the start of desegregation in November 1960. Emile Wagner, Jr., who had opposed even limited student desegregation, finally resigned in August 1962. And several months later Governor Davis appointed Daniel Ellis to serve the remainder of his unexpired term. Two years later, in 1964, Victor Hess and Andrew Rinker won board seats, replacing Ellis and Theodore Shephard. With the election of Robert C. Smith in 1966, Louis Riecke and Lloyd Rittiner were the only board members remaining who had been on the board in November 1960. When Mack J. Spears replaced Riecke in 1968 Rittiner became the lone survivor of the early desegregation crises. But Spears' election signaled more than the passing of another veteran board member, for he was the first black elected to the Orleans Parish School Board. And his election symbolized the already perceptible shift occurring in politics and power in the city, a shift towards increased black political power.[38]

Almost contemporaneous with Spears' election, although not related to it, was the start of federal monetary assistance to the local school board. The national efforts to gain federal dollars for education dated back to the 1870s. But positive action had to await President Lyndon Johnson's Great Society program of the 1960s. Before 1965 the school board received a minuscule amount of money from federal sources. From then on, however, the percentage of the budget derived from federal funds rose steadily. With federal money, of course, came federal regulations. Thus, the combination of increased revenues from the federal government and increased local black political power modified, and eventually altered, the board's stance on race-related issues.[39]

But neither the infusion of federal money nor the election of black board members solved another long-simmering problem in the public school system—low teacher salaries. Throughout the history of the school system, superintendents, board members, community leaders, and teachers themselves had lamented the low salaries and had persistently sought ways to increase them. Although salaries increased during the twentieth century, they still lagged behind those of most Southern cities. And to the chagrin of many New Orleanians, teachers' pay even in other Louisiana cities, such as Shreveport, surpassed teachers' pay in New Orleans. For example, in 1963 the $3,725 a year minimum salary in New Orleans placed Crescent City teachers behind those in Shreveport, who made a minimum of $3,900 a year.[40]

TABLE III[41]

*Teacher Salaries in Selected Southern Cities*

| | | | |
|---|---|---|---|
| Baltimore | $4,800 | Corpus Christi | $4,550 |
| Miami | 4,750 | San Antonio | 4,500 |
| St. Petersburg | 4,750 | Houston | 4,500 |
| Beaumont | 4,700 | Atlanta | 4,440 |
| Lubbock | 4,600 | Tampa | 4,400 |
| El Paso | 4,600 | Austin | 4,400 |
| Dallas | 4,600 | Jacksonville | 4,400 |
| Amarillo | 4,600 | New Orleans | 3,725 |

Source: New Orleans Annual Report, 1963-1964.

Teachers knew that the board needed increased revenues to administer a growing urban school system. They also realized that the board had the unenviable task of trying to reconcile salary needs with other financial obligations. Their sympathy with the board's plight, however, did not prevent them from becoming increasingly vocal on the issue of salaries. Indeed, in 1966 and 1969 teachers used the ultimate employee weapon, a strike, in an attempt to win improved pay. The two strikes, though unsuccessful because of poor community support and a lack of teacher solidarity, indicated a growing militancy within teacher ranks.[42]

The new militancy eventually led, in 1972, to the formation of the United Teachers of New Orleans. UTNO resulted from a rare merger of the local units of two major and rival teacher organizations, the predominantly black Local 527 of the American Federation of Teachers and the predominantly white Orleans Educators Association, a unit of the National Education Association. In its first year of existence, approximately seventeen hundred teachers joined the new union, a number which represented about 38 percent of the teaching staff. UTNO members selected Nat LaCour, a former science teacher and head of Local 527, as president. Cheryl Epling, the former head of the Orleans Educators Association, became vice president of the new organization. LaCour and Epling, both energetic and skilled organizers, became an effective team as they slowly recruited new members and garnered community support for the new organization. Prior to 1978 their biggest victory was winning board approval of UTNO's right to bargain collectively for teachers. By 1978 UTNO was the third largest union in the city. Only the Communication Workers of America and the International Longshoremen's Association had more members.[43]

In April 1978, school officials and UTNO representatives started tentative discussions on the "wage-reopener" provision of the existing contract between teachers and the board. LaCour and his negotiating team asked for a 9 percent pay increase and wanted the board to pay the entire cost of employee health insurance. School officials, led by Superintendent Gene Geisert, pleaded lack of funds but later promised to seek legislative approval to allow citizens to vote on a proposed half-cent sales tax increase. Despite some prior support in the legislature and massive lobbying by teacher groups as well as school officials, the legislators adjourned without passing the tax bill. With that revenue option closed, school board president Mack Spears and the other four members—Mrs. Rose Loving, Lloyd Rittiner, Harwood Koppel, and William Reeves—considered a push to gain support for a property tax increase. Predictably, that idea fizzled, largely because of the historical aversion of New Orleanians to property taxes.[44]

As the city endured its usual hot summer days, little change occurred in the wage and benefit impasse between the board and UTNO. Finally, in August, the board made the union an offer of $800,000, which union leaders rejected. The board raised its offer to one million dollars, which the union called an "insult." Throughout the summer it had become clear that sentiment was growing among the teachers to strike if the board failed to meet their demands.[45]

On August 28, the board issued a letter to all its employees warning them of the possibility of "serious adverse effects resulting from community based opposition to a strike and serious implications for each employee who participates." The letter, signed by Spears, went on to describe in graphic detail the possible consequences teachers faced if they went on strike. He stressed the loss of tenure, salary, fringe benefits, and sabbatical leave. Spears also warned that possibly "teachers and other employees could be held liable for damages in the event that state support for schools in this parish is withdrawn."[46]

Board members sensed, however, that it would take more than threats to avert a strike. After consulting with other board members, Spears authorized Superintendent Geisert to increase the board's offer to $2.5 million. But union leaders rejected it, too. Geisert and Jerry Hart, assistant superintendent for human resources management and a member of the board's negotiating team, indicated the board had made its best and final offer. Faced with accepting the $2.5 million or striking, thousands of teachers and teacher-aides gathered on the morning of August 30 and voted not to return to work until the board met their full demands. That same morning thousands of the city's children started their first day of school without their regular teachers.[47]

Once the strike started, battle lines and strategy became clear. UTNO wanted to disrupt the normal school routine by keeping as many teachers and teachers-aides out of the classrooms as possible. Through meetings and letters, LaCour and his staff kept the union members informed. LaCour refrained from publicly disclosing the percentage of teacher participation in the strike the union needed for it to be successful, but the union probably needed a minimum of 65 percent participation.

The board's strategy called for keeping the schools open at all cost and conducting them on a business-as-usual basis. Both sides wanted and cultivated public support. In order to keep the schools open, the board had to, one, keep some teachers in the schools and, two, keep student attendance low enough for the small staff to handle. On August 29, in anticipation of the strike, Deputy Superintendent Samuel Scarnato gave school principals the authority to hire substitute teachers immediately upon need, without securing central administration approval first. And to entice substitutes to take the jobs, the board announced a $49.00 a day pay-rate for them, nearly double the normal salary. To keep student attendance low, school officials informed parents and students that absences during the strike would not be counted.[48]

On the first day of the strike, 67 percent of the teaching staff was absent from the classrooms. LaCour, Epling, and the rest of UTNO's leadership had reason for cautious optimism. And things looked better the second day, when some 73 percent of the teachers failed to report to work. For the duration of the strike, teacher participation remained above 73 percent, despite a concerted effort by school officials to force the striking teachers back to work.[49]

The conscious effort by union representatives to keep morale high with rallies, picnics, and financial support for teachers proved a wise course because the school board decided to toughen its policy on September 5. Geisert issued an announcement informing striking teachers that they could return to their school on or before September 6 without any disciplinary measures by the board. After that date, however, teachers would have to report to the administrative office to receive an assignment and face possible disciplinary action. The board also reduced its previous offer of $2.5 million to $1.5 million and said it was considering hiring teachers to replace those on strike. But the tactic failed. On the day following Geisert's announcement, 75 percent of the teachers still stayed out.[50]

As the strike continued, both the union and the board faced mounting community pressure to settle it. Students, parents, business leaders, city officials, and the news media urged the two sides to reach an agreement. On September 7, a local editorial declared that "the continuing school strike is clearly developing into a harmful—even dangerous—confrontation in which everyone will lose." The Young Men's Business Club sent telegrams to board members and union officials demanding that they resume negotiations. Mayor Ernest Morial did what he could to help the two sides reach a settlement. Many parents voiced their concerns through various school-based parent-teachers organizations. One group, calling itself the Parent-Community Coalition, demanded greater accountability from the board. The group charged that "the board has not fulfilled its obligation as evidenced by the present state of affairs." Some support also developed for a campaign to recall board members. And not surprisingly, because of their close contact with teachers, students supported the strike. "We are behind our teachers 100 percent," one student leader proclaimed and proceeded to help organize a student boycott of classes.[51]

It was clear by September 7 that Geisert's earlier prediction that teachers would return to work after the Labor Day holiday because their display of union solidarity would crumble as they "begin to consider their economic well-being" was wide of the mark. Teacher absenteeism climbed to 74 percent and above. On September 8 nego-tiations resumed, and three days later the two sides reached a tentative agreement, albeit one that caused almost as much controversy as the strike. The agreement called for 7 percent raises for teachers and an increased contribution by the board for employee health insurance. Teachers-aides, maintenance workers, and bus drivers also received pay and benefit increases. What incensed many New Orleanians was that money to pay for the approximately $6.2 million agreement would have to come from cuts elsewhere in the school budget. In the end, the board voted to trim $1.95 million from the budget, $2.8 million from unallocated funds, and $1.5 million from payroll monies saved during the strike.[52]

"School Board Collapsed," headlined a *New Orleans Times-Picayune* editorial two days following the settlement. "Unless the majority that authorized the settlement can explain its failure satisfactorily," the editor warned, "the board as a forceful policy-making body risks losing what credibility it had." Board member William Reeves, who along with Harwood Koppel had voted against the settlement, bitterly assailed the board's decision and harshly criticized Spears' leadership during the strike. In a "Guest Comment" in the *Times-Picayune*, Reeves branded Spears a pawn in an alledged plan by Mayor Morial to gain control of the school board. He charged that Spears refused to call board meetings to discuss important issues and accused him of not relying on the professional advice of Geisert and Hart. He also criticized Rittiner and Mrs. Loving for their support of the agreement.[53]

Spears answered Reeves and his critics through another local newspaper, *Figaro*. He termed the allegation that he was a Morial pawn "the most preposterous, asinine thing anybody could have conceived." Spears said he supported the settlement because he "became convinced that the alternative was a community without schools for three months and the probability of violence." Increased student involvement and growing parental support, he went on, had convinced him to change his earlier position. And he acknowledged the skill with which union leaders had conducted the strike. To the charge that the settlement cost more in the end than it would have if the board had made it earlier, Spears answered that such was not the case, for conditions had changed as the strike continued.[54]

Despite the *Times-Picayune*'s admonition that "it would be a mistake for anyone, including the teachers union, to view this settlement as a victory," and that "the whole tragic episode could well be just one more nail in the coffin of public education here," the teachers were jubilant. They saw the strike as more than a fight for more money. "I think that teachers can work together outside the classroom. We have a new unity and we will continue working together as one through the union," said one teacher after the strike. Another remarked on the new solidarity discernible among teachers.[55]

During the decade following the strike, school officials spent much of their time searching for ways to efficiently administer an urban school system hampered by community apathy, eroding public support, and dwindling revenues. In 1980, almost as if to start afresh in the new decade, board members decided to replace Superintendent Geisert. They chose Charles Martin, dean of education at the University of New Orleans. Though many black leaders thought the time ripe for naming a black educator to head the school system, few openly criticized Martin's selection. They eventually applauded him for his choice of deputy superintendent. He named to the system's second highest post Maxine Copelin, a black principal who had won praise for her leadership at Carver Middle School, an inner-city school in the city's Ninth Ward.

During Martin's tenure he sought to improve school board financial administration, which had been problem-ridden for a long time. City business and civic groups such as the Young Men's Business Club and the Bureau of Governmental Research had long called for such reform. Stagnant revenues and rising costs made Martin's emphasis on efficiency both sound business practice as well as good public relations. Although city leaders often criticized board policy and low student performance, school officials began to gain increased respect and support from the local business community, which entered cooperative ventures with various schools. Indeed, one of the more important developments in the 1980s was the success of the board's adopt-a-school program.

By the time Everett J. Williams, a veteran teacher and administrator, became the system's first black school superintendent in 1985, the main issue of the preceeding three decades—desegregation—had been replaced by the problem of operating an urban school system amid the many societal ills that plagued New Orleans. When Dr. Williams accepted the challenge of operating one of the South's oldest school systems he realized, as did the board and the community, that urban schools, if they were to succeed or even survive, had to find ways of solving many non-educational problems. Violence, drugs, and teenage pregancy constituted some of the new challenges to the future of education in New Orleans.

Is there hope for the children in our large cities who depend upon public schools for their education? The long travail of the New Orleans schools offers no easy answer. Its one hundred and fifty years of history demonstrate, however, that a large urban public school system never secures an ultimate triumph. The schools either improve or they deteriorate.

Despite some notable achievements, New Orleans public schools have never met the needs of the poorest children of the city, especially the black poor. Individual teachers and schools often demonstrated models of achievement and success, but those isolated efforts could not break the unremitting cycle of poverty and ignorance. From the beginning, issues of race stymied the public will to make any fundamental change. During the 1960s, public and private leaders failed the test of desegregation. For years afterward, most elected officials—particularly mayors and governors—ignored the schools and left them largely adrift, strapped for both human and financial resources. The New Orleans experience shows that, without the crucial leadership of mayors and governors, school officials and parents have not been able to mobilize voters for fundamental and long-term reform.

Yet somehow hope remains. Although federal court orders failed to integrate most classrooms, they redistributed funding for the poor. A greater percentage of black students in New Orleans and in other areas of the South are now graduating from high school and college. Expanded electorates have lessened the worst expressions of racial hatred and oppression. Those electorates have also encouraged public officials to give greater support to public education. In 1989, the nation's governors met in Charlottesville, Virginia, to set some common goals for public schools in the United States. The governors of Louisiana, Mississippi, and Arkansas came not as symbols of neglect and defiance, but as champions of educational reform. Each had made the improvement of public education a key goal of his administration.

Never has the nation reached such a consensus about the objectives of public education. By the year 2000, the governors envisioned that all children would start drug-free schools prepared to learn and that almost all would graduate from high school competent in basic subjects, including math and science.

Some model teachers and schools have always existed in New Orleans and other cities. They show us how to get youngsters ready for school and how to teach them to read, write, and compute. But the challenge still remains for federal and state authorities to help local governments deliver such care and schooling to all children and particularly to the urban poor. In truth, the challenge requires more than just change in public schools. America must rebuild its cities and bring hope to those who reside in them. In New Orleans and in the nation's other major cities lie the destiny of the United States and the quality of its civilization. Whatever is done, urban schools will shape prospects for America's rising generations. Like liberty and democracy, the education of a community requires from its citizens eternal vigilance.

Notes for "A New and Uncertain Era"

[1]Byrd to Erma Landix, March 5, 1953, Byrd Collection.

[2]New Orleans Public Schools, Facts and Finances, 1961-1962, OPSB Collection; *New Orleans Times-Picayune*, September 7, 1961.

[3]*New Orleans Times-Picayune*, April 4, 1962.

[4]Ibid.

[5]OPSB Minutes, April 9, 1962; *Times-Picayune*, April 4, 1962.

[6]*New Orleans Times-Picayune*, April 4, 1962.

[7]Ibid., May 4, 1962.

[8]*New Orleans States-Item*, May 9, 1962.

[9]*New Orleans Times-Picayune*, May 9, 1962.

[10]OPSB Minutes, May 14, 1962.

[11]*New Orleans Times-Picayune*, May 24, 1962.

[12]Facts and Finances, 1962-1963, 1963-1964, 1964-1965.

[13]See, transcript of trial proceedings of April 22 and 23, 1965, in box 46, OPSB Collection.

[14]Ibid. [15]Ibid. [16]Ibid. [17]Ibid.

[18]By January 1962 only twenty students attended McDonogh 19, and the board voted on January 8 to convert the school to black use. That decision, if implemented, would have caused the transfer of the remaining fifteen white students in attendance but would have also relieved overcrowding at several neighboring black schools. Nonetheless, Tureaud, unwilling to concede at such an early date to resegregation, requested and received a restraining order preventing the board from making the change.

[19]Transcript of trial of April 22 and 23, 1965.

[20]Ibid. [21]Ibid.

[22]*New Orleans Times-Picayune*, April 24, 1965.

[23]Facts and Finances, 1961-1962, 1964-1965.

[24]Facts and Finances, 1966-1967.

[25]Facts and Finances, 1960-1961 to 1980-1981.

[26]Facts and Finances, 1969-1970 to 1979-1980.

[27]Samuel Scarnato files, box 16, OPSB Collection. [28]Ibid.

[29]"Informational Report on Staff Desegregation in the School," Scarnato files, box, 16, OPSB Collection.

[30]Ibid.

[31]OPSB Minutes, July 10, 1972.

[32]*New Orleans Times-Picayune*, August 18, 1972.

[33]*Harry G. Caire v. OPSB*, copy of trial transcript in OPSB Collection. [34]Ibid.

[35]William W. Orr to Samuel Rosenberg, November 15, 1972 and December 5, 1972, Alfred Hebeisen to Rosenberg, December 11, 1972, Rosenberg to Lawrence Smith, November 20, 1972, Scarnato files, box 108.

[36]Scarnato files, box 16.

[37]Williams to school principals, January 25, 1973, Scarnato files, box 16.

[38]OPSB Minutes, August 20, 1962, January 14, 1963; Facts and Finances, 1962-1963 to 1968-1969.

[39]Alonzo Hamby, *Liberalism and Its Challengers: FDR to Reagan* (New York, 1985), 259; Allen J. Matusow, *The Unraveling of America: A History of Liberalism in the 1960s* (New York, 1984), 221-26; Facts and Finances, 1964-1965 to 1974-1975.

[40]N. O. Annual Report, 1963-1964. [41]Ibid.

[42]Scarnato files, box 53.

[43]*New Orleans Figaro*, September 6, 1978.

[44]*New Orleans States-Item*, September 15, 1978.

[45]Ibid.

[46]Mack Spears to school board employees, August 28, 1978, Scarnato files, box 53.

[47]*New Orleans Times-Picayune*, September 7, 1978.

[48]Ibid., September 2, 1978.

[49]*New Orleans States-Item*, September 15, 1978.

[50]Superintendent's announcement to teachers, September 5, 1978, Scarnato files, box 53; *New Orleans States-Item*, September 5, 1978; *New Orleans Times Picayune*, September 6, 7, 1978.

[51]*New Orleans Times-Picayune*, September 6, 7, 1978.

[52]Ibid., September 12, 13, 1978.

[53]Ibid., September 13, 21, 1978.

[54]*New Orleans Figaro*, September 20, 1978.

[55]*New Orleans States-Item*, September 12, 1978.

# WHY CAN'T GASTON READ?*

Michael L. Kurtz

Once upon a time, not too many years ago, in a quiet, pleasant little community located somewhere between Grosse Tête and Ville Platte, there lived a little boy named Gaston Troxclair. Gaston grew up amidst the sights, sounds, and aromas of the Atchafalaya Basin, enjoying the frolicking of alligators and nutria beneath the moss-draped cypress, the chirping of birds, the croaking of frogs cavorting in Whiskey Bay, and the alluring scents of the wild honeysuckle and night-blooming jasmine. If this idyllic scene was somewhat marred by the vapors ominously and noxiously emanating from a nearby toxic-waste dump, by the constant roar of the automobile engines on Interstate 10, sarcastically called by the natives, "Acadiana Speedway," and by the pungent stench of the methane gas trapped in the swamps and marshes, Gaston did not seem to mind, for he led a happy home life in a close-knit family. His father worked on an oil rig in the Gulf of Mexico, and his mother kept a neat, clean house and loaded the dinner table with a nightly cornucopia of filé gumbo, crawfish bisque, and his favorite, shrimp jambalaya laced with hot sausage.[1]

After finishing grammar school, Gaston attended the local high school, a shiny new facility replete with the latest equipment and complemented by a brand-new football stadium. His teachers, all certified, instructed him according to the latest methods and innovative teaching techniques, and in their unanimous opinion, Gaston was a bright young man, exhibiting much creativity and demonstrating potential for achieving his educational and vocational objectives. Gaston made steady progress, passing from grade to grade, and bringing home report cards that recorded mainly "A's" and "B's" although the "C's" and "D's" he made in English, Algebra, and Biology lowered his overall grade point average. But Gaston really excelled in those subjects he loved the most: Physical Education; Driver's Ed; automobile repairs; Free Enterprise; and Band. On the night of Gaston's graduation, Mr. and Mrs. Troxclair beamed proudly as he received his diploma

*First published in *Louisiana History*, 26 (1985): 229-39. Reprinted with the kind permission of the author and the Louisiana Historical Association.

from cousin Conrad, the local barber and a duly elected member of the parish school board.[2]

Because he wanted to be a lawyer, Gaston decided to enroll in a state university, so he dutifully took the ACT test required for admission. When he received his test results about six weeks later, he paid little attention to his composite score of 10, and none at all to his inability to read the word "composite," much less comprehend its meaning. After all, it made no difference what score he made on the ACT; under Louisiana law, as a high school graduate, he would automatically gain admission to the state university of his choice. On registration day, Gaston learned that because of his low ACT score, he would have to enter a program called Developmental Education, and take classes in remedial English, Math and Academic Skills, so he could learn how to study. Gaston's parents, however, did not take out a low-interest loan to finance a college education that earned him no credit, so the university, always eager to add to its total of Student Credit Hours Produced (SCH's), permitted him to register for courses in Physical Education (P. E.), Library Science, and American History (he should have taken Western Civilization first, but all the sections in the time slots he wanted were already filled).

As the semester progressed, Gaston could not understand why he kept failing his History tests. He had taken American History in high school, and he had made an "A" in the course, taught by the legendary coach, Maurice Couvillion, affectionately known as "Bulldog" by his legions of admirers. All the kids loved coach "Bulldog's" History class. During football season, he entertained them by reciting from his endless supply of anecdotes from past campaigns and by diagramming plays for Friday night's crucial game. Gaston's college History teacher was quite different, lecturing about such matters as Jonathan Edwards and Henry Clay, and the Missouri Compromise and something called the Wilmot Proviso, and actually testing from a long, dreary textbook filled with names and dates and big words Gaston could not understand. Nor would his instructor, a likeable young graduate assistant, allow him to earn extra credit for building a project on the Civil War for the Social Science Fair.

Gaston managed to survive his first semester. Although he failed History, as a strapping mesomorph, he easily "aced" his weight-lifting P. E. course, and in Library Science, he barely passed because through great effort, he learned the location of the card catalogue and memorized the term "Reader's Guide." He never could comprehend the distinction between the Dewey Decimal and Library of Congress classification systems, but since he never intended to set foot in the facility again, he had no regrets. Having completed the required non-credit courses in Development Education, Gaston now possessed, according to the collective wisdom of the state Board of Regents, academic qualifications for completing a full schedule of regular college classes. In his second semester, he registered for P.E., Art Appreciation, Cheerleading, Marching Band, and freshman English. Of these, only English posed problems. He could easily pass P.E. again, and Cheerleading and Marching Band gave academic credit for performing during football games. Art Appreciation he felt confident of passing, since the course was taught by a professor whose old tests were carefully maintained in the files of his fraternity. Gaston resided in the fraternity house, which had earned a deserved reputation as the "Animal House" of the campus, and he made a big hit with his brothers through his prowess in the house's nightly "chug-a-lug" contests.

Thanks to "B's" in Art Appreciation, Cheerleading, and Marching Band, Gaston also survived his second semester, but he failed P.E. and English, and as a probationary student on appeal, he flunked out of the university the first semester of his sophomore year. But let us not feel too sorry for our fictional friend, Gaston Troxclair. He returned home, married his childhood sweetheart, and they lived on a five-acre farm given them by his parents for a wedding present. Unable to find a steady job, Gaston nevertheless lived comfortably, supporting his growing family through the royalties paid him by Louisiana Land and Exploration for the mineral rights to his land, and through the good graces of cousin Conrad, he supplements this income by serving as a substitute teacher in the parish public schools.

The saga of Gaston Troxclair has a happy ending, but for thousands of young men and women attending school in Louisiana, the future does not hold out the promise of a bonanza from mineral rights or a lucrative job obtained through the intercession of a cousin Conrad. On the contrary, their future appears bleak indeed, for if there is any truth to the adage that "ignorance is bliss," then a large number of young people attending school in Louisiana must be in a state of perpetual ecstasy. But it will soon turn to despondency when, like Gaston Troxclair, they discover that their possession of a diploma certifying their graduation from high school does not attest their mastery of the fundamentals of learning. The statistics speak for themselves. Louisiana has the highest adult illiteracy rate in the nation. Juniors and seniors in state high schools score lower on a watered-down ACT than they did a decade ago, and their average performance on the test ranks second lowest in the nation. Louisiana's high school dropout rate is the highest in the country, and over half of all freshmen entering college must take remedial Math, English, and Reading.[3] College faculty members almost unanimously agree that the academic preparation of their students has declined precipitously in recent years.[4] The dire news and horror stories can be repeated *ad nauseam*, but the point is clear: today's generation of students has been deprived of what by common consent is regarded as a sound education.

For a number of years, I have requested students in my introductory survey courses in American History and Government to take a quiz designed to give me a general idea of their state of preparation in these subjects. The students are fairly representative of Louisiana high school graduates. They come from a broad cross section of ethnic and socio-economic groups, and they have graduated from public and parochial high schools in almost every parish in the state. Their average composite ACT score is 15.8. A sampling of their responses suggests their lack of preparation. One-quarter thought Benjamin Franklin was a president of the United States; two-thirds believed "Stonewall" a nickname for Andrew Jackson; two-fifths thought Herbert Hoover invented the vacuum cleaner; and one quarter believed that he founded the FBI. Over half could not identify the Bill of Rights, the judicial branch of government, and the term "democracy." From Louisiana, over half thought Earl Long was a current United States senator, and over four-fifths could not identify such terms as Code Noir, Reconstruction, and desegregation. The only two native Louisianians of the past whom a majority could correctly identify were Huey Long and Lee Harvey Oswald.[5]

According to Mona J. Davis, the governor's chief education advisor, in Louisiana, "we have the dumbest kids in the country, but the best-fed and the best-transported."[6] Davis's remark did not address the salient issues. None of the available evidence suggests that Louisiana students have innately inferior mental capabilities. The evidence does demonstrate that money spent on schooling in Louisiana is not being spent wisely. In 1984, the state spent $2,821 per student, which ranked it 37th in the country, and teachers' salaries averaged $19,690, 42nd in the nation.[7] Yet student performance has persistently ranked 49th or 50th.[8] Such statistics, of course, can be manipulated to support almost any point of view, but they do demonstrate that the mere infusion of more money into the schools will not necessarily produce an improvement in academic quality.

That improvement will come only if the most serious reasons for the deplorable condition of public schooling in Louisiana are addressed. One of these lies in the inadequate training given teachers. In a recent *Newsweek* article on teachers, the authors called teacher training "the biggest running joke in higher education."[9] ACT and SAT scores for freshmen entering teacher-training programs fall 20 to 30 percent below the national average.[10] In addition, those who complete education curricula undergo what is generally regarded as the least rigorous of all degree programs. The city of New York and the state of New Jersey have permitted college graduates to obtain teaching certificates without having taken the prescribed education courses.[11] At a meeting of the American Association of Colleges for Teacher Education, faculty members, department heads, and deans lamented these policies as leading to an inevitable decline in quality and professionalism in teaching.[12] The fact that such policies have been instituted indicates the deficiencies of the existing certification programs and a need for a drastic overhaul of traditional methods of teacher training.

Unlike universities, where the qualification to teach is certified by a doctorate in an academic discipline, the possession of which attests to its holder's having mastered the subject matter of his teaching field, in grammar and high schools, it is signified by a teaching certificate, the possession of which simply verifies that one has completed a teacher training curriculum, heavily laden with professional education courses. The absence of rigorous standards in such courses as methods, testing and measurement, educational psychology, etc., has been so often and so loudly proclaimed that it need not be repeated here.[13] Suffice it to note that to qualify to teach History in a Louisiana high school, one must major not in History, but in a hydra-headed monster euphemistically labelled Social Studies Education, a hodge-podge of courses in History, Government, Economics, Sociology, and Geography, in addition to a number of education courses.[14]

Once certified in Social Studies, a person is legally qualified to teach any of those five subjects, even though he may have taken as few as three semester hours of it in college.[15] It should be apparent that the essential prerequisite of effective teaching is mastery of the subject matter of one's teaching field, yet the professional education requirements virtually guarantee that a student will graduate without have achieved that mastery.

I have always found it most curious that those of us who teach History, English, Mathematics, Biology, and other academic subjects in college are not legally qualified to teach the same subjects in grades kindergarten through twelve in Louisiana because most of us have never taken courses in "how to teach." One can just image the public outrage if the faculty in our schools of medicine had received most of their training in methods of teaching medicine than in Anatomy, Physiology, Pathology, and Pharmacology. Yet precisely the same principle applies to the instruction of our children in grammar and high school. The problem is compounded by the fact that many teachers are unable to find jobs in their major teaching fields and end up teaching courses in their minor areas of concentration. Further aggravating the situation is the large number of athletic coaches teaching academic subjects. Bulldogs they may be, but most coaches have majored in P.E., yet frequently teach History, Civics, English, Mathematics, Biology, Chemistry, etc. because state policy demands that they spend part of their time in the classroom. Again, imagine the public indignation if teachers of English and French suddenly started coaching football and basketball teams.

All of this, of course, is unfair to the many competent and dedicated teachers in our state, but even they confront obstacles that would tax the abilities of the most gifted of teachers. Salaries are appallingly low, with those in Louisiana $4,000 a year below the national average.[16] School teachers are ordinary men and women trying to earn a living, and very few can manage to maintain a decent standard of living on their salaries. Compared with other professions, teaching is the lowest paid in the country, an obvious deterrent to the desirability of attracting the "best and brightest" young people to select it for a career.[17] With a predicted nationwide shortage of teachers of almost one million by 1990, only substantial increases in pay will attract and retain able teachers.[18] Besides enduring low pay, teachers must also perform a multitude of chores which detract from their professional duties: monitoring cafeteria lines, collecting lunch money, supervising school bus arrivals and departures, chaperoning proms. They must also face the wrath of irate parents for attempting to enforce discipline in the classroom and of angry school boards for introducing "controversial" topics into their courses. Handicapped by outdated textbooks, meager supplies, and an increasing lack of parental cooperation, teachers justifiably complain about the impediments to effective teaching which the system imposes.[19]

Adequate training might serve to compensate for some of this, but most teachers have not received it. With considerable understatement, the dean of a teacher training school in New York described education courses as "unrelievedly boring."[20] Albert Shanker, the president of the American Federation of Teachers, made the same point more forcefully: "Education is the only professional field where after people graduate, they say they would have been better off without the training."[21] When thrust into the real world of the classroom, as opposed to the utopian ideals of the educational psychology texts, the teacher often finds herself confronted with situations for which she is completely unprepared. Problems ranging from soiled underpants to runny noses in the grammar schools and premarital sex and physical violence in the high schools are common. She also discovers that the "methods" of teaching Reading and Social Studies that she learned in her college education courses hardly apply to a class of students unable to read and write, totally unaccustomed to doing homework, and lacking any kind of parental encouragement to do well in school.

Upon completion of the teacher education curriculum, the prospective extinguisher of ignorance must overcome a final obstacle before receiving a teaching certificate: achieving a passing score on the National Teachers Examination (NTE). Hardly an intellectually challenging test, the NTE can in no sense be compared to the Graduate Record Examination, the Law School Admission Test, or the Medical School Admission Test as an accurate measure of one's preparation in an academic discipline, much less as a standard by which potential teaching ability can be gauged. Yet, the state superintendent of education recommended, and the Board of Elementary and Secondary Education approved, a lowering of the NTE passing scores in Social Studies, Mathematics, and other subjects.[22] It is little wonder that less than 10 percent of the nation's teachers believed that their teacher training curricula helped make them better teachers?[23]

In April 1985, Governor Edwin Edwards proposed to the state legislature an education "package" designed to improve the quality of public schools in Louisiana. The most controversial of the proposed bills would provide $1,000 pay raises to all teachers who passed the subject matter test of the NTE, and 15 percent pay raise to teachers who voluntarily relinquished their tenure in return for an evaluation of their teaching performance every five years.[24] Quite understandably, teachers vigorously opposed both measures. Passing the NTE would not improve teaching ability, and the forfeiture of tenure in a state with a long history of political interference in the public schools would remove the security of job permanence from the profession. Superintendent of Education Thomas Clausen proposed a plan whereby one public school in each parish would participate in a pilot program designed to improve the quality of instruction. In those schools, teachers would receive a 10 percent raise at the beginning of the school year, and if the performance of their students improve on certain standardized tests at the end of the year, they would receive an additional 10 percent raise.[25] The Clausen plan has met with much opposition from teachers, primarily because allegations of favoritism in selecting the schools for the program have already surfaced.[26]

It would be easy to stop here, laying the blame for the multitude of problems in our public schools entirely on teacher training programs, state politics, etc. Yet are not those of us in college equally responsible? In the past two decades, American colleges and universities have also contributed to the overall decline in academic quality. The report,

*To Reclaim a Legacy*, by William Bennett, the secretary of education, offers a scathing indictment of the nation's colleges for their failure to provide students with an adequate foundation in the culture and civilization of the society in which they live.[27] Today, it is possible for a person to graduate from 75 percent of American colleges without having taken a single course in Western Civilization, from 72 percent without American History, and from 86 percent without Ancient History.[28] Fewer than half of all colleges now require any study in foreign languages. Some 87 percent of all Humanities courses are taken at the freshman and sophomore survey level, frequently in huge lecture sections taught by graduate assistants, the students' performance almost invariably evaluated by so-called "objective" tests.[29] In short, the Humanities, which by definition entails the study of man, has become the most impersonal of subjects and offers as much humanistic insight as a grade transcript. In our own state, the plight of the Humanities continues to worsen. The study by Judith Gentry and James Dormon documented the large number of degree programs offered by Louisiana colleges that required no History whatsoever and the even larger number that required only a minimum of course work.[30] Accrediting agencies in such disciplines as Business, Music, Social Welfare, and Engineering demand an increasing number of highly specialized courses for degree programs to receive accreditation.[31] These demands force colleges and departments to reduce the number of required courses outside the curriculum, and almost invariably, courses in History, foreign languages, English, and other humanistic disciplines are the first to go. The result is a contemporary pool of college graduates receiving degrees in technical specializations without the broad liberal education traditionally demanded for all.

In college education today, the emphasis is placed increasingly on the peripherals rather than the essentials. The main reason for this trend is intense competition for students. Other than the dedication of a new building, a hefty contribution from a wealthy benefactor, or a winning football season, nothing is more likely to activate the salivary glands of a college president than an increase in SCH's. The more SCH's it produces, the more money a college receives because of a state funding formula that places a premium on the headcount of students rather than on the quality of their instruction. The message filters down through the administrative hierarchy: attract more students. To retain our jobs and win favor with the administration, we faculty members accommodate the perfectly natural and understandable desire of students to accomplish their goals with a minimum of effort by offering gimmicky courses, inflating grades, and generally lowering academic standards. Many junior and senior level courses now require no independent research, and the essay examination appears headed the way of Latin and Greek. It should come as no surprise that in the past two decades, student performance on the Major Subject test of the GRE declined in three-quarters of all disciplines.[32]

Another reason lies in the continuous growth of the administrative bureaucracy of colleges. The perennial complaints by faculty about the excessive funds spent on intercollegiate athletics overlooks a more distressing trend. As a species, college administrators must be the most prolific in history, for they seem to multiply like rabbits. As new administrative positions are established, new secretaries are hired, new Xerox machines purchased, and, of course, new committees organized to study the problem and issue reports to be filed away for future reference. Currently, there seems to be an administrative infatuation with computers. As a "computer illiterate," I admire and respect those proficient in BASIC, FORTRAN, PASCAL, and COBOL, but is it really essential to the academic integrity of a college to outpace its sister institutions in the amount of "state of the art" equipment housed on campus? The groves of academe are rapidly becoming inundated with mainline systems, terminals, modems, software, hardware, logos, passwords, bytes, high resolution monitors, keyboards, floppy discs, magnetic tapes, and systems analysts, and present-day communications apparently cannot survive without the words interface, input, and output. All of this is done in the name of efficiency. In the meantime, faculty members scavenge waste paper baskets for chalk and paper clips, library orders remain unfilled, and academic vacancies are left unfilled.

Many colleges also emphasize faculty research and publication to the detriment of teaching. The new merit raise policies adopted by many of Louisiana's colleges have generated an intense and highly competitive scramble among faculty members to get books and articles published. This is commendable, since research and publication are integral parts of our jobs, but the current policies seem to contend that a scholar who writes a monograph on a topic of interest to perhaps a dozen colleagues makes a greater contribution to knowledge than the instructor teaching a survey course to a hundred students. Faculty members now demand released time, higher salaries, travel funds, and other amenities to do research, and the further removed they are from the classroom, the greater their material rewards. Distinguished professorships and endowed chairs invariably go to those faculty members who spend the least amount of their time in teaching. Those younger members of our profession, required to teach the most difficult sections with the greatest number of students, now bide their time and bite their fingernails while they wait the day when the decision is rendered on whether or not they receive tenure, hoping in the meantime that a sufficient number of us older faculty members will suffer coronary thromboses to open up the tenured positions. By the time they attain that cherished goal, they have endured the "publish or perish" marathon, and they enter into their coveted associate professorships with less and greyer hair and more twitches and rumblings in their gastrointestinal tracts than they deserve.

In an ABC News special television program about American schools, a high school senior in California remarked: "The Revolutionary War. That's over. That's past. I want to know what's going to happen to us." Another high school senior proudly exclaimed: "I don't remember the last book I read. I rarely read books unless they're Harlequin romances."[33] Surely we can do better. The Gaston Troxclairs of our state and our country deserve it.

## Notes for "Why Can't Gaston Read?"

[1]The story of Gaston Troxclair, including all characters depicted therein, is fictional, and resemblance to actual individuals is intended.

[2]Current Louisiana law permits a student to graduate from high school with a 1.0 ("D) average, with 22 units of credit.

[3]*New Orleans Times-Picayune/States-Item*, April 27, 1984, December 19, 1984; *Hammond Daily Star*, February 11, 1985.

[4]Author's informal survey of over one hundred faculty members from all state colleges and universities.

[5]Author's compilation of questionnaire answers from survey courses in American History and Government, 1979-85.

[6]*New Orleans Times-Picayune/States-Item*, March 22, 1985.

[7]*U. S. News & World Report* (May 6, 1985), 16.

[8]*Baton Rouge Morning Advocate*, October 2, 1984.

[9]"Why Teachers Fail," *Newsweek* (September 24, 1984), 64.

[10]Ibid., 64-65.

[11]Ibid., 66-67; see also Neal Pierce, "Teacher Unions Taking Their Lumps," national syndicated column, week of April 7-13, 1985.

[12]Karen J. Winkler, "New Jersey's Schoolteacher Plan Alarms Schools of Education," *Chronicle of Higher Education*, 30 (1985): 18.

[13]Fred M. Hechinger, "The Fate of Pedagoguese," in *The Great Debate: Our Schools in Crisis*, edited by C. Winfield Scott, Clyde M. Hill, and Hobert W. Burns (Englewood Cliffs, N.J., 1959), 29-34; Charles E. Silberman, *Crisis in the Classroom* (New York, 1970), 373-520.

[14]State of Louisiana, State Department of Education, *Certification Requirements for Secondary School Teachers* (Baton Rouge, 1984). The State Department of Education requires only 33 semester hours of Social Studies for certification, although many colleges require more in their Social Studies curricula.

[15]Ibid.

[16]*USA Today*, November 13, 1984.

[17]ABC News Closeup, "Save Our Children: Save Our Schools," September 4, 1984.

[18]*New Orleans Times-Picayune/States-Item*, January 30, 1985.

[19]Author's survey of 287 public school teachers from twelve parishes in southwestern Louisiana.

[20]"Why Teachers Fail," 65.

[21]Ibid.

[22]*Baton Rouge Morning Advocate*, October 25, 1984.

[23]"Save Our Children: Save Our Schools."

[24]*Baton Rouge Morning Advocate*, April 30, 1985.

[25]Ibid., May 5, 1985.

[26]Ibid.

[27]William J. Bennett, *To Reclaim a Legacy* (Washington, 1984).

[28]Ibid., 8.

[29]Ibid., 9.

[30]Judith F. Gentry and James H. Dormon, "Higher Education and Historical Literacy in Louisiana: An Analysis and a Modest Proposal," introduction by Thomas D. Watson, *Louisiana History*, 24 (1983): 345-54.

[31]Report of the Study Group on the Conditions of Excellence in American Higher Education, "Involvement in Learning: Realizing the Potential of American Higher Education," reprinted in *Chronicle of Higher Education*, 30 (1984): 36.

[32]Ibid.

[33]"Save Our Children: Save Our Schools."

# SHREVEPORT GETS A MEDICAL SCHOOL: MEDICAL EDUCATION AND POLITICAL REALITY IN LOUISIANA, 1950-1969*

Brady M. Banta

In August 1994, the Louisiana State University School of Medicine in Shreveport matriculated its twenty-fifth freshman class. That institutional milestone provides an appropriate venue for a retrospective look at the individuals and events that brought the school into existence. Dr. Edgar Hull ranks foremost among the individuals responsible for the school's establishment. Without his visionary leadership, quiet persuasiveness, and the respect that he commanded throughout Louisiana's medical community, the school would not have opened.[1] Hull's notable efforts, however, do not constitute the entire story. A dedicated cadre of Shreveport doctors and the political guidance provided by J. Bennett Johnston, Jr., and John J. McKeithen also deserve mention, for the movement to establish the medical school involved a difficult political campaign that took twenty years to reach fruition.

Dr. Joseph E. Holoubek has suggested that by mid-twentieth century Shreveport was ideally suited for the opening of a medical school.[2] Already something of a regional medical center, Shreveport boasted of five private general hospitals, a Veterans Administration hospital, and the state's second largest charity hospital. Moreover, the city was home to numerous physicians and surgeons who had established private practices in Shreveport upon conclusion of their military service during World War II.[3]

The spark that ignited Shreveport's drive to obtain a medical school occurred in 1950. Having outgrown its 1920s facility, Shreveport had secured construction of a state-of-the-art, 800-bed Charity Hospital.[4] On April 4, 1950, Dr. W. E. Reid, Shreveport Charity's superintendent, proposed to the Shreveport Medical Society that the legislature be asked to appropriate funds for a medical school at the hospital. The medical society referred Reid's proposal to its board of directors.[5] While some board members questioned the need

*First published in *Louisiana History*, 37 (1996): 435-56. Reprinted with the kind permission of the author and the Louisiana Historical Association.

for an additional medical school in Louisiana, the board tentatively agreed to support the proposed school, as long as the Louisiana State University (LSU) Medical School in New Orleans was not adversely impacted.[6]

The medical society's officers subsequently met with Dr. Reid and the Caddo Parish legislative delegation to discuss the prospects of enabling legislation for the proposed medical school. Reid's medical school project emerged from this meeting with supplementary proposals for dental and pharmacy schools. The supplementary proposals appear to have been added to gain a wider base of support, since the only pharmacy and dental schools in Louisiana were both private and located in New Orleans.[7]

Louisiana's political realities forced the medical school's proponents to adopt a more conservative approach in the state legislature. House Concurrent Resolution 12, introduced on May 25, asserted that Louisiana had an acute shortage of doctors, dentists, and pharmacists, particularly in rural areas. Moreover, the state's existing professional schools, all located in New Orleans, were filled to capacity. The resolution asked the governor to appoint a twenty-member committee to investigate the "necessity and advisability" of establishing new state-funded medical training facilities.[8] The resolution moved smoothly through the legislature, but Governor Earl Long ignored it.[9]

Following the ignominious demise of House Concurrent Resolution 12, the campaign for a medical school in Shreveport lay dormant for several years. The crusade was resuscitated on May 5, 1955, at a meeting of the visiting staff of the Confederate Memorial Medical Center, Shreveport's new charity hospital.[10] Addressing the assembled doctors, Dr. Edgar Hull, assistant dean of the Louisiana State University School of Medicine, touted Confederate Memorial as an ideal site for a postgraduate medical education center.[11]

Although the idea had been discussed, at least informally, by the medical school's administrators and some local doctors for several years, Hull's public comments initiated a flurry of activity. The following evening, the Fourth District Medical Society—the regional affiliate of the Louisiana State Medical Society for Northwest Louisiana—assembled to discuss the postgraduate school concept with area legislators. Proponents of the postgraduate school contended that it could be built for approximately two million dollars. Aside from a small support staff of scientists and administrators, the visiting physicians at Confederate Memorial would serve as the proposed school's faculty. This organizational plan was appended to the state government's annual expenses for operating the postgraduate school to a maximum of $250,000. Following a lengthy discussion, the society adopted a resolution endorsing the postgraduate school concept. Legislative support was soon forthcoming, as Senator Charles E. Tooke of Shreveport, chairman of the state's Senate Finance Committee, assured the Shreveport doctors that a "worthwhile" project like this one would get state funding.[12]

Senator Tooke subsequently introduced the necessary legislation during the legislative fiscal session then underway in Baton Rouge. Contending that his bill was fiscal because it provided funds to expand the LSU Medical School, the senator proposed the issuance of

$7 million worth of bonds. Approximately $4.8 million would be used to redeem Confederate Memorial Medical Center construction bonds. The remaining money would fund the postgraduate medical school as well as the thoracic surgery, alcoholic, and psychiatric units at Confederate Memorial.[13]

Less than one week later, the LSU Board of Supervisors convened in Baton Rouge for its regular annual meeting. During a discussion of the postgraduate medical school, university president Gen. Troy Middleton indicated that the New Orleans medical school administrators believed that proposed provision of "the necessary few doctors" to operate the facility was feasible. Having received this limited endorsement, the board gave its support to that portion of Tooke's bill that proposed funding the postgraduate medical school.[14]

On the same day that the LSU Board of Supervisors endorsed Tooke's proposal, the senate referred the Shreveport senator's bill to the Committee on Finance. The measure progressed no farther.[15] Although eventually forced to abandon the senate version of the bill, Tooke continued to support the proposed medical school project. Indeed, on May 29, the Committee on Finance, which Tooke chaired, returned House Bill 68 to the senate floor with amendments. The committee had transformed a bill to appropriate $1,134,370.00 for capital outlay projects at Charity Hospital in New Orleans into a measure authorizing the Louisiana State Building Authority to issue $3,025,000.00 in bonds to "provide for the construction, expansion, improvement and repair of certain charitable institutions of the State. . . ."[16] Moreover, the amended bill "authorized and directed" the building authority to spend up to $1,890,000 of the proceeds from bond sales on the Confederate Memorial Medical Center.[17]

On May 31, the senate approved House Bill 68, as amended, by a vote of 31 to 1.[18] Following negotiations to reconcile differences with the senate version, the house approved the amended bill by a vote of 54 to 18.[19] Governor Robert F. Kennon subsequently approved the measure, now designated Act 30 of 1955.[20] The pace at which this occurred was little short of remarkable. In just over one month enough legislators had been convinced, cajoled, or coerced by Shreveport physicians and their political allies to obtain the State of Louisiana's pledge to provide almost $1.9 million for a post-graduate medical school. The school was to be affiliated with Louisiana State University and to be built adjacent to the Confederate Memorial Medical Center.

With the signing of Act 30, Shreveport-area physicians, working through the Shreveport Medical Society, focused their attention on planning and designing a postgraduate facility. A building committee appointed by Dr. Charles L. Black, president of the Visiting Staff of the Confederate Memorial Medical Center, assumed a leadership role in this phase of the school's development. After designating Dr. Joe E. Holoubek as chairman, Black directed the committee to work in close cooperation with the hospital's board of directors and officials from LSU's School of Medicine.[21]

The committee studied existing postgraduate medical programs and worked with local architects on design concepts throughout the summer of 1955. By late September, the committee members were in agreement that the postgraduate facility at the University of Kansas Medical Center was most nearly like the facility they envisioned for Shreveport.[22] By late November, members of the building committee also reached a consensus regarding the school's location, having determined that the postgraduate facility should not be physically attached to Confederate Memorial Hospital because the two facilities answered to different administrative boards.[23]

The planning of the postgraduate facility was threatened in December by the stunning first-primary gubernatorial triumph of Earl Long, who had opposed establishment of a Shreveport medical school five years earlier. During the campaign, Long had pledged that there would "be no bond issues . . . without submission to the people."[24] This statement was interpreted by medical school supporters as a threat to the project because Act 30 of 1955 did not require voter approval before the State Building Authority sold bonds to finance construction.

A sense of urgency consequently pervaded the building committee. On December 27, Dr. T. J. Smith reported to Confederate Memorial's board of directors that architectural plans for the postgraduate school would not be complete until at least July. Joe Holoubek nevertheless suggested that the facility's cornerstone be laid before Governor Kennon left office in April. The board declined to endorse this proposal.[25]

Undeterred by this setback, concerned supporters of the medical school continued to recommend accelerated construction at subsequent meetings of Confederate Memorial's board of directors. At a special meeting convened on January 13, 1956, project architect Sam Wiener suggested that the State Building Authority be asked to award bids for foundation construction. Wiener indicated that he and his associates would complete detailed construction plans while the foundation was being laid. The board took no immediate action, but requested that Wiener have the foundation plans ready for consideration at the February 28 meeting.[26]

At the February meeting, T. J. Smith reported that the building committee proposed the need to prioritize the three projects sanctioned by Act 30 of 1955 because the legislature had not authorized sufficient funding to complete the project as originally envisioned. The project rankings were as follows: first, the postgraduate medical school; second, the thoracic surgery facility; and third, an alcoholic-psychiatry unit located in the thoracic surgery facility. Sam Weiner insisted that formal designation of the postgraduate medical facility as the top priority was necessary because the State Building Authority was reluctant to authorize construction, even foundation work, unless money was available to complete the project. The board ultimately adopted a resolution requesting that the State Building Authority adopt the construction priorities suggested by the building committee. The hospital directors also recommended that the State Building Authority award contracts for the postgraduate medical school in two stages: foundation and superstructure.[27]

The State Building Authority soon honored the Confederate Memorial board's requests, and by the end of April, it awarded a contract for construction of the postgraduate medical school's foundation.[28]

Meanwhile, the project's proponents prepared to celebrate their achievement. They decided to hold a groundbreaking ceremony on April 22 to coincide with the opening day of Medical Education Week.[29] Utilizing a small appropriation provided by the Shreveport Medical Society, the building committee mailed invitations to more than 1,000 doctors throughout the Ark-La-Tex region and to the deans of medical schools throughout the South. Legislators from northwestern Louisiana, members of the LSU Board of Supervisors, Congressman Overton Brooks, Senator Russell Long, LSU President Troy Middleton, Governor Robert Kennon, and Governor-elect Earl Long were also asked to attend.[30]

On the afternoon of April 22, J. E. Smitherman of Shreveport, a member of the LSU Board of Supervisors, had the honor of turning the first spadeful of dirt at the construction site. In his keynote address, Dr. William Frye, dean of the LSU School of Medicine, stressed the importance of continuing medical education and the contribution that this teaching and research center would make to Louisiana and the nation. It had the potential, Frye contended, to "be a model . . . helping to solve the problems of medicine and medical care in the future."[31]

Governor Kennon was represented at the groundbreaking ceremony by his executive assistant, Wilburn Lunn, but the most conspicuous absentees were General Middleton and Governor-elect Long. The conspicuous absences of these key officials, and the continuing political opposition that they signaled, boded ill for the medical facility's development.

Shreveport physicians had done nothing to ingratiate themselves with Earl Long by hurriedly breaking ground only three weeks before he took office. Indeed, they purposely scheduled the ceremony to occur while Robert Kennon, who had been supportive of their effort, was still governor. They hoped that Long, upon becoming governor, would find it politically unwise to cancel a project that was already under construction.[32] But, as John McKeithen observed in a recent interview, "They didn't know Mister Earl!"[33]

During the first months of his administration, Long did not target the postgraduate school directly, but his actions hinted that trouble loomed ahead. According to Michael Kurtz and Morgan Peoples, Earl Long brought to the 1956 legislative session a package of tax increases that would be needed to fund a wide-ranging program of social programs and capital improvements. He found, however, that the legislators were disinclined to raise taxes, and despite the political leverage at his disposal he could not avoid a political bequest from the Kennon administration—the constitutional requirement that tax increases be approved by a two-thirds majority in each house.

Despite this handicap, Earl Long was able to expand the state's spending for social services because existing tax levies—especially those borne by oil and gas interests—generated steadily increasing revenues between 1956 and 1960. Long could sustain this expansion of social services only by maintaining strict controls over other areas of state spending and, as a rule, the governor opposed the issuance of bonds to fund state capital improvement projects, such as the Shreveport medical school.[34]

Other developments during the summer and fall of 1956 proved equally troublesome for supporters of the medical school. The first of these involved Long's selection of a new superintendent for the Confederate Memorial Medical Center. Kennon had signed legislation making the superintendent an appointee of the hospital's board of directors, but, before taking office, Governor Long had announced his intention to remove Superintendent Dr. Edgar Galloway.[35] Unable to force the existing board of directors to fire Galloway, Long pushed through the 1956 legislative session a measure that increased the size of the board. Long then exercised his appointment authority, and the newly seated board relieved Galloway of his duties, naming Dr. Walter Harmon as the new superintendent.[36] Although Holoubek believes that this squabble over the superintendency had no direct bearing on the developing postgraduate medical school controversy, Governor Long's actions certainly subverted the effort to establish the postgraduate facility. The visiting staff at Confederate Memorial steadfastly resisted his imposition of new leadership at the hospital,[37] and Long surely recognized that the leading proponents of the postgraduate medical school were also prominent members of the visiting staff.

During the summer of 1956, while local attention was focused on Earl Long's administrative appointments at Confederate Memorial hospital, work had continued on the postgraduate medical school. The foundation was completed while the building committee reviewed and revised plans for the superstructure.[38] Meanwhile, LSU administrators subjected the project to an intensive evaluation. An analysis of this study and recommendations based upon it were presented to the LSU Board of Supervisors at its October 1956 meeting by the board's Special Medical School Committee.[39] The administrators's report concluded that "postgraduate education in Medicine can be carried on best and most economically under the auspices of the existing School of Medicine rather than by establishment of a separate School of Postgraduate Medicine."[40]

Financial concerns appear to have prompted this recommendation. Proponents of the postgraduate school assumed that the administrative costs and the salaries of the three or four full-time staff scientists would be provided by the university.[41] The Special Medical School Committee estimated that the initial annual budget for these services would be $186,780. Moreover, they cautioned that it was probable that some of the staff's research would end up being underwritten by the university.[42]

Although the board did not act on this report, it was clear that LSU administrators wanted to avoid any financial obligation to the postgraduate medical school. Moreover, General Middleton wanted to disassociate the university from any request to the legislature for funds to operate the facility. He feared that an appropriation for the postgraduate school would jeopardize legislative funding of the university's budget.[43]

It was also obvious that his exclusion from the planning process had irritated General Middleton. The LSU president's aggravation was symptomatic of more than a bruised ego. Political intervention by special interest groups in recent years had adversely impacted the university's development, as, for example, when the state legislature diverted funds from new library construction to erection of a 10,000-seat addition to Tiger Stadium.[44]

General Middleton's outspoken opposition to the postgraduate school prompted Governor Long to question publicly the wisdom of expending the remaining construction funds on a facility that the university did not wish to support.[45] State Treasurer A. P. Tugwell, acting in his capacity as head of the State Building Authority, consequently withdrew the call for bids to construct the Shreveport facility.[46]

The suspension of bids sparked a flurry of protests from northwestern Louisiana legislators and doctors.[47] These protests only served to harden the governor's opposition to the project.[48] An ignominious end to the postgraduate medical school project came during the legislature's 1958 regular session. In what Representative Jasper K. Smith labeled a "dirty Irish trick," Long's floor leaders obtained legislative approval for a bill transferring to the general fund unexpended money dedicated to the postgraduate school project.[49]

The medical school project lay dormant in the wake of the "dirty Irish trick." Meanwhile, the LSU Medical School's Department of Postgraduate Medicine regularly offered continuing education programs in Shreveport, and the Confederate Memorial Medical Center continued to train doctors in its intern and residency programs. By the early 1960s, however, at least one of these residency training programs faced loss of accreditation, prompting the executive committee of the visiting staff to reassess Confederate Memorial's future as a teaching facility.[50]

The visiting staff consequently asked Dr. Edgar Hull to assess the hospital's relationship with the LSU Medical School. Hull not only offered encouragement and recommendations regarding Confederate Memorial's graduate training programs, but he also urged the Shreveport doctors to consider opening a medical school. In his estimation, the time was ripe, the need existed, and Shreveport had the requisite medical infrastructure.[51]

Hull's response resurrected the medical school project. On November 11, 1963, board president Charles Black informed the directors of the Shreveport Medical Society that he had appointed a special committee to coordinate the renewed effort to obtain a medical school for Shreveport. This special committee, chaired by Holoubek, consisted primarily of individuals who had served on the building committee for the postgraduate medical school.[52]

The timing could hardly have been better as the committee's establishment coincided with the hotly contested second gubernatorial primary campaign between DeLesseps Morrison and John McKeithen. Gubernatorial indifference and opposition had frustrated previous efforts to establish a medical school in Shreveport, but this time both candidates endorsed the medical school project.[53]

In sharp contrast to their inactivity during the general elections of 1951 and 1955, the Shreveport doctors demonstrated considerable political savvy in ingratiating themselves with the two leading 1963 gubernatorial candidates. The committee sought to bolster political support for the project by soliciting endorsements from business and civic organizations.[54] Committee members also invited area representatives and senators to a special meeting of the Shreveport Medical Society on April 8 to discuss the medical school project. Holoubek told the legislators that the country's worsening shortage of doctors could be alleviated only through establishment of new medical schools. Shreveport, he contended, was "the logical place for another medical school in Louisiana. . . ."[55] While the legislators were receptive, they were more interested in a legislative package authorizing the establishment of junior college branches of LSU and Southern in Shreveport. The legislators were reluctant, therefore, to champion the medical school proposal for fear that it might compromise the junior college campaign.[56] Circumstances, however, forced the northwestern Louisiana delegation to take action regarding the medical school during the 1964 legislative session.[57]

During the session there had been speculation that Monroe, Lafayette, and Baton Rouge would attempt to secure a medical school.[58] The first tangible manifestation of these interests came when Representatives Lawrence Gibbs and George Wood introduced a resolution requesting that the Louisiana Department of Hospitals study the need for a medical school at Northeast Louisiana State College in Monroe. Approved by the house and signed by the speaker, the measure became House Resolution 5.[59] The Gibbs-Wood Resolution faded into obscurity, however, with the approval of House Concurrent Resolution 60. Introduced by Representative J. Bennett Johnston, Jr., of Shreveport, it authorized the Louisiana State Medical Society to study the need for another medical school and to determine the best location for the school. The resolution also asked the society to report its findings to the next legislative session.[60]

Although the legislature took no direct action, the campaign to establish a medical school in Shreveport accelerated in 1964. During the legislative session, Governor John McKeithen recounted later, it seemed that every legislator "wanted a medical school or dental school in his backyard."[61] True to his Longite heritage, McKeithen was receptive to the idea of state construction projects. But, unfamiliar with the need to expand the state's medical education facilities, the governor turned to his brother, Dr. A. E. McKeithen of Hodge, Louisiana, for advice. His brother, a supporter of the proposal to build a medical school in Shreveport, suggested that the governor consult Dr. Edgar Hull.

Following his brother's advice, McKeithen met with Hull in early July 1964. The principal topic of their conversation was the medical school proposal. Asked by the governor if Louisiana needed a third medical school, Hull responded that it would "within a very few years." When asked where it should be built, without equivocation Hull suggested Shreveport.[62] Upon receiving Hull's pledge to oversee the school's establishment, the governor said: "Fine! We'll build it."[63]

Armed with Governor McKeithen's endorsement, proponents of the Shreveport medical school project had good reason for optimism. The outlook grew even brighter when the House of Delegates of the Louisiana State Medical Society, meeting in annual convention in New Orleans on May 3-5, 1965, officially recommended the establishment of a medical school in Shreveport.[64] Although the House of Delegates maintained that their recommendation was based upon a study conducted by the state medical society, it actually evolved from data gathered and analyzed by the Study Committee for the Development of a Medical School in Shreveport, a special committee of the Shreveport Medical Society chaired by Dr. Joseph Holoubek.[65]

Having secured the support of the state medical society and the governor, Shreveporters refined their strategy for the upcoming legislative session—once again demonstrating a political acumen lacking in their previous campaigns. Many Shreveport physicians initially wanted the medical school to be independent of LSU, but allied with Confederate Memorial Medical Center. This preference stemmed from LSU's refusal to absorb the postgraduate school's operating costs. To achieve such independence, the bill establishing the school would have to pass both houses of the legislature by a two-thirds majority. If, however, the school were part of LSU, the enabling legislation would need only a simple majority in each house for passage. Aware that interests in other parts of the state coveted this political plum, the medical school supporters sacrificed autonomy.[66]

As introduced by J. Bennett Johnston, House Bill 47 proposed establishment of a medical school in Shreveport as part of the Louisiana State University system and an appropriation of $10,000 to cover the costs of initial planning.[67] The legislative battle commenced on May 25 at a House Appropriations Committee hearing. Accompanied by a large delegation of Shreveport-area doctors, businessmen, educators, and civic leaders, Edgar Hull and Joseph Holoubek repeated the now well worn arguments that Louisiana needed another medical school and that Shreveport was the logical location. The committee took the measure under advisement, but later gave it a favorable report by a six-to-five vote.[68]

The decisive confrontation occurred when the bill came up for final consideration in the house. Lawrence Gibbs, still championing a medical school for Monroe, argued that more time was needed to study the school's location. Jess McLain of St. Tammany protested that Shreveport had received two junior colleges the previous year. These facilities, he maintained, were more than sufficient investment in a parish that had voted Republican in the previous gubernatorial election. Salvador Anzelmo of Orleans Parish and Gordon Causey of Tangipahoa insisted that the state simply could not afford another medical school.

Despite this opposition, the house approved Bill 47 by a vote of 53 to 47. The bill's supporters attributed the victory to Representative Robert Munson of Rapides Parish, a McKeithen floor leader, who asked to be listed as a co-author.[69] Administration support was decisive, but the outcome was never really in doubt. Indeed, recalling the events of that day years later, the governor indicated that he "could of and would of" secured any number of votes needed for passage.[70]

The bill's course through the senate was considerably smoother, the margin of victory being 28 to 9. Garland Bonin of Lafayette and J. D. DeBlieux of Baton Rouge spoke against the bill. Neither disputed the need for another medical school, but both maintained that the state could not afford it. As in the house, key support came from administration floor leader Jamar Adcock of Monroe. Adcock maintained that he bowed to no one in his support of Northeast Louisiana State College, but, he argued, the school's president had given no indication that his institution wanted the medical school. Give Northeast something they can handle, Adcock continued. Awarding it the medical school would be like a "dog chasing a car—they wouldn't know what to do with it if they got it."[71]

Governor McKeithen subsequently signed the bill into law as Act 2 of 1965.[72] The medical school had been created, but no money had been provided for its construction or operation. In addition, although the chief administrators of the medical school, Drs. William Frye and Edgar Hull, were both advocates of the project, neither the LSU president nor the board of supervisors regarded the new medical school as a priority. The apathy of the LSU president and governing board evidently did not concern those championing the medical school project. This cadre of Shreveport physicians shared the feeling that the LSU administrators in Baton Rouge underestimated their resolve, and they believed, according to Holoubek, "that LSU would be happy to get a whole new campus. . . ."[73]

After the signing of Act 2, the Medical School Development Committee of the Shreveport Medical Society began to coordinate planning for the new school's construction and operation. In the summer of 1965, as a first step in this process, twelve local doctors made fact-finding visits to nineteen recently opened or planned medical schools at their own expense.[74] Drawing upon data they gathered, Sam Wiener, the architect working with the Medical School Development Committee, prepared a preliminary construction cost projection. Basing his calculations on a four-year medical school with an enrollment of 250 students, Wiener estimated that it would cost $10.1 million to construct an eight-story, 300,000-square-foot building.[75]

Meanwhile, preparations were made for a delegation from LSU to tour the facilities at Confederate Memorial and to discuss plans for the medical school.[76] On October 20, 1965, Dr. John Hunter, the university president; Dr. Grover Murray, the university vice president; and Drs. William Frye and Edgar Hull from the LSU Medical Center visited Confederate Memorial, met its administrators and medical staff, and attended as honored guests a luncheon held to demonstrate that the project had overwhelming local support. Hunter told those assembled in the Lake Room of the Captain Shreve Hotel that he was optimistic regarding the project; but, he cautioned, there "is the money question."[77]

After the luncheon, the LSU delegation discussed the project with the Medical School Development Committee, local legislators, and representatives of the Shreveport Chamber of Commerce. This was the first time that LSU administrators other than Dr. Hull participated in the planning process. Dr. Hunter focused on the budget. While Wiener had estimated the cost of construction at approximately $10 million, Hunter considered that figure unreasonably low. Indeed, he looked upon that figure as the state's contribution, making the total cost of construction, assuming that the project qualified for a two-to-one federal matching grant, approximately $30 million. Representative J. Bennett Johnston reacted with dismay, and he expressed concern over the governor's continued support of a project that costly.[78]

At the conclusion of these discussions, all in attendance agreed that Governor McKeithen should be consulted soon regarding the administration's support for legislation to fund construction of the medical school. In the interim Representative Johnston drafted a plan to finance the state's share of the construction costs through the sale of bonds backed by a portion of the state's ad valorem tax. Johnston proposed the issuance of $5 million in bonds over the next five years, to be followed by another five-year, $5 million issuance if necessary. Upon being assured that State Treasurer Tugwell and New York bond attorneys had approved the plan, Governor McKeithen heartily endorsed it. Indeed, he told the school's proponents that he foresaw no difficulty getting this package through the legislature. "We'll just raise the $5 million and start building that medical school."[79]

When the legislature convened in May 1966, Representative Johnston introduced a funding bill. Despite the governor's endorsement of the bond issuance, the Legislative Action Committee of Shreveport Chamber of Commerce coordinated an extensive lobbying campaign throughout the spring. Because of the closeness of the house vote on Act 2 of 1965, the medical school proponents determined that neither misunderstanding nor inadequate preparation would jeopardize the funding bill. The committee distributed to every legislator a letter over Chancellor William Frye's signature urging support for Johnston's bill. Similar letters were sent to doctors throughout the state with the request that they lobby their representatives and senators to support the funding legislation.[80] Whether or not its success is attributable to this grassroots campaign, Johnston's funding bill, House Bill 148, moved through the legislature virtually unopposed.[81] Governor McKeithen signed the measure into law as Act 12 of 1966.[82]

Underlying Act 12 was the assumption that the bond revenue would be used to apply for federal matching funds. Upon studying the statute, the procedures for issuing the bonds it authorized, and the rules governing the matching fund programs, attorneys for the LSU Board of Supervisors recommended that the university seek authorization to issue $10 million in bonds immediately. The attorneys contended, and the board of supervisors agreed, that this change would increase the likelihood that the federal matching funds would be awarded.[83]

Responding to this suggestion, Governor McKeithen included a proposal to accelerate the issuance of the bonds in his twenty-one-item call for a special legislative session to convene in December.[84] Following its introduction by Representative Johnston, the bill to reauthorize and consolidate the $10 million bond issue moved through both houses without opposition and became Act 16 of the Extraordinary Session of 1966.[85] The last impediment to the funding of the school appeared to have been removed.

Nearly three years later, the LSU School of Medicine in Shreveport welcomed its inaugural class of thirty-two students to its temporary quarters at the Veterans Administration hospital. The thirty-three months between the special session of 1966 and the opening of the medical school, however, had proved difficult for Dr. Edgar Hull, the school's first dean, and his administrative staff as they struggled to get the school opened and to begin construction of a permanent facility. A lack of money was central to virtually every major problem they confronted.

The legislature had mandated the establishment of the medical school and provided a mechanism for financing its construction, but no money was appropriated for planning and development. These funds had to be obtained from the LSU operating budget. Unfortunately for the Shreveport facility, Dr. Hull requested money to start the Shreveport medical school at the same time that the LSU Board of Supervisors and the system's administrators were struggling to enhance the Baton Rouge campus, to open a school of dentistry in New Orleans, and to support recently opened campuses in New Orleans, Alexandria, Eunice, and Shreveport.

It is not really surprising, therefore, that just seven months before the Shreveport medical school opened, the board of supervisors was debating its ability to operate the institution. Expressing his own personal frustration, but probably also accurately reflecting the thoughts of many of his colleagues on the board, Carlos Spaht said: "We didn't ask for that school in Shreveport. The legislature gave us the school and told us to operate it. . . ."[86] Certainly that sentiment could have been applied to many, if not most, of the other LSU branches established in the late 1950s and early 1960s. It also speaks volumes about the evolution of Louisiana's system of higher education.

Notes for "Shreveport Gets a Medical School: Medical Education and Political Reality in Louisiana, 1950-1969"

[1]Edgar Hull was a faculty member in the Department of Medicine when the Louisiana State University School of Medicine opened in 1931. A gifted clinician and internist, Dr. Hull served for many years as the Chair of the Department of Medicine and eventually became the school's assistant dean. During the thirty-five years that he stayed on the full-time faculty of the school of medicine in New Orleans he earned the respect and admiration of students, colleagues, and associates. By the time he assumed the deanship at the Louisiana State University School of Medicine in Shreveport, he was a living legend in Louisiana medicine.

[2]"Medicine in Small Doses." Videotaped interview of Dr. Joseph E. Holoubek by Dr. Leonard Goldman, Director, Continuing Medical Education, LSU School of Medicine in Shreveport. c. 1979. Louisiana State University Medical Center, Shreveport Archives; hereinafter cited as LSUMC-S Archives.

[3]Interview with Dr. Joseph E. Holoubek, April 3, 1992, LSUMC-S Archives, hereinafter cited as Holoubek Interview (with date).

[4]A state-funded charity hospital had existed in Shreveport since 1876. The first element of the current hospital had been constructed in 1903. Despite renovation and expansion during the 1920s and 1930s, by the early 1940s state hospital officials recognized that the facility was no longer adequate. *Shreveport Times*,

June 1, 1976; Elizabeth Wisner, *Public Welfare Administration in Louisiana*, Social Service Monograph Series, No. 11 (Chicago, 1930), 70 and 74-75; *Shreveport Journal*, June 2, 1953.

[5]Minutes. Shreveport Medical Society Meeting, April 4, 1950, Shreveport Medical Society Records, LSUMC-S Archives.

[6]*The Bulletin of the Shreveport Medical Society*, 1 (1950): 16.

[7]*Shreveport Times*, April 23, 1950.

[8]*Calendar of the House of Representatives of the State of Louisiana at the Fifteenth Regular Session of the Legislature Under the Constitution of 1921. Ending July 6, 1950*, 464, hereinafter cited as *House Calendar* (with appropriate year and/or session).

[9]Ibid.; *Senate Calendar 1950 of the State of Louisiana. Fifteenth Regular Session of the Legislature under the Constitution of 1921. Ending July 6, 1950*, 555, hereinafter cited as *Senate Calendar* (with appropriate year and/or session). The author was unable to find an explanation for the governor's inaction. It may be, however, that even though construction of the new hospital began in 1949, during Long's administration, it had been proposed, authorized, and designed during the Davis administration. Thus, the project was more closely identified with the governor's political opponents.

[10]The name Confederate Memorial Medical Center acknowledges the funding source for the hospital's construction. A surplus accumulating in the state's Confederate Veterans Pension Fund, supported by a three-quarter mill property tax, was used to secure bonds issued to finance the project. *Shreveport Journal*, June 2, 1953.

[11]*Shreveport Times*, May 7, 1955. [12]Ibid.

[13]Ibid., May 11, 18, 1955; *Baton Rouge Morning Advocate*, May 18. 1955. Joining Tooke in sponsoring this measure were Senators John Doles of Plain Dealing, B.H. Rogers of Grand Cane, and Sylvan Friedman of Natchitoches.

[14]Minutes of Regular Annual Meeting of the Board of Supervisors May 23, 1955, *Minutes. Board of Supervisors Louisiana State University*, 17:83, Board of Supervisors Records, University Archives, Louisiana State University Libraries, Baton Rouge.

[15]*Senate Calendar, 1955*, 5. What happened is not in the record, but it is conceivable that Tooke came to realize that he could not muster the votes needed for passage.

[16]*Official Journal of the Proceedings of the House of Representatives of the State of Louisiana at the Eighteenth Regular Session of the Legislature under the Adoption of the Constitution of 1921; Begun and Held in the City of Baton Rouge, May 9, 1955*, 354, hereinafter cited as *House Journal* (with appropriate year and/or session); *Official Journal of the Proceedings of The Senate of the State of Louisiana at the Eighteenth Regular Session of the Legislature Under the Adoption of the Constitution of 1921; Begun and Held in the City of Baton Rouge, May 9, 1955*, 270-71, hereinafter cited as *Senate Journal* (with appropriate year and/or session); *Shreveport Times*, May 30, 1955.

[17]*Senate Journal 1955*, 271.

[18]Ibid., 363-64. The lone dissenting vote came from Senator B.H. Rogers of Grand Cane, one of the co-sponsors of Senate Bill 2. Rogers indicated that he supported the postgraduate medical school, but that he objected to financing its construction through the sale of bonds. *Shreveport Times*, June 1, 1955.

[19]*House Journal 1955*, 708-9.

[20]*State of Louisiana Acts of the Legislature Regular Session 1955*, 30-33, hereinafter cited as *Acts of Louisiana* (with appropriate year and/or session).

[21]Charles L. Black, M.D., President, Visiting Staff to Dear Doctors, June 24, 1955, Box 1, folder 1, Joseph E. Holoubek Papers, LSUMC-S Archives, hereinafter cited as Holoubek Papers. Holoubek was an excellent choice for this responsibility. His interest in developing Shreveport as a center of medical education dated from the late 1940s and stemmed in no small part from a strong personal friendship with and professional respect for Dr. Edgar Hull. Moreover, Holoubek brought to this project levels of commitment and energy that were unsurpassed.

[22]Minutes of the Board of Directors Meeting Confederate Memorial Medical Center, September 27, 1955, 2, Confederate Memorial Medical Center Records, LSUMC-S Archives, hereinafter cited as CMMC Board Minutes (with appropriate date and page). Not only did the University of Kansas Medical Center provide the physical and operational model for the postgraduate medical school, it and the University of Pennsylvania were the conceptual models for the continuing medical education program that Edgar Hull wanted to establish in Shreveport. Edgar Hull to Herbert Tucker, July 23, 1956, Personal Correspondence 1956-57, Edgar Hull Papers, LSUMC-S Archives.

[23]CMMC Board Minutes, August 23, 1955, 5; CMMC Board Minutes, September 27, 1955, 2.

[24]*Shreveport Times*, November 25, 1955.

[25]CMMC Board Minutes, December 27, 1955, 2.

[26]CMMC Board Minutes, January 13, 1956, 4-5. [27]Ibid., February 28, 1956, 1-2.

[28]*Shreveport Times*, April 27, 1956.

[29]CMMC Board Minutes, March 27, 1956, 3; Wynton H. Carroll, M.D., to Dr. C.E. Boyd, President, Shreveport Medical Society, April 19, 1956, Shreveport Medical Society Records, Public Relations and Publicity 1956 file, LSUMC-S Archives.

[30]Minutes of the Meeting of the Shreveport Medical Society, April 3, 1956, LSUMC-S Archives; *Shreveport Times*, April 18, 1956.

[31]Program. Ground Breaking Ceremonies of the Louisiana State University Postgraduate School of Medicine. Shreveport, Louisiana, April 22, 1956, Box 1, folder 1, Holoubek Papers; *Shreveport Times*, April 23, 1956; *Shreveport Journal*, April 23, 1956.

[32]Holoubek Interview, April 3, 1992.

[33]Interview with John J. McKeithen, January 23, 1994, LSUMC-S Archives, hereinafter cited as McKeithen Interview (with date).

[34]Michael L. Kurtz and Morgan D. Peoples, *Earl K. Long: The Saga of Uncle Earl and Louisiana Politics* (Baton Rouge, 1990), 184-85.

[35]Whatever other motives may have influenced Long, clearly politics was a factor. Galloway previously served as superintendent of Shreveport Charity Hospital from 1940 to 1948, during the Sam Jones and Jimmie Davis administrations. Upon assuming the governor's office in 1948, Long replaced him. Galloway returned to Confederate Memorial in 1954 when Governor Robert Kennon found it necessary to replace his brother-in-law, Dr. C. S. Sentell, as hospital director. *Shreveport Times*, March 29, 1961.

[36]CMMC Board Minutes, September 27, 1956, 5.

[37]Holoubek Interview, April 3, 1992.

[38]CMMC Board Minutes, September 27, 1956, 2.

[39]Minutes of the Regular Meeting of the Board of Supervisors October 12-13, 1956. *Minutes. Board of Supervisors. Louisiana State University*, 18:9, Board of Supervisors Records, University Archives, Louisiana State University Libraries, Baton Rouge.

[40]Preliminary Report on the Organization and Administration of Postgraduate Training and Research in Shreveport, Louisiana, Supervised by the Louisiana State University School of Medicine. September 28, 1956, Board of Supervisors Records, University Archives, Louisiana State University Libraries, Baton Rouge, hereinafter cited as Preliminary Report.

[41]Holoubek Interview, April 3, 1992. [42]Preliminary Report, 8 and 11.

[43]*Shreveport Times*, March 1, 1957.

[44]Brady M. Banta, "Football, Fiefdoms, and Frustration: The Political Reality of Planning a New Library for Louisiana State University, 1941-1956," *LLA Bulletin*, 56 (1994): 188.

[45]*Shreveport Times*, February 27, 1957.

[46]Ibid., March 1, 1957; *Shreveport Journal*, March 1, 1957.

[47]*Shreveport Journal*, March 1, 7, and 8, 1957.

[48]*Shreveport Times*, May 11, 15, 1957; *Shreveport Journal*, May 13, 14, 1957.

[49]*Shreveport Times*, February 6, June 27, 1958.

[50]Minutes of the Executive Committee and Chiefs of Staff Confederate Memorial Medical Center, January 15, 1963, Confederate Memorial Medical Center Records, LSUMC-S Archives.

[51]Ibid.; Joseph E. Holoubek, "The Roots of the LSU School of Medicine in Shreveport," *North Louisiana Historical Association Journal*, 17 (1986): 118.

[52]Minutes. Board of Directors Meeting, Shreveport Medical Society, November 11, 1963. Shreveport Medical Society Records, LSUMC-S Archives.

[53]DeLesseps S. Morrison to Dr. Joseph E. Holoubek, December 28, 1963, Box 1, folder 2, Holoubek Papers; John J. McKeithen to Dr. James Eddy, January 4, 1964, Box 2-B, Shreveport Medical Society Records, LSUMC-S Archives.

[54]Joseph E. Holoubek to Dr. Edgar Hull, December 10, 1963, Box 1, folder 2, Holoubek Papers.

[55]James H. Eddy, Jr., to The Honorable Algie D. Brown, April 1, 1964, Box 1, folder 2, Holoubek Papers; *Shreveport Times*, April 9, 1964.

[56]Joseph E. Holoubek to Dr. Edgar Hull, April 22, 1964, Box 1, folder 2, Holoubek Papers; Joseph E. Holoubek to Dr. James Eddy, April 29, 1964, Box 1, folder 2, Holoubek Papers. According to Holoubek, the two campaigns "were almost entirely distinct" until the Caddo Parish legislative delegation, led in their effort by Representative Frank Fulco and Senator Jackson B. Davis, secured the junior colleges. The only local legislator willing to give the medical school project his unqualified support was first-term representative, J. Bennett Johnston, Jr. Holoubek Interview, May 1, 1992.

[57]Joseph E. Holoubek to Dr. Edgar Hull, June 8, 1964, Personal Correspondence 1962-66, Edgar Hull Papers, LSUMC-S Archives.

[58]Ibid.; James H. Eddy, Jr., M.D. to Dr. C. Grenes Cole, June 2, 1964, Box 2-A, Shreveport Medical Society Records, LSUMC-S Archives; Morley Hudson to Dr. James H. Eddy, Jr., June 15, 1964, Box 2-B, Shreveport Medical Society Records, LSUMC-S Archives; *Monroe Morning World*, May 21, 1964.

[59]*House Calendar 1964*, 316.

[60]Ibid., 343; J. Bennett Johnston, Jr., to Dr. C. E. Boyd, July 15, 1964, in *The Bulletin of the Shreveport Medical Society*, 15 (1964), 5.

[61]*Shreveport Times*, May 6, 1973.

[62]Ibid.; Edgar Hull to Dr. Joseph E. Holoubek, July 7, 1964, Box 1, folder 2, Holoubek Papers.

[63]McKeithen Interview, January 25, 1994.

[64]"Abstracted Minutes House of Delegates May, 1965," *The Journal of the Louisiana State Medical Society*, 117 (1965): 207.

[65]This committee sent questionnaires to every undergraduate college in the state that had a pre-medical curriculum. According to their analysis of the data, if in 1970 twenty-five percent of the pre-med students attending Louisiana colleges and universities applied for admission to the two medical schools in Louisiana, there would be three applicants for each available position. The questionnaires and a compilation of the data

are available in Box 1, folders 2 and 3, Holoubek Papers. See also Dr. Joseph E. Holoubek to Dr. Eugene St. Martin, January 15, 1965, Box 1, folder 2, Holoubek Papers; *Shreveport Times*, May 12, 1965.

[66]Graham W. Rogers to J. Bennett Johnston, Jr., May 15, 1965, Box 1, folder 1, Holoubek Papers.

[67]*Shreveport Times*, May 18, 1965; *1965 Legislative Calendar of the State of Louisiana Twenty-Eighth Regular Session of the Legislature under the Constitution of 1921*, 16, hereinafter cited as *Legislative Calendar* (with appropriate year and/or session).

[68]*Shreveport Journal*, May 24, 1965; *Shreveport Times*, May 26, 1965.

[69]*Shreveport Times*, June 1, 1965; *Shreveport Journal*, June 1, 1965; *Monroe Morning World*, June 1, 1965.

[70]McKeithen Interview, January 25, 1994.

[71]*Legislative Calendar, 1965*, 16; *Shreveport Journal*, June 2, 1965; *Shreveport Times*, June 3, 1965; *Monroe Morning World*, June 3, 1965.

[72]*Acts of Louisiana, 1965*, 3. [73]Holoubek Interview, April 10, 1992.

[74]"Medical School Committee Report," *The Bulletin of the Shreveport Medical Society*, 16 (1965): 7, 9. Also see Holoubek correspondence for June and July 1965 in Box 1, folder 3, Holoubek Papers.

[75]Samuel G. Wiener to Dr. Joseph E. Holoubek, September 3, 1965, Box 1, folder 3, Holoubek Papers.

[76]J. Bennett Johnston, Jr., to Dr. Joseph E. Holoubek, September 1, 1965, Joseph E. Holoubek to Dr. William Frye, October 1, 1965, and Joseph E. Holoubek to Dick Thevenot, October 1, 1965, all in Box 1, folder 3, Holoubek Papers; *Minutes. Board of Directors Meeting. Shreveport Chamber of Commerce. September 30, 1965*, 2, film 23, reel 4, Archives and Special Collections, Noel Memorial Library, Louisiana State University in Shreveport.

[77]*Shreveport Journal*, October 20, 21, 1965; *Shreveport Times*, October 21, 1965.

[78]Dick Thevenot to Dr. Joseph E. Holoubek, October 25, 1965, J. Bennett Johnston, Jr. to Dr. William Frye, October 28, 1965, and Joseph E. Holoubek, M.D. to Dr. William W. Frye, November 1, 1965, all in Box 1, folder 3, Holoubek Papers.

[79]*Shreveport Times*, December 7, 1965; *Shreveport Journal*, December 7, 1965. Figuring that the bonds would be retired over twenty years at an expected annual interest rate of 3.75 percent, Johnston later estimated that the bond issue would cost the state $360,000 per year. J. Bennett Johnston, Jr., to Dr. C. E. Boyd, February 14, 1966, Box 3, folder 1, Holoubek Papers.

[80]Dick Thevenot to Dr. Joseph E. Holoubek, March 1, 1966, and Dr. Joseph E. Holoubek to Dr. William Frye, March 7, 1966, in Box 3, folder 2, Holoubek Papers; *Minutes. Board of Directors Meeting. Shreveport Chamber of Commerce*, February 24, 1966, 4, film 23, reel 4, Archives and Special Collections, Noel Memorial Library, Louisiana State University in Shreveport.

[81]*Legislative Calendar, 1966*, 36; *Shreveport Times*, May 11, 18, 27, 1966; *Shreveport Journal*, May 11, 17, 26, 1966. The house approved the measure by a vote of 105 to 0 and the senate added its endorsement by a vote of 29 to 1. J.D. Deblieux of Baton Rouge cast the lone negative vote, maintaining that the money would be better spent at the medical school in New Orleans.

[82]*Acts of Louisiana, 1966*, 95-100; *Shreveport Times*, June 8, 1966.

[83]Minutes of Regular Board Meeting, August 5, 1966. *Board of Supervisors Minutes Books*, 25:253, Board of Supervisors Records, University Archives, Louisiana State University Libraries, Baton Rouge; J. Bennett Johnston, Jr. to Messrs. Wood, King, Dawson & Logan, August 1, 1966, Box 3, folder 2, Holoubek Papers.

[84]*Shreveport Times*, November 23, 1966.

[85]*Legislative Calendar, 37th Extraordinary Session, 1966*, 341-42; *Acts of Louisiana, Extraordinary Session, 1966*, 41-44; *Shreveport Times*, December 6, 1966; *Shreveport Journal*, December 7, 1966.

[86]*Shreveport Times*, March 14, 1969.

# HIGHER EDUCATION AND HISTORICAL LITERACY IN LOUISIANA: AN ANALYSIS AND A MODEST PROPOSAL*

Judith F. Gentry, James H. Dormon, and Thomas D. Watson

## INTRODUCTION

*Professor James Dormon appeared before the meeting of the directors of the Louisiana Historical Association in Hammond on March 24, 1983, and presented a report on the results of a study he and Professor Judith Gentry had conducted on the emphasis—or lack thereof—given to history requirement in baccalaureate curricula by the colleges and universities of Louisiana. The directors resolved to bring the report to the attention of parties responsible for the content of higher education in the state. Accordingly, on June 30 copies of the report were mailed to the governing boards for colleges and universities, university presidents, chancellors, etc.*

*The following article is based on the earlier Dormon and Gentry study. The readers of* Louisiana History, *we speculate, will find it to be both a matter of concern and a timely topic in view of the current national debate on educational priorities. Without doubt a need exists for strengthening the quality of instruction in mathematics and the physical and environmental sciences. However, to do so at the expense of good instruction in the realm of the humanities would be folly.*

*The components of man's cultural environment (*e.g., *political and legal institutions, social and esthetic values) are perhaps more fragile and yet more malleable than those that make up the natural environment. A thorough understanding of* both *are essential to maintaining and improving the quality of human life. Tomorrow's leaders can ill afford to take* either *for granted without incurring the risk of social detriment.*

Thomas D. Watson, *President*
Louisiana Historical Association

*First published in *Louisiana History*, 24 (1983): 345-54. Reprinted with the kind permission of the authors and the Louisiana Historical Association.

It should come as no surprise to the readers of this journal that history as an academic discipline and historians as practitioners of the craft have fallen on hard times. As one of the traditional "humanities"—*i.e.*, one of the collection of disciplines concerned with the study of humankind in its creative and communicative dimensions—history has of late been relegated more often than not to a secondary or tertiary role in college and university curricula, and in the subject-matter preferences of students, throughout the United States.[1] The reasons for this phenomenon are not hard to locate: The domination of high-tech, scientific, and business training in the vocational concerns of college youth; the on-going quest for immediate "relevance" of course work in the values of these same students; the preference of many of them (and of their advisors) for less intellectually rigorous options as "electives" in their college programs. The end result has been over the period from the 1960s to the present a steady decline of the number of students taking history courses, either by necessity or by choice, and hence the steady erosion of history offerings (and of budget considerations to history departments) and an increasing sense, all too often among historians themselves, of the inconsequence and relative insignificance of their discipline and its value in the "real world."[2]

It was thus with a borderline sense of despair that two academic historians—the authors of this report—undertook recently to assess the degree of the problem and the potential of the threat to the discipline here in their own back yard, the state of Louisiana. To be specific, we undertook to examine the curricula of all Louisiana colleges and universities in an effort to ascertain for each school the percentage of the curricula which require no history courses for baccalaureate degrees as well as the percentage of curricula which require at least six hours of history for baccalaureate degrees. Only courses taught by history departments were counted, so courses in college of education on the history of education, for instance, were not considered as history courses. Requirement of a group of courses including history (social studies requirements or humanities requirements, for instance) were not counted, since the student could very well choose other courses in the group and graduate from college without having completed any history courses as such. The results of this study are presented in three tables at the end of this article.

The findings were quite as discouraging as we had anticipated they might be. To take a few cases in point: At Louisiana State University-Baton Rouge, the flagship campus of the state system, 56% of all curricula *require no history at all.* Only 42% of curricula require six or more credit hours in history. At Tulane and Newcomb, the picture is even more bleak. Not *one* curriculum other than that for history majors requires any history courses of students pursuing degrees of whatever sort. Tulane and Newcomb represent the extreme case in point. By comparison, history requirements are somewhat more prevalent at the University of Southwestern Louisiana and the University of New Orleans: USL requires six or more hours of history in 29% of its offering (though 33% of its curricula require no history). The figures for UNO are 22% with history requirements as opposed to 60% with none. Some other representative figures: McNeese State University requires six hours of history in 56% of its offerings while 40% require none. At Louisiana Tech

University, 49% of the curricula require no history; 42% require six or more credits in a history field. Happily, there are some campuses on which the history requirements prevail in *most* curricula. At Southeastern Louisiana University 95% of all curricula require at least one history course, while 65% require six or more hours. Similarly, at Grambling State University 71% of curricula require six or more hours, while only 10% require no history courses. Dillard, Holy Cross, St. Joseph's Seminary, Louisiana College, and Xavier require six hours of history in better than 90% of their curricula. But these are relatively small campuses, and though their standards are to be admired, they represent only a tiny minority of the student body population of the state.[3]

Now, what are we to conclude from these figures? It would appear that those responsible for curriculum development in the universities of this state have patently followed national trends in minimizing or eliminating history requirements, thus depreciating the value of our historical currency. The further question that persists, however, involves the matter of how this trend has affected the university education of students who are deprived of basic historical literacy? Can these students upon graduation claim to be truly "educated"; will they be equipped to handle the civic, social, and political responsibilities of adults in a democratic republic? Or will they graduate and assume their new life roles (to paraphrase Cicero) as perpetual "children," devoid of any awareness of what happened before they were born? Again, the answers seem apparent. And the prospect is not a happy one; it is in fact frightening, and especially so in that our college-educated citizens must assume the leadership roles in American government and society and in the world. But this grim prospect by no means marks the end of the problems created by historical illiteracy. There is also the matter of the maintenance and perpetuation of historically derived institutions, the fundamental institutions of western culture that constitute the basis of our contemporary civilization.

It has been generally acknowledged that republican institutions are uniquely susceptible to the threat of erosion by way of inattention to their historical roots. Jefferson noted that constant vigilance was the prerequisite of continued "liberty," by which he meant attention by the people to the maintenance of the libertarian tradition, the establishment of which constituted the *raison d'être* of the new America. Hamilton believed similarly with reference to institutional continuity. And though the two often differed politically, they agreed that liberty *and* the institutions sustaining liberty (*e. g.*, republican government, the inviolability of property, the separation of powers: the "Lockean Synthesis") depended inordinately upon the awareness of history as the key to both the creation and perpetuation of American institutions—the "last, best hope of mankind."[4] Have we now lost the key? It may well be that we have. We may have lost it in our national preoccupation, a preoccupation bordering on obsession, with the perpetuation of our national dominance in the high-technology fields, and in the utilization of higher education as a form of vocational training for young Americans. As the pundit-historian George Will has recently observed, while we assuredly do need "persons conversant with new technologies," we need even more "a citizenry acquainted with the ancient patrimony of our civilization."[5] "The patrimony," Will continues, "is a renewable resource, but it will not regenerate spontaneously." It requires constant, even "urgent" attention, and especially so when all signs point to an abysmal historical ignorance among American students at all levels. Will notes as a case in point a California college student who asked his professor whether Julius Caesar "resented Shakespeare's portrayal of him."[6] Virtually any Louisiana history professor could match or surpass this example. And given the overwhelming evidence of the decline in history requirements, things are, it seems, destined to grow even worse.

We have, however, a unique opportunity to reestablish the primacy of history in baccalaureate education in the state. At lease in part as a result of the devastating criticism of American education produced by the recent report of the National Committee on Excellence in Education,[7] we are all in the process of taking a long second look at our degree requirements. The curricula of the state's colleges and universities are undergoing close scrutiny by the administrations of the schools, often with an eye to the possibility of creating a "core curriculum," to be pursued by all students preparatory to undertaking their programs in their major specializations.

And now for the "modest proposal": This is the time for the curriculum-makers to be reminded of the need for history in the educational process that will shape the nation's enlightened leadership class. Inclusion of history in a group of optional courses is not an adequate step; rather, as part of the emergent "core" the history requirements must apply, we submit, to *all* university students, regardless of major field of specialization or ultimate career goal. And what, more specifically, must this requirement be? What should all students be required to achieve in the way of familiarity with the historically derived institutions constituting their "patrimony?" The answer seems, once more, self-evident: At an absolute minimum, all curricula must require a full year (two semesters or three quarters) of United States History, covering (in one way or another) the historical backdrop of contemporary American culture. This is the barest minimum. Far more desirable would be a second, additional year of history course requirements in which the student could be afforded the longer view; the view of the formative processes that produced the fundamental institutions, ideas, and values guiding *all* of the great world civilizations, and the nature of the major historical conflicts that have so often divided the world's populations.

Whether we are in fact (as is so often suggested) doomed to repeat our past errors if we know not of them is open to some question, but there can be no doubt whatever that our future leadership elements will benefit by viewing current world problems and issues in the light of the historical record. We simply cannot afford as a nation a generation of college-educated Americans deprived of that light, despite all our concern for occupational vocational training and all our vaunted technical achievements. Of what possible value are such concerns if we must, in achieving them, lose sight of where we came from and what we are? This is the question that must be put before university policymakers immediately and vociferously: To fail this challenge is to fail ourselves at a time of change as great and far-reaching as any since the onset of the Industrial Revolution. An awareness of history, we submit, is, quite simply, essential to cultural continuity and thus to cultural survival.

## APPENDIX[8]

Table I

REQUIRED HISTORY COURSES IN LOUISIANA'S COLLEGES AND UNIVERSITIES

| | REQUIRE 6 OR MORE HOURS HISTORY | REQUIRE NO HISTORY |
|---|---|---|
| LSU System: | | |
| LSU-Baton Rouge | 42% | 56% |
| University of New Orleans | 22% | 60% |
| LSU-Shreveport | 32% | 27% |
| LSU-Alexandria (has only one four-year curriculum) | 0% | 100% |
| Southern System: | | |
| Southern-Baton Rouge | 68% | 23% |
| Southern-New Orleans | 47% | 0% |
| Trustees System: | | |
| Grambling | 71% | 10% |
| Louisiana Tech | 42% | 49% |
| McNeese | 56% | 40% |
| Nicholls | 56% | 2% |
| Northeast | 27% | 16% |
| Northwestern | 21% | 0% |
| Southeastern | 65% | 5% |
| Southwestern | 29% | 33% |
| Private: | | |
| Centenary | 5% | 77% |
| Dillard | 100% | 0% |
| Louisiana College | 98% | 2% |
| Loyola | 26% | 16% |
| Holy Cross | 100% | 0% |
| Newcomb* | 0% | 100% |
| St. Joseph Seminary | 100% | 0% |
| St. Mary's Dominican | 39% | 0% |
| Tulane* | 0% | 100% |
| Xavier | 93% | 4% |

*Excepting history majors

Table II

REQUIRED HISTORY COURSES IN LOUISIANA'S COLLEGES AND UNIVERSITIES

(arranged from highest percentage of curricula requiring 6 or more hours of history to lowest percentage of curricula requiring 6 or more hours of history)

| | REQUIRE 6 OR MORE HOURS HISTORY |
|---|---|
| Dillard | 100% |
| Holy Cross | 100% |
| St. Joseph's Seminary | 100% |
| Louisiana College | 98% |
| Xavier | 93% |
| Grambling | 71% |
| Southern-Baton Rouge | 68% |
| Southeastern | 65% |
| McNeese | 56% |
| Nicholls | 56% |
| Southern-New Orleans | 47% |
| Louisiana Tech | 42% |
| LSU-Baton Rouge | 42% |
| St. Mary's Dominican | 39% |
| LSU-Shreveport | 32% |
| Southwestern | 29% |
| Northeast | 27% |
| Loyola | 26% |
| University of New Orleans | 22% |
| Northwestern | 21% |
| Centenary | 5% |
| Tulane* | 0% |
| Newcomb* | 0% |
| LSU-Alexandria | 0% |

*Excepting history majors

Table III

REQUIRED HISTORY COURSES IN LOUISIANA'S COLLEGES AND UNIVERSITIES

(arranged from highest percentage of curricula requiring no history to lowest percentage of curricula requiring no history)

| | REQUIRE NO HISTORY |
|---|---|
| Tulane* | 100% |
| Newcomb* | 100% |
| LSU-Alexandria | 100% |
| Centenary | 77% |
| University of New Orleans | 60% |
| Northeast | 46% |
| McNeese | 40% |
| Southwestern | 33% |
| LSU-Shreveport | 27% |
| Southern-Baton Rouge | 23% |
| Loyola | 16% |
| Grambling | 10% |
| Southeastern | 5% |
| Xavier | 4% |
| Nicholls | 2% |
| Louisiana College | 2% |
| Dillard | 0% |
| Holy Cross | 0% |
| St. Joseph Seminary | 0% |
| St. Mary Dominican | 0% |
| Northwestern | 0% |
| Southern-New Orleans | 0% |

*Excepting history majors

## Notes for "Higher Education and Historical Literacy in Louisiana: An Analysis and a Modest Proposal"

[1]William J. Bennett, chairman of the National Endowment for the Humanities, has recently made reference to "The Shattered Humanities." See the *Wall Street Journal*, December 31, 1982.

[2]See, e. g., Warren I. Susman, "Annapolis Conference on the Introductory Course," *A. H. A. Prespectives*, 20 (1982): 18-23.

[3]See the appendix to this article for documentation of all figures and a full statistical report.

[4]It is noteworthy that virtually *all* the founding fathers shared these beliefs in the necessity of a knowledge of history to the creation and perpetuation of a viable republican polity.

[5]"Educating the Nation," *New Orleans Times-Picayune*, May 2, 1983.

[6]Ibid.

[7]The National Committee on Excellence in Education, *A Nation at Risk: The Imperative for Educational Reform* (Washington, D.C., 1983).

[8]The three tables constituting this appendix have been prepared from data provided by following catalogues:

LSU General Catalog '82-83
University of New Orleans 1982-83 General Catalog
LSU in Shreveport Bulletin: General Catalog 1982-83
Southern University and A & M College, Main Campus, Baton Rouge, Bulletin 1979-81
Southern University in New Orleans 1981-83 Bulletin
Grambling State University General Catalog 1981-82, 1982-1983 Grambling, Louisiana
Louisiana Tech University 1982-1983 Bulletin
McNeese State University Catalog 1981-83
Nichols State University: Bulletin 1982-83
Northeast Louisiana Catalog: Bulletin 1982-83
Northwestern State University of Louisiana, Bulletin: General Catalog Announcements 1981-83
Southeastern Louisiana University General Catalog 1981-1982: Undergraduate and Graduate Information
The University of Southwestern Louisiana: Bulletin 1981-1983
Centenary College Catalog 1981-83
Dillard University 1982-84 General Catalog
Louisiana College Catalog for 1982-83
Loyola University Bulletin 1981-82 Undergraduate Studies
Our Lady of Holy Cross College 1980-1982 Catalog
St. Joseph Seminary College Bulletin 1982-1983, 1983-1984
St. Mary's Dominican College '78-80 Bulletin
The Sophie H. Newcomb Memorial College for Women 1981-1983
Tulane College of Arts and Sciences 1981-1983
Tulane School of Engineering 1980-82
Xavier University of New Orleans Catalog 1982-84

# PART VI

## Some Reflections on Late Twentieth Century Louisiana

## NEW ORLEANS, USA*

Henry Hurt

### *Camelot and the New Frontier*

The dawn of the sixties was accompanied by two powerful forces that surged through America, pulling and grinding at each other with a passion that can be seen much more clearly a quarter century later. One force was highly visible, the other not so clearly perceived but every bit as potent.

On the one hand, there was the palpable exuberance of that slim majority of American voters who had elected John F. Kennedy. They applauded his promise of a bold and unprecedented new direction for the country and the world. They believed that President Kennedy's vibrant espousal of new ideas would make the world community a better place for everyone—including multitudes of the hungry, ignorant, and sick. His election was seen as a signal that compassion and the sharing of material wealth with those less fortunate, both here and abroad, would be high priorities. There was the fervent belief that this new dimension would foster peace, justice, and equality around the world.

In his inaugural speech, President Kennedy exhorted Americans to "ask not what your country can do for you—ask what you can do for your country."[1] Such ringing phrases evoked wild enthusiasm from Kennedy's constituency, so many of whom were young, charmingly articulate, and wealthy. The men and women in the new Kennedy White House were described at the time as "the richest, prettiest, most interesting young people in the country."[2]

The tone was clearly set for what would come to be called Camelot. But not everyone across the land was pleased. Surging through America with equal intensity was a second force, one overshadowed by the glitter and self-adulation of the highly visible Kennedy supporters. This constituency represented a virtually total dissent from the

*From Henry Hurt, *Reasonable Doubt: An Investigation into the Assassination of John F. Kennedy*. 

frenzied loyalty of the Kennedy people. The dissent by some elements of this constituency was far more sinister than the traditional give-and-take in politics. Inevitably, the voices and tones of this dissent were viewed against the vibrant enthusiasm surrounding the new President. The very eagerness of Kennedy's supporters nourished the feeling that his accomplishments would take a terrible toll from those certain constituencies that were in fundamental opposition to all he stood for. To these opponents, there was a threatening ring in the privileged young President's exhortation that people should ask what they could do for their country. Many of them believed that they already did the maximum for their country, since it unhesitatingly helped itself and others to their wealth.

In an odd way, the enthusiasm for the new President was so ostentatious that it dominated the news here and abroad, as if he had won a mandate, ignoring completely the fact that he had barely squeaked in. Thus, the depth and breadth of his opposition was largely overlooked. So was its intensity, fed by the outrage of powerful adversaries who viewed the young President as having used them to get himself elected, then made political capital by turning against them. The feral intensity of the violent opposition to Kennedy blazed clear at Dealey Plaza. If Kennedy partisans saw in their President the dawn of a new age for America, so did the violent opposition. The question is whether the opponents determined that it was not to be.

In addition to the unsuspected virulence of Kennedy's domestic opposition, he faced opposition around the globe from Communist governments. The most immediate and explosive of these challenges was Fidel Castro, who had taken control of Cuba on January 1, 1959. When Kennedy took office in January 1961, he inherited the heated commitment of U. S. military and intelligence officials to rid the Western Hemisphere of Castro, whom they viewed as a Soviet puppet on the doorstep of the U.S. mainland. There were, of course, no more ardent allies of this official commitment than the thousands of fiery exiles who had sought refuge from Castro in the United States.[3]

The first major effort against Castro was launched in April 1961 with the U.S.-backed invasion by exiles at Cuba's Bay of Pigs. Coming only three months after President Kennedy took office, the invasion was a disaster that humiliated practically everyone connected with it. When the facts began to surface, President Kennedy faced the nearly hysterical wrath of the exiles, who accused him of betrayal by shortchanging them on military support, thus dooming their cause. Many of Kennedy's military and intelligence advisors were also angry at their commander-in-chief for the same reason. On the other side of the coin, Castro directly blamed the President for sponsoring the aborted invasion designed to topple him from power.[4]

Castro's anger toward Kennedy was menacingly intensified by his sure knowledge that official elements of the U.S. government—presumably with the sanction of President Kennedy—were repeatedly trying to assassinate him. Castro ultimately claimed that there were twenty-four U.S. attempts to murder him. In subsequent years a Congressional committee confirmed at least eight U.S. attempts to assassinate the Cuban premier.[5]

In its persistent efforts to murder Castro, the United States reached beyond its routine arsenal of military and intelligence resources. It is now officially conceded that the CIA recruited certain high-level figures from organized crime to carry out murder plots against Castro. As freakish as this collusion appears, both sides had important reasons for wanting to murder the Cuban leader. Not only had he established a hostile Communist government at the edge of the United States, but he had also closed down the narcotics, gambling, and prostitution operations run so lucratively by the U.S. mob. Perhaps it should not be too surprising that these unlikely conspirators had joined forces.[6]

There was an added reason for the mob's willingness to participate in the assassination plots—their desire to turn down the heat from the Justice Department. From the earliest days of the Kennedy administration, the Justice Department, under the direction of Attorney General Robert Kennedy, had exhibited an unparalleled commitment to fight organized crime in the United States. This commitment, taken with the full blessing of the President, particularly puzzled mob bosses, who felt they had virtually delivered the presidency to Kennedy when they brought in the state of Illinois by a whisker—giving him the twenty-seven electoral votes that guaranteed him his razor-thin margin of victory over Richard Nixon in the 1960 presidential election.[7]

In addition to his domestic opposition and that of the pro-Castro and anti-Castro forces, the oil industry had turned savagely against President Kennedy by 1963 because of his support for tax reform that threatened the oil-depletion allowance. This struck at one of the most lucrative tax loopholes ever enjoyed by the fabled oil millionaires of Texas, Louisiana, and other states with substantial oil interests.[8]

Added to this stew of Kennedy opposition were the right-wing extremists and racists, angry over the Kennedy brothers' promise to bring full desegregation to the South. Many feared that desegregation would virtually destroy hallowed traditions involving families, politics, and economics.[9]

All things considered, it is probable that a greater diversity of elements wanted President Kennedy out of office than had been at work during any previous presidency in American history. In simple terms, the most threatening forces boiled down to several darkly potent groups:

* Anti-Castro exiles.
* Pro-Castro elements, including perhaps Castro himself.
* Organized crime.
* Powerful oil interests.
* Right-wing and racist domestic factions.
* Elements of U.S. military and intelligence, enraged over Kennedy's denunciation of their efforts following the Bay of Pigs disaster.

Such forces possessed in abundance the classic ingredients for murder—motive, means, and opportunity. In fact, with such a rare confluence of threatening elements, a great range of shifting opportunities for assassination presented itself, as the President, with increasing frequency during 1963, moved about the country on political trips.

In retrospect, the possibility of a successful political assassination seems immense.

No place in America held a greater concentration of these diverse factions than steamy, seething New Orleans. As a whole, that city has traditionally tolerated, even welcomed, a tantalizing variety of races and creeds, political and social beliefs. The city took delight in its natural diversities, especially during the tumultuous years of the early sixties. This potpourri of diversity—and, by some lights, perversity—had fostered an atmosphere in which almost any extreme—political, philosophical, sexual, artistic, religious, or even criminal—was remarkably at ease. By 1961 the climate of laissez-faire was virtually absolute.

From the earliest days of Castro's power, the city was a major haven for displaced Cubans of all social and economic stripes. Included in the massive influx of hotheaded exiles were many professionals—doctors, lawyers, and bankers.[10] Given this strident Cuban population and an extensive presence of U.S. military and intelligence advisors working in and around New Orleans, it is not surprising that the city became one hub of the efforts by the United States government to stage either the overthrow or assassination of Fidel Castro.[11]

As the major city in one of the largest oil-producing states in the country, New Orleans, like much of Louisiana, was strongly influenced by the attitudes of the powerful companies and men who controlled these vast oil interests. Moreover, cosmopolitan, bohemian New Orleans only superficially escaped the racism and attendant hatred that was so virulent in the Deep South during the early sixties. Even the most prominent of the city's raucous Mardi Gras fetes systematically excluded Negroes and Jews. Beneath a surface of tolerance, many residents harbored the same racist passions that infected so much of the rest of America.

One of the most important factors in any consideration of New Orleans is the powerful presence of Carlos Marcello, the kingpin of organized crime in the south central United States. Marcello, who once admitted to being merely a tomato salesman, had ubiquitous business interests that were intertwined with many aspects of the state's economy—including bars, restaurants, prostitution, transportation, real estate, and tourism. Hundreds of Louisianians worked for him either directly or indirectly, and even the legitimate business people granted him a certain respect, for the power that he represented. A convincing case can be made that for most of the decades of Marcello's power, local and state law-enforcement agencies in Louisiana have rarely taken punitive aim at his wide operations. What legal difficulty Marcello has experienced came from federal authorities, particularly during the Kennedy administration.[12]

Another addition to the volatile mix already described was that New Orleans produced the man the government insisted was the lone assassin of President Kennedy—Lee Harvey Oswald. Not only was Oswald born in New Orleans, he lived there for five months during 1963, until two months before the assassination.[13] In New Orleans, Oswald was associated in varying and confusing ways with elements that would ostensibly benefit from President Kennedy's death.

Finally, it is not surprising that a setting as flamboyant and tawdry as New Orleans should produce the only prosecution in which a man was brought to trial for conspiring to assassinate John F. Kennedy. The prosecution ultimately failed; but it introduced questions and evidence, at a national level, that leave almost any observer certain that *something* connected to the assassination was going on in New Orleans. Just *what* is as confusing a mystery as ever.

### *The Jolly Green Giant*

On February 17, 1967, news began thundering around the world that, for the first time, a duly elected law-enforcement official in the United States was investigating the tangled leads left by the Warren Commission. A few days later, Jim Garrison, the boisterous district attorney of New Orleans, was already promising arrests and prosecution on charges of conspiracy to assassinate the President of the United States. The commission, of course, had found no evidence of a conspiracy. On the surface it appeared odd, if not preposterous, that such an investigation carried no imprimatur of federal sanction. However, there was the wide belief that those vested with the authority to follow the leads three years earlier had failed. Perhaps, it was reasoned, this was the only logical course for the pursuit of truth.[14]

Still, there could have been no more strange, even bizarre, setting for what was about to unfold. The case itself—the JFK assassination—may have been the only one in history that could withstand with even a modicum of seriousness such a sequence of events or so wild a cast of characters. Less than a week after the first confusing reports about the investigation, Jim Garrison confidently told the press that he had "positively solved the assassination of President John F. Kennedy."[15] With this, the bedlam turned into a public frenzy that dwarfed old New Orleans's legendary hysteria for Mardi Gras.[16]

In the beginning, press focus was chiefly on the prosecutor who made the sensational charges, a man of hulking physique, standing six and one-half feet tall and wearing size fourteen shoes. Jim Garrison, a man fond of Shakespeare and good living, was known to both friends and enemies as the Jolly Green Giant. Many years earlier, Garrison, who had worked briefly for the FBI, had shucked his real moniker of Earling Carothers for the simple first name of Jim. A decorated combat flier during World War II, Garrison later acquired a reputation as something of a crusader, for his vice raids on various Bourbon Street enterprises.[17]

While such activity generated considerable publicity, Garrison's critics point out that he customarily avoided any prosecution involving organized crime—a force he asserts did not exist in New Orleans during his years as district attorney. It is significant that in presenting his case, Garrison pointed to certain characters and evidence that even today seem pertinent, but he never once made the obvious connection between them and New Orleans mob boss Carlos Marcello.[18]

Perhaps the best illustration of Garrison's blindness concerning organized crime is seen in his comments on Oswald's killer Jack Ruby, whose organized-crime ties are solidly established. In *Contract on America,* one of the best analyses published on evidence of organized-crime participation in the JFK killing, author David E. Scheim points out:

> Although Garrison made extravagant charges against an assortment of Cuban exiles, CIA agents, Minutemen, White Russians and Nazis, he conspicuously avoided any reference to one prime assassination suspect: the Mafia. . . . In discussing testimony concerning Ruby's anti-Castro activities . . . Garrison described Ruby as a 'CIA bagman' and an 'employee of the CIA.' But Garrison said nothing about Ruby's organized crime involvement.[19]

In this framework, Scheim writes: "It is logical to ask whether [Garrison's] probe was carried out with precisely [the] purpose . . . of deflecting attention from Carlos Marcello."[20]

Aaron Kohn, who for many years was the managing director of the respected private group called the Metropolitan Crime Commission of New Orleans, captured the more common perception when he observed: "Garrison never lets the responsibilities of being a prosecutor interfere with being a politician."[21] Whether or not Kohn's assessment is accurate, it is certain that legions of Garrison's critics agree with that description.

But the world was interested not so much in Jim Garrison as in the evidence he was promising to deliver. In describing the atmosphere after the story broke, one reporter wrote:

> A deluge of frantic incoming calls lighted up the telephone switchboard in the outer office of the district attorney of New Orleans, and for the next month it blazed like a pinball machine gone mad. Day after day, calls poured in from across the U.S., from London, Rome, Paris, Berlin, from South America, Mexico, Japan. At times, the trunk lines jammed completely.[22]

When the story first broke in the *New Orleans States-Item*, it was essentially void of names and details. Several enterprising reporters had pieced together certain facts of the investigation by examining vouchers that showed heavy travel expenses by the district attorney's office to places like Dallas, Houston, and Miami. On the day their story appeared, a man named David William Ferrie contacted the newspaper. He stated that he was a target of Garrison's investigation and that he wanted to talk about it. He said that Garrison's insinuations about him—that he was a getaway pilot for the assassins were groundless.[23]

David Ferrie was, in nearly every sense, a New Orleans-style mad genius—a man to be seized upon by any red-blooded reporter. Rarely has such a wild figure emerged into the light for public scrutiny. Hairless from head to toe as the result of a rare disease, Ferrie compensated for this deficiency by gluing what looked like nothing so much as reddish orange monkey hair on the top of his head. More such hair was used to fashion eyebrows, grotesquely set off by sloppily applied mascara around the eyes. This visage was offset by a beaklike nose on an angular face. A big man of nearly six feet, Ferrie was widely known as an aggressive homosexual who had been arrested several times for molesting young boys. Ferrie, who constantly exhibited his proclivity for foul language, also had a knowledge of medicine. At one time he kept hundreds of mice in his filthy apartment, while working on a private cancer cure he had formulated.[24]

In addition, Ferrie was considered a master hypnotist as well as a student of philosophy, religion, and psychology. Three thousand volumes were crammed into his personal library. He claimed a Ph. D. in psychology and listed himself as a "doctor" in the telephone directory. He was active as a "bishop" in an obscure sect called the Orthodox Old Catholic Church of North America. He made speeches to groups such as the Junior Chamber of Commerce. He was a violent anti-Communist, with prominent connections with the Cuban exile community of New Orleans. Many believe that he served as a CIA contract agent during the height of the Cuban exile activities.[25]

Ferrie was widely considered to be a brilliant pilot of various sorts of aircraft. Until September 1963 Ferrie was employed as a commercial pilot for Eastern Airlines. He was dismissed from Eastern following publicity over his arrest for sodomizing a minor boy. After this, Ferrie worked primarily as a private pilot and as an investigator. On the day of the assassination, he was in a federal courtroom in New Orleans with none other than Carlos Marcello, whose lawyer had retained Ferrie as an investigator.[26]

Ferrie told the newspaper that Garrison seemed to believe that his role in the JFK conspiracy was to be on hand to fly the Dallas assassins to safety outside the country. Ferrie's seemingly ironclad alibi did not deter Garrison, who, it would turn out, was concentrating his case on the act of *conspiracy* to assassinate, rather than actual participation in the murder. Ferrie's comments were the first substantive hint of what Garrison was up to. Investigation by reporters showed that within seventy-two hours of the assassination, Garrison had Ferrie and two friends brought in and then turned over to the FBI and Secret Service—which interviewed them and let them go, a fact duly reflected in the Warren Commission records. Now, three years later, reporters from around the world competed for interviews with the strange, bulbous-eyed man.[27]

One of the reporters who managed to follow Ferrie into his lair was George Lardner, Jr., of the *Washington Post*. He was admitted to Ferrie's apartment around midnight and talked to him for four hours. Lardner later told one of Garrison's investigators that he found Ferrie that night to be "[an] intelligent, well-versed guy [on] a broad range of subjects." Lardner reported that Ferrie was in good spirits when he left him at four o'clock that morning.[28]

Later that day Ferrie's nude, lifeless body was discovered in the apartment. The date was February 22, only five days after the story broke about Garrison's investigation. At the time of his death, Ferrie was forty-nine years old.[29] Two undated notes were found near Ferrie's body—one to a former lover named Al, the other to the world: "To leave this life is, for me, a sweet prospect. I find nothing in it that is desirable, and on the other hand everything that is loathesome."[30]

Despite the note, the coroner ruled that the death was from natural causes, a brain hemorrhage. "There is no indication whatsoever of suicide or murder," stated the coroner.[31] However, Jim Garrison argued that the death was a suicide, and solemnly told the press that David Ferrie was "one of history's most important individuals."[32] Among the peculiar contents of Ferrie's home were three blank U.S. passports—seeming to need only photographs and biographical information to appear valid. There were also a 100-pound bomb and numerous guns and military equipment.[33]

In Washington there was a clear measure of official concern over Garrison's activities. President Johnson telephoned Acting Attorney General Ramsey Clark to inform him of Ferrie's death. Years later an FBI report was disclosed that noted that President Johnson was "very concerned about this matter" and wanted full details about Ferrie's death.[34]

A few days later, when District Attorney Garrison assured reporters that he had "solved" the assassination, he added: "We're working out details of evidence which probably will take months. We know that we're going to be able to arrest every person involved—at least every person who is still living. . . . The key to the whole case is through the looking glass. Black is white; white is black. I don't want to be cryptic, but that's the way it is."[35]

These comments were cryptic indeed. But, by this point, Garrison had a hammerlock on the attention of the Western world. Millions of people eagerly awaited the next development, the next pronouncement from Garrison. The wait was not long.

On March 1, the same day that David Ferrie was buried, Jim Garrison announced the arrest of Clay L. Shaw, a prominent New Orleans business and social figure. Only seventeen months earlier, the city of New Orleans had bestowed upon Shaw its highest honor, a medal for the International Order of Merit. At the time of the arrest, Garrison may have been short on evidence linking Shaw to the assassination, but he made certain the world was informed about some of the strange items his office had turned up in Shaw's home—one chain, five whips, one black hood and cape, and one black gown.[36]

People were outraged at this apparent invasion of Shaw's privacy. He and his friends—and they were numerous and prominent—insisted that the kinky paraphernalia was part of Mardi Gras costumes. Others charged that this was a move on Garrison's part to somehow introduce Shaw's discreet homosexuality into the developing case. Whatever else Jim Garrison's capricious arrest of Shaw accomplished, it earned for Garrison widespread scorn about his motives and called into question the legitimacy of his whole prosecution. At the same time, many observers believed that the fact that Garrison, a man with high political ambitions, would go so far was a solid indication of the strength of the evidence he would present.[37]

The immediate result of Shaw's arrest was frenzied publicity. More than ever, the world's appetite was whetted for the next step the presentation of evidence and the trial of Shaw and his as yet unarrested co-conspirators. Garrison loved the publicity and took to the limelight in a media blitz. He repeatedly asserted in forums all over the country that there would be more arrests and that he was confident of convictions. *Playboy* lent its pages for a full-length interview, and Garrison was invited to appear on Johnny Carson's "Tonight Show." Suddenly, the New Orleans prosecutor was a hot property everywhere.[38]

As Garrison talked, the world—and Clay Shaw—waited. This time, the wait would be a long one.

One of the most curious incidents attendant to Shaw's arrest occurred shortly afterward in Washington. Acting Attorney General Ramsey Clark made the startling statement that the FBI had investigated Shaw in the immediate wake of the assassination and found nothing to pursue. By the FBI's lights, Clark said, Clay Shaw was clean. Later that day, while the FBI officially refused to comment, usually well-informed government sources told the *New York Times* they had no knowledge of such an investigation of Clay Shaw.[39]

As if this were not confusing enough, a Justice Department official then tried to explain Clark's curious statements. In doing so, he managed to introduce a puzzling new name to the confusion. The official told the *New York Times* that the Justice Department "was convinced that Mr. [Clay] Bertrand and Mr. Shaw were the same man." The FBI *did* investigate Clay Bertrand—which probably was the source of the confusion.[40]

By June there was yet another story. The Justice Department, asserting again that Shaw had never been investigated, stated: "The Attorney General has since determined that this was erroneous. Nothing arose indicating the need to investigate Mr. Shaw. . . . Clay Bertrand was not identified as a real person. No evidence was found that Clay Shaw was ever called Clay Bertrand."[41]

It is probably impossible to sift through this morass to find the truth. However, it is certain that, ultimately, a major thrust of Garrison's case against Shaw was predicated on Shaw's alleged use of the alias Clay Bertrand. The aim of the prosecution was to prove that Clay Bertrand was involved in the conspiracy—and then prove that Shaw and Bertrand were one and the same. Shaw, of course, absolutely denied ever using the alias Clay Bertrand. Nonetheless, Shaw was not served well by the confusion raised by Attorney General Ramsey Clark.[42] Clark's motive, curiously enough, seemed to be to offer Shaw support, by saying the FBI investigated him earlier and found him clean.

But all this took place over a period of several months, following Shaw's arrest. Two weeks after the arrest, Garrison presented his charges against Shaw at a preliminary hearing. A three-judge panel was to determine whether there was "sufficient evidence" to go ahead with a trial. For the first time, the public got a glimpse of Garrison's chief witness, as well as the outlines of the case he intended to prove against Shaw.[43]

Perry Raymond Russo, a neatly attired young man of twenty-five who worked as an insurance salesman in Baton Rouge, told the panel of judges of his friendship with David

Ferrie during the early sixties. He swore that in September 1963 he attended a party at Ferrie's home that included an older man called Clem Bertrand and Ferrie's roommate, a young man, with a scraggly beard, called Leon Oswald. Russo, a college graduate, testified that he believed the two were Clay Shaw and Lee Harvey Oswald.[44]

Russo swore that he heard the two men discussing with Ferrie the details of an assassination plot. He heard them use such terms as "diversionary tactics" and "triangulation of cross fire." Russo said that he had never told anyone about his knowledge of the plot until he came forward after hearing about Garrison's investigation.[45]

A second witness, a heroin addict, was used as a backup to link Shaw and Oswald. He testified that one day in 1963, while he was administering drugs to himself at the lakefront, he observed Shaw and Oswald together talking. He said that he watched Shaw give some money to Oswald. He could not, he said, hear what they were talking about.[46]

Based on these witnesses and on Garrison's presentation, the judges ruled that there was sufficient evidence for a trial.[47]

James Phelan, a journalist who was to become significantly involved in the Garrison case, has described in his book *Scandals, Scamps and Scoundrels* what happened next:

> In the public's mind, the judicial ruling . . . was a clear-cut victory for Garrison and gave an aura of substance to his conspiracy solution. . . . No one but Garrison and a few of his top aides knew that he had played all of his evidentiary hole cards. He implied that there was much more to come, and then set out to discover what it was. . .
>
> The preliminary hearing victory made him a national media celebrity, and while his staff was energetically seeking new evidence, [Garrison] embarked on a long series of speeches, talkshow appearances, television, radio and magazine interviews. He had a seemingly endless supply of "new disclosures," all revealed with the . . . confidence of a man who knew exactly what he was doing.[48]

It seems inevitable that in the media circus that followed, Garrison's claims became increasingly far-flung, in terms of the elements he believed to be involved in the assassination. As the months went by, Garrison came up with allusions to dozens of conspirators and numerous theories, including one in which the real killer concealed himself in a manhole in Dealey Plaza, fired a shot into the President's head, and then escaped through the sewer system. In nearly every case, some sort of obscure evidence could be found to support even Garrison's most outlandish assertions. In the end, Garrison settled on a villain that he was comfortable with. He placed the ultimate blame on this country's "military-industrial complex," citing elements of the CIA as being deeply involved in the assassination.[49]

It was becoming increasingly difficult to understand how the defendant, Clay Shaw, fit into such labyrinthine schemes. Garrison insisted that he had the evidence and was anxious to go to trial, where he could present it.[50] But it would be nearly two years before the trial got under way. Meanwhile, the media circus continued, unabated.

Most of what Garrison was saying—and he was spewing out thousands of words for public consumption, while coyly refusing to discuss his "evidence" against Shaw—was indisputably rooted in the gross deficiencies of the Warren Commission. This, of course, was a welcome development for many commission critics, who had been unable to attain a national forum for their findings and suspicions. Ironically, Garrison drew to his cause respectable support from men and women who were often glad for a chance to provide him with their expertise. Few, however, were able to help him with his case against Shaw.[51]

It is impossible to know if Garrison's case would have self-destructed—or whether it was Garrison's clumsy effort to manipulate the press that exploded in his face and wrecked his prosecution. The stage was set when writer James Phelan was dispatched to New Orleans by the *Saturday Evening Post* for a magazine piece on the unfolding Garrison investigation. Phelan had a good relationship with Garrison, from an earlier article he had done about New Orleans, and hoped that he could cajole the district attorney into giving him some special treatment. This was during the two-week period between Shaw's arrest and the preliminary hearing, when no one knew what evidence Garrison had against Shaw.[52]

In his larger-than-life manner, Garrison acceded magnificently. He said he would like to see a major story explaining his case in the magazine. But, he said, things were too hectic in New Orleans for a proper interview; they needed to escape the hordes of reporters from around the world. Garrison told Phelan to pick him up the next day at the airport in Las Vegas, Nevada. They would spend a couple of days there, where, Garrison said, they could talk in peace.[53]

Phelan spent hours in a Las Vegas hotel listening to Garrison, who had agreed to outline "the whole fantastic story" and to reveal to Phelan his evidence against Shaw. It was a reporter's dream, a primary source pouring out exclusive information. But there was a growing difficulty, as Phelan sensed it. The more he listened to Garrison talk, the more uncertain Phelan became that Garrison had much of a case at all. He finally told Garrison that it was clear he had "dug up a lot of odd things, but it comes across as just circumstances, speculation, theory."[54]

It was then that Garrison, with customary self-assurance, told Phelan that he was going to show him "something no one knows about but my top people." According to Phelan, Garrison handed him a packet of documents and stated, "I've got the witness who ties this whole case together. He's my case against Shaw. Here's the evidence my witness is going to present in the Shaw hearing next week."[55]

Back at his hotel Phelan read the papers. There were two documents. One was a 3,500-word memorandum of an interview with Perry Russo conducted by Andrew "Moo Moo" Sciambra, a former boxer and one of Garrison's top assistants. That interview took place on February 25, after Russo read of Ferrie's death and contacted Garrison's office. The second document in Phelan's hands was a stenographic record of what Russo had said when placed under hypnosis several days later.[56]

James Phelan stated: "I read the documents with a deepening sense of horror and disbelief. Russo had told two different stories a few days apart. On the essential issue—the Ferrie, Shaw, Oswald plot to kill Kennedy—they contradicted each other."[57]

The essential point was that in Sciambra's memo of his first interview with Russo, there was not a word about the party where Shaw, Ferrie, and Oswald were supposed to have hatched a plot to kill the President. It was a crucial omission, for that gathering represented the sum of Garrison's evidence tying Shaw to a conspiracy. The conspiracy surfaced in the second document, after Russo had been administered "truth serum," hypnotized, and shown a photograph of Shaw. The transcript showed that it was the hypnotist who introduced the concept that the people at the gathering "are talking about assassinating somebody," which was the first reference to such plans.[58]

After making photocopies of the papers, Phelan returned them to Garrison with as little comment as possible. He said nothing about the terrible gap he had noticed. It was Phelan's belief that Garrison had never bothered to actually read the documents, relying purely on his assistants, who had not warned him of the discrepancy.[59]

A few days after this, Russo appeared at the preliminary hearing and testified that he was at the conspiracy meeting involving Shaw, Ferrie, and Oswald. It was largely this testimony that bound Shaw over for trial. The next day Phelan went to Garrison's home to discuss what Phelan called "a big hole in Russo's testimony." Phelan was about to write his story for the *Saturday Evening Post* and needed Garrison's explanation. When informed, Phelan reports, Garrison became visibly upset and summoned Moo Moo Sciambra to explain it.[60]

Sciambra at first disputed that the conspiracy meeting was not mentioned in his memorandum of the initial interview. Then, when confronted with the fact that Phelan had a copy of it, Sciambra offered elaborate explanations about how he had simply overlooked putting it into the memorandum. He insisted that Russo had reported the conspiracy meeting in the first interview, even if Sciambra had forgotten to include it in his report to Garrison. He argued that he certainly had told Garrison about it, even if it was not in the report.[61]

In the end there was a single compelling point. If Russo actually told Sciambra of the conspiracy meeting with Shaw at their first interview, it is almost impossible to imagine that Sciambra would forget to include it, knowing that the report could well become the centerpiece of Garrison's case against Shaw. (In fact, the report *did* become extremely important, but not for reasons that suited Garrison's office.)[62]

Phelan then sought out Perry Russo and asked him when he first told the Garrison investigators about the actual conspiracy meeting. Without the slightest hesitation, according to Phelan, Russo stated that it was subsequent to his first meeting with Sciambra, *after* he had been placed under hypnosis.[63]

Phelan's article ran as the cover story in the *Saturday Evening Post*. Its revelations gave Clay Shaw his first glimpse of the real nature of Garrison's case against him. Phelan agreed to appear as a defense witness in Shaw's trial.[64]

The revelations of the two documents' damaging inconsistencies did little to diminish public enthusiasm for the case. Garrison by then was talking about even more titillating evidence, as people from around the country poured into his office and blitzed his telephone with claims to strengthen his case against Shaw. Most of the claims, it is now known, were wildly absurd. Still, Garrison had his pick to use as he saw best.[65]

Through this whole period, which was punctuated by intense national publicity, Garrison sought to force certain prospective witnesses to come to New Orleans to give evidence, including federal agents and the former director of the Central Intelligence Agency. By this time, Garrison was claiming that Shaw had, in fact, been an agent of the CIA—an allegation that turned out to have some merit, though of dubious relevance to the case as charged. It is not surprising that there was a general reluctance among federal agencies to cooperate.[66]

Garrison soon moved beyond assertions that the CIA had murdered JFK to claim he had evidence that federal agencies were deliberately executing elaborate machinations to undermine his case. They intended, he said, to abort the emergence of "truth." In the end, some evidence of this was indicated.[67] The reasons, however, may have been more in reaction to Garrison's tactics than anything else. In any event, Garrison managed to alienate himself and the Shaw case from nearly every level of government in the United States.

On January 21, 1969, almost two years after his arrest, Shaw's conspiracy trial opened in New Orleans. The selection of a jury was predictably difficult, in a case of such notoriety. The very first prospective juror examined—a man whose name had been drawn blindly in open court—was promptly excused. His name: John Kennedy.[68]

After nearly 1,200 prospects were examined, the jury was finally seated. Judge Edward A. Haggerty, Jr., told the press that the jurors could be photographed later at their motel, only after putting on dress shirts and ties. "I don't want them looking like the Scopes trial," Judge Haggerty explained. He then announced that he intended to recess court each day by 5:30 P.M. "so we can catch Huntley-Brinkley and Cronkite [to] see what they say about us." These announcements from the judge largely set the tone for the rest of the trial, which lasted thirty-nine days and was one of the best publicized in American history.[69]

Jim Garrison's strongest hand was played before Russo's testimony, on the opening day of the prosecution's presentation. The testimony came from six people who lived at Clinton, Louisiana, a small town about 130 miles from New Orleans. Remarkably diverse witnesses, they testified with impressive consistency that during the late summer of 1963, they had seen three strange men in their town. The three were identified as Lee Harvey Oswald, David Ferrie, and Clay Shaw. Oswald, accompanied by Ferrie and Shaw, seemed to be trying to secure a job. In doing so, he had visited a barber shop and later tried to register to vote. The testimony was a convincing boost to the basic prosecution assertion that Shaw, in contrast to his sworn denials, did know Ferrie and Oswald. The consensus among courtroom observers was that these witnesses were the most persuasive presented by the prosecution. This fresh evidence, never mentioned by the Warren Commission, was Garrison's most valuable contribution to an understanding of Oswald's activities. It was virtually lost in the circus atmosphere that characterized the rest of the trial.

From that point forward, everything was downhill for Garrison's case against Shaw.[70]

Perry Russo, Garrison's star witness, remained the centerpiece of his case to show that Shaw, Ferrie, and Oswald engaged in a conspiracy to assassinate the President. However, Russo's claims were devastated by the testimony of James Phelan. Even worse for Garrison, the defense presented a veteran New Orleans police officer, a lieutenant in the homicide division, who testified that Perry Russo told him that, in truth, Shaw probably was not the man he saw at Ferrie's apartment that night in 1963.[71]

On the other hand, all Clay Shaw could do in his defense was to take the stand and deny that he ever knew Oswald or Ferrie, or that he ever used an alias. He asserted that he had never engaged in a conspiracy to murder the President of the United States. In trying to prove such a negative, there simply was nothing more of substance the defense could do, although witnesses—including Marina Oswald—were summoned to show the unlikely nature of some of the prosecution's basic points.[72]

Before it was all over, Garrison—who hardly ever appeared in the courtroom—struggled mightily to have his assistants put the Warren Commission on trial. Among some forty-five witnesses called by the prosecution, one was a JFK autopsy doctor, and several were FBI agents; numerous witnesses were presented who had been in Dealey Plaza at the time of the assassination. The real highlight of the trial was the showing of the Zapruder film, which the prosecution managed to screen ten times in an effort to show the "triangulation of cross fire" and the devastation to the President. Even Abraham Zapruder, retiring by nature, was on hand to testify that he made the famous home movie and to indicate where he was standing, using an elaborate chart of Dealey Plaza.[73]

The most amusing of the many unusual events at the trial was the prosecution's presentation of a surprise witness from New York City, one Charles I. Spiesel, who stated that he was an accountant. At first Spiesel was a marvelously impressive witness, whose presence sent chills through Shaw's defense. He dressed impeccably and spoke articulately and with calm authority. He testified that during the summer of 1963, while on a visit to see his daughter, who was in school in New Orleans, he attended a party with a man named David Ferrie, whom he had met at a bar. Spiesel then identified the host of the party as Clay Shaw. He calmly swore that he listened quietly as Ferrie and Shaw discussed plans to assassinate the President of the United States.[74]

Jim Garrison's heart must have leaped with joy to discover a witness who shored up the badly tarnished Perry Russo. Spiesel was the perfect witness—up until the moment the prosecution completed its examination.

By the time the defense lawyer concluded his long and gentle questioning of Spiesel, the dapper little man had enthusiastically revealed that, for years, he had been plagued by complete strangers who, at the flick of an eye, could hypnotize him and control his life.

Spiesel guessed that as many as sixty different people had placed him under hypnosis—and that he could never be certain at any given moment whether he was under a hypnotic spell.[75]

Spiesel also acknowledged to the defense lawyer his life-long consuming fear that he was constantly followed by agents of various nefarious groups, among them the Communists seeking to disrupt his life. He stated that he had learned to be so careful that when his daughter visited, he fingerprinted her to make sure she actually was his daughter. He explained that, in this manner, he could be certain she was not some agent merely disguised as his daughter.[76]

Thus, Garrison's only witness to support Russo on the conspiracy point was demolished amid the muffled sniggers of the courtroom. If Garrison was desperate enough to use the pitiable Charles I. Spiesel, it leaves one breathless to consider the quality of witnesses he decided to turn away.[77]

Garrison's evidence on the matter of Shaw's alleged use of the name Clem or Clay Bertrand was a bit more persuasive. He produced a letter carrier who testified that he delivered mail to a Clem Bertrand at a location where Clay Shaw was temporarily receiving his mail. The postman said that none of the several letters he recalled delivering to Clem Bertrand at that address had ever been returned. Garrison also came up with a hostess from a VIP lounge at the New Orleans airport who testified that Clay Shaw was the man she saw sign her guest registry as Clay Bertrand. The guest registry book was produced, and each side presented a handwriting expert to counter the other on whether the writing was that of Clay Shaw.[78]

One of the most tantalizing aspects of the Clem Bertrand evidence concerned the original arrest sheet and fingerprint card, filled out when Shaw was booked following his arrest. The booking officer, a veteran New Orleans police officer named Aloysius J. Habighorst, stated that when he asked Shaw to list any aliases he used, Shaw gave the name Clay Bertrand. (This would have been prior to any wide publicity concerning the notoriety of the name Clem or Clay Bertrand.)[79]

Officer Habighorst claimed he dutifully typed that name onto the card. Clay denied that he provided anyone with that name at the time of his arrest, claiming that the fingerprint card was blank when he signed it. According to the testimony, the card with Shaw's fingerprints—which the judge deemed inadmissible as evidence—showed the name Clay Bertrand in the blank for any alias used by the person arrested. The name Clay Bertrand also appears in the space for aliases on the arrest sheet, which was supposedly filled out in Shaw's presence, but not signed by Shaw.[80]

However, in court, a technical legal debate erupted over whether Habighorst could testify that Shaw gave him the name Clay Bertrand as an alias.[81] Judge Haggerty refused to allow Habighorst to testify before the jury and stated, "Officer Habighorst did not forewarn Shaw of his right to remain silent. Even if Officer Habighorst did question him—and from what I've heard I seriously doubt it—"

"Your honor!" shouted one of the assistant prosecutors. "Are you ruling on the credibility of Habighorst?"

"No jurors are present," answered Judge Haggerty.

"But you are passing on the credibility of a witness before the press and the world," said the prosecutor.

"I don't care," responded the judge. "The whole world can hear that I do not believe Officer Habighorst. I do not believe Officer Habighorst."[82]

The prosecutor then demanded a mistrial, which Judge Haggerty promptly denied. The jury thus never heard the testimony of Habighorst, a veteran policeman, who was prepared to swear that Clay Shaw told him that he used the alias Clay Bertrand.[83]

The dispute over the alias Clay Bertrand may have become academic at the trial, thanks to a lawyer named Dean Andrews. At the heart of an enormous amount of testimony and evidence—going back to what Andrews told the Warren Commission—is the clear fact that Andrews is the first person to introduce the name of Clay or Clem Bertrand into any consideration. Andrews linked Bertrand to Lee Harvey Oswald and several Latin Americans in New Orleans in 1963. Andrews claimed he had done some minor legal work for Oswald and that after the assassination, Clay Bertrand telephoned him and asked him if he would represent Oswald in Dallas.[84] Several years later, Garrison based much of his case on the proposition that Clay Bertrand and Clay Shaw were one and the same—despite the conflicting descriptions of "Bertrand" that Andrews gave at different times. After all, it complemented Perry Russo's allegations perfectly. However, the whole issue came apart at the seams when Andrews, testifying for Shaw's defense, said that the story he gave regarding Clay Bertrand and Oswald was purely a "figment of [his] imagination." (Garrison later charged Andrews with perjury and obtained a conviction.) Andrews's testimony must have had a powerful effect on the jury.[85]

Jim Garrison's performance proved to be disappointing, particularly after months of highly publicized promises of what he would present at the trial. He produced no witnesses to suggest CIA involvement in an assassination conspiracy. He produced nothing, really, that went beyond what had been presented at the preliminary hearing two years earlier. He did not even come to the courtroom to hear Clay Shaw's testimony. He also missed about half of the defense's closing statement.[86]

On the last day of the trial, Garrison appeared to offer the closing argument for the prosecution. In his carefully rehearsed address of twenty-five minutes, Garrison mentioned the name of Clay Shaw only once. His aim, obviously, was to address what he considered to be a larger and more significant point than the charges he had filed against Clay Shaw.[87]

Here are the closing paragraphs of Garrison's final statement to the jury:

> The murder of John Kennedy was probably the most terrible moment in the history of our country. Yet, circumstances have placed you in the position where not only have you seen the hidden evidence but you are actually going to have the opportunity to bring justice into the picture for the first time.

> Now, you are here sitting in judgment on Clay Shaw. Yet you, as men, represent more than jurors in an ordinary case because of the victim in this case. You represent, in a sense, the hope of humanity against government power. You represent humanity, which yet may triumph over excessive government power if you will cause it to be so, in the course of doing your duty in this case.
>
> I suggest that you ask not what your country can do for you but what you can do for your country.
>
> What can you do for your country? You can cause justice to happen for the first time in this matter. You can help make our country better by showing that this is still a government of the people. And if you do that, as long as you live, nothing will ever be more important.[88]

It took the jury only one ballot to find Clay Shaw innocent of conspiracy to assassinate John F. Kennedy. His acquittal came on March 1, 1969, two years to the day after his arrest. Though his horrendous legal expenses had wiped out his personal resources, Shaw seemed to hold no bitterness. Obviously, things could have been worse.[89]

Two days later, Garrison charged Shaw with perjury, claiming he lied when he denied certain points in the trial. Such a move by a prosecutor toward an acquitted person was practically unheard of, raising the serious constitutional question of double jeopardy. Still, Shaw would not be goaded into making a negative comment about Garrison. Five years later, his legal entanglements with Garrison still in the courts, Clay Shaw died of cancer. He was sixty-one.[90]

## *Pearls in the Slime*

The reaction to Jim Garrison's prosecution of Clay Shaw was howling outrage.[91] In a tone that was reflected across the country, the *New Orleans States-Item* demanded that Garrison resign, claiming that he had "perverted the law rather than prosecuted it." Railing against Garrison, the newspaper stated: "This travesty of justice is a reproach to the conscience of all good men. . . . Mr. Garrison stands revealed for what he is: A man without principle who would pervert the legal process to his own ends."[92]

The *New York Times,* accusing Garrison of the "persecution of an innocent man," called the whole episode "one of the most disgraceful chapters in the history of American jurisprudence."[93]

As Garrison was being vilified from every corner of America, Shaw was portrayed as one of the most noble victims in the history of capricious prosecutions.[94] The enumeration of shocking tactics began with Garrison's well-publicized seizure of Shaw's whips and chains on the day of his arrest. This ostentatious performance persisted through the long pretrial period and did not end even with the charge of perjury that followed Shaw's acquittal. To many observers, Jim Garrison seemed obsessed with the destruction of Clay Shaw.[95]

This international vilification never seemed to bother Jim Garrison or, for that matter, the majority of voters of New Orleans. Considering the attention Garrison had directed away from Carlos Marcello, it is not surprising that he continued to coexist peacefully with organized crime. Garrison was handily reelected to his office in 1970, and it is even possible that he was helped locally by the publicity he received over the Shaw trial. In 1973 he lost another bid for reelection.[96]

In 1971 Garrison experienced legal difficulties over federal charges of fraud and conspiracy. Garrison was acquitted of all charges—including an allegation that he accepted payoffs to allow illegal gambling operations—and rather proudly displays these difficulties as scars of his victories over the powers that be. Today, he serves as an appeals judge, an elected office in New Orleans.[97]

In 1981 Garrison reaffirmed to the author his belief that he conducted a just prosecution of Clay Shaw. He reiterated his feeling that the United States government has purposely allowed the JFK case to go unsolved. Garrison said, "The frustrating thing is that really there is no mystery about it at all." With that statement, Garrison launched into a harangue about the military-industrial-intelligence complex and how, he believed (and still believes), it somehow carried off the assassination of President Kennedy.[98]

None of this, however, goes to the heart of Garrison's prosecution of Clay Shaw. Today, in discussing the case, still with considerable enthusiasm, Garrison does not point to specific evidence that he found particularly persuasive against Shaw. Rather, he speaks of the much grander schemes to which he alluded in his closing statement at the trial. He mentions the witnesses he did *not* present—and from there he proceeds to explain his reasons for being certain he does know who killed JFK. He speaks of Clay Shaw's connections with a group that he claims was a CIA operation. He cites his evidence that Shaw was an agent for the CIA. He states his firm belief that Shaw did know Ferrie, and that the two of them associated with Oswald. He speaks of his certainty that Shaw used the alias Clay Bertrand. Garrison's fervor for his case has not diminished.[99]

The fundamental trouble with most of what Garrison says on this point is that it has absolutely nothing to do with the specific conspiracy charge of which Clay Shaw was acquitted. Lee Oswald associated fleetingly with hundreds of people during his short adulthood, and so far not a single one has been proved to have conspired with him to assassinate President Kennedy. It is worth keeping in mind that Shaw could have known Ferrie—and even Oswald, but that alone would not mean that he conspired with them to kill President Kennedy.[100] It could even be established that Shaw is the elusive Clay Bertrand, and that would not prove anything beyond his having a secret life and associations with dubious characters.

At every turn—then and now—Garrison seemed to be telling the world that since he was on to *something*, then it was only right that Shaw, who indeed may have known Oswald and Ferrie, should be convicted. The American judicial system, as the New Orleans jury quickly demonstrated, does not work that way.

But the questions persist. What did Jim Garrison have? Putting aside the matter of his proved innocence, who *was* Clay Shaw? Did he associate with Oswald and David Ferrie? Was he connected to the CIA? The great irony is that Jim Garrison was correct on several points that may well be related to the JFK assassination. He publicly raised questions that still cry out for resolution. Moreover, in one important area concerning Oswald's associations, Garrison today can claim complete vindication by the House Select Committee.

An event in Oswald's life that still challenges comprehension is his presence in Clinton, Louisiana, during the late summer of 1963, when he seemed to be seeking a job. It was perhaps Garrison's most important revelation. In 1978 the Select Committee examined the six Clinton witnesses, who included an elected state representative, a deputy sheriff, and a voting registrar.[101] In its final report, the committee states: "The Committee found that the Clinton witnesses were credible and significant. . . . Some of the witnesses said that Oswald was accompanied by two older men whom they identified as Ferrie and Shaw. If the witnesses were not only truthful but accurate as well in their accounts, they established an association of an undetermined nature between Ferrie, Shaw, and Oswald less than three months before the assassination."[102]

There is virtually no doubt that Oswald, or someone pretending to be Oswald, was in Clinton as described. Given Ferrie's outlandish appearance, it seems certain that the witnesses have properly identified him. As for the third man, cited as Clay Shaw, his identification falls short of the certainty evident in the identification of Oswald and Ferrie. (Oswald actually produced military identification.) The third man was seen only in an automobile, and the cited descriptions could just as well be that of Guy Banister, the former FBI agent and Ferrie associate who will be examined thoroughly in later pages. This possibility has been noted by other writers and critics, who have pointed out that both men were described as being tall and heavily built, with gray hair. As will be seen, it probably makes more sense to believe that the man was Banister rather than Shaw. A prime reason is that Ferrie and Banister are solidly linked in a variety of ways that are unrelated to this incident.[103]

Aside from Garrison's revelation about the Clinton visit, there are several aspects of interest about Shaw. Garrison intimated outside the courtroom that Shaw had been associated with the CIA, a point he did not bring up at the trial.[104] Indeed, Shaw's professional associations are, in this respect, extremely noteworthy. While they have no known connection to an assassination conspiracy, they do raise questions about just who Clay Shaw was and how sensitive the government might have felt about revelations stemming from his prosecution. And, while his sex life is irrelevant to the assassination conspiracy, it, at the same time, may explain misconceptions that have sprung up, some of which may have propelled Garrison along his disastrous course.

Following his distinguished service in Europe during World War II, including combat decorations, Clay Shaw returned to New Orleans. From 1946 until August 1965, he was the managing director of the International Trade Mart, an organization aimed at the development of international trade relations, especially for the Port of New Orleans. In the course of things, Shaw became quite wealthy through his private business dealings, particularly in real estate.[105]

Shaw seems to have done a masterful job for his employers, blending his work as a promoter into his personal life as a writer and patron of the arts. He was at ease in the cultivated social and artistic life of New Orleans and counted among his close friends the most prominent men and women of the city. Stories are told of Shaw's generosity toward friends and his willingness to make sacrifices for others.[106]

Shaw's homosexuality was not an open matter, but rather an aspect of his life that seems not to have interested the people who were his friends and business associates. Even in New Orleans, during those years, it is unlikely that flagrant homosexuality would have been acceptable for a man in Shaw's position. He was, after all, a leading promoter of New Orleans to the outside world. It is not surprising that Shaw's private sex life was not a subject of common knowledge or discussion.[107]

Nor should it be surprising that, indeed, there was a darker side to Shaw's life that he did not flaunt. Given what is known of Hoover's FBI during those years, it is fairly predictable that the sex life of a man of Shaw's stature would come under official scrutiny. As early as 1954, the FBI recorded in its files the report of a New Orleans informant who stated that he "had relations of a homosexual nature with Clay Shaw." The FBI report then notes the informant's report that Shaw was "given to sadism and masochism in his homosexual activities."[108]

In view of this—as well as other unseemly evidence of a similar nature turned up by Garrison's office—it is not outlandish that Shaw might have engaged in a sexual association with David Ferrie. By the same token, he could have been associated with a whole network of homosexual activity that existed in New Orleans's French Quarter, where Shaw lived. It could, indeed, be that Shaw, in a fairly discreet manner, maintained sexual relationships that he very much wanted to conceal—relationships having absolutely nothing to do with a conspiracy to assassinate the President. However, the mere act of concealment—particularly if he falsely denied a relationship in court—could be sufficient to stimulate dark suspicions. Such a hypothesis is enhanced by the fact that Shaw was apparently unhappy over the suggestions of his homosexuality that were bandied about during his two-year nightmare.[109]

In 1977 a CIA document was disclosed that confirmed that Shaw had a relationship with the CIA. The information was contained in a 1967 memorandum prepared by the CIA in response to queries from the justice Department—queries stimulated by Garrison's investigation. It confirmed, at least in part, the connection Shaw had with the agency during his early years with the International Trade Mart.[110]

According to this document, reports from Shaw to the CIA were concerned with international trade as well as with political activities. The reports included various activities in East Germany, Czechoslovakia, Peru, Argentina, and Nicaragua. Between the years 1949 and 1956, according to the document, there were thirty occasions when the agency received information from Shaw.[111]

While the reported contacts stopped in 1956, Shaw apparently continued to enjoy a favorable relationship with the agency. It is not unreasonable to speculate that when the record of reports stopped in 1956, Shaw moved into a more significant role with the CIA—one that no longer went into an accounting in agency files.[112] Even Allen Dulles, the most prominent of the early directors of Central Intelligence, has stated that often no records are kept of the activities of agents.[113]

The apparently favorable relationship between Shaw and the CIA was made manifest in May 1961, when Shaw was asked to introduce the deputy director of the CIA, General Charles P. Cabell, who was in New Orleans to address the Foreign Policy Association. Shaw was program chairman of that group. General Cabell's speech in New Orleans came less than one month after he had personally supervised the disastrous Bay of Pigs invasion.[114] But General Cabell, who later was replaced by President Kennedy, did not use the New Orleans occasion to castigate the President. (Instead, he spoke about how the Soviet system had applied science to further its ideological goals.) The point here is that the selection of Clay Shaw to introduce General Cabell, the second highest figure at the CIA, suggests—in the absence of any record of Shaw's continuing reports to the CIA after 1956—that Shaw continued to enjoy a good relationship with the agency.[115]

Of the legitimate nuggets bandied about by Jim Garrison, none is more significant than the virtually solid evidence of Oswald's association with David W. Ferrie.[116] That link is a taproot from which Oswald's activities run in numerous directions. It is unlikely that the whole truth about Ferrie will ever emerge—or be widely accepted in the event that it does. He is, nonetheless, a significant subject for scrutiny.

Ferrie's known associations form a witch's brew of sinister elements. He can be solidly linked to the mobster Carlos Marcello, with whom he shared an intense hatred for President Kennedy. (See Chapter 8 of Henry Hurt, *Reasonable Doubt: An Investigation into the Assassination of John F. Kennedy* [New York, 1985] for details about Marcello and the Kennedy administration.) For many years Ferrie was closely associated with Guy Banister, a rabid extremist and former FBI man who was deeply involved with government intelligence operations in New Orleans—particularly as they related to Cuban exiles and their plans to "liberate" Cuba. This close association makes it quite possible that it was Bannister who was in Clinton, Louisiana, with Oswald and Ferrie in the summer of 1963.[117]

And there is the possibility of a more direct connection between Ferrie and U.S. intelligence—one that, not surprisingly, has never been confirmed. The most likely role for Ferrie was as a pilot involved in the strategy leading up to the Bay of Pigs invasion.[118] While the HSCA could not confirm such a role, it seemed particularly impressed with the connections between Ferrie and Carlos Marcello. It found that it was likely Ferrie had been a private pilot for Marcello, and the committee even considered "an unconfirmed Border Patrol report" that Ferrie had secretly flown the mobster back to New

Orleans from Guatemala following his sudden deportation by Robert Kennedy in April 1961. However, testifying in an executive session of the HSCA, Marcello denied this. Another interesting link between Ferrie and the New Orleans mob boss is that apparently following the JFK murder, Marcello set up Ferrie with a gas-station franchise—a fact ignored by Garrison in his investigation of Ferrie. If nothing else, the gesture suggested an obligation Marcello felt he owed Ferrie.[119]

Yet another oddity in Ferrie's activities examined by the Select Committee involved a fifteen-minute telephone call he appeared to have made to Jean West in Chicago two months prior to Kennedy's death. On the eve of the assassination, Miss West was in Dallas having drinks with Jack Ruby.[120] While none of this makes a conspiracy, it heightens the provocative interlocking connections that seem to link David Ferrie with various figures, including Marcello, Jack Ruby, and Lee Harvey Oswald.

David Ferrie's most important connection was one that he denied until his death—his suspected association with Oswald. Today the likelihood of that association is greater than ever. In addition to the sighting at Clinton in 1963, Oswald, as a teenager, belonged to Ferrie's unit of the Civil Air Patrol in New Orleans. Today, there are additional eyewitness reports that verify the association.[121]

Despite Ferrie's denial that he knew Oswald, he was plagued with the accusation from the first days of Oswald's notoriety. Even in 1963, the circumstantial evidence against Ferrie was so substantial that he was one of the earliest suspects questioned and released by the FBI.[122] It is worth considering Ferrie's activities—not because they prove anything, but because of the light they shed on this strange man. At the very least, Ferrie had a remarkable penchant for making himself appear to be involved, even if he was not.

During the fall of 1963, David W. Ferrie was supposedly occupied with his work on the immigration case involving Carlos Marcello. Ferrie was employed as an investigator by Marcello's lawyer. During the two weekends prior to the JFK assassination in November, Ferrie was at Churchill Farms, Marcello's 3,000-acre estate just outside New Orleans. Ferrie was supposedly at Marcello's home to participate in strategy sessions for the trial.[123]

That trial ended on November 22, 1963, in a federal courtroom in New Orleans, when Marcello was acquitted. Ferrie was last seen by a reliable witness around midday that Friday, almost at the time word was received that Kennedy had been shot in Dallas.[124] Such a perfectly packaged alibi, it seems, was all too neat for the daring pilot with the orange monkey hair.

Around nine that evening, Ferrie set off on a trip to Texas. He later explained that he wanted to relax after the trial's conclusion; he claimed he first decided to depart New Orleans without firm plans, not really knowing if he was going off "hunting, drinking or driving."[125] This whim took Ferrie and two young male friends on a seven-hour drive through a storm from New Orleans to Houston, a distance of 364 miles.[126]

The sole purpose of this trip, according to Ferrie's later contradictory statements, was to look over an ice rink and to do some skating.[127]

When they reached Houston at 4:30 in the morning, Ferrie and his youthful companions checked into a motel. Telephone records show that while at the motel, Ferrie made four telephone calls to New Orleans—three of them seemingly innocuous. One of the calls, however, was to the headquarters of Carlos Marcello. The purpose of that call, Ferrie claimed, was an attempt to locate the lawyer for whom he worked.[128]

The following day, after getting some rest at the motel, Ferrie and his companions arrived at the Winterland Ice Skating Rink. (The rink's manager told investigators that Ferrie, whom he had never met, had called him from New Orleans to check on his hours of operation.) Upon arriving at the rink, Ferrie introduced himself and told the manager that he and his party would be in and out of the place during the weekend—a weekend that included, among other shattering events, the murder of Oswald by Jack Ruby.[129]

As if Ferrie's presence at the skating rink were not already odd enough, there is another twist. While there, Ferrie never put on a pair of ice skates. Instead, he stayed beside a public telephone for two hours, until he received a call. There is no record of the calls made over that telephone.[130]

When the strange trio left the rink, their first stop was another skating rink in Houston. They then decided to drive on to Galveston before heading back to Louisiana on Sunday night. During this final leg of the trip, Ferrie telephoned a friend in New Orleans who informed him that he was being sought in connection with the assassination of President Kennedy.[131]

In many ways, Ferrie was a predictable suspect. He readily admitted making violent comments suggesting the benefits to America if someone would shoot the President. He had bitterly denounced Kennedy following the Bay of Pigs debacle. On one occasion, Ferrie had to be removed from a speaker's podium at a men's civic club when his comments about Kennedy became violently offensive. Leaders of the group that had invited him to speak felt compelled to squelch his vitriolic and violent bombast.[132]

Much later, in a note apparently written hours before his death, Ferrie reaffirmed his political colors when he wrote that "an electorate cannot be depended on to pick the right man."[133] For all these reasons, it seems certain that Ferrie would not object to the fact or the manner of Kennedy's abrupt removal from office.

Ferrie's reputation as a Kennedy-hater no doubt contributed to the early reports in New Orleans that he had been involved in the assassination.[134] Many knew, too, of his close association with Carlos Marcello, a man with the most intense personal reasons for wanting to see an end to all Kennedy power in the United States.[135]

In any event, the day after his return from the skating escapade in Texas, Ferrie presented himself at the office of the New Orleans district attorney. He was questioned by Jim Garrison's staff and then turned over to the FBI and Secret Service for additional investigation.[136]

The specific reports that led to suspicions of Ferrie came from several sources. One report was that Oswald, when arrested, was carrying Ferrie's New Orleans library card. This apparently was not true. It was also alleged that Ferrie had taught Oswald how to shoot using a telescopic lens when Oswald was a cadet in Ferrie's unit of the Civil Air Patrol.[137]

Ferrie denied that he had ever even met Oswald. He was quickly sent on his way by the FBI and the Secret Service.[138] It was not until three years later that Garrison's office resurrected the whole matter of Ferrie's possible connection to the assassination.

What, though, could Ferrie have been doing at the ice-skating rink in Houston?

Garrison was convinced that the trip was part of the post-assassination phase of the conspiracy. He found that Jack Ruby placed a call to Galveston the night after the assassination, which was during the period of Ferrie's visit there.[139]

Despite intense efforts by Garrison to develop additional evidence to explain Ferrie's reasons for such behavior, the trip remains a mystery. Moreover, there is not the slightest indication that the young men with Ferrie—one of them a high school student—knew what was going on or knew the names of the people Ferrie was talking to on the telephone.[140]

Maybe the whole affair was nothing more than a romp through the rain. Maybe, too, it was something else.

From the moment of Ferrie's death and Clay Shaw's arrest, Jim Garrison saw sinister shadows dancing around (and even within) his prosecution. He believed that he and his office were under extensive surveillance, and he instigated an internal system of code words in an effort to thwart the perceived surveillance. He claimed that the intelligence powers in Washington were working to wreck his case. Garrison also saw evidence of collusion to disrupt his case in the fact that five states refused to extradite certain witnesses. There was the peculiar business of Attorney General Ramsey Clark's leaping into the New Orleans fray with his confused and contradictory statements about Clay Shaw's innocence. Clark's actions, if nothing else, demonstrated that the Justice Department was intent on doing its part to exonerate Shaw. Even President Johnson took a personal interest in the events surrounding the prosecution.[141]

If Garrison had offered a more persuasive case, perhaps some of his subsequent charges could be taken more seriously. Considering the mad atmosphere that marked the whole two-year episode, it is not surprising that five states declined to extradite their residents who did not want to become involved. Moreover, it seems predictable that officials in Washington would be reluctant to testify in such an extravaganza if they could avoid it. While there may have been some technical deficiencies in this lack of cooperation, it is, from a practical standpoint, easy to understand.

However, what is difficult to understand is a report that the CIA, at its highest level, was concerned on a regular basis with the progress of the Garrison case. Victor Marchetti, who resigned from the agency in 1969, served as an executive assistant to the CIA deputy director at the time of the case. Marchetti has told Warren Commission critic

Bernard Fensterwald, Jr., that he heard agency officials, during their regular staff meeting one morning, discuss the need for providing help in the Garrison case. While Marchetti does not claim he heard specific discussion about ways to wreck Garrison's case, he says that the comments, even at the level of director, were in terms of questions like, "Are we giving them all the help they need?"[142]

It is likely that such comments did not refer to helping Garrison. However, what is not known are details of the "help," if any, Shaw may have been provided by the CIA. That was not discussed at the meeting attended by Marchetti. It was also on this occasion that Marchetti heard what would become public many years later—that Clay Shaw had been of service to the agency.[143]

In the final analysis, Jim Garrison never proved a single point in court against Clay Shaw—a fact that is largely responsible for the vilification of Garrison that continues to this day.[144] It will never be known what would have been proved if David Ferrie had lived. Garrison did, however, raise questions that go to the heart of the enduring mystery of the Kennedy assassination. Most of those questions were stimulated by the simple, logical belief of so many—that *something* was going on in New Orleans. Even today, no area of the incomplete investigation is richer than New Orleans in tantalizing irony and coincidence. . . .

## Notes for "New Orleans, USA"

[1]Inaugural speech, January 20, 1961, John F. Kennedy Library.

[2]Ralph G. Martin, *A Hero for Our Time* (New York, 1983), 262.

[3]U.S. House, Select Committee on Assassinations, *Hearings Before the Select Committee: Investigation of the Assassination of President John F Kennedy*, 95th Congress, 2d sess., 5 vols., 1978, and *Appendix to Hearings Before the Select Committee on Assassinations*, 95th Congress, 2d sess., 7 vols., March 1979, (vols. 1-5 from *Investigation*, vols. 6-12 from *Appendix*), 10:6, hereinafter cited as HSCA; U.S. House, Select Committee on Assassinations, *Report of the Select Committee on Assassinations: Findings and Recommendations*, 95th Congress, 2d sess., H. Rpt. 95-1828, part 2, 24, hereinafter cited as HSCR; Richard M. Nixon, "Cuba, Castro, and John F. Kennedy," *Reader's Digest*, November 1964; Warren Hinckle and William Turner, *The Fish Is Red: The Story of the Secret War Against Castro* (New York, 1981), 20-21; Taylor Branch and George Crile III, "The Kennedy Vendetta," *Harper's*, August 1975.

[4]HSCR, 25; Hinckle and Turner, *The Fish Is Red*, 17, 99, 200; HSCA, 4:471; David Scheim, *Contract on America* (Silver Spring, Md., 1983), 156; interview with Dr. Jorge Dominguez, specialist on Cuban affairs, Harvard University, 1984; interview with William Atwood, 1983.

[5]ABC-TV News, "Fidel Castro Speaks," Barbara Walters interview, June 9, 1977; Daniel Schorr, *Clearing the Air* (Boston, 1977), 175; HSCA, 10:181-82; Senate Select Committee to Study Governmental Operations with Respect to Intelligence Activities, *Alleged Assassination Plots Involving Foreign Leaders: An Interim Report*, 94th Congress, 1st sess., November 20, 1975, 71.

[6]HSCA, 9:14; Scheim, *Contract on America*, 160; Senate Select Committee, *Alleged Assassination Plots*, 74-85, 100; G. Robert Blakely and Richard Billings, *The Plot to Kill the President* (New York, 1981), 229-30; Hinckle and Turner, *The Fish Is Red*, 25, 78; Ovid Demaris, *The Last Mafioso* (New York, 1975), 108.

[7]Senate Select Committee, *Alleged Assassination Plots*, 85; HSCR, 33-34; HSCA, 9:60; Scheim, *Contract on America*, 3, 38-39; Harris Wofford, *Of Kennedys and Kings* (New York, 1980), 401, 403; Hinckle and Turner, *The Fish Is Red*, 215; Herbert S. Parmet, *JFK: The Presidency of John F. Kennedy* (New York, 1983), 60; Nixon, "Cuba, Castro, and John F. Kennedy."

[8]Robert Sam Anson, *"They've Killed the President!": The Search for the Murderers of John F. Kennedy* (New York, 1976), 16; Scheim, *Contract on America*, 57-158; "How Tax Changes Split Policy-Makers," *Nation's Business*, November 1962; "Depletion Allowance: Loophole or Merited Relief?", *Business Week*, April 1, 1961; "Kennedy's Latest Word on Tax Cuts," *U.S. News & World Report*, December 24, 1962; spokesman for the Texas Independent Producers and Royalty Owners Association, Austin.

[9]Louis Lomax, "The Kennedys Move in on Dixie," *Harper's*, May 1962; "The South: Crisis in Civil Rights," *Time*, June 2, 1961; Simeon Booker, "What Negroes Can Expect from Kennedy," *Ebony*, January 1961; HSCR, 31; Hinckle and Turner, *The Fish Is Red*, 199.

[10]Spokesman for the Cuban American Foundation, Washington, D.C.

[11]Interview with Aaron Kohn, 1983.

[12]Ibid.; Warren Rogers, "The Persecution of Clay Shaw," *Look*, August 26, 1969; "Carlos Marcello: King Thug of Louisiana," *Life*, September 8, 1967.

[13]U.S. President's Commission on the Assassination of President John F. Kennedy, *Report of the President's Commission on the Assassination of President John F. Kennedy* (Washington, D.C., 1964), 670, 725-31, hereinafter cited as WR for Warren Report.

[14]*New Orleans States-Item*, February 17, 23, and 24, 1967; Rosemary James and Jack Wardlaw, *Plot or Politics?: The Garrison Case and Its Cast* (New Orleans, 1967), 16, 26; "A Taste for Conspiracy," *Newsweek*, March 20, 1967; Joachim Joesten, *The Garrison Enquiry: Truth & Consequences* (London, 1967), 10; Eric Norden, "Playboy Interview: Jim Garrison," *Playboy*, October 1967; Committee to Investigate Assassinations, *Coincidence or Conspiracy?* (New York, 1977), 459; WR, 21; Edward J. Epstein, *Counterplot* (New York, 1969), 21.

[15]*New Orleans States-Item*, February 24, 1967.

[16]"Clay Shaw," *Penthouse*, November 1969; *Washington Post*, March 4, 1969; *New York Post*, March 1, 1969.

[17]James and Wardlaw, *Plot or Politics?*, 16-18, 21-22, 29, 72; *New York Times*, February 25, 1967, March 2, 1969; Rogers, "The Persecution of Clay Shaw"; interview with Kohn, 1983; *Washington Post*, February 23, 1969; James Phelan, "Rush to Judgment in New Orleans," *Saturday Evening Post*, May 6, 1967; *New Orleans States-Item*, February 23, 1967; Jim Garrison, *A Heritage of Stone* (New York, 1970); interview with Jim Garrison; Joesten, *The Garrison Enquiry*, 18-19; FBI memo on the assassination of John Kennedy, February 20, 1967 (HQ 105-82555); Epstein, *Counterplot*, 24; James Kirkwood, *American Grotesque: An Account of the Clay Shaw—Jim Garrison Affair in the City of New Orleans* (New York, 1970), 78; Walter Sheridan, *The Fall and Rise of Jimmy Hoffa* (New York, 1973), 78; Bernard Fensterwald, "Jim Garrison, District Attorney Orleans Parish vs. the Federal Government," *Computers and Automation*, August 1971.

[18]Epstein, *Counterplot*, 25; Sheridan, *The Fall and Rise of Jimmy Hoffa*; Rogers, "The Persecution of Clay Shaw"; G. Robert Blakey and Richard N. Billings, *The Plot to Kill the President* (New York, 1981), 50; *Wall Street Journal*, February 9, 1968; Anson, *"They've Killed the President!"*, 126-27; interview with Kohn, 1983; Kirkwood, *American Grotesque*, 529; James and Wardlaw, *Plot or Politics?*, 26.

[19]Scheim, *Contract on America*, 57.

[20]Ibid., 59.

[21]Interview with Kohn, 1983.

[22]Phelan, "Rush to Judgment in New Orleans."

[23]*New Orleans States-Item*, February 17, 23, 1967; Norden, "Playboy Interview: Jim Garrison"; Phelan "Rush to Judgment in New Orleans"; James and Wardlaw, *Plot or Politics?*, 33-34, 39; Kirkwood, *American Grotesque*, 141; Joesten, *The Garrison Enquiry*, 10, 12; *Dallas Times Herald*, February 19, 1967; FBI memo (HQ 105-82555); statement of George Lardner, Jr., to New Orleans district attorney's office, February 22, 1967.

[24]Kirkwood, *American Grotesque*, 123-26; HSCA, 10:106, 110; Blakely and Billings, *Plot to Kill*, 167; James and Wardlaw, *Plot or Politics?*, 42-43; Joesten, *The Garrison Enquiry*, 11; Harold Weisburg, *Oswald in New*

*Orleans—Case for Conspiracy with the CIA* (New York, 1967), 165-66; FBI memo, DeLoach to Tolson, February 23, 1967 (HQ 62-109060-4582); Warren Commission Document 87, National Archives, hereinafter referred to as CD; interview with Harold Weisburg; Garrison, *A Heritage of Stone*, 121; *New York Times*, February 23, 1967.

[25]Kirkwood, *American Grotesque*, 124; Blakey and Billings, *Plot to Kill*, 167; Phelan, "Rush to Judgment in New Orleans"; James and Wardlaw, *Plot or Politics?*, 43; HSCA, 10:106-107, 109; Weisburg, *Oswald in New Orleans*, 163; Joesten, *The Garrison Enquiry*, 11-12; CD 75, 285-97; *New Orleans States-Item*, February 23, 1967; *Chicago Sun-Times*, March 29, 1967; interview by Bernard Fensterwald of Victor Marchetti, April 22, 1975; Garrison, *A Heritage of Stone*, 122; Committee to Investigate Assassinations, *Coincidence or Conspiracy?*, 298-99; Hinckle and Turner, *The Fish Is Red*, 204; Peter Boyles, "Fear and Loathing on the Assassination Trail," *Denver Magazine*, November 1980.

[26]Blakey and Billings, *Plot to Kill*, 168; HSCA, 10:108, 110; Joesten, *The Garrison Enquiry*, 11; Kirkwood, *American Grotesque*, 123-25; James and Wardlaw, *Plot or Politics?*, 42; *New York Times*, February 23, 1967; HSCA, 10:112; HSCR, 142.

[27]*Dallas Times Herald*, February 19, 1967; Kirkwood, *American Grotesque*, 142; James and Wardlaw, *Plot or Politics?*, 39; *New York Times*, February 23, 1967; Joesten, *The Garrison Enquiry*, 29; HSCR, 39; Phelan, "Rush to Judgment in New Orleans"; *New Orleans States-Item*, February 23, 1967; CD 87; FBI memo, Rosen to Belmont, November 29, 1963; HSCA, 9:103.

[28]*Washington Post*, February 23, 1967, March 1, 1967; statement of Lardner to New Orleans district attorney's office, February 22, 1967; *Chicago Tribune*, February 23, 1967; Kirkwood, *American Grotesque*, 142; James and Wardlaw, *Plot or Politics?*, 40; *New York World Journal Tribune*, February 23, 1967; *Washington Post*, February 23, 1967.

[29]FBI memo (HQ 62-109060-4582); Weisberg, *Oswald in New Orleans*, 163; *New York Times*, February 23, 1967; Kirkwood, *American Grotesque*, 142; James and Wardlaw, *Plot or Politics?*, 40; CD 75, 285-97; FBI teletype, SAC New Orleans to Director, et al. (HQ 62-109060-482).

[30]*Chicago Tribune*, February 23, 1967; *New York World Journal Tribune*, February 23, 1967; *Washington Post*, March 1, 1967; FBI airtel, SAC New Orleans to Director, February 28, 1967 (HQ 62-109060-4579).

[31]*New York World Journal Tribune*, February 23, 24, 1967; Kirkwood, *American Grotesque*, 124; *Washington Post*, March 1, 1967; *Chicago Tribune*, February 23, 1967.

[32]*New York World Journal Tribune*, February 23, 1967; *New Orleans States-Item*, February 23, 1967, January 13, 1979; *New York Times*, February 23, 1967; *Chicago Tribune*, February 23, 1967; Kirkwood, *American Grotesque*, 143.

[33]Weisburg, *Oswald in New Orleans*, 163; *New York World Journal Tribune*, February 28, 1967.

[34]FBI memo (HQ 62-109060-4582).

[35]*New Orleans States-Item*, February 24, 1967.

[36]Kirkwood, *American Grotesque*, 19, 26-27, 145; "Clay Shaw"; Rogers, "The Persecution of Clay Shaw"; FBI memo, Branigan to Sullivan, March 2, 1967 (HQ 105-82555); *The New York Times*, March 2, 3, 1967; Epstein, *Counterplot*, 65; Phelan, "Rush to Judgment in New Orleans"; James and Wardlaw, *Plot or Politics?*, 53.

[37]James and Wardlaw, *Plot or Politics?*, 16-30, 54, 59; *New York Times*, August 16, 1974; Rogers, "The Persecution of Clay Shaw"; "Clay Shaw"; Kirkwood, *American Grotesque*, 27, 80; interview with Kohn, 1983; Anson, *"They've Killed the President!"*, 119.

[38]"Clay Shaw"; Rogers, "The Persecution of Clay Shaw"; Blakey and Billings, *Plot to Kill*, 51; Kirkwood, *American Grotesque*, 154; James and Wardlaw, *Plot or Politics?*, 68; *New York Times*, March 2, 3, 1967, March 2, 1969; Norden, "Playboy Interview: Jim Garrison"; *Los Angeles Free Press*, February 9-15, 1968; Epstein, *Counterplot*, 74.

[39]*New York Times*, March 3, 1967; James and Wardlaw, *Plot or Politics?*, 58.

[40]*New York Times*, March 3, 1967.

[41]Phelan, "Rush to Judgment in New Orleans"; James and Wardlaw, *Plot or Politics?*, 59.

[42]Norden, "Playboy Interview: Jim Garrison." Clark was no longer merely the Acting Attorney General; his appointment was confirmed by the Senate in mid-March 1967.

[43]"Clay Shaw"; *Chicago Sun-Times*, March 29, 1967; *New York Times*, March 18, 1967; Kirkwood, *American Grotesque*, 60, 64-65.

[44]*New York Times*, March 18, 1967; Rogers, "The Persecution of Clay Shaw"; James and Wardlaw, *Plot or Politics?*, 14, 22, 74, 76-78; Kirkwood, *American Grotesque*, 144; *New York Times*, March 16, 1967; Phelan, "Rush to Judgment in New Orleans"; *Dallas Morning News*, March 15, 1967.

[45]"Clay Shaw"; James and Wardlaw, *Plot or Politics?*, 78; *Dallas Morning News*, March 15, 1967; Epstein, *Counterplot*, 55; *New York Times*, March 16, 1967.

[46]Kirkwood, *American Grotesque*, 157, 225; James and Wardlaw, *Plot or Politics?*, 81, 136; *New York Times*, March 18, 1967; Phelan, "Rush to Judgment in New Orleans"; "Clay Shaw."

[47]*New York Times*, March 18, 1967; Phelan, "Rush to Judgment in New Orleans"; Kirkwood, *American Grotesque*, 157; James and Wardlaw, *Plot or Politics?*, 81.

[48]James Phelan, *Scandals, Scamps and Scoundrels: The Casebook of an Investigative Reporter* (New York, 1982), 166-67.

[49]Epstein, *Counterplot*, 70-71; *Washington Post*, February 23, 1969; *New York Post*, February 12, 1968; *New York Times*, September 22, 1967, March 2, 1969; *Cincinnati Enquirer*, September 11, 1967; *Daily Oklahoman*, December 10, 1967; interview with Kohn, 1983; interview with Mary Ferrell; Norden, "Playboy Interview: Jim Garrison"; interview with Jim Garrison; Blakey and Billings, *Plot to Kill*, 50; *Washington Post*, July 13, 1968; Kirkwood, *American Grotesque*, 492.

[50]Anson, *"They've Killed the President!"*, 113-14; interview with Kohn, 1983; *Cincinnati Enquirer*, September 11, 1967.

[51]Harold Weisberg is an excellent example of such a critic. Much of his highly respected, pioneering work on Oswald's ties to some of the figures in Garrison's case is found in his book *Oswald in New Orleans*. Some other critics, however, were more skeptical of Garrison's "evidence." *New York Times*, July 12, 1968; Norden, "Playboy Interview: Jim Garrison"; Rogers, "The Persecution of Clay Shaw"; James and Wardlaw, *Plot or Politics?*, 122, 133; Blakey and Billings, *Plot to Kill*, 45, 51; Anson, *"They've Killed the President!"*, 110; Kirkwood, *American Grotesque*, 178-79; interview with Weisberg; interview with Ferrell; interview with Sylvia Meagher.

[52]Phelan, "Rush to Judgment in New Orleans"; *New Orleans Times-Picayune*, February 27, 1969; Phelan, *Scandals, Scamps and Scoundrels*, 139, 143-45.

[53]Phelan, *Scandals, Scamps and Scoundrels*, 139-45; *New Orleans Times-Picayune*, February 27, 1969; Phelan, "Rush to Judgment in New Orleans."

[54]Phelan, *Scandals, Scamps and Scoundrels*, 142, 145-51; Phelan, "Rush to Judgment in New Orleans."

[55]Phelan, *Scandals, Scamps and Scoundrels*, 151; Phelan, "Rush to Judgment in New Orleans."

[56]*New Orleans Times-Picayune*, February 27, 1969; Phelan, "Rush to Judgment in New Orleans"; Phelan, *Scandals, Scamps and Scoundrels*, 151-52; FBI memo Branigan to Sullivan, February 13, 1969; *New York Times*, February 20, 1969; Kirkwood, *American Grotesque*.

[57]Phelan, *Scandals, Scamps and Scoundrels*, 152.

[58]*Washington Post*, February 23, 1969; Phelan, "Rush to Judgment in New Orleans"; *New Orleans Times-Picayune*, February 27, 1969; FBI memo Branigan to Sullivan, February 13, 1969; Phelan, *Scandals, Scamps and Scoundrels*, 152-54; "Clay Shaw"; Kirkwood, *American Grotesque*, 150.

[59]Phelan, *Scandals, Scamps and Scoundrels*, 154-55; *New Orleans Times-Picayune*, February 27, 1969.

[60]*New Orleans Times-Picayune*, February 27, 1969; Phelan, *Scandals, Scamps and Scoundrels*, 156-58; James and Wardlaw, *Plot or Politics?*, 78, 81; "Clay Shaw"; Kirkwood, *American Grotesque*, 157; *New York Times*, March 18, 1967; Phelan, "Rush to Judgment in New Orleans."

[61]*New Orleans Times-Picayune*, February 27, 1969; Phelan, *Scandals, Scamps and Scoundrels*, 158; Phelan, "Rush to Judgment in New Orleans"; FBI memo Branigan to Sullivan, February 13, 1969.

[62]Kirkwood, *American Grotesque*, 211, 399; Phelan, *Scandals, Scamps and Scoundrels*, 159; Phelan, "Rush to Judgment in New Orleans"; FBI memo Branigan to Sullivan, February 13, 1969.

[63]Phelan, *Scandals, Scamps and Scoundrels*, 159; *New Orleans Times-Picayune*, February 27, 1969.

[64]Phelan, "Rush to Judgment in New Orleans"; "Clay Shaw"; Phelan, *Scandals, Scamps and Scoundrels*, 159-60; James and Wardlaw, *Plot or Politics?*, 79-80; *New York Times*, February 27, 1969; *New Orleans Times-Picayune*, February 27, 1969.

[65]Epstein, *Counterplot*, 75-80; interview with Tom Bethell, researcher for Garrison during Shaw case, 1983; *Dallas Times Herald*, November 21, 1982; interview with Ferrell.

[66]*New York Times*, April 19, 1967, January 27, 1968, November 9, 1968; James and Wardlaw, *Plot or Politics?*, 81, 114; *Atlanta Journal*, May 10, 1967; "Clay Shaw"; interview with Garrison; Epstein, *Counterplot*, 96, 118, 133; *Washington Post*, February 17, 1968; Anson, *"They've Killed the President!"*, 122; FBI memo, Branigan to Sullivan, May 8, 1968 (HQ 62-109060-6404); CIA memo, "Garrison Investigation; Queries from Justice Dept.," September 28, 1967 (CIA 1326-1042); FBI memo, Branigan to Sullivan, May 14, 1968; FBI memo, Branigan to Sullivan, May 13, 1968 (HQ 62-109060-6405).

[67]James and Wardlaw, *Plot or Politics?*, 114; Blakey and Billings, *Plot to Kill*, 50; *Washington Post*, July 13, 1968; *New York Times*, May 10, 1967, June 25, 1967, March 2, 1969; Kirkwood, *American Grotesque*, 492, 535; interview with G. Robert Blakey; *Washington Post*, February 23, 1969; *National Observer*, March 1969; FBI memo, Branigan to Sullivan, May 8, 1968 (HQ 62-109060-6404); Epstein, *Counterplot*, 133; interview with Kohn, 1983; "Clay Shaw."

[68]*Washington Post*, January 21, 1969; *New York Times*, January 21, 22, 1969; "Clay Shaw"; Kirkwood, *American Grotesque*, 62-63.

[69]*Dallas Morning News*, February 2, 1969; "Clay Shaw"; Kirkwood, *American Grotesque*, 62, 187.

[70]*Washington Post*, February 7, 1969; *New Orleans Times-Picayune*, February 22, 1969; HSCR, 142; HSCA, 4:485; Kirkwood, *American Grotesque*, 213-23, Blakey and Billings, *Plot to Kill*, 170; interview with Ferrell.

[71]The one likely explanation for Russo's erratic testimony is, as he told several people privately, that he never dreamed that he was the *only* witness Garrison had to make the conspiracy point. In agreeable innocence, Russo said that he *thought* he saw an older man at a gathering who *could* have been Shaw. At each step, Russo faced the wrath of Garrison's office if he retreated on a point he had been led to previously. Clear indications suggest that Russo was as shocked as anyone to find himself the star witness—the centerpiece around whom the rest of the case revolved.

Kirkwood, *American Grotesque*, 249-50, 290, 399-401, 442, 479, 612; "Clay Shaw"; *Chicago Sun-Times*, March 29, 1967; *New York Times*, February 27, 1969; Rogers, "The Persecution of Clay Shaw"; *New Orleans Times-Picayune*, February 27, 1969; *Dallas Times Herald*, November 21, 1982; *Washington Post*, February 27, 1969.

[72]Kirkwood, *American Grotesque*, 368, 404-7, 410; *New York News*, February 28, 1969; "Clay Shaw"; *New Orleans Times-Picayune*, February 22, 1969; *National Observer*, February 24, 1969.

[73]*Washington Post*, February 14, 1969, March 4, 1969; *National Observer*, February 24, 1969, March 1969; Kirkwood, *American Grotesque*, 97, 311-14, 315, 320-21, 324, 332, 361, 374; *New York Times*, February 16, 25, 26, 1969, March 2, 1969; "Clay Shaw"; interview with Garrison; *New Orleans States-Item*, February 19, 20, 1969; *New Orleans Times-Picayune*, February 26, 1969.

[74]*Washington Post*, February 8, 1969; *New York Times*, February 8, 1969, March 2, 1969; Kirkwood, *American Grotesque*, 231-32; Rogers, "The Persecution of Clay Shaw"; interview with Ferrell.

[75]*New York Times*, February 8, 10, 1969; *Washington Post*, February 8, 1969; Kirkwood, *American Grotesque*, 232, 239; Rogers, "The Persecution of Clay Shaw."

[76]*New Orleans States-Item*, February 20, 1969; *New York Times*, February 8, 1969, March 2, 1969, August 16, 1974; Rogers, "The Persecution of Clay Shaw"; Kirkwood, *American Grotesque*, 235-36.

[77]Kirkwood, *American Grotesque*, 240, 242; interview with Ferrell; Rogers, "The Persecution of Clay Shaw."

[78]Kirkwood, *American Grotesque*, 207, 306-7, 348, 397-98, 423-25; *New Orleans States-Item*, February 19, 20, 26, 1969; *New York Times*, February 20, 26, 1969; *New Orleans Times-Picayune*, February 27, 1969.

[79]Arrest record for Clay Shaw, New Orleans; *New Orleans States-Item*, February 20, 1969; Kirkwood, *American Grotesque*, 353; spokesman for New Orleans Police Department; *New York Times*, February 20, 1969.

[80]Interview with Ferrell; *New Orleans States-Item*, February 20, 1969; *New York Times*, February 20, 1969; Kirkwood, *American Grotesque*, 353.

[81]Kirkwood, *American Grotesque*, 358; *New Orleans States-Item*, February 20, 1969.

[82]*New Orleans States-Item*, February 20, 1969.

[83]Ibid.; *New York Times*, February 20, 1969; Kirkwood, *American Grotesque*, 353-59; spokesman for New Orleans Police Department.

[84]U.S. President's Commission on the Assassination of President John F. Kennedy, *Investigation of the Assassination of President John F. Kennedy: Hearings*, 26 vols. (Washington, D.C., 1964), 11:325-39, 26:771, hereinafter cited as WC; FBI memo Branigan to Sullivan, March 2, 1967 (HQ 105-82555); *New York Times*, March 3, 11, 1967; WC, 23:726; Kirkwood, *American Grotesque*, 130; *New Orleans Times-Picayune*, February 26, 1969; "Clay Shaw"; James and Wardlaw, *Plot or Politics?*, 14, 53.

[85]*New Orleans Times-Picayune*, February 26, 1969; Kirkwood, *American Grotesque*, 139-40, 159-60, 385-95; James and Wardlaw, *Plot or Politics?*, 140; interview with Garrison.

[86]*New York Post*, February 24, 1969; Kirkwood, *American Grotesque*, 404-5, 491; interview with Ferrell; "Clay Shaw."

[87]Interview with Garrison; Kirkwood, *American Grotesque*, 454-60; *Washington Post*, March 2, 1969.

[88]Kirkwood, *American Grotesque*, 459-60.

[89]*National Observer*, March 1969; *Dallas Times Herald*, November 21, 1982; "Clay Shaw"; *Washington Post*, March 2, 1969; Kirkwood, *American Grotesque*, 461, 466, 472-73; *New York Times*, March 4, 1969; *New York News*, March 2, 1969; Rogers, "The Persecution of Clay Shaw."

[90]*New York Times*, March 4, 1969, August 16, 1974; *Washington Post*, March 4, 1969; Kirkwood, *American Grotesque*, 478; "Clay Shaw"; *Dallas Times Herald*, November 21, 1982; *New York Post*, March 7, 1969; interview with Kathryn Kuss, cousin of Clay Shaw, 1983.

[91]*New York Times*, March 4, 1969, November 30, 1969; Kirkwood, *American Grotesque*, 471, 477; *Christian Science Monitor*, March 5, 1969; *Washington Post*, March 4, 1969; *National Observer*, March 1969; *New York Post*, March 1, 3, 7, 1969; *New York News*, March 2, 1969.

[92]*New Orleans States-Item*, March 1, 1969.

[93]*New York Times*, March 2, 1969.

[94]Rogers, "The Persecution of Clay Shaw"; *New York Times*, November 30, 1969; *Christian Science Monitor*, March 5, 1969; *Washington Post*, March 4, 1969; Kirkwood, *American Grotesque*, 471, 477; *New York Post*, March 1, 3, 7, 1969.

[95]Rogers, "The Persecution of Clay Shaw"; *New York Times*, March 3, 1969; Kirkwood, *American Grotesque*, 26-27, 471, 477, 603; Phelan, "Rush to Judgment in New Orleans"; interview with Kohn, 1983.

[96]Rogers, "The Persecution of Clay Shaw"; interview with Kohn, 1983; *New York Times*, November 10, 1969, February 22, 1970, December 17, 1973, March 27, 1974, August 16, 1974; *New Orleans Times-Picayune*, December 19, 1973; Kirkwood, *American Grotesque*, 648.

[97]*Christian Science Monitor*, July 3, 1971; *New York Times*, July 2, 1971; *Wall Street Journal*, May 30, 1972; indictment, *U.S. v. Jim Garrison, et al.*, U.S. District Court, Eastern District of Louisiana, New Orleans Division (CA 71-541); judgment, *U.S. v. Jim Garrison*, U.S. District Court, Eastern District of Louisiana (CA 71-542); judgment, *U.S. v. Jim Garrison*, U.S. District Court, Eastern District of Louisiana (CA 71-541); interview with Garrison; *New York Times*, March 27, 31, 1974, May 29, 1978.

[98]Interview with Garrison.

[99]Ibid.

[100]FBI report, interview of Carroll S. Thomas, New Orleans, March 21, 1967 (N.O. 89-69-1781; HQ 62-109060-4864).

[101]HSCR, 142; Blakey and Billings, *Plot to Kill*, 170; Kirkwood, *American Grotesque*, 213-15.

[102]HSCR, 142-43.

[103]Ibid., 143, 145-46; Blakey and Billings, *Plot to Kill*, 170; Kirkwood, *American Grotesque*, 129, 214-16; Anson, *"They've Killed the President!"*, 121; Anthony Summers, *Conspiracy* (New York, 1981), 335; *New Orleans Times-Picayune*, February 27, 1969; "Clay Shaw"; HSCA, 10:110, 126.

[104]Interview with Garrison; Kirkwood, *American Grotesque*, 574; "Clay Shaw."

[105]*New York Times*, March 2, 3, 1967; Kirkwood, *American Grotesque*, 18-19; James and Wardlaw, *Plot or Politics?*, 55, 63-64, 67; FBI memo, Branigan to Sullivan, March 2, 1967 (HQ 105-82555); "Clay Shaw"; Norden, "Playboy Interview: Jim Garrison"; Committee to Investigate Assassinations, *Coincidence or Conspiracy?*, 451; *New Orleans Times-Picayune*, February 27, 1969.

[106]Norden, "Playboy Interview: Jim Garrison"; interview with Kuss, 1983; Kirkwood, *American Grotesque*; Anson, *"They've Killed the President!"*, 114; interview with Kohn, 1983.

[107]Committee to Investigate Assassinations, *Coincidence or Conspiracy?*, 454; Rogers, "The Persecution of Clay Shaw"; James and Wardlaw, *Plot or Politics?*, 59; interview with Kohn, 1983; interview with Kuss, 1983.

[108]FBI memo, Branigan to Sullivan, March 2, 1967 (HQ 105-82555).

[109]Spokesman for New Orleans Police Department; interview with Kuss, 1983; Rogers, "The Persecution of Clay Shaw."

[110]CIA memo, "Garrison Investigation: Queries from Justice Department," September 28, 1967.

[111]Ibid.

[112]Ibid.

[113]The President's Commission on the Assassination of President John F. Kennedy, *Report of Proceedings*, January 27, 1964, 152.

[114]Today it is known that Cabell and his associates were vehement in their rage toward what they perceived as President Kennedy's "desertion" on the morning of the invasion—the President's refusal to send in military force sufficient to ensure victory. The dispute was so intense that President Kennedy was moved to make his famous comment about wanting to "splinter the CIA in a thousand pieces and scatter it to the winds" over his belief that they had so badly misinformed him about their invasion plans.

Senate Select Committee, *Alleged Assassination Plots*, 91; CIA memo, "Garrison Investigation," September 28, 1967 (CIA 1326-1042); Hinckle and Turner, *The Fish Is Red*, 87, 92, 100; Martin, *A Hero for Our Time*, 329-30; Charles Murphy, "Cuba: The Record Set Straight," *Fortune*, September 1961; Herbert S. Parmet, *JFK: The Presidency of John F. Kennedy* (New York, 1983), 158-59, 169; Arthur M. Schlesinger, Jr., *A Thousand Days: John F. Kennedy in the White House* (Greenwich, Conn., 1965), 256; *New York Times*, April 25, 1966.

[115]It is one of history's odd coincidences that General Cabell's brother, Earle, was the mayor of Dallas in November 1963. He was riding in the motorcade several cars back from the President when Kennedy was struck.

Interview with Ferrell; interview with Paul Hoch; WR, 65; Committee to Investigate Assassinations, *Coincidence or Conspiracy?*, 237; David A. Phillips, *The Night Watch* (New York, 1977), 86.

[116]HSCR, 170.

[117]Ibid., 144, 170-71; HSCA, 10:107, 126; Rogers, "The Persecution of Clay Shaw"; CD 75, 287; Anson, *"They've Killed the President!"*, 121; Kirkwood, *American Grotesque*, 129, 216.

[118]Summers, *Conspiracy*, 329; interview by Fensterwald of Marchetti, April 22, 1975; Committee to Investigate Assassinations, *Coincidence or Conspiracy?*, 302; Hinckle and Turner, *The Fish Is Red*, 204; interview with Marchetti, 1983.

[119]HSCA, 10:109, 111-12; HSCR, 143, 147, 169-70; Rogers, "The Persecution of Clay Shaw"; Anson, *"They've Killed the President!"*, 123; Blakey and Billings, *Plot to Kill*, 50.

[120]Garrison, *A Heritage of Stone*, 124; Summers, *Conspiracy*, 477; HSCA, 4:499; *New Orleans States-Item*, January 3, 1979; WC, 25:190; HSCA, 9: 807.

[121]CD 75, 285-97; James and Wardlaw, *Plot or Politics?*, 12; *New York World Journal Tribune*, February 23, 1967; *Chicago Tribune*, February 23, 1967; HSCA, 9:103-115; HSCR, 145; WC, 22:826.

[122]James and Wardlaw, *Plot or Politics?*, 12, 43; *New York World Journal Tribune*, February 23, 1967; HSCA, 9:103-105; CD 75, 285-97; *Chicago Tribune*, February 23, 1967.

[123]HSCA, 10:110-12; CD 75, 285-97; James and Wardlaw, *Plot or Politics?*, 44; Blakey and Billings, *Plot to Kill*, 168-69; HSCA, 9:75.

[124]Blakey and Billings, *Plot to Kill*, 169; James and Wardlaw, *Plot or Politics?*, 44; CD 75, 219-20, 287; *New York Times*, February 25, 1967; *Chicago Tribune*, February 23, 1967; HSCA, 10:105, 113.

[125]CD 75, 285-97; Scheim, *Contract on America*, 51; HSCA, 10:113; *New York Times*, February 25, 1967.

[126]*New York Times*, February 25, 1967; William W. Turner, "The Garrison Commission on the Assassination of President Kennedy," *Ramparts*, January 1968; Hinckle and Turner, *The Fish Is Red*, 218; CD 75, 285-97; FBI memo, Branigan to Sullivan, February 13, 1969; statement of Alvin R. Beaubouef, Office of the District Attorney, New Orleans, December 15, 1966.

[127]Statement of Beaubouef, December 15, 1966; FBI memo, Branigan to Sullivan, February 13, 1969; CD 75, 287; FBI teletype, SAC New Orleans to Director et al. (HQ 62-109060-482).

[128]CD 75, 285-97; *New York Times*, February 25, 1967; CD 301, 85-87; HSCA, 10:113; Blakey and Billings, *Plot to Kill*, 169; FBI teletype, SAC New Orleans to Director et al. (HQ 62-109060-482).

[129]CD 75, 285-97; CD 301, 85-87; HSCA, 10:113; Hinckle and Turner, *The Fish Is Red*, 221; WR, 216.

[130]Turner, "The Garrison Commission"; Hinckle and Turner, *The Fish Is Red*, 221; Kirkwood, *American Grotesque*, 304.

[131]CD 75, 285-97; HSCA, 10:113; CD 301, 85-87; *New York Times*, February 25, 1967; HSCR, 144.

[132]CD 75, 285-97; Hinckle and Turner, *The Fish Is Red*, 206, 223; HSCR, 170; Blakey and Billings, *Plot to Kill*, 168; Rogers, "The Persecution of Clay Shaw"; HSCA, 10:107; Weisburg, *Oswald in New Orleans*, 65.

[133]FBI airtel from SAC New Orleans to Director, February 28, 1967 (HQ 62-109060-4579).

[134]HSCA, 10:112; CD 75, 309-11.

[135]HSCR, 171; Rogers, "The Persecution of Clay Shaw."

[136]HSCA, 10:113; HSCR, 144.

[137]CD 75, 285-97, 309; FBI airtel, SAC New Orleans to Director, February 24, 1967 (HQ 105-82555-5555); Weisburg, *Oswald in New Orleans*, 176, 183-84; Anson, *"They've Killed the President!"*, 107; HSCR, 144; Hinckle and Turner, *The Fish Is Red*, 221; HSCA, 10:105.

[138]HSCA, 10:105; HSCR, 144-45; *New York Times*, February 23, 1967.

[139]HSCA, 10:113; WC, 25:251; Garrison, *A Heritage of Stone*, 125; letter, Garrison to Sissi Maleki (researcher), February 19, 1984.

[140]HSCA, 10:105; interview with Garrison; interview with Ferrell; CD 75, 307-8.

[141]Interview with Garrison; Kirkwood, *American Grotesque*, 114, 534; *Dallas Times Herald*, November 21, 1982; interview with Ferrell; James and Wardlaw, *Plot or Politics?*, 114; *New York Times*, March 3, 1967, May 10, 1967, June 3, 1967, June 25, 1967; *Washington Post*, February 23, 1969; Committee to Investigate Assassinations, *Coincidence or Conspiracy?*, 452; FBI memo, DeLoach to Tolson, February 23, 1967 (HQ 62-109060-4582).

[142]Interview with Marchetti, 1983; Anson, *"They've Killed the President!"*, 122; interview by Fensterwald of Marchetti, April 22, 1975; Committee to Investigate Assassinations, *Coincidence or Conspiracy?*, 299, 452.

[143]Anson, *"They've Killed the President!"*, 122; Committee to Investigate Assassinations, *Coincidence or Conspiracy?*, 298-99.

[144]Phelan, *Scandals, Scamps and Scoundrels*, 138-76; interview with Ferrell; interview with Kohn, 1983.

# REDUCE LOUISIANA'S MURDER RATE? EXPEL NEW ORLEANS*

Burk Foster

Louisiana's people and political officials are always looking for new ways to reduce our nation-leading homicide rate. We have the toughest homicide laws in the country, giving a few convicted murderers death sentences and punishing the rest with natural life sentences, which has done wonders to build up our prison population but still left us leading the country in the murder rate the last five years. Maybe there is something simple we could do to lower our rate, at least to the level of the other Southern states.

Table 1 shows homicides in Louisiana over the 20 years from 1973 to 1993. The table is broken down into four parts:

1. The number of homicides occurring statewide, and the rate per 100,000. These homicide figures are based on statistics compiled by the Office of Public Health. They are more accurate and also higher—because they include negligent homicides and innocent homicides, such as self-defense killings—than the FBI estimates of murder and man-slaughter that appear in the Uniform Crime Reports.
2. The number of homicides occurring in Orleans Parish, the rate, and the percentage of homicides in Louisiana occurring in just this one parish.
3. The number of homicides occurring in the rest of the state, outside Orleans Parish, and the rate.
4. For reference, the national homicide rate for each year, based on estimates in the Uniform Crime Reports.

*First published in *The Angolite* (March/April 1996), 36-37. Reprinted with the kind permission of the author.

**Homicides in Louisiana, 1973-1993**

| | Homicides in Louisiana | | Orleans Parish | | | Homicides w/o Orleans | | |
|---|---|---|---|---|---|---|---|---|
| Year | Number | Rate (per 100,000) | No. | Percent of State Total | Rate | No. | Rate | U.S. Rate |
| 1973 | 648 | 17.2 | 227 | (35.0%) | 39.1 | 421 | 13.1 | 9.4 |
| 1974 | 659 | 17.5 | 219 | (33.2%) | 38.4 | 440 | 13.5 | 9.8 |
| 1975 | 582 | 15.4 | 183 | (31.4%) | 32.2 | 399 | 12.0 | 9.6 |
| 1976 | 551 | 14.3 | 183 | (33.2%) | 32.2 | 368 | 10.9 | 8.8 |
| 1977 | 631 | 16.1 | 181 | (28.7%) | 32.1 | 450 | 13.0 | 8.8 |
| 1978 | 669 | 16.9 | 217 | (32.4%) | 38.7 | 452 | 12.9 | 9.0 |
| 1979 | 718 | 17.9 | 272 | (37.9%) | 48.8 | 446 | 12.5 | 9.7 |
| 1980 | 666 | 15.9 | 237 | (35.6%) | 42.5 | 429 | 11.7 | 10.2 |
| 1981 | 712 | 16.5 | 246 | (34.6%) | 43.9 | 466 | 12.5 | 9.8 |
| 1982 | 733 | 16.8 | 257 | (35.1%) | 45.6 | 476 | 12.6 | 9.1 |
| 1983 | 672 | 15.1 | 233 | (34.8%) | 41.1 | 439 | 11.5 | 8.3 |
| 1984 | 597 | 13.4 | 222 | (37.2%) | 39.2 | 375 | 9.8 | 7.9 |
| 1985 | 525 | 11.7 | 167 | (31.8%) | 29.6 | 358 | 9.3 | 7.9 |
| 1986 | 622 | 13.8 | 219 | (35.2%) | 38.8 | 403 | 10.5 | 8.6 |
| 1987 | 570 | 12.8 | 221 | (38.8%) | 39.7 | 349 | 9.2 | 8.3 |
| 1988 | 583 | 13.2 | 245 | (42.0%) | 44.9 | 338 | 9.0 | 8.4 |
| 1989 | 685 | 15.6 | 270 | (39.4%) | 50.6 | 415 | 11.2 | 8.7 |
| 1990 | 753 | 17.8 | 312 | (41.4%) | 62.8 | 441 | 11.8 | 9.4 |
| 1991 | 824 | 19.4 | 348 | (42.2%) | 70.0 | 476 | 12.7 | 9.8 |
| 1992 | 786 | 18.3 | 288 | (36.6%) | 58.2 | 498 | 13.1 | 9.3 |
| 1993 | 914 | 21.3 | 385 | (42.1%) | 78.7 | 529 | 13.8 | 9.5 |

Source: Louisiana Department of Health and Hospitals, Office of Public Health, Public Health Statistics; U.S. Bureau of the Census; Uniform Crime Reports; Research Division, College of Administration and Business, Louisiana Tech University

The table shows that the homicide rate in Louisiana was fairly stable for the decade from 1973 to 1983, went down for about five years, then in 1989 began climbing toward new heights. The rate for 1993, 21.3, is not only the highest for any year but it is also the highest for any American state in the history of modern homicide statistics.

How did the murder rate get so high? We cannot definitively consider why it got so high, in a short article, but we can see *where* it got so high: Orleans Parish. Although the population of New Orleans has declined steadily, by about 20 percent since 1960, the number of homicides continues to increase, and the homicide rate has doubled in 20 years. By 1993, New Orleans's population was down to 489,000, only about 12.7 percent of the state total, but its homicides accounted for 42 percent of the state total.

While the homicide rate in New Orleans has doubled in 20 years, the homicide rate for the rest of the state has remained static. It went slowly down, for a time, bottoming out in the latter 1980s, but has come back up again since. The rest of the state, 63 parishes containing 88 percent of the people, are almost exactly where we were 20 years ago. New Orleans has taken a dramatic turn for the worse.

Why does this distinction matter? Legislators pass laws to reflect their perceptions, and their constituents' perceptions, of statewide concerns. The murder rate statewide, while still nothing to be proud of, is not out-of-line with other Southern states. Only when New Orleans is added to the pool do the numbers climb to the top of the charts. The rest of Louisiana, including the other metropolitan areas of Baton Rouge, Shreveport,

Metairie, Lafayette, Alexandria, Monroe, and Houma, has a "typical" Southern murder rate. It is New Orleans's rate that makes the rest of the state look bad.

To dramatically lower Louisiana's murder rate, the legislature ought to first expel New Orleans. Then, after noticing how much safer we are, our political officials and our people would be obliged to quit blaming the rest of the state for the crimes of New Orleans, and we could stop severely punishing criminals in the rest of the state because we are afraid of the criminals of New Orleans.

# ANGOLA IN THE SEVENTIES*

Burk Foster

The picture is of four young men in prison garb crowded together—doing nothing—sitting in a small, bare cell at the Louisiana State Penitentiary at Angola. The caption underneath describes the scene as an isolation cell, where an inmate would normally be kept separate from his fellow prisoners. This photo, from a 1975 issue of *Corrections Magazine*, ironically but accurately describes conditions in Louisiana's prison system in the early 1970s and lends further credence to the ancient Chinese proverb: "One picture is worth more than ten thousand words." It graphically portrayed the problem that would be the subject of considerably more than ten thousand words of litigation, journalism and public debate over the next ten years—prison overcrowding and its effects on the state's correctional system.

The many problems of prison overcrowding were not Louisiana's alone during the seventies. Several states were already under court orders to deal with prison over-population and deteriorating conditions of prison life, and several more would join the list before the decade was out. But because of a persistent inattention to prison needs in Louisiana, a "blind eye" going back to the post-Civil War convict leasing period, Louisiana would have much more to make up for with its reforms. It would find the road to reform slower to travel and would find, ten years after starting out, that rather than the problems being resolved, they were actually intensifying.

LSU history professor Tom Carleton, writing in *Politics and Punishment: The History of the Louisiana State Penal System* in 1971, described the environment that would challenge the prison reform efforts of the seventies: "Underlying and sustaining deficiencies of Louisiana's system have been three interrelated and historically pervasive factors (1) public opinion, the ultimate arbiter of policy formulation in a democracy, has in Louisiana generally ignored the penal system and has been disinclined to bestow upon it the kind of support readily bestowed upon other state agencies; (2) political control of

*First published as Chapter 7 in Burk Foster, Wilbert Rideau, and Douglas Dennis, eds., *The Wall Is Strong: Corrections in Louisiana*, third edition (Lafayette, La.: Center for Louisiana Studies, University of Southwestern Louisiana, 1995), 54-69. Reprinted with the kind permission of the author and the University of Southwestern Louisiana.

the penal system has easily occupied the near-vacuum caused by public apathy, with the result that penal policy on all levels in Louisiana has been formulated exclusively by politicians, who have been able until recently to subordinate completely penological objectives to political considerations of cost, race and patronage; (3) modern penology, with its necessarily higher costs, professional personnel and popularly exaggerated overtones of convict-coddling, has had a difficult time supplanting the old ways in Louisiana, where public officials have preferred to utilize the penal system as a patronage mill, where public opinion has been satisfied when it could be assured that convicts were being punished, and where both officials and public opinion have long agreed that the least expensive penal system is the most desirable one."

Louisiana had passed through the tumultuous decade of the sixties with its old-fashioned prison system relatively intact. The racial antagonisms and political rebellions, the arguments about rehabilitation and reintegration, the deep questioning of the basic role of the prison that occurred in more progressive states never caught on here. In Louisiana prison meant Angola, and Angola was simply a big old prison farm on the Mississippi River where most inmates did agricultural labor.

The only other men's prison in the state, the medium security reformatory officially titled the Louisiana Correctional and Industrial School (LCIS), had opened at DeQuincy in 1957. Most Louisianians did not know it existed.

The state had made a brief feint at modernizing its prison system in the 1950s, when a rash of inmate Achilles tendon-slashings focused attention on Angola and encouraged reform efforts. Professional penologists were imported from the federal system and state politicians pledged to keep their hands off the prison to give new rehabilitation programs a chance to succeed.

In 1962, in the administration of Governor Jimmie Davis, the budget of Angola was cut by about 30 percent. Employees were laid off (inmate guards returning to take their places), programs abandoned and the professional administrators gradually squeezed out. Angola had nine wardens between 1964 and 1968, the year the state Department of Corrections was created. In Louisiana's prisons, it was back to business—and politics—as usual.

The inmate population of Angola held fairly constant during this period, from an average of 3,523 in fiscal year 1962 to 3,463 in fiscal year 1966 to 3,390 in fiscal year 1972. The average cost per day to house inmates remained steady in the $2.50 per day range during the first part of this period and then increased sharply toward the end ($4.86 in fiscal year 1972) as free people were hired to replace the inmate guards.

The prison population's stability or slight decline was not unlike what was going on across the rest of the country, and the trend came to an end in Louisiana at the same time as it did elsewhere—in 1972.

If you were an Angola inmate, 1972 seemed to promise a new period of enlightened prison administration in Louisiana. The populist Edwin Edwards was inaugurated governor and Elayn Hunt, recognized as a progressive in prison reform, was appointed director of corrections. Back-breaking labor in the fields was ended, the use of inmates as guards was stopped, the notorious Red Hat Cell block (where escape artist Charlie Frazier had once been welded inside his seven-by-three-and-a-half foot cell for seven years) was closed, radical revision of the disciplinary procedures occurred and unnecessary restrictions were removed, giving the inmates a little more freedom of choice. In short, life at Angola became less harsh, a little more humane.

Those who anticipated change soon saw it, but in a form different from what they expected. Tougher sentencing practices drove the inmate population up steadily, an average increase of twenty to thirty inmates per month. The legislature failed to appropriate funds to hire new staff or make improvements to the prison's physical plant. And the relaxation of discipline, though more humane in one sense, broke down the old forms of social control: the prisoners ran wild.

From 1972 to 1975, Angola was a full-blown monster, with potential as dangerous as the quality of life in its bowels. It was a particularly vicious period. Forty prisoners were stabbed to death and more than 350 treated with serious knife wounds. It was a dog-eat-dog jungle and having a knife was almost a prerequisite to survival.

Gang wars and clique power struggles kept the stretchers rolling, to the point where "One on the stretcher!" became a morbid call that was soon ignored, generally accepted as a routine risk factor of doing time. One senior correctional officer, who was a rookie guard during this violent era, tells of working the late night shift—often the only guard on duty in a 200-man dormitory. It was a rare day indeed, he says, when he came to work without finding fresh blood on the floor somewhere in the dormitory.

Half the prisoner population wasn't working, dope traffic was rampant, pilferage and exploitation were the rule. The strong ruled, and the weak either served or perished. Sexual abuse and homosexual slavery were widespread, with inmates auctioned, sold and traded like cattle by other inmates. By mid-1975, Angola was the number one prison in America on two counts: with 4,300 inmates, it was the largest, and with one or two inmate stabbing deaths each month, it was also the bloodiest.

State district court Judge Frank Marullo, taking a tour of Angola during this period, described the prison as "essentially unmanageable." He said: "Everyone knows that the mammoth prison must be broken up into several smaller institutions in the future but (they) are unwilling to do anything about Angola today." "Part of the problem," he said, "is educating the general public that improving prisons is not coddling criminals."

Although state officials, including the prison Warden Murray Henderson and corrections director Hunt, were working diligently to correct Angola's problems, the simple fact was that they lacked the resources to undertake substantial lasting reforms. As would be the case in so many other states, it would take federal court intervention to finally bring the prison out of its "dark ages."

A lawsuit filed by prisoner Hayes Williams and other Angola inmates protesting the prison's poor living conditions had been kicking around the federal courts since 1971. United States magistrate Frank Polozola had been designated by federal district judge

Gordon West to look into the complaints, and in late April 1975 he issued his 55-page report. Despite "good faith" efforts by state officials, prison conditions were terrible. Polozola found a lack of adequate physical protection of inmates, including the failure to detect and remove weapons, dormitories beyond capacity, and safety and health hazards in abundance. To clean up these conditions amounting to "cruel and unusual punishment," the report made several recommendations. To the 585 guards then employed, another 365 should be added. More medical personnel, especially physicians, were needed. The physical plant needed to be modernized. And the prison had to work to end the segregation of its predominantly black inmate population.

The state vigorously objected to the report's recommendations, some of which it was already putting into effect and others it said simply could not be done—such as hiring 385 new guards immediately. Mrs. Hunt said there was not enough money available to bring about real prison reform. Even if there was, she said, "The legislature could give me a blank check, and we still couldn't clean up Angola . . . because of where and what it is." She said she wouldn't mind if it was closed down altogether. Her prime hope for prison reform was decentralization, breaking up Angola into smaller prisons closer to cities.

Officials of the Department of Corrections almost seemed to be anticipating Judge West's decision to sign the magistrate's report, thereby giving it the effect of a court order. The judge's action was expected to give them the leverage they needed to get funds from the state legislature.

Judge West did in fact sign the order, on June 10, 1975, and Louisiana's corrections system has not been the same since. In signing the order, Judge West observed that conditions at the prison "not only shock the conscience," but also fragrantly violate basic constitutional requirements. The order touched upon practically every aspect of prison life: security, health and medical care, food service, religion, fire safety, overpopulation, mail service, prison disciplinary procedures and the physical facilities. Some changes were to be made immediately, and state officials were to file long-term improvement plans in his court within 180 days.

Douglas Murphy, writing in the *New Orleans Times-Picayune* on June 12, gave this summary of Judge West's 20-page "Judgment and Order:"

> —that the penitentiary within six months hire about 400 more corrections officers (guards), to bring the staff up to a minimum of 950;
>
> —that at least two guards be placed in each cellblock or dormitory at Angola on a 24-hour a day basis, equipped with walkie-talkies and telephones, to prevent homosexual rapes, fights and gambling in the living areas;
>
> —that the warden immediately remove overt and aggressive homosexuals from the general prison population;
>
> —that inmates known to engage in or constantly cause fights and violence be separated;
>
> —that temporary housing be erected to eliminate as much as possible overcrowding at Angola, which is bulging with some 4,000-plus inmates;

—that Angola immediately hire more and more competent medical personnel, and that doctors at the New General Hospital at the prison be fully licensed by the state of Louisiana;

—that each newly-arrived inmate be examined by a physician within seven days of arrival;

—that all inmates presently held in the so-called 'Psychiatric Unit' at Angola be placed in a 'therapeutic environment' and cared for. The 'PU,' as it is known, has often been described as a 'hellhole.'

The court judgment also ordered that the prison buildings and facilities be brought up to state fire, safety and health standards, something that has so far never been done, according to the inmates and some prison officials.

Perhaps Judge West expected the state to get right to work on prison improvements. If he did, he should have paid close attention to a remark Governor Edwards made on being told the order had been signed. "We didn't take the magistrate's recommendations that seriously," the governor said. "Now that it's been elevated to the status of a formal court order, we'll have to treat it with more deference." How much deference was "more deference?" Not enough to satisfy Judge West apparently. A July newspaper article, titled "Judge Unhappy Over Angola," contains his criticisms of the state legislature, which had just ended its 1975 session without dealing in a substantive way with prison reform.

Judge West was most irritated by the legislature's decision to appropriate funds for expansion of the LSU football stadium while failing to approve additional operating revenues for Angola. State officials told the judge that the prison monies had gotten lost in the maze of bureaucratic procedures through which budget requests had to travel, and consequently no funds were available for the 1975-76 fiscal year. Judge West commented, "I find it's always so easy for people to say what can't be done rather than what can be done." The legislature's only real prison-action—and a portent of things to come—was to appropriate $15 million for prison construction, five million for additions to Angola and ten million for two new first-offender prisons in other parts of the state.

State officials were not so sure they wanted to go ahead with Judge West's reforms—at least according to his time-table. They did what all red-blooded Southerners would do in the face of a federal court order: screamed that the federal courts were interfering in state business and appealed to the Fifth Circuit. They would eventually lose their argument, and in September Judge West turned up the heat. He placed a population limit of 2,640 prisoners on Angola, at a time when the prison had 3,751 inmates officially confined in its cellblocks and dormitories and another 200 in-processing. Prison officials reported a net population increase of 64 a month, 200 coming in and only 136 going out. There could be no new admissions, the judge said, until the population was brought down. The only reply from the legislature, which was not then in session, was silence.

Meanwhile state corrections officials were pursuing their answer to the Angola problem—decentralization. Their idea was to build new prisons across the state, gradually decreasing the reliance on Angola and eventually phasing it out. Let it be a farm again, Mrs. Hunt had said.

Faced with increasing political pressure from Judge West, no proposal to reduce the inmate population was too bizarre to consider. In late September, Mrs. Hunt was reported to be exploring the use of a mothballed U.S. Military Transport Ship for use as a work release center. She had already been to the Norfolk navy yard shopping.

The prison ship idea soon sank without a trace (someone probably ran across the tales of the horrors of the British prison hulks), and so did other hopes for early reforms. Prison reformers and the inmates themselves would later admit that they had been naive—to think that a mere federal court order could overturn a century of prison neglect and bring about quick improvements.

At the end of the crisis year 1975, Angola's population had declined to about 3,500 (causing a backlog to begin building in parish jails). The violence toll for the year: 18 men murdered, 173 verified stabbings with injury. Was the prison any different after the order? One inmate said, "The food got a little better for awhile and nothing really got worse."

As it turned out, 1976 would be the year the prison reform ball really got going. There has never been another year quite like it in the history of Louisiana corrections. The year got off to a bad start when Mrs. Hunt died of pancreatic cancer in early February. The assistant director, Paul Phelps, was appointed to succeed her in March. He continued to move the DOC in the same direction it had been headed under Mrs. Hunt, toward decentralization.

In July 1976 Governor Edwards announced his ten year plan for Louisiana corrections. He called it a decentralization plan, but the original idea had been modified by now, as he found little political support for locating prisons anywhere near urban areas, so a better description would be to call the plan a hybrid—part concentration, part decentralization.

Angola was to house long-term offenders, including violent and sex offenders. Three new outcamps would be built there, to bring the population back up to 4,000 or so. "Only the bad guys would be left," one inmate said.

The "not-so-bad guys" would presumably be dispersed among other facilities, mostly in rural areas: the reformatory at DeQuincy, a medium security prison already under construction at Jackson, a new prison at St. Gabriel to house 500 permanent inmates and another 500 for in-and-out processing, a 500-man prison in Bossier Parish in north Louisiana, and a 250-man work release center at Camp Beauregard in central Louisiana. This was an ambitious plan, made necessary by the DOC's projection that the state prison population would increase by 700 to 800 inmates each year for the foreseeable future.

The state legislature, meeting in regular session in 1976, ignored the governor's plans, the judge's orders, and virtually everything else having to do with prison reform. What everyone was talking about was an incident—almost trivial in itself—that illustrated how totally opposed the public and the legislature were to putting prisoners in the cities.

A nursing home in New Orleans, the Ponchartrain Lodge, was sold to the state which announced plans to begin housing a number of elderly prisoners there, as one of the schemes to reduce Angola's population. The uproar was so great—the viciousness of the response likened to a hurricane's fury—that the state backed off and promised to lease the facility to a church group instead. And the businessman who had sold the property to the state soon came under indictment for allegedly selling and reselling the home to inflate its value. "Don't call us about decentralization," the public seemed to be saying, "we'll call you."

Meanwhile, back on the farm, a new prison warden had brought a new style to Angola. Ross Maggio, who had been in the DOC's agri-business office, had been brought in, it was said, because he had the right attitude to whip the prison into shape—tough, disciplined, no nonsense. An April newspaper article, titled "Prison Warden Forges Ahead, Then Slips Back," pointed out that Maggio was about to get the population down to the court-ordered 2,641. That was some accomplishment, even with 1,200 inmates waiting in the parish prisons. He had hired 200 more guards and was just 150 shy of what the court had ordered. But the turnover rate among guards was 50 percent, and there were few prospective employees left in the remote rural area around Angola. It was truly a "three step forward, two steps back" approach to prison reform.

Problems with prison personnel would continue through the summer as Warden Maggio moved to end corruption and tighten security. The number of guards actually began to decline, and prison officials recognized they could not hire more guards from the surrounding area. Part of Governor Edwards's plan was eventually to increase the population of Angola to 4,000. Warden Maggio, estimating that 2,000 staff members would be needed by then, said that the state would need to spend ten million dollars to build housing for these new employees on the grounds.

Prison critics observed that Maggio was beginning to take control of the giant institution. Only two men were murdered in the first half of 1976. Very few knives were being found in the periodic shakedown searches, down from the "two bushel baskets a day" of a few months earlier.

Inmate Ken Plaisance, who had been at Angola fifteen years, agreed that the level of violence had been drastically reduced. "It is working," he said, "thanks to Judge West's order." The prison was being cleaned up, better medical care provided and safety hazards—human and physical—reduced

It all made good sense, the warden said. "There was nothing in the court order . . . nothing we are now doing to comply with the court order, that wasn't just common sense in running a prison," Maggio said. He conceded it took the order to bring "common sense" into play as an institutional policy.

The state legislature, urged on by the governor and the federal judge, was finally ready to do its part. Meeting in special session beginning on August 15, 1976, in two days it approved $90.6 million in prison bonds: $30.8 million for expansion of Angola, $24 million for the prison and reception center to be built at St. Gabriel, $19.8 million for new highways around Angola, and smaller amounts for improvements at other prisons. The dam had finally been broken; the trickle of prison funds had suddenly become a torrent.

By the latter part of 1976, then, Louisiana had yielded to the irresistible force and begun to modernize its antiquated prison system. The state's initial approach to prison reform could not have been more conventionally simple; as outlined in Governor Edwards's plan, it would add enough new prison beds to relieve overcrowding and keep up with expected population increases.

Over the next seven years, from 1976 to 1983, Louisiana would open four medium security prisons and greatly expand two minimum security work training facilities, increasing the capacity of the system by about 4,500 inmates. The first of the new prisons, the Margaret Dixon Correctional Institute, opened on April 1, 1976, at Jackson, halfway between Baton Rouge and the Mississippi line. The prison grounds had once been part of a mental hospital, the East Louisiana State Hospital, and had been quickly renovated after the court order was imposed.

The prison opened with a maximum intended population of 750, men moved over from Angola. Most of them were quite happy to be moving from the "big farm" to the "funny farm" and so was Warden Hayden Dees, also out of Angola, who said this was the kind of prison that could be used all around the state for 90 percent of the prisoners in Louisiana. Warden Dees even managed to keep the big oaks that provided shade for the yard within Dixon's fences—something that would never have been allowed at Angola.

The next medium security prison to open was the Hunt Prison at St. Gabriel, built on land adjoining the women's prison that had opened in 1973. Named for the recently deceased corrections director, the Hunt prison was always identified as a model facility and often contrasted with Angola. Hunt was designed by former Angola Warden Ross Maggio, who had moved over to build the new prison and open it on January 31, 1979. Its anticipated population was about a thousand men made up of permanent residents and those new inmates just entering the system for classification.

The third new prison, Wade Correctional Institute, located near Haynesville in Claiborne Parish, opened a year-and-a-half later, on December 15, 1980. It was the first prison in north Louisiana. The fourth, called the Washington Parish Prison, was dedicated at Varnado, near the Pearl River in east Louisiana, on May 28, 1983. Its 1600 acre complex was expected to house 1,120 inmates by the end of that year.

The two work training centers, at Camp Beauregard near Alexandria and at Jackson Barracks in New Orleans, were already in use as small work release facilities (along with the State Police Barracks in Baton Rouge and a small section of LCIS at DeQuincy) before 1975. Both were on state-owned property used by the National Guard. The expansion of Camp Beauregard aroused no controversy, but the Jackson Barracks location was bitterly contested: it was the first state prison (to be called a prison, anyway) in an urban area since before the Civil War. New Orleans legislators fought it tooth and nail when the conversion from military to prison use was proposed late in 1976. Three years later, the same legislators were still arguing that it should be shut down and prisoners transferred to the new Hunt Prison.

But prisons, once opened, tend to be impossible to close. Just look at Angola. The old farm, which in 1974 and 1975 everyone wanted to shut down as a blighted anachronism, was suddenly more popular than ever. It was cleaned up, had a new warden, Frank Blackburn replacing Ross Maggio in 1978, new dormitories under construction, hundreds of new employees and a new reputation for safety and security: in 1977 not a single inmate was murdered.

The transformation had come about with almost miraculous speed, and corrections officials had every right to be pleased with their successes. In an interview at the end of 1978, Paul Phelps was optimistic about changes within the system. The state might be released from the federal court orders by 1980, he said, and theoretically should be able to house all state prisoners in local jails by then. The state was even planning to begin the American Correctional Association's accreditation process.

In a speech a few months later, Phelps said of the changes, "I'm of the opinion that we're doing as good a job as anyone in the country. We've come out of the dark past and into the modern-day world in one great big three-year leap."

Change of this magnitude, occurring this quickly, did not come cheap. The Louisiana legislature, once it decided to go along with the program, spent money hand over fist. By 1980, over $300 million had been spent on capital improvements alone—three new outcamps, new dormitories and other renovations at Angola, highway improvements, two new medium security prisons open by that time and another underway, the work training centers—a prison boom unlike anything the state had ever seen.

The DOC's operating budget had skyrocketed, too. In 1971 the state spent seven million dollars to confine 4,000 inmates. By 1975 the budget had increased to $25 million for close to 5,000 inmates, and by 1981 over $100 million for 8,000 inmates. In that one decade, prison expenditures had increased more than tenfold, and corrections officials were coming to be thought of as panhandlers—always going around, hands out, asking for still more money.

Small wonder that the public and the legislature were beginning to protest the high cost of prison operations. If they had been listening carefully, they would have known the day was coming. Paul Phelps had predicted as early as 1976, his first year on the job, that the state would go bankrupt in ten years if it didn't reevaluate its approach to corrections. He suggested the corrections department was in a "futile foot race with the judicial system," which was sentencing 50 more people a month to prison than the state released.

In 1979, speaking before committees in the legislature, Phelps said, "If the state of Louisiana does not change its policies, we are firmly dedicated to building a new prison every other year. Our policy right now is to put everybody in prison."

Legislators were displeased with the huge budget increases Phelps asked for. "Something's got to be done," said Sen. Foster Campbell Jr., of Bossier City. "Pretty soon prisons will be more expensive than schools in this state."

"That's a distinct possibility," Phelps agreed. He argued for more probation officers—three times the 168 then employed—to increase the strictness of probation supervision. But Senator Campbell said he did not believe the voters were ready to broaden probation programs. "I don't think the people of Louisiana are willing to lessen penalties," he said.

Overuse of imprisonment and underuse of probation were themes Phelps would come back to with increasing frequency. "We have to change the concept that the only way you can punish someone is by putting them in jail," he said in 1981. The state had to ask "how much money the public is willing to spend to guarantee that people will be locked up and remain unproductive." He cited figures of $60,000 a bed to build new prisons and $20 a day (which would be up to $30 a day by 1984) to keep men in them once they opened. The public, he said, needs to change its "mental concept of punishment. For a lot of people the worst thing you could do them is to make them get up every morning and go to work."

Although he clearly believed that alternatives to prison were being ignored, Phelps was firmly committed to taking good care of all inmates in state custody. He insisted that the state continue to build and adequately staff the new prisons needed to house the hundreds of new inmates coming in each year.

His position would cause him serious problems as he tried to work in the administration of Dave Treen, the Republican governor who replaced Edwin Edwards in March 1980. Phelps hung on as head of the DOC for eighteen months, then was replaced on September 17, 1981. Was he fired or did he resign, and for what reasons? Phelps would say only that he had been removed, and Treen would never give specific reasons why, speaking only of a "difference in philosophy," mainly over the issue of putting more inmates into existing facilities.

The nature of those differences became more apparent the next month, October 1981, when Phelps's successor, John King, announced a two-year halt in prison construction. The state would hire more guards, reduce the ratio of guards to inmates—from one guard per 3.1 inmates to one per 3.5 in maximum security and 1 to 5.5 in medium security—and use existing facilities more intensively. By reducing the living space allowed dormitory inmates—"double bunking"—King proposed to add more than 4,000 new prison beds.

This was rather an abrupt reversal, for the public to be told after years of publicity about prison overcrowding that Louisiana's prisons weren't really overcrowded after all: it was just that space had not been managed properly.

Louisiana's prisons not overcrowded? That was surely news to the federal courts. Middle District Judge Frank Polozola, the former magistrate who had taken over the court order on his elevation to the bench after Judge West's retirement, took a dim view of the Treen administration's proposal. He asked for more information on how double-bunking would be carried out, reports shuttled back and forth from the DOC to his office for several months, and finally, on December 3, 1982, the judge lowered the boom.

Polozola gave Louisiana officials a four-hour dressing down about failing to come to grips with overcrowding. He wanted concrete data on prison plans; what officials had submitted to him was "garbage." Officials were beginning to get the idea that Polozola was not enthusiastic about double-bunking. Have an alternative plan ready, he told them. And furthermore, they should stop blaming him for the state's prison problems, when it was their own lethargy that was at fault. Warning them that "the credibility of the DOC is at an all-time low with me," Polozola sent the officials away to get down to work.

The announcement that state prisons were not overcrowded had been received with skepticism by another of the DOC's critical audiences, the parish sheriffs, who must have ranked the statement's credibility somewhere up there with Richard Nixon's "peace with honor" Vietnam proclamation. The sheriffs were in the midst of serious jail over-crowding problems of their own, most of them caused by a backlog of state prisoners being held in local jails there since 1975. The state's excuses had been first, no room, and second, not enough guards, to move the prisoners into state custody.

The larger jails had it the worst. Sheriff Charles Foti of Orleans Parish was having lawsuit problems even before Angola was closed to new admissions late in 1975, and those problems would get much worse in the next few years. They would spread across the state as well, as Angola pursued its population-control target by releasing inmates and simply refusing to accept transfers in from local jails. By May 1977, there were 1,867 state prisoners in local jails. State corrections officials were hopeful, however, that nearly all of them would be in state custody by later that summer (when the new dormitory beds at Angola came open).

It never happened. New prison construction would dent the backlog but never completely eliminate it. Sheriffs became accustomed to the cycle: a new prison would open, most of the state prisoners would be taken from the jails and then, inexorably, like flood waters rising toward the top of the levee, the numbers, would begin to inch upward again, each time reaching higher than the time before. The new prisons were like emergency spillways, temporarily relieving the pressure, but the flood of inmates rushing into the system was like the massive deluge engineers say will one day reroute the Mississippi down the center of the state—beyond the means of the system to contain.

Local jail overcrowding would worsen during the Treen administration, which only completed building the prisons begun under Edwards and added no new facilities of its own. Sheriff Foti dramatized the plight of the local authorities in April 1980 by taking 147 state inmates to St. Gabriel and abandoning them in the Hunt Prison parking lot. A grand gesture it was, though Paul Phelps criticized Foti for "blaming the state" instead of trying to solve his problems locally. Phelps pointed out that even though the state might have a few empty bed spaces, it did not have the manpower to guard the prisoners that would fill those spaces.

Several propositions were forthcoming. A New Orleans area legislator proposed that a regional prison be built in the city (or somewhere around it) to hold just those convicted felons on appeal, who by Louisiana law are still the local sheriff's responsibility. Governor Treen, by his count down to 495 state prisoners in local jails by May 14, 1981, promised that all state inmates would be in state facilities by September 1. Had his double-bunking proposal been accepted, sheriffs would have been granted immediate, lasting relief from the problem.

But none of these things happened, and finally, on September 21, 1982, the sheriffs' turn in federal court came: Louisiana became the first state in the nation in which every sheriff was under court order specifying how many prisoners he could house in his jails. Judge Polozola, under authority granted by the Fifth U.S. Circuit Court of Appeals, signed the last of the consent decrees stipulating the number of prisoners to be confined and the number of guards to be employed in every parish prison in Louisiana.

By the end of the next year, Polozola would reach consent decrees with the rest of the DOC's adult prisons, the 105 city jails and the five juvenile training schools. As of December 7, 1983, one federal judge had supervisory authority over the state's entire correctional apparatus, with the exception of local juvenile detention homes.

It should be noted that while the DOC was arousing the ire of some sheriffs by keeping inmates in their jails, it was also contributing to their enrichment by paying them a daily maintenance fee. This fee, which began at $4.50 a day per inmate in the mid-1970s and would eventually increase to $18.25, was a source of considerable income to some sheriffs who had space available. Some of them even enlarged their jails or juggled bed arrangements to house more state prisoners, though any steps causing overcrowding had to cease after the consent decrees were signed.

It was in February 1983, at the beginning of the last year of the Treen Administration, that Judge Polozola approved the comprehensive plan state officials had reworked to submit to him. The plan, as approved on February 11, called for the state to spend $34.1 million to provide pre-fab modular housing additions at several prisons. In return Polozola was to allow limited use of double-bunking at three smaller prisons. The effect of these changes, coupled with the opening of the new Washington Parish Prison, would be to increase the state's prison population from 9,500 to 12,000 by the end of 1983. Governor Treen in announcing the plan said, "At the end of this calendar year, it should give us total relief from our problem." Corrections Secretary King predicted that only 600 to 700 state prisoners would be left in local jails at year's end (of the 1,600 waiting there in February).

It was a good plan; the only thing wrong with it was that the Treen administration forgot to carry it out. Early in 1984, as Dave Treen was preparing to leave office and Edwin Edwards preparing to return as governor, the legislative fiscal office issued a report highly critical of the corrections department as managed by Treen's appointee John King. "The department has not managed its prison construction program in an efficient manner and has failed to adequately plan for future growth." The pre-fab cells authorized in 1983 were never built. The backlog of state inmates in local jails was greater than ever; the jails were very near their stipulated capacity of 9,215.

The fiscal office projected cost figures that were truly staggering: three new prisons needed immediately, at a cost of $170 million; the DOC budget, which stood at $160 million in 1984, projected at $322.5 million in 1989; $240 million, some of it state funds, needed for parish jail expansion.

Running for governor in 1979, Dave Treen had promised to be tough on criminals, and where convicts were concerned he had kept his word: he ignored the problems of prisons, especially after the departure of Paul Phelps, took no action to increase the capacity of the system (other than the double-bunking scheme the federal courts found ludicrous) and then walked away, leaving the chaos to his successor. State Representative Kevin Reilly summed up the mess the DOC created under Treen: "It shows what happens when you have a bunch of amateurs running a department that needs professionals."

When Edwin Edwards was inaugurated to start his third term as governor of Louisiana in March 1984, he reappointed Paul Phelps secretary of corrections. Phelps's mission—sounding like an assignment from the old "Mission: Impossible" television series—was to bring rampaging prison population and cost figures under control.

Phelps hit the trail, sounding in his public statements even more certain than he had been three years before that Louisiana could not continue to send more and more people to prison. It was a straight-forward, repetitious message: the state's oil money was gone, they would have to borrow money, mortgaging their children's future to build new prisons, prison construction and operating costs were continuing to rise, there were 2,500 state inmates in local jails. "How long can we afford it?" Phelps asked. "My concern is that if we don't get away from this lock 'em up business, we're going to go bankrupt."

Hawking intensive probation on the Georgia model, Phelps toured the state. Doomsday headlines—"Corrections Could Bankrupt State," "Louisiana Facing Key Penal Crisis," "Jail Terms Too Costly, Says Phelps"—marked his trail as he tried to sober up a public drunk on locking people up.

This time around Phelps had more help from the governor's mansion. Edwin Edwards himself was more personally involved in publicizing the need for change. Early in his term Edwards said, "You can look forward to an emphasis on prison alternatives, bearing in mind an emphasis on protecting society. Off the top of my head, I'd say there are a significant number of people who could be let go with no danger to society."

The governor appointed two executive committees to consider different aspects of imprisonment. The 80-member Forgotten Man Committee held its first meeting on April 25, 1984. This committee, the reincarnation of a similar committee appointed by Governor Earl Long in the 1950s, was to look into the plight of the "practical lifer," the inmate sentenced to an exceptionally long period of confinement. Angola had 2,500 to

3,000 of these inmates, men ineligible for parole and serving either life sentences or terms so long they could expect to be geriatric cases before they got out.

In the late summer of 1984 Edwards appointed the Governor's Prison Overcrowding Policy Task Force. This group's purpose was pretty much self-explanatory—to investigate possible measures to reduce prison population and make policy recommendations to the governor (and undoubtedly through its hearings to help focus public attention on the crisis). It began meeting in the fall.

Between the start-up dates of these two committees, the 1984 legislative session had come and gone. It had rejected Phelps's package of probation and parole reform bills, reflecting the view that people would prefer to spend money building new jails rather than putting criminals back on the street.

The Overcrowding Task Force encountered similar opinions as it held public meetings around the state in the fall. "We have to develop a rationale to convince the people of this state that there are better, cheaper ways to punish people than to put them in jail," Paul Phelps said.

Persistence at putting people in jail had created an unprecedented prison overcrowding problem in Louisiana. The state prison system was operating at 99.9 percent of capacity (11,118 beds) and there was a backlog of state prisoners (3,161) that consumed one-third of parish jail space—the largest backlog in the U.S. Louisiana's overall incarceration rate—counting all state and local prisoners—was 502 per 100,000, the highest in the nation and nearly twice the national average of 286 (The same year the state ranked only 19th in population and 19th in reported crime).

But Phelps and other members of the task force acknowledged that popular opinion was opposed to alternatives to prison. "In South Louisiana, whenever a crime is committed, the people want to see them in jail," said Minos Hardy, chief of police in Abbeville. "Our legislature is doing what they think the public wants them to do" when lawmakers take a tough line on mandatory sentences, added Frank Serpas, an assistant to the mayor of New Orleans.

In early 1985, as the two committees were preparing interim reports and the legislature was gearing up for another session, Phelps continued emphasizing the economic impact of the continuing high rate of imprisonment. The get-tough on crime policy was all right, he said, long as the oil money was rolling in. But that money was dwindling and there were still 115 more admissions to prison than releases each month. More money needed to be spent on halfway houses, probation and parole. The trouble was, Phelps said, "People think probation and parole is soft on crime." The state legislators have only "reflected the attitudes of their constituencies . . . that the only way to punish people is to lock them up."

It was to the point, he said, that corrections would be taking money from education, highways and other functions of state government. He issued a clear warning: "In 1986, the financial crisis will be so great that the legislature will not have many alternatives."

In their interim reports, submitted in March 1985 before the legislature began meeting on April 15, the two committees said basically the same thing. "Louisiana now faces a set of circumstances that it literally cannot build itself out of—cannot because the numbers are too large, the projected growth too fast and the cost too great," the Forgotten Man Committee wrote in its report. Among this committee's recommendations, and sure to excite controversy, was the proposal to make all prison inmates, including murderers, eligible for release after 20 years in prison.

The Overcrowding Task Force, a group more dominated by professionals in criminal justice, recommended a more conventional approach: more prison and jail construction to alleviate overcrowding until other measures could be developed to correct the problem. The 1985 legislature accepted this recommendation and created a Louisiana Corrections Facility Corporation to sell bonds to finance five more new prisons. The legislature also began a five-year plan of increasing probation and parole supervision by adding the first installment of 100 new field agents. Other major reform measures were either defeated outright or postponed until the 1986 session.

As 1985 came to a close, the Corrections Facility Corporation exercised its bond-selling authority. On December 27 it sold prison bonds in the amount of $156 million, sufficient to build three new prisons and plan two more. These five prisons, all medium security facilities holding 500 beds each, were planned for Avoyelles, Allen, Winn, East Carroll and Union-Ouachita Parishes, all rural parishes where jobs were badly needed.

Thus Louisiana closed out ten years of prison reform preparing for still another round of prison-building. From the date of Judge West's initial court order on Angola, June 10, 1975, through the end of the 1985 fiscal year on June 30, the corrections department's prisoner population had grown by 150 percent, from 5,300 to 13,300. The department's operating budget had grown by nearly 600 percent (from $29 million to $200 million)—a growth rate three times faster than state government overall.

The economists had been mistaken: it wasn't oil that was the state's growth industry, it was prisons. If prison stock had been for sale to the public in 1970, and you had been smart enough to buy, a thousand dollar investment would have been worth $25,000 fifteen years later.

Louisiana remains bullish on prisons. Jim Morris, the head of adult services for the DOC, said late in 1985 that he expected the prison population to continue to increase for the next several years as children of the baby boomers reach young adulthood. Paul Phelps had estimated that the state would need space for 5,300 more prisoners by 1990, when its budget would approach $400 million a year.

How had this ruinous situation come about? How had the state run itself into this predicament? The specific actions are easy to identify: the simplest explanation is to say the state legislature changed the laws to get tougher on criminals. Between 1975 and 1985 it passed at least 47 statutes increasing criminal penalties. Most violent felonies now carry mandatory prison terms. Stricter laws were enacted punishing DWI offenders.

The 1977 legislature passed a law reducing goodtime credit from 25 days a month to 15, obviously an important determinant of how long people remain in prison.

The criminal justice system has made its contribution to the problem. Prosecutors, especially in the New Orleans area, stand on their hard-line approach, judges impose longer sentences, repeat felons are legally forbidden from being placed on probation, even one arm of the DOC helps out. The Parole Board in 1985 was paroling inmates at less than half the rate it had ten years earlier (2,400 parolees to 5,300 inmates in 1975; 2,600 parolees to 13,300 inmates in 1985). Part of the parole situation is due, of course, to legal changes that make an increasing number of inmates ineligible for parole. For many of Louisiana's practical lifers, the only hope of getting out of prison before they are old men lies in executive clemency, the power to commute sentences, which, following Dave Treen's parsimonious example, is also being used much less frequently today than it was in the past.

Is it fair to pin the responsibility on state legislators and criminal justice officials, then? Not really. Officials could act, by changing laws and policies, to reduce the prison population, but they are unlikely to do so in the face of strong public opposition to deinstitutionalization. Public opinion in Louisiana is not apathetic to prison reform (apathy at least allows public officials to do what they think best without interference), it is downright hostile.

In early 1985, after Louisiana's citizens had been exposed to prison problems for a full decade, a public opinion poll commissioned by the *Baton Rouge Morning Advocate* showed that almost 69 percent of the voters preferred increasing taxes to lock up more prisoners. Only 4.2 percent said more prisoners should be let out on parole to alleviate crowding in state prisons. The other 27 percent gave other responses, including "neither," "other," "depends," and "don't know."

A critic of the poll's structure might argue that the question could be reworded to include probation, supervised half-way houses and other options that sound less threatening than parole, but the fact remains that in every section of Louisiana, among male or female, young or old, rich or poor—the ratio is at least 10 to 1 favoring higher taxes over turning prisoners loose on parole. The only exception to this ratio was among blacks, with 61 percent favoring more taxes and 8 percent more parole.

Those seeking to promote prison reforms are well aware of the public's hard-headedness. John Vodicka, who was the director of the Louisiana Coalition on Jails and Prisons during the turbulent period of the late 1970s, said the public's fear, anger and misconceptions about prisons and inmates were blocking meaningful progress in corrections. In Vodicka's view, society needs maturity and self-confidence to develop a rational corrections program. The present prison system, he said, is irrational, an answer to fear and an expression of society's fear and anger.

In a later interview, commenting on the changes Judge West's order had brought about in the DOC, Vodicka said, "It's nice to see the department operating prisons which aren't as brutal as they were in the past. But when you make nice prisons, you just make more of them." Vodicka argued that Judge West's order had trapped the state into spending more and more money only to incarcerate more and more prisoners.

What Louisiana was left with, then, ten years after, was a nicer, safer prison system, one that Paul Phelps could call the best in the South at providing secure custody of inmates, but a system still emphasizing long-term confinement as the appropriate response to crime. Attempts to win acceptance for non-custodial alternatives continue to encounter a stone wall of public opposition which only the most persistent efforts will eventually demolish.

Ask Paul Phelps. He's been trying to knock some holes in the wall for ten years without a whole lot of visible success. A 1985 *New Orleans Times-Picayune* editorial called him "a voice crying in the wilderness." If Phelps has put himself in the position of a prophet trying to prepare the way for real change in Louisiana's approach to corrections, he has yet to receive much of a response from the people he has been preaching to. As he said on the occasion of his removal from office by Governor Treen in 1981, "My basic failure was that I was unable to convince people that locking people up was not the best way to deal with the problem."

Mr. Phelps should not feel so bad: so far no one else has been able to convince the citizens of Louisiana of that, either. His remark stands as the epigraph to a decade of prison building.

# NEW ORLEANS' CHARITY HOSPITAL: A STORY OF PHYSICIANS, POLITICS, AND POVERTY*

John Salvaggio

After the hospital's 250th anniversary in 1986, several events further affected the institution, and its condition continued to worsen. Charles E. "Buddy" Roemer, son of former commissioner of administration Charles Roemer, defeated Edwin Edwards and assumed the office of governor in March, 1988, pledging to "end business as usual in Louisiana politics." Roemer, a young, articulate, dynamic reform governor and Harvard graduate, concentrated his early efforts on fiscal reform. His proposals were designed to change Louisiana's traditional tax base in order to create a favorable business climate and generate more state income. He divided the vast DHHR bureaucracy into two smaller, more manageable agencies: the Department of Health and Hospitals (DHH) and the Department of Social Services. Charity remained under the aegies of the DHH in 1988, since two legislative bills designed to create a separate "Charity Hospital Authority" were deferred. Roemer had many early successes in gaining approval for plans to cut spending and refinance state debt, enacting a strong campaign finance law and public school reform plan, and gaining teacher and Charity resident pay raises at a time of severe budget cuts. His tax reform and revenue generating proposals, however, did not meet with the approval of the Louisiana legislature at a special session on tax reform held in October, 1988. During this stormy session, Roemer's ambitious plans to cut or abolish the homestead tax exemption and increase income taxes was defeated, leaving him to face major budget crisis with totally inadequate finances. He tried again, noting that "in 1988 it was survival. I inherited . . . a bankrupt organization and kept it afloat by crisis management. . . . I'd like to try it [fiscal reform proposals] again . . . better, wiser, and [with proposals] more targeted to jobs."[1] Roemer was forced to trim drastically the state's budget in an effort to control mounting deficits that had accrued mainly because of

*Excerpts first published in John Salvaggio, *New Orleans' Charity Hospital: A Story of Physicians, Politics, and Poverty* (Baton Rouge: © 1992 by Louisiana State University Press), 284-314, 369-71.

decreased oil and gas revenues. In the process, Charity Hospital was forced to accept its share of budget cutbacks, resulting in a number of economy measures. Like several other large urban public hospitals, Charity began to no longer accept "dumping" transfers from private hospitals unless empty beds were available. But its beds remained 100 percent filled, however, effectively ruling out the transfer of deserving indigent patients. A reduction in operating funds and nursing staff also led indirectly to the closure of many hospital beds.

Charity Hospital's bed census was over 3,000 in the 1950s and well over 2,000 as late as 1970. By July, 1987, the number of beds had been reduced to 970; in April, 1988, this figure decreased to 750. The December, 1988, bed census dropped to 645, including beds for all special services such as the AIDS, leukemia, alcohol detoxification, intensive care, rehabilitation units, and 55 nursing bassinets for newborns.

With the failure of Roemer's revenue-generating measures, further bed reductions were virtually assured, even though there was an overwhelming need for hospital beds by seriously ill indigent patients. Nursing shortages became critical in 1987, and in spite of modest pay raises, the hospital remained unable to successfully recruit in this area, a major reason for the drastic reduction in bed numbers. The nursing shortage in New Orleans area hospitals was identified as the worst in a national survey of twenty cities. From 1986 to 1987, the number of local unfilled nursing positions grew from 18.1 to 25.8 percent, and the turnover rate rose from 23.4 to 28.5 percent. The greater New Orleans vacancy rate of 25.8 percent for nursing positions was more than double the national rate of 12 percent. It was also much higher than the vacancy rates in major Texas cities that, like New Orleans, was affected by a slumping oil industry. Nationwide, the number of registered nurses per bed was 97 to 100, but in New Orleans, it was a dismal 1 to 3 or 2 to 3. These conditions are always magnified at Charity Hospital.[2]

In 1988 and 1989 the proud old institution continued to gasp, slowly strangled by the state's purse strings and the lack of community support. Bed closures, technical and physical facility inadequacies, and nursing shortages all affected the hospital's service functions, but they also severely hampered its educational role, since the schools remained inextricably intertwined with Charity and dependent upon it for their educational mission. In March, 1989, LSU dean Robert Daniels publicly warned that further decreases in Charity Hospital's patient population "would be disastrous." He emphasized that the two medical schools were already developing their educational programs at other sites, "particularly university and community hospitals."[3]

Indeed, with Charity Hospital's shrinking bed census, LSU Medical School in particular experienced severe problems in securing an adequate patient-teaching base for its medical students, since it did not have university hospital teaching beds of its own. Tulane had more teaching beds outside of Charity Hospital partly because of its control the medical service at Veterans Hospital and the foresight of [Dr. John] Welsh and others in developing Tulane University's teaching hospital, which was opened with great success under its medical director, Dr. Martin Litwin. Hospital and medical service development, however, were accomplished at the expense of prestigious research and teaching programs at Tulane Medical Center, resulting in some degree of academic erosion. This was particularly evident during the later years of the Walsh regime, when problems, largely beyond his control, with faculty development, filling departmental chairs, the quality of residency teaching, and the number of research grant awards became paramount. Figures from the grants analysis branch of the National Institutes of Health, Division of Research Grants, show that for 1988, Tulane Medical School, traditionally one of the nation's highest ranked academic medical institutions, successfully competed for only $8.8 million of the 2.8 billion awarded in prestigious NIH grants.[4] This was countered by a vigorous and successful effort by Tulane University president Eamon Kelly to develop new medical center leadership and design a strategic plan for expansion of Tulane's research and academic programs.

In 1988 and 1989, Louisiana exported to other states the highest number of medical school graduates in its history. "We're like a developing country," said Robert Suskind, LSU's head of pediatrics, in a March, 1989, newspaper interview. "We're losing residents to other states. . . . The people who are paying for the educational system to train medical students are training them for other states. . . . We're putting money into the system and not coming out where we should." Although a 15 percent pay raise was approved for Charity Hospital's resident trainee physicians as of July, 1988, the LSU and Tulane residency programs, particularly in the large, nonprocedure, primary care areas, continued to perform poorly in "matching" for graduating medical students to enter their residency training programs. In March, 1989, Warren C. Plauche, LSU's associate dean for clinical affairs, emphasized this point: "If you're signing up for a three-or four-year residency program and they can't tell you whether the hospital's going to be operating, you might choose someplace else." Charles V. "Bo" Sanders, who was then the acting chairman of LSU's medicine department, also lamented, "This is robbing Louisiana of some of the best minds of the future. That's what really hurts us." The net result is that in 1988 and 1989, Louisiana's devastated economy and its young physicians' strong desire to avoid further training at Charity Hospital after graduation seriously undermined medical care in Louisiana.[5]

In the 1989 residency "match," LSU and Tulane attracted only ten residents for the more than twenty positions available for their pediatric programs. The situation in the large specialty of internal medicine was even more devastating: LSU attracted only four and Tulane only three residents in the match to fill the more than thirty available positions. Not a single individual from outside Louisiana chose to come to Charity for a medicine residency.[6] This constituted a virtual total rejection of the residency program in internal medicine, the biggest and most important medical specialty. Thus, one of the greatest threats of closure to Charity Hospital in 1989 was the lack of young physicians and nurses to run the institution.

Figures compiled by Charity Hospital's associate director revealed that the overall percentage of local medical graduates remaining in Louisiana for residencies decreased from approximately 70 percent in the early 1980s to 40 percent during the years 1987 and 1988. In 1989, the figures were even worse. Of the 179 LSU Medical School graduates, only 46 percent remained in Louisiana compared with 60 percent in 1986, and only 21 percent of Tulane Medical School's graduates remained in the state. Of those remaining in Louisiana, only 27 percent of LSU's graduates and 17 percent of Tulane's graduates chose to remain at Charity. In spite of resident pay raises, Louisiana still lagged behind other southern hospitals in providing benefits, such as parking and life, health, and disability insurance, for its young resident physicians at Charity.[7] In addition, a barrage of news stories on Charity's dire condition and possible closure led to considerable uncertainty in the minds of the physician trainees about the future of the hospital.

The medical schools had increasing difficulty in attracting not only top quality students and resident trainees but distinguished faculty members as well. During 1987 and 1988, neither LSU nor Tulane medical schools had permanent chairmen for their Internal Medicine and General Surgery departments. All had resigned or retired for various reasons including, most prominently, the frustrations of coping with Charity Hospital's mounting problems and Louisiana's dire financial condition. During this period, several other key administrative positions, including the chair of obstetrics and gynecology and the deanship of the School of Public Health, were unfilled at Tulane, and searches were being conducted for a chancellor to replace Walsh, who was approaching retirement age, and a dean to replace James Hamlin, who had resigned primarily for health reasons.

By late 1989, the situation at Charity became desperate. Talk of cutbacks and of closing the hospital increased, and efforts to recruit nurses remained dismal. Apathy toward the hospital's plight persisted among the upper and middle classes, and neither influential citizens, private corporations, nor the state of Louisiana rallied to the hospital's cause. Throughout 1989, several spirited meetings were organized by diverse groups such as the League of Women Voters and LSU/Tulane medical students to discuss the hospital's plight. Only 1 or 2 of the state's 154 legislators attended these meetings, however, and little was accomplished in terms of concrete action to save the institution. Newspaper headlines noted again that Charity failed to gain accreditation from the Joint Commission on Accreditation of Health Care Organizations because of multiple deficiencies that included staff shortages and a "life threatening situation involving patient safety" in its blood bank, which had only six full-time employees instead of the required seventeen. Charity had been compensating for these vacancies by using part-time employees and even medical students to test donated blood and prepare it for transfusions. Executive director Elliott Roberts was given permission to raise the starting salaries of blood bank personnel by approximately $200 per employee. Even with this increase, the hospital received few commitments to fill these slots. Nursing and other key personnel shortages resulting from budget cuts during the 1980s were also among the prime reasons for the commission's decision. This reprimand further compounded the serious difficulties in recruiting young interns, resident physicians, and other staff members for postgraduate training and patient care.[8]

The gravity of the situation was compounded when the hospital's appeal for full accreditation was denied. In October, 1989, the Health Care Financing Administration (HCFA), a federal agency that certifies reimbursements to hospitals for Medicare and Medicaid expenses incurred by their patients, further reprimanded the hospital. After a five-day inspection, HCFA served notice that Charity would lose these revenues unless severe deficiencies were corrected. In order to meet HCFA standards, Charity was told to hire ten physical therapists and approximately three hundred more nurses and to improve its medical record keeping. Hospital administrators were also admonished to ensure the safety of the patients by making numerous repairs, including the building of a fire stair from the first through the twelfth floors in the very center of the hospital and the installation of fire sprinklers in several areas. These HCFA mandates represented a potential death blow for Charity, since Medicare and Medicaid funds amounted to $77 million of the hospital's $147 million budget for the 1988 to 1989 fiscal year. Roberts stated in exasperation, "We have waltzed around this for lo these many years and now the final boom has been lowered."[9]

News of the hospital's earlier disaccreditation, coupled with the HCFA censure, caused alarm in the New Orleans community and in many areas of the state, particularly in the medical and nursing schools. At Tulane Medical School a new chancellor, Dr. Neal Vanselow, and a new dean, Dr. Vincent Fulginiti, both of whom had outstanding academic and administrative backgrounds, were hired and assumed official duties in 1989 in the midst of the Charity crisis. Recognizing the paramount importance of Charity Hospital for medical student and house officer training, they, together with dean Robert Daniels and chancellor Perry Rigby of LSU School of Medicine, immediately sought meetings with state officials to improve the hospital's financial status and physical plant.

Fulginiti, who assumed his duties in April, 1989, began to work tirelessly to help solve these problems. He remarked that Charity's continuing crises were perhaps most clearly seen by newcomers such as himself, whereas local residents, who had developed an attitude of indifference, accepted these problems as the norm. By October, 1989, Charity had been disaccredited by the JCAH and severely reprimanded by HCFA, and an exasperated Fulginiti, pleading for adequate state funding for the hospital, stated that if he were being recruited at that time for the Tulane deanship, "I would not take the job."[10]

Daniels echoed these words of gloom and pushed for construction of a new, LSU-controlled Charity Hospital, describing the existing facility as "an archaic 50 year old building riddled with asbestos, beset with an aging physical plant, electrical problems, and outmoded equipment." He furthered lamented, "Charity has used up its lifetime. . . . You can't train quality professionals in facilities 25 years behind the times. It's no wonder our students leave." He urged that Charity be placed "at arms length from state government" and called for local planning efforts, a university hospital for LSU, and delivery of some indigent care by local community private hospitals where bed capacity was available. Yet he realized that no hospital wanted to take on more indigent care or "to be the successor of Charity." This point was also made by Dr. George Porter, president of the private Ochsner Foundation, who noted that Ochsner and other community hospitals were "all under the gun to control costs [and] . . . were already giving a large percentage of uncompensated care." Porter did, however, foresee even more charity care in the future, observing that no hospital would "be immune if Charity is restructured. . . . Patients will have to go somewhere, you can't cut off services to the indigent." Vanselow spoke of the hospital's important teaching mission: "Charity is the key hospital in New Orleans in terms of medical education. . . . If it loses its JCAH credit, we can't teach there anymore." He stressed that the period when Charity was widely regarded as premier training ground for young physicians was not ancient history: "[T]he appeal of Charity has always been that it has a large volume of patients with a wide range of diseases, as well as a very strong, very attractive medical program . . . where residents could roll up their sleeves and get a good deal of experience."[11]

At a meeting called by Vanselow on October 26, 1989, to express Tulane Medical Center's concern about the hospital's plight and the need for immediate improvement, DHH secretary David Ramsey, speaking on behalf of Governor Roemer, reaffirmed that the charity hospital system was essential in caring for Louisiana's approximately one million uninsured citizens. Ramsey emphasized that the 1989 budget of $147 million for Charity represented an expenditure by the state of $147 per uninsured citizen—a relatively low amount that could not have been met if the uninsured were cared for in the private sector.[12]

In response to the JCAH and HCFA mandates and continued hard work by Vanselow and other Tulane and LSU medical school officials, $8.1 million in initial funding was approved by the state's Interim Emergency Board on November 30, 1989. The Roemer administration asked the board to allow Charity to exceed its budget by $8.1 million instead of using the board's contingency pool of approximately $6 million. At least $3.5 million was dedicated for salary support and another $3.6 million for safety improvements. The board's action was ratified by a two-thirds vote of both houses of the state legislature. Roemer pledged an increase of $43 million for the system and an additional $14 million in capital outlay funding, pending approval by the legislature.[13]

Meetings were held with the Louisiana Civil Service Commission, and its members voted unanimously to allow Charity Hospital to recruit nurses and respiratory, occupational, and physical therapists in the unclassified range of six months. Medical resident/housestaff salaries were approved by the state legislature for increases to 4.5 percent above the mean salaries of other southern medical schools, and first-year house officers were given an education bonus of $300 per month.[14]

Roemer had spoken about "privatizing" the system and in desperation had removed more than $30 million from the hospital budget in the fiscal year 1988 to 1989 in an attempt to reduce the state's massive deficit. After the HCFA inspection, however, he reversed his position, immediately promising that the state would work with the agency to implement its recommendations and would provide the money to avoid Charity's loss of accreditation. Roemer noted that Charity Hospital should remain a state responsibility, to "take care of the people who are too poor to be sick." He also remarked that some states were coming to Louisiana to look at its state-run medical system, "which was in disrepute a few years ago" (though it was obviously still in disrepute in October, 1989, at the time of his statement).[15] Despite Roemer's optimism, many individuals close to Charity Hospital remained skeptical, believing that his efforts would prove to be too little and too late and that his state administration had a reputation of making definitive promises followed by no definitive action.

In 1989, Roemer established the Louisiana HealthCare Authority (LHCA) and charged it with developing long-range plans to revitalize the entire statewide charity hospital system. This agency held public meetings in several Louisiana cities, including Baton Rouge and New Orleans. During these meetings, hospital employees, medical and nursing school administrators and students, house officers, nurses, and community members urged that the hospital be properly funded and upgraded. The committee reported that the state's charity hospitals were in "extremely critical condition," and it cited a host of structural and physical deficiencies in the system that resulted in relatively low-quality health care. It recommended transfer of authority over the charity hospitals from the DHH to the LHCA. It also proposed major financial reforms, an LHCA board and nine local boards—one for each of the charity hospitals in the system. The boards at first would only be involved in planning. Perry Rigby, an LHCA member, noted that in essence, "the authority didn't have the authority yet," but he looked forward to more dramatic changes that would be made later.[16]

The medical schools were in a schizophrenic situation. They were forced to make contingency plans for moving their physician trainees and faculty members elsewhere in case Charity remained disaccredited or was closed. They continued to stress that these strategies would be employed only as a last resort if the schools' credentials became seriously jeopardized. On October 15, 1989, Vanselow, who championed high-quality educational programs, noted that the Association of American Medical Schools, which holds ultimate responsibility for accrediting medical schools, had warned of accreditation difficulties if the medical schools continued to use a discredited hospital as a major teaching institution. He emphasized: "We feel we have been backed into a corner. . . . There is no such thing in the United States as a nonaccredited medical school." Rigby confirmed that leaving Charity represented a plan no one wanted but added that "our educational program has to come first." In speaking of state and community support, Rigby further stated, "I don't think there is the commitment at this time. Maybe the question of support at Charity has never been asked properly. Maybe other things have taken precedence. Maybe people are not convinced."[17]

Nursing school administrators found themselves in the same quandary. In 1988 and 1989, Louisiana suffered the nation's worst shortage of registered nurses, and the Louisiana State Board of Nursing insisted that teaching hospitals meet HCFA criteria. Federal figures revealed that in 1988, there were only 442 registered nurses per 100,000 residents in Louisiana—the worst ratio in the United States; in 1989, there were 1,000 nursing vacancies in New Orleans alone. Even though the money and the positions were available, the nurses needed to fulfill Charity's requirements could not be found. Like the medical schools, the nursing schools' teaching programs were threatened. They, too, considered withdrawing their students from Charity. At the nursing board's meeting in January, 1990, Barbara Morvant, the board's executive director, simply stated, "It may get to a point where the board has no other option." Helen A. Dunn, dean of the LSU School of Nursing in New Orleans, echoed these remarks. She did not want to remove her students from Charity but would "pull them out if the state board tells me to."[18]

The DHH developed a plan to correct Charity's problems and recommended that the hospital discontinue its nursing education programs in order to allow its regular nursing staff to concentrate on patient care. On December 15, 1989, the state's coordinating board for higher education concurred with the DHH plan and recommended that Charity's 95-year-old nursing education program and four allied health education programs be transferred to Delgado Community College. The recommendation was made because of Charity's budget reductions and declining nursing student enrollment at a time when a critical shortage of registered nurses existed. Under the plan, the nursing students would earn a two-year degree at Delgado, which would also take over the program's $3.5 million budget and the nursing school building and dormitory adjacent to the hospital.[19]

In spite of these heroic efforts, morale remained low at the hospital. Given the funds to hire a sufficient number of nurses and therapists, Charity still faced grave problems in locating and attracting them. As one hospital emergency room nurse reported to the newly formed LHCA, "There is no incentive to come work in this hospital. . . . They [nurses] want to take their experience elsewhere for more money, and who can blame them." The problem of adequate salary was, however, thought by many to be of less importance than was lack of confidence in the Louisiana state government. In Ramsey's words, "In an environment where there is no indication of a future, it's extremely difficult to recruit people."[20]

As 1989 came to an end, HCFA officials again breathed life into Charity Hospital. On December 30, the day after it inspected Charity, HCFA recommended that the hospital continue to receive Medicare and Medicaid money. This ensured the hospital's survival—but at a cost. Since an adequate number of nurses could not be hired, Charity officials resorted once again to reducing the number of beds to match its smaller nurses corps. Thus, while the hospital did not accomplish most of the tasks recommended by the inspection team, it did convince federal officials that it was moving in the right direction, particularly by further cutting the size of its inpatient population. As a result of these measures, the hospital's bed size was reduced to an all time low of 430 beds. Specifically, Charity eliminated 215 beds and began to transfer and reroute emergency room cases to local private hospitals, where a patient-load crisis occurred. By December 18, most of these private hospitals began to turn away emergency patients. The Orleans Parish Medical Society stated that if the volume of bed closures at Charity continued, the emergency medical service of the city would be instructed to ignore ambulance divergences and to bring all emergency patients directly to whatever hospital was deemed appropriate. New Orleans, according to some, was incubating an emergency room crisis, and Charity was forcing other hospitals to bear a burden for which they were not necessarily equipped. This was particularly true regarding severe trauma and acute medical, psychiatric, obstetrical, and cocaine and other narcotic-related emergencies, which were being seen with increasing frequency at Charity (200 cocaine-related admissions per year in 1986, compared with 1,800 per year in 1989).[21]

Some local private hospitals—Tulane, Hotel Dieu, Mercy, Children's, and Touro Infirmary—grudgingly continued to accept Charity transfers, but patients still piled up in Charity's admit room over the 1989 Christmas holidays.[22] As an example, the author, who had been making voluntary ward rounds with residents on the Charity Hospital medical service during this period, admitted eight seriously ill patients on Christmas night. The following day, Dr. Robert Marier phoned to report that there were still sixteen patients on guerneys in the admit room who required admission and could not be transferred because private hospital bed capacities were full. Marier requested that Tulane officials be asked to arrange admission for some of these patients to their hospital. Yet Tulane's hospital was full: Its intensive care unit was already overcrowded with private patients and Charity transfers. Charity Hospital was at one of the lowest points in its history. Many residents and all medical students were on well-deserved Christmas vacations, and a skeleton crew of house officers labored around the clock to care for the patients in the overcrowded admit room. In addition, the worse freeze of the century had hit the city. Temperatures plummeted to ten degrees, and water pipes broke throughout the hospital. Water covered the floors in the rooms and halls on nearly every floor, and sandbags were strategically placed to control flooding—a scene reminiscent of a military field hospital under fire.[23]

These facts notwithstanding, the hospital had survived, though it remained uncertified and disaccredited as of December 30, 1989, its third disaccreditation in fifteen years. It struggled to improve, however, and in accordance with accreditation agency recommendations, it began to recruit respiratory technicians, physical therapists, and nurses and to improve record keeping and maintenance. In addition, a $21.5 million package was put together for physical plant improvements, including the installation of fire alarms and a hallway sprinkler system and the construction of a fire stair from the first floor to the twelfth.

In 1990, uncertainty over Charity's future grew, and public officials vacillated between different approaches to solving the hospital's problems. On February 3, 1990, Roemer stated that his administration was giving serious consideration to "phasing out" the institution. Ramsey, acknowledging that the hospital might be demolished, stated that money spent on hospital repairs was like "pouring money into a hole." He noted that a new hospital could be built and occupied by 1995 for approximately $180 million, whereas the state could spend as much as $270 million to improve the existing, 51-year-old building. Yet Roemer, against the advice of Ramsey and his own appointed health planning group, the Louisiana Health Care Authority, balked at constructing a new Charity Hospital. Roemer stated that it would require $365 million during the next five years to cure defects in the state's health care system.[24]

Roemer favored other alternatives, such as renovating Charity or purchasing the nearby Hotel Dieu Hospital and converting it into a new public hospital, as "better, more palatable economic alternative," given the state's financial crunch. He sought advice from a consulting group on how to solve the hospital problems, and their report was not positive. The state was told that time was running out for corrective measures but that action should be taken.[25] Roemer favored legislative action to enact another task force recommendation, namely, turning the charity hospital system over to a statewide board with local boards running the individual regional hospitals.

The state of emergency existing at the hospital worsened on May 16, when state attorney general William J. Guste, Jr., noted that hospital employees would not be able to collect their pay in two days unless an emergency spending bill was passed by the state senate and signed by the governor. Guste said there were insufficient funds to meet Charity's $3.4 million payroll for its four thousand employees and to pay its other bills. An emergency bill was immediately passed, and the problem was temporarily averted.[26]

In addition to these immediate crises, the LHCA's proposal for a separate statewide board with local boards to run the regional charity hospitals caused considerable turmoil in the state legislature. Some state senators and representatives demanded state control and oversight of all money allocated to the charity system, and others bluntly stated that the LHCA and its proposed board could not manage and distribute the funds any more effectively than could the state. Other civil service supporters lobbied against the bill for fear that any transfer of power from the state to local boards would weaken the civil service system and employee job protection.[27] Clearly, a classic Louisiana political fight was brewing over the legislature's power to control the money and jobs it provided for health care.

Although Roemer's reform measures for the state's health care system were well intentioned, the effects of multiple proposals to close Charity Hospital, transfer its operations to another hospital, build a new facility, or institute a lengthy series of repairs, and to create a new board to manage it—all in the midst of a financial crunch with threats of withholding employee paychecks—proved disastrous to the morale of residents, interns, nurses, other hospital employees, and the students at Tulane and LSU medical schools. This only compounded the previously existing fears of uncertainty and instability.

These crises shed light on the long-standing deficiencies that had been developing slowly and steadily since the early 1960s: lack of money, lack of civic commitment, and years of destructive neglect that cost this once-proud institution and New Orleans preeminence in many fields of medicine. In Houston, civic pride, philanthropy, and state spending built the world's largest medical complex—the Texas Medical Center—which emerged as the dominant force in Houston's economy following the collapse of the oil industry in the mid-1980s. In Atlanta, the city infused large amounts of money into upgrading its large urban teaching hospital, Grady Memorial, and local industry gave massive amounts of money to the overall Emory University medical complex. In Birmingham, visionary physicians built a medical center judged to be one of the best in the United States, surpassed, according to some surveys, only by Mayo Clinic and Massachusetts General Hospital. Vanderbilt University's hospital continued to be a thriving enterprise noted for its support of scholarly and research productivity. By contrast, Charity Hospital remained in the throes of a desperate fight for survival.[28]

Charity's staff declined from 5,000 in 1980 to 3,300 in 1989. The physical structure of the hospital continued to crumble, and because of this deterioration, along with low pay and poor benefits, the majority of new graduates from LSU and Tulane medical schools left Louisiana in 1989 for postgraduate training. The state and Orleans Parish medical societies strongly urged Roemer and the state legislature to support Charity Hospital, and there was overwhelming feeling in New Orleans and throughout the state that the hospital should be supported and fully accredited. Milton C. Chapman, president of the Louisiana State Medical Society, emphasized that "this kind of brain drain will have a definite impact in the future on the quality of medical care that we will be able to provide." Orleans Parish Medical Society president Lynn E. Hickman noted that when attending meetings of the Louisiana Health Care Authority and other public forums, many speakers vented their anger and frustrations: "[T]he words were the same words voiced time and time again over the years . . . talk of band aids and patches to keep the hospital accredited and functioning at minimal standards, but no permanent or long-term solutions." Why have no such solutions been found? According to Hickman, the answer to this question "lies in two powerful words: politics and indifference. . . . Everyone feels that Charity is not their problem, but, in fact, Charity is everybody's problem."[29]

In the late 1980s, Charity Hospital was perhaps in worse shape than ever before. Its staff, residents trainees, and students worked in an obsolete environment. It was heavily ladened with continually increasing layers of bureaucracy, and its finances were the most deplorable of any urban public hospital in the country. This, in turn, burdened the proud local medical schools affiliated with Charity to the point that they no longer attracted residents and were losing many of their renowned faculty members. No one in state and city government, the medical schools, or in the private sector seemed willing to face Charity's problems and provide the leadership, foresight, and funding to reverse the situation.

There have been many warnings through the years of the development of Charity's plight. It is clear that the bell tolled for the current hospital soon after its construction when more than four hundred beds were closed because of political feuds in 1942; when poor finances threatened its closure in 1947; when serious political corruption was again brought to light in 1963; when it began to decline technically in the mid-1960s; when competitive forces became dominant and the HEAL venture failed to revive the Charity-LSU-Tulane medical complex in the early 1970s; when its insured patients were "skimmed" to Tulane and Hotel Dieu beginning in the late 1970s; when it was absorbed into the massive bureaucratic DHHR in 1972; when, together with the medical schools, it became involved in the great Family Health Foundation war of the mid-1970s; when it fought with the medical schools and lost over the affiliation agreement in 1974; and when it lost its accreditation on several occasions in the late 1970s, the early 1980s, and again in 1989. The bell tolled for medical education when the number of intern applicants first began to decrease in 1952 because of poor pay, when Charity's overworked intern and resident corps were spread thin among the many state and private hospitals in the early 1960s, and when local medical graduates began to reject Charity internships in growing numbers in the late 1960s and early 1970s. The bell continued to toll for Charity in the state budget offices in Baton Rouge, in the boardrooms of hospital and residency program accreditation councils, in the ranks of disillusioned Tulane and LSU medical graduates, and in the ever-diminishing medical academic community.

Was anyone listening? Where would it all end? Could this situation be changed? To be sure, it posed a challenging task, since change is the most threatening thing to all human beings and organizations. "It is a paradox," stated Eric Hoffer, "that in our time of rapid drastic change when the future is in our midst devouring the present before our eyes, we have never been less certain of what is ahead of us."[30] Despite our uncertainty, the overwhelming socioeconomic problems at Charity and other large urban public hospitals must be faced. These problems are not only those of the state, hospital staffs, and affiliate medical schools, but of society as a whole. Medicine is a reflection of society. There must be a total commitment to plan and institute the necessary changes, or our system of health care for the indigent will cease to exist, the training of future physicians and other health-care professionals will suffer, and the subsequent quality of health care for all citizens will be reduced.

Notes for "New Orleans' Charity Hospital: A Story of Physicians, Politics, and Poverty"

1"Top Ten Stories of 1988," *New Orleans Times-Picayune*, January 1, 1989.

2Report by Ernst and Whinney and the New Orleans Metropolitan Hospital Council; *New Orleans Times-Picayune*, February 17, 1989.

3Robert S. Daniels, "The Future of Medical Care for the Medically Indigent in Louisiana and Its Relationship to Medical Education," *Journal of the Louisiana State Medical Society*, 141 (1989): 33.

4Data from Grants Analysis Branch of Division of Research Grants, National Institutes of Health, 1988, in NIH headquarters, Bethesda.

5*New Orleans Times-Picayune*, March 26, 1989.

6Ibid.

7James Storer, M.D., interview with author, 1989. Subsequent quotations from Storer are taken from this interview.

8*New Orleans Times-Picayune*, March 4, 1989.

[9]Ibid., October 11, 1989.

[10]Vincent Fulginiti, quoted in John Pope, "Tulane, LSU Medical Schools Ponder alternative to Charity," *New Orleans Times-Picayune*, October 15, 1989.

[11]Jill J. Seider, "Is It Too Late to Rescue Big Charity?" *HealthCare*, 1 (1989): 11, 13, 16.

[12]Minutes of meeting of DHH director David Ramsey with Tulane University School of Medicine Chancellor Neal Vanselow, in Minutes of the Tulane Executive Faculty Committee, October 26, 1989, Dean's Office Files, Tulane University School of Medicine.

[13]*New Orleans Times-Picayune*, December 1, 1989.

[14]Roberts interview.

[15]*New Orleans Times-Picayune*, October 18, 1989.

[16]Andrew Rittenberg, "Baton Rouge Report: Legislature Considers Significant Health Care Related Issues," *HealthCare* (1990): 11-13.

[17]*New Orleans Times-Picayune*, October 15, 1989.

[18]Ibid., October 23, 1989.

[19]Ibid., December 15, 1989.

[20]Ibid., October 15, 1989.

[21]Ibid., December 30, 1989, December 19, 1989; Roberts interview.

[22]Ibid., December 30, 1989.

[23]Ibid.

[24]Ibid., February 3, 1990, March 2, 1990, February 24, 1990.

[25]Ibid., April 7, 1990.

[26]Ibid., May 16, 1990.

[27]Ibid., March 13, 1990.

[28]Ibid., November 5, 1989.

[29]*Capsules*, 12 (1989): 1-3; *Orleans Parish Medical Society Bulletin*, 60 (1989): 5.

[30]Eric Hoffer, *Reflections On the Human Condition* (New York, 1973), 68.

# CANCER IN SOUTH LOUISIANA*

Vivien W. Chen, Elizabeth T.H. Fontham, Jean Fike Craig, Frank D. Groves, Penny Culley, John M. Rainey, Andrew S. Ranier, and Pelayo Correa

Tobacco-related cancers comprise about one third of the newly-diagnosed cancer in South Louisiana. These cancers are three times more common in men then in women. For cancers originating from anatomic sites where there is direct contact with tobacco, ie, lung, larynx, oral cavity, pharynx, and esophagus, incidence rates for blacks are either higher than or similar to the rates for whites. For cancers of the bladder and the kidney, sites which have no direct contact with tobacco products, incidence rates are higher in whites then in blacks. In general, white men in South Louisiana tend to have risk significantly higher than national for tobacco-related cancers, in particular, cancers of the lung (31% higher) and the larynx (42% higher). A similar pattern is observed for white females but is less pronounced. Black men in South Louisiana, on the other hand, have significantly lower rates than the SEER averages for cancers of the esophagus, oral cavity, and pharynx. Risks for other tobacco-related cancers are very comparable. There are very small differences in rates for black women between South Louisiana and SEER areas. Tobacco-related cancers are most preventable. Any effective cancer program in Louisiana must emphasize prevention and cessation of tobacco use.

South Louisiana is the heartland of the Cajun culture and the most heavily industrialized area in the state. Over the last three decades, mortality statistics have consistently shown higher rates for all cancers combined in South Louisiana than the national averages, especially in men.[1] This has led to a general belief that residents of South Louisiana have a higher cancer risk than the rest of the nation. In 1990, cancer incidence data in South Louisiana became more available for the first time. Unlike mortality rates which are affected by survival, cancer incidence rates are a better indicator to measure the risk of developing cancer. They refer to the newly diagnosed cancer cases in a defined geographic area.

*First published in the *Journal of the Louisiana State Medical Society*, 144 (April, 1992): 149-56. Reprinted with the kind permission of Vivien W. Chen and the publisher.

This series of the three papers summarizes and discusses findings from Cancer in Louisiana monographs volumes six and seven of "Cancer Incidence in South Louisiana, 1983-1986."[2] The incidence rates are computed in the Office of Public Health, Department of Health and Hospitals.

## METHODS

*Geographic Area.* South Louisiana includes 35 of the state's 64 parishes and 72% of the population (3.2 million). It is divided into five regions, according the State Health Region System with slight modification. The five regions, the parishes they include, and their corresponding population estimates are shown in Table 1.

Table 1

| Region | Parishes Covered | Population |
|---|---|---|
| New Orleans (Region 1) | Jefferson, Orleans and St. Bernard | 1,107,029 |
| Baton Rouge (Region 2) | Ascension, Assumption, E. Baton Rouge, E. Feliciana Iberville, Livingston, Pointe Coupee, St. Helena, Tangipahoa, W. Baton Rouge and W. Feliciana | 753,866 |
| Southeast Louisiana (Region 3) | Lafourche, Plaquemines, St. Charles St. James, St. John, St. Tammany, Terrebonne and Washington | 501,991 |
| Lafayette (Region 4) | Acadia, Evangeline, Iberia, Lafayette, St. Landry, St. Martin, St. Mary and Vermilion | 583,722 |
| Lake Charles (Region 5) | Allen, Beauregard, Calcasieu, Cameron and Jefferson Davis | 272,267 |

*Data Collection and Quality Control.* Cancer incidence data are collected by the Louisiana Tumor Registry. The LTR is a statewide population based tumor registry. It began its operation in 1974 when cancer incidence was collected for the New Orleans triparish area (Jefferson, Orleans, and St. Bernard) only. In 1983, the LTR expanded its coverage to all of South Louisiana and currently covers the whole state.[3]

In order to have the accurate incidence rates, every case of the newly-diagnosed cancer within the specified geographic area has to be identifed and included in the computation. The LTR screens cancer cases from departments of every hospital in the state as well as from private pathology laboratories and nonhospital affilated radiation centers. In addition, any death certificate which mentions cancer is traced to ensure that the case is not missed by the registry.

Quality control for completeness of case-identification and accuracy of data abstraction is preformed in two levels: at each regional registry and in the central office. This 1983-1986 incidence data set has also been reviewed and evaluated by the International Agency for Research on Cancer of the World Health Organization—the international "gold standard" of tumor registries.

*Computation and Comparison of Rates.* Population estimates for 1984 from the U.S. Bureau of the Census are used as the mid-period population in computing incidence rates. The rates have been age-adjusted to the US 1970 standard population so that the effect of the differences in the age comparison among compared populations is removed. Standard errors and 95% confidence intervals have been computed so that the significance of any rate difference can be assessed.[4]

Cancer incidence rates for South Louisiana in this paper are compared to the combined rates of the Surveillance, Epidemiology and End Results (SEER) area. The SEER program of the National Cancer Institute includes five states (Connecticut, Hawaii, Iowa, New Mexico, and Utah) and four metropolitan areas (Atlanta, Detroit, San Francisco, and Seattle) which represent about 10% of the US population. The combined rates of the SEER areas are often referred to as the "national" average.

*Cancer Sites.* Numerous types of cancers have been found to be associated with tobacco use. The Surgeon General's Report, 1989,[5] summarized the impact of tobacco on health based on evidence from thousands of studies. The cancers for which tobacco has been demonstrated to be the major cause, a major cause, or a major contributory cause are considered as tobacco-related in this manuscipt. These include: cancers of the lung (ICDO=162.0-162.9), larynx (161.0-161.9), oral cavity and pharynx (140.0-149.9), esophagus (150.0-150.9), bladder (188.0-188.9 and 189.3-189.9) and Kidney (189.0-189.2). Cigarette smoking is also a well established risk factor for cancer of the pancreas, but this site will be discussed in the paper on gastrointestinal tract cancers.

# RESULTS

*Lung Cancer.* Lung cancer is the most common cancer in South Louisiana and comprises 20% of the total new cases diagnosed during 1983-1986. Lung cancer is approximately three times more common in men then in women, and the rate is 20% higher for black men then for white men.

White males in South Louisiana have a significant 31% higher incidence rate for lung cancer then white males in the SEER program (Table 2), and this excess is observed in all five regions in South Louisiana (Figure 1). The age-adjusted rate of 108.6/100,000 for all of South Louisiana is also higher than that of any individual tumor registry in the SEER program. The age-specific incidence curve reveals that the excess in white males begins at age 40, but is most evident at age 70 and older. The excess of lung cancer in white females is slight (8%) but ststistically significant. The lung cancer rate for blacks in the combined South Louisiana area is similar to the SEER average for both sexes.

Table 2
Age Adjusted (US 1970) Incidence Rates for Selected Tobacco-Related Cancers By Sex, Race, and Geographic Area, 1983-1986

| | White Males | Black Males | White Females | Black Females |
|---|---|---|---|---|
| Lung | | | | |
| S LA | 108.6* | 129.8 | 38.7 | 40.6 |
| SEER | 82.7 | 132.6 | 35.8 | 39.8 |
| Larynx | | | | |
| S LA | 12.1* | 11.9 | 2.0* | 2.9 |
| SEER | 8.5 | 12.7 | 1.6 | 2.6 |
| Oral Cavity & Pharynx | | | | |
| S LA | 17.6 | 15.9* | 6.0 | 5.0* |
| SEER | 16.9 | 24.3 | 6.5 | 7.2 |
| Esophagus | | | | |
| S LA | 5.1 | 16.4* | 1.3* | 5.2 |
| SEER | 5.1 | 19.6 | 1.6 | 5.1 |
| Bladder | | | | |
| S LA | 29.1* | 15.4 | 7.7 | 5.2 |
| SEER | 31.8 | 16.9 | 8.0 | 6.2 |
| Kidney | | | | |
| S LA | 13.7* | 11.2 | 7.1* | 5.0 |
| SEER | 12.4 | 11.4 | 5.6 | 5.5 |

*Rate is significantly different from the SEER combined rate

Among the five regions in South Louisiana, New Orleans residents (Region 1) have the highest age-adjusted rates in three or four sex-race groups. Black men in New Orleans have the highest lung cancer incidence rate on record.[6] Lake Charles whites (Region V) have the lowest rates among whites for both sexs while blacks residing in Baton Rouge Region (Region II) experience the lowest risk for lung cancer among blacks in South Louisiana.

*Laryngeal Cancer.* Cancer of the larynx is much less frequent than cancer of the lung. It accounts for only 2% of the incidence cases in South Louisiana (2.8% of male cases and 0.8% of female cases). Laryngeal cancer is four to six times more common in males than in females and rates for blacks and whites are comparable. The black preponderance noted nationwide is not observed in South Louisiana.

Rates for laryngeal cancer in South Louisiana are significantly higheer than SEER combined rates for both white males and females, 42% to 25% higher respectivly. However, there is no significant difference in rates found between blacks in South Louisiana and SEER areas. This pattern is similar to that observed for lung cancer.

The highest rates of laryngeal cancer concentrate in the New Orleans region and the lowest rates are clustered in Baton Rouge and Lafayette-Lake Charles area for males and females respectively (Figure 2).

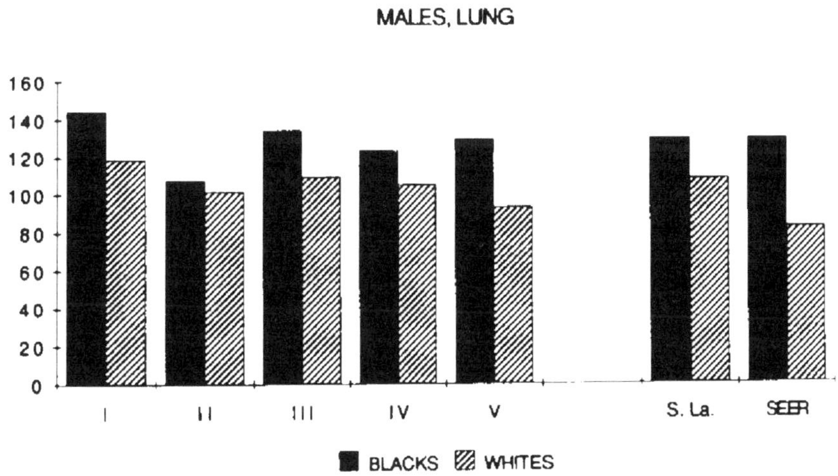


**Figure 1.** Age-Adjusted Incidence Rates of Cancer in S Louisiana by Region and Race, 1983-86

*Cancer of the Oral Cavity and Pharynx.* Cancers of the oral cavity and phaynx comprise about 3% of the total cases during 1983-1986. They are approximately three times more common in South Louisiana men then women. There is no significant racial difference in rates for either sex, in contrast to the SEER program where the rate for black males is 44% higher than that for white males (Figure 3).

When compared to blacks in the SEER areas, South Louisiana blacks have significantly lower rates of cancer of the oral cavity and pharynx. The deficit among black males is significant in each of the five South Louisiana regions. Rates for whites are comparable in the South Louisiana and SEER areas.

New Orleanian men, both blacks and whites, have the highest rates in South Louisiana. There are no regional differences among women of either race.

*Esophageal cancer.* Cancer of the esophagus accounts for only 1.3% of total new cases during the study period. Like most of the tobacco and/or alochol related cancers, esophageal cancer is approximately three times more common in South Louisiana men than in women. A distinct excess risk (about threefold) for blacks is also observed in both sexes.

Unlike cancers of the lung or the larynx, no excess risk for esophageal cancer is found in any sex-race group in South Louisiana. Incidence rates for white males and black females in South Louisiana are virtually identical to those for combined SEER registries. However, black males and white females in South Louisiana have significantly lower rates then their SEER counterparts. Regional variation is minimal and not significant (Figure 4).

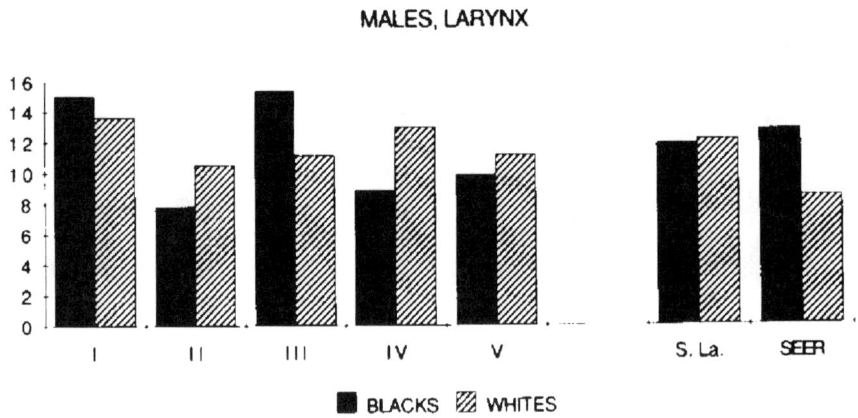


**Figure 2.** Age-Adjusted Incidence Rates of Cancer in S Louisiana by Region and Race, 1983-86

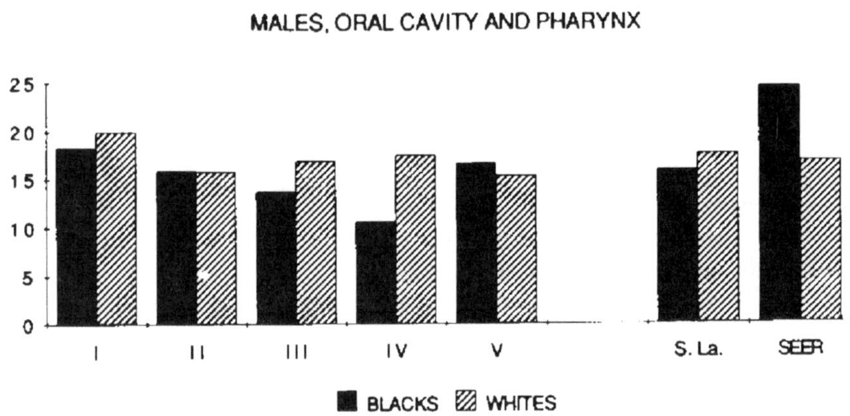


**Figure 3.** Age-Adjusted Incidence Rates of Cancer in S Louisiana by Region and Race, 1983-86

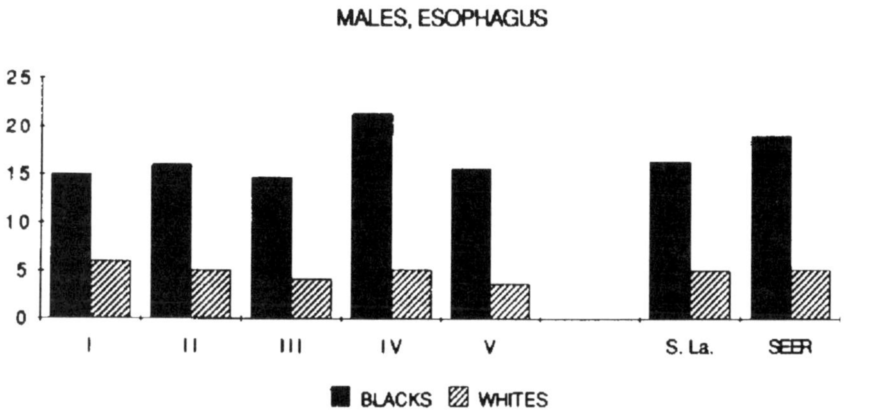


**Figure 4.** Age-Adjusted Incidence Rates of Cancer in S Louisiana by Region and Race, 1983-86

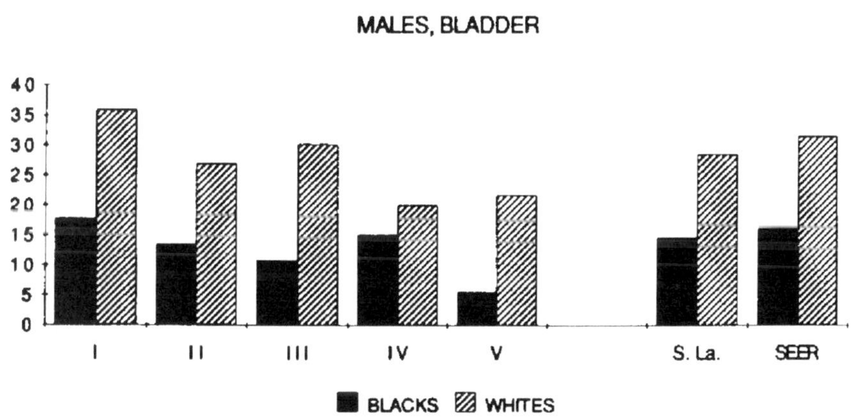


**Figure 5.** Age-Adjusted Incidence Rates of Cancer in S Louisiana by Region and Race, 1983-86

*Bladder and Other Urinary Tract Cancers.* These cancers comprise 4.1% of the newly-diagnosed cases in South Louisiana, 1983-86. Among the four sex-race groups, white males in South Louisiana have the highest incidence rates. The rate of 29.1/100,000 is double the rate for black males (15.4/100,000) and four times the rate for white females (7.7/100,000). These race and gender disparities are also observed in the SEER registries.

Despite the high rate of bladder and urinary tract cancer in South Louisiana white males, they display a small but significant dificit when compared to the SEER rate, 29.1/100,000 vs. 31.8/100,000 (Figure 5). There are no significant differences in rates for black males, white females and black females in South Louisiana and SEER area. The highest rates for bladder cancer are clustered in the New Orleans region. New Orleanian whites have rates significantly higher than those of each individual region as well as the combined South Louisiana rates and SEER rates. Rates for New Orleans blacks show a nonsignificant excess when compared to SEER rates.

*Kidney Cancer.* Cancers of the kidney, renal pelvis and ureter represent 2.4% of total cases in South Louisiana. These cancers accur twice as frequently in means in women and are slighly more common (20-40%) in whites then in blacks.

Unlike bladder cancer, a significant excess risk of kidney cancer is observed for whites in South Louisiana when compared to SEER registries, 13.7 vs. 12.4 and 7.1 vs. 5.6 for males and females respectively. Rates for blacks are very comparable between South Louisiana and SEER areas. In South Louisiana, the highest rates of kidney cancer in males are found in New Orleans for both races, significantly higher than those of Lake Charles region which experiences the lowest rates (Figure 6). The geographic pattern of rates for females differs from males, but is consistent for both races. The highest rates of kidney cancer are found in the Southeast region.

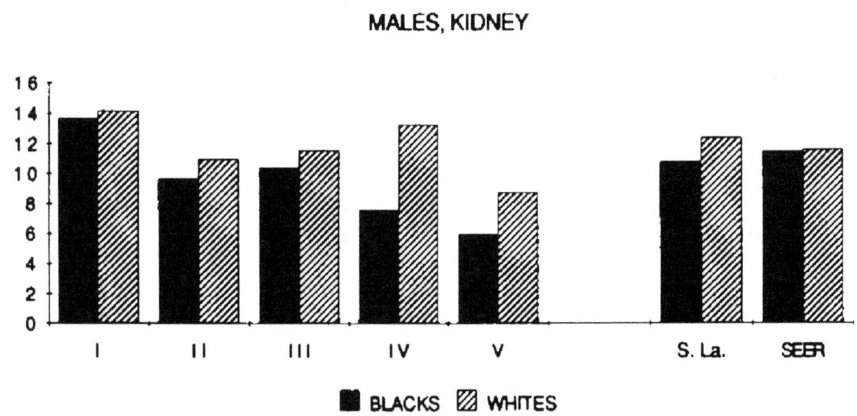


**Figure 6.** Age-Adjusted Incidence Rates of Cancer in S Louisiana by Region and Race, 1983-86

# DISCUSSION

Tobacco use is estimated to account for 30% of all cancer deaths and 87% of lung cancer deaths nationally. Cigarette smoking is the major cause of lung cancer and laryngeal cancer in men and women. It is also a major cause, in addition to alcohol consumption, of oral and esophageal cancer and a contributory cause of blader and renal cancer.[7]

The tobacco-related cancers comprise about one third of the newly-diagnosed cancer in South Louisiana during the period of 1983-1986. These cancers share some similar demographic features. They are approximately three times more common in South Louisiana men then women (ranging from a 2-fold excess for kidney cancer to a 6-fold excess for laryngeal cancer in whtes).

For cancers originating from anatomic sites where there is no direct contact with cigarette smoke or with other forms of tobacco, incidence rates for blacks are either higher than or similar to the rates for whites. Blacks have a threefold risk of esophageal cancer and a 20% higher lung cancer rate than whites. For cancers of the oral cavity, pharynx, and larynx, risk for Louisiana blacks are not higher then whites. These patterns which lack a defined excess risk among blacks are in contrast to the patterns observed nation-wide. Incidence rates for SEER black men are 60% higher then those of their white counterparts for lung cancer, 44% higher for oral cancer, and 50% higher for laryngeal cancer. The phenomenon in South Louisiana is a result of a combination of high rates for white males and much lower rates for black males when compared to the SEER combined rates.

For cancers of the bladder and the kidney (anatomic sites which have no direct contact with tobacco products but with their metabolites), incidence rates are higher in whites then in blacks and are more pronnouced for cancer of the bladder than for cancer of the kidney. This contrasts with other tobacco-related cancers. The higher risk experienced by whites may suggest racial differences in susceptibility to tobacco or differences in exposure to other urineary carcinogens.

Tobacco-related cancers are the most preventable. Studies conducted in South Louisiana and elsewhere in the nation indicate that approxmately 90% of lung cancer is attributed to smoking.[8] That is, if tobacco use is eliminated, 90% of the lung cancer cases could have been avoided. The estimated attributable risk percentages for tobacco-related cancer deaths in the United States, 1985 are shown in Table 3, ranging from 47% to 92% in males and 12% to 87% in females. Any effective cancer prevention and control in South Louisiana must emphasize and be directed toward prevention and cessation of tobacco use.

Table 3
Estimated Attributable Risks (%) For Tobacco-Related Cancer Death From Cigarette Smoking By Sex, United States, 1985

| *Cancer Deaths* | *Males* | *Females* |
|---|---|---|
| | AR% | AR% |
| Lung | 90 (88-92)* | 79 (75-82) |
| Larynx | 81 (57-93) | 87 (56-97) |
| Oral cavity and pharynx | 92 (79-97) | 61 (45-76) |
| Esophagus | 78 (62-89) | 75 (57-87) |
| Bladder | 47 (31-63) | 37 (18-61) |
| Kidney | 48 (32-64) | 12 (3-43) |

*Figures in parentheses are 95% confidence intervals. Source: Report of the Surgeon General 1989.[9]

## Notes for "Cancer in South Louisiana"

[1]L. W. Pickle, T. J. Mason, N. Howard, et al., *Atlas of US Cancer Mortality Among Whites: 1950-1980* (Washington, D. C., 1987), (NIH publication no. 87-2900); Pickle, et al., *Atlas of US Cancer Mortality Among Nonwhites: 1950-1980* (Washington, D. C., 1990), (NIH publication no. 90-1582); P. Correa, Vivien W. Chen, J. F. Craig, et al., *Cancer in Louisiana, Volume 1* (Baton Rouge, 1983).

[2]Vivien W. Chen, J. F. Craig, E. T. Fontham, et al., *Cancer in Louisiana, Volume 6: Cancer Incidence in South Louisiana 1983-1986* (Baton Rouge, 1990); Viven W. Chen, E. T. Fontham, F. P. Groves, et al., *Cancer in Louisiana, Volume 7: Cancer Incidence in South Louisiana 1983-1986* (Baton Rouge, 1991).

[3]J. F. Craig, Viven W. Chen, P. Correa, et al., "Louisiana Tumor Registry," *Journal of the Louisiana State Medical Society*, 140 (1988): 51-54.

[4]International Agency for Research on Cancer. *Cancer Incidence in Five Continents, Volume 5*, C. Muir, J. Waterhouse, T. Mack, eds. (Lyon, 1987), 790-95 (IARC scientific publication no. 88).

[5]U.S. Department of Health and Human Services. *Reducing the Health Consequences of Smoking. 25 Years of Progress—A Report of the Surgeon General, 1989* (Office on Smoking and Health, 1989), (CDC publication no. 89-8411).

[6]Craig, et al., "Louisiana Tumor Registry," 51-54.

[7]U.S. Department of Health and Human Services, *Reducing the Health Consequences of Smoking. . . .*

[8]P. Correa, L. W. Pickle, E. Fontham, et al., "The Causes of Lung Cancer in Louisiana," *Lung Cancer Causes and Prevention* (Deerfield Beach, Fla., 1984), 73-82.

[9]U.S. Department of Health and Human Services, *Reducing the Health Consequences of Smoking. . . .*, 156.

# GOOD-BYE TO MAIN STREET*

Glenn R. Conrad

For over thirty-five years now, I have been conscious, like so many others, of the sometimes slow, sometimes rapid transformation and deterioration of the older commercial districts of Louisiana's cities and small towns. A change that cannot be adjudged good or bad, necessary or not, but one that might be said to be inexorable in the political and economic climate of late twentieth-century America.

Society and "the times" have historically determined the transformation, deterioration, regeneration, and creation of urban commercial districts, whether those districts be the main street of Podunk or the Great White Way of Gotham. Indeed, commercial districts in varying degree have usually been but a reflection of the local community's economic wellbeing, planning, and aesthetics, or the lack of these attributes.

From the historical viewpoint, commercial districts in Louisiana have passed through three major epochs for which we might take labels from the transportation system of the time. The first epoch, the riverboat era, occurred from the time of settlement to the coming of the railroad in the mid-to-late nineteenth century. During this era, most commercial districts, outside of New Orleans, were definitely frontier in character. They were almost always located on the banks of a watercourse, and were composed of a group of wooden structures ranging from log cabins in the early days, to mostly unpainted board-and-batten cypress and pine buildings in the later years of the era.

This early commercial district was usually located on that bank of the stream which was less prone to flooding, and this practice gave rise to such remarkable settlement patterns as one finds along Bayou Teche. There, all early commercial districts are found on the west bank, or higher bank of the stream, from Breaux Bridge to Patterson. As further insurance against flooding, storekeepers usually built their shops on wooden piers. Streets were muddy or dusty depending on the whim of Nature. Animal excrement in the streets, privies behind the shops, smoke from fireplaces, and the ubiquitous tanyard

*A paper presented to the Forum on Regional Architecture on March 21, 1991. Published with the permission of the author.

provided most of these early commercial districts with a vast array of unpleasant odors. People and animals were constant prey of clouds of flies by day and swarms of mosquitoes by day and night. Insects were everywhere, for no opening of any building was as yet screened. Many of the legendary runaways by horses, with or without buggies, were owing to fly torment. Amenities for shoppers were few, only a rare shed to protect the shopper from sun and rain, only an occasional plank substituted for the latter-day sidewalk.

The second epoch in the development of Louisiana's small-town commercial districts dawned after the Civil War as railroads began to crisscross the state. The coming of the railroad gave birth to new towns and sounded the death knell for many older riverboat towns. Happy was the riverboat town that could persuade railroad builders to link it with the outside world by ribbons of steel. Thus, while railroads gave birth to commercial districts oriented toward train freight and passengers, they also tended to reorient the commercial districts of those riverboat towns lucky enough to have train service. Finally, if the situation was one where the railroad passed but a short distance from the old riverboat commercial district, it was not unusual to see the merchants of that district move their shops, lock, stock, and barrel, to a more advantageous site near the railroad.

With the creation or evolution of the railroad town, and the attendant increase in the tempo of economic activity, there appeared, certainly by the 1890s a new commercial architecture employing new building media. Architects and builders now used great amounts of brick and mortar, concrete and glass to provide a far more luxurious scene for shoppers than had been the case before the Civil War and in the years immediately following it.

A major factor contributing to the new brick-and-mortar commercial districts, in addition to an improving economic climate, the appearance of railroads, and growing population, was conflagration. It is absolutely startling to learn of the major fires that destroyed large portions of the old wooden Louisiana towns in the decade or so between 1890 and the early years of the new century. Commercial districts were particularly hard-hit, probably because the early towns were so compact for transportation reasons. Shops, livery stables, hotels, cafes, warehouses, residences, were all crowded into a very small area. Streets were narrow, fire companies were few, structures were highly combustible with wooden walls and wood-shingle roofs. The scenario for tragedy was omni-present. Here in South-central Louisiana, for example, Crowley, Lafayette, New Iberia, Jeanerette, and Franklin were a few of the towns that experienced major downtown fires about a century ago.

Out of the ashes or decay of the wooden towns arose the brick-and-mortar commercial districts so characteristic of the era between 1890 and 1955. Changing times, advancing technology, growing civic pride, several economic booms, particularly those of the 1890s and the years between 1916 and 1923 transformed Main Street. People, now well aware of the catastrophe of fire or the constant threat of it, widened streets to form better firebreaks, built fireproof brick buildings with firewalls forming the common wall between buildings, installed cast-iron facades and metal window blinds as further fire protection, used corrugated iron roofing in place of wooden shingles, and worked with city fathers to install a municipal gravity water system, and employ a full time fire department or a fully reliable volunteer unit.

The brick-and-mortar commercial districts naturally appeared first in the larger communities of Louisiana such as New Orleans and Shreveport. But about a century ago the new commercial architecture began spreading to the larger parish seats and eventually to the smaller, but no less ambitious, towns of the state. I think it is safe to say that the transformation from the old wooden commercial architecture to brick-and-mortar occurred first in those towns having railroad connections, for most bricks were being brought to the rural areas from the larger cities of the state or from out of state. It is true that brick manufacturers existed in rural Louisiana before 1890, but their production was small, and often their product was lacking quality. However, within a decade of the start of the new era, local brickyards sprang up everywhere. Some towns could boast four or five brick manufacturers.

From the beginning of the brick-and-mortar era one can detect a rising tide of civic pride coupled to an awareness of courting the customer that resulted in many civic amenities typical of the era. As the old century closed, many towns were replacing dirt footpaths, planks, or wooden banquettes with concrete sidewalks. Streets were graded to provide better drainage, and in some Louisiana towns, city fathers began to coat streets with a layer of gravel, usually brought to them by the railroad. By the turn of the century many municipalities had garbage collection, albeit usually a one-man operation with a horse and cart. By 1900 any town worth the name, had begun to generate electricity, and the new technology wrought all sorts of changes in downtown.

Shops, cafes, bars, and other enterprises now installed large plate-glass windows to allow for a flood of daylight into the interior of their buildings. Evening shopping became far more agreeable with electric lights and the occasional light bulb lighting the street. Farmers and their families streamed into small-town Louisiana on Saturday afternoon and evening to take advantage of the extended shopping time, usually until 9 or 10 p.m.

Electricity allowed some of the larger Louisiana towns to install streetcar lines, all radiating out from the commercial district and all designed to bring the shopper "downtown" with greater ease and without the trouble of "parking" the horse. Outside of New Orleans, streetcar lines were found in Shreveport, Alexandria, Lake Charles, Baton Rouge, and New Iberia. Although ostensibly a matter of extreme civic pride, streetcars were the objects of much citizen verbal abuse and some litigation whenever a buggy wheel became caught up in the rails and was damaged or pulled off its axle.

By the first decade of the new century there appeared on Main Street that new-fangled contraption called an automobile. It was fully capable of enchanting, amusing, frightening, and frustrating owners and onlookers. Some said it was the wave of the transportation future, others said it was but a passing fancy, few realized that the automobile would be largely responsible for ending the brick-and-mortar era. The telephone was replacing the telegraph as a means of rapid communication, but with electricity and the telephone Main Street suddenly sprouted a forest of less-than-enchanting utility poles: the only American forest that has not been subsequently cut down.

The World War I years and the flapper years of the 1920s were good economic times for small-town Louisiana. By then the brick-and-mortar commercial districts were serving not only growing towns but also a ten-to-twenty-mile radius outside the towns. Parish seats usually developed as the principal town of the area and were fast becoming largely self-sufficient economic units. Ice houses had appeared in small-town Louisiana in the late 1880s, making refrigeration of sorts possible. Wholesale grocery houses in New Orleans and Shreveport established branches in many smaller Louisiana towns, which, in turn, serviced villages and rural communities. Foundries, mills, factories, canneries and other small-scale manufactures, mostly locally owned, provided alternative occupations to farming, fishing, and lumbering as the economic tempo quickened.

The quick end of World War I for the United States, the brilliant victories of American armed forces in France, the experiences engendered in a world beyond the parochial, and "good times," caused many small-town Louisianians to re-think their role in their town of the future. It was clearly a case of rejecting the past as old-fashioned, dull and dreary, completely out of step with the times. The new thinking, as we all know, was quickly revealed in the lifestyle of the Roaring 20s, featuring new fashions, new music, movies, radio, and the improved phonograph and automobile. This new thinking quickly manifested itself in the brick-and-mortar towns and indeed brought them to their heyday.

Chambers of commerce were organized, civic organizations were formed, women's clubs blossomed to address a variety of civic concerns, and hometown newspapers reported every civic improvement in a constant drumbeat of local pride. The commercial district expanded to the streets perpendicular and parallel to Main Street as new businesses opened. In addition to the usual array of food, clothing, and hardware stores, "downtown" now became the haven for car dealerships, larger and more luxurious movie houses, multi-story hotels, and cafes taking on the dimensions of restaurants. New banks appeared, professional people opened downtown offices, and public officials convinced citizens that older city halls, schools, and courthouses had to be replaced by more modern facilities or renovated to keep pace with the times. Dirty and ramshackle were out, clean, neat and shiny were in.

Main Street itself was caught up in the mood of the day. A dirt or gravel main thoroughfare was a thing of the past. Between 1912 and 1925 town after town across Louisiana undertook to pave its main street with bricks or some other all-weather coating. Ramshackle street lighting was replaced with more and better lights, usually atop ornate cast-iron lamp standards. Windows and doors were screened. Flush toilets were installed; cesspools replaced open sewerage ditches; and elementary municipal sewerage systems appeared in some towns. Horses, a transportation thing of the past, were relegated to horse parking lots, usually a block or two from the main shopping district. Curbside parking for automobiles on Main Street was the order of the day. Moreover, every town worth its salt, had a vast parade of weekend drivers motoring up and down Main Street, just seeing the sights.

The Louisiana brick-and-mortar Main Street probably reached the zenith of its development in the late 1920s and thereafter became virtually frozen in time for the next two decades because of two events completely beyond the control of most Americans—the Great Depression and World War II. The Depression was basically a dozen years of a moribund economy not conducive to business expansion and architectural transformation. The war years and the immediate postwar period, while economically stimulating, nevertheless withheld resources for business expansion. Thus, during the Depression and war years, very little was added to the commercial districts of the late 1920s. True, businesses came and went, buildings might be spruced up on the interior and occasionally on the exterior, but the basic streetscape of Main Street remained the same for most of small-town Louisiana until 1950 or thereabouts.

The post-war economic boom not only provided the resources and the financial wherewithal for the expansion of commercial districts, but it also gave to nearly every American family what had been available to a relative few when the Depression began, the opportunity to own an automobile. Now it was possible to go downtown in one's car. Indeed, one still had to go downtown to buy one's car. But the downtowns of Louisiana's small towns were not designed to accommodate automotive traffic that was compounding year after year, they had been designed for the pedestrian. They were therefore compact; and this very compactness with its attendant inability to accommodate the automobile, either on narrow streets or with curbside parking, spelled the beginning of the end for the brick-and-mortar commercial district.

The post-war proliferation of the automobile was also responsible for accelerating a nascent industry of the 1920 and 30s—tourism. Americans were traveling more and as they did so they found the highways always connecting with Main Street, but Main Street was really not geared to the needs of the traveling motorist. Sure, there were service stations downtown dating back to the early years of the automobile, but they were usually small and cramped for space. True, there were nice hotels and restaurants downtown to accommodate the traveler, but there was also a growing chorus of "where do we park the car?" As a result, early on in the postwar era, service stations began to spring up all along the highway route through town and not necessarily in the downtown area. Within five years after V-E day, the overnight accommodation known as a tourist court in the prewar days was rechristened and blossomed forth as the motel. Now the traveler could park his car at his overnight front door.

But the automobile was not the sole factor in the demise of downtown as a viable commercial district. After World War II, but particularly after the Korean War, the evolving American economy brought rapid changes in the field of merchandising. Its hard to point a finger at where it all began because the transition from the compact railroad brick-and-mortar town to the scattershot, automobile town was different in most Louisiana communities. The result, however, has been universal or nearly universal. In some Louisiana towns the first break away from the old commercial district was made by automobile dealerships which had more of their product to display in the post-war years and little room to display it downtown. Thus, the dealership leapfrogged over the residential area adjacent to the old commercial district and set up shop on the edge of town. The dealerships were soon joined in this area by service stations, motels, drive-in theaters, and drive-in food and beverage businesses. The automobile was actually bringing new words into the language. Perhaps more importantly, some downtown businessmen already were finding themselves in competition with other entrepreneurs now strategically located to serve the customer even before he reached the old commercial district.

As American merchandising evolved from the privately owned and operated store to the regional or national chain store, another and very important step was taken in the development of the automobile town, the creation of the shopping center. Without doubt the catalyst for the development of the small-town shopping center was the arrival in town of one of the supermarket chains. Here was mass merchandising of groceries and household items on a scale that few downtown buildings could accommodate, to say nothing of accommodating the motor vehicles of hundreds of customers. Everywhere one heard the truism, "Parking is so convenient." Of course, as we all know the typical strip shopping center of small Louisiana towns developed to incorporate a chain drug store, a chain novelty store, and a branch bank. Like other businesses before them, these mass merchandisers sought the wide open spaces near town to build their buildings and construct their parking lots.

There is no doubt that downtown merchants tried, individually and collectively, to compete with shopping centers. In the matter of accommodating motorists, some brick- and mortar buildings were bought, demolished and the site paved as a parking lot. But painting black stripes on a yellow cat does not make a tiger, and for many motorists the usually smaller downtown parking lots were but poor reflections of the shopping center parking lot. As matters went from bad to worse for downtown merchants, town governments, chambers of commerce, and downtown merchant associations sought other solutions to the problem of runaway customers. Some towns closed off Main Street and converted it into a pedestrian mall, complete with resurfacing, plantings, antique lamp standards, benches, murals, and fountains. Unfortunately for those who made this effort, the result was little more than that found in those towns which could not afford such expensive enticements and had therefore cut barrels in half, filled them with dirt, planted petunias and set them out along Main Street. Individual downtown merchants, still thinking that they could find a cosmetic solution to the problem of shopping centers, tried to zoom into the mid-to-late twentieth-century by covering the brick-and-mortar facade of their downtown store with everything from plastic components to standing red cedar boards. Alas, to little or no avail.

The impact of shopping centers, both from the standpoint of merchandising and motorist accommodation, was traumatic for downtown business people, but the impact became devastating when, in the 1960s and 1970s, into these shopping centers or new ones springing up, came merchandisers like Gibsons and Howard Brothers to be followed and largely replaced in the 70s and 80s by K-Mart and Walmart. Small-town Louisiana would never again be the same. Many to most downtown businesses closed and the stores stand abandoned as local businessmen found it impossible to compete with the prices of the mass-merchandisers and the community could not find a reason to recycle downtown structures. By the late 1980s and early 90s many a brick-and-mortar commercial district in small-town Louisiana stands forlorn. In some towns, only empty shells remain where commerce once flourished. Former shops have been severely vandalized, large plate-glass display windows shattered, doors smashed, and walls that soaked up the small-town gossip of 60 or 70 years ago are currently display areas for contemporary vulgarisms. Many brick-and-mortar buildings, still proudly displaying their birthdate on their facade, have become victims of fire, intentional or otherwise, their fireproof walls testifying to a bygone era. Many buildings simply stand abandoned and gradually collapse under the weight of time and neglect.

Aware of what was happening to the older commercial districts of Louisiana towns, the staff of the Center for Louisiana Studies of the University of Southwestern Louisiana in 1988 undertook a project to photo-document the brick-and-mortar commercial districts of small-town Louisiana. When the project began, all we sought to do was to record in black and white and on color slides what this older commercial architecture was all about. In the end, two years later, the project had succeeded in photographing brick-and-mortar commercial districts of 217 Louisiana towns and producing a photographic archive of about 5000 black-and-white prints and about 3000 color slides. Our project began in April, 1988, in Lake Providence, a one-time riverboat town, a railroad town, and now, perhaps, a town groping for a future in Northeast Louisiana. From there the three-member team crisscrossed the state and in the spring of 1990 completed the photo-documentation aspect of the project in Buras in the Mississippi delta.

From the beginning, however, the project team discovered that we would come to know a great deal more about small-town Louisiana than what was to be found in its near-century-old architecture. Casual observation of many small towns while driving through their streets revealed that they were already suffering a serious malaise that went beyond decaying historical architecture. The observations we made, the information we gathered, the interviews we conducted do not represent in any way a scientific study of small-town Louisiana or of some small towns in Louisiana. Whatever information was offered to us, we accepted. Granted, we looked askance at statements from some vested interest groups who for their own reasons prefer to pretend that the old creaky machine of small-town and rural life in Louisiana is competing favorably with the current lifestyles of the state's and region's larger towns and cities. Local politicians and chambers of commerce nearly always fell into this category. But we also talked with people on the street who, upon learning of our photodocumentation project, eagerly began to talk about the "good old days" and the town they knew. We soon learned, much to our surprise, that these people were describing towns that no longer existed as vital entities; that they were describing municipal amenities which had long since disappeared; and that while bemoaning the loss of a lifestyle, they were now resigned to the fact. We visited many public housing projects and spoke with residents. Their accounts of their lifestyles led members of the project team to conclude that many small towns are today little more than reservations where society warehouses the underprivileged, the unemployed, and the under-employed. We discovered that there is a new bondage loose in the land, the bondage of poverty and ignorance whose victims live out their squalid lives to the drumbeat of drugs, crime, and myriad forms of social degradation.

Basically speaking, what we learned from our small-town informants is that a process which is underway across America, particularly in the Mississippi Valley, is now also well underway in Louisiana, perhaps more so in North Louisiana and the northern tier of Florida Parishes than in Louisiana south of U. S. Highway 190. It appears to us that the population of the state is concentrating in or very near 8 or 9 metropolitan areas: Shreveport, Monroe, Alexandria, Lake Charles, Lafayette, Houma, New Orleans, and Baton Rouge, and, for special reasons, in smaller urban settings such as Ruston, Bastrop, Thibodaux, New Iberia, Hammond, and Bogalusa. The out migration from small towns and rural areas that has been going on now for about 35 years involves those individuals who have the education, talent, and/or ambition to seek job opportunities with corporate America in the metropolitan setting. Job opportunities which range from high tech to fast food.

Job opportunities for the undereducated and undertalented, which were once plentiful in the small-town and rural economies of 50 or 60 years ago have largely vanished today because of many factors, not the least of which are advancing technology which continues to erode the need for muscle work or assembly-line work; the evolution of corporate America, making competition by a locally owned business difficult or impossible; the establishment of a national, indeed international, credit system, which gives the holder instant credit in Tickfaw or Timbuctoo; and finally, the plight of farm families in an economy which depresses the price of raw commodities and inflates the prices of processing, packaging, transportation, and retailing. Adding to the plight of small towns is the fact that wherever locally owned businesses have survived, employment opportunities are usually reserved for family or friends. It should be emphasized that these are only *some* of the factors contributing to the lack of job opportunities in most Louisiana small towns. Needless to say, these factors for unemployment and underemployment are compounded by such major societal problems as drugs, crime, and present-day America's confusion about what constitutes a family unit.

Tears welled into the eyes of a black middle school principal in North Louisiana as he told the project team about the drug problem in his school, a problem which he maintained was of little real concern to his community, beyond a litany of well-rehearsed rhetoric, but a problem which nevertheless leads to poor grades, dropouts, and teenage motherhood. A junior high school principal in one of the western parishes told us of how he and his teachers are constantly encouraging youngsters to stay in school, get an education, and prepare themselves for a job. He shook his head slowly and said, "But, where is the job? Certainly not in this little town that is dying on the vine." Sure, he continued, some graduates can get a job at the local hamburger stand, but their income is little more than change in their pocket. Most have to live at home; few can afford to buy a car, to say nothing of planning for marriage, a home, and a family."

A high-school principal in a parish seat in Acadiana was asked to give some idea of what percentage of his graduating seniors go on to college. He proudly replied that about 30% did. He was then asked how many university-trained persons seek and find jobs or professions in his parish. After some equivocation, he finally stated that there really are not many graduates returning unless they are entering a family business or such things as an established legal firm, medical group, or large-scale farming operation.

Across the state, the project team found that the area of employment opportunity which has grown steadily despite declining populations in small-town and rural Louisiana is government service. Many courthouses, city halls, and school board offices belie the economic and social conditions of their host towns. Almost everywhere in the rural parishes these office buildings appear to be larger and more elegant than they were when small towns began to decline. Many municipal and parochial office buildings seem to have sprouted annexes, appendages, and sundry satellite facilities. All of which, of course, tends to suggest a growing number of people in public service. I recall walking into a North Louisiana parish office of the State Department of Health and Human Resources and being immediately amazed. My amazement was not a result of the number of people in the office seeking help of one kind or another because the apparent economic condition of the town and parish had prepared me for that; rather, I was amazed that every available space in this rather large building that could be occupied by a desk was occupied by a desk with an individual sitting behind it. That night, as the project team discussed the day's activities and my observations in that particular office, a member of the team said something that has stuck with me ever since. "What you describe here and what we have seen elsewhere in this regard is middle-class welfare, particularly designed for those individuals who want to stay in small-town Louisiana. State government knows full well that in small-town and rural Louisiana there are probably few employment opportunities commensurate with these people's education and so they are provided public service jobs."

In a way, the large public payroll in small towns and rural parishes has had an effect beyond maintaining a middle-class way of life for federal, state, parish, and municipal employees. In a few parish seats, for example Homer, in Claiborne Parish, sufficient thought has been given to an eroding parishwide tax base to prompt parish officials to locate parochial offices in renovated former commercial buildings on the square around the courthouse. This congregation of people on the town's central square has, in turn, tended to give new life to some of the older businesses and invites new businesses to establish in renovated brick-and-mortar buildings. In South Louisiana, a similar situation exists in Abbeville where concerned citizens and public officials are doing much to refurbish the old brick-and-mortar part of downtown, especially the transformation of the old Audrey Hotel into a pleasant, spacious City Hall.

An aspect of our study which seems to haunt the members of the project team and which is a topic of conversation whenever we come together will concern my concluding remarks. Throughout rural Louisiana we found evidence of abandoned farmland, shut down mills, factories, and processing plants. The service industry, where it is still to be found, is largely struggling. Medical services are completely lacking in many small towns. The frontier of substandard and marginal housing instead of being ever pushed to obliteration, now flows like a tide into once neat small-town residential neighborhoods. Many long-established small-town amenities are gone, such as parks, swimming pools and other recreational facilities, streetsweepers, sidewalks, and properly functioning sewer systems. In so much of rural Louisiana it appears that the tax base is rapidly eroding and as it does the quality of life in these areas continues to deteriorate. At one of our nightly rap sessions, someone asked the question we all knew was coming sooner or later: "Why?" "Why is there this disparity of opportunity within the state."

On one hand, our growing consensus is not one that is easily accepted because it steps on many vested-interest toes; and, on the other hand, it is easily dismissed by those who claim it is too simplistic to be accepted. Given the scenario I have laid before you here of the flight of the educated and talented population from small-town and rural Louisiana, coupled to the many other factors I have set out, all basically resulting, we believe, from this flight, the project team concurs in the view that the major problem contributing to the plight of small-town and rural Louisiana is declining tax base. A declining tax base, resulting from any number of economic ills or combination of them, not only deprives a small town and rural Louisiana of most of the civic amenities enjoyed by the several metropolitan areas, but, much more importantly, it also condemns a majority of the population of those small towns and rural places to second-class citizenship. Let's look at the obvious example. If educational opportunity is not equal for all Louisianians to enjoy, then we in Louisiana are perpetuating a society composed of privileged and underprivileged. How in the name of all reason can educational opportunity be considered equal for rural and urban children, when the metropolitan area enjoying a healthy tax base can spend greater amounts of money on teachers and educational facilities than can the rural, poor parish? Nearly everyone knows that the best and brightest are drawn toward the greater salary. When the discrepancy in starting teachers' salaries in adjoining parishes, one metropolitan and wealthy, the other rural and "poor," amounts to $4000, there can be no doubt which parish will get the teachers with the highest test scores. I certainly do not denigrate the work, the courage, the dedication of small-town and rural teachers. Many of these dedicated individuals, possessing tremendous talents, are the only beacons for youth in the otherwise culturally bleak landscape of rural Louisiana. I believe that teachers and students alike are victims of the system, a system that might best be described as being as obsolete as the brick-and-mortar commercial district of the 1920s.

What is needed in Louisiana to address the many problems of small towns and rural parishes is a complete administrative restructuring of our state at the local level. There are parishes in Louisiana today that should cease to exist because as a political entity they can no longer provide basic services for their declining population. These parishes appear to exist simply because the administrators have turned them into self-perpetuating entities where administrative salaries remain steady or increase in the face of declining public services. A remedy for much of what diminishes the quality of life in small-town and rural Louisiana might be found in a restructuring of our parochial system to form political and economic regions centered on the several metropolitan areas. In this way, I believe, the human and economic resources of the enlarged administrative unit can be better employed to address the needs of citizens residing in pockets of poverty artificially delimited by what we call parish boundaries. There is no reason to perpetuate a system in which a child living on the "poor" side of a parish line is condemned to fewer educational opportunities than those received by a child living on the "affluent" side of that line. Such a practice only perpetuates classes of citizenship and thereby stifles the individual's right to life, liberty, and the pursuit of happiness.

# NEW ORLEANS MUSEUM OF ART: HISTORY OF THE COLLECTION*

Prescott N. Dunbar

1910 was a propitious year for the founding of an art museum in New Orleans. Historically the most cosmopolitan city in the region, New Orleans was enjoying a new prosperity. Fortunes were being made in shipping, import and export, finance, and agriculture in the City, then the third busiest seaport in the United States with 339,000 inhabitants. Isaac Delgado was one of the most successful of the new generation of civic and business leaders. Born in Jamaica in 1839, Delgado arrived in New Orleans at the age of fourteen, later joining the sugar business founded by his uncle, Samuel Delgado.

A millionaire bachelor with no heirs, Delgado dispersed his fortune to several New Orleans charities. In 1905 he gave $180,000 to Charity Hospital, while he eventually bequeathed the bulk of his estate to establish what is now the Delgado Community College. In February 1910 Delgado offered to donate $150,000 to construct an art museum in City Park. The Commissioners of the City Park Improvement Association accepted his generous gift by providing an appropriate site and a national competition was immediately announced for the design of the building. The winning design, submitted by Samuel A. Marx of the Chicago firm of Lebenbaum & Marx, was for a handsome neo-classic Beaux Arts structure, described by the young architect as, "inspired by the Greek [but] sufficiently modified to give a subtropical appearance."

When the Isaac Delgado Museum of Art was opened to the public on December 16, 1911, it was only the third such institution in the South. Since Delgado had provided no funds for the maintenance of the Museum or for the acquisition of works of art, the City of New Orleans was called upon to provide an annual appropriation for the operating budget, while the exhibition program was sponsored by local art organizations, particularly the Art Association of New Orleans. Works in the inaugural exhibition, including 400 paintings and a number of plaster casts of antique sculptures, were lent

*First published in *New Orleans Museum of Art Handbook of the Collection* (New Orleans: New Orleans Museum of Art, 1995), 7-18. Reprinted with the kind permission of the author and the Museum.

primarily by local collectors. To build its permanent art collection, the Museum had to depend on the generosity of individuals and organizations interested in art.

During the years before World War I, enthusiasm for the Museum ran high in the community and several art collections were donated that served as the core of the permanent holdings for many decades. First, in 1912 Maj. Benjamin M. Harrod bequeathed a group of paintings to the Museum, most by Louisiana artists, including two landscapes by Richard Clague. In 1914 the Museum received the bequest of the Morgan Whitney collection of Chinese jades and other hard stone carvings, which were cataloged and illustrated that year in the Museum's first scholarly publication. Also received in 1914 was a collection of fifty-six pieces of American and European silver, including works by the New Orleans firm of Hyde & Goodrich, the gift of Eugenia U. Harrod. In 1916 Alvin P. Howard gave his collection of Greek vases and ancient glass.

By far the most important art donation received by the Museum during its first forty years was the collection of paintings and sculpture by various nineteenth-century French Salon, Barbizon School and Munich Group artists, bequeathed in 1915 by Mrs. Chapman H. Hyams. The collection of forty-one works, described in the catalog published in 1915 as, "the most important artistic unit south of Washington," included fine paintings by Corot, Vibert, Bouguereau and Gérôme.

The decades of the 1920s and 1930s were static ones for the growth of the Museum's art collection. During this period the Museum and the art world in New Orleans were dominated by Ellsworth Woodward, Professor of Art and dean of the Newcomb College Art School, president of the Art Association of New Orleans, and founder and president of the Southern States Art League. Woodward was one of the nine original trustees of the Delgado Museum and, as the only member with professional art training, served from the first as chairman of the Art Committee. After the death of the Museum's first curator, local artist Charles W. Boyle, Woodward served as volunteer acting director from 1925 to 1939, as well as president of the Board from 1934 to 1939.

Ellsworth Woodward believed that the Museum's first priority was the education and moral uplift of its visitors, while the formation of an art collection of historical scope was secondary. Woodward also took great pride in the resurgent South and used the Museum to foster and promote contemporary Southern artists, who were featured in the majority of the exhibitions at the Museum during his tenure.

While no significant art works were acquired by gift or purchase in the 1920s, the 1930s saw the donation of three important works by Italian old masters, the first of high quality to enter the Museum's collection, from the great New York collector and philanthropist Samuel H. Kress. The first of these paintings, given in 1931, was an early Renaissance *Madonna and Child* by Giovanni del Biondo, followed in 1934 by a *Portrait of Pope Clement XIII,* now attributed to Anton Raphael Mengs, and finally *The Blessing Saviour* by Carpaccio in 1938. Samuel Kress also lent a selection of fifty-two Italian Renaissance and later paintings to the Museum in 1933, the most important special exhibition presented at the Delgado in that decade.

Arthur Feitel, a young New Orleans architect elected to the Museum's Board in 1933, and a few other trustees attempted in the late 1930s to schedule new and stimulating art exhibitions and to reorganize the cluttered galleries. However, real progress and change were only possible after 1939, when Feitel succeeded the late Ellsworth Woodward as volunteer acting director of the Museum and president of the Art Association. While funds for acquisitions were scarce during World War II, Feitel was able to present several important exhibitions that awakened new interest in the Museum. Outstanding among these were *Forty Years of Picasso* from The Museum of Modern Art, which included *Guernica*, and the first American museum exhibition of the work of Hans Hoffman, arranged in 1941 by one of his students, the New Orleans-born artist Fritz Bultman. The only important acquisition of the war years came in 1940 with the purchase of the large Natoire *Toilette of Psyche*, which originally came to New Orleans in 1845 when it was purchased by James Robb from Joseph Bonaparte's collection.

With the quadrupling of the City of New Orleans's annual appropriation to the Museum in 1947, Board President Arthur Feitel was able to realize the long-sought goal of hiring the Museum's first professionally trained director. Alonso Lansford, serving as director from 1948 to 1957, achieved remarkable results in building the permanent collection, acquiring in ten years art works of a far higher quality than most acquired during the Museum's first four decades. Certainly the most important acquisition was the permanent loan and promised gift (finalized in 1961) of twenty-nine Italian old master paintings from the Samuel H. Kress Foundation, part of the dispersement of this huge collection to the National Gallery of Art and selected museums throughout the country. Added to the earlier Kress gifts, this collection allowed the Museum to present for the first time a comprehensive, historical survey of one of the major schools of European art. The Kress Foundation required major renovations to the galleries where its collection was to be displayed, thus beginning long-needed physical improvements to the Delgado Building.

During the 1950s donations of both collections of objects and individual works, as well as several major purchases, occurred with increasing frequency. William E. Campbell, author of such books as *The Bad Seed* under the name William Marsh, gave several fine paintings by American and French artists, including Gottlieb's *Dream* and a Fauve period *Derain*. Unfortunately the bulk of his collection, including nine Soutines, was sold in New York following his premature death in 1954. Several other important twentieth-century works were acquired at this time from members of the Bultman family. In 1955 Mrs. Muriel Bultman Francis donated a Baziotes, while in the following year her father, A. Fred Bultman, Jr., gave Hoffman's doublesided Still Life/Self Portrait and her brother, Fritz Bultman, gave a collection of graphics by German and, later, French artists. The Bultman family's involvement with the Museum continued for many decades, with both A. Fred Bultman, Jr., and Mrs. Francis servings as trustees. During her years on the board, Mrs. Francis regularly donated important art works to the Museum. In a final magnificent gesture of support she bequeathed nearly her entire collection to the Museum in 1986. The Muriel Bultman Francis collection of 185 works was one of the most important art donations in the Museum's history. Particularly rich in drawings, it includes major examples by Ingres, Degas, Redon, Picasso, Matisse, and David Smith.

In 1955 Lansford convinced Melvin P. Billups of New York to donate his large and growing collection of glass to the Museum. By the time the Museum received possession of the Billups collection in 1969 it numbered over 3,000 objects, ranging in time from ancient Egyptian to Victorian—one of the most important such collections in the United States. Among individual donations received during Lansford's directorship were two American works from New Orleans collector William S. Groves, including a George Caleb Bingham portrait. Ten years later Mr. Groves would add substantially to this gift with the donation of a large group of Louisiana paintings. Also given in the mid-fifties was a Max Ernst oil from Mr. and Mrs. Isaac Heller; the Museum's first work by Edgar Degas, a bronze *Walking Horse* from the Musson family; and the first African work to enter the collection, a *Head of an Oba* from the Benin Kingdom of Nigeria. Among acquisitions made during the same period from meager purchase funds were the monumental bronze *Archer* by Bourdelle and paintings by Utrillo and Vlaminck.

During Sue Thurman's brief directorship from 1958 to 1961 few works were acquired for the collection, the Lipchitz bronze being the most important. However, the appointment of James B. Byrnes as director in 1962 marked the beginning of a decade of accelerated growth for the Museum and its art collections. At the start of his directorship, the Museum was able to convince the city administration not only to increase its annual appropriation (thereby expanding the professional staff), but also to give $135,000 to complete the renovation of the Delgado building. The first major additions to the collection under Byrnes began in 1964 with a series of gifts from Mrs. Edgar B. Stern of twentieth-century works by European Constructivists and Op artists, such as Kandinsky, Gabo, Arp, and Vasarely.

Undoubtedly the most important acquisition made during the 1960s was Edgar Degas' Portrait of Estelle Musson Degas, painted during the artist's visit to his maternal relatives in New Orleans in 1872-73. The excitement aroused in completing the Museum's first fund drive to raise the necessary $190,000 to purchase this work in 1964 focused the community's attention and pride on the Museum as never before, making possible further growth and expansion.

While a number of outstanding gifts were made to the collection, the Museum still lacked the funds to make significant art purchases. To begin to remedy this situation, in 1965 a public auction was held of surplus objects, not of Museum quality, from the collection which netted $35,000. Of more lasting importance was the organization of the Women's Volunteer Committee and the start of its annual fundraising benefit the Odyssey Ball. The first Ball was held in November 1966 to open an exhibition of the collection of Mr. and Mrs. Frederick M. Stafford of New York. For the next twenty-two years, proceeds from the Odyssey Ball, totaling $1,750,000, were dedicated to art purchases. The exhibition of the Stafford collection also marked their active involvement and support, which over the years resulted in the gift of numerous art works of great variety and quality by such artists as Bonnard, Miró, Rouault, and objects from Africa, China, Japan, and India. In addition, since 1967 many works from the Stafford collection have remained on extended loan to the Museum and thus broadened its survey of the art of various cultures and national schools.

In 1966 the Museum received a matching grant of $200,000 from The Ella West Freeman Foundation for art acquisitions. The successful completion of the fund drive to match this grant continued the momentum of Museum growth. With major funds now available the director and trustees examined the Museum's future acquisitions policy and determined that an effort should be made to build a cohesive, specialized collection. The area of specialization selected was the arts of the Americas, specifically work produced in North, Central and South America from the pre-Columbian period to the present. During the next five years a great number of works were purchased in this area, resulting in a concentration of Pre-Columbian art from Mexico, particularly from the Maya, and Spanish colonial painting from Peru. In addition, donations of objects from such collectors as Mr. and Mrs. P. Roussel Norman and Mr. and Mrs. Richard McCarthy, Jr. further enriched the Pre-Columbian collection.

An important result of the Freeman grant was the updating of the City of New Orleans's commitment to support the passage of a bond issue to finance Museum expansion. In 1968 the citizens of New Orleans voted in favor of a $1.6 million bond issue to construct a new wing to provide galleries for the permanent collection and special exhibitions. At the same time the Stern Fund provided monies for a separate auditorium and office wing and the Edward Wisner Donation provided funds for an education wing. These three additions tripled the size of the original building. In recognition of the support of the city and other donors since 1910, the trustees voted to change the name to the New Orleans Museum of Art. The new wings were opened in November 1971 with a major loan exhibition, *New Orleans Collects*, which documented the parallel growth of private art collections in the city during the past two decades.

In 1973 the trustees appointed E. John Bullard as director. Building on the accomplishments of the past, Bullard continued the accelerated expansion of the art collection in both old and new areas. Early in 1973, recognizing that photography was then an undervalued art form and that it was possible to build a major, comprehensive collection with limited funds, Bullard convinced the trustees to begin purchasing photographs. As a result the Museum now has one of the country's premier photography collections, numbering nearly 8,000 works. With the generous support of Dr. Kurt A. Gitter and later other donors, in 1973 the Museum also began to build a large and comprehensive collection of Japanese art of the Edo period (1615-1868). Now with over 300 Japanese screens and scrolls, NOMA has built another area of specialization of national stature.

The 1974 bequest of seventeen paintings and sculptures and 180 African and Oceanic objects from Victor K. Kiam was the greatest art donation the Museum had received since the gift of the Kress Collection. Although raised and educated in New Orleans, Mr. Kiam had lived in New York City for many years. However, realizing the importance and place of honor his art collection would have in a regional museum, he decided to bequeath it to NOMA. The Kiam collection significantly increased the Museum's representation of twentieth-century European and American art, with works by Miró, Picasso, Braque, and Pollock among others, while immeasurably broadening and strengthening the African and Oceanic collection. Also received in 1974 was the magnificent collection of 347 English and continental portrait miniatures, the gift of Mrs. Shirley Latter Kaufmann in memory of her parents, Harry and Anna Latter. Collected by Mrs. Kaufmann and her father over many years, it includes examples by Nicholas Hilliard, Samuel Cooper, Richard Cosway, and John Smart.

Having exhausted the Ella West Freeman Foundation Matching Fund some years before, in 1975 the trustees of the Museum launched a major fund drive to raise $2.5 million in art acquisition funds and works of art. The acquisition policy was revised by Bullard, placing emphasis on the acquisition of major works by French artists of the seventeenth through mid-nineteenth centuries to complement the later French art already in the collection and American painting of the eighteenth and nineteenth centuries to further augment the arts of the Americas collection. The Acquisitions Fund Drive was successfully completed in 1978 with the donation of two period rooms of American colonial and Federal furniture and decorative arts, the gift of Emile N. Kuntz, Karolyn Kuntz Westervelt, and Rosemonde Kuntz Capomazza in memory of Rosemonde E. Kuntz, Emile Kuntz, and Felix H. Kuntz. Specially designed galleries to house the Kuntz Collection were opened in 1980. With eventually $1 million in cash received from the 1977 Art Acquisitions Fund Drive the Museum purchased a number of major works by American and French artists, which added new levels of quality to these areas of the collection. The most important of these purchases were Copley's *Portrait of Colonel George Watson*, Peale's *Portrait of Robert Morris*, Sargent's *Portrait of Mrs. Asher B. Wertheimer*, and Claude Lorrain's *Ideal View of Tivoli*.

The presentation of the international blockbuster exhibition, *The Treasures of Tutankhamen*, from September 15, 1977, to January 15, 1978, was the most momentous event in NOMA's history. Seen by over 870,000 visitors and earning $75 million in tourist revenues for the city, the exhibition generated a tremendously increased recognition locally, regionally and nationally of the importance of the Museum. This led to higher levels of support in all areas of the Museum's operation and established NOMA as the prime venue in the South during the next decade for other international exhibitions, including *The Gold of El Dorado*, *The Search for Alexander* and *Carthage: A Mosaic of Ancient Tunisia*.

Although the Louisiana economy was in decline due to the collapse of world oil prices, the 1980s was a decade of incredible growth for NOMA. All areas of the art collection expanded dramatically and several new areas were developed. The period began spectacularly with the long-term loan of the collection of the late Madelyn Kreisler, a native New Orleanian who had lived in New York for many years. With her husband Bernard, she formed an impressive collection of Impressionist and twentieth century works. The loan was made possible by her niece and nephew, New Orleanians Mrs. John N. Weinstock and Richard M. Wise, who donated from the collection in her memory a 1918 Metzinger *Still Life*. In 1993 Mrs. Weinstock made a promised gift to NOMA of her portion of the Kreisler collection, including paintings by Monet, Gauguin, Münter, Vlaminck, Van Dongen, Braque and Chagall.

1981 saw the gift of an important collection of old masters. Bert Piso, born of Dutch parents in Indonesia in 1915, emigrated to the United States after World War II. An early interest in Dutch seventeenth century painting led him to collect works by the "Little Masters," many discovered in antique stores and galleries on his business travels in the South. A discerning eye and scholarly knowledge offset his limited funds and he was able to assemble a collection of quality, which he bequeathed to NOMA. The twenty works in the Piso collection significantly expanded the Museum's representation of the Dutch School and attracted gifts from other collectors, including Dr. and Mrs. Richard W. Levy and Mr. and Mrs. Henry H. Weldon of New York.

Throughout the 1980s the collection of European and American painting continued to expand with both gifts and purchases. Single gifts such as the popular Mary Cassatt, *Mother and Child in the Conservatory*, purchased with funds donated by Mr. and Mrs. Harold Forgotson in 1982, and the "white period" Utrillo of Sacré-Coeur, Montmartre, a 1989 gift of Mrs. Charles Kohlmeyer, Jr., further strengthened the collection of twentieth century masters. Similarly the donation of five Italian, Dutch and French old masters by the Azby Art Fund in memory of Herbert J. Harvey, Jr. and Marion W. Harvey enriched the three national schools that have evolved as NOMA's areas of concentration in European art. With increased purchase funds available from the Odyssey Balls, the director and curators could seek out specific works to fill gaps in the historic survey. Most major purchases of European art were by French masters, including works by Lagilliere, Van Loo, Boucherr, and Vincent. The most spectacular of these acquisitions was the life-size *Portrait of Marie Antoinette, Queen of France*, by Elisabeth Vigée-Lebrun, purchased with funds raised by the Women's Volunteer Committee in honor of the Museum's seventy-fifth anniversary in 1986.

Before 1984 the Museum had an art endowment of less than $100,000. The unexpected bequest of half a million dollars from Miss Carrie B. Heiderich, began a concerted effort by the staff and Board to significantly increase endowment funds for art purchases. With the creation of funds in the names of Robert Gordy, Mervin and Maxine Morais, George S. Frierson, Jr., P. Roussel Norman, Leah Norman Schreier, and most recently, William McDonald and Eva Carol Boles, by gifts and bequests the art endowment has increased to $4 million. With an aggressive planned-giving program, it is expected that this endowment will grow exponentially in the years ahead, thus ensuring a guaranteed source of significant monies to enrich the art collection.

Building on established strengths in the collection, John Bullard and the curators cultivated and encouraged collectors in New Orleans and throughout the country resulting in a steady stream of donations. John W. Keefe, curator of Decorative Arts, through a series of exhibitions focused on local collectors secured a number of gifts which have significantly broadened the holdings of glass, ceramics, and silver. Among these gifts—promised, partial, or completed—are the Irving Gerson collection of Wedgwood, the Elinor Bright Richardson collection of silver by Paul Storr and his contemporaries, the Elizabeth Danos and Paul P. Selley collection of European faience, the Jack Sawyer collection of art glass, and the Harold Newman collection of silvered glass. With limited purchase funds and gifts, Keefe also has developed strong holdings of Old Paris porcelain and American art pottery, two diverse ceramic productions with strong ties to New Orleans.

The collection of Asian art continued to be strengthened in the area of Japanese painting of the Edo period with additional gifts from Dr. Kurt A. Gitter and Mr. and Mrs. George L. Lindemann of New York. The collection of Chinese art attracted important works from past donors, such as Mrs. Frederick M. Stafford and Mr. and Mrs. Moise S. Steeg, Jr., as well as from new ones. Beginning in 1980, NOMA received a number of extraordinary gifts from Jun Tsei Tai, an important connoisseur and dealer in Chinese art in New York. His and his wife's gifts have included archaic bronzes, tomb ceramics, and Buddhist sculptures, particularly a seven-foot high twelfth century *Bodhisattva*, now the centerpiece of the Chinese gallery. The collection of Chinese ceramics was immeasurably strengthened with the partial and promised gift of the Dorothy and Robert Hills collection of blue-and-white porcelains, containing over two hundred fine examples from the Ming and Qing Dynasties. The Museum also has been fortunate to receive from Dr. Robert S. Barron, III, a number of beautiful ceramics of the Song Dynasty, a period of great aesthetic refinement. Most recently the Museum has begun to expand its small collection of the art of India with the support of Dr. Siddharth K. Bhansali, Mrs. Harriett von Breton, and the ever-generous Mrs. Frederick M. Stafford.

The 1974 bequest of Victor Kiam elevated an already fine collection of African art to the rank of one of the country's finest. Since then, with the guidance of William A. Fagaly, NOMA's longtime curator of African Art, this collection has continued to grow both with purchases, made possible in part by the Robert Gordy Endowment, and gifts from numerous collectors locally and nationally. African art has become the special interest in recent years of Mrs. Françoise B. Richardson, a NOMA trustee and past Board president. Her donations have included a number of important works from Nigeria, including a Benin bronze *Leopard Hip Ornament*, a pair of *Ibejis* by the master Yoruba carver, Olowe of Ise, and in 1995 a rare Nok terra cotta *Head of a Court Figure*. Other outstanding works have been given by Dr. H. Russell Albright, Mr. and Mrs. Charles B. Davis, III, Mrs. P. Roussel Norman, Robert Gordy, Helen and Robert Kuhn of Los Angeles, and an anonymous East Coast collector.

In the early 1970s NOMA was one of the pioneers in the acquisition of photography. By the eighties the market for photographs had become world-wide and highly competitive. The resulting increase in prices, with works going from hundreds to tens of thousands of dollars, meant that the Museum's purchases declined from hundreds of prints annually to dozens. Fortunately in the 1980s a number of significant donations were received that further enriched NOMA's already comprehensive collection. In 1982 New Orleans master photographer Clarence John Laughlin gave the Museum his personal collection of 347 photographs by various American and European artists, most of which he obtained by exchanging his own work with his colleagues. The Laughlin gift features work by unknown and famous photographers, which he valued equally, including groups of a dozen or more prints by Cunningham, Bernhard, and Bullock. In 1986 long-time NOMA trustee and patron Mrs. P. Roussel Norman added a large number of photographs to ones previously given, including examples of Adams, Weston, Cunningham, Brassai, Kertész, and Robert Frank. In the same year, Dorothy and Eugene Prakapas of New York gave over 400 nineteenth-century photographs, greatly strengthening the historic part of the collection. In the past ten years, as photography achieved equal status with painting and sculpture, many contemporary artists selected the medium for their most provocative work. The Museum has been able to keep abreast with these cutting edge developments through the ongoing donations of Dr. H. Russell Albright. From his extensive collection NOMA has received work by Cindy Sherman, William Wegman, Robert Mapplethorpe, and David Levinthal, among many others.

During the past fifteen years NOMA has continued its commitment to collect the work of living artists, particularly those working in Louisiana and the Southeast. The 1988 bequest of New Orleans artist Robert Gordy brought the Museum over one hundred paintings, sculptures, drawings, prints and photographs by artists as diverse as Richard Hamilton, Jim Nutt, H. C. Westermann, and William T. Wiley. The 1988 exhibition of selections from the Frederick R. Weisman collection unexpectedly led to the enrichment of the Museum's contemporary collection. Based in Los Angeles, Weisman was one of the country's leading collectors of modern and contemporary art, acquiring thousands of works. An instant love of New Orleans prompted him to purchase a French Quarter house in 1988, which he filled with a small portion of his collection. Following his election to NOMA's Board, Weisman began purchasing works for the Museum, the most visible being the Lin Emery kinetic sculpture installed in the pool at the front entrance. His support of Louisiana artists led him to endow a gallery in the soon-to-be expanded Museum dedicated to the exhibition of such work and to create a fund for future purchases.

In the 1990s there has been a burgeoning interest nationally in the work of contemporary self-taught artists. The South, particularly Louisiana, is home to many of these artists and NOMA in past years has been the first to give shows to artists such as Clementine Hunter, Sister Gertrude Morgan and David Butler. The Museum organized a landmark exhibition of this work in 1994, *Passionate Visions of the American South: Self-Taught Artists from 1940 to the Present*, which toured to five other museums.

NOMA's commitment to this area of contemporary art has resulted in significant gifts from many collectors, particularly, Herbert W. Hemphill, Jr., of New York and Dr. Kurt A. Gitter and Alice Rae Yelen.

By 1979 the Museum clearly recognized the great need to expand in order to properly accommodate its growing collection. While it took nearly fifteen years to achieve this essential goal, the dedication of the staff and trustees finally resulted in the creation of a facility that provided a beautiful setting for a great art collection. Following a national architectural competition in 1986, preliminary plans were developed so that a Capital Campaign could be launched to raise the necessary funds. The fund drive was a classic example of the combination of public and private support that characterizes the history of so many American institutions. In November 1987 the voters of New Orleans overwhelmingly passed a capital bond issue which included $5 million for the Museum. The Capital Campaign, chaired by Louis M. Freeman, was officially launched in April 1988 with commitments of $3 million from three local foundations. By the time ground was broken in January 1991, the campaign had surpassed its goal of $20 million and by the time the doors opened in April 1993 nearly $23 million had been raised. This was almost ten times the amount raised in the 1977 Art Acquisitions Fund Drive, a giant step in the Museum's development efforts and an indication of the high reputation it now enjoys in the community.

Beginning in 1990 in anticipation of the opening of the expanded museum, a major effort co-chaired by Mrs. P. Roussel Norman and Prescott N. Dunbar was made to acquire new art works to inaugurate the new building. This three-year campaign resulted in more than 2,000 new acquisitions by purchase, bequest, and full, partial or promised gift with a value of more than $10 million. Among these many acquisitions were such major works as a Renoir *Vase of Flowers*, from Mrs. Randolph A. Kidder of Washington, D. C.; a 1913 Kirchner landscape given by Eleanor B. Kohlmeyer; *Portrait of a Young Woman* by Modigliani, gift of Majorie Fry Davis and Walter Davis, Jr., through the Davis Family Fund; a Pascin painting done in New Orleans in 1916 from Mr. and Mrs. Moise S. Steeg, Jr.; a 1947 Ralston Crawford oil from Paul J. Leaman, Jr.; and a collection of Native American objects given by Los Angeles artist Emerson Woelffer, to name but a few.

With the opening of forty-six new or renovated galleries, a significant portion of the permanent collection could be seen to its full advantage for the first time. Visitors may now appreciate the many masterworks which highlight the in-depth presentation of world art. With its expanded facility and great collection, the New Orleans Museum of Art has truly become what on the day of its opening in 1911 the *New Orleans Daily Picayune* had described it as being, the "City's splendid possession."

# NEW ORLEANS' ART FOR ARTS' SAKE GALA: A CASE STUDY OF THE CITY'S PENCHANT FOR FESTIVAL*

Ann J. Pond

In the summer 1989 issue of *Art News*, critic and columnist Roger Green described a typical round of Saturday evening art gallery openings in New Orleans. "Yellow light glows through storefront windows, illuminating passing revelers dressed in cocktail regalia. Many of them tote translucent 'go cups,' the ubiquitous plastic receptacles that New Orleanians use to carry alcoholic drinks legally from bar to bar," or in this case gallery to gallery. "Any one gallery," Green went on to say, "might easily serve five cases of white wine, two of red, and eight cases of beer to over a thousand patrons on such an evening." And by the end of the evening, the merrymakers were dancing in every gallery "as bottles and cups collected on table tops—the getdown conclusion to another New Orleans party."[1]

While what Green described is indeed so typical as to be commonplace in New Orleans, it is, nevertheless, unique. Nothing like it, nothing like the veritable festival that accompanies the openings of arts shows, exists anywhere else in the country or, for that matter, in the world.

Even in New Orleans, this phenomenon has not existed very long, at least not in the fully developed form that Green described. In that form it represents the newest of the many festivals that New Orleans has generated over the years, more often than not spontaneously. Because it is only a little over a decade old and because it grew directly out of, and has developed parallel with, the New Orleans Contemporary Art Center, the Art for Arts' Sake gala affords an unusual opportunity for a case study of New Orleans' curious, indeed singular, propensity to generate festivals. Or, put another way, the propensity to celebrate almost any event, even the most trivial or routine occurrences.

*First published in *Louisiana History*, 34 (1993): 411-36. Reprinted with the kind permission of the author and the Louisiana Historical Association.

Far from being on the wane, this long-standing bent for celebration is, if anything, more pronounced now than ever. Within the past decade, the number and size of New Orleans festivals have grown more rapidly than at any point in the past. The French Quarter Festival, the Gumbo Festival, the Tomato Festival, Earth Fest, the Louisiana Black Heritage Festival, and the gay Southern Decadence are only a few of the many secular celebrations that have appeared in recent years.[2]

Outside the city itself a great number of similar festivals have developed, more often than not as spin-offs of New Orleans creations. The little town of Mansura now holds a *Cochon de Lait* Festival which in 1991 attracted 30,000 people for three days of eating and parading.[3] The same year, Lafayette, the Cajun cultural center, was visited by over 350,000 revelers for its *Festival International de Louisiane*, which the New Orleans *Times-Picayune* depicted as a warm-up for the New Orleans Jazz and Heritage Festival to open the next weekend.[4] The Creole Festival of Jeanerette is another boisterous affair held outside the corporate boundaries, as is the Ponchatoula Strawberry Festival. There is even a prison arts and crafts festival, begun in 1985 and held every spring by the inmates of Angola State Penitentiary.[5]

One or more parades is now almost a sine qua non for New Orleans festivals. St. Patrick's Day celebrations seem to have been held in the city since at least 1809. Only in recent years have they become large-scale affairs.[6] Originally restricted to the old "Irish Channel" neighborhood, the festivities today resound through many of the city's neighborhoods, with green beer and cabbage consumed in abundance by thousands. Similarly, St. Joseph's Day festivities, which traditionally involved simply the setting up, by individual families, of St. Joseph's food altars in residence windows or doorways, has recently become an extravagant Italian ethnic celebration, with a many-hours-long parade culminating in a huge food fest in the Piazza d'Italia.[7] The Jazz and Heritage Festival, which has grown to an astonishing size, is now the largest of the city's new celebrations. In 1991, twenty-two years after its establishment, the Jazz and Heritage Festival attracted 38,000 visitors to the Crescent City over the course of its week-long schedule—a period as long as Mardi Gras celebrations when the Jazz and Heritage Festival began. In a 1989 *Esquire* article, Peter Nelson called it "the" festival for Jazz lovers from around the world.[8]

Mardi Gras, which extends back to the founding of the colony at the end of the seventeenth century, is, of course, the grandaddy of all New Orleans festivals.[9] It has been called the "oldest collective function to which any American city may lay claim."[10] Today, more than fifty parades and a hundred balls take place between Twelfth Night in early January and Fat Tuesday which, because it is tied to the church calendar, can fall anywhere from February 3 to March 9.

If Mardi Gras, St. Patrick's, and St. Joseph's Day celebrations have old roots, most of New Orleans' many festivals do not. But it is not their newness that makes the city's festivals unique. It is the sheer number of them—well over twenty-five, an average of over one every two weeks—and, more important, their effortless, unplanned, virtually spontaneous origins.

Spring Fiesta began insignificantly like almost all the others, but, until the Jazz Fest surpassed it around 1980, it ranked second only to Mardi Gras in its command of public attention. In 1937, "Countess" Germain C. Wells, proprietor of Arnaud's Restaurant, began renting a couple of the horse-drawn carriages ferrying tourists about the French Quarter to her house on Esplanade Avenue for lunch.

Her group's arrival and departure from the cathedral and their progress through the Quarter so arrested the attention of churchgoers and passersby that the little spectacle was awaited with much anticipation the following year. When the local newspapers detected the interest and announced the date and time of the procession, the countess added more carriages and some floral decorations: A new festival was born. The following year, 1939, a non-profit organization was formed called the Spring Fiesta Association, and the festival began to expand. By 1950 the affair was second only to Mardi Gras in size and, as Robert Tallant warned, threatened "to become as widespread and complicated."[11] Today, Spring Fiesta comprises a series of events spanning March and April, showcasing tours of historic houses, courtyards, and plantations and a walking tour of the Lower Garden District.[12] Anyone who knows New Orleans is prone to say that because Mardi Gras marks the opening of the Lenten season, it was only logical and natural that another festival—in this case, Spring Fiesta—would develop to mark the end of Lent. But of course there is nothing either logical or natural about it, at least not outside of New Orleans. It happened so easily as to be natural in New Orleans, but would have happened nowhere else.

New Orleans' Art for Arts' Sake also originated as a small, insignificant institutional fundraising event but grew, step by step, into a huge gala that spawned what now amounts to a major annual opening-of-the-art-season festival. The festival spills over from galleries and the Contemporary Arts Center into Julia and Magazine streets and involves thousands of art patron participants and many hundreds more as support personnel, including musicians, singers, caterers, bartenders, guards, traffic policemen, street vendors, acrobats, pantomime artists, and jugglers.

The story of Art for Arts' Sake's development into a festival begins with the New Orleans Contemporary Arts Center, commonly called the C.A.C. In 1979, after much talk and considerable planning, but with many problems (particularly future funding) left unresolved, that institution opened in the K & B Drugstore Chain's old central office building and warehouse at 900 Camp Street. It was conceived as an alternative space devoted not only to the display of visual arts which the New Orleans Museum of Art could no longer adequately accommodate, but also the regional performing arts. Initially, the C.A.C.'s director, Don Marshal, concentrated on the performing arts, mainly because several already-organized local groups—some, such as the Free Southern Theater, with national reputations—needed a home. Development of the Center's visual arts program consequently progressed slowly. In 1980, however, Don Marshal and the board of directors expanded the visual arts program. They hired a coordinator, established a slide registry, scheduled more exhibitions, and launched Art for Arts' Sake.

Diane Whiningder chaired the first Art for Arts' Sake committee. She envisioned the Art for Arts' Sake gala as a means for local artists to give something back to the C.A.C. She realized how difficult it might be for artists to contribute financially to the Center, for most, "don't have much."[13] Their art would be the most practical thing for them to donate.

But Whiningder's plan quickly ran into difficulties, for artists were reluctant to contribute artworks. As George Febres, an artist who exhibited many times with the C.A.C., notes, "artists are rarely generous." Though "it was a bargain for artists to get that kind of exposure for the price of a work of art," Febres went on to say, he could understand that many artists had difficulty feeling a sense of duty to the C.A.C., which, to that point, had done relatively little for the visual arts.[14]

Art galleries echoed the artists' sentiments. Indeed, Sharon Litwin, president at the time, says that she would be at a loss to say who resisted the idea of donating works more, the artists or the galleries.[15] The gallery owners felt that the C.A.C. was competing by selling the artists' works at cheaper rates than they were. Works could be sold at lesser prices by the C.A.C. because one of the basic premises of Art for Arts' Sake in the beginning was to have a $500 limit on the price of the works. Ideally, this would encourage a broader segment of the population to purchase the works of local artists. The C.A.C. gave artists a thirty percent commission on works sold—considerably less than the forty to fifty percent they received from their galleries—and unsold works would be returned to them.[16]

George Febres, assisted by volunteers, undertook the hanging of the first exhibit, an arduous task in the un-airconditioned C.A.C. building on Camp Street.[17] The opening night exhibition included a cash bar and music as well as a "dessert party" at which confectioners' delights were served. The affair ran from 9:00 p.m. to midnight.[18] The list of participating artists comprised 124 names, including such notables as Ida Kohlmeyer, Robert Gordy, George Dureau, Robert Tannen, and George Febres. Artists were selected by the 1980 Art for Arts' Sake committee and sent invitations to exhibit, but uninvited artists were also admitted. Each participant could exhibit up to three art pieces.[19] The overall quality of the works displayed was good in Sharon Litwin's opinion.[20]

To attract the widest possible attention to the exhibition's debut, Diane Whiningder proposed coordinating the Art for Arts' Sake opening with major private gallery openings.[21] A series of meetings were held between C.A.C. and gallery representatives. C.A.C. staff members viewed Art for Arts' Sake as a community effort to raise money for the C.A.C. Gallery representatives, however, had a hard time reconciling this view with their own financial interests. Whiningder said, "It was exciting to have all the galleries coming together, but it was difficult. . . . When we first met with the galleries, they were pulling this concept apart."[22]

Despite these problems, the Art for Arts' Sake exhibit opened as scheduled, on September 13 and proved highly successful, indeed much more successful than anticipated. It generated $15,797 gross, and $6,795 profit from sales of art and alcohol.[23]

The degree of public interest surprised everyone, and prompted some gallery owners to rethink their position. As plans for the following year got underway, Arthur Roger of the Arthur Roger Gallery, and Barbara Muniot of the Galerie Simone Stern asked to meet with Don Marshal to discuss coordinating receptions in their own galleries with the opening night of Art for Arts' Sake. The talks became highly successful and four other galleries, including A Gallery For Fine Photography, also agreed to hold openings of their own the same night as Art for Arts' Sake. The C.A.C. also decided to drop the dessert party in order to create a more public, less intimate image, and, instead, to hold a private "preview" party for C.A.C patrons.

The 1981 Art for Arts' Sake was both more and less successful. It saw an increase of $4,488 in total income,[24] but none of the growth resulted from exhibition sales. Bar sales increased from $1,417 in 1980 to $1,502 in 1981, while sales of works in the exhibit dropped from $14,380 to $9,185. The $9,598 increase came almost entirely from the sale of "artists' portfolios," something new added to the 1981 Art for Arts' Sake. Artist-printer Terry Weldon published a series of large scale prints by six prominent artists: George Dureau, Clifton Webb, Franklin Adams, Ida Kohlmeyer, Richard Johnson, and himself. Sale of these earned more for the C.A.C. than exhibition sales.

What art was sold, moreover, was sold mainly at the patron's party, which had been added to the Saturday night opening. Members of the newly created Century Club (upper level donors), were invited to view the exhibit and given the opportunity to purchase pieces before nine p.m., when the general public was let in. This caused problems. Obviously such an exclusive preview contradicted the stated purpose of offering quality works at low prices to the general public in order to encourage more people to begin collecting contemporary art. "The first people to appear there were the rich, looking to buy the bargains," said George Febres, who had assisted with the hanging of the show again that year. Febres went on to say that "the people they, the C.A.C board and committee, were trying to attract never got a chance to buy anything worthwhile."[25] Sharon Litwin too acknowledged it was a problem that by the time the general public got in, about eighty percent of the works had been sold. But, she reflected, the affair was, after all, a fund raiser, and the only way to raise funds was to appeal to those who were affluent.[26] Others, such as artist Emery Clark, who exhibited often with Art for Arts' Sake, also resigned themselves to the unpleasant reality. "It is just the nature of supporting non-profit businesses," Emery said.[27]

As planning for the next year's 1982 Art for Arts' Sake began, Charlotte Norman and Joel Weinstock agreed to co-chair the steering committee.[28] The organizers decided to put more emphasis on the party aspect of the affair that year. Gallery directors cooperated fully, for they had come to see Art for Arts' Sake as a way of getting more exposure for their own people and boosting their own sales, if not on opening night, certainly in the long run.[29] The full-scale gallery participation marked a turning point in the development of Art for Arts' Sake and headed it in the direction of the festival which it would become. The press releases for the 1982 event are revealing, for as they played up the party aspect of the event, they came close to playing down the art. "To keep an anticipated crowd of over 3,000 in festive spirits," one read, "the Center will provide live music by the Dirty Dozen, dancing, three cash bars, snowballs, and art, of course."[30]

The wording was prophetic. Admission was free and art sales rose twenty percent, from $9,185 in 1981 to $11,587 in 1982—still far short of 1980's $14,380.[31] In a letter to an associate, C.A.C. president Sharon Litwin described the event. "It is, traditionally, the first major opening of the fall season and most New Orleanians visit other art galleries from 7-9 and end up in our gallery from 9-midnight. It is a marvelous evening—lots of fun and a great opportunity for New Orleanians to meet each other."[32] It is significant that she said nothing about art sales.

When planning began for 1983 Art for Arts' Sake, committee members became particularly concerned with the quality of the art to be shown. Except for the first exhibit in 1980, there had been little or no quality control. Chafed by the low commissions and disappointed by the sparse sales, many artists had gradually begun to submit works of lesser quality. Gallery directors, in turn, complained that their artists' works were being hung next to inferior pieces. The show had taken on what one critic called a "garage sale" look.[33] The first thing the steering committee did in its effort to improve that image was to announce that in 1983 they would increase the artists' commissions. An artist would receive fifty percent and the C.A.C. fifty percent, if the artist was not affiliated with a gallery. An affiliated artist would also receive fifty percent of the sales price, but his gallery would receive ten percent and the C.A.C only forty percent.[34] The steering committee also compiled artists' vitae and published them as a directory, which proved attractive to the public and especially to collectors. The directory was pulled together mainly by the efforts of C.A.C. director Don Marshal.

Marshal also worked to make the 1983 Art for Arts' Sake more of a showcase for Louisiana art, which meant establishing quality control.[35] Marshal himself served as curator and, along with visual arts coordinator Alan Gerson, reviewed all slides sent by artists for consideration. The two of them also visited artists' studios in order to examine other works. Marshal and Gerson decided to include some works priced over the old $500 maximum, and to placate gallery owners, they hung the show by galleries, which is to say, each gallery's artists together, with the name of the gallery prominently displayed.

For 1983 the committee also made some changes in the schedule of events to be included. Because, for the past two years, galleries had scheduled their opening receptions from six to nine p.m. on the Saturday opening night, the same hours which the C.A.C. was holding its Century Club preview before the general public was admitted, a certain conflict had developed. The gallery directors suggested, and Art for Arts' Sake committee agreed, to move the Century Club Preview from Saturday night up to Friday night and extend its hours.

Though rescheduling the Century Club Preview solved one problem, it aggravated another, for it further diminished the possibility of realizing the initial concept of making art more accessible to younger, less affluent, potential collectors. Those who were in a position to give substantial financial support to the C.A.C., were given still greater opportunities to pick over the exhibit before the general public was even allowed to see it. Debate over the issue intensified as some art enthusiasts decried the loss of an ideal, while others argued that the C.A.C.'s desperate need of funds justified the move.[36] Big donors, adherents of the latter position stressed, had to be kept happy just as did regular members and artists. Some today still contend that the very success of Art for Arts' Sake can, in some measure, be attributed to the change.[37]

Both sides, however, agreed that the quality of the works exhibited improved greatly in 1983. Art critic Luba Glade wrote at the time that "Art for Arts' Sake, the C.A.C season opener and annual fund-raising event has turned from an ugly duckling into a veritable swan," and credited the work of Don Marshal and Alan Gerson in implementing a more demanding selection process with success.[38]

The public's response to Art for Arts' Sake 1983 also pleased the C.A.C., for attendance increased. Yet profit from art sales still fell below the fundraisers' expectations.[39] The C.A.C. consequently decided to take a larger commission the following year. In 1984, artists received forty percent whether affiliated with galleries or not. If a work was sold by an affiliated artist, his gallery would receive twenty percent and C.A.C. forty. If the artist was unaffiliated, the C.A.C. would keep all sixty percent.[40] The 1984 committee decided to keep the scheduling innovations made the past year. M. K. Wegmann, associate director, in particular, argued for keeping the schedule as it was. "Don't mess with a good thing," she wrote in one of her memos to the committee. Wegmann also urged concentrating on sales and training a more aggressive staff.[41] So, in effect, the committee formulated a policy of more of the same for 1984, with emphasis on the "more."

Opening night of the 1984 Art for Arts' Sake marked a turning point in Art for Arts' Sakes's history. It stunned everyone and alarmed many. Jerah Johnson recalled that it was "one massive traffic jam stretching from the Academy Gallery in the fifty-two hundred block of Magazine all the way down to Arthur Roger's in the three-thousand block—as congested as anything during Mardi Gras season." And because of the crowds on the sidewalks, he said, it took him fifteen minutes to negotiate the hundred feet separating Mario Villa's gallery from Carmen Llewellyn's. When we finally got free and drove to the Center," he continued, "we did not even stop, for we could see that the place was already packed, and another throng was waiting at the door."[42]

Local columnist Errol Laborde, who usually wrote on politics, not art, took similar note of the "exceptional" happening, attributable perhaps at least in part, he said, to the newly popular wine glasses, which enabled people to take their drinks from one gallery to the next. And he reported that flirtatious conversations on that evening assumed the same importance as weighty discussions of art. In summary, he mused, "Somehow there seems to be cause for hope in a city that drinks to art and where the outrageous can be commonplace."[43]

Luba Glade perceptively put her finger on the truth. The opening of the art season in New Orleans, she wrote, now inextricably tied to Art for Arts' Sake had become an "autumnal rite." The whole evening, she said, clearly was primarily a social event, and only secondarily a show of art. She admitted that even she, on that evening, would in no way "ignore friends for art."[44]

From the point of view of the C.A.C., the overwhelming community participation in Art for Arts' Sake was problematic, for fundraising goals remained unmet. The Center's staff had projected $28,000 income. But only $17,023 materialized, though 4,907 visitors jammed the exhibit. The donation box collected only $843.[45] Claudia Barker, development director in 1984, captured the feeling of the C.A.C. Visual Arts Committee. Art for Arts' Sake, she wrote in a memo, "should have been more of a forum for selling art."[46] As a result, the C.A.C. staff launched a series of meetings and discussions to re-evaluate Art for Arts' Sake.

Both Barker and Alan Gerson suggested charging an admission fee to the Saturday night gala. Gerson also felt strongly that the C.A.C. should re-evaluate its relationship with the galleries. The eight galleries involved, he felt, did not give the C.A.C. as much help with their sales as the C.A.C. gave them.[47]

Both Barker and Gerson expressed concern, as well, that there were still too many pieces in the exhibit. Barker believed that the large number of pieces might be keeping potential buyers from focusing on any one piece.

The problem of Center-gallery relations was taken up at a December 1984 meeting, which included representatives from the Academy Gallery, Arthur Roger's, Davis Gallery, Simone Stern, and Tilden-Foley. The gallery owners had three main concerns: the large number of works on exhibit, the varying quality of the works, and "the density of the crowds on Art for Arts' Sake night as this related to the viewing of art work."[48] The owners proposed giving the Center twenty percent of commissions in their galleries for two days in lieu of having their artists exhibit at the C.A.C. as a general solution to the foregoing problems. Don Marshal took this suggestion under advisement, but did not act upon it.[49]

In February 1985, the C.A.C.'s Art for Arts' Sake committee issued its final evaluation of the 1984 event. The committee rated crowding, which had hindered sales, as the event's most pressing problem. In addition, the Center's sales force was inadequately trained. Finally, much of the work in the show was "not of the highest quality."[50]

Having determined the causes of the 1984 exhibition's manifold problems, the Art for Arts' Sake committee took corrective measures. To insure quality at the next exhibition, the committee decided to utilize an outside juror to curate the exhibit in 1985. The committee also decided to create a sales committee which would hold an orientation session for sales personnel the week before Art for Arts' Sake as a means of providing more effective training. Committee members scheduled the 1985 Art for Arts' Sake gala for September 27 and 28, the twentieth anniversary of the National Endowment for the Arts. They also decided to combine the Friday night Century Club preview with the

C.A.C.'s annual party for its theater subscribers, and call the creation "Just Desserts." The idea, developed earlier, of having galleries direct twenty percent of their own sales commissions to the C.A.C. was dropped, primarily because of reservations expressed by Arthur Roger.[51] Artists would continue to receive forty percent commission from C.A.C. sales of their works, the standard set the previous year. In addition, a five-dollar admission fee for non-members was instituted as a means of reducing overcrowding.

The committee then dealt with the exhibition's unwieldy size by breaking it into three separate exhibitions titled respectively, "Louisiana Now," "Artifacts," and "Mini Major Works." The "Louisiana Now" exhibit would be curated by art dealer and former gallery owner Alexandria Monett, whom the committee had selected as juror. Monett would select for this exhibit works priced from $50 to $4,000. "Artifacts," housed in a different part of the C.A.C., would be transformed into a boutique, selling utilitarian pieces of art: clothing, fans, furniture, jewelry, and small design objects. George Febres would assemble this collection. "Mini Major Works," housed in yet another part of the facility, would consist of miniature art works, primarily by Louisiana artists, and would be juried by Don Marshal. "Mini Major Works" had to be less than twelve inches in length and priced at less than $300. "Louisiana Now" was intended to target more "serious" collectors, while the other exhibits appealed to the "general" public.

The 1985 exhibit was impressive. Monett, conscientious sometimes to the point of abrasiveness, assembled an impressive collection which was praised repeatedly.[52] George Febres was acclaimed for his imaginative approach to collecting and displaying the "Artifacts."[53] Indeed, the boutique was so successful that it was kept open for a month following the Art for Arts' Sake opening. Don Marshal's "Mini Major Works," as hoped, was a hit with new collectors.

The public response to the 1985 Art for Arts' Sake—the festival aspect—also blossomed. Some area restaurants began to advertise discounts for patrons with Art for Arts' Sake ticket stubs, and the crowds grew apace.[54]

But, if popular enthusiasm for Art for Arts' Sake was growing, so were new problems, problems that came to a head in 1986. George Febres called 1986 and the few following years "the worst for Art for Arts' Sake."[55] Many people, he continued, began to say the whole affair had become "too messy," by which most meant the crowding and "festivalization," which were beginning to overpower the exhibition's artistic aspects. Others thought Marshal's three-part exhibition was itself "too messy." Some observers thought that Art for Arts' Sake had been much improved by being juried, but others, largely those whose work had been rejected, felt that judging did not work and called it "political."[56] Still others regarded the whole thing as *déclassé,* having become "tacky" with a boutique and mini works.

Also in 1985 the C.A.C. lost both Don Marshal, the director, and Alan Gerson, who had served as visual arts coordinator for four years. M. K. Wegmann had to step in as acting executive director until a replacement for Marshal could be found. Alexandria Monett was retained to generally oversee the next year's gala.

Monett decided, for 1986, to combine the "Mini Major Works" and "Artifacts" exhibits into one show under direction of the curator. The "Louisiana Now" show was to be kept, and the C.A.C. brought in the California museum director, J. David Farmer, as its juror. Little opposition to an out-of-town juror for the exhibition was voiced at the time. But, after he made his selection of works for the show—a limited number of them, resulting in the smallest show ever—protest broke. Even Sharon Litwin voiced concerns about an outside juror for a local art show.[57]

Even installing the 1986 show became a problem. Without Don Marshal and George Febres, whose participation in Center activities declined after Marshal's departure, things ran much less smoothly. Both Marshal and Febres had the ability to commandeer labor and to beg or borrow needed equipment for exhibits. C.A.C. staff member Darrell Brown, who helped to mount the 1986 exhibit, complained about a lack of personnel and materials, even such basic items as display cases and pedestals.[58]

C.A.C. relations with both galleries and artists also degenerated in 1986. In addition to complaints from artists who were not included in the show, many participating artists loudly voiced their dissatisfaction with the forty percent commissions. The C.A.C. staff found the latter complaints disturbing, for they still saw Art for Arts' Sake not as just another exhibit for the benefit of artists, but as a fundraiser for the C.A.C., to which artists, as well as the public, could reasonably be expected to contribute.

Problems with the galleries, on the other hand, stemmed mainly from poor direction and coordination and misunderstandings. For example, Betty Duplantier of Duplantier Gallery complained of a lack of cooperation on the part of the C.A.C. Duplantier, responsible for proofing the Art for Arts' Sake invitation, said she was not shown the invitation, which she deemed of inferior quality, until after it had been printed.[59]

At the Saturday opening on September 27, the ever larger festival crowds jammed the C.A.C.'s foyer to "see and be seen," and the assemblage became an unmovable mass. The art works consequently received little attention from the 2,901 people in attendance. The affair generated $34,549.43, but the C.A.C. committee had expected, or at least hoped, for more.[60]

In the C.A.C. staff "postmortem" evaluations of the 1986 event, a new issue emerged: Should Art for Arts' Sake be mainly a fund-raiser or primarily a showcase for Louisiana art. The latter concept, introduced by Don Marshal in 1983, enjoyed growing popularity. Planning and organization of future exhibitions would naturally differ, depending the goal selected. Litwin suggested making the showcase idea prime, with a rigorously curated 1987 Louisiana exhibit. The Mini-Major exhibit, which would be a sale, would take a secondary place. M. K. Wegmann agreed that Art for Arts' Sake could be restructured strictly as an exhibition with no fundraising element, and suggested that fundraising could be effected in an auction held about a month after the opening. She cited similar successful programs in Washington and Los Angeles.[61] And of course there was the chronic problem of the growing crowds of merrymakers.

The upshot was a compromise. The committee decided to restructure Art for Arts' Sake to permit both fundraising and showcasing, while accommodating the exhibition's traditionally festive atmosphere.[62]

There were four major components of the 1987 Art for Arts' Sake gala. On Sunday, September 23, art aficionados were given the opportunity to participate in a studio tour of artists participating in the exhibition.

A multimedia exhibit opened the following Saturday, September 26. The show, selected by a committee consisting of C.A.C. staff, board members, and "knowledgeable community volunteers,"[63] displayed works by both Louisiana and non-Louisiana artists. The usual forty percent commissions were paid to artists.

Works priced under $50 would be sold directly out of the exhibit. Works priced between $51 and $300 were sold by silent auction (sealed bids to be opened when the exhibit closed). The one hundred or so works in the exhibit priced over $300 were featured in a catalog, which sold for ten dollars and served as admission to a live auction of the high-priced items, to be held at the Westin Canal Place Hotel on October 24. As Alan Gerson observed, the organizers "experimented a lot," for Art for Arts' Sake was "one of those things you kept bandaging."[64]

The Saturday night party, which was in many ways the most troublesome aspect of Art for Arts' Sake because of the thousands of hangers-on it attracted, was also restructured in 1987. The committee extended its hours to 1:00 a.m. and moved it, as much as possible, outside the Center, pursuant to the following guidelines: "The traditional Saturday night Art for Arts' Sake party will be held to open the art season, coordinated with openings at area commercial galleries. . . . Additionally, a band will be hired and a street party held in the C.A.C.'s side parking lot. The street party is to spread out the expected large crowd."[65]

Indeed, the crowd was larger than ever because many of the galleries formerly located uptown on Magazine and Prytania streets had, by then, moved to Julia Street. Delighted with the street party, many, if not most, of the revellers had little interest in venturing inside and were only vaguely aware that an exhibition was on view. They were content to fill their stomachs with drink and food—hot dogs, snowballs, popcorn—now sold by street vendors and dance to the music of the rhythm and blues band, "Oogum Boogum."[66] Yet 3,121 art lovers ventured into the Center, and receipts increased to $36,967.95—over two thousand dollars more than the previous year.[67]

The old, dilapidated K & B Drugstore office and warehouse building which housed the Center had been, up to this point, rented to the C.A.C. for a nominal fee by owner Sidney Besthoff III. The rental agreement did not allow the C.A.C. to undertake any major renovations, but in 1988 Besthoff and the C.A.C. signed a twenty-year lease which gave the Center an option to buy at the end of the period. Besthoff, the owner of a large and impressive art collection, donated $500,000 for refurbishment. Plans were drawn and the project was scheduled for completion in January, 1990.[68]

Because the Center was to be closed for renovations in 1988, the Art for Arts' Sake Committee had to make special arrangements for that year's gala. The committee thus planned an outdoor exhibit of large electric light installations in the Piazza d'Italia, which was also in need of repair. Proceeds would go partially to the C.A.C.'s renovation fund and partially to the Piazza d'Italia's fund for restoration and maintenance.[69]

But the planners had not taken into account the tropical storms that frequently inundate New Orleans in September. Early in the morning of the scheduled opening on September 30, forecasters began predicting cloudbursts for the evening. The organizers hastily convened and decided that the entire exhibit had to be moved. Fortunately for the organizers, construction at the C.A.C. building had not actually begun; hence the Saturday evening opener was moved to the unairconditioned Camp Street building.[70] The unannounced move caused considerable confusion among persons who went to the Piazza d'Italia.[71] Only 1,500 art-lovers made their way to the Center, and no art was sold. The receipts totalled six thousand dollars derived solely from admission fees.[72]

The disappointing 1988 opener prompted organizers to devote particular attention to detail in planning the 1989 gala. The organizers agreed, in January, that all proceeds should go towards C.A.C. renovations. In March it was agreed to have three joint chairpersons for 1989—artist Emery Clark and gallery directors Arthur Roger and Donna Perret. Nina Dunbar was selected as project director to oversee the enterprise in concert with the C.A.C.'s director of development.[73]

The planners also agreed that the exhibit would be a theme show of sorts called "A Palettable Feast." The Center would give to artists small artists' palettes which the artists would have to incorporate into their pieces. Non-Louisiana artists would again be accepted and even encouraged to participate. Because the C.A.C. building was still undergoing repairs, exhibits would be divided between two locations. All proceeds would go to the C.A.C., none to galleries, none to artists. A patron's preview party as well as public festival would be scheduled, the latter including an art show, but not an art sale.[74]

In May 1989, after the basic plans were made but before any of the locations had been identified, the C.A.C. hired Peggy Outon to replace Claudia Barker as development director. Upon arriving in New Orleans, Outon, along with the project director, Nina Dunbar, had only three months to pull the event together. Because no money had been budgeted for rental space, Outon and Barker were compelled to locate and obtain the complimentary use of vacant properties. The New Orleans Union Passenger Train Terminal, at 1001 Loyola Avenue, where the C.A.C. had temporary office space, was secured for the huge public party,[75] while an Historic New Orleans Collection warehouse was used for the smaller patron's party and sales exhibit on September 23.

On Saturday, October 7, twenty-six galleries held coordinated openings between 6:00 p.m. and 9:00 p.m. The "Palettable Feast" exhibit of artists' palettes was still open, as well as another exhibit organized by the C.A.C., "Outta Site: Beyond the Emerging," on display at Simms Gallery nearby. The latter exhibit featured Elizabeth Shannon's and Glen Dugas's sculptures of life-sized figures emerging from boxes, a reference to the

C.A.C.'s living out of boxes in its temporary office at the Union Passenger Terminal, and designed to point thousands of gallery goers towards the Terminal for the big public party that started there at 9:00 p.m. and lasted until 1:00 a.m. It was called "C.A.C. on the Fast Track," and the train steps, platforms, and doorways served as bars and food "stations." The affair reaped $50,784.[76]

The planners of the 1990 Art for Arts' Sake gala recognized the metamorphosis that had transformed the event during its first decade of existence. What began as a fundraiser had grown, by stages, first into a celebration of Louisiana art, then into a New Orleans public festival marking the opening of the art season, ultimately becoming what Luba Glade had, five years earlier, perceived as an "autumnal rite."[77]

The 1990 Art for Arts' Sake comprised eight events spread over ten days and culminated in the Saturday night fest, once again held at the Center, in and around the newly renovated C.A.C. facility. Coordinated gallery openings turned Julia Street into a fair, replete with street vendors and entertainers. Over 6,000 people made their way into the new Center, led by a typical New Orleans parade with a marching band and an ample supply of "throws." Dance music began in the parking lot at 9:00 p.m., and food and drinks were available.

Inside the C.A.C., three exhibits were on display, but profits were derived from the sale of memberships, t-shirts, and posters. Fundraising through the sale of art, the original conception of Art for Arts' Sake, had had to give way to the New Orleans way of life—art for the sake of art and fun for the sake of fun.

Artist Robert Tannen put it best when he said, "it is simply a fact that festival is intimately connected to the way most things happen in New Orleans."[78] Annette Carlozzi, the current C.A.C. director, agreed that the C.A.C. could no longer consider Art for Arts' Sake as a major fundraiser. Any profits generated by the event were "incidental to the celebration."[79] Instead, Art for Arts' Sake had to be thought of as a public statement by and about the New Orleans art community. Tannen's and Carlozzi's sentiments were echoed by artist Elizabeth Shannon, one of the organizers working on the 1991 celebration. "Art for Arts' Sake," she said, "now has its own momentum."[80]

The history of Art for Arts' Sake thus offers a case-study in New Orleans' unique capacity for generating festivals, virtually spontaneously. To distinguish the source of the city's propensity for impromptu celebrations one must determine the distinguishing characteristics of New Orleans festivals. Modern-day "festivals" in other U.S. cities are almost universally conceived, designed, and planned by civic or commercial groups and then staged for the general public. In other words, in those cities, the organization comes first and the festival follows, but in New Orleans the festival emerges and the sustaining organization comes only later. Even in New Orleans, until a festival has become as completely integrated into the fabric of the community as Mardi Gras is, some kind of sustaining organizational or institutional framework is necessary for perpetuation of an event. In the case of the Art for Art's Sake gala, the Contemporary Arts Center provided that necessary framework. But the Center provided that service rather late in the game.

Had the Center decided at some point simply to cancel Art for Arts' Sake, the nascent festival would almost certainly have died, for unlike Mardi Gras, it was not yet—or, for that matter, nor is it now, nor likely will it ever be—sufficiently popular to sustain itself.[81]

The calendar may also have had something to do with the transformation of Art for Arts' Sake. Most older and larger New Orleans festivals occur during the winter, spring, and summer, stretching from the pre-Christmas season through New Years, Mardi Gras, Spring Fiesta, the Jazz Fest, St. Patrick's and St. Joseph's Days to the Fourth of July and Labor Day. There has long been a notable absence of festivals in the fall. The few that occur at that time of year have been small and limited in their appeal. October Fest, for example, has been celebrated mostly by the remnants of New Orleans' German community. It may be that the city's thirst for a fall festival has been quenched, at least in part, by the Art for Arts' Sake outing which involves not only artists and art patrons but a sizeable cross section of the population, many if not most of whom are only vaguely aware that the affair has anything to do with art. Indeed, involvement of such a cross section is another of the defining characteristics of New Orleans public festival. And an art-related event, by nature, facilitates such a social mix. In the art world, the rich and poor, the black and white, the well known and the unknown, buyers and sellers, lookers, and hangers-on easily hob-nob, at least for an evening, in a richly varied and colorful section of the city in which the outrageous is commonplace.

But any New Orleans social mix is unusual. Because the city's status during much of the nineteenth century as a port of immigration second only to New York added layer after ethnic layer to the several already existing ethnic and racial layers inherited from its French and Spanish colonial history, New Orleans has as many and as varied an assortment of racial, ethnic, and cultural components as any city in the United States. Unlike other American cities, however, New Orleans ethnic groups have blended, merged, and quickly melded to form a single new culture that is today commonly called the New Orleans way of life. That melding process meant that in New Orleans a single public culture emerged, one of which all elements and all orders of society felt a part and in which they could all participate. The unifying and public nature of that common culture, helps account for its durability.[82]

All American cities that had populations of varied ethnic groupings also had, during their early histories, numerous fests and festivals, either of a folk nature or, more usually, associated with craftsmen's and artisans' traditional celebrations. But as cities industrialized and labor unionized, the old folk, craft, and artisans' celebrations quickly atrophied and died, or, in some cases, were suppressed by civil and labor union authorities. In most cities such celebrations had ended well before the middle of the nineteenth century.[83]

New Orleans, however, never achieved the degree of industrialization or unionization achieved in other U.S. urban centers. Instead, it remained, economically as well as socially, essentially a pre-industrial city. New Orleans, in social terms, is thus more akin to European cities than to American cities. Alone among American cities, New Orleans, again like European cities, has enjoyed a sedentary population, whereas most American cities have derived much of their population base from rural towns. To find comparisons meaningful for the study of New Orleans, one must necessarily consult literature regarding European cities. Put simply, in New Orleans, older traditions survived because they were not severely challenged by the new industrial order, traditions characterized by what Jerome F. Scott called "stability and coherence," traditions in which community interaction was not at odds with economic development. In such older traditions, he said, "there was no strict separation of work and play," for such a separation is "a feature only of modern industrial society."[84] Or, as George C. Homans noted of pre-industrial European towns: "Sometimes indeed the economic end in view may have been almost incidental to the company to be enjoyed. . . . When . . . a family held a bee, calling in the neighbours to help in some special piece of work . . . the work to be done was little more than an excuse for holding the bee."[85]

Writers such as Robert W. Malcolmson, R. D. Storch, and Edward Palmer Thompson have described the disintegration of customary rituals and recreation in English towns before 1850. In contrast, J. P. Pierrard described the continuation, in France, of workers' festivals throughout the nineteenth century. In R. Bezucha's and Eugene Joseph Weber's studies of the attempts at systematic suppression of workers' festivals by civil authorities in France, one hears distinct echoes of New Orleans authorities' attempts, following the Louisiana Purchase, to suppress such local traditions as Mardi Gras and slave dancing in Congo Square.[86] New Orleans' capacity to "festivalize" lies deeply embedded in the social history of this surviving relic of the pre-industrial age. A fuller answer will require the study of a large number of New Orleans festivals and a consideration of their histories within the framework of the city's social, racial, and ethnic history set against the experience of European—specifically French—cities of the nineteenth century. It is sufficient for present purposes to have sketched the development of one such recently generated festival, to have suggested some probable explanations, and to have identified avenues for further research.

## Notes for "New Orleans' Art for Arts' Sake Gala: A Case Study of the City's Penchant for Festival"

[1]Roger Green, "Party on Julia Street," *Art News* (Summer, 1989): 52.

[2]Some other important festivals to have grown noticeably over the past few years in New Orleans include the Reggae Riddums (a weekend of live, non-stop Reggae and Caribbean music with plenty of traditional arts and Caribbean cuisine), the African-American Jazz Festival, the Asian/Pacific Festival, Carnaval Interamericano, La Cancion Latinoamericana, Cinefest Plus Heritage Celebration, Festa d'Italia, Festival International de Louisiane, the German Heritage Festival, the Greek Festival, Louisiana Heritage Festival, Christmas Under the Oaks, New Orleans Film and Video Festival, Tennessee Williams Literary Festival, The Swamp Festival, Oktoberfest, and the Spanish Food Festival.

[3]*New Orleans Times-Picayune*, April 19, 1991.

[4]Ibid., April 14, 1991.

[5]Ibid., April 12, 1991.

[6]Charles Dufour, "The People of New Orleans," in Henry Krotzer, Roulhac Toledano and Mary Louise Christovich, eds., *250 Years of Life in New Orleans* (New Orleans, n.d.), 37.

[7]Ethelyn Orso, *The St. Joseph Altar Traditions of South Louisiana* (Lafayette, La., 1990). In 1850 the United States census showed New Orleans as having the largest population of Italians (915) of any American city. Between 1880 and 1920 thousands more came to Louisiana, comprising 39% of the population by 1910. During the past thirty years, the Italian tradition of celebrating St. Joseph's Day with an altar feast has greatly expanded. The Feast of St. Joseph occurs on March 19, in the middle of Lent, and is a traditional day for breaking abstinence. It has changed recently from a private indoor celebration to a festival of the public realm including parades. Because it occurs only two days after St. Patrick's Day, the two holidays used to conflict, with the Italians and Irish competing for attention. In 1983, however, a joint Irish-Italian parade was created to quiet the conflict and bridge the gap.

[8]Peter Nelson, "Jazz by the River," *Esquire*, 111-12 (1989): 44.

[9]Thomas Fiehrer and Michael Lodwick, "Carnival in Perspective," *Plantation Society in the Americas* (1990): 5. Ernest G. Vetter, *Fabulous Frenchtown: The Story of the Famous French Quarter of New Orleans* (Washington, 1955) and Lorraine Goreau, "Mardi Gras," *The Past As Prelude 1961-1966* (New Orleans, 1968) are both useful studies of Mardi Gras. Mitchell L. Osborne and Errol Laborde, *Mardi Gras, a Celebration* (New Orleans, 1981) is in many ways the best. No thorough study has yet been written, though Reid Mitchell of Princeton is working on what promises to be a very fine study of the festival since its 1857 Americanization.

[10]Fiehrer and Lodwick, "Carnival in Perspective," 5.

[11]Robert Tallant, *The Romantic New Orleanians* (New York, 1950), 331.

[12]*New Orleans Times-Picayune*, April 12, 1991.

[13]Diane Whiningder, interview by Ann J. Pond, June 20, 1991.

[14]George Febres, interview by Ann J. Pond, June 26, 1991.

[15]Sharon Litwin, interview by Ann J. Pond, July 25, 1991.

[16]"Call to Artists, 1980," the announcement of the show and invitation for artists to submit works, in C.A.C. 1980 publicity file.

[17]George Febres, interview by Ann J. Pond, June 26, 1991.

[18]Invitation to Art for Arts' Sake, September 1980, in C.A.C. 1980 file.

[19]"Call to Artists, 1980" in C.A.C. 1980 file.

[20]Sharon Litwin, interview by Ann J. Pond, July 25, 1991. Alan Gerson, who was a participation artist, felt the same, interview by Ann J. Pond, June 26, 1991. Committee members in this year included, Diane Coleman Whiningder (chairman), Emery Clark (coordinator), George Dureau (design), George Febres (installation), Hane Lowentritt (sales), Betty Moran (preview party), Charlotte Norman (artist contact), and Margery Stich (publicity).

[21]Diane Whiningder, interview by Ann J. Pond, June 20, 1991.

[22]Ibid.

[23]C.A.C. Revenue Report, 1980, in C.A.C. 1980 file.

[24]C.A.C. Revenue Report, 1981, in C.A.C. 1981 file.

[25]George Febres, interview by Ann J. Pond, June 26, 1991.

[26]Sharon Litwin, interview by Ann J. Pond, July 25, 1991.

[27]Emery Clark, interview by Ann J. Pond, August 19, 1991.

[28]Letter from Sharon Litwin to Diane Whiningder, no date 1982, in C.A.C. 1982 correspondence file.

[29]Arthur Roger, interview by Ann J. Pond, February 25, 1991, and Donna Perret, interview by Ann J. Pond, March 9, 1991.

[30]C.A.C. Press Release, in C.A.C. 1982 file.

[31]C.A.C. Revenue Report, in C.A.C. 1982 file.

[32]Letter from Sharon Litwin to Marie-France Colliard, August 2, 1982, in C.A.C. 1982 correspondence file.

[33]Luba Glade, "A Juried Show at the C.A.C.," *New Orleans Gambit*, October 22, 1983.

[34]First Financial Report on Art for Arts' Sake, 1982, in C.A.C. 1982 file.

[35]Alan Gerson, interview by Ann J. Pond, July 26, 1991.

[36]George Febres, interview by Ann J. Pond, June 26, 1991; Sharon Litwin, interview by Ann J. Pond, August 19, 1991.

[37]Emery Clark, interview by Ann J. Pond, August 19, 1991.

[38]Luba Glade, "A Juried Show at the C.A.C." *Gambit*, October 22, 1983.

[39]Available records show no totals for attendance or income for 1983 or 1985.

[40]Art for Art's Sake, Recap of Meeting, 1985, in C.A.C. 1985 file.

[41]Letter form M. K. Wegmann to Don Marshal, no date, 1983, in C.A.C. "1983 correspondence" file.

[42]Jerah Johnson, interview by Ann J. Pond, September 25, 1991.

[43]Errol Laborde, "A Night at the Galleries," *Gambit*, October 6, 1984.

[44]Luba Glade, "The Season Begins," *Gambit*, October 6, 1984.

[45]Art for Arts' Sake 1984 Evaluation, Alan Gerson, December 5, 1984, in C.A.C. 1984 Committee file.

[46]Art for Arts' Sake 1984 Evaluation, Claudia Barker, December 19, 1984, in C.A.C. 1984 Committee file.

[47]Art for Arts' Sake 1984 Evaluation, Alan Gerson, December 5, 1984, in C.A.C. 1984 Committee file.

[48]Arthur Roger, letter to Don Marshal, December 4, 1984, in C.A.C. 1984 Correspondence file.

[49]Ibid.

[50]Cumulative Evaluation Art for Arts' Sake 1984, in C.A.C. 1985 Committee file.

[51]Uptown Gallery Association Meeting Recap, March 1985, in C.A.C. 1985 Committee file.

[52]Sharon Litwin, interview by Ann J. Pond, July 25, 1991; Claudia Barker, interview by Ann J. Pond, July 29, 1991.

[53]*New Orleans Times-Picayune, Dixie*, October 20, 1985.

[54]Riverbend Restaurant Coupon, Fall 1985, in C.A.C. 1986 file.

[55]George Febres, interview by Ann J. Pond, June 26, 1991.

[56]Ibid.

[57]Art for Arts' Sake Evaluation, November 18, 1986, in C.A.C. 1986 Committee file.

[58]Art for Arts' Sake Evaluation, Darrel Brown, 1986, in C.A.C. 1986 Committee file.

[59]Letter from Betty Duplantier to Barbara Lyons, in C.A.C. 1986 Committee file.

[60]Revenue report, 1986, in C.A.C. 1986 financial file.

[61]Art for Arts' Sake Evaluation, November 18, 1986, financial file.

[62]Art for Arts' Sake, Report of 1987 Restructure, no date, in C.A.C. 1987 Committee file.

[63]Ibid.

[64]Alan Gerson, interview by Ann J. Pond, July 26, 1991.

[65]Art for Arts' Sake, Report of 1987 Restructure, no date, in C.A.C. 1987 Committee file.

[66]Ibid.

[67]Revenue Report, 1987, in C.A.C. 1987 financial file.

[68]Roger Green, "C.A.C. Unveils Ambition Renovation Plan," *New Orleans Times-Picayune*, July 15, 1988.

[69]Proposal for Art for Arts' Sake, March 15, 1989, in C.A.C. 1989 Committee file.

[70]Peggy Outon, interview by Ann J. Pond, August 20, 1991.

[71]Minutes of Special Events Committee Meeting, October 20, 1988, in C.A.C. in 1988 file.

[72]Revenue Report, 1988, in C.A.C. 1988 financial file.

[73]Proposal for Art for Arts' Sake, March 15, 1989, in C.A.C. 1989 Committee file.

[74]Ibid.

[75]Peggy Outon, Interview by Ann J. Pond, August 20, 1991.

[76]Revenue Report, 1989, in C.A.C. 1989 financial file.

[77]Luba Glade, "The Season Begins," *Gambit*, October 6, 1984.

[78]Robert Tannen, interview by Ann J. Pond, June 12, 1990.

[79]Annette Carlozzi, interview by Ann J. Pond, June 10, 1990.

[80]Elizabeth Shannon, interview by Ann J. Pond, June 13, 1990.

[81]A revealing example of a would-be-festival that failed is the Crew of Clones and their Beaux Arts Ball, also spin-offs from the C.A.C. In the early 1970s a number of C.A.C. artists, led by Denise Vallon, organized a Mardi-Gras-like parade and an artists ball, both homemade, so to speak, by the artists. The affair grew year by year, and in 1978 the parade took to the streets of the French Quarter, where it delighted, if somewhat mystified, the public, and the riotous ball that followed overflowed the huge C.A.C. garage where it was held. At that point Don Marshal and the C.A.C. staff determined that both the parade and the ball had to somehow be quelled. Another year and it would be out of hand. Consequently, the Center withdrew both support and use of facilities and rechannelled the artists' energies into the more manageable, and more "social," Sweet Arts Ball. Lacking institutional sustenance and a social mix—it involved only artists and their immediate friends, hence was of little interest to patrons and collectors and less to the general public—and being in no way of the people, the near-festival died.

[82]Arnold Hirsh and Joseph Logsdon, eds., *Creole New Orleans: Race and Americanization* (Baton Rouge, 1992): a collection of social and ethnic studies, is the best work yet done on those aspects of the city's history. See also Joseph Logsdon's "Imagination through the Port of New Orleans," in M. Mark Stolarik, ed., *Forgotten Doors* (Philadelphia, 1988).

[83]A number of scholars have explored these developments among whose works, Carl Bridenbaugh, *Cities in Revolt: Urban Life In America, 1743-1776* (New York, 1955): Gary B. Nash, *The Urban Crucible: Social Change, Political Consciousness and the Origins of the American Revolution* (Cambridge, Mass., 1979): and

Sean Wilenz, *Chants Democratic: New York City and Rise of the American Working Class, 1798-1950* (Oxford, Eng., 1984) are notable. Their notes and bibliographies point to a good part of the considerable literature on the subject.

[84]Jerome F. Scott, *The Community Factor in Modern Technology*, 2nd ed. (Paris, 1960).

[85]George C. Homans, *English Villagers of the Thirteenth Century* (Cambridge, Mass., 1941).

[86]R. Bezucha, "Masks of Revolution," in *Revolution and Reaction: 1848 and the Second French Republic*, ed. Richard Price (London, 1975); Robert Malcomson, *Popular Reactions in English Society, 1700-1850* (Cambridge, England, 1973); Pierre Pierrard, *La Vie Ouvrière à Lille sous le Second Empire* (Paris, 1965); Richard Storch, "The Policeman as Domestic Missionary: Urban Discipline and Popular Culture in Northern England 1850-1880," *Journal of Social History*, 9 (1976): 481-509; Edward Palmer Thompson, *The Making of the English Working Class* (New York, 1963); Eugene Weber, *Peasants into Frenchmen: The Modernization of Rural France, 1870-1914* (Stanford, 1976); On Mardi Gras see above, note 8, and on attempts by New Orleans' new American authorities to suppress slave dancing see Jerah Johnson, "New Orleans' Congo Square: An Urban Setting for Early Afro-American Culture Formation," *Louisiana History*, 32 (1991): 117-57.

# RE-VIEWING THE TRADITION OF LOUISIANA WOMEN WRITERS*

Barbara C. Ewell

INEVITABLY, one aspect of a collection defined by region is a forthrightly chauvinistic desire to show off the literary riches of one's homeplace. We plead guilty. Fortunately for us, Louisiana—singularly romantic even among Southern states—has a respectable cache of literary wealth to display. Despite such affluence, few readers actually realize how many writers, male or female, are associated with the state. Not recognizing this literary legacy seems to us a failure of vision, a neglect of the past that distorts our present conceptions of who we are. The most detrimental aspect of this general lapse of consciousness, however, has typically been the systematic exclusion of women (and minorities) from our literary canon. Thus the focus in this collection on writers who are Louisianians (in one way or another) and women (although not often enough nonwhite or lesbian or working-class, pointing up the need for more scholarship on such writers) represents an effort not only to foster a broader appreciation for an overlooked literary tradition of the past, but also to reclaim a diversity that is crucial if we are to redefine our culture flexibly enough to face the challenges of our future together.

The precision of this focus, women writers of a single state—even though it excludes half of the population with one term and relies on arbitrary political boundaries for the other—has another important benefit as well: namely, it highlights thematic and cultural issues that a more inclusive perspective would have diffused. One such issue is the conventionality and deliberate limitation implicit in definitions of gender and place. As Louisianians and as women, the subjects of this volume commonly confront two marginalizing experiences that significantly shape their perspectives and options as writers. The intersection of those experiences provides a provocative context for analysis that allows us to see more clearly the implications of their fictions—and ours.

*First published as the Introduction to Dorothy H. Brown and Barbara C. Ewell, eds., *Louisiana Women Writers: New Essays and a Comprehensive Bibliography* (Baton Rouge: Louisiana State University Press, © 1992), 3-15. Reprinted with the kind permission of the authors and the publisher.

One aspect of such an analysis is a better appreciation of how these essentially restrictive experiences interact, that is, how being a woman is shaped by Louisiana's peculiar brand of Southernness, and how Louisiana—and the South—is constructed by its women. Understanding that interaction could go an important distance toward construing "the female mind of the South," a task that, as Helen Taylor observes, has not yet been adequately undertaken.[1] Certainly, Louisiana women writers represent only a sample of that "mind," and indeed, the authors covered here are only a sample of Louisiana women writers; but the issues raised by their work can help explain an experience that remains subject to a great many myths and far too little understanding.

A natural point of departure is the ambiguity and resonance attached to place, both for women and for the South, as well as for Louisiana women writers. The South, of course, has a notorious "sense of place," one that is reflected by its fictions as well as by its statistics. Rural isolation and a dramatic shared history have contributed much to what Richard Gray calls Southerners' "belief in the power of environment, this feeling of attachment to landscape . . . [which is] one of the structuring principles of Southern myth." And as John Shelton Reed's work suggests, this sense of place endures, even late in this century, in Southerners' preference for their own states or their identification with local communities and systems of kinship.[2] But place in the South also defines social stratification, particularly for African Americans, but also for women, who, like blacks, need to "know their place" as the subordinates of white men in an intensely patriarchal culture.

*Place* for the Southern woman (as for the Southern African American) is thus a loaded and doubled term, expressing both a positive, generally productive relation to a physical and cultural reality and an oppressive, limiting experience of social status. Alice Walker, for example, writes movingly of her efforts as a black Southerner to reclaim the cultural and geographic territory from which racism has displaced her.[3] But that doubleness of place is precisely what eludes most interpreters of Southern women writers. As Helen Taylor observes, many feminist critics, by scrutinizing place as social confinement, have tended to homogenize the specific regional concerns of women writers, subordinating them to formalist and thematic considerations, such as the adoption of certain genres or the modification of female stereotypes, including regionally specific ones—for example, the mammy and the belle. Such emphases, Taylor argues, limit our understanding of how region shapes literary choices. On the other hand, readers without feminist sympathies—sometimes including Southern women writers themselves, who often resist any identification with the women's movement—recognize the power of region for a writer such as Eudora Welty or Flannery O'Connor, but fail or refuse to see how that writer's Southern sense of place is indelibly marked by her experience as a woman who does "know her place," even if she occasionally refuses to stay in it.[4]

Certainly, place is indispensable for writers. It is, as Welty has eloquently explained, the "raw material of writing," serving as a "lesser angel" of inspiration and giving fiction its life and validity. Place imparts to fiction its necessary illusion of reality. The details and specificities of an environment—its colors and oddities, its "named, identified, concrete" elements—furnish, Welty says, "a plausible abode for [fiction's] world of feeling." But most important, she adds, is the fact that evoking that illusion exposes a point of view—what she calls the "burning-glass" of consciousness—framing and disclosing the world before it.[5] What a writer describes, the details of the landscape she selects in order to make the world of feelings credible, also reveals what she sees, what she *can* see. The places of a writer's fiction thus expose both the horizons and the architecture of her vision; they also reveal the adequacy of the fictional furnishings she has selected to accommodate the feelings that are the foundations of her art.

Typically, and as much in their denigration as in their praise, women have been credited with a more precise and searching representation of place than men. William Dean Howells, for example, observed that "the sketches and studies by the women seem faithfuler and more realistic than those of the men, in proportion to their number. Their tendency is more distinctly in that direction, and there is a solidity, an honest observation, in the work of such women . . . which often leaves little to be desired."[6] Howells' approval, of course, reiterates supposed truisms concerning women's eye for detail and their close association with the physical realities of human existence. Generally entrusted with the care and supervision of the places of daily life—the home and its yard, the rooms and furnishings that surround our eating and sleeping and lovemaking and communicating—women are indeed intimates of place, frequently of a single place from which they have neither means nor occasion to wander. That familiarity, enforced or assumed, often—as Howells noted—renders place in women's writing vivid and immediate. But the consciousness or point of view disclosed by those details is distinctive in another way. Whereas men have typically been able to impose individualized perspectives onto their places—their own names, as it were—the shape of places in the writing of women does not always inscribe their personal figures into the design. To the contrary, women's relationship with place, intimate though it be, is usually not one of defining, but of being defined. Their place remains in the home, but the homeplace belongs to someone else.

For women, then, writing about place has frequently involved a discovery of boundaries and confinement—a recognition of the ways in which their lives and vision are constrained by the familial rules that constitute female experience. As Annette Kolodny suggests, unlike men, who tend to find in places projections of filial dependence or eroticized conquest, women find in their places the borders of their domestication. Far from imposing their images on the places they inhabit, women more often reiterate the patterns prescribed by patriarchal custom. However, recognizing limits—like those of mortality—can provide the imagination with a special poignance and power. Judith Fryer, for example, explores the fertile encounters with spatial limits that produced the very different fictions of Edith Wharton and Willa Cather.[7] Obviously, the boundaries women encounter—like the artificial constraints of a sonnet or a short story—can tempt, at least from the gifted writer, an evocation of broad significance from the explicit finiteness of her subject: Jane Austen's "miniatures in ivory."

This challenge of boundaries has likewise shaped the literature of Louisiana as part of the South, a place whose cultural and geographical outlines are as vividly marked in the American imagination as the role of gender in the broader human psyche. Like the narrow place defined for women, the South emerged, especially after the Civil War, as a distinctive, separate locus. Northerners and Southerners alike found reason to foster the notion of a uniquely traditional culture: its aristocratic values and unshaken loyalties in the wake of military defeat offered a consoling alternative to the harsh realities of late nineteenth-century America. As Anne Rowe observes, the shifting political climate that encouraged cooperation by conservatives, North and South, gradually transformed Northern attitudes toward a former enemy "from one of reform and retribution to that of praise and support" and helped to turn the era of Reconstruction into that of Jim Crow, no less virulently in Louisiana than in the rest of the Deep South. That changing political environment, coupled with the nostalgic "pathos and grandeur of a lost civilization" that the South embodied for the contemporary imagination, beset by the destabilizing forces of postwar industrialization and urbanization, ensured the prosperity of the myth of the South. The national acceptance of this myth, bolstered by the region's long-standing need to justify its peculiar institution of slavery and concomitant racism, resulted in the phenomenon—the virtual industry—of Southern literature.[8] Louisiana, thanks to the popularity of George Washington Cable's exotic stories and novels, enjoyed a particular cachet, which opened opportunities for a number of writers, many of them women. But even long after the war, and well into the following century, the primary impulse of much of the region's imaginative and critical writing remained self-definition. What is the South? What is a Southerner? Why is that place so fascinating to us all?

One answer to those questions lies precisely in the limits of the South as a place. As Richard Gray, among others, has noted, the fact of the South as a distinct and homogeneous region has increasingly been called into question, but the *idea* of the South as an identifiable structuring principle of culture remains intact.[9] As such, it offers a singularly—and nearly anachronistic—traditional context: a relatively clear set of social expectations by which the self can or must be identified. These social limits are what has made the South valuable both to individual writers and to the nation as a whole, not least by casting the modern struggle for identity in stark and dramatic terms. To know where we are, at least imaginatively, allows us to figure out a little better just where we can—or cannot—go. If our limits are defined for us, if the social map is a given rather than a riddle, then we can see quite immediately what the possibilities are for accommodation or transgression. In the increasingly disoriented, mobile reality of late nineteenth- and twentieth-century America, such surety was an attractive backdrop for examining identity and "place."

Although, as Michael O'Brien explains, the Southern mid-century literary renascence was not historically unique, it was, for itself at least, a singular conjunction of the isolated modern individual against a stable (and idealized) community.[10] At the same time, this revitalized myth of the South was supported by a tenacious ruralism just as most of America grew urban. This distinctive identity, both within and beyond its borders, thus reinforced the usefulness of the South as an imaginative space. Its remote backwaters and equally remote parlors made the ordinary limits on human behavior—the clogs of prejudice, violence, social stratification—seem somehow less real than they appeared in the complacent and familiar settings of mid-America. Being both part of America and safely separated in its margins, the South offered the nation an exaggerated image of many unacceptable attitudes that Americans disguised from themselves in more familiar environs: a growing consensus condoning racism, a romantic attachment to feudalism and aristocratic status, a nostalgic agrarianism.[11] Sentiments that were inadmissible for a progressive and democratic people, committed to industrialization and urbanization, could be conveniently relegated to a distinct subculture—distinct, at least, from a complacently hegemonic consciousness that was entirely white, mostly male, and predominantly Northeastern. Weaknesses could be shunted off as other—"theirs"—while any virtues could be claimed as the dominant culture's own—"ours." In this role as Other, the South, of course, assumes a very feminine part, for women have consistently been assigned this receptive and distancing function in Western culture. Becoming, like woman, "the space," as Alice Jardine writes, "outside of the conscious subject,"[12] the South thus became America's most fertile imaginative site, the scene of some of our most significant crises of identity.

Louisiana mirrors the complex role that the South has played in the national consciousness. It, too, defines a space that is both psychic and geographic, a site where the Other—of gender, race, religion, sexuality, ethnicity—is often more clearly demarcated than in the rest of America: a place where social boundaries are frequently equated with precise physical limits: the "white" and "colored" water fountains and schools of segregation, the men-only Carnival clubs and state legislatures, the Negro quarters of towns and small cities, the ladies' entrances of certain shops and clubs. Although Louisiana shares many of these narrowly limited spaces with the rest of the South, it has also given them the distinctive shape of its own anomalous history and culture. Primary among the state's anomalies are the strong French and Catholic strains in its character, manifest in its Napoleonic civil code, its festivals of Mardi Gras and All Saints', its devotion to the culinary arts, and its general tolerance of liquor, languor, and lewdness—within limits. Such peculiarities have redefined in Louisiana—sometimes subtly and sometimes sharply—the cultural and geographic places out of which the South has constructed its prevailing mythologies.

But even within the state, these typically Mediterranean influences are unevenly manifest. Louisiana is divided into two quite dissimilar regions: the mostly Protestant and Anglo-Saxon north and the largely Catholic and French south. Significantly, however, the latter area includes New Orleans, which as Louisiana's largest city tends to project its identity onto the whole state—thus the Louisiana hinterland, in this respect at least, shares the fate of downstate Illinois or upstate New York. Marked as much by its atypicality as by its unmistakable Southernness, New Orleans has been an eccentric urban center for the South as a whole as well as for Louisiana. Located at the mouth of North America's greatest river, poised as a border and gateway to the world beyond; with the multiethnic flavor of its French, African, Caribbean, and Spanish influences still pronounced; surrounded by water; at once cosmopolitan and myopically provincial, New Orleans has encouraged conflicting perspectives and definitions. Its divided allegiances were tellingly apparent during the Civil War: never particularly committed to the lost cause, the city fell early in the struggle and escaped many of the worst effects of the South's defining experience. But perhaps more critical to the uniqueness of the city—and thus Louisiana—has been its peculiar treatment of racial difference, the South's most tenacious marker of place. From its earliest period, when the various French colonial proprietors and trading companies responsible for settling the Louisiana territory failed for many years to import sufficient numbers of European women along with male émigrés, the city developed a tacit tolerance for interracial relationships, first with Native Americans and later with Africans from the slave trade. Many of the offspring of such unions remained or became free citizens, constituting a unique social class, *les gens de couleur libre*—free people of color.

Bolstered in the late eighteenth century by free blacks fleeing the insurrections of French Santo Domingo, the *gens de couleur* eventually formed a substantial community in New Orleans, including many individuals of significant wealth and social status. They occupied an anomalous place in Southern culture—not quite parallel to the dominant Euro-American classes, as they were throughout the West Indies, but carefully distinguished from slaves. Their acceptance as part of the city's (and the state's) social fabric did not diminish the institutionalized effects of prejudice, but it did work to blur the lines of racial difference: color could not be wholly synonymous with class here, as it often was elsewhere in the South.[13] Even the elaborate classifications of color—mulatto, quadroon, octoroon, griffe, quinteroon, the "black drop" calculated to distant generations—suggest a reluctance to make otherness absolute, certainly among blacks, and perhaps among whites at least a perverse willingness to acknowledge its relativity. Moreover, encouraged by the cultural variety and economic mobility characteristic of a major port, the ambivalences about race in New Orleans likewise extended to the ethnicity of other European and Euro-American newcomers. Social distinctions were typically identified, and often continue to be identified, with places: Yankees in the Garden District; Irish in the Irish Channel; Cajuns in Marrero, Westwego, and elsewhere on the West Bank (of the river); the French (and later Italians) in the Vieux Carré; Creoles occupying the Seventh Ward (downriver) and, later, New Orleans East, which also now includes substantial Vietnamese and Hispanic populations.

Gathered from and diffused onto Louisiana as a whole, these multiple and intersecting identities have complicated the image of both city and state, making them ripe for literary use. New Orleans in particular has been, as Hamilton Basso once wrote, "a symbol of exotic alienness in the national mind," a source of romance that few writers—within or without the state—have cared to resist."[14] Not surprisingly, given that dominance and appeal, the literary history of Louisiana virtually overlaps that of its principal city, a fact that is apparent throughout this present work, most notably in the paucity of women writers from the state's northern half represented in the selected essays and in the more inclusive Bibliography.

Writing about Louisiana, then, whether about the rural life of Isle Brevelle or the sophisticated cliques of Uptown New Orleans, and writing as a Louisiana woman both imply writing about life at the margins—at the crossroads of dominant and muted cultures, of role definition and identity, of race and class, of place and places. The peculiar otherness of that experience, imposed onto the more familiar layers of Southern myth, gender roles, and color prejudice, is precisely the ingredient that distinguishes the contribution of this group of writers to the fascinating place that Louisiana and its Crescent City occupy in the American psyche.

It has been more than fifty years since anyone has tried to take stock of Louisiana's literary heritage, a serious void that the Bibliography goes a substantial way toward remedying. But even our most rigorous effort at inclusiveness finally demonstrates just how much more work needs to be done. For example, not only the inevitable gaps of data on obscure figures, but the omission even of whole categories—such as that of women writing in French—indicate important scholarship still needed. Both as a research tool and as a challenge to further investigation, the Bibliography is a long-overdue step toward what Adrienne Rich calls the fundamental task of feminist criticism, "re-vision": seeing again what has been written, recognizing what has been lost by unseeing eyes. One dimension of that re-vision is the recovery of many writers whose talents seem undistinguished in isolation, but whose presence among others discloses the essential literary contexts from which writers with greater gifts emerge. As Ellen Moers rightly observed, even Jane Austen could write what she did only because so many others had explored the terrain before her; their failures and partial successes marked the way for her triumphs.[15] Likewise, seeing how many Louisiana women writers there were—and are—makes the achievement of a Chopin or a Grau both less exceptional and more comprehensible. Lesser writers, moreover, can provide valuable cultural data, enriching our understanding of an era, as well as offer glimpses of technique and purpose that their more skillful peers better conceal.

If the Bibliography thus surveys the regions we must traverse, the essays themselves represent a different kind of re-vision, adding evaluation to recovery. Like the Bibliography, they propose another look, often fresh and always perceptive, at the heritage of Louisiana women writers. But their selectiveness also challenges other scholars to pursue the many roads of interpretation that could not all be taken in a single volume. There are, for example, some glaring omissions of writers whose contributions to Louisiana literature are well known: Ruth McEnery Stuart, Anne Rice, Gwen Bristow,

Frances Parkinson Keyes, Valerie Martin, and Lillian Hellman, to name only the most obvious. Much more regrettable to us as editors is the paucity of scholarship on Louisiana's African American women, especially since in the last twenty years that group has produced such a flowering of poets and playwrights, among them Pinkie Gordon Lane, Elizabeth Brown-Guillory, Arthenia Bates Millican, Brenda Marie Osbey, Sybil Kein, Thadious Davis, Gloria Hull, and Mona Lisa Saloy; their work deserves greater critical attention.

Of course, the intent of this volume is not to confirm a canon of Louisiana writers, but to stimulate interest in a rich and vigorous tradition. Obviously, no one collection can encompass the literary variety and wealth that the state has fostered; however, the essays can and do suggest the outlines of that variety. Encouraged only to keep in mind our defining terms, Louisiana and *women,* the essayists approach their subjects from a variety of critical positions. Moreover, whereas unfamiliar writers such as Mollie Moore Davis, Berthe Amoss, or Ada Jack Carver invite introductory or biographical comments, their more famous counterparts such as Chopin or Porter permit more specialized approaches. The consequence is a series of essays whose differing perspectives give glimpses of a continuous tradition, punctuated by perceptive insights into the female mind of Louisiana, and thus of the South.

As one might expect, place resonates for these authors; the culture and geography of Louisiana were indeed, for several, crucial to their opportunities as writers. Local colorists, for example—well represented here by Grace King, Kate Chopin, Mollie Moore Davis, and Alice Dunbar-Nelson—were able to take advantage of the state's popularity as a setting with national audiences in the late 1800s. Even twentieth-century writers such as Ellen Gilchrist, Nancy Lemann, and Shelia Bosworth have successfully capitalized on the state's persistent appeal as setting, although as Randal Woodland points out, not without a distinct awareness of its limitations. The power of Louisiana as an image is directly addressed in the work of Katherine Anne Porter, who spent little time here but whose allusions to the state, as Merrill Skaggs argues, bear important symbolic weight.

The problems of place as social limit are exposed most acutely by the writers of the late nineteenth and early twentieth centuries. Clara Juncker, for example, examines how diarist Sarah Morgan Dawson quietly chafed against the gender roles that wartime Baton Rouge only exacerbated, while Ellen Peel shows how Kate Chopin subtly disclosed the shortcomings of those roles in her tragic portrait of Désirée. But as both essayists suggest, even more unsettling to these writers are the contradictions of race. Linda Coleman addresses the issue most directly in her commentary on the sketches of Grace King, whose sharp realism is consistently distorted by her nostalgic views of blacks. In perhaps the most speculative essay of the collection, Alice Parker ruminates on how Sidonie de la Houssaye, the only representative of Louisiana's important Francophone traditions, usurps the stories of quadroon women to explore territory forbidden to her as a white Victorian woman. Similarly, Elizabeth Meese examines the disruptions in Ada Jack Carver's stories of free people of color in Isle Brevelle, which Carver, like de la

Houssaye, appropriates in order to pass over into another culture. In the fiction of Shirley Ann Grau (as in that of Georgia's Margaret Mitchell, whose epic novel Elzbieta Olesky suggestively compares with Grau's *Keepers of the House*), the conflicts of race are only slightly more submerged than those of gender, although both sharply define the fate of her heroines. Even Berthe Amoss' tales for adolescents, as Sylvia Iskander demonstrates, must confront race and social caste as a consequence of choosing New Orleans as a setting. Conflicts about race and gender are no less apparent in the work of Alice Dunbar-Nelson; however, the lack of a supportive literary community that Dunbar-Nelson experienced in New Orleans as a woman of color—a community that, as Violet Harrington Bryan argues, had it existed, might have enabled her to confront those ambivalences more directly—is made more poignant by the revelation of just such a community's benefits to her older contemporary, Mollie E. Moore Davis. As Patricia Brady's biographical sketch reveals, Davis could and did rely on the privileges of her race and class to shape her life into graceful Southern figures.

That kind of support, shared by most of the white women in this collection, was often essential in creating opportunities to write and publish in a culture that encouraged women to do neither. But reliance on these props frequently obscured the writers' visions of the cramped pedestal of gender that they also occupied. As the essays repeatedly suggest, the failure of King, Chopin, Dawson, Carver, and even Dunbar-Nelson (albeit in a very different way) to extend their tentative analyses of difference to race and gender finally restricted their ability to identify the sources of their constraints as women and as writers. Their consequent ambivalence about redefining their places as Southern women thus underlines the disturbing opacity of their vision of race.

Such disturbances, however, as Linda Coleman reminds us, can be keys to the patterns that blind and entrap entire cultures. Sharing a native or at least a temporary relation to Louisiana, these writers found in the state a fertile imaginative space from which to examine their specific places in a culture whose limits necessarily mark their work. By exposing some of those markings and by revealing the complexity of these different individuals' struggles to claim their places as Louisiana women writers, the essays, together with the Bibliography, attest to the continuing relevance of their achievement. That we might better recognize the full significance of those places is the hope that binds this collection together.

## Notes for "Re-Viewing the Tradition of Louisiana Women Writers"

[1]Helen Taylor, *Gender, Race, and Region in the Writings of Grace King, Ruth McEnery Stuart, and Kate Chopin* (Baton Rouge, 1989), xi. Taylor notes as "pioneering" Anne Goodwyn Jones, *Tomorrow Is Another Day: The Woman Writer in the South, 1859-1936* (Baton Rouge, 1981). Also exceptional in studying southern women is Louise S. Westling, *Sacred Groves and Ravished Gardens: The Fiction of Eudora Welty, Carson McCullers, and Flannery O'Connor* (Athens, Ga., 1985), especially her chapter on "The Blight of Southern Womanhood," 8-35. See also Kathryn Lee Seidel, *The Southern Belle in the American Novel* (Tampa, 1985).

[2]Richard Gray, *Writing the South: Ideas of an American Region* (Cambridge, Mass., 1986), 173. The notion of "sense of place" merits a separate entry in Charles Reagon Wilson and William Ferris, eds., *The Encyclopedia of Southern Culture* (Chapel Hill, 1989), 1137-38. For discussions of the literary sense of place, see Lewis P. Simpson, *The Dispossessed Garden: Pastoral and History in Southern Literature* (Athens, Ga., 1975); and Lucinda Hardwick MacKethan, *The Dream of Arcady: Place and Time in Southern Literature* (Baton Rouge, 1980). John Shelton Reed, "Instant Grits and Plastic Wrapped Crackers: Southern Culture and Regional Development," in Louis D. Rubin, Jr., ed. *American South: Portrait of a Culture* (Baton Rouge, 1980), 35. For a fuller assessment of this phenomenon, see Reed's *Enduring South: Subcultural Persistence in Mass Society* (Lexington, Mass., 1972), especially chapters 4-6.

[3]Alice Walker, "Choosing to Stay at Home: Ten Years After the March on Washington," in *In Search of Our Mothers' Gardens: Womanist Prose* (San Diego, 1983), 158-70.

[4]Taylor, *Gender, Race, and Region*, 21-22. See, for example, Welty's comments in interviews, *Conversations with Eudora Welty*, ed. Peggy Whitman Prenshaw (Jackson, Miss., 1984), especially 54, 136, and 250.

[5]Eudora Welty, "Place in Fiction," in *The Eye of the Story* (New York, 1978), 121-22, 124-25.

[6]See Elaine Showalter, "Women Writers and the Double Standard," in *Women in Sexist Society: Studies in Power and Powerlessness*, ed. Vivian Gornick and Barbara K. Moran (New York, 1971), 474. See also the pointed comments on feminine confinement and materiality by Mary Ellmann, *Thinking About Women* (New York, 1968), 87-93, 97-101. Quotation from William Dean Howells, *Criticism and Fiction* (New York, 1892), 134.

[7]Annette Kolodny, *The Land Before Her: Fantasy and Experience of the American Frontiers, 1630-1860* (Chapel Hill, 1984), 12; Judith Fryer, *Felicitous Spaces: The Imaginative Structures of Edith Wharton and Willa Cather* (Chapel Hill, 1986).

[8]Anne Rowe, *The Enchanted Country: Northern Writers in the South, 1865-1910* (Baton Rouge, 1978), xviii-xix, xix-xx, 138. See also Howard R. Floan, *The South in Northern Eyes, 1831-1861* (Austin, 1958), 184-86; Fred Hobson, Prologue to *Tell About the South: The Southern Rage to Explain* (Baton Rouge, 1983), 3-16; Patrick Gerster and Nicholas Cords, "Northern Origins of Southern Mythology," in their *The New South*, Second ed. (Urbana, 1989), 43-58, Vol. 2 of Gerster and Cords, *Myth and Southern History*, 2 vols.; and Barbara J. Fields, "Ideology and Race in American History" in *Region, Race, and Reconstruction: Essays in Honor of C. Vann Woodward*, ed. J. Morgan Kousser and James M. McPherson (New York, 1982), 143-77. The related issue of southern resistance to "northern" influences is explored in Richard N. Current, *Northernizing the South* (Athens, Ga., 1983).

[9]Gray, *Writing the South*, xxi. A recent summary of this virtual commonplace appears in *Encyclopedia*, ed. Wilson and Ferris, xv-xvi. See also Michael O'Brien, "A Heterodox Note on the Southern Renaissance," in *Rethinking the South: Essays in Intellectual History* (Baltimore, 1988), 166.

[10]O'Brien, "A Heterodox Note," 166.

[11]Gerster and Cords, "Northern Origins of Southern Mythology," 58; Rowe, *Enchanted Country*, xvii-xx.

[12]Alice Jardine, *Gynesis: Configurations of Woman and Modernity* (Ithaca, N.Y., 1985), 114-15.

[13]For an account of the evolution of Louisiana's distinctive African-American castes, see Thomas Marc Fiehrer, "The African Presence in Colonial Louisiana: An Essay on the Continuity of Caribbean Culture," in *Louisiana's Black Heritage*, eds. Robert R. MacDonald, John R. Kemp, and Edward F. Haas (New Orleans, 1979), especially 19-25. See also James R. Frisby, Jr. "New Orleans Writers and the Negro: George Washington Cable, Grace King, Ruth McEnery Stuart, Kate Chopin, and Lafcadio Hearn, 1870-1900" (Ph.D. dissertation, Emory University, 1972), 8-23. Frisby's work is cited by Anna Shannon Elfenbein in her study of

stereotypes in Louisiana writers, *Women on the Color Line: Evolving Stereotypes and the Writings of George Washington Cable, Grace King, Kate Chopin* (Charlottesville, 1989), 12-19.

[14]Hamilton Basso, Introduction to *The World from Jackson Square: A New Orleans Reader*, ed. Etoila S. Basso (New York, 1948), xi. Violet Harrington Bryan's study of the image of New Orleans in literature is forthcoming from the University of Tennessee Press. Two previous works that treat early segments of the city's literary history are Albert Fossier, *New Orleans: The Glamour Period, 1800-1840* (New Orleans, 1957), especially 238-46; and Robert C. Reinders, *End of an Era: New Orleans, 1850-1860* (New Orleans, 1964). The latter is particularly acerbic on the deleterious "emotional female influences in fiction and poetry," 224.

[15]Adrienne Rich, *Lies, Secrets and Silence: Selected Prose, 1966-1978* (New York, 1979), 35; Ellen Moers, *Literary Women: The Great Writers* (New York, 1976), 44.

# WALKER PERCY AND THE SEARCH FOR WISDOM*

Jared W. Bradley

Walker Percy has said, "A novelist should be concerned with what is the case in the world, the facts, the richness, the intricacy and the variety of the way things are."[1] Readers of Percy's novels, *The Moviegoer* (1961), the *Last Gentleman* (1966), and *Love in the Ruins* (1971), will recognize the present-mindedness of his approach to his material. To Percy, his writing is not in the "traditional artistic forms of short stories and classical novels." It is "an exploration of reality."[2]

Reality for Percy is the "everydayness" of life.[3] It is the question which he treats in *Love in the Ruins*: "What if the Bomb should *not* fall? What then?" To Percy, this is the "real anxiety question"—the "what if" life isn't suddenly ended and we have to go on living it out to its end?[4] In choosing to deal with this aspect of man's life in the mid-twentieth century, Percy has addressed himself to that "general and universal physical fear" which William Faulkner referred to in his Nobel Prize acceptance speech in 1950. Unlike Faulkner, however, Percy does not find the locus of that fear so much in the "problems of the heart" as in the "problems of the spirit." Indeed, Faulkner was explicit in his belief that there were "no longer problems of the spirit."[5]

Readers of Percy's fictional pieces may be left with a feeling that he has not provided any ultimate answers. Essentially, this is because of Percy's use of words, which parallels that of the obscure poets who have sought to bring freshness and clarity to literature. Unlike some of the obscure poets, however, Percy will have no truck with that pastime of "rolling out the pretty marbles of word-things to see one catch and reflect the fire of another. . . ." Conscious that "words are potent agents," Percy would have his reader, whom he calls the "Hearer," participate in what he, Percy, has to say: "I would have a horror of finding myself allied with those in the name of instrumentality or inner warmth or whatnot would so attenuate and corrupt truth that it meant nothing."[6]

*First published in *Louisiana Studies*, 12 (1973): 579-90. Reprinted with the kind permission of the author.

Percy's concept of the reader as the "Hearer" is a refinement on the idea of the French writer-philosopher Gabriel Marcel that philosophy is "essentially auditory." To Marcel, man "listens to and responds to 'voice' and 'calls' that make up the symphony of being, which for him is ultimately a supra-national unity beyond images, words, and concepts."[7] To Percy, man today is experiencing action not "on the stage," but "in the privacy of his box."[8] The capacity is that of an observer, but it is also that of the listener, or as Percy said, the "Hearer."

Language, therefore, takes on great significance for Walker Percy. To him, language is a symbol of our comprehension of life around us. It is a metaphysical "inner connection" in its use as a bridge between "traditional empiricism" and "existential insights."[9] However, just as we can never know ourselves as symbolization in the way we can know others and things, we can't see the role which "symbolization plays in cognition" because of its practical necessity, its "indispensability."[10] Thus, Percy sees language as the derivative of "intersubjectivity," which he defines as "that meeting of the minds by which two selves take each other's meaning with reference to the same object beheld in common."[11]

What Percy hopes to do with his selection of words is help his fellow man to know the truth. In this context, Percy's purpose coincides with Faulkner's admonition that it is the "writer's duty . . . to help man endure . . . [and] prevail."[12] Beyond this point, there is little, if any, similarity between the two writers. Percy, with time as his aid, has taken a fuller measure of the "sickness of modern man" than most of the post-World War I writers, the peer group with which William Faulkner is chiefly associated.[13]

The scope of Percy's writing includes not only twentieth century man's "emotional impoverishment," but also "his sense of homelessness in the midst of the very world which he, more than the men of any other time, has made over for his own happiness." As Percy has pointed out, his theme is one which has attracted "existential critics of modern society from Sören Kierkegaard to Gabriel Marcel."[14] The theme has been a popular one since World War II in Europe, particularly France, where writers have sought to unify philosophy and literature for the purpose of exploring reality. Although Percy has said that he reads "Russian novels primarily,"[15] it is the French influence which stands out in his work and particularly the influence of Gabriel Marcel and Henri Bergson. In addition, Percy has been influenced by the ideas of José Ortega y Gasset. Yet, Walker Percy's writing style is in the style and tradition of "The Fugitive Group" which developed around John Crowe Ransom in the years between the two world wars.[16]

Marcel's philosophy has been characterized as one of "exploration and dialogue,"[17] features which perhaps more than any others distinguish Percy's brand of analogy. Percy believes the chief way that modern man can be helped is through identification with one another. Percy's method of providing this assistance is through analogy, or, as he calls it the "cognitive dimension,"[18] a concept borrowed from Ortega y Gasset.[19] As Percy has said, "there must occur a preliminary meeting of the minds and a mutually intended subject before anything can be said at all."[20] Percy, like Marcel, and Bergson before

Marcel, has sought to restore to life some of the mystery which he feels has been lost to the "fragmented and imperiled" contemporary consciousness.[21]

Given Walker Percy's goal and technique in writing, the use of the past in his fiction attracts added interest because of his Southern heritage. Significantly, the past in Percy's novels is not the burden of guilt that the historian C. Vann Woodward referred to, but rather an aid to understanding which Woodward suggested it should be.[22] In this context, Percy, like Faulkner, has employed the "confused mind struggling" for answers in a complex environment to assist his fellow man.[23] As Southerners conscious of their Southern heritage, both Percy and Faulkner have dealt with characters grappling with problems which seem elusive of resolution. However, Faulkner's quest for "final answers in an absurd and chaotic situation"[24] is not that of Walker Percy. Percy casts his characters in a "situation,"[25] but it is a situation identifiable with twentieth century urbanized America. In this sense, Percy's work is not regional. Nonetheless, it is in the vein of the Fugitives because of Percy's concern with the techniques of writing and the use of language.[26] Most importantly, Percy's work is like the Fugitives in his re-affirmation that the spiritual values of the Western cultural tradition are still the means by which man may grasp reality in the modern world.[27] The conversation from *Love in the Ruins* among Dr. Thomas More, the leading character of the novel, and two blacks, Uru and Victor Charles, illustrates Percy's view.

Uru, whose Christian name is Elijah Washington, used to live in Paradise Estates, the setting for the story, but left home to receive his college education with advanced degrees outside the South. He is the leader of the Bantu Rebellion which has just been launched. Victor Charles is almost a stereotype of the faithful and trusty Southern Negro household servant, a man who takes the principles of his Christian religion seriously. In the excerpt, "Doc" More has just been taken prisoner by Victor, who continues to surreptitiously protect More from death.

> "I'll fix you a drink, Doc," says Victor.
>
> "No you won't," says Uru, showing anger for the first time. "You're not his goddamn houseboy."
>
> "You know, my name's Washington, too," Victor tells Uru. "After George Washington Carver."
>
> "Jesus Christ," says Uru. . . .
>
> "Blessed be Jesus," says Victor.
>
> "Look what you done to him," Uru says to me [Doc]
>
> "What he done to me!" cries Victor.
>
> "You did a good job, Doctor. It took you four hundred years but you really did a good job. Let me ask you something."
>
> "All right."
>
> "What would you do about it if you were me? I mean what with the four hundred years and Victor here."

> "What's wrong with Victor?"
>
> "You know what I mean. What would you do about the four hundred years?"
>
> "I'd stop worrying about it and get on with it. To tell you the truth, I'm tired of hearing about the four hundred years." (300-301)

Because of his emphasis upon a meeting of the minds, Percy's novels seem to end on a note of flatness; they appear to have no ending at all, but to offer another beginning, which in truth is what they do. In Percy's opinion, as in Marcel's, life is a perpetual series of starts—some true, more false.[28] The true starts for Percy are dependent upon the establishment of an "I—Thou," as opposed to an "I—It," relationship.[29] Man, Percy says, knows "not as the angels know and not as dogs know but as men who must know one thing through the mirror of another."[30] For Percy, as for Marcel, reality is somehow embodied for man in the daily discoveries in dialogue.[31] The endings of Percy's novels have depended, therefore, upon the Hearer's comprehension of the truism that man needs his fellow man, and his novels abound in vignettes with this message.

In *The Moviegoer*, Binx Bolling marries his neurotically unstable and apparently suicide-bound cousin Kate Cutrer not so much from a feeling of love as from an act of accepting responsibility. From the act, they both begin to learn what compassion and love are. In *The Last Gentleman*, Bibb Barrett is enabled to see the beauty of a Velasquez painting after he and others have reached out to aid a workman who has fallen to the floor of the gallery (25-27). The crash of the fallen worker has the same effect upon Barrett and a few other visitors to the art gallery that the explosion of the Bomb might have if it had been dropped. The wall of silence which enveloped those present and which had sealed them off one from another is shattered. In almost a rush of feeling, Barrett and those who had escaped injury demonstrate their humaneness to the literally fallen fellow man.

Barrett's ability to see beauty in the Velasquez painting is in itself symbolic to Percy. As he remarked in the interview with Carlton Cremeens, "a good bit of *The Last Gentleman* and *The Moviegoer* had to do with the positive values and the beauties of the very things that are made fun of in so much of alienated literature."[32] The compassionate acts of Bolling and Barrett do not immediately reestablish contacts with reality. They are gropings toward reality. This is perhaps most clearly demonstrated in *Love in the Ruins*. In the story, Dr. More finds that recognition of his need for and marriage to Ellen Oglethorpe reduces his "shakes and depressions and unnatural exaltations." (382) Although this is a significant step in healing the psyche, it is only a step. More's problem, the problem of Western man in the twentieth century, is "hermaphroditism of the spirit," which Percy variously calls the "modern Black Death," or "[Sir Thomas] More's syndrome," a "chronic angelism-bestialism that rives soul from body and sets it orbiting the great world as the spirit of abstraction. . . ." (383) Percy, like Bergson and Ortega y Gasset, clearly seeks to restore metaphysics to its proper place in man's life and to free the mind of those abstract "universal laws of truth" which do more to conceal truth than to reveal it.[33] But how is truth, or reality, to be found?

In Walker Percy's novels, the search for reality becomes a mysterious journey. In *The Moviegoer*, Percy has Binx Bolling say to Kate Cutrer, "There is only one thing I can do: listen to people, see how they stick themselves into the world, hand them along a ways in their dark journey and be handed along, and for good and selfish reasons." (233) In Percy's philosophy of life, man is here on earth "as a stranger and as a pilgrim."[34] A major feature of Gabriel Marcel's thinking is the concept of man's life as a "pilgrim in an abidingly mysterious land."[35] Marcel has called this activity "*homo viator*," meaning "man who is always in the process of becoming."[36] Percy used the term in the interview with Carlton Cremeens much as Marcel has employed it.[37] In *The Moviegoer*, Percy called the pilgrimage "rotation," defining it as the "experiencing of the new beyond the expectation of the experiencing of the new." (144) Near the end of *Love in the Ruins*, Tom More is mystified, but happy with his changed circumstances: "What I want is no longer the Nobel, screw prizes, but just to figure out what I've hit on." (383)

Despite the apparent parallel between the philosophical views of Gabriel Marcel and Walker Percy, the rotation concept is not derived only from influences so far from Percy's home environment as France. In *Lanterns on the Levee* (New York, 1941), William Alexander Percy, Walker's father by adoption, spoke of this pilgrimage when he wrote: "Perhaps security is a good thing to seek and a bad thing to find. Perhaps it is never found, and all our best is in the search." (284) Beyond immediate exposure at home to the idea of life as a mysterious journey, Walker Percy clearly is familiar with John Crowe Ransom's definition of the Journey as "rotation." Ransom, the intellectual leader of the Fugitive group at Vanderbilt, was the first to use the term "rotation" in American *belles-lettres*. In "Poets Without Laurels," Ransom wrote: "You may dissociate the elements of experience and exploit them separately. But then at best you go on a schedule of small experiences, taking them in turn, and trusting that when the *rotation* is complete you will have missed nothing."[38] In addition, Percy obviously adheres to viewpoints demonstrated and refined in Ransom's work: interest in language as a tool for exploration; a bent for metaphysics, and, dominant in both men, an "anti-abstractionism manifesting itself as a preoccupation with the uniqueness of individual experience. . . ."[39]

By the ends of Percy's novels thus far, the central characters—Binx Bolling, Kate Cutrer, Bib Barrett, Dr. Sutter Vaught and Dr. Thomas More—usually are able to meet life with a greater sense of security than when they entered our lives. The difference is not a complete transformation of character, however. There is still present a strong feeling of the mirror image: The final scene in *The Moviegoer* has Bolling's unstable Kate nearly pleading with him to think of her in a certain position in the St. Charles Avenue streetcar—sitting "next to the window on the Lake side" with a "cape jasmine in my lap"—as she goes on a brief errand to downtown New Orleans. Binx's assurance that he will visualize Kate just as she tells him she will be sitting gives her the courage to meet life (241-42). A similar constancy of character is demonstrated by Dr. More in *Love in the Ruins*. The novel ends with More still believing that despite the setbacks of five years earlier his Qualitative Quantitative Ontological Lapsometer "can save the world—if I can get it right." (382) Thus, Percy proves the mutability of life, which Ortega y Gasset called upon man to assert, with Percy's demonstration of the philosophy of Bergson, who pointed out the contradictions in man and who chided science for its shortcomings.[40] However, Percy distinguishes himself from not only Bergson, but also later existentialist thinkers in that he does not fault the scientific method for its limitations. Instead, Percy suggests that contemporary man assigns to science a capability it does not have, the capability of supplying the answers in "all sectors of reality."[41]

Children in Percy's novels poignantly make clear the insufficiency of science. As a consequence, these characters are not as life-like as Percy's adults. Children are instruments to press home to the Hearer the sense of mystery about life and man's need for man. These two objectives are attained through the grotesque death of a child. Often, the child's death is immediately preceded by those simple utterances which startle their elders because of the wisdom which the words reflect. In *The Moviegoer*, Binx Bolling's half brother Lonnie Smith, a fourteen-year-old wheelchair-ridden spastic, dies of hepatitis. The crippling and double illness of Lonnie coupled with his death leaves Bolling with the answerless and age old question of why such a thing should happen to a child (238). In *The Last Gentleman*, young Jamie Vaught dies of a "severe and atypical mononucleosis" clutching the hand of the priest who, upon Jamie's request, has just baptized the boy into the church (390). In *Love in the Ruins*, Samantha, Dr. More's daughter, is dying of neuroblastoma which has "pushed one eye out and around the nosebridge so she looked like a Picasso profile." The dying child asks:

> "Just promise me one thing, Papa."
> "What's that?"
> "Don't commit the sin for which there is no forgiveness."
> "Which one is that?"
> "The sin against grace. If God gives you the grace to believe in him and love him and you refuse, the sin will not be forgiven you."
> "I know," answers More. (373-74)

In an age of cynicism, Percy's viewpoint is distinctive, whether considered from the purely literary or philosophical position.[42] Undergirding Percy's controlled flow of well chosen words is a strongly held Christian philosophy of life. The alienation which he writes of "is nothing more or less than a very ancient, orthodox Christian doctrine." What Percy has sought to do is express this orthodoxy in "unorthodox or fresh language."[43] The result is a twentieth century Thomas More who gains relief from his self-induced prison of guilt not through any holocaust brought on by misuse of his Qualitative Quantitative Ontological Lapsometer, but when he accepts the Grace of God.

Because the act of contrition occurs at Christmas, the parallel between the birth of Christ and the rebirth of man suggests itself to the Hearer. Lest the analogy be missed, however, Percy allows his Hearer a glimpse of Tom More's thoughts after he has confessed his sins and donned the symbolic sackcloth: "It is Christmas Day and the Lord is here, a holy night and surely that is all one needs." (402) It is at this point that the similarity between Walker Percy and Gabriel Marcel ends.

Marcel's philosophy is "consistently alien to Thomism and always stops short of being a 'Christian Philosophy,'"[44] but Percy's does not. Most of the English-speaking world continues to be attracted to positivism and linguistic philosophy, but Walker Percy is unabashedly Christian in the Western tradition carved out by Henri Bergson.[45] At the same time, Percy is also eminently Southern. His views on writing hark back to the ideas expressed by John Crowe Ransom in "Poets Without Laurels." In that essay, Ransom lamented the passing of the "old-fashioned moral-beautiful compound" in modern poetry.[46] If Ransom's poetry is the modern version of that tradition, Percy's prose is the modern version of the old-fashioned moral-beautiful compound in the novel.[47] Unlike Ransom, however, Percy accepts, almost welcomes, the irrationality and physical humanness of man.[48] It is all part of the mysterious journey.

Walker Percy's novels are kept from being sentimental and trite because of his understated writing style and realistic use of analogy.[49] In employing the latter, Percy suggested in his essay, "Metaphor as Mistake" that he has sought, like the poet, "to name unmistakably and yet to name by such a gentle analogy that the thing beheld by both of us may be truly formulated for what it is."[50] The following excerpt from *Love in the Ruins* exemplifies this technique. The scene occurs immediately after More has accepted the Grace of God at church. Percy's satire will evoke other nuances of thought, but the over-riding message in the passage, coming as it does immediately after More's acceptance of Grace, is Man's unique destiny. Implicit in the excerpt is Percy's view that this destiny encompassed the relation of man to his fellow man, the relation of man to God, and the need for man to accept increased responsibility in a complex technical age.[51] More is leaving the church when he encounters Victor Charles, who announces that he is running for Congress.

> "The U.S. Congress?"
>
> "Why not?"
>
> He [Charles] wants me [More] to be his campaign manager.
>
> "Why me?"
>
> "I've got the Bantu vote. They've fallen out with each other and are willing to go with me. Chuck Parker's helping me with the swamp people. Max is working on the liberals. Leroy Ledbetter's got the peckerwoods. You could swing the Catholics."
>
> "I doubt that. Anyhow, I'm not much of a politician." I have to laugh. He sounds exactly like a politician from the old Auto Age.

"You organized the SOUP chapter here, didn't you?"

SOUP is Southerners and Others United to Preserve the Union in Repayment of an Old Debt to the Yankees who Saved It Once Before and Are Destroying It Now.

. . . .

"You're a good doctor, Doc. People respect you."

"What's that got to do with politics?"

"Everything, man!"

"You running as Knothead or Left?"

"Doc, I'm running under the old rooster." In Louisiana the rooster stood for old Democratic Party.

I laugh. Victor laughs and claps his hands. It's the same old funny fouled-up coalition. Kennedy, Evers, Goldberg, Stevenson, L. Q. C. Lamar.

"All right."

"All right, what?"

"I will."

We laugh. Why are we laughing? (400-401)

The aesthetic Christian philosophy which Walker Percy adheres to undoubtedly will be important in determining his place in the arts and letters of the future, as will the fact that he addresses himself to suburban America. Although his characters are usually in movement, both literally and figuratively, the backgrounds for his stories are cities: New Orleans, Chicago, New York, Montgomery, Atlanta, Albuquerque, Santa Fe. What undergirds and distinguishes Percy's work now and for all time is his position astride two seemingly divergent worlds: *belles-lettres* and science. Unlike most men of letters, Percy's educational background was in the pure sciences for a career in medicine. Circumstances caused him to relinquish that vocation and led him to become a physician in a broader sense, a writer.[52] Percy is "convinced of the value of the scientific vocation, of the practice of the scientific method," but he emphasizes that the exploration of "man in a concrete situation . . . cannot be done with science or psychology. . . ."[53] In Percy's view, the novel and perhaps the cinema may well be the instruments best suited for exploring what it is to be a man living in the world.[54] Rather than for the laws of know-how, Percy's search, much like Marcel's, has been for wisdom, or as Percy described it in *Love in the Ruins*, "Knowing. . . ." (383)

# Notes for "Walker Percy and the Search for Wisdom"

[1]Carlton Cremeens, "Walker Percy, The Man and the Novelist: An Interview," *The Southern Review*, 4 n.s. (1968): 275. Mr. Cremeens is News Director of television station WAFB (CBS affiliate), Baton Rouge.

[2]Ibid., 287.

[3]Walker Percy, *The Moviegoer* (New York, 1961), 146. This novel won the National Book Award for Fiction in 1962. Percy's second novel, *The Last Gentleman* (New York, 1966), was runner-up for this award in 1967.

[4]Walker Percy, "The Man on the Train: Three Existential Modes," *Partisan Review*, 23 (1956): 479. Walker Percy, *Love in the Ruins* (New York, 1971).

[5]William Faulkner, Nobel Prize Acceptance Speech, reprinted in Thomas D. Young, Floyd C. Watkins and Richmond C. Beatty, eds., *The Literature of the South* (Glenview, Ill., 1968): 1042.

[6]Walker Percy, "Metaphor as Mistake," *The Sewanee Review*, 66 (1958): 89.

[7]Seymour Cain, *Gabriel Marcel* (New York, 1963), 14.

[8]Cremeens, "Walker Percy, The Man and the Novelist," 281.

[9]Percy, "Metaphor as Mistake," 95.

[10]Walker Percy, "Symbol as Hermeneutic in Existentialism: A Possible Bridge from Empiricism," *Philosophy and Phenomenological Research*, 16 (1956): 525.

[11]Walker Percy, "Symbol, Consciousness, and Intersubjectivity," *Journal of Philosophy*, 55 (1958): 631.

[12]Faulkner, Nobel Prize Acceptance Speech, in Young, Watkins and Beatty, eds., *The Literature of the South*, 1042.

[13]Martin Luschei, *The Sovereign Wayfarer; Walker Percy's Diagnosis of the Malaise* (Baton Rouge, 1972), 9, states that Percy was "simply never under Faulkner's influence, though Faulkner often played tennis with his [Percy's] Uncle Will," and despite the fact that Percy admits (Ibid., 10) attempting to imitate Faulkner's writing style while at the University of North Carolina.

Professor Luschei apparently began his search for information on Walker Percy about the time the first version of this essay was written for a course in Southern literature at Louisiana State University, Baton Rouge, in the summer of 1968.

[14]Walker Percy, "The Coming Crisis in Psychiatry," part 1, *America*, 46 (1957): 392.

[15]Cremeens, "Walker Percy, The Man and the Novelist," 286.

[16]Walker Percy, "The Coming Crisis in Psychiatry," part 2, *America*, 46 (1957): 416. Luschei, *The Sovereign Wayfarer*, 6, 8, 15, 19, 39, 83n (see index for other references), sees the philosophical writings of Jean-Paul Sartre, Sören Kierkegaard, Fyodor Dostoevski, Albert Camus, Karl Jaspers and Gabriel Marcel as very important to Percy, but does not mention Henri Bergson or José Ortega y Gasset. Of the Fugitive Group, only Allen Tate is mentioned, but not with reference to Percy's relationship to any member of that group's viewpoints or writings.

[17]Sam Keen, *Gabriel Marcel* (Richmond, 1967), 5.

[18]Percy, "Metaphor as Mistake," 94.

[19]José Ferrater Mora, *Ortega y Gasset, An Outline of His Philosophy* (New Haven, 1957), 63-64.

[20]Percy, "Metaphor as Mistake," 95.

[21]Cremeens, "Walker Percy, The Man and the Novelist," 283.

[22]C. Vann Woodward, *The Burden of Southern History* (New York, 1961), 19-21, 188-91.

[23]Richard Lehan, "The Way Back: Redemption in the Novels of Walker Percy," *The Southern Review*, 4 n.s. (1968): 306.

[24]Ibid.

[25]Cremeens, "Walker Percy, The Man and the Novelist," 280.

[26]Compare Percy's work with the assessment of the Fugitive's works in Louise Cowan, *The Fugitive Group: A Literary History* (Baton Rouge, 1959), 257.

[27]See ibid., 27, 176, 199-201, 224-25, 257, and Louis D. Rubin, Jr.'s, introductory remarks to the Harper Torchbook edition of *I'll Take My Stand: The South and the Agrarian Tradition* (New York, 1962), xii-xiii.

[28]Keen, *Gabriel Marcel*, 7.

[29]Percy, "Symbol as Hermeneutic in Existentialism," 527-29. Compare with Marcel as set forth in Keen, *Gabriel Marcel*, 29-30.

[30]Percy, "Metaphor as Mistake," 99.

[31]Ibid., 93-95; Percy, "Symbol, Consciousness and Intersubjectivity," 636; and Keen, *Gabriel Marcel*, 31.

[32]Cremeens, "Walker Percy, The Man and the Novelist," 284.

[33]Enid Starkie, "Bergson and Literature," in Thomas Hanna, ed., *The Bergsonian Heritage* (New York, 1962), 79-83, and Mora, *Ortega y Gasset*, 34-36.

[34]Cremeens, "Walker Percy, The Man and the Novelist," 284.

[35]Keen, *Gabriel Marcel*, 51.

[36]Ibid., 4, 17. The ontological meaning inherent in Marcel's concept and Percy's utilization of it is greatly reduced if not altogether lost when man is described as little more than a transient. See Luschei, *The Sovereign Wayfarer*, particularly 37-40, 63. See also note 45.

[37]Cremeens, "Walker Percy, The Man and the Novelist," 285.

[38]John Crowe Ransom, *The World's Body* (New York, 1938), 71 (author's italics). Luschei, *The Sovereign Wayfarer*, 15, 103, ignores the obscure poets and sees Walker Percy as stylistically indebted to Albert Camus. Luschei also states, ibid., 10, that W. A. Percy was the "greatest single literary influence" on Walker, but does not reference Will's awareness of the importance of the search for security in life. However, Walker alludes to his uncle's statement about the search for security. See *Love in the Ruins*, 70.

[39]Cowan, *The Fugitive Group*, 27.

[40]Edouard Morot-Sir, "What Bergson Means to Us Today," in Hanna, ed., *The Bergsonian Heritage*, 42-46, and Mora, *Ortega y Gasset*, 34-37.

[41]Walker Percy, "Toward a Triadic Theory of Meaning," *Psychiatry: A Journal for the Study of Interpersonal Processes*, 35 (1972): 17. See also Walker Percy, "Notes for a Novel about the End of the World," *Katallagete* (1967-1968): 11-12, and Luschei, *The Sovereign Wayfarer*, 238-42.

[42]Flannery O'Connor also employed exploration and dialogue in writing. Unlike Walker Percy, Miss O'Connor took the stern Old Testament approach to the question of man's acceptance of the Grace of God. Many of her characters die violently after some incident involving their rejection of God's Grace. E.g., see the ending of "A Good Man Is Hard to Find," in O'Connor, *A Good Man Is Hard to Find and Other Stories* (New York, 1955).

[43]Cremeens, Walker Percy, The Man and the Novelist," 284.

[44]Keen, *Gabriel Marcel*, 1, 3.

[45]Starkie, "Bergson and Literature," 83-84. Luschei, *The Sovereign Wayfarer*, 80-82, 230-31, sees Percy's writing as more secular than I believe it to be.

[46]Ransom, *The World's Body*, 60-61.

[47]The similarities between Walker Percy and Ransom cannot be carried too far. In addition to the differences suggested in the text here and above, Ransom adheres to the concept of Dualism. See Cowan, *The Fugitive Group*, 27, 214. Percy sees language as a symbol which completes a triad between the sender and receiver of sentences. The sentences may deal with dyadic and triadic events. See Percy, "Toward a Triadic Theory of Meaning," 1-9, and Percy, "Symbol, Consciousness and Intersubjectivity," 631-41.

[48]Compare, e.g., the ending of Percy's *Love in the Ruins*, 390-403, with Ransom as set forth in Cowan, *The Fugitive Group*, 27-28, 213-15.

[49]For a different view, see Lehan, "The Way Back: Redemption in the Novels of Walker Percy," 309, 318-19.

[50]Percy, "Metaphor as Mistake," 89.

[51]Percy, "The Coming Crisis in Psychiatry," part 2, 416.

[52]Luschei, *The Sovereign Wayfarer*, 4-5, 11-12, provides the fullest account of this part of Walker Percy's life thus far available.

[53]Cremeens, "Walker Percy, The Man and the Novelist," 282-83. Percy's opinion of the present state of the social sciences is elaborated upon in his two part essay, "The Coming Crisis in Psychiatry," cited in notes 14 and 16 above.

[54]Percy, "Toward a Triadic Theory of Meaning," 17 and Luschei, *The Sovereign Wayfarer*, 239.

# A PLACE IN TIME*

Wiley W. Hilburn, Jr.

## *Storming Down Interstate-20*

June 4, 1978

The authentic North Louisiana thunderstorm starts with a feeling, really, and nothing else; a not unpleasant sensation of tension, of expectation; a sharpened awareness of a yet shapeless something in the atmosphere, the mood and the mind. It is only a feeling, and it comes well before the first tangible signal that something is doing in the weather.

The old collie knows something is brewing out there, too. Restless, she bumps a gray-tawny muzzle against the front door, trying to push it open. The collie can sense a storm when the sky is whole blue and nothing seems astir. But then, after the dog has found her corner refuge, comes the first audible signal that she was right again: a little thump of thunder, away off, like the first note in a great symphony.

With that distant drumroll the tension, felt in a certain closeness, thickens perceptibly. And soon after that it can be seen at last: a huge hump of cloud, still white with a sparkle of sunlight a the top, but, at bottom, sits a mass of purple, pitchforked by lightning.

The storm, I know now, is real, and building; it is tracking east toward me down I-20 in long, splashing strides. Shreveport has taken its rainy licks, the deluge has subsided and the city's gutters and drains are choking on the flood. Taylor and Gibsland are under the hammer. Lincoln Parish, though still dry, is nevertheless under siege.

The tension feels good, like a safe scare in an Alfred Hitchcock movie. Ultimately, with the cloud mushrooming up over the Western horizon, comes the wind—flowing up out of the pasture like a fresh ocean current entering a stagnant lagoon, making old

*First published in Wiley W. Hilburn, Jr., *Fragments: Wiley W. Hilburn's North Louisiana*, edited by Billy H. Gilley (Ruston: McGinty Publications, 1987), 277-313. Reprinted with the kind permission of the editor and publisher.

chimes sing somewhere, rattling sycamore leaves. It is a cool balm, this interlude, and it only lasts for a single moment. I have waited for it. I love it.

But the calm can't last; I know that. The rain smell, a vigorous compound of fresh-plowed soil and cottonseed, is everywhere. The storm has seized the sky now, nearly all of it. Everything is close, close, the moisture, unfallen yet, presses down like a soaking mattress. Then the lightning makes a ripping, tearing path through the tension, spearing across the top of the sky, and the pressure disintegrates, dissolves under that blow.

The crashes fall one on the other, salvos of thunder, and build to a crescendo. It's the last movement of the *1812* Overture out there, and the cannons are all firing. The split sky literally opens. And the rain drives down like a million cold, silver javelins. The tension torn to shreds by the storm, is washed away in a chaos of water; the thunder, muted now, is retreating to the east. The rain slows, too.

At the end the land and the spirit, purged by the storm, are at peace. There is only a dripping solitude in the aftermath of the violence, and a last, filtered light, the color of strawberries.

## *For Christmas: An Old Barn*

December 24, 1978

What I want for Christmas is one of North Louisiana's old barns, preferably seated haphazardly on a slight incline, peering down from the shade of a gnarled hardwood into a low pasture. Granted, that wish isn't likely to turn up in my stocking in the morning, but it doesn't hurt to dream.

Actually, I have been dreaming about old barns, and poking unbidden into their cobwebby innards for years, trespassing on somebody else's forty acres. The raw gash of Interstate 20 in the 1950s exposed dozens of these structures, leaving them caught in the open, dilapidated and deserted, like so many old ladies surprised in curlers and ragged bathrobes.

Yet, like the old ladies that I know and love, there is a dignity and a beauty in their untended decay. Abandoned and unused they are, these leaning and groaning old barns, but even on a gray December afternoon there is the life and smell of memories—memories of vanished, vibrant early farm mornings—within the splintery walls.

This day, dodging bullets of cold rain, we invade just such a place off the Farmerville Road in Lincoln Parish. Inside, there is a musty hay-animal aroma, a not unpleasant odor, and sagging steps leading up to a big loft from a floor of dirt and cow chips.

An old wagon, tongue protruding, loaded with dusty lumber, is forever parked in the past here. Upstairs are empty fifty-pound sacks of range cubes and calf-pellets, old bedsprings, and a roll of barbed wire.

The loft shudders slightly in the brittle winter, but the tin roof shelters us from the thunderous downpour. It is secure and serene up here and this barn, though dying, can still shield us from the weather. It was built with pride and—almost falling down from exhaustion now—it still stands against the elements, and against time.

Outside is a covered well, and under a tough honey locust tree (they made fence posts out of those things) we discover the rusting remains of plows and harrows, an old blacksmith forge, and a set of wheels from an old cotton gin wagon. Again, time stops, and we take a last look before speeding away, toward the present.

It was not our barn, of course, and the sign said "For Sale: 183 Acres." The old barn, we tell each other, can buck the winter wind and rain, but not the bulldozer. And this old lady is perilously close to town.

All the old barns, I fear, are doomed: dinosaurs caught in a shrinking time warp; beautiful old women living out their last days. And if I can't have one for Christmas, then I will look again at Albino Hinojosa's acrylic-on-masonite rendering of two old barns, their tin roofs going red, which hangs on my den wall.

The only thing is, the artist calls his picture "Retired," and that is the sad part of it.

North Louisiana's old barns.

Retired.

That's why I want one, to keep, this Christmas—before it's too late and they are all gone.

## *A Sanctuary for the New Year*

December 31, 1978

The First Presbyterian Church of Ruston is solid against the leaf-swirling winter wind of North Louisiana, rising up out of the early darkness in weathered bricks and great ropes of ivy, its steeple a silhouette against the cold stars.

It sits there serenely, cracked and cobwebbed in places, but somehow proud. Outside the guard is mounted by huge, broken-limbed oak trees. The stained glass windows flicker red and gold, offering a warm invitation to enter.

Once inside, seven tapered candles in each window make a buttery glow that gently defeats the darkness, but lets in long, soft brown shadows that shade the eyes and ease the mind. It is comfortable, even in the solid, hard pine pews.

The roof is high, soaring high, and crisscrossed with massive pine beams. Here is timber, clean-lined and unlaminated and hard, that could—I think—hold up the world. There is strength here, and endurance.

The consciousness drifts in the cadence of the first hymn. I sat here, in this very place, beside my grandfather, holding his gold railroad watch, timing the preacher. I used to kick the bottom of the pew in front, waiting until somebody soundlessly framed an "uh-uh" with their mouth and stopped me with a slight head-shake.

I've dropped many a yellow number two pencil, and heard it roll down the slightly inclined polished hardwood floor, until it sounded—in my ears—like a avalanche. I remember spilling the communion wine in the little church kitchen and getting the black Bible with my name embossed on it in gold.

There was the time, in the high school class, when Bob Barham was innocently giving the opening prayer and I busted him in a tender spot with the red hymnbook. There was also the time when Peg, my grandmother, caught us disrupting a Sunday School class and scolded us all. I still burn with shame at the thought of that.

There was Mr. Davis, magisterial in his black robes; Dr. Thompson, gentle and sincere, who drew Ellen and me, then just dating, to his Sunday night services.

Now there is also my son Greg, and I can hear his voice mingling with my father's when we say the Lord's Prayer. It is a good sound. And there is Kevin, ushering in his new suit, and Anne Marie receiving an award for reciting the Catechism.

This night the congregation is, as usual, rather small. The people here know each other, though, and there is no need to make a fuss—except for a pat on the shoulder, a wink, a handshake behind the pew. The hymns, familiar ones, are sung reverently, with an unhurried grace.

Somebody is playing a fiddle now, and its sharp, clear sounds are enfolded in the deeper, more subtle tones of a new organ in this old church. The air seems fresh, and I detect fresh pine and cedar here and there.

There is an uplifting sense of generations here, a rhythm of time and timelessness, that unites young and old in the candlelight and stained glass and burnished brass, a feeling of continuity and conquered fear.

Here is a sanctuary in the true sense. A place of peace, of rest and renewal, of quiet calm. Outside the winter wind is blowing, and the noise of the New Year—a firecracker and a gunned car engine—intrudes on the Silent Prayer. But the New Year, for all its uncertain hours, can be faced now.

## *February, and Forever, in Boeuf Prairie*

February 4, 1979

It was about this time last year—and it seemed that winter would never end. I was headed for a place called Boeuf Prairie to attend the funeral of the mother of a close friend. Boeuf Prairie? The map didn't list the name, and I stayed on the interstate as long as possible, listening to radio reports of snow and carefully following directions.

In the end, Boeuf Prairie found me this icy winter day, and the result was an editorial in *The Times* "North Louisiana" series. And when that editorial appeared, it turned out that little unmapped Boeuf Prairie had touched a lot of people from the composing room of this newspaper to Washington, D.C.

Blanche Williams of Fort Necessity wrote me an eloquent letter, and she summed up the feelings about Boeuf Prairie and the surrounding Northeast Louisiana region, where she was born and later taught school. "It was the proudest school in the world," she wrote.

The proud people of "The Fort" and Boeuf Prairie remain in my mind, too. A Mr. Ross who shook my hand outside the old church—and then the Daileys, the Buies, the Bonners, the Wooldridges, the Deshas, the Turners, the Masons, the Kincaids, the Pecks and the Moores, and others, they all brought a stranger home.

It's February again, and a good time to revisit Boeuf Prairie as *The Times* North Louisiana series saw it a year ago:

The February snowflakes were big and wet, and they disappeared without a trace into the grainy, gray soil turned fresh out of the gravesite. She had lived out almost a century in this part of Northeast Louisiana, in Franklin Parish, and had not seen a lot change in all that time.

The eulogy was that she had abided deep in the faith, was a strong woman of unadjusted principles, and had raised her children well; children and grandchildren now spread, in their unfolding lives, from Winnsboro to Washington; and, of course, children who had stayed at home, and tended the land.

This day they had all come home, at least in spirit. The priest was not long from Ireland, and his soft lilt lay easy and comforting, like a balm, on the consciousness. After the mass in Winnsboro, the road led directly home—to Fort Necessity.

There followed, almost within sight of her small house and thirty acres, that unforced and unspoken mingling of the faiths for which North Louisiana receives no credit in the great interdenominational church councils, but which is real enough—and common enough—in these parts where neighbors count more than doctrines.

The priest and the Protestant minister said the last words, near a storm-blasted hardwood with the cottonfields as a backdrop, and the final bittersweet parting—because she had given and received a full measure of life—was concluded.

A stranger among the friends and the faithful, we were led to the final ceremony by a Mr. Ross, who in the way of such people made us welcome with the grip of his hand. As we walked, braced against the cold air, he pointed to the clean, white building looming to our right.

"That's my church," he said, in a voice that measured pride on every syllable, and took us to the roots of this whole region. This was Boeuf Prairie, somebody told us then, and we thought of the Boeuf River which flows nearby. And the Methodist Church, we learned then, we raised on this spot before the Civil War.

Tall oaks stood around the church, trailing gray moss. And the churchyard ran right into the cemetery without a gate or a fence to separate them. Here, one saw life and death merge without embarrassment or formality.

It was snowing as we left the church and Fort Necessity—people here call it "The Fort"—and turned up Highway 15 toward Winnsboro and Baskin and Mangham and Alto, headed for Monroe and the interstate, and, ultimately, home.

The cotton left from the autumnal picking hung in limp and sodden shreds in the fields. It was blue-gray outside, and a little snow was beginning to accumulate in the empty fields. But no matter. We kept thinking of the woman who had lived her faith and of the man who said, with utter pride, "That's my church."

Boeuf Prairie was home all the time.

What I saw, that February day in 1978, was the enduring pride of North Louisiana. And North Louisiana, I think as this winter tightens its own grip, is Boeuf Prairie, and Boeuf Prairie is forever.

## *The Free Ferry at Duty*

July 8, 1979

It was Steven Lawson who told me about the free ferry at Duty. He had read one of *The Times* North Louisiana editorials and suggested that the Duty ferry might provide some good material.

Ellen, Aunt Marie, Kevin, Amy Ringheim and I took off on Steve's directions early one Sunday afternoon, and we made good time. The delta roads on both sides of the Ouachita River in Northeast Louisiana are straight and swift, swooping into places like Grayson and Holum and Rosefield on the west and Liddieville and Jigger and Holly Grove on the east.

But Louisiana 559 leaps off the ponderous bow of Route 165 at Columbia like a dusty green arrow. It flies past the McKeithen Plantation, parallels the Ouachita right up to its edge, and knifes through fresh-plowed soybean fields en route to its target and our destination: the ferry at Duty.

And, just as Steve told me, it's a free ferry, right where the arrow of 559 splashes into the river, and it's the only way across—a time warp, an almost literal gap in the river of history, a Ouachita ride on the waters of days forever gone.

The *W. Prescott Foster*, an ancient gray-and-white river tug that once plied the Mississippi out of Baton Rouge, hauled us, our car, and several pick-up trucks across the Ouachita. The old tug heaved and struggled at the ramp, panting black smoke in the strain.

But once in deeper waters the tug moved us all with breast stroking ease. And we could look into the depths of the Ouachita, an obscure, bottom-of-the-bottle green this cool May Sabbath. I let the river passage float me back as we cross—back to cotton instead of soybeans, to old flags and blue bonnets.

It only lasts a moment, that ferry passage, but there is in the mind a sense of history, of something gone and recovered only briefly and lost again, in the crossing—a feeling Amy and Anne Marie and Kevin, caught up in the wonder of the ride, seemed to miss entirely.

The Duty ferry done, we glided through Enterprise and on to Harrisonburg. Just outside this place we climbed out of the flatlands into a high stand of pine trees—the air freshened—and falling away sharply below is Harrisonburg.

There it sits quietly, a church steeple and the columned Catahoula Parish Courthouse, in the embrace of the Ouachita—which, flanked by soybean fields and fringed by willows, meanders on toward Jonesville.

We stopped for cold drinks and conversation at a small Harrisonburg filling station. A snow-haired observer tapped his cane on a bench outside. Then the road was reversed because the children were tired and not looking outside anymore; and because I wanted to ride the Duty ferry one more time.

The kids were reading comic books as the *W. Prescott Foster* pulled us across the river a second time this afternoon. Soon we would ride the 559 arrow toward Interstate 20 and home.

But the gentle current at the Duty ferry had somehow taken me back home, across a great river, one more time. And that passage at Duty, even though Anne Marie and Amy and Kevin don't know it now, is ever so brief.

## *Yes, It Is November in North Louisiana*

November 11, 1979

The summer is only just gone, surely. And September . . . doggone it, September, we hardly knew you. Where are the watermelons and butterbeans? School only just started, it seems; and with the books it was football, and October . . . was there an October?

It was all a blur; a sudden chill-edged morning, a dead battery, a shotgun shell in the woods, a red leaf in the wind, an end to twilight. Yet, the hummingbirds are gone south and the sky—well, the sky is all at once a very intense blue. Blinding almost.

Is it, then, November in North Louisiana? No, it's not November. It could not be November. Yes, face it, before it's too late. November it is; almost two weeks into the eleventh month of the year, at that. Here we are walking the last rickety bridge between autumn and winter. November, as unexpectedly as it arrived, seems old, somehow.

Thanksgiving is almost upon us, for gosh sakes; it's a bare week and a half distant. And those two holidays, Thanksgiving and Christmas, so different in mood and method, are actually jammed one on top of the other. Christmas? Don't even think about it; somebody might string the lights across Main Street, and rob us of yet another passage.

So keep quiet about Christmas. It's still fall, anyway; even if November sneaked up on us and whispered, all soft wind in our ear, "you are missing a whole season." And late fall is the time of collard greens sealed by first frost; the time when collards smell the loudest and taste the best. Mrs. Hilman's wild pear tree is a remarkable red now; before this month is gone its leaves will burn like an oil fire, dark and violent.

Here and there, too, there are glimpses of falling gold, and those thoughts of growing old. From the summit of a hill shown to us by Sonny Barnard we can look far down. It is quiet, and leaves spiral down slowly, rhythmically, not afraid, like children drifting off to sleep.

And in the cool solitude of the woods below, down the cluttered slope to the creek, there are leaves on the water. Viking ships they are in what remains of the child's mind; or, in the adult consciousness, Chinese sampans, floating serenely in the slow but inevitable current. There they go, these ship-leaves, twisting, spinning, turning out of sight toward an unknown destination on the dark, autumnal flow.

They are the last glorious fleet of all, these leaves on the water. They are riding out on sails of amber, orange and lemon, and they are bright and bold. But they are the last ships of the season, these leaves, and soon they will disappear around the bend of the creek on that slow current. Gone.

Maybe we are so slow to notice November because it is the dying season in North Louisiana. But up the bank of the creek, in the mulch of the leaf, is the dormant stuff of life. For under the debris, in a graveyard of bramble, microscopic yet monumental forces are at work.

They are, our neighbor-zoologist John Goertz has told us, forest floor invertebrates; the earthworm, the millipede, the springtail and the familiar rolypoly. This is their world, this rot and ruin, and in the great leaf-fall of November, they eat.

These organisms, unseen and unappreciated, do their crucial work in nature's redemptive cycle; their eating is the breaking-down of material, of mold, so that minerals are returned to the earth. So it is once again that in death, the death of a season, there is life.

Yes, it is November in November Louisiana, and the leaves are on the water. For the leaf-ships of autumn, brilliant in their moment, the final destination is beyond December and January and February; beyond winter even. It is spring, really, that lies around the bend of the creek, sleeping under a quilt of clutter.

It's November all right, and the leaves are on the water.

But that is only the beginning of it all.

## *Milkworms and Magic and Morgan's Pond*

July 13, 1980

"One cannot help but be amused by the armament these fishermen have raised against the wily bass," wrote James Seay in his excellent essay, "The Southern Outdoors: Bass Boats and Bear Hunts," for the book, *The American South*.

That observation took me back a few years to a magical pond just off Highway 80 East outside of Ruston where, armed with milkworms dug out of a pecan orchard and splintery cane poles, Bill Upchurch and I challenged all records for numbers of bluegill, white perch, goggle-eye and bass caught in the course of two childhoods.

This place was called Morgan's Pond, and it was more than a mere fishing hole; it was a way of life for Bill and me. Those July mornings we literally raced separately for the pond; me through a tropical growth that extended from the edge of Marbury Drive to the water's edge and Bill from up and across then-roaring Highway 80 to Monroe.

Once we were established on the dam (where our fishing day always started), the world receded from that piney sanctuary into oblivion; Morgan's Pond was our world, even into the first years of high school when most young lives became automated and thus forever altered. Our friends honked at us from the highway; we distractedly waved them away and checked our tiny blue bream hooks.

We always caught something at Morgan's Pond. The mystery was what species would be dragged out of the water. Dug in 1900, there were actually two ponds separated by a pinestraw-carpeted dam. What we called "the little pond" was scarcely more than a mudhole; it was jammed slam against the highway and sat there still and red like a bowl of Campbell's tomato soup with a little milk added for good measure.

However, even that placid bowl of soup next to the highway held a special prize—incredibly large, red-chested chinquapin bream. Positioning the cork just outside the shade line cast by two enormous pines on the dam guaranteed at least a couple of these fighting, flounder-sized creatures.

But the little pond was only a sideshow. The big pond, a teardrop shaped lagoon of black-green water, dominated our minds. It was a fish cafeteria; decide where to fish and hence what to catch.

The Western bank, a tangle of pine and sweetgum, was designated for speckled perch. We fished the dam for battling, handsized bluegill. The eastern shore was reserved for goggle-eye that fought like banshees, making our light line scream for mercy. The slough, at the tail of the teardrop, raged with largemouth bass.

Bets could be laid on what would be caught out of those particular holes, but part of the fun was that, no, we couldn't be sure, ever, of what was tearing up the water. This was because the ponds were fed by a big underground stream that tunneled under the highway. The underground spring surfaced in a branch on the other side of Old 80 that, in turn, ran into Choudrant Creek.

So, besides the resident bass, bluegill, chinquapin and goggle-eye, Bill and I occasionally landed what we called a sunfish—a creature painted in the hues of broken rainbows, so beautiful we always threw it back.

The appetite of the fish in those ponds, established for well over a half-century when we discovered them, is not a childhood dream. When Bill and I ran out of milkworms—or exhausted the red wrigglers we shoveled out of the Upchurch dogyard—the bluegill went nuts over Holsum bread filched from our mothers' pantries.

Gradually, Bill and I moved up from the cane poles to rods and reels. Bill's dad was an expert angler and his tacklebox bulged with more than three hundred lures. We learned casting on the dam at Morgan's Pond, snagging Hawaiian Wrigglers on the overhanging twin pines.

The first largemouth bass I ever caught blasted a white jitterbug tossed into the far end of the slough, sending up a plume of spray and showing me a green gatemouth that flooded my fourteen-year-old consciousness with awe and amazement.

Bill and I had a series of those arrogant bass snap our lines, including one outraged Moby Dick that surfaced all over the big pond for a full half-hour, trying to spit out an offending Tiny Torpedo.

But my best memories of the rod-and-reel time on Morgan's Pond are focused on a lone stob in the smackdab middle of the big water. Drop a black River Runt an inch to the left or right of that enchanted stob and the result was always the same: reeling in a pound-and-a-half "speck."

It was like pulling in a log, not much of a fight, but the fun was not diminished; it took pinpoint casting to crease the Great Stob. It also took a hard and long throw from the dam to reach that bull's-eye.

Bill's dad introduced him to a Pflueger Supreme reel. On the Upchurchs' good advice, I saved up for a whisper-quiet, green Shakespeare with silk gears. Some of the specks the Shakespeare produced were so large I ran home with them to show my parents.

Before we discovered the rod and reel, Bill and I had already run into trouble in the paradise of Morgan's Pond. It started when we made the mistake of dragging a washtub slick with bluegill through the backyard of one of the owners of the pond—who had spent a week on Black Lake near Natchitoches without achieving half our catch.

The pond was forbidden to me after that, but the ban only added another dimension of attraction to the place. We sneaked down to the dam just as much, and caught almost as many goggle-eye. Daddy added his injunction to the ban on Morgan's Pond, but after Bill and I caught him cleverly camouflaged on the west bank, fishing for those magnificent specks with triple-pronged hooks and minnows, his edict lost all moral force. Mrs. Morgan would sometimes yell us away from her brick house on the hill overlooking the pond, but we always came back.

What finally took me away from Morgan's Pond was a 1957 Chevy, a blond named Ellen and the deadlines of the *Ruston Daily Leader*. My seven-years-younger brother Chet Hilburn inherited my Shakespeare reel (he ruined it) and Morgan's Pond. He regaled me with stories of shark-sized specks when I came home from the graduate school of journalism at LSU. Morgan's Pond slowly receded into a golden childhood and I have never really fished seriously since then.

But, in an era when great impoundments like Toledo Bend and D'Arbonne lakes have turned bassin' into a televised science, I still think longingly of the magic and milkworms of Morgan's Pond where Bill Upchurch and I grew up.

## *A Crazy-Quilt for Thanksgiving*

November 23, 1980

There is a good, high perspective near Gibsland in Bienville Parish. From this summit, in these last autumn hours before Thanksgiving, North Central Louisiana looks like one of Grandmother Kate Trussell's crazy-quilts: haphazard, unsymmetrical patches of amber, red, green, lemon and orange.

It's a perspective that I pull over me like one of those old quilts on Kate's big bed at Antioch from vanished childhood autumns. The quilt was light, but it warmed me—and there was the clean-musty smell of security in those rough covers.

Indeed, there is something secure about the whole Thanksgiving season. A lot of scattered, random, small blessings weave into something solid and warm that, in another season, would go unnoticed and unappreciated.

Around this time of the year, though, I do begin to notice a few little things: like the Air Force-ROTC cadets sounding taps as they carefully pull down the American flag right outside my Kenny Hall office window at Tech. The sound is at once proud, sad, hopeful.

Then, just the other day, a young construction worker on campus caught me at the door of the Karmann Ghia, hog-tied by a typewriter, twenty-two folders and four number two yellow pencils. "Let me get that door for you," he says. I notice that cheerful kindness; it's Thanksgiving season after all.

Suddenly, there is more to notice: six different hues of turning sweetgums counted in an hour between Ruston and Shreveport; the smell of my mother-in-law's collard greens; the golden shower of hickory leaves in the backyard. And there is Daddy in his backyard, strong as ever, grinding up compost for his spring garden. Thanksgiving.

There is the moon coming to life on one side of Black Lake near Natchitoches and the sun dying beyond the other bank. And there is the tough kid from Grant Parish who wrote, "Hey, Hilburn, I'm a closet reader of 'Fragments.' " Thanksgiving.

Ellen is gone for a night, and I miss her. Kevin is on the honor roll at Ruston High School; Greg brings a girl named Cindy home. Anne Marie tells me she will be playing Mary in the eighth-grade Christmas play. "All I have to do is look tranquil all the time," she says, grinning. Thanksgiving.

The ninety-sixth anniversary of Ruston's First Presbyterian Church is celebrated—home-fried chicken, deviled eggs and squash casserole on the grounds—and I talk to a lot of people who raised me in the church. It's Thanksgiving.

Best of all, maybe, the hill country roads are still open to me these cool last hours of November. They are free roads, fair roads and friendly, and blowing with the leaves of the season. It is on such a road near Gibsland, a rising road, that I notice the crazy-quilt perspective of North Louisiana. This is where I remember Kate.

This is where I find Thanksgiving.

# *"'Way up Saline, a Dog Died"*

February 21, 1981

They were 'way up Saline Bayou—past Salsbury Bridge and Sand Point and deep into the still rank-smelling cypress wilderness. The few who come this far don't like to talk about it, for fear that others may start coming in numbers that will rip and tear the heart out of the place.

That's where they first saw the little dog last spring—'way up in the wilderness of the National Forest run of the bayou—wearing a flea collar and gnawing on the last bony remains of an alligator.

The high water had isolated a stretch of ground where the bayou made a big turn. It was a small male dog, evidently very young, with short black hair. Shy and scared, it ran quickly into the brush and disappeared when they called and whistled.

Back at their Saline Lake Camp, the couple speculated that the pup had come in with some other, older dogs and somehow gotten itself stranded on the creek turn. It could easily swim out and find its way back home—or maybe somebody would come looking. The flea collar proved that somebody owned the dog.

The next weekend the pair fished the same wild stretch, and there—stretched out beside the skeleton of the gator—was the same black dog. This time they beached the boat; the dog was obviously lost—lost and trapped.

But, again, the small pup retreated quietly and swiftly into the willows. The dog never barked once, but it moved quickly when they approached. A long search failed to locate him. Wood ducks broke for cover, but the black dog was not to be found.

The third weekend, they had to admit, was reserved not for fishing, but for rescuing the dog—though he assured her that this time the animal would be gone. Surely. They didn't fish at all; it was just a matter of measuring the distance between an abandoned stove, the last sign of civilization, and that turn in the creek.

Guiding the boat past the pipeline, he thought about how much she had worried about this little dog all week. She owned three dogs, loved them, and also specialized in nursing broken-winged birds back to health. Things like this hurt her. Surely, he thought, the dog would be gone this weekend. He hoped so.

They made the turn on Saline, and there was the dog—again lying close to the alligator bones. They raced for the spot, gunned the motor, but again the dog disappeared. This time, though, she noticed that the pup ran very slowly when they approached. Very slowly. "He's starving," she said, tears in her eyes. But another search, pushed nearly to dark, failed to turn up the dog.

The fourth weekend she came prepared with five pounds of dogfood. The trip was the same, with green herons scattering in their hurried wake. She was anxious. And there, in the same place, loomed the turn, the alligator skeleton and—she was elated—the dog. Her partner landed the boat, ramming it up on the bank.

This time, however, the dog did not run. The spring breeze ruffled its black fur, but that special and utter stillness—that unutterable stillness—told the story before they got there. The dog was dead, starved to death, beside the alligator skeleton.

It wasn't a big deal, not a big tragedy, he told her. A dog had died up Saline. She just sat up in the front of the boat, holding five pounds of dogfood. He couldn't see her face. But her shoulders shook all the way back to Saline Lake.

## *Kate's House: The Last Moonrise*

July 26, 1981

It was, I thought at the time, an illusion.

Robert Barham and I were recently parked in the rutted driveway of my Grandmother Kate Trussell's old house at Antioch's four corners, talking quietly and listening to a screech owl over in the pine thicket.

That's when I saw the moonrise, a bright lantern of a moonrise, right through the tin roof of Kate's house. I didn't even tell Bob about it, he thinks I'm crazy, anyway. We left soon on the ten-mile ride back to Ruston, but the moon stayed in my mind.

An illusion.

But then I walked into Shipley's cafe the other morning and Eddie Hood, who was raised in Antioch and knows every redclay sweetgum and gas well in that whole rock-spined territory, told me they were tearing down Kate's old house.

It was a blow, although I tried to hide the disappointment. The moonrise wasn't an illusion, after all. I just saw it through a skeleton of rafters. Kate's house, after all that time, was coming down. And it hurt because I've often stopped there at the four corners.

I don't know why, exactly. Kate has been gone for a long time, and, for years the old house has been a rotting eyesore. It belongs to somebody else. It's just that I could pull up there, near Kate's house, and sift my thoughts and somehow feel better. Consoled.

Crazy, Bob would say—crazy sentimentalism—and he's right. Now, though, I'm not sure where to resolve those restless hours. I used to stop at my other grandparents' old house on West Alabama Street in Ruston before it was torn down, too.

The land sits there at Antioch, of course, and some of it is still in the family. Somehow, though, it won't be the same without the old tin-roofed country house. Maybe I'll go back, after the tearing down is done, but I doubt it.

There was something final about the last moonrise at Kate's house.

The sign says Salem United Methodist Church, and it's a landmark set square against the flying feet of time in the shadowed green hills of North Central Louisiana. The church itself, which stands quietly among a half-dozen regal oak trees at a junction of Louisiana Highway 151 out of Dubach, is made out of native iron ore rock.

In fact, it was about this time in 1939, in the heat of July, when the men of Salem community began to haul the stones out of their fields and woods and to raise them, one by one, with their own hands.

That hard work was completed in September when the first service was held in the ironstone sanctuary. Actually, that new rock building was erected on the same property the Salem Church purchased when it was organized in 1859—the third building, most probably, in all that time. The first Salem Church was a cabin with a split-log floor.

The stones for this last structure were transported to the site in mule-drawn wagons. Then, led by a rock mason from Gibsland named Jones, the Nobles, the Dyes, the Henrys, the Mitchells, the McCrarys—with others, the names of north central Louisiana—labored it up that summer of thirty-nine, rock by rock, sweating, until it was all done by September.

So it stands today, enduring, a cool, cobwebby sanctuary of stone. Inside the ornaments of worship are few, but they are—I notice—made of sturdy wood that will survive. It's small, this church, really small. There is no great organ to sound—no grand cathedral this—but the old hymns will be sung proudly here.

Outside again, within the brown shadow of the church, the light summer wind makes only a small stirring in the old oaks. The dirtdauber nests stuck to the crevices of the rocks are undisturbed. They belong, too.

There is an aura of peace and permanence all about, and Salem United Methodist Church seems to speak to the character of rural North Louisiana: plain and unpretentious, but with a spine of solid iron ore rock that stands against time and the river.

## *Vienna's Syrup Bucket Mystery*

February 28, 1982

Times were hard around Vienna, La., in the early 1930s; times were hard everywhere. The railroad had long since bypassed this North Central Louisiana community for Ruston, and the Depression didn't help matters either. But these were proud hill-country folks—farmers, mostly—and if anybody did go hungry, well, it wasn't something you talked about.

Of course, none of the kids at the Vienna schoolhouse seemed hungry those days; money was non-existent but people had always raised enough food to eat. Or said they did. The school children, in any event, were happily and loudly swapping sandwiches by recess.

The fact that T. C. and his sister wouldn't participate, ever, in the swapping was the start of the problem. Instead of eating with the group, T. C. and his sister unfailingly slipped away from the hilltop school to open the syrup bucket which contained their lunch. They ate alone. Every lunch period. Every day.

It was only natural that the other kids got curious about what T. C. and his sister had in their syrup bucket. T. C. wouldn't answer questions about it and his sister stood shy and silent behind him. But every high noon that rose over Vienna the brother and sister eased off down the hill, past the outhouses to a tangle of pine and sweetgum to eat their lunch. In private.

The mystery of why T. C. and his sister wanted to eat by themselves eventually turned from kidding to open irritation. Spying didn't work and T. C. kept the syrup bucket close to him with the lid on tight. Most of the Vienna kids had plain, spartan fare and speculation grew that T. C. and his sister were eating high on the hog; that maybe there was even fancy store-bought candy in their syrup bucket. It was contrary, even downright mean of old T. C. and his silly kid sister not to share or to swap. That was everybody's feeling, anyway.

Irritation continued to mount and finally a couple of kids tried to take T. C.'s syrup bucket by main force. Well, T. C. fought like somebody possessed, kicking and screaming and biting. He won the fight and hung on to the syrup bucket. And later that day T. C. and his sister slipped down the hill under the barrage of catcalls where, once again, they ate their lunch alone.

What finally happened was inevitable. One of the big, brash kids swiped T. C.'s syrup bucket early in the morning before school started and, with a great yell, pried the lid off while everybody gathered around to see what unsharable goodies were hidden inside.

Then everybody got quiet.

Real quiet.

That surprised, open-mouthed kind of quiet.

Because there was nothing, not a crumb—*nothing*—in T. C.'s bucket.

He lashed out at everybody within reach, cried himself red-eyed down behind the outhouses, and wouldn't come to school until the teacher escorted him in by the ear an hour later. But T. C., even after all that, wouldn't answer any questions and his sister, like always, stood right behind him. Silent.

None of T. C.'s classmates understood it, but a couple of boys went to see their grandmother—one of those great mamaws who knew about everything and everybody. Of course, Mamaw already knew all about T. C., his sister and the empty syrup bucket. She had known all along.

"Boys," Mamaw told them, not unkindly but with a flake or two of flint in her low voice, "every morning when T. C. and his sister left home that syrup bucket was full up to the top. *With pride*." Mamaw let those last two words, *with pride*, come out like hollow-point bullets. They hit home.

"But you and your schoolmates," she finished, "have taken T. C.'s pride away."

The boys understood then, and the mystery of the empty syrup bucket was settled at Vienna school. In fact, nobody ever spoke of it again. Yes, the kids did sort of make a little room for T. C. and his little sister after that—until the circle closed and both of them were just Vienna school kids again. Pride and all.

Was this story of the empty syrup bucket at Vienna made up? Maybe, but it was told to me by Jewette Farley, Lincoln Parish's tax assessor who is a native and still a resident of Vienna, La. The subject came up after my recent column on the depression and the answer to it from area readers.

Jewette, you should know, is Ruston's answer to Will Rogers—full of folk wisdom and tales about the hill-country and proud of his red-clay ancestry. But Jewette swears this is a true story—about T. C. and his empty syrup bucket—and I believe him.

After all, Jewette's grandmother told him the story for the gospel truth, and his grandmother—as everybody in Vienna knows—didn't lie. It doesn't matter anyway. Given the abiding character of North Louisiana, I imagine there were a lot of T. C.'s and empty syrup buckets around these parts during the depression. A lot of pride, too.

## *Let Us Look, Please, Before Winter Comes*

October 30, 1983

*'Slow me down, Lord'*

—Richard Cardinal Cushing

From the end of the dam to the other the little lake reflects the colors of North Louisiana in November; an opaque rendering of reds and russets and lemons that fall out twenty feet from the tree-lined banks.

In the late afternoon, when a rosy flush lights up the landscape, the whole pond is literally a watercolor painting of autumn in mid-course. Of course, winter lies just beyond the horizon; the reflection will dim and disappear with the black limbs and dark torrents of that approaching season.

But for now the colors of fall have dyed the waters. The result is a mirror held to the face of November, a reflection of time and a season—a thing of beauty of which poets speak. Yet, so few of us stop to look.

Slow us down, Lord, and make us look—before winter comes and finally darkens the lights in the water that reflects autumn in North Louisiana.

Legend has it that Davy Crockett stopped at Cloud's Crossing en route to the Alamo; legend also has it that A. V. Tait Jr., our guide for this late October foray into Northwest Louisiana, "heard a whippoorwill sing on Saline, and knew what Hand Williams meant."

Saline Bayou does come singing through Cloud's Crossing, running hard and swift over cypress stumps, dividing Winn and Natchitoches parishes. The crossing stands tall in gum and hickory, its cool floor scattered with hay from trail rides, and Mr. Tait tells us we missed the great autumnal color-turn by a week.

No matter. It's easy to see why Crockett may have camped at this crossing; or why, as also rumored, the James and Dalton gangs rested their horses here. Or why the Taits, and others from as far away as Oregon, light the crossing with their campfires these soft fall weekends.

Cut just into the national forest, Cloud's Crossing has a wildness about it; a deer is almost sure to break across Louisiana 1233. Yet, there is a sheltered look about this place—maybe it's the tall trees—and a good measure of seclusion too. And, as we said, Saline Bayou fairly sings through here.

Mr. Tait has taken us the long way to Cloud's Crossing, he said, because it's nicer. We headed out of Jonesboro on 167 south, took the first right past the Red Barn on Louisiana 126. From there we crossed the Dugdemona River, passed Brewton's mill, and turned left on 1233 into the national forest—and there was Cloud's Crossing.

From Cloud's Crossing, it was straight on to Black Lake, which we crossed with moonrise on one side and sunset on the other. We finally stopped for a supper of catfish and green tomato pickles at Lakewood Inn. The whole tour is recommended—by us and Davy Crockett and Jesse James and A. V. Tait of Jonesboro.

We left Northcentral Louisiana in a spatter of rain last week, under skies the tint and texture of out-of-style gray flannel pants, with the temperature at seventy-eight degrees, and the car air conditioner running.

The calendar said October, but the season was summer, and humidly so. Fall seemed far down the road this soggy early afternoon, despite the number of hunters in their fluorescent caps and green jackets patrolling the woods' rim in Claiborne and Union parishes.

Yet, when we got out of the car not far across the Arkansas line and just a few miles up Highway 167 to shake hands with the Craig Durretts, recently added to *The Times* family and themselves headed for El Dorado, it was—in a rush of north wind and a swirl of sycamore leaves—unmistakably autumn.

Everything was finally altered at that chance meeting the other side of Junction City, and suddenly we were shivering in the short-sleeved shirts that, a season and a half-hour before in Lincoln Parish, had seemed so appropriate. Now headed north for a meeting with the Arkansas Press Women, we changed clothes, moods and climates. It was fall at last.

And crossing the Ouachita at Calion, we ran into signs that confirmed that changing of the seasons. For in southeastern Arkansas, the gums are turning—turning to lemon and russet, and even to deep and burning orange.

The cool wind sharpened our senses, it seemed, and we observed a low-built barn with a moss roof, hay square-baled in the fields, seas of black-eyed susans, and a swaying pick-up truck which advertised: "When you cuss a farmer, don't talk with your mouth full."

We saw the skies clearing, showing an eggshell blue over Hampton's (population 1,601) green water tower and Corner Cafe. Some of the Hamptonites had put on their winter coats and the neighborly talk in this town, even as we zipped through, seemed alert and animated and free of summer.

Of course, the front had pushed the cold air and the season into North Louisiana by the time we got back home, but for us the fall of 1978 was born oh so miraculously, so very swiftly, just across the state line, somewhere between Junction City and El Dorado, Ark.

## *A Book About Us, a Century Ago*

May 27, 1984

In the violent Reconstruction times of North Louisiana, it wasn't the Hatfields against the McCoys but the Grahams against the Greens. It was a lethal time, when armed bands from Lincoln, Claiborne, Union, Jackson and Bienville parishes hunkered down at night in D'Arbonne bottom—braced for an attack from Federal calvary.

E. M. Graham, a Confederate officer in the Civil War, led what was nothing less than a guerrilla war against the forces of Radical Republicanism, headed by former Union loyalist Allen Greene. The battleground, again, was Northcentral Louisiana, and the issue was not completely decided until a Washington political deal ended Reconstruction in 1876.

This dramatic hill country duel is the focal point of Dr. William Y. Thompson's new book, *E. M. Graham: North Louisianian* (Center for Louisiana Studies, University of Southwestern Louisiana, Lafayette, La.). But the full-length view mirrors North Louisiana a century ago as seen through the life of one of this region's most prominent citizens—the same E. M. Graham.

Van Graham, as he was known, rose to prominence as a Confederate colonel, lawyer, judge and political, civil and church leader from the 1860s to the early part of the twentieth century. He lived in Downsville, Vienna, Vernon and Ruston, where he died in 1908—the very epitome of pillar-of-the-community cliche. Graham's Hill is still a Ruston landmark. So is the old First Presbyterian Church, where Graham and his family worshipped.

But, as Thompson points out, it was Graham's "implacable" bid to wrest this region from Radical Republican control, whatever that took, which made his name. He was, writes Thompson, "ever the sober-sided God-fearing and proper man, a stereotyped Victorian who found himself in the pine hills of North Louisiana."

Yet, as Thompson says, the cold and Cromwellian Graham was also a rebel "in the two most important segments of his life, the Civil War and the Reconstruction." In both instances, the unromantic but utterly unafraid Graham was prepared to lay down his life "outside the law."

He was wounded while leading Confederate troops into the flaming mouths of Union cannons at the historically bloody Battle of Franklin, Tenn. Then, ten years later, there was Graham "lying with his friends in D'Arbonne Swamp anticipating an attack by Federal troops."

Graham's archfoe in that last war against Reconstruction was Greene, regarded at the time as a scalawag legislator who had nevertheless brought Lincoln Parish into political being. Thompson, in a balanced judgment, obviously finds Greene the more human of the pair—more gentle and more generous.

In that desperate and often dangerous combat between two so different men—both of whom remained armed even in their homes—Thompson wisely decides against choosing a hero. "Allen Greene . . . was a man ahead of his time, the tolerant, farsighted village sage who sought to heal the wounds of war and welcome the new freedmen into public life, and yet a man whose political self-aggrandizement would call into question . . . his motives."

Graham, on the other side of the schism, is seen as "the man more in keeping with his time . . . his people, who led the struggle against the excesses and sometimes bad government of Reconstruction, and yet a man willing to resort to force and violence to thwart changes . . . that were anathema to him." Graham was respected, even by his enemies, but not loved.

In the end, Thompson finds Graham the "proper rebel, similar to so many of his generation in North Louisiana. . . ." He never doubted, not once, the rectitude of his Presbyterian God nor his political cause. "Of such stuff romantics are not made," acknowledges the author.

"But Graham never pretended to be one (a romantic) and would have been most uncomfortable with such an image," writes Thompson. "He (Graham) may not always have been right. But it is extremely doubtful if he could have been persuaded that he was not. Such was Evander McNair Graham. And so were hundreds of North Louisianians a century ago."

That last line sums up what Thompson has done in his book: That is, to portray upland North Louisiana as it was one hundred years ago, and to hold that mirror up to this very generation. The author would say that Van Graham's life made for that exciting tale, but Thompson is a skillful storyteller, an accomplished *writer* as well as historian who has already produced two other well-received books.

So on that score, he advised: This is *not* yet another local book praising unstinted another local if obscure hero, to be dutifully reviewed by a colleague who has engraved a similar tombstone of a volume. No, Thompson writes the way he teaches as chairman of Tech's history department. He is dramatic in an appropriately low key, possessed of a dark wit and sense of humor, and yet ever the researching scholar.

For example, Thompson fondly dwells on the black sheep of the Graham family. This is a certain Uncle Henry who breaks sober-sided tradition to "drink copiously" and declare that he "did not love his wife as he used to and intended to get a divorce."

As Thompson tells it, the wayward Uncle Henry was finally collared by his Presbyterian clan at a camp rally "up on Hatchet Creek" where he signed an oath promising never to imbibe again. Uncle Henry's "poor wife on hearing it rejoiced aloud" but Thompson recalls that this rebellious Graham soon rebelled again.

This is, then, a well-written and readable book by any measure—one that provides perhaps the first serious historical measure of our own North Louisiana—and it's available in area bookstores. It is, in the end, a book about us, one hundred years ago. I enjoy it.

## *Maybe Some Things Are Forever*

November 25, 1984

In the eye of the poet, "the mighty oak" has ever loomed large and tall, taking on human dimensions of greatness, fortitude, stability and endurance. Nobody will argue those noble personifications.

But as November runs its leafy, sun-blinking course to the far corners of fall, I'm thinking of a pair of big beech trees discovered a half dozen years ago off the Old Vernon Road in Jackson Parish. I wonder now if those beech twins, the subject of an editorial written at the time, are still standing.

Of course, the beech—unlike the oak—is not characteristically associated, in human terms, with strength and stamina. Yet, I consulted the Lincoln Parish Library section on Southern trees and read that beech wood is hard, tight-grained and tough—the stuff of tool handles.

And this matching Jackson Parish pair, which I left guarding a dead spring at the foot of a gentle incline, would hold their bronze and gold leaves as long—or longer—than the most persistent oak in a forest of colored flags.

But there is more to beech wood than toughness and endurance and leaves that defy the winds of November. If the oak is a noble creature, somehow elevated above us mortals, the beech is friendly and sympathetic. A confidant, even.

And though the Jackson beech twins were located well off the beaten path ("don't say exactly where they are," said our guide, "because some idiot may come and cut them down"), they displayed the marks of such contact with humankind.

"Jack Plus Mary" and "Tim Loves Susan" and a dozen other such tributes to romance were engraved on the white-gray trunks of the beech twosome. How many times, I wondered then, had a beech tree acted as a go-between in shy encounters of the heart?

Such beech trees have also preserved many a confidence of secret love, unbetrayed, for all time. Oftentimes a Mary or a Tim never knew that somebody cared, but that love was all the same written on the bark of a beech—there to withstand time and wind and river.

If the two old North Louisiana beeches I saw carried the literal knife-scars of love, they had also heard—and recorded—other human cries. A simple "1950" was carved deep into the great stem of one of the Old Vernon twins—consecrating, in that tranquil and turning wood, some event of gladness or sadness.

I don't know what confidence was poured out—or carved out, in this case—that day in 1950, but the beech tree knew. And if those beeches were engraved with unspoken pleas and prayers, they had also joined in the childhood play and laughter of a whole region.

No, I can't be sure that a gang of fourteen-year-olds dangled from the limbs of the particular Jackson Parish beech pair. But which of us has not, at one time or the other in the bright summer of our youth, hung from the kind arms of a beech that stood, inevitably, over the creek swimming hole?

And if the oak is a thing of beauty, who can deny the impossible balance, the perfect symmetry, of a beech tree's branch-spread? Those beech twins of Old Vernon, standing high in their gold halos, yielded nothing to beauty either—and yet were marked as down-to-earth confidants of humankind.

I think of them—in my mind's eye—as still mounting sentinels, this very hour, over a dry creek bed, and over the sentiments of a whole generation. And I think, picturing the beech pair, that maybe some things are forever. Maybe.

It was Kevin, exploring the rim of a wild-grown pond, who found another beech tree on my in-laws' property off the Rough Edge Road in Lincoln Parish. He showed it to me, just the other day, and I remembered the girl of my dreams.

"Bootsie Loves Ellen," I had carved into that tree, and there it was, worn but still clear.

That message was written on beech bark more than twenty-five years ago, most probably. And now, as the leaves bury this golden autumn of 1984, I think—again—that maybe, just maybe, some things are forever.

# CAJUN MUSIC*

Barry Jean Ancelet

Skeptics wondered at his forsaking current trends, but the recording, an unexpected success, presaged a revival of the earlier styles. Iry LeJeune became a pivotal figure in a revival fueled by the return of homesick GIs seeking to soothe their *mal de pays* in a hot, cultural bath. All over the country, soldiers wanted to eat home cooking. In South Louisiana that meant rice and gravy and gumbo, no more potatoes. And they wanted to hear homemade music. In South Louisiana, that meant Cajun music, no more Hit Parade for a while. These soldiers literally populated the dance halls where they drank and danced to forget the horrors of the war. Dance halls which provided traditional music flourished, and musicians such as Lawrence Walker, Austin Pitre, and Nathan Abshire brought their abandoned accordions out of the closet and once again recorded old-style Cajun music.

The musicians who helped to revive Cajun music in the late 1940s and early 1950s were not only historically important. They were also fine performers and folk poets. The revival of the 1950s consequently produced a corpus of new songs to go along with the retooled traditional sounds. Iry LeJeune adapted many older Amédé Ardoin songs, preserving some elements, such as Ardoin's symbolic mistress Joline, while adding new words and tightening the lyrics. Often working with his friend and producer Eddie Shuler, he also composed a few memorable songs of his own, including "Grand Bosco" and "J'ai fait une grosse erreur."

As a bandleader, Lawrence Walker was a perfectionist. He carefully controlled and crafted the sound of his Wandering Aces band. He was also a gifted singer and composed several Cajun music classics, including "Petits yeux noirs" and the "Reno Waltz." In his "Chère Alice," Walker gave a final form to the story-song about the ill-fated love between Alice Royer and petit Dom Hanks. His "Valse du malchanceux" demonstrates Walker's solid sense of oral poetics.

*Excerpts first published in Barry Jean Ancelet, *Cajun Music: Its Origins and Development* (Lafayette, La.: Center for Louisiana Studies, University of Southwestern Louisiana 1989), 32-51. Reprinted with the kind permission of the author and the University of Southwestern Louisiana.

Nathan Abshire was also influenced by Amédé Ardoin, though more in style than content. Many of his compositions contain a key word which reflects the major characteristic of his music: "Service Blues," "French Blues," "Popcorn Blues," "Offshore Blues," and his signature song, the "Pine Grove Blues."

Another composer of the post-war revival period, Shirley Bergeron created several beautiful songs, including "La Valse de la belle," the "Old Home Waltz," and "Quelle étoile." Other Cajun singers may have been intimidated by Bergeron's soaring high-pitched vocals; few of his songs entered into the standard dance band repertoire despite their moving storylines. His "J'ai fait mon idée" is typical of the poetics of dance band lyrics: brief, impressionistic, and only suggestive, as compared to the longer, more narrative treatment in other forms such as the ballad, or in the legends or tales of spoken tradition.

In the 1950s, a few musicians, such as Joe Bonsall and Rodney LeJeune, whose families had moved to Texas to work in the oil fields and shipyards, set up bands and began playing Cajun music across the Sabine River in what became known as Cajun Lapland (where Cajun culture laps over into Texas). Local recording pioneers such as George Khoury, Eddie Shuler, J. D. Miller, and later, Floyd Soileau and Carol Rachou, picked up the slack left by the national producers who by then had turned exclusively to widely marketable performers. Though bearing the marks of Americanization, Cajun music was making a dramatic comeback just as interest in the culture and language quickened before the 1955 Acadian bicentennial celebration, led by politicians like Dudley J. LeBlanc and Roy Theriot.

In the early 1950s, many dance bands performed as often as seven and eight times a week. Some of these groups developed a tight, well-orchestrated, dance-band style, keeping the successive eight or sixteen bar instrumental rides learned from swing and bluegrass music. (The typical pattern of instrumental rides which developed in Cajun music was: accordion lead, accordion break, vocal lead, steel guitar shuffle, fiddle break, fiddle lead, accordion break, accordion lead.) Groups incorporated palatable elements from various new styles, including early rock-and-roll, to develop new sounds.

Even the names of many of these revived groups reflected the enduring influence of their brush with Americanization. Lawrence Walker's group was called the Wandering Aces. Austin Pitre's was the Evangeline Playboys, after their native Evangeline Parish. Nathan Abshire called his band the Pine Grove Boys, after their regional hit, the "The Pine Grove Blues."

Some began performing on local radio stations; others, such as Aldus Roger and the Lafayette Playboys and Happy Fats and the Mariné Band, were even featured on area television. Most bands were composed of musicians who made a living from other regular jobs, but a few, such as Jimmy C. Newman and Doug Kershaw, became professionals who only played music for a livelihood. They quickly realized that the Louisiana French market was limited and felt they would have to perform in English if they were to attract an audience large enough to support them. Newman continued to sing a few of his native Cajun songs after he moved from Mamou to Nashville, but his direction was clearly toward American country music. He became a regular on the Grand Old Opry with hits such as "Cry, Cry, Darling" (#9 in May 1954) and "A Fallen Star" (#42, June 1957). He eventually hit the country music charts with a few songs that played on Cajun themes such as "Alligator Man" (#22, December 1961), "Bayou Talk" (#12, December 1962), and "Boo Dan" (#31, May 1969). Kershaw recycled older Cajun tunes to produce new songs with English lyrics, like his "I'm Not Strong Enough," which is based on the ancient "Valse du bambocheur," his "Cajun Stripper," a souped-up version of the "Bosco Stomp," and his "Mama Rita in Hollywood," a revival of the traditional "J'ai été-z-au bal." Like Newman, Kershaw also performed original compositions in which he skillfully exploited his Cajun heritage, such as "Cajun Joe" and his best known hits, "Louisiana Man" (#10, February 1961) and "Diggy Liggy Lo" (#14, August 1961). Kershaw developed a small, national following, even appearing on the CBS television network's immensely popular "Ed Sullivan Show."

In the 1950s and '60s, South Louisiana, like the rest of the nation and much of the world, was affected by the emergence of what came to be called rock and roll. The sons and daughters of Cajun musicians followed the musical lead of fellow Louisiana musicians Jerry Lee Lewis and Antoine "Fats" Domino to produce what English author John Broven has called Swamp Pop. More a songwriter than a performer, Bobby Charles (Guidry) gave American popular culture a lasting line with his "See You Later, Alligator" (#30 on the rhythm and blues charts in 1955 and subsequently an international hit for Bill Haley and the Comets). He also wrote songs that became national hits for Clarence "Frogman" Henry ("But I Do") and Fats Domino ("Four Winds," "Walking to New Orleans," and "Before I Grow Too Old"). Within the region, bands with names like Bobby Page (Elwood Dugas) and the Riff Raffs and Clint West (Clinton Guillory) and the Boogie Kings, recorded songs that made the local hit parade. A few South Louisiana musicians even affected the national pop music scene: Warren Storm (Shexnayder), "Prisoner's Song" (#81, August 1958), Cookie (Huey Thierry) and the Cupcakes, "Mathilda" (#47, January 1959), Rod Bernard and the Twisters, "This Should Go On Forever" (#20, March 1959), Johnny Preston (Courville), "Running Bear" (#10, October 1959), among others. Dale (Houston) and Grace (Broussard) reached #1 on the charts with "I'm Leaving It Up to You" (October 1963).

Country music and swamp pop were tempting alternatives and Cajun music was again straying far afield from its traditional sources. Deliberate efforts would be necessary, in Dewey Balfa's words, "to water the roots so that the tree would not die."

The needed impulse came from the national level. Alan Lomax, a member of the Newport Folk Foundation, had become interested in Cajun and Creole music while collecting, in the 1930s, traditional music across the country for the Library of Congress. In the manner prescribed by activist ethnomusicologist Charles Seeger, Lomax sent "cultural guided missles" to document and encourage the preservation of the music during the 1950s. While a professor of English at Louisiana State University in Baton Rouge,

Harry Oster recorded a musical spectrum which ranged from unaccompanied ballads to contemporary dance tunes, especially in Evangeline and Vermilion parishes. His collection, which stressed the evolution of Cajun music, attracted the attention of local activists like Paul Tate and Revon Reed.

The work of Harry Oster and Alan Lomax caught the imagination of the Newport group, and fieldworkers Ralph Rinzler and Mike Seeger were sent to find Cajun musicians for the festival. Cajun dance bands had played at the National Folk Festival as early as the 1930s (when Lawrence Walker accompanied the Broussard family band to the festival in Dallas), but little echo of these performances reached Louisiana. Rinzler and Seeger, seeking the gutsy roots of Cajun music, invited Gladius Thibodeaux, Louis "Vinesse" LeJeune (a cousin of Iry), and Dewey Balfa to represent Louisiana at the 1964 Newport Folk Festival. There alongside nationally known folk revivalists like Joan Baez, Peter, Paul and Mary, and Bob Dylan, they performed the turn-of-the-century, unamplified music which made the Louisiana cultural establishment uneasy. These "unrefined" sounds embarrassed the upwardly mobile "genteel Acadians" who barely tolerated the more polished sounds of popular dance bands like Belton Richard and the Musical Aces. They considered the music chosen for the Newport Festival crude, "nothing but chanky-chank." An editorial by Burton Grindstaff in the *Opelousas Daily World* (October 20, 1965) unabashedly illustrated this sentiment:

> Cajuns brought some mighty fine things down from Nova Scotia with them, including their jolly selves, but their so-called music is one thing I wish they hadn't.
>
> The first time my sensitive ears were shattered by the dissonant squall of a Cajun musician was in Eunice back in 1946. I was told that an acquaintance of mine, a fellow who seemed to be normal in other respects, was going to play an accordion 'Cajun style' at some kind of local program. I was foolish enough to look forward to the event, and even to think I might be in on the discovery of something great that had been hidden from the rest of the country all these years. I broke through a window after the first stanza, went home and doused my head in a bucket of water to drown out the sound. . . .

Grindstaff ended his column with a prediction:

> I suppose there will be no containing them if they get a really bad needle on one of those records the Newport festival people took back with them and some of these modern folk music people get an earful.
>
> All we can do is sit back and wait for the verdict from Newport, scared stiff. I am not sure Cajun music is on trial in Newport. It may be us. Their verdict could subject us to tortures like the world has never known before.

This remarkable tirade was a fairly accurate assessment of the opinion of a certain class of Cajuns and Creoles. Despite Mr. Grindstaff's grim predictions, however, the Newport organizers were intent on showing the beauty and impact of root music. Their instinct proved well-founded as huge crowds gave the old-time music standing ovations.

Two members of the Louisiana group were simply impressed. The third was Dewey Balfa, a fiddler and vocalist in a family band called The Musical Brothers who had accompanied Thibodeaux and LeJeune as a last-minute replacement on guitar. He was so moved by the experience that he returned to Louisiana determined "to bring home the echo of the standing ovation" they had received at the Newport Festival.

Dewey began working on a small scale, among his friends and family in Mamou, Basile and Eunice. Rinzler, who continued his fieldwork through the 1960s, recognized Dewey's budding activism and urged him on. The Newport Folk Festival, under the guidance of Lomax, routed money and fieldworkers into the area through the newly established Louisiana Folk Foundation. Other groups were invited to perform at Newport, including black Creoles (Alphonse Ardoin and Canray Fontenot) as well as Cajuns (Adam and Cyprien Landreneau). Financial support and outside approval brought about gradual changes on the inside. Local activists such as Paul Tate, Revon Reed, Catherine and Edward Blanchet, Milton and Patricia Rickels became involved in preserving the music, language, and culture. Dewey Balfa did not have the educational base of these members of the foundation, but his innate command of the material more than made up for this deficiency, and his clear sense of mission made him an invaluable member of this task force.

With the help of the Newport Folk Festival Foundation, this group organized traditional contests at local events such as the Abbeville Dairy Festival, the Opelousas Yambilee, and the Crowley Rice Festival. Special concerts were presented so that people would have an opportunity to listen to their music without the distractions of a smoke-filled dance hall.

Eventually Dewey convinced Swallow Records, a local company, to release a recording of traditional Cajun music alongside its more modern listings. Superbly performed ancient songs like "La Valse du bambocheur" and "Parlez-nous a boire" which had attracted Rinzler's attention to the Balfa Brothers sound, also proved popular among the heritage-minded Cajuns of the late 1960s, and led to subsequent albums on Swallow and other labels, including Arhoolie (from California), Rounder (Massachusetts), Folkways (New York), Expression Spontanée (France), and Sonet (England). One of the Balfa Brothers' most important contributions was to set the example of looking back to recycle the best of the traditional material. In this effort, they sometimes composed new words for old tunes, such as Will's "Valse de Balfa," a remarkable testimony to undying love. Soon other musicians began searching through their memories to revive old songs instead of only translating outside sources of new material.

In 1968, the state of Louisiana officially recognized the Cajun cultural revival which had been brewing under the leadership of certain musicians and political leaders such as Dewey Balfa and Dudley LeBlanc. In that year, it created the Council for the Development of French in Louisiana (CODOFIL) which, under the chairmanship of James Domengeaux, began its efforts on political, psychological and educational fronts to erase the stigma Louisianians had long attached to the French language and culture. The creation of French classes in elementary schools began to reverse the policy which had barred the language from the schoolgrounds.

Early in the development of CODOFIL's political strategy, Domengeaux had decided that his efforts should be concentrated in the classroom, explaining that if the language could be saved, the rest would follow. He quickly changed his approach, however, when he realized, as he later put it, "that language and culture are inseparable." Influenced by Rinzler and Balfa, CODOFIL organized a first Tribute to Cajun Music festival in 1974 with a three-hour concert designed to present an historical overview of Cajun music from its origins to modern styles. The echo of Newport had finally come home. Dewey Balfa's message of cultural self-esteem was heard by over 12,000 enthusiastic participants, and was heard again and again as the festival subsequently became an annual celebration of Cajun music and culture.

Dewey's message was complex and aimed in many directions at once. The festival not only provided exposure for the musicians but also presented them as cultural heroes and in the same motion made them available to the ones who needed them most. House dances had given way to public dance halls in the 1930s and, especially after Prohibition, only those eighteen years old and older were able to hear Cajun music with any regularity. Young people listened to what music they could hear, usually on records and radio. Festivals helped to close this cultural generation gap by giving young Cajuns the opportunity to hear the music of their heritage. Later, combination restaurant/dance halls such as Mulate's, Randol's, Préjean's and Bélizaire's reinforced the process. Since these dancehalls also served food, children were able to accompany their parents and grandparents to appreciate their music and learn their dances. Many young performers were attracted to the revalidated Cajun music scene and became interested in playing the music of their fathers and grandfathers. At the same time, local French movement officials observing from backstage realized the impact of the grassroots and began to stress the native Louisiana French culture in the revival of French in Louisiana.

Balfa's dogged pursuit of cultural recognition carried him further than he had ever expected. In 1977, he received a Folk Artist in the Schools grant from the National Endowment for the Arts through Atlanta's Southern Folk Revival project to bring his message into elementary school classrooms. He became a regular on the national folk festival touring circuit along with many of his colleagues. Balfa has given workshops in such places as the Smithsonian Institution and the Library of Congress. In 1982, he was presented with the National Heritage Award and in 1986 his album *Souvenirs* was nominated for a Grammy Award in the Ethnic Music category. In 1987, despite his protests that he had little formal education, Balfa was finally convinced to accept a temporary position to teach courses in Cajun music and culture at the University of California at Fresno. The following year, he was appointed Adjunct Professor of Cajun Music at the University of Southwestern Louisiana.

Cajun music seems likely to live for at least another generation. The renewed creativity within the tradition (as opposed to the simple imitation of outside styles) makes earlier predictions of imminent disintegration seem hasty. Camey Doucet has experimented widely with new songs and styles. Recent compositions by musicians such as D. L. Menard, Belton Richard and Ivy Dugas continue to enlarge the stock repertoire of contemporary dance bands. Menard's "La Porte d'en arrière," which almost immediately became an integral part of the standard repertoire when it was released in the early 1960s, reiterates the *l'enfant perdu* theme encountered in many Cajun songs, but treats it in a humorous vein. Members of his group, the Louisiana Aces, found this humorous treatment so unusual that they hesitated at first to record this classic.

Belton Richard's music represents a strong marriage of traditional and swamp pop styles. His translations of contemporary country and pop music hits, such as his versions of "Behind Closed Doors" ("En arrière des portes fermées") and "The Streak" ("La Petite Éclair"), have been successful on the French Louisiana market, but his songwriting abilities are demonstrated most clearly in his original compositions, such as "Le Paradis des musiciens," and "Un autre soir ennuyant."

In addition to obvious translations of top-forty hits such as "Mauvais Leroy Brown," Ivy Dugas has also produced several contemporary Cajun classics, including "La Valse à Mam" and the self-consciously optimistic "Valse de l'Héritage."

On the eastern side of the Atchafalaya Basin, the accordion was briefly popular but faded from the scene during the 1930s and 1940s and did not return after World War II as it did on the southwestern prairies. There is a French music style along Bayous Terrebonne and Lafourche, but it is highly influenced by country and rock sounds. The tradition of the *chansonnier* is especially strong in this region, as heard in the rich baritone voices of singers like Vin Bruce and L. J. Foret. Many songs are adapted from the English, like Vin Bruce's "La Prière de la jeune fille" ("The Maiden's Prayer"). Original compositions such as Bruce's "Dedans la Louisiane" and Foret's "Le Chemin des coeurs cassés" also have a distinct country flavor. Swamp pop performers like Joe Barry and Gene Rodrigue have provided a rock-influenced sound for the region as well.

Back on the southwestern prairies, young Cajuns, discovering local models besides country and rock stars, began performing the music of their heritage. Yet they did not reject modern sounds while adopting older ones. Zachary Richard's first Cajun music recordings reflected his brief flirtation with country sounds in songs like "Marcher le plancher."

He eventually brought rock and pop music trends, as well as additional lyrics, into his arrangements of traditional music, including "Travailler, c'est trop dur" and "L'Arbre est dans ses feuilles." Some of his original compositions, such as "Réveille," "Ballade de Beausoleil," and "Ma Louisiane," reflect the sense of history and cultural activism he encountered in Quebec and the Canadian Maritimes in the early part of his career.

Other songs, such as "Allons Danser" and "Antibone Legbo," show an influence from New Orleans music figures such as Fats Domino, Professor Longhair, Dr. John, and the Neville Brothers. Always the innovator, Richard has even developed Cajun reggae and Cajun rap. Overall, one of Richard's most important contributions was the discovery of new outlets. He found a way to support his career as a professional musician singing in French by reaching out to Quebec and France, where he has had several gold records.

Michael Doucet has incorporated rock, jazz and classical styles into the carefully researched traditional base of his group Beausoleil in songs such as ""Belle", "Je m'endors," "Les Barres de la prison" and "Contredanse de Mamou." He has composed new songs such as "Zydeco gris-gris" and "Hommage aux frères Balfa," arranged instrumental parts for previously unaccompanied songs such as "Pierrot Grouillet et Mademoiselle Josette," and "J'ai marié un ouvrier," and written new original words for traditional instrumentals such as "Le Gigue français," and "Johnnie peut pas danser."

Young performers are making their presence known on the Cajun music scene, gradually replacing older musicians on the weekend dance hall circuit and representing traditional Cajun music at local and national festivals. Some, like Bruce Daigrepont, Wayne Toups and his ZydeCajun band, and Filé are innovating daring new sounds and styles from recombinations of old and new elements. Some of the words of these new songs question the wholesale buying of the American Dream.

Bruce Daigrepont shows much social consciousness in his original compositions. In "Two step de Marksville," he describes the founding of his family's hometown, while in "Disco and Fais do-do," he reflects specifically on the loss of cultural and ethnic roots among young Cajuns and Creoles who missed their water when the well began to run dry.

Wayne Toups came up through the ranks, playing dancehalls in prairie towns like Riceville and Rayne. His heroes include such notables as Iry LeJeune, Nathan Abshire and Belton Richard. On this solid foundation, he is building new structures. Besides adding dynamic new arrangements to Cajun standards, he has learned to create within the tradition. "Soigne mes enfants" and "Mon ami" are among the most beautiful Cajun waltzes of this decade.

Wayne Toups' recent contract with Polygram Records has brought Cajun music to a new segment of the American public, the MTV crowd. Meanwhile, back home in Louisiana, his highly original style has influenced many young musicians who hear in his music a blend of traditional and up-to-the-minute contemporary sounds.

And the beat goes on. One band called Mamou is experimenting with a combination of Cajun and rock without accordions or fiddles. Others, like Steve Riley, Robert Jardell, Felix and Sterling Richard, express a strong interest in reverently preserving the style and repertoires of their mentors, yet even these constantly recharge past songs with the vitality of the present. Some, like Felton LeJeune, Eddie LeJeune, and Ervin LeJeune, unselfconsciously carry on venerable family and neighborhood traditions. A few, such as Joel Sonnier and Bessyl Duhon, have left home for larger markets, but maintain close contact with their roots. Still others, like Jambalaya and Paul Daigle and Cajun Gold, stay home and keep feverishly busy producing new songs for the local music scene where the true value of a song is demonstrated by how many other bands use it in their weekly dance hall performances. Jambalaya combines the creative talents of Terry and Tony Huval, Reggie Matte, Ken David and Bobby Dumatrait on popular new songs such as "La

Mazurka" and "La Belle de la campagne," while Paul Daigle's group has made excellent use of Pierre Varmon Daigle's recent wellspring of new songs, many of which have already become dance band standards, including "La Valse de la vie," "La Nouvelle Valse d'anniversaire," and "La Lumière dans ton chassis."

In the late 1980s, the experimentation process has accelerated. Even a self-avowed traditionalist like Michael Doucet has origins in rock and roll. In the early 1970s, his short-lived group Coteau was one of the first groups to tamper with instrumentation and arrangements, adding hard-driving rock influences to traditional songs. His steady group Beausoleil has long folded jazz and rock into their sound. Doucet has also teamed up with a new group called Cajun Brew, with Pat Breaux on accordion and sax, Jimmy Breaux on drums, Sonny Landreth on electric slide and Steve LaCroix on bass, to record Cajun French versions of 1960s rock songs, such as "Louie Louie" and "Wooly Bully." Mamou, named for the hometown of bandleader Steve Lafleur, has taken the Cajun sound to its current extreme. The style of his electric guitar leads is clearly influenced by rock greats such as Jimi Hendrix and Eric Clapton, yet his rendition of Cajun classics such as "La Valse des Balfa" and "La Danse de Mardi Gras" on his recent album (*Mamou*, Jungle Records 1010) are familiar, not only in melody, but in spirit as well.

Even some of the most conservative elements in Cajun music, like Dewey Balfa himself, insist that tradition is not a product but a process and continue to produce new songs and styles from within the culture. While performing at the 1985 Smithsonian Festival of American Folklife, Dewey surprised the audience by announcing that he was going to play a few original songs from his *Souvenirs* album. He went on to explain:

> Cajun music is like a tree. Its roots have to be watered or it will die. But watering the roots is not all. If a tree is alive, it will grow, and that growth is important, too. Most of the songs I play are about a hundred years old. I'm interested in preserving Cajun music. I've dedicated my life to try to assure that there will be lots of Cajun musicians in another hundred years. But that's not enough. Someone has to provide them with songs to play that will be about a hundred years old then, so I've composed a few that I hope will still be around.

The audience was relieved to hear that these new songs, such as "J'ai pleuré" and "Quand j'étais pauvre," sounded like traditional Cajun music. They sounded that way because they were traditional, coming from the same process which produced the older songs. One of those songs reflects persistent concerns about money and real human values, concerns similar to those expressed by Bruce Daigrepont above, as well as Dewey Balfa's own playful observations about aging and courting.

Purists who would resist new instrumentation, styles and compositions neglect to consider that change and innovation have always been an integral part of Cajun music. Those who want to freeze the tradition at any point lack an historical perspective and share a basic misunderstanding of the importance of improvisation and the creolization process in French Louisiana in general and in Cajun music in particular. The same approach would have barred the borrowing of Anglo-American ballads and Spanish tunes in the eighteenth century, the introduction of the accordion in the nineteenth century, the adding of other instruments in the 1940s and 1950s, the influence of the blues, the addition of swing and country sounds along the way. Today the blending and fusion at the heart of the development of Cajun culture continue to be essential to its music. As Wayne Toups described his own creative input within the traditional context: "There is room to maneuver, but there are clear borders. You can go a long way as long as you respect those borders."

# A CONCISE HISTORY OF JAZZ IN NEW ORLEANS AND NEW ORLEANS JAZZMEN*

Rhodes J. Spedale, Jr.

You have read of the origins of jazz in New Orleans in the preceding chapter, and why it developed here. But *how* did it develop? It is necessary to draw the lines of developments as in the traditional, music school manner here, in order to chart the courses of the development of jazz in New Orleans, separating the *instrumental* development of the form as opposed to its *vocal* tradition.

## The Brass Bands

The brass band tradition was European but was made Orleanian. Now its *de rigeur* to have a brass band "open" any new development. While DeJan's Olympia Bass Band was playing for the groundbreaking of the new Meridién Hotel on Canal Street, The Royal Orleans Hotel lobby was turned into Carnival time as Doc Paulin's Brass Band marched conventioneers from a party in the Esplanade Room to their waiting bus and the Excelsior Brass Band was herded by Teddy Riley and Paul Lentz to the Mayport Jazz Festival in Jacksonville, Florida, to open that event; and the Dirty Dozen Brass Band finally got a steady gig uptown.

Henry "Red" Allen's father headed a brass band in Algiers. The Old Tuxedo Band, The Eagle Brass Band, and The New Reliance—these were all working brass bands in the Twenties and Thirties, and their ranks swelled with such stars as Freddie Keppard, Bunk Johnson, Manuel Perez, Oscar "Papa" Celestine, Lorenzo Tio and Peter Bocage. Many of these brass bands spurred ensembles of smaller numbers and, adding rhythm instruments, they played for other functions (e.g., The Original Tuxedo Jazz Band as sired by Celestine and Bebe Ridgley. The tradition continues today: e.g., Andrew Hall's Society Jazz Band has also a Society Brass Band). These aggregations played for all types of social functions.

*First published in Rhodes Spedale, Jr., *A Guide to Jazz in New Orleans* (New Orleans: Hope Publications, 1984), 28-95. Reprinted with the kind permission of the author.

Brass bands currently performing in the old tradition are Olympia, Onward, and Excelsior Brass Bands (the latter is a good unit which has varying personnel), and Doc Paulin's Brass Band, among others. A distinct departure from this tradition is The Dirty Dozen Brass Band, a group of youngsters including Kirk Joseph and Charles Joseph (progeny of traditional jazz trombonist Walden "Frog" Joseph), Roger Lewis, and Gregory Davis whose repertoire runs the gamut from the Jackson Five, Jimmy Forrest ("Night Train") and Thelonious Monk, to "L'il Liza Jane." Originally it was an imitation instrument group that followed Olympia in parades; but in the 'Eighties they turned it all around and "got serious." Jazz historian, author, and banjoist-guitarist Danny Barker was quoted by Tom Dent in his article, "A Living Tradition of Traditional Jazz," in the 1983 New Orleans Jazz and Heritage Festival Official Program on pages 29-30 follow: "The Dozen has speeded up the beat. I think it comes from the beat of the high school marching bands. Really, it's too fast for a parade beat. They always have to slow down so the parade can catch up." At the same place in the article, Milton Batiste of Olympia says: "The Dozen are ahead of their time. How successful they will be depends upon on whether the people accept them, but they aren't playing marching band music the way it has been played." It's a new viable tradition that the Dirty Dozen has begun. (Methinks I've heard that same controversy over Dizzy Gillespie, Charlie Parker and the Mouldy Fygges in the 'Forties'.)

## The New Orleans Ensemble

From the earliest days in New Orleans Jazz, the most striking feature about the music has been its ensemble—improvisatory as well as written. Again, the developments here took place along the "Uptown—Downtown" lines referred to earlier. Whereas Buddy Bolden's bandsmen were not terribly musically literate, their improvised ensembles were sufficiently strong that even when trombonist Frankie Dusen took over the band following Bolden's mental breakdown it retained popularity. Other contemporaries are epitomized by the John Robichaux Orchestra, a schooled group (discussed in the *One Mo' Time* chapter). Freddie Keppard also led a grand band of improvisers. King Oliver's Creole Jazz Band is generally referred to as the classic New Orleans Jazz ensemble, and the two cornet breaks by Oliver and Armstrong appear to jazz historian Rudi Blesh ("Shining Trumpets") like manna from heaven!

The New Orleans Jazz community from time to time has been rife with controversy over the contribution of early white jazz groups to the development of jazz. Generally the efforts of Nick LaRocca, The Original Dizieland Jazz Band, and the New Orleans Rhythm Kings had been dismissed as "amateurish," posturing, or imitative of black groups. Suffice it to say that all New Orleans Jazzmen are born with "big ears"—that is, they all hear and learn from each other and every other form of music. If there's any generalization one can make about New Orleans Jazzmen it would be that in *the New Orleans Jazz musician is especially attentive and attuned to his surroundings, musical and otherwise.* Everyone in the early days, black and white, was hearing and learning from each other.

It's what was accomplished that counts. Since the black groups had more visibility and since they did pioneer, it was natural that they were models. Nevertheless originality did come out of *all* of these early experiments.

Nick LaRocca claimed he "invented" jazz and there are adherents to his philosophy even today. Nevertheless, Jelly Roll Morton *also* said *he* was the "originator of jazz" and backed it up with his business card. The fact is that *both* of these rugged individualists were true originals, but both were *wrong*. *Jazz evolved; it wasn't invented.*

In that posture, therefore, one can evaluate The Original Dixieland Jazz Band. Their recording of Livery Stable Blues (1917) was the first commercial jazz phonograph record ever produced. I have to believe that social apartheid was the reason they and not Oliver went to New York. Tom Brown's band of about the same vintage, according to reports, was a decidedly inferior ensemble. (Remember also that Freddie Keppard reportedly turned down an early opportunity to record because he didn't want anyone "stealing" his "stuff." Oliver lived and loved like a King in New Orleans; perhaps his complacency maybe as much a reason for the rise of the ODJB as social conditions). The ODJB had a limited repertoire; their recordings include many re-takes with some variance in personnel. There was also a divisive lawsuit which ended with the *obiter dictum* that you can't copyright the blues form that expended much of the group's energy. Nevertheless the ensembles and breaks in such as "At The Jazz Band Ball, Fidgety Feet (War Cloud)," and others are still a standard for the music. LaRocca was a good cornetist and the group presented a legacy which though limited, survives to this day and survives *well*.

The New Orleans Rhythm Kings, on the other hand, were not as ensemble-oriented as ODJB or Oliver. The presence of the superb clarinetist Leon Rapollo, whose lyrical melodicism foreshadowed the sensitivity and dynamics of Bix Biederbecke a few years later has to be a factor. As we have seen, Louis Armstrong broke from the ensemble into the solo regions nationally. At just about the same time Rapollo was showing the possibilities of the soloist *above* and *within* the ensemble in traditional jazz. George Brunies' trombone solo on "Tin Roof Blues" with NORK was widely imitated also.

Tom Brown's Band recorded with Sharkey Bonano on cornet and Harry Shields (brother of ODJB clarinetist Larry Shields) in 1925, though the legendary Emmet Hardy, who was supposed to have been praised by Armstrong as his superior and cited by Biederbecke as an influence, was on the band. Tony Parenti and Bonano are described by critic Samuel Charters in his informative liner notes to *New Orleans Jazz—The '20's* (Folkways RBF 203) as purveying a "less intense style, with many elements of Italian street music which was to become the present day "dixieland" music of New Orleans." (Jazz historian Richard Allen disagrees.) Johnny Bayersdorffer, Charlie Cordilla, and Abbie Brunies sought out the rougher styles of the mid-twenties popular black bands, such as led by Buddy Petit, Punch Miller, and Kid Rena, Charters reports. Louis Duamine's Jazzola Eight included trombonist Earl Humphrey, brother of Willie and Percy Humphrey of Preservation Hall.

The Bebe Ridgley Orchestra grew out of the Tuxedo schism, with Celestine taking one group one way and Ridgley the other. Many famed New Orleans jazz names came out of the Ridgley ranks. Sidney Desvigne and Fate Marable also gave work to jazzmen of New Orleans early on. Another renowned New Orleans ensemble of the twenties was Armond J. Piron's New Orleans Orchestra where the Bocage family was ensconced. Sam Morgan's Jazz Band was another legendary ensemble, with the leader and his brother on cornet, and another brother on tenor, and a young Jim Robinson on trombone. (Robinson was rediscovered with George Lewis and Bunk Johnson in the 1940s revival and they recorded often as the front line.)

Johnny DeDroit, who led a pit band in theaters in the 1920s, was recently recognized by the Tulane Hot Jazz Classic. The New Orleans Owls have liaison with string band music (see later chapter on Hot Strings) as well as contemporary jazz in the city: Their clarinetist, Pinky Vidacovich, was the uncle of one of New Orleans hardest working and currently most active jazz drummers, Johnny Vidacovich. The influences of jazz recordings made elsewhere were heard in the playing of Johnny Hyman (Wiggs), a cornet player spiritually closer to Bix, and Monk Hazel, a drummer who still plays in the '80s sporadically. The later arrangements by King Oliver, Jelly Roll Morton, and Joe Robichaux demonstrate the amalgamation of New Orleans style of the period with later popular big bands and "swing era" modes. The New Leviathan Oriental Foxtrot Orchestra is a relic, a curiosity of the more popular, jazz infused dance music of the era of New Orleans' tango belt of the 1920s. La. Jazz Repertory Ensemble superbly plays early Morton, *etc.* charts today.

Since the rise of the soloist in the mid-twenties foreshadowed the developments of jazz, the following is a thumbnail sketch of the stylistic developments of players on various instruments.

## Trumpet and Cornet

The usual listing of trumpet kings of New Orleans reads: Buddy Bolden, Buddy Petit, Manuel Perez, Freddie Keppard, Joseph "King" Oliver, Bunk Johnson, Emmett Hardy, and finally Louis "Satchmo" Armstrong. The trumpet's role is clearly that of being the *main* horn and leading the ensemble. Louis Armstrong emphasized its *solo* role.

Bolden, Petit and Perez did not record, so far as we know (despite rumors to the contrary). Keppard's rough-hewn blatant trumpet is reputed to be of the Bolden stripe. Oliver's cornet clearly says he's in charge, as does Armstrong's. Johnson's recordings came at a time when he'd passed his prime. The revival of the '40s showed he had a more mellifluous tone than his predecessors; he was definitely ensemble oriented. Kid Shots Madison was of a similar persuasion; he came out of the Original Tuxedo Jazz Band. Oscar "Papa" Celestine, who co-led that ensemble, was gentler of tone, "more pretty," as musicians said as was Hardy, another non-recorder. George Mitchell, a cornetist who recorded with Jelly Roll Morton, was a fine soloist who seemed to stem more from King

Oliver, as did Papa Mutt Carey. Percy Humphrey of Preservation Hall and the Crescent City Joymakers emulates Punch Miller, whose sobriquet was earned by the way he stated and phrased the lead. Kid Thomas Valentine, also a denizen of "The Hall" is brash and driving and is still playing at a high level in the Eighties though he's *well over* 65.

There was a more lyrical, legato style of trumpet development in New Orleans jazz. The line runs from Emmett Hardy through Armstrong (e.g., his early recording of "Between The Devil and The Deep Blue Sea"), *via* Johnny Wiggs and Sharkey Bonano. These were the followers of Bix Biederbecke and Paul Mares of the New Orleans Rhythm Kings. Bix's new style of trumpet was influenced by Leon Rapollo's clarinet work as well as by European impressionist composers (such as Ravel and Debussy, according to his close friend Jimmy McPartland in an interview with this writer in the late 1970s).

There was another kind of tone too: Red Allen buzzed like a bee as did his predecessor, Lee Collins. This was more an outgrowth of Louis Armstrong's authoritative trumpet sound; thus, a line of development can be carried through this offshoot from Armstrong through Celestine and Lee Collins through Red Allen and past Roy Eldridge to Dizzy Gillespie, Wynton Marsalis and beyond.

There are several other players that are harder to categorize. Tommy Ladnier, from Mandeville, worked with King Oliver before teaming with Sidney Bechet in the Thirties and was a 52nd Streeter in the Forties. Perhaps his style stemmed from Oliver, but he spoke no less authoritatively though more softly. Wingy Manone was a lot of fun for a long time; he and the Prima Brothers (Leon and Louis) probably root in Armstrong. Dave Nelson, King Oliver's nephew, was obviously influenced by his uncle; though on recordings he made with the King towards the end discographers continually carp as to who played what where and when. Guy Kelly was a nemesis of Red Allen, Jr. and Chris Kelly was an early legend. I've not heard any recordings by them; but they were reported to be "New Orleans style." Joe Newman stems from Satch and Red Allen but he's of such original bent that these can only be considered as frames of reference. Richard, Merrit, and Abbie Brunies, of that fine New Orleans jazz family, are also players whose recordings are unknown to me but were reputedly similar to the fine Paul Mares of the New Orleans Rhythm Kings.

Frank Assunto, founder of The Dukes of Dixieland, said he cried, "I love Louis" in every note he played on his horn. Whereas that may have been true when Frank came on the scene in the Forties, by the Seventies his flugelhorn work show the taste of Bix and lyricism. George Girard was a contemporary of Assunto with The Basin Street Six (organized by Bunny Franks). Stylistically he looked to Satchmo and Harry James. Thomas Jefferson in the 1950s was a Little Jazz (Eldridge) advocate; his recent recordings and appearances show him more indebted now to Armstrong. Jimmy Ille plays cornet on Bourbon Street and for jazz brunches and seems to look towards McPartland and Bix as does the fine Wes Mix.

Trumpet player Charles Miller, a working New York jazzman, and from New Orleans, recently said in a WWOZ radio interview that Alvin Alcorn's gentle sound reminded him of Miles Davis. Alvin predates Miles by a brace of seasons and plays the prettiest music sounds any jazz bruncher could want to hear. (Cornetist Rex Stewart, himself a great jazzman, listed Alvin as one of the *true originals* he'd ever encountered.) His son, Sam Alcorn, also plays well, soft or loud, traditional or modern. Jack Willis sounds of this persuasion.

Wallace Davenport was an early modernist, leading one of the city's bebop groups. He toured with Basie and Hampton and is extremely popular overseas. He has his own record company and is Armstrong oriented.

Melvin Lastie was a *great* modern jazz cornetist who passed away in the 1970s with too few recordings to show his tremendous ability. (There was a date with Cannonball Adderly and a rare duo with Harold Batiste.) He was a superb jazzman, highly respected locally and a member of a great jazz family.

George Finola is a lyrical cornetist out of the roots of Bix, Bunny, McPartland, Bobby Hackett, Ruby Braff, *et al.* He appears regularly and is a tasteful player. Clyde Kerr, Sr. is a big band veteran who has appeared with his own group and in all star groups at the New Orleans Jazz and Heritage Festival. His son, Clyde Kerr, Jr., takes trumpet steps forward and is more into avant garde. Porgy Jones was a later "Mother Hubbard" supporter.

There's a plethora of fine modern jazz trumpeters working with large groups. Bill Clifford's orchestra houses Emory Thompson (Umar Sharif), who, like jazz, went from New Orleans (he was on the 1964 Big Chief Professor Longhair classic) to Chicago (working with Ellington, Basie and Sun Ra) and back home again. His son (Jamil Sharif) often joins him in the brass section when he's not working with Alvin Batiste's Southern University Jazz Band, the Jaguars. Chuck Easterling is a fine teacher, an ex-Al Belletto sideman, who also had his own larger group. A. J. Pittman and John Brem push Trick Bag along with Jimmy Weber, a fine soloist who has worked with Ed Lewis and recorded with Ronnie Kole. These are basically trained readers who can solo with proficiency. All of the above would have no difficulty working in the brass sections of major national big bands—and many already have. Tony Klatka and Nicky Messina are perfect examples of the New Orleans jazzmen in this category. (Tony will be discussed later in detail.) Herb Tassin, who leads a big band, is a noteworthy soloist.

Bourbon Street has its share of jazz trumpet players that wend their way from group to group, club to club, sometimes leading their own bands. Although they are individuals, they can be grouped under this heading as to characteristics: they all have clean, clear tones and powerful leads. Their solo inventiveness varies, though technique is rarely wanting. Roy Liberto, Clive Wilson, James Davis (who often doubles valve trombone), Eddie Bayard, Tommy Yetta, Jimmy LaRocca (Nick's nephew), Kid Sheik Colar, John Brunious, Murphy Campo (probably the best of the lot), Tex Liuzza, and Connie Jones (replaced Girard in the Basin Street Six and was with Fountain and the Dukes) are all quite proficient and of this stamp. Plato Smith is another breed apart and he will be discussed further on. Dave Bartholomew, who heads a fine big band and did so much work with Fats Domino, and John Horne both play Gillespie model bell-ascendant trumpets but are stylistically mainstream players. (Louis Armstrong is the model for most of these hornmen.) Teddy Riley can play both bop and Bourbon Street.

Al Hirt is much maligned but is a great swing stylist; range, technique, and emotion are his strong suits. Frank Trapani of the Dukes of Dixieland physically resembles Hirt and is a big band veteran. Wendell Brunious is of a Bourbon Street Black family, and a modernist, looking to Gillespie, Clifford Brown, and Freddie Hubbard for inspiration. He can and does play with Brass Bands, Dixieland and Disneyland Bands, and then come and wail on flugelhorn as well as trumpet in a late night jam session. Whereas Ellis Marsalis picked Wendell to play with him and his saxophonist son Branford at the 1982 New Orleans Jazz and Heritage Festival (while Wynton Marsalis was in town), Ellis' son Delfeayo tabbed Leroy Jones to perform at his 1983 New Orleans Jazz and Heritage Festival debut. I've championed Leroy for years, after passing by his bandstand night after night hearing him play Clifford Brown licks on traditional jazz warhorses. He shows his roots on the New Orleans Jazz Repertory Ensemble record. Delf says he's the "best trumpet in the city." (cause Wynton doesn't live here now!)

Wynton Marsalis must have heard Melvin Lastie, due to his father's close association with him during the AFO days. Wynton plays all that's great in jazz trumpet and is a fine classical player also. He is a world-wide star of acclaim. With the exception of Louis Armstrong, he's been called the greatest trumpet ever to come out of New Orleans. Wynton builds on Gillespie, Brown, and Davis, combining the lyrical with the assertive lead style of jazz trumpet. He's a rarity, and he's growing better—and he's in his twenties!

Another top flight trumpeter, formerly with Lionel Hampton, and now with Art Blakely's Jazz Messengers, is Terrence Blanchard, also formerly a member of Ellis Marsalis' Young Generation. Good jazz trumpet, as you see—and—hear is a New Orleans tradition.

## Violin

The violin was originally a lead instrument in the traditional New Orleans Jazz Ensemble, along with the trumpet. (e.g., Peter Bocage, A. J. Piron, etc.) Other than with string bands, its use has fallen by the wayside in New Orleans jazz groups. Jazz historian and composer William Russell (heard often with the New Orleans Ragtime Orchestra), 1983 Grammy award winner Clarence "Gatemouth" Brown, and Ed Wadsworth of Hot Strings are the only local jazzmen on that instrument. Doug Kershaw is of the Cajun music persuasion, but his long lines can swing.

## New Orleans Reedmen

The role of the clarinet is as obligatto to the New Orleans ensemble. It was often used as a lead horn in spasm bands and trios because of its timbre and tone. It was a favorite instrument of the creole downtowners. Lorenzo Tio and his family schooled literally hundreds of New Orleans clarinetists: Sidney Bechet, Barney Bigard, and Louis Cottrell, Jr., to name just three stars.

George Bacquet, Achille Bacquet, and Alphonse Picou were among the earliest jazzmen to gain recognition on the instrument. Scholarly research pins *High Society* on Picou as a composer showing how he took a line from classical music and turned it into a traditional standard. (Others claim Bacquet had a part in its creation; some show that it came from an Ivy League minstrel show.) I first heard Picou on his curved clarinet in the 'Forties as a member of Papa Celestine's Tuxedo Jazz Band. He was an ancient then, but playing with verve and drive. (In fact, he was the first jazz clarinet player I ever saw!) Earl Fouché played expressive alto with Sam Morgan's band, but basically it was a clarinet role that he fulfilled.

Leon Rapollo, as noted earlier, with the New Orleans Rhythm Kings, was known for the melodic nature of his solos which "no doubt" (as Professor Morton would say) influenced Bix. He was a lyrical soloist who took the tradition of Italian street music (noted by Sam Charters previously) and like his late disciple Tony Parenti, adapted to and incorporated these qualities into New Orleans jazz. (The contemporary Tony Mitchell uses these same models.) Johnny Dodds, brother of drummer Baby Dodds, worked with King Oliver and Louis Armstrong in The Creole Jazz Band; he defected with Satchmo, and his especially reedy clarinet tone on Louis' Hot Five sides set the standard for New Orleans clarinet. He was equally adept in ensemble or solo. Sidney Arondin (composer of Lazy River), Charlie Cordilla, Pinky Vidacovich, and Larry and Harry Shields appear to follow him stylistically.

Sidney Bechet was every bit the jazz great on clarinet and soprano saxophone that Louis Armstrong was on cornet and trumpet. His trademark was a big, wide tone on either instrument plus a strong driving attack that was relentless in its swing. New Orleans has never had as dominant a soloist on these instruments as the fine creole gentlemen.

Other early clarinet legends were Lawrence Duhé (also spelled Dewey) one of the first to leave home for the north in the 'Twenties and make good. Similarly, Alcide "Yellow" Nunez preceded ODJB. Big Eye Louis Nelson (aka DeLisle) was an early player of considerable import and influence. Though rediscovered and recorded in the revival, George Lewis took his place on many of those dates. Boyd Senter was a composer who recorded in Chicago with Jelly Roll Morton in 1924, associated with the New Orleans jazz contingent there, and was assimilated.

Jimmy Noone was a bridge between the New Orleans style he espoused (as well as that of his contemporaries Albert Nicholas and Omer Simeon) and the swing clarinet style of Benny Goodman. Simeon and Nicholas were both with King Oliver after Dodds left. (Ed Hall and his brother Herb find their inspiration in these stylists). Barney Bigard played clarinet and tenor saxophone with such a varied gumbo of greats as King Oliver, Louis Armstrong, Sid Catlett and Duke Ellington. He was superior in the lower register, his Chalmeu tone oozing humid warmth. Other fine low register players were Eddie

Miller (primarily a tenor stylist) and Irving Fazola (Pete Fountain's idol) from the Bob Crosby Bobcats. Lester Bouchon and Boojie Centobie, both who doubled clarinet and tenor in 1950s, seem to stem from Fazola.

The 1940s New Orleans revival went back to the roots of New Orleans jazz for its clarinet players. When Dr. Leonard Bechet (a trombonist brother of Sidney) fitted Bunk Johnson with teeth after Bunk was rediscovered on a farm in New Iberia, the clarinet player and real leader of these revivalist recordings was George Lewis, whose soaring creole sound dominated the New Orleans traditional jazz scene for over a quarter century. Only a step behind in talent was Albert Burbank, a mainstay of the Paddock Lounge and Preservation Hall. Willie Humphrey continues this tradition, as did Steve Angrum and Israel Gorman.

Pete Fountain adapted Fazola and Goodman to New Orleans jazz, and he will be covered in detail further on. Other contemporaries of Pete on clarinet were the late Harold Cooper (ex-Dukes of Dixieland, ex-Al Hirt) and Pee Wee Spitalera (ex-Hirt) whose memorable clarinet blues battle at the benefit for Frank Assunto after his death still has local fans talking. Chuck Credo plays in the tradition. René Netto plays all horns well and is of similar stylistic persuasion. The late Louis Cottrell, Jr. was more of the Lewis-Burbank school, with more than a touch of the Noone sweeping line. Orange Kellin takes Noone for a model, but this Scandinavian import goes in a lot of directions as we shall see later. Glen Wilson appears to paraphrase both Fazola and Lewis disciples. Soprano saxist Bill Lee follows Sidney Bechet's example. Chris Burk, an English Emigrant, follows the late Joseph "Cornbread" Thomas stylistically *via* Lewis and Burbank.

Although I've touched saxophonists above only slightly, with few exceptions, until Coleman Hawkins rescued the tenor from comedy acts in the 'Thirties, the primary read soloist in New Orleans jazz was the clarinetist. Davey Jones (heard with Lee Collins), a tenor player in 1929, appears to have a different conception of the role of a tenor as opposed to a clarinet in the traditional ensemble. To that extent Ernest Poree, clearly a senior citizen, is a iconoclast. He's marched with parade bands in the 'Thirties, played with Tony Fougerat's Dixieland Band, but is the earliest vestige of Charlie Parker's alto style extant in the Crescent City. His alto sounds like what Bird played with Jay McShann in Kansas City. Younger New Orleans jazzmen, such as clarinetist Joe Torregano, consider him a legend. He appears now with Andrew Hall's Society Jazz Band and with the revue Oh! Play That Thing. At the same time Captain John Handy, Herman Sherman, and Harold Dejan played traditional jazz alto, by way of contrast.

Clarence Ford played baritone sax on so many Fats Domino dates and has a fine alto solo on the old Ace recording of "Time After Time" that Red Tyler arranged for Frankie Ford. On Bourbon Street and at jazz brunches he plays traditional clarinet and soprano saxophone; but the 1983 New Orleans Jazz And Heritage Festival presented him on flute with Ed Frank, Red Tyler and Clyde Kerr, Jr. and he acquitted himself superbly—better, I feel, than in a traditional context. He was in Wallace Davenport's early bebop band and later has recorded with him in a more traditional setting.

Joseph "Mouse" Bonati, alto saxophone, was a bop pioneer in the city in the 1940s and 1950s. He's now in Las Vegas. Modern tenor giant Brew Moore played New Orleans in the 'forties and left to gain fame on the east coast and in Scandinavia. Benny Clements and Chick Powers, tenor players, were contemporaries but played in a less fervent style. (Interestingly enough, Mouse has recorded recently on tenor.) Al Belletto was the modern jazz alto missionary and mainstay in New Orleans from the 1950s on. Part of his importance is that he was a working modern jazz saxophonist (with Playboy) at a time when this city was not attuned to what was happening in jazz since Parker and Gillespie's advent ("the twentieth century," as Bill Huntington says). Sam Butera took his big-toned tenor west with the Superchief, Louis Prima, where they struck gold in Las Vegas in the 1950s and 1960s.

Nat Perrilliat (tenor sax) is one of the great seminal figures of modern jazz in New Orleans in the 'fifties and 'sixties. Remember, the city was still socially segregated in those days to some degree, so Nat never reached a significant white audience except for those great records for AFO (of Alvin Batiste, Harold Batiste, Melvin Lastie, and Ellis Marsalis) in the 'fifties and a rare date with Cannonball Adderly long out of print. He's still praised by his active contemporaries today long after his passing. Harold Batiste played modern alto and tenor as well as piano and left New Orleans for sunnier financial climes of California, where he was musical director for Sonny and Cher's TV series. He's quite a composer; but his cousin, the monumental Alvin Batiste, leader of the Southern University Jazz Studies Program, a member of the Louisiana Music Commission, and the finest modern jazz clarinetist around, is clearly the superior player. "Bat" has recorded with Alderly and Billy Cobham, among others; he's a superb leader of young players, and I think he could even make Comus swing! Alto saxophonist and clarinetist Don Suhor is also a fine modernist who can play traditional and swing, and has also appeared as soloist with the New Orleans Pops.

Alvin "Red" Tyler is an arranger and a tenor player who has recorded on baritone sax, also. Along with Lee Allen and Robert Parker ('Barefootin") who appear here infrequently (more often abroad), Tyler filled the New Orleans R&B records of the Fifties with big-toned tenor solos of soul. He's likely to appear with Willie Metcalf one night, Germaine Bazzle and The Gentlemen of Jazz the next, do a record date with Gatemouth Brown the following day and help reedmate Wardell Querzque and his arrangements the next day. Adaptability is his middle name, and he's *always* included in all star bop groups where he's usually introduced as "of course, on tenor, Alvin "Red" Tyler, ya'll." Such *pro forma* taking of artistry for granted could make one think that "ya'll" is really Red's last name! The late Alvin Thomas played fine contemporary jazz and soloed on those 1950s R&B records from New Orleans that didn't have Allen, Parker, or Tyler on hand. Gary Brown continues that tradition today with Sea-Saint Studios.

Traditional jazz tenor issues forth with a swing accent from Pud Brown, a rare bird who we catch in flight later on. Michael Sizer plays clarinet and tenor with the Dukes of Dixieland (see infra) and has a split stylistic personality. Bill Kelsey doubles clarinet and tenor, roaring less traditional lines. Baritone sax and clarinet are handled by Oscar Davis in Milton Rich's Jazz Group on Bourbon Street. Otis Bazoon has chosen Pee Wee Russell as his role model on jazz clarinet. Raymond Burke, a superb soloist and senior citizen, is still going strong and should be heard. Michael White is a rarity: a young black clarinetist who plays traditional jazz in Johnny Dodds—Jimmy Noone style. He is a superb craftsman. Norman Meyer is most adept in traditional jazz.

The saxophone section of Bill Clifford's Orchestra at the Blue Room houses impressive players such as Liston Johnson, a Hawk-toned tenor who's recorded on clarinet in a traditional context with young Harry Connick, Jr. Ray Moore has a warm alto sound. Dennis Ruello, along with Roger Lewis (of The Dirty Dozen) lead the city's baritone sax brigade; where the former looks to Serge Challof, the latter takes on Harry Carney and Cecil Payne as sources of inspiration.

Mike Carruba is a veteran with many large organizations and like Ed Lewis represents a more mainstream, 'forties type of tenor soloist. Great James Rivers plays alto and tenor very much along the lines of the late Sonny Stitt. Earl Turbinton, Jr. ("the African Cowboy") plays alto and soprano immensely well and was tabbed for Weather Report. He's recorded sporadically, but is due out soon with new product. He's a *major* soloist, organizer, producer, and scuffler who's not received his due. Cannonball Adderly early on heralded him for greatness. He picks up where Adderly left off and goes into Coltrane's vistas. He appeared in concert with Nat Adderly, Cannon's brother, and it was an eerie aural event—like a rising of a jazz Phoenix. He's well respected nationally. Tenorist David Lastie plays jazz, rock, etc. with equal abandon and excellence in all contexts.

Edward "Kidd" Jordan directs the Southern University Jazz Band in New Orleans and plays free jazz tenor. He's superb in both areas. At the 1983 New Orleans Jazz And Heritage Festival he had the youngsters play a big band free jazz work that was light years away from what a stage band is supposed to do! It was the most exhilarating moment of the festival. He has one son in that ensemble who's a trumpet player and his other son, Kent, is a prominent jazz flutist (now a CBS recording artist) who appears with Ellis Marsalis and has recorded with Jasmine as well as Ellis. He can play free and form. There's an abundance of talent in those jazz families. Branford Marsalis is the alto and tenor progeny of Ellis, a student of Alvin Batiste, and who's taken recent giant steps to New York. Charles Neville appears mainly with his brothers, but when he teams with Ramsey McLean, can play alternatively bone chilling and heart warming jazz on tenor, alto, and soprano in a freer, modern style labeled by some as "loft jazz." His original composition "Ladies" presented in concert with Ramsey is one of the loveliest, most touching works I've ever heard locally in that idiom. Versatile Reggie Houston joins them in The Survivors.

There are fine saxophonists coming out of the UNO and Loyola Jazz Bands. The Loyola Institute of Jazz Studies produced a major soloist and alto saxophonist Charles Pillow, demonstrating how an innate talent can be schooled into a superior artistry. Trick Bag has super sax soloists in heated Bill Gable (alto and baritone), cool tenor Ward Smith, and sometimes on-hand Eric Traub, whose oblique, off-hand tenor sax seems to be all over town. Paul McGinley, ex-Woody Hermanite, teaches at Loyola and plays tenacious, aggressive jazz wherever he's asked. Tony Dagradi is a superb reedman on all horns who leads his own Astral Project and records with Carla Bley, among others. He's tops, and is and will be in the future a major influence on New Orleans modern jazz saxophone for quite sometime. For example, one night I heard him at Tyler's on a stand with three other young saxophonists, and they were all trying to sound like Tony Dagradi. I've also heard Tony Dagradi play clarinet, flute, alto and baritone with no less proficiency. I might also add, that in that instance he wasn't even playing his own horns or mouthpieces!

There are three reedmen who seem to hide their talent under a bush most of the year and only come out at the time of the Jazz and Heritage Festivals and/or Armstrong Park celebrations. Then, they are ubiquitous. Warren Bell has a golden tone on alto, is a modernist, and made some sides with AFO. He's often the part of all star groups at festivals. Fred Kemp is a tenor saxophonist who can play as far out or as far in as you desire. He's got a lot of taste, muscle, and spirit. He has been heard with an all saxophone ensemble, and he blends especially well on a modern front line with such players as Emory Thompson or Wendell Brunious to make a *big* sound. Jacques Gauthé is a chef who has recorded on his own label with his wife Nelly. Both are French, and Jacques shows that he can cook on clarinet as well as in the kitchen. He has been heard doing impassioned playing with such as Sam Alcorn and Freddie Lonzo, as well as The La. Jazz Repertory Ensemble.

Lester Young, the President, a modern jazz giant on tenor saxophone, lived in New Orleans for the first ten years of his life, and his brother, Lee, was born in New Orleans but left here at the age of two. Prez *made* modern jazz tenor saxophone, of course, and his brother was active in studio jobs all over the west coast, and even played some traditional recording dates with Mutt Carey and Bunk Johnson. Another person who gained fame as a modern jazz saxophonist (alto and soprano) was Pony Poindexter. "He was from New Orleans; this was his town," said Jon Hendricks during an interview with the author in August, 1983. Pony was lead alto player with Lionel Hampton's Orchestra, and was better known as modernist in the Bay area in 1950s and 1960s. He moved to Barcelona, Spain and, according to Hendricks suffered a stroke which has confined him to a wheelchair. Pony is not doing much instrumental work these days, "but he still scats!" said Hendricks gleefully.

Looking back on it, reeds and reedman flourish extremely well in the Crescent City. Maybe it has something to do with the water? Oh, yes. James Rivers also has been known to play bagpipes.

## Trombone

The role of the trombone in the New Orleans traditional jazz ensemble is that of a ground bass, to counterpoint and tonally color that ensemble with slurs, smears, slides and all of what the late Branch Rickey referred to as "those important intangibles." The phrase "tailgate" was coined here to describe the practice of touring jazz bands on a wagon seating the trombone player at the rear so he'd be able to maneuver his slide; and, of course, to do so, they had to, like "Tailgate Ramble" says "let the tailgate down." Roy Palmer recorded "Tiger Rag" in 1924 with Jelly Roll Morton's Kings of Jazz and showed smears in his obligatto work. (For an interesting comparison, hear Leon Rapollo's version of that warhorse with the New Orleans Rhythm Kings, where it's a *clarinet* and not a trombone feature.) Other early jazz trombonists in the New Orleans ensemble include Willie Cornish, a powerful man who was on his way to establish a dominant trombone style with Buddy Bolden when he was felled by a stroke, and Frankie Dusen, a sportin' man who took over Bolden's band when it wasn't a world beater for 1900 (cf., *In Search of Buddy Bolden*, by Donald A. Marquis, Louisiana State University Press, Baton Rouge, Louisiana [1978]); Bill (BeBe) Ridgley, of the Original Tuxedo Jazz Orchestra; Tom Brown of Algiers who took the first white "jass" (that's how he spelled it) group to Chicago in 1915; Russ Papalia (basically a pit bandsman but who did play jazz with Leon Prima) and Santo Pecora, an advocate of stand up, no-nonsense slidehorn. Eddie "Daddy" Edwards of the Original Dixieland Jazz Band was on the same mind.

Other trombone pioneers include Jack Carey, older brother of Mutt Carey (famous from the 1940s Kid Ory Band on the Orson Welles broadcast). Carey was so well known in Teens and Twenties that when the crowd wanted to hear the strain which has come to be known as *Tiger Rag*, they'd holler, "Play Jack Carey!" Zue Robertson was a popular New Orleans trombonist in the Twenties and Thirties who recorded with Jelly Roll Morton and Natty Dominique in 1923. The prolific Brunies family had another brassbound player other than those discussed herein: Henry (Trombone), whose work is unfamiliar to me. Oscar "Chicken" Henry was one of the earliest jazz trombonists, basically an ensemble player, and was honored in the 1970s by the New Orleans Jazz And Heritage Festival as a pioneer. Emile Christian, though born in New Orleans, joined the Original Dixieland Jazz Band at Reisenweber's in 1918, went to London, and after a stint with the Memphis Five, stayed in Europe for twenty years. He returned to New Orleans as bassist.

George Brunies, of The New Orleans Rhythm Kings, was a member of the Brunies family; later he changed the spelling of his name to Bruns, moved to Chicago and on to L.A. till his death in 1983. Edward "Kid" Ory and Honore Dutrey (of King Oliver's Creole Jazz Band) were at a par in ensembles; but when Kid joined Satch's Hot Five in 1925 he liberated the trombone from the ensemble and was the first *major* trombone soloist in traditional jazz of New Orleans and hence set the hallmark for the period and the style. Bill Matthews was originally a drummer; hence his was a booting, rhythmic style, foreshadowing the Kansas City sounds of J.C. Higgenbotham. Originally associated with

Papa Celestine and The Tuxedo Jazz Band, he led a band for years at the Paddock Lounge featuring Albert Burbank and Ernie Cagnolatti's clear trumpet.

Big Jim Robinson goes back to the mid-Twenties with Sam Morgan's bunch and was rediscovered in the mid-Forties, taking part with George Lewis in the Bunk Johnson revival records. His specialty was "Ice Cream," and it was his property. (His protégé, Frank Demond of the Preservation Hall Band, plays it in the brash spirit.)

The later 1940s saw a crop of young, talented trombonists come on the scene: Joe Rotis, with the Basin Street Six, was compared by critic George Hoefer with George Brunies of NORK. Freddie Assunto co-founded the Dukes of Dixieland with younger brother Frank and by far outplayed him early in their careers. Freddie had a clipped, staccato, punchy style. Jack Delaney came out of a Jack Teagarden mold, with a legato style that was just plain comfortable in any Dixieland format, be it with Sharkey, Fountain, Alcorn, or Collins—with all of whom he recorded as a sideman.

Older bands were beginning to work more regularly in the Fifties and Sixties. Clem Tervalon doubled bass and trombone and his brash brand was heard with Freddie Kohlman and his own group. (He still wails today and also has a day gig as a Deputy Civil Sheriff.) Preston Jackson returned from Chicago (where his lugubrious sounds has been part of Louis Armstrong's outfits) and moved in on Orleans Street. Louis Nelson, formerly with Ridgley, Fats Pichon, and Sidney Desvigne's organization, worked and most currently has been heard with his warm tone in The New Orleans Joymakers. The Eugene brothers, Wendell and Homer, both loud and loose blowers, were on the scene; theirs was more a Matthews-Higginbotham style. Bob Havens came to the Blue Room with Ralph Flanagan and stayed for years with Al Hirt before going out west to Welkland. Nick Gagliardi was and is heard with The Last Straws.

Waldren "Frog" Joseph stands head and shoulder above all of these. He and his sons (who are with the Dirty Dozen Brass Band) are most active today. He can smear, bray, slide, rip and snort at will. His wry humor recalls Vic Dickenson. He can play a glossary of trombone effects while constructing an organized solo that is in and of itself a composition. Though he didn't copyright it, he's admitted to me that he *did* write "Slide, Frog, Slide." He's a *gem* and works well with a plunger mute too!

Today there are superb trombonists all over the city but most are of the traditional jazz suasion. The exceptions are Freddie Lonzo, who goes from Bunk to Monk; John Dilkey (silky-smooth sliding leader of Tulane University's Jazz Band); and Al Herman, a Tulane physics professor who goes in and out of the city, performing irregularly, but who is one of the many undiscovered great talents kept under a bushel. His modern work with Al Belletto is most fondly remembered. He has received and turned down offers from name bandsmen to leave the city.

Jim Duggan writes, arranges, and plays Bill Clifford's big band. Eric Langstaff is a modern bass trombonist with Trick Bag who gets a lot of session work and has joyful solo voice. Boobie Floyd works with the Dukes. Scotty Hill, who has played with everyone in town, usually leads an impromptu jazz group in fair weather in Jackson

Square, choosing the street musicians life. Bob O'Rourke follows Teagarden and Abe Lincoln stylistically, wrote the tune "Where Y'At," preserving that subculture for posterity, and after stints with Dick Stabile and the Dukes, works Bourbon Street. George Prejan spent an extended period with Al Hirt; and I last saw him with Jim Maxwell's band. J. R. Miller came out of Loyola blowing up a storm and has worked with Stabile. He was last heard with Ed Lewis' band. Mike Guma, Tom Ebert, and Paul Crawford are good traditionalists; Ebert sounds especially good on records. Crawford is a jazz scholar too. Steve Yocum wails with Banu Gibson's group. Frank Naundorf came from Germany, has played with Olympia, but is most often heard with Danny Barker.

Lou Sino left Louis Prima in the Sixties to lead his own group. The man is an entertainer first and foremost, but can play good jazz trombone. Professor Gizmo (Rick Elmore) earned his spurs with west coast traditional clarinetist Rosy McHargue before he came to New Orleans, left for San Francisco, and came back again. Rick can play modern (as well as tailgate) trombone as he demonstrated during his association with Vladmir Vassillief while he was stationed here in the mid-Seventies. Lucien Barbarin keeps the traditional name and flame burning.

Look for young Delfeayo Marsalis (Ellis' son) to take strides forward as a player. Still a teenager, he has heard Bennie Green, and has Bob Brookmeyer's humor. I can't wait till he grows up and wails! He's currently in Boston at Berklee.

Benny Powell, superb ex-Basie trombonist, also came from New Orleans. He's a top Hollywood studio player today, according to ex-Louisianian O. C. Smith in a 1983 interview with the author.

## Banjo and Guitar

As the feature film recites about Emanuel Sayles, "that cat can play anything." He's the outstanding exponent of traditional jazz banjo here in the city and has been since the mid-Twenties. He also plays fine guitar, as does Danny Barker, who's played with everyone from King Oliver to Charlie Parker. Narvin Kimball is also a good banjoist with Preservation Hall. Johnny St. Cyr, formerly with King Oliver and later Satchmo, cut the strings from the rhythm section and made the banjo a solo instrument in the 1925 Hot Five sessions (listen to "Gut Bucket Blues"). The rediscovered Lawrence Marrero in the '40s revival maintained that same posture in the Bunk Johnson and George Lewis sessions. John Chaffe drives the Louisiana Jazz Repertory Ensemble today. Neal Unterseher, Frankie Lynne, and Buzz Podewell all work regularly today.

Until 1925 the banjo and/or guitar was purely a rhythmic accompaniment to the New Orleans ensemble. There's a world of difference between Bill Johnson with King Oliver's Creole, Jazz Band and Johnny St. Cyr with the same group. St. Cyr isn't just "chunk chunk" in the background. Joe Capraro (*sic* Capero) and Nappy Lamare (before the Bobcats) made memorable sides with Monk Hazel in the 1920s. The New Orleans Owls of 1928 had a stellar pairing when Monk Smith put down his tenor saxophone and played guitar duets with Rene Gelpi's banjo. This foreshadowed the DeGruy-Mackie moments with Hot Strings. Creole George Guesnon was recorded with Riverside Records in the 1950s and showed his craft. The legendary Snoozer Quinn recorded with Wiggs.

A thirteen-year-old Bill Huntington recorded on banjo for Folkways Records with Ed "Montudi" Garland, Buddy Bolden's bassist. Huntington developed into a superb bassist and was one of the city's first modern jazz guitarists, playing long-lined solos that hearkened to Jimmy Raney in their thoroughness and consistency. Justin Adams was the guitarist with his family band (pianist Dolly, drummer (now bassist) Placide, and bassist Gerald); he's now heard often with Alvin Alcorn at jazz brunches, with Andrew Hall Society Jazz Band, and on innumerable R&B sides from the '50s on, especially with Dave Bartholomew, with whom he still also appears. His is a more blues-based style. Edgar Blanchard and his guitar were prominent on 1950s R&B recordings as was Ernest McLean with Dave Bartholomew, and Walter "Papoose" Nelson and Ray Montrell with Fats Domino and Professor Longhair. Adaptable Erving "Buddy" Charles plays in all styles everywhere, with anyone!

There are more good guitarists in the city now than ever before, given the popularity of the instrument in the current rock genre. Charlie Brent (leader, writer, and arranger) of Trick Bag should give us more of his funky solo work. Ditto Sal Gentile, who's from the West Bank, another underrated player, though he's often added to the Blue Room band when a competent accompanist and soloist is called for by a visiting fireman. Cranston Clements (Ed Lewis' son) of The Rockabyes can whine and wail in a modern vein as can Scott Godeau (listen to his "Hot Stuff" solo on Chris Owen's album of the same name). Allen Toussaint is a good guitar soloist, not merely competent, though modern jazz is not necessarily his métier.

Gene Pelas is one of the those individuals for unknown reasons who hides his talent under a bushel. He's a Johnny Smith fan, but rarely appears. Gary Hulette has all the technique in the world, but doesn't want to work in a jazz context. Listeners have complained that when he gets started, he needs editing, 'cause he plays the history of jazz guitar in every number. He's a great example of unbridled talent who could be a major jazz soloist here.

On the other hand, the disciplined Steve Masakowski (who also doubles electric bass) is a soloist *par excellence*. He leads Mars and has appeared with everyone, from James Black to Jimmy Smith to "The Girl From Ipanema," Astrud Gilberto. He's contemporary to the core. Leo Nocentelli is called "the best damn guitarist in the whole damn world" by Meters fans; and, I've heard him play fearsome jazz even in a rock format.

Phil DeGruy and Hank Mackie are treated separately and together in the Hot Strings article. Emily Remler perked the Percolators and left for the Concord gold on the west coast. Walter Washington, the Wolf Man, wails, as do Gatemouth Brown and Deacon John Moore in more of a rock idiom. George Davis who played rock and jazz, left with Dizzy Gillespie in the Sixties, has comfortably ensconced in New York and has a studio. Jimmy Robinson is a fleet soloist who recalls Pat Metheny as he leads Woodenhead.

And Father Al Lewis, a traditional jazz banjoist, whose solo style comes from Earl Hines, still plects away at Preservation Hall.

## Bass and Tuba

Although Ed "Montudi" Garland worked with Buddy Bolden, it was "Pops" Foster who slapped and plucked the string bass into popularity here and in New York. In a WWOZ radio interview Danny Barker related how *all* of the New York tuba players lined up outside Pop's door for OJT (on the job training) and quickie-type instruction during Pop's tenure there in the Twenties. Again, we're speaking mainly of a *rhythmic* accompaniment. The tuba and its cousin, the sousaphone, have had somewhat more currency lately locally. Danny Rubio anchors the Dukes of Dixieland with a flowing tuba bass line. The Dirty Dozen uses the sousaphone of Kirk Joseph (Frog's son) like the string bass in a modern jazz combo; hence the Dirty Dozen plays a faster rhythm, as has been noted elsewhere. Olympia's Fats Lacen and Preservation Hall's Allen Jaffe are traditional tuba and bass horn players working today; TV newsman Bill Yeager also works occasionally on his big horn. Recently Phil Darois and Rick Elmore have been heard doubling tuba.

Chink Martin was an old line tuba player with NORK but later switched to bass. Bunny Franks organized the Basin Street Six, played with just about every local Dixie band and Forties and Fifties and still is in demand today. Emile Christian, one of the jazz pioneers, switched from trombone to string bass sometime in the 40s. Sherwood Mangiapane worked for a bank by day and plucked bass at night up and down Bourbon Street and in and out of Southland Recording Studios. Phil Darois, formerly of the Dukes, has gone from string bass to electric bass. Arnold Loyacano, of a prolific New Orleans jazz family, was the bassist with the New Orleans Rhythm Kings' predecessor, The Friars, and an active player in the 1920s and 1930s, following Steve Brown, a local legend who gained fame with NORK, Whiteman and Goldkette.

Richie Payne long worked with Belletto at the Playboy Club and with the New Orleans Symphony in the 1950s. Gerald and brother Placide Adams played both traditional and more modern dates. Chuck Badie took part in early Fifties modern jazz sessions for AFO Records and has recently started playing in earnest again.

Bill Huntington had the steadiest work, with Dick Stabile, Al Belletto, the Dukes and Hirt for extended periods, and there were few better players and no better soloists during the 1950s and 1960s. Lloyd Lambert (Phamous' brother) works Bourbon Street. George French plays electric bass almost exclusively; though early on his orientation was primarily as a singer, he is now a powerful ensemble and solo voice. Oliver Felix provides a bottom for Hirt and later Fountain and soloed well. Walter Payton works Bourbon Street on bass and tuba and modern gigs elsewhere. He's also a great teacher for young students in public schools. Everett Link was the bassist with Ronnie Kole.

In the 1970s Rusty Gilder came to town after working with Marian and Jimmy McPartland, Jimmy Rowles, and the Ellingtonians and was much in demand. Al Bernard

Jr. worked with Rene Netto, the Stabile Band, the Dukes, Bourbon Street, and is now back in the Blue Room with Bill Clifford's Orchestra. Frank Fields came from Plaquemine, Louisiana, and gigged up and down Bourbon Street. Chris Severin is a youngster who's gained experience with Ellis Marsalis and bears watching. For a time he was the house bassist at the Hyatt Regency LeClub and has appeared with, among others, Red Norvo and Earl Hines.

Over the past several years in almost every context the call has been for Jimmy James Singleton to play bass with the group. He came here with Gatemouth Brown, but is now so much a part of the city and its jazz scene. Fans have watched him grow from a rebellious kid with enthusiasm, long hair, and great technique and ideas going in every direction into a mature, accomplished jazz soloist on upright who can play bop, free, fusion, funk and anything. He's a clear cut superstar that is often part of Ellis Marsalis' group, Astral Project, Mike Pellara's Trio, and every other good band you can name. Ramsey McLean, who leads the Lifers, is more oriented to free jazz. He is admired by Sam Rivers and other New York players. He's our local answer to the music Charlie Mingus made.

The venerable Chester Zardis and James Prevost are still playing Preservation Hall today and carrying on the tradition of Alcide "Slow Drag" Pavegeau, the revivalist discovery of the 1940s.

Electric bassists of note in the city include the adaptable Jim Markway (with Jasmine), Edgar Lips (with Woodenhead) and the redoubtable David Lee Watson (of Trick Bag) whose lines are object lessons in now to swing and yet give a solid bottom to a brass heavy group. David has recorded with Professor Longhair and has the best sound in town on the electric instrument. George Porter (ex-Meter) is primarily a rock bassist, but he plays just the right notes economically. Cranston Clements, primarily a guitarist, has played jazz gigs on electric bass also. Elton Herron is heard exclusively with Edward "Kidd" Jordan's ultra contemporary group. Julius Farmer, an ex-Southern Jaguar, and active locally in the Seventies is reportedly in Los Angeles with pianist Henry Butler and guitarist Victor Sirker, ex-Orleanians. Joseph Hebert heads up the Loyola Jazz Studies program and performs on acoustic and electric bass with the Loyola University Faculty Jazz group and with Jubilation.

## Drums

Baby Dodds' "Spooky Drums" solo from 1946 has been cited by many as showing the African influence of rhythm and drums in jazz. I don't necessarily agree. Berendt, Collier, and other jazz scholars have pointed out the basic rhythmic difference in African drumming and jazz drumming. But, the role of the jazz drummer in the traditional New Orleans group evolved from that of a *time-keeper* who kept the beat to a *rhythm maker* accenting the beat, to a soloist flowing above and around the beat. Although Dodds was the premier timekeeper and occasional soloist for the Creole Jazz Band days of the Twenties, Louis Cottrell, Sr. of A. J. Piron's Orchestra was admired by no less than

Armstrong himself. Cornelius Tillman, Buddy Bolden's drummer, left the jazz business shortly after Buddy went insane (1907).

The parade march beat tempered by ragtime and the popular dance tempi of the day melded into the rhythms utilized by jazz drummers in the early years in New Orleans. Revered drummers of the Twenties were Abbie Foster of the Original Tuxedo Band of Celestine and Ridgley, Josiah "Cie" Frazier, who later joined Celestine's offshoot of the band in 1927 and *still* plays Preservation Hall today, and Monk Hazel, who played with the Wiggs, Nappy Lamare, Sidney Arondin and Sharkey Bonano in the late Twenties.

The other local tower of strength in drumming of this period was "Drumface", Zutty Singleton, who refined Dodd's style into his own. Even in early recordings with Fate Marable, whose Society Syncopaters played the Streckfus Line, you could hear the unaccented four beats that Sam Chartres claims some feel came from Memphis ("Memphis time") but which was a Zutty trademark with its unrelenting drive. Zutty later went on to fame with Armstrong, Bechet, and leading his own group, even recording with modernist Charlie Parker in the 1940s! The Barbarin brothers, Paul and Lewis, were especially active throughout this period; frankly, they were both great and there was little to choose between them.

Others also on the scene were Abbie Brunies, plus one of the New Orleans brother acts: Minor "Ram" Hall and Tubby Hall, brothers who played with Frank Dusen's Eagle Band, King Oliver, Kid Ory, and then in Chicago in the Twenties with Noone. All of these names were rediscovered by the revivalists in the Forties. Ray Bauduc had gone west with the Bobcats after stints with the Dorseys and Joe Venuti.

It was in the Forties that the role of the drummer New Orleans ensembles seemed to change. Listen to the Oscar "Papa" Celestine recordings where Christopher "Black Happy" Goldston is on hand. One hears the beats being accented sometimes erratically, a departure from Zutty's credo. I'm told by New Orleans jazzmen that these are important recordings and Goldston was very influential among the young crop of drummers. The Riverside Records revival of the 1960s trouped out drummers who had been playing well since the Thirties and Forties—Frazier, Alfred Williams, Sammy Penn, and Albert Jiles. Charlie Duke was with the Basin Street Six in the Forties. Phil Zito discovered two youngsters, named George Girard and Pete Fountain in the Forties and had them, along with Joe Rotis, for the front line in his Dixieland combo even before the advent of the Basin Street Six of Bunny Franks.

The advent of New Orleans rhythm and blues recordings in the Fifties greatly influenced the beat of New Orleans jazz. "Fusion" started *here*, right at the drum stool. Smoky Johnson played R&B sessions at Cosimo's Studios by day and often Dixieland at night. His later appearances with Bourbon Street Dixieland combos and the Dukes of Dixieland demonstrate how such fusion of rock and jazz came to be. Since that time the city has been awash with drummers who can play New Orleans style along with many other styles. Frank Parker played R&B and jazz dates. Vernell Fournier left for Chicago where he sparked the Ahmad Jamal Trio and in an interview with this author, Ahmad recalled how Vernell often utilized his New Orleans "roots" in performances.

There were drummers in the Fifties and Sixties who, although they worked Bourbon Street, were not strictly two-or-four beaters: Louis Timken, Bill Hawkins, Paul Edwards, Milton Rich, Dick Johnson with the Dukes of Dixieland, Paul Edwards with Pete Fountain and Al Hirt and Freddie Kohlman with his own group and others of note, before his stint at Chicago's Jazz Limited. Reed Vaughan was an early modernist; and ex-Stan Kenton sideman, he joined pianist Joe Burton's trio and later moved into the Blue Room where he played till 1983 (I saw him working Bourbon Street in the summer of 1983). Earl Palmer was also on the scene recording R&B dates with Lee Allen and jazz with Jack Martin (of the Al Belletto band) and Mouse Bonati. Earl later left for California where he's been much in demand for studio work, has gigged with Buddy Collette, and then became an official in the Musician's Union. Tony Bazley left the city with the Johnson Brothers Band in 1951, went to the west coast and worked with Eric Dolphy, and recorded with Leroy Vinnegar and returned to the Crescent City in the 1970s. Paul Ferrara worked two bass drums (*á la* Louis Bellson) with Hirt, The Dukes, and Murphy Campo.

The 1960s and 1970s saw the rise of many good drummers in the city. Dicky Taylor pushed the Ronnie Kole Trio. John Boudreaux was with the AFO group; his LeJohn recording with Melvin Lastie is well described by annotator Harold Batiste as "drums, drums all over the place." Along came James Black, the youngest lion in the AFO pride. Young, gifted, and black, after some superb compositions and recordings (e.g. Monkey Puzzle) he toured with ultra-modern (for the time) Yuseff Lateef and Horace Silver went to the Big Apple and found it rotten to the core. He came back home in the mid-Seventies. He is one of the most sought after and pre-eminent local drummers. He played the "One Mo Time Show and Shangri-La." He has appeared on club dates and at the New Orleans Jazz And Heritage Festival with national stars of the stripe of organist Jimmy Smith and worked locally with Belletto, Marsalis, Jasmine, and other modern groups as well as leading his own ensemble. He not only keeps great time; he colors the beat, shading it to perfection. His compositional talents are boundless; his "Little Boy Man" is still performed locally, as is "Monkey Puzzle," and "Magnolia Triangle," a 5/4 composition that doesn't ape Brubeck-Desmond's Take Five. He deserves national recognition; and nobody plays a better set of fours than James Black.

Al Belletto also plucked another gem in Johnny Vidacovich, out of Loyola's School of Music, and made him his regular drummer while Johnny was still a teenager. Vidacovich's uncle, a traditionalist, would be proud to hear Johnny's New Orleans drums on a recent Ronnie Kole Dixieland recording; but Johnny V. is a superb modernist who *composes* a drum solo, building on it musically and emotionally. He's played with Joe Williams, Eddie Harris, Sam Rivers, Mose Allison,—the list is endless! He's "first call," as they say. He toured with Professor Longhair, interned in Italy, matured, and came back with renewed vigor. With Jimmy Singleton and David Torkanowsky, they formed the

New Orleans rhythm section that can—and does—play in Astral Project and several other modern jazz groups around town.

Another great drummer to come to the fore with AFO, moved away to the west coast where he became famous with Ornette Coleman (who has spent some time here in New Orleans); he makes occasional visitations back here: Edward Blackwell. A master percussionist who has unfortunately been ill for several years, he, Black, and Boudreaux helped New Orleans jazz drummers turn the corner into modern jazz.

Bob Breaux, another Loyola Jazz Band alum, was active in New Orleans in the 1970s and 1980s, teaching at Loyola's Institute of Jazz Studies, working with Al Belletto and Al Hirt and appearing with Art Pepper in 1979 on a local date. After the 1983 NOJHF he headed for the studios in Texas, but returns often. Ricky Sebastian played jazz with pianist Chuck Berlin's Trio and with Belletto and filled in with Leigh Harris (Little Queenie), and recorded with The Lifers and "jazz poet" Ron Cuccia. In June, 1983, he moved to New York. Joseph "Zigaboo" Modeliste is such an accomplished drummer in R&B and when the Meters have David Torkanowsky on keyboards he shows his jazz side. Jeff Boudreaux, a youngster, has worked with Ronnie Kole and Mose Allison. Alvin Fielder lives in Mississippi at last report, but visits here often enough with Ramsey McLean and The Lifers and Kidd Jordan (with whom he's recorded) to be considered a "home boy." He's an ex-associate of the avant-garde Art Ensemble of Chicago.

Special mention should be made of Idris Muhamud, a New Orleans drummer also known as Leo Morris, who has gone on to international jazz fame. He says, and there's no gainsaying it, that when he went to New York in the late 'Sixties and early 'Seventies, he introduced the New Orleans beat—that funky, parade-born pulse from the swamp—to The Apple. Julian Garcia, a fine local modernist, is adept and adaptable and follows in that style.

Other drummers active in the Seventies and Eighties include the late Popee Lastie (of that fine Bourbon Street Black family, who could drive a band by dint of his own personality); Alonzo Stewart, Duke Barker, Ernest Elly (ex-Ray Charles and Dukes of Dixieland), Stanley Williams, British import Trevor Richard, Howie Kadison, Ken Allen, and June Gardner (ex-Lionel Hampton). These mainly worked in the traditional and/or Dixieland (Bourbon Street) context, but some (especially Barker, Elly and Gardner) have been heard playing more contemporary rhythms with authority. Allyn Robinson drives Trick Bag relentlessly. Bill Clifford's Orchestra has Vic Zipeto, an adaptable, ex-Belletto Sideman, on its drum stool. Frank Vicari is often heard with Ed Lewis and Harry Morel's bands.

Herlin Riley, of the Lastie family (Melvin's nephew) is a superb young drummer (now with Ahmad Jamal) who I first heard with Vladmir Vassilief's Latin-based group and later with Johnny Bachemin's Trio. He's been coveted by many local leaders and has appeared in modern jazz and traditional context as well as rock. Another fine young player is Noel Kendrick, with Delfeayo Marsalis's group at the New Orleans Jazz And

Heritage Festival in 1983; he also plays both contemporary and classic New Orleans rhythms. James Comiskey (of Woodenhead) is a youngster to watch also.

A special mention should be made for percussionist Mark Sanders, who appears with Caliente (his own combo), Woodenhead, Astral Project, Jasmine, and others. He's a student of Latin rhythms and adds judicious percussive color to whatever context in which he appears.

## Piano

If Storyville had a positive side for jazz, its most salutory effect was on pianists; for it gave them many varied venues for employment, from Lulu White's Establishment to Tom Brown's Cafe. And the king of Storyville was Professor Antoine Jackson, Jr., self-taught, known to history as Tony Jackson, composer of "Pretty Baby."[1] Clarence Williams played Storyville, soaking up blues and atmosphere, led various recording groups, but made his name as a publisher and promoter, as did Richard "Trouble In Mind" Jones. Jelly Roll Morton bridged ragtime and blues and his Library of Congress recordings evoke memories of those early formative years of jazz. A superb orchestrator as well as pianist, the Winin' Boy, despite his flamboyance, never failed to make good any boasts. His Red Hot Peppers are one of the classic traditional jazz groups and Jelly's compositions are evergreens.

These pianists in Storyville were called "Professors." Perhaps none was as more renowned and has more lived up to his name than 'Fess Manuel Manetta, who in 1907 was at Willie Piazza's and in the 1960s on public television series with Armand Hug teaching the roots of New Orleans jazz piano. Before his death in 1969 he had taught scores of New Orleans pianists. Isadore "Tuts" Washington played Storyville then and often plays the Fairmont Court today.

There were other Storyville Professors chronicled in Al Rose's history cited above: John The Baptist, Buddy Carter, Kid Ross, Albert Cahill (aka Carrol aka Carell), Sammy Lewis, Mamie Desdoumes (who taught Jelly), Frank "Dude" Amacker, Steve Lewis, who later joined A. J. Piron's Orchestra. These were essentially blues and ragtime solo-ists who could "jazz up" on occasional ballad of the day. Few were probably schooled; Lewis was the exception—he could and did perform with others (like Piron in 1925).

In the 1920s jazz piano in New Orleans was manned by Henry Ragas and J. Russell Robinson with the Original Dixieland Jazz Band; Sweet Emma Barrett with The Original Tuxedo Jazz Orchestra who played till the Eighties in and around the nation and the city (even after a stroke) with Preservation Hall Bands; Bill Eastwood with the Original New Orleans Rhythm Kings as well as Elmer Schoebel and Mel Stitzel (before he went to Chicago); Norman Brownlee with Emmett Hardy and Tom Brown; Johnny Miller with Johnny Bayersdorffer; Morris Rouse with trumpeter Louis Dumaine's Jazzola Eight, Walter Decou with Sam Morgan; Fate Marable with his orchestra on the Streckfus Line Boats; Bill Whitmore with the Halfway House band of Abbie Brunies; Johnny Riddick with the Arcadian Serenaders; Zefried (aka Sigfried) Christensen with the New Orleans

Owls; Jeanette Salvant (now Kimball) with Papa Celestine (she's still quite active today); and Joe Robichaux among others. These were essentially band pianists who could solo with authority, but were not known as singular stylists (though many, like Sweet Emma and Jeanette Kimball grew into that role). There were also the legendary barrelhouse pianists, like Drive'em Down, admired by Champion Jack Dupree.

In the 1940s, during the renaissance of New Orleans jazz, the archivists re-discovered Alton Purnell, who took part in George Lewis and Bunk Johnson sessions; Bert Peck, who had played with Emmett Hardy; Stanley Mendelson, grossly underrated as soloist and a band pianist; the late Armand Hug, a talented link between the immediate past and that present who could play in all styles and did successfully till the 1970s; Quentin Batiste with Freddie Kohlman; Roy Zimmerman with the Basin Street Six; Walter Lewis, and Octave Crosby, who worked with Sidney Desvigne and Papa Celestine; Jeff Riddick, who despite looking like Harry Truman, was a fine jazz player in the tradition.

The advent of modern jazz in the mid-Forties and Fifties led to a new crop of jazz pianists. The odysseys of Roger Dickerson and Ellis Marsalis are covered in separate vignettes. Frank Strazzeri ventured through town in the 1950s and recorded with Jack Martin and left. Freddie Crane was an important cog with Al Belletto before going to Texas to make a mint in the studios. Fats Pichon and LaVergne Smith played more traditional stride and cafe society solo piano at the Old Absinthe House during this decade; Fats, formerly with Luis Russell, was a Gershwin favorite, and could play stride, while LaVergne could give Dorothy Donegan a run for her money at that juncture. These were all post-1940s jazz oriented players.

Snookum Russell left the territory band bushes (he'd discovered Ray Brown, Tommy Turrentine, Fats Navarro, J. J. Johnson, and Joe Harris) and hustled a job, working solo at the Paddock for years, till ill health, and finally death stilled the spirit of Fats Waller that Snookum played so well. He only recorded a couple of times, more's the pity. Ed Frank was a superb modernist of this era. He suffered a stroke, is still active today, and is a good player. "But," a contemporary of his opines, "you should a heard him *before* the stroke." He wrote, arranged, and conducted one of the finest aggregations of New Orleans contemporary jazzmen at the 1980 New Orleans Jazz And Heritage Festival as the New Orleans Be Bop All Stars.

The 1960s saw Al Belletto with a fine group of pianists coming in and out of the Playboy Club, such Johnny Probst and Buddy Prima. Henry Butler left for the west coast after being coached by Alvin Batiste. Frank Puzzullo worked with Belletto, taught at Loyola's Institute of Jazz Studies, and is now in jazz education in the mid-west. Antonio York joined the Blue Room band and stayed from Stabile through Bill Clifford.

More into the Seventies came Billy Meynier with various Bourbon Street groups and The Dukes of Dixieland, where he replaced Tim Herbez. David Thomas Roberts occasioned into town to play ragtime. John Royen and Steve Pistorius are covered as is Lars Edegran. Harvey Rubin and Phil Morgan worked Bourbon Street playing a lot more than traditional jazz piano. Roosevelt Sykes brought his Honeydripper home to roost as did cousin Joe (Pleasant Joseph), both veterans of numerous jazz and blues recordings in New York, Chicago, and overseas. Johnnie Bachemin, a dancer, and self-taught, played driving, popularly accessible jazz piano at the Monteleone. Bobby Broockmann had been playing cocktail piano; but after jamming at the benefit concert for Frank Assunto, turned to jazz full-time. Olivia Cook Charlot recorded gospel and worked Bourbon Street. Bob Discon, who'd recorded with George Girard, played solo gigs mainly for hotel traffic; Don Ewell, the internationally renowned stride-master (who died in August, 1983) did a turn with Frank Assunto's Dukes, then solo at the Royal Orleans, and left for Florida. Frank "Lil Daddy" Moliere worked Bourbon Street; Pete Montelone, The Top of The Mart. Wilson Turbinton (Willie Tee) played jazz with his brother Earl and funk with everyone else. Emile Vinette worked jazz brunches with various traditional groups and is a powerful player. Ronnie Kole cut a popular trail with Everett Link (b) and Dicky Taylor (drums) in the 1960s and 1970s.

Those were the traditional and modern (contemporary jazz) pianists of the Fifties, Sixties, and Seventies. There were also a group of pianists closely aligned (like Wille Tee) who were into "a whole 'nother bag; *viz*." New Orleans Rhythm and Blues; from the 1950s on, this city did to R&B what Nashville did to country—shaped, marketed, and sold it. Most important pianists of genre R&B are led by the unique Henry Roland Byrd, aka Professor Longhair (or 'Fess), whose piano style based from boogie, blues, and Caribbean idiosyncrasy into an intensively rhythmic entity. Fats Domino, Huey "Piano" Smith, Tommy Ridgley, Paul Gayton, Clarence "Frogman" Henry, Lawrence Cotton, Archibald, and Sugar Boy Crawford are of this same stripe. Allen Toussaint and Mac Rebennack (Dr. John) are of a somewhat later period, as are Art Neville, Al Farrell, and James Booker. These are talented players who specialize in a type of music that is more akin to jazz; it is an important facet of the jazz spectrum.[2] Without New Orleans Rhythm and Blues of the 1950s what goes under the title of "fusion" music today would not exist.

In the 1980s pianists find themselves called upon to play a variety of jazz styles and a variety of keyboard instruments. James Singleton says that "New Orleans is now a piano player's town." Especially active on the scene today in contemporary jazz is James Drew, a noted classical composer who also teaches at Loyola's Institute of Jazz Studies. He can play in a variety of styles with uncanny lyricism. David Torkanowsky plays jazz, rock, and traditional with great finesse and adaptability. He's worked with everyone from Frank Trapani, to George Porter, Allen Toussaint, Astral Project, and with every major, nationally known jazz instrumentalist or vocalist who's visited New Orleans in the past five years. With Singleton and Vidacovich they constitute New Orleans' version of the All-American rhythm section. Harry Connick, Jr. was subjected to indulgent Dixieland recordings while a sub-teen with old-line jazzmen; but, after a stint with Ellis Marsalis at the New Orleans Center For The Creative Arts he was a prize-winning soloist at the National Association of Jazz Educators Conference in 1983. Willie Metcalf came from the Detroit scene and was closely associated with Barry Harris, that area's piano master.

The late Eddie Collins played New Orleans traditional staples (remember his Someday You'll Be Sorry?) but was more at home with Germaine Bazzle, Red Tyler, and The Gentlemen of Jazz. Alan White broadcasts mornings over WWOZ and works evenings at Windsor Court Hotel, though he's served time with Bobby Byrne's Big Band in the New York City area. Dr. Chuck Berlin heads L.S.U. Medical School's Speech and Hearing Center, but has performed solo around Baltimore and with a trio locally, as well as in concert. Ronnie Dupont was one of the first I heard doing modern insertions with Al Hirt; he's worked conventions with a trio and can play Hines, Wilson, and Bud Powell sounds. Phamous Lambert is discussed in the vignette of the Dukes of Dixieland. A. J. Loria is a talented composer and vocalist. Larry Sieberth is a most contemporary keyboard player. Phil Parnell accompanies singers Lady B.J. and Leslie Smith.

Jim Moore, a talented baritone sax player, has played Bourbon Street and at The Top Of The Mart, with the S-Mart Guys, as a pianist. Banu Gibson has a youngster well versed in tradition and stride: David Boedinghaus, who is drawing rave reviews deservedly.

The newest returnee to the city, and one of the busiest, is Mike Pellara, formerly with Woody Herman and Buddy Rich. Mike has a steady gig with his trio, backing Germaine Bazzle, and with Earl Turbinton. He's quite a player and has a great sense of humor in his style.

All of the above have some familiarity with various keyboards, with Al Farrell, Allen Toussaint, and Lawrence Cotton probably the earliest to switch-hit on acoustic and electric. David Torkanowsky is especially adept. Allen Toussaint is the sole Liberation soloist I've seen on the scene. Willie Tee, Art Neville, and Ivan Neville double effectively. Ray Morvant is heard on keyboards with Chris Owens. He's her musical director and has arranged jazz charts for the Loyola Jazz Band and Ronnie Kole.

## Vocalists

Although, as we've seen, jazz in New Orleans developed out of gospel, blues, hollers, and ethnic songs, the early days of New Orleans jazz didn't emphasize vocal contributions. Lorenzo Staultz, a guitarist, is reported to have improvised some obscene lyrics from "Buddy Bolden's Blues" while with Buddy's 1906 band.[3] Jelly Roll Morton was a charming vocalist in Storyville as was Tony Jackson—in fact, many of the Storyville Professors sang; but, as Al Rose notes, "The type of vocal blues made famous by Ma Rainey, Bessie Smith . . . was not indigenous to New Orleans and prominent in Storyville's musical picture, but at least one such singer, Ann Cook, did perform in the district. . . ."

Of course, the players themselves sang. One of the very important byproducts of Louis Armstrong's Hot Five recordings were his vocals, jazz vocals, some with improvised "scat" singing, wordless vocalese imitative of instrumental sounds. In fact, if you hear Armstrong's trumpet and then hear his voice, it is undoubtedly the ideation of the same person. Similarly, Kid Ory played and sang, including some "sanitized" blues from

Storyville and creole patois tunes like "Eh, la, bas!" Cousin Joe (Pleasant Joe aka Joseph Pleasants) recorded with great jazzmen in New York after gigging here in the city as did Champion Jack Dupree, a boxer turned blues singer in the 1930s, who also attended the same waif's home as Satchmo. Lizzie Miles in the 1940s began to attract attention in radio broadcasts as a blue belter in English and Cajun French with Sharkey Bonano's band. Papa Celestine on the same broadcasts sang in his own gentle style, which was more conversational in its approach.

Then there was Blue Lu Barker, originally a dancer, with her husband Danny Barker, banjoist and jazzman extraordinare. They had a hit with the somewhat risque, "Don't You Feel My Leg" (also recorded by Big Joe Turner [also a New Orleans resident in the Fifties] as "Don't You Make Me High") and censors banned it from broadcast in the Thirties.

Blanche Thomas, niece of Lizzie Miles, came to prominence in the Fifties and was finally beginning to get a deserved audience when she died in the 1970s. She had the Empress of the Blues disposition to go with her talent. Alto saxist-vocalist Louis Jordan of this city made "Caldonia" a national hit and, Bobby Mitchell said, "opened the doors" for a lot of rhythm and blues artists.

Strangely enough, it was that "new" music that evolved out of the 1950s rhythm and blues sessions in New Orleans that gave the city its vocal surge that still obtains today. The Fats Domino, Smiley Lewis, Huey Smith, Al Johnson, Lee Dorsey, et al. sessions gave rise to a new crop of rhythm and blues-based vocalists who also had a toehold on jazz, such as Johnny Adams, who has held his own in sets with vocalese master Bobby McFerrin at the 1983 New Orleans Jazz And Heritage Festival. Barbara George, Annie Laurie, the Dixie Kups were contemporaries of Irma Thomas, a lady who went west and then came home to rediscovery. *She's* still going strong. The Meters (Art Neville, Leo Nocentelli, George Porter, and Zigaboo Modeliste) foresaw fusion back in 1969. Aaron Neville's golden tones preserved telling it like it is still today and 'Fess told us about Tipitina's. The Nevilles with the Wild Tchoupitoulas made Mardi Gras Indian music and chant meaningful all year long and showed another of the roots of jazz in New Orleans. And though Frankie Ford (Guzzo) could give us motion sickness in "Sea Cruise," on "Time After Time" he showed he could have taken the path and been a good jazz vocalist. A. J. Loria sings his own material well.

Tami Lynn recorded with her discoverer, Red Tyler, on the old AFO label, went to L.A., New York, London, and was last heard with Dr. John and in her own Dinah Washington tribute program. Germaine Bazzle, a superb vocalist today, is the subject of further discussion herein. Angelle Trosclair was discovered and featured with Al Belletto. After a west coast recording career, she's back in New Orleans much the wiser. Joanna Martin, a statuesque redhead who is jazz influenced, sang ballads well with Belletto in Fat City. Coco York made big sounds with a big voice and was last heard of in Holland after moving from Australia. LaVergne Smith sang in the French Quarter in a Sarah Vaughn mode for some time. She died in 1983.[4] LaVerne Butler is now with Jasmine; a stunningly beautiful lady, her vocal artistry is no less arresting. Banu Gibson sings traditional jazz brassily and happily, and makes the good times roll! Mary Bonnett is heard with James Black.

Luther Kent is a blues brawler; with Trick Bag and Charlie Brent, he's in a superb element. Lady B. J. Crayton has all the tools, experience and appearance, but needs direction. Leslie Smith works regularly as does Sandy Hancock, who I heard doing great work with clarinetist Frank Mannino's Big Band. (Some say Frank could give Pete Fountain a run for his money!) Allen Toussaint's new vocalist Carla Baker just signed with Island Records, and has shown she can do more than just contemporary popular music. Linda Aubert plays bass and piano and sings jazz. Sally Townes has a deft touch on keyboard instruments and her sound system; she went through the jazz program at North Texas State. Stephanie Sieberth is one of the more forward looking vocal artists on the scene, building on the past with a view ahead. Nelly Gauthé sings early blues. Helen Matthews sang gospel with The Southern Harps. She went to Broadway as Linda Hopkins singing Bessie Smith in "Me and Bessie."

The Pfister Sisters have proven crowd pleasers at the New Orleans Jazz And Heritage Festival and have a regular Sunday gig, as of this writing. They perform Boswell Sisters repertory better than the original New Orleans girls did themselves. Granted, Connee, et al., were hampered by the commercial demands of sweetness and light of the Thirties and Forties and never individually or as a group were able to make the vocal style take off and fly. The Pfisters, however, soar more often than not, unhampered by any Bing Crosby philosophy. They also perform more contemporary material.

Many contemporary singers here in New Orleans are perhaps better described as jazz influenced. I'm not going to stir up the controversy as to what makes a jazz singer. Let me say, though, I consider Mel Tormé to be a jazz singer just as much as Bessie Smith—if not more so. Thus, my observations on that vocal art are rather catholic—even for an instrumentalist!

## Passin' Thru

There are several other jazzmen who made New Orleans for a short period of time and then moved elsewhere, often to greater fame and fortune. I've mentioned some as I've gone along. Some of their visits and stays are apocryphal (e.g., Ornette Coleman is reported to have done yard work and manual labor according to liner notes to his first contemporary records album, with few playing gigs). Vladimir Vassillief, who is recounted earlier, came with Charo, stayed and worked in Latin and Dixieland Bands and left. Rick Kriska, a fine tenor player in the Eighties, worked locally till "Dancin'" stole him for the pit band. Lon Price, who was ubiquitous in the Seventies on tenor and soprano on modern jazz gigs, moved to California.

Earlier, in the 1950s and 1960s, the Playboy Club, under the musical directorship of Al Belletto, was a haven for jazzmen passin' thru. Trombonist Roger DeLillo graduated from Berklee School of Music, gigged here for several seasons, then went back to

Philadelphia where he was musical director of the Mike Douglas TV show. Bob Teeters was a modern trumpet player with him at that time. Willie Thomas worked with Al Belletto's group and was called by many the finest modern jazz trumpet in the area in the late 1950s. He's now an outstanding member of the National Association Of Jazz Educators in Valdosta, Georgia. Freddie Crane played piano and arranged for Belletto and is now in Texas with a jingle empire. Ed Fenasci was a good modern jazz pianist at the club. Jack Martin played French horn, composed and arranged for Belletto and is now out of state.

Rudy Aikels was a Florida A&M graduate who came, played modern jazz bass at the Playboy Club with pianist Buddy Prima, and then became the first modern electric bassist with Frank Assunto and The Dukes of Dixieland. He's now active in Las Vegas, working with his wife, vocalist Edie Aikels, according to B. B. King (with whom he was formerly employed) in a 1983 interview with the author. Larry Muhoberac, pianist, vocalist, and arranger, had a Belletto-like group in Baton Rouge that played the Starmist Lounge, played New Orleans, and later was heard recording with Barbara Streisand and Ray Conniff.

Pianist Joe Burton spent a stint in the city in the 1960s with his own club at the corner of Jefferson Davis and Canal. Jay Cave, formerly of Ralph Sharon's trio, was a bassist with the group. He later went to the Playboy Hutch and left town. Bob Ciccarelli was another bassist the often erratic Burton employed. Bob was last reported in the Los Angeles area. Jimmy Fox was a drummer with several local groups and once had the distinction of replacing Buddy Rich in 1960s in Buddy's own group at the Dream Room, playing with Carmen Leggio, John Bunch, et al., when Buddy's plane didn't arrive on time. I've asked numerous musicians as to his whereabouts to no avail; he's also worked with Roger Dickerson and Earl Williams, but isn't even listed in the AFM directory now. Trumpeter Warren Leuning, Jr. is a studio man out west.

In 1983, Joe Pass, the great jazz guitarist, recounted in an interview that he was here for ten months in 1949, coming to town with the Stylists at the Monteleone. He stayed, playing for strippers at the Gunga Den on Bourbon Street because, after 3:00 A.M. "we could jam, and that's what kept me here," he recalls. He mentioned Johnny Elgin, a pianist from Chicago (that Belletto says now is in Florida), as being active on that scene, along with the tenor player, Pete Kowchak, as well as Benny Clements, and the great Brew Moore "off and on." "In 1949 there was as much good jazz and good players happening here as in, say, Chicago; 'cause you could live here relatively cheap and you could play—all night and all day!" Going further back Luis Russell came from Panama in the Twenties and played locally before heading north and later east to New York to records and recognition. Another pianist, Henry Butler, was a Southern University Jaguar, gigged locally, won a grant to study with McCoy Tyner in the Seventies and now makes the west coast his home. And we all know the heights to which the great vocalist Bobby McFerrin has soared since he spent seasons here with Astral Project! Earl Bostic was taught alto sax by a nun at Xavier and turned that knowledge into an international career. Wellman Braud, a mainstay bassist of early Duke Ellington orchestras, toured nationally and internationally. Donald Harrison played tenor at NOCCA with the Marsalis clan and now gigs in New York.

These jazzmen all flavored jazz in New Orleans and all over the world—and vice versa.

Notes for "A Concise History of Jazz in New Orleans and New Orleans Jazzmen"

[1]See Al Rose, *Storyville, New Orleans* (University, Ala., 1974) for a fine vignette of this early monarch, with tributes from Johnny St. Cyr, Bunk Johnson, Alberta Hunter, and two of his most famous followers, Plaquemine, Louisiana's Clarence Williams and Jelly Roll Morton.

[2]For a thorough history of this aspect of New Orleans music, see John Broven, *Rhythm And Blues In New Orleans* (Gretna, La., 1978).

[3]See Don Marquis, *In Search of Buddy Bolden's Band* (Baton Rouge, La., 1978), 78-79.

[4]Ibid.

# DIDN'T HE RAMBLE?*

Laurence Bergreen

Louis was in Spoleto, Italy, that night for a performance, and became seriously ill. Alerted, Dr. Schiff found him on his knees, grasping the bed, and immediately called an ambulance. During the ride, Louis said, "I don't know why they are taking me to the hospital. I'm fine," but the physicians who examined him described his condition as "grave." In the hospital, he ran a fever of 104 degrees, and an attendant was about to give him an injection of penicillin, to which he was allergic, when Dr. Schiff ran into the room and shattered the syringe.

As the news that he was stricken spread to newspapers worldwide, everyone around Louis went into denial. Dr. Schiff declared that his patient had not suffered a heart attack; the diagnosis, he said, was pneumonia. The Italian doctors concurred. Louis simply refused to believe that after all the Swiss Kriss he had ingested to cleanse his bowels and marijuana he had inhaled to relax his mind, he could possibly have had a heart attack. Nevertheless, that was precisely what had happened to him. Even when forced to confront the truth, he disputed its meaning. "Man, a heart attack is nothing but so much *gas* accumulated and bubbled over," he said.

Under the cover story that he was recovering from a bout of pneumonia, Louis remained in the hospital until the end of the month. From Spoleto, he went to Rome, where he visited St. Peter's and rested in his hotel room, still insisting that he had not had a heart attack. He flew home to New York and stunned everyone by appearing, unannounced, in the middle of a concert at Lewisohn Stadium on July 4, his ceremonial birthday. "If there had been a roof, it would have been blown off," said the reviewer from the *New York Times*. He blew for fifteen minutes or so, taking it easy with tunes like "When It's Sleepy Time Down South," and after his brief set ended, he declared, "I didn't come here to prove I'm not sick. I came just to play." By September, he was back on

*From Laurence Bergreen, *Louis Armstrong*. Copyright © 1997 by Laurence Bergreen. Used by permission of Broadway Books, a division of Bantam Doubleday Dell Publishing Group.

the road with a limited performing schedule, and seemed so much his old self that he managed to convince everyone that the heart attack had never occurred.

In the months to come, people close to Louis would question the wisdom of Joe Glaser's working his renowned client almost to death. Louis went along with the plan; as far as he was concerned, if he was too feeble to stand up in front of an audience and blow, he might just as well be dead. Accordingly, Glaser booked more movies and record dates and television appearances, and everything was as it had been before the heart attack, except that Louis was tired all the time. He was often late for engagements, and sequestered himself in his dressing room with Dr. Schiff, rather than holding court as he once had. No longer an energetic jazz sprite, he began to age quickly and visibly. His eyes became rheumy, and when he wasn't on stage, blowing and beaming, he seemed frail, far older than his fifty-eight years. Only his smile remained unchanged, electric as ever.

He tried to resume his former pace. In October 1959, he returned to Ghana with the All Stars, dancing and carrying on with Prime Minister Nkrumah, but the tour failed to recapture the spontaneous ebullience of his first visit. In Nigeria, a crowd of fifteen thousand assembled to see him and departed well before the end of his set. The following week, in the Congo (now Zaïre), he received a warmer reception, as local dignitaries swapped their normal Western attire for more exotic garb, including spears and headdresses, and the good times returned for a while. He hobnobbed with Moïse Tshombé, who would soon be the country's leader, and even criticized Tshombé to his face, to the consternation of the other band members, who knew Tshombé's reputation and feared he would poison Louis. But the two of them got along like a house on fire, and even after Tshombé was arrested and charged with the murder of his political adversary, Patrice Lumumba, Louis remained loyal to his pal. "I pray each night they won't kill him," he said. "That cat was *so* nice to me. Kept me in his big palace and all, fed me good, stayed up all night gassing. I had this little tape recorder that cost me several big bills and Tshombé dug it so much I laid it on him."

Throughout the tour, he took grief from no one. When the All Stars swung into Beirut for a performance, Trummy Young said, "some newspaper guys came in the basement dressing room and said, 'How come you're going to play for them damn Jews in Israel?' So Louis looked at them, and he said, 'Let me tell you something. When I go down there, the first thing they are going to ask me is, 'How come you played for them damn Arabs?' That horn, you see that horn? That horn ain't prejudiced. A note's a note in any language.'" Sure enough, when he arrived in Israel, journalists posed the same question, and Louis gave them the same answer. "So ain't none of you no better than the other one," he lectured, as the All Stars laughed in delight at his *chutzpah*.

The laughter ended abruptly. Shortly before the All Stars left Africa, Velma Middleton, the oversized, lively singer whom Louis loved and the critics despised, suffered a stroke while performing. She was taken to a local hospital, and Glaser ordered the band to continue the tour without her. She lingered for a brief while, and then word came that

Velma had died in the hospital. Shock and dismay spread among the All Stars, and Barney Bigard remarked bitterly, "I'll never forgive Joe Glaser and Louis for that, because they said it would take too many people to lift her on the plane to France. I said to myself, 'This woman gave her all, and they just leave her in some little African town.'"

Louis returned to the United States in March 1960, rested briefly, and went back on the road with the All Stars, whose ranks now included Velma's replacement, Jewell Brown.

In April 1960, Glaser unexpectedly pulled Louis off the road for a unique recording event. He was to collaborate with the other great survivor of the Jazz Age, Duke Ellington. Although Ellington was as active and energetic as Louis, the only other figure in the jazz world to equal him, the two maintained only a cordial, arm's-length relationship. Duke had his orchestra, Louis his All Stars, and the two units went their separate ways. Even now, their collaboration was carried out under curious circumstances.

The celebrities did not record for a major label, as might be expected. Instead, they circumvented their contracts to record for tiny Roulette Records, a label whose boss, Morris Levy, was later revealed to have strong ties to organized crime. Fortunately, a credible producer was in charge, Bob Thiele, who enlivened Roulette during its brief heyday. "The miasmal hoodlum atmosphere at Roulette Records was so heavily oppressive that it was often difficult for me to concentrate on the musical matters that were my direct and only responsibilities," Thiele said later. "Everyone was diligently circumspect about my 'civilian' status and left me alone, even though every day I felt I was trapped in a grade B gangster epic." Glaser allowed Louis and Duke just two days, April 3 and 4, to make their recordings.

Despite the discouraging circumstances, Thiele worked wonders with his aging and fatigued stars, who, for all their experience, were insecure about the collaboration. He struck a balance by persuading Louis to perform songs written by Duke, and he convinced Duke to play the piano backed not by his own orchestra but by the All Stars. For this recording, the lineup consisted only of Barney Bigard on clarinet, Trummy Young on trombone, Mort Herbert on bass, and Danny Barcelona on drums.

The musicians convened in the RCA studios in New York, and although he managed to smile for photographers, Louis was uncomfortable. His lip was down, and worse, he was recording material that was new to him. Duke, meanwhile, was suffering from a persistent headache. No matter. Their performances were perfect—there is no other word to describe them. Louis sang and blew his way through the Ellington standards, "C Jam Blues," "I'm Just a Lucky So and So," "Cottontail," "Drop Me Off in Harlem" (with updated lyrics), and "It Don't Mean a Thing." The session closed with "Azalea," a song Duke had written years before, thinking of Louis, a tune mixing memory and desire. Duke had recorded some of these numbers dozens of times, but with Louis on board, they sounded fresh and different. He treated every syllable and note, no matter how simple, as if it contained essential truths, and in the process, demonstrated his uncanny knack for transforming familiar material into something special. Fatigue and acceptance of mortality are present in his voice, but so is a lifetime of experience. When he was done, Louis didn't bother to assess the quality of the recordings, which resulted in two albums. To him, it was just another recording date, perhaps best forgotten. Late that afternoon, he was back on the bus, nursing his sore chops with ointments and salves, as he hurried to another live performance.

Racism continued to plague him even now. On a tour that took him through Connecticut, he asked the driver to stop so he could use the bathroom. It was a sunny Saturday afternoon. "I was stunned when the owner of a restaurant, clearly on the basis of race, refused him use of otherwise available facilities," said Herb Snitzer, a photographer who accompanied the band. "I will never forget the look on Louis's face. Hero that he was, world-famous, a favorite to millions of people, America's single most identifiable entertainer, and yet excluded in the most humiliating fashion from a common convenience." Among the most visible and popular of all blacks, he was still, after all these years, condemned to this treatment—not in Louisiana, Alabama, or Mississippi, but in Connecticut.

Back in New York, Glaser was still contending with the southern promoters who canceled Louis's dates when they realized he performed with an integrated band. At the same time, another hot Glaser client, Dave Brubeck, suffered the cancellation of an entire southern tour once promoters discovered that his band was not all white. Brubeck became indignant on behalf of both himself and Louis and wanted to compose a work addressing the cruel irony of the American ambassador to the world who could not use a rest room in his own land. "I had read about what Louis Armstrong had done on his tours," Brubeck said, "and it seemed that jazz, stemming from World War II, had become a real symbol of freedom for many Europeans. I felt that real jazz had never been presented in a Broadway show. So my wife, Iola, and I thought of the idea of the musicians themselves being on stage and playing themselves, and they would get into a cultural exchange program." To star in their musical, the Brubecks wanted Louis Armstrong, "the epitome of jazz, not only to us, but to Europeans." They set to work and wrote the score and libretto. At one point, Louis would be called on to declaim, *"They said I look like God. Could God be black? My God. If both are made in the image of Thee, would Thou perchance a zebra be?"* It was a solemn and high-minded work, not really in Louis's rambunctious vein, but it belonged to the moment when Civil Rights came to the top of the national agenda.

The Brubecks took their idea to Glaser, who represented them all. Joe had no interest in sticking Louis in a Broadway show, which would prevent him from touring and tie up all his time, but a recording might be a possibility. Even there Joe had his doubts, for he still was looking exclusively for hits, and *The Real Ambassadors*, as Brubeck called his work, did not promise to be a toe-tapping jamboree. Still, he couldn't just stifle his two important clients. He suggested that Brubeck find Louis and talk it over with him.

Brubeck caught up with his star in a Chicago hotel, and talked his way past several gatekeepers into Louis's suite, where he anxiously presented his idea. To his delight, Louis endorsed it. "What I want you to do is go play all these pieces on the piano and put them on tape, and I will learn them," he said to Dave. He also wanted Brubeck to print the lyrics in large type. Louis would then paste the lyrics to the mirror and memorize them while he shaved. He went around telling people, "Brubeck's written me an opera."

With Louis on board, Brubeck dashed back to New York to nail down a recording date with his label, Columbia, which also viewed the project with skepticism. Like Glaser, the company wanted hits, and though it agreed to the project in the end, it devoted scant resources to the making or the selling of the album. Louis came off the road in September 1961 to record it with an orchestra and the singer Carmen McRae. Time was short as always, but to Brubeck's surprise, "Louis was prepared. It's amazing how well he did and how musical that guy is. When the time came to sing harmony, where we had written Louis to sing the lead, Carmen said, 'Pops, please, you sing the harmony and let me sing the lead.' Without any rehearsal, he jumps right in and does it. He was amazing to work with."

Despite the optimism and idealism surrounding the project, the resulting album attracted little attention—in part because Columbia did not promote it, and in part because it was unlike anything else Louis had done. It was, truth to tell, obvious and a bit strained. Nonetheless, *The Real Ambassadors* enjoyed a reprise the following year, at the Monterey Jazz Festival. Glaser meddled as usual, and refused to allow the performance to be filmed or recorded. To complicate matters further, the Brubecks wanted Louis to dress the part of an ambassador, with a top hat. At first he balked, but then relented, and when he made his entrance and heard the applause, he paused at Dave's piano and whispered, "Am I hamming it up enough to suit you, Pops?" Unlike the stiff recording that had preceded it, the performance itself, according to those present, was moving and deeply felt. This was the only live performance of *The Real Ambassadors*.

Joe Glaser appeared to be in full control of Louis's career at this point, but he was, in reality, engaged in a losing battle with the mob. People in the entertainment industry were aware of his former associations with the Capone syndicate in Chicago, and Glaser helped to keep the rumors alive, but there was much more to the story. Glaser kept in touch with Al Capone's stylish successor, Murray "The Camel" Humphreys, who now ran the Chicago syndicate. Humphrey's every move was shadowed by the FBI, and many of his supposedly secret business meetings were surreptitiously recorded by enterprising FBI agents. Among those tracking Humphreys was FBI agent William Roemer, a charter member of J. Edgar Hoover's "Top Hoodlum Program" in Chicago. In this capacity, Roemer listened to thousands of hours of conversation picked up by the hidden microphone nicknamed "Little Al," after Al Capone, planted in Celano's Custom Tailor Shop at 620 North Michigan Avenue. The tailor shop served as the Outfit's headquarters.

"One day in 1960," Roemer said, "Murray The Camel Humphreys and an associate, Frankie Strongie Ferraro, were discussing bringing an entertainer to Joe Glaser because they had an association with him and felt he could properly represent the performer. Humphreys had a working relationship with Glaser. He could present a situation to Glaser and get what he wanted from Glaser."

Glaser's mob connections occasionally had a direct bearing on Louis's engagements. In Philadelphia, he was unhappy about having to play at Ciro's, a nightclub owned by hoodlums. He was accustomed to dealing with gangsters, and while he didn't let his resentment show as he grinned and signed autographs, he ultimately got his revenge. "Louis is the king of scat. With an extra twist," said a musician who sat in with him. "Somehow, in the middle of these choruses he manages to keep saying, 'Kiss my ass, kiss my ass, kiss my ass.' Over and over. I hear it plain as day but nobody in that bunch digs what he's putting down. He's looking right at them, smiling his famous smile, scatting, 'Kiss my ass, kiss my ass.'"

Glaser's control over Associated Booking faltered when Sidney Korshak, one of the most feared men in the entertainment industry, entered his life. Like Glaser, Korshak came out of Chicago, where he, too, had formed ties to the Capone syndicate, but then Korshak headed to Los Angeles, where as a labor lawyer and power broker he moved in the highest circles in Hollywood. At the same time, he maintained a close relationship with the Chicago syndicate, according to the FBI. William Roemer, who supervised the FBI's file on Korshak, confirmed that the lawyer's direct link to the Chicago mob was Gussie Alex, who was Murray Humphrey's first lieutenant. "Korshak always did what the mob told him to do," Roemer said, and he recalled something Alex once said to Korshak: "You're our guy, we raised you up. When we call you, you call us." (For the record, Korshak denied he knew Alex, though he did admit that their wives, both models, were friends.) In a 1976 exposé of Korshak, the *New York Times* reported. "Federal officials contend that he has been involved in such activities as bribery, kickbacks, extortion, fraud and labor racketeering." The IRS had been on his case since 1942. He was even responsible for successfully blackmailing Senator Estes Kefauver, who at the time was leading a congressional inquiry into organized crime in Chicago, by photographing the senator in bed with a woman "supplied by the Chicago underworld."

Given this reputation, no one wanted to get on the wrong side of Sidney Korshak, not even Joe Glaser. When Korshak decided to bring Associated Booking and its roster of famous artists into his sphere of influence, Glaser had no choice but to acquiesce. In 1962, he assigned control over the agency, the nation's third largest, to both Korshak and himself. No one realized that Glaser had actually taken a much more powerful partner into the business. To the outside world, it seemed that Sidney Korshak was, at most, the company's legal counsel. When Joe Glaser died in 1969, Korshak demonstrated his authority by assuming complete control over ABC.

Since the entire transaction was conducted in secret, it is highly unlikely that Louis or any other ABC client realized how large a role Korshak played in the company. Given

Louis's lifelong affinity for hoodlum-managers, it is unlikely he would have minded even if he had known.

Throughout this period, Louis continued to blow, but as the 1960s turned confrontational and shrill, his brand of jazz came to sound like distant music. The British invasion and the rise of rock and roll in 1963 pushed him to the periphery of the popular music world he had dominated so many decades ago. To make matters worse, jazz was becoming more specialized and losing its audience, just as he had prophesied in 1947. The few vital musicians who were around, people such as Miles Davis and John Coltrane, were taking jazz to a level of sophistication that Louis couldn't hope to match. They were pushing the limits and setting new standards for hipness, while he was blowing endless choruses of "When It's Sleepy Time Down South" and "Back Home in Indiana." It seemed that his day had passed.

At the end of 1963, Glaser directed Louis to record a song. It was just a demo, no guarantee that it would ever be released. The tune, "Hello, Dolly," came from a musical by the same name, which had yet to open. The music publisher wanted to enlist Louis to record it simply as a way to plug the show, which had nothing to do with jazz. On December 4, 1963, Louis and the All Stars went into the studio. Louis found the song lifeless and trite, and in a last-minute effort to inject some zip into the proceedings, the recording company dubbed a banjo introduction. Louis promptly forgot about the session and went back on the road.

When Glaser heard the demo, he exclaimed, "It's a fucking hit!" and pushed like mad to get the song released. The demo tape eventually found its way to Jack Kapp, the founder of Decca, who now ran his own label, and he swiftly released it. Jazz purists gagged when they heard "Hello, Dolly." It supplied further proof, if any were needed, that Louis had lost all connection with the jazz world. Its provenance was suspect, for it came from a Broadway show, and the recording contained a banjo and strings, both of which marked it as a novelty number, at best. What the purists didn't realize—though Glaser did—was that "Hello, Dolly" was Louis's best single in donkey's years. The vocal featured exquisite timing, and Louis's trumpet playing contained a striking, improvised passage. In addition, the song had excellent self-promotion possibilities, for Louis changed a lyric to include his name: "This is Louis, Dolly." Not "Lou-ie," but "Lou-*is*," the way he always pronounced his own name. By drawing himself into the tune, he turned it into a paean to the long-lost persona of Louis Armstrong, who had so much history behind him, and who was still out there singing and blowing.

*Hello, Dolly!*, the musical, opened on Broadway in January 1964, and it became a major hit. Louis's demo recording followed suit. It appeared on the charts in February, and on May 9 the song astounded the music industry, to say nothing of the jazz world, by reaching the number-one spot for one gorgeous week, at a time when the Beatles and other British rock groups were thought to have an absolute lock on the charts.

Louis missed all the hoopla. He was on the road, playing Puerto Rico, when Glaser's office called down to tell the All Stars to start playing their new smash hit "Hello, Dolly." The musicians, Louis included, were perplexed. They didn't even have the music. "Any you guys remember this damn tune?" Louis gently inquired. No one did. They raced all over San Juan trying to find the sheet music, without success, and finally a copy arrived from New York, and the band learned it. The first time they played it, in San Juan, they were a bit skeptical about whether it was a bona fide hit, but when the audience made Louis take eight curtain calls, they damn well knew Glaser was right: it really was a fucking hit.

Kapp capitalized on the success of "Hello, Dolly" by hauling Louis back into the studio for an album consisting of remakes of earlier hits, and in June, the album also reached the number-one position. Louis basked in the glow of his sudden, unexpected popularity. He was all over the radio, and all over television, on *The Ed Sullivan Show*, and just about every other variety and talk show. Later, he appeared in the movie, singing "Hello, Dolly" to Barbara Streisand, his version of the song largely responsible for building the Hollywood version of the show into yet another hit. At sixty-three, after years of riding the bus, touring, blowing, and singing, in good times and bad, Louis enjoyed a personal triumph the likes of which he had never expected to see.

The only problem with Louis's hit was that it supplanted his earlier, more distinguished work in the public mind. For millions, especially younger listeners, "Hello, Dolly" was their first exposure to Louis Armstrong. They knew him not as the heroic and volatile personification of jazz, but as the charming old man who sang "Hello, Dolly," in that funny, gravelly voice. He had succeeded in reinventing himself at the cost of obscuring his earlier achievements. The audience he won with "Hello, Dolly" overlooked his discography, one of the biggest and richest in the business. Since his first sessions with King Oliver, he had recorded over a thousand tunes, some many times over. There were nearly a hundred versions of his "When It's Sleepy Time Down South," for instance, and more than fifty renditions of "When the Saints Go Marching In." He recorded "Basin Street Blues," "Muskrat Ramble," and "Mack the Knife," to name but a few, more than forty times each.

Despite his unequaled longevity and fertility, not to mention his recent number-one hit, record label executives remained skeptical about his appeal. Shortly after "Hello, Dolly," Bob Thiele, who had produced the distinguished Armstrong-Ellington albums, came to Louis with a ballad called "What a Wonderful World." Louis instantly fell in love with the song, and he agreed to record it with Thiele, who was now at ABC Records. For once, Louis didn't play his horn, he simply sang. Since the recording required the added expense of strings, cellos, and other musicians, he even agreed to forego his usual advance and work for scale—$250.

When the company president, Larry Newton, heard the recording, he hated it. He hated Armstrong, the song, and Thiele. A distraught Glaser offered to buy the recording from ABC Records, but Newton insisted on releasing it without any promotion. It sold fewer than a thousand copies, while "Hello, Dolly" had sold millions. In England, however, "What a Wonderful World" quickly sold six hundred thousand copies and went to the top of the charts, and its popularity spread to other countries as well, everywhere except the United States. Newton predictably did an about-face and demanded that Louis make an entire "What a Wonderful World" album for five hundred dollars. When he heard that, Glaser told Thiele, "You tell that fat bastard to fuck himself and give us twenty-five thousand dollars for eight more sides." Newton returned the compliment, saying that Glaser could go fuck himself, too.

Ultimately Glaser prevailed and Louis recorded the album for the full twenty-five thousand dollars. When it was released, Newton was showered with accolades for his brilliant and innovative exploitation of Louis Armstrong. But the song didn't find a wide audience in America until it was featured on the soundtrack of the movie, *Good Morning, Vietnam*, more than twenty years later.

Louis's enhanced popularity and income during the mid-1960s had little effect on the way he lived. By this point in his life, he was who he was, and he was damned if he was going to change to suit anyone, not even his wife Lucille. Not surprisingly, she had become impatient with their modest house in Corona, Queens, and yearned for the lush green expanses of suburban Long Island. With Glaser's help, she located a posh dwelling complete with swimming pool, not far from Jackie Robinson's home, but Louis wouldn't have any of it. "We're right out here with the rest of the colored folk and the Puerto Ricans and Italians and the Hebrew cats," he said of life in Corona. "We don't need to move out in the suburbs to some big mansion with lots of servants and yardmen and things. What for? What the hell do I care about living in a 'fashionable' neighborhood? Ain't nobody cutting off the lights and gas here 'cause we didn't pay the bills. The frigidaire is full of food. What more do we need?" Asked why he didn't live in Beverly Hills with other celebrities, Louis carefully explained that he never felt a part of Hollywood. He had been to a few Hollywood parties, and people were polite to him, but frequently someone who'd had a few too many would come up to him and say, "You know, I used to have a colored mammy." He didn't consider the movie stars his friends, not even those who admired or imitated him. "Even though I've played with a lot of them—Danny Kaye, Sinatra—I don't even know where they live," he said. "In fact, I've never been invited to the home of a movie star, not even Bing's." He knew he would never feel at home in Hollywood.

He liked to do his own shopping, to visit the local barbershop, to buy ice cream cones from the Good Humor Man for the kids in the neighborhood every afternoon at 3:15. Sometimes, the kids came into the living room and watched television with him in the late afternoon; he favored Westerns. "We've seen three generations grow up on our block," he said, looking back over his twenty-odd years in Corona. "White and black, and those kids when they grew up and got married, their children still come around to our house and visit their friends Louis and Lucille. That's how close they feel towards us." This, he knew, was the way life should be.

Kids weren't the only visitors to the house in Corona. Jazz musicians and critics frequently dropped in on Pops, even at the price of participating in his obsession with Swiss Kriss. His old nemesis Dizzy Gillespie, who lived nearby, became a friend and frequent visitor. Diz realized Louis was still the hippest cat in jazz; he had never been the Uncle Tom of the boppers' imaginings. He had risked everything when he had taken on Ike over school desegregation in 1957, and although the public at large quickly forgot the controversy, the jazz world remembered his stand. Musicians like Diz, and even Miles, came to understand how much they owed to Louis's music and his career. Diz would come by, usually with Clark Terry, the trumpet player, and they would say, "Pops, we came to get our batteries charged."

Inside, the rooms were large and immaculate, and the bathrooms resplendent, with mirrors and gold-plated fixtures. In the den, Louis stored his mammoth collection of reel-to-reel tapes of the All Star performances. He owned almost none of the records he had made; the live music held more appeal for him. In his spare time, he decorated the tape boxes with bold collages of photos and headlines clipped from newspapers, and later he compiled a 175-page catalog of his tape collection. Lucille, for her part, furnished the living room in contemporary French decor, and she continued to cook for Louis in the large kitchen, which was equipped with an oversized stove. She hung paintings by Leroy Neiman on the walls. A blowup of Louis's 1935 *Vanity Fair* portrait hung over the fireplace. And she made sure to display their marriage license in the hallway.

Meanwhile, Louis's sister lived on in New Orleans, proudly and defiantly remaining in a shabby neighborhood. Mama Lucy was nearly a foot taller than her brother, with the same rumbling voice and stubborn independence. "I got my grave, my tombstone, and my funeral's all paid," she declared. "I don't need no help from no one, no how." She refused to take money from Louis, and she actually sent him food to make sure he was eating enough up north. Photographs of him were displayed throughout her home. There was little love lost between Lucille and Mama Lucy, though the older woman did admit, "My brother was married four times, but he has only one wife." On hearing that remark, Lucille said, "You know, that was the first time Mama Lucy ever said anything nice about me."

Beneath the superficial tranquillity of Louis's life, his iconoclastic spirit boiled away. He refused to hobnob with the wealthy and powerful, black or white. On learning that Howard University wished to confer an honorary doctorate on him, he sighed and lamented, "Where were they forty years ago when I needed them?" And in 1969, when Richard Nixon, newly elected president, dispatched an emissary to invite Louis to the White House, Armstrong gave short shrift to an honor few would refuse. "Fuck that shit," he said. "Why didn't they do it before? The only reason he would want me to play there now is to make some niggers happy."

He was ambivalent about living this *haute bourgeois* existence with Lucille. They fought occasionally in front of friends. Once they got into a scuffle on a train, and Louis became so enraged he drove his fist through the glass window. Afterward, he muttered dark words about divorcing Lucille, and even mentioned the idea to several friends. "If I had to make a choice between my wife and my little trumpet," he told William Russell, the jazz critic, "I'll take my little trumpet." Russell added, "He really meant it." Once he had finished ventilating his rage and frustration with the constraints of marriage, and Lucille's unwillingness to embrace the wilder side of life, he returned to speaking of her in tender, passionate tones. "We're *still* married and still at it. Yes, Lord, it's ALL SEX," he wrote in 1969.

> Can you imagine these kids of my neighborhood at my home listening and grinning as I was telling them about Aunt Lucille's and my beautiful life together? I commenced to calling Lucille 'Moms.' My Moms. She's so attentive, and she reminds me and does a lot of things just like my mother, Mary Ann. And since she passed in 1927, it seems as if Lucille has features just like Mayann. Some of Lucille's ways and little gestures are just like my mother.

During the late '60s, Louis was beset with minor ailments, but he kept touring with the zeal and humility of a young cat trying to make a name for himself. The man who refused to play the White House came to Iowa in 1968 to perform at Grinnell College. "Nearly two-dozen intellectuals and artists were on campus to participate in a series of discussions and to receive honorary degrees, yet the college refused to award one to Armstrong," wrote the jazz critic Gary Giddins, who, as a Grinnell student, had been responsible for inviting Louis to the campus. "Outside the gymnasium where he performed, a handful of students picketed because they wanted a rock group." Giddins was even more disquieted when he approached the great man of jazz: "There he was, an old man in a loose tuxedo, his brown coloring tinctured with gray, his eyes slightly rheumy, the scar on his upper lip alarmingly raw." On stage that night, though, "he appeared transfigured. The ashen color was gone, the eyes blazed, the smile blinded. . . . His huge tone was as gold and unspotted as ever."

Many of Louis's admirers wondered why he drove himself this way. He didn't need the money, he had every accolade that could come the way of a jazz musician, his reputation as a cultural force and jazz icon was secure. Why did he do it? "People are quick to forget you if you don't keep your name before the public," he insisted, evoking the tragic end of his mentor, Joe Oliver. He didn't want to become just a name in the history books, an occasion for nostalgia; he was determined to blow till he dropped. Glaser still drove him at a cruel pace. After all these decades, Louis was still doing one-nighters, as he always had. It was the life he knew, and it was the routine that Joe Glaser knew. Louis occasionally quoted Bert Williams's lament, "In show business, you've got to die to prove that you're sick," but then he would pick up his horn, and for an hour or two he would forget about the inescapable fact of his mortality. So he hauled himself to

Las Vegas, or Atlantic City, to play for jaded audiences, and was transported the moment he began to blow.

Despite his ebbing strength, he kept devising ways to inject new energy into the material he performed. In 1968, he recorded his most surprising album, "Disney Songs the Satchmo Way," a children's collection bursting with affecting vocals and surprising solos, all of them recorded when Louis was obviously fatigued and uncomfortable. Even so, his rendition of "Chim Chim Cher-ee," for instance, showed that he still had the power to invest a familiar song with haunting emotional urgency and musical finesse.

In September 1968, he appeared in the office of his doctor, Gary Zucker, short of breath. When Dr. Zucker ordered him to proceed directly to Beth Israel Hospital. Louis could not bring himself to enter the hospital. Unable to let go of life and all its pleasures, he dropped out of sight for two weeks. He spent his time in Harlem, carousing, seeing old friends, being himself, denying his mortality. Meanwhile, his condition worsened, and his limbs swelled ominously. Eventually, he was forced to go to Beth Israel. His heart and his kidneys were failing. He was suffering from a lifetime of very hard living, of driving himself incessantly, of gaining and losing weight, not to mention more than forty years of marijuana. Chronic use of the drug that Louis insisted was necessary to his well-being leads to lung disease, mild depression, and disorientation—all of which plagued him now.

Rest and treatment in the form of diuretics helped him to regain his health, and he was able to go home, only to return to Beth Israel in February 1969 with more heart and kidney problems. This time, he stayed for two wrenching months. He underwent emergency surgery to clear his lungs of fluid, and his doctors tried to make him understand that he could no longer return to his old life of one-nighters; in fact, he couldn't even blow his horn anymore. It was too hard on his weakened lungs. These restrictions were more than Louis could bear. "He made it abundantly clear that the only thing that was important was to make music," said his doctor. "If he couldn't make music, then he was through."

Even Joe Glaser was telling his star client that it was time to retire.

Before he could enforce his will, Glaser suffered a debilitating stroke in the elevator of his office building. He was taken to Beth Israel for treatment. Louis was still there, undergoing treatment, but Lucille decided not to tell him about Glaser, for fear of upsetting her husband. He found out anyway, when Dizzy Gillespie came to visit Louis and mentioned he was going to give blood for Mr. Glaser.

"Blood for Joe Glaser for what?" Louis asked.

"Why, man, Joe Glaser's sick as a dog right around the corner in the hospital here."

Incensed, Louis insisted on visiting Glaser, and was taken in a wheelchair to see his manager, who lay in a coma in an intensive care unit. Louis returned from the visit badly shaken. "He didn't know me," he said to Lucille.

As Louis continued to languish in his hospital room, he sought consolation in memories of his youth, of Storyville and its prostitutes, his mother and sister and boyhood friends. On March 31, 1969, Louis, "ill in his bed at the Beth Israel Hospital," as he described himself, penned an affecting memoir of his days with the Karnoffsky family, and, making an associative leap, dedicated the piece to the dying Joe Glaser, "the best friend that I've ever had. May the Lord bless him, watch over him always." He signed it, "His boy and disciple who loved him dearly, Louis Satchmo Armstrong."

Glaser never awoke from his coma. He died on June 6. His passing was a devastating blow for Louis, who faced the prospect of living on without the spiritual father who had filled such a large void in his career, and in his heart. He recovered sufficiently to go home, and tried to make the best of what was left of his life. Looking back on this terrible period in July, Louis wrote a friend, "It was a toss up between us, who would cut out first. Man, it broke my heart that it was him. I love that man, which the world already knows. I prayed, as sick as I was, that he would make it. God bless his soul. He was the greatest for me and all the spades that he handled."

Associated Booking continued to manage Louis's career and finances. He resumed a limited performing and recording schedule, singing, but not blowing, always conscious of his health, and growing increasingly dependent on the doctors who tended to him. Every appearance he made now had the air of a valedictory about it. In May 1970, he returned to the studio to record an album entitled "With Friends." The friends included some of the leading lights of jazz, many of whom had either disdained or evolved far beyond him. Eddie Condon, Miles Davis, and Ornette Coleman were there; old friends like Bobby Hackett came along; even a few jazz critics, such as Stanley Dance, turned up—all of them backing Louis in a chorus. Even George Wein joined in. The event was a bit show-business sappy, but everyone realized that Louis wasn't going to be around forever, and they wanted one last memory of him, a memory he was happy to supply.

On his ceremonial seventieth birthday, July 4, 1970, he sat for an introspective, somber interview with the *New York Times*. He sounded as if he had come to terms with the prospect of his own death. "I think I had a beautiful life. I didn't wish for anything I couldn't get, and I got pretty near everything I wanted because I worked for it." He talked about his own funeral, visualizing it as a traditional New Orleans sendoff. "They're going to enjoy blowing over me, ain't they?" he remarked.

> Cats will be coming from California and everywhere else just to play. . . . If anybody plans a bad note, Lucille'll slap'em right in the face. She'll take care of that for me. I don't want no part of it. Once I cut out, forget it. It'll be good if I can get to the Pearly Gates upstairs. Saint Peter will have all those good things written down. He ain't got no business with the bad things up there. . . . I listen to my idols, I ain't going to worry about their personals, their living. Just the music, that's all I'm interested in. . . . You have to have something to die with, Pops.

Later that summer, George Wein organized a birthday tribute to Louis at the Newport Jazz Festival. The occasion proved bittersweet, because Louis was very frail by this time, emaciated and unable to climb a short staircase without a boost. In rehearsal, he looked distinctly retired, puttering around in his shorts and a white baseball cap with the visor turned to one side. His voice was, if possible, more gravelly than ever, and doctor's orders forbade him from blowing. Troubled by the memory of Louis's famous ruckus at Newport back in 1959, Wein was attentive to his star's needs, but they disagreed on the staging of the show. Louis wanted to come out singing "When It's Sleepy Time Down South," just as he always did, to demonstrate that nothing had changed, he was still the same, but Wein urged Louis simply to walk out on stage and stand beneath a spotlight, unannounced, to what Wein was certain would be an ovation. The idea made Louis nervous. What if no one recognized him? What if they didn't applaud? Ultimately, Wein got his way, and when Louis appeared on stage after a series of trumpet tributes, the effect was electric. He did look transformed, straight and strong in an impeccable bronze-colored suit, his cufflinks gleaming, and for the time being, he was still the king of the trumpet, and the king of jazz. He sang "Mack the Knife," and his gruff voice glided through surprisingly mellifluous passages. His horn was gone, but his voice was still going, and his timing remained as startling as ever. Once again, he *was* the music.

Invigorated by his success at Newport, he planned a comeback. Against doctor's orders, he began practicing the trumpet, but only in the bathroom, where he thought no one would hear him. In September 1970, he played a two-week stand in Las Vegas with a reconstituted All Stars. The good times, it seemed, were back. He was on the road again, spending October in England, and December in Vegas. In February 1971, he went on network television, singing "Pennies from Heaven" with Bing Crosby. He recorded "The Night Before Christmas." There was no more talk of dying.

At home, feeling cocky, he spent his time answering the voluminous mail elicited by his illness and remarkable comeback, stuffing his letters into envelopes imprinted with the infamous photograph of Satchmo on the toilet. To a friend he wrote, "Your boy Satchmo is getting pretty sassy these days. Blowing his black ass off. I knew I could, all the time. My fans and friends, quite naturally they'd be a little uneasy about things, but as for me, they're my chops. I wear them 24 hours a day, and I keep them in good trim." He was still in love with his Lucille, in his slightly crazy way: "We shares everything in life from soup to nuts, especially the latter. Ha. Ha. Ya dig?"

In March, he played a two-week engagement—"just another hustle"—in the Waldorf-Astoria's Empire Room. Before his first show, his doctor, Gary Zucker, issued a dire warning: "You could drop dead while you're performing."

"Doc, you don't understand. My whole life, my whole soul, my whole spirit is to blow that horn," Louis said. "I've got to do it."

On opening night, he received a devastating review. After he read it, he turned to Joe Sully, a representative from his manager's office, and asked, "But you'll still book me, huh, Joe?"

As soon as the engagement ended, he returned to Beth Israel, having suffered another heart attack. The press kept watch over Louis, and bulletins about his condition regularly appeared in the papers. He underwent a tracheotomy to ease congestion in his lungs and bronchial tubes, and in mid-June, he went home again to recover whatever was left of his health.

For a time, he seemed to rally. On his ceremonial birthday, July 4, 1971, television crews and interviewers came to visit him in Corona. In a soft voice, with Lucille at his side, he declared his intention to resume performing as soon as he was able. The next day, he told the All Stars to prepare for a rehearsal. He had another gig coming up, and he was very excited about it.

At 5:30 the next morning, July 6, 1971, Louis Armstrong died at his home, in bed, in his sleep.

His last rites in New York were splendid and dignified, but nothing like the festive jazz funeral he had imagined for himself. The roster of "honorary pallbearers"—including the likes of John Lindsay, the Mayor of New York City; Johnny Carson; Earl Wilson, the gossip columnist; Dick Cavett; and Merv Griffin—sparked controversy. People in the jazz world wondered what these prominent white figures had to do with Louis, or with jazz. His body reposed in an open coffin at the Seventh Regiment Armory at Park Avenue and 66th Street in Manhattan. An estimated twenty-five thousand mourners waited in line to pay their last respects. Again, there were rumblings in the jazz world because many of the musicians who had known Louis in the old days couldn't afford to come to New York to say good-bye. On July 9, his funeral took place at the Corona Congregational Church, and there was, astonishingly, no music. He was buried in Flushing Cemetery.

Two days later, an old-fashioned raucous jazz funeral took place in New Orleans. An immense parade in Louis's honor wound its way through the streets of the city, streets that he had celebrated in his music. The Onward Brass Band, successor to the marching bands in which Louis had played as a young man, pounded out the old familiar tunes: *"Oh, didn't he ramble? . . . He rambled everywhere . . . He rambled till the butcher cut him down. . . ."*

Amid the clamor attendant on his death, Lil Hardin, Louis's second wife, went overlooked. Lil still lived in the house at 421 East 44th Street in Chicago, where she and Louis had once spent so many happy hours, and played so much music. The years had done nothing to lessen the tie she felt to him, and she still considered herself Mrs. Armstrong.

Several weeks after his death, on August 28, 1971, she emerged from semiretirement to play in a televised memorial concert at the Civic Center Plaza, an outdoor arena in Chicago. After waiting impatiently for her turn, she was introduced to the crowd and began to play the "St. Louis Blues" as if it were still in 1924, and she was the same "Hot

Miss Lil." She exuded joy and smiled broadly as the music poured forth. Then, suddenly, she began gasping for breath and collapsed in front of the audience. She had suffered a massive heart attack.

With cameras mercilessly bearing down on the scene, a rescue worker attempted mouth-to-mouth resuscitation, and finally an ambulance took her to a nearby hospital. Doctors tried to revive her, without success, and pronounced her dead. To some, the manner of her passing seemed grotesque, too public, while others considered it altogether fitting that Lil died performing in honor of her late husband.

Louis left an estate valued at $530,775. The amount was formidable for a jazz man, but it was hardly the millions people supposed he had amassed. Joe Glaser, for example, was a far wealthier man and left an estate valued at more than $3,000,000. For decades, rumors had circulated that Glaser had stolen Louis blind. Associated Booking insisted that was not the case, that the agency took a standard 15 percent fee. Lucille, for her part, affirmed that Joe Glaser always kept half of Louis's earnings.

Louis's will, dated February 10, 1970, bequeathed nearly all his assets to his wife. Clarence and Mama Lucy each received five thousand dollars. Louis had never legally adopted Clarence, and he lived on in obscurity. After her husband's death, Lucille stayed in the house in Corona, Queens, preserving it as a memorial to her husband. During the ensuing decade, she received royalties averaging seventy-three thousand dollars a year, and her assets approached a million dollars. She was now wealthy, but she lived as she always had, devoted to her husband's memory, no matter what trials he had put her through during their years together.

At the beginning of October 1983, she journeyed to Boston to attend a fund-raising concert at Brandeis University in honor of her late husband. She suffered a seizure in her hotel room and died at Beth Israel Hospital in Boston on October 5, at the age of sixty-nine. Lucille was buried beside Louis, as if to maintain an everlasting vigil over his restless spirit.

# Index

Governor Charles
"Buddy" Roemer III
1988-1992

Governor David C. Treen
1980-1984